Y0-AER-568

REFERENCE
DOES NOT CIRCULATE

Historic Documents
of 2019

Sara Miller McCune founded SAGE Publishing in 1965 to support the dissemination of usable knowledge and educate a global community. SAGE publishes more than 1000 journals and over 600 new books each year, spanning a wide range of subject areas. Our growing selection of library products includes archives, data, case studies and video. SAGE remains majority owned by our founder and after her lifetime will become owned by a charitable trust that secures the company's continued independence.

Los Angeles | London | New Delhi | Singapore | Washington DC | Melbourne

Historic Documents
of 2019

Heather Kerrigan, Editor

$SAGE reference |

FOR INFORMATION:

CQ Press

An Imprint of SAGE Publications, Inc.

2455 Teller Road

Thousand Oaks, California 91320

E-mail: order@sagepub.com

SAGE Publications Ltd.

1 Oliver's Yard

55 City Road

London EC1Y 1SP

United Kingdom

SAGE Publications India Pvt. Ltd.

B 1/I 1 Mohan Cooperative Industrial Area

Mathura Road, New Delhi 110 044

India

SAGE Publications Asia-Pacific Pte. Ltd.

18 Cross Street #10-10/11/12

China Square Central

Singapore 048423

SAGE Editor: Laura Notton

Editor: Heather Kerrigan

Managing Editor: Linda Grimm

Contributors: Anastazia Clouting

Melissa Feinberg

Linda Grimm

Robert William Howard

Megan Howes

Heather Kerrigan

Gia Miller

Lyndi Schrecengost

Production Editor: Tracy Buyan

Copy Editor: Talia Greenberg

Typesetter: C&M Digitals (P) Ltd.

Proofreader: Lawrence Baker

Indexer: Joan Shapiro

Cover Designer: Glenn Vogel

Copyright © 2020 by CQ Press, an Imprint of SAGE Publications, Inc. CQ Press is a registered trademark of Congressional Quarterly Inc.

All rights reserved. Except as permitted by U.S. copyright law, no part of this work may be reproduced or distributed in any form or by any means, or stored in a database or retrieval system, without permission in writing from the publisher.

All third-party trademarks referenced or depicted herein are included solely for the purpose of illustration and are the property of their respective owners. Reference to these trademarks in no way indicates any relationship with, or endorsement by, the trademark owner.

Printed in the United States of America

ISBN 978-1-5443-8466-5
ISSN 0892-080X

This book is printed on acid-free paper.

20 21 22 23 24 10 9 8 7 6 5 4 3 2 1

Contents

JANUARY

A statement by President Donald Trump on January 8, 2019, on the
crisis at the U.S.–Mexico border and federal government shutdown; a
January 8, 2019, statement by Sen. Chuck Schumer, D-N.Y., and Rep.
Nancy Pelosi, D-Calif., on the federal shutdown and the president's call
for border wall funding; a January 14, 2019, tweet from Trump calling
on Democrats to end the shutdown; a January 20, 2019, tweet from
Pelosi asking Trump to put federal employees back to work; and a
January 25, 2019, statement by Trump announcing a deal to
temporarily reopen the federal government.

A resolution approved by the Organization of American States on
January 10, 2019, not recognizing President Nicolas Maduro's second
term; the Venezuela National Assembly's declaration on January 15,
2019, that Maduro's government was illegitimate; a statement released
by President Donald Trump on January 23, 2019, announcing the
United States' recognition of Juan Guaidó as the interim president of
Venezuela; a statement by Lima Group members on February 4, 2019,
recognizing Guaidó as interim president; a statement issued by
Norway's Foreign Ministry on May 17, 2019, announcing the start of
talks between Maduro's government and opposition leaders; and
Executive Order 13884, issued on August 5, 2019, which imposed
additional U.S. sanctions on the government of Venezuela.

A proclamation by Washington governor Jay Inslee on January 25, 2019, declaring a local public health emergency after a measles outbreak; a March 26, 2019, press release from Rockland County, New York, announcing a state of emergency related to a measles outbreak; an April 29, 2019, public health emergency declaration in New York City; a May 30, 2019, press release from the Centers for Disease Control and Prevention detailing measles case growth in the United States in 2019; and a press release from the Department of Health and Human Services on October 4, 2019, announcing that the United States would maintain its measles elimination status.

FEBRUARY

The text of President Donald Trump's February 5, 2019, State of the Union address; and the text of the Democratic response delivered by Stacey Abrams, the former Democratic candidate for Georgia governor and State House minority leader, also on February 5, 2019.

A press release issued by NASA on February 13, 2019, announcing the end of the Mars Opportunity rover mission; a memorandum signed by President Donald Trump on February 19, 2019, to establish a new U.S. Space Force; remarks delivered by Vice President Mike Pence on March 26, 2019, in which he announced an accelerated timeline for NASA's new lunar program; and remarks by President Trump on August 29, 2019, at his signing of an executive order creating U.S. Space Command.

A tweet posted by White House press secretary Stephanie Grisham on February 14, 2019, announcing Attorney General William Barr's confirmation; a tweet posted by EPA administrator Andrew Wheeler on February 28, 2019, in response to his confirmation; the resignation letter of DHS secretary Kirstjen Nielsen, dated April 7, 2019; the resignation letter of Labor secretary Alexander Acosta, submitted on July 12, 2019; President Donald Trump's responses to reporter questions about DHS staffing during an exchange on September 18, 2019; and Energy secretary Rick Perry's resignation letter from October 17, 2019.

MARCH

JUNE

JULY

SEPTEMBER

OCTOBER

issued by the World Food Programme on December 6, 2019, announcing an increase in food assistance to Haiti; and a tweet posted by President Jovenel Moïse on January 12, 2020, on opportunities for political change.

NOVEMBER

DECEMBER

Thematic Table of Contents

GOVERNMENT AND POLITICS

HEALTH AND SOCIAL SERVICES

INTERNATIONAL AFFAIRS

AFRICA

INTERNATIONAL AFFAIRS

ASIA

INTERNATIONAL AFFAIRS

AUSTRALIA AND NEW ZEALAND

INTERNATIONAL AFFAIRS

EUROPE

INTERNATIONAL AFFAIRS

LATIN AMERICA AND THE CARIBBEAN

INTERNATIONAL AFFAIRS

MIDDLE EAST

INTERNATIONAL AFFAIRS

RUSSIA AND THE FORMER SOVIET REPUBLIC

INTERNATIONAL AFFAIRS

GLOBAL ISSUES

NATIONAL SECURITY AND TERRORISM

RIGHTS, RESPONSIBILITIES, AND JUSTICE

List of Document Sources

CONGRESS

EXECUTIVE DEPARTMENTS, AGENCIES, FEDERAL OFFICES, AND COMMISSIONS

INTERNATIONAL GOVERNMENTAL ORGANIZATIONS

INTERNATIONAL NONGOVERNMENTAL ORGANIZATIONS

JUDICIARY

NONGOVERNMENTAL ORGANIZATIONS

NON-U.S. GOVERNMENTS

U.S. STATE AND LOCAL GOVERNMENTS

WHITE HOUSE AND THE PRESIDENT

Executive Office of the President. "Remarks with Chairman of the State
     Affairs Commission Kim Jong Un of North Korea and President Moon
     Jae-in of South Korea and an Exchange with Reporters in Panmunjom, Korean
     Demilitarized Zone." June 30, 2019. *Compilation of Presidential
     Documents* 2019, no. 00446 (June 30, 2019).   121
Executive Office of the President. "Statement Announcing United States
     Recognition of National Assembly President Juan Gerardo Guaidó
     Márquez as Interim President of Venezuela." January 23, 2019. *Compilation of
     Presidential Documents* 2019, no. 00046 (January 23, 2019).   23
Executive Office of the President. "Statement on Signing Fiscal Year 2020
     Appropriations Legislation." December 20, 2019. *Compilation of Presidential
     Documents* 2019, no. 00879 (December 20, 2019).   607
Executive Office of the President. "Statement on the Liberation of Territory
     Controlled by the Islamic State of Iraq and Syria Terrorist Organization."
     March 23, 2019. *Compilation of Presidential Documents* 2019, no. 00169
     (March 23, 2019).   205
Executive Office of the President. "Statement on Turkey's Actions in
     Northeast Syria." October 14, 2019. *Compilation of Presidential Documents*
     2019, no. 00721 (October 14, 2019).   206
Stephanie Grisham (@PressSec). Twitter post. February 14, 2019.   75
The White House. "Memorandum of Telephone Conversation." July 25, 2019.
     Declassified September 24, 2019.   518
The White House. "Press Briefing by USCIS Acting Director Ken Cuccinelli."
     August 12, 2019.   407
The White House. "Remarks by Vice President Pence at the Fifth Meeting of
     the National Space Council." March 26, 2019.   68

Preface

The impeachment of President Donald Trump, his fight for the construction of a border wall, the release of the Mueller report, political turmoil in South America, a continued Brexit showdown in the United Kingdom, the revocation of Kashmir autonomy in India, and Supreme Court decisions on political gerrymandering and administrative processes for updating the U.S. Census are just a few of the topics of national and international significance chosen for discussion in *Historic Documents of 2019*. This edition marks the forty-seventh volume of a CQ Press project that began with *Historic Documents of 1972*. This series allows students, librarians, journalists, scholars, and others to research and understand the most important domestic and foreign issues and events of the year through primary source documents. To aid research, many of the lengthy documents written for specialized audiences have been excerpted to highlight the most important sections. The official statements, news conferences, speeches, special studies, and court decisions presented here should be of lasting public and academic interest.

Historic Documents of 2019 opens with an "Overview of 2019," a sweeping narrative of the key events and issues of the year that provides context for the documents that follow. The balance of the book is organized chronologically, with each article comprising an introduction titled "Document in Context" and one or more related documents on a specific event, issue, or topic. Often, an event is not limited to a particular day. Consequently, readers will find that some events include multiple documents that may span several months. Their placement in the book corresponds to the date of the first document included for that event. The event introductions provide context and an account of further developments during the year. A thematic table of contents (page xix) and a list of documents organized by source (page xxiii) follow the standard table of contents and assist readers in locating events and documents.

As events, issues, and consequences become more complex and far-reaching, these introductions and documents yield important information and deepen understanding about the world's increasing interconnectedness. As memories of current events fade, these selections will continue to further understanding of the events and issues that have shaped the lives of people around the world.

How to Use This Book

Each of the entries in this edition consists of two parts: a comprehensive introduction followed by one or more primary source documents. The articles are arranged in chronological order by month. Articles with multiple documents are placed according to the date of the first document. There are several ways to find events and documents of interest:

By date: If the approximate date of an event or document is known, browse through the titles for that month in the table of contents. Alternatively, browse the tables of contents that appear at the beginning of each month's articles.

By theme: To find a particular topic or subject area, browse the thematic table of contents.

By document type or source: To find a particular type of document or document source, such as the White House or Congress, review the list of document sources.

By index: The index allows researchers to locate references to specific events or documents as well as entries on the same or related subjects.

An online edition of this volume, as well as an archive going back to 1972, is available and offers advance search and browse functionality.

Each article begins with an introduction. This feature provides historical and intellectual contexts for the documents that follow. Documents are reproduced with the original spelling, capitalization, and punctuation of the original or official copy. Ellipsis points indicate textual omissions (unless they were present in the documents themselves, indicating pauses in speech), and brackets are used for editorial insertions within documents for text clarification. The excerpting of Supreme Court opinions has been done somewhat differently from other documents. In-text references and citations to laws and other cases have been removed when not part of a sentence to improve the readability of opinions. In those documents, readers will find ellipses used only when sections of narrative text have been removed.

Full citations appear at the end of each document. If a document is not available on the Internet, this too is noted. For further reading on a particular topic, consult the "Other Historic Documents of Interest" section at the end of each article. These sections provide cross-references for related articles in this edition of *Historic Documents* as well as in previous editions. References to articles from past volumes include the year and page number for easy retrieval.

Overview of 2019

In the United States, the year began with partisan wrangling to end the longest federal government shutdown in history that lasted for five weeks from December 2018 into January 2019. The disagreement between Congress and the White House over how to fund the government revolved around President Donald Trump's request for more than $5 billion to fund the construction of a wall along the U.S.–Mexico border. The final fiscal year 2019 funding bill provided only a fraction of that amount, leading the president to declare a national emergency along the southern border that allowed him to redirect funds to wall construction. That decision was one of a number of immigration-related orders released by the president during the year. He also set limits on who could apply for a green card or asylum and sought to change regulations on how long a migrant minor can be held in detention. All of the president's immigration orders were challenged in court.

In March, former Federal Bureau of Investigation (FBI) director Robert Mueller finished his nearly two-year-long review of possible coordination between the campaign of President Trump and the Russian government during the 2016 election. Mueller concluded that there was no collaboration between the campaign and the Russian government, though Russia had attempted to influence the U.S. presidential election. The report's release did not stop some Democrats from calling for ongoing investigations into the president's activities as well as his impeachment.

House Speaker Nancy Pelosi, D-Calif., resisted those calls until September 2019, when she announced the start of an impeachment inquiry. Her decision was based on a whistle-blower complaint about a July phone call alleging that the president attempted to withhold aid to Ukraine until the president of that country announced an investigation into former vice president Joe Biden. The House conducted weeks of public and closed-door hearings related to the president's conduct with regards to Ukraine. Ultimately, on December 18, the House voted to impeach the president. The Senate took up the two articles of impeachment in February 2020 but voted not to remove the president from office.

In the states, abortion prohibitions and the ongoing opioid crisis characterized the year. A dozen states passed strict abortion legislation, primarily banning abortion after the detection of a fetal heartbeat. Alabama went beyond that, banning all abortion in the state unless a mother's life was in danger or the fetus had a fatal abnormality. Some of the states enacting new abortion bans admitted that their legislation contradicted *Roe v. Wade*, but their intent was to draw a lawsuit that would eventually result in the Supreme Court reconsidering abortion regulations. State and local governments were also grappling with the toll opioid abuse was taking on their populations and coffers. Oklahoma sued pharmaceutical manufacturers for their role in the opioid crisis, seeking to extract funds it could use to pay for services for opioid users and their families. Hundreds of local governments and individuals followed suit, and their cases against drug manufacturers, pharmaceutical companies, distributors, and doctors were consolidated into a nationwide litigation with new trials expected to begin in 2020.

Internationally, the United Kingdom's departure from the European Union (known as Brexit) continued to dominate headlines, as Prime Minister Theresa May repeatedly failed to push a Withdrawal Agreement through parliament. With support waning, May announced her resignation, paving the way for Boris Johnson, a pro-Brexit politician and former member of May's administration, to become prime minister. Johnson negotiated a revised agreement with the European Union that won parliament's approval, and the United Kingdom withdrew from the union in January 2020.

The year was also marked by major public protests in South America, Africa, and the Middle East. While many demonstrations were sparked by unpopular policy proposals, underlying economic concerns fueled the unrest, as did allegations of government corruption and attempts to cling to power. Peruvian president Martín Vizcarra dissolved Congress amid an unfolding corruption scandal. Congress suspended Vizcarra's presidency in response, setting up a political showdown while Peruvians rallied to support Vizcarra. In Chile, students protested a proposed subway fare increase, but the demonstrations soon became a broader call for greater income equality. President Sebastián Piñera reshuffled his cabinet, launched social reform efforts, and laid groundwork for a constitutional rewrite in response. Ecuadorian president Lenín Moreno's proposed austerity measures ignited public frustrations with the faltering economy. Demonstrations ended after an unprecedented televised negotiation between the president and protest leaders. Bolivian president Evo Morales was ousted after an audit of the country's general election had been manipulated in his favor. Many Bolivians took to the street to demand Morales's resignation, while others rallied to show support for the embattled leader.

In Africa, mass protests preceded changes in leadership in Algeria and Sudan. Algerian president Abdelaziz Bouteflika rescinded his candidacy for a fifth term, and new elections were called after thousands demanded his resignation and major reforms. Military leaders removed Sudanese president Omar al-Bashir from office following months of protest over austerity measures. After violent clashes and alleged human rights abuses, military officials and opposition leaders came together to form a joint military–civilian transitional council that would oversee the establishment of Sudan's first all-civilian government. A coup attempt occurred in a major region of Ethiopia, as well, and five government officials were assassinated in related attacks. Ethnic tensions flared and new protests broke out when an opponent of Prime Minister Abiy Ahmed claimed police tried to allow an attack against him, but Ahmed continued pushing his reform agenda.

Iran and Iraq both experienced periods of intense public disquiet in 2019. In November, Iranians protested increased fuel prices and other measures meant to offset the harsh economic impact of U.S. sanctions. Demands included an end to foreign meddling in Iraq's affairs. U.S. attacks on Iranian proxies in Iraq sparked further backlash, including a major breach of security at the U.S. embassy in Baghdad. Meanwhile, the United States withdrew from the Syrian conflict, allowing Turkey to invade Kurdish-held territory in Syria's northeast and Russia to expand its role as a regional powerbroker. Some analysts argued the move could also create opportunities for a resurgence of the Islamic State of Iraq and the Levant (ISIL), despite a successful U.S. raid that killed the group's leader.

Domestic Issues

President Declares a National Emergency

From December 22, 2018, through January 25, 2019, the federal government experienced its longest shutdown in history. For thirty-five days, Democrats and Republicans argued over how to address President Trump's request for $5.7 billion to build a portion of a wall along the U.S.–Mexico border. In the end, the two sides agreed to provide $1.375 billion for steel border fencing. The president signed the legislation to reopen the government but said he would seek alternate methods to fund the border wall. On February 15, 2019, the president declared a national emergency along the U.S.–Mexico border. That announcement allowed the president to circumvent Congress and redirect federal funds from other projects to the wall construction. The decision drew condemnation from both parties in Congress, and in March the body passed a bipartisan resolution revoking the national emergency. President Trump vetoed the legislation, and the House and Senate failed to overturn the veto.

The national emergency drew a number of lawsuits, including one from a coalition of sixteen states arguing that the president's declaration was in direct violation of the Constitution's separation of powers. While a U.S. District Court judge ruled in favor of the states, the U.S. Supreme Court picked up the case without an appeal from the administration and handed a victory to President Trump when it decided 5–4 that the states did not have standing to bring the case. That ruling allowed the president to move ahead with the diversion of billions of dollars from other projects, primarily funds initially allocated to military construction, to the border wall.

Trump Administration Releases Immigration Orders

The national emergency was one of a series of actions by the Trump administration in 2019 to crack down on immigration. In July, the president announced a change to U.S. immigration law that would limit which immigrants along the southern U.S. border would be permitted to apply for asylum. Any migrant who reached the United States after crossing through Mexico or another country who had not applied for and been denied asylum in one of those countries would not be permitted to apply in the United States. The change was challenged by the American Civil Liberties Union, Southern Poverty Law Center, and Center for Constitutional Rights. A federal court granted an injunction, arguing that the administration's decision did not align with existing federal law and that the public was not provided the requisite time for comment before implementation. The Trump administration appealed to the Supreme Court, which lifted the injunction while the case made its way through the courts.

In August, the Trump administration announced its intent to replace the *Flores* settlement. *Flores* sets standards of care for migrant minors in detention and states that they cannot be held for more than twenty days. The new regulations sought by the Trump administration would eliminate the twenty-day cap and remove a requirement that migrant minors can only be held in state-licensed facilities, instead replacing that with federal licensing guidelines. The decision was quickly challenged in court, and in September, a federal judge ruled that the original *Flores* settlement and its requirements for the detention of minors could only be repealed by an act of Congress.

The Trump administration also unveiled changes to the public charge policy, a long-standing rule that allows the United States to deny a green card to anyone who would primarily be dependent on federal social programs to survive. Under the original rule, immigration officials were prohibited from considering health, nutrition, or housing programs as part of their green card determination. The changes sought by the administration broadened what could be considered to include those three categories, along with other new factors regarding age, income, and health. These changes were disputed in court; ultimately, the Supreme Court allowed the changes to go into effect while appeals were ongoing.

Russia Inquiry Concludes

In May 2017, the Justice Department launched an investigation into possible coordination between the Trump campaign and Russian government. The investigation was led by former FBI director Mueller. For nearly two years, Mueller's team sifted through thousands of documents, conducted hundreds of interviews, and issued indictments against thirty-four people and three businesses, including members of the Trump presidential campaign and White House advisers.

On March 22, 2019, Mueller submitted his report to the Justice Department. The final, redacted report was made public on April 18. It was divided into two volumes; the first addressed possible coordination between the Trump campaign and Russian government during the 2016 election, and the second looked at whether President Trump had attempted to obstruct Mueller's work. Mueller's team concluded that the Russian government tried to influence the U.S. presidential election. However, Mueller's team did not find any coordination with the Trump campaign. Mueller further concluded that there was not enough evidence to determine whether President Trump attempted to obstruct justice and interfere with the work being done by the Mueller team.

The lack of clarity on obstruction led Attorney General William Barr to declare in a letter to Congress that he and his deputy, Rod Rosenstein, determined that there was no evidence supporting the conclusion that the president should be charged with obstruction. Mueller took issue with that in both a letter to Barr and during his testimony before Congress. Mueller said his team had not decided one way or the other on obstruction because there were too many issues complicating charging a sitting president with obstruction.

Health Concerns Impact Communities Nationwide

From late 2018 through fall 2019, a measles outbreak swept across the United States. The Centers for Disease Control and Prevention (CDC) confirmed more than 1,200 individual cases, the biggest outbreak in twenty-five years. The outbreak resulted in action at the state and local level to encourage more individuals to be vaccinated against deadly diseases like measles. In California, a law banning religious and personal exemptions to vaccines was expanded to stop doctors from issuing unnecessary medical exemptions to families. A new law in Washington State banned philosophical and personal exemptions to the measles, mumps, and rubella (MMR) vaccine for all children attending public and private schools or daycares. In Maine, which has one of the highest vaccine opt-out rates, the governor signed a bill into law removing personal and religious exemptions for all vaccines required for children to attend school. That law faced a referendum in March 2020 but was ultimately upheld by voters. In nearby New York, the governor signed into law a bill removing the religious belief exemption for vaccines for all children in public schools.

By mid-2019, two other public health crises were gaining widespread attention: e-cigarette use and opioid abuse. According to the CDC, a growing number of young people were arriving at emergency rooms with severe respiratory distress brought on by the use of e-cigarette products. Federal officials struggled throughout the year to pinpoint what ingredient in e-cigarettes was causing users to develop lung disease. As they investigated, the president announced his support for a ban on flavored e-cigarette products, which tend to appeal to younger customers. The president, along with the Food and Drug Administration, thought such a ban could help reduce the high number of middle and high school students using e-cigarettes. Some public health experts expressed concern with the ban, cautioning that it could drive more teens to replace e-cigarettes with traditional tobacco. E-cigarette sellers and users also launched a campaign to encourage the president to reconsider. It was not until early January 2020 when the administration finalized a ban on most e-cigarette flavors.

Opioid abuse also made headlines when the state of Oklahoma launched one of the first federal cases seeking to hold pharmaceutical companies responsible for their role in the opioid crisis. A number of named defendants in the case settled out of court, but Johnson & Johnson opted to go to trial. The state alleged that the company used deceptive marketing techniques to encourage doctors to overprescribe opioid medications to patients while downplaying the risks. Johnson & Johnson denied that it had any role in the crisis, noting that its opioids made up only a small percentage of those prescribed in the state and that those prescriptions are highly regulated. The judge agreed with the state, ruling that Johnson & Johnson had perpetuated a "public nuisance" that contributed to Oklahoma's opioid crisis. The judge ordered the company to pay a $465 million fine, which Johnson & Johnson appealed.

The Oklahoma trial was followed by the start of a nationwide consolidated case brought by more than 2,000 local governments against pharmaceutical companies, physicians, and distributors. Pretrial motions in National Prescription Opiate Litigation would be heard in the federal court for the Northern District of Ohio before being returned to their original courts for the full trial to be carried out. The first cases, brought by Summit and Cuyahoga Counties in Ohio, were supposed to be heard in October 2019, but the defendants reached a last-minute settlement. New trials are expected to be scheduled in 2020.

States Enact New Abortion Measures

In 2019, a dozen states passed new laws limiting a woman's ability to access an abortion. Most of these were so-called heartbeat bills that prohibit a doctor from performing the procedure after a fetal heartbeat is detected, often as early as six weeks into a pregnancy. Many of these laws included an exception for cases when the mother is in danger of death or severe physical impairment but did not permit abortion for instances of rape or incest. Physicians who performed an abortion after detecting a heartbeat could be penalized with loss of licensure, fines, and jail time. Most heartbeat bills were challenged in court.

Missouri initially considered heartbeat language but ultimately passed a bill structured to avoid legal challenges by building in a tiered abortion ban. At the start, the bill prohibited abortion after eight weeks, except to prevent physical impairment or death of the mother. If that was blocked by a court, the law then moved to a fourteen-week ban. If that was challenged, an eighteen-week ban would go into effect, followed by a twenty-week ban. A judge blocked nearly all of the law, except for a provision banning abortion based on fetal race, sex, or Down syndrome diagnosis. The state appealed the decision.

Alabama passed, and the governor signed, the nation's strictest abortion legislation, banning virtually all abortions at any point in a pregnancy unless the woman's life was in danger or the fetus had a fatal abnormality. Alabama's governor admitted that the law was likely incongruent with *Roe v. Wade*, a Supreme Court decision from the 1970s that allowed women to terminate a pregnancy for any reason until a fetus could survive outside the womb. The state's intent was to draw a challenge that would eventually force the now conservative-majority Supreme Court to reconsider *Roe*. Alabama's law was quickly challenged in court, and a preliminary injunction blocking it from taking effect was issued. The state promised to appeal.

In October, the Supreme Court announced its intent to hear an abortion case brought against a 2014 Louisiana law that requires abortion doctors to have admitting procedures at a nearby hospital. Supporters of the law said it ensured protection for the mother, while opponents argued that the licensing restrictions were an attempt to outlaw abortion in the state. Arguments in the case were heard in March 2020.

House Votes to Impeach President Trump

In August 2019, a whistleblower filed a complaint against President Trump alleging that during a July phone call, the president attempted to withhold aid from Ukraine until the country announced an investigation into a political rival, former vice president Joe Biden, who at the time was campaigning to be the 2020 Democratic presidential nominee. This prompted Speaker Pelosi to launch an impeachment inquiry in September into the president's conduct. On October 31, a vote in the House formalized the inquiry and set rules for the work that would be carried out by the House Judiciary and Intelligence Committees. The president frequently lashed out against Democrats in the House, criticizing the inquiry as a "witch hunt" and "hoax."

The Intelligence Committee began the formal impeachment proceedings with public and closed-door testimony over the course of two weeks, hearing from current and former federal officials about the president's dealings with Ukraine. Once its hearings were complete, the Intelligence Committee sent a report to the House Judiciary Committee, where additional public hearings began on December 3. That committee heard from law professors about whether the president's alleged conduct amounted to an impeachable offense. They also heard testimony from Democratic and Republican counsel on the Intelligence and Judiciary Committees to discuss the findings from the Intelligence Committee report.

Based on the work being done by the committees, on December 5, Pelosi called on the Judiciary Committee to draft formal articles of impeachment against President Trump. The Democrats drafted two articles, one on abuse of power and the other on obstruction of Congress. The Judiciary Committee passed the two articles to the full House on December 13.

On December 18, 2019, after six hours of debate, the House voted 230–197–1 on the first article and 229–198–1 on the second. The vote to impeach the president was almost entirely along party lines. President Trump was the third sitting president to be impeached. Democrats in the House waited until January 15, 2020, to vote to send the articles of impeachment to the Senate. There, the Senate would hear arguments from the House impeachment managers as well as the president's defense team before making a decision about whether the president should be removed from office. A two-thirds majority was needed to remove the president. The Senate heard forty-eight hours of testimony and participated in a day of question-and-answer before voting 52–48 to reject the first article and 53–47 to reject the second article. Again, the vote was almost entirely along party lines.

SUPREME COURT DECISIONS

The U.S. Supreme Court issued rulings in several noteworthy cases during its 2018–2019 term, including the highly anticipated *Department of Commerce v. New York*. This case involved the Trump administration's effort to reinstate a citizenship question on the 2020 Census questionnaire. Commerce secretary Wilbur Ross claimed the addition had been requested by the Department of Justice and that the question would support enforcement of the Voting Rights Act and protections for minority voters. However, it was later revealed that Ross had pushed Department of Justice officials to request the citizenship question. The Court ruled on June 27 that the administration had provided insufficient rationale for adding the question and sent the case back to the district court. The administration took no further action and a citizenship question was not included in the 2020 Census.

The same day as the Census verdict, the Court issued a major decision in the case of *Rucho v. Common Cause*. The Court ruled that oversight of partisan gerrymandering of congressional districts fell outside the jurisdiction of federal courts and that any issues surrounding the makeup of those districts should be resolved by the states or federal lawmakers. The case centered on voters' legal challenges to congressional districting maps in North Carolina and Maryland, where lower courts ruled that the maps unconstitutionally advantaged one political party. While the Court has ruled on racial gerrymandering and said it could not condone "excessive" partisan gerrymandering, its opinion in this case effectively rejected future review of partisan gerrymandering cases and opened the door for state legislatures to redraw politically favorable districts following the 2020 Census.

Another noteworthy decision came on November 12, in *Remington Arms v. Soto*. Gun manufacturer Remington Arms Co. asked the Court to review a decision by a state court that would allow the families of victims in the Sandy Hook Elementary School shooting to sue the company, which makes one of the guns used in the tragedy. The families alleged that Remington's marketing of the gun violated Connecticut's unfair trade practices law by specifically targeting disturbed young men and promoting the gun's use against other people in nonmilitary contexts. Remington claimed the suit went against a law that protects gun manufacturers and sellers from prosecution when their products are used to commit crimes. In its ruling, the Court denied Remington's request for review, meaning the families could pursue their lawsuit against the company.

FOREIGN AFFAIRS

Brexit Finalized

A January vote on the Withdrawal Agreement outlining the terms of the United Kingdom's split from the European Union (EU) was the first of three failures by Prime Minister May to secure parliament's approval of the deal. A provision called the "backstop" was particularly controversial because some lawmakers believed it would give the European Union a mechanism to keep the United Kingdom in the union indefinitely. The backstop gave the European Union and United Kingdom two years to negotiate a free trade deal that would avoid a hard border between Northern Ireland (part of the United Kingdom) and Ireland (an EU member). If a deal was not reached by the deadline, the United Kingdom would temporarily remain in the EU customs union until an agreement was concluded.

Although May succeeded in obtaining a binding commitment from the European Union that the backstop would be temporary, it was not enough to reassure lawmakers. A second and third vote on the Withdrawal Agreement failed by significant margins. Meanwhile, May twice requested extensions of the original withdrawal deadline—March 29, 2019—from the European Union to allow more time for internal talks and avoid a "hard Brexit," or a withdrawal without a deal. The European Union agreed to both extension requests, setting a new deadline of October 31, 2019. The prime minister sought another vote on a revised Brexit plan in late May but withdrew it from consideration following intense backlash over her proposal that members of parliament vote on holding a second referendum. Unable to deliver Brexit, May resigned.

The Conservative Party chose former foreign secretary and prominent pro-Brexit campaigner Johnson as its new leader, and thus the United Kingdom's new prime minister. Johnson pledged to seek a better Withdrawal Agreement with the European Union while declaring the United Kingdom would leave the bloc by October 31 with or without a deal. Johnson pressed the European Union to consider "alternative arrangements" to the backstop and successfully negotiated a new Withdrawal Agreement that allowed Northern Ireland to remain in the UK's customs territory while abiding by select EU trading rules and regulations. The deal was announced on October 17, but lawmakers delayed consideration of the agreement until related implementation legislation could also be passed. Johnson was forced by parliament to request another deadline extension from the European Union, getting a reprieve until January 31, 2020. With a new deal and an extension secured, the opposition Labour Party agreed to support Johnson's call for snap elections. A poll was conducted in mid-December and resulted in a decisive victory for the Conservatives at Labour's expense. Johnson's Brexit deal was approved by both chambers of parliament on January 22, 2020, and the United Kingdom formally withdrew from the European Union on January 31.

South Americans Protest Corruption, Faltering Economies

Hundreds of thousands of South Americans took to the streets in 2019 to protest against government corruption and policy proposals that were expected to have a disproportionate impact on low-income families. In Peru, President Vizcarra dissolved Congress, claiming the action was necessary to overcome lawmakers' staunch resistance to his proposed anticorruption measures and calling of fresh elections. Dozens of sitting members of Congress had been implicated in a widespread corruption scandal involving a Brazil-based construction company that paid bribes and made illegal campaign contributions in exchange for public construction contracts. Opposition lawmakers retaliated by voting to suspend Vizcarra's presidency and nominating Vice President Mercedes Aráoz as acting president, prompting public demonstrations in support of Vizcarra. Peru's Constitutional Tribunal subsequently affirmed that Vizcarra's dissolution of Congress was legal, allowing legislative elections to be held in January 2020.

In Chile, Ecuador, and Bolivia, public frustrations with faltering economies also fueled unrest. Students in Chile were the driving force behind mass protests against the government's increase of subway fares for the Santiago metro system. Many Chileans viewed the price increase as yet another example of the country's systemic inequality, and protesters' demands expanded from a reversal of the fare hike to include a higher minimum wage, changes to the pension system, and a new constitution. While most protests were peaceful, violence broke out in the city as subway stations were set on fire and public and private buildings were vandalized. After weeks of protests, President Piñera dismissed his cabinet, announced a program of new social reforms, and worked with lawmakers to organize a constitutional referendum that would be held in April 2020.

Similarly, major protests were sparked by Ecuadorian president Moreno's announcement that government-funded fuel subsidies would end. The policy change was one of several austerity measures Moreno's government sought to implement in order to receive more than $4 billion in International Monetary Fund loans to shore up the economy. Indigenous groups, long a force for change in Ecuador, became the primary organizers of nationwide protests that led Moreno to declare a state of emergency and relocate the capital due to security concerns. Protest-related violence and riots killed at least nine people and injured more than 1,500 others. Facing pressure at home and from the United Nations, Moreno met with indigenous leaders during a televised negotiation that concluded with an agreement to restore fuel subsidies.

Economic troubles were also a factor in Bolivian president Morales's significant loss of public support in 2019, as were his continued efforts to consolidate political power. After eliminating presidential term limits, Morales announced his intent to run for a fourth term in the 2019 general election. Bolivia's Supreme Electoral Tribunal began publishing vote counts after polls closed the evening of October 20 but suddenly stopped releasing updates for almost twenty-four hours. Before the pause in results, Morales did not have enough votes to win a first-round vote outright; once vote counts resumed, Morales was projected to win by a narrow margin. Allegations of vote tampering triggered mass protests and led to an election audit by the Organization of American States (OAS). The OAS team found significant irregularities in the electoral processes and vote tallies, concluding that results had been manipulated. Morales and many other high-ranking government officials subsequently resigned.

Political Change Takes Shape in Africa

Changes in leadership also took place in Algeria and Sudan following periods of intense public unrest. Like Morales, Algerian president Bouteflika announced his intention to run for another term—his fifth—in the April 2019 election. The protests prompted by his announcement were reportedly among the largest public demonstrations in Algeria's history. Protesters opposed Bouteflika's candidacy—blaming him for Algeria's flagging economy and citing past allegations of election rigging—but also called for major political and constitutional reforms, as well as an end to the military's influence over government. The president's eventual resignation failed to quell unrest, and the country struggled to organize new elections. Many Algerians rejected the December vote, which featured only candidates with connections to Bouteflika, and the official results.

A military coup removed Sudanese president al-Bashir from office following months of protests against emergency austerity measures implemented by the government in 2018 to stem an economic crisis. These protests later evolved to call for al-Bashir's resignation and a new, civilian-led government. Military leaders established the Transitional Military Council (TMC) after the coup to oversee a two-year transition to a full civilian government. Talks between the TMC and protest movement leaders collapsed shortly before paramilitary forces led a deadly raid on a peaceful sit-in—an incident that drew global condemnation and increased pressure on the TMC. Fresh talks mediated by the African Union and Ethiopia resulted in an agreement to form a joint civilian–military transitional government that would work toward an all-civilian government within a roughly three-year period.

Ethiopian prime minister Ahmed, in office for less than a year, continued to push an ambitious agenda of political reforms in 2019, despite flares in ethnic violence and an attempted overthrow of a regional government that resulted in the deaths of three officials. Two other senior officials close to Ahmed were murdered in the capital. The prime minister also faced fresh protests in several cities following claims by a prominent opponent that the police had tried to facilitate an attack against him. Meanwhile, Ahmed moved forward with dismantling the political coalition that had ruled Ethiopia for more than twenty-five years, replacing it with a single political party intended to represent all Ethiopians.

Tensions Flare across the Middle East

The Middle East remained a volatile region throughout 2019 amid shifting U.S. foreign policy and ongoing proxy conflicts. President Trump surprised U.S. and foreign leaders by announcing in October 2019 that the United States would withdraw all military personnel from Syria. The U.S. troop presence had been reduced earlier in the year after Trump declared that ISIL had been defeated, but about 1,000 soldiers remained in Syria. Critics of the withdrawal argued it would leave the United States' Kurdish partners vulnerable to attacks by the Turkish government, which views its own Kurdish minority as disloyal and had declared its intent to invade northeastern Syria to create a buffer zone between the two countries. A temporary cease-fire ultimately allowed some Kurds to retreat from the territory. The U.S. draw down allowed the government of Syrian president Bashar al-Assad to regain control over some territories while also expanding Russia's power in the region and potentially benefiting Iran. Meanwhile, the United States relied on intelligence information provided by the Kurds to execute a military raid that killed Abu Bakr al-Baghdadi, the head of ISIL, on October 27.

U.S. troops that had been in Syria were temporarily redeployed to Iraq, without the government's permission, at a time when Iraq was swept up in violent protests against corruption, a weak economy, and foreign interference in Iraqi affairs—unrest that eventually pushed Prime Minister Adel Abdul Mahdi out of office. While initially focused on Iran's efforts to exert influence in the region, public hostility toward foreign involvement shifted to target the United States after the military conducted retaliatory airstrikes against Iranian proxies in Iraq. Thousands of protesters breached the outer walls of the U.S. embassy in Baghdad and set fires in the compound. U.S. officials responded by beefing up security measures to protect American personnel while blaming Iran for inciting conflict and orchestrating the embassy attack.

The United States and its allies also blamed Iran for attacks against four oil tankers off the coast of the United Arab Emirates (UAE) in May. These incidents contributed to UAE officials' decision to withdraw troops from Yemen, where they were supporting the fight against Iranian-backed Houthi rebels, amid growing concerns about Iranian retaliation. Iran was accused of launching attacks against Saudi Arabian oil facilities in September as well, even though the Houthis claimed responsibility. At the same time, Iran was facing new U.S. sanctions for violating the terms of the Joint Comprehensive Plan of Action—an agreement that remained in effect despite the United States' withdrawal. These sanctions and others have had a significant impact on the Iranian economy, contributing to the government's decision in November 2019 to raise fuel prices and introduce petrol rationing. These measures were necessary, officials said, to help generate funds that could support the poorest Iranians. The announcement triggered an intense period of unrest that was met by a brutal government crackdown on protesters.

—Linda Grimm and Heather Kerrigan

January

President Trump and Congressional Leaders Remark on Border Wall Funding Fight and Government Shutdown

JANUARY 8, 14, 20, AND 25, 2019

The longest federal government shutdown in history stretched from December 22, 2018, to January 25, 2019, costing the federal government billions of dollars, hampering projected economic growth, and leaving federal workers without a paycheck. The thirty-five-day lapse in funding began because of a disagreement between Democrats and Republicans over President Donald Trump's request for $5.7 billion to fund a wall along the U.S.–Mexico border (according to the Office of Management and Budget, those funds would build approximately 234 miles of new steel barrier). Democrats refused to include any funding for the wall in the temporary measure that reopened the government in January, and the final fiscal 2019 spending bill included only $1.375 billion for steel border fencing, leaving the president to seek other methods—including the declaration of a national emergency related to immigration—to obtain funding for his key campaign promise.

BORDER WALL DEFINES EARLY NEGOTIATIONS

During his campaign for president, Trump promised to build a wall along the U.S.–Mexico border to deter illegal immigration and stop what he saw as an unfettered flow of criminals and drugs into the United States. Initially, Trump promised that he would force Mexico to pay for the wall, an idea the Mexican government refused to entertain. After taking office, Trump began requesting funding through the normal congressional appropriations process to build the wall. The actual structure went through various iterations, including the president's preferred concrete wall to steel slats or bollards.

After the government shut down at midnight on December 22, 2018, Trump refused to sign any funding bill that did not include some form of funding for his wall. Democrats, who won a majority of House seats in the November 2018 election, would not budge from their position that funding would be better spent on high-tech surveillance and other means to detect and deter border crossers than on a wall.

On January 8, 2019, Trump—and subsequently House Speaker Nancy Pelosi, D-Calif., and Senate minority leader Chuck Schumer, D-N.Y.—addressed the nation on the border issue. In his address, the president spoke of the "growing humanitarian and security crisis at our southern border." The border wall was critical to addressing a number of issues, the president said, including the thousands of illegal immigrants and vast amounts of deadly drugs coming into the United States each day. Uncontrolled illegal immigration "strains public resources and drives down jobs and wages," Trump stated. The president said that his administration had provided to Congress a multipronged proposal to secure the border that included new technology, additional border agents and immigration judges, more detention center beds, closing border security loopholes, and $5.7 billion in funding for a border wall. "The border wall would very quickly pay for itself," the president said, with a price tag far lower than the estimated $500 billion annual cost of illegal drugs. And, he added, "the wall will also be paid for, indirectly, by the great new trade deal we have made with Mexico." The president accused Democrats of failing to recognize the crisis along the border, and he suggested they had previously advocated for a border wall prior to his taking office. "The Federal Government remains shut down for one reason and one reason only: because Democrats will not fund border security," which the president said "could be solved in a 45-minute meeting."

In the joint Democratic address, Pelosi accused the president of holding hostage "critical services for the health, safety, and well-being of the American people" for border wall funding. Schumer agreed: "The President of the United States—having failed to get Mexico to pay for his ineffective, unnecessary border wall, and unable to convince the Congress or the American people to foot the bill—has shut down the government." Both Pelosi and Schumer noted a shared opinion among Democrats and Republicans that something needs to be done about illegal immigration, but that a wall was not the best way. "There is an obvious solution," Schumer said. "Separate the shutdown from the arguments over border security." Schumer and Pelosi expressed a preference for additional personnel and surveillance equipment to secure the border. "We can secure our borders without an expensive, ineffective wall. And we can welcome legal immigrants and refugees without compromising safety and security," Schumer said, adding, "The symbol of America should be the Statue of Liberty, not a thirty-foot wall."

PARTIES REACH AGREEMENT ON STOPGAP MEASURE, PASS FULL BUDGET

The shutdown was unique not only in its length, but also in that it spanned two sessions of Congress with differing party control. When negotiations began on the fiscal 2019 budget, Republicans controlled both the House and Senate, but when the 116th Congress was seated, Democrats held the majority in the House.

On assuming the Speakership, Pelosi made clear that her first priority was to reopen the government. On January 3, 2019, the day the new Congress was seated, bills were placed on the floor for consideration. One would fund the Department of Homeland Security (DHS) through February 8, while another set of measures funded the remaining federal agencies for the rest of fiscal 2019. These bills contained no funding for the border wall. Despite passing the House on a party-line vote, the bills were not considered in the Republican-controlled Senate.

The Senate failed to pass two of its own bills on January 24. One measure, backed by President Trump, would provide the requested $5.7 billion in funding for the border wall in exchange for more protection for undocumented immigrants, specifically those covered under the Obama-era Deferred Action for Childhood Arrivals (DACA) program. That bill failed, 50–47. A second bill, backed by Democrats, would reopen the government without any funding for the border wall and without any other protections for or restrictions on immigrants. That bill failed, 52–44. Some Republicans in the Senate voiced concern that they had lost their bargaining position. According to those familiar with a closed-door Republican luncheon, Sen. Johnny Isakson, R-Ga., noted the party had "already lost" and it was now "a matter of the extent we want to keep losing."

Conference Committee Debates Detention Beds

On January 25, the House and Senate temporarily broke the impasse and agreed to a three-week continuing resolution that would reopen the government but provide no money for the border wall. Trump signed the bill only after securing promises from congressional leaders that they would work over the next few weeks to negotiate money for the wall in the final fiscal 2019 funding bill. "If we don't get a fair deal from Congress, the government will either shut down on February 15, or I will use the powers afforded to me under the laws and Constitution of the United States to address this emergency," the president said in a Rose Garden ceremony on January 25.

Democrats and Republicans chose seventeen members for the conference committee that would negotiate the bill. Talks revolved not only around funding for the wall but also detention beds. In a January letter to Congress, the White House had asked for funding for an additional 52,000 detention beds; Democrats sought to cap the number at 16,500. According to Rep. Lucille Roybal-Allard, D-Calif., a member of the joint conference committee, the cap proposed by Democrats was meant to ensure Trump administration deportation policies targeted "violent felons and other people who pose security risks for deportation, instead of pursuing reckless mass deportation policies that actually make us less safe." Republicans hit back, asserting that the Democrats sought to let an uncontrolled number of illegal immigrants enter and remain in the United States. "The Democrats do not want us to detain, or send back, criminal aliens! This is a brand new demand. Crazy!" the president tweeted on February 11, 2019.

On February 11, the conference committee announced it had reached "an agreement in principle" on a fiscal 2019 funding package that included $1.375 billion for fifty-five miles of steel border fencing. In a reversal, Democrats dropped their demands to significantly reduce the number of Immigration and Customs Enforcement (ICE) beds. Instead, funding was set at a level that would encourage ICE to reduce the number of those in detention facilities to 40,520 by the end of 2019 and curb the vastly expanding detention program pursued by the Trump administration. At the time the conference committee released its draft bill, ICE was holding more than 50,000 detainees per day.

The measure overwhelmingly passed both the House and Senate on February 14. The White House announced the president would sign the bill, but that he would subsequently take executive action to secure border wall funding, which Schumer and Pelosi called "a lawless act, a gross abuse of the power of the presidency." On February 15, 2019, the same day he signed the budget bill, the president declared a national emergency along the U.S.–Mexico border in an attempt to secure the funds necessary for the wall. That proclamation quickly drew condemnation and a spate of lawsuits.

Impact of the Shutdown

An estimated 800,000 federal workers felt the impact of the five-week shutdown. More than half of them were expected to report to work without pay, including those deemed critical for national health and safety, such as border patrol agents, federal prison guards, and Transportation Security Administration (TSA) agents. These workers were guaranteed back pay under an earlier bill, but many faced financial hardship in the immediate term.

The Coast Guard, which is structured under DHS and not the Department of Defense (the latter was funded prior to the shutdown), was unable to pay its service members. Coast Guard commandant Adm. Karl Schultz called it "unacceptable that USCG members must rely on food pantries and donations to get through day-to-day life" during the shutdown. Coast Guard civilian employees received a tip sheet on weathering the shutdown, which included holding a garage sale or finding ways to monetize hobbies.

Some federal workers who were forced to remain on the job called in sick, including air traffic controllers who called off in such a significant number that they slowed air travel. The president of the Association of Flight Attendants called for a strike in support of furloughed federal workers and joined a statement by the National Air Traffic Controllers Association and Air Line Pilots Association noting, "We cannot even calculate the level of risk currently at play, nor predict the point at which the entire system will break."

Outside of the federal government, Americans felt the impact of the shutdown. The National Parks Service was forced to close many of its locations or significantly cut back on staff, resulting in cancelled vacations and weddings and vandalism at some locations. Those who rely on federal assistance like housing subsidies and the Supplemental Nutrition Assistance Program (SNAP) worried they would not continue to receive these vital benefits.

Standard and Poor's estimated the shutdown cost the federal government at least $6 billion. The Congressional Budget Office (CBO) reported gross domestic product growth would be 0.2 percentage points lower for the fourth quarter of 2018 and 0.4 percentage points lower for the first quarter of 2019 due to the shutdown. The CBO also estimated the impact on the private sector could be "significant" due to factors like reduced access to loans and delayed federal permits. Larry Kudlow, director of the White House National Economic Council, sought to downplay the CBO's report, noting there was "certainly no permanent damage to the economy."

—Heather Kerrigan

Following is a statement by President Donald Trump on January 8, 2019, on the crisis at the U.S.–Mexico border and federal government shutdown; a January 8, 2019, statement by Sen. Chuck Schumer, D-N.Y., and Rep. Nancy Pelosi, D-Calif., on the federal shutdown and the president's call for border wall funding; a January 14, 2019, tweet from Trump calling on Democrats to end the shutdown; a January 20, 2019, tweet from Pelosi asking Trump to put federal employees back to work; and a January 25, 2019, statement by Trump announcing a deal to temporarily reopen the federal government.

President Trump Addresses the Nation on Immigration and Government Shutdown

DOCUMENT

January 8, 2019

My fellow Americans, tonight I am speaking to you because there is a growing humanitarian and security crisis at our southern border.

Every day, Customs and Border Patrol agents encounter thousands of illegal immigrants trying to enter our country. We are out of space to hold them, and we have no way to promptly return them back home to their country.

America proudly welcomes millions of lawful immigrants who enrich our society and contribute to our Nation. But all Americans are hurt by uncontrolled, illegal migration. It strains public resources and drives down jobs and wages. Among those hardest hit are African Americans and Hispanic Americans.

Our southern border is a pipeline for vast quantities of illegal drugs, including meth, heroin, cocaine, and fentanyl. Every week, 300 of our citizens are killed by heroin alone, 90 percent of which floods across from our southern border. More Americans will die from drugs this year than were killed in the entire Vietnam War.

In the last 2 years, ICE officers made 266,000 arrests of aliens with criminal records, including those charged or convicted of 100,000 assaults, 30,000 sex crimes, and 4,000 violent killings. Over the years, thousands of Americans have been brutally killed by those who illegally entered our country, and thousands more lives will be lost if we don't act right now.

This is a humanitarian crisis, a crisis of the heart and a crisis of the soul. Last month, 20,000 migrant children were illegally brought into the United States, a dramatic increase. These children are used as human pawns by vicious coyotes and ruthless gangs. One in three women are sexually assaulted on the dangerous trek up through Mexico. Women are—children are the biggest victims, by far, of our broken system. This is the tragic reality of illegal immigration on our southern border. This is the cycle of human suffering that I am determined to end.

My administration has presented Congress with a detailed proposal to secure the border and stop the criminal gangs, drug smugglers, and human traffickers. It's a tremendous problem. Our proposal was developed by law enforcement professionals and border agents at the Department of Homeland Security. These are the resources they have requested to properly perform their mission and keep America safe, in fact, safer than ever before.

The proposal from Homeland Security includes cutting-edge technology for detecting drugs, weapons, illegal contraband, and many other things. We have requested more agents, immigration judges, and bed space to process the sharp rise in unlawful migration fueled by our very strong economy. Our plan also contains an urgent request for humanitarian assistance and medical support.

Furthermore, we have asked Congress to close border security loopholes so that illegal immigrant children can be safely and humanely returned back home.

Finally, as part of an overall approach to border security, law enforcement professionals have requested $5.7 billion for a physical barrier. At the request of Democrats, it will be a steel barrier rather than a concrete wall. This barrier is absolutely critical to border security. It's also what our professionals at the border want and need. This is just common sense.

The border wall would very quickly pay for itself. The cost of illegal drugs exceeds $500 billion a year, vastly more than the $5.7 billion we have requested from Congress. The wall will also be paid for, indirectly, by the great new trade deal we have made with Mexico.

Senator Chuck Schumer—who you will be hearing from later tonight—has repeatedly supported a physical barrier in the past, along with many other Democrats. They changed their mind only after I was elected President.

Democrats in Congress have refused to acknowledge the crisis. And they have refused to provide our brave border agents with the tools they desperately need to protect our families and our Nation. The Federal Government remains shut down for one reason and one reason only: because Democrats will not fund border security.

My administration is doing everything in our power to help those impacted by the situation. But the only solution is for Democrats to pass a spending bill that defends our borders and reopens the Government. This situation could be solved in a 45-minute meeting. I have invited congressional leadership to the White House tomorrow to get this done. Hopefully, we can rise above partisan politics in order to support national security.

Some have suggested a barrier is immoral. Then, why do wealthy politicians build walls, fences, and gates around their homes? They don't build walls because they hate the people on the outside, but because they love the people on the inside. The only thing that is immoral is the politicians to do nothing and continue to allow more innocent people to be so horribly victimized.

America's heart broke the day after Christmas when a young police officer in California was savagely murdered in cold blood by an illegal alien, who just came across the border. The life of an American hero was stolen by someone who had no right to be in our country.

Day after day, precious lives are cut short by those who have violated our borders. In California, an Air Force veteran was raped, murdered, and beaten to death with a hammer by an illegal alien with a long criminal history. In Georgia, an illegal alien was recently charged with murder for killing, beheading, and dismembering his neighbor. In Maryland, MS–13 gang members who arrived in the United States as unaccompanied minors were arrested and charged last year after viciously stabbing and beating a 16-year-old girl.

Over the last several years, I've met with dozens of families whose loved ones were stolen by illegal immigration. I've held the hands of the weeping mothers and embraced the grief-stricken fathers. So sad. So terrible. I will never forget the pain in their eyes, the tremble in their voices, and the sadness gripping their souls.

How much more American blood must we shed before Congress does its job? To those who refuse to compromise in the name of border security, I would ask: Imagine if it was your child, your husband, or your wife whose life was so cruelly shattered and totally broken? To every Member of Congress, pass a bill that ends this crisis.

To every citizen: Call Congress and tell them to finally, after all of these decades, secure our border. This is a choice between right and wrong, justice and injustice. This is about whether we fulfill our sacred duty to the American citizens we serve. When I took the oath of office, I swore to protect our country. And that is what I will always do, so help me God. Thank you, and goodnight.

SOURCE: Executive Office of the President. "Address to the Nation on Border Security." January 8, 2019. *Compilation of Presidential Documents* 2019, no. 00009 (January 8, 2019). https://www.govinfo.gov/content/pkg/DCPD-201900009/pdf/DCPD-201900009.pdf.

Senator Schumer and Representative Pelosi Remark on Shutdown

January 8, 2019

PELOSI: Good evening. I appreciate the opportunity to speak directly to the American people tonight about how we can end this shutdown and meet the needs of the American people.

Sadly, much of what we have heard from President Trump throughout this senseless shutdown has been full of misinformation and even malice.

The President has chosen fear. We want to start with the facts.

The fact is: On the very first day of this Congress, House Democrats passed Senate Republican legislation to re-open government and fund smart, effective border security solutions.

But the President is rejecting these bipartisan bills which would re-open government—over his obsession with forcing American taxpayers to waste billions of dollars on an expensive and ineffective wall—a wall he always promised Mexico would pay for!

The fact is: President Trump has chosen to hold hostage critical services for the health, safety and well-being of the American people and withhold the paychecks of 800,000 innocent workers across the nation—many of them veterans.

He promised to keep government shutdown for "months or years"—no matter whom it hurts. That's just plain wrong.

The fact is: We all agree that we need to secure our borders, while honoring our values: we can build the infrastructure and roads at our ports of entry; we can install new technology to scan cars and trucks for drugs coming into our nation; we can hire the personnel we need to facilitate trade and immigration at the border; and we can fund more innovation to detect unauthorized crossings.

The fact is: the women and children at the border are not a security threat, they are a humanitarian challenge—a challenge that President Trump's own cruel and counterproductive policies have only deepened.

And the fact is: President Trump must stop holding the American people hostage, must stop manufacturing a crisis, and must re-open the government.

Thank you.

SCHUMER: Thank you, Speaker Pelosi.

My fellow Americans, we address you tonight for one reason only: the President of the United States—having failed to get Mexico to pay for his ineffective, unnecessary border wall, and unable to convince the Congress or the American people to foot the bill—has shut down the government.

American democracy doesn't work that way. We don't govern by temper tantrum. No president should pound the table and demand he gets his way or else the government shuts down, hurting millions of Americans who are treated as leverage.

Tonight—and throughout this debate and his presidency—President Trump has appealed to fear, not facts. Division, not unity.

Make no mistake: Democrats and the President both want stronger border security. However, we sharply disagree with the President about the most effective way to do it.

So, how do we untangle this mess?

There is an obvious solution: separate the shutdown from the arguments over border security. There is bipartisan legislation—supported by Democrats and Republicans—to re-open government while allowing debate over border security to continue.

There is no excuse for hurting millions of Americans over a policy difference. Federal workers are about to miss a paycheck. Some families can't get a mortgage to buy a new home. Farmers and small businesses won't get loans they desperately need.

Most presidents have used Oval Office addresses for noble purposes. This president just used the backdrop of the Oval Office to manufacture a crisis, stoke fear, and divert attention from the turmoil in his Administration.

My fellow Americans, there is no challenge so great that our nation cannot rise to meet it. We can re-open the government AND continue to work through disagreements about policy. We can secure our border without an expensive, ineffective wall. And we can welcome legal immigrants and refugees without compromising safety and security.

The symbol of America should be the Statue of Liberty, not a thirty-foot wall.

So our suggestion is a simple one: Mr. President: re-open the government and we can work to resolve our differences over border security. But end this shutdown now.

Thank you.

SOURCE: Office of Speaker of the House Nancy Pelosi. "Pelosi, Schumer Remarks Responding to Presidential Address on Trump Shutdown." Delivered January 8, 2019 (text released January 9, 2019). https://www.speaker.gov/newsroom/1819-2.

 ## President Trump Calls on Democrats to End Shutdown

January 14, 2019

Nancy and Cryin' Chuck can end the Shutdown in 15 minutes. At this point it has become their, and the Democrats, fault!

SOURCE: Donald Trump on Twitter (@realDonaldTrump). January 14, 2019. https://twitter.com/realDonaldTrump/status/1084788796011491330?s=20.

 ## Speaker Pelosi Asks President to Reopen the Government

January 20, 2019

@realDonaldTrump, 800,000 Americans are going without pay. Re-open the government, let workers get their paychecks and then we can discuss how we can come together to protect the border. #EndTheShutdown

SOURCE: Nancy Pelosi on Twitter (@SpeakerPelosi). January 20, 2019. https://twitter.com/SpeakerPelosi/status/1086994625615839232.

 ## President Trump Announces End of Shutdown

January 25, 2019

Thank you very much. My fellow Americans, I am very proud to announce today that we have reached a deal to end the shutdown and reopen the Federal Government. As everyone knows, I have a very powerful alternative, but I didn't want to use it at this time. Hopefully, it will be unnecessary.

I want to thank all of the incredible Federal workers and their amazing families, who have shown such extraordinary devotion in the face of this recent hardship. You are fantastic people. You are incredible patriots. Many of you have suffered far greater than anyone but your families would know or understand. And not only did you not complain, but in many cases you encouraged me to keep going, because you care so much about our country and about its border security.

Again, I thank you. All Americans, I thank you. You are very, very special people. I am so proud that you are citizens of our country. When I say "Make America Great Again," it could never be done without you. Great people.

In a short while, I will sign a bill to open our Government for 3 weeks until February 15. I will make sure that all employees receive their backpay very quickly or as soon as possible. It will happen fast. I am asking Senate Majority Leader Mitch McConnell to put this proposal on the floor immediately.

After 36 days of spirited debate and dialogue, I have seen and heard from enough Democrats and Republicans that they are willing to put partisanship aside—I think—and put the security of the American people first. I do believe they're going to do that. They have said they are for complete border security, and they have finally and fully acknowledged that having barriers, fencing, or walls—or whatever you want to call it—will be an important part of the solution.

A bipartisan conference committee of House and Senate lawmakers and leaders will immediately begin reviewing the requests of our Homeland Security experts—and experts they are—and also law enforcement professionals, who have worked with us so closely. We want to thank Border Patrol, ICE, and all law enforcement. Been incredible. Based on operational guidance from the experts in the field, they will put together a Homeland Security package for me to shortly sign into law.

Over the next 21 days, I expect that both Democrats and Republicans will operate in good faith. This is an opportunity for all parties to work together for the benefit of our whole beautiful, wonderful nation. If we make a fair deal, the American people will be proud of their Government for proving that we can put country before party. We can show all Americans, and people all around the world, that both political parties are united when it comes to protecting our country and protecting our people.

Many disagree, but I really feel that, working with Democrats and Republicans, we can make a truly great and secure deal happen for everyone.

Walls should not be controversial. Our country has built 654 miles of barrier over the last 15 years, and every career Border Patrol agent I have spoken with has told me that walls work. They do work. No matter where you go, they work. Israel built a wall—99.9 percent successful. Won't be any different for us.

They keep criminals out. They save good people from attempting a very dangerous journey from other countries—thousands of miles—because they think they have a glimmer of hope of coming through. With a wall, they don't have that hope. They keep drugs out, and they dramatically increase efficiency by allowing us to patrol far larger areas with far fewer people. It's just common sense. Walls work.

That's why most of the Democrats in Congress have voted in the past for bills that include walls and physical barriers and very powerful fences. The walls we are building are not medieval walls. They are smart walls designed to meet the needs of frontline border agents and are operationally effective. These barriers are made of steel, have see-through visibility, which is very important, and are equipped with sensors, monitors, and cutting-edge technology, including state-of-the-art drones.

We do not need 2,000 miles of concrete wall from sea to shining sea—we never did; we never proposed that; we never wanted that—because we have barriers at the border where natural structures are as good as anything that we can build. They're already there. They've been there for millions of years.

Our proposed structures will be in predetermined, high-risk locations that have been specifically identified by the Border Patrol to stop illicit flows of people and drugs. No border security plan can ever work without a physical barrier. Just doesn't happen.

At the same time, we need to increase drug detection technology and manpower to modernize our ports of entry, which are obsolete. The equipment is obsolete. They're old. They're tired. This is something we have all come to agree on and will allow for quicker and safer commerce. These critical investments will improve and facilitate legal trade and travel through our lawful ports of entry.

Our plan also includes desperately needed humanitarian assistance for those being exploited and abused by coyotes, smugglers, and the dangerous journey north.

The requests we have put before Congress are vital to ending the humanitarian and security crisis on our southern border, absolutely vital. It will not work without it.

This crisis threatens the safety of our country and thousands of American lives. Criminal cartels, narcoterrorists, transnational gangs like MS–13, and human traffickers are brazenly violating U.S. laws and terrorizing innocent communities.

Human traffickers—the victims are women and children. Maybe to a lesser extent, believe or not, children. Women are tied up. They're bound, duct tape put around their faces, around their mouths; in many cases, they can't even breathe. They're put in the backs of cars or vans or trucks. They don't go through your port of entry. They make a right turn going very quickly. They go into the desert areas or whatever areas you can look at. And as soon as there's no protection, they make a left or a right into the United States of America. There's nobody to catch them. There's nobody to find them.

They can't come through the port, because if they come through the port, people will see four women sitting in a van with tape around their face and around their mouth. We can't have that. And that problem, because of the internet, is the biggest problem—it's never been like this before—that you can imagine. It's at the worst level—human trafficking—in the history of the world. This is not a United States problem, this is a world problem. But they come through areas where they have no protection, where they have no steel barriers, where they have no walls. And we can stop almost a hundred percent of that.

The profits reaped by these murderous organizations are used to fund their malign and destabilizing conduct throughout this hemisphere.

Last year alone, ICE officers removed 10,000 known or suspected gang members, like MS–13 and members as bad as them: horrible people, tough, mean, sadistic. In the last two years, ICE officers arrested a total of 266,000 criminal aliens inside of the United States, including those charged or convicted of nearly 100,000 assaults, 30,000 sex crimes, and 4,000 homicides or, as you would call them, violent, vicious killings. It can be stopped.

Vast quantities of lethal drugs—including meth, fentanyl, heroin, and cocaine—are smuggled across our southern border and into U.S. schools and communities. Drugs kill much more than 70,000 Americans a year and cost our society in excess of $700 billion.

The sheer volume of illegal immigration has overwhelmed Federal authorities and stretched our immigration system beyond the breaking point. Nearly 50 migrants a day are being referred for medical assistance—they are very, very sick—making this a health crisis as well. It's a very big health crisis. People have no idea how big it is, unless you're there.

Our backlog in the immigration courts is now far greater than the 800,000 cases that you've been hearing about over the last couple of years. Think of that though: 800,000 cases, because our laws are obsolete. So obsolete. They're the laughing stock all over the world. Our immigration laws, all over the world—they've been there for a long time—are the laughing stock, all over the world.

We do not have the necessary space or resources to detain, house, vet, screen, and safely process this tremendous influx of people. In short, we do not have control over who is entering our country, where they come from, who they are, why they are coming.

The result, for many years, is a colossal danger to public safety. We're going to straighten it out. It's not hard. It's easy, if given the resources.

Last month was the third straight month in a row with 60,000 apprehensions on our southern border. Think of that: We apprehended 60,000 people. That's like a stadium full of people, a big stadium.

There are many criminals being apprehended, but vast numbers are coming, because our economy is so strong. We have the strongest economy now in the entire world. You see what's happening. We have nowhere left to house them and no way to promptly remove them. We can't get them out, because our laws are so obsolete, so antiquated, and so bad.

Without new resources from Congress, we will be forced to release these people into communities—something we don't want to do—called catch-and-release. You catch them. Even if they are criminals, you then release them. And you can't release them from where they came, so they go into our country and end up in places you would least suspect. And we do as little releasing as possible, by they're coming by the hundreds of thousands.

I have had zero Democrat lawmakers volunteer to have them released into their districts or States. And I think they know that, and that's what we're going to be discussing over the next 3 weeks. The painful reality is that the tremendous economic and financial burdens of illegal immigration fall on the shoulders of low-income Americans, including millions of wonderful, patriotic, law-abiding immigrants who enrich our Nation.

As Commander in Chief, my highest priority is the defense of our great country. We cannot surrender operational control over the Nation's borders to foreign cartels, traffickers, and smugglers. We want future Americans to come to our country legally and through a system based on merit. We need people to come to our country. We have great companies moving back into the United States. And we have the lowest employment and the best employment numbers that we've ever had. There are more people working today in the United States than have ever worked in our country. We need people to come in to help us—the farms, and with all of these great companies that are moving back. Finally, they're moving back. People said it couldn't happen. It's happening.

And we want them to enjoy the blessings of safety and liberty and the rule of law. We cannot protect and deliver these blessings without a strong and secure border.

I believe that crime in this country can go down by a massive percentage if we have great security on our southern border. I believe drugs, large percentages of which come through the southern border, will be cut by a number that nobody will believe.

So let me be very clear: We really have no choice but to build a powerful wall or steel barrier. If we don't get a fair deal from Congress, the Government will either shut down on February 15, again, or I will use the powers afforded to me under the laws and the Constitution of the United States to address this emergency. We will have great security.

And I want to thank you all very much. Thank you very much.

SOURCE: Executive Office of the President. "Remarks on the Federal Government Shutdown." January 25, 2019. *Compilation of Presidential Documents* 2019, no. 00049 (January 25, 2019). https://www.govinfo.gov/content/pkg/DCPD-201900049/pdf/DCPD-201900049.pdf.

OTHER HISTORIC DOCUMENTS OF INTEREST

FROM THIS VOLUME

FROM PREVIOUS *HISTORIC DOCUMENTS*

Venezuelan President Declared Illegitimate; Opposition Leader Recognized

JANUARY 10, JANUARY 15, JANUARY 23, FEBRUARY 4, MAY 17, AND AUGUST 5, 2019

In January 2019, Venezuelan president Nicolas Maduro began his second term in office despite widespread allegations of election fraud and denunciations by dozens of foreign leaders. Just a few days into his term, however, the National Assembly declared Maduro's government "illegitimate" and its leader, Assembly president Juan Guaidó, later declared himself to be the interim president of Venezuela. The United States quickly recognized Guaidó as interim president, with officials stating "all options are on the table" for removing Maduro from office, and was soon followed by leaders in dozens of other countries. Opposition momentum waned as the year progressed and talks between opposition leaders and the government have since broken down.

MADURO SWORN IN FOR SECOND TERM

At an inauguration ceremony on January 10, Maduro was sworn in as president for a second term. "I want a change and profound correction of the errors of the revolution," he said. "Rest assured, as we have in our twenty years of revolution, we will know how to overcome the obstacles, the difficulties and we're going to come out of this victorious." Within hours, officials from countries around the world denounced Maduro's government. The Permanent Council of the Organization of American States (OAS) passed a resolution agreeing "to not recognize the legitimacy of Nicolas Maduro's new term" and that "only through a national dialogue with the participation of all Venezuelan political actors and stakeholders can national reconciliation be achieved." The resolution also called for new presidential elections and urged OAS member states and permanent observers to adopt "diplomatic, political, economic and financial measures . . . to contribute to the prompt restoration of the democratic order of Venezuela." A statement from the Council of the European Union said Maduro's inauguration "only pushes further away the possibility of a constitutional negotiated solution while the political, economic, and social situation in the country keeps getting worse." Officials in Paraguay said they would remove their embassy from Caracas, Venezuela's capital.

This response was not surprising: dozens of countries refused to recognize the 2018 presidential election that granted Maduro a second term, with some, such as the United States, declaring the outcome invalid even before the vote took place due to allegations of fraud and election rigging. The vote had been scheduled for December 2018, but the National Constituent Assembly—comprised entirely of Maduro supporters—voted unanimously in January of that year to move the election up to April. This was followed by a

Supreme Court ruling that prohibited the main opposition coalition, the Democratic Unity Roundtable (MUD), from registering for the election. MUD leaders planned to field only one candidate for all its member parties. The court ruling and National Constituent Assembly vote left the opposition scrambling to determine which parties would register which candidates in a significantly shortened campaign period.

Opposition leaders decried the decision to reschedule the election as yet another attempt to keep Maduro in power. The National Electoral Council and the Supreme Court are also stacked with Maduro loyalists, and, together with the National Constituent Assembly and the president, have worked to strip power from the opposition-controlled National Assembly and limit the opposition's ability to participate in elections. Additionally, the National Electoral Council suspended MUD's pursuit of a recall referendum against Maduro in 2016, citing claims by pro-Maduro governors that several thousand signatures gathered by the coalition in support of its petition were fraudulent.

MUD boycotted the election and encouraged voters to stay home. Maduro faced two challengers but still won 68 percent of the vote, according to election officials. However, reports of voting irregularities and allegations of election fraud were rampant and included evidence that the government used food aid to pressure voters into supporting Maduro. Turnout was also notably low, with less than half of registered Venezuelans casting a vote. Despite these considerations, officials in some countries did accept the election results, including members of the Chinese, Cuban, and Russian governments.

Opposition Declares Maduro "Illegitimate"

The day after Maduro's inauguration, National Assembly president Juan Guaidó stated he would be willing to serve as interim president and call new elections if he had the support of Venezuelans and the military. (Per the Venezuelan Constitution, the leader of the National Assembly is tapped to fill a presidential vacancy until new elections are held.) Guaidó had been sworn in as Assembly president on January 5. An industrial engineer, he helped found the centrist opposition party Popular Will in 2009 with well-known opposition leader Leopoldo López. Unlike his mentor, Guaidó was relatively unknown, even after becoming a full member of the Assembly in 2016, but his announcement—and his arrest two days later—earned him notoriety. Reports indicated agents with the Venezuelan intelligence service briefly detained Guaidó on January 13. Guaidó told the *New York Times* in an exclusive interview that the agents questioned him about his plans to become the interim president and call new elections, then let him go. Some observers speculated Guaidó's quick release was a sign of wavering support for Maduro among members of the country's security forces, but Communications Minister Jorge Rodriguez claimed the arrest was a rogue operation.

On January 15, the National Assembly declared Maduro's administration to be illegitimate, arguing the president had violated the constitution by usurping powers from the National Assembly, the courts, and other government entities. Guaidó and other opposition leaders called for Venezuelans to take to the streets on January 23 to show their support for Guaidó's interim presidency.

Hundreds of thousands of people answered that call in the first major showing of public dissatisfaction since the government's violent crackdown on anti-Maduro demonstrations in 2017. Protestors demanded that Maduro leave office and called for sweeping changes to improve the country's deteriorating situation. Some of Venezuela's economic challenges stretch back for decades, but the current crisis is widely attributed to poor policy decisions and mismanagement by—and corruption within—both Maduro's government and that of his predecessor, the late Hugo Chávez. The economy has been in free fall since Maduro took office, and Venezuela is today plagued by hyperinflation; an almost completely devalued currency; severe shortages of food, medicine, and other goods; and recurring power and water outages. According to the United Nations, more than three million Venezuelans have fled the country in search of food, medicine, and a better quality of life.

News media reported clashes between protestors and the military, the latter of which used tear gas to dispel the demonstrations. Foro Penal, a Venezuelan human rights group, said seven people were killed in protests outside of the capital. A smaller rally of Maduro supporters was held outside the Miraflores presidential palace.

That same day, Guaidó declared himself to be the interim president of Venezuela and took an oath of office in front of thousands of supporters in Caracas. "Today, January 23, 2019, in my capacity as president of the National Assembly, before God Almighty, Venezuela and my fellow deputies, I swear to formally assume the powers of the national executive as the president in charge of Venezuela," he said.

Foreign Leaders Recognize Guaidó as Interim President

Shortly after Guaidó's announcement on January 23, President Donald Trump issued a statement recognizing him as Venezuela's interim president. "In its role as the only legitimate branch of government duly elected by the Venezuelan people, the National Assembly invoked the country's constitution to declare Nicolas Maduro illegitimate and the office of the Presidency therefore vacant," the statement read. "The people of Venezuela have courageously spoken out against Maduro and his regime and demanded freedom and the rule of law." Trump promised to "use the full weight of United States economic and diplomatic power to press for the restoration of Venezuelan democracy." He added that the United States would continue to hold Maduro's administration "directly responsible for any threats it may pose to the safety of the Venezuelan people."

On February 4, eleven of the Lima Group's fourteen members—Argentina, Brazil, Canada, Chile, Colombia, Costa Rica, Guatemala, Honduras, Panama, Paraguay, and Peru—issued a joint declaration recognizing and supporting Guaidó as interim president. The seventeen-point document also called for free and fair presidential elections, condemned human rights violations, and urged that freedom of the press be restored. The group further stated that "attempts for dialogue" made by international actors had been "manipulated by the Maduro regime, transforming them into delaying tactics in order for him to remain in power," and that any diplomatic or political solution to the current leadership crisis must support a constitutional roadmap that "seeks a peaceful transition for Venezuelans, will result in the exit of the dictatorial regime of Maduro, allow for holding of elections and the restoration of democracy in Venezuela." Officials in Bolivia, Cuba, and Turkey were some of those supporting Maduro. "Maduro, brother, stand tall. Turkey stands with you," said Turkish president Recep Tayyip Erdoğan.

Responding to the news, Maduro vowed to stay in office, declaring "the imperialist U.S. government is directing an operation to impose through a coup a puppet government" to advance its own interests. "No one here is surrendering," he said. "We're going to combat until victory." The president also ordered all U.S. diplomats to leave Venezuela within seventy-two hours. Shortly thereafter, Guaidó tweeted an open letter to all foreign embassies in Venezuela, stating all diplomats were welcome to stay. "Any messages to the contrary lack any validity, since they come from people or entities that have been characterized as usurpers," he wrote. U.S. secretary of state Mike Pompeo said Maduro did not have "the legal authority" to cut diplomatic ties with the United States and the Trump administration would maintain relations with Venezuela through Guaidó's government.

Norway Brokers Talks between Government and Opposition

Recognizing the power of the military's continued support for Maduro, Guaidó repeatedly called on soldiers and military leaders to abandon the president, promising amnesty for any who did. On the morning of April 30, Guaidó called for a military uprising against Maduro and said some "brave soldiers, brave patriots, brave men attached to the Constitution" had already followed his call. Maduro's administration swiftly accused the opposition of promoting a coup and said it was "confronting and deactivating a small group of military traitors." Some officials accused the United States of encouraging the coup.

Later that day, Guaidó attended a protest in Caracas where he declared Maduro no longer had the military's support. Yet there was no protest action on military bases, and no military leaders issued statements supporting him or came to the protest; some actually expressed their opposition to Guaidó instead. In the days following the failed uprising attempt, reports indicated that, while under house arrest, Leopoldo Lopez met with and obtained agreements from key Maduro supporters in the military that they would publicly abandon the president in order to retain their current positions in a Guaidó-led interim government. The opposition had been expecting these leaders to issue public statements on April 30, but they never came.

Roughly two weeks later, Norway's Ministry of Foreign Affairs announced it had "preliminary contacts with representatives of the main political actors of Venezuela, as part of an exploratory phase, with the aim of contributing to finding a solution to the situation in the country." Representatives of the opposition and the Maduro government participated in this first round of a series of negotiations mediated by the Norwegian government. Opposition leaders said they sought an agreement that would include the formation of a transition government with lawmakers from all parties and, most critically, a new election. Those representing the Venezuelan government called for U.S. and other sanctions to be lifted. While they did not publicly indicate openness to a new presidential election, they did propose early legislative elections—a proposal rejected as insufficient by the opposition.

Several unsuccessful rounds of talks had taken place when, on August 5, President Trump issued an executive order freezing all assets of the Venezuelan government within the United States' control and prohibiting transactions with Venezuelan officials and government entities. The order also prohibited any Venezuelans who had previously been sanctioned by the United States, including Maduro and his wife, from entering the country. Exceptions were made for the provision of humanitarian aid to Venezuela.

Maduro's administration characterized the executive order as a "brutal and grave aggression" against the Venezuelan people, and the president announced the government's withdrawal from talks. "The people have asked me why I'm in a dialogue with people who have tried to assassinate, overthrow, and fill the country with violence, but we have still done it," Maduro said. "In this case, we cannot sit down with people who celebrate this criminal economic blockade that the U.S. has imposed on us."

On September 15, Guaidó declared the talks had ended "after more than 40 days during which he [Maduro] refused to continue." He accused Maduro and his supporters of "refusing to discuss and agree on a sensible proposal." The next day, members of several small opposition parties (they held less than one-tenth of National Assembly seats) signed an agreement with Maduro's government to begin negotiations separate from the Norway-led talks. The new negotiations would be focused on reforming the National Electoral Council and finding ways to balance legislative power between the National Assembly and the National Constituent Assembly. There was no indication from either the opposition parties or the government that a transitional government or a new election would be discussed. Also on September 16, Communications Minister Jorge Rodriguez said the government was considering sending some Socialist Party lawmakers back to the National Assembly. (Socialist lawmakers left the Assembly in 2017 after government efforts to strip the body of its authority and create the National Constituent Assembly.) Thirty-eight of these lawmakers returned to the Assembly on September 24.

The future of the opposition movement and Maduro's tenure as president remains unclear. Guaidó and his supporters have struggled to maintain momentum since the January announcements, and they have so far been unsuccessful in turning military commanders and other senior officials against Maduro. However, the National Assembly ratified Guaidó as interim president on September 17, suggesting he will continue to lead the legislative body after his one-year term ends in January 2020.

—Linda Grimm

Following is a resolution approved by the Organization of American States on January 10, 2019, not recognizing President Nicolas Maduro's second term; the Venezuela National Assembly's declaration on January 15, 2019, that Maduro's government was illegitimate; a statement released by President Donald Trump on January 23, 2019, announcing the United States' recognition of Juan Guaidó as the interim president of Venezuela; a statement by Lima Group members on February 4, 2019, recognizing Guaidó as interim president; a statement issued by Norway's Foreign Ministry on May 17, 2019, announcing the start of talks between Maduro's government and opposition leaders; and Executive Order 13884, issued on August 5, 2019, which imposed additional U.S. sanctions on the government of Venezuela.

Organization of American States Resolution Not to Recognize Maduro's Government

DOCUMENT

January 10, 2019

The Permanent Council of the Organization of American States (OAS) today agreed "to not recognize the legitimacy of Nicolas Maduro's new term as of the 10th of January of 2019." The resolution was approved with 19 votes in favor, 6 against, 8 abstentions and one absent.

Following is the complete text of the resolution:

RESOLUTION ON THE SITUATION IN VENEZUELA

(Adopted by the Permanent Council at its special meeting held on January 10, 2019)

THE PERMANENT COUNCIL OF THE ORGANIZATION OF AMERICAN STATES,

REAFFIRMING the right of the peoples of the Americas to democracy and the obligation of their governments to promote and defend it as reflected in Article 1 of the Inter-American Democratic Charter,

RECALLING that, through resolution AG/RES. 2929 (XLVIII-O/18) of June 5, 2018, the General Assembly declared that the May 20, 2018 electoral process in Venezuela lacked legitimacy for not having met the participation of all Venezuelan political actors, its failure to comply with international standards, and for being carried out without the necessary guarantees for a free, fair, transparent, and democratic process,

CONSIDERING that the 2019–2025 presidential period beginning in Venezuela on the 10th of January of 2019 is the result of an illegitimate electoral process,

UNDERSCORING the constitutional authority of the democratically elected National Assembly.

REITEREITING ITS DEEP CONCERN about the worsening political, economic, social and humanitarian crisis in Venezuela resulting from the breakdown of democratic order and serious human rights violations in that state, and the government of Venezuela's negligence to meet the fundamental Inter-American standards of human rights and democracy;

RECOGNIZING that, as a consequence, a significant number of Venezuelans are being forced to flee the country because their basic needs have not been met.

REITEREITING its serious concern about the collapse of Venezuela's health-care system, which has led to a reemergence of previously eradicated infectious diseases across Venezuela and into neighboring countries and the wider region.

NOTING that the exodus of Venezuelans is having an impact on the capacity of countries in the region to meet their humanitarian needs and poses challenges to public health and security.

TAKING NOTE, in this regard, of the Quito Declaration on the human mobility of Venezuelan citizens in the region, of September 4th 2018, and its Plan of Action adopted on November 23rd 2018.

CONDEMNING in the strongest terms the arbitrary detentions, lack of due process and the violation of other human rights of political prisoners by the Government of Venezuela.

UNDERSCORING that the Permanent Council and the Meeting of Consultation of Foreign Ministers remain ready to engage in diplomatic initiatives, including good offices, aimed at promoting dialogue in Venezuela, with a view to arriving at a political solution to the crisis in that country.

RESOLVES:

To not recognize the legitimacy of Nicolas Maduro's new term as of the 10th of January of 2019.

To reaffirm that only through a national dialogue with the participation of all Venezuelan political actors and stakeholders can national reconciliation be achieved and the necessary conditions agreed upon for holding a new electoral process that truly reflects the will of the Venezuelan citizens and peacefully resolves the current crisis in that country.

To urge all Member States and invite Permanent Observers of the OAS to adopt, in accordance with international law and their national legislation, diplomatic, political, economic and financial measures that they consider appropriate, to contribute to the prompt restoration of the democratic order of Venezuela.

To call for new Presidential elections with all necessary guarantees of a free, fair, transparent, and legitimate process to be held at an early date attended by international observers.

To invite Member States and Permanent Observers to implement measures to address the humanitarian crisis in Venezuela and impacted countries, through the support to appropriate international and regional organizations.

To urge the Venezuelan regime to allow the immediate entry of humanitarian aid to the people in Venezuela, including epidemiological surveillance, to prevent the aggravation of the humanitarian and public health crisis, particularly against the reappearance and propagation of diseases.

To demand the immediate and unconditional release of all political prisoners.

To express the Organization's ongoing solidarity with the Venezuelan people and its commitment to remain seized of the situation in Venezuela and to support diplomatic measures that facilitate the restoration of democratic institutions and the full respect for human rights.

To instruct the Secretary General to transmit the text of this resolution to the Secretary General of the United Nations.

SOURCE: General Secretariat of the Organization of American States. "OAS Permanent Council Agrees 'to Not Recognize the Legitimacy of Nicolas Maduro's New Term.'" January 10, 2019. https://www.oas.org/en/media_center/press_release.asp?sCodigo=E-001/19.

National Assembly Declares Usurpation of Maduro

January 15, 2019

In its ordinary session of this Tuesday, the National Assembly (NA) approved an agreement in which it formally declared the usurpation by Nicolás Maduro of the position of President of the Republic.

The approved document also emphasized the application of the Constitution of the Bolivarian Republic of Venezuela (CBRV) so as to restore its validity. In the agreement, the NA invokes Articles 233, 333, and 350 with the purpose of adopting measures so as to restore the constitutional order, the cessation of the usurpation, the conformation of the transitional government as well as convoking to free elections.

Before the approval of the agreement, it developed a debate started by deputy Jorge Millán. "Today we have to declare that we do not have a President of the Republic, at least not a democratic and legitimate one. What we have is a man usurping the position." The deputy pointed out that the NA must do whatever is necessary to recover the government by means of elections. "We must pose a democratic transition process which will lead us to elections and to freedom." Millán addressed the soldiers of the Homeland, " . . . those who in their hearths still resides the heroism of the fathers who founded the nation, to step forward and avoid being the barrier between an oppressed people and some oppressing troglodytes."

On his part, the deputy Juan Pablo García emphatically reiterated that Maduro is not the President of the Republic. "There is a power vacuum in the country and on January 11 of this year Juan Guaidó, our President of the NA, so bravely assumed." In his view, this act is not sufficient for either the international community or for the population. "It is necessary to invoke the 233. We count on the support of the international community and of the legitimate High Court of Justice (HCJ). But we have to do what is necessary to do because we cannot fail them." García ended his intervention by addressing the head of the NA: "Juan Guaidó, not only are you the President of the NA, today you are the President of the Republic and the Chief Commander of the National Armed Force."

The deputy Dennis Fernández also intervened and stressed to her colleagues the need to apply political intelligence. "These are hours to think, to be coherent and to apply political intelligence. The objective is to conquer freedom and democracy. We must proceed with knowledge and political intelligence." She pointed out that the country can count on a President of the NA who is eager, together with its 112 deputies, to assume this country with courage as well as to follow the procedures stated in the CBRV. "That is what we have to do, with courage and with political intelligence. We are going to agree to the usurpation of the power (sic) and continue with all the procedures that we have to follow."

Afterward, the deputy José Pratt stressed that the cessation of the usurpation is not going to fall from heaven. "We have to create a force so as to apply the CBRV and for that we need coherence, clarity in the message and determination in the action, and we have seen those three elements in Guaidó." Pratt highlighted that there was risk in delaying and he believes that internal unity and expeditious channels must exist. "The people do ask their leadership for clear messages. We need total support for the restitution of the democracy to Venezuela."

Meanwhile, making use of his right to speak, the deputy Juan Andrés Mejía indicated that Maduro usurped the position because in his capacity there have been neither answers nor solutions to the country's severe crisis. He believes that Article 233 of the CBRV established the path. "It is not true that there is an elected President in Venezuela. Experts know that this article is the one closest to resolving the change in the country. Beware of excuses." Mejía called for the support of Article 233 and addressed the people, the international community, and the National Armed Forces (NAF) to exhort them to fight together for this constitutional section, for a transitional government to be installed and, afterwards, for a legitimate government in Venezuela. "I invite you to have confidence in Juan Guaidó, who is not only the President of this NA, but of the whole Venezuela."

Finally, deputy Elimar Díaz took the floor to mention that Maduro represents the backwardness of the country. "He is not only the usurper, but the continuous diaspora. He represents the high cost of living, the collapse of the public services and that shows us that Venezuelans have a great responsibility." He added that the NA became the mechanism to solve the severe crisis. "We must be reasonable and not 'escape through the green roads' (emigrate). We have to guarantee the people that after the usurpation we are going to lead them to electoral processes that are fair and free."

SOURCE: National Assembly of Venezuela. "AN Formally Declared the Usurpation of Maduro in the Position of President of the Republic." January 15, 2019. Translated by SAGE Publishing. http://www .asambleanacional.gob.ve/noticias/an-declaro-formalmente.

United States Recognizes Juan Gerardo Guaidó Márquez as Interim President of Venezuela

January 23, 2019

Today I am officially recognizing the President of the Venezuelan National Assembly, Juan Guaidó, as the Interim President of Venezuela. In its role as the only legitimate branch of government duly elected by the Venezuelan people, the National Assembly invoked the country's constitution to declare Nicolas Maduro illegitimate and the office of the Presidency therefore vacant. The people of Venezuela have courageously spoken out against Maduro and his regime and demanded freedom and the rule of law.

I will continue to use the full weight of United States economic and diplomatic power to press for the restoration of Venezuelan democracy. We encourage other Western Hemisphere governments to recognize National Assembly President Guaidó as the Interim President of Venezuela, and we will work constructively with them in support of his efforts to restore constitutional legitimacy. We continue to hold the illegitimate Maduro regime directly responsible for any threats it may pose to the safety of the Venezuelan people. As Interim President, Guaidó noted yesterday: "Violence is the usurper's weapon; we only have one clear action: to remain united and firm for a democratic and free Venezuela."

Source: Executive Office of the President. "Statement Announcing United States Recognition of National Assembly President Juan Gerardo Guaidó Márquez as Interim President of Venezuela." January 23, 2019. *Compilation of Presidential Documents* 2019, no. 00046 (January 23, 2019). https://www.govinfo.gov/content/pkg/DCPD-201900046/pdf/DCPD-201900046.pdf.

Lima Group Declaration Recognizing Guaidó

February 4, 2019

The Governments of Argentina, Brazil, Canada, Chile, Colombia, Costa Rica, Guatemala, Honduras, Panama, Paraguay, Peru, members of the Lima Group, express the following:

1.   They reiterate their recognition and support for Juan Guaidó as the Interim President of the Bolivarian Republic of Venezuela as per its Constitution. Salute the growing number of countries which have recognized interim President Guaidó and call upon the international community to give its strongest support to Interim President Guaidó and the National Assembly in their efforts to establish a government of democratic transition in Venezuela.

2. Accept with great pleasure the request from interim President to incorporate the legitimate government of Venezuela in the Lima Group and welcome him amongst us.

3. They agree to recognize and work with the representatives designated by the government of Interim President Juan Guaidó in their respective countries.

4. They note that the attempts for dialogue initiated by various international actors have been manipulated by the Maduro regime, transforming them into delaying tactics in order for him to remain in power and, consequently, consider that any political or diplomatic initiative that is developed must aim to support the constitutional roadmap presented to the National Assembly and interim President Juan Guaidó, which seeks a peaceful transition for Venezuelans, will result in the exit of the dictatorial regime of Maduro, allow for holding of elections and the restoration of democracy in Venezuela.

5. They call for the immediate re-establishment of democracy in Venezuela through the holding of free and fair elections called by the legitimate authorities, according to international standards as soon as possible. These elections should be conducted with sufficient guarantees, with the participation of all political leaders and with international observation, including the appointment of a new National Electoral Council.

6. They condemn the persistent and serious violations of human rights in Venezuela. In this regard, they reject acts of violence and repression of popular demonstrations by the security forces which have caused many deaths, injuries and detentions.

7. Urge the restoration of full freedom of the press, the end [of] censorship and to the normalization of the functions of the media whose operations [have] been arbitrarily impeded by the Maduro regime.

8. They reiterate the importance of effectively applying the Resolution of the United Nations Human Rights Council approved on September 27, 2018, "Promotion and Protection of Human Rights in the Bolivarian Republic of Venezuela". They urge the United Nations' High Commissioner for Human Rights to respond immediately to the serious human rights situation in the country.

9. They express their deep concern for the situation of all political prisoners in Venezuela and demand their immediate release; further they demand guarantees for the physical safety of members of the National Assembly.

10. They reiterate their deep concern about the serious humanitarian situation in Venezuela caused by the Maduro regime. They consider it imperative that access to humanitarian assistance be guaranteed in order to respond to the urgent needs of Venezuelans. They call upon the United Nations and its agencies and the international community to be prepared to provide humanitarian assistance to vulnerable populations in that country, whenever possible, and based on their needs.

11. They call upon the National Armed Forces of Venezuela to demonstrate their loyalty to the Interim President in his constitutional functions as their Commander in Chief. Similarly, they urge the National Armed Forces not to impede the entry and transit of humanitarian assistance to Venezuelans.

12. They reiterate their concerns regarding the migration caused by the political, economic and social crisis in Venezuela, and highlight its direct connection with the break of the constitutional order. Similarly, they recognize the efforts of host countries and underscore the need to support and strengthen their capacity for the humanitarian response by facilitating their access to the necessary resources.

13. They take note of Resolution 1/2019 of the Inter-American Commission on Human Rights (IACHR) that grants precautionary measures for Juan Guaidó and his family and demand their immediate implementation.

14. They reject the steps taken by the Supreme Court of Justice, as controlled by the Maduro regime, to prohibit the travel of Juan Guaido and the freezing of his bank accounts and assets in Venezuela.

15. They acknowledge the fundamental role the legitimate Supreme Court of Justice has played in initiating support for the democratic transition.

16. They call on members of the international community to take measures to prevent the Maduro regime from conducting financial and trade transactions abroad, from having access to Venezuela's international assets and from doing business in oil, gold and other assets.

17. Finally, they reiterate their support for a process of peaceful transition through political and diplomatic means without the use of force.

SOURCE: Global Affairs Canada. "Lima Group Declaration February 04, 2019." February 4, 2019. https://www.canada.ca/en/global-affairs/news/2019/02/lima-group-declaration-february-04-2019.html.

Norway Announces Start of Talks with Venezuelan Leaders

May 17, 2019

Norway announces that it has had preliminary contacts with representatives of the main political actors of Venezuela, as part of an exploratory phase, with the aim of contributing to finding a solution to the situation in the country.

Norway commends the parties for their efforts. We reiterate our willingness to continue supporting the search for a peaceful solution for the country.

SOURCE: Norway Ministry of Foreign Affairs. "Statement on Venezuela." May 17, 2019. https://www.regjeringen.no/en/aktuelt/statement-on-venezuela/id2645675/.

Executive Order 13884—Blocking Property of the Government of Venezuela

August 5, 2019

By the authority vested in me as President by the Constitution and the laws of the United States of America, including the International Emergency Economic Powers Act (50 U.S.C. 1701 *et seq.*) (IEEPA), the National Emergencies Act (50 U.S.C. 1601 *et seq.*), section 212(f) of the Immigration and Nationality Act of 1952 (8 U.S.C. 1182(f)), and section 301 of title 3, United States Code,

I, Donald J. Trump, President of the United States of America, in order to take additional steps with respect to the national emergency declared in Executive Order 13692 of March 8, 2015 (Blocking Property and Suspending Entry of Certain Persons Contributing to the Situation in Venezuela), as amended, as relied upon for additional steps taken in subsequent Executive Orders, and in light of the continued usurpation of power by Nicolas Maduro and persons affiliated with him, as well as human rights abuses, including arbitrary or unlawful arrest and detention of Venezuelan citizens, interference with freedom of expression, including for members of the media, and ongoing attempts to undermine Interim President Juan Guaido and the Venezuelan National Assembly's exercise of legitimate authority in Venezuela, hereby order:

Section 1. (a) All property and interests in property of the Government of Venezuela that are in the United States, that hereafter come within the United States, or that are or hereafter come within the possession or control of any United States person are blocked and may not be transferred, paid, exported, withdrawn, or otherwise dealt in.

(b) All property and interests in property that are in the United States, that hereafter come within the United States, or that are or hereafter come within the possession or control of any United States person of the following persons are blocked and may not be transferred, paid, exported, withdrawn, or otherwise dealt in: any person determined by the Secretary of the Treasury, in consultation with the Secretary of State:

    i.   to have materially assisted, sponsored, or provided financial, material, or technological support for, or goods or services to or in support of, any person included on the list of Specially Designated Nationals and Blocked Persons maintained by the Office of Foreign Assets Control whose property and interests in property are blocked pursuant to this order; or

    ii. to be owned or controlled by, or to have acted or purported to act for or on behalf of, directly or indirectly, any person whose property and interests in property are blocked pursuant to this order.

(c) The prohibitions in subsections (a)–(b) of this section apply except to the extent provided by statutes, or in regulations, orders, directives, or licenses that may be issued pursuant to this order, and notwithstanding any contract entered into or any license or permit granted prior to the effective date of this order.

Sec. 2. The unrestricted immigrant and nonimmigrant entry into the United States of aliens determined to meet one or more of the criteria in section 1(b) of this order would be detrimental to the interests of the United States, and entry of such persons into the United States, as immigrants or nonimmigrants, is hereby suspended, except when the Secretary of State determines that the person's entry would not be contrary to the interests of the United States, including when the Secretary so determines, based on a recommendation of the Attorney General, that the person's entry would further important United States law enforcement objectives. In exercising this responsibility, the Secretary of State shall consult the Secretary of Homeland Security on matters related to admissibility or inadmissibility within the authority of the Secretary of Homeland Security. Such persons shall be treated in the same manner as persons covered by section 1 of Proclamation 8693 of July 24, 2011 (Suspension of Entry of Aliens Subject to United Nations Security Council Travel Bans and International Emergency Economic Powers Act Sanctions). The Secretary of State shall have the responsibility for implementing this section pursuant to such conditions and procedures as the Secretary has established or may establish pursuant to Proclamation 8693.

Sec. 3. The prohibitions in section 1 of this order include:

(a) the making of any contribution or provision of funds, goods, or services by, to, or for the benefit of any person whose property and interests in property are blocked pursuant to this order; and

(b) the receipt of any contribution or provision of funds, goods, or services from any such person.

Sec. 4. (a) Any transaction that evades or avoids, has the purpose of evading or avoiding, causes a violation of, or attempts to violate any of the prohibitions set forth in this order is prohibited.

(b) Any conspiracy formed to violate any of the prohibitions set forth in this order is prohibited.

Sec. 5. Nothing in this order shall prohibit:

(a) transactions for the conduct of the official business of the Federal Government by employees, grantees, or contractors thereof; or

(b) transactions related to the provision of articles such as food, clothing, and medicine intended to be used to relieve human suffering.

Sec. 6. For the purposes of this order:

(a) the term "person" means an individual or entity;

(b) the term "entity" means a partnership, association, trust, joint venture, corporation, group, subgroup, or other organization;

(c) the term "United States person" means any United States citizen, permanent resident alien, entity organized under the laws of the United States or any jurisdiction within the United States (including foreign branches), or any person in the United States; and

(d) the term "Government of Venezuela" includes the state and Government of Venezuela, any political subdivision, agency, or instrumentality thereof, including the Central Bank of Venezuela and Petroleos de Venezuela, S.A. (PdVSA), any person owned or controlled, directly or indirectly, by the foregoing, and any person who has acted or purported to act directly or indirectly for or on behalf of, any of the foregoing, including as a member of the Maduro regime. For the purposes of section 2 of this order, the term

"Government of Venezuela" shall not include any United States citizen, any permanent resident alien of the United States, any alien lawfully admitted to the United States, or any alien holding a valid United States visa.

Sec. 7. For those persons whose property and interests in property are blocked pursuant to this order who might have a constitutional presence in the United States, I find that because of the ability to transfer funds or other assets instantaneously, prior notice to such persons of measures to be taken pursuant to this order would render those measures ineffectual. I therefore determine that for these measures to be effective in addressing the national emergency declared in Executive Order 13692, there need be no prior notice of a listing or determination made pursuant to section 1 of this order.

Sec. 8. The Secretary of the Treasury, in consultation with the Secretary of State, is hereby authorized to take such actions, including promulgating rules and regulations, and to employ all powers granted to the President by IEEPA as may be necessary to implement this order. The Secretary of the Treasury may, consistent with applicable law, redelegate any of these functions within the Department of the Treasury. All agencies of the United States Government shall take all appropriate measures within their authority to carry out the provisions of this order.

Sec. 9. (a) Nothing in this order shall be construed to impair or otherwise affect:

- i.   the authority granted by law to an executive department or agency, or the head thereof; or
- ii. the functions of the Director of the Office of Management and Budget relating to budgetary, administrative, or legislative proposals.

(b) This order shall be implemented consistent with applicable law and subject to the availability of appropriations.

(c) This order is not intended to, and does not, create any right or benefit, substantive or procedural, enforceable at law or in equity by any party against the United States, its departments, agencies, or entities, its officers, employees, or agents, or any other person.

Sec. 10. This order is effective at 9:00 a.m. eastern daylight time on August 5, 2019.

SOURCE: Executive Office of the President. "Executive Order 13884—Blocking Property of the Government of Venezuela." August 5, 2019. *Compilation of Presidential Documents* 2019, no. 00539 (August 5, 2019). https://www.govinfo.gov/content/pkg/DCPD-201900539/pdf/DCPD-201900539.pdf.

OTHER HISTORIC DOCUMENTS OF INTEREST

FROM PREVIOUS *HISTORIC DOCUMENTS*

State, County, and Federal Officials Respond to Measles Outbreak

JANUARY 25, MARCH 26, APRIL 9, MAY 30, AND OCTOBER 4, 2019

Between January 1 and October 4, 2019, the Centers for Disease Control and Prevention (CDC) confirmed 1,249 individual cases of measles throughout the United States, the highest since 1992. While cases were reported in thirty-one states, 75 percent were linked to outbreaks in two Orthodox Jewish communities in New York. The outbreak renewed the national debate over the importance of vaccinations, and some state legislatures moved to amend their vaccine opt-out policies for school-age children.

MEASLES SPREADS, PUBLIC HEALTH EMERGENCIES DECLARED

Measles is considered one of the most infectious viruses on the planet. Up to 90 percent of nonimmunized individuals who come in contact with one contagious person will contract measles. It spreads rapidly partly because it is contagious before symptoms appear. When a person contracts the virus, it lives inside the body for up to two weeks without any signs or symptoms. Initial symptoms, such as a cough, runny nose, sore throat, or conjunctivitis, are often mistaken for a common cold. Approximately three days after those symptoms begin, the identifiable measles symptoms appear: fever, itchy rash beginning on the face and then the hands and feet, and bluish-white spots in the mouth. Those infected are contagious four days before and up to four days after the rash first appears. The virus can cause serious complications, including permanent hearing loss, blindness, pneumonia, seizures, and encephalitis.

The 2019 outbreak actually began in September 2018 in the Brooklyn, New York, neighborhood of Williamsburg after unvaccinated members of ultra-Orthodox Jewish communities traveled from Israel to the United States after contracting the virus. The virus quickly spread in the tight-knit populace, which does not approve of vaccinations on religious grounds. That community, and one other Hasidic neighborhood in New York, would account for the vast majority of measles cases. In total, thirty-one states would report at least one confirmed case of the virus in 2019, and at more than 1,000 total cases, the CDC reported that it was the biggest outbreak in twenty-five years.

During the year, approximately 10 percent of those infected with measles were hospitalized, while about half that number reported complications from the virus. The virus's rise threatened the country's measles elimination status, earned in 2000, and considered one of the most significant achievements in U.S. public health. A World Health Organization (WHO) policy requires removing a country's elimination designation once the virus has spread continuously for a year, of which the United States came just one month shy.

HEALTH EMERGENCIES DECLARED

On January 25, Washington governor Jay Inslee declared a public health emergency with regards to the virus after over two dozen cases of measles were confirmed in his state. In his proclamation, he directed the state's agencies and departments to "utilize state resources and to do everything reasonably possible to assist" affected areas. The declaration also allowed Washington to request medical resources from other states.

Two months later, on March 26, after 153 cases were confirmed in Rockland County, New York, County Executive Ed Day declared a local state of emergency and banned unvaccinated individuals under the age of eighteen from public places. The penalty for failure to comply was a maximum six months in jail and/or a $500 fine. To determine whether someone had violated the order, the county planned to use standard investigative procedures to identify where the infected individual was exposed and then correlate that with possibly unvaccinated people. The order was immediately met with resistance. A judge lifted the ban on April 5, and an appellate court upheld that decision less than two weeks later. The state of emergency was renewed on April 25, but without a prohibition on unvaccinated individuals in public places.

On April 9, New York City mayor Bill de Blasio declared a public health emergency. By that point the city had confirmed more than 285 cases since the fall of 2018. In an effort to stop the virus from spreading further, the declaration required all unvaccinated people who lived in the Williamsburg neighborhood of Brooklyn to be vaccinated against measles. Failure to comply could result in a $1,000 fine. This was de Blasio's second attempt to stop the outbreak; a December 2018 order banning unvaccinated students from attending certain schools had proved ineffective.

ANTI-VACCINATION MOVEMENT RECEIVES GLOBAL ATTENTION

Throughout 2018 and 2019, the majority of measles cases were found in people who were not vaccinated against the virus. The CDC recommends that a minimum of 95 percent of kindergarten children need to receive the measles, mumps, and rubella (MMR) vaccine to protect others with compromised immune systems and infants from the disease. During the 2018–2019 school year in the United States, only 94.7 percent of kindergarteners had received both doses of the MMR vaccine.

The movement against vaccinating children has been around for more than 200 years. But it took off in 1998 following a study by Andrew Wakefield that concluded that the childhood MMR vaccination causes autism spectrum disorder. Wakefield's study of twelve children has since been retracted and disproven, and his team found guilty of ethical violations, scientific misrepresentation, and deliberate fraud. Despite numerous studies to the contrary, many parents still adhere to Wakefield's findings and refuse to vaccinate their children.

The ongoing failure of some parents to vaccinate their children led the World Health Organization in 2019 to list the anti-vaccination movement as one of the ten threats to global health. The body noted that vaccines had saved two to three million lives per year and could save an estimated 1.5 million more if vaccination rates increased.

STATES REWRITE VACCINE OPT-OUT LAWS

The measles outbreak and its link to a failure to vaccinate also resulted in a number of states changing their vaccination exemption laws. California—which in 2015 voted to disallow religious or personal exemptions for vaccinations—chose to expand its law in April 2019, tightening the medical exemption provision to create a new standardized request form in an effort to stop doctors from giving families phony medical exemptions. The law also permits the state's health department to review medical exemptions at schools with a vaccination rate below 95 percent and for any doctors who write five or more exemptions in a year. Backlash was swift, with protesters shutting down both chambers of the state legislature during bill consideration and surrounding the governor's office. But the bill easily passed and was signed by the governor on September 9.

On April 25, Governor Inslee signed House Bill 1638 into law, which noted, "A philosophical or personal objection may not be used to exempt a child from the measles, mumps, and rubella vaccine." All children attending public and private schools or day care centers were included. Protesters there cited questionable safety standards for vaccines and expressed a belief that parents should be given the choice to vaccinate their children if there is any potential risk involved. Rep. Paul Harris, a Republican supporting the bill, said, "There's a lot of misinformation out there, and people either don't believe in science or think there are more vaccine injuries than are being reported." He received death threats from some anti-vaxxers.

Just one month later, on May 24, Governor Janet Mills of Maine signed House Bill 586 into law, removing the personal and religious belief exemptions for all vaccines required for a child to attend school. Maine has one of the nation's highest vaccine opt-out rates, but as in other states, dissent among the public was swift, arguing that the law infringed on personal liberty. An effort to overturn the legislation collected enough signatures to place a referendum on the March 2020 ballot that will ask voters whether the law should stand.

And, on June 13, New York governor Andrew Cuomo signed Senate Bill 2994, which removed the religious belief exemption for all vaccines for children attending public school. "Although freedom of religious expression is a founding tenet of this nation, there is longstanding precedent establishing that one's right to free religious expression does not include the right to endanger the health of the community, one's children, or the children of others," the New York bill read, in part.

The federal government also took note of the ongoing vaccine debate. In an October 4 press release, Health and Human Services secretary Alex Azar commented on the "dangers of vaccine hesitancy and misinformation" and committed to continue promoting vaccination as a simple way to keep people healthy and safe.

MEASLES OUTBREAK RAISES QUESTION ABOUT 2020 OLYMPIC GAMES

The United States was not the only country to experience a measles outbreak. In Japan, 566 people were infected between January and May 2019, more than double the total for 2018. Some of the outbreak was linked to a religious group in Mie, Japan, but after members were infected, the group agreed to receive vaccinations for a variety of diseases, including measles. A number of cases in Japan were also the result of a school field trip to the Philippines, a country that had an alarming rise in measles in 2019, with more than 9,000 cases and 146 deaths reported in just the first six weeks of the year. That marked a 266 percent increase over the same period in 2018.

With the 2020 Olympics and Paralympics planned to take place in Tokyo, several countries, including the United States, expressed concern regarding the drastic rise in cases of both measles and rubella in Japan. In response, the Japanese government announced plans to encourage all people involved in the events—including government employees and those in the private sector—to get the measles and rubella vaccinations. And, as an attempt to stop new viruses from entering the country, Japan's health officials began to monitor all ports of entry using thermography to measure body temperature.

—Gia Miller

Following is a proclamation by Washington governor Jay Inslee on January 25, 2019, declaring a local public health emergency after a measles outbreak; a March 26, 2019, press release from Rockland County, New York, announcing a state of emergency related to a measles outbreak; an April 9, 2019, public health emergency declaration in New York City; a May 30, 2019, press release from the Centers for Disease Control and Prevention detailing measles case growth in the United States in 2019; and a press release from the Department of Health and Human Services on October 4, 2019, announcing that the United States would maintain its measles elimination status.

DOCUMENT

Governor Inslee Declares Public Health Emergency

January 25, 2019

PROCLAMATION BY THE GOVERNOR 19-01

WHEREAS, Clark County has declared a local public health emergency beginning January 18, 2019, after identifying an outbreak of measles that creates a substantial likelihood of risk to the citizens of Clark County and the seven cities therein; and

WHEREAS, The Washington State Department of Health has confirmed the existence of 25 cases of the measles in Clark County and one case in King County as of January 24, 2019; and

WHEREAS, The measles virus is a highly contagious infectious disease that can be fatal in small children, and the existence of 26 confirmed cases in the state of Washington creates an extreme public health risk that may quickly spread to other counties; and

WHEREAS, The measles vaccine is effective at preventing the disease when given prior to exposure, and proactive steps to provide the vaccination and other measures must be taken quickly to prevent further spread of the disease; and

WHEREAS, The Washington State Department of Health has instituted an infectious disease Incident Management Structure to manage the public health aspects of the incident; and

WHEREAS, The Washington State Military Department, State Emergency Operations Center, is coordinating resources to support the Department of Health and local officials in alleviating the impacts to people, property and infrastructure and is assessing the magnitude and long-term effects of the incident with the Department of Health; and

WHEREAS, The measles outbreak and its effects impact the life and health of our people, as well as the economy of Washington State, and is a public disaster that affects life, health, property or the public peace.

NOW, THEREFORE, I, Jay Inslee, Governor of the state of Washington, as a result of the above-noted situation, and under Chapters 38.52 and 43.06 RCW, do hereby proclaim that a State of Emergency exists in all counties in the state of Washington, and direct the plans and procedures of the Washington State Comprehensive Emergency Management Plan be implemented. State agencies and departments are directed to utilize state resources and to do everything reasonably possible to assist affected political subdivisions in an effort to respond to and recover from the incidents.

Signed and sealed with the official seal of the State of Washington this 25th day of January, A.D, Two Thousand and Nineteen at Olympia, Washington.

By:
Jay Inslee, Governor

Source: State of Washington Office of the Governor. "Proclamation by the Governor 19-01." January 25, 2019. https://www.governor.wa.gov/sites/default/files/proclamations/19-01%20State%20of%20Emergen cy.pdf?utm_medium=email&utm_source=govdelivery.

Rockland County Declares State of Emergency for Measles Outbreak

March 26, 2019

County Executive Ed Day declared a county wide State of Emergency relating to the ongoing measles outbreak. Effective at the stroke of midnight, Wednesday, March 27, anyone who is under 18 years of age and unvaccinated against the measles will be barred from public places until this declaration expires in 30 days or until they receive the MMR vaccination.

This declaration was issued under New York State Executive Law § 24 and is attached.

"Every action we have taken since the beginning of this outbreak has been designed to maximize vaccinations and minimize exposures. We are taking the next step in that endeavor today," said County Executive Day. "This is an opportunity for everyone in our community to do the right thing for their neighbors and come together. We must do everything in our power to end this outbreak and protect the health of those who cannot be vaccinated for medical reasons and that of children too young to be vaccinated."

In this emergency declaration, public places are defined as: a place where more than 10 persons are intended to congregate for purposes such as civic, governmental, social, or religious functions, or for recreation or shopping, or for food or drink consumption, or awaiting transportation, or for daycare or educational purposes, or for medical treatment. A place of public assembly shall also include public transportation vehicles, including but not limited to, publicly or privately owned buses or trains, but does not include taxi or livery vehicles.

"As this outbreak has continued our inspectors have begun to meet resistance from those they are trying to protect. They have been hung up on or told not to call again. They've been told "we're not discussing this, do not come back," when visiting the homes of infected individuals as part of their investigations. This type of response is unacceptable and irresponsible. It endangers the health and well-being of others and displays a shocking lack of responsibility and concern for others in our community," said Day.

Law enforcement will not be patrolling or asking for vaccination records but those found to be in violation will be referred to the Rockland County District Attorney's Office.

The Rockland County Department of Health will host a free MMR vaccination clinic from 1–3 pm, Wednesday, March 27 on the 2nd floor of Building A, Robert L. Yeager Health Complex, 50 Sanatorium Road, Pomona, NY.

"We must not allow this outbreak to continue indefinitely. We will not sit idly by while children in our community are at risk. This is a public health crisis, and it is time to sound the alarm, to ensure that everyone takes proper action to protect themselves and their neighbors; for the health and safety of all of us in Rockland," concluded County Executive Day.

SOURCE: Rockland County. "State of Emergency Declared." March 26, 2019. http://rocklandgov.com/departments/county-executive/press-releases/2019-press-releases/state-of-emergency-declared/.

New York City Issues Public Health Emergency Declaration

April 9, 2019

The de Blasio Administration today declared a public health emergency in select zip codes in Williamsburg, following a measles outbreak affecting the Orthodox Jewish community. As part of the declaration, unvaccinated individuals living in those ZIP codes who may have been exposed to measles will be required to receive the measles-mumps-rubella (MMR) vaccine in order to protect others in the community and help curtail the ongoing outbreak.

Under the mandatory vaccinations, members of the City's Department of Health and Mental Hygiene will check the vaccination records of any individual who may have been in contact with infected patients. Those who have not received the MMR vaccine or do not have evidence of immunity may be given a violation and could be fined $1,000.

"There's no question that vaccines are safe, effective and life-saving," said Mayor de Blasio. "I urge everyone, especially those in affected areas, to get their MMR vaccines to protect their children, families and communities."

"Measles is a dangerous, potentially deadly disease that can easily be prevented with vaccine," said Deputy Mayor for Health and Human Services Dr. Herminia Palacio. "When people choose not to get their children vaccinated, they are putting their children and others—such as pregnant women, people on chemotherapy, and the elderly—at risk of contracting measles. The City has worked aggressively to end this outbreak, and today's declaration of a public health emergency and new vaccine mandate, in combination with the blanket Commissioner's Orders for yeshivas, ensures we are using every tool to protect New Yorkers."

"As a pediatrician, I know the MMR vaccine is safe and effective. This outbreak is being fueled by a small group of anti-vaxxers in these neighborhoods. They have been spreading dangerous misinformation based on fake science," said Health Commissioner Dr. Oxiris Barbot. "We stand with the majority of people in this community who have worked hard to protect their children and those at risk. We've seen a large increase in the number of people vaccinated in these neighborhoods, but as Passover approaches, we need to do all we can to ensure more people get the vaccine."

This public health emergency declaration comes after the NYC Health Department issued Commissioner's Orders last week to all yeshivas and day care programs serving the Orthodox Jewish community in Williamsburg, doubling down on their order to exclude unvaccinated students or face violations and possible closure, first announced in December. Now any school out of compliance will immediately be issued a violation and could be subject to closure.

To date, 285 cases have been confirmed since the beginning of the outbreak in October, with many of these new cases being confirmed in the last two months. The vast majority of cases are children under 18 years of age (246 cases), and 39 cases are adults. Most of these measles cases were unvaccinated or incompletely vaccinated individuals. There have been no deaths associated with this outbreak, although there have been complications, including 21 hospitalizations and five admissions to the intensive care unit.

Measles is a highly contagious disease and can cause severe complications such as pneumonia, encephalitis (swelling of the brain), and death. Measles is easily preventable with the safe and effective MMR vaccine. Newborns, pregnant individuals, and those with weakened immune systems cannot get vaccinated, so it is important that everyone around them be vaccinated in order to protect them from contracting the virus and prevent severe complications in these susceptible populations.

While the MMR vaccine is the safest and most effective method of prevent measles, it is only 97 percent effective, so population-wide immunity is a key component to protecting our most at risk New Yorkers from measles. Pregnant women—even if they have received the MMR vaccine—are still at risk of complications including birth defects or loss of pregnancy.

In February, the Department expanded vaccination recommendations for providers serving the Orthodox Jewish community to include an early, extra dose of the MMR vaccine for children between the ages of 6 months to 11 months who live in Williamsburg and Borough Park.

Precautions New Yorkers Should Take

- Measles can be prevented through vaccinations. New Yorkers should call 311 to access a list of facilities that can provide MMR at low or no cost.

- There are large outbreaks of measles in Europe and Israel, as well as in countries in South America, Africa, and Asia. New Yorkers should make sure they have been vaccinated with MMR vaccine before traveling to Europe or Israel. Infants ages 6 to 11 months should also be vaccinated prior to international travel.

- New Yorkers who believe they were exposed to measles or who have symptoms of measles should contact their health care provider before seeking care to prevent exposure to other patients.

For more information, New Yorkers can visit the Health Department's Measles page.

SOURCE: New York City Office of the Mayor. "De Blasio Administration's Health Department Declares Public Health Emergency Due to Measles Crisis." April 9, 2019. https://www1.nyc.gov/office-of-the-mayor/news/186-19/de-blasio-administration-s-health-department-declares-public-health-emergency-due-measles-crisis#/0. April 9, 2019, press release of Mayor Bill de Blasio of New York City is used with permission of the City of New York.

DOCUMENT *CDC on Measles Case Growth*

May 30, 2019

Today, CDC is reporting 971 cases of measles in the United States thus far in 2019. This is the greatest number of cases reported in the U.S. since 1994, when 963 cases were reported for the entire year.

CDC continues to work with affected state and local health departments to get ongoing outbreaks under control.

"Measles is preventable and the way to end this outbreak is to ensure that all children and adults who can get vaccinated, do get vaccinated. Again, I want to reassure parents that vaccines are safe, they do not cause autism. The greater danger is the disease the vaccination prevents," said CDC Director Dr. Robert Redfield, M.D. "Your decision to vaccinate will protect your family's health and your community's well-being. CDC will continue working with public health responders across our nation to bring this outbreak to an end."

Outbreaks in New York City and Rockland County, New York have continued for nearly 8 months. If these outbreaks continue through summer and fall, the United States may lose its measles elimination status. That loss would be a huge blow for the nation and erase the hard work done by all levels of public health. The measles elimination goal, first announced in 1966 and accomplished in 2000, was a monumental task. Before widespread use of the measles vaccine, an estimated 3 to 4 million people got measles each year in the United States, along with an estimated 400 to 500 deaths and 48,000 hospitalizations.

We were able to eliminate measles in the United States for two main reasons:

- Availability and widespread use of a safe and highly effective measles vaccine, and

- Strong public health infrastructure to detect and contain measles

CDC encourages parents with questions about measles vaccine to consult with their child's pediatrician, who know the children and community, and want to help parents better understand how vaccines can protect their children. Concerns based on misinformation about the vaccine safety and effectiveness, as well as disease severity, may lead parents to delay or refuse vaccines.

All parents want to make sure their children are healthy and are interested in information to protect them. We have to work to ensure that the information they are receiving to make health decisions for their children is accurate and credible.

Everyone 6 months and older should be protected against measles before traveling internationally. Babies 6 to 11 months old need one dose of measles vaccine before traveling. Everyone 12 months and older needs two doses. International travelers unsure of their vaccination status should consult with their healthcare provider before traveling. Information can be found at http://www.cdc.gov/travel.

SOURCE: Centers for Disease Control and Prevention. "U.S. Measles Cases in First Five Months of 2019 Surpass Total Cases per Year for Past 25 Years." May 30, 2019. https://www.cdc.gov/media/releases/2019/p0530-us-measles-2019.html.

HHS Announces U.S. Retention of Measles Elimination Status

October 4, 2019

The United States has maintained its measles elimination status of nearly 20 years. The New York State Department of Health yesterday declared the end of the state's nearly year-long outbreak that had put the U.S. at risk of losing its measles elimination status.

"We are very pleased that the measles outbreak has ended in New York and that measles is still considered eliminated in the United States. This result is a credit to the cooperative work by local and state health departments, community and religious leaders, other partners, and the CDC," said HHS Secretary Alex Azar. "But this past year's outbreak was an alarming reminder about the dangers of vaccine hesitancy and misinformation. That is why the Trump Administration will continue making it a priority to work with communities and promote vaccination as one of the easiest things you can do to keep you and your family healthy and safe."

The CDC confirmed 1,249 cases of measles between January 1 and October 4, 2019. This year marks the greatest number of measles cases in the country since 1992. While cases have been reported in 31 states, 75% of measles cases were linked to outbreaks in New York City and New York state, most of which were among unvaccinated children in Orthodox Jewish communities. These outbreaks have been traced to unvaccinated travelers who brought measles back from other countries at the beginning of October 2018.

Since measles outbreaks continue to occur in countries around the world, there is always a risk of measles importations into the U.S. When measles is imported into a highly vaccinated community, outbreaks either do not happen or are usually small. However, if measles is introduced into an under-vaccinated community, it can spread quickly and it can be difficult to control. Measles elimination status is lost immediately if a chain of transmission in a given outbreak is sustained for more than 12 months. CDC has been working with the Pan American Health Organization (PAHO) throughout the year to keep stakeholders updated on measles surveillance. CDC will also meet with PAHO's Regional Verification Commission in the coming months to review the U.S. surveillance data and verify measles elimination status.

In the last year, the United Kingdom, Greece, Venezuela, and Brazil have lost their measles elimination status. Data from the World Health Organization indicates that during the first six months of the year there have been more measles cases reported worldwide than in any year since 2006. From January 1–July 31, 2019, 182 countries reported 364,808 cases of measles. That increase is part of a global trend seen over the past few years as other countries struggle with achieving and maintaining vaccination rates.

A significant factor contributing to the outbreaks this year has been misinformation in some communities about the safety of the measles-mumps-rubella (MMR) vaccine. Some organizations are deliberately targeting these communities with inaccurate and misleading information about vaccines. CDC continues to encourage parents to speak to their family's healthcare provider about the importance of vaccination. CDC also encourages local leaders to provide accurate, scientific-based information to counter misinformation.

"Our Nation's successful public health response to this recent measles outbreak is a testament to the commitment and effectiveness of state and local health departments, and engaged communities across the country," said CDC Director Robert R. Redfield, M.D. "CDC encourages Americans to embrace vaccination with confidence for themselves and their families. We want to emphasize that vaccines are safe. They remain the most powerful tool to preserve health and to save lives. The prevalence of measles is a global challenge, and the best way to stop this and other vaccine preventable diseases from gaining a foothold in the U.S. is to accept vaccines."

Before the measles vaccine was introduced in the U.S., nearly all children got measles by the time they were 15 years of age. It is estimated three to four million people were infected, and among the 500,000 measles cases reported annually, 48,000 were hospitalized and 500 people died.

SOURCE: U.S. Department of Health and Human Services. "With End of New York Outbreak, United States Keeps Measles Elimination Status." October 4, 2019. https://www.hhs.gov/about/news/2019/10/04/end-new-york-outbreak-united-states-keeps-measles-elimination-status.html.

OTHER HISTORIC DOCUMENTS OF INTEREST

FROM PREVIOUS *HISTORIC DOCUMENTS*

February

State of the Union Address
and Democratic Response

FEBRUARY 5, 2019

Less than two weeks after the longest federal government shutdown in U.S. history came to an end, President Donald Trump stood before a joint session of Congress to deliver the annual State of the Union address. The president stuck to the themes that had characterized his presidency, including immigration, the economy, and strengthening the U.S. position abroad. He gave only a brief nod to the ongoing investigation into possible links between his campaign and the Russian government, calling "ridiculous, partisan investigations" one of the only things that could derail the progress his administration was making.

Stacey Abrams of Georgia, who lost her race for governor in 2018, was chosen to give the Democratic response. She used her speech to call for a greater partnership between the president, Republicans, and Democrats to improve wages, health care, voting rights, and immigration.

TRUMP SPEECH DELAYED

The president is invited each year by letter from the Speaker of the House to deliver the State of the Union address before a joint session of Congress. A resolution is then approved by both the House and Senate dictating the date and time for the address in the House chamber. On January 3, Speaker Nancy Pelosi, D-Calif., invited President Trump to deliver the address on January 29. But due to the ongoing government shutdown, on January 16, Pelosi asked the president either to delay his speech until after the government reopened or deliver it to Congress in writing. Pelosi cited the cost of providing security at a time when federal agencies were already stretched without their annual appropriation. "I suggest that we work together to determine another suitable date after government has reopened," Pelosi wrote. She stopped short, however, of outright rescinding her earlier invitation.

The president responded that he would either find another venue suitable for his speech or would defy Pelosi's suggestion and arrive at the Capitol for the speech as planned on January 29. Various Republicans in state legislatures around the country offered their own chambers for the president's address, and the White House was also reportedly considering holding the speech in a southern state along the U.S.–Mexico border or in the Senate chamber. In response to Trump's refusal to postpone, Pelosi said she would not bring a motion to the floor to vote on the resolution for the joint session. "I think that's a great blotch on the incredible country that we all love," Trump said.

The president backed down on January 24, admitting that "no venue that can compete with the history, tradition, and importance of the House Chamber" could be located.

Calling the date change Pelosi's "prerogative," Trump said on Twitter that he looked "forward to giving a 'great' State of the Union Address in the near future!"

After the federal government temporarily reopened with a three-week continuing resolution while negotiators sorted out the final fiscal 2019 funding bill, on January 28, Pelosi reissued her invitation to the president to deliver his address on February 5. "It is my great honor to accept," the president wrote in response. "We have a great story to tell and yet, great goals to achieve!"

TRUMP TOUTS HIS ECONOMIC RECORD

In a break with tradition, after the president entered the House chamber and arrived at the lectern to deliver his address on February 5, he immediately began speaking, instead of waiting for the Speaker of the House to introduce him. In the audience, the president was greeted by a sea of white, with female members of the Democratic Caucus choosing to wear the color to represent both the 100th anniversary of women gaining the right to vote and the historic number of women elected to serve in the 116th Congress, a point Trump celebrated in the middle of his address.

As most presidents do, Trump began his speech on a lofty, bipartisan note. "We meet tonight at a moment of unlimited potential. As we begin a new Congress, I stand here ready to work with you to achieve historic breakthroughs for all Americans," the president said. "Millions of our fellow citizens are watching us now, gathered in this great Chamber, hoping that we will govern not as two parties, but as one Nation. The agenda I will lay out this evening is not a Republican agenda or a Democrat agenda. It's the agenda of the American people."

Throughout his eighty-two minute speech—the third-longest State of the Union in U.S. history—President Trump focused on his primary areas of concern from the first two years of his presidency: the economy and immigration. The president touted his economic record, "a boom that has rarely been seen before," citing 5.3 million jobs created, including 600,000 in the manufacturing industry. He also noted that under his administration wages were quickly rising, which was lifting millions of Americans off food stamps, and that unemployment was at its lowest level in fifty years. "After 24 months of rapid progress, our economy is the envy of the world," the president said.

Fact-checkers were quick to take issue with some of the president's economic claims. For example, they noted that job growth, while impressive, was actually slightly lower than the president stated at 4.9 million total jobs created since January 2017, 436,000 of which were manufacturing jobs. President Trump's figures, while true, count job growth from Election Day 2016 rather than his first day in office. Furthermore, although 3.6 million individuals had stopped receiving benefits from the Supplemental Nutrition Assistance Program (SNAP), formerly known as food stamps, low unemployment and increasing wage growth were only part of the story. The number of individuals receiving benefits has been steadily declining since 2014, some states have decreased the number of weeks individuals can receive benefits, and some media reports indicate that immigrants are no longer applying for assistance for fear of Trump administration backlash. Whether Trump's claim on wage growth was correct depends on whether one accounts for inflation, and although his unemployment claim was true in 2018, in January 2019 unemployment actually rose slightly to 4 percent, equivalent to the rate in March and June 2018.

President Remains Committed to Border Wall

Turning to immigration, the president called on Democrats and Republicans to come together to "confront an urgent national crisis" and "secure our very dangerous southern border." The president announced he was sending an additional 3,750 troops to the U.S.–Mexico border to provide assistance in dealing with the flow of immigrants across the border, which had reached an estimated 2,000 per day. Trump called addressing the U.S. immigration system a "moral issue." He cited the importance of improved immigration policies to ensure working-class Americans do not lose their jobs or experience reduced wages due to illegal immigrants, and also to ensure the security of children being brought across the border and those smuggled in by sex traffickers.

President Trump said that addressing immigration was also vital to stop the flow of deadly drugs and criminals into the United States. "Year after year, countless Americans are murdered by criminal illegal aliens," he said. The president's guests at the State of the Union address illustrated his points on immigration and included the family of a couple who was killed in Nevada by an illegal immigrant, as well as an Immigration and Customs Enforcement (ICE) officer who legally immigrated to the United States as a child. According to Trump, ICE had made 266,000 arrests of criminal aliens in 2017 and 2018. Fact-checks on this portion of the president's speech primarily pointed to evidence that illegal immigrants are less likely to commit crimes than the native-born American population and that economists tend to believe immigration is a net positive for the American economy, though it does disproportionately impact specific sectors of the workforce, primarily less-educated, low-skill, and low-wage workers.

"My administration has sent to Congress a commonsense proposal to end the crisis on the southern border. It includes humanitarian assistance, more law enforcement, drug detection at our ports, closing loopholes that enable child smuggling, and plans for a new physical barrier, or wall, to secure the vast areas between our ports of entry," Trump said. His comments came while Congress was in the midst of a three-week continuing resolution that had reopened the government on January 25 after a thirty-five-day shutdown predicated on a refusal by Democrats in Congress to provide funds for a wall along the U.S.–Mexico border. Trump maintained in the address that the wall would be built, because many members of Congress had previously supported similar measures.

Foreign Policy Receives Brief Nod

President Trump touched only briefly on foreign affairs, focusing on two key trade deals his administration was working on—one with China and another to replace the North American Free Trade Agreement (NAFTA)—and protecting American interests abroad. On the former, Trump said he would keep imposing tariffs on China if they continued to steal American intellectual property and commit other unfair trade practices. And he encouraged Congress to pass the U.S.–Mexico–Canada (USMCA) trade agreement "so that we can bring back our manufacturing jobs in even greater numbers, expand American agriculture, protect intellectual property, and ensure that more cars are proudly stamped with our four beautiful words: Made in the U.S.A."

President Trump committed to continuing his work to bring more U.S. troops home and end the ongoing wars in Iraq and Afghanistan and the engagement in Syria. He also committed to confronting state sponsors of terrorism, such as Iran, where the United States had in late 2018 imposed new sanctions after leaving the multination Iranian nuclear agreement. In what he called "a bold new diplomacy," Trump announced he would again meet with North Korean chairman Kim Jong-un within the next few weeks in Vietnam. "If I had not been elected President of the United States, we would right now, in my opinion, be in a major war with North Korea. Much work remains to be done," Trump said.

ABRAMS DELIVERS REBUTTAL

Stacey Abrams, the former Democratic candidate for Georgia governor and a rising star in the Democratic Party, was chosen to deliver the party's response to the president's speech. Abrams's gubernatorial race was one of the most closely watched in 2018, and if elected, she would have become the nation's first black female governor. Abrams faced off against Republican secretary of state Brian Kemp in a race that drew a litany of lawsuits alleging voter suppression. Ultimately, Kemp's 55,000-vote margin of victory was too large for an automatic recount.

Abrams began her address by talking about the importance of Americans supporting one another, illustrated by stories from her childhood about growing up both poor and working class. "In these United States, when times are tough, we can persevere because our friends and neighbors will come for us," Abrams said. Her criticism of the president focused first on economic security and immigration. Abrams claimed that Republican policies, and more specifically the 2017 tax bill, left working-class citizens further behind. "Rather than bringing back jobs, plants are closing, layoffs are looming, and wages struggle to keep pace with the actual cost of living," Abrams said. She noted optimism that Democrats and Republicans could work together to build a better immigration system, adding that "America is made stronger by the presence of immigrants, not walls."

She also called on the president and congressional leaders to address the high cost of health care and climate change but noted that these ambitious goals, among others, are not "possible without the bedrock guarantee of our right to vote." She said that "voter suppression is real," citing laws that make it harder to register to vote, voters removed improperly from the rolls, moving polling locations, and rejecting properly cast ballots. "The foundation of our moral leadership around the globe is free and fair elections, where voters pick their leaders, not where politicians pick their voters," Abrams said.

Despite vast disagreement with the president's policies, Abrams closed by noting that "even as I am very disappointed by the president's approach to our problems, I still don't want him to fail. But we need him to tell the truth and to respect his duties and respect the extraordinary diversity that defines America." She added, "America wins by fighting for our shared values against all enemies, foreign and domestic. That is who we are, and when we do so, never wavering, the state of our union will always be strong."

—Heather Kerrigan

Following is the text of President Donald Trump's February 5, 2019, State of the Union address; and the text of the Democratic response delivered by Stacey Abrams, also on February 5, 2019.

President Trump Delivers
State of the Union Address

February 5, 2019

The President. Madam Speaker, Mr. Vice President, Members of Congress, the First Lady of the United States, and my fellow Americans: We meet tonight at a moment of unlimited potential. As we begin a new Congress, I stand here ready to work with you to achieve historic breakthroughs for all Americans.

Millions of our fellow citizens are watching us now, gathered in this great Chamber, hoping that we will govern not as two parties, but as one Nation. The agenda I will lay out this evening is not a Republican agenda or a Democrat agenda. It's the agenda of the American people.

Many of us have campaigned on the same core promises: to defend American jobs and demand fair trade for American workers; to rebuild and revitalize our Nation's infrastructure; to reduce the price of health care and prescription drugs; to create an immigration system that is safe, lawful, modern, and secure; and to pursue a foreign policy that puts America's interests first.

There is a new opportunity in American politics, if only we have the courage, together, to seize it. Victory is not winning for our party, victory is winning for our country.

This year, America will recognize two important anniversaries that show us the majesty of America's mission and the power of American pride.

In June, we mark 75 years since the start of what General Dwight D. Eisenhower called the Great Crusade, the Allied liberation of Europe in World War II. On D-day, June 6, 1944, 15,000 young American men jumped from the sky, and 60,000 more stormed in from the sea, to save our civilization from tyranny. Here with us tonight are three of those incredible heroes: Private First Class Joseph Reilly, Staff Sergeant Irving Locker, and Sergeant Herman Zeitchik. Please. Gentlemen, we salute you.

In 2019, we also celebrate 50 years since brave young pilots flew a quarter of a million miles through space to plant the American flag on the face of the Moon. Half a century later, we are joined by one of the *Apollo 11* astronauts who planted that flag: Buzz Aldrin. Thank you, Buzz. This year, American astronauts will go back to space on American rockets.

In the 20th century, America saved freedom, transformed science, redefined the middle class, and when you get down to it, there's nothing anywhere in the world that can compete with America. Now we must step boldly and bravely into the next chapter of this great American adventure, and we must create a new standard of living for the 21st century. An amazing quality of life for all of our citizens is within reach.

We can make our communities safer, our families stronger, our culture richer, our faith deeper, and our middle class bigger and more prosperous than ever before. But we must reject the politics of revenge, resistance, and retribution, and embrace the boundless potential of cooperation, compromise, and the common good.

Together, we can break decades of political stalemate. We can bridge old divisions, heal old wounds, build new coalitions, forge new solutions, and unlock the extraordinary promise of America's future. The decision is ours to make. We must choose between greatness or gridlock, results or resistance, vision or vengeance, incredible progress or pointless destruction. Tonight I ask you to choose greatness.

Over the last 2 years, my administration has moved with urgency and historic speed to confront problems neglected by leaders of both parties over many decades. In just over 2 years since the election, we have launched an unprecedented economic boom, a boom that has rarely been seen before. There's been nothing like it. We have created 5.3 million new jobs and, importantly, added 600,000 new manufacturing jobs, something which almost everyone said was impossible to do. But the fact is, we are just getting started.

Wages are rising at the fastest pace in decades and growing for blue-collar workers, who I promised to fight for. They're growing faster than anyone else thought possible. Nearly 5 million Americans have been lifted off food stamps. The U.S. economy is growing almost twice as fast today as when I took office. And we are considered, far and away, the hottest economy anywhere in the world. Not even close.

Unemployment has reached the lowest rate in over half a century. African American, Hispanic American, and Asian American unemployment have all reached their lowest levels ever recorded. Unemployment for Americans with disabilities has also reached an alltime low. More people are working now than at any time in the history of our country: 157 million people at work.

We passed a massive tax cut for working families and doubled the child tax credit. We virtually ended the estate tax—or death tax, as it is often called—on small businesses, for ranchers, and also for family farms. We eliminated the very unpopular Obamacare individual mandate penalty. And to give critically ill patients access to lifesaving cures, we passed, very importantly, "right to try."

My administration has cut more regulations in a short period of time than any other administration during its entire tenure. Companies are coming back to our country in large numbers thanks to our historic reductions in taxes and regulations. And we have unleashed a revolution in American energy. The United States is now the number-one producer of oil and natural gas anywhere in the world. And now, for the first time in 65 years, we are a net exporter of energy.

After 24 months of rapid progress, our economy is the envy of the world, our military is the most powerful on Earth, by far, and America is again winning each and every day. Members of Congress: The state of our union is strong.

Audience members. U.S.A.! U.S.A.! U.S.A.!

The President. That sounds so good. [*Laughter*]

Our country is vibrant, and our economy is thriving like never before. On Friday, it was announced that we added another 304,000 jobs last month alone, almost double the number expected. An economic miracle is taking place in the United States, and the only thing that can stop it are foolish wars, politics, or ridiculous, partisan investigations. If there is going to be peace and legislation, there cannot be war and investigation. [*Laughter*] It just doesn't work that way.

We must be united at home to defeat our adversaries abroad. This new era of cooperation can start with finally confirming the more than 300 highly qualified nominees who are still stuck in the Senate, in some cases, years and years waiting. Not right. The Senate has failed to act on these nominations, which is unfair to the nominees and very unfair to our country. Now is the time for bipartisan action. Believe it or not, we have already proven that that's possible. In the last Congress, both parties came together to pass unprecedented legislation to confront the opioid crisis, a sweeping new farm bill, historic

VA reforms. And after four decades of rejection, we passed VA Accountability so that we can finally terminate those who mistreat our wonderful veterans.

And just weeks ago, both parties united for groundbreaking criminal justice reform. They said it couldn't be done. Last year, I heard, through friends, the story of Alice Johnson. I was deeply moved. In 1997, Alice was sentenced to life in prison as a first-time nonviolent drug offender. Over the next 22 years, she became a prison minister, inspiring others to choose a better path. She had a big impact on that prison population and far beyond.

Alice's story underscores the disparities and unfairness that can exist in criminal sentencing and the need to remedy this total injustice. She served almost that 22 years and had expected to be in prison for the remainder of her life.

In June, I commuted Alice's sentence. When I saw Alice's beautiful family greet her at the prison gates, hugging and kissing and crying and laughing, I knew I did something right. Alice is with us tonight, and she is a terrific woman. Terrific. Alice, please. Alice, thank you for reminding us that we always have the power to shape our own destiny. Thank you very much, Alice. Thank you very much.

Inspired by stories like Alice's, my administration worked closely with members of both parties to sign the First Step Act into law. Big deal. It's a big deal. This legislation reformed sentencing laws that have wrongly and disproportionately harmed the African American community. The First Step Act gives nonviolent offenders the chance to reenter society as productive, law-abiding citizens. Now States across the country are following our lead. America is a nation that believes in redemption.

We are also joined tonight by Matthew Charles from Tennessee. In 1996, at the age of 30, Matthew was sentenced to 35 years for selling drugs and related offenses. Over the next two decades, he completed more than 30 Bible studies, became a law clerk, and mentored many of his fellow inmates. Now Matthew is the very first person to be released from prison under the First Step Act. Matthew, please. Thank you, Matthew. Welcome home.

Now Republicans and Democrats must join forces again to confront an urgent national crisis. Congress has 10 days left to pass a bill that will fund our Government, protect our homeland, and secure our very dangerous southern border. Now is the time for Congress to show the world that America is committed to ending illegal immigration and putting the ruthless coyotes, cartels, drug dealers, and human traffickers out of business.

As we speak, large, organized caravans are on the march to the United States. We have just heard that Mexican cities, in order to remove the illegal immigrants from their communities, are getting trucks and buses to bring them up to our country in areas where there is little border protection. I have ordered another 3,750 troops to our southern border to prepare for this tremendous onslaught.

This is a moral issue. The lawless state of our southern border is a threat to the safety, security, and financial well-being of all America. We have a moral duty to create an immigration system that protects the lives and jobs of our citizens. This includes our obligation to the millions of immigrants living here today who followed the rules and respected our laws. Legal immigrants enrich our Nation and strengthen our society in countless ways. I want people to come into our country in the largest numbers ever, but they have to come in legally. Tonight I am asking you to defend our very dangerous southern border out of love and devotion to our fellow citizens and to our country. No issue better illustrates the divide between America's working class and America's political class than illegal immigration. Wealthy politicians and donors push for open borders while living their lives behind walls and gates and guards.

Meanwhile, working-class Americans are left to pay the price for mass illegal immigration: reduced jobs, lower wages, overburdened schools, hospitals that are so crowded you can't get in, increased crime, and a depleted social safety net. Tolerance for illegal immigration is not compassionate; it is actually very cruel.

One in three women is sexually assaulted on the long journey north. Smugglers use migrant children as human pawns to exploit our laws and gain access to our country. Human traffickers and sex traffickers take advantage of the wide-open areas between our ports of entry to smuggle thousands of young girls and women into the United States and to sell them into prostitution and modern-day slavery.

Tens of thousands of innocent Americans are killed by lethal drugs that cross our border and flood into our cities, including meth, heroin, cocaine, and fentanyl.

The savage gang, MS-13, now operates in at least 20 different American States, and they almost all come through our southern border. Just yesterday an MS-13 gang member was taken into custody for a fatal shooting on a subway platform in New York City. We are removing these gang members by the thousands. But until we secure our border, they're going to keep streaming right back in.

Year after year, countless Americans are murdered by criminal illegal aliens. I've gotten to know many wonderful Angel moms and dads and families. No one should ever have to suffer the horrible heartache that they have had to endure.

Here tonight is Debra Bissell. Just 3 weeks ago, Debra's parents Gerald and Sharon were burglarized and shot to death in their Reno, Nevada, home by an illegal alien. They were in their eighties and are survived by 4 children, 11 grandchildren, and 20 great-grandchildren. Also here tonight are Gerald and Sharon's granddaughter Heather and great-granddaughter Madison.

To Debra, Heather, Madison, please stand. Few can understand your pain. Thank you. And thank you for being here. Thank you very much. I will never forget, and I will fight for the memory of Gerald and Sharon that it should never happen again. Not one more American life should be lost because our Nation failed to control its very dangerous border.

In the last 2 years, our brave ICE officers made 266,000 arrests of criminal aliens, including those charged or convicted of nearly 100,000 assaults, 30,000 sex crimes, and 4,000 killings or murders. We are joined tonight by one of those law enforcement heroes: ICE Special Agent Elvin Hernandez. When Elvin—[applause]—thank you. When Elvin was a boy, he and his family legally immigrated to the United States from the Dominican Republic. At the age of 8, Elvin told his dad he wanted to become a Special Agent. Today, he leads investigations into the scourge of international sex trafficking.

Elvin says that "If I can make sure these young girls get their justice, I've really done my job." Thanks to his work, and that of his incredible colleagues, more than 300 women and girls have been rescued from the horror of this terrible situation, and more than 1,500 sadistic traffickers have been put behind bars. Thank you, Elvin. We will always support the brave men and women of law enforcement, and I pledge to you tonight that I will never abolish our heroes from ICE. Thank you.

My administration has sent to Congress a commonsense proposal to end the crisis on the southern border. It includes humanitarian assistance, more law enforcement, drug detection at our ports, closing loopholes that enable child smuggling, and plans for a new physical barrier, or wall, to secure the vast areas between our ports of entry.

In the past, most of the people in this room voted for a wall, but the proper wall never got built. I will get it built. This is a smart, strategic, see-through steel barrier, not just a simple concrete wall. It will be deployed in the areas identified by the border agents as having the greatest need. And these agents will tell you: Where walls go up, illegal crossings go way, way down.

San Diego used to have the most illegal border crossings in our country. In response, a strong security wall was put in place. This powerful barrier almost completely ended illegal crossings.

The border city of El Paso, Texas, used to have extremely high rates of violent crime, one of the highest in the entire country, and considered one of our Nation's most danger- ous cities. Now, immediately upon its building, with a powerful barrier in place, El Paso is one of the safest cities in our country. Simply put: Walls work, and walls save lives. So let's work together, compromise, and reach a deal that will truly make America safe.

As we work to defend our people's safety, we must also ensure our economic resur- gence continues at a rapid pace. No one has benefited more from our thriving economy than women, who have filled 58 percent of the newly created jobs last year.

[At this point, Democratic congresswomen joined other Members of Congress, Cabinet members, and attendees in a standing ovation.]

You weren't supposed to do that. Thank you very much. Thank you very much. [Laughter]

All Americans can be proud that we have more women in the workforce than ever before.

[Democratic congresswomen joined other Members of Congress and others in another standing ovation.]

Don't sit yet. You're going to like this. [Laughter]

And exactly one century after Congress passed the constitutional amendment giving women the right to vote, we also have more women serving in Congress than at any time before.

Audience members. U.S.A.! U.S.A.! U.S.A.!

The President. That's great. Really great. And congratulations. That's great.

As part of our commitment to improving opportunity for women everywhere, this Thursday we are launching the first-ever Governmentwide initiative focused on economic empowerment for women in developing countries.

To build on—[applause]—thank you. To build on our incredible economic success, one priority is paramount: reversing decades of calamitous trade policies. So bad.

We are now making it clear to China that, after years of targeting our industries and stealing our intellectual property, the theft of American jobs and wealth has come to an end. Therefore, we recently imposed tariffs on $250 billion of Chinese goods, and now our Treasury is receiving billions and billions of dollars.

But I don't blame China for taking advantage of us; I blame our leaders and represen- tatives for allowing this travesty to happen. I have great respect for President Xi, and we are now working on a new trade deal with China. But it must include real, structural change to end unfair trade practices, reduce our chronic trade deficit, and protect American jobs. [Applause] Thank you.

Another historic trade blunder was the catastrophe known as NAFTA. I have met the men and women of Michigan, Ohio, Pennsylvania, Indiana, New Hampshire, and many other States whose dreams were shattered by the signing of NAFTA. For years, politicians promised them they would renegotiate for a better deal, but no one ever tried, until now.

Our new U.S.–Mexico–Canada Agreement, the USMCA, will replace NAFTA and deliver for American workers like they haven't had delivered to for a long time. I hope you can pass the USMCA into law so that we can bring back our manufacturing jobs in even greater numbers, expand American agriculture, protect intellectual property, and ensure that more cars are proudly stamped with our four beautiful words: Made in the U.S.A.

Tonight I am also asking you to pass the United States Reciprocal Trade Act so that if another country places an unfair tariff on an American product, we can charge them the exact same tariff on the exact same product that they sell to us.

Both parties should be able to unite for a great rebuilding of America's crumbling infrastructure. I know that Congress is eager to pass an infrastructure bill, and I am eager to work with you on legislation to deliver new and important infrastructure investment, including investments in the cutting-edge industries of the future. This is not an option, this is a necessity.

The next major priority for me, and for all of us, should be to lower the cost of health care and prescription drugs and to protect patients with preexisting conditions. Already, as a result of my administration's efforts, in 2018, drug prices experienced their single largest decline in 46 years.

But we must do more. It's unacceptable that Americans pay vastly more than people in other countries for the exact same drugs, often made in the exact same place. This is wrong, this is unfair, and together, we will stop it, and we'll stop it fast.

I am asking Congress to pass legislation that finally takes on the problem of global freeloading and delivers fairness and price transparency for American patients, finally. We should also require drug companies, insurance companies, and hospitals to disclose real prices to foster competition and bring costs way down.

No force in history has done more to advance the human condition than American freedom. In recent years, we have made remarkable progress in the fight against HIV and AIDS. Scientific breakthroughs have brought a once-distant dream within reach. My budget will ask Democrats and Republicans to make the needed commitment to eliminate the HIV epidemic in the United States within 10 years. We have made incredible strides. Incredible. Together, we will defeat AIDS in America and beyond.

Tonight I am also asking you to join me in another fight that all Americans can get behind: the fight against childhood cancer. Joining Melania in the gallery this evening is a very brave 10-year-old girl, Grace Eline. Every birthday—[applause]. Hi, Grace. [Laughter] Every birthday since she was 4, Grace asked her friends to donate to St. Jude's Children's Hospital. She did not know that one day she might be a patient herself. That's what happened.

Last year, Grace was diagnosed with brain cancer. Immediately, she began radiation treatment. At the same time, she rallied her community and raised more than $40,000 for the fight against cancer. When Grace completed treatment last fall, her doctors and nurses cheered—they loved her; they still love her—with tears in their eyes as she hung up a poster that read: "Last day of chemo." Thank you very much, Grace. You are a great inspiration to everyone in this room. Thank you very much.

Many childhood cancers have not seen new therapies in decades. My budget will ask Congress for $500 million over the next 10 years to fund this critical lifesaving research.

To help support working parents, the time has come to pass school choice for Americans' children. I am also proud to be the first President to include in my budget a plan for nationwide paid family leave so that every new parent has the chance to bond with their newborn child.

Audience member. Yes!

The President. There could be no greater contrast to the beautiful image of a mother holding her infant child than the chilling displays our Nation saw in recent days. Lawmakers in New York cheered with delight upon the passage of legislation that would allow a baby to be ripped from the mother's womb moments from birth. These are living, feeling, beautiful babies who will never get the chance to share their love and their dreams with the world. And then, we had the case of the Governor of Virginia where he stated he would execute a baby after birth.

To defend the dignity of every person, I am asking Congress to pass legislation to prohibit the late-term abortion of children who can feel pain in the mother's womb. Let us work together to build a culture that cherishes innocent life. And let us reaffirm a fundamental truth: All children—born and unborn—are made in the holy image of God.

The final part of my agenda is to protect American security. Over the last 2 years, we have begun to fully rebuild the United States military, with $700 billion last year and $716 billion this year.

We are also getting other nations to pay their fair share. Finally. [*Applause*] Finally. For years, the United States was being treated very unfairly by friends of ours, members of NATO. But now we have secured, over the last couple of years, more than $100 billion of increase in defense spending from our NATO Allies. They said it couldn't be done.

As part of our military buildup, the United States is developing a state-of-the-art missile defense system.

Under my administration, we will never apologize for advancing America's interests.

For example, decades ago, the United States entered into a treaty with Russia in which we agreed to limit and reduce our missile capability. While we followed the agreement and the rules to the letter, Russia repeatedly violated its terms. It's been going on for many years. That is why I announced that the United States is officially withdrawing from the Intermediate-Range Nuclear Forces Treaty, or INF Treaty. Perhaps—[*applause*]—we really have no choice. Perhaps we can negotiate a different agreement, adding China and others, or perhaps we can't, in which case, we will outspend and outinnovate all others by far.

As part of a bold new diplomacy, we continue our historic push for peace on the Korean Peninsula. Our hostages have come home, nuclear testing has stopped, and there has not been a missile launch in more than 15 months. If I had not been elected President of the United States, we would right now, in my opinion, be in a major war with North Korea. Much work remains to be done, but my relationship with Kim Jong Un is a good one. Chairman Kim and I will meet again on February 27 and 28 in Vietnam.

Two weeks ago, the United States officially recognized the legitimate Government of Venezuela and its new President, Juan Guaidó. We stand with the Venezuelan people in their noble quest for freedom, and we condemn the brutality of the Maduro regime, whose socialist policies have turned that nation from being the wealthiest in South America into a state of abject poverty and despair.

Here in the United States, we are alarmed by the new calls to adopt socialism in our country.

Audience members. Boo!

The President. America was founded on liberty and independence and not Government coercion, domination, and control. We are born free, and we will stay free.

Audience members. U.S.A.! U.S.A.! U.S.A.!

The President. Tonight we renew our resolve that America will never be a socialist country.

Audience members. U.S.A.! U.S.A.! U.S.A.!

The President. One of the most complex set of challenges we face, and have for many years, is in the Middle East. Our approach is based on principled realism, not discredited theories that have failed for decades to yield progress. For this reason, my administration recognized the true capital of Israel and proudly opened the American Embassy in Jerusalem.

Our brave troops have now been fighting in the Middle East for almost 19 years. In Afghanistan and Iraq, nearly 7,000 American heroes have given their lives. More than 52,000 Americans have been badly wounded. We have spent more than $7 trillion in fighting wars in the Middle East.

As a candidate for President, I loudly pledged a new approach. Great nations do not fight endless wars. When I took office, ISIS controlled more than 20,000 square miles in Iraq and Syria, just 2 years ago. Today, we have liberated virtually all of the territory from the grip of these bloodthirsty monsters. Now, as we work with our allies to destroy the remnants of ISIS, it is time to give our brave warriors in Syria a warm welcome home.

I have also accelerated our negotiations to reach—if possible—a political settlement in Afghanistan. The opposing side is also very happy to be negotiating. Our troops have fought with unmatched valor. And thanks to their bravery, we are now able to pursue a possible political solution to this long and bloody conflict.

In Afghanistan, my administration is holding constructive talks with a number of Afghan groups, including the Taliban. As we make progress in these negotiations, we will be able to reduce our troop's presence and focus on counterterrorism. And we will indeed focus on counterterrorism. We do not know whether we'll achieve an agreement, but we do know that, after two decades of war, the hour has come to at least try for peace. And the other side would like to do the same thing. It's time.

Above all, friend and foe alike must never doubt this Nation's power and will to defend our people. Eighteen years ago, violent terrorists attacked the USS *Cole*. And last month, American forces killed one of the leaders of that attack.

We are honored to be joined tonight by Tom Wibberley, whose son, Navy Seaman Craig Wibberley, was one of the 17 sailors we tragically lost. Tom, we vow to always remember the heroes of the USS *Cole*. Thank you, Tom.

My administration has acted decisively to confront the world's leading state sponsor of terror: the radical regime in Iran. It is a radical regime. They do bad, bad things. To ensure this corrupt dictatorship never acquires nuclear weapons, I withdrew the United States from the disastrous Iran nuclear deal. And last fall, we put in place the toughest sanctions ever imposed by us on a country.

We will not avert our eyes from a regime that chants "Death to America" and threatens genocide against the Jewish people. We must never ignore the vile poison of anti-Semitism or those who spread its venomous creed. With one voice, we must confront this hatred anywhere and everywhere it occurs.

Just months ago, 11 Jewish Americans were viciously murdered in an anti-Semitic attack on the Tree of Life synagogue in Pittsburgh. SWAT Officer Timothy Matson raced into the gunfire and was shot seven times chasing down the killer. And he was very successful. Timothy has just had his 12th surgery, and he is going in for many more. But he made the trip to be here with us tonight. Officer Matson, please. Thank you. We are forever grateful. Thank you very much.

Tonight we are also joined by Pittsburgh survivor, Judah Samet. He arrived at the synagogue as the massacre began. But not only did Judah narrowly escape death last fall, more than seven decades ago, he narrowly survived the Nazi concentration camps. Today is Judah's 81st birthday.

[*Audience members sang "Happy Birthday."*]

The President. [*Laughter*] Great.

Pittsburgh, PA, resident Judah Samet. Thank you! [*Laughter*]

The President. They wouldn't do that for me, Judah. [*Laughter*]
Judah says he can still remember the exact moment, nearly 75 years ago, after 10 months in a concentration camp, when he and his family were put on a train and told they were going to another camp. Suddenly, the train screeched to a very strong halt. A soldier appeared. Judah's family braced for the absolute worst. Then, his father cried out with joy: "It's the Americans! It's the Americans!" [*Applause*] Thank you.

A second Holocaust survivor who is here tonight, Joshua Kaufman, was a prisoner at Dachau. He remembers watching through a hole in the wall of a cattle car as American soldiers rolled in with tanks. "To me," Joshua recalls, "the American soldiers were proof that God exists, and they came down from the sky." They came down from Heaven. I began this evening by honoring three soldiers who fought on D-day in the Second World War. One of them was Herman Zeitchik. But there is more to Herman's story. A year after he stormed the beaches of Normandy, Herman was one of the American soldiers who helped liberate Dachau. He was one of the Americans who helped rescue Joshua from that hell on Earth.

Almost 75 years later, Herman and Joshua are both together in the gallery tonight, seated side by side, here in the home of American freedom. Herman and Joshua, your presence this evening is very much appreciated. Thank you very much. [*Applause*] Thank you.

When American soldiers set out beneath the dark skies over the English Channel in the early hours of D-day, 1944, they were just young men of 18 and 19, hurtling on fragile landing craft toward the most momentous battle in the history of war. They did not know if they would survive the hour. They did not know if they would grow old. But they knew that America had to prevail. Their cause was this Nation and generations yet unborn.

Why did they do it? They did it for America. They did it for us. Everything that has come since—our triumph over communism, our giant leaps of science and discovery, our unrivaled progress towards equality and justice—all of it is possible thanks to the blood and tears and courage and vision of the Americans who came before.

Think of this Capitol. Think of this very Chamber, where lawmakers before you voted to end slavery, to build the railroads and the highways and defeat fascism, to secure civil rights, and to face down evil empires.

Here tonight, we have legislators from across this magnificent republic. You have come from the rocky shores of Maine and the volcanic peaks of Hawaii; from the snowy woods of Wisconsin and the red deserts of Arizona; from the green farms of Kentucky and the golden beaches of California. Together, we represent the most extraordinary nation in all of history.

What will we do with this moment? How will we be remembered? I ask the men and women of this Congress: Look at the opportunities before us. Our most thrilling achievements are still ahead. Our most exciting journeys still await. Our biggest victories are still to come. We have not yet begun to dream.

We must choose whether we are defined by our differences or whether we dare to transcend them. We must choose whether we squander our great inheritance or whether we proudly declare that we are Americans. We do the incredible. We defy the impossible. We conquer the unknown.

This is the time to reignite the American imagination. This is the time to search for the tallest summit and set our sights on the brightest star. This is the time to rekindle the bonds of love and loyalty and memory that link us together as citizens, as neighbors, as patriots. This is our future, our fate, and our choice to make. I am asking you to choose greatness. No matter the trials we face, no matter the challenges to come, we must go forward together.

We must keep America first in our hearts, we must keep freedom alive in our souls, and we must always keep faith in America's destiny that one Nation, under God, must be the hope and the promise and the light and the glory among all the nations of the world.

Thank you, God bless you, and God bless America. Thank you very much. Thank you.

SOURCE: Executive Office of the President. "Address before a Joint Session of the Congress on the State of the Union." February 5, 2019. *Compilation of Presidential Documents* 2019, no. 00063 (February 5, 2019). https://www.govinfo.gov/content/pkg/DCPD-201900063/pdf/DCPD-201900063.pdf.

Stacey Abrams Delivers Democratic Response to the State of the Union

February 5, 2019

As Prepared for Delivery

Good evening my fellow Americans and happy Lunar New Year. I'm Stacey Abrams and I'm honored to join the conversation about the state of our union.

Growing up, my family went back and forth between lower middle class and working class, yet even when they came home weary and bone tired my parents found a way to show us all who we could be.

My librarian mother taught us to love learning. My father, a shipyard worker, put in overtime and extra shifts. And they made sure we volunteered to help others. Later, they both became United Methodist ministers, an expression of the faith that guides us.

These were our family values. Faith, service, education, and responsibility.

Now, we only had one car, so sometimes my dad had to hitchhike and walk long stretches during the 30 mile trip home from the shipyards. One rainy night, my mom got worried. We piled in the car and went out looking for him, and we eventually found my dad making his way along the road, soaked and shivering in his shirt sleeves.

When he got in the car, my mom asked if he had left his coat at work. He explained that he'd given it to a homeless man he'd met on the highway. When we asked why he'd given away his only jacket, my dad turned to us and said, "I knew when I left that man, he'd still be alone, but I could give him my coat, because I knew you were coming for me."

Our power and strength as Americans lives in our hard work and our belief in more. My family understood firsthand that while success is not guaranteed, we live in a nation where opportunity is possible.

But we do not succeed alone.

In these United States, when times are tough, we can persevere because our friends and neighbors will come for us. Our first responders will come for us. It is this mantra, this uncommon grace of community that has driven me to become an attorney, a small-business owner, a writer, and most recently the Democratic nominee for governor of Georgia.

My reason for running was simple. I love our country and its promise of opportunity for all. And I stand here tonight because I hold fast to my father's credo.

Together, we are coming for America. For a better America.

Just a few weeks ago, I joined volunteers to distribute meals to furloughed federal workers. They waited in line for a box of food and a sliver of hope since they hadn't received paychecks in weeks.

Making livelihoods of our federal workers a pawn for political games is a disgrace. The shutdown was a stunt, engineered by the president of the United States, one that defied every tenant of fairness and abandoned not just our people, but our values.

For seven years, I led the Democratic Party in the Georgia House of Representatives. I didn't always agree with the Republican speaker or governor, but I understood that our constituents didn't care about our political parties.

They cared about their lives.

So when we had to negotiate criminal justice reform or transportation or foster care improvements, the leaders of our state didn't shut down. We came together and we kept our word.

It should be no different in our nation's capital. We may come from different sides of the political aisle, but our joint commitment to the ideals of this nation cannot be negotiable. Our most urgent work is to realize Americans' dreams of today and tomorrow, to carve a path to independence and prosperity that can last a lifetime.

Children deserve an excellent education from cradle to career. We owe them safe schools and the highest standards, regardless of ZIP code.

Yet this White House responds timidly, while first graders practice active shooter drills and the price of higher education grows ever steeper. From now on, our leaders must be willing to tackle gun safety measures and face the crippling effect of educational loans. To support educators and invest what is necessary to unleash the power of America's greatest minds.

In Georgia and around the country, people are striving for a middle class where a salary truly equals economic security. But instead, families' hopes are being crushed by Republican leadership that ignores real life or just doesn't understand it.

Under the current administration, far too many hard-working Americans are falling behind, living paycheck to paycheck, most without labor unions to protect them from even worse harm.

The Republican tax bill rigged the system against working people. Rather than bringing back jobs, plants are closing, layoffs are looming, and wages struggle to keep pace with the actual cost of living.

We owe more to the millions of everyday folks who keep our economy running, like truck drivers forced to buy their own rigs, farmers caught in a trade war, small business owners in search of capital and domestic workers serving without labor protections.

Women and men who could thrive if only they had the support and freedom to do so.

We know bipartisanship could craft a 21st century immigration plan, but this administration chooses to cage children and tear families apart.

Compassionate treatment at the border is not the same as open borders. President Reagan understood this. President Obama understood this. Americans understand this and the Democrats stand ready to effectively secure our ports and borders.

But we must all embrace that from agriculture to health care to entrepreneurship, America is made stronger by the presence of immigrants, not walls.

And rather than suing to dismantle the Affordable Care Act as Republican attorneys general have, our leaders must protect the progress we've made and commit to expanding health care and lowering cost for everyone.

My father has battled prostate cancer for years. To help cover the cost, I found myself sinking deeper into debt, because while you can defer some payments, you can't defer cancer treatment.

In this great nation, Americans are skipping blood pressure pills, forced to choose between buying medicine or paying rent.

Maternal mortality rates show that mothers, especially black mothers, risk death to give birth and in 14 states, including my home state, where a majority want it, our leaders refuse to expand Medicaid, which could save rural hospitals, save economies, and save lives.

We can do so much more, take action on climate change, defend individual liberties with fair-minded judges. But none of these ambitions are possible without the bedrock guarantee of our right to vote.

Let's be clear. Voter suppression is real. From making it harder to register and stay on the rolls, to moving and closing polling places to rejecting lawful ballots, we can no longer ignore these threats to democracy.

While I acknowledge the results of the 2018 election here in Georgia, I did not and we cannot accept efforts to undermine our right to vote. That's why I started a nonpartisan organization called Fair Fight to advocate for voting rights. This is the next battle for our democracy, one where all eligible citizens can have their say about the vision we want for our country.

We must reject the cynicism that says allowing every eligible vote to be cast and counted is a power grab. Americans understand that these are the values that our brave men and women in uniform and our veterans risk their lives to defend.

The foundation of our moral leadership around the globe is free and fair elections, where voters pick their leaders, not where politicians pick their voters.

In this time of division and crisis, we must come together and stand for and with one another. America has stumbled time and again on its quest towards justice and equality. But with each generation, we have revisited our fundamental truths, and where we falter, we make amends.

We fought Jim Crow with the Civil Rights Act and the Voting Rights Act. Yet we continue to confront racism from our past and in our present, which is why we must hold everyone from the highest offices to our own families accountable for racist words and deeds and call racism what it is, wrong.

America achieved a measure of reproductive justice in *Roe v. Wade*, but we must never forget, it is immoral to allow politicians to harm women and families, to advance a political agenda. We affirmed marriage equality, and yet the LGBTQ community remains under attack.

So even as I am very disappointed by the president's approach to our problems, I still don't want him to fail. But we need him to tell the truth and to respect his duties and respect the extraordinary diversity that defines America. Our progress has always been found in the refuge, in the basic instinct of the American experiment, to do right by our people.

And with a renewed commitment to social and economic justice, we will create a stronger America together.

Because America wins by fighting for our shared values against all enemies, foreign and domestic. That is who we are, and when we do so, never wavering, the state of our union will always be strong.

Thank you and may God bless the United States of America.

SOURCE: Office of Speaker of the House Nancy Pelosi. "Former Georgia State House Minority Leader Stacey Abrams' Democratic Response to President Trump's State of the Union." Delivered February 5, 2019 (text released February 6, 2019). https://www.speaker.gov/newsroom/2519-3.

OTHER HISTORIC DOCUMENTS OF INTEREST

FROM THIS VOLUME

- President Trump and Congressional Leaders Remark on Border Wall Funding Fight and Government Shutdown, p. 3
- President Trump Declares a National Emergency on the Southern Border, p. 89
- U.S. and North Korean Leaders Hold Summit; North Korea Renews Missile Tests, p. 113

FROM PREVIOUS *HISTORIC DOCUMENTS*

- U.S. and Chinese Officials Respond to Trade Dispute, *2018*, p. 163
- President Trump and European Leaders on Decision to Remove the U.S. from the Iran Nuclear Deal, *2018*, p. 288
- President Trump, Chairman Kim Remark on Historic Summit, *2018*, p. 347
- President Trump on New Trade Pact with Mexico and Canada, *2018*, p. 489
- Donald Trump and Nancy Pelosi Respond to Midterm Elections, *2018*, p. 646

President Trump, Vice President Pence, and NASA Remark on Space Program Efforts

FEBRUARY 13, FEBRUARY 19, MARCH 26, AND AUGUST 29, 2019

The U.S. space program and military space activities were the focus of several important developments in 2019. In February, the National Aeronautics and Space Administration (NASA) announced the conclusion of its long-running Mars Opportunity rover mission. The following month, Vice President Mike Pence directed the agency to accelerate the timeline for its new lunar program by four years and to use any means necessary to send Americans back to the moon's surface by 2024. At the same time, President Donald Trump continued taking steps to establish a new U.S. Space Force and U.S. Space Command to better address emerging national security concerns in space.

Mars Opportunity Rover Mission Comes to an End

On February 13, 2019, NASA officials announced the end of the space agency's nearly fifteen-year Mars Opportunity rover mission. NASA reported that the rover got caught in a "severe Mars-wide dust storm" in June 2018 that covered the craft's solar panels. Without power, the rover could not continue communicating with Earth. Engineers at NASA's Jet Propulsion Laboratory made more than 1,000 attempts to restore contact with the rover over an eight-month period, but none of them worked. The rover's last transmission was sent on June 10, 2018, from a location known as Perseverance Valley.

"It is because of trailblazing missions such as Opportunity that there will come a day when our brave astronauts walk on the surface of Mars," said NASA administrator Jim Bridenstine in the announcement. "And when that day arrives, some portion of that first footprint will be owned by the men and women of Opportunity, and a little rover that defied the odds and did so much in the name of exploration."

Opportunity launched from Cape Canaveral Air Force Station in Florida on July 7, 2003, landing on the planet's surface approximately seven months later, in January 2004. Its arrival followed that of its twin rover, named Spirit, which landed on the opposite side of Mars. The Opportunity rover far exceeded expectations for its mission: it traveled more than twenty-eight miles across the planet's surface, when it was designed to travel less than one mile, and overwhelmingly surpassed its life expectancy of ninety Martian days, which are only about forty minutes longer than Earth days. By contrast, the Spirit rover traveled roughly five miles and concluded its mission in May 2011. Among Opportunity's key achievements, NASA listed the discovery of hematite, a mineral that forms in water, at the rover's landing site; the return of more than 217,000 images; the analysis and sampling of more than 120 Martian rocks; and the discovery of evidence that ancient water similar to a terrestrial pond or lake may have existed in Mars's Endeavour Crater. NASA said the data collected by Opportunity suggested that Mars may have been habitable at some point in its history.

NASA's exploration of the Martian service continues through the Curiosity rover and InSight lander missions. The agency also plans to launch a new Mars rover in July 2020 that will look for "signs of past microbial life."

TRUMP ADMINISTRATION TAKES STEP TOWARD SPACE FORCE ESTABLISHMENT

On February 19, President Trump signed a memorandum directing the Department of Defense "to marshal its space resources to deter and counter threats in space, and to develop a legislative proposal to establish a United States Space Force as a sixth branch of the United States Armed Forces within the Department of the Air Force." Trump first raised the prospect of a new Space Force early in March 2018; three months later, he ordered the Pentagon to "immediately begin the process" necessary for creating the force.

The 2019 memorandum, known as Space Directive 4, took a step further by laying out how Space Force might be organized and what a proposal to Congress, which must approve—and agree to fund—new military entities, might look like. The positioning of Space Force under the Air Force's oversight was notable, since Trump's 2018 announcement suggested it would be an independent, sixth branch of the military. However, the memo did state that the secretary of defense would conduct periodic reviews to determine whether Space Force should become a separate entity. The memo said Space Force would be "authorized to organize, train, and equip military space forces of the United States to ensure unfettered access to, and freedom to operate in, space." It would be led by a civilian undersecretary of the Air Force for space and a four-star general who would be Space Force's chief of staff. This general would also become a member of the Joint Chiefs of Staff. The administration proposed that all civilian and military personnel "conducting and directly supporting space operations" for the Department of Defense be transferred to Space Force, and that the new force assume responsibility for any major space acquisition programs. NASA, the National Reconnaissance Office, and the National Oceanic and Atmospheric Administration would not be incorporated into Space Force.

While Trump declared the creation of Space Force to be "very important," critics say it would create unnecessary bureaucracy and could strain defense resources. Others have expressed concern that Space Force could spark another space race or militarize an area where peaceful collaboration has been effective. Most observers speculated that even if Congress signed off, it would take years to fully set up Space Force, in part because it may require substantial increases in space budget and military space personnel. It would also involve significant realignment within the armed forces to centralize all military space functions. The Air Force is currently responsible for most military space activity, but the Navy and Army also maintain space-related commands.

Trump followed Space Directive 4's issuance with the signing of an executive order creating United States Space Command on August 29. "As the newest combatant command, SPACECOM will defend America's vital interests in space—the next warfighting domain," said Trump at the signing ceremony. Trump noted how U.S. combatant commands have been created to respond to specific threats, highlighting the 2009 creation of U.S. Cybercommand to protect against cybersecurity threats as an example. (U.S. Cybercommand was elevated to a combatant command in 2018.) SPACECOM was necessary, he said, because "those who wish to harm the United States seek to challenge us in the ultimate high ground of space," and these adversaries are "weaponizing Earth's orbits with new technology targeting American satellites that are critical to both battlefield operations and our way of life at home." (A 2018 U.S. intelligence threat assessment had projected that China and Russia would be capable of shooting down U.S. satellites in two to three years.) Trump also announced that Gen. Jay Raymond, then the head of Air Force Space Command, would be tapped to lead SPACECOM.

In interviews following the announcement, General Raymond told reporters that one of his priorities will be building alliances with other militaries that have identified security concerns in outer space. He also said that SPACECOM would have about 300 staff to start, most of whom were already working on space-related missions for U.S. Strategic Command, which oversees nuclear operations and deterrence, among other matters. As with other combatant commands, SPACECOM will be able to draw from troops in other military branches for defense needs.

On December 11, the House passed the broadly bipartisan 2020 National Defense Authorization Act, which included a provision creating Space Force under the Air Force's oversight. A chief of space operations will lead Space Force and will serve on the Joint Chiefs of Staff while reporting to the secretary of the Air Force. The Senate approved the bill on December 17, sending it on to President Trump for signature.

LUNAR PROGRAM TIMELINE ACCELERATED

In addition to preparing for missions to Mars, NASA has been working to develop a new lunar program since Trump signed Space Directive 1 in December 2017. That memo directed the agency to send Americans back to the moon "for long-term exploration and use" before traveling on to Mars. NASA was targeting a crewed mission to the moon by 2028, reports indicated, but on March 26, 2019, Vice President Mike Pence told agency staff "that's just not good enough."

Delivering remarks before the fifth meeting of the National Space Council, which he chairs, Pence said NASA had been lacking a clear direction or focus and that "bureaucratic inertia" kept the agency from making acceptable progress in developing the technologies and spacecraft to return to the moon. He expressed disappointment with "years of cost overruns and slipped deadlines," saying that NASA and the United States were "better than that." Pence declared the United States was once again in a space race, noting that China landed on the far side of the moon in December 2018 and that American astronauts had to rely on Russia for transport to the International Space Station. "Urgency must be our watchword," he said. "I'm here, on the President's behalf, to tell the men and women of the Marshall Space Flight Center and the American people that, at the direction of the President of the United States, it is the stated policy of this administration and the United States of America to return American astronauts to the Moon within the next five years." He added, "And let me be clear: The first woman and the next man on the Moon will both be American astronauts, launched by American rockets, from American soil." Pence said National Space Council would soon make specific recommendations to NASA to guide its return to the moon, including a recommendation that the first crewed mission land near the moon's south pole, where water ice has been found in lunar craters.

NASA affirmed its commitment to the new timeline in early April, indicating the Artemis program would essentially consist of two phases: an initial phase focused on quickly landing astronauts on the moon by 2024, and a second phase that would develop a "sustained human presence on and around the moon" by 2028. Each phase will in turn be comprised of different missions. The first two Artemis missions will involve an unmanned test of *Orion* spacecraft atop a Space Launch System rocket and a manned orbital flight, respectively, but astronauts will not land on the moon until Artemis III. NASA has also released plans for what it calls the Gateway: a space station–like outpost that will orbit the moon long-term and provide a jumping-off point for lunar exploration, as well as a pit stop for crews on future missions to Mars. NASA plans to launch the first element of the Gateway system by December 2022.

—Linda Grimm

Following is a press release issued by NASA on February 13, 2019, announcing the end of the Mars Opportunity rover mission; a memorandum signed by President Donald Trump on February 19, 2019, to establish a new U.S. Space Force; remarks delivered by Vice President Mike Pence on March 26, 2019, in which he announced an accelerated timeline for NASA's new lunar program; and remarks by President Trump at the White House Rose Garden August 29, 2019, on his signing of an executive order creating U.S. Space Command.

NASA's Mars Rover Mission Ends

February 13, 2019

One of the most successful and enduring feats of interplanetary exploration, NASA's Opportunity rover mission is at an end after almost 15 years exploring the surface of Mars and helping lay the groundwork for NASA's return to the Red Planet.

The Opportunity rover stopped communicating with Earth when a severe Mars-wide dust storm blanketed its location in June 2018. After more than a thousand commands to restore contact, engineers in the Space Flight Operations Facility at NASA's Jet Propulsion Laboratory (JPL) made their last attempt to revive Opportunity Tuesday, to no avail. The solar-powered rover's final communication was received June 10.

"It is because of trailblazing missions such as Opportunity that there will come a day when our brave astronauts walk on the surface of Mars," said NASA Administrator Jim Bridenstine. "And when that day arrives, some portion of that first footprint will be owned by the men and women of Opportunity, and a little rover that defied the odds and did so much in the name of exploration."

Designed to last just 90 Martian days and travel 1,100 yards (1,000 meters), Opportunity vastly surpassed all expectations in its endurance, scientific value and longevity. In addition to exceeding its life expectancy by 60 times, the rover traveled more than 28 miles (45 kilometers) by the time it reached its most appropriate final resting spot on Mars—Perseverance Valley.

"For more than a decade, Opportunity has been an icon in the field of planetary exploration, teaching us about Mars' ancient past as a wet, potentially habitable planet, and revealing uncharted Martian landscapes," said Thomas Zurbuchen, associate administrator for NASA's Science Mission Directorate. "Whatever loss we feel now must be tempered with the knowledge that the legacy of Opportunity continues—both on the surface of Mars with the Curiosity rover and InSight lander—and in the clean rooms of JPL, where the upcoming Mars 2020 rover is taking shape."

The final transmission, sent via the 70-meter Mars Station antenna at NASA's Goldstone Deep Space Complex in California, ended a multifaceted, eight-month recovery strategy in an attempt to compel the rover to communicate.

"We have made every reasonable engineering effort to try to recover Opportunity and have determined that the likelihood of receiving a signal is far too low to continue recovery efforts," said John Callas, manager of the Mars Exploration Rover (MER) project at JPL.

Opportunity landed in the Meridiani Planum region of Mars on Jan. 24, 2004, seven months after its launch from Cape Canaveral Air Force Station in Florida. Its twin rover, Spirit, landed 20 days earlier in the 103-mile-wide (166-kilometer-wide) Gusev Crater on the other side of Mars. Spirit logged almost 5 miles (8 kilometers) before its mission wrapped up in May 2011.

From the day Opportunity landed, a team of mission engineers, rover drivers and scientists on Earth collaborated to overcome challenges and get the rover from one geologic site on Mars to the next. They plotted workable avenues over rugged terrain so that the 384-pound (174-kilogram) Martian explorer could maneuver around and, at times, over rocks and boulders, climb gravel-strewn slopes as steep as 32-degrees (an off-Earth record), probe crater floors, summit hills and traverse possible dry riverbeds. Its final venture brought it to the western limb of Perseverance Valley. . . .

More Opportunity Achievements

- Set a one-day Mars driving record March 20, 2005, when it traveled 721 feet (220 meters).

- Returned more than 217,000 images, including 15 360-degree color panoramas.

- Exposed the surfaces of 52 rocks to reveal fresh mineral surfaces for analysis and cleared 72 additional targets with a brush to prepare them for inspection with spectrometers and a microscopic imager.

- Found hematite, a mineral that forms in water, at its landing site.

- Discovered strong indications at Endeavour Crater of the action of ancient water similar to the drinkable water of a pond or lake on Earth.

All of the off-roading and on-location scientific analyses were in service of the Mars Exploration Rovers' primary objective: To seek out historical evidence of the Red Planet's climate and water at sites where conditions may once have been favorable for life. Because liquid water is required for life, as we know it, Opportunity's discoveries implied that conditions at Meridiani Planum may have been habitable for some period of time in Martian history. . . .

JPL managed the Mars Exploration Rovers Opportunity and Spirit for NASA's Science Mission Directorate in Washington. For more information about the agency's Mars Exploration program, visit: https://www.nasa.gov/mars.

Source: National Aeronautics and Space Administration. "NASA's Record-Setting Opportunity Rover Mission on Mars Comes to End." February 13, 2019. https://www.nasa.gov/press-release/nasas-record-setting-opportunity-rover-mission-on-mars-comes-to-end.

Trump Administration Issues Memo on Establishing a U.S. Space Force

February 19, 2019

Space Policy Directive–4

Memorandum for the Vice President, the Secretary of State, the Secretary of Defense, the Secretary of Commerce, the Secretary of Labor, the Secretary of Transportation, the Secretary of Homeland Security, the Director of the Office of Management and Budget, the Director of National Intelligence, the Assistant to the President for National Security Affairs, the Director of the Office of Science and Technology Policy, the Chairman of the Joint Chiefs of Staff, the Administrator of the National Aeronautics and Space Administration, and the Deputy Assistant to the President for Homeland Security and Counterterrorism

Subject: Establishment of the United States Space Force

 Section 1. Introduction. Space is integral to our way of life, our national security, and modern warfare. Although United States space systems have historically maintained a technological advantage over those of our potential adversaries, those potential adversaries are now advancing their space capabilities and actively developing ways to deny our use of space in a crisis or conflict. It is imperative that the United States adapt its national security organizations, policies, doctrine, and capabilities to deter aggression and protect our interests. Toward that end, the Department of Defense shall take actions under existing authority to marshal its space resources to deter and counter threats in space, and to develop a legislative proposal to establish a United States Space Force as a sixth branch of the United States Armed Forces within the Department of the Air Force. This is an important step toward a future military department for space. Under this proposal, the United States Space Force would be authorized to organize, train, and equip military space forces of the United States to ensure unfettered access to, and freedom to operate in, space, and to provide vital capabilities to joint and coalition forces in peacetime and across the spectrum of conflict.

 Sec. 2. Definitions. For the purposes of this memorandum and the legislative proposal directed by section 3 of this memorandum, the following definitions shall apply:

 (a) The term "United States Space Force" refers to a new branch of the United States Armed Forces to be initially placed by statute within the Department of the Air Force.

 (b) The term "Department of the Space Force" refers to a future military department within the Department of Defense that will be responsible for organizing, training, and equipping the United States Space Force.

 (c) The term "United States Space Command" refers to a Unified Combatant Command to be established pursuant to the Presidential memorandum of December 18, 2018 (Establishment of United States Space Command as a Unified Combatant Command), that will be responsible for Joint Force space operations as will be assigned in the Unified Command Plan.

 Sec. 3. Legislative Proposal and Purpose. The Secretary of Defense shall submit a legislative proposal to the President through the Office of Management and Budget that would establish the United States Space Force as a new armed service within the Department of the Air Force.

The legislative proposal would, if enacted, establish the United States Space Force to organize, train, and equip forces to provide for freedom of operation in, from, and to the space domain; to provide independent military options for national leadership; and to enhance the lethality and effectiveness of the Joint Force. The United States Space Force should include both combat and combat support functions to enable prompt and sustained offensive and defensive space operations, and joint operations in all domains. The United States Space Force shall be organized, trained, and equipped to meet the following priorities:

(a) Protecting the Nation's interests in space and the peaceful use of space for all responsible actors, consistent with applicable law, including international law;

(b) Ensuring unfettered use of space for United States national security purposes, the United States economy, and United States persons, partners, and allies;

(c) Deterring aggression and defending the Nation, United States allies, and United States interests from hostile acts in and from space;

(d) Ensuring that needed space capabilities are integrated and available to all United States Combatant Commands;

(e) Projecting military power in, from, and to space in support of our Nation's interests; and

(f) Developing, maintaining, and improving a community of professionals focused on the national security demands of the space domain.

Sec. 4. Scope. (a) The legislative proposal required by section 3 of this memorandum shall, in addition to the provisions required under section 3 of this memorandum, include provisions that would, if enacted:

(i) consolidate existing forces and authorities for military space activities, as appropriate, in order to minimize duplication of effort and eliminate bureaucratic inefficiencies; and

(ii) not include the National Aeronautics and Space Administration, the National Oceanic and Atmospheric Administration, the National Reconnaissance Office, or other non-military space organizations or missions of the United States Government.

(b) The proposed United States Space Force should:

(i) include, as determined by the Secretary of Defense in consultation with the Secretaries of the military departments, the uniformed and civilian personnel conducting and directly supporting space operations from all Department of Defense Armed Forces;

(ii) assume responsibilities for all major military space acquisition programs; and

(iii) create the appropriate career tracks for military and civilian space personnel across all relevant specialties, including operations, intelligence, engineering, science, acquisition, and cyber.

Sec. 5. United States Space Force Budget. In accordance with the Department of Defense budget process, the Secretary of Defense shall submit to the Director of the Office of Management and Budget a proposed budget for the United States Space Force to be included in the President's Fiscal Year 2020 Budget Request.

Sec. 6. United States Space Force Organization and Leadership. (a) The legislative proposal required by section 3 of this memorandum shall create a civilian Under Secretary of the Air Force for Space, to be known as the Under Secretary for Space, appointed by the President by and with the advice and consent of the Senate.

(b) The legislative proposal shall establish a Chief of Staff of the Space Force, who will be a senior military officer in the grade of General or Admiral, and who shall serve as a member of the Joint Chiefs of Staff.

Sec. 7. Associated Elements. (a) A Unified Combatant Command for space, to be known as the United States Space Command, will be established consistent with law, as directed on December 18, 2018. This command will have all of the responsibilities of a Unified Combatant Command in addition to the space-related responsibilities previously assigned to United States Strategic Command. It will also have the responsibilities of the Joint Force provider and Joint Force training for space operations forces. Moving expeditiously toward a Unified Combatant Command reflects the importance of warfighting in space to the Joint Force. The commander of this command will lead space warfighting through global space operations that may occur in the space domain, the terrestrial domains, or through the electromagnetic spectrum.

(b) With forces provided by the United States Space Force and other United States Armed Forces, the United States Space Command shall ensure unfettered access to, and freedom to operate in, space and provide vital effects and capabilities to joint and coalition forces during peacetime and across the spectrum of conflict. . . .

[Sections 8 and 9 discussing the Space Force's relationship with National Intelligence and its operational authorities have been omitted.]

Sec. 10. Periodic Review. As the United States Space Force matures, and as national security requires, it will become necessary to create a separate military department, to be known as the Department of the Space Force. This department will take over some or all responsibilities for the United States Space Force from the Department of the Air Force. The Secretary of Defense will conduct periodic reviews to determine when to recommend that the President seek legislation to establish such a department. . . .

[Section 11 detailing general provisions has been omitted.]

SOURCE: Executive Office of the President. "Memorandum on Establishment of the United States Space Force." February 19, 2019. *Compilation of Presidential Documents* 2019, no. 00088 (February 19, 2019). https://www.govinfo.gov/content/pkg/DCPD-201900088/pdf/DCPD-201900088.pdf.

Vice President Pence Remarks on the U.S. Space Program

March 26, 2019

. . . Fifty years ago, "one small step for man" became "one giant leap for mankind." But now it's come the time for us to make the next "giant leap" and return American astronauts to the Moon, establish a permanent base there, and develop the technologies to take American astronauts to Mars and beyond. That's the next "giant leap."

And as we'll hear today from these members of the National Space Council and our distinguished panelists, under the leadership of President Trump and with the strong support of NASA's 13th Administrator, we've made great progress toward renewing America's proud legacy of leadership in space. . . .

Today we stand at the dawn of a new era of space exploration—an era that will bring untold new challenges and opportunities, and it will demand the best of us. It will demand new ideas, renewed energies, courage, and bold action.

After spending more than 45 years in low-Earth orbit, President Trump and our entire administration believe that it is time to push onward to new horizons and new destinations.

And that's why, under the President's leadership, we've taken decisive action to propel human space exploration missions further into the depths of our solar system, and we've unleashed America's private pioneers to cultivate the vast expanses of low-Earth orbit.

Last year, NASA and American innovators began designing the precursor to outposts on the Moon and the mission to Mars, the Lunar Gateway. And we are rallying the world to join us in this vital work. This month, Canada became our first international partner and announced a 24-year commitment to cooperate on the Lunar Gateway.

And, as we speak, we're working with Congress to provide $500 million to get an American crew aboard this lunar-orbiting platform in the coming years. . . .

And, of course, in December of 2017, the President signed Space Policy Directive-1 to return Americans to the moon and prioritize crewed missions to the lunar surface.

SPD-1, as it's come to be known, marked a watershed moment for America's space enterprise. Since the disastrous decision to cancel the Constellation Program in 2010, the truth is NASA's exploration efforts were left adrift with no clear direction, focus, or mission.

To your great credit, the men and women of the Marshall Space Flight Center never gave up. You persevered with distinction through a time of indecision at the highest levels of our national government. And you continued to do your best, which is to build the greatest and most powerful rockets ever known to man. . . .

With Space Policy Directive-1, President Trump finally gave NASA the clear direction and clear mission that it needs. And as President Trump said, we will return "American astronauts to the Moon for the first time since 1972 for long-term exploration and use." And as he said, not only to, quote, "plant our flag and leave our footprint[s]," but to "establish a foundation [on the Moon] for an eventual mission to Mars." (Applause.) . . .

But to achieve our objectives, I came here today to say that NASA must meet that new spirit with new urgency and the focus that it all deserves. . . .

The truth is, despite the dedication of the men and women who are designing and building and testing the SLS, you all know the program has been plagued by bureaucratic inertia, by what some call the "paralysis of analysis." The nation actually learned, with great disappointment, in recent weeks, that the date for its first flight for the SLS has been pushed back yet again, to 2021.

You know, after years of cost overruns and slipped deadlines, we're actually being told that the earliest we can get back to the moon is 2028. Now, that would be 18 years after the SLS program was started and 11 years after the President of the United States directed NASA to return American astronauts to the Moon.

Ladies and gentlemen, that's just not good enough. We're better than that. It took us eight years to get to the Moon the first time, 50 years ago, when we had never done it before, and it shouldn't take us 11 years to get back. . . .

We have the technology to return to the Moon and renew American leadership in human space exploration. What we need now is urgency.

Now, make no mistake about it: We're in a space race today, just as we were in the 1960s, and the stakes are even higher.

Last December, China became the first nation to land on the far side of the Moon and revealed their ambition to seize the lunar strategic high ground and become the world's preeminent spacefaring nation.

And for more than seven years, without a viable human space launch program of our own, Russia has been charging the United States more than $80 million a seat every time an American astronaut travels to the International Space Station.

But it's not just competition against our adversaries; we're also racing against our worst enemy: complacency. And the truth is, we've been here before. . . .

And I'm here, on the President's behalf, to tell the men and women of the Marshall Space Flight Center and the American people that, at the direction of the President of the United States, it is the stated policy of this administration and the United States of America to return American astronauts to the Moon within the next five years. (Applause.)

And let me be clear: The first woman and the next man on the Moon will both be American astronauts, launched by American rockets, from American soil.

But to accomplish this, we must redouble our efforts here in Huntsville and throughout this program. We must accelerate the SLS program to meet this objective. But know this: The President has directed NASA and Administrator Jim Bridenstine to accomplish this goal by any means necessary. . . .

Urgency must be our watchword. Failure to achieve our goal to return an American astronaut to the Moon in the next five years is not an option. . . .

You know, urgency has always been in the DNA of Rocket City. And the men and women of the Marshall Space Flight Center know exactly what it takes to be first—to be first in space because you've been doing it for generations. . . .

President Trump knows that meeting this challenge will require a great national investment of time, talent, and resources. But the costs of inaction are greater.

The United States must remain first in space, in this century as in the last, not just to propel our economy and secure our nation, but above all because the rules and values of space, like every great frontier, will be written by those who have the courage to get there first and the commitment to stay. . . .

But, as I said, mission success will require more than just money. And that's why, today, the National Space Council will send recommendations to the President that will launch a major course correction for NASA and reignite that spark of urgency that propelled America to the vanguard of space exploration 50 years ago.

As you will hear, in these recommendations, we will call on NASA not just to adopt new policies but to embrace a new mindset. That begins with setting bold goals and staying on schedule. To reach the Moon in the next five years, we must select our destinations now. NASA already knows that the lunar South Pole holds great scientific, economic, and strategic value. But now it's time to commit to go there.

And today, the National Space Council will recommend that when the first American astronauts return to the lunar surface, that they will take their first steps on the Moon's South Pole.

But in order to accomplish this, NASA must transform itself into a leaner, more accountable, and more agile organization. If NASA is not currently capable of landing

American astronauts on the Moon in five years, we need to change the organization, not the mission.

To continue to build a world-class workforce, NASA needs the authority to recruit, train, and motivate the world's best and brightest scientists, engineers, and managers, and to remove any barriers standing in their way. And that includes building new and renewed partnerships with America's pioneering space companies and entrepreneurs.

And in this century, we're going back to the Moon with new ambitions, not just to travel there, not just to develop technologies there, but also to mine oxygen from lunar rocks that will refuel our ships; to use nuclear power to extract water from the permanently shadowed craters of the South Pole; and to fly on a new generation of spacecraft that will enable us to reach Mars not in years but in months.

To develop these new technologies, NASA must adopt an all-hands-on-deck approach to procurement, contracts, and its partnerships. If a commercial company can deliver a rocket, a lunar lander, or any other capability faster and at a lower cost to the taxpayer than the status quo, then NASA needs to have the authority and the courage to change course quickly and decisively to achieve that goal. . . .

I leave here with confidence that with the leadership of President Donald Trump, with our renewed commitment to space, with the courage and ingenuity of this new generation of explorers, and with God's help, that America will once against astonish the world with the heights we reach and the wonder we achieve. And we will lead the world in human space exploration once again.

Now let's get to work. Thank you all. God bless you.

SOURCE: The White House. "Remarks by Vice President Pence at the Fifth Meeting of the National Space Council." March 26, 2019. https://www.whitehouse.gov/briefings-statements/remarks-vice-president-pence-fifth-meeting-national-space-council-huntsville-al/.

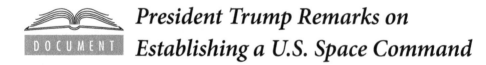

President Trump Remarks on Establishing a U.S. Space Command

August 29, 2019

THE PRESIDENT: Thank you very much. It's a great honor. What a beautiful day in the Rose Garden. Please sit. Thank you. . . .

We're gathered here in the Rose Garden to establish the United States Space Command. It's a big deal. As the newest combatant command, SPACECOM will defend America's vital interests in space—the next warfighting domain. And I think that's pretty obvious to everybody. It's all about space. . . .

We're especially grateful to welcome the new leader of SPACECOM, General Jay Raymond, a highly respected man within the military, joined this afternoon by his wife Mollie—thank you . . . General Raymond, congratulations. So important. I know he's going to do a fantastic job. Thank you very much.

The United States combatant commands were developed to join branches of our armed forces in common cause across diverse fields of battle.

Each of the United States military's combatant commands has an area of responsibility, from CENTCOM, which oversees our mission in the Middle East, to our most recent, CYBERCOM, which we established just last year to protect Americans from the most advanced cyber threats and also to create very, very severe and powerful offensive threats, should we need them. The dangers to our country constantly evolve, and so must we.

Now, those who wish to harm the United States to—seek to challenge us in the ultimate high ground of space. It's going to be a whole different ballgame.

Our adversaries are weaponizing Earth's orbits with new technology targeting American satellites that are critical to both battlefield operations and our way of life at home. Our freedom to operate in space is also essential to detecting and destroying any missile launched against the United States.

So, just as we have recognized land, air, sea, and cyber as vital warfighting domains, we will now treat space as an independent region overseen by a new unified geographic combatant command. The establishment of the 11th Combatant Command is a landmark moment. This is a landmark day—one that recognizes the centrality of space to America's national security and defense.

Under General Raymond's leadership, SPACECOM will boldly deter aggression and outpace America's rivals, by far. . . .

SPACECOM will soon be followed, very importantly, by the establishment of the United States Space Force as the sixth branch of the United States Armed Forces. And that's really something, when you think about it. The Space Force will organize, train, and equip warriors to support SPACECOM's mission.

With today's action, we open another great chapter in the extraordinary history of the United States military. SPACECOM will ensure that America's dominance in space is never questioned and never threatened, because we know the best way to prevent conflict is to prepare for victory.

From our nation's first days, America's military blazed the trails and crossed the frontiers that secured our nation's future. No adversary on Earth will ever match the awesome courage, skill, and might of American Armed Forces. Today, we salute the heroic men and women who will serve in SPACECOM and keep America's horizons forever bright and forever free. . . .

I would now like to ask Secretary Esper to sign documents formally establishing the United States Space Command. Thank you. . . .

I'd now like to like to now [*sic*] invite Chief Master Sergeant Roger Towberman to the stage to unfurl the flag of the United States Space Command. Thank you very much. . . .

SOURCE: Executive Office of the President. "Remarks on the Establishment of the United States Space Command." August 29, 2019. *Compilation of Presidential Documents* 2019, no. 00577 (August 29, 2019). https://www.govinfo.gov/content/pkg/DCPD-201900577/pdf/DCPD-201900577.pdf.

OTHER HISTORIC DOCUMENTS OF INTEREST

FROM PREVIOUS *HISTORIC DOCUMENTS*

- NASA Announces Launch of New Mission to Mars; European Scientists Find Martian Lake, *2018*, p. 281

Trump Administration Officials Comment on Personnel Changes

FEBRUARY 14, FEBRUARY 28, APRIL 7, JULY 12,
SEPTEMBER 18, AND OCTOBER 17, 2019

The number of leadership and personnel changes in U.S. president Donald Trump's administration have attracted significant attention since the beginning of his first year in office, particularly changes that involved personal or professional scandals. High-level confirmations and departures continued throughout 2019, with some analyses indicating Trump's administration had more turnover than any other recent president. The ongoing churn and widespread vacancies raised questions about the effectiveness and quality of the administration's policymaking efforts and prompted some federal employees to express their frustrations.

CABINET-LEVEL CONFIRMATIONS AND DEPARTURES

The Trump administration celebrated two cabinet-level confirmations early in 2019. First, William Barr was confirmed as the next attorney general on February 14, in what White House press secretary Stephanie Grisham declared "a major victory for justice and the rule of law in America." Barr replaced acting attorney general Matthew Whitaker, who had assumed the role after Jeff Sessions was pushed out in November 2018. Two weeks later, the Senate confirmed Andrew Wheeler as Environmental Protection Agency (EPA) administrator. Wheeler had been serving in an acting role since the summer of 2018, after former administrator Scott Pruitt resigned amid multiple investigations into his alleged legal and ethical violations. "I am deeply honored, and I look forward to continuing the President's agenda and the work of the Agency alongside all my EPA colleagues," said Wheeler. Other noteworthy confirmations in 2019 included that of David Bernhardt as interior secretary on April 11. Previously the department's deputy secretary, Bernhardt had served as its interim leader since former secretary Ryan Zinke resigned under pressure—while also facing allegations of ethics violations—in December 2018. On June 23, Mark Esper was confirmed as the new defense secretary, becoming the Defense Department's third leader in six months. Former defense secretary Jim Mattis had resigned in protest over the president's decision to withdraw U.S. troops from Syria, prompting Trump to name Patrick Shanahan, then Mattis's deputy, as acting secretary. But Shanahan resigned in June amid reports of past domestic violence incidents involving his family.

One of the highest-profile—and most anticipated—departures of 2019 was Department of Homeland Security (DHS) secretary Kirstjen Nielsen, who submitted her resignation on April 7 at Trump's request. Nielsen had become the public face of the administration's widely criticized and legally challenged immigration actions, specifically its implementation of a policy that separated migrant families arriving illegally at the U.S.–Mexico border. Trump had been openly critical of Nielsen for months and pushed her to be more aggressive in stopping the flow of illegal immigrants. "Despite our progress in reforming homeland security for a new age, I have determined it is the right time for me to step aside," Nielsen wrote in her resignation letter. "I hope the next Secretary will have the support of Congress and the courts in fixing the laws which have impeded our ability to fully secure America's borders." There was no deputy secretary in place at DHS at the time, meaning that Claire Grady, undersecretary for management and acting deputy secretary, should have been tapped to fill Nielsen's role temporarily, per the Federal Vacancies Reform Act. Instead, Trump fired Grady and named Kevin McAleenan, the commissioner of U.S. Customs and Border Protection (CBP), as acting secretary.

Nielsen was followed by Labor Secretary Alexander Acosta, who submitted his resignation on July 12. Acosta had come under fresh scrutiny for his handling of a case against New York financier Jeffrey Epstein—who in July 2019 was charged with child sex trafficking—in 2008 when Acosta was a federal prosecutor in Florida. The case alleged Epstein had sexually abused dozens of young women and girls. Acosta agreed to a plea deal with Epstein's lawyers, resulting in thirteen months of jail time for the financier, which he claimed was the best option for ensuring Epstein went to jail. The secretary said he was resigning because the scandal had become a distraction. "I agreed to serve so that I could implement your agenda," he wrote to the president. "Your agenda, putting the American people first, must avoid any distractions."

In September, National Security Advisor John Bolton left the administration over disagreements with the president about U.S. policy toward Afghanistan, Iran, and North Korea. Bolton claimed he quit, but Trump said he was fired. Charles Kupperman, Bolton's deputy, became the acting national security advisor—Trump's fourth since taking office. No other president has had as many national security advisors in his first three years in office. Department of Energy secretary Rick Perry was the next to go, resigning in mid-October. Trump reportedly blamed Perry for arranging the call with Ukrainian president Volodymyr Zelenskiy that became the subject of a whistleblower complaint that prompted Democrats to launch an impeachment inquiry against the president. Perry said he had wanted the two leaders to discuss strengthening energy business ties. "The opportunity to serve in your Cabinet as the Secretary of Energy of the United States has been an extreme honor," Perry said in his resignation letter. "Your leadership has positively changed the course of this country, and there is much to be proud of, especially in the energy sector." Trump nominated Deputy Secretary Dan Brouillette to take Perry's place.

REPORTS FIND RECORD TURNOVER, HIGH VACANCY RATES IN TRUMP ADMINISTRATION

These changes in cabinet-level positions were echoed by departures and reassignments within the Executive Office of the President. Press Secretary Sarah Huckabee Sanders, Deputy Chief of Staff and Communications Director Bill Shine, Director of National Intelligence Dan Coats, and Council of Economic Advisors chair Kevin Hassett were among those who left the administration in 2019.

These and other personnel changes have led the Trump administration to "record-setting turnover," according to Kathryn Dunn Tenpas, a nonresident senior fellow at the Brookings Institution. In 2019, Brookings published an analysis by Tenpas in which she found that Trump has already had higher turnover in his first term than any of the previous five presidents did in their first (or only) term. As of November 22, 2019, 80 percent of the sixty-five positions on Trump's "A Team" had turned over. Tenpas defined the

A Team as comprising the "most influential positions within the Executive Office of the President," such as the White House chief of staff and communications director, and directors of the Central Intelligence Agency and the Office of Management and Budget. The two most recent presidents, Barack Obama and George W. Bush, had 71 percent and 63 percent turnover, respectively, in their A Teams. Tenpas further found that 33 percent of Trump's A Team positions have experienced "serial turnover," meaning they have been occupied by more than two individuals. Additionally, Tenpas found that within Trump's cabinet, there have been ten changes in the leadership of executive departments, as compared to three and two such changes in the Obama and Bush administrations, respectively.

Other analyses pointed to a high number of vacancies within the Trump administration. According to a database maintained by *The Washington Post* and the nonprofit, nonpartisan Partnership for Public Service, 492 of 742 "key" administration positions requiring Senate approval had been confirmed as of December 9, 2019. Candidates for another 103 of these positions had been formally nominated, while eight positions are awaiting formal nominations (meaning a candidate has been announced but not sent to the Senate). The remaining 140 open positions do not have a nominee. DHS had the highest number of vacancies among federal agencies as of December 9, with 47 percent of key positions confirmed. Positions tracked by this database include cabinet secretaries, deputy and assistant secretaries, general counsels, heads of agencies, and ambassadors, among others.

Max Stier, president and CEO of the Partnership for Public Service, said the number of "consistent vacancies" across the Trump administration is "unprecedented." He also observed that "an element of musical chairs—filling one job and creating a vacancy somewhere else" has contributed to the administration's gaps in staffing. This was the case when Trump tapped McAleenan to replace Nielsen; McAleenan's new assignment created a vacancy at CBP. Underscoring this point, a separate analysis published by the Brookings Institution in July 2019 found that in his first two and a half years in office, Trump had twenty-eight acting secretaries—twenty-five of whom served for at least ten days. Trump's count of acting officials is not only higher than that of the five previous presidents, the analysis found, but his acting secretaries have also served longer tenures.

IMPLICATIONS OF HIGH TURNOVER

Many political analysts say that such high turnover could have a significant impact on the administration's ability to pursue Trump's agenda. Acknowledging that "some staff changes no doubt rid the White House staff of bad apples," Tenpas observed that any leadership departure can create uncertainty and instability and may deprive the administration of the former official's relationships. It can also disrupt the policymaking process. "Any vacancy requires hiring a replacement, helping the replacement learn the ropes, and other staff shouldering more work until the new hire is up-to-speed," she wrote. Martha Joynt Kumar, director of the White House Transition Project, says that turnover also results in lost continuity. "What happens is you lose the possibility of having a memory," she says. "You can't start in a positive way and then move forward and build on it."

Similarly, Anne Joseph O'Connell, a law professor at Stanford University, argued that acting officials—and vacancies, generally—have "significant consequences for public policy" because they contribute to "agency inaction, confusion among nonpolitical workers, and decreased agency accountability." O'Connell acknowledged that even though acting officials have not been "vetted" by the Senate and may therefore be seen as unqualified, they often have the skills and knowledge necessary for their temporary posts. However, Stier has argued that no matter an acting leader's qualifications, they are "akin to the substitute teacher" who is treated poorly by students who doubt the substitute's authority. "They certainly don't have long-term tenure, and as a result, they themselves typically don't take on the hard challenges or view the choices that they're making from that long-term lens," Stier says. "And the people around them understand that any choice they make may be changed by the full-time leadership as it comes in."

Connor Raso, an attorney with the Securities and Exchange Commission, suggested that personnel challenges—particularly in understaffed agencies—may be contributing to a "significantly reduced" volume of agency rulemaking under Trump, as compared to prior administrations. The Trump administration pursued 1,293 rules during the president's first year in office, Raso found in a 2018 analysis. By contrast, the Obama administration issued 2,024 rules in the president's first year, while George W. Bush pursued 3,374 rules.

Rachel Augustine Potter, an assistant professor of politics at the University of Virginia, suggested that personnel issues may also be a cause of the Trump administration's "regulatory corner-cutting." She noted that federal agencies under Trump have in some instances delayed the effective or compliance dates of regulations finalized by the Obama administration, manipulating cost-benefit analyses to support the administration's policy positions during rules analysis and limiting public comment periods below federal or agency guidelines. Difficulty filling positions, high turnover, and a lack of government experience among those in leadership positions mean "some appointees may choose to undercut the system rather than work through it, while others may be too inexperienced to appreciate the procedural intricacy and value of process in rulemaking," Potter said, adding that their quality of work may also be lower. "That means agencies may be producing rules that are not as coherent or able to effectively achieve the intended policy outcomes."

Reported comments by some anonymous federal agency staffers appear to support these concerns. "Frankly, the White House is just not interested in policy analysis," one Office of Management and Budget staff member told *Washingtonian* magazine. "They send us work to review that clearly has not been through a very rigorous clearance process." Others note the change in priorities that may occur when new leaders step in, and the uncertainty that creates. "We're still reeling from the big reorganization that [former secretary Rex] Tillerson was supposed to do but never happened," said one State Department employee in the same *Washingtonian* report. "Office mergers have been pending as imminent for months, and no one has really told us why or if anything is going to happen."

"We do need stability with DHS," a CBP agent told the *Los Angeles Times,* referring to a purge and reshuffling of DHS leadership that has been ongoing since Nielsen's resignation. Between April and July, both U.S. Immigration and Customs Enforcement and CBP had three different acting directors each. In May, Trump fired the head of U.S. Customs and Immigration Services (USCIS), L. Francis Cissna. The president nominated Ken Cuccinelli, former Virginia attorney general, as acting head of USCIS even though Republican leaders in the Senate said they would not confirm him. Then, in October, McAleenan resigned. Chad Wolf, DHS under secretary for strategy, policy, and plans, was named acting secretary the following month. A CBP official told *Politico* the many leadership changes were "awful for morale," adding that each time a new leader is named, "we're back to square one, getting a new person briefed. . . . It's like starting all over in a transition."

In some instances, the administration has employed creative staffing maneuvers to keep acting leaders in place. Per the Federal Vacancies Reform Act, acting secretaries and deputies can serve up to 300 days in a president's first year and 210 days in subsequent years. Acting deputy secretary of the Veterans Administration (VA) Jim Byrne reached his 210-day limit in January 2019; VA secretary Robert Wilkie subsequently reassigned Byrne as a "general counsel, performing the duties of the deputy secretary," allowing him to continue filling the acting role. Similarly, prior to Bernhardt's confirmation, the Department of the Interior delegated the responsibilities of vacant positions requiring Senate confirmation to other staff who were not subject to the Vacancies Act because they were not given an "acting" title. According to a Congressional Research Service report, "an action taken by any person who" is not in compliance with the Vacancies Act "in the performance of any function or duty of a vacant office . . . shall have no force or effect." This may lead to a greater risk of legal challenges to policies pursued and actions taken by acting officials.

The Trump administration has appeared unconcerned by these potential impacts. When asked about the high turnover, White House spokesperson Judd Deere said the president had "assembled an incredible team" and has had "undeniable success." The president has also asserted his administration has "tremendous stability" and that having acting personnel gives him flexibility. "The reason they're acting is because I'm seeing how I like them," he said. "We also have people that I've let go that have been here for many, many years and have done a bad job, and I let them go," he added. "I really don't say that's turmoil. I say that's being smart."

—Linda Grimm

Following is a tweet posted by White House press secretary Stephanie Grisham on February 14, 2019, announcing Attorney General William Barr's confirmation; a tweet posted by EPA Administrator Andrew Wheeler on February 28, 2019, in response to his confirmation; the resignation letter of DHS secretary Kirstjen Nielsen, dated April 7, 2019; the resignation letter of Labor Secretary Alexander Acosta, submitted on July 12, 2019; President Donald Trump's responses to reporter questions about DHS staffing during an exchange on September 18, 2019; and Energy Secretary Rick Perry's resignation letter from October 17, 2019.

DOCUMENT

White House Press Secretary Announces Attorney General Confirmation

February 14, 2019

A major victory for justice and the rule of law in America: the Senate just confirmed President @realDonaldTrump's outstanding nominee William Barr as Attorney General

SOURCE: Stephanie Grisham (@PressSec). Twitter post. February 14, 2019. https://twitter.com/PressSec/status/1096108854557982720.

Andrew Wheeler Comments on Confirmation as EPA Administrator

February 28, 2019

It is truly humbling to serve the American public as EPA Administrator. I want to thank President Trump for nominating me and Leader McConnell and Chairman Barrasso for navigating my confirmation through the Senate.

I am deeply honored, and I look forward to continuing the President's agenda and the work of the Agency alongside all my EPA colleagues.

SOURCE: Andrew Wheeler (@EPAAWheeler). Twitter post. February 28, 2019. https://twitter.com/EPAA Wheeler/status/1101186957080780801 and https://twitter.com/EPAAWheeler/status/1101186958024470534.

Homeland Security Secretary Nielsen Resignation Letter

April 7, 2019

Mr. President,

I hereby resign from the position of Secretary of the U.S. Department of Homeland Security (DHS), effective April 7th, 2019. It has been my great honor to lead the men and women of the Department as its sixth Secretary. I could not be prouder of and more humbled by their service, dedication, and commitment to keep our country safe from all threats and hazards. I join all Americans in thanking them for their sacrifices and those of their families.

For more than two years of service beginning during the Presidential Transition, I have worked tirelessly to advance the goals and missions of the Department. I am immensely proud of our successes in transforming DHS to keep pace with our enemies and adversaries—whether it is in cyberspace or against emerging threats from new technologies.

Despite our progress in reforming homeland security for a new age, I have determined it is the right time for me to step aside. I hope the next Secretary will have the support of Congress and the courts in fixing the laws which have impeded our ability to fully secure America's borders and which have contributed to discord in our nation's discourse. Our country—and the men and women of DHS—deserve to have all the tools and resources they need to execute the mission entrusted to them.

I can say with confidence our homeland is safer today than when I joined the Administration. We have taken unprecedented action to protect Americans. We have implemented historic efforts to defend our borders, combat illegal immigration, obstruct the inflow of drugs, and uphold our laws and values. We have responded decisively to record-breaking natural disasters and helped Americans rebuild. We have prevented the disruption of U.S. elections and guarded against foreign interference in our democracy. We have replaced complacency with consequences in cyberspace, we are holding digital intruders accountable, and we are stepping up our protection of American networks. We have thwarted terrorist plotting against our homeland and launched new efforts to block terrorists and criminals from reaching our shores. And we have ramped up security measures to make it harder for our enemies and adversaries to attack us, whether it is with drones, chemical and biological weapons, or through other means.

Thank you again for the privilege to serve the American people and to lead the outstanding men and women of the Department of Homeland Security. Supporting these patriots has been the honor of a lifetime.

Sincerely,
Kirstjen M. Nielsen
Secretary of Homeland Security.

SOURCE: Kirstjen M. Nielsen (@SecNielsen). Twitter post. April 7, 2019. https://twitter.com/SecNielsen/status/1115027149054992384.

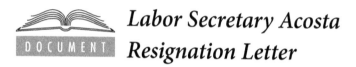

Labor Secretary Acosta Resignation Letter

July 12, 2019

Dear Mr. President,

My parents left Cuba as refugees in search of freedom to make a better life in the greatest country in the world, the United States of America.

They worked hard and wanted the best opportunities for their son and grandchildren. In one generation, their dreams were more than surpassed when you offered me the honor of a lifetime to serve as a member of your Cabinet, as Secretary of Labor.

From our first meeting, you offered me the opportunity to move consequential work forward on behalf of the American workforce. We have millions of new jobs, fewer injuries and fatalities on the job, record low unemployment, less regulation, and new family-sustaining career opportunities for the future. I have traveled from Alaska to Florida and from Maine to California to bring to the growers, miners, makers, movers, and servers your message that your presidency is focused on delivering for them. You are delivering for them. You have made America great again.

It has meant so much to me that you have offered your steadfast support in our private discussions and in your public remarks. That support notwithstanding, I agreed to serve so that I could implement your agenda. Your agenda, putting the American people first, must avoid any distractions. A Cabinet position is a temporary trust. I must set aside the part of me that wants to continue my service with the thousands of talented professionals at the Department of Labor.

Therefore, I am offering, and wish for you to accept, my resignation as United States Secretary of Labor effective one week from today.

My resignation from this position will not diminish my support for you and your agenda. I believe you have done an incredible job and have the right vision for our nation by putting working American families at the center of your presidency. When that vision is complete in the middle of the next decade, your successor will inherit an America that will be an even greater nation than it is today.

On behalf of my family, I thank you and will always treasure the opportunity to serve my fellow citizens of this shining city upon a hill.

Sincerely,
R. Alexander Acosta

SOURCE: U.S. Department of Labor. "Secretary Acosta Letter to President Trump." July 12, 2019. https://www.dol.gov/sites/dolgov/files/OPA/newsreleases/SecretaryAcostaLetterToPresidentTrump.pdf.

President Trump Comments on Department of Homeland Security Staffing

September 18, 2019

[The following comments were excerpted from a question-and-answer session with reporters while visiting a border wall site in California.]

Q. Mr. President, there has been a great deal of turmoil at the Department of Homeland Secretary the last several months.

The President. I don't think there has.

Q. Pretty much every person——

The President. Yes.

Q. ——leading that agency is in an acting capacity. Are you going to be——

The President. Well, being fired, because they weren't doing jobs. And some of them were there for a long time.

Q. When will you make permanent appointments there, nominations?

The President. Yes, I'm very happy, I can say. I haven't announced it yet, but I'm very happy with many of the people there. And we'll be announcing things in the future. I mean, there were many people that were there for a long period of time, and I wasn't happy with the job they were doing. And who could be happy? They were there for many years. They weren't doing their job. And we've made some incredible replacements. And yes, I'll be announcing permanents in the—pretty soon.

Q. But should the American people expect——

The President. I like—you know that—you know, Phil, I like—I like having nonpermanent, to a certain extent. It gives me more flexibility. I like having acting. I like the word "acting," because it gives me great flexibility. But at a certain period of time, we'll be making permanent positions.

Q. Is it unfair for the American people to expect some stability now——

The President. No, I think we have tremendous stability.

Q. ——in that agency, especially if there's a national emergency going on?

The President. I think we have tremendous—I mean, that's the way you write. But I think we have tremendous stability. I think we've never had a border—when this is completed, there won't be a border anywhere that's a border like this.

And a big beneficiary, frankly, is going to be Mexico. And one of the things that is happening—and I've heard it from the top echelons of Mexico—is, they're breaking up the cartels. The cartels have been disaster. And that's a good thing for Mexico because they have their own problems.

No, we have acting people. And the reason they're acting is because I'm seeing how I like them. And I'm liking a lot of them very, very much. We also have people that I've let go that have been here for many, many years and have done a bad job, and I let them go. And if you call that turmoil—I don't call it [turmoil]—I really—I really don't say that's turmoil. I say that's being smart. And that's what we do.

SOURCE: Executive Office of the President. "Remarks at the Otay Mesa Border Wall Site and an Exchange with Reporters in San Diego, California." September 18, 2019. *Compilation of Presidential Documents* 2019, no. 000627 (September 18, 2019). https://www.govinfo.gov/content/pkg/DCPD-201900627/pdf/DCPD-201900627.pdf.

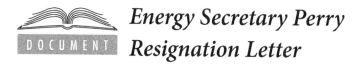

Energy Secretary Perry Resignation Letter

October 17, 2019

Dear Mr. President,

The opportunity to serve in your Cabinet as the Secretary of Energy of the United States has been an extreme honor. The citizens of this country will continue to benefit greatly from the policies and accomplishments of your Administration for years to come. Your leadership has positively changed the course of this country, and there is much to be proud of, especially in the energy sector.

Mr. President, for decades, American Presidents have talked about the importance of energy independence. Under your watch, it has finally been achieved. We no longer depend on other nations for our energy supply—nor are we beholden to the geopolitics of other world leaders for our energy security. Instead, we arrive in their capitals espousing the benefits of American energy resources, technology and services. I can attest first hand that the demand for our product is stronger than it has ever been, and under your leadership that will only multiply.

Across the world, we are competing like we never have before. Not long ago, America was an importer of energy. Now, the U.S. private sector is leading the world in energy production, exploration and exports. This historic success speaks to your leadership and willingness to go places where other leaders never thought possible. Today, when the world looks for energy, they can now think of America first.

The work being done across the Department of Energy and throughout our national labs to develop more abundant, less expensive and cleaner energy is world-class. From reviving our commercial nuclear energy industry to producing historic levels of domestic oil and gas and renewable energy, America has seen a remarkable turnaround in our energy industry.

The Department of Energy has also embraced, with success, the national security mission of modernizing our nuclear enterprise to make sure our weapons are safe and work as designed. We have also achieved unprecedented success in the clean-up of our nuclear facilities.

Mr. President, the American energy story is being written every day by millions of men and women in the workforce who are innovating and dedicating themselves to achieving greatness.

A perfect example of this are the men and women who are part of the DOE mission. They will be the ones who are at the forefront of innovation, such as with artificial intelligence and cyber security.

I am proud to have established the Office of Cybersecurity, Energy Security and Emergency Response and the Office of Artificial Intelligence and Technology. These new offices will help to provide the underlying research and building blocks for government and the private sector to work together in tackling challenges and pursuing opportunities.

An important part of the American energy story is what we are doing with science and technology to make our air cleaner. Greenhouse gas emissions have fallen dramatically, with remissions from the electric power sector at their lowest levels since 1987. During the same time, energy-related carbon emissions fell at an even greater pace. This was achieved through American innovation

Now more than ever, I believe strongly in the mission of the Department of Energy. The people across the enterprise have a sincere commitment to this country. I feel comfortable that the Department is well prepared to continue this mission with new leadership at the helm.

It has been a tremendous honor to serve our country in your administration in such a meaningful way. Anita and I will be forever grateful for this opportunity and I look forward to further supporting you and advancing American leadership in significant ways as a private citizen.

Please accept this letter as my official notification that I plan to resign at a date later this year.

Most respectfully,
Rick Perry

Source: U.S. Department of Energy. "Secretary Perry Announces Resignation, Effective Later This Year." October 17, 2019. https://www.energy.gov/articles/secretary-perry-announces-resignation-effective-later-year.

OTHER HISTORIC DOCUMENTS OF INTEREST

FROM THIS VOLUME

FROM PREVIOUS *HISTORIC DOCUMENTS*

Democrats Revise Primary Debate Rules

FEBRUARY 14, 2019

The Democratic presidential primary campaign began in earnest in early 2019, with more than two dozen candidates entering the race before the year's end. Frontrunner status, at least in public polling, was consistently held by former vice president Joe Biden, although his fundraising lagged that of other candidates and his candidacy did not readily ignite parts of the Democratic base frustrated by how the 2016 presidential primary process played out. To address concern that the party's primary process was undemocratic and did not reflect the views of all facets of the party, the Democratic National Committee (DNC) announced in February that it was making changes to the primary debate process to allow more voices to be heard. The result was twenty candidates debating across two nights during the first two events, a number winnowed to ten by the third. Pundits criticized the format for failing to give any clarity to the field, and voters polled after each event did not indicate much movement in their preferences.

DNC Revises Primary Debate Rules

After the 2016 presidential election, the Democratic Party faced sharp criticism that it favored Hillary Clinton, the eventual nominee, in the primary process over Sen. Bernie Sanders, I-Vt., who had a strong grassroots following. In an effort to avoid similar backlash, on February 14, 2019, DNC chair Tom Perez announced a plan to amend how candidates are selected to take part in the primary debates to increase the number of debate participants. The DNC said the intent was to: "(1) give the grassroots a bigger voice than ever before; (2) showcase our candidates on an array of media platforms; (3) present an opportunity for vigorous discussion about issues, ideas and solutions; and (4) reach as many potential voters as possible." Perez stated that "campaigns are won on the strength of their grassroots" so the changes were "giving all types of candidates the opportunity to reach the debate stage and giving small-dollar donors a bigger voice in the primary than ever before."

In the first two debates, a total of twenty candidates would be permitted to qualify by either earning 1 percent support in three qualifying polls or meeting a fundraising requirement of 65,000 individual donors with a minimum of 200 unique donors per state in at least twenty states. Given the expectation that a large number of candidates would qualify for the early debates, the DNC intended to divide the first two between separate nights. A lottery process would be used to determine which candidates would appear on which night, rather than having a "tiered" system that Republicans relied on in the lead-up to the 2016 election in which the most popular candidates held one debate, and the least popular were given a later debate time.

The primary debate policy was one of a number of changes implemented by the DNC in response to criticism over the way it handled the 2016 election. Another, voted on in mid-2018, lessened the power of superdelegates, unpledged individuals who can vote for any candidate of their choosing during the nominating convention. In future conventions, superdelegates will only be permitted to cast a vote on the first ballot if the outcome is already ensured (if there is only one frontrunner) or if the convention moves to a second ballot, which is rare. In addition, states that utilize caucuses rather than primaries to select a party's presidential nominee would be required to accept absentee votes instead of asking all participants to be at the caucus in person, the latter of which some have argued makes the process less democratic. Perez said the changes would ensure the production of a stronger candidate.

Democrats Hold Early Debates, Key Issues Emerge

Debates were scheduled for June, July, September, October, November, and December 2019, as well as January, February, March, and April 2020. Twenty candidates qualified for the first debate of the 2020 presidential election cycle. They included Colorado Senator Michael Bennet, former vice president Joe Biden, New Jersey senator Cory Booker, South Bend mayor Pete Buttigieg, former secretary of Housing and Urban Development Julián Castro, New York City mayor Bill de Blasio, Maryland representative John Delaney, Hawaii representative Tulsi Gabbard, New York senator Kirsten Gillibrand, California senator Kamala Harris, former Colorado governor John Hickenlooper, Washington governor Jay Inslee, Minnesota senator Amy Klobuchar, former Texas representative Beto O'Rourke, Ohio representative Tim Ryan, Vermont senator Bernie Sanders, California representative Eric Swalwell, Massachusetts senator Elizabeth Warren, author Marianne Williamson, and businessman Andrew Yang. The DNC tightened its rules for subsequent debates to narrow the number of candidates who would qualify, doubling the polling and fundraising requirements. Still, the second debate featured twenty candidates, but the third and fifth cut the field in half with only ten candidates, which allowed the debate to take place on one night (the fourth debate had twelve candidates and took place on one night).

Candidates in the first five debates tried to differentiate themselves from one another, while also criticizing the current administration and the Democratic frontrunner: Biden. Some candidates on the debate stage advocated for a move away from the politics of the Obama administration, policies that Biden frequently cited. "Every time something good about Barack Obama comes up, he says, 'Oh, I was there, I was there, that's me, too,'" said Castro. "And then every time somebody questions part of the administration that we were both part of, he says, 'Well, that was the president.'" Biden argued back that he stood by the president, "good, bad, and indifferent." Others, including Warren, asserted that Obama had not gone far enough in his policies, especially on health care, and her administration would build on his work. "The question is, how best can we improve on it?" she asked.

Each early debate set up a clash between the moderate and progressive wings of the party, from which a few key themes began to emerge that would characterize the lengthy 2020 primary process. These included health care, child care, and strengthening the middle class. On the latter, most candidates vowed to eliminate the 2017 tax cuts supported by President Donald Trump, which they felt unfairly benefited the wealthy. "Donald Trump has put us in a horrible situation. . . . I would be going about eliminating Donald Trump's tax cut for the wealthy," Biden said. Harris promised to repeal the tax cuts on the first day of her administration, which she would replace with a tax credit of up to $500 per month for those making less than $100,000 per year.

Another major issue among Democratic candidates on the primary stage was universal health care, especially in light of changes made to the 2010 Patient Protection and Affordable Care Act (ACA) in 2017. Then, as part of a larger tax cut package, Republicans voted to zero out the penalty taxpayers were penalized with if they did not have a qualifying health insurance plan. All of the early Democrat candidates asserted a belief that health care is a human right, and many endorsed varying degrees of an idea known as Medicare for All. Such a program would eliminate the private health insurance market and replace it with a government-run program (either Medicare or something similar to it). "Health care is an American right, and the current system is definitely wrong. I believe the best way to get there is by having Medicare for all," Booker said, while Harris called having Medicare for all "the bottom line" in improving the U.S. health care system. A few, including Bennet, Gillibrand, and Biden, would instead give all Americans the option of either purchasing their own private health insurance or getting coverage through Medicare.

Senator Warren's campaign made child care and early childhood education a key focus of the Democratic primary. She proposed instituting a universal child care model, similar to what the United States had during World War II, that would provide free or heavily subsidized child care to all families, regardless of income. Warren actually introduced a bill in the 116th Congress to institute such a model. The Universal Child Care and Early Learning Act would create in- and out-of-home child care centers and preschools where families would pay no more than 7 percent of their income. Any family earning less than 200 percent of the federal poverty level would receive free care. All centers would be held to a set of national quality standards.

To fund her program, which was estimated to cost $70 billion per year, Warren would impose a 2 percent tax on households earning more than $50 million and 3 percent on those earning more than $1 billion. "Access to affordable and high-quality childcare and early education should be a right for all families rather than a privilege for only the rich," said Warren. Warren's proposal was backed by fellow candidates Booker and Ryan, who also cosponsored the bill in Congress. Her plan faced criticism from the right, which claimed not only that it was unaffordable but there was no guarantee it would improve quality; furthermore, studies in other countries where universal care was implemented found harm to children and parents.

Other candidates expressed support for affordable care and better early childhood education, but stopped short of a universal care model. Gillibrand's Family Bill of Rights, for example, included public prekindergarten. A variety of candidates also backed expanding the existing Child Care and Dependent Tax Credit, which provides a refundable credit of up to $2,000 to help cover the cost of child care, or instituting new programs under the U.S. tax code that would financially support parents and caregivers.

FRONTRUNNERS TAKE SHAPE, TRUMP CHALLENGERS STRUGGLE

By late 2019, fifteen candidates remained in the primary race, but clear frontrunners were emerging in Biden, Warren, and Sanders, who all consistently ranked in the double digits in national polls, though Buttigieg was strong in the polls in the early primary states of Iowa and New Hampshire. The South Bend, Indiana, mayor ranked first in a poll of likely Iowa voters conducted by Monmouth November 7–11, 2019. Looking solely at fundraising strength in 2019, Biden was in fourth, bringing in $15.7 million from July through September, while Buttigieg brought in $19.1 million, Warren $24.6 million, and Sanders $25.2 million. Where Biden relied on big-dollar donors, other candidates surpassed his fundraising totals by collecting smaller amounts, much of it through social media campaigns.

In his tweets and at rallies, President Trump displayed no concern about any of the frontrunners. "Sleepy Joe," as President Trump called Biden, was one of his most heavily attacked opponents. Biden "was never considered a good senator," Trump said, noting he was only a good vice president because he was a yes man for President Obama. By mid-year, Trump renewed his feud with Warren as she gained in the polls. The two had sparred previously over Warren's insinuation that she had Native American heritage. While calling himself "so great looking and smart, a true Stable Genius!" he referred to Warren in the same series of tweets as "a very nervous and skinny version of Pocahontas."

Trump also did not express concern about the handful of Republicans who intended to challenge the president. One such challenger was former congressman and South Carolina governor Mark Sanford, who announced his bid in September. Sanford intended to focus on financial issues, citing his long-running record as a fiscal conservative. Although it grabbed some media attention, Sanford's bid was short-lived, and he withdrew his name from consideration on November 12, citing the Democratic-led impeachment inquiry in Congress that was making it difficult for his campaign to gain traction. Other Republican candidates seeking to become their party's nominee included former Massachusetts governor Bill Weld and former congressman Joe Walsh of Illinois. Neither gained much traction, and it was unlikely that they could mount a serious threat to the president's nomination because in January 2019, the RNC adopted a resolution to give "undivided support" to the president ahead of his 2020 election. That announcement faced pushback from some Republicans, including Maryland governor Larry Hogan, who called it "unprecedented," and accused the party of an attempt to block any potential primary challengers.

—Heather Kerrigan

Following is the text of an announcement from the Democratic National Committee on February 14, 2019, announcing the revised process for candidates to qualify for 2020 presidential primary debates.

Democrats Announce Revised Debate Format

February 14, 2019

NBC News, MSNBC and Telemundo to host first debate in June; CNN to host second in July

Last year, DNC Chair Tom Perez announced that his goals for the Democratic presidential primary debates are to (1) give the grassroots a bigger voice than ever before; (2) showcase our candidates on an array of media platforms; (3) present an opportunity for vigorous discussion about issues, ideas and solutions; and (4) reach as many potential voters as possible. Perez announced 12 presidential primary debates to be held over the course of the 2020 cycle, with the first two occurring in June and July of 2019.

Today, the DNC is proud to announce NBC News, MSNBC and Telemundo as its partner for the first debate and CNN as its partner for the second debate. To accommodate what is expected to be a historically large primary field, both debates will have the option of occurring over consecutive nights in prime time to make room for as many as twenty candidates, with the lineups for each night determined at random. This approach will provide each candidate with a fair opportunity to make his or her case to a large, national audience.

This agreement is unprecedented—no debate has ever aired in prime time on back-to-back nights. Both debates will be streamed online for free.

The DNC also announced the qualification criteria for candidates' participation in the first two debates—a two-path system that employs both a polling threshold and a grassroots fundraising threshold, and uses the two measures in combination in the event that more than 20 candidates qualify.

"As Chair of the DNC, I am committed to running an open and transparent primary process. To that end, we've spent months working with media partners to provide this unprecedented opportunity for candidates and voters to get to know each other. Because campaigns are won on the strength of their grassroots, we also updated the threshold, giving all types of candidates the opportunity to reach the debate stage and giving small-dollar donors a bigger voice in the primary than ever before."—DNC Chair Tom Perez

DETAILS ON MEDIA PARTNERS:

The DNC will partner with NBC News, MSNBC and Telemundo to host the first debate of the 2020 Democratic presidential primary process. The debate will be broadcast simultaneously on all three networks, with real-time Spanish translations on Telemundo, in prime time on back-to-back weeknights in June. The debate will also be streamed for free on NBC News' digital platforms including NBCNews.com, MSNBC.com, NBC News Mobile App, and OTT apps in addition to Telemundo's digital platforms.

The July debate will be broadcast on CNN, CNN International, and CNN en Español in prime time on back-to-back weeknights if more than one night is needed. An unauthenticated live stream of the debate will also be available for all users on CNN's website, mobile apps and connected TVs via CNNgo.

Both agreements are unprecedented—no debate has ever aired in prime time on back-to-back nights before.

Location, venue, moderators, date and time, format and logistics of the first and second debates will be announced at a later date.

DETAILS ON THRESHOLD FOR PARTICIPATION:

Democratic candidates may qualify for the first and second debate by meeting one of the two following sets of criteria:

Polling Method: Register 1% or more support in three polls (which may be national polls, or polls in Iowa, New Hampshire, South Carolina, and/or Nevada) publicly released between January 1, 2019, and 14 days prior to the date of the Organization Debate. Qualifying polls will be limited to those sponsored by one or more of the following organizations/institutions: Associated Press, ABC News, CBS News, CNN, *Des Moines Register*, Fox News, *Las Vegas Review Journal*, Monmouth University, NBC News, *New York Times*, National Public Radio (NPR), Quinnipiac University, Reuters, University of New

Hampshire, *Wall Street Journal, USA Today, Washington Post*, Winthrop University. Any candidate's three qualifying polls must be conducted by different organizations, or if by the same organization, must be in different geographical areas.

Grassroots Fundraising Method. Candidates may qualify for the debate by demonstrating that the campaign has received donations from at least (1) 65,000 unique donors; and (2) a minimum of 200 unique donors per state in at least 20 U.S. states. To demonstrate that the fundraising threshold has been reached, candidates must provide verifiable evidence, which they may do by authorizing ActBlue and/or NGP VAN to provide that evidence.

If more than 20 candidates qualify for the debate, the top 20 candidates will be selected using a methodology that gives primacy to candidates meeting both thresholds, followed by the highest polling average, followed by the most unique donors.

TIEBREAKING SYSTEM

If more than 20 candidates qualify for the June or July debates, then the media partner, in coordination with the DNC, will select only the top 20 qualifying candidates to participate in each debate (over two nights, as described above) under the following methodology:

a) Candidates who qualify for the debate under both the Polling and Grassroots Fundraising Method will be the first to qualify for the debate. If more than 20 candidates all qualify under both the Polling and Grassroots Fundraising Methods, such candidates with the highest polling averages will be included in the debate, as calculated pursuant to the formula described below.

b) If fewer than 20 candidates qualify for the debate by meeting both the Polling and Grassroots Fundraising Methods, but at least 20 candidates have qualified via the Polling Method, the remaining slots up to a maximum of 20 will be filled by the candidates with the highest polling averages who failed to qualify under the Grassroots Fundraising Method.

c) If fewer than 20 candidates qualify for the debate by meeting both the Polling and Grassroots Fundraising Method and fewer than 20 candidates have qualified for the debate under the Polling Method, then every candidate who has qualified using the Polling Method will be invited to participate in the debate and the remainder of the 20 slots will be filled by candidates who have qualified under the Grassroots Fundraising Method in descending order based on the highest number of unique donors.

CALCULATING POLLING AVERAGE

For the purposes of resolving tiebreaking scenarios, "highest polling average" is calculated by adding the top three polling results for each candidate (using the top-line number listed in the original public release from the approved sponsoring organization/ institution, whether or not it is a rounded or weighted number), and dividing by three. The resulting number will be rounded to the nearest tenth of a percentage point.

In the event that the top twenty candidates cannot be identified using this approach because multiple candidates are tied for the final qualifying spot(s), candidates who are initially tied for the final qualifying spots will be ranked according to the total number of qualifying polls submitted by each candidate for purposes of determining who is in the top 20. The total number of qualifying polls for each candidate will be calculated by tallying the total number of polls in which each candidate received 1% or more support.

SOURCE: Democratic National Committee. "DNC Announces Details for the First Two Presidential Primary Debates." February 14, 2019. https://democrats.org/news/dnc-announces-details-for-the-first-two-presidential-primary-debates.

OTHER HISTORIC DOCUMENTS OF INTEREST

FROM THIS VOLUME

- Whistleblower Complaint Filed against President Trump, p. 511

FROM PREVIOUS *HISTORIC DOCUMENTS*

- RNC and DNC Leaders Remark on Super Tuesday; Trump and Clinton Accept Nominations, *2016*, p. 127
- Donald Trump Elected U.S. President, *2016*, p. 612

President Trump Declares a National Emergency on the Southern Border

FEBRUARY 15, FEBRUARY 18, AND MARCH 15, 2019

On February 15, 2019, after struggling to fund his signature agenda item over his first two years in office, President Donald Trump declared an emergency on the U.S.–Mexico border, empowering his administration to circumvent Congress to fund a border wall. The move was met with swift, bipartisan condemnation from Congress. Democrats saw the move as an abuse of power. Republicans expressed similar concerns and worried about the precedent it would set for future administrations, including Democratic ones. A month after the proclamation, Congress passed a bipartisan resolution revoking the national emergency yet failed to gain veto-proof majorities in either chamber, setting up Trump's first presidential veto. Outside of Congress, the proclamation sparked legal challenges, most notably from a coalition of states led by California. While a lower court ruled in favor of the coalition states, the U.S. Supreme Court sided with the Trump administration, effectively ending any challenge to the constitutionality of the proclamation. The administration soon began to divert $8 billion from other programs to fund the wall's construction.

CONGRESS DENIES TRUMP REQUEST FOR WALL FUNDING

One of Trump's biggest promises to the American people during his 2016 presidential campaign was to build a wall along the southern border to prevent immigrants from entering the country illegally. Yet despite complete Republican control of Washington during the first two years of his term, Trump was unable to secure funding for the border wall. With a new Democratic majority in the U.S. House of Representatives following the 2018 midterm elections, convincing Congress to allocate funding became more difficult.

In late 2018, the issue came to a head. House Democrats, led by House Speaker Nancy Pelosi, D-Calif., refused to allocate a budget for a border wall in a bill funding the federal government through fiscal year 2019. Senate Republicans, led by Senate majority leader Mitch McConnell, R-Ky., signaled they wanted to move beyond the border wall fight. Yet Trump remained steadfast, stating publicly and privately that he would not sign a government funding bill that did not include money for a wall. The standoff, which lasted thirty-four days, sparked the longest government shutdown in American history. Although the president eventually capitulated, he threatened a new, controversial approach—to declare a national emergency on the southern border and redirect funds that had already been appropriated by Congress to address it.

TRUMP DECLARES A "BORDER SECURITY AND HUMANITARIAN CRISIS"

On February 15, 2019, one day after signing a bipartisan funding bill that did not contain money for a border wall, Trump followed through on his warning. Calling the southern border a "a major entry point for criminals, gang members, and illicit narcotics," and criticizing "large-scale unlawful migration" that has "worsened in certain respects in recent years," he issued a proclamation invoking the National Emergencies Act to address what his administration described as "a border security and humanitarian crisis that threatens core national security interests and constitutes a national emergency." Altogether the administration stated it would reapportion about $8 billion to wall construction—more than the $5.7 billion that Congress refused to give him.

In remarks, the president focused on the threats posed by illicit drugs, crime, and illegal immigration to justify his decision. "We have tremendous amounts of drugs flowing into our country, much of it coming from the southern border," Trump said. The president also argued that securing ports of entry was not enough. Crime was flowing "through areas where you have no wall"—a seeming rebuttal of congressional Democrats' claim that a wall would be ineffective because most narcotics came into the United States through ports of entry. "A big majority of the big drugs—the big drug loads—don't go through ports of entry," Trump said, adding, "You can't take human traffic—women and girls—you can't take them through ports of entry."

Official statistics and immigration experts painted a different picture. Crossings at the U.S.–Mexico border are at their lowest levels in nearly fifty years, according to data from U.S. Customs and Border Protection (CBP). Only 4 percent of the hundreds of thousands of people CBP has encountered were convicted of a crime, whether in the United States or abroad, and only 0.1 percent were considered gang members. Meanwhile, public polling revealed a majority of Americans disapproved of the measure.

Proclamation Garners Bipartisan Condemnation

Lawmakers responded swiftly to Trump's announcement, offering sharp criticism that crossed party lines. Congressional Democrats condemned the move as unlawful, citing Congress's traditional power over the federal purse and accusing the administration of overreach. "Declaring a national emergency would be a lawless act, a gross abuse of the power of the presidency and a desperate attempt to distract from the fact that President Trump broke his core promise to have Mexico pay for his wall," Speaker Pelosi and Senate minority leader Chuck Schumer, D-N.Y., said in a joint statement. "It is yet another demonstration of President Trump's naked contempt for the rule of law. This is not an emergency, and the president's fear-mongering doesn't make it one," they added.

Congressional Republicans also expressed concerns, focusing on the precedent the proclamation could set. "I think it's a dangerous step," Sen. John Cornyn, R-Tex., said. "To me it has nothing to do with immigration. It has to do with whether or not the president can spend money that Congress didn't give to him," said Rep. Rand Paul, R-Ky. In a statement, Rep. Cathy McMorris Rodgers, R-Wash., said, "I do not support this decision because declaring a national emergency sets a very dangerous precedent that undermines our constitutional separation of powers. By circumventing Congress and Article I of the Constitution, President Trump is opening the door for any future president to act alone without congressional approval." Representative Rodgers summarized many Republicans' angst over the proclamation when she added, "If elected president, how would Elizabeth Warren or Bernie Sanders use this precedent for a national disaster declaration to force the Green New Deal on the American people?" (The Green New Deal is a proposed climate action plan favored by some Democrats.)

Lawsuits Challenge Constitutionality

Trump's proclamation also prompted immediate challenges in court. Sixteen states, led by California and New York, sued the administration on the grounds that the move abused the Constitution's separation of powers because Congress controls federal spending. "President Trump is manufacturing a crisis and declaring a made-up 'national emergency' in order to seize power and undermine the Constitution," said California governor Gavin Newsom upon announcing the suit. "We're suing President Trump to stop him from unilaterally robbing taxpayer funds lawfully set aside by Congress for the people of our states," California attorney general Xavier Becerra added. Specifically, the states' filing read that the plaintiffs were suing to protect their residents, natural resources, and economic interests. "Contrary to the will of Congress, the president has used the pretext of a manufactured 'crisis' of unlawful immigration to declare a national emergency and redirect federal dollars appropriated for drug interdiction, military construction and law enforcement initiatives toward building a wall on the United States–Mexico border," the lawsuit read. The American Civil Liberties Union, on behalf of the Sierra Club and the Southern Border Communities Coalition, filed a similar suit, as did various nonprofit watchdog groups representing landowners and environmental groups.

In June, U.S. district judge Haywood Gilliam ruled in favor of the states. Trump, speaking after the Group of 20 summit in Japan, called the ruling "a disgrace" and said the administration would be "immediately appealing." A month later, the U.S. Supreme Court overturned the lower court's ruling. In a 5–4 vote that fell along ideological lines, the Court said it was ruling before it heard an appeal because the government had made a "sufficient showing" that the plaintiffs did not have standing. The ruling cleared the way for the administration to begin using funds for border wall construction and effectively ended the debate over the constitutionality of the president's emergency declaration.

Congressional Resolution Draws Trump's First Veto

As the various lawsuits worked their way through the courts, Congress took its own action. On March 14, nearly one month to the day after the president issued his proclamation, the Senate passed a House-approved resolution to overturn the emergency declaration.

Trump had threatened to veto the resolution if it made it to his desk. He sought to frame the vote as a demonstration of personal loyalty to him, putting pressure on Senate Republicans expected to face difficult reelection fights in 2020. "It's pure and simple: It's a vote for border security; it's a vote for no crime," he said. In an op-ed published in *The Washington Post*, Sen. Thom Tillis, R-N.C., characterized the political bind in which many Senate Republicans found themselves. Senator Tillis explained that he supported the president's vision for the border but would vote against the measure because of his concerns about the separation of powers. Despite this very public declaration, Senator Tillis reversed course amid intense pressure from the White House and conservatives in his home state.

While facing similarly intense lobbying from the administration, nearly a quarter of Senate Republicans joined Senate Democrats in supporting the House-passed resolution of disapproval, a rarity in an increasingly polarized Washington. "Our nation's founders gave to Congress the power to approve all spending so that the president would not have too much power. This check on the executive is a crucial source of our freedom," said Sen. Lamar Alexander, R-Tenn. But the resolution failed to muster a veto-proof margin in either chamber.

The next day, Trump issued his promised veto, the first of his presidency. Flanked by Vice President Mike Pence, Attorney General William Barr, and Homeland Security secretary Kirstjen Nielsen, the president denounced the resolution as "dangerous," "reckless," and a "vote against reality." He added, "Congress has the freedom to pass this resolution, and I have the duty to veto it."

WALL CONSTRUCTION BEGINS

As the dust settled from the legal and congressional challenges, more details emerged from the administration about the impact of Trump's proclamation and the funding to be tapped to build the wall. The administration reallocated $3.6 billion from military construction appropriations, $2.5 billion from the Department of Defense's counter-drug activities, and $600 million from the Department of the Treasury's drug-asset forfeiture funds to the southern border. The Pentagon announced that 127 military construction projects would be effectively defunded, affecting projects in nearly half of the fifty states, three territories, and twenty countries.

As construction of the border wall proceeds, constitutional scholars and academics continue to question the long-term implications. For many, the emergency declaration amounted to an executive branch overreach that would permanently and vastly expand the power of the presidency. Questions remain about whether future presidents will use the precedent set by the Trump administration to achieve their respective policy agenda.

—Robert Howard

Following is a statement by President Donald Trump on February 15, 2019, announcing a national emergency concerning the southern border of the United States; the text of Proclamation 9844, issued on February 15, 2019, declaring a national emergency along the U.S.–Mexico border; a press release issued by California attorney general Xavier Becerra's office on February 18, 2019, announcing a lawsuit challenging Trump's declaration; and remarks by Trump on March 15, 2019, on his veto of a congressional resolution revoking the national emergency.

DOCUMENT

President Trump Declares National Emergency at Southern Border

February 15, 2019

[The president's opening remarks on U.S.–China trade relations, Brexit, the Islamic State in Iraq and the Levant, and North Korea have been omitted.]

Border Security
    . . . Today I'm announcing several critical actions that my administration is taking to confront a problem that we have right here at home. We fight wars that are 6,000 miles away, wars that we should have never been in, in many cases. But we don't control our own border.

So we're going to confront the national security crisis on our southern border. And we're going to do it one way or the other—we have to do it—not because it was a campaign promise, which it is. It was one of many, by the way, not my only one. We're rebuilding the military; our economy is thriving like never before. . . .

But one of the things I said I have to do and I want to do is border security, because we have tremendous amounts of drugs flowing into our country, much of it coming from the southern border. When you look and when you listen to politicians—in particular, certain Democrats—they say it all comes through the port of entry. It's wrong. It's wrong. It's just a lie. It's all a lie.

They say walls don't work. Walls work a hundred percent. Whether it's El Paso—I really was smiling, because the other night I was in El Paso—we had a tremendous crowd and—tremendous crowd. And I asked the people—many of whom were from El Paso, but they came from all over Texas. And I asked them. I said, "Let me ask you, as a crowd: When the wall went up, was it better?" You were there, some of you. It was not only better; it was like a hundred percent better. You know what they did.

But that's only one example. There are so many examples. In El Paso, they have close to 2,000 murders right on the other side of the wall. And they had 23 murders. It's a lot of murders, but it's not close to 2,000 murders right on the other side of the wall, in Mexico.

So everyone knows that walls work. And there are better examples than El Paso, frankly. You just take a look, almost everywhere. Take a look at Israel. They're building another wall. Their wall is 99.9-percent effective, they told me—99.9 percent. That's what it would be with us too.

The only weakness is, they go to a wall, and then they go around the wall. They go around the wall and in. Okay? That's what it is. Very simple. And a big majority of the big drugs—the big drug loads—don't go through ports of entry. They can't go through ports of entry. You can't take big loads, because you have people—we have some very capable people; the Border Patrol, law enforcement—looking.

You can't take human traffic—women and girls—you can't take them through ports of entry. You can't have them tied up in the back seat of a car or a truck or a van. They open the door. They look. They can't see three women with tape on their mouth or three women whose hands are tied.

They go through areas where you have no wall. Everybody knows that. Nancy knows it. Chuck knows it. They all know it. It's all a big lie. It's a big con game.

You don't have to be very smart to know: You put up a barrier, the people come in, and that's it. They can't do anything unless they walk left or right and they find an area where there's no barrier, and they come into the United States. Welcome. . . .

We've detained more people. Our border agents are doing such incredible work. Our military has been incredible. We put up barbed wire on top of certain old walls that were there. We fixed the wall, and we load it up with barbed wire. It's very successful.

But our military has been fantastic, and I want to thank them. And it's very necessary. We've broken up two caravans that are on their way. They just are breaking. They're in the process of breaking up. We have another one that we haven't been able to break up yet.

We've been actually working with Mexico much better than ever before. I want to thank the President. I want to thank Mexico. They have their own problems. They have the largest number of murders that they've ever had in their history, almost 40,000 murders. Forty thousand. And they got to straighten that out, and I think they will.

But I just want to thank the President, because he's been helping us with these monstrous caravans that have been coming up. We had one that it was up to over

15,000 people. It's largely broken up. Others have gotten through. And in Tijuana, you have a lot of people staying there. If we didn't have the wall up, and if we didn't have the wall secured and strengthened, they would have walked right through; they'd be welcomed to the United States.

One of the things we'd save tremendous—just a tremendous—amount on would be sending the military. If we had a wall, we don't need the military, because we'd have a wall.

So I'm going to be signing a national emergency. And it's been signed many times before. It's been signed by other Presidents from 1977 or so. It gave the Presidents the power.

There's rarely been a problem. They sign it; nobody cares. I guess they weren't very exciting. But nobody cares. They sign it for far less important things, in some cases, in many cases. We're talking about an invasion of our country with drugs, with human traffickers, with all types of criminals and gangs. . . .

And by signing the national emergency—something signed many times by other Presidents—many, many times. President Obama—in fact, we may be using one of the national emergencies that he signed, having to do with cartels. Criminal cartels. It's a very good emergency that he signed. And we're going to use parts of it in our dealings on cartels. So that would be a second national emergency. But in that case, it's already in place.

And what we want—really want to do is simple. It's not like it's complicated. It's very simple: We want to stop drugs from coming into our country. We want to stop criminals and gangs from coming into our country. Nobody has done the job that we've ever done. I mean, nobody has done the job that we've done on the border.

And in a way, what I did by creating such a great economy—and if the opposing party got in, this economy would be down the tubes. You know, I hear a lot of people say, "Oh, well, but maybe the previous administration"—let me tell you, the previous administration, it was heading south, and it was going fast. We would have been down the tubes. The regulations were strangling our country. Unnecessary regulations.

By creating such a strong economy—you just look at your televisions or see what's going on today; it's through the roof. What happens is, more people want to come, so we have far more people trying to get into our country today than probably we've ever had before. And we've done an incredible job in stopping them, but it's a massive number of people.

If we had the wall, it would be very easy. We would make up for the cost of the wall just in the cost of the fact that I would be able to have fewer people. We wouldn't need all of this incredible talent, some of whom are sitting in the first row. You wouldn't need all of this incredible talent. We would get thousands of law enforcement people, including Border Patrol. You put them in different areas; you have them doing different things. Law enforcement and Border Patrol.

And I want to thank law enforcement, and I want to thank Border Patrol, and I want to thank ICE. ICE is abused by the press and by the Democrats. And by the way, we're going to be taking care of ICE. You know, we talk about the new bill. We're going to be taking care of ICE. They wanted to get rid of ICE. And the bill is just the opposite of that. A lot of good things happened.

So that's the story. We want to have a safe country. I ran on a very simple slogan: "Make America Great Again." If you're going to have drugs pouring across the border, if you're going to have human traffickers pouring across the border in areas where we have no protection, in areas where we don't have a barrier, then very hard to make America great again. . . .

So the order is signed. And I'll sign the final papers as soon as I get into the Oval Office. And we will have a national emergency, and we will then be sued, and they will sue us in the Ninth Circuit, even though it shouldn't be there. And we will possibly get a bad ruling, and then we'll get another bad ruling. And then, we'll end up in the Supreme Court, and hopefully, we'll get a fair shake. And we'll win in the Supreme Court, just like the ban. They sued us in the Ninth Circuit, and we lost, and then we lost in the appellate division, and then we went to the Supreme Court, and we won. . . .

[Reporter questions and the president's responses have been omitted.]

SOURCE: Executive Office of the President. "Remarks on Declaring a National Emergency Concerning the Southern Border of the United States and an Exchange with Reporters." February 15, 2019. *Compilation of Presidential Documents* 2019, no. 00079 (February 15, 2019). https://www.govinfo.gov/content/pkg/DCPD-201900079/pdf/DCPD-201900079.pdf.

Proclamation 9844 Declaring a National Emergency at the Southern Border

February 15, 2019

The current situation at the southern border presents a border security and humanitarian crisis that threatens core national security interests and constitutes a national emergency. The southern border is a major entry point for criminals, gang members, and illicit narcotics. The problem of large-scale unlawful migration through the southern border is long-standing, and despite the executive branch's exercise of existing statutory authorities, the situation has worsened in certain respects in recent years. In particular, recent years have seen sharp increases in the number of family units entering and seeking entry to the United States and an inability to provide detention space for many of these aliens while their removal proceedings are pending. If not detained, such aliens are often released into the country and are often difficult to remove from the United States because they fail to appear for hearings, do not comply with orders of removal, or are otherwise difficult to locate. In response to the directive in my April 4, 2018, memorandum and subsequent requests for support by the Secretary of Homeland Security, the Department of Defense has provided support and resources to the Department of Homeland Security at the southern border. Because of the gravity of the current emergency situation, it is necessary for the Armed Forces to provide additional support to address the crisis.

Now, Therefore, I, Donald J. Trump, by the authority vested in me by the Constitution and the laws of the United States of America, including sections 201 and 301 of the National Emergencies Act (50 U.S.C. 1601 *et seq.*), hereby declare that a national emergency exists at the southern border of the United States, and that section 12302 of title 10, United States Code, is invoked and made available, according to its terms, to the Secretaries of the military departments concerned, subject to the direction of the Secretary of Defense in the case of the Secretaries of the Army, Navy, and Air Force. To provide additional authority to the Department of Defense to support the Federal Government's response to the emergency at the southern border, I hereby declare that this emergency requires use of the Armed Forces and, in accordance with section 301 of the National Emergencies Act (50 U.S.C. 1631), that the construction authority provided in section 2808 of title 10, United States Code, is invoked and made available, according to its terms, to the Secretary of Defense and, at the discretion of the Secretary of Defense, to the Secretaries of the military departments. I hereby direct as follows:

Section 1. The Secretary of Defense, or the Secretary of each relevant military department, as appropriate and consistent with applicable law, shall order as many units or members of the Ready Reserve to active duty as the Secretary concerned, in the Secretary's discretion, determines to be appropriate to assist and support the activities of the Secretary of Homeland Security at the southern border.

Sec. 2. The Secretary of Defense, the Secretary of the Interior, the Secretary of Homeland Security, and, subject to the discretion of the Secretary of Defense, the Secretaries of the 2 military departments, shall take all appropriate actions, consistent with applicable law, to use or support the use of the authorities herein invoked, including, if necessary, the transfer and acceptance of jurisdiction over border lands.

Sec. 3. This proclamation is not intended to, and does not, create any right or benefit, substantive or procedural, enforceable at law or in equity by any party against the United States, its departments, agencies, or entities, its officers, employees, or agents, or any other person.

In Witness Whereof, I have hereunto set my hand this fifteenth day of February, in the year of our Lord two thousand nineteen, and of the Independence of the United States of America the two hundred and forty-third.

SOURCE: Executive Office of the President. "Proclamation 9844—Declaring a National Emergency Concerning the Southern Border of the United States." February 15, 2019. *Compilation of Presidential Documents* 2019, no. 00080 (February 15, 2019). https://www.govinfo.gov/content/pkg/DCPD-201900080/pdf/DCPD-201900080.pdf.

California, Partner States Announce Lawsuit Challenging Emergency Declaration

February 18, 2019

California Governor Gavin Newsom and Attorney General Xavier Becerra, leading a 16-state coalition, today filed a lawsuit in the U.S. District Court for the Northern District of California challenging President Trump's declaration of a national emergency and his attempt to divert funding appropriated by Congress for other purposes. In the complaint, the coalition alleges that the Trump Administration's emergency declaration and diversion of funds is unconstitutional and otherwise unlawful. The states seek to block the Trump Administration's emergency declaration, the unauthorized construction of the border wall, and any illegal diversion of Congressionally-appropriated funds.

"President Trump is manufacturing a crisis and declaring a made-up 'national emergency' in order to seize power and undermine the Constitution," said Governor Newsom. "This 'emergency' is a national disgrace. Rather than focusing on fighting the real vulnerabilities facing Americans, the President is using the powers of America's highest office to fan the flames of nativism and xenophobia. Our message to the White House is clear: California will not be part of this political theater. We will see you in court."

"President Trump treats the rule of law with utter contempt. He knows there is no border crisis, he knows his emergency declaration is unwarranted, and he admits that he will likely lose this case in court. He is willing to manipulate the Office of the Presidency to engage in unconstitutional theatre performed to convince his audience that he is committed to his 'beautiful' border wall," said Attorney General Becerra. "Today, on Presidents Day, we take President Trump to court to block his misuse of presidential power. We're suing President Trump to stop him from unilaterally robbing taxpayer funds lawfully set aside by Congress for the people of our states. For most of us, the Office of the Presidency is not a place for theatre."

The complaint filed today alleges that the Trump Administration's action declaring a national emergency due to a purported border crisis is unlawful and unconstitutional. President Trump's hyped crisis is a pretext to justify redirecting congressionally-appropriated funds to pay to build a wall along the southern border after he failed to get Congress—or Mexico—to pay for it. The facts do not support President Trump's rhetoric or his declaration. Unlawful southern border entries are at their lowest point in 20 years, immigrants are less likely than native-born citizens to commit crimes, and illegal drugs are more likely to come through official ports of entry. There is no credible evidence to suggest that a border wall would decrease crime rates.

The states allege that the Trump Administration's action exceeds the power of the executive office, violates the U.S. Constitution and federal statutes, and would illegally and unconstitutionally divert federal funds appropriated by Congress for other purposes. The suit seeks declaratory and injunctive relief to block the emergency declaration, the construction of the wall, and any illegal diversion of congressionally-appropriated funds.

Joining Attorney General Becerra in filing the lawsuit are the attorneys general of Colorado, Connecticut, Delaware, Hawai'i, Illinois, Maine, Maryland, Michigan, Minnesota, Nevada, New Jersey, New Mexico, New York, Oregon, and Virginia.

SOURCE: Office of California Attorney General Xavier Becerra. "Governor Newsom, Attorney General Becerra, and 15 Partner States File Lawsuit Challenging President Trump's Contrived Declaration of National Emergency at the Southern Border." February 18, 2019. https://oag.ca.gov/news/press-releases/governor-newsom-attorney-general-becerra-and-15-partner-states-file-lawsuit.

President Trump Remarks on Veto of Congressional Resolution Revoking National Emergency

March 15, 2019

[Opening remarks on the shooting in Christchurch, New Zealand, and acknowledging Vice President Mike Pence have been omitted.]

. . . As President, the protection of the Nation is my highest duty. Yesterday, Congress passed a dangerous resolution that, if signed into law, would put countless Americans in danger—very grave danger. The Democrat-sponsored resolution would terminate vital border security operations by revoking the national emergency issued last month. It is definitely a national emergency. Rarely have we had such a national emergency.

Therefore, to defend the safety and security of all Americans, I will be signing and issuing a formal veto of this reckless resolution—and that's what it was. And I have to, in particular, thank the Republican—strong, wonderful people—the Republican Senators that were on our side and on the side of border security and on the side of doing what they have to to keep our Nation safe. They were very courageous yesterday, and I appreciate that very much.

Congress's vote to deny the crisis on the southern border is a vote against reality. It's against reality. It is a tremendous national emergency. It is a tremendous crisis.

Last month, more than 76,000 illegal migrants arrived at our border. We're on track for a million illegal aliens to rush our borders. People hate the word "invasion," but that's what it is. It's an invasion of drugs and criminals and people. We have no idea who they are, but we capture them because border security is so good. But they're put in a very bad position, and we're bursting at the seams. Literally, bursting at the seams. What Border Patrol is able to do is incredible. . . .

We've really nowhere left to hold all of the people that were captured. And we're at a point where we're just going to have to say, with these horrible decisions that we've been handed by people that aren't living in reality, that there's nothing we can do. There's absolutely nothing we can do. We're bursting at the seams. You can only do so much. And the only option then is to release them, but we can't do that either. Because when you release them, they come into our society, and in many cases they're stone-cold criminals. And in many cases, and in some cases, you have killers coming in and murderers coming in, and we're not going to allow that to happen. Just not going to allow it to happen.

There has been a nearly 2,000-percent increase in border-related asylum claims over the last decade. Part of the reason is because our country is doing so well economically that people are coming up in droves. The vast majority are rejected, but smuggling organizations—making a tremendous amount of money, like they've never made before—are using these people to crash the system. Our immigration system is stretched beyond the breaking point.

And as I said, nothing much we can do. We can just do our job and do it well. But there's a point at which, if the Democrats would—we'd get in, we'd be able to make a deal. Literally, in 15 minutes, we could make a deal on changing catch and release; changing the horrible asylum laws that are so unfair; changing visa lottery, chain migration. These laws are just horrendous. I won't explain them, but everybody standing behind me knows exactly what they are: They're dangerous for our country, and they're inspired by Democrats who have to change.

One in three migrant women is sexually assaulted on the journey north. The border crisis is driving the drug crisis. Seventy thousand Americans a year are killed by drugs, including meth, heroin, cocaine, and fentanyl. And the 70,000 people is a number that's so low that it probably shouldn't even be used anymore.

The mass incursion of illegal aliens, deadly drugs, dangerous weapons, and criminal gang members across our borders has to end.

We are bringing out thousands and thousands a year of MS-13 gang members, and other gang members that are just as bad, where they come into our country, they're able to skirt the border, come through areas where we don't have proper wall, where we don't have any wall at all. And they get into the country and they do a lot of damage, in many cases. But we get them out by the thousands, and we bring them back or we incarcerate them.

The national emergency I declared last month was authorized by Congress under the 1976 National Emergencies Act. And there haven't been too many that are a bigger emergency than we have right at our own border.

Consistent with the law and the legislative process designed by our Founders, today I am vetoing this resolution. Congress has the freedom to pass this resolution, and I have the duty to veto it. And I'm very proud to veto it. And I'm very proud, as I said, of a lot of Republican Senators that were with me. And I'm also very proud of the House. The Republicans in the House voted overwhelmingly in favor of a secure border.

Since 1976, Presidents have declared 59 national emergencies. They often involved protecting foreign citizens in far-off lands, yet Congress has not terminated any of them. Every single one of them is still in existence. And yet, we don't worry about our land; we worry about other people's lands. That's why I say "America first." If that's okay: "America first."

The only emergency Congress voted to revoke was the one to protect our own country. So, think of that: With all of the national emergencies, this was the one they don't want to do. And this is the one, perhaps, they should most do. . . .

As I said, I was elected on a very—by a very, very great group of American people—millions and millions of people—because they want security for our country. And that's what we're going to have. . . .

[Remarks by Secretary of Homeland Security Kirstjen Nielson, Attorney General William Barr, Pence, and state and county law enforcement officials have been omitted.]

Thank you very much. Thank you. That's a big—a big step. We're building a lot of wall right now. It's started. A lot of people are saying, "Well, gee, you took down wall and you're building new." Well, we took down wall that almost didn't exist. It was like paper. And we're replacing it with, in many cases, 30-foot bollards. And, in many cases, we're replacing it with 18-foot wall.

But we have a lot of—we have many miles under construction right now, and we're going to be signing contracts over the next couple of days for literally hundreds of miles of wall. And it's being built in the right places, and it's doing the job. It's doing the job. . . .

This wall is a beautiful-looking structure. It's much stronger. And you can build it faster and cheaper. Other than that, what can I say, right?

It's a—it's going to be great, and it's going to have a tremendous impact. . . .

So with that, I just want to thank everybody for being here. In particular, I want to thank you, folks, because you have been—and please say "hello" to all of your friends that have been with us, really, from day one. What you've gone through is unthinkable, and I appreciate it.

And you're strong people. You're strong and you're proud. And your kids are, you know, looking down on you right now and they're—they're very proud of their moms and their dads. You know that, right? They're very proud. Thank you very much.

And, again, to those Republican Senators that did what they had to do yesterday, I want to thank them. They're very special friends and very special people. And they want to see borders that are strong, where we don't allow drugs and crime and all of the problems coming into our country.

Thank you all very much. Thank you. . . .

[Reporter questions and the president's answers have been omitted.]

SOURCE: Executive Office of the President. "Remarks on Signing a Message to the House of Representatives Returning without Approval Legislation to Terminate the National Emergency Concerning the Southern Border of the United States and an Exchange with Reporters." March 15, 2019. *Compilation of Presidential Documents* 2019, no. 00150 (March 15, 2019). https://www.govinfo.gov/content/pkg/DCPD-201900150/pdf/DCPD-201900150.pdf.

OTHER HISTORIC DOCUMENTS OF INTEREST

FROM THIS VOLUME

- President Trump and Congressional Leaders Remark on Border Wall Funding Fight and Government Shutdown, p. 3
- Trump Administration and Supreme Court Issue Immigration Orders, p. 400

FROM PREVIOUS *HISTORIC DOCUMENTS*

- Trump Administration Remarks on U.S. Immigration Policy, *2018*, p. 221
- Federal Officials Remark on Immigration Procedures; Supreme Court Denies Asylum Policy Stay, *2018*, p. 631
- President Trump Issues Immigration Orders, *2017*, p. 42
- U.S. Government Seeks to Impose New Immigration Limits, *2017*, p. 417

Former Trump Lawyer Testifies before Congress; Democrats Announce Trump Inquiry

FEBRUARY 27, MARCH 4, AND MAY 20, 2019

In February and March 2019, President Donald Trump's former lawyer and self-professed "fixer" testified before Congress both publicly and behind closed doors on the alleged wrongdoings he witnessed during his time with the president. Michael Cohen's credibility was immediately challenged by Republicans, who asserted that Cohen admitted to lying to Congress before and was in fact going to prison for that and other issues that he pleaded guilty to in 2018. Republicans also questioned the Democrats' lengthy attempt to link the president to a crime, despite repeatedly coming up empty. Shortly after Cohen's testimony, Democrats announced their intent to launch an investigation into the president, which many believed would be the underpinnings of a formal impeachment inquiry.

COHEN ATTACKS TRUMP IN PUBLIC TESTIMONY

In his opening statement, Cohen said he was "ashamed" that he worked for President Trump and took part in what he described as "concealing Mr. Trump's illicit acts." Cohen went on: "I am ashamed because I know what Mr. Trump is. He is a racist. He is a conman. He is a cheat."

Cohen's testimony took place as former Federal Bureau of Investigation (FBI) director Robert Mueller continued his work on the nearly two-year investigation into alleged links between the Trump campaign and Russia. The testimony provided no definitive proof that President Trump colluded with the Russian government during the 2016 presidential election, and Cohen in fact admitted he had no "direct evidence" of such. He did speak to two claims previously surfaced during the Mueller investigation—first, that Trump knew about a June 2016 meeting at Trump Tower in New York City between Trump's son Donald Jr., son-in-law Jared Kushner, campaign chair Paul Manafort, and Russians who claimed to have dirt on Democratic presidential nominee Hillary Clinton, and second, that Trump knew in advance, through his adviser Roger Stone, that WikiLeaks had and would be releasing e-mails and other information damaging to the Clinton campaign.

Unrelated to Russia, Cohen made a number of other claims about the president and his associates that could be utilized in investigations carried out by Congress or federal prosecutors. Among these was the allegation that then-candidate Trump directed Cohen to make a hush money payment to Stormy Daniels, an adult-film actress who said she had an affair with Trump. Cohen said he made the payment of $130,000 with a home-equity line of credit, and was later reimbursed by Trump. Cohen also indicated he was aware of other illegalities carried out by Trump, but that "those are part of the investigation that's currently being looked at by the Southern District of New York" and he therefore could not comment on them.

To support his testimony, Cohen provided a series of documents to the committee, including a copy of a check from Trump to Cohen, allegedly partial reimbursement for the hush money payment; financial statements meant to indicate that Trump had inflated his assets to secure loans from Deutsche Bank to buy a football team; copies of letters written by Cohen at the direction of Trump to his alma maters threatening action if they released his grades or SAT scores; and a document indicating Trump had misused charitable funds to reimburse a straw bidder at an auction to ensure a Trump portrait would be the highest-priced portrait at the event.

REPUBLICANS QUESTION COHEN'S CREDIBILITY

The February testimony marked the second time Cohen testified before Congress. During his 2017 appearance, which looked into Trump's possible connection to Russia during the 2016 presidential election, Cohen stated the Trump team stopped negotiating with Russia to build a Trump hotel in Russia in January 2016. During his 2019 testimony, Cohen admitted that he lied. "The last time I appeared before Congress, I came to protect Mr. Trump. Today, I'm here to tell the truth about Mr. Trump," Cohen said. Cohen said he was never directly told by the president to lie under oath, but that personal statements made by Trump to Cohen indicated "that he wanted me to lie." According to Cohen, Trump's desire was clarified when Trump's personal lawyer edited Cohen's 2017 testimony before it was provided to Congress.

This factor was key to the Republican line of questioning during the hearing. According to an analysis by *The Washington Post*, more than two-thirds of Republican time in the hearing was committed to attacking Cohen rather than defending the president. This began with the opening statement of the committee's ranking member, Rep. Jim Jordan, R-Ohio. "I want everyone in the room to think about this: The first announced witness for the 116th Congress is a guy who is going to prison in two months for lying to Congress," Jordan said. Rep. Carol Miller, R-W.V., echoed that. "You're about to go to prison for lying. How can we believe anything you say? The answer is we can't," she said. Various members also asked Cohen to produce hard evidence of the allegations he made during the hearing, which Cohen in many cases admitted he could not.

Cohen responded to allegations from Republicans that he was not a credible witness, noting, "For those who question my motives for being here today, I understand. I have lied, but I am not a liar. I have done bad things, but I am not a bad man. I have fixed things, but I am no longer your 'fixer,' Mr. Trump." Cohen added that he was accepting responsibility for his actions. "I have done things I am not proud of, and I will live with the consequences of my actions for the rest of my life. But today, I get to decide the example I set for my children and how I attempt to change how history will remember me. I may not be able to change the past, but I can do right by the American people here today," Cohen said in closing.

COHEN CLOSED-DOOR TESTIMONY RELEASED

After publicly addressing the House Committee on Oversight and Reform, Cohen participated in closed-door hearings with the House and Senate Intelligence Committees. It was widely believed that, although the public hearing would likely produce sound bites helpful to Democrats and Republicans with their own base, the more vital information would be addressed behind closed doors because committee members would be able to ask questions related to Mueller's ongoing investigation into alleged connections between the Trump campaign and the Russian government.

On May 20, in a 12–7 party-line vote, the House Permanent Select Committee on Intelligence voted to release hundreds of pages of transcripts and materials related to Cohen's February and March closed-door testimonies. Rep. Adam Schiff, D-Calif., chair of the committee, announced the release, stating, "The public should judge for themselves both the evidence released today in conjunction with Cohen's testimony related to Trump, his troubling relationship with Russia, and the efforts by Trump and those close to him to hide the relationship and potential business deals. The public also deserves the chance to judge Cohen's credibility for themselves, including by examining some of the evidence he provided to the Committee." Schiff noted that the committee felt compelled to release the information now that Mueller had completed and released his work.

A bulk of the closed-door testimony focused on a meeting between members of Trump's campaign and Russians about information to discredit Clinton as well as the timing of negotiations with Russia over a possible Moscow hotel. Cohen noted he had discussed a presidential pardon with Trump attorney Jay Sekulow and other members of the Trump team in exchange for saying in his 2017 testimony that the hotel negotiations ended in January 2016, before the Iowa caucuses. Cohen alleged in his closed-door testimony that it was Sekulow who edited his 2017 remarks.

Sekulow denied the allegations. "Cohen's alleged statements are more of the same from him and confirm the observations of prosecutors in the Southern District of New York that Cohen's 'instinct to blame others is strong,'" Sekulow's attorneys said in a statement. "That this or any Committee would rely on the word of Michael Cohen for any purpose—much less to try and pierce the attorney-client privilege and discover confidential communications of four respected lawyers—defies logic, well-established law and common sense," they added.

Democrats Announce Inquiry into President Trump

On March 4, Rep. Jerry Nadler, D-N.Y., announced the House Judiciary Committee would open an investigation "into the alleged obstruction of justice, public corruption, and other abuses of power by President Trump, his associates, and members of his Administration." Democrats on the committee sought to determine whether the president had improperly leveraged the power of his office for personal gain or committed any other criminal acts. In his announcement, Nadler said the investigation was "an obligation of Congress and a core function of the House Judiciary Committee. We have seen the damage done to our democratic institutions in the two years that the Congress refused to conduct responsible oversight. Congress must provide a check on abuses of power."

The announcement—which joined a host of other congressional investigations into the president—was coupled with a request for documents from eighty-one individuals and organizations affiliated with Trump, including the Trump Organization, White House, FBI, and Trump's sons. Democrats hoped these documents would help build a case of possible misdeeds committed by the president that they could present to the American people. It was widely expected that the individuals and organizations would either refuse to comply or delay providing the requested documents. Notably, despite rumblings in the Democratic Caucus, Nadler's announcement did not include the word *impeachment*, but it was widely believed that the information collected could be used as the impetus for such proceedings, which typically originates in the House Judiciary Committee.

Republicans and the White House condemned the announcement. "The Democrats are not after the truth," said White House press secretary Sarah Huckabee Sanders. "They are after the president." On Twitter, President Trump called the investigation "Ridiculous," and later noted, "You know, the beautiful thing? No collusion. It's all a hoax." Many accused Nadler and the Democrats of failing to respect the ongoing investigation by Mueller's team. "We don't even know what the Mueller report says, but Democrats are already hedging their bets," said Rep. Doug Collins, R-Ga. "The scope of the Democrats' race to find something bad on this president is getting more and more concerning. . . . Where are they willing to stop?" Collins asked.

—Heather Kerrigan

Following is the edited text of a testimony delivered by Michael Cohen before the House Oversight and Reform Committee on February 27, 2019; a March 4, 2019, statement from House Judiciary Committee chair Jerry Nadler, D-N.Y., announcing a congressional investigation into President Donald Trump and his associates; and a May 20, 2019, statement from the House Permanent Select Committee on Intelligence announcing the release of Cohen's closed-door testimony transcripts and related documents.

Michael Cohen Testifies before Congress

DOCUMENT

February 27, 2019

Chairman Cummings, Ranking Member Jordan, and Members of the Committee, thank you for inviting me here today.

I have asked this Committee to ensure that my family be protected from Presidential threats, and that the Committee be sensitive to the questions pertaining to ongoing investigations. Thank you for your help and for your understanding.

I am here under oath to correct the record, to answer the Committee's questions truthfully, and to offer the American people what I know about President Trump.

I recognize that some of you may doubt and attack me on my credibility. It is for this reason that I have incorporated into this opening statement documents that are irrefutable, and demonstrate that the information you will hear is accurate and truthful.

Never in a million years did I imagine, when I accepted a job in 2007 to work for Donald Trump, that he would one day run for President, launch a campaign on a platform of hate and intolerance, and actually win. I regret the day I said "yes" to Mr. Trump. I regret all the help and support I gave him along the way.

I am ashamed of my own failings, and I publicly accepted responsibility for them by pleading guilty in the Southern District of New York.

I am ashamed of my weakness and misplaced loyalty—of the things I did for Mr. Trump in an effort to protect and promote him.

I am ashamed that I chose to take part in concealing Mr. Trump's illicit acts rather than listening to my own conscience.

I am ashamed because I know what Mr. Trump is. He is a racist.

He is a conman.

He is a cheat.

He was a presidential candidate who knew that Roger Stone was talking with Julian Assange about a WikiLeaks drop of Democratic National Committee emails.

I will explain each in a few moments. . . .

[A list of documents provided by Cohen has been omitted.]

I hope my appearance here today, my guilty plea, and my work with law enforcement agencies are steps along a path of redemption that will restore faith in me and help this country understand our president better.

***

Before going further, I want to apologize to each of you and to Congress as a whole.

The last time I appeared before Congress, I came to protect Mr. Trump. Today, I'm here to tell the truth about Mr. Trump.

I lied to Congress about when Mr. Trump stopped negotiating the Moscow Tower project in Russia. I stated that we stopped negotiating in January 2016. That was false—our negotiations continued for months later during the campaign.

Mr. Trump did not directly tell me to lie to Congress. That's not how he operates.

In conversations we had during the campaign, at the same time I was actively negotiating in Russia for him, he would look me in the eye and tell me there's no business in Russia and then go out and lie to the American people by saying the same thing. In his way, he was telling me to lie.

There were at least a half-dozen times between the Iowa Caucus in January 2016 and the end of June when he would ask me "How's it going in Russia?"—referring to the Moscow Tower project.

You need to know that Mr. Trump's personal lawyers reviewed and edited my statement to Congress about the timing of the Moscow Tower negotiations before I gave it.

To be clear: Mr. Trump knew of and directed the Trump Moscow negotiations throughout the campaign and lied about it. He lied about it because he never expected to win the election. He also lied about it because he stood to make hundreds of millions of dollars on the Moscow real estate project.

And so I lied about it, too—because Mr. Trump had made clear to me, through his personal statements to me that we both knew were false and through his lies to the country, that he wanted me to lie. And he made it clear to me because his personal attorneys reviewed my statement before I gave it to Congress.

****

[Cohen's brief description of his background has been omitted.]

. . . last fall I pled guilty in federal court to felonies for the benefit of, at the direction of, and in coordination with Individual #1.

For the record: Individual #1 is President Donald J. Trump.

It is painful to admit that I was motivated by ambition at times. It is even more painful to admit that many times I ignored my conscience and acted loyal to a man when I should not have. Sitting here today, it seems unbelievable that I was so mesmerized by Donald Trump that I was willing to do things for him that I knew were absolutely wrong.

For that reason, I have come here to apologize to my family, to the government, and to the American people.

***

Accordingly, let me now tell you about Mr. Trump.

I got to know him very well, working very closely with him for more than 10 years, as his Executive Vice President and Special Counsel and then personal attorney when he became President. When I first met Mr. Trump, he was a successful entrepreneur, a real estate giant, and an icon. Being around Mr. Trump was intoxicating. When you were in his presence, you felt like you were involved in something greater than yourself—that you were somehow changing the world.

I wound up touting the Trump narrative for over a decade. That was my job. Always stay on message. Always defend. It monopolized my life. At first, I worked mostly on real estate developments and other business transactions. Shortly thereafter, Mr. Trump brought me into his personal life and private dealings. Over time, I saw his true character revealed.

Mr. Trump is an enigma. He is complicated, as am I. He has both good and bad, as do we all. But the bad far outweighs the good, and since taking office, he has become the worst version of himself. He is capable of behaving kindly, but he is not kind. He is capable of committing acts of generosity, but he is not generous. He is capable of being loyal, but he is fundamentally disloyal.

Donald Trump is a man who ran for office to make his brand great, not to make our country great. He had no desire or intention to lead this nation—only to market himself and to build his wealth and power. Mr. Trump would often say, this campaign was going to be the "greatest infomercial in political history."

He never expected to win the primary. He never expected to win the general election. The campaign—for him—was always a marketing opportunity.

I knew early on in my work for Mr. Trump that he would direct me to lie to further his business interests. I am ashamed to say, that when it was for a real estate mogul in the private sector, I considered it trivial. As the President, I consider it significant and dangerous.

But in the mix, lying for Mr. Trump was normalized, and no one around him questioned it. In fairness, no one around him today questions it, either.

A lot of people have asked me about whether Mr. Trump knew about the release of the hacked Democratic National Committee emails ahead of time. The answer is yes.

As I earlier stated, Mr. Trump knew from Roger Stone in advance about the WikiLeaks drop of emails.

In July 2016, days before the Democratic convention, I was in Mr. Trump's office when his secretary announced that Roger Stone was on the phone. Mr. Trump put Mr. Stone on the speakerphone. Mr. Stone told Mr. Trump that he had just gotten off the phone with Julian Assange and that Mr. Assange told Mr. Stone that, within a couple of days, there would be a massive dump of emails that would damage Hillary Clinton's campaign.

Mr. Trump responded by stating to the effect of "wouldn't that be great."

Mr. Trump is a racist. The country has seen Mr. Trump court white supremacists and bigots. You have heard him call poorer countries "shitholes."

In private, he is even worse.

He once asked me if I could name a country run by a black person that wasn't a "shithole." This was when Barack Obama was President of the United States.

While we were once driving through a struggling neighborhood in Chicago, he commented that only black people could live that way.

And, he told me that black people would never vote for him because they were too stupid.

And yet I continued to work for him.

Mr. Trump is a cheat. . . .

[References to the documents provided by Cohen have been omitted.]

Mr. Trump is a conman.

He asked me to pay off an adult film star with whom he had an affair, and to lie to his wife about it, which I did. Lying to the First Lady is one of my biggest regrets. She is a kind, good person. I respect her greatly—and she did not deserve that.

I am giving the Committee today a copy of the $130,000 wire transfer from me to Ms. Clifford's attorney during the closing days of the presidential campaign that was demanded by Ms. Clifford to maintain her silence about her affair with Mr. Trump. This is Exhibit 4 to my testimony.

Mr. Trump directed me to use my own personal funds from a Home Equity Line of Credit to avoid any money being traced back to him that could negatively impact his campaign. I did that, too—without bothering to consider whether that was improper, much less whether it was the right thing to do or how it would impact me, my family, or the public.

I am going to jail in part because of my decision to help Mr. Trump hide that payment from the American people before they voted a few days later. . . .

The President of the United States thus wrote a personal check for the payment of hush money as part of a criminal scheme to violate campaign finance laws. You can find the details of that scheme, directed by Mr. Trump, in the pleadings in the U.S. District Court for the Southern District of New York.

So picture this scene—in February 2017, one month into his presidency, I'm visiting President Trump in the Oval Office for the first time. It's truly awe-inspiring, he's showing me around and pointing to different paintings, and he says to me something to the effect of . . . Don't worry, Michael, your January and February reimbursement checks are coming. They were Fed-Exed from New York and it takes a while for that to get through the White House system. As he promised, I received the first check for the reimbursement of $70,000 not long thereafter. . . .

The sad fact is that I never heard Mr. Trump say anything in private that led me to believe he loved our nation or wanted to make it better. In fact, he did the opposite.

When telling me in 2008 that he was cutting employees' salaries in half—including mine—he showed me what he claimed was a $10 million IRS tax refund, and he said that he could not believe how stupid the government was for giving "someone like him" that much money back.

During the campaign, Mr. Trump said he did not consider Vietnam Veteran, and Prisoner of War, Senator John McCain to be "a hero" because he likes people who weren't captured. At the same time, Mr. Trump tasked me to handle the negative press surrounding his medical deferment from the Vietnam draft.

Mr. Trump claimed it was because of a bone spur, but when I asked for medical records, he gave me none and said there was no surgery. He told me not to answer the specific questions by reporters but rather offer simply the fact that he received a medical deferment.

He finished the conversation with the following comment. "You think I'm stupid, I wasn't going to Vietnam."

I find it ironic, President Trump, that you are in Vietnam right now. And yet, I continued to work for him.

***

Questions have been raised about whether I know of direct evidence that Mr. Trump or his campaign colluded with Russia. I do not. I want to be clear. But, I have my suspicions.

Sometime in the summer of 2017, I read all over the media that there had been a meeting in Trump Tower in June 2016 involving Don Jr. and others from the campaign with Russians, including a representative of the Russian government, and an email setting up the meeting with the subject line, "Dirt on Hillary Clinton." Something clicked in my mind. I remember being in the room with Mr. Trump, probably in early June 2016, when something peculiar happened. Don Jr. came into the room and walked behind his father's desk—which in itself was unusual. People didn't just walk behind Mr. Trump's desk to talk to him. I recalled Don Jr. leaning over to his father and speaking in a low voice, which I could clearly hear, and saying: "The meeting is all set." I remember Mr. Trump saying, "Ok good . . . let me know."

What struck me as I looked back and thought about that exchange between Don Jr. and his father was, first, that Mr. Trump had frequently told me and others that his son Don Jr. had the worst judgment of anyone in the world. And also, that Don Jr. would never set up any meeting of any significance alone—and certainly not without checking with his father.

I also knew that nothing went on in Trump world, especially the campaign, without Mr. Trump's knowledge and approval. So, I concluded that Don Jr. was referring to that June 2016 Trump Tower meeting about dirt on Hillary with the Russian representative when he walked behind his dad's desk that day—and that Mr. Trump knew that was the meeting Don Jr. was talking about when he said, "That's good . . . let me know."

***

Over the past year or so, I have done some real soul searching. I see now that my ambition and the intoxication of Trump power had much to do with the bad decisions I made.

To you, Chairman Cummings, Ranking Member Jordan, the other members of this Committee, and the other members of the House and Senate, I am sorry for my lies and for lying to Congress.

To our nation, I am sorry for actively working to hide from you the truth about Mr. Trump when you needed it most.

For those who question my motives for being here today, I understand. I have lied, but I am not a liar. I have done bad things, but I am not a bad man. I have fixed things, but I am no longer your "fixer," Mr. Trump.

I am going to prison and have shattered the safety and security that I tried so hard to provide for my family. My testimony certainly does not diminish the pain I caused my family and friends – nothing can do that. And I have never asked for, nor would I accept, a pardon from President Trump.

And, by coming today, I have caused my family to be the target of personal, scurrilous attacks by the President and his lawyer—trying to intimidate me from appearing before this panel. Mr. Trump called me a "rat" for choosing to tell the truth—much like a mobster would do when one of his men decides to cooperate with the government. . . .

I never imagined that he would engage in vicious, false attacks on my family—and unleash his TV-lawyer to do the same. I hope this committee and all members of Congress on both sides of the aisle will make it clear: As a nation, we should not tolerate attempts to intimidate witnesses before congress and attacks on family are out of bounds and not acceptable. . . .

I am not a perfect man. I have done things I am not proud of, and I will live with the consequences of my actions for the rest of my life.

But today, I get to decide the example I set for my children and how I attempt to change how history will remember me. I may not be able to change the past, but I can do right by the American people here today.

Thank you for your attention. I am happy to answer the Committee's questions.

SOURCE: House Committee on Oversight and Reform. "Testimony of Michael D. Cohen." February 27, 2019. https://docs.house.gov/meetings/GO/GO00/20190227/108969/HHRG-116-GO00-Wstate-CohenM-20190227.pdf.

House Judiciary Chair Announces Trump Investigation

DOCUMENT

March 4, 2019

Today, House Judiciary Chairman Jerrold Nadler (D-NY) unveiled an investigation by the House Judiciary Committee into the alleged obstruction of justice, public corruption, and other abuses of power by President Trump, his associates, and members of his Administration. As a first step, the Committee has served document requests to 81 agencies, entities, and individuals believed to have information relevant to the investigation.

"Over the last several years, President Trump has evaded accountability for his near-daily attacks on our basic legal, ethical, and constitutional rules and norms," said Chairman Jerrold Nadler. "Investigating these threats to the rule of law is an obligation of Congress and a core function of the House Judiciary Committee. We have seen the damage done to our democratic institutions in the two years that the Congress refused to conduct responsible oversight. Congress must provide a check on abuses of power. Equally, we must protect and respect the work of Special Counsel Mueller, but we cannot rely on others to do the investigative work for us. Our work is even more urgent after senior Justice Department officials have suggested that they may conceal the work of the Special Counsel's investigation from the public.

"We have sent these document requests in order to begin building the public record. The Special Counsel's office and the Southern District of New York are aware that we are taking these steps. We will act quickly to gather this information, assess the evidence, and follow the facts where they lead with full transparency with the American people. This is a critical time for our nation, and we have a responsibility to investigate these matters and hold hearings for the public to have all the facts. That is exactly what we intend to do."

The Committee's investigation will cover three main areas:

- Obstruction of Justice, including the possibility of interference by the President and others in a number of criminal investigations and other official proceedings, as well as the alleged cover-up of violations of the law;

- Public Corruption, including potential violations of the emoluments clauses of the U.S. Constitution, conspiracy to violate federal campaign and financial reporting laws, and other criminal misuses of official positions for personal gain; and

- Abuses of Power, including attacks on the press, the judiciary, and law enforcement agencies; misuse of the pardon power and other presidential authorities; and attempts to misuse the power of the Office of the Presidency.

[A list of individuals and corporations receiving requests has been omitted.]

SOURCE: House Committee on the Judiciary. "House Judiciary Committee Unveils Investigation into Threats against the Rule of Law." March 4, 2019. https://judiciary.house.gov/news/documentsingle .aspx?DocumentID=1502.

DOCUMENT

Democrats Announce Intent to Release Cohen Closed-Door Testimony Transcripts

May 20, 2019

Today, the House Permanent Select Committee on Intelligence voted to release Michael Cohen's testimony and related exhibits to the public by a vote of 12–7.

Afterwards, Chairman Adam Schiff (D-CA) made the following statement:

"With the completion of Special Counsel Mueller's work and the release of his report, it is critically important that the Committee, and the Congress, make public as much information as possible that bears on Mueller's findings, explain the evidence he uncovered, and expose the obstructive actions taken by this President and those who surround him.

"It is in this light that the Committee today releases the transcripts of two days of interviews of Trump's former personal lawyer Michael Cohen.

"Cohen's February and March 2019 testimony corroborate information previously received by the Committee, including the Trump Tower Moscow deal under negotiation throughout the 2016 election season by then-candidate Donald Trump. Cohen also presented significant and troubling new detail regarding the false statement that he provided to our Committee in August 2017 and for which, in part, he is now in prison. Since Cohen's testimony, the Committee has already begun to follow up on information that Cohen provided related to attorneys for others involved in a joint defense agreement—including Jared Kushner and Donald Jr. and Ivanka Trump—to determine whether they aided in Cohen's obstruction of the Committee's investigation.

"Cohen also testified that throughout the 2016 election, candidate Trump was actively kept apprised of a potential licensing agreement on a building to be erected in the heart of Moscow—a deal for which Mr. Trump and his family would have personally earned millions and would have required active participation by the Kremlin to get final approval. Cohen testified that while Trump continued to falsely claim that he had no business deals with Russia, Cohen was actively pursuing the deal through summer 2016.

"Trump and his associates sought to ensure that false narrative continued. Cohen testified Trump urged him to 'stay on message, which is there's no Russia, there's no collusion, there's no business deals.' Cohen also said that the president's personal attorney, Jay Sekulow, also directed him to 'stay on message,' in part by encouraging Mr. Cohen to falsely claim to Congress that the Trump Tower Moscow deal ended in January 2016, before the Iowa caucuses. According to Mr. Cohen, attorneys for Kushner, Trump Jr., Ivanka Trump, and the Trump Organization also reviewed the statement before it was provided to Congress and raised no concerns with its false content.

"The obstructive acts did not stop there. After the raid of Cohen's hotel and office, Trump's legal team, according to Cohen, again interjected—this time coaxing Cohen not to cooperate with authorities through implicit promises of a future pardon. Cohen testified that he had several conversations with Sekulow through July 2018 about pardons, and with an intermediary for the president's personal attorney, Rudy Giuliani. When Cohen no longer chose to toe the party line on President Trump's relationship with Russia, the president and his allies trained their fire on Cohen and his family through a campaign of public intimidation to silence his testimony before several congressional committees—quintessential witness intimidation.

"The public should judge for themselves both the evidence released today in conjunction with Cohen's testimony related to Trump, his troubling relationship with Russia, and the efforts by Trump and those close to him to hide the relationship and potential business deals. The public also deserves the chance to judge Cohen's credibility for themselves, including by examining some of the evidence he provided to the Committee.

"The Committee will continue its investigation, continue to pursue additional evidence related to Cohen's testimony, and present to the American people what we find.

"But make no mistake, any attempt by the President, his associates or Administration to suborn perjury, obstruct our investigation or mislead the public will not be tolerated—and will be exposed."

[The unclassified, closed-door testimony Cohen gave before the House Permanent Select Committee on Intelligence on February 28, 2019, can be found at https://docs.house.gov/ meetings/IG/IG00/20190520/109549/HMTG-116-IG00-20190520-SD002.pdf; the unclassified transcript of the March 6, 2019 closed-door hearing can be found at https://docs.house .gov/meetings/IG/IG00/20190520/109549/HMTG-116-IG00-20190520-SD001.pdf.]

Source: House Permanent Select Committee on Intelligence. "Chairman Schiff Statement on Release of Michael Cohen Testimony and Documents." May 20, 2019. https://intelligence.house.gov/news/docu mentsingle.aspx?DocumentID=644.

OTHER HISTORIC DOCUMENTS OF INTEREST

FROM THIS VOLUME

- Department of Justice Releases Mueller Report, p. 179
- House Passes Articles of Impeachment against President Trump; President Responds, p. 667

FROM PREVIOUS *HISTORIC DOCUMENTS*

- Cohen, Manafort Reach Plea Agreements in Special Counsel Probe, *2018*, p. 460
- Former FBI Director Robert Mueller Appointed Special Counsel on U.S. Election-Russia Investigation, Issues Indictments, *2017*, p. 270

U.S. and North Korean Leaders Hold Summit; North Korea Renews Missile Tests

FEBRUARY 27, MARCH 2, JUNE 28, AND JUNE 30, 2019

As a follow-up to their historic summit in 2018, U.S. president Donald Trump and North Korean chairman Kim Jong-un met again in February 2019 to discuss a path toward ending North Korea's nuclear weapons program. Hopes for a concrete agreement were dashed when Trump ended talks early, stating the United States could not agree to North Korea's demand for sanctions relief until Kim made greater commitments to dismantle more of its nuclear facilities. The two men met again in June—when Trump became the first sitting president to enter North Korea—and agreed to continue discussions through teams of negotiators. Meanwhile, North Korea resumed testing of various missiles and conventional weapons, raising questions about Kim's trustworthiness and the viability of further talks. North Korean officials also threatened punitive action against the United States unless it cancelled all joint military exercises with South Korea.

PRESIDENT TRUMP AND CHAIRMAN KIM MEET IN VIETNAM

Trump and Kim convened for their second meeting in Hanoi, Vietnam, on February 27, 2019. The two leaders previously came together for a historic summit in June 2018—the first time a sitting U.S. president and North Korean chair met. Trump had declared the 2018 summit a success, but many international analysts and some members of Congress criticized the president for legitimizing a dictator and for not pressing Kim to make concrete commitments on denuclearization. Kim instead offered a vague promise to "work toward complete denuclearization of the Korean Peninsula." A joint statement issued at the conclusion of the summit indicated the countries' intent to continue working together on the nuclear issue in return for "security guarantees" from the United States. Talks between the two countries occurred infrequently in the second half of the year. The parties remained far apart, with North Korean officials insisting the United States lift sanctions before it ceased all nuclear activities, and U.S. officials stipulating that denuclearization had to come first. Over time, Trump increasingly highlighted his relationship with Kim as the measure of the talks' success, rather than denuclearization commitments.

In Hanoi, Trump and Kim met for one-on-one discussions before dining with White House chief of staff Mick Mulvaney, U.S. secretary of state Mike Pompeo, and two of Kim's top advisors. Speaking to the press before dinner, the leaders praised each other. "I truly believe that this successful and great meeting that we are having today is thanks to the courageous decision—political decision—that your team, Mr. President, reached," said Kim. Trump observed that North Korea had "tremendous economic potential" and that Kim would "have a tremendous future with your country," calling him a great leader. "I look forward to watching it happen and helping it to happen," he added.

Despite this promising talk, Trump ended the talks early on February 28 after North Korean negotiators demanded the removal of all U.S. sanctions. Trump said Kim had offered to begin dismantling the country's Yongbyon nuclear facility—the primary source of fuel for the country's nuclear weapons program—but this was not enough of a commitment for the United States to lift sanctions. The president observed that U.S. negotiators "brought many points up that [North Korean negotiators] were surprised that we knew," intimating that U.S. officials had information about other, secret nuclear facilities that they wanted North Korea to shut down before providing sanctions relief. "Sometimes you have to walk. This was just one of those times," Trump explained at a post-summit news conference, adding that "it was a very friendly walk." Trump sought to position the talks as "productive" and another step in what he has repeatedly said would be a long process to convince Kim to end his country's nuclear program. The president acknowledged that the United States and North Korea did not have the same definition of denuclearization, "but it's a lot closer than it was a year ago and I think eventually we'll get there." Trump also said Kim had promised that North Korea would not resume its nuclear or long-range-missile tests.

TRUMP CROSSES KOREAN BORDER IN HISTORIC MOMENT

Trump and Kim met again briefly on June 30 at the Demilitarized Zone separating North and South Korea. After greeting Kim, Trump stepped over the border and shook hands with the chair, becoming the first sitting U.S. president to set foot in North Korea. The occasion also marked the first time U.S. and North Korean heads of state met at the border since the Armistice Agreement ending fighting in the Korean War was signed in 1953. The two men then crossed into South Korea and shook hands again. "Big moment, big moment," said Trump. "It's a great honor to be here." Kim told reporters that Trump's action was "an expression of his willingness to eliminate all the unfortunate past and open a new future." Trump and Kim met for a few minutes with South Korean president Moon Jae-in, then proceeded to the Inter-Korean House of Freedom for bilateral talks lasting about one hour. At the end of the meeting, Trump said he and Kim had agreed to establish teams of negotiators to "work out some details" and "see if we can do a really comprehensive, good deal."

The border meeting was announced hours before it happened and followed Trump's seemingly impromptu outreach to Kim via social media while attending the Group of 20 summit in Japan two days prior. "After some very important meetings, including my meeting with President Xi of China, I will be leaving Japan for South Korea (with President Moon)," Trump wrote on Twitter. "While there, if Chairman Kim of North Korea sees this, I would meet him at the Border/DMZ just to shake his hand and say Hello(?)!" Some observers were skeptical the meeting had actually been that spontaneous, noting the many complexities involved in organizing such an event and suggesting it was political theater meant to convey diplomatic progress in the absence of concrete commitments from North Korea.

NORTH KOREA RESUMES MISSILE TESTS

Although North Korea voluntarily placed a moratorium on nuclear and long-range-missile tests in April 2018, it did not halt all of its weapons programs. At the beginning of March 2019, reports from U.S. and South Korean military and intelligence officials indicated North Korea had begun rebuilding some of the facilities it uses to build intercontinental ballistic missiles (ICBMs) and launch satellite-carrying rockets. Officials' conclusions were based on an analysis of commercial satellite images suggesting construction activity at the Sohae Satellite Launching Station. North Korea had dismantled some components of the site following the 2018 Trump–Kim summit and had offered to completely demolish the station in September 2018 during a meeting with Moon. News reports said that South Korea's National Intelligence Service had also collected information suggesting North Korea had begun rebuilding the facilities before Trump and Kim met in Vietnam.

In mid-April, North Korean state media reported that the country had tested a new "tactical guided weapon." Defense and intelligence officials said there was no evidence the test involved nuclear weapons or an ICBM. Observers speculated it was probably a test of artillery or antiaircraft systems and was meant to be a signal to Trump that unless negotiations continued, North Korea would find another way to protect itself from the United States. Around the same time, Kim said he was open to a third summit and would give the United States until the end of the year to come up with an agreement that included sanctions removal.

Then on May 4, news came that North Korea had tested several short-range missiles. A statement from the South Korean military said the missiles flew 70–200 km before landing in the sea between North Korea and Japan. Since these launches did not involve ICBMs, they technically did not violate the testing moratorium. International analysts speculated the tests were meant to pressure the Trump administration to reconsider its denuclearization-first negotiating position and demonstrate North Korea's commitment to continuing its weapons program until—or unless—a diplomatic solution was agreed upon. The tests also raised questions about Kim's trustworthiness and how willing Trump would be to accept this seemingly antagonistic behavior.

North Korea proceeded to conduct further tests throughout the year, with news reports indicating that at least eight missile launches took place between May and early September. At the beginning of October, North Korean officials confirmed the country had test-fired a ballistic missile from a submarine. Responding to the news, the U.S. State Department urged North Korea to "refrain from provocations" and "remain engaged in substantive and sustained negotiations." Trump has generally dismissed the importance of these tests (though he has acknowledged their potential violation of United Nations Security Council resolutions), which some analysts suggest has given North Korea leeway to continue developing and testing its short-range weapons systems.

UNITED STATES CANCELS SOME MILITARY EXERCISES WITH SOUTH KOREA

Since the 1950s, the U.S. and South Korean militaries have engaged in periodic joint exercises both to maintain the readiness levels of their fighting forces and deter North Korea from taking aggressive actions in the region. Following the 2018 Trump–Kim summit, the two countries have cancelled or scaled back many of these exercises in support of the ongoing diplomatic efforts between the United States and North Korea, though smaller exercises have continued.

On March 2, 2019, the United States and South Korea announced the cancellation of two annual, large-scale joint exercises known as Key Resolve and Foal Eagle. These exercises typically involve thousands of ground, air, and naval troops from the United States, South Korea, Australia, Britain, France, and other allies. The U.S. Defense Department provided a readout of a call between acting defense secretary Patrick Shanahan and South

Korean minister of national defense Jeong Kyeong-doo in which the two officials agreed to conduct smaller trainings instead. The men reportedly "reaffirmed their commitment to ensuring the continued combined defense posture of U.S.–Republic of Korea combined forces to meet any security challenge, and agreed to maintain firm military readiness through newly designed Command Post exercises and revised field training programs." They also stated that changes to the joint training program reflected their "desire to reduce tension and support our diplomatic efforts to achieve complete denuclearization of the Korean Peninsula in a final, fully verified manner."

A two-week joint drill took place in early August but was not officially announced or widely publicized. The drill reportedly involved mostly computer simulations, rather than in-field training. Regardless, the North Korean Foreign Ministry denounced the drills, and officials accused the United States and South Korea of inciting tensions in the region. In November, U.S. and South Korean officials announced the large-scale aerial exercise known as Vigilant Ace would be suspended for a second year, but they would proceed with a "Combined Flying Training Event" instead. North Korean state media published a statement from the country's powerful State Affairs Commission saying such a drill would violate agreements between Kim and Trump. "The U.S. had better behave itself with prudence at a sensitive time when the situation on the Korean Peninsula could go back to the starting point due to the joint military drills," the statement read. The United States, the statement continued, "will face greater threat and be forced to admit its failure, being put into trouble before long if it doesn't do anything to change the trend of the present situation."

Return to Talks Possible

The future of U.S.–North Korean talks remains in question. U.S. and North Korean negotiators resumed their discussions on October 4, meeting for working-level talks in Stockholm, Sweden. However, talks were called off the following day. Trump administration officials said negotiators had "good discussions," but North Korea's Foreign Ministry called them "sickening." Kim Myong Gil, the chief negotiator for North Korea, said the breakdown was "entirely due to the United States' failure to abandon its outdated viewpoint and attitude." Officials reiterated Kim's end-of-year deadline. In mid-November, Kim Myong Gil released a statement that the United States had proposed to resume talks in December 2019 but did not indicate whether North Korea intended to accept the offer.

—Linda Grimm

Following are remarks by U.S. president Donald Trump and North Korean chairman Kim Jong-un on February 27, 2019, at the start of their Vietnam summit; a readout of a March 2, 2019, call between acting U.S. defense secretary Patrick Shanahan and South Korean minister of national defense Jeong Kyeong-doo in which they discussed joint military exercises; a tweet posted by Trump on June 28, 2019, asking if Kim would like to meet; and remarks by Trump and Kim before and following the U.S. president's crossing of the Korean border on June 30, 2019.

President Trump and Chairman Kim
Remarks at Meeting in Vietnam

February 27, 2019

Chairman Kim. So it's exactly 261 days since we met last time in Singapore, in June, last year.

President Trump. Yes.

Chairman Kim. And I truly believe that this successful and great meeting that we are having today is thanks to the courageous decision—political decision—that your team, Mr. President, reached.

So, during that 261 days since we last met, there have been some misunderstandings. There have been all these eyes from the world who are misunderstanding the situation. But—and there was some hostility that still remained from the very, very past period that—from the outside.

President Trump. Right.

Chairman Kim. But, however, we have been able to overcome all those obstacles, and here we are today after 261 days, in Hanoi together. And I truly believe that those 261 days were the days which were—and during which a lot of painstaking efforts were necessary and also a lot of patience were needed.

But here we are today sitting next to each other, and that gives us a hope that we will be successful with time. And I would really make—try to make that happen.

President Trump. Thank you very much. That's really nice. Thank you.

Well, I want to just say it's an honor to be with Chairman Kim. It's an honor to be together in, really, a country, Vietnam, where they've really rolled out the red carpet, and they've—they're very honored to have us. And it's great to be with you.

We had a very successful first summit. I felt it was very successful, and some people would like to see it go quicker. I'm satisfied; you're satisfied. We want to be happy with what we're doing. But I thought the first summit was a great success. And I think this one, hopefully, will be equal or greater than the first. And we made a lot progress, and I think the biggest progress was, our relationship is really a good one.

And as I've said many times—and I say it to the press; I say it to anybody that wants to listen—I think that your country has tremendous economic potential. Unbelievable. Unlimited. And I think that you will have a tremendous future with your country—a great leader. And I look forward to watching it happen and helping it to happen. And we will help it to happen.

[At this point, President Trump and Chairman Kim shook hands.]

President Trump. Thank you all very much. We appreciate it. And we're going to go have dinner, and then we have some big meetings scheduled for tomorrow. And we'll see you, I guess, at a news conference at some point during the day. Thank you very much. . . .

SOURCE: Executive Office of the President. "Remarks in a Meeting with Chairman of the State Affairs Commission Kim Jong Un of North Korea and an Exchange with Reporters in Hanoi, Vietnam." February 27, 2019. *Compilation of Presidential Documents* 2019, no. 00103 (February 27, 2019). https://www.gov info.gov/content/pkg/DCPD-201900103/pdf/DCPD-201900103.pdf.

Readout of Acting Defense Secretary Shanahan's Call with South Korean Minister of National Defense

March 2, 2019

During a phone call on March 2, Minister of National Defense Jeong Kyeong-doo and the Acting Secretary of Defense Patrick Shanahan assessed the outcomes of the Summit between President Trump and Chairman Kim and discussed the further coordination of measures to establish complete denuclearization and lasting peace on the Korean Peninsula, as well as steps to maintain the readiness of combined forces.

Secretary Shanahan reviewed the results of the U.S.–DPRK Summit, and, Minister Jeong expressed his regrets that a complete agreement was not reached while also noting his hopes for the U.S. and the DPRK to continue further vigorous conversations based on the discussion results of the Summit. Both the Minister and Secretary agreed that close coordination between the military activities of the United States and Republic of Korea will continue to support diplomatic efforts.

The Secretary and Minister reviewed and approved the Alliance decisions recommended by the Commander of U.S. Forces Korea and the Republic of Korea Joint Chiefs of Staff on the combined exercise and training program. Following close coordination, both sides decided to conclude the KEY RESOLVE and FOAL EAGLE series of exercises.

The Minister and Secretary reaffirmed their commitment to ensuring the continued combined defense posture of U.S.–ROK combined forces to meet any security challenge, and agreed to maintain firm military readiness through newly designed Command Post exercises and revised field training programs. The Secretary and Minister both affirmed their continued support for the ROK and U.S. armed forces, the Combined Force Command, and the United Nations Command in support of peace and security in the region.

The Minister and Secretary made clear that the Alliance decision to adapt our training program reflected our desire to reduce tension and support our diplomatic efforts to achieve complete denuclearization of the Korean Peninsula in a final, fully verified manner.

The Secretary and Minister share the understanding that the two countries' communication is more robust than ever in the midst of changes in the security environment of the Korean Peninsula. Both agreed to continue strengthening coordination and cooperation by meeting one another in person in the near future to further deepen the ROK–U.S. Alliance and ensure peace and security on the Korean Peninsula.

SOURCE: U.S. Department of Defense. "Readout of Minister of National Defense Jeong Kyeong-doo's Phone Call with Acting Secretary of Defense Patrick Shanahan." March 2, 2019. https://www.defense .gov/Newsroom/Releases/Release/Article/1773294/readout-of-minister-of-national-defense-jeong- kyeong-doos-phone-call-with-actin/.

President Trump Requests Meeting with Chairman Kim

June 28, 2019

After some very important meetings, including my meeting with President Xi of China, I will be leaving Japan for South Korea (with President Moon). While there, if Chairman Kim of North Korea sees this, I would meet him at the Border/DMZ just to shake his hand and say Hello(?)!

SOURCE: Donald Trump (@realDonaldTrump). Twitter post. June 28, 2019. https://twitter.com/realdon aldtrump/status/1144740178948493314?lang=en.

Remarks by President Trump, Chairman Kim, and President Moon at Meeting in the Demilitarized Zone

June 30, 2019

[Prior to greeting Chairman Kim at the line of demarcation, the president walked from the Freedom House, paused at the curb separating South and North Korea, and waited as Chairman Kim approached. He then greeted Chairman Kim as follows.]

President Trump. My friend.

Chairman Kim. It is good to see you again. I've never expected to meet you at this place.

President Trump. That's good. It's my honor. Would you like me to step across? [Inaudible] Would you like me to?

Chairman Kim. If you—[inaudible]—take a step forward, you will be the first U.S. President to cross the border. Good luck.

President Trump. I'm okay with that. I'd be very proud. I'd be very proud to do that. Okay. Let's do it. Come on.

[At this point, the President crossed briefly into North Korean territory, walking with Chairman Kim. They then turned, shook hands, spoke briefly, and returned to the line of demarcation, where they paused for photographs.]

Chairman Kim. This is a great moment.

President Trump. Big moment, big moment. Big progress. Tremendous progress.

[The President and Chairman Kim walked together into South Korean territory and continued their conversation.]

President Trump. So I was in Japan, and then it was Seoul. [Inaudible]—and you said yes. And I said, "Great."

Q. How do you feel?

President Trump. It's great. I feel great. It's a great honor to be here.

Chairman Kim. As you can see, this shows that nobody has expected this moment.

Q. Chairman Kim, how do you feel?

Chairman Kim. President Trump has just walked across the demarcation line. That made him the first U.S. President to visit our country. I believe just looking at this action, this is an expression of his willingness to eliminate all the unfortunate past and open a new future.

President Trump. I just want to say that this is my honor. I didn't really expect it. We were in Japan for the G–20. We came over, and I said: "Hey, I'm over here. I want to call up Chairman Kim." And we got to meet. And stepping across that line was a great honor. A lot of progress has been made. A lot of friendships have been made. And this has been in particular a great friendship. So I just want to thank you. That was very quick notice, and I want to thank you.

So we're going to go inside. We're going to talk for a little while about different things. And a lot of really positive things are happening, and I'm glad you could be here to see it. But tremendous positivity. Really great things are happening and—in a lot of places. But we met, and we liked each other from day one, and that was very important.

Thank you, everybody. Thank you.

Q. Would you invite him to the U.S.?

President Trump. I would invite him right now—to the White House. Absolutely.

[President Trump and Chairman Kim approached the Freedom House, where they greeted President Moon and continued their conversation.]

President Moon. I'd really like to pay my tribute to the efforts of you two. You have really made a historic moment today.

President Trump. Thank you. I think it is. And it's a great day for a lot of people. It's a great day, really, for the world, if you think about it. Beyond North Korea, South Korea, it's a great day for the world, and it's an honor for me to be here. And thank you both very much.

President Moon. The two leaders have just presented such a big hope to the 80,000 Korean people as well as to the whole world. So I do look forward to great progress being made in your subsequent dialogue.

President Trump. Well, I want to thank everybody. Thank you all for being here. I have to say that when I first became President of the United States, there was great conflict in this area. Great, great conflict. And now we have just the opposite. And it's my honor. And it's the Chairman's honor, I can say. We work well together. And, Mr. President, thank you.

Chairman Kim. I would like to also take this opportunity to express my gratitude for all your assistance in having such a good opportunity.

President Trump. Thank you very much. Thank you very much. Thank you all.

SOURCE: Executive Office of the President. "Remarks with Chairman of the State Affairs Commission Kim Jong Un of North Korea and President Moon Jae-in of South Korea and an Exchange with Reporters in Panmunjom, Korean Demilitarized Zone." June 30, 2019. *Compilation of Presidential Documents* 2019, no. 00446 (June 30, 2019). https://www.govinfo.gov/content/pkg/DCPD-201900446/pdf/DCPD-201900446.pdf.

President Trump and Chairman Kim Comment on Meeting in Demilitarized Zone

DOCUMENT

June 30, 2019

Chairman Kim. It's always special, and I want to thank you—[inaudible]—for having me.

President Trump. I want to thank you. Because—[inaudible.] It was great. Look, I mean, the world is watching, and it's very important for the world.

Chairman Kim. And also, the place of our meeting is special. That is why it aroused the attention of so many people. Some people say as if this meeting was prearranged through the letters you have sent me. But myself was surprised yesterday morning when you expressed a willingness to meet with me here and also when we got the official confirmation late yesterday afternoon.

And also, I'm always grateful to meet with you again. And this place of our meeting is a symbol of the separation between the North and South and also a reminder of unfortunate past. And as the two countries, we share a long unfortunate past, meeting at such place shows that we are willing to put an end to the unfortunate past and also open a new future and provide positive opportunities in the future.

If it was not for our excellent relation between the two of us, it would have not been possible to have this kind of opportunity. So I would like to use this strong relation to create more good news, which nobody expects in the past and also to propel the good relations between our countries—[inaudible].

President Trump. Well, I want to thank you, Chairman. You hear the power of that voice.

Nobody has heard that voice before. He doesn't do news conferences, in case you haven't heard. And this was a special moment. This is, I think, really—as President Moon said, this is a historic moment, the fact that we're meeting.

And I want to thank Chairman Kim for something else. When I put out the social media notification, if he didn't show up, the press was going to make me look very bad. So you made us both look good, and I appreciate it.

But we've developed a great relationship. I really think that, if you go back 2½ years, and you look at what was going on prior to my becoming President, it was a very, very bad situation, a very dangerous situation for South Korea, for North Korea, for the world.

And I think the relationship that we've developed has meant so much to so many people. And it's just an honor to be with you, and it was an honor that you asked me to step over that line. And I was proud to step over the line. I thought you might do that; I wasn't sure. But I was ready to do it. And I want to thank you. It's been great. It's been great.

A very historic meeting. We were just saying—one of the folks from the media was saying this could to be a very historic moment, and I guess that's what it is. But I enjoyed being with you, and thank you very much.

SOURCE: Executive Office of the President. "Remarks in a Meeting with Chairman of the State Affairs Commission Kim Jong Un of North Korea in Panmunjom, Korean Demilitarized Zone." June 30, 2019. *Compilation of Presidential Documents* 2019, no. 00447 (June 30, 2019). https://www.govinfo.gov/content/pkg/DCPD-201900447/pdf/DCPD-201900447.pdf.

Other Historic Documents of Interest

From previous *Historic Documents*

March

International Leaders Respond to Protests in Algeria

MARCH 11, MARCH 12, MARCH 27, AND APRIL 25, 2019

Simmering dissatisfaction with Algeria's stagnant economy and the ruling political party's grip on power boiled over into nationwide protests following the announcement that President Abdelaziz Bouteflika would run for a fifth term in 2019. The peaceful demonstrations spread in size and demands, with protestors continuing to call for an overhaul of the country's political system even after Bouteflika resigned. Foreign officials commended the Algerians for expressing themselves peacefully and offered support for their desire for change without intervening in the situation.

Bouteflika Announces Reelection Run

On February 9, the state-run Algeria Press Service published an announcement that President Bouteflika would seek a fifth term in the election scheduled for April 18, 2019. Bouteflika was eighty-one years old at the time of the announcement and had been serving as president since 1999. Widely credited with negotiating an end to the country's civil war, in which at least 100,000 Algerians were killed, Bouteflika had enjoyed years of support from the public, labor unions, and businesses, as well as alliances with other political parties.

However, Bouteflika's government had also been criticized for Algeria's flagging economy, which relies heavily on oil and gas exports to generate revenue. For decades the country's lack of economic diversification has contributed to higher unemployment, inflation, and rising costs for basic goods. In 2011 and 2012, a wave of protests broke out across Algeria, with tens of thousands of people calling for economic and political change. Bouteflika's government cut rising food costs, increased spending for public programs, and ended the state of emergency that had been in place since 1992, when the civil war began. Yet none of these or other economic policies—including one program that offered low-interest loans to help young people start businesses—helped to reduce unemployment. The economy was also hit by the global drop in oil prices that occurred in 2015 and 2016. The resulting drop in energy sector revenue prompted the Algerian government to cut spending, including budgets for public assistance programs.

Bouteflika's presidency was also marked by claims of election rigging. In 1999, he ultimately ran unchallenged after all opposition candidates withdrew due to concerns that it would not be a fair election. Four opposition parties boycotted the 2002 legislative elections claiming the vote was a sham, which allowed Bouteflika's party, the National Liberation Front (FLN), to triple the number of seats it held in parliament. Fraud allegations were also made in the 2012 parliamentary election and the 2014 vote for president. Bouteflika's victory in the 2014 election gave rise to a public protest movement known as "Barakat," or "Enough."

Additionally, since 2013, speculation had been mounting that Bouteflika was no longer capable of serving in office. That year, the president suffered a stroke that paralyzed him and left him wheelchair bound. His public appearances have grown increasingly rare, and he has not addressed the Algerian people since his stroke.

If Bouteflika won a fifth term in 2019, it would be his last. When he first took office in 1999, presidents were limited to two five-year terms, but Algerian lawmakers amended the constitution in 2008 to remove the term limit and allow Bouteflika to run a third time. However, lawmakers voted to reinstate the two-term limit in 2016 amid mounting public pressure for reforms. The change allowed Bouteflika to run for one final term in 2019.

ALGERIANS TAKE TO THE STREETS

Bouteflika's announcement sparked nationwide protests, with several reports indicating they were some of the biggest public demonstrations in Algeria's history. Protests began on February 22 and continued weekly, with Algerians leveraging social media to organize peaceful demonstrations across the country. Most observers noted that Algerian youth played a major role in driving the protests, citing a lack of job opportunities as their key motivation. Unemployment was particularly high among Algerians under the age of thirty; in September 2018, the government's National Statistics Bureau reported that nearly 30 percent of people aged sixteen to twenty-four were unemployed. Older Algerians and some analysts also observed that young people were not dissuaded by government officials' claims that changes in leadership would lead to another civil war, in part because they did not experience the "Black Decade."

Although they initially mobilized to oppose Bouteflika's reelection, protestors also sought major political reforms, including the ouster of all Bouteflika appointees and allies, the formation of transitional institutions to replace the existing system of government, constitutional reforms, and an end to the military's power over politics. "Algerians don't want a replacement of a façade," said Rachid Chaibi, a member of the Socialist Forces Front opposition party, in an interview with *The Washington Post*. "They want to rebuild their country's political and social system from ground zero."

Protestors' disaffection extended beyond Bouteflika to the FLN, which has controlled the presidency and parliament since Algeria won its independence from France in 1962. A thirteen-year ban on all political parties except the FLN helped to cement the party's dominance. Opposition parties remain weak and often struggle to attract significant support. Protestors' demands for change also targeted a broader network of military leaders, intelligence officers, lawmakers, business executives, and other Bouteflika allies—a group known in Algeria as *le pouvoir,* or the power. All of these individuals needed to be removed from their positions of influence in order for a new, civilian, and democratic government to take shape, protestors argued.

BOUTEFLIKA STEPS DOWN

Despite the ongoing demonstrations, Bouteflika filed required election paperwork with Algeria's constitutional council in early March, confirming he still intended to run. A statement issued to state media promised that if he won, Bouteflika would organize new elections—in which he would not be a candidate—within one year. The public was not appeased, however, and protests continued.

Days later, on March 11, Bouteflika reversed course. In a letter to the country published by state news agency APS, Bouteflika wrote, "There will be no fifth term and there has never been any question for me, since my health condition and my age assign me as an ultimate duty, to the Algerian people." He added that "the new generations of Algerians" would build a new republic. Bouteflika also announced that the April 18 election would be postponed and a constitutional convention would be convened, but he did not identify a date when either event would take place. Opposition leaders claimed the move was another attempt by the president to remain in power, since Bouteflika stated he would stay in office until a successor was chosen.

On the international stage, reaction to Bouteflika's announcement was generally measured. Most foreign officials characterized the developments in Algeria as an internal situation that must be handled by the Algerian people and their government. "France expresses hope that a new dynamic capable of responding to the deepest aspirations of the Algerian people will swiftly emerge," said Jean-Yves Le Drian, France's minister for Europe and foreign affairs. He also said, "It is up to the Algerian people to choose their leaders and decide their future." U.S. State Department deputy spokesperson Robert Palladino said the United States supported "the rights of the Algerians to assemble and peacefully express their views" and their right to "vote in a free and fair election." European Union (EU) officials echoed these sentiments, adding that they would help with new elections and a government transition if Algeria asked for it. "We should encourage a free, fair, and inclusive election of Algeria's next president. . . . We should also support the call for the broader reform and transition process," said Johannes Hahn, EU commissioner for European neighborhood policy and enlargement negotiations, in remarks before the European Parliament. "The European Union stands ready to accompany Algeria in this process if the Algerians request it." Hahn also noted that the demonstrations in Algeria "have been largely peaceful and the response by the security services has been very measured," despite the protests' massive scale. "This is highly commendable and restraint should continue."

Back in Algeria, the protests continued and Bouteflika's allies started to distance themselves from the president. Gen. Ahmed Gaid Salah, chief of the Algerian Army, pushed lawmakers to declare Bouteflika unfit for office. On April 2, Salah publicly called for the president to step down. Hours later, Bouteflika announced his resignation. Per the country's constitution, the chair of the upper house of parliament, Abdelkader Bensalah, became the interim president, with a set term of ninety days. On April 10, Bensalah announced the postponed election would be held on July 4 and pledged it would be a free and fair poll.

PROTESTS CONTINUE

Bouteflika's resignation failed to quell the protests and tens of thousands of Algerians continued to demonstrate in the capital and other parts of the country. They added to their calls for reform a demand that Bensalah, Prime Minister Noureddine Bedoui, and Constitutional Council head Tayeb Belaiz resign. Responding to the ongoing protests, Minister of Communication Hassane Rabehi, the government's spokesperson, called for Algeria "to give shape to the demands expressed by millions of Algerians in peaceful demonstrators and transform them into proposals for serious dialogue, with the participation of all, including the political parties and associations." The goal of such a dialogue, he said, would be "to elaborate a consensus action plan to direct the country to a safe harbor, through the organization of a free, democratic and transparent presidential election."

The protestors also took aim at Gaid Salah, who had begun claiming that Algeria's enemies were manipulating the protestors. Gaid Salah was also pushing for a new election as soon as possible, while protestors sought a further postponement until all Bouteflika administration officials and supporters were removed from power. In addition, the army chief initiated a crackdown on protests, ordering police to stop and seize vehicles caught transporting demonstrators to the capital. A growing number of protestors were arrested and imprisoned, including a well-known opposition member, Karim Tabou, who was accused of undermining the military. Reports by Human Rights Watch and others indicated some of the protestors who were arrested were simply standing peacefully, holding signs or waving Algerian flags. Other reports stated police had established checkpoints throughout the capital in an effort to prevent protestors from attending demonstrations. At the same time, Gaid Salah led a push to arrest senior officials and other Bouteflika allies on fraud and corruption charges. This effort, combined with the crackdown on protests, was characterized by many observers as a "carrot-and-stick" strategy for ending the demonstrations.

ELECTION POSTPONED AGAIN

Only two candidates filed to run in the rescheduled presidential election and both were rejected by election officials. The Constitutional Council did not explain why the candidates had been rejected in its official statement, saying simply that because of the decision, it would be "impossible" to conduct the election as planned, causing the vote to be postponed yet again. In mid-September, Bensalah, who had by then exceeded his ninety-day term limit, announced the election would take place on December 12. Bensalah also persuaded lawmakers to establish a new entity to oversee the election process and ensure transparency. Though characterized as an independent body, Karim Younes, a former speaker of the lower house of parliament and Bouteflika supporter, was appointed to direct the group, raising objections from the opposition.

Five candidates, all of whom had connections to Bouteflika, were certified by electoral officials to stand in the December vote. Ali Benflis and Abdelmadjid Tebboune, both former prime ministers under Bouteflika, were among the candidates and were considered frontrunners. Algerians protested the vote and called for a boycott, claiming the election was a sham. Widespread demonstrations occurred on Election Day. In some locations, protestors reportedly stormed polling places. Various reports said police beat and kicked protestors in their efforts to break up the demonstrations. Election officials declared Tebboune the winner with roughly 58 percent of the vote on December 13. The official voter turnout was said to be about 40 percent, but some observers suggested actual turnout had been much lower, particularly in the cities. The announcement of the results prompted fresh protests, with participants reportedly chanting, "We didn't vote." Antigovernment protests are expected to continue.

—Linda Grimm

Following is a letter from President Abdelaziz Bouteflika to the Algerian people, published on March 11, 2019, announcing he would not seek a fifth term; a statement issued by French minister for Europe and foreign affairs Jean-Yves Le Drian on March 11, 2019, in response to Bouteflika's announcement; a brief exchange between U.S. State Department deputy spokesperson Robert Palladino and reporters on March 12, 2019, on the situation in Algeria; remarks by EU commissioner for

European Neighbourhood policy and enlargement negotiations Johannes Hahn on March 27, 2019, opening and closing the European Parliament's plenary debate on developments in Algeria; and an April 25, 2019, statement from Algeria's minister of communication Hassane Rabehi on the demands of protestors.

President Bouteflika Announces Postponement of 2019 Presidential Election

March 11, 2019

President of the Republic Abdelaziz Bouteflika sent Monday a message to the nation in which he announced the postponement of the Presidential Elections of 18 April 2019, and his decision to renounce his bid to seek a 5th term as president.

President Bouteflika also announced the holding of the Presidential Election an extension of the National Inclusive and Independent Conference as well as the formation of a government of the national competences.

Here is the full text of the message:

Algeria is living through a sensitive stage of its History. On March 8, for the third consecutive Friday, major popular marches took place across the country. I have followed these developments, and as I already announced on March 3rd, I do understand the motivations of the numerous compatriots who choose this way of expression of which I once again hail the peaceful nature.

I particularly understand the message given by youth, in terms of anxiety and ambition for their own future and that of the country. I also understand the gap which may have been the source of concern, between the holding of the Presidential Election on a technically appropriate date, as a milestone of governance in the institutional and political life, and the opening, without delay of a large and high priority undertaking at the political level.

It concerns the conception and the conduct of deep reforms in the political, institutional, economic and social fields, with the largest possible and most representative participation of the Algerian society, with the just share that should be dedicated to women and youth.

I understand that the renovating project of our State-Nation, which I announced the key lines, would benefit from more explanations and preparations, so to clear doubts by providing the conditions for its approval by all the Algerian society's categories and the nation's components.

Loyal to the oath I took before the Algerian people to protect and promote in all the circumstances the interests of our country, and after the institutional consultations needed under the Constitution,

I invoke the grace and support of Almighty God to avail myself of the higher values of our people, our glorious martyrs and brave Mujahedeen to announce to you the following decisions:

First: There will be no fifth term and there has never been any question for me, since my health condition and my age assign me as an ultimate duty, to the Algerian people; the contribution to the foundations of a new Republic as part of the new Algerian system that we all strive for. This new Republic and this new system will be in the hands of the new generations of Algerians, men and women, who will naturally be the main actors and beneficiaries of public life and sustainable development in the Algeria of tomorrow.

Second: There will be no Presidential Election on April 18th. This is to meet a pressing request that [many of you have expressed] to me in your concern to remove any misunderstanding as to the desirability and irreversibility of the generational transmission to which I am committed. It is also a matter of making prevail the noble purpose of the legal devices which resides in a sound regulation of the institutional life and in the harmony of the socio-political interactions, on a rigid fulfillment of pre-established rendezvous.

The postponement of the Presidential Election that has been demanded comes therefore to ease the apprehensions that have been expressed in order to pave the way for spreading serenity, tranquility and public security, with the aim of undertaking together the actions of paramount importance which will make it possible to prepare as quickly as possible the advent of a new era in Algeria.

Third: With a view to greater mobilization from the public authorities and enhancing the effectiveness of the State's action in all areas, I decided to make capital changes within the Government in the near future. These changes are set to be an adequate response to the expectations you voiced to me, as well as an illustration of my receptivity to the requirement of accountability and rigorous assessment, as part of the exercise of senior positions at all levels and in all sectors.

Fourth: The Inclusive and Independent National Conference will be a forum with all the forces necessary for debating, developing and adopting all types of reforms, which are meant to be the foundation for the new system for launching the process of transforming our nation-state, which I consider to be my ultimate mission in completing the work the Almighty God has given me the capacity and the Algerian people have given me the opportunity to do.

This conference will be equitably representative of the Algerian society as well as its trends. Its proceedings will be overseen by a plural presidential body, chaired by an independent, consensual and experienced national figure. The conference should strive to complete its mandate by the end of 2019. The draft Constitution emanating from the Conference will be submitted to a popular referendum. The National Independent Conference will fix the date of the presidential election, in which I will not be candidate.

Fifth: The Presidential Election, which will take place in the wake of the Inclusive and Independent national conference, will be organized under the exclusive authority of an Independent National Electoral Commission whose mandate, composition and mode of operation will be codified in a legislative text, based on the most established experiences and practices in the world.

The creation of an Independent National Electoral Commission is decided in response to a demand largely upheld by the Algerian political parties as well as to a constant recommendation of the electoral observation missions of the international and regional organizations, invited and received by Algeria during the previous elections.

Sixth: In order to optimally contribute to the holding of the presidential election under indisputable conditions of freedom, regularity and transparency, a Government of national competencies will be formed with the support of the components of the National Conference.

This Government will supervise the missions of the public administration and the security services and will fully collaborate with the Independent National Electoral Commission. For its part, the Constitutional Council will assume, in complete independence, the powers conferred on it by the Constitution and the law on the presidential elections.

Seventh: I solemnly pledge before the Almighty God and in front of the Algerian people to spare no effort so that the State institutions, structures, dismemberments and local authorities mobilize to contribute to the full success of this action plan. I also undertake to ensure that all the constitutional institutions of the Republic scrupulously pursue the accomplishment of their respective missions and exercise their respective authorities in the exclusive service of the Algerian people and the Republic.

Finally, I pledge to hand over the prerogatives of the President of the Republic to the successor that the Algerian people will freely elect.

SOURCE: Algeria Press Service. "President Bouteflika Announces Postponement of 2019 Presidential Election." March 11, 2019. http://www.aps.dz/en/algeria/28311-president-bouteflika-announces-postponement-of-presidential-elections.

Algerian President Will Not Seek Another Term

March 11, 2019

I welcome the statement by President Bouteflika announcing that he will not seek a fifth term and vowing measures to update the Algerian political system.

Following massive protests, which took place in a calm and dignified manner throughout Algeria, France expresses the hope that a new dynamic capable of responding to the deepest aspirations of the Algerian people will swiftly emerge.

France reaffirms its attachment to its ties of friendship with Algeria, offering its best wishes for peace, stability and prosperity for all its people.

SOURCE: French Ministry for Europe and Foreign Affairs. "Algeria—Statement by Jean-Yves Le Drian, Minister for Europe and Foreign Affairs (11 March 2019)." March 11, 2019. https://www.diplomatie.gouv.fr/en/country-files/algeria/events/article/algeria-statement-by-jean-yves-le-drian-minister-for-europe-and-foreign-affairs.

U.S. State Department Remarks on Situation in Algeria

March 12, 2019

[The following questions and answers have been excerpted from the transcript of a press briefing.]

. . . **QUESTION:** Could you give us your reaction, the U.S. reaction, on President Bouteflika of Algeria not to seek a fifth term but to stay—to postpone the election and to stay in power, at least until the end of the year and probably after that?

MR. PALLADINO: We support efforts in Algeria to chart a new path forward based on dialogue that reflects the will of all Algerians and their aspirations for a peaceful and prosperous future.

QUESTION: That's all?

MR. PALLADINO: Well, we respect the rights of the Algerians to assemble and peacefully express their views, and we're closely monitoring reports that Algeria's elections have been postponed. We support the right of the Algerian people to vote in a free and fair election, as we do around the world.

QUESTION: You think it's a good thing that he's not seeking a fifth term?

MR. PALLADINO: We support efforts in Algeria to chart a new path forward, and I'll leave it at that. . . .

Source: U.S. Department of State. "Department Press Briefing—March 12, 2019." March 12, 2019. https://www.state.gov/briefings/department-press-briefing-march-12-2018/.

DOCUMENT *EU Official on Situation in Algeria*

March 27, 2019

Thank you Madame Chair, Honourable Members of the European Parliament,

We have been witnessing a new dynamic in recent weeks starting on 22 February with massive, nation-wide demonstrations in Algeria. These were prompted by the announcement that incumbent President [of Algeria, Abdelaziz] Bouteflika would run for a fifth mandate in the Presidential election initially set for 18 April. Since then, demonstrations have continued virtually every day, and have grown in size. Besides opposing a new mandate for President Bouteflika, the protestors are demanding a broader reform of Algeria's political system. Notwithstanding their massive scale, the demonstrations have been largely peaceful and the response by the security services has been very measured.

Official communication from the government in recent weeks, following the nomination of a new Prime Minister and Deputy Prime Minister, stresses the necessity to consult and listen to the people with a view to introducing significant reforms.

Algeria is a key partner for the European Union. We have important political, economic and people-to-people interests in the country and in the region, where Algeria is a stabilizing factor. Our bilateral relations have progressed positively in recent years and we expect that to continue. High Representative/Vice-President Federica Mogherini met Minister of State [of Algeria, Ramtane] Lamamra in Brussels on 7 March to discuss the situation in the country, before his subsequent appointment as Deputy Prime Minister and Foreign Minister. I also had the opportunity to talk to him.

The demonstrations have so far been peaceful, and the response by security services has been measured. This is highly commendable and restraint should continue.

As you all know, the situation is currently very fluid. We have been following today's developments very closely. It is key now that there should be a positive response to the people's aspirations: their call for reform of governance, for greater political openness, and for more economic and social opportunities, especially for the young. Any process has to be transparent and include all sections of Algerian society.

During this period, it is important to remember that it is for the Algerians to decide for themselves, and among themselves, how to make this transition happen. On the EU side, we should encourage a free, fair and inclusive election of Algeria's next president, to be organized within a reasonable timeframe. The EU is ready to support the election with technical expertise and will consider fielding an Electoral Observation Mission, of course, if Algeria requests this and if the conditions of the process are met. I count on Parliament's support in this regard.

We should also support the call for the broader reform and transition process. A National Conference could be the platform for discussing this, as long as it is genuinely inclusive, representative and designed to ensure political legitimacy. It is important to make quick progress on this. Citizens' initiatives for a peaceful solution are also circulating, and we understand there is willingness on both sides to define a common way forward. We hope that a consensus crystallises around a roadmap for the transition, as well as on who should be in charge of carrying it out. Whatever process is followed, it must be one that is accepted by Algerians as expressing their will. And, as we have stated publicly, the European Union stands ready to accompany Algeria in this process if the Algerians request it.

The EU should continue to support Algeria in its socio-economic reforms, and the shaping of perspectives that match the desires and ambitions of the population, especially the young.

All this will be done in full respect of Algeria's sovereignty and in a spirit of partnership as it is defined in our Neighbourhood Policy concepts. The events over the past four weeks have tested political maturity in Algeria and we count on all concerned to face up to the call for change and to bring a peaceful transition to fruition. . . .

We will continue to monitor all developments in Algeria, a key partner to our South. As I said, we hope that the situation remains peaceful, and we believe it is vital that the legitimate aspirations of the Algerian people are addressed. At the same time, I believe we can agree that the best we can do right now is not to interfere in an internal process.

We should be ready to provide support to the consensus and the ensuing process when the moment is ripe, while following closely the various steps on the way and remembering it is for the Algerians to decide for themselves and among themselves how to make this transition happen.

Allow me therefore to express my appreciation for your attention and support in giving this important file the considerate approach it deserves and to stay vigilant on this subject.

Thank you very much.

SOURCE: European Union, European External Action Service. "Speech on Behalf of the High Representative/Vice-President at the European Parliament Plenary Debate on the Situation in Algeria." March 27, 2019. https://eeas.europa.eu/headquarters/headquarters-homepage/60298/speech-behalf-high-representativevice-president-european-parliament-plenary-debate-situation_en.

Algerian Minister of Communication Comments on Protests, Need for Dialogue

April 25, 2019

Minister of Communication, spokesman of the Government, Hassane Rabehi, called on Wednesday in Algiers for "giving shape to the demands expressed during Algerian peaceful protests and transforming them into proposals for serious dialogue."

"Currently, Algeria needs to give shape to the demands expressed by millions of Algerians in peaceful demonstrators and transform them into proposals for serious dialogue, with the participation of all, including the political parties and associations," Rabehi told a news conference following the Government Council meeting.

In this regard, he insisted on the importance of "choosing competent figures to represent the demonstrators in this dialogue" which goal would be "to elaborate a consensus action plan to direct the country to a safe harbor, through the organization of a free, democratic and transparent presidential election."

The Government's spokesman who deemed "meaningless" to exclude the State from the dialogue, said that "all the proposals are welcome, as long as they serve the best interests of the country."

"The high authorities of the country advocate consensus and the protection of Algeria from all dangers," said the Communication Minister, warning against "constitutional vacuum."

Rabehi called on the Algerian people to "stand firm against the attempts at the stability of the country."

Speaking about the consultation meeting organized Monday by the presidency of the Republic, Rabehi said that the participating parties "have their rightful place, as being representative, authorized and free in the expression of their views."

Regarding the absence of the Head of State in this meeting, the Government's spokesman said that "Bensalah, head of the State in virtue of the Constitution, has huge responsibilities and his absence is the result of his willingness to provide the conditions conducive to inclusive dialogue."

Hailing the last statement of Lt General Ahmed Gaïd Salah, Deputy Minister of National Defence, Chief of Staff of the People's National Army (ANP), who referred to some voices who do want to harm Algeria, and who impel the people to be stubborn and hinder State officials' activities, the Communication Minister called for "avoiding those who disseminate prejudices against State officials and government staff."

About some municipal elected officials who refuse to participate in the organization of the July 4 presidential election, he said that, as a minister, he cannot "attack their positions," calling upon those officials "to assume their full responsibility and show vigilance and wisdom for the good of the country."

Answering a question on the investigations launched by the Judiciary and the arrest of many senior State officials and businessmen, Rabehi said that "Algeria entered era of democracy," adding that "Justice is above all and its mission is to probe into the cases that have harmed the national economy and the stability of the country."

"We need to let justice do its job, we must respect the privacy of the individuals (who are allegedly involved in these cases), far from any defamation and prejudices," he said.

"The Government cannot ban citizens or the media from being present at the courts before which these defendants appear," he added.

To a question about the partial reshuffle conducted by the head of state among Governors, the Government spokesman affirmed that "this reshuffle is a response to the requirements of the situation."

SOURCE: People's Democratic Republic of Algeria Ministry of Communication. "Minister of Communication, Spokesman of the Government Called for Giving Shape to People's Demands as Proposals for Dialogue." April 25, 2019. http://www.ministerecommunication.gov.dz/en/node/6267.

OTHER HISTORIC DOCUMENTS OF INTEREST

FROM PREVIOUS *HISTORIC DOCUMENTS*

Prime Minister May Reacts to Ongoing Brexit Negotiations, Resigns

MARCH 12, MARCH 20, MAY 22, AND MAY 24, 2019

When 2019 began, United Kingdom prime minister Theresa May was preparing for a critical vote in parliament on an agreement outlining the terms of the UK's withdrawal from the European Union, more commonly known as Brexit. Despite her efforts to secure binding commitments from the EU that a Northern Ireland "backstop" negotiated as part of the Withdrawal Agreement would be temporary, and thus assuage pro-Brexit lawmakers' concerns with the mechanism, May's proposed Brexit deal was soundly defeated three times. The impasse in parliament pushed May to request two extensions of the Brexit deadline—originally set for March 29—from EU officials and open talks with the opposition Labour Party. After talks faltered, the prime minister put forward her fourth and final proposal with a number of concessions designed to attract Labour support. Instead, May's proposal prompted a major backlash across political parties, causing her to resign days later.

A Looming Deadline

The UK was due to leave the EU by March 29, 2019, two years after Prime Minister May formally initiated the member withdrawal process by invoking Article 50 of the EU Treaty. Once Article 50 has been triggered, the withdrawing member country must leave the EU within two years regardless of whether an agreement outlining the terms of withdrawal has been concluded. Talks between EU and UK negotiators were halting throughout 2017, but progress was made on key issues in 2018. Notable agreements included settling on a "divorce bill," or the sum the UK would pay the EU—in this case, approximately 50 billion pounds (USD $59 billion)—in exchange for continued access to the EU single market during a transition period ending on December 31, 2020. The two parties also agreed to grant "settled status" to the roughly three million EU citizens living in the UK, and UK citizens living in EU member states.

Negotiators also reached agreement on a potentially fraught issue related to Northern Ireland's status. Northern Ireland is part of the UK, but the Republic of Ireland is not and intended to remain in the EU. Since the rest of the UK is an island, this meant that Northern Ireland would be the UK's only land border with the EU after Brexit. May had rejected the possibilities of the UK staying in the EU's customs union or single market, which would have allowed people and goods to freely flow across the border with Northern Ireland. She also dismissed establishing an arrangement between Northern Ireland and the EU that was different than the arrangement for the rest of the UK. This appeared to leave only one option for managing the EU–UK land border: establishing border controls, including checkpoints, in Northern Ireland. Doing so, however, would violate the government's legal obligations under the 1998 Good Friday Agreement that ended a bloody thirty-year conflict between Irish nationalists and UK unionists. (The agreement guarantees the continued free flow of people and goods in Ireland.)

In October 2018, negotiators developed a solution dubbed the "backstop." During the transition period, the UK and EU would work to reach a free trade agreement that would avoid border checks in Northern Ireland. If they did not reach an agreement by December 31, 2020, all of the UK would temporarily remain in the EU customs union until a deal could be concluded. In relaying the details to members of parliament, Prime Minister May stressed the arrangement would be temporary but also acknowledged the EU did not make a legally binding commitment to the backstop's temporary nature.

EU leaders approved the Withdrawal Agreement in November 2018, but anti-EU lawmakers in the UK grew concerned that the UK would become permanently stuck in the customs union. Parliament was supposed to vote on the Withdrawal Agreement in December 2018, but, sensing she was about to lose, May postponed the vote to January, hoping the delay would give her time to obtain firmer commitments on the backstop from the EU and shore up support among lawmakers at home.

May Struggles to Garner Support

The Withdrawal Agreement vote took place on January 15, 2019. In what some reports characterized as the most significant government defeat in decades, 432 Members of Parliament (MPs) voted against the agreement, with 202 MPs voting in its favor. Labour Party leader Jeremy Corbyn called for a vote of no confidence in May's government; the prime minister narrowly survived. May had faced a similar challenge the month before, when the Conservative Party conducted a vote of no confidence among its own MPs.

May continued her efforts to secure further EU commitments on the backstop issue, announcing on March 11 that negotiators had agreed on a "legally binding" instrument that could be used to initiate a dispute against the EU if it tried to keep the UK in the customs union indefinitely. Yet this was not enough to assuage lawmakers' concerns. MPs rejected the Withdrawal Agreement again on March 12, this time by a vote of 391–242. Addressing the House of Commons after the vote, May said, "I profoundly regret the decision that this House has taken tonight. I continue to believe that by far the best outcome is that the UK leaves the EU in an orderly fashion with a deal, and that the deal we have negotiated is the best and indeed the only deal available." May acknowledged she had also struggled with the public's decision to leave the EU but declared she was "passionate about delivering the result of the referendum" and affirmed her belief that a majority of MPs agreed it was better to have a deal in place with the EU than not.

On March 20, May wrote to European Council president Donald Tusk to request an extension of the Brexit deadline until June 30, 2019. Noting the two failed votes in the House of Commons, May stated it remained her intention to bring the deal back before parliament. "If the motion is passed, I am confident that Parliament will proceed to ratify the deal constructively. But this will clearly not be completed before 29 March 2019," she wrote. May further explained the extension was necessary because both houses of parliament would need to approve the deal and "the timetable for this is inevitably uncertain at this stage." That same day, in brief remarks outside 10 Downing Street, May explained her appeal for the extension to the public and tried to cast blame on MPs. "You the public have had enough," she said. "You want this stage of the Brexit process to be over and done with. I agree. I am on your side. It is now time for MPs to decide." May said parliament had "done everything possible to avoid making a choice" and would only say what they did not want.

May's frustrations with the Brexit process appeared to be shared by the public. On March 23, hundreds of thousands of people protested in London to demand a referendum on the Withdrawal Agreement. Around the same time, former UK Independence Party leader and prominent Brexit supporter Nigel Farage was leading a "March to Leave" across the UK. Additionally, more than four million people signed a petition calling for the government to revoke or cancel Article 50 and stay in the EU.

EU GRANTS BREXIT EXTENSIONS

EU leaders agreed on March 21 to extend the Brexit deadline but made it conditional upon a third vote in parliament. If MPs approved the Withdrawal Agreement the following week, the UK would leave the EU by May 22. If MPs rejected the deal, the UK would either need to leave the EU without an agreement or present a new plan to EU officials by April 12.

Parliament voted for a third time on the Brexit deal on March 29. This time, MPs were asked only to consider the Withdrawal Agreement, with a separate vote to be scheduled on the agreement's companion political declaration. (MPs had previously voted on both documents at the same time.) A required document, the declaration states that the EU and UK will negotiate a future relationship after Brexit is complete and provides an outline of what that relationship could look like. Earlier in the month, Speaker of the House of Commons John Bercow ruled that parliament would not consider May's Brexit proposal a third time unless it had substantially changed. By essentially splitting the deal into two pieces, the government met Bercow's criteria and was able to bring the proposal forward again. In the days leading up to the vote, May told Conservative Party members she would resign if parliament approved the agreement. This reportedly won the prime minister support from some hard-line pro-Brexit MPs, but it was still not enough. The agreement was rejected a third time, by a vote of 344–286, meaning the UK would need to revoke Article 50, seek another extension, or leave the EU without a deal.

On April 2, May announced she would request another extension from the EU and offered to meet with Labour Party leaders to come up with a compromise deal. Cross-party talks continued for about six weeks, with the Labour Party seeking changes such as a preservation of the customs union, alignment with the EU single market, and assurances that environmental and employee protections would not be rolled back. Reports suggested the government was unwilling to compromise on many of these points and wanted to preserve the existing Brexit terms. Labour Party officials called off the talks on May 17. "The talks have been detailed, constructive and have involved considerable effort for both our teams," Corbyn wrote in a letter to May. "However, it has become clear that, while there are some areas where compromise has been possible, we have been unable to bridge important policy gaps between us."

MAY ANNOUNCES A NEW BREXIT DEAL

Days after talks faltered, May addressed the House of Commons to outline what she described as a new Brexit deal. "It is clear that the only way forward is leaving with a deal—but it is equally clear that this will not happen without compromise on all sides of the debate," she said. "Having listened to the Opposition, to other party leaders, to the devolved administrations, to business leaders, trade unionists and others, we are now making a 10-point offer to Members across the House."

May's ten-point plan included measures legally obligating the government to conclude "alternative arrangements" to replace the Northern Ireland backstop by December 2020 so that it would never be used. Negotiation objectives and final treaties governing the UK's future relationship with the EU would need to be approved by MPs, she said. The revised plan would call for a new Workers' Rights Bill to ensure "hard-won protections for employees" were not rolled back. It would also create a new Office of Environmental Protection and provide assurances there would be no change in the "level of environmental protection" in the UK after Brexit. The most significant concession, however, was the inclusion of a measure requiring MPs to vote on whether to hold a referendum on the deal. May said she remained opposed to a second referendum, asking, "What would it say about our democracy if the biggest vote in our history were to be re-run because this House didn't like the outcome?"

The new proposal was meant to attract the support of Labour Party MPs, but it sparked harsh reactions from all sides. Corbyn called the proposal a "rehash" and "a repackaging of the same old bad deal, rejected three times by parliament." Democratic Unionist Party member Nigel Dodds said May's backstop-related proposals "serve as an attempt through domestic law to mitigate a bad deal whereas the focus should be on getting a better deal," adding that "the fatal flaws of the draft treaty remain." Many Conservatives were outraged by the idea of a second referendum. Simon Clarke, a Conservative Party MP, said he had supported May's efforts to complete Brexit by the original deadline, but "this speech from the PM means there is no way I will support the Withdrawal Agreement Bill." The Conservative leader of the House of Commons, Andrea Leadsom, resigned on May 22, saying she could not support the government "willingly facilitating" another referendum and that there had been a "complete breakdown" in government processes and responsibilities.

May's government had been pushing for a vote on the new Brexit deal the first week of June, but amid the growing and heated backlash, the proposal was withdrawn on May 23. The prime minister announced her resignation the following day. "I feel as certain today as I did three years ago that in a democracy, if you give people a choice you have a duty to implement what they decide," she said. "I have done my best to do that." She added that it would "always remain a matter of deep regret for me that I have not been able to deliver Brexit." May said she would step down as the Conservative Party's leader on June 7, with the selection of her successor to take place the following week. At least four candidates had declared their intent to run, with former foreign secretary Boris Johnson emerging as the front-runner. The incoming prime minister would be charged with meeting a new Brexit deadline: October 31, 2019.

—Linda Grimm

Following is a statement by Prime Minister Theresa May before the House of Commons on March 12, 2019, responding to parliament's first rejection of the Withdrawal Agreement; a letter sent by May to European Council president Donald Tusk on March 20, 2019, requesting a Brexit extension; remarks made by May on March 20, 2019, on the status of Brexit; a speech by May before the House of Commons on May 22, 2019, in which she announced the details of a new Brexit deal; and May's statement of resignation, delivered on May 24, 2019.

Prime Minister May's Statement to the House of Commons

March 12, 2019

On a point of order, Mr. Speaker,

I profoundly regret the decision that this House has taken tonight.

I continue to believe that by far the best outcome is that the UK leaves the EU in an orderly fashion with a deal, and that the deal we have negotiated is the best and indeed the only deal available.

Mr. Speaker, I would like to set out briefly how the Government means to proceed.

Two weeks ago, I made a series of commitments from this despatch box regarding the steps we would take in the event that this House rejected the deal on offer. I stand by those commitments in full.

Therefore, tonight we will table a motion for debate tomorrow to test whether the House supports leaving the European Union without a deal on 29 March.

The Leader of the House will shortly make an emergency business statement confirming the change to tomorrow's business.

This is an issue of grave importance for the future of our country. Just like the referendum, there are strongly held and equally legitimate views on both sides.

For that reason, I can confirm that this will be a free vote on this side of the House.

I have personally struggled with this choice as I am sure many other Honourable Members will. I am passionate about delivering the result of the referendum. But I equally passionately believe that the best way to do that is to leave in an orderly way with a deal and I still believe there is a majority in the House for that course of action. And I am conscious also of my duties as Prime Minister of the United Kingdom of Great Britain and Northern Ireland and of the potential damage to the Union that leaving without a deal could do when one part of our country is without devolved governance.

I can therefore confirm that the motion will read:

> That this House declines to approve leaving the European Union without a Withdrawal Agreement and a Framework on the Future Relationship on 29 March 2019; and notes that leaving without a deal remains the default in UK and EU law unless this House and the EU ratify an agreement.

I will return to the House to open the debate tomorrow and to take interventions from Honourable Members. And to ensure the House is fully informed in making this historic decision, the Government will tomorrow publish information on essential policies which would need to be put in place if we were to leave without a deal. These will cover our approach to tariffs and the Northern Ireland border, among other matters.

If the House votes to leave without a deal on 29 March, it will be the policy of the Government to implement that decision.

If the House declines to approve leaving without a deal on 29 March, the Government will, following that vote, bring forward a motion on Thursday on whether Parliament wants to seek an extension to Article 50.

If the House votes for an extension, the Government will seek to agree that extension with the EU and bring forward the necessary legislation to change the exit date commensurate with that extension.

But let me be clear. Voting against leaving without a deal and for an extension does not solve the problems we face. The EU will want to know what use we mean to make of such an extension.

This House will have to answer that question. Does it wish to revoke Article 50? Does it want to hold a second referendum? Or does it want to leave with a deal but not this deal?

These are unenviable choices, but thanks to the decision the House has made this evening they must now be faced.

SOURCE: UK Prime Minister's Office. "PM Statement in the House of Commons: 12 March 2019." March 12, 2019. https://www.gov.uk/government/speeches/pm-statement-in-the-house-of-commons-12-march-2019.

Prime Minister May's Letter to European Council President Tusk

March 20, 2019

Dear Donald,

The UK Government's policy remains to leave the European Union in an orderly manner on the basis of the Withdrawal Agreement and Political Declaration agreed in November, complemented by the Joint Instrument and supplement to the Political Declaration President Juncker and I agreed on 11 March.

You will be aware that before the House of Commons rejected the deal for a second time on 12 March, I warned in a speech in Grimsby that the consequences of failing to endorse the deal were unpredictable and potentially deeply unpalatable. The House of Commons did not vote in favour of the deal. The following day it voted against leaving the EU without a negotiated deal. The day after that it supported a Government motion that proposed a short extension to the Article 50 period if the House supported a meaningful vote before this week's European Council. The motion also made clear that if this had not happened, a longer extension would oblige the UK to call elections to the European Parliament. I do not believe that it would be in either of our interests for the UK to hold European Parliament elections.

I had intended to bring the vote back to the House of Commons this week. The Speaker of the House of Commons said on Monday that in order for a further meaningful vote to be brought back to the House of Commons, the agreement would have to be "fundamentally different—not different in terms of wording, but different in terms of substance." Some Members of Parliament have interpreted that this means a further change to the deal. This position has made it impossible in practice to call a further vote in advance of the European Council. However, it remains my intention to bring the deal back to the House.

In advance of that vote, I would be grateful if the European Council could therefore approve the supplementary documents that President Juncker and I agreed in Strasbourg, putting the Government in a position to bring these agreements to the House and confirming the changes to the Government's proposition to Parliament. I also intend to bring forward further domestic proposals that confirm my previous commitments to protect our internal market, given the concerns expressed about the backstop. On this basis, and in the light of the outcome of the European Council, I intend to put forward a motion as soon as possible under section 13 of the Withdrawal Act 2018 and make the argument for the orderly withdrawal and strong future partnership the UK economy, its citizens' security and the continent's future, demands.

If the motion is passed, I am confident that Parliament will proceed to ratify the deal constructively. But this will clearly not be completed before 29 March 2019. In our legal system, the Government will need to take a Bill through both Houses of Parliament to enact our commitments under the Withdrawal Agreement into domestic law. While we will consult with the Opposition in the usual way to plan the passage of the Bill as quickly and smoothly as possible, the timetable for this is inevitably uncertain at this stage. I am therefore writing to inform the European Council that the UK is seeking an extension to the Article 50 period under Article 50(3) of the Treaty on European Union, including as applied by Article 106a of the Euratom Treaty, until 30 June 2019.

I would be grateful for the opportunity to set out this position to our colleagues on Thursday.

Yours ever,
Theresa May

Source: UK Prime Minister's Office. "PM to President of the European Council." March 20, 2019. https://assets.publishing.service.gov.uk/government/uploads/system/uploads/attachment_data/file/787434/PM_to_President_of_the_European_Council.pdf.

Prime Minister May Remarks on Brexit Status

DOCUMENT

March 20, 2019

Nearly three years have passed since the public voted to leave the European Union.

It was the biggest democratic exercise in our country's history.

I came to office on a promise to deliver on that verdict.

In March 2017, I triggered the Article 50 process for the UK to exit the EU—and Parliament supported it overwhelmingly.

Two years on, MPs have been unable to agree on a way to implement the UK's withdrawal.

As a result, we will now not leave on time with a deal on 29 March.

This delay is a matter of great personal regret for me.

And of this I am absolutely sure: you the public have had enough.

You are tired of the infighting.

You are tired of the political games and the arcane procedural rows.

Tired of MPs talking about nothing else but Brexit when you have real concerns about our children's schools, our National Health Service, and knife crime.

You want this stage of the Brexit process to be over and done with.

I agree. I am on your side.

It is now time for MPs to decide.

So today I have written to Donald Tusk, the President of the European Council, to request a short extension of Article 50 up to the 30 June to give MPs the time to make a final choice.

Do they want to leave the EU with a deal which delivers on the result of the referendum—that takes back control of our money, borders and laws while protecting jobs and our national security?

Do they want to leave without a deal?

Or do they not want to leave at all, causing potentially irreparable damage to public trust—not just in this generation of politicians, but to our entire democratic process?

It is high time we made a decision.

So far, Parliament has done everything possible to avoid making a choice.

Motion after motion and amendment after amendment have been tabled without Parliament ever deciding what it wants.

All MPs have been willing to say is what they do not want.

I passionately hope MPs will find a way to back the deal I have negotiated with the EU.

A deal that delivers on the result of the referendum and is the very best deal negotiable.

I will continue to work night and day to secure the support of my colleagues, the DUP and others for this deal.

But I am not prepared to delay Brexit any further than 30 June.

Some argue that I am making the wrong choice, and I should ask for a longer extension to the end of the year or beyond, to give more time for politicians to argue over the way forward.

That would mean asking you to vote in European Elections, nearly three years after our country decided to leave.

What kind of message would that send?

And just how bitter and divisive would that election campaign be at a time when the country desperately needs bringing back together?

Some have suggested holding a second referendum.

I don't believe that is what you want—and it is not what I want.

We asked you the question already and you gave us your answer.

Now you want us to get on with it.

And that is what I am determined to do.

SOURCE: UK Prime Minister's Office. "PM Statement on Brexit: 20 March 2019." March 20, 2019. https://www.gov.uk/government/speeches/pm-statement-on-brexit-20-march-2019.

Prime Minister May Discusses New Brexit Deal

May 22, 2019

With permission, Mr. Speaker, I would like to make a statement on the Government's work to deliver Brexit by putting forward a new deal that members of this House can stand behind.

We need to see Brexit through, to honour the result of the referendum, and to deliver the change the British people so clearly demanded.

I sincerely believe that most members of this House feel the same.

That, for all our division and disagreement, we believe in democracy.

That we want to make good on the promise we made to the British people when we asked them to decide on the future of our EU membership.

As to how we make that happen, recent votes have shown that there is no majority in this House for leaving with no deal.

And this House has voted against revoking Article 50.

It is clear that the only way forward is leaving with a deal—but it is equally clear that this will not happen without compromise on all sides of the debate.

That starts with the Government, which is why we have just held six weeks of detailed talks with the Opposition—talks that the Leader of the Opposition chose to end before a formal agreement was reached, but which nonetheless revealed areas of common ground.

And having listened to the Opposition, to other party leaders, to the devolved administrations, to business leaders, trade unionists and others, we are now making a 10-point offer to Members across the House.

Ten changes that address the concerns raised by Hon and Rt Hon Members.

Ten binding commitments that will be enshrined in legislation so they cannot simply be ignored.

And 10 steps that will bring us closer to the bright future that awaits our country once we end the political impasse and get Brexit done.

First, we will protect British jobs by seeking as close to frictionless trade in goods with the EU as possible while outside the single market and ending free movement.

The government will be placed under a legal duty to negotiate our future relationship on this basis.

Second, we will provide much-needed certainty for our vital manufacturing and agricultural sectors by keeping up to date with EU rules for goods and agri-food products that are relevant to checks at the border.

Such a commitment—which will also be enshrined in legislation—will help protect thousands of skilled jobs that depend on just-in-time supply chains.

Third, we will empower Parliament to break the deadlock over future customs arrangements.

Both the Government and Opposition agree that we must have as close as possible to frictionless trade at the UK–EU border—protecting the jobs and livelihoods that are sustained by our existing trade with the EU.

But while we agree on the ends, we disagree on the means.

The Government has already put forward a proposal which delivers the benefits of a customs union but with the ability for the UK to determine its own trade and development policy.

The Opposition are both sceptical of our ability to negotiate that and don't believe an independent trade policy is in the national interest. They would prefer a comprehensive customs union—with a UK say in EU trade policy but with the EU negotiating on our behalf.

As part of the cross-party discussions the government offered a compromise option of a temporary customs union on goods only, including a UK say in relevant EU trade policy, so that the next government can decide its preferred direction.

But we were not able to reach agreement—so instead we will commit in law to let Parliament decide this issue, and to reflect the outcome of this process in legislation.

Fourth, to address concerns that a future government could roll back hard-won protections for employees, we will publish a new Workers' Rights Bill.

As I have told the House many times, successive British administrations of all colours have granted British workers' rights and protections well above the standards demanded by Brussels.

But I know that people want guarantees, and I am happy to provide them.

If passed by Parliament, this Bill will guarantee that the rights enjoyed by British workers can be no less favourable than those of their counterparts in the EU—both now and in the future.

And we will discuss further amendments with trade unions and business.

Fifth, the new Brexit deal will also guarantee there will be no change in the level of environmental protection when we leave the EU. And we will establish a new and wholly independent Office of Environmental Protection, able to uphold standards and enforce compliance.

Sixth, the Withdrawal Agreement Bill will place a legal duty on government to seek changes to the political declaration that will be needed to reflect this new deal—I am confident we will be successful in doing so.

Seventh, the Government will include in the Withdrawal Agreement Bill at introduction a requirement to vote on whether to hold a second referendum.

I have made my own view clear on this many times—I am against a second referendum.

We should be implementing the result of the first referendum, not asking the British people to vote in a second one.

What it would say about our democracy if the biggest vote in our history were to be re-run because this House didn't like the outcome?

What would it do to that democracy, what forces it would unleash?

But I recognise the genuine and sincere strength of feeling across the House on this important issue.

So to those MPs who want a second referendum to confirm the deal, I say: you need a deal and therefore a Withdrawal Agreement Bill to make it happen.

Let it have its Second Reading and then make your case to Parliament.

If this House votes for a referendum, it would require the Government to make provisions for such a referendum—including legislation if it wanted to ratify the Withdrawal Agreement.

Eighth, Parliament will be guaranteed a much greater role in the second part of the Brexit process: the negotiations over our future relationship with the EU.

In line with the proposal put forward by the Hon Members for Wigan and Stoke-on-Trent Central, the new Brexit deal will set out in law that the House of Commons will approve the UK's objectives for the negotiations.

And MPs will also be asked to approve the treaty governing that relationship before the Government signs it.

Ninth, the new Brexit deal will legally oblige the government to seek to conclude the Alternative Arrangements process by December 2020, avoiding any need for the Northern Ireland backstop coming into force.

This commitment is made in the spirit of the amendment tabled by my Hon Friend the Member for Altrincham and Sale West, passed by this House on 29 January.

And while it is not possible to use Alternative Arrangements to replace the backstop in the Withdrawal Agreement, we will ensure they are a viable alternative.

And finally, 10th, we will ensure that, should the backstop come into force, Great Britain will stay aligned with Northern Ireland.

We will prohibit the proposal that a future Government could split Northern Ireland off from the UK's customs territory.

And we will deliver on our commitments to Northern Ireland in the December 2017 Joint Report in full.

We will implement paragraph 50 of the Joint Report in law.

The Northern Ireland Assembly and Executive will have to give their consent on a cross-community basis for new regulations which are added to the backstop.

And we will work with our Confidence and Supply Partners on how these commitments should be entrenched in law, so that Northern Ireland cannot be separated from the United Kingdom.

Following the end of EU election purdah, the Withdrawal Agreement Bill will be published on Friday so the House has the maximum possible time to study its detail.

If Parliament passes the Bill before the summer recess, the UK will leave the EU by the end of July.

We will be out of the EU political structures, out of ever closer union.

We will stop British laws being enforced by a European court.

We will end free movement.

We will stop making vast annual payments to the EU budget.

By any definition, that alone is delivering Brexit.

And by leaving with a deal we can do so much more besides.

We can protect jobs, guarantee workers' rights, maintain the close security partnerships that do so much to keep us all safe.

We will ensure that there is no hard border between Northern Ireland and Ireland.

And we can bring an end to the months—years—of increasingly bitter argument and division that have both polarised and paralysed our politics.

We can move on, move forwards, and get on with the jobs we were sent here to do, what we got into politics to do.

That is what we can achieve if we support this new deal.

Reject it, and all we have before us is division and deadlock.

We risk leaving with no deal, something this House is clearly against.

We risk stopping Brexit altogether, something the British people would simply not tolerate.

We risk creating further division at a time when we need to be acting together in the national interest.

And we guarantee a future in which our politics become still more polarised and voters increasingly despair as they see us failing to do what they asked of us.

None of us want to see that happen.

The opportunity of Brexit is too large and the consequences of failure too grave to risk further delay.

So in the weeks ahead there will be opportunities for MPs on all sides to have their say, to table amendments, to shape the Brexit they and their constituents want to see.

Mr. Speaker, in time another Prime Minister will be standing at this despatch box.

But while I am here, I have a duty to be clear with the House about the facts.

If we are going to deliver Brexit in this Parliament we are going to have to pass a Withdrawal Agreement Bill.

And we will not do so without holding votes on the issues that have divided us the most—that includes votes on customs arrangements and on a second referendum.

We can pretend otherwise and carry on arguing and getting nowhere.

But in the end our job in this House is to take decisions, not to duck them.

So I will put those decisions to this House.

Because that is my duty.

And because it is the only way that we can deliver Brexit.

So let us demonstrate what this House can achieve.

Let's come together, honour the referendum, deliver what we promised the British people, and build a successful future for our whole country.

And I commend this statement to the House.

SOURCE: UK Prime Minister's Office. "PM Statement on New Brexit Deal: 22 May 2019." May 22, 2019. https://www.gov.uk/government/speeches/pm-statement-on-new-brexit-deal-22-may-2019.

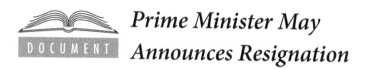

Prime Minister May Announces Resignation

May 24, 2019

Ever since I first stepped through the door behind me as Prime Minister, I have striven to make the United Kingdom a country that works not just for a privileged few, but for everyone.

And to honour the result of the EU referendum.

Back in 2016, we gave the British people a choice.

Against all predictions, the British people voted to leave the European Union.

I feel as certain today as I did three years ago that in a democracy, if you give people a choice you have a duty to implement what they decide.

I have done my best to do that.

I negotiated the terms of our exit and a new relationship with our closest neighbours that protects jobs, our security and our Union.

I have done everything I can to convince MPs to back that deal.

Sadly, I have not been able to do so.

I tried three times.

I believe it was right to persevere, even when the odds against success seemed high.

But it is now clear to me that it is in the best interests of the country for a new Prime Minister to lead that effort.

So I am today announcing that I will resign as leader of the Conservative and Unionist Party on Friday 7 June so that a successor can be chosen.

I have agreed with the Party Chairman and with the Chairman of the 1922 Committee that the process for electing a new leader should begin in the following week.

I have kept Her Majesty the Queen fully informed of my intentions, and I will continue to serve as her Prime Minister until the process has concluded.

It is, and will always remain, a matter of deep regret to me that I have not been able to deliver Brexit.

It will be for my successor to seek a way forward that honours the result of the referendum.

To succeed, he or she will have to find consensus in Parliament where I have not.

Such a consensus can only be reached if those on all sides of the debate are willing to compromise. . . .

As we strive to find the compromises we need in our politics—whether to deliver Brexit, or to restore devolved government in Northern Ireland—we must remember what brought us here.

Because the referendum was not just a call to leave the EU but for profound change in our country.

A call to make the United Kingdom a country that truly works for everyone. I am proud of the progress we have made over the last three years.

We have completed the work that David Cameron and George Osborne started: the deficit is almost eliminated, our national debt is falling and we are bringing an end to austerity.

My focus has been on ensuring that the good jobs of the future will be created in communities across the whole country, not just in London and the South East, through our Modern Industrial Strategy.

We have helped more people than ever enjoy the security of a job.

We are building more homes and helping first-time buyers onto the housing ladder—so young people can enjoy the opportunities their parents did.

And we are protecting the environment, eliminating plastic waste, tackling climate change and improving air quality. . . .

Our politics may be under strain, but there is so much that is good about this country. So much to be proud of. So much to be optimistic about.

I will shortly leave the job that it has been the honour of my life to hold—the second female Prime Minister but certainly not the last.

I do so with no ill-will, but with enormous and enduring gratitude to have had the opportunity to serve the country I love.

SOURCE: UK Prime Minister's Office. "Prime Minister's Statement in Downing Street: 24 May 2019." May 24, 2019. https://www.gov.uk/government/speeches/prime-ministers-statement-in-downing-street-24-may-2019.

OTHER HISTORIC DOCUMENTS OF INTEREST

FROM PREVIOUS *HISTORIC DOCUMENTS*

- Prime Minister May, EU Remark on Brexit Negotiations, *2018*, p. 531
- British Prime Minister Triggers Exit from European Union, *2017*, p. 198
- British Prime Minister, European Union Leaders Remark on Continuation of Brexit Negotiations, *2017,* p. 524
- Britons Vote to Exit the European Union, *2016*, p. 280

FAA Orders Grounding of MAX Jet; Ethiopia Releases Crash Report

MARCH 13 AND APRIL 4, 2019

More than 150 people were killed on March 10, 2019, when Ethiopian Airlines Flight 302 crashed into a field minutes after takeoff. It was the second deadly accident in five months to involve a Boeing 737 MAX 8 aircraft, raising significant questions about the plane's safety and prompting many international aviation authorities to ground it, including the U.S. Federal Aviation Administration (FAA). A preliminary investigation report released by Ethiopian officials identified a faulty sensor and a feature of the aircraft's automated flight system as the likely cause of the crash.

ETHIOPIAN AIRLINES FLIGHT 302 CRASHES MINUTES AFTER TAKEOFF

Ethiopian Airlines Flight 302 was scheduled to fly from Addis Ababa, Ethiopia, to Nairobi, Kenya, on the morning of March 10, 2019. Roughly six minutes after taking off, the plane crashed into a farm field, traveling nearly 700 miles per hour. All 157 people on board were killed, including more than 20 United Nations–affiliated passengers who were traveling to attend the international body's Environment Assembly.

Tewolde Gebremariam, the group chief executive of Ethiopian Airlines, extended his "profound sympathy and condolences to the families and loved ones" of those who died in the crash. He noted that the four-month-old aircraft involved had "no known technical problems" and had flown only 1,200 hours, adding that the pilot had an "excellent flying record." The office of Ethiopian prime minister Abiy Ahmed issued a statement expressing "deepest condolences to the families of those that have lost their loved ones," and a national day of mourning was declared on March 11. The prime minister also called for a "full and timely" investigation of the incident.

The airplane's black boxes, which record flight data as well as voices and other noises in the cockpit, were retrieved from the crash site the same day and were later sent to France's Bureau of Enquiry and Analysis for Civil Aviation Safety in Paris for analysis. (Information collected from black boxes is often used by investigators to determine the cause of a plane crash.) Officials stated the boxes had to be sent to France because they were too badly damaged for Ethiopian investigators to read.

Notably, the tragedy followed another deadly crash involving a Boeing 737 MAX aircraft. Lion Air Flight 610 had crashed into Indonesia's Java Sea on October 29, 2019, approximately thirteen minutes after taking off from Jakarta's Soekarno–Hatta International Airport, killing 189 passengers and crew. In a preliminary report released the following month, the Indonesian National Transportation Safety Committee said its initial investigation found that a device known as an Angle of Attack (AOA) sensor sent faulty information about the angle at which the plane was flying to the aircraft's flight control system. These inaccurate data caused the automated system to push the plane's nose down. The report said the pilot tried to correct the issue, but the system continued to force the nose down multiple times, eventually causing the plane to crash.

FAA Declares Boeing 737 MAX Safe to Fly

With two fatal accidents occurring five months apart, questions were soon raised about the safety of the Boeing 737 MAX aircraft. Ethiopian Airlines suspended operation of its 737 MAX planes the day of the crash. Aviation authorities around the world also moved quickly to ground the planes, including those in Australia, Brazil, Canada, China, the European Union, India, Indonesia, New Zealand, South Korea, and Turkey.

The FAA was a notable holdout among aviation officials. An agency team comprised of FAA and National Transportation Safety Board (NTSB) officials arrived onsite in Addis Ababa on March 11 to assist with the investigation. (International protocol dictates that officials from the country where the crash occurred lead the investigation, but that U.S. officials participate in investigations involving aircraft built by an American company.) "We are collecting data and keeping in contact with international civil aviation authorities as information becomes available," the FAA said in a statement, adding that if the agency identified an issue that affects safety, it would "take immediate and appropriate action."

Later that day, the FAA issued a Continued Airworthiness Notification to the International Community stating the 737 MAX fleet was safe to fly. The document acknowledged that comparisons were being made between the Ethiopian Airlines and Lion Air accidents but said the "investigation has just begun and to date we have not been provided data to draw any conclusions or take any actions." It also highlighted several actions taken by the FAA and commitments from Boeing that were intended to improve the safety of 737 MAX aircraft following the Lion Air crash, including the FAA-issued emergency Airworthiness Directive 2018-23-51. Released on November 7, 2018, the directive mandated design changes to enhance the flight control system of the 737 MAX to address concerns about faulty AOA sensors.

The FAA continued to call the 737 MAX airworthy on March 12; however, the agency reversed course the following afternoon and ordered the temporary grounding of all 737 MAX aircraft operated by U.S. airlines or in U.S. territory because it had "determined that an emergency exists related to safety in air commerce." The FAA order stated the investigation had revealed new information that "indicates some similarities between the ET302 and JT610 [Lion Air] accidents that warrant further investigation of the possibility of a shared cause." Speaking at a press conference, FAA acting administrator Daniel K. Ewell said the path of the Ethiopian Airlines flight "was very close—and behaved very similarly" to the Lion Air flight.

Ethiopian Government Releases Initial Investigation Findings

The Ethiopian Ministry of Transport's Aircraft Accident Investigation Bureau released a preliminary accident report on April 4. The findings were similar to those of the initial Lion Air investigation.

According to the report, one of Flight 302's AOA sensors sent faulty information to the Maneuvering Characteristics Augmentation System (MCAS)—an automated component of the aircraft's flight control system—shortly after takeoff. These data indicated the plane was flying too steeply and was about to stall, causing the MCAS to force the plane's nose downward. (Nosing down is a technique for reengaging engines.) The plane's second AOA sensor indicated a flight path that was nearly 60 degrees less steep than the first sensor's reading; however, the MCAS can be activated by just one sensor. The report indicated the captain and first officer attempted to pull the plane's nose up three times, but each time the MCAS forced the plane to angle back down. The crew tried to turn the MCAS off and adjust the aircraft's flight path manually, but the plane was traveling too fast for that to work. They requested and received approval to turn back to the Addis Ababa airport from air traffic control, but in the process of turning the plane around, the MCAS pushed the aircraft into a steep descent. The plane was traveling too fast for the pilots to recover. "The aircraft impacted in a farm field and created a crater approximately 10 meters deep, with a hole of about 28 meters width and 40 meters length," the report read. "Most of the wreckage was found buried in the ground."

The report ruled out other contributing factors such as weather, engine failure, and runway conditions. It noted Ethiopian Airlines had updated the aircraft flight manual and the flight crew operation manual with information and response procedures for "uncommanded horizontal stabilizer trim movement," as mandated by the FAA's 2018 Airworthiness Directive. Furthermore, the report stated the crew had the necessary licenses and experience to fly the plane. "The crew performed all the procedures repeatedly provided by the manufacturer but were not able to control the aircraft," said Ethiopian minister of transport Dagmawit Moges at a news conference releasing the report.

The report outlined two safety recommendations based on the investigation's initial findings. "Since repetitive un-commanded aircraft nose down conditions are noticed in this preliminary investigation, it is recommended that the aircraft flight control system related to flight controllability shall be reviewed by the manufacturer," the report stated. "Aviation Authorities shall verify that the review of the aircraft flight control system related to flight controllability has been adequately addressed by the manufacturer before the release of the aircraft to operations."

The final investigation report was expected to be released in spring 2020.

BOEING, FAA WORK TO CORRECT FLIGHT SYSTEM ISSUES AND CERTIFICATION PROCESS

Responding to the report's release, Boeing CEO Dennis Muilenburg said in a recorded statement that it was apparent the MCAS had "activated in response to erroneous" data in both the Ethiopian Airlines and Lion Air flights. "It's our responsibility to eliminate that risk," he said. "We own it, and we know how to do it."

In a separate statement, Boeing said it was developing a software update to the MCAS and a related pilot training to "ensure unintended MCAS activation will not occur again." The software update had to be reviewed and approved by the FAA before it could be installed on the 737 MAX aircraft. The update will reportedly require the MCAS to compare data from both of the aircraft's AOA sensors, and the system will only activate if the data agree. The MCAS will only activate once based on AOA data, and will move the plane's nose down more slowly, giving pilots more time to react and readjust if necessary. Other update features will reportedly generate new visual alerts for pilots if the plane's external sensors show different readings than the MACS, and will disengage the MACS if there is a significant discrepancy in sensor readings.

Boeing was slated to submit the update to the FAA at the end of March, but the FAA announced a delay on April 1. "Time is needed for additional work by Boeing as the result of an ongoing review of the 737 Max Flight Control System to ensure that Boeing has identified and appropriately addressed all pertinent issues," the agency said in a statement. Boeing reported on May 16 that it had finished the software update and completed the required tests but had to provide more information to the FAA before it could be approved. In late June, the company stated the FAA had "identified an additional requirement" in its review of the MCAS update that must be addressed before the aircraft can be certified and return to flight.

Meanwhile, the FAA established a Joint Authorities Technical Review to conduct "a comprehensive review of the certification of the [Boeing 737 MAX] automated flight control system" to assess the certification process's regulatory compliance and identify any enhancements necessary. Led by former NTSB chair Chris Hart, the group was comprised by representatives of the FAA, NASA, and international aviation authorities from Australia, Brazil, Canada, China, the EU, Indonesia, Japan, Singapore, and the United Arab Emirates. The group submitted its final report to the FAA on October 11, 2019, providing several recommendations for modernizing and improving the FAA's certification process. These included considering whether the process adequately addresses overall safety, not just compliance with federal regulations and standards, because as the complexity of flight systems increases, it is unlikely that regulations and standards alone will cover every possible scenario. Other recommendations said the FAA should ensure aircraft have fail-safe mechanisms incorporated into their design, and that the agency should revisit its standards for the time needed by pilots to identify and respond to problems with an aircraft.

Separately, the NTSB also submitted to the FAA several recommendations for improving flight safety. NTSB chair Robert Sumwalt said the recommendations focused on addressing the agency's observation that both Boeing and the FAA made certain assumptions about pilot behavior and response when designing and certifying the 737 MAX— assumptions that proved not to be true in both the Ethiopian Airlines and Lion Air incidents. The NTSB recommendations included developing and using tools to validate assumptions about pilot response.

Additionally, Boeing launched an internal independent review of company policies and processes for designing and developing airplanes. On September 30, the company announced several organizational changes it would implement immediately as a result of this review, such as the creation of a new Product and Services Safety organization that would centralize all of the company's safety-related work, rather than have a patchwork of teams and units be responsible for different aspects of aircraft safety. Boeing's board of directors fired Muilenberg on December 23 for failing to stem the reputational crisis facing the company after the crash. In a statement, the company said, "a change in leadership was necessary to restore confidence."

At the time of writing, the FAA grounding order remained in place and it was unclear when the 737 MAX may be recertified. Boeing officials said they were aiming for a return to service by the end of 2019, but on December 11, FAA administrator Stephen Dickson said in an interview with CNBC that the agency would not clear the aircraft for flight until 2020, noting a number of milestones that still needed to be completed before it could do so. "We're going to do it diligently because safety is absolutely our priority with this airplane," he said. Boeing said it would "continue to work closely with the FAA and global regulators toward certification and the safe return to service of the MAX." Among U.S. carriers, United Airlines and American Airlines has cancelled flights on the 737 MAX through June 4, 2020. Southwest Airlines has removed the aircraft from its flight schedule through mid-April 2020.

—Linda Grimm

Following is an emergency order issued by the Federal Aviation Administration on March 13, 2019, grounding Boeing 737 MAX aircraft in the United States; and the preliminary investigation report released on April 4, 2019, by the Ethiopian Ministry of Transport.

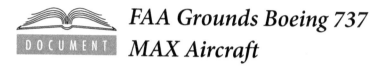

FAA Grounds Boeing 737 MAX Aircraft

March 13, 2019

Operators of Boeing Company
Model 737-8 and
Boeing Company Model 737-9
Airplanes

EMERGENCY ORDER OF PROHIBITION

This Emergency Order of Prohibition is issued by the Federal Aviation Administration (FAA) pursuant to 49 U.S.C. § 40113(a) and § 46105(c). Effective immediately, this Order prohibits the operation of Boeing Company Model 737-8 and Boeing Company Model 737-9 airplanes by U.S. certificated operators. This Order also prohibits the operation of Boeing Company Model 737-8 and Boeing Company Model 737-9 series airplanes in the territory of the United States. Airplanes covered by this Order, if in flight at the time this Order is issued, may proceed to and complete their soonest planned landing, but may not again takeoff. . . .

[The section outlining the FAA's authority has been omitted.]

SCOPE AND EFFECT

This Order applies to all persons operating the Boeing Company Model 737-8 and Boeing Company Model 737-9 airplanes in the territory of the United States, and to U.S. certificated operators conducting flights with Boeing Company Model 737-8 and Boeing Company Model 737-9 airplanes. These airplanes are hereinafter referred to as the Boeing 737 MAX series airplanes.

This Order is effective immediately. This Order prohibits the operation of Boeing 737 MAX series airplanes by U.S. certificated operators. This Order also prohibits the operation of Boeing 737 MAX series airplanes in the territory of the United States. Boeing 737 MAX series airplanes covered by this Order, if in flight at the time this Order is issued, may proceed to and complete their soonest planned landing, but may not again takeoff. Special flight permits may be issued in accordance with 14 C.F.R. § 21.197 and § 21.199, including to allow non-passenger carrying flights, as needed, for purposes of flight to a base for storage, production flight testing, repairs, alterations, or maintenance.

Experimental airworthiness certificates may be issued in accordance with 14 C.F.R § 21.191 to support certification of design changes.

This Order remains in effect until the issuance of an applicable FAA order rescinding or modifying this Order. The Administrator will rescind or modify this Order, as appropriate, if the Administrator determines that the prohibitions prescribed herein are no longer necessary to address an emergency related to safety in air commerce.

BASIS FOR ORDER

Based on the initial investigations and the reliable and credible evidence presently available, the Acting Administrator finds that:

1. On October 29, 2018, a Boeing Company Model 737-8 operated by Lion Air as flight JT610 crashed after taking off from Soekamo-Hatta Airport in Jakarta, Indonesia. Flight JT610 departed from Jakarta with an intended destination of Pangkal Pinang, Indonesia. It departed Jakarta at 6:20 a.m. (local time), and crashed into the Java Sea approximately 13 minutes later. One hundred and eighty-four passengers and five crewmembers were on board. There were no survivors. An Indonesian-led investigation into the cause of this accident is ongoing, supported by the National Transportation Safety Board (NTSB), FAA, and Boeing.

2. On March 10, 2019, Ethiopian Airlines flight ET302, also a Boeing Company Model 737-8, crashed at 8:44 a.m. (local time), six minutes after takeoff. The flight departed from Bole International Airport in Addis Ababa, Ethiopia with an intended destination of Nairobi, Kenya. The accident site is near Bishoftu, Ethiopia. One hundred and forty-nine passengers and eight crewmembers were on board. None survived. An Ethiopian-led investigation into the cause of this accident is ongoing, supported by the NTSB, FAA, and Boeing.

3. The Boeing Company Model 737-8 and the Boeing Company Model 737-9 comprise the Boeing 737 MAX series, sharing nearly identical design features. The Boeing 737 MAX series airplanes are narrow-body airplanes with two high-bypass turbofan engines. The Boeing 737 MAX series airplanes are used for passenger carrying operations and are equipped with new CFM LEAP-lB engines and larger cockpit displays.

Under 49 U.S.C. § 46105(c), the Acting Administrator has determined that an emergency exists related to safety in air commerce. On March 13, 2019, the investigation of the ET302 crash developed new information from the wreckage concerning the aircraft's configuration just after takeoff that, taken together with newly refined data from satellite-based tracking of the aircraft's flight path, indicates some similarities between the ET302 and JT610 accidents that warrant further investigation of the possibility of a shared cause for the two incidents that needs to be better understood and addressed. Accordingly, the Acting Administrator is ordering all Boeing 737 MAX airplanes to be grounded pending further investigation.

This Order is effective immediately. While this Order remains in effect, the FAA intends to initiate a proceeding, as appropriate, to address the factors that contributed to the two previously discussed accidents involving Boeing 737 MAX series airplanes.

CONSEQUENCES OF FAILURE TO COMPLY WITH THIS ORDER

Any person who fails to comply with this Order is subject to a civil penalty for each flight found not to comply. Small business concerns and individuals (other than persons serving as an airman) are subject to a civil penalty of up to $13,333 per flight. See 49 U.S.C. § 46301(a)(5)(A)(ii), 14 CFR 13.301. A person serving as an airman on a flight operated in violation of this Order is subject to a civil penalty of up to $1,466 per flight or a certificate action, up to and including revocation. See 49 U.S.C. §§ 46301(a)(l)(B) and 44709(b)(l)(A), 14 CFR 13.301. An air carrier violating this Order is subject to certificate action, up to and including revocation. See id. Any person failing to comply with this Order may be subject to a cease and desist order or a civil action in a United States district court to ensure compliance. See 49 U.S.C. §§ 44103(a) and 46106. . . .

[Sections on interested parties' right to review and emergency contact details have been omitted.]

Dated March 13, 2019

Daniel K. Elwell
Acting Administrator
Federal Aviation Administration

SOURCE: Federal Aviation Administration. "Emergency Order of Prohibition." March 13, 2019. https://www.faa.gov/news/updates/media/Emergency_Order.pdf.

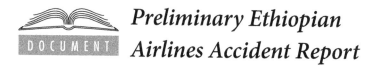

Preliminary Ethiopian Airlines Accident Report

April 4, 2019

[The first seven pages of the report have been omitted and contain the foreword, list of acronyms, executive summary, table of contents, and information on the investigation's organization.]

History of Flight

On March 10, 2019, at about 05:44 UTC1, Ethiopian Airlines flight 302, a Boeing 737-8 (MAX), Ethiopian registration ET-AVJ, crashed near Ejere, Ethiopia, shortly after takeoff from Addis Ababa Bole International Airport (HAAB), Ethiopia. The flight was a regularly scheduled international passenger flight from Addis Ababa to Jomo Kenyatta International Airport (HKJK), Nairobi, Kenya. There were 157 passengers and crew on board. All were fatally injured, and the Aircraft was destroyed.

The following is based on the preliminary analysis of the DFDR, CVR and ATC communications. As the investigation continues, revisions and changes may occur before the final report is published.

At 05:37:34, ATC issued take off clearance to ET-302 and to contact radar on 119.7 MHz.

Takeoff roll began from runway 07R at a field elevation of 2333.5 m at approximately 05:38, with a flap setting of 5 degrees and a stabilizer setting of 5.6 units. The takeoff roll appeared normal, including normal values of left and right angle-of-attack (AOA). During takeoff roll, the engines stabilized at about 94% N1, which matched the N1 Reference recorded on the DFDR. From this point for most of the flight, the N1 Reference remained about 94% and the throttles did not move. The N1 target indicated non data pattern 220 seconds before the end of recording. According to the CVR data and the control column forces recorded in DFDR, captain was the pilot flying.

At 05:38:44, shortly after liftoff, the left and right recorded AOA values deviated. Left AOA decreased to 11.1° then increased to 35.7° while value of right AOA indicated 14.94°. Then after, the left AOA value reached 74.5° in ¾ seconds while the right AOA reached a maximum value of 15.3°. At this time, the left stick shaker activated and remained active until near the end of the recording. Also, the airspeed, altitude and flight director pitch bar values from the left side noted deviating from the corresponding right side values. The left side values were lower than the right side values until near the end of the recording.

At 05:38:43 and about 50 ft radio altitude, the flight director roll mode changed to LNAV.

At 05:38:46 and about 200 ft radio altitude, the Master Caution parameter changed state. The First Officer called out Master Caution Anti-Ice on CVR. Four seconds later, the recorded Left AOA Heat parameter changed state.

At 05:38:58 and about 400 ft radio altitude, the flight director pitch mode changed to VNAV SPEED and Captain called out "Command" (standard call out for autopilot engagement) and an autopilot warning is recorded.

At 05:39:00, Captain called out "Command".

At 05:39:01 and about 630 ft radio altitude, a second autopilot warning is recorded.

At 05:39:06, the Captain advised the First-Officer to contact radar and First Officer reported SHALA 2A departure crossing 8400 ft and climbing FL 320.

Between liftoff and 1000 ft above ground level (AGL), the pitch trim position moved between 4.9 and 5.9 units in response to manual electric trim inputs. At 1000 ft AGL, the pitch trim position was at 5.6 units.

At 05:39:22 and about 1,000 feet the left autopilot (AP) was engaged (it disengaged about 33 seconds later), the flaps were retracted and the pitch trim position decreased to 4.6 units.

Six seconds after the autopilot engagement, there were small amplitude roll oscillations accompanied by lateral acceleration, rudder oscillations and slight heading changes. These oscillations continued also after the autopilot was disengaged.

At 05:39:29, radar controller identified ET-302 and instructed to climb FL 340 and when able right turns direct to RUDOL and the First-Officer acknowledged.

At 05:39:42, Level Change mode was engaged. The selected altitude was 32000 ft. Shortly after the mode change, the selected airspeed was set to 238 kt.

At 05:39:45, Captain requested flaps up and First-Officer acknowledged. One second later, flap handle moved from 5 to 0 degrees and flaps retraction began.

At 05:39:50, the selected heading started to change from 072 to 197 degrees and at the same time the Captain asked the First-Officer to request to maintain runway heading.

At 05:39:55, Autopilot disengaged.

At 05:39:57, the Captain advised again the First-Officer to request to maintain runway heading and that they are having flight control problems.

At 05:40:00 shortly after the autopilot disengaged, the FDR recorded an automatic aircraft nose down (AND) activated for 9.0 seconds and pitch trim moved from 4.60 to 2.1 units. The climb was arrested and the aircraft descended slightly.

At 05:40:03 Ground Proximity Warning System (GPWS) "DON'T SINK" alerts occurred.

At 05:40:05, the First-Officer reported to ATC that they were unable to maintain SHALA 1A and requested runway heading which was approved by ATC.

At 05:40:06, left and right flap position reached a recorded value of 0.019 degrees which remained until the end of the recording.

The column moved aft and a positive climb was re-established during the automatic AND motion.

At 05:40:12, approximately three seconds after AND stabilizer motion ends, electric trim (from pilot activated switches on the yoke) in the Aircraft nose up (ANU) direction is recorded on the DFDR and the stabilizer moved in the ANU direction to 2.4 units. The Aircraft pitch attitude remained about the same as the back pressure on the column increased.

At 05:40:20, approximately five seconds after the end of the ANU stabilizer motion, a second instance of automatic AND stabilizer trim occurred and the stabilizer moved down and reached 0.4 units.

From 05:40:23 to 05:40:31, three Ground Proximity Warning System (GPWS) "DON'T SINK" alerts occurred.

At 05:40:27, the Captain advised the First-Officer to trim up with him.

At 05:40:28 Manual electric trim in the ANU direction was recorded and the stabilizer reversed moving in the ANU direction and then the trim reached 2.3 units.

At 05:40:35, the First-Officer called out "stab trim cut-out" two times. Captain agreed and First-Officer confirmed stab trim cut-out.

At 05:40:41, approximately five seconds after the end of the ANU stabilizer motion, a third instance of AND automatic trim command occurred without any corresponding motion of the stabilizer, which is consistent with the stabilizer trim cutout switches were in the "cutout" position.

At 05:40:44, the Captain called out three times "Pull-up" and the First-Officer acknowledged.

At 05:40:50, the Captain instructed the First Officer to advise ATC that they would like to maintain 14,000 ft and they have flight control problem.

At 05:40:56, the First-Officer requested ATC to maintain 14,000 ft and reported that they are having flight control problem. ATC approved.

From 05:40:42 to 05:43:11 (about two and a half minutes), the stabilizer position gradually moved in the AND direction from 2.3 units to 2.1 units. During this time, aft force was applied to the control columns which remained aft of neutral position. The left indicated airspeed increased from approximately 305 kt to approximately 340 kt (VMO). The right indicated airspeed was approximately 20–25 kt higher than the left.

The data indicates that aft force was applied to both columns simultaneously several times throughout the remainder of the recording.

At 05:41:20, the right overspeed clacker was recorded on CVR. It remained active until the end of the recording.

At 05:41:21, the selected altitude was changed from 32000 ft to 14000 ft.

At 05:41:30, the Captain requested the First-Officer to pitch up with him and the First-Officer acknowledged.

At 05:41:32, the left overspeed warning activated and was active intermittently until the end of the recording.

At 05:41:46, the Captain asked the First-Officer if the trim is functional. The First-Officer has replied that the trim was not working and asked if he could try it manually. The Captain told him to try. At 05:41:54, the First-Officer replied that it is not working.

At 05:42:10, the Captain asked and the First-Officer requested radar control a vector to return and ATC approved.

At 05:42:30, ATC instructed ET-302 to turn right heading 260 degrees and the First-Officer acknowledged.

At 05:42:43, the selected heading was changed to 262 degrees.

At 05:42:51, the First-Officer mentioned Master Caution Anti-Ice. The Master Caution is recorded on DFDR.

At 05:42:54, both pilots called out "left alpha vane".

At 05:43:04, the Captain asked the First Officer to pitch up together and said that pitch is not enough.

At 05:43:11, about 32 seconds before the end of the recording, at approximately 13,4002 [sic] ft, two momentary manual electric trim inputs are recorded in the ANU direction. The stabilizer moved in the ANU direction from 2.1 units to 2.3 units.

At 05:43:20, approximately five seconds after the last manual electric trim input, an AND automatic trim command occurred and the stabilizer moved in the AND direction from 2.3 to 1.0 unit in approximately 5 seconds. The aircraft began pitching nose down. Additional simultaneous aft column force was applied, but the nose down pitch continues, eventually reaching 40° nose down. The stabilizer position varied between 1.1 and 0.8 units for the remainder of the recording.

The left Indicated Airspeed increased, eventually reaching approximately 458 kts and the right Indicated Airspeed reached 500 kts at the end of the recording. The last recorded pressure altitude was 5,419 ft on the left and 8,399 ft on the right. . . .

Personnel Information

Pilot in Command

According to Ethiopian Airlines records, the captain has the following flight experience:

- Total hours: 8122
- Total hours in B737: 1417
- Total hours in B737-8 MAX: 103
- Flight time in previous 90 days: 266 hours and 9 minutes
- Flight time in previous 7 days: 17 hours and 43 minutes
- Flight time in previous 72 hours: no flight time

The pilot in command was 29 years old. According to Ethiopian Civil Aviation Authority (ECAA) records, the Captain's most recent simulator training experience was September 30, 2018, and his most recent simulator proficiency check was October 1, 2018. The captain completed the Ethiopian Aviation Academy on July 23, 2010. A review of the captain's training records indicated that he received his 737-800 First Officer type rating on January 31, 2011 and completed his PIC type rating for the 737-800 October 26, 2017. 737MAX differences training on 3 July, 2018.

The pilot in command is type rated as a First Officer of the following types of aircrafts: B737-7/800, B767/757, B777 and B787. As pilot in command, he is rated on B737-7/800 and B737MAX.

The pilot's ECAA license allowed him to act as pilot-in-command in commercial air transport operations in a Boeing 737-7/800 (dated October 26, 2017) and Boeing 737 MAX (dated July 3, 2018.)

The pilot had a first-class medical certificate with no limitations dated December 12, 2018. A review of the medical exam that resulted in the issuance of this certificate showed no vision or hearing deficiencies, and on the certificate application, the pilot stated he was taking no prescription or non-prescription medications. He reported no medical conditions.

First Officer

According to Ethiopian Airlines records, the First-Officer has the following flight experience:

- Total hours: 361

- Total hours in B737: 207

- Total hours in B737-8 MAX: 56

- Flight time in previous 90 days: 207 hours and 26 minutes

- Flight time in previous 7 days: 10 hours and 57 minutes

- Flight time in previous 72 hours: 5 hours and 25 minutes

The first-officer was 25 years old. According to ECAA records, the first-officer's most recent simulator event was listed as a proficiency check and occurred on December 3, 2018. His line training/check (conducted in the B737 aircraft) was completed on January 31, 2019.

The first-officer's ECAA license allowed him to act as first-officer in commercial air transport operations in Boeing 737-7/800 (dated December 12, 2018) and Boeing 737 MAX (dated December 12, 2018.)

The first-officer had a first-class medical certificate with no limitations dated July 30, 2018. A review of the medical exam that resulted in the issuance of this certificate showed no vision or hearing deficiencies, and on the certificate application, the pilot stated he was taking no prescription or non-prescription medications. He reported no medical conditions.

[Five pages providing general information about the aircraft and its flight control system have been omitted.]

Engines

. . . Both engines were found buried in the ground at a depth of approximately 10 meters. To access the buried wreckage (engines, aircraft structure and components), backhoes were used to remove the wreckage from the area around the impact point.

The field investigation did not find evidence of any non-containment event (engine components ejected out of the side of the engine), or any other anomalies with either engine that would have precluded their normal operation. Evidence of the field investigation indicated that the LP and HP spools of both engines were rotating, evidence of high-speed axial compression of the both engines, and the engine was operating at power at the time of impact. . . .

Aircraft Flight and Maintenance Log

The Maintenance Log Book (MLB) was reviewed in detail for the last 39 flights from 26 February 2019 until 09 March 2019 (previous flight to the accident flight). In addition, the records were reviewed for the 1A check conducted in early February.

Over the previous 39 flights, the MLB cited in particular: Captain's flight compartment PC power outlet has no power; the crew oxygen cylinder was replaced due to low pressure; and the APU would not start. All three issues led to maintenance actions and did not reoccur.

In addition, the MLB was reviewed at a higher level for all flights back to the delivery flight in November 2018. Maintenance actions of relevance occurred in early December 2018 and involved several write-ups involving temporary erratic airspeed and altitude fluctuations as well as a report of the aircraft rolling during autopilot operation and altitude and vertical speed indication on the PFD showed an erratic and exaggerated indication. Maintenance actions were performed and none were reported to have reoccurred.

The only scheduled check of the Aircraft occurred from 01 February and 04 February 2019. This is a routine check and General Visual Inspection (GVI) of various areas of the airframe. No major discrepancies or repairs were noted for this check.

[Three pages with information about weather and runway conditions, communications, and aircraft flight recorders have been omitted.]

Wreckage and Impact Information

The accident site was located near Ejere, Ethiopia with a GPS location of approximately 8.8770 N, 39.2516 E.

The Aircraft impacted in a farm field and created a crater approximately 10 meters deep (last aircraft part found) with a hole of about 28 meters width and 40 meters length. Most of the wreckage was found buried in the ground; small fragments of the aircraft were found scattered around the site in an area by about 200 meters width and 300 meters long.

The damages to the aircraft are consistent with a high energy impact. . . .

Ethiopian Airlines Aircraft Flight Manual (AFM)

A check of the AFM provided by Ethiopian Airlines showed that the airline had incorporated the revisions A180625 on November, 11 2018 required by Airworthiness Directive 2018-23-51. . . .

FCOM Bulletin Issued by Boeing to Ethiopian Airlines

An FCOM bulletin issued by Boeing to Ethiopian Airlines (ETH-12) regarding uncommanded nose-down stabilizer trim required Ethiopian Airlines to insert the bulletin in their B737MAX FCOM. The US Ops/hp technical advisors were provided an electronic copy of the Airline's B737MAX FCOM, and the bulletin was found to be incorporated per Boeing directions. . . .

Initial Findings

On the basis of the initial information gathered during the course of the investigation, the following facts have been determined:

- The Aircraft possessed a valid certificate of airworthiness;
- The crew obtained the license and qualifications to conduct the flight;
- The takeoff roll appeared normal, including normal values of left and right angle-of-attack (AOA).
- Shortly after liftoff, the value of the left angle of attack sensor deviated from the right one and reached 74.5 degrees while the right angle of attack sensor value was 15.3 degrees; then after, the stick shaker activated and remained active until near the end of the flight.
- After autopilot engagement, there were small amplitude roll oscillations accompanied by lateral acceleration, rudder oscillations and slight heading changes; these oscillations also continued after the autopilot disengaged.
- After the autopilot disengaged, the DFDR recorded an automatic aircraft nose down (AND) trim command four times without pilot's input. As a result, three motions of the stabilizer trim were recorded. The FDR data also indicated that the crew utilized the electric manual trim to counter the automatic AND input.
- The crew performed runaway stabilizer checklist and put the stab trim cutout switch to cutout position and confirmed that the manual trim operation was not working.

Safety Actions Taken

The day of the accident, the operator decided to suspend operation of B737-8MAX.

On 14th March 2019, Ethiopian Civil Aviation Authority issued NOTAM regarding "The operation of Boeing B737-8 'MAX' and Boeing B737-9 'MAX' aircraft from, into or over the Ethiopian airspace, which is still active at the date of this report publication.

Safety Recommendations

- Since repetitive un-commanded aircraft nose down conditions are noticed in this preliminary investigation, it is recommended that the aircraft flight control system related to flight controllability shall be reviewed by the manufacturer.
- Aviation Authorities shall verify that the review of the aircraft flight control system related to flight controllability has been adequately addressed by the manufacturer before the release of the aircraft to operations.

[Report appendices have been omitted.]

Source: Federal Democratic Republic of Ethiopia, Ministry of Transport, Aircraft Accident Investigation Bureau. "Aircraft Accident Investigation Preliminary Report, Ethiopian Airlines Group, B737-8 (MAX) Registered ET-AVJ, 28 NM South East of Addis Ababa, Bole International Airport, March 10, 2019." April 4, 2019. http://www.ecaa.gov.et/home/wp-content/uploads/2019/07/Preliminary-Report-B737-800MAX-ET-AVJ.pdf.

OTHER HISTORIC DOCUMENTS OF INTEREST

New Zealand Prime Minister Remarks on Mosque Shooting and Gun Legislation

MARCH 15, MARCH 16, MARCH 21, AND MAY 15, 2019

On March 15, 2019, a gunman attacked two mosques in the city of Christchurch, New Zealand, killing fifty people and wounding dozens of others. The tragedy prompted Prime Minister Jacinda Ardern to call for new gun regulations, resulting in parliament's fast and near-unanimous approval of a ban on military style semi-automatic weapons and assault rifles. The shooter's use of social media to livestream a portion of the attack—and to share an anti-immigrant, anti-Muslim manifesto—also prompted Ardern and her government to take a closer look at the platforms' role in the incident and lead a global push to stop the spread of violent and extremist content online.

TRAGEDY IN CHRISTCHURCH

The shooting began around the time of midday Friday prayers at the Al Noor Mosque in Christchurch, New Zealand's third-largest city. After killing dozens of people, the shooter drove to nearby Linwood Mosque, where he opened fire again. A total of fifty people were killed, with nearly fifty more injured. Police arrested three people in connection with the tragedy, including a white man in his late twenties who was charged with murder. (The other two individuals were released.)

In a statement characterizing March 15 as "one of New Zealand's darkest days," Ardern said, "Many of the people affected by this act of extreme violence will be from our refugee and migrant communities. New Zealand is their home. They are us." She added, "The person or people who carried out this act of unprecedented violence are not. There is no place in our home for them." The shooter's chosen targets fueled immediate speculation that the tragedy was linked to growing nationalism and white supremacism in New Zealand. A manifesto by the suspected killer, published online shortly before the shooting began, appeared to confirm this motive. He expressed anti-immigrant and anti-Muslim sentiments in addition to identifying his white nationalist heroes. The shooter posted links to the manifesto on both Twitter and 8chan, an online forum known for message boards used by white supremacists and others to share extreme and violent views.

Ardern and her government made a concerted effort to keep the shooter's name out of the news. "He is a terrorist. He is a criminal. He is an extremist," Ardern said in remarks before parliament on March 19. "But he will, when I speak, be nameless." She encouraged others to focus on the victims and speak their names, adding the shooter "may have sought notoriety, but we in New Zealand will give him nothing." The shooter was later identified in court filings as Brenton Harrison Tarrant, a twenty-eight-year-old personal trainer originally from Australia. Tarrant was charged with 50 counts of murder and 39 counts of attempted murder at the end of March. Seeming to follow Ardern's lead, the judge presiding over the case approved suppression orders to limit news reporting of court proceedings, including requiring any images of Tarrant to be pixelated before being published and prohibiting the taking of pictures or recording of audio or video in court. On May 21, New Zealand authorities also charged Tarrant with carrying out a terrorist act, as well as one additional murder count for a victim who died from his wounds in the hospital. Tarrant pleaded not guilty on June 14. The judge said the court had reviewed reports on Tarrant's mental health and found "no issues" regarding his fitness to enter a plea and stand trial. The trial is scheduled to begin on June 2, 2020.

GOVERNMENT ANNOUNCES BAN ON CERTAIN FIREARMS

The day following the shooting, Ardern declared, "Our gun laws will change." The last mass shooting in New Zealand occurred in 1997, when six people were killed and four wounded. The deadliest incident took place in 1990; a man killed thirteen people after a dispute with a neighbor. The country's gun laws had been tightened after the 1990 shooting, and at the time of the Christchurch incident, any New Zealander wishing to buy and own a gun needed to be licensed. The licensing process typically took months to complete and included a review of an applicant's criminal record and mental health and a visit to their residence to confirm a safe storage mechanism. The applicant also had to complete a gun safety program and provide an explanation of how the gun would be used. Certain classes of firearms had additional permitting, storage, and inspection requirements.

Ardern said the terrorist attack had "exposed a range of weaknesses in New Zealand's gun laws" and announced on March 18 that her cabinet had made "in-principle decisions" around the laws' reform. Three days later, Ardern joined with Police Minister Stuart Nash to announce a proposed ban on all "military style semi-automatic and assault rifles." The ban would also apply to high-capacity magazines and parts used to convert firearms into military style semi-automatic weapons. Limited exemptions were to be provided for "legitimate business use" of guns, including professional pest control and policing and defense functions. Exemptions were also provided for two classes of firearms commonly used for farming and hunting, although the proposed reforms would limit the magazine capacity for these guns to five or ten rounds of ammunition.

Ardern acknowledged the reforms would require parliament to approve legislation before the ban could be implemented. "That legislation has now been drafted and will be introduced under urgency," she said, adding she expected the ban to be in place by April 11. In the meantime, she said, the government had taken an "interim measure" to ensure "irresponsible dealers" did not continue to sell firearms that would soon be banned. She explained that Governor-General Dame Patsy Redd had signed an Order in Council to reclassify military style semi-automatic weapons and assault rifles as firearms requiring the harder-to-obtain E-Category gun license. Prior to this order, New Zealanders could purchase military style semi-automatic weapons with a standard gun license (A-Category).

Ardern and Nash said anyone owning a banned gun would have three options for coming into compliance with the new law: surrender their firearm to the police for safe disposal, sell or gift the firearm to someone with the correct license, or fill out an online form to arrange for the police to collect their weapon during a planned buyback period. Both officials encouraged New Zealanders to turn their guns in to police before the buyback began, noting that some had already done so.

The Christchurch shooter had primarily used two assault rifles that he bought with an A-Category license. He had modified the guns with large-capacity magazines purchased online, enabling him to shoot continuously and for longer periods. The proposed gun reforms, Ardern said, would "ban every semi-automatic weapon used in the terrorist attack." The prime minister sought to reassure "owners who have legitimate uses for their guns" that the gun law changes were "not because of you and are not directed at you."

The first of three readings of the bill in parliament took place on April 2 and was followed by a near-unanimous vote in favor of the reform package. The one vote against the ban was cast by David Seymour, a lawmaker belonging to the conservative ACT New Zealand party. Seymour said his objections had more to do with the speed at which the government was seeking to push the bill through parliament than the bill's content. The bill was read a third and final time and was approved in a vote of 119–1 on April 10. Governor-General Redd signed the bill into law on April 11.

The government initiated its planned buyback program on June 20. It is scheduled to run through December 20, 2019. Nash announced on October 31 that more than 32,000 licensed firearms and 120,000 "prohibited parts such as high-capacity magazines" had been bought back. At the time of writing, a second round of government-proposed gun reforms—including creation of a national gun registry—was being considered by parliament.

Tech Companies, World Leaders Sign the Christchurch Call

Ardern's government also focused its attention on the shooter's use of social media and the role social platforms play in facilitating extreme speech. The shooter used Facebook's livestreaming service to broadcast about seventeen minutes of his killing spree. Facebook representatives said the New Zealand police informed them of the livestream shortly after it started, at which point the company "quickly removed both the shooter's Facebook and Instagram accounts and the video" and began working to remove "any praise or support for the crime and the shooter." The company later reported that in the twenty-four hours following the attack, it had blocked more than 1.2 million attempts to upload video of the shooting and had pulled down another 300,000 uploads. The video was also shared on Twitter, YouTube, WhatsApp, Reddit, and Instagram. Reddit banned two channels that had shown the video, and the country's three largest broadband providers—VodafoneNZ, Spark, and 2degrees—said they had suspended access to websites that were hosting the video.

The New Zealand police said they were trying to get the video removed from the Internet and asked people not to share it. On March 18, officials announced that possession or sharing of the shooting video had been classified as a criminal offense. "If you have a record of it, you must delete it," said David Shanks, chief censor in the Office of Film & Literature Classification. "If you see it, you should report it." At least two people have since been charged under New Zealand's Films, Videos, and Publications Classification Act, which made possession of "an objectionable publication" an offense. Several days later, Shanks announced the shooter's manifesto had also been classified as "objectionable" material. "There is an important distinction to be made between 'hate speech,' which may be rejected by many right-thinking people, but which is legal to express, and this type of publication, which is deliberately constructed to inspire further murder and terrorism," he said. "It crosses the line."

Ardern called for an investigation into social media's role in the attack and for changes to the online platforms. "We cannot simply sit back and accept that these platforms just exist and that what is said on them is not the responsibility of the place where they are published," she said in remarks to parliament. "They are the publisher, not just the postman."

In April, Ardern began working with French president Emmanuel Macron to develop a document called the Christchurch Call, which sought a number of nonbinding commitments from social media companies and governments. Ardern and Macron wanted social media companies to share more data among themselves and with government officials to help eradicate the spread of extreme material online, ensure robust enforcement of their terms of service, reexamine the algorithms that push people to extremist content, and take measures to redirect people searching for extremist content. For governments, commitments included adopting and enforcing laws banning objectionable content and setting guidelines for news media on reporting about terrorism without amplifying it. The document did not prescribe enforcement or regulatory measures for carrying out these commitments, leaving it up to the individual companies and countries to determine their own next steps. Ardern explained that the pledge was focused specifically on violent and extreme content so as to avoid a broader debate on hate speech and mitigate concerns about potential impingements of free speech.

On May 15, Ardern and Macron cohosted a summit with ministers from G7 members and leaders of major tech companies to discuss and sign the document. Government signatories included representatives from Australia, Canada, Germany, India, Indonesia, Ireland, Italy, Japan, Jordan, the Netherlands, Norway, Senegal, Spain, Sweden, and the United Kingdom. The United States declined to sign the pledge. A statement from the administration of President Donald Trump explained the United States "is not currently in a position to join the endorsement" and that the "best tool to defeat terrorist speech is productive speech."

Amazon, Facebook, Google, Microsoft, and Twitter signed the pledge, saying in a joint statement that "it is right that we come together" after the "horrifying tragedy" in Christchurch. The day before the summit, Facebook had separately announced new restrictions on its livestreaming service. If a user violated the rules for broadcasting content on Facebook Live, the company said, that user would be temporarily barred from the service. (Previously, a user would need to have multiple offenses before being barred from Facebook Live.) If the user was a repeat offender or posted particularly egregious content, they could be banned from Facebook. The company also announced new partnerships with the University of Maryland, Cornell University, and the University of California, Berkeley, to develop new technology for detecting and removing images and videos of concern. Acknowledging a desire by some for Facebook to simply shut down its livestreaming service, Guy Rosen, the company's vice president of integrity, explained that Facebook's goal was "to minimize risk of abuse on Live while enabling people to use Live in a positive way every day."

—Linda Grimm

Following is a statement by New Zealand prime minister Jacinda Ardern on March 15, 2019, responding to the Christchurch shooting; remarks by Ardern on March 16, 2019, in which she provided various updates on the shooting; a press release issued by Ardern's government on March 21, 2019, announcing a proposed ban on military style semi-automatic weapons and assault rifles; remarks by Ardern and Police Minister Stuart Nash on March 21, 2019, about the ban; and the May 15, 2019, text of the Christchurch Call.

Prime Minister Ardern Addresses the Christchurch Shooting

March 15, 2019

Prime Minister Jacinda Ardern has expressed her horror at the events that are currently unfolding in Christchurch.

"This was an act of extraordinary and unprecedented violence. It has no place in New Zealand.

"It is one of New Zealand's darkest days.

"Many of the people affected by this act of extreme violence will be from our refugee and migrant communities.

"New Zealand is their home. They are us.

"The person or people who carried out this act of unprecedented violence are not.

"There is no place in our home for them.

"My thoughts, and I know all New Zealanders' thoughts, are with those affected and with the people of Christchurch.

"To those who are in lockdown and separated from their families, stay safe and stay inside, follow instructions and be assured the police are actively managing the situation."

SOURCE: Government of New Zealand. "Statement from Jacinda Ardern on Christchurch Shootings." March 15, 2019. https://www.beehive.govt.nz/release/statement-jacinda-ardern-christchurch-shootings.

Prime Minister Ardern Provides Updates on Christchurch Shooting

March 16, 2019

I have just been briefed by officials and agency representatives and can provide the following update.

A total now of 49 people have been killed—work is under way to confirm their identities as quickly as possible.

41 people died at Deans Avenue Mosque, 7 at the Linwood Avenue Mosque—and 1 person has since died in hospital.

Over 40 people are being treated for injuries at Christchurch hospital—they have all been identified and those names have been shared with members of the community.

Two of those are in critical condition and this includes a 4-year-old child who has been transported today to Starship Hospital in Auckland.

This is the only transfer that has taken place. I am advised that the hospital is coping well—there are available beds and 7 acute theatres for those in need.

Pathologists from throughout the country have made themselves available, and we have additional pathologists coming in from Australia.

Three people have been arrested in relation to this event.

One Australian citizen will appear in court today charged with murder.

This individual has travelled around the world with sporadic periods of time spent in New Zealand. They were not a resident of Christchurch. In fact they were currently based in Dunedin.

Enquires are ongoing to establish whether the other two were directly involved with this incident.

The fourth person who was arrested yesterday was a member of the public who was in possession of a firearm, but with the intention of assisting police. They have since been released.

Police are working to build a picture of anyone who might be involved and all of their activities prior to this event.

None of those apprehended had a criminal history either here, or in Australia. As I said last night, they were not on any watch lists either here, or in Australia.

I want to be very clear that our intelligence community and police are focused on extremism of every kind.

Given global indicators around far-right extremism, our intelligence community has been stepping up their investigations in this area.

The individual charged with murder had not come to the attention of the intelligence community nor the police for extremism.

I have asked our agencies this morning to work swiftly on assessing whether there was any activity on social media or otherwise that should have triggered a response. That work is already under way.

Today as the country grieves, we are seeking answers.

I want to speak specifically about the firearms used in this terrorist act.

I'm advised that there were five guns used by the primary perpetrator. There were two semi-automatic weapons, and two shotguns. The offender was in possession of a gun licence.

I'm advised that this was acquired of November 2017.

A lever action firearm was also found.

While work is being done as to the chain of events that led to both the holding of this gun licence, and the possession of these weapons, I can tell you one thing right now. Our gun laws will change.

There have been attempts to change our laws in 2005, 2012 and after an inquiry in 2017.

Now is the time for change.

There are obviously questions being asked of how this person was able to enter the country and undertake this act of terror.

I have instructed ODESC to report to Cabinet on Monday on this sequence of events with a view to strengthening our systems on a range of fronts including but not limited to, firearms, border controls, enhanced information sharing with Australia and any practical reinforcement of our watch list processes.

I want to come now to what people can expect over the course of the day and beyond.

The safety of New Zealanders is our highest priority.

New Zealand Police remain on high alert.

Christchurch residents are strongly urged to stay home if possible and stay safe. Please monitor the Police website and social media for further information.

If you see something suspicious then call 111 immediately. . . .

If anyone needs to speak to someone or if they are feeling distressed, I encourage you to call or text 1737. There are extra staff available. That number is available to everyone.

Police are aware of distressing material relating to this event being online and are reminding people it is an offence to distribute objectionable material. . . .

I want to finish by saying that while the nation grapples with a form of grief and anger that we have not experienced before, we are seeking answers.

After this media conference I will board a defence force plane and travel to Christchurch. I will have other political leaders with me including the Leader of the Opposition.

As is the entire nation, we are all unified in grieving together.

SOURCE: Government of New Zealand. "Statement from Jacinda Ardern on Christchurch Mass Shooting–9am 16 March." March 16, 2019. https://www.beehive.govt.nz/release/statement-jacinda-ardern-christchurch-mass-shooting-%E2%80%93-9am-16-march.

Prime Minister Ardern Announces Ban on Semi-Automatic and Assault Rifles

DOCUMENT

March 21, 2019

Military style semi-automatics and assault rifles will be banned in New Zealand under stronger new gun laws announced today, Prime Minister Jacinda Ardern says.

"On 15 March our history changed forever. Now, our laws will too. We are announcing action today on behalf of all New Zealanders to strengthen our gun laws and make our country a safer place," Jacinda Ardern said.

"Cabinet agreed to overhaul the law when it met on Monday, 72 hours after the horrific terrorism act in Christchurch. Now, six days after this attack, we are announcing a ban on all military style semi-automatics (MSSA) and assault rifles in New Zealand.

"Related parts used to convert these guns into MSSAs are also being banned, along with all high-capacity magazines.

"An amnesty will be put in place for weapons to be handed in, and Cabinet has directed officials to develop a buyback scheme. Further details will be announced on the buyback in due course.

"All semi-automatic weapons used during the terrorist attack on Friday 15 March will be banned.

"I strongly believe that the vast majority of legitimate gun owners in New Zealand will understand that these moves are in the national interest and will take these changes in their stride.

"When Australia undertook similar reforms, their approach was to allow for exemptions for farmers upon application, including for pest control and animal welfare. We have taken similar action to identify the weapons legitimately required in those areas and preclude them.

"Legislation to give effect to the ban will be introduced when Parliament sits in the first week of April. We will provide a short, sharp Select Committee process for feedback on the technical aspects of the changes. We are looking to progress the amendments to this legislation under urgency and expect these amendments to the Arms Act to be passed within the next session of Parliament," Jacinda Ardern said.

"The Bill will include narrow exemptions for legitimate business use, which would include professional pest control. Police and the Defence Force will also have exemptions. Issues like access for mainstream international sporting competitions are also being worked through," Police Minister Stuart Nash said.

"We have also acknowledged that some guns serve legitimate purposes in our farming communities and have therefore set out exemptions for 0.22 calibre rifles and shotguns commonly used for duck hunting. These will have limitations around their capacity.

"While the legislation is being drafted, I am announcing the Government will take immediate action today to restrict the potential stock-piling of these guns and encourage people to continue to surrender their firearms.

Earlier this afternoon, an Order in Council under section 74A(c) of the Arms Act was signed by the Governor-General to reclassify a wider range of semi-automatic weapons under the Act. It came into effect at 3pm today.

"This interim measure will ensure that all of the weapons being banned under amendments to the Arms Act are now categorised as weapons requiring an E endorsement on a firearms licence.

"The effect of this is that it will prevent the sale of MSSAs and assault rifles to people with A category gun licences. The Order in Council is a transitional measure until the wider ban takes effect.

"We are introducing transitionary measures for gun owners to hand in their guns to Police to hold until details of a buy-back are announced. Likewise, the Police continue to accept guns for destruction.

"Again, we encourage gun owners to phone in to Police ahead of time to advise them they are bringing their guns in to the station," Stuart Nash said.

"The actions announced today are the first step of the Government's response. We will continue to develop stronger and more effective licensing rules, storage requirements and penalties for not complying with gun regulations. It is the Government's intention that these amendments will go through the full legislative process," Jacinda Ardern said.

"To owners who have legitimate uses for their guns, I want to reiterate that the actions being announced today are not because of you and are not directed at you. Our actions, on behalf of all New Zealanders, are directed at making sure this never happens again."

Questions and Answers

1. What semi-automatic firearms will be affected by the ban?

The ban will apply to all firearms now defined as Military Style Semi-Automatics (MSSAs) and will also include assault rifles.

2. What semi-automatic firearms will NOT be affected by the ban?

There is a balance to be struck between public safety and legitimate use. The changes exclude two general classes of firearms which are commonly used for hunting, pest control, stock management on farms, and duck shooting:

- Semi-automatic .22 calibre rimfire firearms with a magazine which holds no more than ten rounds
- Semi-automatic and pump action shotguns with a non-detachable tubular magazine which holds no more than five rounds

3. What semi-automatic firearms are affected by today's Order in Council?

Two types of firearms are now defined as Military Style Semi-Automatics (MSSAs):

- A semi-automatic firearm capable of being used with a detachable magazine which holds more than five cartridges
- A semi-automatic shotgun capable of being used with a detachable magazine which holds more than five cartridges

4. I have an A-Category firearms licence and now own MSSAs. What should I do?

It would normally be an offence for an A-Category licence holder to possess an MSSA, punishable by up to three years in prison or a $4000 fine. However, a transitional period gives time for people to comply with the law, if they take certain steps. The transitional period will be confirmed next month. Firearms owners who unlawfully possess an MSSA now have three options:

- Voluntarily surrender the firearm to Police for safe disposal.
- Complete an online form on the Police website to arrange for the MSSA to be collected, while details are finalised for compensation under a buy back scheme
- Sell or gift the firearm to a person who has an E-Category licence and a 'permit to procure' the weapon

5. Are Police geared up to receive large numbers of MSSAs?

Yes. They will work with the New Zealand Defence Force to enable safe storage, transport and destruction of MSSAs. Police are establishing an online form which will make it easier for firearms owners to arrange for Police to collect the MSSAs. The online form will go live over the weekend. It will not be practicable for firearms owners to physically return their weapons to Police stations without prior approval. Where extra administrative staff are required they will be hired on fixed-term contracts.

6. Will this lead to stockpiling of semi-automatics?

No. The changes under the Order in Council take effect immediately. Anyone who now unlawfully has an MSSA, which yesterday was a lawful firearm, needs to take steps to comply with the law.

7. Will some firearms dealers be breaking the law if they have these MSSAs in stock?

Some firearms dealers only hold A-category licences. In order to comply with the law, they could sell their stock of semi-automatics to a Category E licence holder or return them to their supplier.

8. What are the statistics for firearms licences and firearms in circulation?

- There are 245,000 firearms licences
- Of these, 7,500 are E-Category licences; and 485 are dealer licences
- There are 13,500 firearms which require the owner to have an E-Cat licence, this is effectively the known number of MSSAs before today's changes
- The total number of firearms in New Zealand is estimated to be 1.2–1.5 million

9. What further issues are being considered?

Cabinet will consider further steps on 25 March. These will include measures to:

- Tighten firearms licensing and penalties
- Impose greater controls over a range of ammunition

- Address a number of other issues relevant to special interest groups such as international sports shooters and professional pest controllers, such as DoC.

- Future proof the Arms Act to ensure it is able to respond to developments in technology and society

10. How will the buyback work, and who will administer it?

Police, the Treasury and other agencies are working through the detail. More information will be available when the legislation is introduced next month. The compensation will be fair and reasonable based on firearm type, average prices and the age of firearms.

11. What is the cost of the buyback likely to be?

That is very difficult to judge, given the limited information about the total number of firearms affected by this change. Preliminary advice suggests it could be in the range of $100m–$200m. The buyback will ensure these weapons are taken out of circulation and that we fulfil our obligations under the law.

Source: Government of New Zealand. "New Zealand Bans Military Style Semi-automatics and Assault Rifles." March 21, 2019. https://www.beehive.govt.nz/release/new-zealand-bans-military-style-semi-automatics-and-assault-rifles.

Prime Minister Ardern Comments on Gun Ban

March 21, 2019

Welcome everyone.

On 15 March the nation witnessed a terrorist attack that demonstrated the weakness of New Zealand's gun laws.

New Zealand's regulation of arms primarily dates back to 1983. Sadly, since that time the most substantive changes to our laws came following the Aramoana shootings.

Those changes however did not go far enough. Successive attempts have been made and failed to change our laws since then.

Those attempts were in 1999, 2005, 2012, and more recently through a select committee inquiry in early 2017. And still none of the changes that have been made in the past dealt with one of the most glaring issues we have that sets New Zealand apart from many other nations. The availability of military style semi-automatic weapons.

The attacker on 15 March took a significant number of lives using primarily two guns. They were assault rifles and they were purchased legally on an A-Category gun licence. The standard license held by gun owners in New Zealand.

The capacity of these assault rifles was then enhanced using 30–plus-round magazines, essentially turning them into military style semi-automatic weapons. While the modification of these guns was illegal, it was done easily through a simple online purchase. The guns used in this terrorist attack had important distinguishing features. First, their capacity and also their delivery. They had the power to shoot continuously but they also had large capacity magazines.

I absolutely believe there will be a common view amongst New Zealanders, those who use guns for legitimate purposes, and those who have never touched one that the time for the mass and easy availability of these weapons must end. And today they will.

Today I'm announcing that New Zealand will ban all military style semi-automatic weapons. We will also ban all assault rifles. We will ban all high capacity magazines. We will ban all parts with the ability to convert semi-automatic or any other type of firearm into a military style semi-automatic weapon. We will ban parts that cause a firearm to generate semi-automatic, automatic, or close to automatic gunfire. In short, every semi-automatic weapon used in the terrorist attack on Friday will be banned in this country.

These changes will require legislation. That legislation has now been drafted and will be introduced under urgency. A shortened select committee process will apply. So I encourage all those who wish to submit to start now. My expectation is that the law will be in place by the end of the next two-week sitting session, which is by the 11th of April.

As a Government, however, we did not wish to allow a situation where irresponsible dealers continue to sell weapons that will be banned within a few weeks. That is why we have taken an interim measure. As at 3:00 pm today an order in council took effect. These changes to our regulations will ensure virtually all of the weapons I have announced [have] been banned will be categorized as weapons that require an E-Class endorsement.

The effect of this will mean that no one will be able to buy these weapons without a permit to procure from the police. I can assure people that there is no point in applying for such a permit. This is an interim measure to ensure the trade of these weapons ceases from 3 p.m. today.

As a Government we acknowledge that there will be gun owners who have legitimately purchased weapons we have now moved to ban. Some, for instance, will use them for large scale culling such as DOC. We will, as a Cabinet, work through legalised exemptions for these purposes but they will be tightly regulated. For others, these guns will now come out of circulation.

I acknowledge and thank those retailers who have voluntarily ceased to sell military style semi-automatic and assault rifles. You will have seen the collective issues we face as a country and reacted swiftly and I thank you for that. For other dealers, sales should essentially now cease. My expectation is that these weapons will be returned to your suppliers and never enter into the New Zealand market again.

For current owners of the weapons we have moved to ban, I acknowledge that many of you will have acted within the law. In recognition of that and to incentivise their return, we will be establishing a buy-back scheme. The details of the scheme are being developed in parallel to the drafting of the legislation to enforce the ban.

In the meantime we are asking all current holders of military style semi-automatic weapons and assault rifles to visit www.police.govt.nz. There they will find details of the weapons included in the ban, and the next 48 hours a form will be available on the site that we are asking these gun owners to complete, identifying what banned guns they hold. The police will then arrange for these weapons to be handed over and eventually destroyed. Details of the weapons handed back by owners that are covered by the ban will also be taken to ensure that fair and reasonable compensation is paid once the buy-back is in place.

If owners are unable to complete the online form, they are able to contact the police on the phone to arrange the handover of these now banned guns. I do want to emphasise: to manage the flow of information to the police, online is the best way to arrange the return of your weapons. Do not arrive at the police station unannounced with these weapons in your possession.

As the legislation has developed, we will determine the time available for the return of military style semi-automatic weapons and assault rifles and the duration of the buyback scheme. I can assure people that there will be time for the returns to be made and that they will not be criminalised overnight. After a reasonable period for returns those who continue to possess these guns will be in contravention of the law.

Currently the penalties for this range from fines of up to $4,000 and/or three years in prison. The draft legislation will look to increase these penalties. I want to acknowledge that the weapons available in New Zealand are only part of the problem and loopholes with our current law continue to exist.

On Monday, Cabinet will receive and consider further amendments to our gun laws. These proposals will, however, go through a more fulsome process. But be assured, this is just the beginning of the work we need to do.

Finally, I want to repeat a message I have consistently shared since announcing our laws would change. We do have guns in New Zealand that are used for legitimate purposes by responsible owners every single day and that includes our rural community. They manage pests. They use for animal welfare and also for recreation. I've been steadfast in my belief that the vast majority of these owners will support what we are doing here today because it's about all of us. It's in the national interest and it's about safety. I will work hard to retain that support as we work on the remaining tranches of reform that we must make to prevent an act of terror happening in our country ever again. . . .

SOURCE: Government of New Zealand. "PM Statement on Christchurch Mosques Terror Attack—21 March." March 21, 2019. https://www.beehive.govt.nz/release/pm-statement-christchurch-mosques-terror-attack-21-march.

DOCUMENT   *Christchurch Call*

May 15, 2019

A free, open and secure internet is a powerful tool to promote connectivity, enhance social inclusiveness and foster economic growth.

The internet is, however, not immune from abuse by terrorist and violent extremist actors. This was tragically highlighted by the terrorist attacks of 15 March 2019 on the Muslim community of Christchurch—terrorist attacks that were designed to go viral.

The dissemination of such content online has adverse impacts on the human rights of the victims, on our collective security and on people all over the world.

Significant steps have already been taken to address this issue by, among others: the European Commission with initiatives such as the EU Internet Forum; the G20, and the G7, including work underway during France's G7 Presidency on combating the use of the internet for terrorist and violent extremist purposes; along with the Global Internet Forum to Counter Terrorism (GIFCT); the Global Counterterrorism Forum; Tech Against Terrorism; and the Aqaba Process established by the Hashemite Kingdom of Jordan.

The events of Christchurch highlighted once again the urgent need for action and enhanced cooperation among the wide range of actors with influence over this issue, including governments, civil society, and online service providers, such as social media companies, to eliminate terrorist and violent extremist content online.

The Call outlines collective, voluntary commitments from Governments and online service providers intended to address the issue of terrorist and violent extremist content online and to prevent the abuse of the internet as occurred in and after the Christchurch attacks.

All action on this issue must be consistent with principles of a free, open and secure internet, without compromising human rights and fundamental freedoms, including freedom of expression. It must also recognise the internet's ability to act as a force for good, including by promoting innovation and economic development and fostering inclusive societies.

To that end, we, the Governments, commit to:

Counter the drivers of terrorism and violent extremism by strengthening the resilience and inclusiveness of our societies to enable them to resist terrorist and violent extremist ideologies, including through education, building media literacy to help counter distorted terrorist and violent extremist narratives, and the fight against inequality.

Ensure effective enforcement of applicable laws that prohibit the production or dissemination of terrorist and violent extremist content, in a manner consistent with the rule of law and international human rights law, including freedom of expression.

Encourage media outlets to apply ethical standards when depicting terrorist events online, to avoid amplifying terrorist and violent extremist content.

Support frameworks, such as industry standards, to ensure that reporting on terrorist attacks does not amplify terrorist and violent extremist content, without prejudice to responsible coverage of terrorism and violent extremism.

Consider appropriate action to prevent the use of online services to disseminate terrorist and violent extremist content, including through collaborative actions, such as:

- Awareness-raising and capacity-building activities aimed at smaller online service providers;
- Development of industry standards or voluntary frameworks;
- Regulatory or policy measures consistent with a free, open and secure internet and international human rights law.

To that end, we, the online service providers, commit to:

Take transparent, specific measures seeking to prevent the upload of terrorist and violent extremist content and to prevent its dissemination on social media and similar content-sharing services, including its immediate and permanent removal, without prejudice to law enforcement and user appeals requirements, in a manner consistent with human rights and fundamental freedoms. Cooperative measures to achieve these outcomes may include technology development, the expansion and use of shared databases of hashes and URLs, and effective notice and takedown procedures.

Provide greater transparency in the setting of community standards or terms of service, including by:

- Outlining and publishing the consequences of sharing terrorist and violent extremist content;
- Describing policies and putting in place procedures for detecting and removing terrorist and violent extremist content.

Enforce those community standards or terms of service in a manner consistent with human rights and fundamental freedoms, including by:

- Prioritising moderation of terrorist and violent extremist content, however identified;
- Closing accounts where appropriate;
- Providing an efficient complaints and appeals process for those wishing to contest the removal of their content or a decision to decline the upload of their content.

Implement immediate, effective measures to mitigate the specific risk that terrorist and violent extremist content is disseminated through livestreaming, including identification of content for real-time review.

Implement regular and transparent public reporting, in a way that is measurable and supported by clear methodology, on the quantity and nature of terrorist and violent extremist content being detected and removed.

Review the operation of algorithms and other processes that may drive users towards and/or amplify terrorist and violent extremist content to better understand possible intervention points and to implement changes where this occurs. This may include using algorithms and other processes to redirect users from such content or the promotion of credible, positive alternatives or counter-narratives. This may include building appropriate mechanisms for reporting, designed in a multi-stakeholder process and without compromising trade secrets or the effectiveness of service providers' practices through unnecessary disclosure.

Work together to ensure cross-industry efforts are coordinated and robust, for instance by investing in and expanding the GIFCT, and by sharing knowledge and expertise.

To that end, we, Governments and online service providers, commit to work collectively to:

Work with civil society to promote community-led efforts to counter violent extremism in all its forms, including through the development and promotion of positive alternatives and counter-messaging.

Develop effective interventions, based on trusted information sharing about the effects of algorithmic and other processes, to redirect users from terrorist and violent extremist content.

Accelerate research into and development of technical solutions to prevent the upload of and to detect and immediately remove terrorist and violent extremist content online, and share these solutions through open channels, drawing on expertise from academia, researchers, and civil society.

Support research and academic efforts to better understand, prevent and counter terrorist and violent extremist content online, including both the offline and online impacts of this activity.

Ensure appropriate cooperation with and among law enforcement agencies for the purposes of investigating and prosecuting illegal online activity in regard to detected and/or removed terrorist and violent extremist content, in a manner consistent with rule of law and human rights protections.

Support smaller platforms as they build capacity to remove terrorist and violent extremist content, including through sharing technical solutions and relevant databases of hashes or other relevant material, such as the GIFCT shared database.

Collaborate, and support partner countries, in the development and implementation of best practice in preventing the dissemination of terrorist and violent extremist content online, including through operational coordination and trusted information exchanges in accordance with relevant data protection and privacy rules.

Develop processes allowing governments and online service providers to respond rapidly, effectively and in a coordinated manner to the dissemination of terrorist or violent extremist content following a terrorist event. This may require the development of a shared crisis protocol and information-sharing processes, in a manner consistent with human rights protections.

Respect, and for Governments protect, human rights, including by avoiding directly or indirectly contributing to adverse human rights impacts through business activities and addressing such impacts where they occur.

Recognise the important role of civil society in supporting work on the issues and commitments in the Call, including through:

- Offering expert advice on implementing the commitments in this Call in a manner consistent with a free, open and secure internet and with international human rights law;
- Working, including with governments and online service providers, to increase transparency;
- Where necessary, working to support users through company appeals and complaints processes.

Affirm our willingness to continue to work together, in existing fora and relevant organizations, institutions, mechanisms and processes to assist one another and to build momentum and widen support for the Call.

Develop and support a range of practical, non-duplicative initiatives to ensure that this pledge is delivered.

Acknowledge that governments, online service providers, and civil society may wish to take further cooperative action to address a broader range of harmful online content, such as the actions that will be discussed further during the G7

Biarritz Summit, in the G20, the Aqaba Process, the Five Country Ministerial, and a range of other fora.

SOURCE: New Zealand Ministry of Foreign Affairs and Trade. "Christchurch Call to Eliminate Terrorist and Violent Extremist Content Online." May 15, 2019. https://www.christchurchcall.com/call.html.

OTHER HISTORIC DOCUMENTS OF INTEREST

FROM PREVIOUS *HISTORIC DOCUMENTS*

- French President Responds to Attack on *Charlie Hebdo* Headquarters, *2015,* p. 10
- Norwegian Government on Oslo and Utøya Terrorist Attack, *2011,* p. 415

Department of Justice Releases Mueller Report

MARCH 22, 24, AND 27, 2019

After twenty-two months of investigation, on March 22, 2019, Special Counsel Robert Mueller provided the Department of Justice his final report related to the investigation into Russian interference in the 2016 election and possible coordination between Russian officials and the campaign of President Donald Trump. The report concluded that, while the Russian government had tried to influence the U.S. election, there was no coordination with the Trump campaign, nor was there enough evidence to establish whether the president attempted to obstruct justice by interfering with the Mueller investigation. Mueller's work spawned a number of federal investigations into individuals both affiliated and unaffiliated with the Trump campaign, and Democrats committed to continuing their own work to determine whether President Trump had in fact acted to obstruct justice and whether his actions were worthy of an impeachment inquiry.

MUELLER OPENS INVESTIGATION INTO POSSIBLE TRUMP–RUSSIA LINK

On May 17, 2017, the Department of Justice announced it would appoint former Federal Bureau of Investigation (FBI) director Mueller as special counsel to lead an investigation into "any links and/or coordination between the Russian government and individuals associated with the campaign of President Donald Trump." Mueller and his team, made up of staff from the Department of Justice, were also authorized "to prosecute federal crimes arising from the investigation of these matters." The announcement was made by Deputy Attorney General Rod Rosenstein, who said he found the appointment of a special counsel necessary "in order for the American people to have full confidence in the outcome" of the FBI's investigation into a link between Russia and Trump, first launched in July 2016. Rosenstein also cautioned his announcement did not represent a "finding that crimes have been committed or that any prosecution is warranted."

President Trump responded that the investigation would clear his campaign of any wrongdoing, noting "there was no collusion between my campaign and any foreign entity." In the intervening months, the president and his allies frequently took to the airwaves and Twitter to air their grievances about the investigation, which the president repeatedly referred to as a "witch hunt" orchestrated by the Democrats to bring down his administration. He regularly accused former Democratic presidential nominee Hillary Clinton of committing wrongdoings that should be scrutinized, and he called on the Department of Justice to reprise the investigation into her use of a private e-mail server during her time as secretary of state. "Wow, FBI confirms report that James Comey drafted letter exonerating Crooked Hillary Clinton long before investigation was complete," Trump tweeted in reference to a 2015–2016 investigation into Clinton's e-mails and the letter written by then–FBI director Comey released days before Election Day clearing Clinton of any wrongdoing. "All of the Crimes were committed by Crooked Hillary, the Dems, the DNC and Dirty Cops—and we caught them in the act!" Trump would later tweet in 2019.

Mueller's nearly two-year investigation was carried out largely in secret, with few leaks coming from the team, resulting in wild speculation about what might have been uncovered. Mueller's team conducted hundreds of interviews, reviewed thousands of documents, and issued indictments against thirty-four individuals and three companies. Some of those indictments targeted individuals who worked for the president's campaign or in the White House. These included Michael Flynn, a Trump campaign advisor and the White House national security advisor who pleaded guilty to lying to the FBI about conversations he had with the Russian ambassador prior to Trump's inauguration, and Paul Manafort, Trump's campaign chair, who was convicted on eight counts, including tax and bank fraud. By the time Mueller concluded his investigation in March, his work had already garnered a total of seven guilty pleas and one conviction.

Mueller Report Released

On March 22, Mueller announced the end of his investigation and provided the long-awaited final report of his findings to the Department of Justice. Attorney General William Barr subsequently notified Congress that the report had been received but provided no additional details. The only information made public on the day the report was released was that Mueller would not recommend any additional indictments related to his investigation.

Two days after Mueller delivered his report, Barr sent a four-page letter to Congress summarizing the findings. Barr's letter quoted from the report, noting that Mueller's investigation "did not establish that members of the Trump Campaign conspired or coordinated with the Russian government in its election interference activities." Barr's summary also stated that, while Mueller's team did not reach the conclusion that President Trump attempted to obstruct justice by interfering with the special counsel's investigation, Barr and Rosenstein determined there was not enough evidence "to establish that the President committed an obstruction of justice offense." Mueller later sent his own letter to Barr, writing that the summary "did not fully capture the context, nature, and substance" of the investigation. "There is now public confusion about critical aspects of the results of our investigation. This threatens to undermine a central purpose for which the Department appointed the Special Counsel: to assure full public confidence in the outcome of the investigations," Mueller wrote.

The 448-page report was divided into two volumes. The first detailed Russian interference in the 2016 presidential election and answered the question of whether the Trump campaign coordinated with the Russians. The second volume looked at the question of whether President Trump tried to obstruct the Mueller investigation.

Mueller Report Volume I: Coordination between Trump Campaign and Russia

At the start of the first volume, the Mueller team took issue with a word frequently used by the president: *collusion*. The president frequently asserted there was no collusion between his campaign and Russian officials during the 2016 election. However, Mueller's team noted that "collusion" is not a legal term. "In evaluation of whether evidence about collective action of multiple individuals constituted a crime, we applied the framework of conspiracy law, not the concept of 'collusion,'" the report stated, adding, "Collusion is not a specific offense or theory of liability found in the United States Code, nor is it a term of art in federal criminal law." Instead, the Mueller team looked at whether the Trump campaign *coordinated* with Russian officials in support of Trump's candidacy. "We understood coordination to require an agreement—tacit or express—between the Trump Campaign and the Russian government on election interference," the report states. Any such agreement would have required both the Trump campaign and the Russian government to take actions "informed by or responsive to the other's actions or interests." Using that definition, the investigation "did not establish that members of the Trump campaign conspired or coordinated with the Russian government in its election interference activities."

The investigation did, however, uncover numerous instances in which Russian operatives interacted with those associated with the campaign. The report noted that the Russian government knew it would benefit from a Trump presidency and that the campaign understood that Trump's electability stood to gain from any information Russia released to discredit Clinton. However, the investigation failed to establish whether members of the Trump campaign actually knew they were interacting with Russian government officials who had criminal intent. Additionally, the report noted that Russian operatives relied heavily on social media to recruit Americans unaffiliated with the campaign to spread their messaging and participate in pro-Trump political events and rallies. Again, Americans were largely unaware they were supporting a Russian effort.

The report also delved into the question about whether members of the Trump campaign worked with Russia to help disseminate Clinton's e-mails and other information released by WikiLeaks in the summer of 2016. Here, the report noted, "Under applicable law, publication of these types of materials would not be criminal unless the publisher also participated in the underlying hacking conspiracy." As such, the Mueller team did not find that any member of the Trump campaign illegally disseminated these materials.

MUELLER REPORT VOLUME II: OBSTRUCTION OF JUSTICE

In Volume II, Mueller looked at ten separate actions by President Trump and his associates to subvert the Mueller investigation to determine whether the president acted to obstruct justice. These actions included firing former FBI director Comey because, according to the report, Comey refused to exonerate the president of any wrongdoing during the 2016 election. Trump had been highly critical of Comey and the work he did on the Clinton e-mail investigation, and he asserted when he fired Comey in May 2017 that he did so on the recommendation of Rosenstein and then–attorney general Jeff Sessions because Comey was "not able to effectively lead the bureau." Other actions reviewed by the special counsel included instances of the president asking White House counsel Don McGahn to fire Mueller, pressuring Sessions to reverse his decision to recuse himself from the Russia inquiry, and attempts to hide details of a meeting at Trump Tower between members of the Trump campaign and those affiliated with the Russian government. The report stated these efforts to undermine Mueller's investigation "were mostly unsuccessful, but that is largely because the persons who surrounded the President declined to carry out orders or accede to his requests."

The Mueller report noted that it would be difficult to make an accusation of obstruction of justice against a sitting president because it "would place burdens on the president's capacity to govern and potentially preempt constitutional process for addressing presidential misconduct." In the end, Mueller's team declined to make a determination about whether obstruction of justice occurred. "The evidence we obtained about the president's actions and intent presents difficult issues that would need to be resolved if we were making a traditional prosecutorial judgement," the report stated. "At the same time, if we had confidence after a thorough investigation of the facts that the president clearly did not commit obstruction of justice, we would so state. Based on the facts and the applicable legal standards, we are unable to reach that judgement. Accordingly, while this report does not conclude that the president committed a crime, it also does not exonerate him."

DEMOCRATS, REPUBLICANS RESPOND TO REPORT'S RELEASE

President Trump immediately celebrated the report's release. "I'm having a good day. . . . It's called 'no collusion, no obstruction.' There never was, by the way, and there never will be," Trump said. "This should never happen to another president again, this hoax," he added. Later, the president wrote in two tweets, "This was an Illegally Started Hoax that never should have happened, a . . . big, fat waste of time, energy and money." He said that those who were attempting to bring down his presidency were "some very sick and dangerous people who have committed very serious crimes, perhaps even Spying or Treason." Vice President Mike Pence also rallied around the president. Mueller's findings confirmed "what the president and I have said since Day 1: There was no collusion between the Trump campaign and Russia and there was no obstruction of justice," Pence said.

Other Republicans took a different tact, focusing on the attempts by Russia to undermine a U.S. election. "We should ALL be alarmed at how effective Putin was & we should ALL be relieved, not disappointed, that President [Trump] didn't collaborate with him," tweeted Sen. Marco Rubio, R-Fla. Sen. Rob Portman, R-Ohio, admitted the report "documents a number of actions taken by the president or his associates that were inappropriate," but that none of them rose to the criminal level. Sen. Mitt Romney, R-Utah, a frequent critic of President Trump, had a different response. "I am sickened at the extent and pervasiveness of dishonesty and misdirection by individuals in the highest office of the land, including the president," Romney said. The report "is a sobering revelation of how far we have strayed from the aspirations and principles of the founders," he added.

Democrats in Congress took the report as marching orders to hold President Trump accountable. "The Mueller report outlines disturbing evidence that President Trump engaged in obstruction of justice and other misconduct," said Rep. Jerry Nadler, D-N.Y., chair of the House Judiciary Committee. "The Special Counsel made clear that he did not exonerate the President," Nadler said. Democrats also decried the variation between Barr's four-page summary of the Mueller report and the report itself. "As we continue to review the report, one thing is clear: Attorney General Barr presented a conclusion that the president did not obstruct justice while Mueller's report appears to undercut that finding," House Speaker Nancy Pelosi, D-Calif., and Senate minority leader Chuck Schumer, D-N.Y., said in a joint statement.

Many Democratic leaders stopped short of signaling the information presented in the Mueller report was grounds for impeachment or they would quickly begin impeachment proceedings, saying instead they needed to gather additional information and review the full report. Nadler in April issued a subpoena to the Department of Justice to provide the unredacted report for review by Congress; that release was blocked by an appeals court in October. According to a *Washington Post* analysis, 39 percent of the report's pages had at least some redaction. Most of the redactions were in Volume I, and according to Barr fell into four categories: information related to ongoing investigations, information from grand jury trials, secret material, and details that would "unduly infringe on the personal privacy and reputational interests of peripheral third parties." More progressive members of the Democratic Caucus, however, were ready to immediately remove the president from office. Freshman representative Rashida Tlaib, D-Mich., circulated an impeachment resolution that was joined by a number of her colleagues, including Rep. Alexandria Ocasio-Cortez, who tweeted, "While I understand the political reality of the Senate + election considerations, upon reading the DoJ report, which explicitly names Congress in determining obstruction, I cannot see a reason for us to abdicate from our constitutionally mandated responsibility to investigate."

MUELLER TESTIFIES BEFORE CONGRESS

On July 24, Mueller was called to testify before the House Judiciary and Intelligence Committees. Over the course of nearly seven hours, Mueller detailed the work of his team but rarely strayed from the text of the report, offering little fodder for either Democrats or Republicans. Mueller frequently refused to engage in partisan lines of questioning and often responded with one-word answers or directed the questioner to the report. "As I said on May 29: the report is my testimony. And I will stay within that text," Mueller said.

Mueller was asked why he did not subpoena the president for an in-person testimony but instead accepted his written responses. Mueller admitted it was because it would have taken additional time in court "litigating the interview with the President." Mueller also indicated the president's written responses might have been untruthful. Rep. Val Demings, D-Fla., asked, "Director Mueller, isn't it fair to say that the president's written answers were not only inadequate and incomplete, because he didn't answer many of your questions, but where he did his answers showed that he wasn't always being truthful?" Mueller replied, "I would say generally."

Mueller noted his report and testimony were not the product of "a witch hunt" as the president had asserted, and he also reiterated the investigation did not reach a conclusion on obstruction of justice but "the president was not exculpated for the acts that he allegedly committed." Mueller called Trump's activities under investigation "problematic" but gave little pushback to Republicans who questioned some of the tactics of his investigation, specifically why he relied on the much-maligned Steele dossier, a privately produced intelligence report funded in part by the Democratic National Committee (DNC) in support of Clinton's campaign seeking evidence of a link between Russia and the Trump campaign.

The former FBI director expressed strong emotion only a few times, including when his investigation team was attacked as being politically biased. "We strove to hire those individuals that could do the job," Mueller said. "I have been in this business for almost 25 years. And in those 25 years I have not had occasion, once, to ask somebody about their political affiliation. It is not done. What I care about is the capability of the individual to do the job and do the job quickly and seriously and with integrity," he said. Mueller also sought to stress his concern that Russia would continue to undermine U.S. elections. "I hope this is not the new normal. But I fear it is," Mueller said, adding, "They're doing it as we sit here."

ONGOING CASES RELATED TO THE MUELLER INVESTIGATION

Although the Mueller investigation had reached its conclusion, federal prosecutors were pursuing fourteen other investigations referred by Mueller's office. Two of those—one related to Michael Cohen, Trump's former personal lawyer, and another against former Obama-era

White House counsel Gregory Craig—were mentioned in the report, while the remaining twelve were redacted to prevent any harm to the ongoing investigation. Another eleven cases started by the Mueller team were transferred to federal investigators to complete; in most instances, these were cases where the defendant was awaiting trial or prosecution.

One of the more high-profile cases transferred was related to longtime Trump advisor Roger Stone, who was charged with seven counts including obstruction of justice, witness tampering, and lying to Congress. Prosecutors in the case sought to closely link Stone with alleged wrongdoing by Trump and his associates. Stone worked closely with Trump beginning in 1980, and although Stone was a member of the campaign team early in Trump's run, they parted ways before the election but remained in touch. According to prosecutors, Stone and Trump talked dozens of times throughout 2016.

The case against Stone centered partly on the information dump that came from WikiLeaks ahead of Election Day 2016. According to prosecutors, Stone failed to provide information to Congress during their 2017 investigation into Russian interference confirming he sought information from WikiLeaks and was in communication with the organization. Prosecutors said this resulted in an inaccurate final House report on Russian interference in the election.

Rick Gates, Trump's former deputy campaign chair who himself had pleaded guilty to crimes related to the Mueller investigation, was a key witness for the prosecution, alleging Stone knew about the coming WikiLeaks disclosure well before April 2016, the timeline offered by the Mueller investigation, and had shared that information with Trump. Trump asserted in his written responses to Mueller that he didn't recall speaking with Stone or discussing the WikiLeaks hack of DNC servers.

On November 15, after a brief jury deliberation, Stone was found guilty on all seven counts against him. The prosecution sought to have Stone immediately taken into custody, arguing he had violated his gag order by contacting a member of the media ahead of the ruling. The judge declined. Stone's sentencing date was set for February 6, 2020.

—Heather Kerrigan

Following are the executive summaries of Volumes I and II of the report delivered by Special Counsel Robert Mueller following his investigation into Russian efforts to interfere in the 2016 election, possible coordination between the campaign of Donald Trump and Russian officials, and attempts by President Trump to obstruct the investigation. The reports were submitted to the Department of Justice on March 22, 2019, and made public on April 18, 2019. Also included below is the text of Attorney General William Barr's four-page summary of the Mueller report, sent to members of Congress on March 24, 2019, and Mueller's letter, written March 27, 2019, in response to Barr's summary.

Mueller Report Volume I: Effort to Undermine U.S. Elections

March 22, 2019

[Only the Executive Summary of Volume I has been included; all other material has been omitted.]

EXECUTIVE SUMMARY TO VOLUME I

RUSSIAN SOCIAL MEDIA CAMPAIGN

The Internet Research Agency (IRA) carried out the earliest Russian interference operations identified by the investigation—a social media campaign designed to provoke and amplify political and social discord in the United States. The IRA was based in St. Petersburg, Russia, and received funding from Russian oligarch Yevgeniy Prigozhin and companies he controlled. Prigozhin is widely reported to have ties to Russian President Vladimir Putin, [redacted]

In mid-2014, the IRA sent employees to the United States on an intelligence-gathering mission with instructions [redacted]

The IRA later used social media accounts and interest groups to sow discord in the U.S. political system through what it termed "information warfare." The campaign evolved from a generalized program designed in 2014 and 2015 to undermine the U.S. electoral system, to a targeted operation that by early 2016 favored candidate Trump and disparaged candidate Clinton. The IRA's operation also included the purchase of political advertisements on social media in the names of U.S. persons and entities, as well as the staging of political rallies inside the United States. To organize those rallies, IRA employees posed as U.S. grassroots entities and persons and made contact with Trump supporters and Trump Campaign officials in the United States. The investigation did not identify evidence that any U.S. persons conspired or coordinated with the IRA. Section II of this report details the Office's investigation of the Russian social media campaign.

RUSSIAN HACKING OPERATIONS

At the same time that the IRA operation began to focus on supporting candidate Trump in early 2016, the Russian government employed a second form of interference: cyber intrusions (hacking) and releases of hacked materials damaging to the Clinton Campaign. The Russian intelligence service known as the Main Intelligence Directorate of the General Staff of the Russian Army (GRU) carried out these operations.

In March 2016, the GRU began hacking the email accounts of Clinton Campaign volunteers and employees, including campaign chairman John Podesta. In April 2016, the GRU hacked into the computer networks of the Democratic Congressional Campaign Committee (DCCC) and the Democratic National Committee (DNC). The GRU stole hundreds of thousands of documents from the compromised email accounts and networks. Around the time that the DNC announced in mid-June 2016 the Russian government's role in hacking its network, the GRU began disseminating stolen materials through the fictitious online personas "DCLeaks" and "Guccifer 2.0." The GRU later released additional materials through the organization WikiLeaks.

The presidential campaign of Donald J. Trump ("Trump Campaign" or "Campaign") showed interest in WikiLeaks's releases of documents and welcomed their potential to damage candidate Clinton. Beginning in June 2016, [redacted] forecast to senior Campaign officials that WikiLeaks would release information damaging to candidate Clinton. WikiLeaks's first release came in July 2016. Around the same time, candidate Trump announced that he hoped Russia would recover emails described as missing from a private server used by Clinton when she was Secretary of State (he later said that he was speaking sarcastically). [redacted] WikiLeaks began releasing Podesta's stolen emails on October 7, 2016, less than one hour after a U.S. media outlet released video considered damaging to candidate Trump. Section III of this Report details the Office's investigation into the Russian hacking operations, as well as other efforts by Trump Campaign supporters to obtain Clinton-related emails.

RUSSIAN CONTACTS WITH THE CAMPAIGN

The social media campaign and the GRU hacking operations coincided with a series of contacts between Trump Campaign officials and individuals with ties to the Russian government. The Office investigated whether those contacts reflected or resulted in the Campaign conspiring or coordinating with Russia in its election-interference activities. Although the investigation established that the Russian government perceived it would benefit from a Trump presidency and worked to secure that outcome, and that the Campaign expected it would benefit electorally from information stolen and released through Russian efforts, the investigation did not establish that members of the Trump Campaign conspired or coordinated with the Russian government in its election interference activities.

The Russian contacts consisted of business connections, offers of assistance to the Campaign, invitations for candidate Trump and Putin to meet in person, invitations for Campaign officials and representatives of the Russian government to meet, and policy positions seeking improved U.S.–Russian relations. Section IV of this Report details the contacts between Russia and the Trump Campaign during the campaign and transition periods, the most salient of which are summarized below in chronological order.

Some of the earliest contacts were made in connection with a Trump Organization real-estate project in Russia known as Trump Tower Moscow. Candidate Trump signed a Letter of Intent for Trump Tower Moscow by November 2015, and in January 2016 Trump Organization executive Michael Cohen emailed and spoke about the project with the office of Russian government press secretary Dmitry Peskov. The Trump Organization pursued the project through at least June 2016, including by considering travel to Russia by Cohen and candidate Trump.

Spring 2016. Campaign foreign policy advisor George Papadopoulos made early contact with Joseph Mifsud, a London-based professor who had connections to Russia and traveled to Moscow in April 2016. Immediately upon his return to London from that trip, Mifsud told Papadopoulos that the Russian government had "dirt" on Hillary Clinton in the form of thousands of emails. One week later, in the first week of May 2016, Papadopoulos suggested to a representative of a foreign government that the Trump Campaign had received indications from the Russian government that it could assist the Campaign through the anonymous release of information damaging to candidate Clinton. Throughout that period of time and for several months thereafter, Papadopoulos worked with Mifsud and two Russian nationals to arrange a meeting between the Campaign and the Russian government. No meeting took place.

Summer 2016. Russian outreach to the Trump Campaign continued into the summer of 2016, as candidate Trump was becoming the presumptive Republican nominee for President. On June 9, 2016, for example, a Russian lawyer met with senior Trump Campaign officials Donald Trump Jr., Jared Kushner, and campaign chairman Paul Manafort to deliver what the email proposing the meeting had described as "official documents and information that would incriminate Hillary." The materials were offered to Trump Jr. as "part of Russia and its government's support for Mr. Trump." The written communications setting up the meeting showed that the Campaign anticipated receiving information from Russia that could assist candidate Trump's electoral prospects, but the Russian lawyer's presentation did not provide such information.

Days after the June 9 meeting, on June 14, 2016, a cybersecurity firm and the DNC announced that Russian government hackers had infiltrated the DNC and obtained access to opposition research on candidate Trump, among other documents.

In July 2016, Campaign foreign policy advisor Carter Page traveled in his personal capacity to Moscow and gave the keynote address at the New Economic School. Page had lived and worked in Russia between 2003 and 2007. After returning to the United States, Page became acquainted with at least two Russian intelligence officers, one of whom was later charged in 2015 with conspiracy to act as an unregistered agent of Russia. Page's July 2016 trip to Moscow and his advocacy for pro-Russian foreign policy drew media attention. The Campaign then distanced itself from Page and, by late September 2016, removed him from the Campaign.

July 2016 was also the month WikiLeaks first released emails stolen by the GRU from the DNC. On July 22, 2016, WikiLeaks posted thousands of internal DNC documents revealing information about the Clinton Campaign. Within days, there was public reporting that U.S. intelligence agencies had "high confidence" that the Russian government was behind the theft of emails and documents from the DNC. And within a week of the release, a foreign government informed the FBI about its May 2016 interaction with Papadopoulos and his statement that the Russian government could assist the Trump Campaign. On July 31, 2016, based on the foreign government reporting, the FBI opened an investigation into potential coordination between the Russian government and individuals associated with the Trump Campaign.

Separately, on August 2, 2016, Trump campaign chairman Paul Manafort met in New York City with his longtime business associate Konstantin Kilimnik, who the FBI assesses to have ties to Russian intelligence. Kilimnik requested the meeting to deliver in person a peace plan for Ukraine that Manafort acknowledged to the Special Counsel's Office was a "backdoor" way for Russia to control part of eastern Ukraine; both men believed the plan would require candidate Trump's assent to succeed (were he to be elected President). They also discussed the status of the Trump Campaign and Manafort's strategy for winning Democratic votes in Midwestern states. Months before that meeting, Manafort had caused internal polling data to be shared with Kilimnik, and the sharing continued for some period of time after their August meeting.

Fall 2016. On October 7, 2016, the media released video of candidate Trump speaking in graphic terms about women years earlier, which was considered damaging to his candidacy. Less than an hour later, WikiLeaks made its second release: thousands of John Podesta's emails that had been stolen by the GRU in late March 2016. The FBI and other U.S. government institutions were at the time continuing their investigation of suspected Russian government efforts to interfere in the presidential election. That same day, October 7, the Department of Homeland Security and the Office of the Director of National Intelligence issued a joint public statement "that the Russian Government directed the recent compromises of e-mails from US persons and institutions, including from US political organizations." Those "thefts" and the "disclosures" of the hacked materials through online platforms such as WikiLeaks, the statement continued, "are intended to interfere with the US election process."

Post-2016 Election. Immediately after the November 8 election, Russian government officials and prominent Russian businessmen began trying to make inroads into the new administration. The most senior levels of the Russian government encouraged these efforts. The Russian Embassy made contact hours after the election to congratulate the President-Elect and to arrange a call with President Putin. Several Russian businessmen picked up the effort from there.

Kirill Dmitriev, the chief executive officer of Russia's sovereign wealth fund, was among the Russians who tried to make contact with the incoming administration. In early December, a business associate steered Dmitriev to Erik Prince, a supporter of the Trump Campaign and an associate of senior Trump advisor Steve Bannon. Dmitriev and Prince later met face-to-face in January 2017 in the Seychelles and discussed U.S.-Russia relations. During the same period, another business associate introduced Dmitriev to a friend of Jared Kushner who had not served on the Campaign or the Transition Team. Dmitriev and Kushner's friend collaborated on a short written reconciliation plan for the United States and Russia, which Dmitriev implied had been cleared through Putin. The friend gave that proposal to Kushner before the inauguration, and Kushner later gave copies to Bannon and incoming Secretary of State Rex Tillerson.

On December 29, 2016, then-President Obama imposed sanctions on Russia for having interfered in the election. Incoming National Security Advisor Michael Flynn called Russian Ambassador Sergey Kislyak and asked Russia not to escalate the situation in response to the sanctions. The following day, Putin announced that Russia would not take retaliatory measures in response to the sanctions at that time. Hours later, President-Elect Trump tweeted, "Great move on delay (by V. Putin)." The next day, on December 31, 2016, Kislyak called Flynn and told him the request had been received at the highest levels and Russia had chosen not to retaliate as a result of Flynn's request.

* * *

On January 6, 2017, members of the intelligence community briefed President-Elect Trump on a joint assessment—drafted and coordinated among the Central Intelligence Agency, FBI, and National Security Agency—that concluded with high confidence that Russia had intervened in the election through a variety of means to assist Trump's candidacy and harm Clinton's. A declassified version of the assessment was publicly released that same day.

Between mid-January 2017 and early February 2017, three congressional committees—the House Permanent Select Committee on Intelligence (HPSCI), the Senate Select Committee on Intelligence (SSCI), and the Senate Judiciary Committee (SJC)—announced that they would conduct inquiries, or had already been conducting inquiries, into Russian interference in the election. Then-FBI Director James Comey later confirmed to Congress the existence of the FBI's investigation into Russian interference that had begun before the election. On March 20, 2017, in open-session testimony before HPSCI, Comey stated:

> I have been authorized by the Department of Justice to confirm that the FBI, as part of our counterintelligence mission, is investigating the Russian government's efforts to interfere in the 2016 presidential election, and that includes investigating the nature of any links between individuals associated with the Trump campaign and the Russian government and whether there was any coordination between the campaign and Russia's efforts. . . . As with any counterintelligence investigation, this will also include an assessment of whether any crimes were committed.

The investigation continued under then-Director Comey for the next seven weeks until May 9, 2017, when President Trump fired Comey as FBI Director—an action which is analyzed in Volume II of the report.

On May 17, 2017, Acting Attorney General Rod Rosenstein appointed the Special Counsel and authorized him to conduct the investigation that Comey had confirmed in his congressional testimony, as well as matters arising directly from the investigation, and any other matters within the scope of 28 C.F.R. § 600.4(a), which generally covers efforts to interfere with or obstruct the investigation.

President Trump reacted negatively to the Special Counsel's appointment. He told advisors that it was the end of his presidency, sought to have Attorney General Jefferson (Jeff) Sessions unrecuse from the Russia investigation and to have the Special Counsel removed, and engaged in efforts to curtail the Special Counsel's investigation and prevent the disclosure of evidence to it, including through public and private contacts with potential witnesses. Those and related actions are described and analyzed in Volume II of the report.

* * *

THE SPECIAL COUNSEL'S CHARGING DECISIONS

In reaching the charging decisions described in Volume I of the report, the Office determined whether the conduct it found amounted to a violation of federal criminal law chargeable under the Principles of Federal Prosecution. See Justice Manual § 9-27.000 et seq. (2018). The standard set forth in the Justice Manual is whether the conduct constitutes a crime; if so, whether admissible evidence would probably be sufficient to obtain and sustain a conviction; and whether prosecution would serve a substantial federal interest that could not be adequately served by prosecution elsewhere or through non-criminal alternatives. See Justice Manual § 9-27.220.

Section V of the report provides detailed explanations of the Office's charging decisions, which contain three main components.

First, the Office determined that Russia's two principal interference operations in the 2016 U.S. presidential election—the social media campaign and the hacking-and-dumping operations—violated U.S. criminal law. Many of the individuals and entities involved in the social media campaign have been charged with participating in a conspiracy to defraud the United States by undermining through deceptive acts the work of federal agencies charged with regulating foreign influence in U.S. elections, as well as related counts of identity theft. See *United States v. Internet Research Agency, et al.,* No. 18-cr-32 (D.D.C.). Separately, Russian intelligence officers who carried out the hacking into Democratic Party computers and the personal email accounts of individuals affiliated with the Clinton Campaign conspired to violate, among other federal laws, the federal computer-intrusion statute, and they have been so charged. See *United States v. Netyksho, et al.,* No. 18-cr-215 (D.D.C.). [redacted]

Second, while the investigation identified numerous links between individuals with ties to the Russian government and individuals associated with the Trump Campaign, the evidence was not sufficient to support criminal charges. Among other things, the evidence was not sufficient to charge any Campaign official as an unregistered agent of the Russian government or other Russian principal. And our evidence about the June 9, 2016 meeting and WikiLeaks's releases of hacked materials was not sufficient to charge a criminal campaign-finance violation. Further, the evidence was not sufficient to charge that any member of the Trump Campaign conspired with representatives of the Russian government to interfere in the 2016 election.

Third, the investigation established that several individuals affiliated with the Trump Campaign lied to the Office, and to Congress, about their interactions with Russian-affiliated individuals and related matters. Those lies materially impaired the investigation of Russian election interference. The Office charged some of those lies as violations of the federal false-statements statute. Former National Security Advisor Michael Flynn pleaded guilty to lying about his interactions with Russian Ambassador Kislyak during the transition period. George Papadopoulos, a foreign policy advisor during the campaign period, pleaded guilty to lying to investigators about, inter alia, the nature and timing of his interactions with Joseph Mifsud, the professor who told Papadopoulos that the Russians had dirt on candidate Clinton in the form of thousands of emails. Former Trump Organization attorney Michael Cohen pleaded guilty to making false statements to Congress about the Trump Moscow project. [redacted] And in February 2019, the U.S. District Court for the District of Columbia found that Manafort lied to the Office and the grand jury concerning his interactions and communications with Konstantin Kilimnik about Trump Campaign polling data and a peace plan for Ukraine.

* * *

The Office investigated several other events that have been publicly reported to involve potential Russia-related contacts. For example, the investigation established that interactions between Russian Ambassador Kislyak and Trump Campaign officials both at the candidate's April 2016 foreign policy speech in Washington, D.C., and during the week of the Republican National Convention were brief, public, and non-substantive. And the investigation did not establish that one Campaign official's efforts to dilute a portion of the Republican Party platform on providing assistance to Ukraine were undertaken at the behest of candidate Trump or Russia. The investigation also did not establish that a meeting between Kislyak and Sessions in September 2016 at Sessions's Senate office included any more than a passing mention of the presidential campaign.

The investigation did not always yield admissible information or testimony, or a complete picture of the activities undertaken by subjects of the investigation. Some individuals invoked their Fifth Amendment right against compelled self-incrimination and were not, in the Office's judgment, appropriate candidates for grants of immunity. The Office limited its pursuit of other witnesses and information—such as information known to attorneys or individuals claiming to be members of the media—in light of internal Department of Justice policies. See, e.g., Justice Manual §§ 9-13.400, 13.410. Some of the information obtained via court process, moreover, was presumptively covered by legal privilege and was screened from investigators by a filter (or "taint") team. Even when individuals testified or agreed to be interviewed, they sometimes provided information that was false or incomplete, leading to some of the false-statements charges described above. And the Office faced practical limits on its ability to access relevant evidence as well—numerous witnesses and subjects lived abroad, and documents were held outside the United States.

Further, the Office learned that some of the individuals we interviewed or whose conduct we investigated—including some associated with the Trump Campaign—deleted relevant communications or communicated during the relevant period using applications that feature encryption or that do not provide for long-term retention of data or communications records. In such cases, the Office was not able to corroborate witness statements through comparison to contemporaneous communications or fully question witnesses about statements that appeared inconsistent with other known facts.

Accordingly, while this report embodies factual and legal determinations that the Office believes to be accurate and complete to the greatest extent possible, given these identified gaps, the Office cannot rule out the possibility that the unavailable information would shed additional light on (or cast in a new light) the events described in the report.

SOURCE: U.S. Department of Justice. "Report on the Investigation into Russian Interference in the 2016 Presidential Election. Volume I of II." March 22, 2019. https://www.justice.gov/storage/report.pdf.

Mueller Report Volume II: Efforts to Obstruct Mueller Investigation

March 22, 2019

[Only the Executive Summary of Volume II has been included; all other material has been omitted.]

EXECUTIVE SUMMARY TO VOLUME II

Our obstruction-of-justice inquiry focused on a series of actions by the President that related to the Russian-interference investigations, including the President's conduct towards the law enforcement officials overseeing the investigations and the witnesses to relevant events.

FACTUAL RESULTS OF THE OBSTRUCTION INVESTIGATION

The key issues and events we examined include the following:

The Campaign's response to reports about Russian support for Trump. During the 2016 presidential campaign, questions arose about the Russian government's apparent support for candidate Trump. After WikiLeaks released politically damaging Democratic Party emails that were reported to have been hacked by Russia, Trump publicly expressed skepticism that Russia was responsible for the hacks at the same time that he and other Campaign officials privately sought information (b) (6), (b) (7)(A), (b) (7)(B), (b) (7)(C) about any further planned WikiLeaks releases. Trump also denied having any business in or connections to Russia, even though as late as June 2016 the Trump Organization had been pursuing a licensing deal for a skyscraper to be built in Russia called Trump Tower Moscow. After the election, the President expressed concerns to advisors that reports of Russia's election interference might lead the public to question the legitimacy of his election.

Conduct involving FBI Director Comey and Michael Flynn. In mid-January 2017, incoming National Security Advisor Michael Flynn falsely denied to the Vice President, other administration officials, and FBI agents that he had talked to Russian Ambassador Sergey Kislyak about Russia's response to U.S. sanctions on Russia for its election interference. On January 27, the day after the President was told that Flynn had lied to the Vice

President and had made similar statements to the FBI, the President invited FBI Director Comey to a private dinner at the White House and told Comey that he needed loyalty. On February 14, the day after the President requested Flynn's resignation, the President told an outside advisor, "Now that we fired Flynn, the Russia thing is over." The advisor disagreed and said the investigations would continue.

Later that afternoon, the President cleared the Oval Office to have a one-on-one meeting with Comey. Referring to the FBI's investigation of Flynn, the President said, "I hope you can see your way clear to letting this go, to letting Flynn go. He is a good guy. I hope you can let this go." Shortly after requesting Flynn's resignation and speaking privately to Comey, the President sought to have Deputy National Security Advisor K.T. McFarland draft an internal letter stating that the President had not directed Flynn to discuss sanctions with Kislyak. McFarland declined because she did not know whether that was true, and a White House Counsel's Office attorney thought that the request would look like a quid pro quo for an ambassadorship she had been offered.

The President's reaction to the continuing Russia investigation. In February 2017, Attorney General Jeff Sessions began to assess whether he had to recuse himself from campaign-related investigations because of his role in the Trump Campaign. In early March, the President told White House Counsel Donald McGahn to stop Sessions from recusing. And after Sessions announced his recusal on March 2, the President expressed anger at the decision and told advisors that he should have an Attorney General who would protect him. That weekend, the President took Sessions aside at an event and urged him to "unrecuse." Later in March, Comey publicly disclosed at a congressional hearing that the FBI was investigating "the Russian government's efforts to interfere in the 2016 presidential election," including any links or coordination between the Russian government and the Trump Campaign. In the following days, the President reached out to the Director of National Intelligence and the leaders of the Central Intelligence Agency (CIA) and the National Security Agency (NSA) to ask them what they could do to publicly dispel the suggestion that the President had any connection to the Russian election-interference effort. The President also twice called Comey directly, notwithstanding guidance from McGahn to avoid direct contacts with the Department of Justice. Comey had previously assured the President that the FBI was not investigating him personally, and the President asked Comey to "lift the cloud" of the Russia investigation by saying that publicly.

The President's termination of Comey. On May 3, 2017, Comey testified in a congressional hearing, but declined to answer questions about whether the President was personally under investigation. Within days, the President decided to terminate Comey. The President insisted that the termination letter, which was written for public release, state that Comey had informed the President that he was not under investigation. The day of the firing, the White House maintained that Comey's termination resulted from independent recommendations from the Attorney General and Deputy Attorney General that Comey should be discharged for mishandling the Hillary Clinton email investigation. But the President had decided to fire Comey before hearing from the Department of Justice. The day after firing Comey, the President told Russian officials that he had "faced great pressure because of Russia," which had been "taken off" by Comey's firing. The next day, the President acknowledged in a television interview that he was going to fire Comey regardless of the Department of Justice's recommendation and that when he "decided to just do it," he was thinking that "this thing with Trump and Russia is a made-up story." In response to a question about whether he was angry with Comey about the Russia investigation, the

President said, "As far as I'm concerned, I want that thing to be absolutely done properly," adding that firing Comey "might even lengthen out the investigation."

The appointment of a Special Counsel and efforts to remove him. On May 17, 2017, the Acting Attorney General for the Russia investigation appointed a Special Counsel to conduct the investigation and related matters. The President reacted to news that a Special Counsel had been appointed by telling advisors that it was "the end of his presidency" and demanding that Sessions resign. Sessions submitted his resignation, but the President ultimately did not accept it. The President told aides that the Special Counsel had conflicts of interest and suggested that the Special Counsel therefore could not serve. The President's advisors told him the asserted conflicts were meritless and had already been considered by the Department of Justice.

On June 14, 2017, the media reported that the Special Counsel's Office was investigating whether the President had obstructed justice. Press reports called this "a major turning point" in the investigation: while Comey had told the President he was not under investigation, following Comey's firing, the President now was under investigation. The President reacted to this news with a series of tweets criticizing the Department of Justice and the Special Counsel's investigation. On June 17, 2017, the President called McGahn at home and directed him to call the Acting Attorney General and say that the Special Counsel had conflicts of interest and must be removed. McGahn did not carry out the direction, however, deciding that he would resign rather than trigger what he regarded as a potential Saturday Night Massacre.

Efforts to curtail the Special Counsel's investigation. Two days after directing McGahn to have the Special Counsel removed, the President made another attempt to affect the course of the Russia investigation. On June 19, 2017, the President met one-on-one in the Oval Office with his former campaign manager Corey Lewandowski, a trusted advisor outside the government, and dictated a message for Lewandowski to deliver to Sessions. The message said that Sessions should publicly announce that, notwithstanding his recusal from the Russia investigation, the investigation was "very unfair" to the President, the President had done nothing wrong, and Sessions planned to meet with the Special Counsel and "let [him] move forward with investigating election meddling for future elections." Lewandowski said he understood what the President wanted Sessions to do.

One month later, in another private meeting with Lewandowski on July 19, 2017, the President asked about the status of his message for Sessions to limit the Special Counsel investigation to future election interference. Lewandowski told the President that the message would be delivered soon. Hours after that meeting, the President publicly criticized Sessions in an interview with the *New York Times*, and then issued a series of tweets making it clear that Sessions's job was in jeopardy. Lewandowski did not want to deliver the President's message personally, so he asked senior White House official Rick Dearborn to deliver it to Sessions. Dearborn was uncomfortable with the task and did not follow through.

Efforts to prevent public disclosure of evidence. In the summer of 2017, the President learned that media outlets were asking questions about the June 9, 2016 meeting at Trump Tower between senior campaign officials, including Donald Trump Jr., and a Russian lawyer who was said to be offering damaging information about Hillary Clinton as "part of Russia and its government's support for Mr. Trump." On several occasions, the President directed aides not to publicly disclose the emails setting up the June 9 meeting, suggesting that the emails would not leak and that the number of lawyers with access to them should be limited. Before the emails became public, the President edited a press statement for

Trump Jr. by deleting a line that acknowledged that the meeting was with "an individual who [Trump Jr.] was told might have information helpful to the campaign" and instead said only that the meeting was about adoptions of Russian children. When the press asked questions about the President's involvement in Trump Jr.'s statement, the President's personal lawyer repeatedly denied the President had played any role.

Further efforts to have the Attorney General take control of the investigation. In early summer 2017, the President called Sessions at home and again asked him to reverse his recusal from the Russia investigation. Sessions did not reverse his recusal. In October 2017, the President met privately with Sessions in the Oval Office and asked him to "take [a] look" at investigating Clinton. In December 2017, shortly after Flynn pleaded guilty pursuant to a cooperation agreement, the President met with Sessions in the Oval Office and suggested, according to notes taken by a senior advisor, that if Sessions unrecused and took back supervision of the Russia investigation, he would be a "hero." The President told Sessions, "I'm not going to do anything or direct you to do anything. I just want to be treated fairly." In response, Sessions volunteered that he had never seen anything "improper" on the campaign and told the President there was a "whole new leadership team" in place. He did not unrecuse.

Efforts to have McGahn deny that the President had ordered him to have the Special Counsel removed. In early 2018, the press reported that the President had directed McGahn to have the Special Counsel removed in June 2017 and that McGahn had threatened to resign rather than carry out the order. The President reacted to the news stories by directing White House officials to tell McGahn to dispute the story and create a record stating he had not been ordered to have the Special Counsel removed. McGahn told those officials that the media reports were accurate in stating that the President had directed McGahn to have the Special Counsel removed. The President then met with McGahn in the Oval Office and again pressured him to deny the reports. In the same meeting, the President also asked McGahn why he had told the Special Counsel about the President's effoli to remove the Special Counsel and why McGahn took notes of his conversations with the President. McGahn refused to back away from what he remembered happening and perceived the President to be testing his mettle.

Conduct towards Flynn, Manafort, [redacted]. After Flynn withdrew from a joint defense agreement with the President and began cooperating with the government, the President's personal counsel left a message for Flynn's attorneys reminding them of the President's warm feelings towards Flynn, which he said "still remains," and asking for a "heads up" if Flynn knew "information that implicates the President." When Flynn's counsel reiterated that Flynn could no longer share information pursuant to a joint defense agreement, the President's personal counsel said he would make sure that the President knew that Flynn's actions reflected "hostility" towards the President. During Manafort's prosecution and when the jury in his criminal trial was deliberating, the President praised Manafort in public, said that Manafort was being treated unfairly, and declined to rule out a pardon. After Manafort was convicted, the President called Manafort "a brave man" for refusing to "break" and said that "flipping" "almost ought to be outlawed.". . .

Conduct involving Michael Cohen. The President's conduct towards Michael Cohen, a former Trump Organization executive, changed from praise for Cohen when he falsely minimized the President's involvement in the Trump Tower Moscow project, to castigation of Cohen when he became a cooperating witness. From September 2015 to June 2016, Cohen had pursued the Trump Tower Moscow project on behalf of the Trump Organization and had briefed candidate Trump on the project numerous times, including discussing whether Trump should travel to Russia to advance the deal. In 2017, Cohen provided false testimony to Congress about the project, including stating that he had only briefed Trump on the project three times and never discussed travel to Russia with him, in an effort to adhere to a "party line" that Cohen said was developed to minimize the President's connections to Russia. While preparing for his congressional testimony, Cohen had extensive discussions with the President's personal counsel, who, according to Cohen, said that Cohen should "stay on message" and not contradict the President. After the FBI searched Cohen's home and office in April 2018, the President publicly asserted that Cohen would not "flip," contacted him directly to tell him to "stay strong," and privately passed messages of support to him. Cohen also discussed pardons with the President's personal counsel and believed that if he stayed on message he would be taken care of. But after Cohen began cooperating with the government in the summer of 2018, the President publicly criticized him, called him a "rat," and suggested that his family members had committed crimes.

Overarching factual issues. We did not make a traditional prosecution decision about these facts, but the evidence we obtained supports several general statements about the President's conduct.

Several features of the conduct we investigated distinguish it from typical obstruction-of-justice cases. First, the investigation concerned the President, and some of his actions, such as firing the FBI director, involved facially lawful acts within his Article II authority, which raises constitutional issues discussed below. At the same time, the President's position as the head of the Executive Branch provided him with unique and powerful means of influencing official proceedings, subordinate officers, and potential witnesses—all of which is relevant to a potential obstruction-of-justice analysis. Second, unlike cases in which a subject engages in obstruction of justice to cover up a crime, the evidence we obtained did not establish that the President was involved in an underlying crime related to Russian election interference. Although the obstruction statutes do not require proof of such a crime, the absence of that evidence affects the analysis of the President's intent and requires consideration of other possible motives for his conduct. Third, many of the President's acts directed at witnesses, including discouragement of cooperation with the government and suggestions of possible future pardons, took place in public view. That circumstance is unusual, but no principle of law excludes public acts from the reach of the obstruction laws. If the likely effect of public acts is to influence witnesses or alter their testimony, the harm to the justice system's integrity is the same.

Although the series of events we investigated involved discrete acts, the overall pattern of the President's conduct towards the investigations can shed light on the nature of the President's acts and the inferences that can be drawn about his intent. In particular, the actions we investigated can be divided into two phases, reflecting a possible shift in the President's motives. The first phase covered the period from the President's first interactions with Comey through the President's firing of Comey. During that time, the President had been repeatedly told he was not personally under investigation. Soon after the firing of Comey and the appointment of the Special Counsel, however, the President became aware that his own conduct was being investigated in an obstruction-of-justice inquiry. At that point, the President engaged in a second phase of conduct, involving public attacks on the investigation, non-public efforts to control it, and efforts in both public and private to encourage witnesses not to cooperate with the investigation. Judgments about the nature of the President's motives during each phase would be informed by the totality of the evidence.

STATUTORY AND CONSTITUTIONAL DEFENSES

The President's counsel raised statutory and constitutional defenses to a possible obstruction-of-justice analysis of the conduct we investigated. We concluded that none of those legal defenses provided a basis for declining to investigate the facts.

Statutory defenses. Consistent with precedent and the Department of Justice's general approach to interpreting obstruction statutes, we concluded that several statutes could apply here. See 18 U.S.C. §§ 1503, 1505, 1512(b)(3), 1512(c)(2). Section 1512(c)(2) is an omnibus obstruction-of-justice provision that covers a range of obstructive acts directed at pending or contemplated official proceedings. No principle of statutory construction justifies narrowing the provision to cover only conduct that impairs the integrity or availability of evidence. Sections 1503 and 1505 also offer broad protection against obstructive acts directed at pending grand jury, judicial, administrative, and congressional proceedings, and they are supplemented by a provision in Section 1512(b) aimed specifically at conduct intended to prevent or hinder the communication to law enforcement of information related to a federal crime.

Constitutional defenses. As for constitutional defenses arising from the President's status as the head of the Executive Branch, we recognized that the Department of Justice and the courts have not definitively resolved these issues. We therefore examined those issues through the framework established by Supreme Court precedent governing separation-of-powers issues. The Department of Justice and the President's personal counsel have recognized that the President is subject to statutes that prohibit obstruction of justice by bribing a witness or suborning perjury because that conduct does not implicate his constitutional authority. With respect to whether the President can be found to have obstructed justice by exercising his powers under Article II of the Constitution, we concluded that Congress has authority to prohibit a President's corrupt use of his authority in order to protect the integrity of the administration of justice.

Under applicable Supreme Court precedent, the Constitution does not categorically and permanently immunize a President for obstructing justice through the use of his Article II powers. The separation-of-powers doctrine authorizes Congress to protect official proceedings, including those of courts and grand juries, from corrupt, obstructive acts regardless of their source. We also concluded that any inroad on presidential authority that would occur from prohibiting corrupt acts does not undermine the President's ability to fulfill his constitutional mission. The term "corruptly" sets a demanding standard. It requires a concrete showing that a person acted with an intent to obtain an improper advantage for himself or someone else, inconsistent with official duty and the rights of others. A preclusion of "corrupt" official action does not diminish the President's ability to exercise Article II powers. For example, the proper supervision of criminal law does not demand freedom for the President to act with a corrupt intention of shielding himself from criminal punishment, avoiding financial liability, or preventing personal embarrassment. To the contrary, a statute that prohibits official action undertaken for such corrupt purposes furthers, rather than hinders, the impartial and evenhanded administration of the law. It also aligns with the President's constitutional duty to faithfully execute the laws. Finally, we concluded that in the rare case in which a criminal investigation of the President's conduct is justified, inquiries to determine whether the President acted for a corrupt motive should not impermissibly chill his performance of his constitutionally assigned duties. The conclusion that Congress may apply the obstruction laws to the President's corrupt exercise of the powers of office accords with our constitutional system of checks and balances and the principle that no person is above the law.

CONCLUSION

Because we determined not to make a traditional prosecutorial judgment, we did not draw ultimate conclusions about the President's conduct. The evidence we obtained about the President's actions and intent presents difficult issues that would need to be resolved if we were making a traditional prosecutorial judgment. At the same time, if we had confidence after a thorough investigation of the facts that the President clearly did not commit obstruction of justice, we would so state. Based on the facts and the applicable legal standards, we are unable to reach that judgment. Accordingly, while this report does not conclude that the President committed a crime, it also does not exonerate him.

SOURCE: U.S. Department of Justice. "Report on the Investigation into Russian Interference in the 2016 Presidential Election. Volume II of II." March 22, 2019. https://www.justice.gov/storage/report_volume2.pdf.

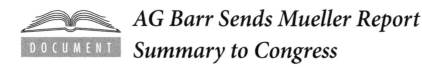

AG Barr Sends Mueller Report Summary to Congress

March 24, 2019

[Addresses for the four members in receipt of the letter have been omitted.]

Dear Chairman Graham, Chairman Nadler, Ranking Member Feinstein, and Ranking Member Collins:

As a supplement to the notification provided on Friday, March 22, 2019, I am writing today to advise you of the principal conclusions reached by Special Counsel Robert S. Mueller III and to inform you about the status of my initial review of the report he has prepared.

The Special Counsel's Report

On Friday, the Special Counsel submitted to me a "confidential report explaining the prosecution or declination decisions" he has reached, as required by 28 C.F.R. 600.8(c). This report is entitled "Report on the Investigation into Russian Interference in the 2016 Presidential Election." Although my review is ongoing, I believe that it is in the public interest to describe the report and to summarize the principal conclusions reached by the Special Counsel and the results of his investigation.

The report explains that the Special Counsel and his staff thoroughly investigated allegations that members of the presidential campaign of Donald J. Trump, and others associated with it, conspired with the Russian government in its efforts to interfere in the 2016 U.S. presidential election, or sought to obstruct the related federal investigations. In the report, the Special Counsel noted that, in completing his investigation, he employed 19 lawyers who were assisted by a team of approximately 40 FBI agents, intelligence analysts, forensic accountants, and other professional staff. The Special Counsel issued more than 2,800 subpoenas, executed nearly 500 search warrants, obtained more than 230 orders for communication records, issued almost 50 orders authorizing use of pen registers, made 13 requests to foreign governments for evidence, and interviewed approximately 500 witnesses.

The Special Counsel obtained a number of indictments and convictions of individuals and entities in connection with his investigation, all of which have been publicly disclosed. During the course of his investigation, the Special Counsel also referred several matters to other offices for further action. The report does not recommend any further indictments, nor did the Special Counsel obtain any sealed indictments that have yet to be made public. Below, I summarize the principal conclusions laid out in the Special Counsel's report.

Russian Interference in the 2016 U.S. Presidential Election. The Special Counsel's investigation determined that there were two main Russian efforts to influence the 2016 election. The first involved attempts by a Russian organization, the Internet Research Agency (IRA), to conduct disinformation and social media operations in the United States designed to sow social discord, eventually with the aim of interfering with the election. As noted above, the Special Counsel did not find that any U.S. person or Trump campaign official or associate conspired or knowingly coordinated with the IRA in its efforts, although the Special Counsel brought criminal charges against a number of Russian nationals and entities in connection with these activities.[1]

The second element involved the Russian government's efforts to conduct computer hacking operations designed to gather and disseminate information to influence the election. The Special Counsel found that Russian government actors successfully hacked into computers and obtained emails from persons associated with the Clinton campaign and Democratic Party organizations, and publicly disseminated those materials through various intermediaries, including WikiLeaks. Based on these activities, the Special Counsel brought criminal charges against a number of Russian military officers for conspiring to hack into computers in the United States for the purposes of influencing the election. But as noted above, the Special Counsel did not find that the Trump campaign, or anyone associated with it, conspired or coordinated with the Russian government in these efforts, despite multiple offers from Russian-affiliated individuals to assist the Trump campaign.

Obstruction of Justice. The report's second part addresses a number of actions by the President—most of which have been the subject of public reporting—that the Special Counsel investigated as potentially raising obstruction-of-justice concerns. After making a "thorough factual investigation" into these matters, the Special Counsel considered whether to evaluate the conduct under Department standards regarding prosecution and conviction but ultimately determined not to make a traditional prosecutorial judgment. The Special Counsel therefore did not draw a conclusion—one way or the other—as to whether the examined conduct constituted obstruction. Instead, for each of the relevant actions investigated, the report sets out evidence on both sides of the question and leaves unresolved what the Special Counsel views as "difficult issues" of law and fact concerning whether the President's actions and intent could be viewed as obstruction. The Special Counsel's report states that "while this report does not conclude that the President committed a crime, it also does not exonerate him."

---

[1] In assessing potential conspiracy charges, the Special Counsel also considered whether members of the Trump campaign "coordinated" with Russian election interference activities. The Special Counsel defined "coordination" as an "agreement—tacit or express—between the Trump Campaign and the Russian government on election interference."

The Special Counsel's decision to describe the facts of his obstruction investigation without reaching any legal conclusions leaves it to the Attorney General to determine whether the conduct described in the report constitutes a crime. Over the course of the investigation, the Special Counsel's office engaged in discussions with certain Department officials regarding many of the legal and factual matters at issue in the Special Counsel's obstruction investigation. After reviewing the Special Counsel's final report on these issues; consulting with Department officials, including the Office of Legal Counsel; and applying the principles of federal prosecution that guide our charging decisions, Deputy Attorney General Rod Rosenstein and I have concluded that the evidence developed during the Special Counsel's investigation is not sufficient to establish that the President committed an obstruction-of-justice offense. Our determination was made without regard to, and is not based on, the constitutional considerations that surround the indictment and criminal prosecution of a sitting president.[2]

In making this determination, we noted that the Special Counsel recognized that "the evidence does not establish that the President was involved in an underlying crime related to Russian election interference," and that, while not determinative, the absence of such evidence bears upon the President's intent with respect to obstruction. Generally speaking, to obtain and sustain an obstruction conviction, the government would need to prove beyond a reasonable doubt that a person, acting with corrupt intent, engaged in obstructive conduct with a sufficient nexus to a pending or contemplated proceeding. In cataloguing the President's actions, many of which took place in public view, the report identifies no actions that, in our judgment, constitute obstructive conduct, had a nexus to a pending or contemplated proceeding, and were done with corrupt intent, each of which, under the Department's principles of federal prosecution guiding charging decisions, would need to be proven beyond a reasonable doubt to establish an obstruction-of-justice offense.

Status of the Department's Review

The relevant regulations contemplate that the Special Counsel's report will be a "confidential report" to the Attorney General. See Office of Special Counsel, 64 Fed. Reg. 27,038, 37,040-41 (July 9, 1999). As I have previously stated, however, I am mindful of the public interest in this matter. For that reason, my goal and intent is to release as much of the Special Counsel's report as I can consistent with applicable law, regulations, and Departmental policies.

Based on my discussions with the Special Counsel and my initial review, it is apparent that the report contains material that is or could be subject to Federal Rule of Civil Procedure 6(e), which imposes restrictions on the use and disclosure of information relating to "matter[s] occurring before [a] grand jury." Fed. R. Crim. P. 6(e)(2)(B). Rule 6(e) generally limits disclosure of certain grand jury information in a criminal investigation and prosecution. Id. Disclosure of 6(e) material beyond the strict limits set forth in the rule is a crime in certain circumstances. See, e.g., 18 U.S.C. 401(3). This restriction protects the integrity of grand jury proceedings and ensures that the unique and invaluable investigative powers of a grand jury are used strictly for their intended criminal justice function.

---

[2] See A Sitting President's Amenability to Indictment and Criminal Prosecution, 24 Op. O.L.C, 222 (2000).

Given these restrictions, the schedule for processing the report depends in part on how quickly the Department can identify the 6(e) material that by law cannot be made public. I have requested the assistance of the Special Counsel in identifying all 6(e) information contained in the report as quickly as possible. Separately, I also must identify any information that could impact other ongoing matters, including those that the Special Counsel has referred to other offices. As soon as that process is complete, I will be in a position to move forward expeditiously in determining what can be released in light of applicable law, regulations, and Departmental policies.

***

As I observed in my initial notification, the Special Counsel regulations provide that "the Attorney General may determine that public release of" notifications to your respective Committees "would be in the public interest." 28 C.F.R. 600.9(c). I have so determined, and I will disclose the letter to the public after delivering it to you.

Sincerely,
William P. Barr
Attorney General

Source: U.S. Department of Justice. "Attorney General's Letter to House and Senate Judiciary Committee." March 24, 2019. https://www.justice.gov/ag/page/file/1147981/download.

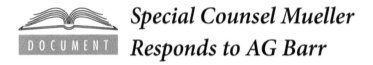

Special Counsel Mueller Responds to AG Barr

March 27, 2019

The Honorable William P. Barr
Attorney General of the United States
Department of Justice
Washington, D.C.

Re: Report of the Special Counsel on the Investigation Into Russian Interference in the 2016 Presidential Election and Obstruction of Justice (March 2019)

Dear Attorney General Barr:

I previously sent you a letter dated March 25, 2019, that enclosed the introduction and executive summary for each volume of the Special Counsel's report marked with redactions to remove any information that potentially could be protected by Federal Rule of Criminal Procedure 6(e); that concerned declination decisions; or that related to a charged case. We also had marked an additional two sentences for review and have now confirmed that these sentences can be released publicly.

Accordingly, the enclosed documents are in a form that can be released to the public consistent with legal requirements and Department policies. I am requesting that you provide these materials to Congress and authorize their public release at this time.

As we stated in our meeting of March 5 and reiterated to the Department early in the afternoon of March 24, the introductions and executive summaries of our two-volume report accurately summarize this Office's work and conclusions. The summary letter the Department sent to Congress and released to the public late in the afternoon of March 24 did not fully capture the context, nature, and substance of this Office's work and conclusions. We communicated that concern to the Department on the morning of March 25. There is now public confusion about critical aspects of the results of our investigation. This threatens to undermine a central purpose for which the Department appointed the Special Counsel: to assure full public confidence in the outcome of the investigations. See Department of Justice, Press Release (May 17, 2017).

While we understand that the Department is reviewing the full report to determine what is appropriate for public release—a process that our Office is working with you to complete—that process need not delay release of the enclosed materials. Release at this time would alleviate the misunderstandings that have arisen and would answer congressional and public questions about the nature and outcome of our investigation. It would also accord with the standard for public release of notifications to Congress cited in your letter. See 28 C.F.R. 609(c) ("the Attorney General may determine the public release" of congressional notifications "would be in the public interest").

Sincerely yours,
Robert S. Mueller, III
Special Counsel

SOURCE: U.S. Department of Justice. "Letter from Special Counsel Robert Mueller to Attorney General William Barr." March 27, 2019.

OTHER HISTORIC DOCUMENTS OF INTEREST

FROM THIS VOLUME

- House Passes Articles of Impeachment against President Trump; President Responds, p. 667

FROM PREVIOUS *HISTORIC DOCUMENTS*

- Cohen, Manafort Reach Plea Agreements in Special Counsel Probe, *2018*, p. 460
- FBI Director Fired, Testifies before Congress, *2017*, p. 247
- Former FBI Director Robert Mueller Appointed Special Counsel on U.S. Election–Russia Investigation, Issues Indictments, *2017*, p. 270

President Trump Announces Victory against ISIL, Syria Troop Withdrawal

MARCH 23 AND OCTOBER 14, 2019

On March 23, 2019, President Donald Trump announced the United States and its partners had defeated the Islamic State of Iraq and the Levant (ISIL) in Syria. At the time, there were 1,000 U.S. service members still in the country, who partnered with Syrian Defense Forces to ensure the terrorist group would not regain its foothold. In October, surprising military leaders, members of Congress, and some in his own cabinet, President Trump announced he was withdrawing U.S. troops from northeastern Syria and ceding the responsibility for protecting the area against ISIL to Turkey, which had just announced its intent to invade a portion of Syria where pro-U.S. Kurdish forces were located. The decision drew sharp backlash from both Democrats and Republicans, who accused the president of deserting the Kurds, a key partner in the fight against ISIL.

U.S. AND TURKISH POLICY TOWARD SYRIA

From the onset of Syria's civil war in 2011, American engagement in the country lacked a clear strategy. The United States first imposed sanctions in 2011 as a perfunctory response to reported war crimes. Two years later, then-president Barack Obama described the use of chemical weapons against civilians in Syria as a "red line" that would provoke a U.S. reprisal against the government of Syrian president Bashar al Assad. When evidence indicated Assad had used such weapons that summer, the Obama administration considered a range of options for military action but ultimately opted for a Russia-brokered deal to eliminate the majority of the Assad government's chemical weapons stockpiles.

President Obama acknowledged his fluid policy response to Syrian chemical attacks would likely diminish perceived U.S. credibility in the region. However, he held the decision ensured a more comprehensive cleanup of Syria's weapons than an American military campaign, something that had scant support from the U.S. public or Congress.

American troops would eventually arrive in Syria in 2014. Their involvement began as an air campaign against ISIL in September 2014, a spillover from U.S. operations against the terrorist group that had commenced a month earlier in Iraq. U.S. forces subsequently joined the Syrian Democratic Forces (SDF) on the ground. The SDF, comprised of Kurdish and Arab fighters, was formed in 2015 under the Kurdish leadership of the People's Protection Units (YPG). With U.S. support and coalition air cover, the SDF cleared ISIL strongholds from Syria by March 2019, sustaining thousands of casualties in the process.

Turkey, heretofore a secondary player in the conflict, had long designated the YPG as a terrorist organization. Turkish president Recep Tayyip Erdoğan initially called for Syria's Assad to step down. As civil war took hold, Erdoğan later sought to leverage Turkey's status as a host country for Syrian refugees by lobbying for a safe zone on the other side of its border with Syria. This provided a pretext for sporadic Turkish campaigns against

Kurdish-majority towns in the area. (Turkey views its own Kurdish minority as disloyal to the Erdoğan government.)

President Trump Declares Victory in Syria

In his campaign to succeed President Obama, Trump endorsed a U.S. retreat from conflicts in the Middle East. In December 2018, he floated the idea of a U.S. withdrawal from Syria following a phone call with Erdoğan. By March 2019, President Trump announced victory over ISIL in Syria and Iraq.

In announcing that the "caliphate" had been defeated, he warned that ISIL could "resurface" but noted "they have lost all prestige and power. They are losers and will always be losers." The president promised the United States would partner with other nations to eliminate terrorist networks around the globe and would "remain vigilant against ISIS by aligning global counterterrorism efforts to fight ISIS until it is finally defeated wherever it operates." With victory declared, 1,000 U.S. troops would be left in place along the Syria–Turkey border to deter any new conflict.

Over the course of 2019, the SDF complied with American requests to fill in the barricades between their towns and the Turkish border, and undertook joint border patrols with U.S. troops. The SDF effectively governed one-third of Syria, with Turkey holding small gains by the northwest border. The Assad government regained control of the remaining territories.

This new normal was upended on October 6, when President Erdoğan informed President Trump that Turkish forces would invade Syria to secure a roughly twenty-mile-deep buffer-zone between the two countries for which Erdoğan had unsuccessfully lobbied for Turkish control in international forums. President Trump responded by pulling out the remaining 1,000 U.S. troops from Syria, arguing Turkey needed the border in northeastern Syria to be "cleaned out."

The announcement caught both U.S. military personnel and foreign partners by surprise. The Pentagon had been slow to respond to previous declarations for troop withdrawal in Syria, seeking to protect ethnic Kurds in the northeastern part of the country near Turkey, who were a key U.S. ally in the fight against ISIL. This time, troops staged a haphazard exit, sometimes under fire and with interrupted supply lines, as Turkey moved in. Concurrently, videos from the area appeared to indicate Russian soldiers had moved into the vacated U.S. bases.

After their withdrawal, U.S. troops were redeployed at least temporarily to western Iraq, without the permission of the Iraqi government. The Iraqi president, Barham Salih, described plans for the sudden pullout as creating "a perfect storm" in his region that empowered subdued terrorist groups to pose a fresh threat to Iraq's sovereignty. The timing of the redeployment also coincided with widespread public demonstrations in Iraq against corruption and stagnant living standards, which called for the removal of the government.

Swift International Criticism Draws U.S. Response

Facing bipartisan domestic criticism of the sudden policy reversal that put a U.S. ally— the Kurds—in the crosshairs, President Trump dispatched Vice President Mike Pence and Secretary of State Mike Pompeo to negotiate with Turkey. Turkey agreed to suspend operations for 120 hours to allow the Kurds to retreat from targeted territory. Media reports suggested the cease-fire was loosely adhered to by all parties concerned; however, as attacks continued, many Kurdish militias opted to remain in place and defend their villages. Still, upwards of 200,000 people in northeast Syria were displaced by Turkey's October campaign.

After U.S. troops left, the SDF cooperated with Syrian government forces to push back against Turkish troops. Erdoğan took his negotiations for additional land and power in Syria to Russia's president, Vladimir Putin, the region's emerging powerbroker. On October 22, the two parties agreed that Russian troops would take over the patrols previously conducted by U.S. forces, to be performed in tandem with the Turkish military in the new buffer zone. Under Russian control, the fate of the Kurds remains uncertain, though some have speculated that one possible outcome could be their integration in the 5th Corps, an international unit in the Syrian Army directed by Russia.

Impact of U.S. Withdrawal

International analysts expect the U.S. withdrawal from Syria will empower Russia along with other U.S. rivals. Iran, also a supporter of the Assad government, could gain another overland access route for supplying its Hezbollah allies in Lebanon. ISIL also stands to benefit: ISIL fighters and their family members are detained in Kurdish prisons. As Kurdish officers drew down from their positions, some militants were able to escape, and the fear is they could either reactivate local sleeper cells or surreptitiously return to their countries of origin to execute attacks.

Strategic adversaries of the United States, including Iran, Russia, and myriad militant groups, all stand to gain from its disorganized disengagement from Syria and the sudden dissolution of its alliance with the SDF. The crisis is likely to push Turkey further into Russia's orbit and drive another cleavage through the North Atlantic Treaty Organization (NATO), a key Russian foreign policy objective. The United States is also exposed to new risks in the event of a regional altercation, in part because Turkey, an erstwhile ally in NATO, stores a regional supply of U.S. nuclear weapons. Turkey's campaign against the SDF, which it considers a terrorist group, increases its tolerance of retaliatory sanctions and the threat of bilateral conflict. Meanwhile, disputes between overlapping Turkish and Syrian forces are being routed through Russian intermediaries, who have succeeded U.S. officials in the borderlands.

In vacating Syrian territory, the United States also surrendered an intelligence network informed by the SDF. Information provided by the group was critical to planning the October 27 raid that killed Abu Bakr al-Baghdadi, the head of ISIL. The raid was expedited by military personnel after the withdrawal was announced, in order to execute the maneuver while they still had a footprint and informants. President Trump later praised Russia and Turkey for facilitating the operation by opening their airspace but only briefly thanked the Kurds for providing "some information that turned out to be helpful."

Toward the end of October, President Trump appeared to reconsider a complete exit from Syria, suggesting the Syrian oilfields could be leveraged to repay the United States for wartime expenses. The suggestion is precluded by international law, however. Additionally, private sector investors have claims that predate the war, and the oilfields themselves are too dilapidated after years of turmoil even to meet local supply demands.

—Anastazia Clouting

Following is a statement by President Donald Trump on March 23, 2019, on the liberation of ISIL-controlled territory in Syria; and an October 14, 2019, statement on Turkey's military actions in Syria, noting that President Trump had ordered all U.S. troops out of the area.

President Trump Declares ISIL Defeat

March 23, 2019

I am pleased to announce that, together with our partners in the Global Coalition To Defeat ISIS, including the Iraqi Security Forces and the Syrian Democratic Forces, the United States has liberated all ISIS-controlled territory in Syria and Iraq, 100 percent of the "caliphate."

Just 2 years ago, ISIS controlled a vast amount of territory in both Iraq and Syria. Since then, we have retaken more than 20,000 square miles of land and liberated millions of Syrians and Iraqis from ISIS's "caliphate." ISIS's loss of territory is further evidence of its false narrative, which tries to legitimize a record of savagery that includes brutal executions, the exploitation of children as soldiers, and the sexual abuse and murder of women and children. To all of the young people on the internet believing in ISIS's propaganda, you will be dead if you join. Think instead about having a great life.

While on occasion these cowards will resurface, they have lost all prestige and power. They are losers and will always be losers. We will remain vigilant against ISIS by aligning global counterterrorism efforts to fight ISIS until it is finally defeated wherever it operates. The United States will defend American interests whenever and wherever necessary. We will continue to work with our partners and allies to totally crush radical Islamic terrorists.

SOURCE: Executive Office of the President. "Statement on the Liberation of Territory Controlled by the Islamic State of Iraq and Syria Terrorist Organization." March 23, 2019. *Compilation of Presidential Documents* 2019, no. 00169 (March 23, 2019). https://www.govinfo.gov/content/pkg/DCPD-201900169/pdf/DCPD-201900169.pdf.

President Trump Comments on Turkey's Actions in Syria

October 14, 2019

I will soon be issuing an Executive order authorizing the imposition of sanctions against current and former officials of the Government of Turkey and any persons contributing to Turkey's destabilizing actions in northeast Syria. Likewise, the steel tariffs will be increased back up to 50 percent, the level prior to reduction in May. The United States will also immediately stop negotiations, being led by the Department of Commerce, with respect to a $100 billion trade deal with Turkey.

This order will enable the United States to impose powerful additional sanctions on those who may be involved in serious human rights abuses, obstructing a cease-fire, preventing displaced persons from returning home, forcibly repatriating refugees, or threatening the peace, security, or stability in Syria. The order will authorize a broad range of consequences, including financial sanctions, the blocking of property, and barring entry into the United States.

Since my first day in office, the Trump administration has worked tirelessly to preserve the safety and security of the United States and its citizens. The United States and our partners have liberated 100 percent of ISIS's ruthless territorial caliphate. Turkey must not put these gains in jeopardy. Turkey must also prioritize the protection of civilians, particularly vulnerable ethnic and religious minorities in northeast Syria. Indiscriminate targeting of civilians, destruction of civilian infrastructure, and targeting of ethnic or religious minorities is unacceptable. Additionally, the return of refugees must be conducted in a safe, voluntary, and dignified manner.

Turkey's military offensive is endangering civilians and threatening peace, security, and stability in the region. I have been perfectly clear with President Erdoğan: Turkey's action is precipitating a humanitarian crisis and setting conditions for possible war crimes. Turkey must ensure the safety of civilians, including religious and ethnic minorities, and is now, or may be in the future, responsible for the ongoing detention of ISIS terrorists in the region. Unfortunately, Turkey does not appear to be mitigating the humanitarian effects of its invasion.

As I have said, I am withdrawing the remaining United States servicemembers from northeast Syria. As United States forces have defeated the ISIS physical caliphate, United States troops coming out of Syria will now redeploy and remain in the region to monitor the situation and prevent a repeat of 2014, when the neglected threat of ISIS raged across Syria and Iraq. A small footprint of United States forces will remain at Al Tanf Garrison in southern Syria to continue to disrupt remnants of ISIS.

The United States will aggressively use economic sanctions to target those who enable, facilitate, and finance these heinous acts in Syria. I am fully prepared to swiftly destroy Turkey's economy if Turkish leaders continue down this dangerous and destructive path.

SOURCE: Executive Office of the President. "Statement on Turkey's Actions in Northeast Syria." October 14, 2019. *Compilation of Presidential Documents* 2019, no. 00721 (October 14, 2019). https://www.gov info.gov/content/pkg/DCPD-201900721/pdf/DCPD-201900721.pdf.

OTHER HISTORIC DOCUMENTS OF INTEREST

FROM THIS VOLUME

FROM PREVIOUS *HISTORIC DOCUMENTS*

- President Trump, United Nations Respond to Chemical Attack in Syria, *2017*, p. 224
- Syria Peace Talks Begin, *2016*, p. 68
- Aleppo Returned to Syrian Government Control; Russia Backs New Trilateral Talks, *2016*, p. 655
- United Nations–Brokered Syrian Peace Talks Conclude without Agreement, *2014*, p. 31
- President Obama Remarks on Conflict in Syria, *2013*, p. 411

April

Facebook, Twitter, and Google Executives Testify on Hate Speech and Conservative Bias

APRIL 9 AND 10, 2019

In April 2019, representatives from Facebook, Google, and Twitter testified in two separate hearings before the House and Senate to address hate speech and an alleged bias toward liberal content. In the House Judiciary Committee, Facebook and Google executives addressed criticism that they were not doing enough to combat hate speech and the spread of white nationalism on their platforms. Both representatives explained that the companies had, in recent years, increased the hiring of content reviewers and implemented new artificial intelligence tools to identify content for removal. However, the social media giants admitted that the sheer volume of content makes it difficult to locate everything. One day later, Twitter and Facebook spoke before the Senate Judiciary Committee Subcommittee on the Constitution, where they were accused by Republican members of suppressing conservative content from being shared on their platforms. Both representatives vehemently denied that they actively removed content based solely on the political leaning of the message.

SOCIAL MEDIA PLATFORMS WORK TO ELIMINATE HATEFUL CONTENT

Throughout 2019, Facebook, Twitter, and YouTube (which is owned by Google) all expanded policies and announced new plans to combat the proliferation of hate speech on their platforms. In March, Facebook announced it was enhancing its effort to ban white nationalism and separatism—not just white supremacy, which it had previously banned. Two months later, the company began removing the accounts of far-right figures for violating its hate speech policies. Deactivated accounts included those held by InfoWars founder Alex Jones (and all InfoWars fan pages); conservative commentators Milo Yiannopoulos, Paul Joseph Watson, and Laura Loomer; and Nation of Islam leader Louis Farrakhan. In an announcement, Facebook defended the move, saying it has "always banned individuals or organizations that promote or engage in violence and hate, regardless of their ideology." Jones called the decision "authoritarian," while Watson told followers on Twitter, "In an authoritarian society controlled by a handful of Silicon Valley giants, all dissent must be purged."

In June, YouTube expanded its own long-standing policy against hate speech. "We're taking another step in our hate speech policy by specifically prohibiting videos alleging that a group is superior in order to justify discrimination, segregation or exclusion based on qualities like age, gender, race, caste, religion, sexual orientation or veteran status." The announcement said the platform would also "remove content denying that well-documented violent events, like the Holocaust or the shooting at Sandy Hook Elementary, took place." YouTube expressed a hope that this expanded policy would add to the success of its earlier regulation, introduced in 2017, that limited the ability to share and comment on white supremacist content. According to the company, that policy reduced views of videos supporting white supremacy by an average of 80 percent.

In July, Twitter issued a policy on hate speech that targets religious groups to better fall in line with regulations already in place on Facebook and YouTube. Citing evidence that dehumanizing language increases the risk of offline violence against certain groups, Twitter said, "We're expanding our rules against hateful conduct to include language that dehumanizes others on the basis of religion." Twitter also indicated that it would in the future consider banning hateful content targeted at marginalized groups, including homosexuals or racial minorities, but that it needed first to identify the most sensitive way to do that. "There are additional factors we need to better understand and be able to address before we expand this rule to address language directed at other protected groups," the company said. In October, Twitter released a policy addressing hate speech by world leaders, making clear that those individuals "are not above our policies entirely." Therefore, it would remove content or entire accounts held by world leaders if their content fell into a set of categories, including promotion of terrorism, direct threats of violence, encouraging self-harm, or posting a private individual's personal information. "In other cases involving a world leader, we will err on the side of leaving the content up if there is a clear public interest in doing so," Twitter said. That last statement drew the ire of some on the left, who were pushing the social media company to remove content shared by President Donald Trump that it claimed incites violence. In response, Twitter said that decisions about content or account removal are "not that simple" and that "the actions we take and policies we develop will set precedent around online speech and we owe it to the people we serve to be deliberate and considered in what we do," adding that "context matters."

GOOGLE AND FACEBOOK TESTIFY BEFORE THE HOUSE

The House Judiciary Committee's announcement of a hearing on hate speech on social media platforms came just after the Christchurch shooting at two mosques in New Zealand that killed more than fifty people. The shooting was livestreamed on Facebook before the content was caught and pulled down. At the same time, the United States was experiencing its own rise in hate crimes. According to the Southern Poverty Law Center, hate crimes rose 30 percent from 2015 through 2017, and there were more than 1,000 known hate groups operating in the country. In organizing the hearing, the panel said it would review "the impact white nationalist groups have on American communities and the spread of white identity ideology" and "what social media companies can do" to stop its spread.

Testifying at the House hearing were Neil Potts, Facebook's public policy director, and Alexandria Walden, a counsel for free expression and human rights at Google. In opening the hearing, Rep. Jerry Nadler, D-N.Y., called white supremacy an "urgent crisis in our country" and said that social media sites serve "as conduits to spread vitriolic hate messages to every home." Congress, he added, "has failed to take seriously the threat." Both Potts and Walden explained to the committee the lengths to which their platforms go in an effort to stop hateful messaging but expressed that these efforts must be balanced against a respect for free speech.

"I want to state clearly that every Google product that hosts user content prohibits incitement to violence and hate speech against individuals or groups based on particular attributes, including race, ethnicity, gender, religion, and veteran status. We view both as grave social ills," Walden said in her opening statement. But, she added, "YouTube's commitment to free expression and access to information means that we sometimes preserve views that may be objectionable or offensive." To achieve balance, the company relies heavily on both humans and machines to help identify content that violates their hate speech policies. The decision to permanently remove content is always made by an individual reviewer because machines can sometimes incorrectly flag content that may be questionable but that does not truly violate any policies. In the fourth quarter of 2018, Google was able to remove 58,000 videos flagged for review as hateful or harassing.

Potts echoed Walden's remarks, noting that as a community of two billion monthly users, the site must constantly evolve to balance free speech with protection. "I want to be clear: There is no place for terrorism and hate on Facebook. We remove content that incites violence, or that bullies, harasses, or threatens others when we become aware of it," Potts said. However, he added that "determining what content should and should not be removed is not always simple." In addition to relying on artificial intelligence, employees, and volunteer staff to evaluate whether content is allowed, Facebook is also in the process of creating a review board so that content creators can easily appeal any removal decisions. Potts also called for industry-wide standards to make it easier for social media platforms to determine how to review, allow, or remove content in a standardized way.

Although some Republican members of the panel shared the Democrats' concern about the rise of hate speech, a few denounced remarks by their Democratic colleague Rep. Ilhan Omar, D-Minn., as hate speech. The freshman representative was accused of anti-Semitism after comments she made about the American Israel Public Affairs Committee, a powerful lobbying group that supports pro-Israel policies. This sparked a particularly contentious moment during the hearing, which was broken only when Nadler was given a news report indicating that YouTube had to shut down a livestream of the hearing shortly after it began because of the hateful comments coming in. Nadler read some of the comments out loud, and then said, "This just illustrates part of the problem we're dealing with." Rep. Louie Gohmert, R-Tex., responded, "Could that be another hate hoax?" and urged colleagues to "keep an open mind."

Senate Holds Hearing on Social Media Bias

On April 10, the Senate Judiciary Committee's Subcommittee on the Constitution held a separate hearing related to social media companies, this time on whether the platforms actively suppressed conservative voices. Facebook and Twitter were invited to testify. Google was expected to join them and proposed sending its head of conservative outreach, but according to media reports Sen. Ted Cruz, R-Tex., the committee chair, rejected the idea as a violation of committee requirements regarding seniority and the committee instead planned to hold a separate hearing with Google only on the subject of political bias at a later date.

This was not the first time Republicans in Congress sought to address their concerns about liberal bias in Silicon Valley and its impact on the content permitted on social media platforms. In July 2018, Facebook, Google, and Twitter testified before the House Judiciary Committee on their filtering policies that remove certain types of content. The platforms admitted that neither the human reviewers nor automated algorithms are perfect, but that they have not worked to eliminate conservative voices. Suppression of conservative views is also a favorite talking point of President Trump, who in March tweeted that social media harbors a hatred for a "certain group of people that happen to be in power, that happen to have won the election."

Cruz, who led the more than three-hour April 2019 hearing, opened by saying that "not only does big tech have the power to silence voices with which they disagree, but big tech has the power to collate a person's feed in a way that agrees with their political agenda." He added that multiple reports show a "consistent pattern of political bias and censorship on the part of big tech." Sen. Marsha Blackburn, R-Tenn., characterized this bias by telling the committee that a campaign ad she posted was barred by Twitter before being later allowed on the site. Twitter's representative, Carlos Monje, apologized on behalf of the company, adding that Twitter has removed both liberal and conservative content—sometimes in error—and later reversed its decision.

Facebook denied it actively attempted to stop conservative messaging from spreading on its platform, calling that "directly contrary to Facebook's mission." Twitter came armed with data to disprove the Republican argument. It had tracked tweets by Republican and Democratic members of Congress during the five weeks leading up to the hearing and found no difference in the reach of messages shared by either party.

While Democrats dismissed the hearing as nothing more than politics and criticized Republicans for failing to pay better attention to the rise of hate speech and disinformation, which they viewed as the larger problem, Cruz proposed that Congress could take regulatory action to require social media platforms to allow both liberal and conservative ideas to be equally shared. His suggestions included ensuring the companies could not be held liable for content their users post and share, and looking more carefully at antitrust issues related to the social media giants. However, Cruz cautioned, he did not want the government to become the "speech police."

—Heather Kerrigan

Following are the opening statements delivered before the House Judiciary Committee hearing on the spread of hate speech on social media on April 9, 2019, by Alexandria Walden of Google and Neil Potts of Facebook; and the opening statements of Potts and Twitter's Carlos Monje on April 10, 2019, before the Senate Committee on the Judiciary Subcommittee on the Constitution hearing regarding conservative bias on social media.

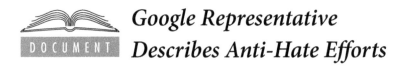

Google Representative Describes Anti-Hate Efforts

April 9, 2019

I. INTRODUCTION

Chairman Nadler, Ranking Member Collins, and members of the Committee: Thank you for the opportunity to appear before you today. I appreciate your leadership on the important issues of hate speech and free expression online, and welcome the opportunity to discuss Google's work in these areas.

My name is Alexandria Walden, and I serve as the global policy lead for human rights and free expression for Google. Throughout my career, I have worked on a number of issues in the civil and human rights field, including criminal justice reform, violence against women, and voting rights. In my work at Google, and specifically with YouTube, I advise the company on how we can preserve our deep commitment to free expression and access to information in a complicated global operating environment. As part of these efforts, I am especially mindful of how these concepts can be a cornerstone for human rights defenders around the world.

Broadly, the Internet has been a force for creativity, learning, and access to information. At Google, supporting this free flow of ideas is core to our mission to organize and make the world's information universally accessible and useful. We build tools that empower users to access, create, and share information like never before—giving them more choice, opportunity, and exposure to a diversity of opinions. Products like YouTube, for example, have expanded economic opportunity for small businesses to market and sell their goods; have given artists, creators, and journalists a platform to share their work, connect with an audience, and enrich civic discourse; and have enabled billions to benefit from a bigger, broader understanding of the world. In addition, digital platforms like YouTube have long been a place for breaking news, exposing injustices, and sharing content from places without access to other forms of media. The economic benefits have also never been clearer: many creators make a living through the content they post on the platform. YouTube channels making over six figures in revenue are up 40 percent over the last year.

This openness has democratized how stories, and whose stories, get told. It has created a space for communities to tell their own stories. And it has created a platform where anyone can be a creator and can succeed. Around 2 billion people come to YouTube every month. We see over 500 hours of video uploaded every minute—making it one of the largest living collections of human culture ever assembled in one place. The vast majority of this content is positive—ranging from how-to videos, family vloggers, and funny pet videos, to educational and cultural content and more. In fact, learning and educational content drives over a billion views on YouTube every single day.

We strive to make information from the web available to all our users, but not all speech is protected. We respect the laws of the nearly 200 countries and territories in which we offer services. Once we are on notice of content that may violate local law, we evaluate it and block it for the relevant jurisdiction. For many issues, such as privacy, defamation, or hate speech, our legal obligations may vary country by country as different jurisdictions have come to different conclusions about how to deal with these complex issues. In the case of all legal removals, we share information about government requests for removal in our Transparency Report.

We know, however, that the very platforms that have enabled these societal benefits may also be abused, ranging from the annoying, like spam, to the criminal, like child pornography. This is why in addition to being guided by local law, we have Community Guidelines our users have to follow.

Before I explain how we enforce our policies, I want to state clearly that every Google product that hosts user content prohibits incitement to violence and hate speech against individuals or groups based on particular attributes, including race, ethnicity, gender, religion, and veteran status. We view both as grave social ills, so our policies go well beyond what the United States requires.

We are deeply troubled by the recent increase in hate and violence in the world, particularly by the acts of terrorism and violent extremism in New Zealand. We take these issues seriously and want to be a part of the solution.

II. YOUTUBE ENFORCEMENT

Tough policies have to be coupled with tough enforcement. Over the past two years, we have invested heavily in machines and people to quickly identify and remove content that violates our policies against incitement to violence and hate speech:

1) YouTube's enforcement system starts from the point at which a user uploads a video. If it is somewhat similar to videos that already violate our policies, it is sent for humans to review. If they determine that it violates our policies, they remove it and the system makes a "digital fingerprint" or hash of the video so it can't be uploaded again. In the fourth quarter of 2018, over 70% of the more than 8 million videos reviewed and removed were first flagged by a machine, the majority of which were removed before a single view was received.

2) Machine learning technology is what helps us find this content and enforce our policies at scale. But hate and violent extremism are nuanced and constantly evolving, which is why we also rely on experts to find videos the algorithm might be missing. Some of these experts sit at our intel desk, which sits in-house and proactively looks for new trends in content that might violate our policies. We also allow expert NGOs and governments to notify us of bad content in bulk through our Trusted Flagger program. We reserve the final decision on whether to remove videos they flag, but we benefit immensely from their expertise.

3) Finally, we go beyond enforcing our policies by creating programs to promote counterspeech on our platforms to present narratives and elevate the voices that are most credible in speaking out against hate, violence, and terrorism.

a) For example, our Creators for Change program supports creators who are tackling tough issues, including extremism and hate, by building empathy and acting as positive role models. There are 60 million video views of Creators for Change content to date; 731,000 total watch time hours of Creators for Change content; and through "Local chapters" of Creators for Change, creators tackle challenges specific to different markets.

b) Google's Jigsaw group, an incubator to tackle some of the toughest global security challenges, has deployed the Redirect Method, which uses Adwords targeting tools and curated YouTube playlists to disrupt online radicalization. The method is open to anyone to use, and we know that NGOs have sponsored campaigns against a wide-spectrum of ideologically-motivated terrorists.

It is also important to note that hate speech removals can be particularly complex compared to other types of content. Hate speech, because it often relies on spoken cues rather than visual ones, is sometimes harder to detect than some forms of branded terrorist propaganda. It is intensely context specific and it can be contentious as there is often disagreement on what could be considered political speech. On the opposite end, overaggressive enforcement can also inadvertently silence voices that are using the platform to make themselves heard about important issues. That's why we've also invested heavily here to use our automated flagging technology to quickly send potential hate speech for review by our human review teams. In the fourth quarter of 2018, we removed nearly 58,000 videos for hate and harassment compared to 49,000 for violent extremism.

Often times in this space, we have found that content can sit in a gray area that comes up right against the line and may be offensive, but does not directly violate YouTube's policies against incitement to violence and hate speech. When this occurs, we have built a policy to drastically reduce a video's visibility by making it ineligible for ads, removing its comments, and excluding it from our recommendation system. In particular, we understand the issues around YouTube's recommendation system have been top of mind. This is why several months ago, we also updated our recommendation systems to begin reducing recommendations of even more borderline content or content that can misinform users in harmful ways.

Before I conclude, I'd like to say a final word about Neo-Nazism and white supremacist content. We block Nazi content in countries where it is illegal. Furthermore, a lot of content produced by Neo-Nazis and white supremacists violates our policies on hate speech or violence and is removed globally. For borderline content, we take measures to hamper its dissemination by ensuring it cannot be recommended, monetized, or commented on. YouTube's commitment to free expression and access to information means that we sometimes preserve views that may be objectionable or offensive—but we are also willing to revisit where we draw that line in consultation with experts on civil rights, civil liberties, hate, terrorism, and representatives from impacted communities.

III. CONCLUSION

As I mentioned at the start, we build our products for all of our users from all political stripes around the globe. The long-term success of our business is directly related to our ability to earn and maintain the trust of our users. We have a natural and long-term incentive to make sure that our products work for users of all viewpoints. We will continue to pursue that trust by encouraging and acting on feedback about ways we can improve.

We also understand that people will value these services only so long as they continue to trust them to work well and provide them with the most relevant and useful information. That is why hate speech and violent extremism have no place on YouTube. We believe we have developed a responsible approach to address the evolving and complex issues that manifest on our platform.

In formulating and applying our policies, YouTube seeks to balance and preserve "Four Freedoms"—freedom of expression, freedom of information, freedom of opportunity and freedom to belong. It also seeks to balance free expression with preventing the spread of content that violates its Community Guidelines in order to maintain a vibrant community. Striking this balance is never easy, especially for a global platform operating in societies that have different standards for when speech crosses the line.

Thank you for the opportunity to outline our efforts in this space. I'm happy to answer any questions you might have.

SOURCE: House Committee on the Judiciary. "Testimony of Alexandria Walden, Global Human Rights & Free Expression Policy Counsel, Google." April 9, 2019. https://docs.house.gov/meetings/JU/JU00/20190409/109266/HHRG-116-JU00-Wstate-WaldenA-20190409.pdf.

Facebook Representative Describes Efforts to Ban Hate Speech

April 9, 2019

I. Introduction

Chairman Nadler, Ranking Member Collins, and distinguished members of the Committee, thank you for the opportunity to appear before you today. My name is Neil Potts, and I am a Director at Facebook with oversight of the development and implementation of Facebook's Community Standards, which serve as Facebook's rules for what types of content are allowed on our platform. I am a graduate of the United States Naval Academy and the University of Virginia School of Law. Prior to joining Facebook, I served as a ground intelligence officer in the United States Marine Corps and was deployed in support of Operation Enduring Freedom and Operation Iraqi Freedom.

I want to start by saying that all of us at Facebook stand with the victims, their families, and everyone affected by the horrific terrorist attack in New Zealand. In the aftermath of such heinous acts, it is more important than ever to stand against hate and violence. We continue to make that a priority in everything we do at Facebook.

Facebook's mission is to give people the power to build community and to bring the world closer together. Over two billion people come to our platform every month to stay connected with friends and family, to discover what's going on in the world, to build their businesses, to volunteer or donate to organizations they care about, to help in a crisis, and to share billions of pictures, stories, and videos about their lives and their beliefs each day. The diversity of viewpoints, expression, and experiences on our platform every day highlight much of what is best about Facebook.

We firmly believe that technology has the power to do good. We also recognize that bad actors may seek to use our platform in unacceptable ways, and we take seriously our responsibility to stop them. As we work to connect people, we strive to make sure those connections remain positive. As we give people a voice, we want to make sure they are not using that voice to hurt others. That is why we have longstanding policies against terrorism and hate, and that is also why last month we instituted a prohibition on praise, support, and representation of white nationalism and white separatism.

I want to be clear: There is no place for terrorism and hate on Facebook. We remove content that incites violence, or that bullies, harasses, or threatens others when we become aware of it.

But determining what content should and should not be removed is not always simple. These decisions can be both far-reaching and novel: how to improve the quality of the discourse on a site as voluminous and varied as ours, how to keep hateful content off the site, and how to do so without hampering free expression. As Mark Zuckerberg noted in his recent op-ed, we should not make so many important decisions about speech on our own and everyone in the social media space should strive to do everything they can to keep the amount of harmful content to a minimum.

For our part, Facebook is creating an independent body so people can appeal our decisions. And we are working with governments on ensuring the effectiveness of our content review systems. But we need a standardized, industry-wide approach for determining the guidelines by which potentially harmful content is reviewed, and by which we assess issues as critical as election integrity, privacy, and data portability.

The rules of the Internet should reflect our society's values for a safe and open Internet. We care about updating these rules because we believe that technology should serve everyone. Conversations like the ones we will have here today are an important part of making that belief a reality, and we appreciate the opportunity to take part in it.

First, I would like to provide you with information about the significant progress we have made in preventing terrorist content from appearing on our platform, and the continuing improvements we intend to make going forward. Second, I want to provide more details about our ban on praise, support, or representation of white supremacy, white nationalism, or white separatism, as well as our other work in keeping hateful content off our platform. And finally, I would like to tell you more about our content moderation policies and our efforts to keep Facebook a safe and welcoming environment for everyone while embracing diverse views and protecting the freedom of speech.

II. Terrorism, Hate Crimes, and Violence

Facebook is meant to be a place for people to express themselves and connect with one another. But unfortunately, there are those who would use the platform instead to spread hatred, violence, and terror. We are committed to protecting the safety of our community, and we remove content threatening that safety.

To do so, Facebook employs more than 30,000 people across the globe focused on safety and security, including blocking and removing terrorist and extremist accounts and their content. And we have specific protocols in place to pass on threats of imminent harm to law enforcement as soon as we become aware of them.

We also are proud to have co-launched the Global Internet Forum to Counter Terrorism (GIFCT) more than two years ago to help fight terrorism and extremism online alongside our peers at other technology companies, including Google, YouTube, Microsoft, and Twitter. GIFCT was the culmination of years of informal partnerships among our companies on these issues, and the group has created a shared industry database of "hashes"—unique digital "fingerprints"—for violent terrorist imagery that we have removed from our services.

Sharing information allows all of us to identify more quickly and more accurately potential extremist content on our respective platforms. Most importantly, it also allows smaller companies the ability to take advantage of our technology and tactics, even with fewer people and resources. We believe that terrorism and extremism are shared problems that require shared solutions, and we encourage all tech companies to join us in our efforts to keep such violence and hate off of online communities.

Since the tragic events in Christchurch, Facebook has been working closely with the New Zealand Police to respond to the attack. At the same time, we have been working to understand how our platform was used so we can prevent such use in the future. I would like to share some of our goals moving forward in this area.

First, we are exploring restrictions on who can go Live depending on factors such as prior Community Standards violations. We also want to improve our matching technology to detect and stop the spread of horrific viral videos. Our current technology can recognize spliced or edited content, but we know that some versions of the New Zealand attacker's video temporarily slipped our detection. This is a sensitive discussion that we want to avoid having publicly because we know that terrorists follow our statements to try to identify ways to circumvent our systems.

Second, we want to react faster to harmful content on live-streamed video. This includes scrutinizing how to employ AI more effectively and encouraging our users to report content faster. But this is not an easy problem to solve, and we do not expect easy or immediate solutions. What we do expect, and what we will do, is work tirelessly to improve our abilities in these areas, so that we can prevent our platform from playing any role in such horrific acts.

Third, we will continue to proactively detect and combat hate speech and terrorism of all kinds on our platform. We have developed a number of techniques to counter ISIS and al-Qaeda, and we began deploying those techniques against a wider range of terrorist and hate organizations last year.

Fourth, we are expanding our industry collaboration through the GIFCT, and intend to refine and improve our ability to collaborate in a crisis. We have also begun experimenting with sharing URLs systematically rather than just content hashes and are working to address the range of terrorists and violent extremists operating online.

We have made significant progress in our efforts to stamp out hate and violence on our platform, but we know we have more work to do. We will continue to review our policies constantly, to develop and adopt further technical solutions, and to strengthen our partnerships with external stakeholders, all of which will allow us to find more effective ways to combat terrorism, extremism, and hate.

III. Hate Speech and White Supremacy, White Nationalism, and White Separatism

Hate can take many forms beyond overt terrorism and none of it is permitted in our community. We do not allow hate speech on our platform because it creates an environment of intimidation and exclusion that limits people's willingness to communicate and share with one another. We remove hate speech whenever we become aware of it, and we are continually working on developing new or improved technologies that let us more quickly and more accurately identify and eliminate such content. For example, in the first three quarters of 2018, we took action on about 8 million pieces of content containing hate speech.

In fact, Facebook rejects not just hate speech, but all hateful ideologies. Our rules have always been clear that white supremacists are not allowed on our platform under any circumstances, and we have banned more than 200 white supremacist groups under our Dangerous Organizations policy. But even under that policy, we had previously viewed white nationalism and white separatism as distinct from white supremacy. While we removed content from white nationalist or white separatist groups that violated our policies, we did not remove the accounts of such groups wholesale.

We were reluctant to ban such groups outright because we did not want to ban all nationalist and separatist ideas—recognizing that patriotism, for example, is an important part of many people's identities. But after meeting with experts in race relations around the world and conducting our own review of hate figures and organizations, we are convinced that white supremacy cannot be meaningfully separated from white nationalism and white separatism.

Therefore, we announced that we are updating our policies to make it clear that all praise, support, and representation of white nationalism and white separatism violates our rules. We will now use our Dangerous Organizations policy to remove any praise, support, or representation of white nationalism and white separatism from our platform.

But our efforts to combat hate do not stop there. We will also start connecting people who search for terms associated with white supremacy, white nationalism, or white separatism to resources focused on helping people leave behind hate groups. People searching for these terms will be directed to Life After Hate, an organization founded by former violent extremists that provides crisis intervention, education, support, and outreach. We believe that by connecting individuals to Life After Hate, we can try to address the root of the problem in addition to addressing the hateful and dangerous actions that can result.

We recognize the serious harm that hateful content can inflict in any community, including ours, and we continue to be committed to finding new and better ways to combat hate on Facebook and to keep our community one that is always welcoming and safe.

IV. Content Moderation and Neutrality

Our Community Standards and related policies work to balance our goals of giving people a place to express themselves genuinely while also promoting a welcoming and safe environment for everyone.

We created our Community Standards in an effort to standardize our content removal decisions. Our Standards outline publicly and transparently what is and is not allowed on Facebook. They apply around the world to all types of content and are designed so they can be applied consistently and fairly to a community that transcends regions, cultures, and languages.

At the same time, we believe in embracing diverse views. Unless we are confronted with a specific potential harm, we tend to err on the side of allowing content, even when some people find it objectionable or offensive. These can be difficult decisions, and we will not get them all right, but we strive to apply our policies consistently and fairly to a global and diverse community.

To be clear, our Community Standards do not prohibit discussing controversial topics or espousing a debated point of view; nor do they favor opinions on one end of the political spectrum or the other. We believe that such discussion is critical to promoting greater understanding among members of our community.

But our process for gauging what meets and what does not meet those Standards is not perfect. We have made mistakes. We know that there have been a number of high-profile content removal incidents affecting individuals across the political spectrum. My colleague, Monika Bickert, spoke with you last year about some of the concerns such incidents had raised. Today, I wanted to provide you with a brief update about some of the actions we have taken to address those concerns:

- We have created an appeals process for content that was removed from our platform as hate speech and are working to create an independent oversight board of experts on free speech and safety to decide those appeals transparently.

- We now publish a Community Standards Enforcement Report that describes the amount and types of content we have taken action against, as well as the amount of content we have proactively flagged for review.

- We have asked former Senator Jon Kyl to advise the company on any potential bias against conservative voices.

- Laura Murphy, a national civil liberties and civil rights leader, as part of an independent civil rights audit, is coordinating with civil rights groups to help advise

Facebook on how to empower users with a diversity of opinions while encouraging civil discourse.

- We have partnered with over 100 groups across the political spectrum. We believe that these groups' input will help us to improve over time and ensure we can most effectively serve our diverse community.

- And we are continuing to expand our list of outside partner organizations so that we regularly receive feedback on our content policies from a diverse set of viewpoints.

While we will continue to take steps on our own to improve, we hope that we have a broader discussion with the industry regarding decisions about what speech is harmful. People should be able to expect that companies will address these issues in a consistent way. We should have a broader debate about what we want as a society and how regulation can help. We believe Facebook has a responsibility to help address these issues, and we are looking forward to discussing them with lawmakers around the world, including during our discussion here today.

V. Conclusion

In closing, I want to reiterate our deep commitment to building a community that encourages and fosters free expression, as well as to stopping terrorists, extremists, and hate groups from using our platform to promote abhorrent ideologies. We want Facebook to be a place where individuals with diverse viewpoints can connect and exchange ideas. There is a lot more to do, but we are proud of the significant progress we have made over the last few years. Still, we know that people have questions about what we are doing to continue that progress, and we are looking forward to working with the members of this Committee, other policymakers, and others in the tech industry and civil society to continue the dialogue around these issues. I appreciate the opportunity to be here today, and I look forward to your questions.

SOURCE: House Committee on the Judiciary. "Testimony of Neil Potts, Public Policy Director, Facebook." April 9, 2019. https://docs.house.gov/meetings/JU/JU00/20190409/109266/HHRG-116-JU00-Wstate-PottsN-20190409.pdf.

Twitter Representative Addresses Congress on Anti-Conservative Bias

April 10, 2019

Chairman Cruz, Ranking Member Hirono, and Members of the Subcommittee:

Thank you for the opportunity to appear before you today.

Twitter is an American company, and Twitter's purpose is to serve the public conversation. Twitter is an open communications platform. We welcome perspectives and insights from diverse sources and embrace being a platform where the open and free exchange of ideas can occur. Every day on Twitter we see this play out on topics as diverse as sporting events, award shows, natural disasters, political movements, and the latest music.

We put the people who use our service first in every step we take. To support the many voices on Twitter, we have rules in place that are designed to ensure the safety and security of the people who come to our service. Safety and free expression go hand in hand, both online and in the real world. If people do not feel safe to speak, they very often will not.

These two guideposts, free expression for all perspectives and rules of the road to promote safety, are not only in our users' interests, but also paramount to sustaining our business. People come to Twitter to discover and talk about what is happening, and they want to hear from multiple perspectives. Conversely, people will not use our service if it is not a healthy space.

Today, I hope my testimony before the Committee will demonstrate our commitment to the free flow of information and the sharing of diverse perspectives and viewpoints. We want to communicate how our platform works in a clear and straightforward way.

Let me be clear about some important and foundational facts: Twitter does not use political viewpoints, perspectives, or party affiliation to make any decisions, whether related to automatically ranking content on our service or how we develop or enforce our rules. Our rules are not based on ideology or a particular set of beliefs. Instead, the Twitter Rules are based on behavior.

We believe strongly in being impartial, and we strive to enforce our rules dispassionately. We work extremely hard to make sure our algorithms are fair and endeavor to be transparent and fix issues when we make mistakes. The open nature of Twitter means that our enforcement actions are plainly visible to the public, even when we cannot always reveal the private details of individual accounts who have broken our rules. We do this to protect the privacy of the individuals who use our platform. And we strive to become more transparent when we remove a Tweet by providing explanations to individuals regarding which specific rules were broken.

My testimony today will provide important information about our service: (1) protecting diverse perspectives on Twitter; (2) additional context on some high-profile incidents; (3) the algorithms that shape the experience of individuals who use Twitter; and (4) Twitter's application of rules and policies.

I. PROTECTING DIVERSE PERSPECTIVES ON TWITTER

Every day, we see elected representatives around the world using Twitter to communicate with their constituents, fellow elected representatives, and with international leaders. In the United States, every senator, governor, House member, and mayors of the 25 largest cities have Twitter accounts. Millions of people around the globe have taken to Twitter to engage in local, national, and global conversations on a wide range of issues of civic importance. We also partner with news organizations to live-stream prominent congressional hearings and political events, providing the public access to important developments in our democracy. The notion that we would silence any political perspective is antithetical to our commitment to free expression.

Twitter continues to be one of the most popular platforms for conservative voices and movements in the United States. For example, in 2018, there were 32.6 million Tweets about Make America Great Again or MAGA. It was the fifth most Tweeted hashtag in the

U.S. in 2018. Globally, the top 10 most mentioned accounts in 2018 included @realdon aldtrump and @POTUS, accounts for President Donald Trump. And Twitter's political sales team works with hundreds of active conservative advertisers.

Our Government and Elections Team also provides Twitter support and regular best-practices trainings for members of Congress—on both sides of the aisle. Providing this support to all elected officials, regardless of political party, is consistent with our commitment to serving the public conversation around political speech from various viewpoints.

Twitter also supports the White House and media broadcasters to have a dynamic experience on Twitter, publishing live video event pages to millions of people on Twitter during President Trump's State of the Union address in 2019. In total, more than 22 media broadcasters including ABC, CBS, NBC News, PBS NewsHour, Reuters, Univision, and *USA Today* participated, reaching approximately 2.7 million live viewers. Additionally, the White House and Senate GOP both published the entire live video on Twitter reaching more than 4.6 million viewers. There were 5 million Tweets regarding the 2019 State of the Union. As a subset of that total, Twitter developed an emoji hashtag #SOTU that was Tweeted nearly 1.7 million times. The purpose of an emoji hashtag is to make it easier for people to discover and participate in the conversation about this topic. Although emoji hashtags are typically created as a paid advertisement, Twitter provided it without charge to encourage open discourse.

In preparation for this hearing and to better inform the members of the Subcommittee, our data scientists analyzed Tweets sent by all members of the House and Senate that have Twitter accounts for a five-week period spanning February 7, 2019, until March 17, 2019. We learned that, during that period, Democratic members sent 8,665 Tweets and Republican members sent 4,757. Democrats on average have more followers per account and have more active followers. As a result, Democratic members in the aggregate receive more impressions or views than Republicans.

Despite this greater number of impressions, after controlling for various factors such as the number of Tweets and the number of followers, and normalizing the followers' activity, we observed that there is no statistically significant difference between the number of times a Tweet by a Democrat is viewed versus a Tweet by a Republican. In aggregate, controlling for the same number of followers, a single Tweet by a Republican will be viewed as many times as a single Tweet by a Democrat, even after all filtering and algorithms have been applied by Twitter. Our quality filtering and ranking algorithms do not result in Tweets by Democrats or Tweets by Republicans being viewed any differently. Their performance is the same because the Twitter platform itself does not take sides.

II. ADDITIONAL CONTEXT TO HIGH-PROFILE INCIDENTS

A. Auto-Suggest Issue

In July 2018, we acknowledged that some accounts (including those of Republicans and Democrats) were not being auto-suggested when people were searching for their specific name. This happened because Twitter had made a change to how one of our behavior-based algorithms worked in search results. A more detailed explanation of our behavior-based algorithms is included in Section III. When people used search, our algorithms were filtering out of auto-complete those accounts that had a higher likelihood of being abusive. Those search results remained visible if someone turned off the quality filter in search, and they were also visible elsewhere throughout the product.

Our change in the usage of the behavioral signals within search was causing this to happen. To be clear, this only impacted our search auto-suggestions. The accounts, their Tweets, and surrounding conversation about those accounts were still available in search results. Once identified, this issue was resolved within 24 hours. In addition to fixing the search auto-suggestion function, we continue to carefully evaluate potential product changes for unintended consequences such as this.

This issue impacted 600,000 accounts across the globe. The vast majority of impacted accounts were not political in nature. The issue impacted 53 accounts of politicians in the U.S., representing 0.00883 percent of total affected accounts. This subset of affected accounts includes 10 accounts of Republican Members of Congress. The remainder of impacted political accounts relate to campaign activity and affected candidates across the political spectrum.

An analysis of accounts for Members of Congress that were affected by this search issue demonstrates there was no negative effect on the growth of their follower counts. To the contrary, follower counts of those Members of Congress spiked. Twitter has made this internal analysis available to the House Committee on Energy and Commerce, and we have submitted copies to this Subcommittee.

This functionality was not what we intended, and we removed this signal from our search suggestions as soon as we became aware of this issue.

It is important to note that these behavior-based algorithms are designed to reduce the visibility of abusive content, and the initial results of these behavioral filters showed a reduction in abuse reports of 8 percent from conversations and 4 percent drop in abuse reports from search results. But this technology is constantly evolving, and we know that we will continually learn and adapt to achieve the best outcome for our users. As always, we will continue to refine our approach, evaluate unintended consequences, and will be transparent about the reasons underpinning our decisions.

B. Rules Violations

Twitter takes violations of the Twitter Rules and Terms of Service seriously. We want to ensure that we police our platform in meaningful ways using automated systems, and those efforts are not always visible to the public. Additionally, we do not always share publicly the reason we take action on a particular account to protect the privacy of our users.

In the recent instance regarding the account @UnplannedMovie, the account was caught in our automated systems used to detect ban evasion. Ban evasion occurs when an individual registers for a new account despite having been suspended previously for breaking our rules. We reinstated the @UnplannedMovie account as soon as it was brought to our attention that the new account was not intended for similar violative activity. Followers of a specific account are replenished over time following reinstatement, and we are not hiding follower counts or disallowing certain people from following this account. If users searched for and followed the account during this time, it appeared as if the account was unfollowed. Individuals who followed the account during that time period were automatically restored as a follower to that account once it stabilized. Ultimately, the hashtag #unplannedmovie became a trending topic on Twitter.

In other instances, Twitter employs extensive content detection technology to identify and police harmful and abusive content embedded in various forms of media on the platform. We use PhotoDNA and hash matching technology, particularly in the context of child sexual exploitation material and terrorism. From January to June 2018, we removed 487,363 unique accounts due to violations of our rules prohibiting child sexual exploitation material, 97 percent of which were identified through our internal tools. Additionally, during the same period, we suspended 205,156 accounts as violations of our prohibitions regarding promotion of terrorism, 91 percent of which were identified internally. We do not share publicly the reasons an individual's account has been removed in most of these cases for privacy reasons and to ensure we do not interfere with a potential investigation by law enforcement.

C. Sensitive Content Controls

Some commentators have raised concerns about the limiting of specific Tweets that fall under our "sensitive" content controls. The Twitter Rules and Twitter Media Policy limit the types of content that may be shared on Twitter and describe requirements for users who choose to share potentially sensitive content on Twitter. For example, when adult content, graphic violence, or hateful imagery appears in Tweets, we may place this content behind an interstitial advising viewers to be aware that they will see sensitive media if they click through. This allows us to identify potentially sensitive content that some people may not wish to see.

Every user has the ability to mark their account as "sensitive" based on the content they share, and every user has the choice of whether they will see a warning for sensitive content or not. When an individual on Twitter has this setting enabled, people who visit a specific profile may see a message that the account may include potentially sensitive content and inquiring if the individual wants to view it. This setting enables individuals on Twitter to control their own experience and protects them from seeing sensitive content without first having made a choice to click through the warning, or to never see warnings.

D. Political Advertisements

We develop policies governing advertisements that run on Twitter that strive to balance allowing our advertisers to communicate their message with protecting individuals on the platform from potentially distressing content. Striking the right balance is particularly challenging in the realm of political advertising. We see a range of groups across the political spectrum utilize our advertising products, and all are bound by the same Ads Policies and Twitter Rules.

Some critics have raised concerns regarding Twitter's error in initially delaying a political advertisement promoted by Senator Marsha Blackburn. The advertisement ultimately ran on Twitter, the initial video was never blocked, and her original Tweet was never censored.

In the advertisement, Senator Blackburn referenced ending the "sale of baby body parts" by Planned Parenthood, and Twitter reviewers responded to user reports that the ad was inflammatory. Our team made the wrong call. Following an appeal from Senator Blackburn's media firm, we reviewed the initial decision. We relied upon additional context that there were no graphic images portrayed and that the concerning language was a very small portion of the overall advertisement. We then reversed the decision and apologized.

III. ALGORITHMS SHAPING THE TWITTER EXPERIENCE

We want Twitter to provide a useful, relevant experience to all people using our service. With hundreds of millions of Tweets every day on Twitter, we have invested heavily in building systems that organize content on Twitter to show individuals using the platform the most relevant information for that individual first. With 126 million people using Twitter each day in dozens of languages and countless cultural contexts, we rely upon machine learning algorithms to help us organize content by relevance. If an individual wants to see Twitter without any algorithms applied, they have a single accessible control in order to view their timeline in reverse chronological order.

To preserve the integrity of our platform and to protect conversations on the platform from manipulation, Twitter also employs tools and technology to detect and minimize the visibility of certain types of abusive and manipulative behaviors on our platform.

A. Timeline Ranking and Filtering

For nearly a decade, the Twitter home timeline displayed Tweets from accounts an individual follows in reverse chronological order. When individuals originally opened Twitter, they saw the most recently posted Tweet first. As the volume of content on Twitter increased, individuals using the platform told us they were not always seeing useful or relevant information or were missing important Tweets. Based on this feedback, in 2016 we introduced a new ranking feature to the home timeline. This feature creates a better experience for people using Twitter by showing people the Tweets they might find most interesting first.

In December 2018, Twitter introduced a sparkle icon located at the top of individuals' timelines to more easily switch on and off reverse chronological timeline. As described above, the algorithms we employ are designed to help people see the most relevant Tweets. The icon now allows individuals using Twitter to easily switch to chronological order ranking of the Tweets from only those accounts they follow. This improvement allows individuals on Twitter to see how algorithms affect what they see, and enables greater transparency into the technology we use to rank Tweets.

In addition to the home timeline, Twitter has a notification timeline that enables people to see who has liked, Retweeted and replied to their Tweets, as well as who mentioned or followed them. We give individuals on Twitter additional controls over the content that appears in the notifications timeline, since notifications may contain content an individual on Twitter has not chosen to receive, such as mentions or replies from someone the individual does not follow. By default we filter notifications for quality, and exclude notifications about duplicate or potentially spammy Tweets. We also give individuals on the platform granular controls over specific types of accounts they might not want to receive notifications from, including new accounts, accounts the individual does not follow, and accounts without a confirmed phone or email address.

B. Conversations

Conversations are happening all the time on Twitter. The replies to any given Tweet are referred to as a "conversation." Twitter strives to show content to people that we think they will be most interested in and that contributes meaningfully to the conversation. For this reason, the replies, grouped by sub-conversations, may not be in chronological order. For example, when ranking a reply higher, we consider factors such as if the original Tweet author has replied, or if a reply is from someone the individual follows.

C. Safe Search

Twitter's search tools allow individuals on Twitter to search every public Tweet on Twitter. There are many ways to use search on Twitter. An individual can find Tweets from friends, local businesses, and everyone from well-known entertainers to global political leaders. By searching for topic keywords or hashtags, an individual can follow ongoing conversations about breaking news or personal interests. To help people understand and organize search results and find the most relevant information quickly, we offer several different versions of search.

By default, searches on Twitter return results in "Top mode." Top Tweets are the most relevant Tweets for a search. We determine relevance based on the popularity of a Tweet (e.g., when a lot of people are interacting with or sharing via Retweets and replies), the keywords it contains, and many other factors. In addition, "Latest mode" returns real-time, reverse-chronological results for a search query.

We give people control over what they see in search results through a "Safe Search" option. This option excludes potentially sensitive content from search results, such as spam, adult content, and the accounts an individual has muted or blocked. Individual accounts may mark their own posts as sensitive as well. Twitter's safe search mode excludes potentially sensitive content, along with accounts an individual may have muted or blocked, from search results in both Top and Latest. Safe Search is enabled by default, and people have the option to turn safe search off, or back on, at any time.

D. Behavioral Signals and Safeguards

Twitter also uses a range of behavioral signals to determine how Tweets are organized and presented in the home timeline, conversations, and search based on relevance. Twitter relies on behavioral signals—such as how accounts behave and react to one another—to identify content that detracts from a healthy public conversation, such as spam and abuse. Unless we have determined that a Tweet violates Twitter policies, it will remain on the platform. Where we have identified a Tweet as potentially detracting from healthy conversation (e.g., as potentially abusive), it will only be available to view if an individual clicks on "Show more replies" or choose to see everything in his or her search setting.

Some examples of behavioral signals we use, in combination with each other and a range of other signals, to help identify this type of content include: an account with no confirmed email address, simultaneous registration for multiple accounts, accounts that repeatedly Tweet and mention accounts that do not follow them, or behavior that might indicate a coordinated attack. Twitter is also examining how accounts are connected to those that violate our rules and how they interact with each other. The accuracy of the algorithms developed from these behavioral signals will continue to improve over time.

These behavioral signals are an important factor in how Twitter organizes and presents content in communal areas like conversation and search. Our primary goal is to ensure that relevant content and Tweets contributing to healthy conversation will appear first in conversations and search. Because our service operates in dozens of languages and hundreds of cultural contexts around the globe, we have found that behavior is a strong signal that helps us identify bad faith actors on our platform. The behavioral ranking that Twitter utilizes does not consider in any way political views or ideology. It focuses solely on the behavior of all accounts. Twitter is always working to improve our behavior-based ranking models such that their breadth and accuracy will improve over time. We use thousands of behavioral signals in our behavior-based ranking models—this ensures that no one signal drives the ranking outcomes and protects against malicious attempts to manipulate our ranking systems.

Through early testing in markets around the world, Twitter has already seen a recent update to this approach have a positive impact, resulting in a 4 percent drop in abuse reports from search and 8 percent fewer abuse reports from conversations. That metric provided us with strong evidence that fewer people are seeing Tweets that disrupt their experience on Twitter.

Some critics have described the sum of all of this work as a banning of conservative voices. Once again, we restate that this is unfounded and false. In fact, our approach of focusing on behavior is a robust defense against bias, as it requires us to define and act upon bad conduct, not any specific language or type of speech. Our purpose is to serve the conversation, not to make value judgments on personal beliefs.

IV. TWITTER'S APPLICATION OF RULES AND POLICIES

Content moderation on a global scale is a new challenge not only for our company, but also across our industry. While we continue to improve in efficiency and effectiveness in our content moderation practices, mistakes do occur. When we become aware of mistakes, we act promptly to correct them. We now offer people who use Twitter the ability to more easily file an appeal from within the Twitter app when we tell them which Tweet has broken our rules. This makes the appeal process quicker and easier for users. We also allow individuals to file a report through a web form that can be accessed at http://help .twitter.com/appeals. We also continue to improve our transparency around the actions we take, including better in-app notices where we have removed Tweets for breaking our rules. We also communicate with both the account who reports a Tweet and the account which posted it with additional detail on our actions. These steps are all a part of our continued commitment to transparency, and we will continue to better inform individuals who use Twitter on our work in these areas.

As policymakers and experts examine policies around content moderation, it is critical to note the importance of preserving Section 230 of the Communications Decency Act (CDA § 230). When it enacted CDA § 230 more than 20 years ago as part of the Telecommunications Act of 1996, Congress made the judgment that companies like Twitter that host content provided by others should have the latitude to make editorial decisions without becoming legally responsible for that content. CDA § 230 is a foundational law that has enabled American leadership in the tech sector worldwide.

It is the protection that allows us to proactively moderate content around activities such as child sexual exploitation, terrorism, voter suppression, and illicit drug sales. Without these tools, platforms would either cease to moderate content, including content that could relate to offline harm, or over-moderate content, resulting in less speech. Some lawmakers have suggested carving out CDA § 230 for political speech, and I want to be clear that any such measures could have unwanted consequences for people across the political spectrum who use Internet platforms to share their views. Eroding CDA § 230 creates risks of liability for companies that make good-faith efforts to moderate bad faith actors and could result in greater restrictions around free expression.

***

The purpose of Twitter is to serve the public conversation, and we do not make value judgments on personal beliefs. We are focused on making our platform—and the technology it relies upon—better and smarter over time and sharing our work and progress with everyone. Simply put: Twitter would not be Twitter if everyone had the same viewpoints and ideology. We strive to balance the safety of Twitter users and freedom of expression every day. We are working to be more clear about our rules and transparent about our enforcement.

Thank you, and I look forward to your questions.

SOURCE: Senate Committee on the Judiciary. Subcommittee on the Constitution. "Testimony of Carlos Monje, Director, Public Policy and Philanthropy, Twitter, Inc." April 10, 2019. https://www.judiciary.sen ate.gov/imo/media/doc/Monje%20Testimony.pdf.

Facebook Testifies on Social Media Conservative Bias

April 10, 2019

I. Introduction

Chairman Cruz, Ranking Member Hirono, and distinguished members of the Subcommittee, thank you for the opportunity to appear before you today. My name is Neil Potts, and I am a Director at Facebook with oversight of the development and implementation of Facebook's Community Standards, which serve as Facebook's rules for what types of content are allowed on our platform. I am a graduate of the United States Naval Academy and the University of Virginia School of Law. Prior to joining Facebook, I served as a ground intelligence officer in the United States Marine Corps and was deployed in support of Operation Enduring Freedom and Operation Iraqi Freedom.

Facebook's mission is to give people the power to build community and bring the world closer together. Over two billion people come to our platform every month to connect with friends and family, to discover what's going on in the world, to build their businesses, to volunteer or donate to organizations they care about, and to help those in need. Our users share billions of pictures, stories, and videos about their lives and their beliefs each day.

The diversity of viewpoints, expression, and experiences on our platform highlights much of what is best about Facebook. But it also presents challenges when deciding what content should and should not be allowed on our platform.

Facebook's most important responsibility is keeping people safe, both online and off.

But we also strive to foster a diversity of viewpoints and experiences on our platform. To create a place that is safe for such a variety of people, we have to make hard decisions about what can and cannot be allowed on our platform.

We created our Community Standards to standardize our content removal decisions. Our Standards outline publicly and transparently what content is permissible. They apply around the world to all types of content and are designed to be applied consistently and fairly to a community that transcends regions, cultures, religions, and languages. At our scale, we are not always going to get the enforcement decision right. But I would like to state unequivocally that Facebook does not favor one political viewpoint over another, nor does Facebook suppress conservative speech. Our Community Standards have been carefully designed to ensure that content is reviewed in a neutral way, focused on what is necessary to keep our users safe. Our systems and human reviewers work in concert to identify and remove violent, hateful, or dangerous content.

But these decisions can be both far-reaching and novel: how to improve the quality of the discourse on a site as voluminous and varied as ours, how to keep hateful content off that site, and how to do so without hampering free expression. As Mark Zuckerberg noted in his recent op-ed, we should not make so many important decisions about speech on our own and everyone in the social media space should strive to do everything they can to keep the amount of harmful content to a minimum.

For our part, Facebook is creating an independent body so people can appeal our decisions. And we are working with governments on ensuring the effectiveness of our content review systems. But we need a standardized, industry-wide approach for determining the guidelines by which potentially harmful content is reviewed, and by which we assess issues as critical as election integrity, privacy, and data portability.

The rules of the Internet should reflect our society's values for a safe and open Internet. We care about updating these rules because we believe that technology should serve everyone, whatever their background, whatever their politics. Conversations like the ones we will have here today are an important part of making that belief a reality, and we appreciate the opportunity to take part in it.

I would like to begin by telling you more about our efforts to ensure that our content moderation policies are viewpoint neutral and designed to encourage dialogue and the free flow of ideas.

II. Content Moderation and Neutrality

Our content policies are the centerpiece of our efforts to keep people safe. Our Community Standards and related policies work to balance our goals of giving people a place to express themselves genuinely while also promoting a welcoming and safe environment.

At the same time, we believe in embracing diverse views. Indeed, one of Facebook's foundational principles is to be a platform for diverse ideas. Suppressing content on the basis of political viewpoint or preventing people from seeing what matters most to them is directly contrary to Facebook's mission. We want Facebook to be a place where people can discover a greater diversity of news and information than they could otherwise. Therefore, unless we are confronted with a specific potential harm, we tend to err on the side of allowing content, even when some people find it objectionable or offensive.

Research shows that social media platforms provide more information diversity than traditional media ever has. A 2017 Reuters digital news report concluded that, on average, people who use social media, aggregators, and search engines experience more information diversity than non-users. Similarly, a Pew Research Center survey found that more than half of Facebook users report that there are a range of political beliefs among their Facebook friends.

Our Community Standards do not prohibit users from discussing controversial topics or supporting a debated point of view. Nor do they favor opinions on one end of the political spectrum or the other. We believe that such discussion is critical to promoting greater understanding among members of our community.

But given the amount of content on our platform, content reviewers must respond to millions of reports each week from all over the world, and we do not always get it right. We know that there have been a number of high-profile content removal incidents affecting individuals across the political spectrum, and we are taking a variety of steps to respond to the concerns raised by this Subcommittee and others.

We want to make sure our community understands the systems and processes that lead to our content removal decisions. Transparency is the key to fostering that understanding, and as part of our annual Transparency Report, we publish a Community Standards Enforcement Report describing the amount and types of content we have taken action against, as well as the amount of content that we have proactively flagged for review.

We currently publish our report every six months, but we soon expect to do so every quarter. In addition, we publish comprehensive guidelines to provide more clarity around where we draw lines on these complex and evolving issues. We hope that by sharing this information, we can encourage all stakeholders to contribute to an ongoing dialogue around our decisionmaking processes and help us improve our efforts to develop and enforce our standards.

We have also solicited external feedback on our content moderation policies from sources across the political spectrum. We have partnered with over 100 groups across the political spectrum, and we are continuing to expand our list of outside partner organizations to ensure we receive feedback on our content policies from a diverse set of viewpoints. The input we receive from these groups will help us to improve over time and ensure we can most effectively serve our diverse community.

For example, former Senator Kyl is gathering insights from members of Congress and a number of conservative groups and is assessing whether the company is unintentionally biased against conservative points of view. Senator Kyl and his team at Covington & Burling have talked to over 130 groups and individuals to understand how our policies and enforcement are affecting different people and communities. Having wrapped up the first phase of the project, which was focused on this external engagement, Senator Kyl and his team are now reviewing our external and internal policies. While conducting this review, Senator Kyl and his team have also been engaged in reviewing and providing insights into future policy changes under consideration. After Senator Kyl has reviewed our policies and internal guidelines, he and his team will share feedback and suggestions for improvements.

Another example of external feedback we have solicited is that of Laura Murphy, a national civil liberties and civil rights leader, who, as part of an independent civil rights audit, is coordinating with civil rights groups to help advise Facebook on how to empower users with a diversity of opinions while encouraging civil discourse. And Relman, Dane & Colfax, a respected civil rights law firm, is in the process of carrying out a comprehensive civil rights assessment of Facebook's services and internal operations.

We also created an appeals process for content that was removed from our platform as hate speech because we recognize that we sometimes make enforcement errors. We are working to extend this process further, by making appeals available not just for content that was taken down, but also for content that was reported and nonetheless left up, and by creating an independent oversight board of experts on free speech and safety to render binding and transparent decisions on these appeals. Through efforts like these, we will continue improving our systems and processes to correct for and minimize mistakes in the future.

And we are continuing our work to refine and enhance the quality of our machine learning, which is a first line of defense for content assessment on our platform. We hope that these improvements and safeguards will help ensure that Facebook remains a platform for a wide range of ideas and enables the broadest spectrum of free expression possible, while still keeping our space welcoming and safe for our entire community.

While we will continue to take steps on our own to improve, we hope that we have a broader discussion with the industry regarding decisions about what speech is harmful. People should be able to expect that companies will address these issues in a consistent way. We should have a broader debate about what we want as a society and how regulation can help. We believe Facebook has a responsibility to help address these issues, and we are looking forward to discussing them with lawmakers around the world, including during our discussion here today.

III. Terrorism, Violence, and Hate Speech

While I know that we are here today to discuss our efforts to encourage a diversity of views and to ensure we remain politically neutral in our efforts to create a safe and welcoming environment for our community, I would also appreciate the opportunity to discuss our efforts to stamp out the use of our platform by terrorists and other extremists, particularly in light of the despicable acts perpetrated recently in Christchurch.

Since the terrorist attack, Facebook has been working closely with the New Zealand Police. At the same time, we have been working to understand how we can prevent such use in the future. Those efforts include exploring restrictions on who can go Live depending on factors such as prior Community Standards violations, working to improve our matching technology to detect and stop the spread of horrific viral videos, and developing methods to react faster when harmful content is video live-streamed.

More broadly, Facebook employs over 30,000 people across the country and around the world focused on safety and security, including those that block and remove terrorist and extremist accounts and their content. That group includes engineers who every day are building new, automated systems to identify and remove this material—often at upload, before it can be viewed by our community. And we have specific protocols in place to pass on threats of imminent harm to law enforcement as soon as we become aware of them.

We are also expanding our industry collaboration through the Global Internet Forum to Counter Terrorism (GIFCT), which we co-launched more than two years ago to help fight terrorism and extremism online alongside our peers at other technology companies, including Google, YouTube, Microsoft, and Twitter. The information made available through GIFCT allows smaller companies the ability to take advantage of our technology and tactics, even with fewer people and resources.

But hate can take many forms and none of it is permitted in our community. We disallow hate speech because it creates an environment of intimidation and exclusion that limits people's willingness to communicate and share with one another. In fact, Facebook rejects not just hate speech, but all hateful ideologies. That means that white supremacists are not allowed on our platform under any circumstances, and we have recently announced a ban on white nationalism and white separatism as well. We will therefore now use our Dangerous Organizations policy to remove from our platform praise, support, or representation of white supremacy, as well as of white nationalism or white separatism, because both ideologies are inextricably linked with white supremacy and with violence more generally. We have already banned more than 200 white supremacist groups because of our Dangerous Organizations policy.

We recognize the serious harm that hateful content can inflict in any community, including ours, and we continue to be committed to finding new and better ways to combat hate on Facebook.

V. Conclusion

In closing, I want to reiterate our deep commitment to building a community that encourages and fosters free expression, as well as to stopping terrorists, extremists, and hate groups from using our platform to promote abhorrent ideologies. We want Facebook to be a place where individuals with diverse viewpoints can connect and exchange ideas. There is a lot more to do, but we are proud of the significant progress we have made over the last few years. Still, we know that people have questions about what we are doing to continue that progress, and we are looking forward to working with the members of this Committee, other policymakers, and others in the tech industry and civil society to continue the dialogue around these issues. I appreciate the opportunity to be here today, and I look forward to your questions.

SOURCE: Senate Committee on the Judiciary. Subcommittee on the Constitution. "Testimony of Neil Potts, Public Policy Director, Facebook." April 10, 2019. https://www.judiciary.senate.gov/imo/media/doc/Potts%20Testimony.pdf.

OTHER HISTORIC DOCUMENTS OF INTEREST

FROM THIS VOLUME

FROM PREVIOUS *HISTORIC DOCUMENTS*

Sudanese and UN Leaders Remark on Violence and Government Overthrow

APRIL 11, JUNE 3, JULY 5, AND AUGUST 21, 2019

In April 2019, Sudanese president Omar al-Bashir was removed from office by military coup following months of protests calling for him to step down and demanding the formation of a civilian-led government. Protesters continued to press their demands for change after al-Bashir's removal, despite a violent crackdown by the transitional military government that resulted in dozens of deaths. Negotiations mediated by the African Union and Ethiopian officials led to a major agreement between the military and the pro-democracy movement that paved the way for a new civilian–military transitional government that would serve as a steppingstone to an all-civilian government.

NATIONWIDE PROTESTS PROMPT PRESIDENT'S OUSTER

Protests have been erupting across Sudan since December 2018 following the government's implementation of emergency austerity measures in the face of an economic crisis. The Sudanese economy has struggled to recover from years of U.S. sanctions, most of which were lifted in 2017. South Sudan's 2011 separation from the northern part of the country to become an independent state dealt a further blow to the Sudanese economy in the form of lost oil revenues. (Approximately three-quarters of Sudan's oil fields were located in the south.) Additionally, Sudan remains on the U.S. list of state sponsors of terrorism, which renders it ineligible for debt relief and other funds from global organizations and makes it difficult to attract foreign investment.

The austerity measures imposed in 2018 included cuts to food and fuel subsidies as well as a devaluation of Sudan's currency, causing the costs of basic commodities to rise significantly. The Sudanese initially took to the streets to protest their economic struggles but soon began to call for al-Bashir to leave office and demand a new, civilian-led government. (A military coup installed former army commander al-Bashir as president in 1989. While he oversaw the peace deal that ended the country's bitter civil war and led to South Sudan's independence, he has also been charged with genocide, war crimes, and crimes against humanity by the International Criminal Court. An international warrant for his arrest has been issued.) While protesters represent Sudanese of every age and lifestyle, demonstrations have primarily been organized by the Sudanese Professionals Association (SPA), an umbrella organization comprised of associations representing doctors, health workers, lawyers, and teachers, among other professionals. The SPA and other pro-democracy groups came to be known collectively as the Forces for Freedom and Change (FFC).

Instead of capitulating to the protesters' demands, al-Bashir declared a yearlong state of emergency in February 2019, dissolved the federal and provincial governments, and appointed various military and security officers to replace state governors. At the time, human rights organizations estimated that about forty protesters had been killed and more than 1,000 Sudanese arrested since demonstrations began.

The Sudanese were not dissuaded, however, and a period of heightened protest kicked off on April 6—a date chosen to coincide with the anniversary of a successful, peaceful uprising against former dictator Jaafar Nimeiri in 1985. Tens of thousands of people joined the protests, with some staging a sit-in outside the army's headquarters in Khartoum, the capital. The United Nations (UN) later reported that more than twenty people were killed and at least another hundred wounded between April 6 and April 11. The National Intelligence and Security Services allegedly used tear gas and live ammunition to disperse protesters participating in the sit-in, with other reports detailing widespread arrests and attacks against journalists. UN officials condemned the "excessive use of force against peaceful protests in Sudan." Michael Forst, the UN special rapporteur on the situation of human rights defenders, said the Sudanese people "have the right to express their views and concerns through peaceful means, in particular on issues concerning fundamental rights."

On April 11, First Vice President and Minister of Defense Lt. Gen. Awad Ibn Auf appeared on state television to announce that al-Bashir's government had been replaced by a Transitional Military Council (TMC) and that the ousted president had been detained "in a secure place." Ibn Auf said the army would lead a transitional government for two years while overseeing the changeover to a full civilian government. (Ibn Auf resigned as head of the TMC twenty-four hours after announcing al-Bashir's removal, and Lt. Gen. Abdel Fattah Abdelrahman Burhan was named the new leader.)

In a statement, Moussa Faki Mahamat, the chair of the African Union (AU) Commission, expressed the organization's "conviction that the military take-over is not the appropriate response to the challenges facing Sudan and the aspirations of its people." He appealed to all stakeholders in the conflict to "engage in an inclusive dialogue to create the conditions that will make it possible to meet the aspirations of the Sudanese people to democracy, good governance and well-being and restore constitutional order as soon as possible." UN Secretary-General António Guterres shared similar sentiments, stating that the "democratic aspirations" of the people needed to be realized through "an appropriate and inclusive transition process." He also called for calm and "utmost restraint."

Government Cracks Down as Protests Continue

The protesters were not satisfied with al-Bashir's removal from office, and they continued to demand the formation of a civilian government. SPA leaders argued that the military officers who led the coup and now sat on the TMC were part of the problems the Sudanese were protesting, and also needed to be removed. The movement's demands further expanded to include the withdrawal of the Rapid Support Forces (a paramilitary group better known as the Janjaweed) from cities; the release of political prisoners; assistance for unarmed civilians who had been attacked during protests; and for those who had killed, hurt, or abused peaceful protesters to face justice.

The sit-in at army headquarters continued during this time. On June 3, the Rapid Support Forces led a violent raid of the protesters' camp, using live fire to try to disperse sit-in participants. Reports by independent medical groups and human rights organizations said protesters were beaten, raped, and subject to humiliations such as being urinated on by militia members or forced to wade through sewer water. Other reports suggested the Rapid Support Forces chased protesters into hospitals while continuing to shoot at them, blocked entrances and exits to the camp before opening fire, and burned protesters' camps and makeshift clinics. Independent groups estimated that more than 120 people were killed and hundreds more were wounded.

The raid occurred following the collapse of initial talks between the TMC and the FFC, which failed due to a disagreement over whether a civilian or a soldier should lead a new transitional governing body. Several days before the raid, the TMC claimed the ongoing sit-in had become "a danger" to national security and warned that action may be taken against "unruly elements."

World leaders and independent organizations decried the crackdown. The AU's Mahamat "strongly condemns the violence," the commission said, and called for "an immediate and transparent investigation in order to hold those all responsible accountable." He also called for "all international partners to reinforce common efforts towards the immediate cessation of the violence and rapid resumption of negotiations for a political settlement." The AU suspended Sudan's membership several days later. The TMC expressed "sorrow for the way events escalated," claiming the operation had targeted "trouble makers and petty criminals." Government prosecutors later produced an inquiry concluding "rogue" military personnel were responsible for the raid.

The SPA remained undeterred, calling for a blockade of roads and bridges to "paralyze public life" in response to the violence. "It is imperative to go out to the streets to protect the revolution and the remaining dignity," it said in a statement. Major protests resumed later that month, with tens of thousands of Sudanese once again taking to the streets on June 30, despite efforts by security forces to dispel them with tear gas. The acting under secretary for health reported that at least seven people died and nearly two hundred were injured during this round of demonstrations.

Agreement on Transitional Government Reached

After the deadly raid on June 3, officials from the AU and Ethiopia stepped in to mediate renewed talks between the TMC and the FFC. On July 5, the parties to the talks announced they had reached a deal to form a joint civilian–military transitional government as a next step toward the installation of an all-civilian administration. The deal called for a Sovereign Council comprised of six civilians and five military officers. The Council president would be a military officer for the first twenty-one months of a thirty-nine-month transition period; a civilian would hold the presidency for the remaining eighteen months. At the end of the designated transition period, new elections would be held. In addition to the Sovereign Council, the agreement called for the creation of a Sovereign Cabinet and legislative assembly. Eighteen of the twenty cabinet positions would be appointed by the pro-democracy movement; the ministers of defense and interior would be chosen by the military. The legislative assembly would be comprised of 300 members, the parties agreed. A majority of seats (67 percent) would be given to the FFC to fill. The remaining seats would be filled by members of political groups not associated with al-Bashir. In addition, the pro-democracy movement would nominate a prime minister to lead the cabinet.

The agreement was heralded as an important victory for the Sudanese people and their push for democracy. Mahamat applauded the people of Sudan on their "important breakthrough" and their "commitment to the peaceful expression of their legitimate aspirations" for peace and democracy in Sudan. Guterres said he was "encouraged by the agreement," urging stakeholders "to ensure the timely, inclusive, and transparent implementation of the agreement" and to continue dialogue to resolve outstanding issues.

Those outstanding issues included the future of the Rapid Support Forces and immunity for military officers but were resolved over two days of additional talks in August. It was decided that the Rapid Support Forces would move under the oversight of the Sudanese army and that military generals could be prosecuted for past actions if such legal proceedings were approved by the forthcoming legislative body. On August 4, the TMC and the FFC signed a constitutional declaration affirming the terms of their agreement. "Today, we turn a conflict-ridden page in Sudan's history," said TMC deputy chief Lt. Gen. Mohamed Hamdan at the signing ceremony. Lt. Gen. Burhan declared it to be "the agreement the Sudanese people have been waiting for" since the country gained its independence from Britain in 1956.

The new Sovereign Council assumed governing responsibilities from the TMC on August 20. The next day, Abdullah Hamdouk was sworn in as prime minister. Hamdouk was an economist who had previously served as the deputy executive secretary of the UN Economic Commission for Africa. He also held positions at the International Labor Organization and the African Development Bank. His selection signaled to many observers that Sudan's transitional government would focus on addressing the country's economic woes. In remarks following his swearing-in, Hamdouk affirmed that improving the economy and reform of state institutions would be top priorities, along with "stopping the war and achieving a comprehensive and just peace." Hamdouk said the government would work to "build a national economy based on production and not donations and aid," declaring, "We are a rich country, we can rely on our own resources." The prime minister announced the appointment of eighteen cabinet ministers on September 5, pledging the government would begin working immediately "in a harmonious and collective way." The remaining two cabinet ministers were appointed mid-October. At the time of writing, Sudan's new legislative body had not been formed.

—Linda Grimm

Following is a United Nations news story published on April 11, 2019, with statements from UN secretary-general António Guterres and human rights experts on the coup and violence in Sudan; a statement by African Union chair Moussa Faki Mahamat from April 11, 2019, on President Omar al-Bashir's removal from office; a statement by Mahamat on June 3, 2019, condemning violence against Sudanese protesters; statements by Guterres and Mahamat on July 5, 2019, in response to the transitional government agreement; and remarks by Sudanese prime minister Abdullah Hamdouk following his swearing-in on August 21, 2019.

UN Secretary-General Guterres
Responds to President al-Bashir's Ouster

DOCUMENT

April 11, 2019

UN chief António Guterres said on Thursday that the "democratic aspirations of the Sudanese people" need to be realized through "an appropriate and inclusive transition process," following the overthrow and arrest of President Omar al-Bashir by order of the country's new military governing council.

In a statement issued in New York by his Spokesperson, the Secretary-General said he would continue to follow development "very closely" and reiterated his call for calm and "utmost restraint by all."

In announcing the end of Mr. Bashir's rule via State television, Sudan's defence minister said that he was being held "in a secure place," and the army would now oversee a two-year period of transition back to full civilian rule.

But on Thursday night, according to news reports, thousands of Sudanese in the capital Khartoum defied a military curfew which was supposed to keep citizens off the streets from 10pm until 4am, raising fears of fresh violence between security forces and protesters, as well as possible clashes between militia and army units.

An official message carried on State-run media stated that "the armed forces and security council will carry out its duty to uphold peace," protect citizens' security, and "citizens' livelihoods."

Mr. Guterres said in his statement that the UN "stands ready to support the Sudanese people as they chart a new way forward." Earlier in the day, a group of UN human rights experts condemned reports of "excessive use of force against peaceful protesters in Sudan" during the past six days of heightened protest leading up to the overthrow of President Bashir, when tens-of-thousands took to the streets, holding a sit-in outside army headquarters in central Khartoum.

"While taking note of the latest reports that a military council is being formed," the experts called on the authorities to respond to "the legitimate grievances of the people."

More than 20 killed, 100 injured in protests

More than 20 people have been killed and over 100 injured since 6 April, the experts said, adding they had also received reports of widespread arrests and attacks on journalists by the security forces.

At the sit-in prior to the military takeover, the National Intelligence and Security Services used live ammunition and tear gas to disperse protesters, prompting the army to move in to protect them.

"In this moment of crisis, the exercise of the rights to freedom of expression and freedom of peaceful assembly needs to be protected and guaranteed," said the UN Special Rapporteur on the rights to freedom of peaceful assembly and of association, Clément Nyaletsossi Voule, and the Special Rapporteur on the right to freedom of opinion and expression, David Kaye.

Protests erupted nearly four months ago when the Government attempted to raise the prices of bread and basic commodities.

"I urge the authorities to lift the national state of emergency and respond to the legitimate grievances of the Sudanese people through inclusive peaceful political process," Mr. Voule said. "The Sudanese people, including human rights defenders, have the right to express their views and concerns through peaceful means, in particular on issues concerning fundamental rights," added Michel Forst, UN Special Rapporteur on the situation of human rights defenders.

The UN Independent Expert on the situation of human rights in Sudan, Aristide Nononsi, said the State's institutions are obliged to protect civilians and respect the people's legitimate demands and constitutional rights.

"I call on State authorities to uphold their primary responsibility to protect the civilian population in Sudan, and I strongly urge the Sudanese military and security forces to exercise the utmost restraint to avoid further escalation of violence and to take immediate measures to protect the constitutional rights of the Sudanese," Mr. Nononsi said.

Rapid-response aid, from UN's emergency fund

Also on Thursday, Emergency Relief Coordinator Mark Lowcock released a $26.5 million Rapid Response allocation from the UN's Central Emergency Response Fund to provide life-saving food, livelihood, nutrition, health, water and sanitation assistance to over 800,000 people affected by a worsening economic crisis and food insecurity across seven states in Sudan, over the next six months.

"The economic crisis has had knock-on effects on the wider humanitarian situation that go beyond food insecurity. Higher food prices mean that families are eating less nutritious food and more young children and pregnant women are getting sick. Families struggle to afford even limited medical treatment," said Mr. Lowcock.

The CERF allocation will target internally displaced people, refugees, host communities, and vulnerable residents in areas with some of the largest increases in food insecurity, including in East, North, South and West Darfur, Red Sea, West Kordofan and White Nile states.

SOURCE: United Nations News. "'Democratic Aspirations of the Sudanese People' Must Be Met Urges Guterres, Following Military Removal of al-Bashir from Power." April 11, 2019. https://news.un.org/en/story/2019/04/1036551.

AU Commission Chair Statement on al-Bashir Removal

April 11, 2019

The Chairperson of the African Union Commission, Moussa Faki Mahamat, is closely monitoring the ongoing developments in Sudan, in particular the announcement of the First Vice President and Minister of Defence Lt. General Awad Ibn Auf on the suspension of the Constitution, the dissolution of the National Assembly, the formation of a military-led transitional government which will rule for two years, and the arrest of President Omar Al Bashir, as well as the imposition of a state of emergency for three months.

The Chairperson expresses the African Union conviction that the military take-over is not the appropriate response to the challenges facing Sudan and the aspirations of its people.

The Chairperson recalls the 2000 Lomé Declaration on the unconstitutional change of Government and the African Charter on Democracy, Elections, and Governance, which strongly condemn any unconstitutional change of Government and commit member states to the respect of the rule of law, democratic principles and human rights. In view of the ongoing developments, the Chairperson reiterates these provisions, and looks forward to the Peace and Security Council meeting swiftly to consider the situation and take the appropriate decisions.

In the meantime, the Chairperson urges all concerned to exercise calm and utmost restraint and to respect the rights of citizens, foreign nationals and private property in the interest of the country and its people.

The Chairperson further appeals to all stakeholders to engage in an inclusive dialogue to create the conditions that will make it possible to meet the aspirations of the Sudanese people to democracy, good governance and well-being and restore constitutional order as soon as possible.

The Chairperson expresses the African Union solidarity with the people of Sudan, and pledges its commitment and readiness to support Sudan during this period, in line with the relevant AU instruments and principles.

SOURCE: African Union. "Statement of the Chairperson of the Commission on the Situation in Sudan." April 11, 2019. https://au.int/sites/default/files/pressreleases/36376-pr-36377-pr-statement_of_the_chairperson_of_the_commission_on_the_situation_in_sudan-1.pdf.

AU Commission Chair Condemns Violence against Sudanese

DOCUMENT

June 3, 2019

The Chairperson of the African Union Commission, Moussa Faki, strongly condemns the violence that erupted today which led to reported deaths and several civilian injuries. In this regard, he calls for an immediate and transparent investigation in order to hold those all responsible accountable. The Chairperson calls on the Transitional Military Council to protect the civilians from further harm.

The Chairperson wishes to recall the African Union Peace and Security Council (AU PSC) Communique of 30 April 2019 on Sudan, which demanded all Sudanese stakeholders to return to the negotiations urgently in order to arrive at an inclusive accord, which paves the way for a civilian-led Transitional Authority.

Furthermore, the Chairperson calls on all international partners to reinforce common efforts towards the immediate cessation of the violence and rapid resumption of negotiations for a political settlement.

Given the tense situation in the country, the Chairperson calls on all concerned to exercise outmost restraint and to respect the rights of citizens, in the interest of the country and its people.

The Chairperson reiterates the African Union's determination to continue to engage and accompany the Sudanese people to support the consolidation of a political agreement in line with the relevant AU Peace and Security Council decisions.

SOURCE: African Union. "Statement of the Chairperson on the Situation in Sudan." June 3, 2019. https://au.int/en/pressreleases/20190603/statement-chairperson-situation-sudan.

UN Secretary-General Guterres
Statement on Agreement in Sudan

July 5, 2019

The Secretary-General is encouraged by the agreement reached between the Forces for Freedom and Change and the Transitional Military Council on 5 July towards the establishment of transitional governing bodies. He congratulates the African Union and Ethiopia for their role in mediating the Sudanese-led talks and commends the Inter-Governmental Authority on Development (IGAD) for its support to the process.

The Secretary-General encourages all stakeholders to ensure the timely, inclusive, and transparent implementation of the agreement and resolve any outstanding issues through dialogue. He also welcomes the parties' commitment to conducting an independent investigation into the violence perpetrated against peaceful protesters, including the events on 3 June.

The Secretary-General expresses his solidarity with the people of Sudan and reiterates the commitment of the United Nations to assist in the transition process.

SOURCE: United Nations Secretary-General. "Statement Attributable to the Spokesman for the Secretary-General—on Sudan." July 5, 2019. https://www.un.org/sg/en/content/sg/statement/2019-07-05/statement-attributable-the-spokesman-for-the-secretary-general-sudan.

AU Commission Chair Statement
on Agreement in Sudan

July 5, 2019

The Chairperson highly commends the people of Sudan on the occasion of this important breakthrough and recognizes their commitment to the peaceful expression of their legitimate aspirations for a peaceful and democratic Sudan.

The Chairperson wishes to make a special mention of congratulations to his Special Envoy Professor Mohamed el Hacen Lebatt and the Special Envoy of Ethiopia's Prime Minister Dr. Abiy Ahmed, Ambassador Mahmoud Dirir, and their teams, for their exemplary and patient mediation efforts. The support and collaboration of the International Governmental Authority on Development (IGAD) and the neighboring countries of Sudan in this regard, is also highly appreciated.

The Chairperson also extends his gratitude to the international community for their support to a Sudanese-led process and the African mediation process that led to this positive outcome for the country, the region and the Continent.

The Chairperson urges the national parties to maintain this spirit of compromise and responsibility for the national interests of Sudan.

The Chairperson further reiterates the steadfast and continued commitment of the African Union to accompany the Sudanese people in their pursuit towards a democratic Sudan.

SOURCE: African Union. "Statement of the Chairperson of the AU Commission on the Situation in Sudan." July 5, 2019. https://au.int/sites/default/files/pressreleases/36976-pr-auc-sudan_05072019_.pdf.

Sudanese Prime Minister Hamdouk Comments on Government Priorities

August 21, 2019

Sudanese Prime Minister Dr. Abdullah Hamdouk revealed the priorities of his government during the transitional period, and stressed that stopping the war and achieving a comprehensive and just peace are the most important priorities besides the economic file and the reform of state institutions and the fight against corruption and achieving the rule of law and transparency and creating balanced external relations that take into account the interests of the country.

The prime minister said on a press statement after his swearing-in as Prime Minister at the Presidential Palace, "My nomination is by the forces of freedom and change but after taking the oath I will be prime minister for all the Sudanese," Hamdouk added.

"The legacy is overloaded, and we don't have 'Moses' stick,' but with the popular consensus we will cross our country forward armed with our consensus."

Mr. Hamdouk pointed out that the slogan of the revolution "freedom, peace and justice" will form the program of the next transitional period, and he said "We will work to stop the suffering of our people in the refugee camps and displacement and address the economic crisis and build a national economy based on production and not donations and aid. We are a rich country we can rely on our own resources."

He assured that the chosen ministers are competency-based, he points that as agreed with freedom and change forces that three names will be nominated for the position, and he stressed that if the competency criterion did not apply to the three candidates, he would return the list to select others eligible for the position.

The prime minister assured of the women representation in the coming government, he said that women were in the front line of the revolution but they didn't have their rights in the group of delegations, pointing that women representative in the government is a basic right.

Mr. Hamdouk called for organizing multiple democratic system adding that "let us [agree how to govern Sudan and we leave the question of who rules Sudan to its great people]."

He pledged that to give hand to those who affected by torrents and rains by harnessing the possibilities [*sic*].

SOURCE: Council of Ministers of the Republic of the Sudan. "Prime Minister: 'I Will Be Prime Minister for All Sudanese.'" August 21, 2019. http://www.sudan.gov.sd/index.php/en/home/news_details/1476.

OTHER HISTORIC DOCUMENTS OF INTEREST

FROM PREVIOUS *HISTORIC DOCUMENTS*

May

State Leaders Sign Stringent Abortion Legislation; Courts Weigh In

MAY 15, MAY 24, AND OCTOBER 29, 2019

In 2019, a dozen states passed laws limiting the ability of women to seek an abortion. A majority of these were known as so-called heartbeat bills, which penalized doctors with fines, loss of licensure, and prison time for performing an abortion after a fetal heartbeat could be detected. The most stringent law passed was in Alabama, where the legislature did not use the heartbeat standard but instead banned all abortion, with exceptions only in instances of fatal fetal abnormality or when a mother's life would be in danger if the pregnancy were carried to term. In most states, the Republican leaders driving the legislation admitted that they were likely incongruent with *Roe v. Wade*, the 1973 Supreme Court decision that allows women to terminate a pregnancy for any reason until a fetus would be considered viable outside the womb. Their intent in passing these laws was to draw court cases that would eventually result in a reconsideration of *Roe* by the now-conservative-majority high court. Liberal organizations including the American Civil Liberties Union (ACLU) and Planned Parenthood filed suit on behalf of women in the states where restrictive abortion legislation was passed, promising to keep these laws from going into effect. Ongoing judicial review meant that by the close of 2019, abortion was still legal in all fifty states, though at varying times during a pregnancy.

ALABAMA GOVERNOR SIGNS STRICT ANTIABORTION LEGISLATION

On May 15, 2019, Alabama's Republican governor, Kay Ivey, signed the Human Life Protection Act, a bill banning nearly all abortions and one of the strictest pieces of abortion legislation in the United States. The law made it a crime for doctors to perform an abortion at any stage of pregnancy, unless the woman's life was threatened or the fetus had a fatal abnormality; for mental illness to qualify a woman for an abortion, two doctors would need to agree that the emotional condition was serious enough that either the woman or fetus could die as a result. The law made a fetus a legal person "for homicide purposes," but women seeking an abortion would not be held liable for their action. The doctor performing the procedure, however, could be punished with a maximum sentence of ninety-nine years in jail. The law made no exception for rape or incest, which was a point of contention among Republicans, with some arguing that a fetus is a person with rights and all abortion is murder, and others that a carve-out was necessary to protect women who were victims of a crime.

Ivey admitted that the legislation was likely unenforceable under *Roe* but said during a ceremony signing the bill that its supporters and sponsors "believe that it is time, once again, for the U.S. Supreme Court to revisit this important matter, and they believe this act may bring about the best opportunity for this to occur." The National Organization for Women (NOW) criticized the legislation as an "unconstitutional measure" that "would send women in the state back to the dark days of policymakers having control over their bodies, health, and lives." The group added that they "strongly oppose this bill and the other egregious pieces of legislation that extremist lawmakers are trying to pass in what they claim is an attempt to force the Supreme Court to overturn *Roe*."

Less than two weeks after the bill was signed, Planned Parenthood, the ACLU, and the ACLU of Alabama filed a lawsuit on behalf of Alabama abortion providers to challenge the new law. According to the complaint, the law would "inflict immediate and irreparable harm on plaintiffs' patients by violating their constitutional rights, threatening their health and well-being, and forcing them to continue their pregnancies to term against their will." In late October, Judge Myron H. Thompson of the U.S. District Court for the Middle District of Alabama issued a preliminary injunction blocking the law from going into effect on November 15. The judge argued that the law violates the Supreme Court precedents set in *Roe* and later cases such as *Planned Parenthood v. Casey*. The state's attorney general, Steve Marshall, promised to appeal the decision. "As we have stated before, the state's objective is to advance our case to the U.S. Supreme Court," Marshall said, arguing "the Constitution does not prohibit states from protecting unborn children from abortion."

States Pass Heartbeat Abortion Legislation

In recent years, a growing number of states led by conservative legislatures have limited access to abortion through a variety of means, including reducing the time frame during a pregnancy when abortion is legal, increasing waiting periods between when a woman seeks abortion treatment and when the procedure can be performed, and adding medical requirements for doctors and building standards for clinics. In 2019, these activities continued. Arkansas and Utah each passed—and the governors signed—legislation banning abortion at eighteen weeks, which was quickly challenged in court. The governors in Indiana and North Dakota signed legislation banning the dilation and evacuation abortion procedure, which is used primarily in second-trimester abortions and which effectively outlawed any second-trimester abortions. A preliminary injunction was issued against the Indiana law, and groups in North Dakota were considering a challenge.

The most frequently passed abortion-related legislation in 2019 were "heartbeat" bills, which banned abortion once a doctor could detect a fetal heartbeat, sometimes as early as six weeks into the pregnancy. Medical experts argue that what the laws designate as a heartbeat really is not one, because at that point, a fetus does not truly have a heart. Instead, ultrasounds at that time detect a flickering of the fetal tissue that will eventually become the heart in the course of development. Dr. Ted Anderson, president of the American College of Obstetricians and Gynecologists, said calling it a heartbeat bill is "out of step with the anatomical and clinical realities of that stage of pregnancy."

Mississippi was the first to pass a heartbeat bill in 2019, its second abortion ban in as many years. The 2018 legislation banned abortion after fifteen weeks, but a temporary injunction was issued in December 2018, preventing the law from going into effect while appeals were pursued in court. The March 2019 law relied on the heartbeat standard for when an abortion could no longer be performed and included exceptions for danger to the life of or severe physical impairment of the mother, but it had no exception for rape or incest. Physicians performing an abortion after the cutoff would lose their license. The Center for Reproductive Rights, which filed the lawsuit targeting the 2018 law, quickly expanded its complaint to include the new heartbeat legislation.

In April, Ohio governor Mike DeWine signed heartbeat legislation that the state legislature had been attempting to enact for a number of years. In 2016 and 2018, the legislature passed similar bills, but they were vetoed by then–Republican governor John Kasich, who refused to sign the legislation because he considered it unconstitutional. Like Mississippi, the law included no exception for rape or incest, but it did allow for abortion in order to prevent death or irreversible physical impairment of the mother. Doctors who performed an abortion after the detection of a heartbeat, or who failed to look for one before performing the procedure, would be guilty of a fifth-degree felony and could be charged $20,000 for each violation; they would also be open to wrongful death lawsuits from the mother. The ACLU, ACLU of Ohio, and Planned Parenthood filed a lawsuit against the legislation on May 15. Undeterred by the legal challenge, the state legislature continued through the summer and fall to work on additional abortion legislation, including a bill that would require doctors to try to "reimplant an ectopic pregnancy into the woman's uterus." The text of the bill drew near-immediate scorn from the medical community, which dismissed it as dangerous misinformation and "science fiction."

Missouri was among the other states that considered heartbeat legislation. Although an original draft of the bill included heartbeat language, it was pulled before final consideration and passage by the state legislature in May. Instead, the bill was structured to avoid legal challenges by setting different time limits at which abortion would be legal, each of which would go into effect if a previous time limit was struck down by the courts. To begin, the bill sought an eight-week near-total abortion ban, which included no carve-out for rape or incest and only permitted abortion after that time to prevent physical impairment or death of the mother. If a court blocked that from going into effect, the law would move to a fourteen-week ban, then an eighteen-week ban, and finally a twenty-week ban. In signing the Missouri Stands for the Unborn Act, Republican governor Mike Parson said the state was "sending a strong signal to the nation that, in Missouri, we stand for life, protect women's health, and advocate for the unborn." Like other laws, it was quickly challenged by abortion proponents, and a judge blocked almost all of the law in August, with the exception of a provision that bans abortion based on a fetus's race, sex, or a possible Down syndrome diagnosis. The court's decision is being appealed.

SUPREME COURT AGREES TO HEAR ABORTION CASE

In October, the Supreme Court announced it would hear an abortion case, *June Medical Services v. Gee*, a challenge to a 2014 Louisiana law that placed strict licensing requirements on abortion doctors. Specifically, any doctor performing the procedure needed to have admitting privileges at a nearby hospital. Since it went into effect, only one doctor in the state met the qualifications. The abortion providers challenging the law state that the licensing requirements are not meant to protect the health of women but are instead a backdoor attempt to ban abortion in Louisiana.

The law's supporters argue that requiring doctors to have hospital-admitting privileges ensures not only a certain level of competency among abortion providers but also that women can access emergency medical assistance if the procedure goes wrong. Opponents point to data indicating that abortion rarely results in hospitalization. According to a study published by the peer-review medical journal *BMC Medicine*, "Abortion-related ED [emergency department] visits comprise a small proportion of women's ED visits. . . . Given the low rate of major incidents, perceptions that abortion is unsafe are not based on evidence."

Louisiana's law was upheld in 2018 by a three-judge panel in the Fifth Circuit Court of Appeals, with Judge Jerry E. Smith writing for the majority that the law provides "some evidence of a minimal benefit" that "promotes the well-being of women seeking abortion." The case is likely to be closely watched because the Supreme Court struck down a similar law out of Texas in 2016. Then, the Court avoided a deadlock (it was short one member following the death of Justice Antonin Scalia) and reached a 5–3 decision when Justice Anthony Kennedy joined the four more liberal justices to rule against the Texas law. The seats held by both Scalia and Kennedy were replaced by more conservative justices in 2017 and 2018, making the outcome far less certain. Alexis McGill Johnson, acting president of Planned Parenthood, said of the case, "Access to abortion is hanging by a thread in this country, and this case is what could snap that thread."

—Heather Kerrigan

Following is the text of Governor Kay Ivey's statement from May 15, 2019, on signing the Alabama Human Life Protection Act; Governor Mike Parson's May 24, 2019, statement on signing the Missouri Stands for the Unborn Act; and the text of the October 29, 2019, ruling in Robinson v. Marshall *by the U.S. District Court of the United States for the Middle District of Alabama, Northern Division, which placed a temporary injunction on the state's abortion ban.*

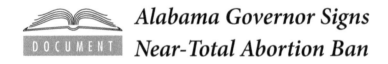

Alabama Governor Signs Near-Total Abortion Ban

May 15, 2019

Governor Kay Ivey on Wednesday signed into law the Alabama Human Life Protection Act, after both houses of the Alabama Legislature passed HB314.

Upon signing the bill, Governor Ivey released the following statement:

"Today, I signed into law the Alabama Human Life Protection Act, a bill that was approved by overwhelming majorities in both chambers of the Legislature. To the bill's many supporters, this legislation stands as a powerful testament to Alabamians' deeply held belief that every life is precious and that every life is a sacred gift from God.

To all Alabamians, I assure you that we will continue to follow the rule of law.

In all meaningful respects, this bill closely resembles an abortion ban that has been a part of Alabama law for well over 100 years. As today's bill itself recognizes, that long-standing abortion law has been rendered "unenforceable as a result of the U.S. Supreme Court decision in *Roe v. Wade.*"

No matter one's personal view on abortion, we can all recognize that, at least for the short term, this bill may similarly be unenforceable. As citizens of this great country, we must always respect the authority of the U.S. Supreme Court even when we disagree with their decisions. Many Americans, myself included, disagreed when *Roe v. Wade* was handed down in 1973. The sponsors of this bill believe that it is time, once again, for the

U.S. Supreme Court to revisit this important matter, and they believe this act may bring about the best opportunity for this to occur.

I want to commend the bill sponsors, Rep. Terri Collins and Sen. Clyde Chambliss, for their strong leadership on this important issue.

For the remainder of this session, I now urge all members of the Alabama Legislature to continue seeking the best ways possible to foster a better Alabama in all regards, from education to public safety. We must give every person the best chance for a quality life and a promising future."

SOURCE: Office of the Governor of Alabama. "Governor Ivey Issues Statement after Signing the Alabama Human Life Protection Act." May 15, 2019. https://governor.alabama.gov/statements/governor-ivey-issues-statement-after-signing-the-alabama-human-life-protection-act.

Missouri Governor Signs Abortion Legislation

May 24, 2019

This morning at the State Capitol, Governor Parson joined with House and Senate members and pro-life coalition leaders to sign House Bill 126. The bill was passed by super-majorities in both the House and the Senate.

"By signing this bill today, we are sending a strong signal to the nation that, in Missouri, we stand for life, protect women's health, and advocate for the unborn," said Governor Mike Parson. "All life has value and is worth protecting."

HB 126, also known as the "Missouri Stands for the Unborn Act," prohibits an abortion in a non-medical emergency past eight weeks of gestational age and ensures the protection of women's safety. HB 126 prohibits an individual from performing or inducing an abortion solely because of a diagnosis of potential for Down Syndrome in an unborn child or because of the race or sex of the unborn child.

HB 126 contains an emergency clause that requires written notification of a parent or guardian by the custodial parent or guardian of consent for an abortion to be performed on a minor. The bill expands the definition of a pregnancy resource center for tax credit purposes to include facilities that provide assistance to families as well. In addition, this bill removes the sunset and cumulative tax credit cap beginning in FY 2021 and increases the pregnancy resource center tax credit from 50 percent to 70 percent beginning January 1, 2021.

The Governor encourages all Missourians to get involved in efforts to support life in their communities, whether that's opening your family's home to adoption to assist children in need, volunteering at your local pregnancy resource center, or joining with your faith community to provide the necessary support to help individuals choose life.

Governor Parson continued, "Thanks to decades of pro-life leadership, Missouri recently hit an all-time low for the number of abortions. We've gone from a high of more than 20,000 in our state, to now below 3,000. By working together, we can continue to assist more Missourians in choosing life."

The Governor also signed SB 21, which adds the cities of Portageville, Riverside, and Fayette to the list of cities authorized to propose a sales tax for the purposes of improving public safety. The sales tax cannot exceed a rate of 0.5 percent. This bill also modifies the City Sales Tax Act to allow cities to propose a sales tax for general city purposes at a rate not to exceed 1 percent instead of at a rate of 0.5 percent, 0.875 percent, or 1 percent. SB 21 bill contains an emergency clause and will become law upon the Governor's signature.

SOURCE: Office of the Governor of Missouri. "Governor Parson Signs House Bill 126 and Senate Bill 21." May 24, 2019. https://governor.mo.gov/press-releases/archive/governor-parson-signs-house-bill-126-and-senate-bill-21.

Federal Court Temporarily Blocks Alabama Abortion Law

October 29, 2019

[Footnotes and in-text references have been omitted.]

IN THE DISTRICT COURT OF THE UNITED STATES FOR THE MIDDLE DISTRICT OF ALABAMA, NORTHERN DIVISION

YASHICA ROBINSON, M.D., et al., on behalf of themselves, their patients, physicians, clinic administrators, and staff,

    Plaintiffs,

    v.

STEVEN MARSHALL, in his official capacity as Alabama Attorney General,

    Defendant.

CIVIL ACTION NO.
2:19cv365-MHT (WO)

OPINION

This lawsuit challenges a 2019 Alabama statute, Ala. Act No. 2019–189, that imposes criminal liability on abortion providers for nearly all abortions, completed or attempted, regardless of fetal viability. In essence the Act imposes a near-total ban on abortion. It is set to take effect on November 15, 2019.

The plaintiffs are providers of abortion services: Dr. Yashica Robinson, M.D.; Alabama Women's Center; Planned Parenthood Southeast, Inc.; Reproductive Health Services; and West Alabama Women's Center. They sue on behalf of their patients claiming that the Act is unconstitutional under the Due Process of the Fourteenth Amendment, as enforced through 42 U.S.C. §1983 because it violates their patients' substantive-due-process rights to liberty and privacy. They also sue on behalf of themselves. The defendant is the State Attorney General, sued in his official capacity. This court's jurisdiction is proper under 28 U.S.C. §1331 (federal question) and 28 U.S.C. §1343(a)(3) & (4) (civil rights).

The case is now before the court on the plaintiffs' motion for a preliminary injunction (doc. no. 50). For the reasons detailed below, the motion will be granted with respect to any and all applications of the Act to pre-viability abortion.

I. LEGAL STANDARDS

To show that a preliminary injunction is appropriate, the plaintiffs must demonstrate that (1) there is a substantial likelihood that they ultimately will prevail on the merits of the claim; (2) they will suffer irreparable injury unless the injunction issues; (3) the threatened injury to them outweighs whatever damage the proposed injunction may cause the defendant; and (4) the public interest will not be harmed if the injunction should issue. The plaintiffs bear the burden to make each showing.

Here, in order to demonstrate substantial likelihood of success on the merits, the plaintiffs must show that the Act is likely to violate the substantive-due-process rights of individuals seeking abortions in Alabama. The Fourteenth Amendment to the United States Constitution protects a woman's right to terminate her pregnancy. "The woman's right to terminate her pregnancy before viability," the Supreme Court has stated, is "a rule of law and a component of liberty we cannot renounce." The Supreme Court "has determined and then redetermined that the Constitution offers basic protection to the woman's right to choose."

This right, however, has limits. As the Court recognized in *Casey*, the State has legitimate interests in protecting maternal health and the potential life of the fetus. A State may regulate abortion to further those interests but only if the laws in question do not pose an "undue burden" to a woman's right to end her pregnancy. "An undue burden exists, and therefore a provision of law is invalid, if its purpose or effect is to place a substantial obstacle in the path of a woman seeking an abortion before the fetus attains viability." In evaluating regulations of pre-viability abortion, then, courts must "consider[ ] the burdens a law imposes on abortion access together with benefits those laws confer."

But unlike laws that *regulate* the performance of pre-viability abortion, *bans* on pre-viability abortion require no balancing at all. The United States Constitution forbids the prohibition of abortion prior to fetal viability. "Before viability, the State's interests are not strong enough to support a prohibition of abortion. . . ." This bright-line rule governs bans, rather than mere regulations, of pre-viability abortion.

II. DISCUSSION

A. Substantial Likelihood of Success on the Merits

1. Justiciability

As a threshold matter, the plaintiff's success on the merits requires a justiciable case. Here, clear case law supports the plaintiffs' standing to bring suit—a fact that the defendant has acknowledged.

The plaintiffs sue in part on behalf of their patients. They argue that the Act threatens their patients' substantive-due-process rights, which are guaranteed under the Fourteenth Amendment to the United States Constitution.

Federal courts, including the Supreme Court, routinely allow providers to challenge abortion laws on behalf of patients. These cases emphasize "the central role of the physician, both in consulting with the woman about whether or not to have an abortion, and in determining how any abortion was to be carried out." Such a relationship similarly supports standing for the plaintiffs at bar—all are intimately involved in patients' decisions regarding abortion and reproductive health.

In sum, under precedent that the Supreme Court has repeatedly reaffirmed, abortion providers may assert the substantive-due-process rights of their patients. The plaintiffs may do so here. The court thus turns to the constitutional arguments that they raise in favor of a preliminary injunction.

2. Substantive Due Process

The court is persuaded that the plaintiffs are likely to succeed in showing that the Act violates an individual's constitutional right to obtain a pre-viability abortion, and thus that it violates her constitutional rights. And the defendant agrees.

The Act imposes criminal liability on any person who "intentionally perform[s] or attempt[s] to perform an abortion," with limited exceptions for serious health risks to the mother. It does so without regard to the viability of the fetus.

This fact alone makes an injunction appropriate. As stated previously, banning abortion before viability violates Supreme Court precedent.

Thus, as a ban on pre-viability abortion, the Act contravenes established law. The plaintiffs have shown a substantial likelihood of success on the merits of their claim.

B. Irreparable Harm

The plaintiffs' alleged injury is concrete and imminent. Enforcement of the ban would yield serious and irreparable harm, violating the right to privacy and preventing women from obtaining abortions in Alabama.

First, any ongoing violation of the constitutional right to privacy constitutes "irreparable injury." The nature of the violation thus counsels in favor of an injunction.

Even apart from this general principle, the enforcement of the Act would irreparably harm those who contemplate or seek, but cannot lawfully obtain, a pre-viability abortion. A near-total ban imposes substantial costs on women, including those who are unable to obtain an abortion and those who "desperately seek to exercise their ability to decide whether to have a child" and thus "would take unsafe measures to end their pregnancies."

Finally, the law's limited exceptions do not alter the court's conclusion. "[A] medical exception cannot save an otherwise unconstitutional ban." This is especially so when the exceptions are narrow, arguably ambiguous, or validated post-hoc.

The court thus finds that, if not enjoined, the Act's near-total ban on abortion would impose a substantial and irreparable harm, leaving many patients without recourse. This factor, too, points toward a preliminary injunction.

C. The Balance of Hardships

The balance of hardships tilts in favor of the plaintiffs. Because the Act prohibits nearly all pre-viability abortions, the outcome is simple: no state interest can prevail in this context.

Moreover, because the law will almost certainly be found unconstitutional, any cost to the State is slight: Alabama has "no legitimate interest in enforcing an unconstitutional [law]." The balance of equities favors an injunction.

D. The Public Interest

Fourth, and finally, a preliminary injunction furthers the public interest. A preliminary injunction prohibiting enforcement of the Act will preserve the status quo, allowing the court to make a full ruling on the merits of the case without subjecting the plaintiffs, their patients, or the public to the ban's potential impact.

Further, "the public interest is promoted by the robust enforcement of constitutional rights." In contrast, the public has no interest in enforcing an unconstitutional statute, particularly when "the legislation seems designed, as here, as a protest against Supreme Court decisions." A preliminary injunction supports the public interest, and so the fourth factor counsels in favor of an injunction.

III. CONCLUSION

Alabama's abortion ban contravenes clear Supreme Court precedent. It violates the right of an individual to privacy, to make "choices central to personal dignity and autonomy." It diminishes "the capacity of women to act in society, and to make reproductive decisions." It defies the United States Constitution.

The court will, therefore, enter an appropriate order preliminarily enjoining enforcement of the Act as applied to pre-viability abortion. . . .

DONE, this the 29th day of October, 2019.

/s/ Myron H. Thompson
United States District Judge

SOURCE: U.S. District Court for the Middle District of Alabama, Northern Division. *Robinson v. Marshall.* Civil Action No. 2:19cv365-MHT(WO). October 29, 2019. http://www.almd.uscourts.gov.

OTHER HISTORIC DOCUMENTS OF INTEREST

FROM PREVIOUS *HISTORIC DOCUMENTS*

Israeli Knesset Votes to Dissolve
and Hold New Elections

MAY 28, MAY 30, OCTOBER 3, AND NOVEMBER 21, 2019

The Israeli government marked two significant firsts in 2019: the first dissolution of a newly elected legislature before a government was formed, and the first sitting prime minister to face criminal charges. Prime Minister Benjamin Netanyahu's indictment on bribery, fraud, and breach of trust charges contributed to his inability to forge a coalition government following the April 2019 legislative election, as did a contentious proposal to change the country's military draft that divided his right-wing allies. Both Netanyahu and his primary opponent, the Blue and White alliance's Benny Gantz, failed to form a coalition after a second election was held in September, leaving the future of the Israeli government in limbo.

NETANYAHU FAILS TO FORM COALITION GOVERNMENT

Israel's legislative election took place on April 9, 2019. Netanyahu's conservative Likud Party secured 35 of the Knesset's 120 seats, as did the centrist Blue and White, an alliance of three political parties. (Blue and White was established just before the April election, but its strong showing in the election—winning more than one million votes—pushed the alliance into the role of primary opposition.)

Both Netanyahu and Blue and White leader Benny Gantz claimed victory. "This is a night of tremendous victory," said Netanyahu, adding that it was "a golden opportunity to turn our country into a strong nation, among the strongest nations of the world." He said he would form a new coalition with Likud's "natural partners" in the right wing, but that he would be the prime minister of all Israelis. Gantz declared, "We are the winners!" He also pledged to be the "prime minister of everyone and not just of those who voted for us."

Since no party secured a majority in the Knesset, a coalition government was necessary. Although Likud and Blue and White won an equal number of seats, Netanyahu was asked by President Reuven Rivlin to form a coalition government because he had a larger base of potential support. (Right-wing and conservative parties allied with Likud held sixty-five seats in the Knesset.) Coalition governments are the norm in Israel, and Netanyahu has earned the nickname "the magician" for his ability to unite enough lawmakers behind him to remain in office. It was therefore shocking when Likud announced on May 29, the deadline for forming a government, that it had the support of only sixty lawmakers—falling one seat shy of the sixty-one lawmakers required for a coalition.

When one party is unable to form a coalition government, the president typically tasks a different leader to pursue the same goal. However, as the deadline approached, Likud lawmakers introduced and quickly advanced a bill to dissolve the Knesset and schedule new elections in case Netanyahu was unsuccessful. This would prevent Rivlin, whom Netanyahu considers to be a political foe, from giving Gantz or another rival the opportunity to form a government. "Anyone who votes against the dissolution of the Knesset will ensure the creation of a left-wing government headed by Benny Gantz," said Miki Zohar, Likud lawmaker and author of the dissolution bill. "Those who vote for dissolution will, on the contrary, ensure the continuation of the rule of the Right," he continued. The bill passed its first reading on May 28, by a vote of 66–44, with one abstention. The bill's third and final reading took place on May 30. Seventy-four lawmakers voted to dissolve the Knesset and hold a second election on September 17, 2019, marking the first time in Israel's history that a new legislature voted to dissolve itself before a government was formed.

Netanyahu blamed Avigdor Lieberman, leader of the ultranationalist Yisrael Beiteinu Party, for his inability to form a government. Yisrael Beiteinu had joined Netanyahu's government in 2016 and Lieberman served for roughly two years as defense minister. But Lieberman resigned in protest in November 2018 over a cease-fire agreement between the government and Palestinians in the Gaza Strip, and he withdrew his party from Netanyahu's coalition. Lieberman said Yisrael Beiteinu would not rejoin the coalition unless Netanyahu supported his proposal to change Israel's military draft. Introduced to the Knesset in 2018, Lieberman's proposal would end the exemption of ultra-Orthodox Jewish men from the draft, which allows them to study at a yeshiva instead of joining the military, and replace it with a quota system that would require at least some ultra-Orthodox men to enlist. If quotas were not met, fines and other penalties would be imposed. Israel's Supreme Court ruled in 2017 that the blanket exemption for ultra-Orthodox men was discriminatory and unconstitutional (most Jewish men who are age eighteen or older are drafted for more than two years), giving lawmakers one year to draft a new law. But Lieberman's proposal was divisive, causing a split between the right wing's secular ultranationalists and ultra-Orthodox members. Lieberman insisted his proposal be passed without amendment; religious parties wanted to soften the bill's language. (In fact, lawmakers' inability to agree on changes to the military draft was one factor that caused the government to call elections earlier than planned. A new legislature was not due to be selected until November 2019, but the Knesset voted to dissolve itself at the end of December, prompting the April poll.)

"Lieberman never intended to reach an agreement," Netanyahu said. "He clearly wanted to shoot down this government and he is doing so because he reckons he will receive a few more votes." Lieberman claimed Netanyahu was "capitulating to the ultra-Orthodox," adding that members of his party were "natural partners for a right-wing government but not for a government based on Jewish law."

PRIME MINISTER FACES INDICTMENT

A pending indictment of Netanyahu also contributed to the prime minister's inability to form a coalition government. On February 28, 2019, Attorney General Avichai Mandelblit announced his intention to indict Netanyahu, pending a hearing. His announcement followed a two-year investigation into allegations of the prime minister's impropriety and appeared to embrace the findings of two police reports that recommended Netanyahu's indictment.

The prime minister faced potential charges of bribery, fraud, and breach of trust in three cases in which Netanyahu was said to have traded political favors for expensive gifts and flattering news coverage. In one case, Netanyahu and his wife, Sara, allegedly received hundreds of thousands of dollars' worth of expensive gifts from a Hollywood producer. In exchange, Netanyahu sought to extend a ten-year tax exemption for Israeli expatriates returning to the country, which could have benefited the producer. In another case, Netanyahu reportedly used his post as communications minister (a role he filled while serving as prime minister) to help an Israeli media tycoon sell one of his companies for millions of dollars more than it was worth. In return, the tycoon used another one of his media properties to push complimentary news coverage of Netanyahu and his wife while also suppressing or softening negative coverage. The third case involved allegations that Netanyahu made a deal with a leading newspaper publisher to promote legislation that would damage a competing publication in exchange for favorable news coverage.

Netanyahu claimed the charges were politically motivated and denied any wrongdoing. "I tell you, citizens of Israel, this whole tower of cards will collapse," he said. "I intend to serve as your prime minister for many years." Netanyahu also said he would remain in office while the charges were pending and even if he was indicted, which is permitted under Israeli law unless the Supreme Court intervenes. (He would be required to step down if convicted of the charges.)

The Blue and White alliance refused to form a government with a prime minister who was facing indictment, meaning Netanyahu could not look to Gantz for support in the Knesset. Gantz called for Netanyahu to "come to your senses and show national responsibility and resign," adding that Israel deserved better than a prime minister who spent most of his time "dealing with his legal situation" instead of governing.

Many observers questioned the timing of the attorney general's announcement, with the election roughly one month away. Some legal experts said it was necessary for Mandelblit to make his announcement before the election because if he waited until after the vote, he likely would have been accused of misleading the public. Israelis should know about the legal challenges their prime minister might face before they cast their vote, these experts said. Others said the announcement would unfairly damage Netanyahu's chances in the election. The prime minister's lawyers reportedly asked Mandelblit several times to delay his announcement, but the attorney general refused.

Mandelblit did agree to delay Netanyahu's hearing, originally planned for the summer, until the fall, though the prime minister's lawyers had pushed for a May 2020 date. The hearing began on October 2 and lasted for four days. On November 21, Mandelblit announced an official indictment of Netanyahu, making him the first Israeli prime minister to face criminal charges while in office. A statement from the state prosecution's office said that "after all claims were reviewed, it was found that there were no claims that arose at the hearing to change the offenses attributed to the prime minister." Mandelblit called it "a difficult and sad day." He said that based on the evidence, he determined there was "a reasonable likelihood of conviction" and thus it was his "duty by law to indict."

Netanyahu decried the indictment as a "witch hunt" and called Mandelblit weak. "Tonight we are witnesses to a coup attempt against a prime minister through an investigation process which is contaminated and tendentious," he said. Netanyahu's political opponents called for him to step down. Mandelblit affirmed that Netanyahu was not required to resign as prime minister but did need to relinquish his ministerial portfolios, which cover agriculture, welfare, health, and diaspora affairs. Deputy Health Minister Yaakov Litzman was promoted to full health minister on December 29. Netanyahu announced his resignation of his welfare, agriculture, and diaspora affairs portfolios on January 1, 2020. New ministers have not yet been appointed to these posts. The same day, the prime minister announced he would ask the Knesset for immunity from prosecution. However, Netanyahu withdrew his request several weeks later, stating that it would not have received a fair hearing. Mandelblit formally filed his indictment in Jerusalem District Court on January 28.

SECOND ELECTION INCONCLUSIVE

The second legislative election took place as planned on September 17. Official results were not announced until one week later. This time, Blue and White won thirty-three seats, compared to Likud's thirty-two seats. However, fifty-five lawmakers had expressed support for Netanyahu, giving him a one-seat advantage over Gantz, who had fifty-four supporters in the Knesset. Rivlin once again invited Netanyahu to make the first attempt at forming a government.

While negotiations between the various parties proceeded, the twenty-second session of the Knesset had its inaugural sitting on October 3. Knesset Speaker Yuli-Yoel Edelstein implored party leaders to come together to find a solution to the political impasse. "The citizens of Israel want unity!" Edelstein declared. "They want this House to reflect the common denominator between them. They want us to find a way to integrate their various priorities." He addressed Netanyahu and Gantz directly, telling them, "It is not too late! My office . . . is at your disposal, even today." He encouraged the men to sit and talk and "leave no stone unturned until you find the formula for a solution." During a reception following the inaugural sitting, Netanyahu acknowledged that "the people have spoken clearly, but unfortunately the effort towards unity has not yet come to fruition," adding that Israel "cannot afford another election campaign." Calling a "broad and stable" government "the need of the hour," Netanyahu said, "we have to proceed together, to end the rejection and boycotts of publics and individuals."

Despite the calls for unity, Lieberman remained an obstacle for Netanyahu. He continued to insist that a coalition government be formed with his party, Likud, and Blue and White. But Netanyahu declined to cut ties with right-wing religious parties, and Gantz was still reluctant to work with the prime minister. On October 21, Netanyahu informed Rivlin that he was unable to form a government. Two days later, Rivlin asked Gantz to try. Accepting the mandate from Rivlin, Gantz said he would invite Likud to be a part of his government, suggesting for the first time a willingness to collaborate with Netanyahu regardless of his legal troubles.

Gantz did not succeed where Netanyahu had failed. On November 20, the Blue and White alliance said Gantz had not formed a coalition after nearly thirty days of unsuccessful negotiations. Lieberman—the purported "kingmaker"—refused to back either man. Gantz's failure kicked off a three-week period during which a majority of lawmakers had to come together to support Gantz, Netanyahu, or any other member of the Knesset as prime minister, or else a third election would be called. This deadline passed on December 11, and the Knesset dissolved itself once again. A new election will likely be held on March 2, 2020.

—Linda Grimm

Following are press releases issued by the Israeli Knesset on May 28 and May 30, 2019, announcing passage of a bill dissolving the legislature and scheduling new elections; remarks by Knesset Speaker Yuli-Yoel Edelstein on October 3, 2019, calling for a unity government; remarks by Prime Minister Benjamin Netanyahu on October 3, 2019, on the need for a broad coalition government; and a press release from State Attorney General Dr. Abihai Mandelblit's office on November 21, 2019, summarizing the decision to indict the prime minister.

Israeli Knesset Votes on Proposal to Dissolve

May 28, 2019

By a vote of 66 to 44, with one abstention, the Knesset plenum early Tuesday morning passed in its first reading a proposal to disperse the 21st Knesset—about a month after it was sworn in—and hold elections for the 22nd Knesset on Tuesday, September 17.

Prior to the vote, the bill's author MK Miki Zohar (Likud) said, "Anyone who votes against the dissolution of the Knesset will ensure the creation of a left-wing government headed by [Blue and White chairman MK] Benny Gantz. Those who vote for dissolution will, on the contrary, ensure the continuation of the rule of the Right."

"It is with great sadness and regret that I ask you to support the dissolution of the Knesset," he told the plenum, adding that the special committee he chairs will convene Tuesday at 11 am to prepare the bill for its second and third readings.

Following MK Zohar's remarks, the debate turned heated, as MK Zohar and members of Blue and White exchanged accusations.

SOURCE: The Knesset. "Approved in First Reading: 21st Knesset Will Disperse, Elections for 22nd Knesset to Be Held on September 17." May 28, 2019. https://main.knesset.gov.il/EN/News/PressReleases/Pages/28519o.aspx.

Lawmakers Dissolve Knesset and Schedule New Election

May 30, 2019

The Knesset plenum late Wednesday night passed the bill to disperse the 21st Knesset, just over a month after it was sworn in, and hold general elections for the 22nd Knesset on Tuesday, September 17.

The bill, submitted by MK Miki Zohar (Likud), passed its third and final reading by a vote of 74–45, with one MK absent (Kulanu's Roy Folkman).

The previous elections were held on April 9, 2019.

SOURCE: The Knesset. "Knesset Votes to Disperse; Elections Set for Sept. 17." May 30, 2019. https://main.knesset.gov.il/EN/News/PressReleases/Pages/press30519f.aspx.

Speaker of the Knesset Comments on Inaugural Sitting of New Session

October 3, 2019

The 22nd Knesset officially began its term on Thursday with a festive ceremony during which the MKs pledged their allegiance to the State of Israel and vowed to fulfill their duties in the Israeli parliament. Acting Speaker of the Knesset MK Yuli-Yoel Edelstein (Likud) read the declaration: "I commit to being faithful to the State of Israel and faithfully fulfill my duties in the Knesset." The MKs responded, separately: "I commit."

The ceremony was held in the presence of President Reuven Rivlin, who was greeted at the Knesset by an honor guard and then signed the Knesset's "Book of Presidents."

Prior to the ceremony, the members of the 22nd Knesset, some of whom arrived with their families, received their Knesset identification cards, and boutonnières to wear.

Following the inaugural sitting, President Rivlin and the leaders of the various parliamentary groups were scheduled to head to the Knesset's Chagall Hall to raise a celebratory glass of wine and pose for the traditional group photo.

During the inaugural sitting, Speaker of the Knesset Yuli-Yoel Edelstein (Likud) said "The attempt to establish a Jewish sovereign state in the Land of Israel failed twice. Twice the beginning was promising, and twice the failure was bitter. The glory days of David and Solomon came to an end when the kingdom split; when the one nation became tribes; when the capital city was divided in two. A thousand years passed, and the Hasmonean state was established. In the days when they fought with joined forces, they succeeded in banishing the empires from here. But when a civil war broke out—everything collapsed like a house of cards. Unjustified hatred destroyed the Temple, even before the first Roman broke through the walls of Jerusalem. 2,000 years later—the State of Israel was founded."

"This is the third attempt: Like those which preceded it, this one also carries with it great promise. Like [the attempts] which came before it, its success depends solely on us: on our ability to live in unity; our hope for a shared future; and our belief that despite all the differences, we are not separate tribes, but one nation."

In his speech, Speaker Edelstein said the results of the recent elections reflected the differences in the priorities of Israel's citizens, as well as the citizens' dreams and fears. "For some, bolstering security is the most important task. There are those for whom social issues top the list [of priorities]. As always, and as it should be, it was not just one note that was coming from the ballot boxes. The citizens of Israel spoke in many voices and different accents. Not all of these [voices and accents] are always clear, but they are all loved. They are all legitimate. They are all part of the Israeli story. And everyone realizes that we will achieve a balance between this abundance of priorities only with genuine, honest and complete unity."

"The citizens of Israel want unity!" Speaker Edelstein declared. "They want this House to reflect the common denominator between them. They want us to find a way to integrate their various priorities."

"National unity is a difficult task," Speaker Edelstein told his fellow MKs. "We've failed at it twice before in our history. At times it appears that achieving it is as complex as moving mountains. It is particularly difficult because there is no partial unity. There is no 'as if' unity. There is no unity that consists of exclusions—unity with this part but not with the other. We either move the mountain or we don't."

"Unity that is combined with the disqualification of sectors in Israel, unity that is blended with the tarnishing of entire publics, will never be real unity," Speaker Edelstein proclaimed. "We need unity which will seat at one table all those who believe in the State of Israel—Jewish and democratic. We need a unity of all those who are willing to do everything to ensure that in our third attempt to establish an exemplary state in the land of our fathers, we will never fail."

Speaker Edelstein further told his fellow lawmakers that "the citizens of Israel will never forgive us if we fall into the abyss of another election campaign."

Turning directly to Prime Minister MK Benjamin Netanyahu (Likud) and Blue and White Chairman MK Benny Gantz, Speaker Edelstein said "It is not too late! My office, located just a few meters from here, is at your disposal, even today. Sit! Talk! Leave no stone unturned until you find the formula for a solution. The gaps can be bridged. The tears can be mended. It is possible—of course it is possible—to achieve unity."

SOURCE: The Knesset. "22nd Knesset Is Officially Sworn In; Interim Speaker Edelstein Says 'Citizens of Israel Want Unity.'" October 3, 2019. https://main.knesset.gov.il/EN/News/PressReleases/Pages/press31019s.aspx.

Prime Minister Netanyahu Calls for Unity Government

October 3, 2019

Shortly after the inaugural sitting of the 22nd Knesset concluded on Thursday, the heads of the various parliamentary groups, along with President Reuven Rivlin, Acting Speaker of the Knesset Yuli-Yoel Edelstein (Likud) and Supreme Court President Esther Hayut convened at the Knesset's Chagall Hall to raise a celebratory glass of wine and pose for the traditional group photo.

During the reception, Acting Speaker Edelstein wished the 22nd Knesset success, "in the hope that we will form a broad coalition and a stable government, and that we will be able to serve the public that sent us here."

Prime Minister MK Benjamin Netanyahu (Likud) said, "More than a million people voted for me directly, and another million indirectly, but it wasn't enough. And many people voted for (Blue and White Chairman MK) Benny Gantz as well, but that was not enough in order for him to form a left-wing government. The country cannot afford another election campaign, and I am doing all I can to avoid it."

"We are facing an enormous security challenge that is intensifying from week to week," said the Prime Minister. "This isn't spin, it's not a whim; this is not 'Netanyahu trying to scare us.' Anyone with eyes in his head sees that Iran continues to arm itself. It attacks and sends terror emissaries everywhere and says that Israel will disappear. This reality requires [Israel to arm itself] and invent defensive and offensive tools of a quality we have not had until now; to allocate billions more for our security needs and make difficult and complex decisions the likes of which we have not made in decades."

"The people have spoken clearly, but unfortunately the effort towards unity have not yet come to fruition," PM Netanyahu stated. "I have invested considerable efforts in order to form a broad and stable government. I repeat, such a government is the need of the hour. I had an honest and non-defiant conversation with [Yisrael Beitenu chairman] Avigdor Lieberman today, and I told him what I tell my colleagues in the camp: we have to proceed together, to end the rejection and boycotts of publics and individuals. Whoever accepts a Jewish and democratic state is acceptable to us. Mr. President, I adhere to the standpoint that there is no alternative to the outline that you proposed—a broad national unity government. If we do not achieve it now, we shall achieve it later on, after both of us, myself and Benny Gantz, return the mandate and go back to the starting point."

SOURCE: The Knesset. "PM Netanyahu after 22nd Knesset Is Sworn In: 'Unity Government Is the Need of the Hour.'" October 3, 2019. https://main.knesset.gov.il/EN/News/PressReleases/Pages/press31019k .aspx.

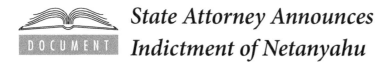

State Attorney Announces Indictment of Netanyahu

November 21, 2019

The attorney general, Dr. Avichai Mandelblit, has decided to issue an indictment against the prime minister, MK Benjamin Netanyahu, for offenses of accepting a bribe and of fraud and breach of trust in Case 4000 and for offenses of fraud and breach of trust in Cases 1000 and 2000, which he allegedly committed during his service as prime minister and as minister of communications.

The attorney general has thus adopted the recommendation of State Attorney Shai Nitzan and the recommendation of Tel Aviv District Attorney for Taxation and Economics Liat Ben Ari Shwekey, who recommended after the hearing that he issue the indictment for the above offenses.

A notice regarding the decision of the attorney general and a copy of the indictment have been submitted to the representatives of the prime minister.

Further, pursuant to Section 4 of the Knesset Members Immunity Act, a copy of the indictment has been submitted to the speaker of the Knesset so that the prime minister will have the opportunity to inform the Knesset of whether he wishes to request that it grant him immunity from criminal prosecution.

The attorney general has further decided, in accordance with the recommendation of the Office of the State Attorney, to issue an indictment against the couple Shaul and Iris Elovitch as well, for offenses of bribery, obstruction of justice, and subordination in connection with an investigation in Case 4000, and for additional offenses against Shaul Elovitch.

The attorney general has further decided, in accordance with the recommendation of the Office of the State Attorney, to issue an indictment against the controlling shareholder and managing editor of the Yedioth Ahronoth Group, Arnon (Noni) Mozes, as well, for an offense of offering a bribe in Case 2000.

Notices to this effect have been submitted to the representatives of those implicated.

The decision of the attorney general concerning the prime minister was made following a comprehensive and thorough examination of the many arguments raised by the prime minister's representatives over the course of the four days of the hearing held in early October 2019. All of the arguments were examined in depth over the course of an orderly work process spread out over very many work hours, during which hundreds of pages of in-depth opinions relating to the arguments raised in the hearing were submitted by the Office of the State Attorney.

Once all of the arguments had been examined, it was found that the arguments raised in the hearing did not suffice to change the offenses imputed to the prime minister in the notice of intent to indict. Notwithstanding, some of the arguments brought about changes in the indictment, albeit not changes in the offense clauses as such.

Concurrently, all arguments raised in the hearings held for Mr. Shaul Elovitch, Ms. Iris Elovitch, and Mr. Arnon Mozes were examined, and the aforementioned decision was made.

The investigations in these cases were managed by the Lahav 433 unit of the Israel Police (the National Economic Crimes Unit and the National Fraud Investigations Unit) and the Investigations, Intelligence, and Market Surveillance Department of the Israel Securities Authority, facilitated by the Office of the Attorney for Taxation and Economics.

The decision to consider issuing an indictment against all of the above parties, subject to a hearing, was made on February 28, 2019, following some three months of deliberations on the matter, after the investigative cases were transferred to the Office of the State Attorney and residual parts of the investigation were completed, near the end of 2018.

The timing of the hearing for the prime minister was initially set for July 2019, and was postponed at his request to the beginning of October 2019.

Study of the material submitted by the representatives of the prime minister, and the deliberations that took place, extended over some six weeks.

Summary of first indictment: Case 4000

During the period from December 2012 to January 2017, Netanyahu had authority to grant approvals and licenses for various commercial activities performed by the Bezeq Group by virtue of holding the office of prime minister and subsequently by virtue of holding the office of minister of communications as well. Netanyahu further was able to influence government matters affecting the Bezeq Group.

During the relevant period, Elovitch was the controlling shareholder of the Bezeq Group, and thus was able to influence the character and nature of news publications on the Walla website, which is controlled by Bezeq.

The matter of news coverage was of great significance for Netanyahu and members of his family, and he saw it as decisively important in all matters relating to his political future.

Against this background, a give-and-take relationship between Netanyahu and Elovitch formed on the basis of their mutual understanding that each of them had a significant interest that the other party was able to advance. In this context, at a joint supper of the Netanyahus and the Elovitches in 2012, during the election campaign for the 19th Knesset, it was agreed that Netanyahu and his wife would be able to make of the Elovitches demands concerning the nature of news coverage that they received on the Walla website.

The relationship between Netanyahu and the Elovitches was characterized by an intense and ongoing affiliation conducted directly and through intermediaries. In this relationship, Netanyahu and his family made of the Elovitches various demands concerning the nature of news coverage that they received on the Walla website, and also made demands concerning the coverage of Netanyahu's political rivals. The Elovitches brought heavy and continuous pressure to bear on the CEO of Walla at the time, Ilan Yeshua, to accede to these demands. As a result, Yeshua directed the editors and journalists at Walla to change publications on the website in a way that corresponded to Netanyahu's demands. Examples illustrating Netanyahu's demands for intervention in publications on the website and the nature of the exceptional acquiescence to them are given in Annex A of the indictment.

Throughout the relevant period, as part of the mutual give-and-take relationship, the Elovitches generally acceded to Netanyahu's demands as given and made every effort to implement them. In a significant part of the cases, their efforts for Netanyahu also bore fruit. Netanyahu knew that the degree of the Elovitches' commitment and acquiescence to his demands was exceptional, significant, and extensive and that it was given to him in exchange for the performance of actions related to his public office. The Elovitches acceded to his demands for intervention in publications on the website and also made it their business to ensure that Netanyahu was aware of the degree of their acquiescence to his demands.

In the context of the give-and-take relationship that developed between Netanyahu and the Elovitches, Netanyahu used his power and authority as a public servant to advance matters whose advancement was of interest to Elovitch—for him, for Bezeq, and for various companies in the Eurocom Group, through which he controlled Bezeq and Walla. In so doing, concurrently with his demands of Elovitch concerning coverage on the Walla website, Netanyahu dealt by virtue of his public offices, in several cases, with Elovitch's regulatory affairs and performed actions that advanced significant commercial interests of his, with a scope of colossal sums. Netanyahu performed his actions to benefit Elovitch in consideration of benefits that he obtained from the Elovitches having to do with coverage, as noted, while acting with deference and placing himself in a conflict of interest between his public duties and his personal interests, and while acting improperly.

Elovitch explicitly linked the manner in which Netanyahu was covered on Walla to the regulatory decisions that Netanyahu made and actions that he was supposed to perform while carrying out his public duties. Similarly, Iris Elovitch too linked the acquiescence to the demands of Netanyahu and his wife for intervention in publications to the manner in which Netanyahu handled Bezeq's regulatory interests. The Elovitches also clarified to various actors at Walla that coverage of Netanyahu and his family members was to be improved in order to bring about regulatory decisions to their liking.

Netanyahu systematically and consistently hid his relationship with the Elovitches from an array of officials, to whom he gave partial and misleading information about the nature of his relationship with Elovitch.

To conceal their relationship with Netanyahu, the Elovitches took action to destroy evidence found on mobile telephones in their possession and instructed Yeshua to act similarly, as well as directed him to give false statements concerning their involvement in changing the publications on the Walla website, their relationship with Netanyahu, and his demands for their intervention in the various publications.

Summary of second indictment: Case 2000

Over the years, there has been a profound rivalry between Netanyahu and Mozes. Notwithstanding, over the course of the years the two held three series of meetings: in 2008–2009, in 2013, and in 2014. Over the course of each of these series of meetings,

Netanyahu and Mozes conducted a discourse about the advancement of their mutual interests: improving the manner in which Netanyahu was covered in media belonging to the Yedioth Ahronoth Group; imposing limitations on *Israel Hayom*, a matter of great economic significance for Mozes and for the Yedioth Ahronoth Group.

At one of the meetings that took place on December 4, 2014, ahead of the election campaign for the 20th Knesset, Mozes offered Netanyahu a bribe: he would bring about a conspicuous change for the better in the line governing coverage of Netanyahu and his family and the manner of this coverage in media belonging to the Yedioth Ahronoth Group, and a change for the worse in the manner in which his political rivals were covered, to the point of an "earthquake" or "turning around the ship," as stated in their conversation. Mozes proposed that he do so in such a way as to ensure that Netanyahu would continue to serve as prime minister for a lengthy time, in consideration of which Netanyahu would exploit his influence as prime minister to advance legislation that would impose limitations on *Israel Hayom* and bring about significant economic benefits for Mozes and his business.

Netanyahu did not reject the offer of a bribe and did not consequently end the conversation with Mozes, and although he did not intend to advance the bill, he continued to conduct with Mozes a long and detailed conversation about the elements of the offer and represented to him that there was a real possibility that he would use his governmental power to advance legislation benefiting Mozes. Netanyahu acted as stated in order to extend the discourse and thus to cause Mozes to positively influence the manner in which he was covered in media belonging to the Yedioth Ahronoth Group during the election period and to cause Mozes to take action to prevent negative publications damaging to him or his family, at least in this period and so long as the conversations between them were ongoing.

Pursuant to this meeting, to keep Mozes under the impression that he was examining the feasibility of advancing the said legislation, Netanyahu met with the coalition chairman, Zeev Elkin, and the chairman of the House Committee of the Knesset, Yariv Levin, with attention to the possibility that the fact of its occurrence would become known to Mozes. At the meeting, Elkin and Levin made clear to Netanyahu that it would not be possible to advance the legislation at the time. Subsequently, Netanyahu took the initiative to hold an additional meeting with Mozes, during which he represented to him that he would act to advance the legislation after the elections, with the goal of extending the discourse with him about the offer of a bribe.

By thus acting, Mozes offered Netanyahu a bribe.

By thus acting, Netanyahu committed a breach of trust fundamentally damaging public trust in public servants and elected officials and in their integrity. By exploiting his position and the power of the post to obtain personal benefit, and as the most senior elected official, he sent a message that offers of bribes are a tool that can be used for the advancement of the mutual interests of senior public servants and businesspersons and that there is no defect in bribery transactions.

Summary of third indictment: Case 1000

Since 1999, Netanyahu and businessman Arnon Milchan have had a personal relationship, including various links and associations, in which during the relevant period to the charge, Netanyahu and his wife received from Milchan various benefits. In 2013, Milchan introduced Netanyahu to Australian businessman James Packer. In 2014–2016, Netanyahu and his wife received from Packer various benefits.

Benefits from Milchan and Packer, primarily boxes of cigars and cases of champagne, were given to Netanyahu and his wife continuously, in response to requests and even demands, inter alia in deliveries, even when Milchan and Packer were not present in Israel, to the extent that they became a kind of "supply line." The scope of the benefits reached a sum of approximately NIS 700,000. The benefits were given to Netanyahu in connection with his public offices and his status as the prime minister of Israel.

In view of the multitude of links between Netanyahu and Milchan, Netanyahu should have entirely avoided dealing with Milchan's interests in the context of his duties. Nevertheless, during the period between October 2011 and December 2016, Netanyahu took action while fulfilling his public duties to benefit Milchan in the following cases: in 2013–2014, Netanyahu interceded with individuals in the American government so that Milchan would be granted a visa to enter the United States, on two occasions; in 2013, Netanyahu approached the minister of finance at the time, Yair Lapid, with regard to extending the length of the exemption given to returning residents from reporting and paying income tax, which Milchan enjoyed; and in 2015, Netanyahu acted personally and directed the director general of the Ministry of Communications at the time, Shlomo Filber, to assist Milchan in matters related to regulation, in connection with a merger deal between communications companies Reshet and Keshet, so that an investment that Milchan was at the time considering would be economically worthwhile for him.

According to the indictment, by thus acting, Netanyahu committed breaches of trust fundamentally damaging public trust and integrity, inasmuch as he maintained for years an illegitimate relationship with Milchan and Packer in which Netanyahu and his wife received from them benefits of very great scope in connection with his public duties and his status as the prime minister of Israel. Netanyahu similarly committed breaches of trust fundamentally damaging public trust, integrity, and proper administrative conduct by pursuing his public duties while having a severe and ongoing conflict of interest between his personal obligation to Milchan and his obligation to the public.

SOURCE: Government of Israel. Department of Justice. State Attorney's Office. "The Court Decided to Indict Prime Minister Benjamin Netanyahu." November 21, 2019. Translated by SAGE Publishing. https://www.gov.il/he/departments/news/21-11-2019-05.

OTHER HISTORIC DOCUMENTS OF INTEREST

FROM PREVIOUS *HISTORIC DOCUMENTS*

June

U.S. and International Officials Respond to Extreme Weather Events and Climate Change

JUNE 10, JULY 2, SEPTEMBER 22, DECEMBER 11 AND 15, 2019

Throughout much of 2019, the midwestern and southeastern United States experienced historic flooding that devastated communities, destroyed infrastructure, and hampered agricultural productivity, while in Europe, a deadly heatwave took hold, with many countries seeing triple-digit temperatures. Climate change experts warned that as global temperatures continue to rise, these extreme weather events will become more common unless nations can significantly limit greenhouse gas emissions. In December, world leaders came together at the annual United Nations Climate Change Summit, the twenty-fifth meeting of the Conference of the Parties (COP25), to discuss their plans for limiting global temperature rise in line with the 2015 Paris Agreement. The conference was criticized by UN secretary-general António Guterres—and a number of world leaders—for failing to advance the efforts of the global community to tackle climate change.

FLOODING SPREADS ACROSS THE MIDWEST AND SOUTHEASTERN UNITED STATES

After a historically wet winter throughout the midwestern United States, the National Oceanic and Atmospheric Administration predicted that a significant portion of the nation would face a serious flood risk. "This is shaping up to be a potentially unprecedented flood season, with more than 200 million people at risk for flooding in their communities," said Ed Clark, director of NOAA's National Weather Center. The severity of that prediction became readily apparent in March, as heavy rains began to fall in areas where the ground was still frozen. The saturation resulted in what the *New York Times* would dub "The Great Flood of 2019."

The problem was not just the homes, businesses, and roads under water. For midwestern states, it was also farmland. According to a Reuters analysis, at least one million acres of farmland were flooded by late March, many just weeks before spring planting was set to begin. If farmers were unable to plant their crops on time, they would be barred from full crop insurance coverage, which ensures farmers receive a minimum price for their crop sales. Although the affected land is a small portion of the 240 million acres used to grow crops like corn, soybean, wheat, rice, cotton, sorghum, and barley, the farmers hit by the floods were already suffering from oversupplied markets, tumbling crop prices, and the trade war with China.

Many farmers had a significant crop supply in storage that was destroyed by floodwaters. While the federal government can compensate farmers for damage to farmland, it had no mechanism to do so for stored crops. "This is really going to hurt a lot of farmers," said Brett Adams, a Nebraska and Missouri farmer. "Commodity prices are already low, and then you throw this on top of it. And it's a bad deal," he added. To provide some relief, in the late spring President Donald Trump signed legislation that would compensate farmers for damages suffered from flooding and the ongoing trade war.

The flooding did not impact only midwestern states. In New Orleans, water levels remained above flood stage longer than at any time since 1927. The water flowing downstream from the Midwest also carried with it fertilizers from farms, lawns, and other sources, which flowed into the Gulf of Mexico and created a near-record dead zone—an area that cannot support marine life—the size of New Hampshire.

An estimated 14 million people were affected by the 2019 floods. A total of 19.3 million acres of crops went unplanted, and dozens of states and counties issued disaster and emergency declarations. In Nebraska, Bryan Tuma, the assistant director of the state's Emergency Management Agency, called the flooding "biblical." The problem seemed far from over by the close of 2019. Meteorologists predicted another wet winter for the Midwest, and the Army Corps of Engineers was continuing to release water from upstream dams into the Missouri River in anticipation of more wet weather into the spring of 2020, meaning that flooding could continue into the new year.

HEATWAVE TEARS ACROSS EUROPE

Across the Atlantic, Europe was experiencing some of its warmest months on record. France recorded a June temperature of 46°C, while in July the Netherlands broke a seventy-five-year record at 39.3°C and Belgium hit 39.9°C. The heatwave resulted in thousands of deaths, though fewer than the tens of thousands killed in the 2003 heatwave. In France, drownings were up 30 percent compared to the previous year because unexperienced swimmers were seeking relief from the heat.

Extreme heat in Europe is especially deadly because the countries and their citizens are ill prepared to handle the high temperatures. Less than 5 percent of European households have air conditioning. Furthermore, nearly three-quarters of all Europeans live in urban areas that are full of asphalt and concrete. These materials trap the heat, meaning that nighttime temperatures stay high. The result was closed nuclear power plants and schools, and trains cancelled due to breakdown and risk of derailment. Participants in the annual Tour de France cycling race were pictured wearing vests packed with ice to keep cool.

A group of European university and government climate scientists warned that the extreme heat could become the new normal. In a report published by World Weather Attribution, the group said that if the current warming patterns seen around the world continue, deadly heatwaves could occur more frequently. According to the study, "Every heatwave occurring in Europe today is made more likely and more intense by human-induced climate change. How much more depends very strongly on the event definition: location, season, intensity and duration." Others agreed that climate change was the driving factor. "Such intense and widespread heatwaves carry the signature of man-made climate change," said Johannes Cullmann, director of the World Meteorological Organization's (WMO) climate and water department.

WORLD METEOROLOGICAL ORGANIZATION DOCUMENTS RISING TEMPERATURES

The impact of climate change was not limited to the United States or Europe. Around the globe, changing weather patterns resulted in intense storms, like the hurricanes that swept across the Bahamas and typhoons in the Pacific that were among some of the strongest on record. In September, the WMO released a report on climate change spanning 2015 through mid-2019. WMO researchers found that global temperatures had increased 1.1°C since pre-industrial levels and 0.2°C compared to the period from 2011 to 2015. That increase, according to researchers, was a driving factor in the deadly climate events seen in 2019.

WMO secretary-general Petteri Taalas warned that "[i]t is highly important that we reduce greenhouse gas emissions, notably from energy production, industry, and transport. This is critical if we are to mitigate climate change and meet the targets set out in the Paris Agreement," the international treaty agreed to in 2015 during the United Nations Framework Convention on Climate Change (UNFCCC) to keep global temperature rise below 2°C above pre-industrial levels during this century, with a target of 1.5°C. Taalas noted that to achieve that goal, "the level of ambition needs to be tripled." The goal was in question because President Trump announced that the United States would leave the agreement. Furthermore, the United Nations was already reporting that even if the Paris Agreement signatories were able to meet their individual greenhouse gas goals, global temperatures during the century would still rise to more than the 1.5°C target. In December, on the release of the WMO's annual climate report, Taalas warned that climate change was only getting worse, and "the only solution is to get rid of fossil fuels in power production, industry, and transportation." The report found that the decade from 2010 to 2019 was likely to be the warmest on record, and the impact would be quickly rising and warming seas, melting arctic ice, and ground warming that would further exacerbate extreme weather events.

WORLD LEADERS DISCUSS CLIMATE CHANGE

In 2019, a sixteen-year-old climate change activist named Greta Thunberg became the face of the climate change movement. She first drew attention in her home country of Sweden when she protested outside the nation's parliament during school hours to call for action on global warming. Other students—both in Sweden and around the world—joined her, organizing what became known as Fridays for Future, a global school climate strike. In 2019, Thunberg made a carbon-neutral transatlantic crossing to New York, where she spoke at the UN Climate Action Summit ahead of the September General Assembly meeting. In her speech, Thunberg criticized world leaders for their failure to act on climate change: "You have stolen my dreams and my childhood with your empty words. And yet I'm one of the lucky ones. People are suffering. People are dying. Entire ecosystems are collapsing. We are in the beginning of a mass extinction, and all you can talk about is money and fairy tales of eternal economic growth. How dare you!" Trump, who has repeatedly claimed that climate change is a hoax, mocked Thunberg on Twitter, calling her a "very happy young girl looking forward to a bright and wonderful future."

At the September climate change summit, more than 100 nations announced they were either making plans to or were working on reducing greenhouse gas emissions, some to net zero. China, the European Union, and India all committed to releasing new plans in 2020 detailing how they intend to cut carbon emissions, and Greece committed to phasing out the use of coal power plants by 2028. Less than three months later, world leaders again gathered to discuss climate change, this time at COP25. Initially planned for Chile, the conference was moved to Spain at the last minute because of unrelated protests in the South American nation.

At the opening of COP25, UN secretary-general Guterres said, "Climate-related natural disasters are becoming more frequent, more deadly, more destructive, with growing human and financial costs." The 2019 meeting of world leaders was the longest UN climate conference in history, running two days past its scheduled end to allow negotiators more time to extract agreements from the nations present. The conference was widely criticized as failing to meet its primary goals, including pushing the world's largest polluters to make bigger commitments on capping carbon emissions. Although seventy-three countries announced their intent to submit enhanced plans for addressing climate change within their borders, Guterres said he was "disappointed with the results" of the conference. However, he added that the outcome made him "more determined than ever to work for 2020 to be the year in which all countries commit to do what science tells us is necessary to reach carbon neutrality in 2050."

—Heather Kerrigan

Following is a statement from Secretary of Agriculture Sonny Perdue on June 10, 2019, announcing federal relief for farmers; a July 2, 2019, press release from the World Meteorological Organization (WMO) on the European heatwave; a September 22, 2019, report from the WMO detailing climate change trends; a December 11, 2019, press release from the United Nations Climate Change Conference (COP25) announcing the events' outcomes; and a December 15, 2019, statement by UN secretary-general António Guterres expressing disappointment at the outcome of the COP25 meetings.

U.S. Agriculture Secretary Announces Relief for Farmers

June 10, 2019

U.S. Secretary of Agriculture Sonny Perdue issued the following statement on disaster and trade-related assistance:

"Whether it's because of natural disasters or unfair retaliatory tariffs, farmers across the country are facing significant challenges and tough decisions on their farms and ranches. Last month, immediately upon China reneging on commitments made during the trade talks, President Trump committed USDA to provide up to $16 billion to support farmers as they absorb some of the negative impact of unjustified retaliation and trade disruption. In addition, President Trump immediately signed into law the long-awaited disaster legislation that provides a lifeline to farmers, ranchers, and producers dealing with extensive damage to their operations caused by natural disasters in 2018 and 2019.

"Given the size and scope of these many disasters, as well as the uncertainty of the final size and scope of this year's prevented planting acreage, we will use up to $16 billion in support for farmers and the $3 billion in disaster aid to provide as much help as possible to all our affected producers.

"I have been out in the country this spring and visited with many farmers. I know they're discouraged, and many are facing difficult decisions about what to do this planting season or if they've got the capital to stay in business, but they shouldn't wait for an announcement to make their decisions. I urge farmers to plant for the market and plant what works best on their farm, regardless of what type of assistance programs USDA is able to provide.

"In the coming weeks, USDA will provide information on the Market Facilitation Program payment rates and details of the various components of the disaster relief legislation. USDA is not legally authorized to make Market Facilitation Program payments to producers for acreage that is not planted. However, we are exploring legal flexibilities to provide a minimal per acre market facilitation payment to folks who filed prevent plant and chose to plant an MFP-eligible cover crop, with the potential to be harvested and for subsequent use of those cover crops for forage."

Background:

For frequently asked questions regarding the USDA Risk Management Agency's prevented planting policy and losses resulting from floods, please visit the USDA RMA Flooding page. For several frequently asked questions regarding how USDA will treat prevented planting acres with regard to the recently announced 2019 Market Facilitation Program and 2018/2019 disaster relief legislation, see below.

1. What is the purpose of the Market Facilitation Program? What is the legal authority?

- The Market Facilitation Program (MFP) assists farmers with the additional costs of adjusting to disrupted markets, dealing with surplus commodities, and expanding and developing new markets at home and abroad, consistent with the authorities of the Commodity Credit Corporation (CCC) Charter Act.

2. Last year, soybeans had the highest MFP payment per bushel, should I plant soybeans this year to get the highest payment if I have the opportunity?

- You should plant what works best for your operation and what you would plant in any other year, absent any assistance from USDA. 2019 MFP assistance is based on a single county payment rate multiplied by a farm's total plantings to the MFP-eligible crops (outlined below) in aggregate in 2019. *Those per acre payments are not dependent on which of those crops are planted in 2019*, and therefore will not distort planting decisions. Your total payment-eligible plantings cannot exceed your total 2018 plantings.

- 2019 MFP-eligible non-specialty crops: alfalfa hay, barley, canola, crambe, dry peas, extra-long staple cotton, flaxseed, lentils, long grain and medium grain rice, millet, mustard seed, dried beans, oats, peanuts, rapeseed, rye, safflower, sesame seed, small and large chickpeas, sorghum, soybeans, sunflower seed, temperate japonica rice, triticale, upland cotton, and wheat.

- 2019 MFP-eligible specialty crops: tree nuts, fresh sweet cherries, cranberries, and fresh grapes.

3. My fields never dried out enough to get *any* crop in, do I get a 2019 Market Facilitation Program payment?

- No, USDA does not have the legal authority to make MFP payments to producers for acreage that is not planted. To qualify for a 2019 MFP payment, you must have planted a 2019 MFP-eligible crop. Producers unable to plant their crop should work with their crop insurance agent to file a claim.

4. I filed a prevented planting claim and I am going to plant a cover crop to prevent erosion, does that count for 2019 MFP if it's on the 2019 MFP-eligible list you announced in May?

- If you choose to plant a cover crop with the potential to be harvested, because of this year's adverse weather conditions, you may qualify for a minimal amount of 2019 MFP assistance. You must still comply with your crop insurance requirements to remain eligible for any indemnities received.

5. I heard that I could get 90% of my crop insurance guarantee as a prevented planting payment through the disaster bill, is that true?

- The Additional Supplemental Appropriations for Disaster Relief Act of 2019 gives the USDA the authority to compensate losses caused by prevented planting in 2019 up to 90%. While the authority exists, USDA must operate within finite appropriations limits. It is highly unlikely that the supplemental appropriation will support that level of coverage in addition to crop insurance. Congress appropriated $3.005 billion in assistance for a wide array of losses resulting from disasters throughout 2018 and 2019, requiring USDA to prioritize how it is allocated. The Department plans to provide assistance on prevented planting losses within the confines of our authority.

6. If I plant a second crop or cover crop, can I still get my full prevented planting payment? What about an MFP payment?

- You must comply with crop insurance requirements to remain eligible for a full prevented planting indemnity. USDA encourages you to visit with your crop insurance agent to ensure you are aware of those various options for your operation. If you choose to plant a cover crop with the potential to be harvested, because of this year's adverse weather conditions, you may qualify for a minimal amount of 2019 MFP assistance.

7. I have heard that only acreage in a declared disaster area will qualify for prevented planting under the Disaster Relief Act. Is that true?

- USDA is currently evaluating the new authority provided under the Additional Supplemental Appropriations for Disaster Relief Act of 2019. However, it is generally true that producers with qualifying losses in a Secretarial or Presidentially-declared disaster area will be eligible for Disaster Relief Act assistance. Producers with qualifying losses outside of those areas will have eligibility determined on a case-by-case basis.

8. I have a revenue protection policy with a "harvest price option," do I get the higher of the projected price or harvest price for my prevented planting payment?

- The Additional Supplemental Appropriations for Disaster Relief Act of 2019 gives the USDA the authority to compensate losses caused by prevented planting in 2019 and also provides additional authority to compensate producers on the higher of the projected price or harvest price. USDA is currently exploring legal flexibility to provide assistance that better utilizes the harvest price in conjunction with revenue and prevent planting policies.

9. If I am prevented from planting but manage to get a cover crop or a forage in the ground, am I able to hay or graze that prior to November 1, given the forage shortage we're going to experience?

- USDA encourages you to visit with your crop insurance agent to ensure you are aware of those various prevented planting, cover crop, and harvest options for your operation. USDA is currently reviewing the prevented planting restrictions in the Federal Crop Insurance Act to determine what options may be available to address this and other issues. Further clarity regarding this haying and grazing date will be forthcoming.

10. What if I don't have crop insurance? How do MFP and disaster relief programs work for me if I'm prevented from planting due to natural disasters?

- Crop insurance is not required to qualify for 2019 MFP assistance. However, USDA requires that a producer plant a 2019 MFP-eligible crop to qualify for the 2019 MFP assistance.

- If you choose to plant a cover crop with the potential to be harvested, because of this year's adverse weather conditions, you may qualify for a minimal amount of 2019 MFP assistance.

- The Additional Supplemental Appropriations for Disaster Relief Act of 2019 gives the USDA the authority to compensate losses caused by prevented planting in 2019. Producers with qualifying losses in a Secretarial or Presidentially-declared disaster area will be eligible for Disaster Relief Act assistance. Producers with qualifying losses outside of those areas will have eligibility determined on a case-by-case basis.

SOURCE: U.S. Department of Agriculture. "Secretary Perdue Statement on Disaster and Trade-Related Assistance." June 10, 2019. https://www.usda.gov/media/press-releases/2019/06/10/secretary-perdue-statement-disaster-and-trade-related-assistance.

WMO Remarks on Record Temperatures in Europe

July 2, 2019

An unusually early and exceptionally intense heatwave has set new temperature records in Europe and ensuring that the month of June was the hottest on record for the continent, with the average temperature of 2° Celsius above normal. The high temperatures pose a major threat to people's health, agriculture and the environment, but initial reports indicated that heat-health early warnings successfully limited the death toll.

Such heatwaves are consistent with climate scenarios which predict more frequent, drawn out and intense heat events as greenhouse gas concentrations lead to a rise in global temperatures.

"Every heatwave occurring in Europe today is made more likely and more intense by human-induced climate change," said a study published by scientists at World Weather Attribution on the human contribution to record-breaking June 2019 heatwave in France.

"The observations show a very large increase in the temperature of these heatwaves. Currently such an event is estimated to occur with a return period of 30 years, but similarly frequent heatwaves would have likely been about 4ºC cooler a century ago. In other words, a heatwave that intense is occurring at least 10 times more frequently today than a century ago," it said.

The five days of unusually high temperatures followed days with record-breaking temperatures further east in Europe. This led to the month as a whole being around 1°C above the previous record for June, set in 1999, and about 1°C higher than expected from the trend in recent decades, according to the European Centre for Medium Range Weather Forecast (ECMWF) Copernicus Climate Change Service.

Météo-France verified a new national temperature record of 46°C in Vérargues and a temperature of 45.9° Celsius in nearby Gallargues-le-Montueux on 28 June. It was the first time in modern French history that 45°C has been exceeded.

Such temperatures are more typical of August in Furnace Creek, Death Valley, California (which holds the record as the world's hottest place), commented Météo-France.

Some 13 observing stations broke the previous national heat record of 44.1°C set during the August 2003 heatwave. Many observing stations broke all-time maximum temperature station records, or June records. Numerous overnight minimum temperature records were broken. A new national average temperature record (including daytime and overnight) of 27.9°C was set on 27 June.

Spain also reported widespread temperatures above 40 degrees from 27 to 30 June. Very high to extreme fire risk continues in North Eastern Spain as a result. The Spanish national meteorological and hydrological agency AEMET issued a detailed article on the "June 2019 heatwave in the context of the climate crisis."

The Deutscher Wetterdienst said that a new national June temperature record of 39.6°C was set on 30 June. It said that 243 observing stations set new June temperature records, with many of these being all-time temperature records, and that 223 stations reported 35.0°C or above.

Austria is expected to have its warmest June on record, 4.5°C above the long-term average and ahead of 2003, according to the national meteorological and hydrological service ZAMG.

More than half of Switzerland's observing stations measured new June temperature records on Wednesday. Out of 85 stations, 43 recorded June temperature records and six saw an absolute record. This includes Davos at 1594 meters with a temperature of 29.8°C. The heatwave in Switzerland peaked on 30 June.

In the Czech Republic, a new national June temperature record was set, at 38.9°C, Doksany, 26/06/2019, and Poland also reported records. Hungary saw its warmest June on record.

Temperatures above 40°C were recorded in some places in In North Africa. Serious concerns have been raised about the well-being of players at the ongoing Africa Cup of Nations in Egypt as a consequence of extreme heat. . . .

[The remainder of the press release, detailing expected temperatures in the coming weeks and health risks posed by extreme heat, has been omitted.]

SOURCE: World Meteorological Organization. "European Heatwave Sets New Temperature Records." July 2, 2019. https://public.wmo.int/en/media/news/european-heatwave-sets-new-temperature-records.

Global Scientists Release Climate Change Trend Report

September 22, 2019

[The table of contents and opening letters and statements have been omitted, along with all figures and references to them.]

Key Messages

The Global Climate in 2015–2019

- Average global temperature for 2015–2019 is on track to be the warmest of any equivalent period on record. It is currently estimated to be 1.1°C above pre-industrial (1850–1900) times and 0.2°C warmer than 2011–2015

- Observations show that global mean sea level rise is accelerating and an overall increase of 26% in ocean acidity since the beginning of the industrial era

Global Fossil CO_2 Emissions

- CO_2 emissions from fossil fuel use continue to grow by over 1% annually and 2% in 2018 reaching a new high

- Growth of coal emissions resumed in 2017

- Despite extraordinary growth in renewable energy, fossil fuels still dominate the global energy system

Greenhouse Gas Concentrations

- Increases in CO_2 concentrations continue to accelerate

- Current levels of CO_2, CH_4 and N_2O represent 146%, 257% and 122% respectively of pre-industrial levels (pre-1750)

Emissions Gap

- Global emissions are not estimated to peak by 2030, let alone by 2020

- Implementing current unconditional NDCs would lead to a global mean temperature rise between 2.9°C and 3.4°C by 2100 relative to pre-industrial levels, and continuing thereafter

- The current level of NDC ambition needs to be roughly tripled for emission reduction to be in line with the 2°C goal and increased fivefold for the 1.5°C goal. Technically it is still possible to bridge the gap

Intergovernmental Panel on Climate Change 2018 & 2019 Special Reports

- Limiting temperature to 1.5°C above pre-industrial levels would go hand-in-hand with reaching other world goals such as achieving sustainable development and eradicating poverty

- Climate change puts additional pressure on land and its ability to support and supply food, water, health and wellbeing. At the same time, agriculture, food production, and deforestation are major drivers of climate change

Climate Insights

- Growing climate impacts increase the risk of crossing critical tipping points

- There is a growing recognition that climate impacts are hitting harder and sooner than climate assessments indicated even a decade ago

- Meeting the Paris Agreement requires immediate and all-inclusive action encompassing deep decarbonisation complemented by ambitious policy measures, protection and enhancement of carbon sinks and biodiversity, and effort to remove CO_2 from the atmosphere

Global Framework for Climate Services

- Climate and early warning information services should underpin decision-making on climate action for adaptation

- The capacities of countries to deliver climate and early warning information services varies across regions

The Global Climate in 2015–2019

Warmest five-year period on record

The average global temperature for 2015–2019 is on track to be the warmest of any equivalent period on record. It is currently estimated to be 1.1°Celsius (± 0.1 °C) above pre-industrial (1850–1900) times and 0.20 ±0.08 °C warmer than the global average temperature for 2011–2015.

The 2015–2019 five-year average temperatures were the highest on record for large areas of the United States, including Alaska, eastern parts of South America, most of Europe and the Middle East, northern Eurasia, Australia, and areas of Africa south of the Sahara. July 2019 was the hottest month on record globally.

Sea-level rise is accelerating, sea water is becoming more acidic

The observed rate of global mean sea-level rise increased from 3.04 millimeters per year (mm/yr) during the period 1997–2006 to approximately 4 mm/yr during the period 2007–2016. The accelerated rate in sea level rise as shown by altimeter satellites is attributed to the increased rate of ocean warming and land ice melt from the Greenland and West Antarctica ice sheets.

The ocean absorbs nearly 25% of the annual emissions of anthropogenic CO_2 thereby helping to alleviate the impacts of climate change on the planet. The absorbed CO_2 reacts with seawater and increases the acidity of the ocean.

Observations show an overall increase of 26% in ocean acidity since the beginning of the industrial era. The ecological cost to the ocean, however, is high, as the changes in acidity are linked to shifts in other carbonate chemistry parameters, such as the saturation state of aragonite. This process, detrimental to marine life and ocean services, needs to be constantly monitored through sustained ocean observations.

Continued decrease of sea ice and ice mass

The long-term trend over the 1979–2018 period indicates that Arctic summer sea-ice extent has declined at a rate of approximately 12% per decade. In every year from 2015 to 2019, the Arctic average summer minimum and winter maximum sea-ice extent were well below the 1981–2010 average. The four lowest values for winter sea-ice extent occurred in these five years.

Summer sea ice in Antarctica reached its lowest and second lowest extent on record in 2017 and 2018, respectively. The second lowest winter extent ever recorded was also experienced in 2017. Most remarkably sea ice extent values for the February minimum (summer) and September maximum (winter) in the period from 2015–2019 have been well below the 1981–2010 average since 2016. This is a sharp contrast with the 2011–2015 period and the long term 1979–2018 values that exhibited increasing trends in both seasons.

Overall, the amount of ice lost annually from the Antarctic ice sheet increased at least six-fold between 1979 and 2017. The total mass loss from the ice sheet increased from 40 Gigatons (Gt) average per year in 1979–1990 to 252 Gt per year in 2009–2017.

Sea level rise contribution from Antarctica averaged 3.6 ± 0.5 mm per decade with a cumulative 14.0 ± 2.0 mm since 1979. Most of the ice loss takes place by melting the ice shelves from below, due to incursions of relatively warm ocean water, especially in West Antarctica and to a lesser extent along the Peninsula and in East Antarctica.

Analysis of long-term variations in glacier mass often relies on a set of global reference glaciers, defined as sites with continuous high-quality in situ observations of more than 30 years. Results from these time series are, however, only partly representative for glacier mass changes at the global scale as they are biased to well-accessible regions such as the European Alps, Scandinavia and the Rocky Mountains. Nevertheless, they provide direct information on the year-to-year variability in glacier mass balance in these regions. For the period 2015–2018, data from the World Glacier Monitoring Service (WGMS) reference glaciers indicate an average specific mass change of –908 mm water equivalent per year. This depicts a greater mass loss than in all other five-year periods since 1950, including the 2011–2015 period. Warm air from a heatwave in Europe in July 2019 reached Greenland, sending temperature and surface melting to record levels.

Intense heatwaves and wild fires

Heatwaves were the deadliest meteorological hazard in the 2015–2019 period, affecting all continents and setting many new national temperature records. Summer 2019 saw unprecedented wildfires in the Arctic region. In June alone, these fires emitted 50 megatons (Mt) of carbon dioxide into the atmosphere. This is more than was released by Arctic fires in the same month from 2010 to 2018 put together.

There were multiple fires in the Amazon rainforest in 2019, in particular in August.

Costly tropical cyclones

Overall, the largest economic losses were associated with tropical cyclones.

The 2018 season was especially active, with the largest number of tropical cyclones of any year in the twenty-first century. All Northern Hemisphere basins experienced above-average activity—the Northeast Pacific recorded its largest Accumulated Cyclone Energy (ACE) value ever.

The 2017 Atlantic hurricane season was one of the most devastating on record with more than US$ 125 billion in losses associated with Hurricane Harvey alone. Unprecedented back-to-back Indian Ocean tropical cyclones hit Mozambique in March and April 2019.

Food insecurity increasing

According to the Food and Agriculture Organization of the United Nations (FAO) report on the State of Food Security and Nutrition in the World, climate variability and extremes are among the key drivers behind the recent rises in global hunger after a prolonged decline and one of the leading contributors to severe food crises. Climate variability and extremes are negatively affecting all dimensions of food security—food availability, access, utilization and stability. The frequency of drought conditions from 2015–2017 show the impact of the 2015–2016 El Niño on agricultural vegetation. The following map shows that large areas in Africa, parts of central America, Brazil and the Caribbean, as well as Australia and parts of the Near East, experienced a large increase in frequency of drought conditions in 2015–2017 compared to the 14-year average.

Overall risk of climate-related illness or death increasing

Based on data and analysis from the World Health Organisation (WHO), between 2000 and 2016, the number of people exposed to heatwaves was estimated to have increased by around 125 million. The average length of individual heatwave events was 0.37 days longer, compared to the period between 1986 and 2008, contributing to an increased risk of heat-related illness or death.

Gross domestic product is falling in developing countries due to increasing temperatures

The International Monetary Fund found that for a medium and low-income developing country with an annual average temperature of 25°C, the effect of a 1°C increase in temperature is a fall in growth by 1.2%. Countries whose economies are projected to be hard hit by an increase in temperature accounted for only about 20% of global Gross Domestic Product (GDP) in 2016. But they are home to nearly 60% of the global population, and this is expected to rise to more than 75% by the end of the century.

[Sections documenting fossil fuel emissions and greenhouse gas concentration have been omitted.]

The Emissions Gap—Where we are and where we need to be

Global emissions show no sign of peaking

Global greenhouse gas emissions have grown at a rate of 1.6% per year from 2008 to 2017, reaching a record high of 53.5 Gigatons of CO_2 equivalent ($GtCO_2e$) in 2017, including emissions from land-use change. Preliminary findings from the Emission Gap Report 2019 indicate that emissions continued to rise in 2018. Global emissions are not estimated to peak by 2030, let alone by 2020, if current climate policies and ambition levels of the Nationally Determined Contributions (NDCs) are continued.

Collectively, G20 members are projected to achieve the Cancun pledges, which consist of economy-wide emission reduction targets, by 2020, but they are not yet on track to realize their NDCs for 2030.

Concerns about the current level of both ambition and action are amplified in the 2018 and forthcoming 2019 Emissions Gap Reports compared to previous reports.

The gap is larger than ever

The emissions gap in 2030 between emission levels under full implementation of conditional NDCs and levels consistent with least-cost pathways to the 2°C target is 13 $GtCO_2e$. If only the unconditional NDCs are implemented, the gap increases to 15 $GtCO_2e$. The gap in the case of the 1.5°C target is 29 $GtCO_2e$ and 32 $GtCO_2e$ respectively. The gap numbers 40 increased in 2018 compared with 2017, mainly as a result of the more detailed and diverse literature on 1.5°C and 2°C pathways prepared for the IPCC Special Report on 1.5°C. Only minor changes to the gap numbers are expected in the 2019 report.

The current NDCs are estimated to lower global emissions in 2030 by up to 6 $GtCO_2e$ compared to a continuation of current policies. This level of ambition needs to be roughly tripled to be aligned with the 2°C goal and increased around fivefold to align with the 1.5°C goal.

Implementing the unconditional NDCs, and assuming that climate action continues consistently throughout the twenty-first century, would lead to a global mean temperature rise between 2.9°C and 3.4°C by 2100 relative to pre-industrial levels, and continuing thereafter. Implementation of the conditional NDCs would reduce these estimates by 0.2°C in 2100.

Technically, it is still possible to bridge the gap in 2030 to ensure global warming stays below 2°C and 1.5°C. The sectoral emission reduction potential in 2030 is estimated to be up to between 30 and 40 $GtCO_2e$.

However, if NDC ambitions are not increased urgently and backed up by immediate action, exceeding the 1.5°C goal can no longer be avoided. If the emissions gap is not closed by 2030, it is very plausible that the goal of a well-below 2°C temperature increase is also out of reach.

A substantial part of the technical potential can be realized through scaling up and replicating existing, well-proven policies that simultaneously contribute to key sustainable development goals. Remarkably, the potential available in just six relatively well-developed areas as shown (below left) present a combined potential of up to 21 $GtCO_2e$ per year by 2030.

The use of carbon pricing to reduce greenhouse gas emissions is still only emerging in many countries and is generally not applied at a sufficient level to facilitate a real shift towards low-carbon societies. Even when considering energy-specific taxes together with explicit carbon pricing policies, half of the emissions from fossil fuels are not priced at all, and only 10% of global emissions from fossil fuels are estimated to be priced at a level consistent with limiting global warming to 2°C.

If all fossil fuel subsidies were phased out, it would lead to a reduction of global carbon emissions of up to about 10% by 2030.

At the global scale, the stock of coal-fired power plants is still increasing, as are emissions from coal. The existing stocks, in combination with what is currently planned and under construction (assuming standard lifetimes and usage rates), account for a significant share of the available carbon budget for a 2°C target, and would make a 1.5°C target infeasible.

Avoiding further lock-in and facilitating a balanced transition out of coal for power production will therefore be essential for the success of global mitigation efforts.

Finally, non-state and subnational action plays an important role in delivering national pledges. Emission reduction potential from non-state and subnational action could ultimately be significant, allowing countries to raise ambition, but currently such impacts are extremely limited and poorly documented. Coordinated, comparable and transparent reporting and verification of actions by all actors is essential to clarify effects and possible overlaps.

[The remainder of the report, documenting recommended WMO strategies for combating climate change, has been omitted.]

Source: World Meteorological Organization. "United in Science." September 22, 2019. https://ane4bf-datap1.s3-eu-west-1.amazonaws.com/wmocms/s3fs-public/ckeditor/files/United_in_Science_ReportFINAL_0.pdf?XqiG0yszsU_sx2vOehOWpCOkm9RdC_gN.

Coalition of COP25 Attendees Commits to New Climate Action Plans

December 11, 2019

In Madrid today, the President [of] COP25, Minister Carolina Schmidt, presented a renewed alliance of countries and Non-State Actors who determined to follow the recommendations of science as regards climate change. Chile has led this alliance after a request of the Secretary General of the United Nations, António Guterres, in the context of the 2019 Climate Summit.

Minister Schmidt announced that 73 nations have signaled their intention to submit an enhanced climate action plan (or Nationally Determined Contribution), and she acknowledged those 11 nations who have started an internal process to boost ambition and have this reflected in their national plans by 2020, as established in the Paris Agreement (full list in Annex 1).

She also stated that 73 Parties to the UNFCCC, 14 regions, 398 cities, 786 businesses and 16 investors are working towards achieving net-zero CO_2 emissions by 2050. This demonstrates clearly that both State and non-State actors recognize the urgent need to take ambitious action to address the climate change emergency (full list in Annex 2).

Minister Schmidt expressed that "Today we are strengthening our global push for more ambition. More and more leaders are joining this effort to demonstrate that boosting NDC ambition is both necessary and possible. We are here to listen to what our people are demanding its leaders to do."

Minister Schmidt also indicated that Chile and the United Kingdom will join efforts to mobilize additional actors to join the alliance on the road towards COP26. The Alliance will also strengthen its work on adaptation and the involvement of the private sector. All efforts will aim to accelerate the transformation needed to meet the goals of the Paris Agreement and ultimately stabilize global temperature rise at 1.5°C.

"Led by Chile, the Climate Ambition Alliance was launched at the Climate Action Summit in New York," the United Nations Secretary-General, António Guterres, said at COP25. "I am deeply encouraged by the growth [in the Ambition Alliance]. The shift from the grey to the green economy is on, and it is gathering pace. As we look ahead to 2020, there is much to be done."

UN Climate Change Executive Secretary Patricia Espinosa said, "Joining the Chile-driven Climate Ambition Alliance is a concrete way to demonstrate that the world is united behind the imperative to boost ambition. Under this Alliance, nations can publicly commit to enhancing their national climate plans by 2020."

As we urgently increase our efforts to reduce emissions, we must also give equal and increased urgency to adapt to climate impacts and build resilience for the future. Communities that are vulnerable to the impacts of climate change face an existential threat. The IPCC Special Report on the Impacts of Global Warming of 1.5°C states that both urgent and transformational adaptation action is needed to reduce climate-related risk. The scale of expected impacts is such that business as usual is no longer an option for any country, community, business or financial institution. The Call for Action on Adaptation and Resilience was launched at the UN Climate Action Summit and has been signed by 118 countries. The call marks the beginning of a paradigm shift in the way we all build adaptation and resilience.

"The UK is hugely determined and committed to work together with our global part-ners to tackle the climate crisis. Every country must come forward as soon as possible in 2020 with a more ambitious NDC. Sixty-six Parties joined the Climate Ambition Alliance at UNCAS through commitments to going net zero. I commend the leadership of Chile in launching the Alliance. We only have this planet, and we all have a duty to do everything we can to leave it a better place than we found it," said Claire O'Neill, COP26 President Designate of UK.

For mitigation, the Climate Ambition Alliance will focus on the submission of enhanced Nationally Determined Contributions; reaching new commitments to achieve Net Zero by 2050; and the implementation of measures to strengthen the protection of forests and oceans.

For adaptation, the Climate Ambition Alliance, will focus on strong actions to improve the management of water, resilience in infrastructure and the sustainability of cities.

It's time for action.

[Annexes 1 and 2 have been omitted but are available online at https://cop25.cl/#/cop-news/6uwx6gJHfSFV5TdOF6r9.]

SOURCE: United Nations Climate Change Conference. "Climate Ambition Alliance: Nations Renew Their Push to Upscale Action by 2020 and Achieve Net Zero CO_2 Emissions by 2050." December 11, 2019. https://unfccc.int/news/climate-ambition-alliance-nations-renew-their-push-to-upscale-action-by-2020-and-achieve-net-zero.

DOCUMENT

UN Secretary-General Comments on COP25 Outcome

December 15, 2019

"I am disappointed with the results of #COP25.

The international community lost an important opportunity to show increased ambi-tion on mitigation, adaptation & finance to tackle the climate crisis.

But we must not give up, and I will not give up.

I am more determined than ever to work for 2020 to be the year in which all countries commit to do what science tells us is necessary to reach carbon neutrality in 2050 and a no more than 1.5 degree temperature rise."

SOURCE: United Nations Climate Change Conference. "Statement by the UN Secretary-General António Guterres on the Outcome of COP25." December 15, 2019. https://unfccc.int/news/statement-by-the-un-secretary-general-antonio-guterres-on-the-outcome-of-cop25.

OTHER HISTORIC DOCUMENTS OF INTEREST

FROM PREVIOUS *HISTORIC DOCUMENTS*

- United States Withdraws from the Paris Climate Accord, *2017*, p. 323
- United Nations Climate Change Conference Reaches Historic Agreement, *2015*, p. 656

New President Takes Office in Kazakhstan; EU and UN Detail Election and Protests

JUNE 12, SEPTEMBER 2, OCTOBER 4, AND OCTOBER 6, 2019

Kazakhstan president Nursultan Nazarbayev's surprising resignation in March 2019 set the stage for an early presidential election that handed his chosen successor, Senate chair Kassym-Jomart Tokayev, an overwhelming victory. Accusations of election-rigging and a growing desire among some Kazakhs for political change prompted rare demonstrations in major cities, challenging the country's tight restrictions on public assembly. Despite calls for dialogue and cooperation, the new president has overseen an ongoing suppression of dissent while promising a continuation of Nazarbayev's policies.

A PRESIDENT STEPS ASIDE, A PROTÉGÉ TAKES OVER

Nazarbayev announced his resignation on March 19, 2019, surprising many observers and the people he served. He was the only leader Kazakhstan had had since it became an independent country following the collapse of the Soviet Union in the 1990s. He first took power in 1989, as the first secretary of the Central Committee for the Communist Party of Kazakhstan. Nazarbayev won five electoral victories to remain president, the latest of which occurred in 2015, though international observers say none of these elections were fair and only pitted the president against token opponents. Nazarbayev had been accused of corruption and human rights abuses by his critics, but his supporters credited him with maintaining peace among Kazakhstan's diverse ethnic groups and overseeing rapid economic growth in the oil-rich nation.

While many did not expect Nazarbayev's announcement, the president indicated his transition out of power had been planned for more than three years. He said the decision was "not easy" but that "I see my task now in facilitating the rise of a new generation of leaders who will continue the reforms that are under way in the country." Nazarbayev said Tokayev would serve as interim president for the remainder of his term, ending in 2020. Tokayev was widely characterized as the outgoing president's protégé. In addition to leading the Senate twice, Tokayev had served as prime minister from October 1999 to January 2002. He was also the former director-general of the United Nations Office at Geneva.

Tokayev said he would continue Nazarbayev's policies as interim president and consult with him on policy matters. He did not make any major policy or personnel changes during his early days in office, though he did name several new deputy ministers. One of these first acts as president was to rename Kazakhstan's capital city, Astana, as Nur-Sultan as a tribute to Nazarbayev.

Tokayev Calls Snap Election

Another of Tokayev's early actions was to call snap presidential elections. (The next presidential election was not due to be held until 2020.) Tokayev claimed the early vote was needed to eliminate political uncertainty. "We must continue to work on the implementation of the strategy of [Nazarbayev]," he said. "This can be done only by the direct expression of the will of the people." He added a guarantee that "the elections will be held honestly, openly, and fairly."

Seven candidates, including Tokayev, were registered for the short and largely uneventful campaign. Tokayev's primary challenger was Amirjan Qosanov, a journalist and veteran opposition leader. Qosanov's candidacy marked the first time since 2005 that someone claiming to represent the opposition was included on the presidential ballot. Also making history was Dania Espaeva. A member of the Mazhilis, the lower chamber of Kazakhstan's parliament, Espaeva was the country's first female presidential candidate.

The election took place on June 9, with nearly 78 percent of registered Kazakhs turning out to vote. The Central Election Commission announced Tokayev as the winner, with about 71 percent of the vote, the next day. Qosanov received roughly 16 percent of the vote; Espaeva was the third-highest vote getter, receiving 5 percent of the vote. In remarks at his swearing-in on June 12, Tokayev affirmed his intent to continue implementing Nazarbayev's policies. "It has to be recognized that, in these elections, citizens voted for the continuation of the course of the [Leader of the Nation]," he said.

However, the poll was widely dismissed as fraudulent, including by the Organisation for Security and Co-operation in Europe (OSCE), which sent more than 300 election observers to Kazakhstan to monitor the vote. In a statement issued on June 10, the OSCE said the vote took place "in a political environment dominated by the ruling party" and had been compromised by "irregularities on Election Day and a disregard for formal procedures." In its final report on the election proceedings, issued October 4, the OSCE said the vote had been "tarnished by violations of fundamental freedoms as well as pressure on critical voices," stating that "considerable restrictions on the right to stand and limits to peaceful assembly and expression inhibited genuine political pluralism." The OSCE said the election was "efficiently organized," but "significant irregularities were observed on Election Day, including cases of ballot box stuffing, and a disregard of counting procedures meant that an honest count could not be guaranteed." Responding to the report, the European External Action Service said, "We expect Kazakhstan to address these violations, as well as the controlled legal and political electoral framework, as they run counter to the country's OSCE commitments and international obligations."

Kazakhs Push for Change

The vote's validity was also challenged by certain segments of the Kazakh population. Many had hoped Nazarbayev's resignation would be an opportunity for change. While the country's economy had prospered for nearly two decades, its recent stagnation caused frustrations over lower living standards and fed the public's complaints about poor social services. Nazarbayev had reportedly fired his cabinet the month prior to his resignation for failing to address these social problems.

But hopes for change quickly waned as it became clear that Nazarbayev and his allies sought to stay in control. Although Nazarbayev resigned, he retained the formal title "Leader of the Nation"; remained head of the governing political party, Nur Otan; and kept his position as head of the powerful Security Council. Additionally, the president's daughter, Dariga Nazarbayeva, took over the Senate chairship from Tokayev, leading to speculation the former president had a long-term plan for a dynastic succession. Many Kazakhs also took the renaming of the capital without public consultation as a sign that the government wanted to maintain the status quo. In this environment, the snap election was widely decried as a sham by the government's opponents.

Kazakhstan has a history of strict suppression of dissent, even though its Constitution grants citizens "the right to peacefully and without arms assemble, hold meetings, rallies and demonstrations, street processions and pickets." The parliament is largely devoid of opposition to Nur Otan, the government controls the news media, and social media and other websites are regularly blocked. The government has also adopted restrictions on public demonstrations: those wishing to stage a protest must apply to local officials ten days in advance; if the application is approved, protesters are typically confined to a few select areas. This low tolerance for opposing viewpoints was underscored by the government's response to the small protests that popped up before the presidential election. In one instance, two activists were charged with violating public assembly laws and sentenced to fifteen days in prison for displaying a banner reading "You won't run away from the truth" during a marathon in Kazakhstan's largest city, Almaty. Another protester was arrested on charges of hooliganism after hanging a banner reading "The only source of the state power is the people," which is a quote from the Kazakhstan Constitution. In another widely publicized incident, police arrested a man who stood in a public square with a blank sign. The man told reporters he wanted to show the government's tolerance for public demonstrations was so low, the police would detain him even if he wasn't saying anything. When asked by a journalist why the man was being detained, police responded that they would "sort that out later." The protests began to grow in size, with participants calling for a boycott of the upcoming election. Dozens of people were arrested at protest marches in Nur-Sultan and Almaty. Government officials said the protests were unnecessary because the vote would let the people make a real choice among the largest and most diverse field of presidential candidates Kazakhstan had seen.

On June 9 and 10, the largest demonstrations the country had seen in several years took place in Nur-Sultan and Almaty, with protesters declaring the election had been rigged for Tokayev. Hundreds of protesters were arrested at what First Deputy Interior Minister Marat Kozhayev described as "unsanctioned rallies." Kozhayev and other officials blamed the protests on Democratic Choice of Kazakhstan, a banned group the government had labeled as extremist. Kozhayev said "fugitive leaders of this organization" had orchestrated "socially disruptive rallies" and "embarked on a major propaganda push to discredit the authorities." Tokayev seemed undisturbed by the demonstrations, saying it was the "people's choice" to protest, though elections should not be a "battlefield."

Citing information from independent organizations, the UN Office of the High Commissioner for Human Rights reported that at least 1,000 protesters, including journalists, had been arrested by police—550 of whom were charged and punished for "participating in an unauthorized assembly." The UN was also "made aware" of expedited judicial proceedings against protesters being held at police stations, at night, and often without defense lawyers present. Ryszard Komenda, head of the UN Human Rights Office for Central Asia, said the government's actions against protesters were "extremely regrettable" and "an apparent contradiction with Kazakhstan's obligations under international human rights law." Komenda urged the government to "fulfill its legal obligations to respect and protect the rights to freedom of peaceful assembly, expression, and ensure the right to meaningful political participation."

Periodic protests have continued since the election, including multicity demonstrations staged on Nazarbayev's birthday in July.

Tokayev Outlines Vision for Future

On September 2, in his first major address as president, Tokayev outlined his various policy priorities and a vision for Kazakhstan's future. Tokayev cautioned against "unsystematic political liberalization," declaring that global experience shows such "explosive" change leads to "destabilization of the domestic political situation and even to the loss of statehood." He pledged to pursue political reforms "consistently, persistently and thoughtfully," without "running ahead."

Tokayev called for cooperation between Nur Otan and other political parties to develop constructive policies that benefit all of society. He said it was his duty to foster a multiparty political system and pluralism of opinions, noting that legislative elections scheduled for 2020 would provide another opportunity to further develop political competition. "Our common task is to implement the concept of a state capable of hearing, which quickly and efficiently responds to all constructive requests of citizens," he said, continuing, "Only through a constant dialogue of power and society can a harmonious state be built in the context of modern geopolitics." Tokayev added that societal problems should not be decided "in the streets" but rather "discussed and find their solution in the Parliament and in the framework of civil dialogue."

—Linda Grimm

Following is President Kassym-Jomart Tokayev's inaugural address on June 12, 2019; a June 12, 2019, press release from the UN Human Rights Office in response to a crackdown on protesters in Kazakhstan; the text of President Tokayev's State of the Nation address delivered on September 2, 2019; and statements by the OSCE and EU, released on October 4, 2019, and October 6, 2019, respectively, regarding election conduct in Kazakhstan.

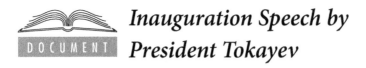

Inauguration Speech by President Tokayev

June 12, 2019

Dear *Leader of Nation*,

Dear Compatriots,

First of all, I would like to express my profound thanks to Kazakhstan's nation, which has supported me during the campaign and placed their faith in my presidency.

The elections reinforced our country's principles of democracy. There was a fair and open competition at the polling stations.

Politicians from all sides engaged in the process. It was an open contest where political parties and politicians were judged on their merits.

There is a common saying that "Elections are simply a race of opinions."

Indeed, this is a fair comparison.

In the most important political race in our nation's history; the wisdom and good judgment of our nation prevailed.

This victory is a victory for all our people!

As a progressive, unified nation, we have collectively chosen the way forward for Kazakhstan's future growth.

The opinion of each citizen who voted for a bright future on June 9 matters. It matters to us.

After all, our most important, common values are the peace, unity and solidarity of our people. Protecting these values should be a priority for all of us.

Therefore, as Kazakhstan's newly elected President, I would like to say the following to our people:

My ultimate goal is to protect the interests of every citizen. I will not allow anyone or anything to drive a wedge between us, based on a difference of political views or positions.

I will consider the valuable proposals and initiatives which are put forward by various political and community leaders.

We will continue to work openly and fairly. . . .

In these elections our citizens voted to support the strategic direction of the First President!

Nursultan Nazarbayev has built a model of development that was recognized worldwide. Thanks to him, the pale-blue flag of Kazakhstan is waving around the world. . . .

The progress of modern Kazakhstan is, first and foremost, thanks to the work and dedication of the First President.

Leader of Nation is the founder of the Kazakh state, a statesman on a global scale. And so it is written in world history.

It is a common duty for all of us to respect the great service the First President has done for our people and the global community.

Dear Compatriots!

During the election campaign, I visited many parts of the country.

My political platform has been developed in response to the main requests of our citizens.

First, I will work on the implementation of the Third Modernization in Kazakhstan, Five Institutional reforms and other important strategic state projects. In other words, I am going to work to deliver on the First President's long-term Strategy.

New approaches and new solutions are needed for the country to reach the next level of sustainable development. They will soon be made public.

Secondly, I plan to specifically address acute social problems, providing assistance to those most in need.

The government will take concrete steps to achieve tangible results in this area. We need to make serious changes to our social policy. We need to systematically reform our social policies.

Third, I will support Kazakh entrepreneurs, attract and protect investments, stimulate business activity, and expand our broad middle class.

Fourth, my goal is to ensure the unity of society and protect the rights of every citizen.

And finally, always and forever, I will defend the national interests of Kazakhstan.

Today, the world has entered an era of rapid change.

Technology, economies and social order are changing. The youth's vision is changing.

Kazakhstan faces new challenges and threats. As a long-term student of international relations, I feel the advent of a new era approaching.

Trade wars, tensions in international relations, the breakdown of previous security mechanisms, the growth of regional conflicts—this is the new geopolitical reality.

Over the coming years, the leading issues of our time will come to the fore: which countries will be able to effectively adapt and integrate to the new global realities, and who will be left on the sidelines of world development.

Economic, social and political progress is our only correct response to the challenges of our time.

We are open to the world, striving to secure the best achievements and advanced technologies. Creative change for the benefit of all our people is how I view progress.

At the same time, the authorities are obliged to hear people's demands, solve problems on the ground, and must be accountable to the citizens.

Not promising, but acting! This rule should be followed by all Cabinet members and the regional mayors across the country.

As President, the most important measure of progress is not the overall figure of economic development, but the real well-being of all citizens.

Therefore, when making decisions on strategic issues, the view of the people will be considered.

The formula of our state governance: a strong, empowered President—an influential, capable Parliament—the Cabinet accountable to the people.

It is this political system that best meets the needs of our state, responds to complex geopolitical realities and contributes to the implementation of the strategic tasks facing us.

At the same time, the political transformation of society will keep on.

The political structures and institutions must align with wide-ranging economic transformations, otherwise the reforms may be stifled.

This is clearly evidenced by international experience.

Only decent, educated people, appointed based on meritocracy, should work within public administration. There can be no other principle of recruitment.

Overall, we must raise the responsibility of the authorities to the needs of people. Special attention will be paid to the development of civil society.

Dear people,

My pre-election campaign focused on a wide-ranging public consultation. . . .

What is the public most concerned about today?

Firstly, citizens want justice everywhere.

The citizens require state bodies to provide proper service that starts, first of all, from social policy.

The main issue of concern is reduced incomes.

The destabilisation of international financial markets and the devaluation of the tenge (KZT) had a negative impact on people's incomes.

More than a million of our citizens had to take a loan from a bank.

The gap between high- and low-income citizens is another pressing issue that concerns society.

Of course, such challenges are present in every nation, but we cannot stand aside and let this issue go unaddressed.

Therefore, we must take action in the medium term to address these acute socio-economic and political problems.

The current poor state of the environment is another matter of public concern.

Therefore, we need to develop and adopt a single environmental policy.

A new environmental code would give impetus to a system of environmental protection.

The next problem is access to the water supply.

Every home, every family shall have access to clean drinking water.

Another important issue of public concern is quality of roads.

That is why improving road conditions is one of our main goals.

One of the biggest challenges that we face in the 21st c. is digitization.

We must embrace it in all spheres of our life starting with the provision of public services through to the creation of the new branches in the future economy.

The development of the country, including political progress is directly connected to digitization.

It will improve the relationship between the state and society.

Therefore, the state program Digital Kazakhstan first introduced by Leader of the Nation must be completed.

Our citizens are deeply concerned about the development of dialogue between the government and the society.

This dialogue should be based on the recognition of pluralism of opinion. Different views, but one united nation—this is the main guideline.

That is why I have decided to establish the National Council of Public Trust.

This Council shall embrace all the representatives of society, including the youth.

The first meeting of the National Council of Public Trust will take place in August this year.

The authorities are obliged to fulfill their promises which they made to the people. It is our primary mission. It is the only way to strengthen the unity of the nation and maintain stability in the country.

Therefore, a substantial program regarding the implementation of my election platform shall be developed.

The best ideas and initiatives put forward by the people will be reflected in this document. . . .

Dear Compatriots,

We have a great task before our nation!

Our goal is clear, and our path is open!

Kazakhstan has become a country of new opportunities and prospects.

Our youth and future generations will reap the benefits of these opportunities.

We are a nation that honors the traditions of our ancestors while striving for the best global achievements.

This is the pillar of our strength.

We are going to overcome all the challenges ahead.

We will work together for the development of a strong and prosperous Kazakhstan.

Faithfulness to my oath and a firm commitment to the obligation is my duty to the nation.

I promise to work hard for the bright future of Kazakhstan, for the nation.

I wish all of you good health and happiness.

Long live our beloved Motherland—the Republic of Kazakhstan!

Source: President of the Republic of Kazakhstan. "Statement from Kassym-Jomart Tokayev, Official Inauguration Ceremony of the Elected President of Kazakhstan." June 12, 2019. http://www.akorda.kz/en/speeches/internal_political_affairs/in_speeches_and_addresses/statement-from-kassym-jomart-tokayev-official-inauguration-ceremony-of-the-elected-president-of-kazakhstan.

UN Human Rights Office Responds to Crackdown on Protesters in Kazakhstan

DOCUMENT

June 12, 2019

"Kazakhstan's actions against peaceful protestors, activists and journalists during and after the presidential elections on 9 June are extremely regrettable," Mr. Ryszard Komenda, Head of the UN Human Rights Office for Central Asia said on Tuesday. "The freedom of expression and peaceful assembly are the building blocks of successful and vibrant societies. Any attempt to restrict them unnecessarily and without proper justification constitute risks for stability and social cohesion."

On 9 and 10 June, various independent sources reported at least 1000 arrests of peaceful protesters—among them journalists—in Nur-Sultan, Almaty and Shymkent. Officials confirmed that 550 individuals were charged and penalized for "participating in an unauthorised assembly"—an administrative offence in Kazakhstan. The UN Human Rights Office was also made aware about numerous expedited court proceedings held on the premises of police stations, conducted at night and in many instances without the presence of defence lawyers.

The UN Human Rights Office is concerned about the significant scale of arrests and convictions for peaceful and legitimate expression of political opinion and dissent. "This is an apparent contradiction with Kazakhstan's obligations under international human rights law," said Mr. Komenda. "I urge Kazakhstan to fulfil its legal obligations to respect and protect the rights to freedom of peaceful assembly, expression, and ensure the right to meaningful political participation."

Source: United Nations Office of the High Commissioner for Human Rights. "UN Human Rights Office Calls on Kazakhstan to Respect Freedoms of Peaceful Assembly, Expression and Right to Political Participation." June 12, 2019. https://www.ohchr.org/EN/NewsEvents/Pages/DisplayNews.aspx?NewsID=24691&LangID=E.

President Tokayev Gives
State of the Nation Address

September 2, 2019

Dear compatriots!

Dear members of parliament and government!

Congratulations on the beginning of the new parliamentary season!

We are approaching the important part in the newest history of our country.

Approximately thirty years ago, we proclaimed our independence thus fulfilling the dream that our ancestors had for centuries.

Since that time, under the leadership of the First President of Kazakhstan—the Leader of the Nation Nursultan Nazarbayev, our country has become a stable and reputable state in the world.

Thanks to the solid unity of our nation, we have strengthened our independence and created opportunities for improving the wellbeing of our people.

It was a time of creation and progress, peace and harmony.

The whole world recognized the way of development of the country and called it the Kazakhstan model or the Nazarbayev model.

Today, we are able to double the achievements of our independence and to bring our country to a qualitatively new stage of development.

We can achieve this by maintaining the continuity of the policy of the Leader of the Nation and through systemic reforms. . . .

I. MODERN EFFECTIVE STATE.

The political transformation I promised will be gradually and steadily carried out taking into account the interests of our state and people.

World experience shows that explosive, unsystematic political liberalisation leads to the destabilisation of the domestic political situation and even to the loss of statehood.

Therefore, we will carry out political reforms without "running ahead of ourselves," but consistently, persistently and thoughtfully. Our fundamental principle: successful economic reforms are no longer possible without the modernisation of the country's sociopolitical life. . . .

Our common task is to implement the concept of the "Listening State," which quickly and efficiently responds to all constructive citizen requests. Only through a constant dialogue between the Government and society can a harmonious state be built in the context of modern geopolitics.

Therefore, it is necessary to maintain and strengthen civil society, to involve it in the discussion of the most urgent national tasks in order to solve them.

It is for this purpose that the National Council of Public Trust, representative in composition, was created, which will work on a rotational principle.

In the near future, we all have to implement the following measures.

First. Continue the process of party building.

The Nur Otan party, thanks to our Leader and its Chairman, Nursultan Abishevich Nazarbayev, is consistently carrying out the difficult and responsible mission of the country's leading political force.

We must cooperate with other political parties and movements that pursue a constructive policy for the benefit of society.

The main problems that concern our society should be discussed and their solutions should be found in Parliament and in the framework of civil dialogue, but not on the streets.

Deputies can and should use their legal rights, including by sending inquiries to the Government on pressing issues and requiring it to take specific measures.

At the same time, relations between the legislative and executive powers should be mutually respectful, business-like, without artificial confrontation.

As Head of State, I see my task as contributing to the development of a multi-party system, political competition and pluralism of opinions in the country.

This is important for the stability of the political system in the long run.

The upcoming elections to the Mazhilis of Parliament and maslikhats should contribute to the further development of the multi-party system in the country.

Second. Effective citizen feedback.

Public dialogue, openness, quick response to the needs of people are the main priorities for the activities of state bodies.

A department has been created in the Presidential Administration that will monitor the quality of reviewing citizens' requests by state bodies and take prompt measures on them.

Often people are forced to turn to the President because of the "deafness" and closed-off national and local officials.

Repeated complaints about the unfairness of decisions in a particular area mean systemic problems in a particular Government agency or region. Now this should be viewed in this way, and appropriate actions should be taken.

In order to increase the efficiency of the work of civil servants, it is necessary to attract trained young personnel into their ranks.

At the same time, starting in 2020, we will begin to gradually reduce the number of civil servants, and we will use the released funds to provide material incentives for the most useful staff.

By 2024, the number of civil servants and employees of national companies should be reduced by 25 percent.

Third. Improving the legislation on rallies.

According to the Constitution, our citizens have the right to freedom of expression.

If peaceful protests do not pursue the goal of violating the law and the peace of citizens, then they should be embraced and given approval for them to be carried out in the manner prescribed by law, to allocate special places for this. And not in the outskirts of cities.

But any calls for unconstitutional and hooligan actions will be dealt with within the framework of the law.

Fourth. Strengthening the public consensus.

The harmony between social and ethnic groups is the result of the joint work of the whole society.

In this regard, it is necessary to analyse political tendencies and take concrete measures to strengthen our unity.

We need, taking into account the role of the Kazakh people as a nation-building people, to continue building inter-ethnic concord and inter-religious understanding.

Our position: the unity of the nation is in its diversity. . . .

I believe it is necessary to enhance the image of non-governmental organisations in the creation of an active civil society.

Therefore, in the near future, we need to elaborate and adopt the Concept of Civil Society Development until 2025. . . .

II. ENSURING RIGHTS AND SECURITY OF CITIZENS.

A key factor in enhancing the protection of citizens' rights and their security is the substantial reform of the judicial and law enforcement systems.

A number of serious measures must be taken to improve the quality of court decisions.

The right of a judge to make a decision based on law and internal convictions remains unshakable. However, a thorough analysis of court decisions should be carried out and the uniformity of judicial practice should be ensured.

In public law disputes, when appealing against decisions and actions of authorities, citizens are not on equal footing. Their capabilities are incommensurable with the resources of the state apparatus.

Therefore, it is necessary to introduce administrative justice, as a special dispute resolution mechanism, levelling this difference.

Henceforth, when resolving disputes, the court will have the right to initiate the collection of additional evidence, the responsibility for the collection of which lies with the state body, and not with the citizen or business.

All contradictions and ambiguities of the legislation should be interpreted in favour of citizens. . . .

The principle of the presumption of innocence must be fully respected.

One of the most pressing tasks remains a full-fledged reform of the law enforcement system.

The image of the police, as a power tool of the state, will gradually become a thing of the past; it will become a body providing services to citizens to ensure their safety.

At the first stage, it is necessary to reorganise the work of the Committee of Administrative Police by the end of 2020. This must be done qualitatively and without a gung-ho approach.

The effectiveness of the work of the police depends on the reputation of the police service itself.

Over the next three years, 173 billion tenge will be allocated to reform the Ministry of Internal Affairs.

These funds will be used to increase wages, provide accommodation, and the creation of modern front-line police offices on the principle of public service centres. . . .

III. DEVELOPED AND INCLUSIVE ECONOMY.

Kazakhstan's economy is moving forward despite the global challenges.

From the start of the year its growth has been higher than the world average.

If necessary structural adjustments can be implemented, by 2025, annual sustainable growth of gross domestic product can reach 5% or higher.

In order to give a new impetus to the development of the economy, the Presidential Administration and the Government should carefully analyse the work of domestic and foreign experts.

We need to implement a number of structural tasks in line with the Long-term Development Strategy 2050 and the Plan of the Nation proposed by Elbasy.

First. Abandonment of the raw material–based mentality and diversification of the economy.

The "knowledge economy," increased labour productivity, innovation development and the introduction of artificial intelligence have become major factors in global progress.

In the course of the third five-year plan of industrialisation, we should take into account the mistakes and shortcomings that have been made earlier.

The Government should take into account all my comments and fully implement the relevant instructions in these matters.

We need to increase real labour productivity by at least 1.7 times.

Raising our reputation in Central Asia as a leader in the region is a strategic task.

This is our political course determined by Elbasy.

Second. Increased returns from the quasi-public sector.

Our state-owned companies have become bulky conglomerates whose international competitiveness is in doubt.

In order to reduce the unjustified presence of the state in the economy, I decided to introduce a moratorium on the creation of quasi-state-owned companies.

We need to understand the genuine contribution of the Sovereign Wealth Fund to the growth of the welfare of the people over the past 14 years since its creation.

The Government, together with the Accounts Committee, must conduct an analysis of the effectiveness of state holdings and national companies within three months.

Quasi-state companies often compete with each other on the same field. In the field of housing policy, for example, seven state operators are operating simultaneously, and this is only at the national level!

The number of state-owned companies can and should be reduced.

At the same time, one should carefully approach the activities of state-owned companies operating in strategic sectors.

State control over them should be maintained. Otherwise, instead of state monopolists, we will get private monopolists with all the ensuing consequences.

The Government needs to systematically and substantively deal with pricing and tariff issues. This also applies to the goods and services of natural monopolists. It is no secret that prices in our country are high—from food and clothing to the cost of various services. . . .

Third. Effective small and medium sized businesses are a solid foundation for the development of cities and villages.

Small enterprises, especially micro-businesses, play an important role in the socio-economic and political life of the country. . . .

Therefore, the state will continue to support businesses.

Around 100 billion tenge has been allocated from the National Fund for this purpose.

However, according to experts, financial support is only received by the businesses affiliated with local authorities.

In fact, new companies and jobs should have been created within the new projects.

This is directly related to "the economy of simple things."

However, local akims have not fulfilled the organisational work.

As a consequence, conditions were not created to increase the tax base, pension contributions, and strengthen the local budget.

In this regard, I instruct the Accounts Committee and the Ministry of Finance to take strict control over the expenditure of funds.

There are plenty of examples of entrepreneurship development in our country. Our whole society needs to support small businesses.

I instruct the Government to develop a legislative framework to exempt micro and small business companies from paying income tax for a period of three years.

Corresponding amendments to the legislation should enter into force from 2020.

My decision for a three-year ban on inspections of micro and small business entities will come into force from January 2020.

We believe in the integrity and law-abiding nature of our businesses, which should have responsibility towards consumers and citizens. During the moratorium, it is necessary to activate the tools of self-regulation and public control.

In cases of violation by business entities of the prescribed norms and rules, especially in the sanitation and contagious diseases sphere, such companies will be closed, their owners will be held accountable.

We are thus reducing the burden on businesses.

At the same time, there are still numerous problems associated with the actions of law enforcement and regulatory authorities.

Cases of raiding against SMEs have become more frequent.

My position on this issue is well known: any attempts to hinder the development of business, especially small and medium-sized ones, should be considered crimes against the state.

In this regard, additional legislative measures are needed. Parliament and the Government should propose a solution to this problem.

At the same time, it is necessary to strengthen opposition to the shadow economy, to tighten the fight against the capital flight and tax evasion.

Furthermore, the system of state financial support for SMEs needs to be "rebooted," giving priority to new projects.

I instruct the Government to allocate an additional 250 billion tenge for the next three years under the new "Business Roadmap."

It is necessary to actively introduce new forms of business support with an emphasis on social aspects—the creation of family businesses, primarily for large and low-income families.

Particular attention should be paid to the development of tourism, especially eco- and ethno-tourism, as an important area of the economy. . . .

Fourth. Support for national businesses in international markets.

It is necessary to drastically increase the effectiveness of state support for exporting companies.

I speak, first of all, about medium-sized business.

Meanwhile, we do not have effective state support measures for this particular segment of entrepreneurs, especially regarding the sale of products. We need to support our SMEs.

I instruct the Government, within the framework of the State Programme for Industrial and Innovative Development, to develop a set of measures to support high-performance medium-sized businesses, including through tax, financial, and administrative incentives.

It is necessary to seriously intensify efforts to attract foreign direct investment, without which the potential for further economic growth will be limited. This is one of the priority tasks of the executive branch.

Within the framework of the Strategic Plan for the Development of Kazakhstan until 2025, appropriate targets are set for each industry and region.

Their achievement is the direct responsibility of the heads of state bodies, especially regional akims.

Kazakhstan has embarked on developing a digital economy.

There is a lot of work to do. Our task is to strengthen our leadership in the region in terms of the development of info-communication infrastructure.

The Government will have to adapt the legislation to new technological innovations: 5G, Smart Cities, Big Data, blockchain, digital assets, and new digital financial instruments.

Kazakhstan should have the reputation as an open jurisdiction for technological partnership, construction and placement of data centres, development of data transit, participation in the global digital services market.

The Government should continue to support the activities of the Astana International Financial Centre (AIFC), which, in essence, has acquired constitutional status. The AIFC could become a platform for the development of the latest digital technologies together with the Nazarbayev University.

Fifth. Developed agricultural industry.

. . . Furthermore, we need to move away from only exporting raw materials, which reached 70%, while the load of processing enterprises is only 40%.

An urgent task is to attract foreign investors to the agricultural sector. Discussions are already underway; the Government needs to achieve concrete results.

I would like to specifically address an issue that is of public concern.

As Head of State I repeat: our land is not for sale to foreigners. This is not allowed.

All insinuations on this issue must end. At the same time, our task is to ensure the effective use of land.

The issue of inefficient use of land resources is becoming increasingly relevant.

The situation is compounded by the low level of direct taxes on land.

Many of those who received land leases for free from the state keep the land for future use without working on it. . . .

It is time to begin the seizure of unused agricultural land.

Land is our common wealth and must belong to those who work on it. . . .

Sixth. Fair taxation and sound financial regulation.

. . . I believe it is necessary to modernize the tax system with a focus on a more equitable distribution of the national income.

The Government should also pay attention to the growing volume of social contributions.

On the one hand, they ensure the stability of social and pension systems.

However, there are risks that employers will lose incentives to creating jobs and increasing wages. Businesses will go into the shadow.

Therefore, I instruct the Government to postpone the introduction of additional pension contributions in the amount of 5% until 2023. We will then return to this question.

During this time, the Government, business representatives and experts should calculate the options and come to an agreed decision taking into account the interests of both future pensioners and employers.

The Government must impose a ban on all payments and fees that are not provided for by the Tax Code. These are, in fact, additional taxes.

A separate problem is improving the quality of the current tax system.

It should stimulate companies to invest in human capital, in raising labour productivity, technical re-equipment and exports.

Non-cash payments should be introduced everywhere, eliminating the constraining factor—a high banking commission. To achieve this, it is necessary to actively develop non-banking payment systems with relevant regulatory rules. With the obvious simplicity and attractiveness of this segment, it should not become a channel for money laundering and capital flight from the country. The National Bank should establish effective control in this area.

The next issue is the support for the export of non-oil products. The issue of applying simpler and faster VAT refund procedures needs to be considered.

One of the most problematic issues in our economy is the insufficient volume of lending. Over the past five years, the total volume of lending to legal entities, as well as small and medium-sized businesses, has decreased by more than 13%.

Second-tier banks cite a shortage of good borrowers and make provisions for excessive risks in the cost of credit.

The problem of quality borrowers, of course, exists. But you can't just pass on your responsibility and take only the easy route.

I expect the well-coordinated and effective work of the Government and the National Bank on this issue.

Another problem—debt load, especially of socially vulnerable segments of the population,—has led to the need for emergency measures. You are aware of this.

This problem has gained social and political urgency.

Therefore, I entrust the Government and the National Bank to prepare within two months for the implementation of mechanisms that are guaranteed to prevent the repetition of this situation.

The lack of effectiveness of monetary policy is becoming one of the obstacles to the country's economic development.

Lending to businesses should be ensured by second-tier banks on acceptable and long-term terms. By the end of the year, the National Bank needs to complete an independent assessment of the quality of assets of second-tier banks. . . .

["Seventh. Effective use of the National Fund" has been omitted.]

Eighth. Increase of salaries.

As the success of large mining companies increases, we see that the wages of our citizens have not significantly grown.

As this concerns the social welfare of the population, the Government must remain persistent in this regard.

I instruct the Government to consider the issue of incentives for employers to increase wages.

IV. NEW STAGE OF SOCIAL MODERNISATION

The country's budget should be focused on two main objectives—the development of the economy and solving social problems.

The social sphere should focus on the following areas.

First. Improving the quality of education.

The effective methodology of accounting for the balance of labour resources has not yet been developed in our country.

In fact, the domestic training system is out of touch with the real labour market.

Around 21,000 school graduates annually do not have access to vocational and higher education.

This group of young people is the basis of the unemployed and marginalised. Many of them are exposed to criminal and extremist movements' influence.

We need to identify the pupils' abilities and move towards a career guidance policy.

This policy should be the basis of the national standard of secondary education.

Demand for technicians in our economy is very high, but capabilities of the national education system are low. Enterprises have to invite relevant professionals from abroad. We need to correct this situation quickly.

The difference in quality of secondary education is growing between urban and rural schools.

The main problem is the deficit of qualified teachers in rural areas.

Therefore, we need to expand the scope of the program "With diploma to the village" and continue the work on a new level. I task the Government to finance the programme with up to $20 billion tenge next year.

It is necessary to select talented rural youth and prepare them for domestic and foreign higher education institutions.

I task the Government to develop a roadmap to support gifted children from less well off and large families.

Governments and akims should have the opportunity to make such children attend youth clubs and centres and summer camps.

Now I want to focus on the quality of the higher education.

Only half of the country's higher education institutions ensure a 60 per cent employment rate for their graduates.

Therefore, it is necessary to consider the reduction of their number.

It is no secret that there are universities that are engaged in selling diplomas instead of quality education.

By banning them, we should strive to improve the quality of the teaching in educational institutions.

Another problem with education is the uneven financing and the inefficiency of the modern regional governance system.

It is necessary to transfer the functions of managing the education departments and administration of budgetary funds from the district level to the regional level.

It is necessary to introduce a special financing order at all levels of education. . . .

These measures are not going to have an effect if we do not improve the social standing of teachers.

That's why I have instructed, at the August conference, the doubling of teachers' salaries over the next four years. This means that next year salaries of teachers will grow by 25%. . . .

["Second. Support for the institution of family and childhood, the creation of an inclusive society" has been omitted.]

Third. Ensuring the quality and accessibility of medical services.

We are still seeing regional imbalances in the health of our population, especially in maternal and infant mortality.

Yes, these gaps are decreasing, but they remain large and significantly exceed those in developed countries.

The Government must create a list of health priorities for each region and introduce a budget based on such a list.

On January 1, 2020, Kazakhstan will launch a system of compulsory social health insurance.

I want to re-assure everyone: the state will maintain a guaranteed amount of free medical care. More than 2.8 trillion tenge will be allocated for its financing over the next three years.

The implementation of the compulsory social medical insurance is designed to improve the quality and accessibility of medical services.

Under the three-year budget, an additional $2.3 trillion tenge will be allocated for the development of our healthcare system.

The Government needs to be extremely responsive in implementing the social health insurance scheme to prevent its further discrediting.

We no longer have room for mistake. . . .

["Fourth. Support for those who work in culture and the arts" has been omitted.]

Fifth. Further development of the social support system.

The state is taking measures to support citizens in need.

But a number of decisions were not fully thought through.

As a result, we face a serious increase in dependency attitudes. Over the past 5 years, the number of recipients of targeted social assistance in Kazakhstan has grown from 77,000 to more than 1.4 million.

The amount of funds allocated from the budget for social support since 2017 has increased more than 17 times.

In other words, more and more people choose not to work or, even worse, hide their income to receive social assistance. Cases of wealthy families receiving social assistance have been covered in the media.

Once again, I note. As set out in our Constitution, the state is focused on social welfare and must fulfil its obligations to citizens.

The Government is obliged to proceed from this principle in its work, and additional funds must be found by eradicating wasteful expenditure and by increasing revenues.

Reserves for this, of course, are available. The Ministry of Finance is working to increase revenue. But more effort is needed including in areas such as customs.

Elbasy at a meeting of the Nur Otan political council drew special attention to streamlining the public procurement process. The Ministry of Finance has begun improving procurement, but legislative measures are also needed.

Public procurement is a field where money is wasted—according to some estimates, up to 400 billion tenge per year—which could go towards finding the solution of acute social issues.

In 2018, 4.4 trillion tenge was spent on public procurement, of which 3.3 trillion tenge or 75% took place in a non-competitive way with only one supplier.

It is time to end this "feeding trough" for officials and "clingers-on" of various kinds.

Returning to targeted social assistance, the Government should adjust the way it is allocated so that it becomes transparent, fair and encourages people to seek work rather than pursue an idle lifestyle.

Assistance should mainly be given to those who work.

At the same time, we need to take care of children from low-income families.

They require the introduction of a guaranteed social package. This should include help for preschool children, free hot meals for all schoolchildren, the provision of school supplies and uniforms, payment of medical, including dental care and reimbursement of public transport travel expenses.

All these measures should come into effect on January 1, 2020.

The Government, together with the Atameken National Chamber of Entrepreneurs, is required within a month to develop a special programme for the participation of mothers of large families in micro and small businesses, including through home working.

Sixth. I would also like to draw attention to the development of our domestic pension system where serious problems have accumulated.

At the moment, the funding of pensions is sufficient. But in 10 years, this situation may change.

The number of working citizens making pension savings will decrease significantly while the number of pensioners will increase.

At the same time, the amount of investment income received from pension assets remains low.

Therefore, the Government, together with the National Bank, should carry out substantial work to increase the effectiveness of the pension system.

Currently, a working person can only access his pension savings on retirement. But the desire of people to use these funds during their working lives is understandable.

I instruct the Government by the end of the year to consider how the targeted use by working citizens of part of their pension savings, for example, for buying a house or getting an education might be achieved.

In order to reduce costs and improve the quality of investment asset management, I instruct the Government to look at consolidating the extra-budgetary social security system by creating a unified social fund and introducing one social payment. . . .

[Section V, discussing housing and infrastructure, has been omitted.]

Dear compatriots!

We have entered a new stage in reforming the country. We must fulfil these important tasks to a high standard.

Every citizen of the country should feel positive changes. . . .

I invite all of you to contribute to our national prosperity.

A constructive public dialogue is the basis of peace and stability. . . .

Elbasy's message "The unity of the people is our most valuable treasure" remains our guiding principle.

Harmony and unity, wisdom and mutual understanding help our nation move forward.

Our destination is clear, and our way is open.

I hope that together, the country will achieve even greater success!

I wish all of you wellbeing and success.

SOURCE: President of the Republic of Kazakhstan. "President of Kazakhstan Kassym-Jomart Tokayev's State of the Nation Address, September 2, 2019." September 2, 2019. http://www.akorda.kz/en/addresses/addresses_of_president/president-of-kazakhstan-kassym-jomart-tokayevs-state-of-the-nation-address-september-2-2019.

OSCE Announces Findings of Election Monitoring Report

October 4, 2019

Following Kazakhstan's early presidential election on 9 June 2019, the OSCE Office for Democratic Institutions and Human Rights (ODIHR) has published its final report. While the election was an opportunity for potential political reforms, it was tarnished by violations of fundamental freedoms as well as pressure on critical voices. There were seven candidates, including a woman for the first time ever, but considerable restrictions on the right to stand and limits to peaceful assembly and expression inhibited genuine political pluralism. The election was efficiently organized. However, significant irregularities were observed on election day, including cases of ballot box stuffing, and a disregard of counting procedures meant that an honest count could not be guaranteed. There were widespread detentions of peaceful protesters on election day in major cities.

Key recommendations include:

- Lifting restrictions on legislation related to constitutionally guaranteed fundamental rights and freedoms

- Amending the election law to guarantee an inclusive and broad representation of political parties in election commissions at all levels

- Ensuring universal suffrage by revising the blanket withdrawal of voting rights of citizens serving prison sentences and abolishing the norms disenfranchising people with disabilities

- Removing the residency, language and professional experience requirements for candidate eligibility and ensuring that any restrictions on the right to stand for those with criminal convictions are proportionate to the severity of the offence

- Ensuring that election campaigning is conducted in an atmosphere free from intimidation and fear of retribution and amending the law on peaceful assemblies to require a simple notification procedure for holding a public gathering

- Repealing criminal provisions on defamation, insult and spreading of false information, in favour of civil sanctions designed to restore the reputation harmed, rather than compensate the plaintiff or punish the defendant

- Enhancing transparency and safeguarding the integrity of election results by publishing disaggregated polling station protocols on the website of the Central Election Commission.

ODIHR deployed an Election Observation Mission on 8 May 2019 to observe the early presidential election. All 57 participating States across the OSCE region have formally committed to following up promptly on ODIHR's election assessments and recommendations.

SOURCE: Organization for Security and Co-operation in Europe. "Kazakhstan Early Presidential Election 2019: ODIHR Observation Mission Final Report." October 4, 2019. https://www.osce.org/odihr/elections/kazakhstan/434465.

EU Statement on Presidential Elections in Kazakhstan

October 6, 2019

Presidential elections took place in the Republic of Kazakhstan on 9 June 2019 with Kassym-Jomart Tokayev voted into his first term as President. According to the preliminary findings of the internationally-recognised OSCE/ODIHR Election Observation Mission, the election offered an important moment for potential political reforms, but it was tarnished by clear violations of fundamental freedoms as well as pressure on critical voices. There were widespread detentions of peaceful protesters on election day.

Overall, the OSCE/ODIHR Election Observation Mission recognised that elections were administered efficiently by the Central Electoral Commission, but significant irregularities were observed across the country, including cases of ballot box stuffing, group voting and series of identical signatures on voter lists. The count was also negatively assessed in more than half of observations.

In the light of the shortcomings reported by the OSCE/ODIHR Mission, we expect Kazakhstan to address these violations, as well as the controlled legal and political electoral framework, as they run counter to the country's OSCE commitments and international obligations. In the framework of our Enhanced Partnership and Cooperation Agreement with Kazakhstan, the European Union stands ready to further support reforms to strengthen the promotion and protection of fundamental freedoms and human rights, the respect for democratic principles, the rule of law and good governance. We look forward to working with the new President in this regard, as well as to advance EU–Kazakhstan relations more broadly.

SOURCE: European Union. European External Action Service. "Statement by the Spokesperson on the Presidential Elections in the Republic of Kazakhstan." October 6, 2019. https://eeas.europa.eu/headquar ters/headquarters-homepage/63895/statement-spokesperson-presidential-elections-republic-kazakh stan_en.

OTHER HISTORIC DOCUMENTS OF INTEREST

FROM PREVIOUS *HISTORIC DOCUMENTS*

▦ End of the Soviet Union and Gorbachev's Rule, *1991,* p. 786

Hong Kong Government
Responds to Protests

JUNE 16, JULY 9, AND SEPTEMBER 4, 2019

A proposal by the Hong Kong government to allow accused criminals to be sent to countries with which the territory does not have extradition agreements—including China—set off a wave of massive public protests against the bill in 2019. The movement grew to encompass additional demands, including a call for greater autonomy from mainland China, and persisted even after the government withdrew the extradition bill.

EXTRADITION LEGISLATION FEEDS CONCERNS OVER CHINESE INFLUENCE

Hong Kong was a British colony for approximately 150 years before the territory was given back to China on July 1, 1997. According to the Sino-British Joint Declaration authorizing the handover, China is to govern the Hong Kong Special Administrative Region under a principle of "one country, two systems" until 2047. This policy provides Hong Kong with significant autonomy, allowing the city to maintain its capitalist economic system, an independent government and judicial system, and a police force, as well as its own currency. Hongkongers also have greater freedoms than citizens on the Chinese mainland, including rights to free speech and free assembly. However, China retains a number of important controls over the territory, including the authority to interpret (and reinterpret) Basic Law, which effectively functions as Hong Kong's Constitution. Additionally, while the head of Hong Kong's government—known as the chief executive—is indirectly elected by the people, this person must be formally appointed by the Chinese central government. China loyalists also dominate the current Legislative Council.

As a younger, politically outspoken generation has increasingly engaged in the public discourse, frustration and discontent over China's involvement in the territory have grown. Many Hongkongers believe that China is working to slowly erode the territory's autonomy, pointing to such interventions as China's invalidation of the election of three pro-democracy lawmakers in 2016. (The three lawmakers used their oaths of office to express their contempt for China.) Many also believe that Hong Kong's government will do anything the Chinese government asks it to do.

In February 2019, the Hong Kong government introduced legislation that fed public concerns about growing Chinese influence. The proposed legislation, the Extradition Law Amendment Bill, would have permitted the transfer of accused criminals to countries with which Hong Kong does not have an extradition treaty, including China. Chief Executive Carrie Lam and other officials said the bill would ensure that Hong Kong did not become a haven for criminals. They cited the recent case of a man who allegedly murdered his girlfriend in Taiwan, then fled to Hong Kong to avoid prosecution, as an example of why the bill was necessary. The bill's critics claimed it would allow China to target dissidents in the territory by filing false charges and would amount to a further erosion of Hongkongers' liberties. The proposal was instantly contentious, to the point of causing scuffles between pro-China and pro-democracy lawmakers in the Legislative Council building.

A PROTEST MOVEMENT EMERGES

The proposal was also unpopular among many Hongkongers, with people taking to the streets twice in the spring to voice their discontent. On June 9, the scale of public opposition to the bill became clear as an estimated one million people—or roughly one in seven Hongkongers—protested throughout the city. A second major protest took place on June 12, as lawmakers were due to debate the extradition bill. The protest was largely peaceful, though some reportedly tried to storm the Legislative Council building while throwing umbrellas and other projectiles at officers. The police responded by firing rubber bullets, bean bag rounds, and tear gas at this smaller group, but they also used pepper spray, batons, and more than 150 canisters of tear gas to disperse the other protesters. The protesters and their supporters claimed the police had used excessive force against unarmed people and drew comparisons to the use of tear gas against pro-democracy student protesters in 2014. (Public outcry over police actions in that incident gave rise to the Umbrella Movement, which sought greater autonomy for Hong Kong.)

Facing mounting public pressure and increased scrutiny of the police, the government announced a suspension—but not a withdrawal—of the extradition bill on June 15 in hopes of "restoring calmness in society as soon as possible." The government said Lam "clearly heard the views expressed in a peaceful and rational manner" and acknowledged that protesters "embodied the spirit of Hong Kong as a civilised, free, open and pluralistic society that values mutual respect, harmony and diversity." Lam also apologized for "deficiencies in the government's work" that had led to dissatisfaction, the government statement read, and pledged "to adopt a most sincere and humble attitude to accept criticisms and make improvements." Separately, Lam stated she could not completely withdraw the bill because then the public would claim the proposal had been groundless.

But the suspension did not satisfy protesters. An estimated two million Hongkongers staged a peaceful march through the city in response—the largest protest in Hong Kong's history. They called for the bill to be fully withdrawn and for Lam to step down as chief executive. "Postponement is temporary. It's just delaying the pain," said Claudia Mo, a pro-democracy lawmaker. "We demand a complete scrapping of this controversial bill."

PROTESTERS' DEMANDS GROW AS VIOLENCE SURGES

Demonstrations continued with an emphasis on the extradition bill, but the movement soon evolved into a broader protest of China's power in Hong Kong. Protesters' demands expanded to include greater autonomy for Hong Kong and direct elections for the chief executive and all lawmakers, as well as an independent investigation into police use of force against protesters and amnesty for those arrested during the demonstrations. Some pro-China lawmakers even came forward to encourage the government to listen to the protesters and consider their demands.

The vast majority of protests have been nonviolent, but an uptick in violence occurred as the summer wore on, with some participants—particularly young people—throwing bricks and other projectiles at police, hitting officers with sticks, setting debris on fire, and throwing gasoline bombs. Many of these protesters defended their actions by saying the government was not listening to peaceful protests, so new tactics were necessary. On July 1, hundreds of protesters broke into the Legislative Council building, occupying and vandalizing the premises for several hours. The incident followed a day of peaceful protests involving hundreds of thousands of people. A few days later, the Hong Kong University of Science and Technology student union said Lam had proposed a private meeting to discuss youth concerns, but said it declined the invitation because any discussion with the government must be open to the public and allow for representation of all protesters. In a speech on July 9, Lam said she would "welcome and agree to do this open dialogue with our student representatives" and that the government would follow up with the student union. In the same remarks, Lam said she was "saddened and shocked by recent events" and made "a very sincere plea" that "if anyone in Hong Kong has any different views, especially those about Hong Kong Government's policies, please continue to uphold the value of expressing it in a peaceful and orderly manner." She also declared the extradition bill "dead."

Clashes continued, however. After a peaceful protest on July 21, thousands of demonstrators continued beyond the end of the official march route and blockaded several roads, with some vandalizing the office of the Chinese government's liaison to Hong Kong. Police fired tear gas to dispel the protesters. That evening, a mob of masked men attacked antigovernment protesters and passersby at a train station, following people as they tried to flee and beating them with sticks. The police were reportedly delayed in arriving at the train station and did not make any arrests, leading to allegations that they had allowed the attack to happen.

On August 5, protesters led a general strike, blocking roads and rail lines, occupying shopping malls, and holding mass demonstrations across the city. Several police stations were also vandalized. Responding to the strike, Lam said the city had "become unsafe and unstable" and that "a series of extremely violent acts are pushing Hong Kong into very precarious circumstances." In mid-August, police clashed with protesters in Hong Kong's airport after a few participants attacked a man they accused of being a Chinese police officer in disguise. The incident caused hundreds of flight delays and a short suspension of operations at the airport. At the end of the month, police arrested three pro-democracy lawmakers, two pro-democracy activists, and the former leader of the banned Hong Kong National Party, drawing comparisons to China's suppression of dissent. Officials also denied protesters permission to hold a demonstration on August 31 to coincide with the five-year anniversary of China's decision to limit direct elections in Hong Kong. That protest proceeded without official authorization, leading to more violent clashes between protesters and police.

Chinese officials have repeatedly warned protesters that they will face consequences for their actions. "Those who play with fire will perish by it," said Yang Guang, a spokesperson for China's Hong Kong and Macau Affairs Office. "At the end of the day, they will eventually be punished." China also deployed propaganda to portray the protesters as gangsters and terrorists and has at times hinted that its military could be called in to quell the movement. However, the central government has largely yielded the response to Lam and the local government.

GOVERNMENT WITHDRAWS EXTRADITION PROPOSAL

On September 4, Lam announced the government was formally withdrawing the extradition bill "to fully allay public concerns." Acknowledging that "after more than two months of social unrest, it is obvious to many that discontentment extends far beyond the bill,"

Lam said her office would reach out to the community to discuss solutions and invited recommendations from community leaders, professionals, and academics. "We cannot agree or accept that violence is a solution to our problems," Lam said, adding that the government's first priority was to end violence and "safeguard the rule of law." Regarding the movement's other demands, Lam said it was not possible to provide amnesty for arrested protesters because it was "contrary to the rule of law, and is not acceptable." She also stated that "matters relating to police enforcement actions are best handled by the existing and well-established Independent Police Complaints Council (IPCC), which was set up for exactly this purpose." She noted the IPCC had already initiated an investigation into "the handling of large-scale public order events that took place after June 9" and claims against individual police officers, adding that the government would fully support the IPCC's work in this area.

But the demonstrations and the violence continued. The next major protest took place on October 1 to coincide with China's celebration of seventy years of Communist Party rule. The protest was notable for its timing, but also because it was the first instance in which police fired live ammunition at a participant: an eighteen-year-old protester was shot in the shoulder. A spokesperson for the Hong Kong Police Force said the shot was fired in self-defense as "rioters" attacked police officers. A video posted online appeared to show the protester as part of a mob who chased an officer and tackled him before beating him with metal pipes. Police commissioner Stephen Lo said the officer gave the protester a verbal warning before shooting him, so he had acted in a "legal and reasonable" manner.

Three days later Lam used her office's emergency powers to impose a ban on face masks. Such masks were used by most protesters to protect themselves from tear gas, and by some to hide their identity and avoid potential retaliation. Violators could receive up to one year of jail time and be fined. Lam said she was issuing the rule in response to "a state of serious danger" and out of particular concern for the young people participating in the protests. "As a responsible government, we have a duty to use all available means to stop the escalating violence and restore calmness in society." The announcement set off another wave of protests, with many participants wearing face masks in defiance of the government.

According to government data, more than 4,300 people have been arrested in connection with the protests and 2,600 have sought medical treatment for protest-related injuries at public hospitals. Dissatisfaction with the government helped pro-democracy candidates win a landslide victory in district council elections on November 24; roughly 90 percent of the 452 district council seats are now held by pro-democracy officials, meaning they now control all but one of Hong Kong's district councils. Following the vote, Lam promised to "listen to the opinions of members of the public humbly and seriously reflect," but it is so far unclear whether the government will take further action to meet protesters' demands. A demonstration involving an estimated 800,000 participants took place on December 9 to mark six months of protest.

—Linda Grimm

Following is a statement by Hong Kong chief executive Carrie Lam on June 16, 2019, announcing the suspension of the Extradition Law Amendment Bill; remarks by Lam on July 9, 2019, on the ongoing demonstrations and protesters' demands; and remarks by Lam on September 4, 2019, announcing the bill's withdrawal.

Chief Executive Lam Announces Suspension of Extradition Amendment

June 16, 2019

In response to the public procession today (June 16), a Government spokesman said the following:

Over the past two Sundays, a large number of people have expressed their views during public processions. The Government understands that these views have been made out of love and care for Hong Kong.

The Chief Executive clearly heard the views expressed in a peaceful and rational manner. She acknowledged that this embodied the spirit of Hong Kong as a civilised, free, open and pluralistic society that values mutual respect, harmony and diversity. The Government also respects and treasures these core values of Hong Kong.

Having regard to the strong and different views in society, the Government has suspended the legislative amendment exercise at the full Legislative Council with a view to restoring calmness in society as soon as possible and avoiding any injuries to any persons. The Government reiterated that there is no timetable for restarting the process.

The Chief Executive admitted that the deficiencies in the Government's work had led to substantial controversies and disputes in society, causing disappointment and grief among the people. The Chief Executive apologised to the people of Hong Kong for this and pledged to adopt a most sincere and humble attitude to accept criticisms and make improvements in serving the public.

SOURCE: Government of the Hong Kong Special Administrative Region. "Government Response to Public Procession." June 16, 2019. https://www.info.gov.hk/gia/general/201906/16/P2019061600803.htm.

Chief Executive Lam Remarks on Demonstrations and Responds to Protesters' Demands

July 9, 2019

Following is the transcript of remarks by the Chief Executive, Mrs. Carrie Lam, at a media session before the Executive Council meeting this morning (July 9):

Let me say a few words in English. I am sure many people in Hong Kong, including myself, are saddened and shocked by recent events in the past few weeks. I have fully reflected on the people's concerns, and I noticed that there are two entirely different situations in the many protests and marches that we have seen. On the one hand, hundreds of thousands of people from all sorts of background have taken part in marches in a peaceful and orderly manner. I think this again reflects the core value of Hong Kong, that we all have this freedom to express our views. I am also very proud of the quality of the Hong Kong people. But on the other hand, a very small minority of protesters have used the occasion to resort to violent acts and vandalism. We are sad to see these violent acts because they undermine the rule of law in Hong Kong. So I make a very sincere plea here, that in future, if anyone in Hong Kong has any different views, especially those about Hong Kong Government's policies, please continue to uphold the value of expressing it in a peaceful and orderly manner.

On June 18, I have tendered my most sincere apology for the disturbances, tensions and confrontations caused by our work in amending the Fugitive Offenders Ordinance. Since then, in the past few weeks, I have met a lot of people and listened to their views. I just want to give a brief account of our views now.

First of all, the cause of all these grievances and confrontations is an exercise to amend the Fugitive Offenders Ordinance. I have almost immediately put a stop to the amendment exercise, but there are still lingering doubts about the Government's sincerity, or worries whether the Government will restart the process in the Legislative Council. I reiterate here there is no such plan—the bill is dead. As regards the other demands, myself, the Secretary for Justice, the Secretary for Security and the Chief Secretary for Administration, have responded on different occasions. In brief, we have not given a label to what took place on June 12. Whatever label given by whoever is not going to have any impact on the ultimate prosecution decision because prosecutions in Hong Kong are undertaken independently by the Department of Justice in accordance with the evidence, the law and also the Prosecution Code.

Secondly, any demand that we should grant an amnesty at this stage, in other words, we will not follow up on investigations and prosecutions of offenders, is not acceptable, because that bluntly goes against the rule of law in Hong Kong and also deviates from the very important principle laid down in the Basic Law that no one should interfere with the Department of Justice's prosecutorial decisions.

As regards the setting up of an independent Commission of Inquiry, we have all noticed that on Friday last week, the statutory Independent Police Complaints Council (IPCC) has already unanimously decided that they will conduct a fact-finding study on the events that have taken place during the period from June 9 to July 2, with a view to finding out the facts and providing the true situation to members of the public. They are appealing for members of the public, the policemen and the journalists to provide information to this fact-finding study. I am very grateful that IPCC has taken on my views or wishes that they will try to finish this independent study report within six months, submit the report with recommendations to myself and make the report open, so that everyone will know what had happened during that period.

I fully understand that the responses of the Government may not have fully met the wishes of the people, especially the protesters who have gone on the streets several times to express their views. I just want to reiterate that this is nothing to do with my own pride or arrogance. This is the Government's full deliberations of the various concerns and factors, and it comes to the conclusion that the responses are practical measures for us to move ahead. My sincere plea is, please give us an opportunity, the time, the room, to take Hong Kong out of the current impasse and try to improve the current situation.

The Government has the most important duty to improve the situation, so on July 1 I announced in my speech that we would adopt a new governance style in order to ensure that we are able and capable of listening to views from different sectors before we implement policies. I want to make some concrete follow-up to those suggestions.

One is we will listen more extensively to people from different backgrounds with different ideas so that we have a better grasp of public opinion. This work will be carried out not only by myself, it's also to be carried out by my political team, including the Principal Officials, the Under Secretaries, the Political Assistants, and also by my senior civil servants whom I have met over the last few weeks. They are all very willing to help by displaying that same sincerity to consult and listen. As for the role of the Executive Council in this particular aspect, I will enhance the role of the Executive Council, that is the Non-Official Members of the Executive Council, so that they also shoulder an important responsibility in engaging public opinions and reflecting those opinions to me.

The second concrete measure is we will reform the existing consultative machinery, which basically comprises a large number of consultative advisory committees with members appointed by the Government into these committees to offer us advice. I feel that we need to be more innovative. In other words, sometimes we may not need a formal committee—we should build more open platforms to facilitate dialogues in a very frank manner, and to make sure that whoever joins the committees or these dialogues come from different backgrounds, so they are not homogeneous of one group. They should come from a more diverse background so that we can really receive views from a wider spectrum of society. One of the important committees that will undergo I would say a major overhaul will be the Youth Development Commission (YDC), because this commission was set up to co-ordinate initiatives relating to young people and to address young people's concern. I hope that the YDC will undergo a major changeover to a more open dialogue platform to listen to views from young people of various backgrounds.

The third concrete initiative is when I said that in rolling out policies the Government should have more thorough deliberations. We should not be guided just by executive efficiency or an end date for achieving a particular target. I have invited all my Principal Officials to revisit and re-examine some of the controversial policy initiatives under their respective jurisdiction, and consider whether we should redo or enhance the consultation and discussions with the people so that at the end of the day we could have an initiative which has more broad-based support, and in doing so I hope we could restore some of the trust in the Government amongst our people.

And finally, I said on July 1 that I will reach out to more young people of different backgrounds to hear them out, and that's why last week I contacted the presidents of two universities, the Hong Kong University of Science and Technology and the Chinese University of Hong Kong to seek their help in arranging smaller sessions, closed-door sessions, so that we can listen without any sort of constraints. I realise that this idea is not welcomed by the student unions. They instead counter-proposed that we should have an open dialogue. I now readily welcome and agree to do this open dialogue with our student representatives, and we will follow up. I hope this open dialogue will be conducted without any prerequisites on my part or on the part of the students.

To conclude, I want to say this really from the bottom of my heart. Five years ago, I was one of the Principal Officials involved in Occupy Central. Now five years later, as the Chief Executive, I was overseeing this Fugitive Offenders Ordinance amendment. Both exercises have caused a lot of grievances, unhappiness and tensions in society. I believe they reflect not only one incident but some fundamental and deep-seated problems in Hong Kong. Five years ago, we finished Occupy Central, we moved on without addressing those fundamental problems. But this time, I don't think we could continue to ignore those fundamental and deep-seated problems in Hong Kong society. I hope together with Hong Kong community we could really go deep into those fundamental issues and try to find solutions. In recent days, several university presidents, religious leaders and social and community leaders have spoken to me on the idea of creating an open, constructive, interactive platform for dialogue with people from different backgrounds, especially with young people, to jointly understand and identify those deep-seated issues with a view that they could identify also some solutions for us to move forward. I certainly welcome this idea, which I hope will not only provide some relief to the current tense situation in Hong Kong but also help to mend the rift in society. I support this piece of work and hope that it could be started as soon as possible. Since the proponents told me that they preferred this dialogue to be created through community efforts, the Government will not go in to direct how this dialogue should be established, but whenever I and my officials are needed to take part in the dialogue, we are very happy to do so. While the dialogue is being established, meanwhile the Hong Kong SAR Government and myself will continue to address the social, economic and livelihood problems in Hong Kong with a view to resolving some of the current difficulties.

Reporter: Mrs. Lam, you said you have to address issues leftover from the Occupy Movement in 2014, you said you have to address the leftover issues, are you saying that the Government will restart political reform and grant Hong Kong a genuine universal suffrage in the near future? Also, you said you are going to listen to a wide variety of views. Andrew Li, the former Chief Justice, said today that there should be a Commission of Inquiry (CoI) into the clashes in the recent protests, have his views not fallen on deaf ears? What are you saying—that there shouldn't be such an investigation?

Chief Executive: On the second question first. Over the past few weeks, there have been very different views from various quarters about the setting up of an independent Commission of Inquiry. There have also been very concrete steps taken by the statutory Independent Police Complaints Council on how they could help us and help society at large to address this concern—that is through a very detailed fact-finding study. While I respect the views expressed by different quarters, as I have mentioned in my introductory remarks, at the end of the day, it is not a personal preference for going which way. It is the Government, taking into account various factors and concerns, coming to a view on what is in the best interest of Hong Kong. While I respect the views of the Honourable Andrew Li, and also thank him for his support for me to continue to serve Hong Kong, I'm afraid on this particular issue of an independent CoI, the view has been taken for the IPCC to perform this role in accordance with their statutory functions under the ordinance in order to provide a report on what has happened during that period for the public to understand.

I mentioned Occupy Central and the relationship to the current exercise, not targeting a particular issue as you have put it. But it would be a bit simplistic, or even naive, for the Government to feel that this is an isolated incident—that once we addressed the crisis or once the protest subsided, there will no longer be any problem in Hong Kong. I'm telling you most sincerely that I do not take that view. I come to the conclusion that there are some fundamental deep-seated problems in Hong Kong society. They could be economic problems, they could be livelihood issues, they could be political divisions in society. The first thing we should do is to identify those fundamental issues and hopefully to find some solutions to move forward.

SOURCE: Government of the Hong Kong Special Administrative Region. "Transcript of Remarks by CE at Media Session before ExCo Meeting (with Video)." July 9, 2019. https://www.info.gov.hk/gia/general/201907/09/P2019070900608.htm.

Chief Executive Lam Withdraws Extradition Amendment

DOCUMENT

September 4, 2019

Following is the full text of the video address by the Chief Executive, Mrs. Carrie Lam, to members of the public today (September 4):

Fellow citizens,

For more than two months, protests arising from the Fugitive Offenders Bill have continued. Our citizens, police and reporters have been injured during violent incidents. There have been chaotic scenes at the airport and MTR stations; roads and tunnels have been suddenly blocked, causing delay and inconvenience to daily life. Visitors wonder whether our city is still a safe place for travel or business. Families and friends have been under stress, and arguments have flared. We have also seen abuse and bullying in some schools and on the Internet. For many people, Hong Kong has become an unfamiliar place.

Incidents over these past two months have shocked and saddened Hong Kong people. We are all very anxious about Hong Kong, our home. We all hope to find a way out of the current impasse and unsettling times.

Of the "five demands" raised by the public, we have in fact responded on various occasions:

(i) First, on withdrawing the Bill. On June 15 I announced that the Bill was suspended and later reiterated that "the Bill is dead" and that all the legislative work had come to a complete halt;

(ii) Second, on setting up a Commission of Inquiry. The Government believes that matters relating to police enforcement actions are best handled by the existing and well-established Independent Police Complaints Council (IPCC), which was set up for exactly this purpose. In addition to handling complaints against individual police officers, the IPCC has undertaken a fact-finding study, under its powers, on the handling of large-scale public order events that took place after June 9. One focus will be the Yuen Long incident on July 21 which attracted serious public concern. The study aims to ascertain the facts, to assess the police handling of protests, and to make recommendations to the Government. The IPCC has established a panel of international experts to assist in its work and will make its findings and recommendations public;

(iii) Third, on the matter of the protest being a riot. We have explained that in fact there is no legal effect on how such incidents are described or categorised. The Department of Justice has assured the public that each and every prosecution decision is based on the evidence collected, and is in strict accordance with the relevant law and the Prosecution Code;

(iv) Fourth, on dropping charges against protesters and rioters and shelving prosecutions. I have explained that this is contrary to the rule of law, and is not acceptable. It also goes against the Basic Law, which states that criminal prosecutions must be handled by the Department of Justice, free from any interference;

(v) Fifth, on implementing universal suffrage. Indeed, this is the ultimate aim laid down in the Basic Law. As we said before, if we are to achieve this, discussions must be undertaken within the legal framework, and in an atmosphere that is conducive to mutual trust and understanding, and without further polarising society.

Our responses to the five demands have been made with full consideration of different constraints and circumstances. I recognise that these may not be able to address all the grievances of people in society. However, should we all think deeply whether escalating violence and disturbances is the answer? Or whether it is better to sit down to find a way out through dialogue.

Many would say that we need a common basis to start such a dialogue, and that this has to start with the Chief Executive. I now present four actions to initiate this dialogue.

First, the Government will formally withdraw the Bill in order to fully allay public concerns. The Secretary for Security will move a motion according to the Rules of Procedure when the Legislative Council resumes.

Second, we will fully support the work of the IPCC. In addition to the overseas experts, I have appointed two new members to the IPCC, namely Mrs. Helen Yu Lai Ching-ping and Mr. Paul Lam Ting-kwok, SC. I pledge that the Government will seriously follow up the recommendations made in the IPCC's report.

Third, from this month, I and my Principal Officials will reach out to the community to start a direct dialogue. People from all walks of life, with different stances and backgrounds are invited to share their views and air their grievances. We must find ways to address the discontent in society and to look for solutions.

Fourth, I will invite community leaders, professionals and academics to independently examine and review society's deep-seated problems and to advise the Government on finding solutions. After more than two months of social unrest, it is obvious to many that discontentment extends far beyond the Bill. It covers political, economic and social issues, including the oft-mentioned problems relating to housing and land supply, income distribution, social justice and mobility, and opportunities for our young people, as well as how the public could be fully engaged in the Government's decision-making. We can discuss all these issues in our new dialogue platform.

Fellow citizens, lingering violence is damaging the very foundations of our society, especially the rule of law. Some people, though not many, attacked the Central Government's office in Hong Kong and vandalised the national flag and national emblem. This is a direct challenge to "One Country, Two Systems". Both have put Hong Kong in a highly vulnerable and dangerous situation. Irrespective of our grievances, or the depth of discontentment towards the Government, we cannot agree or accept that violence is a solution to our problems. Our foremost priority now is to end violence, to safeguard the rule of law and to restore order and safety in society. As such, the Government has to strictly enforce the law against all violent and illegal acts.

My team and I hope that the four actions just announced can help our society to move forward. Let's replace conflicts with conversations, and let's look for solutions.

SOURCE: Government of the Hong Kong Special Administrative Region. "Video Address by CE to Members of the Public (with Video)." September 4, 2019. https://www.info.gov.hk/gia/general/201909/04/P2019090400666.htm.

OTHER HISTORIC DOCUMENTS OF INTEREST

FROM PREVIOUS *Historic Documents*

- China Invalidates Seats of Hong Kong Legislators, *2016*, p. 597
- Chinese Standing Committee Reviews Universal Suffrage in Hong Kong, *2014*, p. 428
- Agreement on Return of Hong Kong to China, *1984*, p. 1046

World Leaders React to Ongoing War in Yemen

JUNE 21, JUNE 24, AUGUST 9, AND OCTOBER 30, 2019

Yemen's civil war stretched into its fourth year in 2019, fueling a humanitarian crisis the United Nations (UN) has described as the worst in the world. In June, UN officials announced the partial suspension of food aid deliveries, citing interference by the antigovernment Houthi rebels. That same month, the United Arab Emirates (UAE), a key player in the Saudi Arabia–led coalition backing the Yemeni government, began withdrawing its troops from the country. Internal developments and external pressures eventually led to new, informal talks between the Houthis and the Saudis that many hope will bring peace to the war-ravaged nation.

A Protracted Civil War

Yemen has been embroiled in an internal conflict since early 2015, when the Arab Spring–deposed former president, Ali Abdullah Saleh, aligned with a growing insurgency against the new president, Abdu Rabbu Mansour Hadi. Led by the Houthis, the insurgency sparked a civil war that forced Hadi into exile and pushed his government out of the capital city, Sana'a, which is now controlled—along with large swaths of Yemen—by Houthi rebels. The ongoing conflict is widely viewed as a proxy war between Iran, which is backing the Houthi rebels, and Saudi Arabia, which is leading a coalition of primarily Sunni Arab states in support of the Hadi government. Outside of the region, the United States and the United Kingdom are among the countries providing logistical and intelligence assistance to the Saudi-led coalition, in a bid to stop Iran from gaining broader influence in the Middle East. Efforts to negotiate cease-fires or broker a political solution to the internal crisis have largely failed.

UN Suspends Some Relief Efforts

As the war dragged on, Yemen's humanitarian crisis deepened. Tens of thousands of Yemenis have been killed in the conflict, and the majority of the population lacks sufficient access to food, clean water, and medicine. A September 2019 report by the UN Development Programme stated that more than 80 percent of Yemen's thirty million people required humanitarian assistance and protection. An estimated 36 percent of Yemenis were malnourished, the report said, and 75 percent lived in poverty.

The UN accused the Houthis of hampering relief efforts by blocking aid convoys and diverting aid from the neediest families. On June 21, 2019, the UN World Food Programme (WFP) announced a "partial suspension" of aid to parts of Yemen controlled by the Houthis, including Sana'a. WFP executive director David Beasley told UN Security Council members that aid may be suspended entirely because there was "serious evidence" that food was being misappropriated and taken "from the mouths of hungry little boys and girls." WFP spokesperson Hervé Verhoosel said the UN was trying to reach an agreement with local Houthi authorities that would "protect the Yemeni families we serve" and ensure food aid reached the families who needed it most. In a joint statement, the governments of Saudi Arabia, the UAE, the United Kingdom, and the United States expressed concern about the suspension of food deliveries. "We call on the Houthis to immediately end all restrictions on aid agencies to ensure the delivery of life-saving assistance to those Yemenis most in need," they said.

In August, WFP announced it would resume aid deliveries to the capital after receiving "written guarantees from the Houthis" that supplies would reach those in need. WFP began implementing a smartcard system to register roughly nine million Yemenis living in Houthi-controlled areas to receive aid. UN officials said they would continue working to scale up aid efforts in hopes of reaching twelve million Yemenis per month.

UAE Withdraws Troops

The UAE has played a critical role in the Saudi-led coalition, contributing weapons, money, and thousands of soldiers to fight the Houthis. But in June 2019, amid mounting pressure from Western allies to end the war and growing concerns about Iranian retaliation, the UAE began drawing down its forces in Yemen. (Attacks against four oil tankers off the UAE's coast in May—which Saudi and U.S. officials blamed on Iran—contributed to the unease at home.) UAE officials also said the drawdown was intended to support a cease-fire agreement in the port city of Hudaydah that had been on shaky ground since its negotiation in December 2018.

The phased withdrawal concluded in October, when the UAE announced its departure from the southern port city of Aden. A statement from the General Command of the UAE Armed Forces published by state media said UAE troops had "accomplished their role in liberating and stabilizing Aden" and had transferred control of the city to Saudi and Yemeni soldiers. The General Command would continue its fight against "terrorist forces" in South Yemen and other areas, the statement added.

Saudi Arabia Steps in to Broker New Talks

On September 14, the Houthis claimed responsibility for a damaging assault on Saudi oil facilities. U.S. officials and most observers claimed Iran orchestrated the attack, citing its sophistication and evidence the assault launched from the north, not the south. Six days later, the Houthis announced a voluntary suspension of their drone and missile strikes against Saudi Arabia. In return, the Houthis wanted Saudi airstrikes to end and restrictions on access to northern Yemen lifted. Saudi Arabia did not end its airstrikes, but it did reduce them significantly: a November 22 report by the UN's envoy to Yemen, Martin Griffiths, found that coalition airstrikes had decreased by roughly 80 percent in the prior two weeks. Saudi officials also allowed fuel shipments to some Houthi-controlled areas to resume.

This easing of tensions created a diplomatic opportunity. In mid-November, reports revealed the Saudi government had been engaged in informal, indirect talks with the Houthis since late September. The talks are reportedly focused on achieving short-term goals, such as the reopening of the international airport in Sana'a, with the ultimate objective of negotiating a cease-fire agreement.

The Saudis were bolstered in their talks with the Houthis by their diplomatic success in another matter. Early in November, the Yemeni government and the separatist Southern Transitional Council (STC) signed an agreement ending a power struggle that had been raging in the southern part of the country. Backed by the UAE before its withdrawal from Yemen, the STC had been part of the coalition fighting against the Houthis but turned against Hadi's government in August, seizing territory in the port of Aiden and trying to extend its reach throughout the south. The shift not only caused a rift between the UAE and Saudi Arabia, it also threatened to open a new front in the war. The UAE's departure set the stage for the Saudi-brokered truce, dubbed the Riyadh Agreement. Under the deal, the STC would join a new cabinet in Hadi's government that would have equal representation of northern and southern regions, would participate in any talks to negotiate a political solution to end the war, and would bring its troops under the government's control.

In addition to these efforts, U.S. officials indicated their intent to open direct talks with the Houthis that would also involve the Saudis. Lawmakers increasingly pressured the Trump administration to scale back U.S. support for the Saudi coalition, which included assistance with bombing campaigns, deployment of small special operations teams, and intelligence gathering. Support for the Saudi coalition waned steadily in the United States, primarily due to a high number of civilian deaths caused by Saudi airstrikes. According to the Armed Conflict Location and Event Data Project, such strikes had killed more than 8,000 civilians since 2015. In April 2019, Congress passed a bipartisan measure seeking to end U.S. involvement in the war, but the president vetoed it. "The United States should not be led into a war by a despotic, undemocratic, murderous regime," said Sen. Bernie Sanders, I-Vt., the resolution's author. "What we're seeing now in Yemen is an unparalleled humanitarian disaster."

—Linda Grimm

Following is an announcement by the UN World Food Programme on June 21, 2019, that it was partially suspending aid to Yemen; a joint statement released by Saudi Arabia, the United Arab Emirates, the United States, and the United Kingdom on June 24, 2019, about the situation in Yemen; an announcement by the UN World Food Programme on August 9, 2019, that it was resuming food aid deliveries to Yemen; and a statement by the General Command of the UAE Armed Forces on October 30, 2019, that it had withdrawn all troops from Yemen.

DOCUMENT

UN World Food Programme Announces Withdrawal of Aid from Yemen

June 21, 2019

The World Food Programme (WFP), the UN's emergency food relief agency, confirmed on Friday in a statement that it has started a "partial suspension" of aid to areas of Yemen controlled by Houthi opposition forces, including the capital, Sana'a.

Spokesperson Hervé Verhoosel briefed journalists in Geneva that the agency took the decision after efforts failed to prevent aid being diverted from those who need it most, despite repeated warnings:

"In any conflict areas, some individuals seek to profit from preying on the vulnerable and diverting food away from where it is most needed," he said. "WFP has been seeking the support of the Sana'a-based authorities to introduce a biometric registration system that would prevent diversion and protect the Yemeni families we serve, ensuring food reaches those who need it most. Unfortunately, we are yet to reach agreement."

In a briefing in New York on Monday, David Beasley, the head of WFP, warned the Security Council that a suspension of aid was likely, because there was "serious evidence" that food was being misappropriated, and being taken "from the mouths of hungry little boys and little girls," and that deals signed by Houthi leaders were being flouted on the ground.

Mr. Beasley, during his blunt address, said that no one associated with the UN should stand "idly by" as some in the Houthis forces look to obstruct and delay WFP aid efforts, in order to make a profit.

Friday's development means that aid will be cut to the capital region, which could affect some 850,000 people; although Mr. Verhoosel insisted that WFP will maintain nutrition programmes for malnourished children, pregnant and nursing mothers.

In total, WFP estimates that around three-quarters of the people in Yemen who do not have reliable access to food, some nine million, are in areas controlled by Houthis, who have been fighting forces loyal to President Abrdabbuh Mansour Hadi for more than four years.

Back in May, WFP's Spokesperson said that the greatest challenge the agency faced in getting aid to Houthi-held areas does not come from guns, but rather "the obstructive and uncooperative role of some of the Houthi leaders in areas under their control." He said humanitarians working in Yemen were being denied access to the hungry, with aid convoys blocked, and local authorities interfering with who gets food.

Source: United Nations News. "UN Food Agency Begins 'Last Resort' Partial Withdrawal of Aid to Opposition-Held Yemeni Capital." June 21, 2019. https://news.un.org/en/story/2019/06/1041021.

Saudi Arabia, UAE, UK, and United States Remark on Situation in Yemen

June 24, 2019

The text of the following statement on Yemen was released by the Governments of Saudi Arabia, the United Arab Emirates, the United Kingdom, and the United States.

The Kingdom of Saudi Arabia, the United Arab Emirates, the United Kingdom and the United States of America express their concern over escalating tensions in the region and the dangers posed by Iranian destabilizing activity to peace and security both in Yemen and the broader region, including attacks on the oil tankers at Fujairah on 12 May and in the Gulf of Oman on 13 June. These attacks threaten the international waterways that we all rely on for shipping. Ships and their crews must be allowed to pass through international waters safely. We call on Iran to halt any further actions which threaten regional stability, and urge diplomatic solutions to de-escalate tensions.

We further note with concern the recent escalation in Houthi attacks on Saudi Arabia using Iranian made and facilitated missiles and Unmanned Aerial Vehicles. In particular, we condemn the Houthi attack on Abha civilian airport on 12 June, which injured 26 civilians. We express full support for Saudi Arabia and call for an immediate end to such attacks by the Iranian-backed Houthis.

The Quad members express concern that the World Food Program has been forced to suspend food deliveries to Sanaa due to Houthi interference in aid delivery. We call on the Houthis to immediately end all restrictions on aid agencies to ensure the delivery of life-saving assistance to those Yemenis most in need.

We reiterate our commitment to the Yemeni peace process and relevant Security Council Resolutions, including UNSCR 2216. We express our full support for the UN Special Envoy Martin Griffiths. In this regard, we call on the Yemeni parties to engage constructively with the Special Envoy to accelerate implementation of the agreements reached in Stockholm. We call on the Houthis to facilitate full and unhindered access for UNMHA, UNDP and UNVIM.

We call on the Yemeni parties to participate constructively in the joint Redeployment Coordination Committee to accelerate implementation of the Hodeidah Agreement, which includes agreeing [on] the Concept of Operations and tripartite monitoring, as well as engaging constructively on local security issues. We call on the Houthis to withdraw fully from the ports of Hodeidah, Ras Issa and Saleef. We look to the Security Council to review progress when they meet on 17 July.

The Quad nations note that implementation of the Stockholm Agreement will give the opportunity to start a comprehensive political process which can lead to an enduring political settlement that will end the conflict in Yemen.

SOURCE: U.S. Department of State. "Joint Statement by Saudi Arabia, the United Arab Emirates, the United Kingdom, and the United States on Yemen and the Region." June 24, 2019. https://www.state.gov/joint-statement-by-saudi-arabia-the-united-arab-emirates-the-united-kingdom-and-the-united-states-on-yemen-and-the-region/.

UN Announces Resumption of Food Aid to Yemen

August 9, 2019

Life-saving food aid distribution is set to resume to 850,000 people in the Yemeni capital, Sana'a, following guarantees by Houthi opposition forces that the supplies will reach those who need them most, the World Food Programme (WFP) said on Friday.

Under a deal that ends a partial two-month break in WFP assistance to Houthi-held areas of the war-torn country after the agency said that humanitarians were being denied access and local authorities were interfering with deliveries, spokesperson Hervé Verhoosel insisted that a new registration process had been agreed [to].

"We have written guarantees from the Houthis," he said, in reference to a document signed with the Sana'a-based authorities, on Saturday 3 August.

The announcement that WFP food aid will resume after the Eid Al Adha festival next Monday follows the signing of key technical annexes, the last of which was inked on Thursday, the agency spokesperson explained.

"The Houthis have been engaging with us in the last few weeks to negotiate the document that we have signed together and more importantly to also agree on the technical terms," he said.

Under the terms of the deal, WFP will use a smartcard system to register nine million people in areas controlled by the Houthis, although aid will be delivered to those whose details have not yet been recorded.

"The people in Sana'a . . . will start receiving food even before we start the registration process", Mr. Verhoosel told journalists in Geneva. "These are people to whom we stopped providing food (for the past) two months waiting for the agreement, or the document, to be signed. . . . That food will be distributed to them, we will start the process then next week."

The humanitarian operation in Yemen is WFP's largest. It maintains that the new measures are needed to ensure the protection and privacy of those in need, and the independence of its distribution teams.

The development means that WFP can continue to scale up operations in a bid to reach 12 million people a month across Yemen, where more than four years of conflict between the Houthis and Government forces that are supported by a Saudi-led Coalition are estimated to have left thousands of civilians dead and pushed people to the brink of famine.

SOURCE: United Nations News. "UN Food Aid to Yemen Will Fully Resume after Two-Month Break, as Houthis 'Guarantee' Delivery." August 9, 2019. https://news.un.org/en/story/2019/08/1044011.

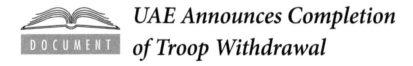

UAE Announces Completion of Troop Withdrawal

DOCUMENT

October 30, 2019

The General Command of the UAE Armed Forces has announced the return of its troops from the Aden Governorate in Yemen after having successfully accomplished their role in liberating and stabilising Aden, and transferring its charge to Saudi and Yemeni forces, who will now maintain the security and stability of the Governorate.

The UAE troops were received by Mohammed bin Ahmed Al Bowardi, Minister of State for Defence Affairs, and Lt. General Hamad Mohammed Thani Al Rumaithi, Chief of Staff of the UAE Armed Forces.

The General Command said in a statement today that the UAE forces had completed the process of hand over responsibly as per a military strategy with a view to guarantee the consolidation of the military gains.

The statement explained that the forces returning from Aden had liberated the city from both the Houthis and terrorist actors on 17th July 2015.

"Thereafter, the Saudi-led Arab Coalition forces spread out from Aden and liberated many other areas of Yemen from the Houthi rebels, foiling Iranian attempts to infiltrate Yemen and dominate its affairs," it added.

The General Command recalled that the UAE and Saudi forces had worked on securing and stabilising Aden after its liberation, uprooting the terrorists and neutralising all security threats.

"As a result, security and stability were restored across the Governorate. The forces also armed and trained the Yemeni forces in a way that would enable them to discharge their military responsibilities independently. The Yemeni forces thus trained are highly competent, professional and capable of maintaining security and stability," the UAE military pointed out.

The statement added that the UAE forces would resume, jointly with their allies, their fight against terrorist forces in South Yemen and other regions.

The General Command commended the heroic role the UAE forces played since the liberation of Aden in 2015 as they fought many battles against the Houthis and the terrorist outfits. The Command also recalled the sacrifices made by the martyrs who laid down their lives fighting for their country, defending the truth and their brothers.

The statement concluded by emphasising the commitment of the UAE Armed Forces as part of the Arab Coalition to extend all possible support to protect the interests of the people of Yemen.

SOURCE: Emirates News Agency. "UAE Troops Return after Successful Liberation, Stabilisation of Aden." October 30, 2019. https://wam.ae/en/details/1395302798764.

OTHER HISTORIC DOCUMENTS OF INTEREST

FROM PREVIOUS *HISTORIC DOCUMENTS*

UN, AU, and Ethiopian Leaders on Violence and New Government

JUNE 23 AND 25, 2019

After months of pursuing political reforms, the government of Ethiopian prime minister Abiy Ahmed faced new challenges in the form of an attempted overthrow of regional leaders, the assassination of several senior officials, and fresh protests sparked by claims of opposition suppression. Despite the challenges, Ahmed pushed forward with planned changes, including the replacement of a long-dominant political coalition with a single political party meant to represent all of Ethiopia's diverse ethnic groups.

NEW LEADERSHIP PROMOTES REFORM BUT FAILS TO QUELL UNREST

Ahmed took office in April 2018 following the resignation of Prime Minister Hailemariam Desalegn. Three years of antigovernment protests preceded Desalegn's decision to step down as the head of state and chair of the ruling Ethiopian People's Revolutionary Democratic Front (EPRDF). The demonstrations reportedly began over land rights issues and were initially focused in the Oromia and Amhara regions but soon spread to other parts of the country, with protesters calling for broader political and economic reforms. Human rights groups estimated that hundreds of Ethiopians were killed and tens of thousands arrested in the violent government crackdown on dissent that ensued.

Upon becoming prime minister, Ahmed moved quickly to usher in major political reforms. He lifted the state of emergency declared by EPRDF after Desalegn's resignation, released political prisoners, lifted bans on political parties, and invited exiled opposition leaders to return to Ethiopia. He also reestablished relations with Eritrea, a neighboring country with whom Ethiopia had been engaged in a twenty-year conflict. The two countries reached a peace agreement and formally declared an end to hostilities in June 2018. For this achievement, Ahmed received the 2019 Nobel Peace Prize.

While Ahmed's reforms were welcomed by many, the prime minister made enemies by replacing senior officers in the military and intelligence services. (He also fired several senior prison officials for alleged human rights abuses.) Ahmed survived an alleged assassination attempt at a rally in June 2018; nine police officers were arrested for their suspected involvement in the attack. In October 2018, a group of soldiers marched on the capital to demand pay raises. Ahmed reportedly defused the situation by doing pushups with the men.

Ahmed also faces growing pressure from regional and ethnic group leaders who are fighting each other and the federal government for more power. Ethiopia is organized into nine ethnically based regions that are overseen by a highly centralized federal government; regional governments control local taxes, education, and local security forces. The regions are led by the largest of the country's more than eighty ethnic groups. Some regional leaders seek greater autonomy from the central state, while other ethnic groups claim they should be given regional governments of their own. There are also ongoing disputes over regional borders and land ownership. Inter-ethnic conflicts have plagued Ethiopia for years and have displaced approximately three million people within the country's borders, but fighting flared after Ahmed took office. Many observers speculate that the increased violence is linked to the government's reforms and its relaxation of long-held control.

COUP ATTEMPT ENDS IN ASSASSINATIONS

On June 23, 2019, the government reported that an attempted coup against leaders of the Amhara regional government had been foiled. Dr. Ambachew Mekonnen, the regional government president and an ally of Ahmed's, and Ezez Wassie, the regional government's office advisor, were both shot and killed during the incident in Amhara's capital. Regional attorney general Migbaru Kebede also suffered "heavy injuries"; he died of his wounds on June 24. The government accused Brig. Gen. Asaminew Tsige, head of the regional government's Peace and Security Bureau, of orchestrating the attack and said he, along with several suspected collaborators, had been arrested. (The next day state media reported that Tsige had been killed.) Officials said regional leaders were in a meeting to discuss how to stop Tsige from openly recruiting ethnic Amhara militias when the attempted coup took place. The week before, Tsige had released a video calling for the Amhara people to arm themselves and prepare to fight other ethnic groups. The government also reported a second attack that took place on the same day, this time targeting Gen. Seare Mekonnen, the chief of staff of the Ethiopian National Defense Forces and another Ahmed supporter. Mekonnen's bodyguard was arrested and accused of murdering the general and retired major general Gezai Abera, who was visiting Mekonnen at his home in Addis Ababa. The government said these killings were related to the coup attempt but did not specify how. (Addis Ababa is in the Oromia region.)

Ahmed said the federal government was collaborating with the Amhara regional government and had the situation "under full control." The government remained "committed to ensuring national security," he said, adding a call for Ethiopians to "be guardians of peace and support all efforts in holding suspected individuals accountable." He also expressed his "deepest sympathies and condolences to the family and friends of the deceased." Moussa Faki Mahamat, the chair of the African Union (AU) Commission, offered condolences as well and reiterated the AU's "steadfast support" for Ahmed and his government "in their pursuit of the national reform and reconciliation agenda in the country." United Nations secretary-general António Guterres said he was "deeply concerned by the weekend's deadly incidents." He called on "all Ethiopian stakeholders to demonstrate restraint, prevent violence and avoid any action that could undermine the peace and stability of Ethiopia."

AHMED CRITIC SPARKS NEW PROTESTS

Fresh protests broke out in Addis Ababa and some regional cities on October 23 and 24 after Jawar Mohammed, owner of an independent media network and a prominent political activist, claimed the police tried to remove the government security detail from his home so as to facilitate an attack against him. (Mohammed used his influential media network to help install Ahmed in the prime minister's office, but he had become critical of some of Ahmed's policies, particularly those that promote a single, national identity over greater ethnic and regional autonomy.) In remarks to parliament the day before, Ahmed accused "media owners who don't have Ethiopian passports" of "playing both ways" and said if they "undermine the peace and existence of Ethiopia," the government would "take measures." Many observers believed this to be a reference to Mohammed, who has dual American citizenship. Mohammed declined to "say for certain" that Ahmed was responsible for the actions taken by the police but said it was possible "loyalists in the security services thought they had a green light from what he was saying in Parliament." The protesters who gathered outside Mohammed's home and elsewhere declared that Ahmed had betrayed the people by threatening a critic. Shimelis Abdisa, the Oromia region's deputy president, told reporters the police visit to Mohammed's home was "a major mistake" that would be investigated, adding that the federal and regional government would work on ensuring Mohammed's safety and that of other formerly exiled individuals.

The protests ended after Mohammed held a news conference in which he called on his supporters to "open the blocked roads, clean the towns of barricades, treat those who have been injured during the protests and reconcile with those you have quarreled with." Police later reported the multiday protests resulted in the deaths of sixty-seven people. Kefyalew Tefera, Oromia's regional police commissioner, said thirteen people were killed by security forces while the rest were killed in fighting that broke out among different groups involved in the protests. Subsequent news reports detailed ethnic clashes that had sprung out of the protests in various cities, including attacks against some churches and mosques. The death toll was raised to eighty-six on November 3. A government spokesperson said more than 400 people had been detained. "We have to stop those forces who are trying pull us two steps back while we are going one step forward," said Ahmed. He pledged "to bring the perpetrators to justice" and urged Ethiopians to unite to protect against further instability.

RULING COALITION DISSOLVED

In another step toward reform, Ahmed announced in November that the EPRDF would be dissolved and replaced with the Prosperity Party—a unified political party designed to represent the interests of all Ethiopians. The EPRDF was a coalition comprised of the Oromo People's Democratic Organization (OPDO), the Amhara National Democratic Movement (ANDM), the Tigray People's Liberation Front (TPLF), and the Southern Ethiopian People's Democratic Movement (SEPDM). It ran Ethiopia's government for more than twenty-five years and completely controlled the parliament since 2015. The coalition was originally formed by the TPLF when its leader, Meles Zalawi, was the prime minister, with the goal of broadening the group's appeal beyond the Tigray people and undercutting other parties' power. The TPLF was historically the most dominant member of the coalition, despite its inclusion of the country's largest ethnic groups, the Oromo and Amhara. (The Oromo comprise about 35 percent of Ethiopia's population while the Amhara make up roughly 27 percent.) This had fueled claims by the Oromo and Amhara that they have been marginalized economically, politically, and culturally by the minority Tigrayans.

On November 21, the OPDO, AMDM, and SEPDM voted overwhelmingly in support of merging their groups into one political party to replace the EPRDF. "The unanimous decision passed today to merge the Party is a crucial step in harnessing our energy to work toward a shared vision," Ahmed said in a tweet following the vote. "Prosperity Party is committed to strengthening & applying a true Federal system which recognizes the diversity and contributions of all Ethiopians." Ahmed characterized the decision as unanimous because the TPLF boycotted the meeting and the vote. Party leaders argued that the merger was rushed and undemocratic. It "weakens the federal system and takes away the rights of people to self-administration," said Debretsion Gebremichael, the TPLF chair. "The drive to form a united party does not consider the existing situations in the country." The Prosperity Party has since moved ahead with preparing "a clear program and bylaws as well as a ten-year plan that leads Ethiopia to prosperity," according to Ahmed.

Observers say the move is intended to help change the image of a coalition that has been associated with human rights abuses and oppression and win over voters ahead of the planned 2020 election. Some support Ahmed's decision, claiming it is a critical step toward unifying the country and removing the system of ethnic federalism that has caused many of Ethiopia's troubles. Others note that it may be unpopular with voters who have a strong attachment to their ethnicity and want greater autonomy for their ethnic community, while still belonging to the state. Echoing one of the TPLF's concerns, some observers say that while the merger may be a positive step, it was poorly timed; the government must focus on completing Ethiopia's transition to a democracy and meeting the varied demands of its people before trying to change the party structure. Ahmed's minister of defense, Lemma Megerssa, even noted that "merging this party is not timely as there are many dangers." The government is working on "borrowed time," he said. Mohammed has announced his intent to challenge Ahmed by running for election, although his dual citizenship may disqualify him.

—Linda Grimm

Following is a press release issued by the office of Prime Minister Abiy Ahmed on June 23, 2019, reporting on the coup attempt and assassination of senior officials; a statement by UN secretary-general António Guterres on June 23, 2019, condemning the violence; and a statement from African Union Commission chair Moussa Faki Mahamat on June 25, 2019, responding to the attacks.

Ethiopian Prime Minister Reports Coup Attempt and Assassinations

June 23, 2019

In the early evening of June 22, 2019, an orchestrated coup attempt occurred on the executive leadership of the Amhara Regional Government. During attacks in this coup attempt, H. E. Dr. Ambachew Mekonnen, President of the Amhara Regional Government and H. E. Ezez Wassie, Amhara Regional Government Office Advisor, were killed from gunshot injuries sustained. The Regional Attorney General Migbaru Kebede has also sustained heavy injuries and is currently undergoing medical treatment.

The attempted coup and attacks on the leadership of the Amhara Regional Government President was orchestrated by Brigadier General Asaminew Tsige who has been serving as the regional government's Peace and Security Bureau head, in collaboration with other individuals. Many of the individuals involved in the attacks have been arrested and there is an ongoing operation to arrest the remaining. It is to be recalled that Brigadier General Asaminew Tsige was given amnesty and released from imprisonment last year.

The situation in the Amhara Region is currently under full control by the Federal Government in collaboration with the Regional Government, which in accordance with the constitution is being led by the Vice President, Lake Ayalew. The Federal Government remains committed to ensuring national security and through the command of Prime Minister Abiy Ahmed, various tasks are underway. In this regard, we encourage citizens to also be guardians of peace and support all efforts in holding suspected individuals accountable.

In relation to the coup attempt in Amhara region, the Chief of Staff of the Ethiopian National Defense Forces, General Seare Mekonnen, together with retired Major General Gezai Abera, were also killed yesterday night in Addis Ababa within the residence of General Seare. This fatal attack was committed by General Seare's bodyguard who has also been arrested. A national committee has been formed to organize military funeral honors for General Seare Mekonnen and retired Major General Gezai Abera. The committee will update and provide further information as needed.

The Amhara Regional Government will provide further information on funeral arrangements for Dr. Ambachew Mekonnen and Ezez Wassie.

Prime Minister Abiy Ahmed, on behalf of the Federal Government of Ethiopia, conveys his deepest sympathies and condolences to the family and friends of the deceased.

SOURCE: Office of the Prime Minister of Ethiopia (@PMEthiopia). Twitter post. June 23, 2019. https://twitter.com/PMEthiopia/status/1142720512109494272.

UN Secretary-General Condemns Assassinations in Ethiopia

June 23, 2019

The assassination of the chief of staff of the Ethiopian army and killing of a regional governor in what the Government has described as a regional coup attempt has been condemned by the UN Secretary-General.

In a statement released on Sunday, António Guterres said he was "deeply concerned by the weekend's deadly incidents." The Governor of the restive Amhara National Region was killed along with an adviser, while in the capital Addis Ababa, another key ally of Prime Minister Abiy Ahmed, Chief of Staff General Seare Mekonnen, was shot, along with another senior officer.

Mr. Guterres called on "all Ethiopian stakeholders to demonstrate restraint, prevent violence and avoid any action that could undermine the peace and stability of Ethiopia."

According to news reports, the Government has said the situation is now under control, which the Prime Minister addressed the nation on television urging Ethiopians to unite in the face of the "evil" coup attempt in Amhara. The region has been a hotspot of inter-ethnic violence, and the Government reportedly believes that the assassinations are linked. Many of those involved in the alleged coup attempt have been arrested, said Mr. Abiy's office.

The Prime Minister has made sweeping changes to the politics of the fast-growing African nation since taking office in April last year, transforming relations with neighbouring Eritrea, and making a series of bold internal reforms.

The Secretary General said in his statement that he "welcomed the commitment of the Prime Minister and Government of Ethiopia to ensure that the perpetrators of these actions are brought to justice. The United Nations remains committed to supporting the Government of Ethiopia in its efforts to address ongoing challenges."

Around three million people have been displaced within Ethiopia, due to long-standing ethnic disputes, usually involving land ownership and rights.

SOURCE: United Nations News. "Assassinations in Ethiopia amidst Regional 'Coup' Attempt, Condemned by UN Chief." June 23, 2019. https://news.un.org/en/story/2019/06/1041121.

 # Statement of the AU Commission Chair Regarding the Situation in Ethiopia

June 25, 2019

The Chairperson of the African Union Commission, Moussa Faki Mahamat, wishes to express his deepest condolences to the families of the national figures killed in the tragic events that occurred on Saturday 22 June 2019 in the Amhara region and in the capital Addis Abeba.

The Chairperson also wishes to reiterate the steadfast support of the African Union Commission to Prime Minister Abiy Ahmed and the government of the Federal Democratic Republic of Ethiopia in their pursuit of the national reform and reconciliation agenda in the country.

SOURCE: African Union. "Statement of the Chairperson Regarding the Situation in Ethiopia." June 25, 2019. https://au.int/en/pressreleases/20190625/statement-chairperson-regarding-situation-ethiopia.

OTHER HISTORIC DOCUMENTS OF INTEREST

FROM THIS VOLUME

- Ethiopian Prime Minister Awarded Nobel Peace Prize, p. 708

FROM PREVIOUS *HISTORIC DOCUMENTS*

- Ethiopian Prime Minister Resigns, *2018*, p. 148

President Trump Announces Sanctions against Iran

JUNE 24, 2019

The United States' 2018 withdrawal from the multilateral nuclear deal with Iran and its reimposition of sanctions against the Islamic republic further strained already tense relations between the two countries and created difficulties for the remaining parties to the accord. Iran resumed some of the activities restricted by the agreement at various points throughout 2019 in an effort to push European signatories to soften the impact of U.S. sanctions. These violations and Iran's involvement in regional hostilities—including its shooting down of a U.S. drone and alleged role in attacking several oil tankers—prompted President Donald Trump and his administration to introduce new sanctions.

IRAN STATES INTENT TO VIOLATE NUCLEAR AGREEMENT

China, France, Germany, Iran, Russia, the United Kingdom, and the United States signed the Joint Comprehensive Plan of Action (JCPOA) in 2015. Under the agreement, Iran accepted limits on certain nuclear activities and increased monitoring by the International Atomic Energy Agency (IAEA) in exchange for the lifting of U.S., European Union, and United Nations sanctions.

Trump was sharply critical of the nuclear deal as a presidential candidate and continued to attack the agreement after taking office. In October 2017, the president declined to certify to Congress Iran's compliance with the JCPOA and the deal's value to U.S. national security. (Congress passed a law in 2015 requiring the president to recertify the agreement every ninety days.) Trump said he was directing his administration to work closely with lawmakers and U.S. allies to fix the JCPOA's "many serious flaws," warning that if an improved agreement could not be reached, the United States would withdraw from the deal. Trump again declined to certify the deal in January 2018, saying he was giving lawmakers and allies a "last chance" to come up with a better deal. On May 8, Trump announced he was removing the United States from the JCPOA and putting U.S. sanctions against Iran back in place. The president cited the JCPOA's shortcomings, Iran's development of ballistic missiles, and its support for "destabilizing activities" in the Middle East—such as its involvement in conflicts in Iraq, Syria, and Yemen—as reasons for the withdrawal. Administration officials said they were open to negotiating a new agreement but identified a dozen elements they insisted be included, such as a requirement that Iran completely end its uranium enrichment activities, that many analysts said were unrealistic.

The other parties to the JCPOA assailed the U.S. decision to withdraw from the deal. Officials from France, Germany, Russia, and the UK said their countries would honor their commitment to the agreement's implementation while continuing a dialogue with Iran. For their part, Iranian officials said they would continue to abide by the terms of the

JCPOA but could resume some of the activities suspended by the deal if the remaining parties did not provide the economic benefits they had promised.

On June 17, 2019, Atomic Energy Organization of Iran spokesperson Behrouz Kamalvandi stated that Iran would soon exceed the JCPOA's uranium enrichment limits. (The JCPOA allowed Iran to stockpile up to 300 kilograms of enriched uranium. Another provision stated that Iran's level of uranium enrichment could not exceed 3.67 percent.) "We have quadrupled the rate of enrichment and even increased it more recently, so that in 10 days it will bypass the 300 kg limit," he said. Kamalvandi added that Iran may also exceed the agreed-upon enrichment level, noting that 5 percent enriched uranium was needed for the Bushehr Nuclear Power Plant and that the Tehran Research Reactor required uranium enriched to a level of 20 percent. However, he also stated that if European countries made "their best efforts" to provide more sanctions relief and "carry out their commitments," Iran would not violate the agreement any further.

Iranian officials met with their British, Chinese, French, German, and Russian counterparts in Vienna on June 28 to discuss how to keep the JCPOA in place and ensure all parties' compliance with its terms. During the meeting, Iranian officials said they were proceeding with plans to exceed the uranium stockpile cap and could take more significant action unless the Europeans made progress in developing a trade mechanism to mitigate the impact of U.S. sanctions on Iran. European officials confirmed that the mechanism, Instex, was operational and had begun processing some transactions. (Instex was designed to allow trade between European and Iranian companies without requiring monetary transfers in dollars. Effectively operating as a barter system, Instex would circumvent the United States' so-called "secondary sanctions" that punish foreign entities that trade with Iran.) The Iranians said this was a positive step forward but was insufficient to meet their expectations.

On July 1, Iranian officials and IAEA inspectors confirmed the stockpile limit had been exceeded. The Trump administration pledged to continue pressuring Iran until it ended "its nuclear ambitions and its malign behavior" and called for a ban on all uranium enrichment, but the remaining parties to the JCPOA said they would not reimpose sanctions.

Iran continued to reduce its compliance with the deal as the year progressed. On September 7, Kamalvandi announced that Iran had restarted its advanced centrifuges to enrich uranium. The JCPOA allowed Iran to continue using about 5,000 first-generation centrifuges; at the time of Kamalvandi's announcement, Iran had begun using 40 advanced centrifuges that were capable of producing enriched uranium five to ten times as fast as the first-generation equipment. Roughly two months later, on November 5, Iranian officials said they had begun injecting uranium gas into centrifuges at the Fordow nuclear facility, though it was unclear from the announcement whether enrichment activities had also resumed at the plant. The JCPOA expressly prohibited any uranium enrichment at Fordow. The once-secret facility has been of particular concern to Western officials since it was revealed in 2009, primarily because its location under a mountain would make it difficult to destroy with military resources. Iranian president Hassan Rouhani made it clear that renewed activity at Fordow was being used as a bargaining chip. "We know their sensitivity with regard to Fordow," he said, "but at the same time when they uphold their commitments we will cut off the gas again." "Iran has no credible reason to expand its uranium enrichment program, at the Fordow facility or elsewhere other than a clear attempt at nuclear extortion that will only deepen its political and economic isolation," said the U.S. State Department in a statement. While the other parties to the JCPOA raised some concerns about Iran's latest violations, they continued to resist the resumption of sanctions.

Attacks in Persian Gulf Region Inflame Tensions

Iran's reduction in JCPOA compliance occurred against a backdrop of increasing tensions around the Persian Gulf. In May and June, six oil tankers were damaged in the Gulf of Oman. U.S. and Saudi Arabian officials claimed Iran was behind those attacks as well as drone strikes against Saudi oil facilities in May. Iranian officials denied any involvement in these incidents. These developments prompted the United States to deploy an additional 2,500 troops to the Middle East in May and June. "The recent Iranian attacks validate the reliable, credible intelligence we have received on hostile behavior by Iranian forces and their proxy groups that threaten United States personnel and interests across the region," said acting defense secretary Patrick Shanahan, adding that the "United States does not seek conflict with Iran."

On June 20, the Iran Revolutionary Guard Corps (IRGC) shot down an unmanned U.S. surveillance drone that was flying over the Strait of Hormuz. (Located at the mouth of the Persian Gulf, the strait is a strategically important shipping lane through which approximately 20 percent of the global oil supply is transported.) A statement by the IRGC claimed the drone "violated Iran's airspace and engaged in information gathering and spying." Gen. Hossein Salami, IRGC commander, said Iran's borders were a "red line" and that "any enemy that violates the borders will be annihilated." U.S. officials maintained it was "an unprovoked attack" in international airspace. Air Force Lt. Gen. Joseph Guastella, commander of U.S. Central Command, said the drone was at least thirty-four kilometers away from Iranian territory when it was shot down. Trump approved retaliatory airstrikes against Iran but called them off at the last minute, later explaining that the deaths of an estimated 150 people would not be "proportionate to shooting down an unmanned drone."

U.S. officials announced on July 18 that an Iranian drone had been taken down over international waters in the Strait of Hormuz. A Department of Defense spokesperson said the unmanned drone had "closed within a threatening range" of a U.S. amphibious assault ship. The ship's jamming equipment had been used to cause the drone to lose control and crash. Trump said the drone flight was "the latest of many provocative and hostile actions by Iran." Iranian foreign minister Mohammed Javad Zarif said the incident was being investigated but that officials had "no information about losing a drone," seeming to cast doubt on the Americans' claims.

U.S. Imposes New Sanctions

Throughout 2019, the United States engaged in a "maximum pressure" campaign to push Iran to forgo its nuclear program and end its involvement in regional conflicts. This included the April 22 announcement that the United States would stop granting exemptions from sanctions prohibiting imports of Iranian oil to certain countries. Sanctions waivers given to China, India, Japan, South Korea, and Turkey would expire on May 2, said Secretary of State Mike Pompeo. After that date, any companies or banks in those countries that continued to be involved in importing Iranian oil would face economic penalties. (Iran exports roughly one million barrels of oil per day, about half of which are purchased by China.) Iran threatened to close the Strait of Hormuz in response but did not.

On June 24, Trump announced new sanctions targeting Iranian supreme leader Ali Khamenei and the Office of the Supreme Leader. Executive Order 13876 blocked Khamenei and other Iranian leaders from using the U.S. financial system or accessing assets held in the United States. It also threatened economic penalties against any foreign financial institutions that conducted "significant transactions" with sanctioned individuals. Additionally, the executive order authorized the Department of the Treasury to issue sanctions against any officials appointed to their position by Khamenei or individuals who provide material support to the Office of the Supreme Leader. "The Supreme Leader of Iran is one who ultimately is responsible for the hostile conduct of the regime," said Trump before signing the executive order. "His office oversees the regime's most brutal instruments, including the Islamic Revolutionary Guard Corps." Adding that the United States did not "seek conflict with Iran or any other country," Trump said he looked forward "to the day when sanctions can be finally lifted and Iran can become a peaceful, prosperous, and productive nation." In a separate statement, Pompeo claimed Khamenei's office "sits atop a vast network of tyranny and corruption" and had "enriched itself at the expense of the Iranian people." The new sanction would deny Iran's leadership "the financial resources to spread terror and oppress the Iranian people," he said.

The same day, the Department of the Treasury announced sanctions against eight senior IRGC commanders for their oversight of the forces' "malicious regional activities." Additional sanctions were announced on July 18, this time against "a network of front companies and agents involved in the procurement of sensitive materials" for Iran's nuclear program. The Department of the Treasury's sanctions targeted individuals and entities based in Belgium, China, and Iran that officials said had acted as a procurement network for Iran's Centrifuge Technology Company, which produces centrifuges for uranium enrichment. "Iran cannot claim benign intent on the world stage while it purchases and stockpiles products for centrifuges," said Treasury Secretary Steven Mnuchin. "The U.S. government is deeply concerned by the Iranian regime's uranium enrichment and other provocative behaviors, and will continue to target all who provide support to Iran's nuclear program." Sanctions against the Central Bank of Iran and the National Development Fund of Iran were announced on September 20. Five days later, the United States sanctioned several Chinese companies for allegedly transporting Iranian oil in violation of U.S. sanctions.

—Linda Grimm

Following are Executive Order 13876 and remarks by President Donald Trump on signing the order to impose sanctions on Iran, both dated June 24, 2019.

Trump Issues Executive Order 13876—Imposing Sanctions with Respect to Iran

June 24, 2019

By the authority vested in me as President by the Constitution and the laws of the United States of America, including the International Emergency Economic Powers Act (50 U.S.C. 1701 *et seq.*) (IEEPA), the National Emergencies Act (50 U.S.C. 1601 *et seq.*), section 212(f) of the Immigration and Nationality Act of 1952 (8 U.S.C. 1182(f)), and section 301 of title 3, United States Code,

I, Donald J. Trump, President of the United States of America, in order to take additional steps with respect to the national emergency declared in Executive Order 12957 of March 15, 1995, in light of the actions of the Government of Iran and Iranian-backed proxies, particularly those taken to destabilize the Middle East, promote international terrorism, and advance Iran's ballistic missile program, and Iran's irresponsible and provocative actions in and over international waters, including the targeting of United States military assets and civilian vessels, hereby order:

Section 1. (a) All property and interests in property that are in the United States, that hereafter come within the United States, or that are or hereafter come within the possession or control of any United States person of the following persons are blocked and may not be transferred, paid, exported, withdrawn, or otherwise dealt in:

(i) the Supreme Leader of the Islamic Republic of Iran and the Iranian Supreme Leader's Office (SLO); or

(ii) any person determined by the Secretary of the Treasury, in consultation with the Secretary of State:

(A) to be a person appointed by the Supreme Leader of Iran or the SLO to a position as a state official of Iran, or as the head of any entity located in Iran or any entity located outside of Iran that is owned or controlled by one or more entities in Iran;

(B) to be a person appointed to a position as a state official of Iran, or as the head of any entity located in Iran or any entity located outside of Iran that is owned or controlled by one or more entities in Iran, by any person appointed by the Supreme Leader of Iran or the SLO;

(C) to have materially assisted, sponsored, or provided financial, material, or technological support for, or goods or services to or in support of any person whose property and interests in property are blocked pursuant to this section;

(D) to be owned or controlled by, or to have acted or purported to act for or on behalf of, directly or indirectly any person whose property and interests in property are blocked pursuant to this section; or

(E) to be a member of the board of directors or a senior executive officer of any person whose property and interests in property are blocked pursuant to this section.

(b) The prohibitions in subsection (a) of this section apply except to the extent provided by statutes, or in regulations, orders, directives, or licenses that may be issued pursuant to this order, and notwithstanding any contract entered into or any license or permit granted before the date of this order.

Sec. 2. (a) The Secretary of the Treasury, in consultation with the Secretary of State, is hereby authorized to impose on a foreign financial institution the sanctions described in subsection (b) of this section upon determining that the foreign financial institution has knowingly conducted or facilitated any significant financial transaction for or on behalf of any person whose property and interests in property are blocked pursuant to section 1 of this order.

(b) With respect to any foreign financial institution determined by the Secretary of the Treasury in accordance with this section to meet the criteria set forth in subsection

(a) of this section, the Secretary of the Treasury may prohibit the opening, and prohibit or impose strict conditions on the maintaining, in the United States of a correspondent account or a payable-through account by such foreign financial institution.

(c) The prohibitions in subsection (b) of this section apply except to the extent provided by statutes, or in regulations, orders, directives, or licenses that may be issued pursuant to this order, and notwithstanding any contract entered into or any license or permit granted before the date of this order.

Sec. 3. I hereby determine that the making of donations of the types of articles specified in section 203(b)(2) of IEEPA (50 U.S.C. 1701(b)(2)) by, to, or for the benefit of any person whose property and interests in property are blocked pursuant to section 1 of this order would seriously impair the President's ability to deal with the national emergency declared in Executive Order 12957, and I hereby prohibit such donations as provided by section 1 of this order.

Sec. 4. The prohibitions in section 1 of this order include:

(a) the making of any contribution or provision of funds, goods, or services by, to, or for the benefit of any person whose property and interests in property are blocked pursuant to this order; and

(b) the receipt of any contribution or provision of funds, goods, or services from any such person.

Sec. 5. The unrestricted immigrant and nonimmigrant entry into the United States of aliens determined to meet one or more of the criteria in subsection 1(a) of this order would be detrimental to the interests of the United States, and the entry of such persons into the United States, as immigrants or nonimmigrants, is hereby suspended. Such persons shall be treated as persons covered by section 1 of Proclamation 8693 of July 24, 2011 (Suspension of Entry of Aliens Subject to United Nations Security Council Travel Bans and International Emergency Economic Powers Act Sanctions).

Sec. 6. The Secretary of the Treasury, in consultation with the Secretary of State, is hereby authorized to take such actions, including adopting rules and regulations, to employ all powers granted to the President by IEEPA as may be necessary to carry out the purposes of this order, other than the purposes described in section 5 of this order. The Secretary of the Treasury may, consistent with applicable law, redelegate any of these functions within the Department of the Treasury. All departments and agencies of the United States shall take all appropriate measures within their authority to implement this order.

Sec. 7. (a) Any transaction that evades or avoids, has the purpose of evading or avoiding, causes a violation of, or attempts to violate any of the prohibitions set forth in this order is prohibited.

(b) Any conspiracy formed to violate any of the prohibitions set forth in this order is prohibited.

Sec. 8. For the purposes of this order:

(a) the term "person" means an individual or entity;

(b) the term "entity" means a partnership, association, trust, joint venture, corporation, group, subgroup, or other organization;

(c) the term "foreign financial institution" means any foreign entity that is engaged in the business of accepting deposits, making, granting, transferring, holding, or brokering loans or credits, or purchasing or selling foreign exchange, securities, commodity futures or options, or procuring purchasers and sellers thereof, as principal or agent. The term includes, but is not limited to, depository institutions, banks, savings banks, money service businesses, trust companies, securities brokers and dealers, commodity futures and options brokers and dealers, forward contract and foreign exchange merchants, securities and commodities exchanges, clearing corporations, investment companies, employee benefit plans, dealers in precious metals, stones, or jewels, and holding companies, affiliates, or subsidiaries of any of the foregoing. The term does not include the international financial institutions identified in 22 U.S.C. 262r(c)(2), the International Fund for Agricultural Development, the North American Development Bank, or any other international financial institution so notified by the Secretary of the Treasury;

(d) the term "knowingly," with respect to conduct, a circumstance, or a result, means that a person has actual knowledge, or should have known, of the conduct, the circumstance, or the result; and

(e) the term "United States person" means any United States citizen, permanent resident alien, entity organized under the laws of the United States or any jurisdiction within the United States (including foreign branches), or any person in the United States.

Sec. 9. For those persons whose property and interests in property are blocked pursuant to this order who might have a constitutional presence in the United States, I find that because of the ability to transfer funds or other assets instantaneously, prior notice to such persons of measures to be taken pursuant to this order would render those measures ineffectual. I therefore determine that for these measures to be effective in addressing the national emergency declared in Executive Order 12957, there need be no prior notice of a listing or determination made pursuant to section 1 of this order.

Sec. 10. (a) Nothing in this order shall be construed to impair or otherwise affect:

(i) the authority granted by law to an executive department or agency, or the head thereof; or

(ii) the functions of the Director of the Office of Management and Budget relating to budgetary, administrative, or legislative proposals.

(b) This order shall be implemented consistent with applicable law and subject to the availability of appropriations.

(c) This order is not intended to, and does not, create any right or benefit, substantive or procedural, enforceable at law or in equity by any party against the United States, its departments, agencies, or entities, its officers, employees, or agents, or any other person.

Sec. 11. The measures taken pursuant to this order are in response to actions of the Government of Iran occurring after the conclusion of the 1981 Algiers Accords, and are intended solely as a response to those later actions.

SOURCE: Executive Office of the President. "Executive Order 13876—Imposing Sanctions with Respect to Iran." June 24, 2019. *Compilation of Presidential Documents* 2019, no. 00417 (June 24, 2019). https://www.govinfo.gov/content/pkg/DCPD-201900417/pdf/DCPD-201900417.pdf.

President Trump Remarks on Signing the Executive Order Sanctioning Iran

June 24, 2019

The President. Okay, thank you very much. In a few moments, I'll be signing an Executive order imposing hard-hitting sanctions on the Supreme Leader of Iran and the office of the Supreme Leader of Iran and many others.

Today's action follows a series of aggressive behaviors by the Iranian regime in recent weeks, including shooting down of U.S. drones. They shot down the drone. It's—I guess everyone saw that one. And many other things. They've done many other things aside from the individual drone. You saw the tankers, and we know of other things that were done also, which were not good and not appropriate.

The Supreme Leader of Iran is one who ultimately is responsible for the hostile conduct of the regime. He's respected within his country. His office oversees the regime's most brutal instruments, including the Islamic Revolutionary Guard Corps.

Sanctions imposed through the Executive order that I'm about to sign will deny the Supreme Leader and the Supreme Leader's office, and those closely affiliated with him and the office, access to key financial resources and support. The assets of Ayatollah Khamenei and his office will not be spared from the sanctions.

These measures represent a strong and proportionate response to Iran's increasingly provocative actions. We will continue to increase pressure on Tehran until the regime abandons its dangerous activities and its aspirations, including the pursuit of nuclear weapons, increased enrichment of uranium, development of ballistic missiles, engagement in and support for terrorism, fueling of foreign conflicts, and belligerent acts directed against the United States and its allies.

The agreement that was signed was a disaster. It was not doing what it was supposed to do. Many bad things were taking place. And most importantly, it was so short term that, within a very short number of years, they would be able to make nuclear weapons. And that's unacceptable.

Never can Iran have a nuclear weapon.

Also included in this is, we want the stoppage immediately of their sponsoring of terrorism. They sponsor terrorism at a level that nobody has ever seen before, and that's been over the last number of years. And they've taken all of that money that was given to them by the past administration, and much of it was given out to terrorist organizations.

In fact, I remember when John Kerry was asked a question about whether or not this money will be spent for terror. He actually said "yes"—or at least he was referring to some of it. But he said, "Yes, it will be used for terror," with—if you can believe that. We're giving them money. We're saying, "Yes, it can be used for terror." That was not a good answer, but that was the least of it, frankly.

So America is a peace-loving nation. We do not seek conflict with Iran or any other country.

I look forward to the day when sanctions can be finally lifted and Iran can become a peaceful, prosperous, and productive nation. That can go very quickly; it can be tomorrow. It can also be in years from now.

So I look forward to discussing whatever I have to discuss with anybody that wants to speak.

In the meantime, who knows what's going to happen. I can only tell you we cannot ever let Iran have a nuclear weapon. And it won't happen.

And secondly, and very importantly, we don't want money going out to sponsor terror. And they are the number-one sponsor of terror anywhere in the world.

So I'll sign this order right now. And I want to thank our military. I want to thank all of the people that have been working with me over the last number of months on this. I think a lot of restraint has been shown by us. A lot of restraint. And that doesn't mean we're going to show it in the future.

But I felt that we want to give this a chance—give it a good chance—because I think Iran, potentially, has a phenomenal future.

Just—and I say that about North Korea too. I've said it about North Korea. I think North Korea has a phenomenal future. And I think Iran also has a phenomenal future. And we would like to—I think a lot of people would like to see them get to work on that great future.

So I'll sign this now. And I appreciate you all being here. Thank you.

[The President signed the Executive order and related documents.]

Okay. Thank you very much, everybody.

Diplomatic Efforts with Iran/Joint Comprehensive Plan of Action

Q. Mr. President, is your goal to negotiate a new deal with Iran?

The President. We would love to be able to negotiate a deal if they want to. If they don't want to, that's fine too. But we would love to be able to. And frankly, they might as well do it soon.

But obviously, the people of Iran are great people. You know, I know many of them. I lived in New York. I haven't been there very much the last 2½ years, but I know many Iranians living in New York, and they're fantastic people. I have many friends that are Iranian, and it's just very sad what's happening to that country.

The deal should've never been done. It wasn't ratified by Congress. It wasn't properly done, as you know. As a treaty, it wasn't properly done. It was incorrectly done. But we'll get it properly done.

So we'll see what happens. I hope it's going to be for the good. But the people in Iran are great people, and all of the people I know—so many, in New York—these are great people. Okay. Anything else?

Q. Sir, just to be clear, is this the U.S. response to the Iranians shooting down the drone?

The President. This, you can probably, Steve [Steve A. Holland, Reuters], add that into it, but basically, this is something that was going to happen anyway.

Q. Okay.

Q. If they reach the uranium limits on the 27th, will you take additional action?

The President. I won't say what I'll do, but I don't think they should do it.

Q. What is your message for the Supreme Leader? And do you want a meeting with him one on one?

The President. Just—my only message is this: He has the potential to have a great country, and quickly. Very quickly. And I think they should do that rather than going along this very destructive path. Destructive for everybody. Destructive for everybody.

We can't let them have a nuclear weapon. He said he doesn't want nuclear weapons. It's a great thing to say. But a lot of things have been said over the years, and it turns out to be not so. But he said very openly and plainly for everyone to hear that he does not want to have nuclear weapons. So if that's the case, we can do something very quickly. Okay?

Thank you very much, everybody. . . .

SOURCE: Executive Office of the President. "Remarks on Signing the Executive Order on Iran Sanctions and an Exchange with Reporters." June 24, 2019. *Compilation of Presidential Documents* 2019, no. 00416 (June 24, 2019). https://www.govinfo.gov/content/pkg/DCPD-201900416/pdf/DCPD-201900416.pdf.

OTHER HISTORIC DOCUMENTS OF INTEREST

FROM PREVIOUS *HISTORIC DOCUMENTS*

- President Trump and European Leaders on Decision to Remove U.S. from the Iran Nuclear Deal, *2018*, p. 288
- Decertification of Iranian Nuclear Deal, *2017*, p. 536
- Iranian Nuclear Deal Takes Effect, *2016*, p. 43
- Iranian Nuclear Deal Reached, *2015*, p. 148

Supreme Court Rules on Census Immigration Question

JUNE 27, 2019

On June 27, 2019, in the highly anticipated case of *Department of Commerce v. New York*, the Supreme Court effectively put an end to the Trump administration's plan to add a controversial citizenship question to the upcoming 2020 Census questionnaire. The fractured opinion, written by Chief Justice John Roberts, found that the explanation the government had given for adding the citizenship question "seems to have been contrived." The opinion provided no definitive legal conclusion on the validity of reinstating a citizenship question, only that such an action must be supported by a "reasoned explanation." The Court sent the case back to the district court to determine if the government could provide an adequate rationale. What resulted was confusion about whether the administration had time to take further action on a citizenship question and an announcement by the president that he might attempt adding a question via executive order. However, in the end, the Trump administration took no action and the 2020 Census would not include a question about citizenship.

COMMERCE SECRETARY ANNOUNCES CITIZENSHIP QUESTION

In March 2018, Secretary of Commerce Wilbur Ross announced his decision to reinstate a question about citizenship on the 2020 Census. Such a question had last appeared in the short-form questionnaire that goes to all families in 1950, although the question remained on the long-form questionnaire sent to a smaller number of families. In sworn testimony before Congress, Secretary Ross stated that he sought to add the question "solely" because he had received a request from the Department of Justice (DOJ) stating that it needed the citizenship information to better enforce the Voting Rights Act (VRA) to protect minority voters. The secretary of commerce overruled the unanimous advice of Census Bureau experts who predicted that the action would make the census "less accurate, not more." Ross acknowledged that adding such a question could have "some impact on responses," but he felt that the information was "of greater importance than any adverse effect that may result from people violating their legal duty to respond."

Eighteen states, the District of Columbia, various counties and cities, and other organizations filed a case in the federal district court in New York. They alleged that Ross's decision violated several provisions of the Constitution as well as the requirements of the Administrative Procedure Act. In response to a request for all records supporting the decision to add the citizenship question, the government submitted the December 2017 letter from the DOJ requesting the addition. Later, however, at the urging of the DOJ, in order to provide "further background and context," the government provided a supplemental memo revealing that it was Ross who had originally asked the DOJ to request the citizenship question.

Determining that the secretary's original submission was incomplete and in bad faith, the district court ordered the government to provide the complete administrative record. The new filing included e-mails and other records revealing that, in fact, Ross was determined to add the citizenship question from the time he was confirmed in early 2017. Ross engaged in multiple discussions about the subject with former White House strategist Stephen Bannon as well as hardline immigration opponent Stephen Miller. He instructed his staff to find a way to make the change happen and reached out to several other agencies, including the Department of Homeland Security and DOJ's Office for Immigration Review, asking them to request census-based citizenship data before subsequently contacting DOJ's Civil Rights Division. The VRA rationale only emerged late in the process.

The district court held a bench trial and ruled that the secretary's action was arbitrary and capricious, based on a pretextual rationale, and violated certain provisions of the Census Act. On these statutory claims, the court blocked the secretary from reinstating the citizenship question until it resolved these "legal defects." The court rejected an Equal Protection claim, concluding that the plaintiffs had not proved that the secretary was motivated by discriminatory animus.

The government appealed the case directly to the Supreme Court because "the case involved an issue of imperative public importance, and the census questionnaire needed to be finalized for printing by the end of June 2019."

After the Supreme Court heard oral arguments in the case, but before it ruled, the plaintiffs petitioned to return the case to the district court because of newly discovered evidence. The daughter of a recently deceased Republican redistricting strategist, Thomas Hofeller, found files on his hard drive arguably showing that he had "played a significant, previously undisclosed role in orchestrating" the inclusion of the citizenship question. His files included memos in which he argued that adding a citizenship question would advantage Republicans and white voters in future elections.

The Supreme Court did not grant the motion to remand the case for further consideration of these new revelations, but judges in both New York and Maryland said that they would consider these revelations as evidence that Ross violated the Equal Protection Clause of the Constitution, claims that the courts had previously ruled were not supported by sufficient evidence. A week before the Supreme Court ruled, the Maryland district court judge wrote that the new evidence "potentially connects the dots between a discriminatory purpose—diluting Hispanics' political power—and Secretary Ross's decision."

When the Supreme Court ruled on June 27, no opinions mentioned this new evidence.

SUPREME COURT ISSUES A SPLINTERED OPINION

Much of Roberts's opinion sounded like a victory for the government. He first ruled that the Constitution and long historical practice support the right of the secretary of commerce "to inquire about citizenship on the census questionnaire." He next ruled that the Administrative Procedure Act allows for review of the secretary's decision under a narrow and deferential "arbitrary and capricious" standard, which he found was satisfied in this case. Next, Roberts reversed the lower court ruling that the secretary had violated the Census Act, finding any violation to be merely "technical" and any error "surely harmless." Roberts also was not moved with the fact that Ross had an intention to add the question from the time he entered office, finding that "[i]t is hardly improper for an agency head to come into office with policy preferences and ideas."

However, in the last section of his opinion, the chief justice addressed the question of whether the stated reason for adding the citizenship question was pretextual and concluded that "viewing the evidence as a whole, we share the District Court's conviction that the decision to reinstate a citizenship question cannot be adequately explained in terms of DOJ's request for improved citizenship data to better enforce the VRA." The sole justification offered by the Department of Commerce was that it was merely responding to a request from another agency and this, the opinion found, was at odds with all the evidence that "Commerce went to great lengths to elicit the request from DOJ (or any other willing agency)." The opinion variously refers to Secretary Ross's explanation for his actions as "incongruent," "contrived," and "a distraction." These cannot satisfy the requirement of administrative law that government action be supported by a "reasoned explanation," a requirement that, Roberts explained, "is meant to ensure that agencies offer genuine justifications for important decisions, reasons that can be scrutinized by courts and the interested public."

The opinion did not find that it was necessarily wrong to include the citizenship question, only that agencies are required by law to have a reason for their actions: "If judicial review is to be more than an empty ritual, it must demand something better than the explanation offered for the action taken in this case." With that, Chief Justice Roberts sent the case back to the district court.

TIMELINE AND TWEET CREATE CONFUSION AFTER OPINION

The Supreme Court remanded the case back to the lower court, but there was very little time before the census questionnaire would be finalized and sent to printers. On July 2, the Census Department announced that it would honor the Court's opinion and begin printing the census without the citizenship question. President Donald Trump surprised officials by tweeting in response that this was "FAKE," and that he was "absolutely moving forward" with the citizenship question. DOJ lawyers told the federal courts on July 4 that they had been asked "to reevaluate all available options." On July 5, President Trump told reporters that he was considering four or five options to add the citizenship question, including the use of an executive order.

On July 11, 2019, President Trump and Attorney General William Barr appeared in the Rose Garden to announce that the administration would no longer seek the inclusion of the citizenship question. The president stressed that he was not "backing down on our efforts" to gather citizenship data but would instead order all federal agencies to provide the Department of Commerce with citizenship data from existing government records. He promised, "We will leave no stone unturned."

While the 2020 Census itself will not ask about citizenship, the quest to determine the citizen status of the population has continued in other ways. In mid-October, for instance, the Census Bureau announced that it is asking states to voluntarily turn over driver's license records, which typically include citizenship data.

PARALLEL INVESTIGATIONS IN THE HOUSE OF REPRESENTATIVES

As the legal case worked its way through the judicial system, the House Oversight Committee, headed by Rep. Elijah E. Cummings, D-Md., began investigating the origins of the administration's efforts to add the citizenship question to the census. The committee issued subpoenas for documents relevant to their inquiry to Barr and Ross, both of whom refused to produce anything after President Trump issued a blanket assertion of executive privilege. On July 17, 2019, the House voted to hold Barr and Ross in criminal contempt of Congress for defying congressional subpoenas. This move, though largely symbolic because the Department of Justice refused to enforce the citation, marked only the second time in U.S. history that Congress held a sitting cabinet official in contempt.

—Melissa Feinberg

Following is the edited text of the Supreme Court's June 27, 2019, ruling in Department of Commerce v. New York, *in which the Court struck down the Trump administration's attempt to add a question to the decennial census about an individual's citizenship.*

Supreme Court Issues Ruling on Census Citizenship Question

June 27, 2019

[Footnotes have been omitted.]

SUPREME COURT OF THE UNITED STATES

No. 18–966

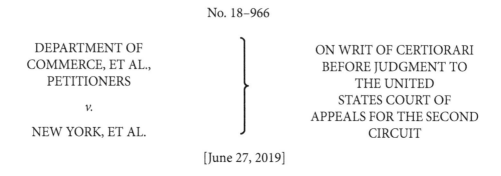

DEPARTMENT OF COMMERCE, ET AL., PETITIONERS *v.* NEW YORK, ET AL.	ON WRIT OF CERTIORARI BEFORE JUDGMENT TO THE UNITED STATES COURT OF APPEALS FOR THE SECOND CIRCUIT

[June 27, 2019]

CHIEF JUSTICE ROBERTS delivered the opinion of the Court.

The Secretary of Commerce decided to reinstate a question about citizenship on the 2020 census questionnaire. A group of plaintiffs challenged that decision on constitutional and statutory grounds. We now decide whether the Secretary violated the Enumeration Clause of the Constitution, the Census Act, or otherwise abused his discretion.

I

A

[Background about the census has been omitted.]

B

In March 2018, Secretary of Commerce Wilbur Ross announced in a memo that he had decided to reinstate a question about citizenship on the 2020 decennial census questionnaire. The Secretary stated that he was acting at the request of the Department of Justice (DOJ), which sought improved data about citizen voting-age population for purposes of enforcing the Voting Rights Act (or VRA)—specifically the Act's ban on diluting the influence of minority voters by depriving them of single-member districts in which they can elect their preferred candidates. App. to Pet. for Cert. 548a. DOJ explained that federal courts determine whether a minority group could constitute a majority in a particular district by looking to the citizen voting-age population of the group. . . .

[A discussion of opinions analyzed by the Census Bureau has been omitted.]

C

Shortly after the Secretary announced his decision, two groups of plaintiffs filed suit in Federal District Court in New York, challenging the decision on several grounds. The first group of plaintiffs included 18 States, the District of Columbia, various counties and cities, and the United States Conference of Mayors. They alleged that the Secretary's decision violated the Enumeration Clause of the Constitution and the requirements of the Administrative Procedure Act. The second group of plaintiffs consisted of several nongovernmental organizations that work with immigrant and minority communities. They added an equal protection claim. The District Court consolidated the two cases. Both groups of plaintiffs are respondents here.

The Government moved to dismiss the lawsuits, arguing that the Secretary's decision was unreviewable and that respondents had failed to state cognizable claims under the Enumeration Clause and the Equal Protection Clause. The District Court dismissed the Enumeration Clause claim but allowed the other claims to proceed. 315 F. Supp. 3d 766 (SDNY 2018).

In June 2018, the Government submitted to the District Court the Commerce Department's "administrative record": the materials that Secretary Ross considered in making his decision. That record included DOJ's December 2017 letter requesting reinstatement of the citizenship question, as well as several memos from the Census Bureau analyzing the predicted effects of reinstating the question. Shortly thereafter, at DOJ's urging, the Government supplemented the record with a new memo from the Secretary, "intended to provide further background and context regarding" his March 2018 memo. App. to Pet. for Cert. 546a. The supplemental memo stated that the Secretary had begun considering whether to add the citizenship question in early 2017, and had inquired whether DOJ "would support, and if so would request, inclusion of a citizenship question as consistent with and useful for enforcement of the Voting Rights Act." *Ibid.* According to the Secretary, DOJ "formally" requested reinstatement of the citizenship question after that inquiry. *Ibid.*

Respondents argued that the supplemental memo indicated that the Government had submitted an incomplete record of the materials considered by the Secretary. They asked the District Court to compel the Government to complete the administrative record. The court granted that request, and the parties jointly stipulated to the inclusion of more than 12,000 pages of additional materials in the administrative record. Among those materials were emails and other records confirming that the Secretary and his staff began exploring the possibility of reinstating a citizenship question shortly after he was confirmed in early 2017, attempted to elicit requests for citizenship data from other agencies, and eventually persuaded DOJ to request reinstatement of the question for VRA enforcement purposes.

[A procedural history of the issue before the Court has been omitted, as has Section II, which covers the basis of jurisdiction.]

III

The Enumeration Clause of the Constitution does not provide a basis to set aside the Secretary's decision. The text of that clause "vests Congress with virtually unlimited discretion in conducting the decennial 'actual Enumeration,'" and Congress "has delegated its broad authority over the census to the Secretary." *Wisconsin*, 517 U. S., at 19. . . .

[The Court's legal analysis has been omitted.]

. . . In light of the early understanding of and long practice under the Enumeration Clause, we conclude that it permits Congress, and by extension the Secretary, to inquire about citizenship on the census questionnaire. We need not, and do not, decide the constitutionality of any other question that Congress or the Secretary might decide to include in the census.

IV

The District Court set aside the Secretary's decision to reinstate a citizenship question on the grounds that the Secretary acted arbitrarily and violated certain provisions of the Census Act.

[A legal discussion about the Administrative Procedure Act has been omitted.]

At the heart of this suit is respondents' claim that the Secretary abused his discretion in deciding to reinstate a citizenship question. We review the Secretary's exercise of discretion under the deferential "arbitrary and capricious" standard. . . .

The District Court set aside the Secretary's decision for two independent reasons: His course of action was not supported by the evidence before him, and his stated rationale was pretextual. We focus on the first point here and take up the question of pretext later.

The Secretary examined the Bureau's analysis of various ways to collect improved citizenship data and explained why he thought the best course was to both reinstate a citizenship question and use citizenship data from administrative records to fill in the gaps. He considered but rejected the Bureau's recommendation to use administrative records alone. . . .

The District Court overruled that choice, agreeing with the Bureau's assessment that its recommended approach would yield higher quality citizenship data on the whole. But the choice between reasonable policy alternatives in the face of uncertainty was the Secretary's to make. He considered the relevant factors, weighed risks and benefits, and articulated a satisfactory explanation for his decision. In overriding that reasonable exercise of discretion, the court improperly substituted its judgment for that of the agency.

[Additional legal factors considered by the Court have been omitted.]

V

We now consider the District Court's determination that the Secretary's decision must be set aside because it rested on a pretextual basis, which the Government conceded below would warrant a remand to the agency.

We start with settled propositions. First, in order to permit meaningful judicial review, an agency must "disclose the basis" of its action. *Burlington Truck Lines, Inc.* v. *United States*, 371 U. S. 156, 167–169 (1962) (internal quotation marks omitted); see also *SEC* v. *Chenery Corp.*, 318 U. S. 80, 94 (1943) ("[T]he orderly functioning of the process of review requires that the grounds upon which the administrative agency acted be clearly disclosed and adequately sustained.").

Second, in reviewing agency action, a court is ordinarily limited to evaluating the agency's contemporaneous explanation in light of the existing administrative record. *Vermont Yankee Nuclear Power Corp.* v. *Natural Resources Defense Council, Inc.*, 435 U. S. 519, 549 (1978); *Camp* v. *Pitts*, 411 U. S. 138, 142–143 (1973) (*per curiam*). That principle reflects the recognition that further judicial inquiry into "executive motivation" represents "a substantial intrusion" into the workings of another branch of Government and should normally be avoided. *Arlington Heights* v. *Metropolitan Housing Development Corp.*, 429 U. S. 252, 268, n. 18 (1977); see *Overton Park*, 401 U. S., at 420.

Third, a court may not reject an agency's stated reasons for acting simply because the agency might also have had other unstated reasons. See *Jagers* v. *Federal Crop Ins. Corp.*, 758 F. 3d 1179, 1185–1186 (CA10 2014) (rejecting argument that "the agency's subjective desire to reach a particular result must necessarily invalidate the result, regardless of the objective evidence supporting the agency's conclusion"). Relatedly, a court may not set aside an agency's policymaking decision solely because it might have been influenced by political considerations or prompted by an Administration's priorities. Agency policy-making is not a "rarified technocratic process, unaffected by political considerations or the presence of Presidential power." *Sierra Club* v. *Costle*, 657 F. 2d 298, 408 (CADC 1981). Such decisions are routinely informed by unstated considerations of politics, the legislative process, public relations, interest group relations, foreign relations, and national security concerns (among others).

Finally, we have recognized a narrow exception to the general rule against inquiring into "the mental processes of administrative decisionmakers." *Overton Park*, 401 U. S., at 420. On a "strong showing of bad faith or improper behavior," such an inquiry may be warranted and may justify extra-record discovery. *Ibid.*

The District Court invoked that exception in ordering extra-record discovery here. Although that order was premature, we think it was ultimately justified in light of the expanded administrative record. Recall that shortly after this litigation began, the Secretary, prodded by DOJ, filed a supplemental memo that added new, pertinent information to the administrative record. The memo disclosed that the Secretary had been considering the citizenship question for some time and that Commerce had inquired whether DOJ would formally request reinstatement of the question. That supplemental memo prompted respondents to move for both completion of the administrative record and extra-record discovery. The District Court granted both requests at the same hearing, agreeing with respondents that the Government had submitted an incomplete administrative record and that the existing evidence supported a *prima facie* showing that the VRA rationale was pretextual.

The Government did not challenge the court's conclusion that the administrative record was incomplete, and the parties stipulated to the inclusion of more than 12,000 pages of internal deliberative materials as part of the administrative record, materials that the court later held were sufficient on their own to demonstrate pretext. The Government did, however, challenge the District Court's order authorizing extra-record discovery, as well as the court's later orders compelling depositions of the Secretary and of the Acting Assistant Attorney General for DOJ's Civil Rights Division.

We agree with the Government that the District Court should not have ordered extra-record discovery when it did. At that time, the most that was warranted was the order to complete the administrative record. But the new material that the parties stipulated should have been part of the administrative record—which showed, among other things, that the VRA played an insignificant role in the decisionmaking process—largely justified such extra-record discovery as occurred (which did not include the deposition of the Secretary himself). We accordingly review the District Court's ruling on pretext in light of all the evidence in the record before the court, including the extra-record discovery.

That evidence showed that the Secretary was determined to reinstate a citizenship question from the time he entered office; instructed his staff to make it happen; waited while Commerce officials explored whether another agency would request census-based citizenship data; subsequently contacted the Attorney General himself to ask if DOJ would make the request; and adopted the Voting Rights Act rationale late in the process. In the District Court's view, this evidence established that the Secretary had made up his mind to reinstate a citizenship question "well before" receiving DOJ's request, and did so for reasons unknown but unrelated to the VRA. 351 F. Supp. 3d, at 660.

The Government, on the other hand, contends that there was nothing objectionable or even surprising in this. And we agree—to a point. It is hardly improper for an agency head to come into office with policy preferences and ideas, discuss them with affected parties, sound out other agencies for support, and work with staff attorneys to substantiate the legal basis for a preferred policy. The record here reflects the sometimes involved nature of Executive Branch decisionmaking, but no particular step in the process stands out as inappropriate or defective.

And yet, viewing the evidence as a whole, we share the District Court's conviction that the decision to reinstate a citizenship question cannot be adequately explained in terms of DOJ's request for improved citizenship data to better enforce the VRA. Several points, considered together, reveal a significant mismatch between the decision the Secretary made and the rationale he provided.

The record shows that the Secretary began taking steps to reinstate a citizenship question about a week into his tenure, but it contains no hint that he was considering VRA enforcement in connection with that project. The Secretary's Director of Policy did not know why the Secretary wished to reinstate the question, but saw it as his task to "find the best rationale." *Id.*, at 551. The Director initially attempted to elicit requests for citizenship data from the Department of Homeland Security and DOJ's Executive Office for Immigration Review, neither of which is responsible for enforcing the VRA. After those attempts failed, he asked Commerce staff to look into whether the Secretary could reinstate the question without receiving a request from another agency. The possibility that DOJ's Civil Rights Division might be willing to request citizenship data for VRA enforcement purposes was proposed by Commerce staff along the way and eventually pursued.

Even so, it was not until the Secretary contacted the Attorney General directly that DOJ's Civil Rights Division expressed interest in acquiring census-based citizenship data to better enforce the VRA. And even then, the record suggests that DOJ's interest was directed more to helping the Commerce Department than to securing the data. The December 2017 letter from DOJ drew heavily on contributions from Commerce staff and advisors. Their influence may explain why the letter went beyond a simple entreaty for better citizenship data—what one might expect of a typical request from another agency— to a specific request that Commerce collect the data by means of reinstating a citizenship question on the census. Finally, after sending the letter, DOJ declined the Census Bureau's offer to discuss alternative ways to meet DOJ's stated need for improved citizenship data, further suggesting a lack of interest on DOJ's part.

Altogether, the evidence tells a story that does not match the explanation the Secretary gave for his decision. In the Secretary's telling, Commerce was simply acting on a routine data request from another agency. Yet the materials before us indicate that Commerce went to great lengths to elicit the request from DOJ (or any other willing agency). And unlike a typical case in which an agency may have both stated and unstated reasons for a decision, here the VRA enforcement rationale—the sole stated reason—seems to have been contrived.

We are presented, in other words, with an explanation for agency action that is incongruent with what the record reveals about the agency's priorities and decisionmaking process. It is rare to review a record as extensive as the one before us when evaluating informal agency action—and it should be. But having done so for the sufficient reasons we have explained, we cannot ignore the disconnect between the decision made and the explanation given. Our review is deferential, but we are "not required to exhibit a naiveté from which ordinary citizens are free." *United States* v. *Stanchich*, 550 F. 2d 1294, 1300 (CA2 1977) (Friendly, J.). The reasoned explanation requirement of administrative law, after all, is meant to ensure that agencies offer genuine justifications for important decisions, reasons that can be scrutinized by courts and the interested public. Accepting contrived reasons would defeat the purpose of the enterprise. If judicial review is to be more than an empty ritual, it must demand something better than the explanation offered for the action taken in this case.

In these unusual circumstances, the District Court was warranted in remanding to the agency, and we affirm that disposition. See *Florida Power & Light Co.* v. *Lorion*, 470 U. S. 729, 744 (1985). We do not hold that the agency decision here was substantively invalid. But agencies must pursue their goals reasonably. Reasoned decisionmaking under the Administrative Procedure Act calls for an explanation for agency action. What was provided here was more of a distraction.

* * *

The judgment of the United States District Court for the Southern District of New York is affirmed in part and reversed in part, and the case is remanded for further proceedings consistent with this opinion.

It is so ordered.

JUSTICE THOMAS, with whom JUSTICE GORSUCH and JUSTICE KAVANAUGH join, concurring in part and dissenting in part.

. . . Our only role in this case is to decide whether the Secretary complied with the law and gave a reasoned explanation for his decision. The Court correctly answers these questions in the affirmative. *Ante*, at 11–23. That ought to end our inquiry.

The Court, however, goes further. For the first time ever, the Court invalidates an agency action solely because it questions the sincerity of the agency's otherwise adequate rationale. Echoing the din of suspicion and distrust that seems to typify modern discourse, the Court declares the Secretary's memorandum "pretextual" because, "viewing the evidence as a whole," his explanation that including a citizenship question on the census would help enforce the Voting Rights Act (VRA) "seems to have been contrived." *Ante*, at 23, 26, 28. The Court does not hold that the Secretary merely had *additional*, unstated reasons for reinstating the citizenship question. Rather, it holds that the Secretary's stated rationale did not factor *at all* into his decision.

[The remainder of the opinion, along with an opinion written by Justice Breyer and another by Justice Alito, concurring in part and dissenting in part, has been omitted.]

SOURCE: Supreme Court of the United States. *Department of Commerce v. New York.* 588 U.S. ___ (2019). https://www.supremecourt.gov/opinions/18pdf/18-966_bq7c.pdf.

OTHER HISTORIC DOCUMENTS OF INTEREST

FROM THIS VOLUME

▪ State of the Union Address and Democratic Response, p. 41

FROM PREVIOUS *HISTORIC DOCUMENTS*

▪ President Trump Issues Immigration Orders, *2017*, p. 42

Supreme Court Rules on Partisan Gerrymandering

JUNE 27, 2019

On June 27, 2019, in a 5–4 landmark decision likely to impact elections nationwide, the Supreme Court ruled that federal courts have no role to play in the policing of partisan gerrymandering of political districts. "We conclude," Chief Justice John Roberts wrote for the majority in *Rucho v. Common Cause*, "that partisan gerrymandering claims present political questions beyond the reach of the federal courts." This ruling effectively ended decades of struggle by the federal courts to determine whether election maps could be so partisan that they rise to the level of a constitutional violation. Roberts did not deny that "excessive partisanship in districting leads to results that reasonably seem unjust." However, the majority ruled that these "unjust" results fall outside the jurisdiction of the federal judiciary and should instead be left to the states or Congress to solve. A strong dissent from Justice Elena Kagan accused the majority of "abandon[ing] the Court's duty to declare the law."

PARTISAN GERRYMANDERING AND THE COURTS

Every ten years, after the federal census, state governments redraw voting district lines to ensure districts of roughly the same population size. Whichever party controls the state legislature at that time has enormous power to draw lines in a way that benefits their continued power. When those drawing the lines do so to further entrench the party in power, it is referred to as "partisan gerrymandering."

The Supreme Court first addressed the legality of purely partisan gerrymandering in a 2004 case. Although the Court was unable to reach a consensus on the issue at the time, then-justice Anthony Kennedy held out hope in a concurring opinion that "in another case a standard might emerge" to hold that extreme partisan gerrymandering could run afoul of constitutional rights. *Rucho v. Common Cause* presented the Court with that opportunity, only this time with Justice Kennedy's replacement, Justice Brett Kavanaugh.

Rucho combines two cases in which voters had successfully challenged their states' congressional districting maps for unconstitutional partisan gerrymandering. The first arose from the appeal of a North Carolina court decision that the state district maps unconstitutionally benefited Republicans; in the second case, a Maryland court had held that the state's maps had unconstitutionally benefited Democrats. The cases had both previously been appealed to the Supreme Court, but while they were pending, in June 2018 the Court decided a different partisan gerrymandering case out of Wisconsin, *Gill v. Whitford*. In that case, the Court did not decide the merits of the partisan gerrymander challenge, instead finding that the parties bringing the challenge did not have the requisite "standing" to bring the case. The Court then sent the cases out of Maryland and North Carolina back to the lower courts for reconsideration in light of the *Gill* decision.

On remand, the district courts of both states again found the voting maps to present unconstitutional partisan gerrymanders. In North Carolina, the mapmaker had admitted drawing district lines purely for partisan advantage. In 2016, Republicans, who won 53 percent of the statewide vote, earned ten out of thirteen seats in the state's congressional delegation (77 percent) and, in 2018, they received nine out of twelve seats (one race was thrown out after allegations of ballot tampering; a revote was held in 2019 and the seat was won by a Republican), despite receiving only 50 percent of the vote. On August 27, 2018, the North Carolina federal judges issued a new opinion, again holding that "the General Assembly's predominant intent was to discriminate against voters who supported or were likely to support non-Republican candidates," and to "entrench Republican candidates" in violation of the Fourteenth Amendment's Equal Protection Clause, the First Amendment, and Article I of the U.S. Constitution.

In Maryland, former governor Martin O'Malley, a Democrat, redrew the district map in 2011, with what he admitted was partisan intent to increase the Democratic advantage in districts from six out of eight to seven out of eight. The state did so by moving 360,000 voters out of one of the Republican voting districts, and moving in 350,000 new voters, leading to a successful and enduring flip of the seat to Democratic. A panel of federal judges held that this map violated the U.S. Constitution and ordered Maryland to adopt a new plan for the 2020 election.

The defendants in both cases appealed the decisions directly to the Supreme Court, which consolidated the cases and heard oral argument on March 26, 2019.

Supreme Court Ends Challenges to Partisan Gerrymanders

The majority opinion, written by Chief Justice Roberts and joined by Justices Clarence Thomas, Samuel Alito, Neil Gorsuch, and Kavanaugh, did not spend much time detailing the impact of the partisan gerrymanders at issue on the voters in Maryland and North Carolina. In fact, the opinion conceded that the Court could not "condone excessive partisan gerrymandering," acknowledging that such practice results in seemingly unjust outcomes that are "incompatible with democratic principles." Instead, the majority focused on a jurisdictional issue to reach its conclusion that partisan gerrymandering claims present "political" and not "legal" questions and, as such, do not belong to the judiciary, "the unelected and politically unaccountable branch of the Federal Government."

Article III of the Constitution gives federal courts the power to decide "cases" and "controversies," and there is a long history of jurisprudence fine-tuning the meaning of this limitation on judicial power. While the famous case of *Marbury v. Madison* in 1803 first declared that it is "the province and duty of the judicial department to say what the law is," sometimes courts have held that an issue is "entrusted to one of the political branches or involves no judicially enforceable rights." Such cases are said to present "political questions" and are not justiciable by the courts. Roberts framed the issue in *Rucho* as questioning "whether there is an 'appropriate role for the Federal Judiciary' in remedying the problem of partisan gerrymandering—whether such claims are claims of *legal* right, resolvable according to *legal* principles, or political questions that must find their resolution elsewhere."

Before answering that question, the majority opinion looked to history to examine how partisan gerrymandering existed and was debated prior to independence. In the first congressional elections, George Washington accused Patrick Henry of attempting to gerrymander Virginia's districts against Washington's preferred candidates. The Framers of the Constitution gave the power to regulate the election of members of Congress to state legislatures in the Elections Clause of the Constitution, but they also gave Congress the power to "make or alter" any such regulations for reasons that contemporaneous debate shows to have explicitly included the need to counter "malapportionment" by state legislatures. In the *Rucho* decision, the majority emphasized that throughout the relevant history "[a]t no point was there a suggestion that the federal courts had a role to play."

The Supreme Court, nevertheless, has weighed in on some districting issues, repeatedly finding, for example, that racial gerrymandering is impermissible. However, the case of extreme partisan gerrymandering is, according to Roberts, more complicated and unmanageable. The Framers of the Constitution gave the power to draw district lines to political entities understanding that they would take their partisan interests into account. The "central problem," Roberts wrote, then becomes "determining when political gerrymandering has gone too far." This is a question of degree—that is, how much is too much. "At what point," Roberts asks, "does permissible partisanship become unconstitutional?"

Answering this question would require standards that are "clear, manageable, and politically neutral," Roberts wrote. According to the majority opinion, no such "discernible and manageable standards" exist. Without clear constitutional authorization or workable standards to limit and direct legal intervention, the Supreme Court pulled itself out of the role of policing partisan gerrymandering claims entirely. Such questions are "political" and "beyond the reach of the federal courts," the majority determined.

Claiming that this ruling does not "condemn complaints about districting to echo into a void," Roberts concluded by listing various state proposals to address the issue, including state courts striking down districting plans for violating state laws, state constitutional amendments to prohibit partisanship in redistricting, and voter initiatives in Michigan and Colorado to create independent commissions to create district maps. He also acknowledged that the Framers gave Congress the power to do something about partisan gerrymandering, and he listed bills introduced in the House that seek to do that.

DISSENT ACCUSES MAJORITY OF ABDICATING RESPONSIBILITY

The majority opinion asserted, "No one can accuse this Court of having a crabbed view of the reach of its competence." But that is exactly what the dissent in this case did. Justice Kagan, in a dissent joined by Justices Ruth Bader Ginsburg, Stephen Breyer, and Sonia Sotomayor, wrote, "For the first time in this Nation's history, the majority declares that it can do nothing about an acknowledged constitutional violation because it has searched high and low and cannot find a workable legal standard to apply." She described the majority's reliance on the long history of gerrymandering as creating an ill-placed complacency. The big data and modern technology, unmentioned in the majority opinion, have the effect of making gerrymanders exponentially more effective and durable. "These are not," she wrote, "your grandfather's—let alone the Framers'—gerrymanders."

Throughout the dissent, Justice Kagan described how the partisan gerrymanders at issue in this case "debased and dishonored our democracy, turning upside-down the core American idea that all governmental power derives from the people." Not only that, but they may "irreparably damage our system of government," Kagan wrote. And, she argued that "the majority misses something under its nose: What it says can't be done *has* been done." Federal courts across the country have "largely converged on a standard for adjudicating partisan gerrymandering claims."

Reading from the bench, and at times emotional, Justice Kagan concluded her dissent not with the standard language, "I respectfully dissent," but with a conclusion signifying her disappointment, "With respect but deep sadness, I dissent."

COURT RULING RAISES QUESTIONS ON FUTURE GERRYMANDERING

Rucho v. Common Cause, et al., shut the door to any further federal court review of partisan gerrymandering, immediately impacting Maryland, Michigan, Ohio, and North Carolina, presidential battleground states previously ordered to change their maps by lower federal courts. Looking forward, this decision raises the stakes for the 2020 vote, another census year election. Whichever party wins control of state legislatures will be able to redraw both state and federal district lines for the next decade without any fear of judicial oversight, no matter how partisan. Currently, Republicans control both the governorship and legislature in twenty-one states, compared with fifteen for Democrats. The remaining states have split-party rule.

At the same time, public outrage over partisan gerrymandering is increasing. In 2018, five states passed voter referendums limiting the power of state legislatures in the district drawing process or creating independent commissions for redistricting. State courts have also stepped into the fray. In North Carolina, after the Supreme Court dismissed the gerrymandering challenge, the state court, this time relying on the state constitution, again threw out the challenged voter map.

—Melissa Feinburg

Following is the edited text of the June 27, 2019, Supreme Court ruling in Rucho v. Common Cause, *in which the Court determined that it could not rule on partisan gerrymandering, instead leaving oversight for the issue to states and Congress.*

Supreme Court Rules on
Partisan Gerrymanders

June 27, 2019

SUPREME COURT OF THE UNITED STATES

Nos. 18–422, 18–726

ROBERT A. RUCHO, ET AL., APPELLANTS	LINDA H. LAMONE, ET AL., APPELLANTS
18–422 *v.*	18–726 *v.*
COMMON CAUSE, ET AL.; AND	O. JOHN BENISEK, ET AL.
ON APPEAL FROM THE UNITED STATES DISTRICT COURT FOR THE MIDDLE DISTRICT OF NORTH CAROLINA	ON APPEAL FROM THE UNITED STATES DISTRICT COURT FOR THE DISTRICT OF MARYLAND

[June 27, 2019]

CHIEF JUSTICE ROBERTS delivered the opinion of the Court.

Voters and other plaintiffs in North Carolina and Maryland challenged their States' congressional districting maps as unconstitutional partisan gerrymanders. The North Carolina plaintiffs complained that the State's districting plan discriminated against Democrats; the Maryland plaintiffs complained that their State's plan discriminated against Republicans. The plaintiffs alleged that the gerrymandering violated the First Amendment, the Equal Protection Clause of the Fourteenth Amendment, the Elections Clause, and Article I, §2, of the Constitution. The District Courts in both cases ruled in favor of the plaintiffs, and the defendants appealed directly to this Court.

These cases require us to consider once again whether claims of excessive partisanship in districting are "justiciable"—that is, properly suited for resolution by the federal courts. This Court has not previously struck down a districting plan as an unconstitutional partisan gerrymander, and has struggled without success over the past several decades to discern judicially manageable standards for deciding such claims. The districting plans at issue here are highly partisan, by any measure. The question is whether the courts below appropriately exercised judicial power when they found them unconstitutional as well.

[A description of the parties in the case has been omitted.]

II

A

Article III of the Constitution limits federal courts to deciding "Cases" and "Controversies." We have understood that limitation to mean that federal courts can address only questions "historically viewed as capable of resolution through the judicial process." *Flast* v. *Cohen*, 392 U. S. 83, 95 (1968). In these cases we are asked to decide an important question of constitutional law. "But before we do so, we must find that the question is presented in a 'case' or 'controversy' that is, in James Madison's words, 'of a Judiciary Nature.'" *DaimlerChrysler Corp.* v. *Cuno*, 547 U. S. 332, 342 (2006) (quoting 2 Records of the Federal Convention of 1787, p. 430 (M. Farrand ed. 1966)).

[Further discussion of justiciability standards has been omitted, as has a history of gerrymandering.]

B

Partisan gerrymandering claims rest on an instinct that groups with a certain level of political support should enjoy a commensurate level of political power and influence. Explicitly or implicitly, a districting map is alleged to be unconstitutional because it makes it too difficult for one party to translate statewide support into seats in the legislature. But such a claim is based on a "norm that does not exist" in our electoral system—"statewide elections for representatives along party lines." *Bandemer*, 478 U. S., at 159 (opinion of O'Connor, J.).

Partisan gerrymandering claims invariably sound in a desire for proportional representation. As Justice O'Connor put it, such claims are based on "a conviction that the greater the departure from proportionality, the more suspect an apportionment plan becomes." *Ibid.* "Our cases, however, clearly foreclose any claim that the Constitution requires proportional representation or that legislatures in reapportioning must draw district lines to come as near as possible to allocating seats to the contending parties in proportion to what their anticipated statewide vote will be." *Id.*, at 130 (plurality opinion). See *Mobile v. Bolden*, 446 U. S. 55, 75–76 (1980) (plurality opinion) ("The Equal Protection Clause of the Fourteenth Amendment does not require proportional representation as an imperative of political organization.").

The Founders certainly did not think proportional representation was required. For more than 50 years after ratification of the Constitution, many States elected their congressional representatives through at-large or "general ticket" elections. Such States typically sent single-party delegations to Congress. See E. Engstrom, Partisan Gerrymandering and the Construction of American Democracy 43–51 (2013). That meant that a party could garner nearly half of the vote statewide and wind up without any seats in the congressional delegation. The Whigs in Alabama suffered that fate in 1840: "their party garnered 43 percent of the statewide vote, yet did not receive a single seat." *Id.*, at 48. When Congress required single-member districts in the Apportionment Act of 1842, it was not out of a general sense of fairness, but instead a (mis)calculation by the Whigs that such a change would improve their electoral prospects. *Id.*, at 43–44.

Unable to claim that the Constitution requires proportional representation outright, plaintiffs inevitably ask the courts to make their own political judgment about how much representation particular political parties *deserve*—based on the votes of their supporters—and to rearrange the challenged districts to achieve that end. But federal courts are not equipped to apportion political power as a matter of fairness, nor is there any basis for concluding that they were authorized to do so. As Justice Scalia put it for the plurality in *Vieth*:

> "'Fairness' does not seem to us a judicially manageable standard. . . . Some criterion more solid and more demonstrably met than that seems to us necessary to enable the state legislatures to discern the limits of their districting discretion, to meaningfully constrain the discretion of the courts, and to win public acceptance for the courts' intrusion into a process that is the very foundation of democratic decision-making." 541 U. S., at 291.

The initial difficulty in settling on a "clear, manageable and politically neutral" test for fairness is that it is not even clear what fairness looks like in this context. There is a large measure of "unfairness" in any winner-take-all system. Fairness may mean a greater number of competitive districts. Such a claim seeks to undo packing and cracking so that supporters of the disadvantaged party have a better shot at electing their preferred candidates. But making as many districts as possible more competitive could be a recipe for disaster for the disadvantaged party. As Justice White has pointed out, "[i]f all or most of the districts are competitive . . . even a narrow statewide preference for either party would produce an overwhelming majority for the winning party in the state legislature." *Bandemer*, 478 U. S., at 130 (plurality opinion).

On the other hand, perhaps the ultimate objective of a "fairer" share of seats in the congressional delegation is most readily achieved by yielding to the gravitational pull of proportionality and engaging in cracking and packing, to ensure each party its "appropriate" share of "safe" seats. See *id.*, at 130–131 ("To draw district lines to maximize the representation of each major party would require creating as many safe seats for each party as the demographic and predicted political characteristics of the State would permit.");

Gaffney, 412 U. S., at 735–738. Such an approach, however, comes at the expense of competitive districts and of individuals in districts allocated to the opposing party.

Or perhaps fairness should be measured by adherence to "traditional" districting criteria, such as maintaining political subdivisions, keeping communities of interest together, and protecting incumbents. See Brief for Bipartisan Group of Current and Former Members of the House of Representatives as *Amici Curiae*; Brief for Professor Wesley Pegden et al. as *Amici Curiae* in No. 18–422. But protecting incumbents, for example, enshrines a particular partisan distribution. And the "natural political geography" of a State—such as the fact that urban electoral districts are often dominated by one political party—can itself lead to inherently packed districts. As Justice Kennedy has explained, traditional criteria such as compactness and contiguity "cannot promise political neutrality when used as the basis for relief. Instead, it seems, a decision under these standards would unavoidably have significant political effect, whether intended or not." *Vieth*, 541 U. S., at 308–309 (opinion concurring in judgment). See *id.*, at 298 (plurality opinion) ("[P]acking and cracking, whether intentional or no, are quite consistent with adherence to compactness and respect for political subdivision lines").

Deciding among just these different visions of fairness (you can imagine many others) poses basic questions that are political, not legal. There are no legal standards discernible in the Constitution for making such judgments, let alone limited and precise standards that are clear, manageable, and politically neutral. Any judicial decision on what is "fair" in this context would be an "unmoored determination" of the sort characteristic of a political question beyond the competence of the federal courts. *Zivotofsky* v. *Clinton*, 566 U. S. 189, 196 (2012).

And it is only after determining how to define fairness that you can even begin to answer the determinative question: "How much is too much?" At what point does permissible partisanship become unconstitutional? If compliance with traditional districting criteria is the fairness touchstone, for example, how much deviation from those criteria is constitutionally acceptable and how should mapdrawers prioritize competing criteria? Should a court "reverse gerrymander" other parts of a State to counteract "natural" gerrymandering caused, for example, by the urban concentration of one party? If a districting plan protected half of the incumbents but redistricted the rest into head to head races, would that be constitutional? A court would have to rank the relative importance of those traditional criteria and weigh how much deviation from each to allow.

If a court instead focused on the respective number of seats in the legislature, it would have to decide the ideal number of seats for each party and determine at what point deviation from that balance went too far. If a 5–3 allocation corresponds most closely to statewide vote totals, is a 6–2 allocation permissible, given that legislatures have the authority to engage in a certain degree of partisan gerrymandering? Which seats should be packed and which cracked? Or if the goal is as many competitive districts as possible, how close does the split need to be for the district to be considered competitive? Presumably not all districts could qualify, so how to choose? Even assuming the court knew which version of fairness to be looking for, there are no discernible and manageable standards for deciding whether there has been a violation. The questions are "unguided and ill suited to the development of judicial standards," *Vieth*, 541 U. S., at 296 (plurality opinion), and "results from one gerrymandering case to the next would likely be disparate and inconsistent," *id.*, at 308 (opinion of Kennedy, J.).

[A discussion of how the standards for one-person-one-vote and racial gerrymandering cases are relatively easy to administer compared to partisan gerrymandering cases, along with the rejection of tests proposed by the appellees and the dissent, has been omitted.]

V

Excessive partisanship in districting leads to results that reasonably seem unjust. But the fact that such gerrymandering is "incompatible with democratic principles," *Arizona State Legislature*, 576 U. S., at ___ (slip op., at 1), does not mean that the solution lies with the federal judiciary. We conclude that partisan gerrymandering claims present political questions beyond the reach of the federal courts. Federal judges have no license to reallocate political power between the two major political parties, with no plausible grant of authority in the Constitution, and no legal standards to limit and direct their decisions. "[J]udicial action must be governed by *standard*, by *rule*," and must be "principled, rational, and based upon reasoned distinctions" found in the Constitution or laws. *Vieth*, 541 U. S., at 278, 279 (plurality opinion). Judicial review of partisan gerrymandering does not meet those basic requirements.

Today the dissent essentially embraces the argument that the Court unanimously rejected in *Gill*: "this Court *can* address the problem of partisan gerrymandering because it *must*." 585 U. S., at ___ (slip op., at 12). That is not the test of our authority under the Constitution; that document instead "confines the federal courts to a properly judicial role." *Town of Chester* v. *Laroe Estates, Inc.*, 581 U. S. ___, ___ (2017) (slip op., at 4).

What the appellees and dissent seek is an unprecedented expansion of judicial power. We have never struck down a partisan gerrymander as unconstitutional—despite various requests over the past 45 years. The expansion of judicial authority would not be into just any area of controversy, but into one of the most intensely partisan aspects of American political life. That intervention would be unlimited in scope and duration—it would recur over and over again around the country with each new round of districting, for state as well as federal representatives. Consideration of the impact of today's ruling on democratic principles cannot ignore the effect of the unelected and politically unaccountable branch of the Federal Government assuming such an extraordinary and unprecedented role. See *post*, at 32–33.

Our conclusion does not condone excessive partisan gerrymandering. Nor does our conclusion condemn complaints about districting to echo into a void. The States, for example, are actively addressing the issue on a number of fronts. In 2015, the Supreme Court of Florida struck down that State's congressional districting plan as a violation of the Fair Districts Amendment to the Florida Constitution. *League of Women Voters of Florida* v. *Detzner*, 172 So. 3d 363 (2015). The dissent wonders why we can't do the same. See *post*, at 31. The answer is that there is no "Fair Districts Amendment" to the Federal Constitution. Provisions in state statutes and state constitutions can provide standards and guidance for state courts to apply. (We do not understand how the dissent can maintain that a provision saying that no districting plan "shall be drawn with the intent to favor or disfavor a political party" provides little guidance on the question. See *post*, at 31, n. 6.) Indeed, numerous other States are restricting partisan considerations in districting through legislation. One way they are doing so is by placing power to draw electoral districts in the hands of independent commissions. . . .

Other States have mandated at least some of the traditional districting criteria for their mapmakers. Some have outright prohibited partisan favoritism in redistricting. . . .

As noted, the Framers gave Congress the power to do something about partisan gerrymandering in the Elections Clause. . . .

We express no view on any of these pending proposals. We simply note that the avenue for reform established by the Framers, and used by Congress in the past, remains open.

***

No one can accuse this Court of having a crabbed view of the reach of its competence. But we have no commission to allocate political power and influence in the absence of a constitutional directive or legal standards to guide us in the exercise of such authority. "It is emphatically the province and duty of the judicial department to say what the law is." *Marbury* v. *Madison*, 1 Cranch, at 177. In this rare circumstance, that means our duty is to say "this is not law."

The judgments of the United States District Court for the Middle District of North Carolina and the United States District Court for the District of Maryland are vacated, and the cases are remanded with instructions to dismiss for lack of jurisdiction.

It is so ordered.

JUSTICE KAGAN, with whom JUSTICE GINSBURG, JUSTICE BREYER, and JUSTICE SOTOMAYOR join, dissenting.

For the first time ever, this Court refuses to remedy a constitutional violation because it thinks the task beyond judicial capabilities.

And not just any constitutional violation. The partisan gerrymanders in these cases deprived citizens of the most fundamental of their constitutional rights: the rights to participate equally in the political process, to join with others to advance political beliefs, and to choose their political representatives. In so doing, the partisan gerrymanders here debased and dishonored our democracy, turning upside-down the core American idea that all governmental power derives from the people. These gerrymanders enabled politicians to entrench themselves in office as against voters' preferences. They promoted partisanship above respect for the popular will. They encouraged a politics of polarization and dysfunction. If left unchecked, gerrymanders like the ones here may irreparably damage our system of government.

And checking them is *not* beyond the courts. The majority's abdication comes just when courts across the country, including those below, have coalesced around manageable judicial standards to resolve partisan gerrymandering claims. Those standards satisfy the majority's own benchmarks. They do not require—indeed, they do not permit—courts to rely on their own ideas of electoral fairness, whether proportional representation or any other. And they limit courts to correcting only egregious gerrymanders, so judges do not become omnipresent players in the political process. But yes, the standards used here do allow—as well they should—judicial intervention in the worst-of-the-worst cases of democratic subversion, causing blatant constitutional harms. In other words, they allow courts to undo partisan gerrymanders of the kind we face today from North Carolina and Maryland. In giving such gerrymanders a pass from judicial review, the majority goes tragically wrong.

[The body of the dissent has been omitted.]

Of all times to abandon the Court's duty to declare the law, this was not the one. The practices challenged in these cases imperil our system of government. Part of the Court's role in that system is to defend its foundations. None is more important than free and fair elections. With respect but deep sadness, I dissent.

SOURCE: Supreme Court of the United States. *Rucho v. Common Cause.* 588 U.S. __ 2019. https://www .supremecourt.gov/opinions/18pdf/18-422_9oll.pdf.

OTHER HISTORIC DOCUMENTS OF INTEREST

FROM PREVIOUS *HISTORIC DOCUMENTS*

- Federal Court and Supreme Court Issue Rulings on Gerrymandering, *2018,* p. 13
- Supreme Court Rules on Gerrymandering, *2017,* p. 293

July

Boris Johnson Remarks on Election and Brexit Negotiations

JULY 24, AUGUST 19, OCTOBER 17, AND DECEMBER 13, 2019

Following Prime Minister Theresa May's resignation in the spring, the United Kingdom's (UK) Conservative Party chose former London mayor and prominent pro-Brexit campaigner Boris Johnson as its new leader, installing him at 10 Downing Street in late July. Johnson pledged to deliver Brexit by the extended October 31 deadline granted by the European Union (EU), with or without an approved withdrawal agreement. The projected economic impact of a "no deal" Brexit concerned many opposition lawmakers, who pushed Johnson to request more time from the EU and in some cases called for a second Brexit referendum. Through political maneuvering—including a suspension of parliament and call for snap elections—and continued negotiations with the EU, Johnson was able to secure both a commanding Conservative majority in parliament and an amended withdrawal agreement that gained lawmakers' approval in early 2020.

CONSERVATIVE PARTY SELECTS A NEW LEADER

Since May resigned midterm, the Conservative Party was able to choose a new leader—and thus a new prime minister—without holding new elections. Of the eight candidates seeking to replace May, Johnson emerged as a clear front-runner early in the campaign since he had secured support from different factions within the party. Johnson ran on a campaign promising to "deliver Brexit, unite the country and defeat Jeremy Corbyn," the Labour Party leader. Five rounds of voting among Conservative members of parliament (MPs) winnowed the list of candidates down to Johnson and Foreign Secretary Jeremy Hunt. On July 23, roughly 87 percent of the party's nearly 160,000 dues-paying members had the opportunity to cast their ballot for one of the two candidates. Johnson emerged victorious, winning about 66 percent of the vote.

Opposition lawmakers—particularly Corbyn—were critical of the selection process, noting that Johnson was chosen by "fewer than 100,000" party members to lead a country of approximately 66 million people. "The people of our country should decide who becomes the prime minister in a general election," Corbyn said. Several cabinet ministers and senior government officials resigned shortly before and immediately following Johnson's selection, stating they could not work with the prime minister because they did not agree with his approach to Brexit. Notable departures included Education Minister Anne Milton, Chancellor of the Exchequer Philip Hammond, Secretary of State for Justice David Gauke, Foreign Office Minister Alan Duncan, and International Development Secretary Rory Stewart. Britons also appeared divided on Johnson. A survey conducted by polling firm YouGov days before the party vote found that 58 percent of respondents had a negative opinion of Johnson. (A similar YouGov survey found that 36 percent of Britons viewed May unfavorably when she took office in August 2016.) Others congratulated

Johnson, including May, who offered her "full support from the backbenches." Hunt said he was "very disappointed" in the outcome but that Johnson would do "a great job." The European Commission's Brexit negotiator, Michel Barnier, said he looked forward to working with Johnson "to facilitate the ratification of the withdrawal agreement and achieve an orderly Brexit."

In a series of formal events on July 24, May held her final session of prime minister's questions in the House of Commons before heading to Buckingham Palace to deliver her resignation to Queen Elizabeth II. Johnson arrived at the palace minutes later for an audience with the queen, who invited him to form a government. Johnson then gave his first speech as prime minister in front of 10 Downing Street. "There are pessimists at home and abroad who think that after three years of indecision that this country has become a prisoner to the old arguments of 2016 and that in this home of democracy, we are incapable of honouring a basic democratic mandate," Johnson said. "The people who bet against Britain are going to lose their shirts," he went on, declaring that "we are going to fulfil the repeated promises of parliament to the people and come out of the EU on October 31, no ifs or buts."

JOHNSON PUSHES FOR ALTERNATIVE TO CONTROVERSIAL "BACKSTOP"

Throughout his campaign to become the new prime minister, Johnson repeatedly said delivering Brexit by October 31 was "do or die," meaning the UK would leave the EU without a deal if an agreement could not be reached by the deadline. Johnson also declared the withdrawal agreement negotiated by May "dead" since it was rejected by parliament three times, and he said he would seek a new and better deal that addressed MPs' concerns.

Chief among those concerns was the proposed "backstop" provision, which would prevent the need for post-Brexit border controls between Northern Ireland (part of the UK) and Ireland (an EU member) and fulfill the British government's legal obligations under the 1998 Good Friday Agreement. (The agreement guarantees the continued free flow of people and goods in Ireland.) The backstop established a transition period during which the UK and EU would work on a free trade agreement that negated the need for Irish checkpoints. If an agreement was not reached by the end of the transition period, the entire UK would temporarily remain in the EU customs union until a deal was made. The provision was controversial because the EU did not make a legally binding commitment to the backstop's temporary nature; therefore, pro-Brexit lawmakers were concerned the EU could effectively keep the UK in its customs union indefinitely. May tried unsuccessfully to assuage these concerns by negotiating a legally binding dispute mechanism that could be triggered if the EU did not make a good faith effort to negotiate a permanent solution.

Johnson's government took a different approach. In an August 19 letter to European Council president Donald Tusk, Johnson proposed replacing the backstop with "alternative arrangements" for "managing the customs and regulatory differences contingent on Brexit." Johnson declared the backstop to be "anti-democratic and inconsistent with the sovereignty of the UK as a state" because of its potential to lock it into the EU customs union indefinitely. Johnson further noted "the simple political reality that it has three times been rejected by the House of Commons," adding, "the truth is that it is simply unviable."

Tusk rejected Johnson's proposal, saying the backstop would avoid "a hard border" in Ireland. "Those against the backstop and not proposing realistic alternatives in fact support re-establishing a border," he said, "even if they do not admit it." A statement from the European Commission also noted that Johnson did "not provide a legal operational solution" to replace the backstop and did "not set out what any alternative arrangements could be." A separate document distributed by the EU to member states asserted that many claims in Johnson's letter were "incorrect" or "misleading."

Johnson blamed efforts by some Conservative MPs to prevent a no-deal Brexit for Tusk's rejection of his backstop proposal, claiming the lawmakers had undermined his negotiating position. (Concerns about the economic impacts of a no-deal Brexit—which were projected to include food, fuel, and medicine shortages, among other issues—were leading factors in lawmakers' opposition to a no-deal Brexit.) "As long as [EU officials] think there's a possibility that Parliament will block Brexit they are unlikely to be minded to make the concessions that we need," he said.

Suspended by Johnson, Parliament Forces Brexit Delay

On August 27, news broke that the Labour Party had agreed with other opposition lawmakers to pass a bill requiring Johnson to seek another extension from the EU if a Brexit deal had not been approved by October 31. Johnson, who continued to insist that a no-deal Brexit option had to be on the table as a bargaining chip, moved to undercut this strategy by asking the queen to suspend parliament. This would give lawmakers as little time as possible to force a delay or come up with an alternative to a no-deal Brexit. Lawmakers were due to return from August recess and resume session for the first two weeks of September, then take a three-week break for annual political party conferences before reconvening on October 9. But the queen granted Johnson's request, approving a suspension to begin between September 9 and September 12 and end on October 14. Labour's Corbyn decried the move as "reckless" and a "smash and grab on our democracy to force through a no deal." John Bercow, speaker of the House of Commons, called it a "constitutional outrage" with a "blindingly obvious" purpose of preventing parliament from debating Brexit and "performing its duty in shaping a course for the country."

Not to be outdone, the House of Commons voted on September 3 to take control of parliament's agenda, allowing them to propose legislation delaying Brexit without the government's approval. At the same time, Conservative MP Phillip Lee opted to quit the party and join the anti-Brexit Liberal Democrats, costing Johnson his working majority in parliament. In response, Johnson pledged to bring a motion calling for an early general election and threatened to expel any Conservative MPs who voted against the government. The next day, the House of Commons approved a bill requiring the government to request and accept a deadline extension from the EU if the UK could not agree on a withdrawal deal before October 31. The House of Lords passed the extension bill two days later. Meanwhile, Johnson failed to secure approval for a snap election from the required two-thirds of lawmakers. Johnson was later rebuked by the UK's Supreme Court, which declared his suspension of parliament unlawful on September 24. Parliament reconvened shortly thereafter.

Negotiations with the EU continued amid these political maneuvers, and Johnson and EU officials announced on October 17 that a revised withdrawal agreement had been reached. Under the new deal, Northern Ireland would remain within the UK's customs territory. It would be required to comply with European rules, regulations, and procedures for tariffs and would have to follow EU single market rules for industrial and agricultural products. Goods would be subject to customs checks as they passed between Britain and Northern Ireland, effectively establishing a soft border in the middle of the Irish Sea instead of a hard border with Ireland. Lawmakers in Northern Ireland would also get a say on whether to remain in the deal, via a vote held every two years. If officials decided to withdraw from the arrangement, EU trade rules would remain in place for two years while a new solution that avoided a hard border was negotiated. "This deal represents a very good deal both for the EU and for the UK," Johnson said. "And it's a reasonable, fair outcome." Tusk also endorsed the compromise agreement, noting it would allow the EU to avoid a hard border between Ireland and Northern Ireland while ensuring the integrity of the union's single market. "Today we have a deal, which allows us to avoid chaos and an atmosphere of conflict between the EU27 and the United Kingdom," he said. European Commission president Jean-Claude Juncker said the new deal was a "testament to the commitment and willingness of both sides to do what is best for EU and UK citizens." However, Northern Ireland's Democratic Unionist Party refused to support the agreement, saying it "drives a coach and horses through the professed sanctity" of the Good Friday Agreement and would harm the region's economy.

The House of Commons took up consideration of the new Brexit deal on October 19. Lawmakers moved to pass an amendment to the withdrawal agreement bill delaying its final approval until parliament had also passed the detailed implementation legislation required to enact it. Some expressed a concern that without this amendment, the government would try to rush the Brexit deal through without giving lawmakers sufficient time to scrutinize its terms. Some reports also hinted at concerns that hardline pro-Brexit lawmakers would try to block passage of implementing legislation, thereby forcing a no-deal withdrawal.

With the number of days to the October 31 deadline dwindling, Johnson appealed to the EU for another extension. While the EU considered the extension, the House of Commons voted 329–299 to approve the Brexit deal on its second reading, signaling agreement with its terms in principle, but also passed a motion extending the timeline for its further consideration beyond October 31. Johnson had proposed pushing the bill through the House of Commons in three days, threatening to scrap the deal entirely and demand new elections if lawmakers did not accept that timeline. Instead, Johnson opted to "pause" the agreement until the EU decided on an extension.

That decision came on October 28. Tusk announced the EU would grant the UK a "flextension" until January 31, 2020, which gave the UK the option to leave earlier—on December 1 or January 1—if parliament had approved a deal by then. The following day, Corbyn announced that the Labour Party would support Johnson's call for a new election. "I have consistently said that we are ready for an election and our support is subject to a 'no deal' Brexit being off the table," he said, reasoning that the new extension meant that "for the next three months, our condition of taking No Deal off the table has now been met."

CONSERVATIVES WIN BIG IN SNAP ELECTION

The Conservative Party won a decisive victory in the Brexit-focused election held on December 12, gaining forty-seven seats, and therefore a majority, in the House of Commons. The Labour Party was dealt a major blow, losing fifty-nine seats. "Getting Brexit done is now the irrefutable, irresistible, unarguable decision of the British people," Johnson said, adding that the election put to rest once and for all the idea of holding a second referendum on Brexit. Corbyn said that while he would remain an MP, he would not lead the party in future general election campaigns.

The House of Commons passed Johnson's Brexit deal on January 9 by a vote of 330–231. The House of Lords sought to amend the bill, but these changes were rejected by the lower chamber. The agreement was finally approved by both chambers on January 22 and received royal assent on January 23. The UK formally withdrew from the EU at 11:00 p.m. on January 31.

—Linda Grimm

Following is the text of Prime Minister Boris Johnson's first speech after assuming office on July 24, 2019; a letter sent by Johnson to European Council president Donald Tusk on August 19, 2019, requesting that the Irish backstop be removed from the Withdrawal Agreement; remarks by Tusk on October 17, 2019, about the European Council's endorsement of the revised Withdrawal Agreement; a press release issued by the European Commission on October 17, 2019, announcing its approval of the new Withdrawal Agreement; and remarks by Johnson on December 13, 2019, following the snap election.

DOCUMENT

Boris Johnson's First Speech as Prime Minister

July 24, 2019

Good afternoon.

I have just been to see Her Majesty the Queen who has invited me to form a government and I have accepted.

I pay tribute to the fortitude and patience of my predecessor and her deep sense of public service but in spite of all her efforts it has become clear that there are pessimists at home and abroad who think that after three years of indecision that this country has become a prisoner to the old arguments of 2016 and that in this home of democracy we are incapable of honouring a basic democratic mandate.

And so, I am standing before you today to tell you the British people that those critics are wrong.

The doubters, the doomsters, the gloomsters—they are going to get it wrong again.

The people who bet against Britain are going to lose their shirts because we are going to restore trust in our democracy and we are going to fulfil the repeated promises of parliament to the people and come out of the EU on October 31, no ifs or buts, and we will do a new deal, a better deal that will maximise the opportunities of Brexit while allowing us to develop a new and exciting partnership with the rest of Europe based on free trade and mutual support.

I have every confidence that in 99 days' time we will have cracked it, but you know what—we aren't going to wait 99 days because the British people have had enough of waiting.

The time has come to act, to take decisions, to give strong leadership and to change this country for the better, and though the Queen has just honoured me with this extraordinary office of state, my job is to serve you, the people, because if there is one point we politicians need to remember it is that the people are our bosses.

My job is to make your streets safer—and we are going to begin with another 20,000 police on the streets and we start recruiting forthwith.

My job is to make sure you don't have to wait 3 weeks to see your GP and we start work this week with 20 new hospital upgrades and ensuring that money for the NHS really does get to the front line.

My job is to protect you or your parents or grandparents from the fear of having to sell your home to pay for the costs of care and so I am announcing now—on the steps of Downing Street—that we will fix the crisis in social care once and for all with a clear plan we have prepared to give every older person the dignity and security they deserve.

My job is to make sure your kids get a superb education wherever they are in the country and that's why we have already announced that we are going to level up per pupil funding in primary and secondary schools and that is the work that begins immediately behind that black door and though I am today building a great team of men and women I will take personal responsibility for the change I want to see.

Never mind the backstop—the buck stops here.

And I will tell you something else about my job. It is to be Prime Minister of the whole United Kingdom, and that means uniting our country, answering at last the plea of the forgotten people, and the left behind towns by physically and literally renewing the ties that bind us together so that with safer streets and better education and fantastic new road and rail infrastructure and full fibre broadband we level up across Britain.

With higher wages, and a higher living wage, and higher productivity we close the opportunity gap, giving millions of young people the chance to own their own homes and giving business the confidence to invest across the UK. Because it is time we unleashed the productive power not just of London and the South East, but of every corner of England, Scotland, Wales and Northern Ireland, the awesome foursome that are incarnated in that red white and blue flag who together are so much more than the sum of their parts, and whose brand and political personality is admired and even loved around the world for our inventiveness, for our humour, for our universities, our scientists, our armed forces, our diplomacy, for the equalities on which we insist—whether race or gender or LGBT or the right of every girl in the world to 12 years of quality education, and for the values we stand for around the world.

Everyone knows the values that flag represents.

It stands for freedom and free speech and habeas corpus and the rule of law and above all it stands for democracy. And that is why we will come out of the EU on October 31 because in the end Brexit was a fundamental decision by the British people that they wanted their laws made by people that they can elect, and they can remove from office, and we must now respect that decision and create a new partnership with our European friends—as warm and as close and as affectionate as possible.

And the first step is to repeat unequivocally our guarantee to the 3.2 m EU nationals now living and working among us. And I say directly to you—thank you for your contribution to our society, thank you for your patience and I can assure you that under this government you will get the absolute certainty of the rights to live and remain.

And next I say to our friends in Ireland, and in Brussels and around the EU, I am convinced that we can do a deal without checks at the Irish border, because we refuse under any circumstances to have such checks and yet without that anti-democratic backstop and it is of course vital at the same time that we prepare for the remote possibility that

Brussels refuses any further to negotiate and we are forced to come out with no deal not because we want that outcome—of course not but because it is only common sense to prepare.

And let me stress that there is a vital sense in which those preparations cannot be wasted and that is because under any circumstances we will need to get ready at some point in the near future to come out of the EU customs union and out of regulatory control fully determined at last to take advantage of Brexit because that is the course on which this country is now set.

With high hearts and growing confidence we will now accelerate the work of getting ready, and the ports will be ready, and the banks will be ready, and the factories will be ready, and business will be ready, and the hospitals will be ready, and our amazing food and farming sector will be ready and waiting to continue selling ever more not just here but around the world.

And don't forget that in the event of a no deal outcome we will have the extra lubrication of the £39 bn.

And whatever deal we do we will prepare this autumn for an economic package to boost British business and to lengthen this country's lead as the number one destination in this continent for overseas investment and to all those who continue to prophesy disaster.

I say yes—there will be difficulties, though I believe that with energy and application they will be far less serious than some have claimed. But if there is one thing that has really sapped the confidence of business over the last three years, it is not the decisions we have taken, it is our refusal to take decisions.

And to all those who say we cannot be ready, I say do not underestimate this country.

Do not underestimate our powers of organisation and our determination, because we know the enormous strengths of this economy in life sciences, in tech, in academia, in music, the arts, culture, financial services.

It is here in Britain that we are using gene therapy, for the first time, to treat the most common form of blindness, here in Britain that we are leading the world in the battery technology that will help cut CO_2 and tackle climate change and produce green jobs for the next generation.

And as we prepare for a post-Brexit future it is time we looked not at the risks but at the opportunities that are upon us.

So let us begin work now to create freeports that will drive growth and thousands of high-skilled jobs in left behind areas.

Let's start now to liberate the UK's extraordinary bioscience sector from anti genetic modification rules and let's develop the blight-resistant crops that will feed the world.

Let's get going now on our own position navigation and timing satellite and earth observation systems—UK assets orbiting in space with all the long term strategic and commercial benefits for this country.

Let's change the tax rules to provide extra incentives to invest in capital and research.

And let's promote the welfare of animals that has always been so close to the hearts of the British people.

And yes, let's start now on those free trade deals, because it is free trade that has done more than anything else to lift billions out of poverty.

All this and more we can do now and only now, at this extraordinary moment in our history, and after three years of unfounded self-doubt it is time to change the record, to recover our natural and historic role as an enterprising, outward-looking and truly global Britain, generous in temper and engaged with the world.

No one in the last few centuries has succeeded in betting against the pluck and nerve and ambition of this country. They will not succeed today.

We in this government will work flat out to give this country the leadership it deserves, and that work begins now.

Thank you very much.

SOURCE: UK Prime Minister's Office. "Boris Johnson's First Speech as Prime Minister: 24 July 2019." July 24, 2019. https://www.gov.uk/government/speeches/boris-johnsons-first-speech-as-prime-minister-24-july-2019.

Prime Minister Johnson Requests Removal of Irish Backstop

August 19, 2019

Dear Donald,

The date of the United Kingdom's (UK) exit from the European Union (EU), 31 October, is fast approaching. I very much hope that we will be leaving with a deal. You have my personal commitment that this Government will work with energy and determination to achieve an agreement. That is our highest priority.

With that in mind, I wanted to set out our position on some key aspects of our approach, and in particular on the so-called "backstop" in the Protocol on Ireland/Northern Ireland in the Withdrawal Agreement. Before I do so, let me make three wider points.

First, Ireland is the UK's closest neighbour, with whom we will continue to share uniquely deep ties, a land border, the Common Travel Area, and much else besides. We remain, as we have always been, committed to working with Ireland on the peace process, and to furthering Northern Ireland's security and prosperity. We recognise the unique challenges the outcome of the referendum poses for Ireland, and want to find solutions to the border which work for all.

Second, and flowing from the first, I want to re-emphasise the commitment of this Government to peace in Northern Ireland. The Belfast (Good Friday) Agreement, as well as being an agreement between the UK and Ireland, is a historic agreement between two traditions in Northern Ireland, and we are unconditionally committed to the spirit and letter of our obligations under it in all circumstances—whether there is a deal with the EU or not.

Third, and for the avoidance of any doubt, the UK remains committed to maintaining the Common Travel Area, to upholding the rights of the people of Northern Ireland, to ongoing North–South cooperation, and to retaining the benefits of the Single Electricity Market.

The changes we seek relate primarily to the backstop. The problems with the backstop run much deeper than the simple political reality that it has three times been rejected by the House of Commons. The truth is that it is simply unviable, for these three reasons.

First, it is anti-democratic and inconsistent with the sovereignty of the UK as a state.

The backstop locks the UK, potentially indefinitely, into an international treaty which will bind us into a customs union and which applies large areas of single market legislation in Northern Ireland. It places a substantial regulatory border, rooted in that treaty, between Northern Ireland and Great Britain. The treaty provides no sovereign means of exiting unilaterally and affords the people of Northern Ireland no influence over the legislation which applies to them. That is why the backstop is anti-democratic.

Second, it is inconsistent with the UK's desired final destination for a sustainable long-term relationship with the EU. When the UK leaves the EU and after any transition period, we will leave the single market and the customs union. Although we will remain committed to world-class environmental, product and labour standards, the laws and regulations to deliver them will potentially diverge from those of the EU. That is the point of our exit and our ability to enable this is central to our future democracy.

The backstop is inconsistent with this ambition. By requiring continued membership of the customs union and applying many single market rules in Northern Ireland, it presents the whole of the UK with the choice of remaining in a customs union and aligned with those rules, or of seeing Northern Ireland gradually detached from the UK economy across a very broad range of areas. Both of those outcomes are unacceptable to the British Government.

Accordingly, as I said in Parliament on 25 July, we cannot continue to endorse the specific commitment, in paragraph 49 of the December 2017 Joint Report, to "full alignment" with wide areas of the single market and the customs union. That cannot be the basis for the future relationship and it is not a basis for the sound governance of Northern Ireland.

Third, it has become increasingly clear that the backstop risks weakening the delicate balance embodied in the Belfast (Good Friday) Agreement. The historic compromise in Northern Ireland is based upon a carefully negotiated balance between both traditions in Northern Ireland, grounded in agreement, consent, and respect for minority rights. While I appreciate the laudable intentions with which the backstop was designed, by removing control of such large areas of the commercial and economic life of Northern Ireland to an external body over which the people of Northern Ireland have no democratic control, this balance risks being undermined.

The Belfast (Good Friday) Agreement neither depends upon nor requires a particular customs or regulatory regime. The broader commitments in the Agreement, including to parity of esteem, partnership, democracy, and to peaceful means of resolving differences, can best be met if we explore solutions other than the backstop.

Next Steps

For these three reasons the backstop cannot form part of an agreed Withdrawal Agreement. That is a fact we must both acknowledge. I believe the task before us is to strive to find other solutions, and I believe an agreement is possible.

We must, first, ensure there is no return to a hard border. One of the many dividends of peace in Northern Ireland and the vast reduction of the security threat is the disappearance of a visible border. This is something to be celebrated and preserved. This Government will not put in place infrastructure, checks, or controls at the border between Northern Ireland and Ireland. We would be happy to accept a legally binding commitment to this effect and hope that the EU would do likewise.

We must also respect the aim to find "flexible and creative" solutions to the unique circumstances on the island of Ireland. That means that alternative ways of managing the customs and regulatory differences contingent on Brexit must be explored. The reality is that there are already two separate legal, political, economic, and monetary jurisdictions on the island of Ireland. This system is already administered without contention and with an open border.

The UK and the EU have already agreed that "alternative arrangements" can be part of the solution. Accordingly:

- I propose that the backstop should be replaced with a commitment to put in place such arrangements as far as possible before the end of the transition period, as part of the future relationship.

- I also recognise that there will need to be a degree of confidence about what would happen if these arrangements were not all fully in place at the end of that period. We are ready to look constructively and flexibly at what commitments might help, consistent of course with the principles set out in this letter.

Time is very short. But the UK is ready to move quickly, and, given the degree of common ground already, I hope that the EU will be ready to do likewise. I am equally confident that our Parliament would be able to act rapidly if we were able to reach a satisfactory agreement which did not contain the "backstop": indeed it has already demonstrated that there is a majority for an agreement on these lines.

I believe that a solution on the lines we are proposing will be more stable, more long lasting, and more consistent with the overarching framework of the Belfast (Good Friday) Agreement which has been decisive for peace in Northern Ireland. I hope that the EU can work energetically in this direction and for my part I am determined to do so.

I am copying this letter to the President of the European Commission and members of the European Council.

Yours ever,
Boris

Source: UK Prime Minister's Office. "PM Letter to His Excellency Mr. Donald Tusk." August 19, 2019. https://assets.publishing.service.gov.uk/government/uploads/system/uploads/attachment_data/file/826166/20190819_PM_letter_to_His_Excellency_Mr_Donald_Tusk.pdf.

European Council President Tusk Remarks on Revised Withdrawal Agreement

October 17, 2019

We have concluded a discussion among the leaders about the Brexit deal that our negotiator agreed with the UK government earlier today. First of all, many thanks to Michel Barnier and his team for your outstanding work. The European Council endorsed this deal and it looks like we are very close to the final stretch. Why has a deal that was impossible yesterday, become possible today?

Firstly, the new version of the deal has been positively assessed by Ireland. I've said from the beginning that we would always stand behind Ireland, and not force a deal unfavourable to Dublin.

Secondly, the deal has been positively assessed by the European Commission. This gives us certainty that it is favourable and safe for the citizens of the European Union.

The key change in comparison with the earlier version of the deal is Prime Minister Johnson's acceptance to have customs checks at the points of entry into Northern Ireland. This compromise will allow us to avoid border checks between Ireland and Northern Ireland, and will ensure the integrity of the Single Market.

The reality is that today we have a deal, which allows us to avoid chaos and an atmosphere of conflict between the EU27 and the United Kingdom. Therefore, the European Council invited the Commission, the European Parliament and the Council to ensure that this agreement can enter into force on the 1st of November 2019. Now we are all waiting for the votes in both Parliaments.

On a more personal note, what I feel today is sadness. Because in my heart, I will always be a Remainer. And I hope that if our British friends decide to return one day, our door will always be open.

SOURCE: European Council. "Remarks by President Donald Tusk after the Meeting of the European Council (Art. 50) on 17 October 2019." October 17, 2019. https://www.consilium.europa.eu/en/press/press-releases/2019/10/17/remarks-by-president-donald-tusk-after-the-meeting-of-the-european-council-art-50-on-17-october-2019.

European Commission Recommends Endorsement of New Brexit Deal

October 17, 2019

The European Commission has today recommended the European Council (Article 50) to endorse the agreement reached at negotiator level on the Withdrawal Agreement, including a revised Protocol on Ireland / Northern Ireland, and approve a revised Political Declaration on the framework of the future EU–UK relationship. The Commission also recommends that the European Parliament give its consent to this agreement. This follows a series of intensive negotiations between the European Commission and UK negotiators over the past few days.

Jean-Claude Juncker, President of the European Commission, said: "This agreement is a fair compromise between the EU and the UK. It is testament to the commitment and willingness of both sides to do what is best for EU and UK citizens. We now have a newly agreed Protocol that protects peace and stability on the island of Ireland and fully protects our Single Market. I hope that we can now bring this over the line and provide the certainty our citizens and businesses so deserve."

Michel Barnier, the European Commission's Chief Negotiator, said: "We had difficult discussions over the past days. We have managed to find solutions that fully respect the integrity of the Single Market. We created a new and legally operative solution to avoid a hard border, and protect peace and stability on the island of Ireland. It is a solution that works for the EU, for the UK and for people and businesses in Northern Ireland."

The revised Protocol provides a legally operational solution that avoids a hard border on the island of Ireland, protects the all-island economy and the Good Friday (Belfast) Agreement in all its dimensions and safeguards the integrity of the Single Market. This solution responds to the unique circumstances on the island of Ireland with the aim of protecting peace and stability.

All other elements of the Withdrawal Agreement remain unchanged in substance, as per the agreement reached on 14 November 2018. The Withdrawal Agreement brings legal certainty where the UK's withdrawal from the EU created uncertainty: citizens' rights, the financial settlement, a transition period at least until the end of 2020, governance, Protocols on Gibraltar and Cyprus, as well as a range of other separation issues.

The revised Withdrawal Agreement

In terms of regulations, Northern Ireland will remain aligned to a limited set of rules related to the EU's Single Market in order to avoid a hard border: legislation on goods, sanitary rules for veterinary controls ("SPS rules"), rules on agricultural production/ marketing, VAT and excise in respect of goods, and state aid rules.

In terms of customs, the EU–UK Single Customs Territory, as agreed in November 2018, has been removed from the Protocol on Ireland / Northern Ireland, at the request of the current UK government. EU and UK negotiators have now found a new way to achieve the goal of avoiding a customs border on the island of Ireland, while at the same time ensuring Northern Ireland remains part of the UK's customs territory. This agreement fully protects the integrity of the EU's Single Market and Customs Union, and avoids any regulatory and customs checks at the border between Ireland and Northern Ireland.

Finally, the EU and the UK have agreed to create a new mechanism on 'consent', which will give the Members of the Northern Ireland Assembly a decisive voice on the long-term application of relevant EU law in Northern Ireland. The Commission has been in close contact with the Irish government on this point.

The revised Political Declaration

The main change in the Political Declaration relates to the future EU–UK economic relationship where the current UK government has opted for a model based on a Free Trade Agreement (FTA). The Political Declaration provides for an ambitious FTA with zero tariffs and quotas between the EU and the UK. It states that robust commitments on a level playing field should ensure open and fair competition. The precise nature of commitments will be commensurate with the ambition of the future relationship and take into account the economic connectedness and geographic proximity of the UK.

Next steps

It is for the European Council (Article 50) to endorse the revised Withdrawal Agreement in its entirety, as well as approve the revised Political Declaration on the framework of the future relationship.

Before the Withdrawal Agreement can enter into force, it needs to be ratified by the EU and the UK. For the EU, the Council of the European Union must authorise the signature of the Withdrawal Agreement, before sending it to the European Parliament for its consent. The United Kingdom must ratify the agreement according to its own constitutional arrangements.

SOURCE: European Commission. "Brexit: European Commission Recommends the European Council (Article 50) to Endorse the Agreement Reached on the Revised Protocol on Ireland/Northern Ireland and Revised Political Declaration." October 17, 2019. https://ec.europa.eu/commission/presscorner/detail/en/ip_19_6120.

Prime Minister Statement on Election Outcome and Future of Brexit

December 13, 2019

This morning I went to Buckingham Palace and I am forming a new government.

And on Monday MPs will arrive at Westminster to form a new parliament and I am proud to say that members of our new one nation government—a people's government—will set out from constituencies that have never returned a Conservative MP for 100 years.

And yes, they will have an overwhelming mandate, from this election, to get Brexit done, and we will honour that mandate by Jan 31.

And so in this moment of national resolution I want to speak directly to those who made it possible, and to all those who voted for us, for the first time, all those whose pencils may have wavered over the ballot, and who heard the voices of their parents and their grandparents whispering anxiously in their ears. I say thank you for the trust you have placed in us and in me and we will work round the clock to repay your trust and to deliver on your priorities with a parliament that works for you.

And then I want to speak also to those who did not vote for us or for me and who wanted and perhaps still want to remain in the EU.

And I want you to know that we in this one nation conservative government will never ignore your good and positive feelings—of warmth and sympathy towards the other nations of Europe because now is the moment—precisely as we leave the EU—to let those natural feelings find renewed expression in building a new partnership, which is one of the great projects for next year and as we work together with the EU as friends and sovereign equals in tackling climate change and terrorism, in building academic and scientific cooperation, redoubling our trading relationship.

I frankly urge everyone on either side of what after three and a half years after all an increasingly arid argument I urge everyone to find closure and to let the healing begin because I believe, in fact I know, because I have heard it loud and clear from every corner of the country that the overwhelming priority of the British people now is that we should focus above all on the NHS, that simple and beautiful idea that represents the best of our country with the biggest ever cash boost, 50,000 more nurses, 40 new hospitals as well as providing better schools, safer streets.

And in the next few weeks and months we will be bringing forward proposals to transform this country with better infrastructure, better education, better technology.

And if you ask yourselves what is this new government going to do, what is he going to do with his extraordinary majority, I will tell you that is what we are going to do we are going to unite and level up—unite and level up, bringing together the whole of this incredible United Kingdom, England, Scotland, Wales, Northern Ireland together, taking us forward unleashing the potential of the whole country delivering opportunity across the entire nation.

And since I know that after five weeks frankly of electioneering this country deserves a break from wrangling, a break from politics, and a permanent break from talking about Brexit, I want everyone to go about their Christmas preparations happy and secure in the knowledge that here in this people's government the work is now being stepped up to make 2020 a year of prosperity and growth and hope and to deliver a Parliament that works for the people.

Thank you all very much and happy Christmas.

SOURCE: UK Prime Minister's Office. "PM Statement in Downing Street: 13 December 2019." December 13, 2019. https://www.gov.uk/government/speeches/pm-statement-in-downing-street-13-december-2019.

OTHER HISTORIC DOCUMENTS OF INTEREST

FROM THIS VOLUME

FROM PREVIOUS *HISTORIC DOCUMENTS*

Federal Reserve Cuts Interest Rate

JULY 31, SEPTEMBER 18, AND OCTOBER 30, 2019

In July, September, and October 2019, the Federal Reserve Board of Governors Federal Open Market Committee (FOMC) voted to cut its benchmark interest rate. The July reduction was the first since December 2008, when the Fed attempted to restart economic growth during the recession. While drawing criticism from President Donald Trump, who sought more aggressive rate cuts, Federal Reserve chair Jay Powell wanted to avoid panic by saying that the economy was still strong, but the FOMC wanted flexibility in case it needed to respond to stalled growth in the near future.

FEDS CONSIDER ACTION TO MAINTAIN RECORD-SETTING ECONOMY

The Federal Reserve's primary role is to maintain economic stability by ensuring maximum employment and stable prices. To do this, it raises and lowers the federal funds rate, which is the interest rate banks charge when lending to another banking institution. This cost is then passed on to consumers through both the interest rates they pay on financial instruments such as loans but also the return they receive on savings and investments.

During the 2007–2009 recession, the FOMC decided to cut the benchmark short-term interest rate to near zero, an unprecedented move intended to slowly boost economic growth by encouraging banks to expand lending. It was not until 2015 that the FOMC voted to begin gradually raising interest rates, an indication that the economy had regained much of its strength lost during the recession. Rate hikes continued through December 2018, when the target rate reached a range of 2.25 percent to 2.5 percent, the highest level since 2008.

The U.S. economy was strong throughout most of 2019. Stocks were at record highs and unemployment was near an all-time low at 3.5 percent by December. Based on early Bureau of Economic Analysis estimates, gross domestic product (GDP) rose 2.3 percent in 2019, compared to 2.9 percent in 2018. Economic analysts anticipated the slowdown because of weakening global markets and uncertainty surrounding trade. Inflation was also persistently sluggish, below the 2 percent target the Fed set in 2012, and slow price gains were making it difficult for employers to raise wages.

To hasten economic expansion, President Trump suggested that the Fed should drastically reduce the federal funds rate, or even enact a negative rate, the latter of which Powell said was "not at the top of the list" of FOMC considerations. "The Federal Reserve should get our interest rates down to ZERO, or less, and we should then start to refinance our debt. . . . The USA should always be paying the lowest rate. No Inflation!" Trump tweeted. According to the president, if the target rate were lower, growth would be well above 4 percent. The president frequently criticized Powell (whom he nominated to lead the Federal Reserve Board of Governors in 2017) and the Federal Reserve as a whole, alternately calling them "boneheads," "crazy," and the "greatest threat" to U.S. economic growth. Powell has maintained that the FOMC acts without regard for political considerations or pressure from national leaders.

July Anticipated Interest Rate Cut

The July 31, 2019, announcement that the Federal Reserve voted to reduce its benchmark rate to a range of 2 percent to 2.25 percent was widely expected by economists. Although consumer spending was strong and the stock market continued to reach record highs, business investment had weakened, manufacturing was slowing, and fears were growing over a global economic slowdown precipitated on trade wars, China's weakening economy, and political turmoil in Europe and South America. The FOMC minutes note, "Members who voted for the policy action sought to better position the overall stance of policy to help counter the effects on the outlook of weak global growth and trade policy uncertainty, insure against any further downside risks from those sources, and promote a faster return of inflation" to the 2 percent target. Two of the ten FOMC members voted against the rate cut: Boston Federal Reserve president Eric Rosengren and Kansas City Federal Reserve president Esther George, both of whom indicated a belief that the rate should remain unchanged.

During a press conference after the FOMC announcement, Powell called the cut an insurance policy against any dips in the economy. "There is really no reason why the expansion can't keep going," and "there's no sector that's booming and therefore might bust," Powell said. In its statement, the FOMC explained the decision to cut the rate "supports the Committee's view that sustained expansion of economy activity, strong labor market conditions, and inflation near the Committee's symmetric 2 percent objective are the most likely outcomes, but uncertainties about this outlook remain." The committee left the door open for additional 2019 rate cuts, noting in its statement that "it will continue to monitor the implications of incoming information for the economic outlook" before making any decisions. But Powell cautioned in his press conference that the July decision to raise rates would not mark "the beginning of a long series of rate cuts."

At its July meeting, the FOMC also decided to stop selling its $3.8 trillion in certain assets earlier than anticipated in a bid to further ease the economy and guard against a downturn. A majority of those funds were left over from the 2007–2009 recession when the Fed bought Treasury bonds and mortgage-backed securities to help keep interest rates low.

The rate cut, the first in more than a decade, followed years of rate increases intended to stop the economy from growing at an unsustainable rate that could lead to recession. Despite economists and investors anticipating the cut, the stock market reacted negatively to the FOMC news. The Dow closed 333.75 points—or 1.2 percent—lower, and the S&P 500 and Nasdaq both lost more than 1 percent of their value. Some analysts cited Powell's uncertainty over future rate increases as a possible reason for the market response.

Trump said that the cuts should have been more aggressive. "What the Market wanted to hear from Jay Powell and the Federal Reserve was that this was the beginning of a lengthy and aggressive rate-cutting cycle that would keep pace with China, The European Union and other countries around the world," the president tweeted. "As usual, Powell let us down, but at least he is ending quantitative tightening, which shouldn't have started in the first place—no inflation. We are winning anyway, but I am certainly not getting much help from the Federal Reserve!" he added.

Additional Rate Cuts in September and October

At both its September and October meetings, the FOMC again voted to cut the benchmark rate by another 25 basis points, first in September to a range of 1.75 percent to 2 percent, and then in October to a range of 1.50 percent to 1.75 percent.

In his September remarks after the official announcement, Powell again stressed that the economy was strong and unemployment was low but that the committee felt the cuts were necessary "to help keep the U.S. economy strong in the face of some notable developments and to provide insurance against ongoing risks." Powell specifically cited conversations with business leaders who explained that uncertainty about the Trump administration's trade policy was discouraging them from making investments in their companies.

Powell hinted at additional cuts, saying, "There may come a time when the economy weakens and we would then have to cut more aggressively." But, he added, "We don't know. We're going to be watching things carefully, the incoming data and the evolving situation." Only seven of the ten committee members voted for the September rate cut. Two, Rosengren and George, wanted to maintain the rate, while James Bullard, president of the Federal Reserve Bank of St. Louis, wanted a more extensive cut. This marked the most no votes at a single FOMC meeting since 2016, and Powell admitted the committee had entered "a time of difficult judgments."

Again, Trump lashed out at Powell. "Jay Powell and the Federal Reserve Fail Again. No 'guts,' no sense, no vision! A terrible communicator," the president tweeted. Powell, in turn, said Fed decisions would not be swayed by the president's beliefs. "I continue to believe that the independence of the Federal Reserve from direct political control has served the public well over time," Powell said, adding, "I assure you that my colleagues and I will continue to conduct monetary policy without regard to political considerations."

On October 30, Powell announced the year's third cut, citing "weakness in global growth and trade developments" that posed a risk to ongoing U.S. economic expansion. Again, George and Rosengren dissented, wanting to see a more significant dip in the U.S. economy before acting. At his press conference, Powell said he considered the October rate cut to be the last in the near term. "We see the current stance of monetary policy as likely to remain appropriate as long as incoming information about the economy remains broadly consistent with our outlook," Powell said. But, he added, "If developments emerge that cause a material reassessment of our outlook, we would respond accordingly. Policy is not on a pre-set course."

—Heather Kerrigan

Following are three statements released by the Federal Reserve on July 31, September 18, and October 30, 2019, announcing cuts to the short-term target range for the federal funds rate.

Federal Reserve Announces First Rate Cut in Eleven Years

July 31, 2019

Information received since the Federal Open Market Committee met in June indicates that the labor market remains strong and that economic activity has been rising at a moderate rate. Job gains have been solid, on average, in recent months, and the unemployment rate has remained low. Although growth of household spending has picked up from earlier in the year, growth of business fixed investment has been soft. On a 12-month basis, overall inflation and inflation for items other than food and energy are running below 2 percent. Market-based measures of inflation compensation remain low; survey-based measures of longer-term inflation expectations are little changed.

Consistent with its statutory mandate, the Committee seeks to foster maximum employment and price stability. In light of the implications of global developments for the economic outlook as well as muted inflation pressures, the Committee decided to lower the target range for the federal funds rate to 2 to $2^1/_4$ percent. This action supports the Committee's view that sustained expansion of economic activity, strong labor market conditions, and inflation near the Committee's symmetric 2 percent objective are the most likely outcomes, but uncertainties about this outlook remain. As the Committee contemplates the future path of the target range for the federal funds rate, it will continue to monitor the implications of incoming information for the economic outlook and will act as appropriate to sustain the expansion, with a strong labor market and inflation near its symmetric 2 percent objective.

In determining the timing and size of future adjustments to the target range for the federal funds rate, the Committee will assess realized and expected economic conditions relative to its maximum employment objective and its symmetric 2 percent inflation objective. This assessment will take into account a wide range of information, including measures of labor market conditions, indicators of inflation pressures and inflation expectations, and readings on financial and international developments.

The Committee will conclude the reduction of its aggregate securities holdings in the System Open Market Account in August, two months earlier than previously indicated.

Voting for the monetary policy action were Jerome H. Powell, Chair; John C. Williams, Vice Chair; Michelle W. Bowman; Lael Brainard; James Bullard; Richard H. Clarida; Charles L. Evans; and Randal K. Quarles. Voting against the action were Esther L. George and Eric S. Rosengren, who preferred at this meeting to maintain the target range for the federal funds rate at $2^1/_4$ to $2^1/_2$ percent.

SOURCE: Board of Governors of the Federal Reserve System. "Federal Reserve Issues FOMC Statement." July 31, 2019. https://www.federalreserve.gov/monetarypolicy/files/monetary20190731a1.pdf.

 **Federal Reserve Announces**
DOCUMENT **Second 2019 Rate Cut**

September 18, 2019

Information received since the Federal Open Market Committee met in July indicates that the labor market remains strong and that economic activity has been rising at a moderate rate. Job gains have been solid, on average, in recent months, and the unemployment rate has remained low. Although household spending has been rising at a strong pace, business fixed investment and exports have weakened. On a 12-month basis, overall inflation and inflation for items other than food and energy are running below 2 percent. Market-based measures of inflation compensation remain low; survey-based measures of longer-term inflation expectations are little changed.

Consistent with its statutory mandate, the Committee seeks to foster maximum employment and price stability. In light of the implications of global developments for the economic outlook as well as muted inflation pressures, the Committee decided to lower the target range for the federal funds rate to $1^3/_4$ to 2 percent. This action supports the Committee's view that sustained expansion of economic activity, strong labor market conditions, and inflation near the Committee's symmetric 2 percent objective are the most likely outcomes, but uncertainties about this outlook remain. As the Committee contemplates the future path of the target range for the federal funds rate, it will continue to monitor the implications of incoming information for the economic outlook and will act as appropriate to sustain the expansion, with a strong labor market and inflation near its symmetric 2 percent objective.

In determining the timing and size of future adjustments to the target range for the federal funds rate, the Committee will assess realized and expected economic conditions relative to its maximum employment objective and its symmetric 2 percent inflation objective. This assessment will take into account a wide range of information, including measures of labor market conditions, indicators of inflation pressures and inflation expectations, and readings on financial and international developments.

Voting for the monetary policy action were Jerome H. Powell, Chair; John C. Williams, Vice Chair; Michelle W. Bowman; Lael Brainard; Richard H. Clarida; Charles L. Evans; and Randal K. Quarles. Voting against the action were James Bullard, who preferred at this meeting to lower the target range for the federal funds rate to $1^1/_2$ to $1^3/_4$ percent; and Esther L. George and Eric S. Rosengren, who preferred to maintain the target range at 2 percent to $2^1/_4$ percent.

SOURCE: Board of Governors of the Federal Reserve System. "Federal Reserve Issues FOMC Statement." September 18, 2019. https://www.federalreserve.gov/monetarypolicy/files/monetary20190918a1.pdf.

Federal Reserve Announces Third and Final 2019 Rate Cut

October 30, 2019

Information received since the Federal Open Market Committee met in September indicates that the labor market remains strong and that economic activity has been rising at a moderate rate. Job gains have been solid, on average, in recent months, and the unemployment rate has remained low. Although household spending has been rising at a strong pace, business fixed investment and exports remain weak. On a 12-month basis, overall inflation and inflation for items other than food and energy are running below 2 percent. Market-based measures of inflation compensation remain low; survey-based measures of longer-term inflation expectations are little changed.

Consistent with its statutory mandate, the Committee seeks to foster maximum employment and price stability. In light of the implications of global developments for the economic outlook as well as muted inflation pressures, the Committee decided to lower the target range for the federal funds rate to $1^1/_2$ to $1^3/_4$ percent. This action supports the

Committee's view that sustained expansion of economic activity, strong labor market conditions, and inflation near the Committee's symmetric 2 percent objective are the most likely outcomes, but uncertainties about this outlook remain. The Committee will continue to monitor the implications of incoming information for the economic outlook as it assesses the appropriate path of the target range for the federal funds rate.

In determining the timing and size of future adjustments to the target range for the federal funds rate, the Committee will assess realized and expected economic conditions relative to its maximum employment objective and its symmetric 2 percent inflation objective. This assessment will take into account a wide range of information, including measures of labor market conditions, indicators of inflation pressures and inflation expectations, and readings on financial and international developments.

Voting for the monetary policy action were Jerome H. Powell, Chair; John C. Williams, Vice Chair; Michelle W. Bowman; Lael Brainard; James Bullard; Richard H. Clarida; Charles L. Evans; and Randal K. Quarles. Voting against this action were: Esther L. George and Eric S. Rosengren, who preferred at this meeting to maintain the target range at $1^3/_4$ percent to 2 percent.

SOURCE: Board of Governors of the Federal Reserve System. "Federal Reserve Issues FOMC Statement." October 30, 2019. https://www.federalreserve.gov/monetarypolicy/files/monetary20191030a1.pdf.

OTHER HISTORIC DOCUMENTS OF INTEREST

FROM PREVIOUS *HISTORIC DOCUMENTS*

- Fed Hikes Interest Rate; Treasury Secretary Remarks on Economy, *2018*, p. 714
- Federal Reserve Announces Interest Rate Hike, *2015*, p. 672
- Unemployment Rate Falls; Federal Reserve Ends Controversial Bond Buying Program, *2014*, p. 485

August

India Revokes Kashmir Autonomy

AUGUST 5 AND OCTOBER 29, 2019

The government of Indian prime minister Narendra Modi delivered on a key promise to supporters in 2019 by revoking an article of the Indian Constitution that granted special autonomy to Kashmir, a disputed territory at the center of multiple wars and violent cross-border conflict between India and Pakistan. The revocation prompted a major backlash by Pakistani officials and protests from Kashmiri leaders, but a government-imposed communications lockdown and a tightening of security measures across the region prevented major demonstrations from occurring.

A CONTESTED TERRITORY

The Kashmir region has long been disputed territory, with China, India, and Pakistan all laying claim to the land. Kashmir was an independent state for a brief period in 1947—the year India and Pakistan won independence from Britain—but an invasion by Pakistani militants pushed the region's leaders to seek protection from India. The Kashmiris agreed their land would become part of India on the condition that Article 370 be added to the Indian Constitution. Article 370 granted Kashmir a special autonomous status: Kashmir had its own flag and constitution, the ability to write its own laws, input on which federal laws could be imposed on the territory, and special property rights that prevented non-Kashmiris from owning land in the territory. Despite the agreement, Pakistan refused to recognize Kashmir's accession to India, igniting a roughly year-long war between the two countries.

The Indo-Pakistani War of 1947 was the first of several wars in which control of Kashmir was a central issue. China seized a northeastern portion of the territory, known as Asksai Chin, during the Sino-Indian War of 1962. Ten years and two wars later, India and Pakistan signed the Simla Accord, establishing an agreed-upon Line of Control between the two countries in Kashmir. Since then, Pakistan has controlled the northwestern areas of Gilgit-Baltistan and Azad Kashmir, while India controls the south and southeastern portion known as Jammu and Kashmir.

However, the agreement did not bring peace to the region, and soon the rise of anti-India Kashmiri insurgent groups spurred fresh violence. India claims these insurgents receive training, weapons, and other material support from Pakistan and that some militants operate from within Pakistani-controlled territory. A cease-fire negotiated in 2003 remains in place but has failed to quell the conflict. More than 300 militants and security personnel and roughly 100 civilians were killed in the region in 2018 alone. In February 2019, a Kashmiri militant drove a vehicle carrying explosives into a convoy of Indian paramilitary forces, killing forty soldiers. India pointed a finger at Pakistan, recalling its ambassador and ending preferential trade status for the neighboring country, but Pakistani officials denied involvement. A Pakistan-based terrorist group, Jaish-e

Muhammad, later claimed responsibility for the attack. The incident sparked a military standoff between the two countries. On February 26, India launched an airstrike against a purported "terrorist camp" in Pakistan. The next day, Pakistani fighter jets shot down two Indian military planes; an Indian pilot was subsequently captured and briefly detained by Pakistan.

A desire to end the ongoing violence and Pakistan's influence in Kashmir was a leading factor in a long-standing effort by India's Hindu nationalists to end the territory's special status. (The conflict has largely driven Kashmir's Hindu minority out of the region. The territory is primarily Muslim.) Prime Minister Narendra Modi, leader of a Hindu nationalist political party, was elected in 2014 on a platform promising to crack down on anti-India militant groups and to take a tougher stance in dealings with Pakistan. Revocation of Article 370, and thus Kashmir's autonomy, was a key campaign promise of Modi's when he ran for reelection in 2019.

ARTICLE 370 REVOKED

On August 5, 2019, the Indian government issued an order revoking Article 370 of the Indian Constitution, ending more than seventy years of Kashmiri autonomy. The move effectively repealed roughly 150 state laws implemented under Article 370 and made about 100 federal laws, including India's penal code, applicable in the territory. The government also revoked Kashmiris' special property rights, opening the door for nonresidents of Jammu and Kashmir to purchase property. Modi and other officials claimed these changes would bring peace to the region and spur economic development. "Article 370 was a hurdle for development of Kashmir" and "gave only separatism, nepotism, and corruption to the people," said Modi. Amit Shah, minister of home affairs, cited internal security concerns "fueled by cross-border terrorism" as a key consideration in issuing the revocation order.

Political leaders in Kashmir denounced the revocation as illegal and unconstitutional. Hasnain Masoodi, a member of Indian parliament representing Kashmir, called the order a "massive assault on the identity and autonomy of the state," saying the region had been "reduced to a municipality" after decades of independence. "Everyone has a sense of bitterness," he said. "There is a sense of injustice, disillusionment, and humiliation."

Pakistani leaders also reacted sharply. Prime Minister Imran Khan said the revocation could lead to yet another war. He also claimed India was acting on a "racist ideology" and warned that Modi's government "may initiate ethnic cleansing in Kashmir to wipe out the local population." (Claims of ethnic cleansing are based on a belief that the loss of autonomy will cause Kashmir to be overrun by an influx of Hindus who will push out the Muslim population.) Echoing Khan's concerns, Minister for Human Rights Shireen Mazari equated India's order with "war crimes" and accused Modi's government of violating UN Security Council resolutions recognizing Kashmir as a disputed territory. On August 7, Pakistan formally downgraded its diplomatic ties and suspended trade with India. Foreign Minister Shah Mahmood Qureshi said Pakistan's ambassador and senior diplomats in India would be recalled and that "their counterparts here will also be sent back." Officials said they would file a formal protest with the UN and review all bilateral agreements with India. Parliament later unanimously passed a resolution condemning the revocation as an "illegal, unilateral, reckless, and coercive attempt to alter the disputed status of Indian occupied Kashmir." The Pakistani government has also led public protests and rallies to show solidarity with Kashmir.

At Pakistan's request, China called a meeting of the UN Security Council on August 16 to discuss the situation in Kashmir. Indian ambassador Syed Akbaruddin explained his country's position "was, and remains, that matters related to Article 370 of the Indian Constitution are entirely an internal matter of India," adding that "of particular concern is that one state is using terminology of jihad against and promoting violence in India." The Pakistani ambassador, Maleeha Lodhi, countered that the fact the meeting took place "is testimony to the fact that this is an international dispute" and said it was allowing "the voice of the people of the occupied Kashmir" to be heard in "the highest diplomatic forum of the world."

In addition to the revocation order, on August 5 the upper house of India's parliament approved a bill to divide Jammu and Kashmir into two distinct territories. The first, named Ladakh, will have an estimated population of 300,000. (This area is considered a Buddhist enclave.) It will be directly controlled by the federal government, have a lieutenant governor, and get one representative in India's legislature. The second territory will still be known as Jammu, and Kashmir and will have an estimated population of 12.2 million people. Jammu and Kashmir will have its own state assembly, a governor, and five representatives in India's legislature, but it will mostly be controlled by the federal government. This division took effect on October 31, as did the revocation order.

India Blocks Communications, Makes Mass Arrests in Kashmir

Anticipating a Kashmiri backlash against the revocation, the Indian government sent thousands of additional soldiers to the region. Schools were closed, tourists were evacuated, and public gatherings of more than four people were prohibited. Curfews were imposed, and roadblocks and checkpoints restricted Kashmiris' movement. The government also blocked Internet access, phone use (both mobile and land line), and some television broadcasts in an effort to quell potential protests before they began. A petition challenging these restrictions was filed with the Supreme Court of India, but Justice Arun Mishra ruled on August 13 that they could remain in place because the government needed more time to restore order. "The situation is such that nobody knows what is going on," Mishra said. "We should give them time to restore normalcy. Nobody can take one percent of chance."

The communications blockade continued for months. Some mobile and landline phone services were restored in October; text messaging was restored at the end of December. On January 10, 2020, the Supreme Court of India ordered the government to review the ongoing Internet suspension, noting that Internet access is guaranteed under the constitution's protections of freedom of speech. The government announced on January 15 that Internet services would be restored to hospitals, banks, government offices, hotels, and tour and travel companies via new Internet kiosks. However, personal use of the Internet and social media is still prohibited, and the designated kiosks can only access pre-approved websites. The Ministry of Home Affairs explained the continued Internet suspension was necessary to stop "sustained efforts being made by the terrorists to infiltrate from across the border, reactivate their cadres and scale up anti-national activities in Kashmir." The UN Office of the High Commissioner for Human Rights (OHCHR) is among the international organizations and human rights groups that have called for a complete end to the blockade. "We are extremely concerned that the population of Indian-Administered Kashmir continues to be deprived of a wide range of human rights and we urge the Indian authorities to unlock the situation and fully restore the rights that are currently being denied," a spokesperson said.

In a further bid to tamp down opposition, Indian security forces arrested several prominent Kashmiri leaders, including Mehbooba Mufti, the chief minister of Jammu and Kashmir. "The fifth of August is the blackest day of Indian democracy when its Parliament, like thieves, snatched away everything from the people of Jammu and Kashmir," Mufti said. Other notable figures who were arrested included Farooq Abdullah, president of Kashmir's oldest political party and a representative of the region in India's parliament; Omar Abdullah, a former chief minister of Jammu and Kashmir; and Syed Ali Geelani, a former Kashmiri lawmaker and a member of the separatist Joint Resistance Leadership.

Mass arrests were soon reported throughout Kashmir. According to a government document reported on by Reuters, more than 3,800 people had been arrested in Kashmir as of September 6. Of those, roughly 2,600 people were released, although dozens of new arrests were being reported each day. The tally included more than 200 Kashmiri politicians, over 100 separatist leaders and activists, and about 150 people accused of being affiliated with anti-Indian militant groups. Reuters reported that most of those who were detained were described as "stone pelters and other miscreants" and that some were being held under the Public Safety Act, which allows India to detain people for up to two years without filing charges. Various reports indicated that Indian security officials were conducting night raids on private homes and arresting dozens of young people. Other reports suggested widespread abuse and torture of Kashmiris by Indian forces.

There have been some reports of protests in Kashmir since the region's autonomy was revoked; however, the communications lockdown has made it difficult to confirm how many protests have occurred, how many people have participated, and how interactions between police and protestors have unfolded. "There have been several allegations of excessive use of force including the use of pellet-firing shotguns, tear gas, and rubber bullets by security forces during sporadic protests, with unconfirmed reports of at least six civilian killings and scores of serious injuries," said a spokesperson for the OHCHR. "We have also received a number of allegations of torture and ill-treatment of people held in detention," the spokesperson continued. "These must be independently and impartially investigated. Torture is totally and unequivocally prohibited under international law."

—Linda Grimm

Following is the text of the August 5, 2019, government order revoking Article 370 of the Indian Constitution; and a press briefing note issued by the UN Office of the High Commissioner for Human Rights on October 29, 2019, identifying human rights concerns in Kashmir.

Presidential Order Revoking Kashmir Autonomy

August 5, 2019

MINISTRY OF LAW AND JUSTICE

(Legislative Department)

NOTIFICATION

New Delhi, the 5th August, 2019

G.S.R .551(E).—the following Order made by the President is published for general information:

THE CONSTITUTION (APPLICATION TO JAMMU AND KASHMIR) ORDER, 2019

C.O. 272

In exercise of the powers conferred by clause (1) of article 370 of the Constitution, the President, with the concurrence of the Government of State of Jammu and Kashmir, is pleased to make the following Order:—

1. (1) This Order may be called the Constitution (Application to Jammu and Kashmir) Order, 2019.

(2) It shall come into force at once, and shall thereupon supersede the Constitution (Application to Jammu and Kashmir) Order, 1954 as amended from time to time.

2. All the provisions of the Constitution, as amended from time to time, shall apply in relation to the State of Jammu and Kashmir and the exceptions and modifications subject to which they shall so apply shall be as follows:—

To article 367, there shall be added the following clause, namely:—

"(4) For the purposes of this Constitution as it applies in relation to the State of Jammu and Kashmir—

(a) references to this Constitution or to the provisions thereof shall be construed as references to the Constitution or the provisions thereof as applied in relation to the said State;

(b) references to the person for the time being recognized by the President on the recommendation of the Legislative Assembly of the State as the Sadar-i-Riyasat of Jammu and Kashmir, acting on the advice of the Council of Ministers of the State for the time being in office, shall be construed as references to the Governor of Jammu and Kashmir;

(c) references to the Government of the said State shall be construed as including references to the Governor of Jammu and Kashmir acting on the advice of his Council of Ministers; and

(d) in proviso to clause (3) of article 370 of this Constitution, the expression "Constituent Assembly of the State referred to in clause (2)" shall read "Legislative Assembly of the State".'"

RAM NATH KOVIND,
President.

Source: Government of India. Ministry of Electronics and Information Technology. National Informatics Centre. "The Constitution (Application to Jammu and Kashmir) Order, 2019 C.O. 272." August 5, 2019. http://egazette.nic.in/WriteReadData/2019/210049.pdf.

UN Comments on Human Rights Situation in Kashmir

October 29, 2019

We are extremely concerned that the population of Indian-Administered Kashmir continues to be deprived of a wide range of human rights and we urge the Indian authorities to unlock the situation and fully restore the rights that are currently being denied.

Twelve weeks ago, on 5 August, the Government of India revoked constitutional provisions granting partial autonomy to the state of Jammu and Kashmir and announced the creation of two separate federally-administered Union Territories, which will come into effect this Thursday (October 31). At the same time, very restrictive measures were imposed. Although some of these measures have been relaxed, their impact on human rights continues to be widely felt.

The undeclared curfew imposed by the authorities in the region was lifted from much of Jammu and Ladakh region within a few days, but is reportedly still in place in large parts of the Kashmir Valley, preventing the free movement of people, as well as hampering their ability to exercise their right to peaceful assembly, and restricting their rights to health, education and freedom of religion and belief.

There have been several allegations of excessive use of force including the use of pellet-firing shotguns, tear gas and rubber bullets by security forces during sporadic protests, with unconfirmed reports of at least six civilian killings and scores of serious injuries in separate incidents since 5 August.

We have also received reports of armed groups operating in Indian-Administered Kashmir threatening residents trying to carry out their normal business or attend school, as well as several allegations of violence against people who have not complied with the armed groups' demands. At least another six people have been killed and over a dozen injured in alleged attacks by armed group members since 5 August.

Hundreds of political and civil society leaders, including three former Chief Ministers of Jammu and Kashmir, have been detained on a preventative basis. While some political workers have reportedly been released, most senior leaders—especially those from the Kashmir Valley—remain in detention.

We have also received a number of allegations of torture and ill-treatment of people held in detention. These must be independently and impartially investigated. Torture is totally and unequivocally prohibited under international law.

While restrictions on landline telephones were eventually lifted, and a state-run telecom company allowed to resume partial mobile services, all Internet services remain blocked in the Kashmir Valley. Media outlets continue to face undue restrictions, with at least four local journalists allegedly arrested in the past three months.

The Supreme Court of India has been slow to deal with petitions concerning habeas corpus, freedom of movement and media restrictions. The Jammu and Kashmir State Human Rights Commission, the State Information Commission (which implements the right-to-information laws) and the State Commission for Protection of Women and Child Rights are among key institutions being wound up, with the new bodies to replace them yet to be established.

Meanwhile, major political decisions about the future status of Jammu and Kashmir have been taken without the consent, deliberation or active and informed participation of the affected population. Their leaders are detained, their capacity to be informed has been badly restricted, and their right to freedom of expression and to political participation has been undermined.

SOURCE: United Nations Office of the High Commissioner for Human Rights. "Press Briefing Note on Indian-Administered Kashmir." October 29, 2019. https://www.ohchr.org/en/NewsEvents/Pages/DisplayNews.aspx?NewsID=25219&LangID=E.

OTHER HISTORIC DOCUMENTS OF INTEREST

FROM THIS VOLUME

FROM PREVIOUS *HISTORIC DOCUMENTS*

New Governor Takes Office in Puerto Rico

AUGUST 8, 2019

In July 2019, Puerto Rican governor Ricardo Rosselló and nine other officials became embroiled in a scandal involving inappropriate chat messages that disparaged segments of the island nation's population and elected officials. News of the scandal broke shortly after two former high-level government officials were indicted on corruption charges. Angered by these developments and other long-simmering frustrations with the government, Puerto Ricans took to the streets to demand Rosselló's resignation. Rosselló eventually capitulated, but his successor, Justice Secretary Wanda Vázquez, is also unpopular and has already faced calls for her resignation.

CORRUPTION CHARGES, "CHATGATE" ROIL PUERTO RICO

Dissatisfaction with Rosselló's government grew steadily in Puerto Rico after Hurricane Maria devastated the island in September 2017. Nearly 3,000 people were killed by the storm and the longer-term problems it caused, such as widespread flooding and blackouts, food and water shortages, and hospital closures due to storm damage. Many Puerto Ricans said Rosselló did not do enough to address the U.S. government's slow response to the disaster, or to challenge President Donald Trump's controversial statements about the storm and its impact. (The initial, official death toll was sixty-four people, but Trump declared that no more than eighteen Puerto Ricans were killed. He rejected the much higher tally, calculated by an independent organization, as an effort by the Democratic Party to "make me look as bad as possible." He also claimed federal relief efforts were successful but had been unappreciated, in part because of incompetent Puerto Rican officials.) Puerto Ricans also linked Rosselló to the unpopular fiscal oversight board appointed by the federal government to oversee the island's finances as part of a 2016 deal that allowed the commonwealth to restructure most of its tens of billions of dollars in debt. Since the board's creation, the government has taken steps to shore up finances by laying off thousands of public employees, raising tuition rates, closing schools, and cutting public services—none of which have been welcomed by Puerto Ricans.

A series of developments over the summer of 2019 brought public frustrations to a head. In late June, Puerto Rican treasury secretary Raúl Maldonado Gautier told a reporter that officials in his department were being investigated for corruption, calling them an "institutional mafia." He further claimed that some of these officials had tried to extort him. Gautier was subsequently fired. On July 10, former education secretary Julia Keleher and former executive director of the Health Insurance Administration Angela Avila-Marrero were arrested along with two government contractors and two private businessmen in connection with a federal indictment. Keleher and Avila-Marrero were accused of directing up to $15.5 million in government funds to contractors with political connections to the leading New Progressive Party. The indictment included thirty-two counts of money laundering, conspiracy, and wire fraud, although the U.S. attorney for Puerto Rico said neither Keleher nor Avila-Marrero directly benefitted from the scheme. Rosselló declared that his administration "will not tolerate corruption" and promised to cooperate with law enforcement officials on the matter.

Then on July 13, a scandal known as "Chatgate" broke. That day, the Puerto Rican Center for Investigative Journalism published nearly 900 pages of messages sent between Rosselló and nine other government officials via the messaging app Telegram. The messages disparaged women, homosexuals, and artists, and appeared to show a lack of concern for the victims of Hurricane Maria. In one exchange, Secretary of State Luis Rivera Marín joked about the storm's rising death toll and the island's overwhelmed morgues. Another official joked about shooting San Juan mayor Carmen Yulín Cruz, to which Rosselló responded, "You'd be doing me a huge favor." A sexual slur was used against the former speaker of the New York City Council, Melissa Mark-Viverito, who was born in Puerto Rico, and offensive language and imagery were used to refer to the fiscal oversight board. Some of the messages had already been leaked by bloggers and other journalists, but the center's explosive report magnified the scandal. Chief Financial Officer Christian Sobrino, also among the officials involved, and Marín quickly resigned, and Rosselló apologized as soon as the messages began to leak. "Yes, I use bad language, I send memes, I send sarcastic things," he said. "I'm not proud of that and when these things happen, I start by saying that I apologize."

PROTESTS BEGIN, CALL FOR ROSSELLÓ'S RESIGNATION

To Puerto Ricans, the Chatgate messages provided yet another example of how Rosselló and his political allies viewed themselves as superior to the people and cared little for the public's welfare. They began protesting in front of the governor's residence in San Juan and marching through the streets, demanding that Rosselló resign. Notable Puerto Ricans—including pop music star Ricky Martin, actor Benicio Del Toro, and rap artist Bad Bunny—traveled to the island to participate in the protests. "They mocked our dead, they mocked women, they mocked the LGBT community, they made fun of people with physical and mental disabilities, they made fun of obesity. It's enough," said Martin. Many elected officials joined the call for Rosselló to step down, while others suggested he be impeached. "The events of the past two weeks have worsened, even more so over the last six days, paralyzing economic activity and government activity, portraying an anarchic Puerto Rico to the rest of the world," said Jenniffer González-Colón, Puerto Rico's nonvoting resident commissioner in Congress. "This is not sustainable."

After a week of persistent demonstrations, Rosselló announced that he would step down as leader of the New Progressive Party and would not run for reelection in 2020, but he refused to resign. "To every Puerto Rican—I have heard you, I have committed errors, but I am a good man who has a great love for his island and its people," he said. "I recognize that apologizing is not enough. Only my work will help restore the confidence of those sectors and get us on the path to true reconciliation."

The people were not satisfied. On July 22, hundreds of thousands of Puerto Ricans staged a mass protest in San Juan. Students, retirees, trades workers, and professionals of all ages marched together with well-known Puerto Rican artists and athletes down the Expreso Las Américas highway. The city's biggest shopping mall closed, as did some banks and universities. Cruise ships were also diverted from the city's port. A front-page editorial published by leading newspaper *El Nuevo Día* declared, "Governor, it's time to listen to the people. You must resign."

With pressure building, a growing number of top government aides resigned, including Rosselló's chief of staff. On July 24, the president of Puerto Rico's House of Representatives, Carlos Méndez Núñez, called for the Legislative Assembly to begin impeachment proceedings against the governor. Attorneys retained by Méndez Núñez had reportedly identified five impeachable offenses committed by the governor, including the use of public resources for partisan purposes and allowing government officials and contractors to misuse public funds. Méndez Núñez said he would call off the impeachment proceedings if Rosselló resigned but would still refer the attorneys' report to the appropriate authorities for further investigation. Late that evening, Rosselló announced his resignation. "My mandate is over, and the most I wish for is peace and progress for our people," he said. Rosselló added that continuing on as governor "would endanger the successes we have achieved." Rosselló said his resignation would take effect on August 2, at which point Justice Secretary Wanda Vázquez would likely be sworn in as governor. (The secretary of state is first in Puerto Rico's constitutional line of succession to the governor's office; the justice secretary is second.) In a separate statement, Vázquez said Rosselló had "made the right decision, for the good of both his family and for Puerto Rico" and promised to work with him on ensuring a smooth transition. She added that she would be ready to serve as interim governor "if necessary," suggesting that someone else might be named as Rosselló's successor. (Vázquez previously stated that she had no interest in becoming governor.)

Two New Governors in One Week

On July 31, Rosselló nominated Pedro Pierluisi, a former resident commissioner to Congress, to fill the vacant secretary of state position, and therefore become Puerto Rico's new governor. Rosselló said Pierluisi would finish the outgoing governor's term but did not intend to run for office in 2020. "His aspiration is to complete this term, so that the successes we have achieved do not disappear," Rosselló said. "The electoral process that will begin in the coming months will allow other highly qualified leaders to put their ideas and character to the people's consideration, as Pierluisi and I did in the last primary."

The House of Representatives approved Pierluisi's nomination on August 2. Senate president Thomas Rivera Schatz said there would not be enough votes in his chamber to confirm Pierluisi's appointment but scheduled a hearing for August 5. Rosselló and Pierluisi claimed that Puerto Rican statute did not require a secretary of state to be confirmed by the Legislative Assembly in order to become governor, and Pierluisi was sworn in without a Senate vote. Schatz filed a request with the Puerto Rican Supreme Court to grant a preliminary injunction preventing Pierluisi from acting as governor. "His swearing-in is null. He is acting illegally as governor," Schatz said. "It is my duty to take him to court."

The court's nine justices ruled unanimously on August 7 that Pierluisi had been sworn in on unconstitutional grounds. The court called for a new governor—one who followed the constitutional line of succession—to take office. Vázquez was sworn in later that day. In remarks following the ceremony, the new governor acknowledged that "the last weeks have been highly painful for the people of Puerto Rico" and that "we have all experienced the anxiety provoked by instability and uncertainty." But, she noted, they had also seen "a nation that has not lost its faith and hope in its own abilities and potential to advance." Vázquez said it was her duty to assume the governor's office, but that she also sought to "respond to a collective situation which demands the provision of stability to our governmental institutions . . . and widespread participation of all the sectors in the demo-cratic exercise which is the governance of a nation." Vázquez promised to meet with "the most diverse sectors of the civil society and the political parties, as well as community, entrepreneur, civic, and religious leaders" to have "a constructive dialogue for the sake of Puerto Rico." Once she had listened to all points of view, Vázquez said, she would work on "all that which links us together and seek consensus for all the issues we disagree on."

While Puerto Ricans celebrated Rosselló's resignation, they soon began protesting against Vázquez as well. Many believe she has too many connections to Rosselló's admin-istration, and her tenure as justice secretary has been criticized. Some claim she did not do enough to investigate allegations the government mishandled hurricane relief supplies. She has also been accused of intervening in a case on her daughter's behalf.

—Linda Grimm

Following are remarks by Puerto Rican governor Wanda Vázquez on August 8, 2019, after being sworn into office.

Swearing-in Statement by Gov. Wanda Vázquez

August 8, 2019

Good afternoon people of Puerto Rico,

Today I am addressing all Puerto Ricans who, the same as I do, feel an immense love for this beautiful isle.

The Constitution of the Commonwealth of Puerto Rico, inspired by the vision of our Founding Fathers, laid the foundations of our democratic co-existence. That same Constitution guarantees and protects the rights of the people to the freedom of speech and their right to show their agreement and disagreement to the activities of all the leaders elected in the genuine democratic exercise at the polls.

The last weeks have been highly painful for the people of Puerto Rico, and I have personally felt the same way. We have all experienced the anxiety provoked by instability and uncertainty.

However, this historical scenario has shown to the world a nation that has not lost its ability to vindicate its rights, a nation which demands action and which presses for public issues to be dealt with in total adherence to law.

Likewise, we have seen a nation that has not lost its faith and hope in its own abilities and potential to advance.

The highest forum has expressed itself and with its decision, the Supreme Court has given certainty to the order of succession stated by the Constitution of the Commonwealth of Puerto Rico in Article IV, Section 7, and Law Number 7 of July 24, 1952, as amended, known as the "Law for providing the Succession and Substitution order for the position of Governor."

Our Constitution states an order of succession in case there is a permanent vacancy in the position of Governor. Since the position of Secretary of State was vacant, and due to the fact that I occupied the position of Secretary of Justice, our legal system imposes on me the duty of leading the destiny of this nation.

Today, apart from responding to a duty, I respond to a collective situation which demands the provision of stability to our governmental institutions, cleanliness in the processes and widespread participation of all the sectors in the democratic exercise which is the governance of a nation.

I assume the position of Governor with the certainty that history has brought me here without any political aspiration, but with the firm wish of fully complying with the People. I am a lawyer, I have never pursued a political position. I have always been a public servant who, for 32 years, has complied with my duties, with an unflagging commitment to justice.

Therefore, before this enormous challenge and before God, I step forward without any other interest but to serve the nation as I have been doing for all of my life. I accept the duty with the highest sense of responsibility and social awareness.

We are facing new challenges which demand an unwavering commitment to governing with responsibility, with openness and in convergence, times in which the demands for results by the nation to its leaders are even more evident.

Social justice, education, health, security and economic growth are the issues that are set at the highest priority of my attention immediately after assuming this position.

In the following days I will be summoning the most diverse sectors of the civil society and the political parties, as well as community, entrepreneur, civic and religious leaders so as to listen directly to their thoughts and to learn the inputs which they may present for the benefit of the country. Likewise, I will have meetings with the leaders of the legislative bodies so as to have a constructive dialogue for the sake of Puerto Rico.

Once we have completed this x-ray, and as part of a conciliatory and inclusive dialogue, we will work on all that which links us together and seek consensus for all the issues we disagree on. The times so demand it. It is necessary to provide stability to the country, certainty to the markets as well as guarantee the funds for the reconstruction.

I acknowledge that I have not been elected by the people for this position, but that I came to the position by mandate of our Constitution, though I come from that very same people. I am a product of the public school, here I grew and here I developed as a professional. I know what it means to work hard, always serving in an honorable manner. Those who know me can attest to my unwavering commitment to justice.

As a Puerto Rican, I feel great love for Puerto Rico and I will strive and devote my best efforts to make the island continue steadily on its road towards total recovery. The historical moment so requires it, since we are before a situation in which the respect for the will of the people shall be the base for the reconstruction of our isle.

Governance is not a unilateral exercise; it requires the legitimate participation of the People in the decisions. Supported by the rights, liberties and responsibilities enshrined in the Constitution, we shall always govern aiming at the justice, the equality and the welfare of all the inhabitants of this blessed island.

I can assure that I will devote all my energy and my hearth to steer Puerto Rico towards a productive society where it is possible to achieve the stability we all long for. To the People, I ask you not to lose faith in the persons and in their capabilities. You have already shown your resilience and value when facing great challenges. I am convinced that putting together all those wills shall enable us to bring the country back on track and achieve the long-awaited stability and progress the people deserve and wait for.

It will be so with the help of God and of all those who inhabit this blessed island. God bless you and God bless Puerto Rico.

SOURCE: Office of the Governor of Puerto Rico. "Message from Wanda Vázquez Garced, the Governor of Puerto Rico." August 8, 2019. Translated by SAGE Publishing. https://www.fortaleza.pr.gov/content/mensaje-de-la-gobernadora-de-puerto-rico-wanda-v-zquez-garced.

HISTORIC DOCUMENTS OF INTEREST

FROM PREVIOUS *HISTORIC DOCUMENTS*

- President Trump, Vice President Pence Visit Texas, Florida, and Puerto Rico after Hurricanes, *2017*, p. 457
- President Obama Signs PROMESA into Law, *2016*, p. 303
- American and Puerto Rican Leaders Remark on Island Nation's Default, *2015*, p. 537

Trump Administration and Supreme Court Issue Immigration Orders

AUGUST 12, AUGUST 14, SEPTEMBER 11, AND
OCTOBER 4, 2019

With Congress stalled on the comprehensive immigration reform sought by President Donald Trump, the administration used the power of the presidency to enact restrictions on who can enter the United States. This included releasing an expanded version of the "public charge" rule that limits asylum applications from immigrants who might rely on public assistance, a presidential proclamation banning entry into the United States for immigrants who would require government-funded health care, and a ban on asylum seekers who arrived in the United States by way of a third country who did not first attempt to apply for asylum in that country. These presidential actions contributed to a decline in the number of people apprehended crossing the U.S. border in 2019.

TRUMP ADMINISTRATION BARS CERTAIN ASYLUM SEEKERS

On July 15, 2019, the Trump administration announced a change in asylum policy, one that would significantly limit immigration by families from Central America. Since 1980, American asylum law, rooted both in international treaty and in U.S. immigration law, has provided the right to apply for asylum to all foreign nationals, whether already in the country or at the border, who have a "credible fear" of persecution and violence in their home countries. Those fleeing persecution and violence at home have had the right to apply for asylum and prove their concerns before a judge, regardless of how they got to the border. In July, the Trump administration added an exception to this rule, announcing that any immigrants who arrive at the southern U.S. border, after first traveling through Mexico or another third country, will only be able to apply for asylum if they were first denied asylum in one of the countries through which they traveled. Effectively, this sweeping rule bans the vast majority of refugees who seek asylum at the southern border, most of whom arrive from Central America and must pass through Mexico or Guatemala to reach the United States.

The American Civil Liberties Union (ACLU), Southern Poverty Law Center, and Center for Constitutional Rights immediately filed suit to have the new rule declared unlawful. A federal court granted an injunction against its implementation, after finding the change to be inconsistent with federal immigration law and noting that the administration had failed to provide the advance notice and opportunity for public comment required by federal law. The Trump administration made an emergency application directly to the Supreme Court to lift the injunction, arguing that foreign affairs were at issue and that the new policy was necessary to avoid "an additional surge of asylum seekers." On September 11, 2019, the Supreme Court, with a short, unsigned statement, lifted the lower court's injunction while the case works its way through the courts. The administration immediately began denying asylum claims from migrants who pass through third countries without first seeking asylum there.

Justice Sonia Sotomayor, joined by Justice Ruth Bader Ginsberg, dissented from the Court's action, arguing that the lower court decisions "warrant respect" and the legal intervention sought by the government should be an "extraordinary" judicial act. Especially so, Sotomayor writes, given the nature of the new policy, which "topples decades of settled asylum practices and affects some of the most vulnerable people in the Western Hemisphere—without affording the public a chance to weigh in."

The Trump administration's reaction to the decision came in a tweet from the president: "BIG United States Supreme Court WIN for the Border on Asylum!" The case is likely to return to the Supreme Court when the legal challenges are completed in the lower courts.

TRUMP ADMINISTRATION, MEXICO REACH DEAL TO CURB IMMIGRATION

Almost a million migrants arrived at America's southern border in 2018, more than 90 percent of whom were from the Central American countries of El Salvador, Guatemala, and Honduras. These migrants must pass through Mexico to reach the border with the United States.

Before President Trump declared a rule change requiring new asylum seekers from Central America to first apply for asylum in Mexico or another third country, he tried to get Mexican president Andrés Manuel López Obrador to agree to a "safe-third-country" designation that under international law would require Mexico to handle any asylum claims from U.S.-bound migrants. To bring the Mexican president to the negotiating table, Trump threatened to impose tariffs on hundreds of billions of dollars in goods from Mexico. He tweeted, "On June 10th, the United States will impose a 5% Tariff on all goods coming into our Country from Mexico, until such time as illegal migrants coming through Mexico and into our Country, STOP." According to the president's tweet, the tariffs would go up every month until they hit 25 percent in October. The announcement triggered a rapid drop-off in global stock markets, leading to the Dow's longest weekly losing streak since 2011.

While Mexico continued to resist a safe-third-country designation, the country did reach an agreement to try to prevent people fleeing persecution in Central America from reaching the United States. On June 7, the president announced in a pair of tweets, "I am pleased to inform you that The United States of America has reached a signed agreement with Mexico. The Tariffs scheduled to be implemented by the U.S. on Monday, against Mexico, are hereby indefinitely suspended. Mexico, in turn, has agreed to take strong measures to . . . stem the tide of Migration through Mexico, and to our Southern Border."

Under the deal, Mexico agreed to form a new National Guard unit of 6,000 troops to be stationed around the country with many placed along Mexico's southern border with Guatemala. The troops would cut off the northward flow of migrants from Central America and dismantle trafficking organizations. In addition, Mexico agreed to build more migrant detention centers and checkpoints. By the end of June, President Trump renewed pressure on Mexico to slow immigration, and Mexico sent an additional 15,000 troops—both National Guard and military—to the U.S. border.

As part of the deal, the United States continued to expand its Migration Protection Protocols, more commonly known as the "Remain in Mexico" policy, across the entire U.S. border with Mexico. This policy represents a shift in the processing of asylum claims. Now, most non-Mexican asylum seekers wait in Mexico while their cases move through the immigration courts in the United States, a process that can take months or years. In 2019, more than 50,000 migrants who had started the asylum process in the United States were returned to Mexican border towns to wait while their immigration proceedings continued.

NEW TRUMP ADMINISTRATION REGULATION SEEKS TO TERMINATE *FLORES* SETTLEMENT

In 1997, the U.S. government settled a class action lawsuit that had arisen from the treatment of migrant children held in federal detention. Fifteen-year-old Jenny Lisette Flores was the named plaintiff in the lawsuit and gave her name to the consent decree agreed to by the parties to end the lawsuit. Under the terms of the *Flores* settlement, the government agreed to specific standards for the detention of migrant minors. Children must be held in state-licensed facilities, treated with a mandated level of care, and released "expeditiously"—in most cases within twenty days. This agreement has been upheld in dozens of cases. As recently as August 15, 2019, a federal appeals court relied on the *Flores* settlement to reject a Trump administration argument that it did not need to provide children with access to soap and toothbrushes or with adequate sleep at Border Patrol facilities. *Flores*, the court held, authorized the lower court to specify what will satisfy the "safe and sanitary conditions" requirement of the settlement. Moreover, the appellate court asserted, "Assuring that children eat enough edible food, drink clean water, are housed in hygienic facilities with sanitary bathrooms, have soap and toothpaste, and are not sleep-deprived are without doubt essential to the children's safety."

Less than a week after this ruling, on August 21, the Trump administration announced plans to replace the *Flores* rule with regulations that would allow children and their parents to be held in detention indefinitely, eliminating the existing twenty-day limit for minors. Additionally, the newly proposed rule would remove the state-licensing requirement for facilities housing children. Such licensing generally would come with stringent schooling, health, and recreation requirements. Instead, the Trump regulation would create a government-run licensing project. Acting Department of Homeland Security (DHS) secretary Kevin McAleenan tweeted that the "Flores Final Rule" allows "DHS to keep families together during fair and expeditious immigration proceedings and eliminates a key incentive that encourages traffickers to exploit children." The government could, under this new regulation, hold children and their families in detention until their asylum cases can be finally decided. By the end of 2019, there was a backlog of more than one million cases pending in immigration courts.

The announcement drew widespread criticism from immigration and human rights advocates. RAICES, a nonprofit group providing legal services to immigrants, tweeted, "It's cruel beyond imagination," and pointed out that at least seven children had died in detention. The American Association of Pediatrics, as well as other medical organizations, spoke out against the change. "No amount of time in detention is safe for a child. When children are detained, they experience physical and emotional stress, placing them at risk for serious short- and long-term health problems, such as developmental delays, poor psychological adjustment, anxiety, depression, and suicidal ideation," the organization said in a statement.

The new ruling was challenged in the same California federal court that has been overseeing the *Flores* litigation for years and, on September 27, 2019, Federal Judge Dolly Gee of the Central District of California again upheld the continuing validity of the *Flores* settlement. She noted that *Flores* is a "binding contract" and a "final binding judgment" that can only be repealed by an act of Congress. The administration, she ruled, "cannot simply impose their will by promulgating regulations that abrogate the consent decree's most basic tenets. That violates the rule of law. And that this Court cannot permit." It is likely the case will eventually reach the Supreme Court.

ADMINISTRATION BROADENS "PUBLIC CHARGE" RULE

On August 12, 2019, the Trump administration unveiled an overhaul of the long-standing "public charge" policy that, for more than 100 years, has provided authorities with the grounds to deny applications for green cards or for entry into the United States to those "likely to become a public charge." As applied in the past, the rule would only exclude immigrants who were found to be "primarily dependent on the government for subsistence." Regulations interpreting the rule specified that the government would not consider the use of health, nutrition, and housing programs in making a public charge assessment. Under the rule published in the *Federal Register* on August 14, 2019, titled "Inadmissibility on Public Charge Grounds," the definition of "public charge" was broadened to include anyone receiving public benefits for more than twelve months in any thirty-six-month period, and officials could now consider previously excluded programs, such as Medicaid, food stamps, and housing subsidies. The new rule also allows immigration officers to consider other factors in making the determination of whether an applicant is likely to be a public charge at any time in the future. These factors include age and health, and establish a new income standard of 125 percent of the federal poverty line.

Ken Cuccinelli, the acting director of U.S. Citizenship and Immigration Services (USCIS), stated that the new rule "encourages and ensures self-reliance and self-sufficiency for those seeking to come to, or to stay in, the United States." Others have predicted that the rule is likely to lead to a decrease in participation in Medicaid and other programs among immigrant families, most of whom live in mixed-status households, often with citizen children. According to the Kaiser Family Foundation, a nonpartisan health policy group, "Previous experience and recent research suggest that the rule will lead individuals to forgo enrollment in or disenroll themselves and their children from public programs because they do not understand the rule's details and fear their own or their children's enrollment could negatively affect their or their family members' immigration status."

In October, Trump issued a proclamation piggybacking on the public charge expansion, suspending entry into the United States for any immigrant who would burden the health care system. According to the proclamation, the already stretched health care system is harmed "by admitting thousands of aliens who have not demonstrated any ability to pay for their healthcare costs. Notably, data show that lawful immigrants are about three times more likely than United States citizens to lack health insurance. Immigrants who enter this country should not further saddle our healthcare system, and subsequently American taxpayers, with higher costs."

That same month, a handful of district courts had granted injunctions against the new public charge rule, ordering DHS not to implement or enforce it pending a final ruling. In December, two appellate courts ruled for the government, reversing these decisions. However, injunctions remained in cases filed in Illinois and New York. In January 2020, the Trump administration petitioned the Supreme Court to allow the public charge rule to go into effect. A coalition of technology companies, including Facebook, Google, Amazon, and dozens of others filed an amicus brief with the Court opposing the rule, calling it "unconscionable" and arguing that it will make it harder to hire talent from abroad. On January 27, 2020, the Supreme Court issued a brief order allowing the public charge rule to go into effect while awaiting the outcome of appeals.

PRESIDENT DIVERTS FUNDING TO PAY FOR BORDER WALL AND DETENTION

When the 2019 budget passed by Congress provided only $1.4 billion to fund the construction of a wall along the U.S.–Mexico border, significantly less than the $5 billion requested, President Trump declared a national emergency in order to access billions of additional dollars in federal funding that did not require congressional approval.

President Trump looked first to the Pentagon to find border wall funding and initially identified $2.5 billion in Department of Defense funds that had been allocated for military personnel. The funds were funneled through a counternarcotic account, and the government asserted that 120 miles of border wall were necessary to interdict drugs entering the country. A lawsuit challenging this diversion of funds is pending as of this writing; however, on July 26, 2019, the Supreme Court ruled that the money could be used for border wall construction while the court case is heard. In addition, on September 4, 2019, Defense Secretary Mark Esper signed off on transferring another $3.6 billion in defense funds, this time earmarked for military construction, to build another 175 miles of border wall. The funds were initially set aside for projects such as schools on military bases, road repairs, and those meant to prevent fire danger at ship maintenance buildings in Virginia. Members on both sides of the aisle were critical of the decision, arguing that the White House was usurping the power of Congress. Sen. Jack Reed, D-R.I., the top Democrat on the Senate Armed Services Committee, said the raiding of defense funds "should be struck down by the courts"; otherwise, "future Presidents will make similar end-runs to try and tap defense dollars for anything a President wants to label a 'national emergency.'" Rep. Mac Thornberry, R-Texas, top Republican on the House Armed Services Committee, called the move "contrary to Congress's constitutional authority."

On August 27, DHS announced that it would transfer $155 million from the Federal Emergency Management Administration (FEMA) disaster relief fund to pay for more detention beds and hearing facilities at the U.S.–Mexico border. DHS described the move as necessary to deal with a "security and humanitarian crisis," stemming from an "influx of migrants from U.S. Customs and Border Protection apprehensions." According to DHS, additional funds would be repurposed from the Coast Guard, Transportation Security Administration, Cybersecurity and Infrastructure Security Agency, DHS management accounts, and several other offices within DHS.

—Melissa Feinberg

Following is the text of a statement delivered by U.S. Citizenship and Immigration Services acting director Ken Cuccinelli on August 12, 2019, describing the Trump administration's expansion of the public charge rule; the summary text of the expanded public charge rule published in the Federal Register *on August 14, 2019; the Supreme Court's September 11, 2019, preliminary stay related to asylum seekers; and an October 4, 2019, proclamation by President Donald Trump suspending the entry into the United States by immigrants who would require publicly funded health care services.*

Acting USCIS Director Describes
Public Charge Rule

August 12, 2019

ACTING DIRECTOR CUCCINELLI: Good morning. It's a pleasure to be here with you today. I'm Ken Cuccinelli. I'm head of the United States Citizenship and Immigration Services. And President Trump has once again delivered on his promise to the American people to enforce longstanding immigration law.

Today, USCIS, the agency I head as part of the Department of Homeland Security, has issued a rule that encourages and ensures self-reliance and self-sufficiency for those seeking to come to, or to stay in, the United States. It will also help promote immigrant success in the United States as they seek opportunity here.

Throughout our history, self-reliance has been a core principle in America. The virtues of perseverance, hard work, and self-sufficiency laid the foundation of our nation and have defined generations of immigrants seeking opportunity in the United States.

Our current law, which is generations old, recognizes that some new arrivals to our country need the help of their family and community. It requires some of those, who seek to live and remain in the United States, to have a sponsor who will be financially responsible for them.

In the case of my own family, my Italian grandfather played this role, sponsoring two of his cousins, Mario and Silvio, to come to America. Once they arrived, my grandfather wanted to make sure his cousins spoke English—certainly well enough to work—and listed my father in that effort, as well, to make sure they could speak English well enough to work. And they did.

My family worked together to ensure that they could provide for their own needs, and they never expected the government to do it for them. And the same hardworking spirit shared by countless immigrants who've made the U.S. their home is central to our American identity.

This spirit has also been rooted for over a century—well over a century—in our immigration laws, going back to the 1800s.

Since 1996, the law has required foreign nationals to rely on their own capabilities and the resources of their families, sponsors, and private organizations in their communities to succeed. However, Congress has never defined the term "public charge" in the law, and that term hadn't been clearly defined by regulation. Well, that is what changes today with this rule.

Through the public charge rule, President Trump's administration is reinforcing the ideals of self-sufficiency and personal responsibility, ensuring that immigrants are able to support themselves and become successful here in America.

Our rule generally prevents aliens, who are likely to become a public charge, from coming to the United States or remaining here and getting a green card. Public charge is now defined in a way that ensures the law is meaningfully enforced and that those who are subject to it are self-sufficient.

Under the rule, a public charge in now defined as an individual who receives one or more designated public benefits for more than 12 months in the aggregate within any 36-month period. For instance, receipt of two different benefits in one month counts as two months.

A public charge in an admissibility determination is prospective and looks at whether an individual is likely, at any point in the future, to become a public charge as we define it in the regulation.

Public benefits are defined as federal, state and local, as well as tribal, cash assistance for income maintenance and small list of non-cash benefits.

Some examples of the public benefits that are part of the rule are general assistance, SSI, SNAP, most forms of Medicaid, and certain subsidized housing programs. Significantly, the rule does not consider many forms of government assistance that protect children and pregnant women's health as public benefits.

Generally, this includes emergency medical assistance, disaster relief, national school lunch programs, WIC, CHIP, Medicaid received by people under the age of 21 or pregnant women, as well as foster care and adoption subsidies, student and mortgage loans, energy assistance, food pantries, homeless shelters, and Head Start.

It's important to note this rule will apply prospectively only to applications and petitions received starting on October 15th of this year. Once this rule is implemented and effective on October 15th, USCIS Career Immigration Services Officers—what we call ISOs—will generally consider an alien's current and past receipt of the designated public benefits while in the United States as a negative factor when examining applications. However, receipt of certain non-cash benefits received before October 15th will not be considered as a negative factor.

The underlying statute passed on a bipartisan basis also requires officers to assess, at a minimum, each applicant's age, health, family status, assets, resources and financial status, and their education and skills, as well as other factors set forth in the rule in the totality of the circumstances. The totality of the circumstances means that officers will assess all of the evidence related to these factors, and no one factor alone will decide an applicant's case.

Most of these factors are the ones Congress mandated us to review when considering immigration benefit applications. Under this final rule, USCIS will be able to objectively determine whether an applicant is likely at any time in the future to receive public benefits above the designated threshold.

Importantly, this final rule has no impact on humanitarian-based immigration programs for refugees and asylees. No impact on refugees or asylees. And it clarifies the exemption for trafficking victims and victims of domestic violence. Congress has long carved out exemptions for these categories. And our regulation adheres strictly to the laws as written.

The final rule also excludes from consideration public benefits received by certain members of the U.S. Armed Forces and their spouses and children, as well as Medicaid benefits for emergency medical services.

Lastly, under the final rule, USCIS can permit an applicant seeking a green card from inside the United States, who is inadmissible only on the public charge ground, to adjust their status to that of a legal permanent resident if they will post a public charge bond.

So, to conclude, I'd just note again that generations of immigrants have strengthened the foundation of our country and making positive contributions today, and we expect that to continue in the future.

Through faithful execution of our nation's longstanding laws, President Trump's public charge inadmissibility rule better ensures that immigrants are able to successfully support themselves as they seek opportunity here in America. Throughout our history, Americans and legal immigrants have pulled themselves up by their bootstraps to pursue their dreams and the opportunity of this great nation.

As President Trump delivers on his promise to uphold the rule of law, this administration is promoting our shared history and encouraging the core values needed to make the American dream a reality. And with that, I'm happy to take some questions.

[The Q&A with reporters has been omitted.]

SOURCE: The White House. "Press Briefing by USCIS Acting Director Ken Cuccinelli." August 12, 2019. https://www.whitehouse.gov/briefings-statements/press-briefing-uscis-acting-director-ken-cuccinelli-081219/.

Final Public Charge Rule Released

August 14, 2019

DEPARTMENT OF HOMELAND SECURITY

8 CFR Parts 103, 212, 213, 214, 245 and 248

[CIS No. 2637–19; DHS Docket No. USCIS–2010–0012]

RIN 1615–AA22

Inadmissibility on Public Charge Grounds

AGENCY: U.S. Citizenship and Immigration Services, DHS.

ACTION: Final rule.

SUMMARY: This final rule amends DHS regulations by prescribing how DHS will determine whether an alien applying for admission or adjustment of status is inadmissible to the United States under section 212(a)(4) of the Immigration and Nationality Act (INA or the Act), because he or she is likely at any time to become a public charge. The final rule includes definitions of certain terms critical to the public charge determination, such as "public charge" and "public benefit," which are not defined in the statute, and explains the factors DHS will consider in the totality of the circumstances when making a public charge inadmissibility determination. The final rule also addresses USCIS' authority to issue public charge bonds under section 213 of the Act in the context of applications for adjustment of status. Finally, this rule includes a requirement that aliens seeking an extension of stay or change of status demonstrate that they have not, since obtaining the nonimmigrant status they seek to extend or change, received public benefits over the designated threshold, as defined in this rule.

This rule does not create any penalty or disincentive for past, current, or future receipt of public benefits by U.S. citizens or aliens whom Congress has exempted from the public charge ground of inadmissibility. This rule does not apply to U.S. citizens, even if the U.S.

citizen is related to an alien subject to the public charge ground of inadmissibility. The rule also does not apply to aliens whom Congress exempted from the public charge ground of inadmissibility (such as asylees, refugees, or other vulnerable populations listed as exempt in this final rule). Nor does this rule apply to aliens for whom DHS has statutory discretion to waive this ground of inadmissibility, if DHS has exercised such discretion.

In addition, this includes special provisions for how DHS will consider the receipt of public benefits, as defined in this rule, by certain members of the U.S. Armed Forces and their families; certain international adoptees; and receipt of Medicaid in certain contexts, especially by aliens under the age of 21, pregnant women (and women for up to 60 days after giving birth), and for certain services funded by Medicaid under the Individuals with Disabilities Education Act (IDEA) or in a school setting. Aliens who might qualify for these exemptions should study the rule carefully to understand how the exemptions work.

This final rule also clarifies that DHS will only consider public benefits received directly by the alien for the alien's own benefit, or where the alien is a listed beneficiary of the public benefit. DHS will not consider public benefits received on behalf of another. DHS also will not attribute receipt of a public benefit by one or more members of the alien's household to the alien unless the alien is also a listed beneficiary of the public benefit.

This final rule supersedes the 1999 Interim Field Guidance on Deportability and Inadmissibility on Public Charge Grounds.

DATES: This final rule is effective at 12:00 a.m. Eastern Time on October 15, 2019. DHS will apply this rule only to applications and petitions postmarked (or, if applicable, submitted electronically) on or after the effective date. Applications and petitions already pending with USCIS on the effective date of the rule (i.e., were postmarked before the effective date of the rule and were accepted by USCIS) will not be subject to the rule. . . .

SOURCE: Government Printing Office. *Federal Register.* Vol. 84, no. 157. August 14, 2019. https://www .govinfo.gov/content/pkg/FR-2019-08-14/pdf/2019-17142.pdf.

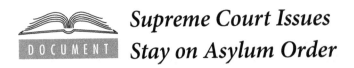

Supreme Court Issues
Stay on Asylum Order

September 11, 2019

[All citations have been omitted.]

WILLIAM P. BARR,
ATTORNEY GENERAL, ET AL.

v.

EAST BAY SANCTUARY
COVENANT, ET AL.

ON APPLICATION
FOR STAY

[September 11, 2019]

The application for stay presented to JUSTICE KAGAN and by her referred to the Court is granted. The district court's July 24, 2019 order granting a preliminary injunction and September 9, 2019 order restoring the nationwide scope of the injunction are stayed in full pending disposition of the Government's appeal in the United States Court of Appeals for the Ninth Circuit and disposition of the Government's petition for a writ of certiorari, if such writ is sought. If a writ of certiorari is sought and the Court denies the petition, this order shall terminate automatically. If the Court grants the petition for a writ of certiorari, this order shall terminate when the Court enters its judgment.

JUSTICE SOTOMAYOR, with whom JUSTICE GINSBURG joins, dissenting from grant of stay.

Once again the Executive Branch has issued a rule that seeks to upend longstanding practices regarding refugees who seek shelter from persecution. Although this Nation has long kept its doors open to refugees—and although the stakes for asylum seekers could not be higher—the Government implemented its rule without first providing the public notice and inviting the public input generally required by law. After several organizations representing immigrants sued to stop the rule from going into effect, a federal district court found that the organizations were likely to prevail and preliminarily enjoined the rule nationwide. A federal appeals court narrowed the injunction to run only circuit-wide, but denied the Government's motion for a complete stay.

Now the Government asks this Court to intervene and to stay the preliminary decisions below. This is an extraordinary request. Unfortunately, the Court acquiesces. Because I do not believe the Government has met its weighty burden for such relief, I would deny the stay.

The Attorney General and Secretary of Homeland Security promulgated the rule at issue here on July 16, 2019. In effect, the rule forbids almost all Central Americans—even unaccompanied children—to apply for asylum in the United States if they enter or seek to enter through the southern border, unless they were first denied asylum in Mexico or another third country.

The District Court found that the rule was likely unlawful for at least three reasons. First, the court found it probable that the rule was inconsistent with the asylum statute. . . . Section 1158 generally provides that any noncitizen "physically present in the United States or who arrives in the United States . . . may apply for asylum." And unlike the rule, the District Court explained, the statute provides narrow, carefully calibrated exceptions to asylum eligibility. As relevant here, Congress restricted asylum based on the possibility that a person could safely resettle in a third country. The rule, by contrast, does not consider whether refugees were safe or resettled in Mexico—just whether they traveled through it. That blunt approach, according to the District Court, rewrote the statute.

Second, the District Court found that the challengers would likely prevail because the Government skirted typical rulemaking procedures. The District Court noted "serious questions" about the rule's validity because the Government effected a sea change in immigration law without first providing advance notice and opportunity for public comment. The District Court found the Government's purported justifications unpersuasive at the preliminary-injunction stage.

Last, the District Court found the explanation for the rule so poorly reasoned that the Government's action was likely arbitrary and capricious. On this score, the District Court addressed the Government's principal justifications for the rule: that failing to seek asylum while fleeing through more than one country "raises questions about the validity and urgency" of the asylum seeker's claim; and that Mexico, the last port of entry before the United States, offers a feasible alternative for persons seeking protection from persecution. The District Court examined the evidence in the administrative record and explained why it flatly refuted the Government's assumptions. A "mountain of evidence points one way," the District Court observed, yet the Government "went the other—with no explanation."

After the District Court issued the injunction, the Ninth Circuit declined the Government's request for a complete stay, reasoning that the Government did not make the required "'strong showing'" that it would likely succeed on the merits of each issue. Narrowing the injunction to the Circuit's borders, the Ninth Circuit expedited the appeal and permitted the District Court to consider whether additional facts would warrant a broader injunction.

The lower courts' decisions warrant respect. A stay pending appeal is "extraordinary" relief. Given the District Court's thorough analysis, and the serious questions that court raised, I do not believe the Government has carried its "especially heavy" burden. The rule here may be, as the District Court concluded, in significant tension with the asylum statute. It may also be arbitrary and capricious for failing to engage with the record evidence contradicting its conclusions. It is especially concerning, moreover, that the rule the Government promulgated topples decades of settled asylum practices and affects some of the most vulnerable people in the Western Hemisphere—without affording the public a chance to weigh in.

Setting aside the merits, the unusual history of this case also counsels against our intervention. This lawsuit has been proceeding on three tracks: In this Court, the parties have litigated the Government's stay request. In the Ninth Circuit, the parties are briefing the Government's appeal. And in the District Court, the parties recently participated in an evidentiary hearing to supplement the record. Indeed, just two days ago the District Court reinstated a nationwide injunction based on new facts. Notably, the Government moved to stay the newest order in both the District Court and the Ninth Circuit. (Neither court has resolved that request, though the Ninth Circuit granted an administrative stay to allow further deliberation.) This Court has not considered the new evidence, nor does it pause for the lower courts to resolve the Government's pending motions. By granting a stay, the Court simultaneously lags behind and jumps ahead of the courts below. And in doing so, the Court side-steps the ordinary judicial process to allow the Government to implement a rule that bypassed the ordinary rulemaking process. I fear that the Court's precipitous action today risks undermining the interbranch governmental processes that encourage deliberation, public participation, and transparency.

* * *

In sum, granting a stay pending appeal should be an "extraordinary" act. Unfortunately, it appears the Government has treated this exceptional mechanism as a new normal. Historically, the Government has made this kind of request rarely; now it does so reflexively. Not long ago, the Court resisted the shortcut the Government now invites. I regret that my colleagues have not exercised the same restraint here. I respectfully dissent.

SOURCE: Supreme Court of the United States. *Barr v. East Bay Sanctuary Covenant*. 588 U.S. __ (2019). September 11, 2019. https://www.supremecourt.gov/opinions/18pdf/19a230_k53l.pdf.

DOCUMENT

President Trump Issues Immigration Proclamation 9945

October 4, 2019

By the President of the United States of America

A Proclamation

Healthcare providers and taxpayers bear substantial costs in paying for medical expenses incurred by people who lack health insurance or the ability to pay for their healthcare. Hospitals and other providers often administer care to the uninsured without any hope of receiving reimbursement from them. The costs associated with this care are passed on to the American people in the form of higher taxes, higher premiums, and higher fees for medical services. In total, uncompensated care costs—the overall measure of unreimbursed services that hospitals give their patients—have exceeded $35 billion in each of the last 10 years. These costs amount to approximately $7 million on average for each hospital in the United States, and can drive hospitals into insolvency. Beyond uncompensated care costs, the uninsured strain Federal and State government budgets through their reliance on publicly funded programs, which ultimately are financed by taxpayers.

Beyond imposing higher costs on hospitals and other healthcare infrastructure, uninsured individuals often use emergency rooms to seek remedies for a variety of non-emergency conditions, causing overcrowding and delays for those who truly need emergency services. This non-emergency usage places a large burden on taxpayers, who reimburse hospitals for a portion of their uncompensated emergency care costs.

While our healthcare system grapples with the challenges caused by uncompensated care, the United States Government is making the problem worse by admitting thousands of aliens who have not demonstrated any ability to pay for their healthcare costs. Notably, data show that lawful immigrants are about three times more likely than United States citizens to lack health insurance. Immigrants who enter this country should not further saddle our healthcare system, and subsequently American taxpayers, with higher costs.

The United States has a long history of welcoming immigrants who come lawfully in search of brighter futures. We must continue that tradition while also addressing the challenges facing our healthcare system, including protecting both it and the American taxpayer from the burdens of uncompensated care. Continuing to allow entry into the United States of certain immigrants who lack health insurance or the demonstrated ability to pay for their healthcare would be detrimental to these interests.

Now, Therefore, I, Donald J. Trump, by the authority vested in me by the Constitution and the laws of the United States of America, including sections 212(f) and 215(a) of the Immigration and Nationality Act (8 U.S.C. 1182(f) and 1185(a)) and section 301 of title 3, United States Code, hereby find that the unrestricted immigrant entry into the United States of persons described in section 1 of this proclamation would, except as provided for in section 2 of this proclamation, be detrimental to the interests of the United States, and that their entry should be subject to certain restrictions, limitations, and exceptions. I therefore hereby proclaim the following:

Section 1. Suspension and Limitation on Entry. (a) The entry into the United States as immigrants of aliens who will financially burden the United States healthcare system is hereby suspended and limited subject to section 2 of this proclamation. An alien will financially burden the United States healthcare system unless the alien will be covered by approved health insurance, as defined in subsection (b) of this section, within 30 days of the alien's entry into the United States, or unless the alien possesses the financial resources to pay for reasonably foreseeable medical costs.

(b) Approved health insurance means coverage under any of the following plans or programs:

(i) an employer-sponsored plan, including a retiree plan, association health plan, and coverage provided by the Consolidated Omnibus Budget Reconciliation Act of 1985;

(ii) an unsubsidized health plan offered in the individual market within a State;

(iii) a short-term limited duration health policy effective for a minimum of 364 days—or until the beginning of planned, extended travel outside the United States;

(iv) a catastrophic plan;

(v) a family member's plan;

(vi) a medical plan under chapter 55 of title 10, United States Code, including coverage under the TRICARE program;

(vii) a visitor health insurance plan that provides adequate coverage for medical care for a minimum of 364 days—or until the beginning of planned, extended travel outside the United States;

(viii) a medical plan under the Medicare program; or

(ix) any other health plan that provides adequate coverage for medical care as determined by the Secretary of Health and Human Services or his designee.

(c) For persons over the age of 18, approved health insurance does not include coverage under the Medicaid program.

Sec. 2. Scope of Suspension and Limitation on Entry. (a) Section 1 of this proclamation shall apply only to aliens seeking to enter the United States pursuant to an immigrant visa.

(b) Section 1 of this proclamation shall not apply to:

(i) any alien holding a valid immigrant visa issued before the effective date of this proclamation;

(ii) any alien seeking to enter the United States pursuant to a Special Immigrant Visa, in either the SI or SQ classification, who is also a national of Afghanistan or Iraq, or his or her spouse and children, if any;

(iii) any alien who is the child of a United States citizen or who is seeking to enter the United States pursuant to an IR–2, IR–3, IR–4, IH–3, or IH–4 visa;

(iv) any alien seeking to enter the United States pursuant to an IR–5 visa, provided that the alien or the alien's sponsor demonstrates to the satisfaction of the consular officer that the alien's healthcare will not impose a substantial burden on the United States healthcare system;

(v) any alien seeking to enter the United States pursuant to a SB–1 visa;

(vi) any alien under the age of 18, except for any alien accompanying a parent who is also immigrating to the United States and subject to this proclamation;

(vii) any alien whose entry would further important United States law enforcement objectives, as determined by the Secretary of State or his designee based on a recommendation of the Attorney General or his designee; or

(viii) any alien whose entry would be in the national interest, as determined by the Secretary of State or his designee on a case-by-case basis.

(c) Consistent with subsection (a) of this section, this proclamation does not affect the entry of aliens entering the United States through means other than immigrant visas, including lawful permanent residents. Further, nothing in this proclamation shall be construed to affect any individual's eligibility for asylum, refugee status, withholding of removal, or protection under the Convention Against Torture and Other Cruel, Inhuman or Degrading Treatment or Punishment, consistent with the laws and regulations of the United States.

Sec. 3. Implementation and Enforcement. (a) An alien subject to this proclamation must establish that he or she meets its requirements, to the satisfaction of a consular officer, before the adjudication and issuance of an immigrant visa. The Secretary of State may establish standards and procedures governing such determinations.

(b) The review required by subsection (a) of this section is separate and independent from the review and determination required by other statutes, regulations, or proclamations in determining the admissibility of an alien.

(c) An alien who circumvents the application of this proclamation through fraud, willful misrepresentation of a material fact, or illegal entry shall be a priority for removal by the Department of Homeland Security.

Sec. 4. Reports on the Financial Burdens Imposed by Immigrants on the Healthcare System. (a) The Secretary of State, in consultation with the Secretary of Health and Human Services, the Secretary of Homeland Security, and the heads of other appropriate agencies, shall submit to the President a report regarding:

(i) the continued necessity of and any adjustments that may be warranted to the suspension and limitation on entry in section 1 of this proclamation; and

(ii) other measures that may be warranted to protect the integrity of the United States healthcare system.

(b) The report required by subsection (a) of this section shall be submitted within 180 days of the effective date of this proclamation, with subsequent reports submitted annually thereafter throughout the effective duration of the suspension and limitation on entry set forth in section 1 of this proclamation. If the Secretary of State, in consultation with the heads of other appropriate executive departments and agencies, determines that circumstances no longer warrant the continued effectiveness of the suspension or limitation on entry set forth in section 1 of this proclamation or that circumstances warrant additional measures, the Secretary shall immediately so advise the President.

(c) The Secretary of State and Secretary of Health and Human Services shall coordinate any policy recommendations associated with the reports described in subsection (a) of this section.

Sec. 5. Severability. It is the policy of the United States to enforce this proclamation to the maximum extent possible to advance the interests of the United States. Accordingly:

(a) if any provision of this proclamation, or the application of any provision to any person or circumstance, is held to be invalid, the remainder of the proclamation and the application of its other provisions to any other persons or circumstances shall not be affected thereby; and

(b) if any provision of this proclamation, or the application of any provision to any person or circumstance, is held to be invalid because of the failure to follow certain procedures, the relevant executive branch officials shall implement those procedural requirements to conform with existing law and with any applicable court orders.

Sec. 6. General Provisions. (a) Nothing in this proclamation shall be construed to impair or otherwise affect:

(i) United States Government obligations under applicable international agreements;

(ii) the authority granted by law to an executive department or agency, or the head thereof; or

(iii) the functions of the Director of the Office of Management and Budget relating to budgetary, administrative, or legislative proposals.

(b) This proclamation shall be implemented consistent with applicable law and subject to the availability of appropriations.

(c) This proclamation is not intended to, and does not, create any right or benefit, substantive or procedural, enforceable at law or in equity by any party against the United States, its departments, agencies, or entities, its officers, employees, or agents, or any other person.

Sec. 7. Effective Date. This proclamation is effective at 12:01 a.m. eastern daylight time on November 3, 2019.

In Witness Whereof, I have hereunto set my hand this fourth day of October, in the year of our Lord two thousand nineteen, and of the Independence of the United States of America the two hundred and forty-fourth.

DONALD J. TRUMP

SOURCE: Executive Office of the President. "Proclamation 9945—Suspension of Entry of Immigrants Who Will Financially Burden the United States Healthcare System, in Order to Protect the Availability of Healthcare Benefits for Americans." October 4, 2019. *Compilation of Presidential Documents* 2019, no. 00699 (October 4, 2019). https://www.govinfo.gov/content/pkg/DCPD-201900699/pdf/DCPD-201900699 .pdf.

OTHER HISTORIC DOCUMENTS OF INTEREST

FROM THIS VOLUME

FROM PREVIOUS *HISTORIC DOCUMENTS*

United Nations and Pacific Regional Leaders Call for End of Violence in Indonesia

AUGUST 16 AND SEPTEMBER 4, 2019

Indonesia was racked by several periods of public unrest in 2019, from protests challenging the outcome of general elections in April to student-led demonstrations against a perceived weakening of the country's anticorruption commission and other legislative actions. In August, racial slurs spoken against students from Indonesia's Papua region sparked two weeks of often-violent protests, with Papuans calling for an end to the discrimination they faced and some demanding independence. Clashes between protesters and Indonesian security forces, as well as a government-imposed Internet blackout, drew the attention of United Nations (UN) officials and experts, who pushed for an end to the violence and the preservation of human rights.

PRESIDENTIAL CHALLENGER PROTESTS ELECTION OUTCOME

Indonesia's restive year included protests challenging the reelection of President Joko Widodo, who first took office in 2014. Widodo had cultivated an image as a "man of the people" and is widely credited with spurring economic growth in the country. However, he faced criticism for failing to make progress in addressing Indonesia's human rights violations, and his efforts to court major infrastructure investments from China were controversial. Widodo's opponent was former general Prabowo Subianto, a former commander of Indonesia's special forces. Subianto had been accused of complicity in human rights abuses committed by General Suharto, a dictator who ruled Indonesia for thirty years, but he maintained his innocence. (Subianto is married to Suharto's daughter.) Subianto sought to distance himself from the former dictator and the country's political elites during his campaign. Notably, Subianto and Widodo had run against each other in 2014. When Widodo was announced the winner, Subianto challenged the result in Indonesia's constitutional court, but lost.

The election took place on April 17, 2019. An early quick count of election results showed Widodo was the likely winner, but Subianto declared victory and accused the president of cheating. "We got evidence of widespread cheating at the village, sub-district and district levels across Indonesia," he claimed. These allegations appeared to contradict reports from private pollsters who counted a sample of votes and also determined Widodo was likely to win. Various independent observers also stated the election had been free and fair. Official results were released by the General Elections Commission (KPU) on May 21, and Widodo had received 55.5 percent of the vote, commissioners reported. Subianto rejected the result and said he would pursue "legal avenues" to challenge the outcome.

Meanwhile, Subianto and his supporters called for protests in front of the KPU building in the capital of Jakarta. More than 30,000 armed police equipped with tear gas and water cannon were deployed around the KPU office and that of the Election Supervisory Body in anticipation of the protests. Demonstrations began the day that results were announced and were mostly peaceful. However, law enforcement officials reported that around 11:00 p.m., a mob of protesters tried to enter the office of the Election Supervisory Body. Police pushed the crowd away from the building but then were reportedly attacked with fireworks and stones. The mob also set fire to various debris, cars, and a police dormitory. The police used tear gas to dispel protesters and arrested roughly 100 people. The next morning, Jakarta governor Anies Baswedan reported that six people had been killed and 200 people injured in clashes between police and rioters. These totals were later increased to eight deaths and more than 600 injuries. Protests continued on May 22 and periodically became violent, with protesters reportedly throwing stones and burning tires. The government temporarily prohibited the sending of photos and videos via social media, with officials saying they did not want "hoaxes" to be spread to incite further rioting.

Papuans Protest Discrimination, Seek Independence

Amid Independence Day celebrations on August 17, allegations that Papuan university students desecrated an Indonesian flag emerged. Some accounts indicated the students bent a flagpole outside their dormitory in the East Java city of Surabaya, while others suggested they had thrown the flag on the ground. News of the incident spread quickly on social media, drawing a mob—including members of some nationalist groups—to the students' dorm. Members of the mob shouted anti-Papuan statements, and some called the students "monkeys," "pigs," and "dogs." When police arrived later, they fired tear gas into the building before arresting forty-three of the students. Some accounts indicated police used the slurs as well. The students were questioned briefly, then released.

The incident inflamed tensions in a region marked by clashes between Indonesian security forces and Papuan separatists. The Papua and West Papua provinces were part of a Dutch colony until they declared independence in 1961 but have formed the easternmost part of Indonesia since 1969, when Papuans voted to become part of the country's archipelago. Although recognized by the UN, the vote was widely considered a sham because only about 1,000 Papuans were allowed to participate. These Papuans were allegedly handpicked by Indonesian military officials and were threatened with violence if they did not vote in favor of joining the country. As a result, Papuans believed the vote was invalid and have pushed for independence ever since. Most Papuans are ethnic Melanesian and Christian, which makes them both ethnically and religiously distinct from the vast majority of Indonesia's population. (About 80 percent of Indonesians are Muslim, and of the country's more than 300 ethnic groups, Javanese make up about 40 percent of the population.) The Papuans say this has led to racial and ethnic discrimination. Indonesian security forces have also been accused of abusing Papuans' rights, including through arbitrary arrests and extrajudicial killings, in their efforts to quell unrest. Additionally, the Papua provinces are among the poorest parts of Indonesia despite the region's wealth of natural resources, such as the world's largest gold mine. This further contributed to discontent among Papuans. A weak separatist movement emerged and periodically challenges Indonesian security forces in the region. Papua has seen an uptick in violence since December 2018, when separatists attacked and killed nineteen people who were building infrastructure for a government contractor. The military crackdown that ensued, and ongoing clashes between the troops and separatists, displaced tens of thousands of people. The government took some steps to try to ease tensions, such as giving the region more autonomy, increasing government funds allocated to Papua, and scheduling more presidential visits to the area.

Against this backdrop, the August 17 incident sparked protests by thousands of Papuans angered by the slurs shouted at the students. In the cities of Sorong and Manokwari, the capital of West Papua province, protesters blocked roads as well as burned tires and tree branches. Manokwari deputy governor Mohamad Lakotani said protesters also set fire to the local parliament and office buildings, in addition to pulling down powerline poles and burning cars. In Sorong, protesters reportedly vandalized some parts of the airport. Protests also took place in Jayapura, the capital of Papua province, but reports indicated those demonstrations were largely peaceful.

Papua governor Lukas Enembe explained that the people were angry because of "the extremely racist words used by East Java people, the police, and military." Benny Wenda, the exiled West Papuan leader, said what happened to the students was "just one example of what we have experienced daily for nearly 60 years." He added, "Indonesians see our black skin as less than equal; they do not see us as human beings." Khofifah Indar Parawansa, governor of East Java province, apologized for the incident, saying it did "not represent the voice of the people of East Java." Then Coordinating Minister for Political, Legal, and Security Affairs Wiranto promised that the Indonesian government would conduct a "complete and fair" investigation into the incident, while Widodo appealed for calm. "It's okay to be emotional, but it's better to be forgiving," he said. "Patience is also better."

More than 1,200 police and soldiers were deployed to the region to help restore order. The government also blocked Internet access on August 22, stating the shutdown was necessary to stop the spread of disinformation that could inflame tensions. Internet service was partially restored in early September, though it remained suspended in cities where protests had been the most violent. But demonstrations continued, spreading to other cities and growing in size. Some turned deadly: on August 28, six protesters and one military officer were killed amid clashes in Deiyai. And in Jayapura on August 30, protesters set fire to the Papua People's Assembly and threw rocks at other buildings. In response, the government deployed an additional 1,250 police to the city.

In addition to demanding a recognition of and an end to discrimination against Papuans, many protesters called for a new independence referendum and self-determination for the region. The government has repeatedly rejected requests for a referendum. "Indonesia's unity is non-negotiable," said Wiranto. In late August, the government announced that five security personnel had been suspended by East Javan officials while allegations they had engaged in racial abuse were investigated. Separately, Wiranto said that police had identified two mob participants who were suspected of using hate speech.

Commenting on the ongoing unrest, UN high commissioner for human rights Michelle Bachelet said she was "disturbed by escalating violence" in Papua and West Papua, and particularly by the deaths of some protesters and security personnel. "There should be no place for such violence in a democratic and diverse Indonesia, and I encourage the authorities to engage in dialogue with the people of Papua and West Papua on their aspirations and concerns, as well as to restore internet services and refrain from any excessive use of force," she said. Bachelet noted that racism and discrimination were "a long-standing, serious issue" in the provinces and expressed concern that "nationalist militias and groups are also actively involved in the violence." She urged that "local human rights defenders," as well as students and journalists, be protected from threats and violence.

Regional leaders and advocates for the Papuans have repeatedly called for Bachelet's office to investigate alleged human rights abuses in the region. On August 16, one day before the Papuan students' arrest, leaders participating in the Pacific Islands Forum issued a communiqué strongly encouraging Indonesia to arrange a visit for Bachelet's office to investigate reported abuses and provide an "evidence-based, informed report" within a year. The leaders "reaffirmed recognition of Indonesia's sovereignty over West Papua" but acknowledged "the reported escalation in violence and continued allegations of human rights abuses" in the region. "Leaders called on all parties to protect and uphold the human rights of all residents and to work to address the root causes of the conflict by peaceful means," the communiqué stated.

Indonesia invited UN human rights officials to visit the country and the UN said it will send representatives, but there has not been an agreement on dates. Earlier in 2019, a UN spokesperson said there had been "a fair bit of back and forth" between the UN and Indonesia in relation to the proposed visit. "In the UN Human Rights office, we always insist on unfettered, unconditional access when we do get access, which means we should be able to meet with not only government officials but also civil society activists, of our choosing and we should be able to visit without any undue constraint," she added.

The Indonesian government banned violent protests and the public promotion of separatism on September 2, announcing at the same time that it was deploying an additional 6,000 police and military personnel to Papua and West Papua. Despite the ban, new protests broke out in the town of Wamena on September 23. Protesters set fire to a government office and other buildings, and gunfire between security personnel and "armed separatists" was reported. Twenty-eight people were killed and sixty-six were injured in the violence. The protests followed news that a local teacher had used racial slurs against a student, but Widodo and local government officials claimed that was "fake news." Roughly two weeks later, with protests and clashes ongoing, military officials reported that more than 16,000 people had fled Wamena to escape the violence.

STUDENTS PUSH FOR CHANGE

A fresh wave of protests began on September 24 as students in cities across the country rallied against parliament's approval of changes to the Corruption Eradication Commission. This independent agency had been established in 2002 after General Suharto's overthrow to combat what is widely seen as rampant government corruption. A law ratified by legislators on September 17 sought to reduce the commission's independence by making it a government entity, establishing a council to oversee the commission, and requiring the commission to receive state approval for certain investigative actions, such as conducting wiretaps. Students claimed these changes would significantly weaken the commission and called for the law's revocation or replacement. But, over several days of protests, their demands soon expanded to include calls for parliament to delay considering legislation that would criminalize or increase the penalties for certain sexual activities, including premarital sex. The students also pushed to delay bills on labor, environmental, and other issues, citing various problematic provisions.

Amid the public outcry, Widodo asked parliament to delay planned votes on Indonesia's criminal code and the other bills of concern to the students, and lawmakers agreed. However, the president said the government will not reverse changes to the corruption commission. The students pledged to continue their protests.

—Linda Grimm

Following is an excerpt from the Fiftieth Pacific Islands Forum Communique, issued on August 16, 2019, addressing the situation in West Papua; and a statement by UN high commissioner for human rights Michelle Bachelet on September 4, 2019, calling for an end to violence in Indonesia.

Leaders of Pacific Islands Call for Dialogue and Investigation

August 16, 2019

[The following statements specific to West Papua have been excerpted from a broader communiqué issued by participants in the Fiftieth Pacific Islands Forum.]

West Papua (Papua)

Leaders reaffirmed recognition of Indonesia's sovereignty over West Papua (Papua).

Leaders acknowledged the reported escalation in violence and continued allegations of human rights abuses in West Papua (Papua) and agreed to re-emphasise and reinforce the Forum's position of raising its concerns over the violence.

Leaders called on all parties to protect and uphold the human rights of all residents and to work to address the root causes of the conflict by peaceful means. Further, Leaders agreed to maintain open and constructive dialogue with Indonesia on the issue of alleged human rights abuses and violations in West Papua (Papua).

Leaders welcomed the invitation by Indonesia for a mission to West Papua (Papua) by the UN High Commissioner for Human Rights, and strongly encouraged both sides to finalise the timing of the visit and for an evidence-based, informed report on the situation be provided before the next Pacific Islands Forum Leaders meeting in 2020.

SOURCE: Pacific Islands Forum Secretariat. "Forum Communiqué." August 16, 2019. https://www.forum sec.org/wp-content/uploads/2019/08/50th-Pacific-Islands-Forum-Communique.pdf.

Statement by UN High Commissioner for Human Rights on the Situation in Indonesia

DOCUMENT

September 4, 2019

"I have been disturbed by escalating violence in the past two weeks in the Indonesian provinces of Papua and West Papua, and especially the deaths of some protestors and security forces personnel. This is part of a trend we have observed since December 2018, and we have been discussing our concerns with the Indonesian authorities. There should be no place for such violence in a democratic and diverse Indonesia, and I encourage the authorities to engage in dialogue with the people of Papua and West Papua on their aspirations and concerns, as well as to restore internet services and refrain from any excessive use of force. Blanket internet shutdowns are likely to contravene freedom of expression and limiting communications may exacerbate tensions.

"I welcome the appeals made by President Widodo and other high-level figures against racism and discrimination—a long-standing, serious issue in Papua and West Papua provinces—and their calls for dialogue and calm. I note that some arrests have been made and some members of security forces have been suspended in relation to the original violent attacks on Papuan students in Surabaya and Malang, but I am concerned about reports that nationalist militias and groups are also actively involved in the violence. Local human rights defenders, students and journalists have been facing intimidation and threats and should be protected."

SOURCE: From "Comment by UN High Commissioner for Human Rights Michelle Bachelet on Indonesia (Papua and West Papua)," September 4, 2019, by Office of the UN High Commissioner for Human Rights ©2019 United Nations. Reprinted with the permission of the United Nations. https://ohchr.org/EN/NewsEvents/Pages/DisplayNews.aspx?NewsID=24942&LangID=E.

OTHER HISTORIC DOCUMENTS OF INTEREST

FROM PREVIOUS HISTORIC DOCUMENTS

Trump Administration Announces Regulatory Changes to the Endangered Species Act

AUGUST 12, 2019

On August 12, 2019, the U.S. Fish and Wildlife Service (USFWS) and the National Oceanic and Atmospheric Administration's National Marine Fisheries Service (NOAA Fisheries) jointly announced several significant revisions to the Endangered Species Act (ESA) regulations that alter how the federal government implements that law. While the administration promoted these changes as an effort to modernize the framework, improve efficiency and transparency, and reduce regulatory constraints, critics maintained that the changes weaken the ESA's power to protect vulnerable species and habitats. A broad coalition of environmental advocacy organizations, Democratic members of Congress, and more than a dozen states challenged the new rules through lawsuits and legislative action.

ESA: The Legal Bedrock of Conservation

In response to the bald eagle's rapid population decline caused by DDT pesticide, and amid growing public concern over environmental degradation, Congress passed the ESA with overwhelming bipartisan support in 1973. For almost fifty years, the law has been a powerful regulatory tool for conservation, balancing the needs of plant and animal species against pressures of industrial development. The ESA has prevented extinction of wildlife such as the peregrine falcon, humpback whale, Tennessee purple coneflower, and numerous other species that are endemic and integral to functioning ecosystems across the country. Despite insufficient funding for conservation efforts, the law has been remarkably effective in its mandate to prevent extinction: of more than 1,600 species listed, only 11 have become extinct, and more than 55 have been recovered and delisted (including the bald eagle in 2007).

USFWS and NOAA Fisheries are responsible for using the best available science to identify species that are at risk of extinction based on population status and current threats. Those species that are found to be in danger of extinction are listed as endangered, and those at less imminent risk of extinction, but "likely to become endangered within the foreseeable future," are listed as threatened. When a species is listed, a critical habitat designation establishes protections for specific areas with physical and biological features necessary for recovery. Species on both lists are managed through recovery plans that are largely implemented by wildlife agencies at the state level.

According to a 2018 poll by researchers at The Ohio State University, about 80 percent of Americans (including a majority of conservatives) support the law. Despite its popularity among the general public, the ESA has long drawn the ire of those who perceive it as being overly restrictive to business and landowners. Supporters of the law acknowledge its shortcomings, and while modernizing the act has been discussed by both parties and among career staff at federal and state agencies, there is disagreement about the direction these efforts should take. Republicans maintain a goal to narrow the scope of the law and improve efficiency, while Democrats emphasize the need to ensure effectiveness, particularly given the growing uncertainty and urgency presented by climate change.

ESA Regulation Revisions

In 2017, USFWS sought public input on how the ESA's regulatory frameworks could be improved. After two years of review and revisions, the long-anticipated changes were jointly announced by the Departments of Interior and Commerce. The final rules include nearly all of the key changes the USFWS proposed in July 2018, in response to which more than 200,000 public comments were received. These changes, which apply only to future listing decisions and are not retroactive, are some of the most sweeping revisions ever made to the way the law is implemented.

One of the most contentious changes allows regulating agencies greater freedom to "compile" and "present" economic impacts when deciding whether a species warrants protection. The regulation retains language stating that a determination should be made "solely on the basis of the best scientific and commercial information," but it removes a key phrase that decisions be "made without reference to possible economic or other impacts." USFWS acknowledged that many public comments expressed opposition to removing this provision. The agency maintained that the revision improves transparency and does not signal any difference in how the rule will be implemented, but it is uncertain whether that stated intent will hold true because publishing economic impacts of potential development and opportunity costs could agitate public and industry opposition to a future listing proposal.

The administration also established restrictions requiring tighter causal links between threats and necessary protections. USFWS eliminated its "blanket rule" under section 4(d), where previously the same protections were given to endangered and threatened species alike, unless otherwise specified. NOAA Fisheries, which enforces the ESA for coastal and marine species, has always designated protections for threatened species and their habitats on a case-by-case basis, and this change promotes greater alignment between the agencies in their application of the provision. A related change could make removing species from the list easier, as the new regulations related to "de-listing" no longer mention the term *recovery*.

The new regulations limit the ability of an agency to weigh impacts of climate change when making listing assessments. To merit consideration, impacts of climate change will require higher levels of certainty in the "foreseeable future," and the regulating agency has significant discretion in interpreting what "foreseeable future" means, as well as the scientific data to be considered "best available." Many public comments expressed concern that under the proposed framework, the USFWS would not consider the probable threat of climate change as immediate or operative enough, or would otherwise elect to disregard relevant climate models. These heightened standards make it more difficult to designate an area that may be critical to a species survival as "critical habitat" if the species does not occupy that area at the time of evaluation. Species that are at risk of habitat loss and shifting migration patterns due to climate change in the coming decades are most vulnerable in this situation. For example, under this framework, it would have been much more difficult to list the polar bear as threatened in 2010. Because of the loss of sea ice, their critical habitat designation included nearly 200,000 square miles of barrier islands in Alaska based on climate models predicting how rapid warming in the Arctic could impact polar bear habitat in the coming decades.

At the same time the administration was considering revisions to the ESA, the United Nations Intergovernmental Science Policy Platform on Biodiversity and Ecosystem Services (IPBES) released a comprehensive report presenting a biodiversity crisis that threatens every ecosystem on Earth. The assessment found that upward of one million plant and animal species are at risk of extinction, some within decades. According to the report, this is being accelerated by factors including mass industrialization and climate change and will carry consequences for global food and water security and human health.

Despite warnings such as the United Nations assessment, the ESA revisions have long been a priority for conservatives, particularly in rural states, who see it as a regulatory burden that unfairly restricts land use and hinders economic growth. Republican lawmakers and industry groups applauded the changes. Rep. Rob Bishop, R-Utah, ranking member of the House Natural Resources Committee, said, "These final revisions are aimed at enhancing interagency cooperation, clarifying standards, and removing inappropriate one-size-fits-all practices." Others felt the overhaul of the regulatory framework did not go far enough. Sen. John Barrasso, R-Wyo., said in a statement, "These final rules are a good start, but the administration is limited by an existing law that needs to be updated. We must modernize the Endangered Species Act in a way that empowers states, promotes the recovery of species, and allows local economies to thrive."

ESA Changes Challenged in Congress and the Courts

The final rules were challenged in Congress and in the courts on grounds that the changes substantially weaken how protections are considered and enforced, and thus violate the ESA's mandate to prevent extinction and recover endangered populations. About a week after the changes were announced, a coalition of national environmental and conservation advocacy organizations, led by Earthjustice, filed a lawsuit against the Trump administration for violation of the language and purpose of the ESA on multiple counts—and violation of the National Environmental Policy Act—by failing to publicly disclose and analyze potential harms and impacts of some changes that were included in the final rules but were not subject to public comment. "The new rules move the Endangered Species Act dangerously away from its grounding in sound science that has made the Act so effective—opening the door to political decisions couched as claims that threats to species are too uncertain to address," said Sierra Club staff attorney Karimah Schoenhut in a press release.

This legal challenge was followed by a similar suit filed by a coalition of seventeen state attorneys general, led by Massachusetts and California. Maura Healey, attorney general of Massachusetts, explained the states were "suing to defend federal law and protect our imperiled wildlife and environment," telling *The Washington Post* that the "the way this was done was illegal under federal laws and this is an administration that needs to be held accountable." In court, the administration will be required to present a reasoned basis for the changes and demonstrate consistency with the underlying law. This will likely require a court to overrule a long-standing precedent: the 1978 Supreme Court case of *Tennessee Valley Authority v. Hill* ruled that under the ESA, costs associated with conservation efforts are "legally irrelevant" and that conservation of a species was the highest priority of the law.

These changes are subject to opposition under the Congressional Review Act, which gives Congress broad authority to assess and invalidate rules established by federal agencies. Sen. Tom Udall, D-N.M., ranking member of the appropriations subcommittee that oversees the Department of the Interior's budget, said in a statement, "The Trump administration issued regulations that take a wrecking ball to one of our oldest and most effective environmental laws. . . . As we have seen time and time again, no environmental protection—no matter how effective or popular—is safe from this administration." On September 17, 2019, Senator Udall and House Natural Resources Committee chair Raúl Grijalva, D-Ariz., each introduced legislation to nullify the rules.

—Megan Howes

Following is the text of a press release from the Department of the Interior on August 12, 2019, detailing the changes made to the Endangered Species Act (ESA).

DOCUMENT

Changes to the Endangered Species Act Announced

August 12, 2019

In its more than 45-year history, the Endangered Species Act (ESA) has catalyzed countless conservation partnerships that have helped recover some of America's most treasured animals and plants from the bald eagle to the American alligator. Today, U.S. Secretary of the Interior David Bernhardt unveiled improvements to the implementing regulations of the ESA designed to increase transparency and effectiveness and bring the administration of the Act into the 21st century.

"The best way to uphold the Endangered Species Act is to do everything we can to ensure it remains effective in achieving its ultimate goal—recovery of our rarest species. The Act's effectiveness rests on clear, consistent and efficient implementation," said Secretary Bernhardt. "An effectively administered Act ensures more resources can go where they will do the most good: on-the-ground conservation."

"The revisions finalized with this rulemaking fit squarely within the President's mandate of easing the regulatory burden on the American public, without sacrificing our species' protection and recovery goals," said U.S. Secretary of Commerce Wilbur Ross. "These changes were subject to a robust, transparent public process, during which we received significant public input that helped us finalize these rules."

The changes finalized today by Interior's U.S. Fish and Wildlife Service and Commerce's National Marine Fisheries Service apply to ESA sections 4 and 7. Section 4, among other things, deals with adding species to or removing species from the Act's protections and designating critical habitat; section 7 covers consultations with other federal agencies.

The ESA directs that determinations to add or remove a species from the lists of threatened or endangered species be based solely on the best available scientific and commercial information, and these will remain the only criteria on which listing determinations will be based. The regulations retain language stating, "The Secretary shall make a [listing] determination solely on the basis of the best scientific and commercial information regarding a species' status."

The revisions to the regulations clarify that the standards for delisting and reclassification of a species consider the same five statutory factors as the listing of a species in the first place. This requirement ensures that all species proposed for delisting or reclassification receive the same careful analysis to determine whether or not they meet the statutory definitions of a threatened or endangered species as is done for determining whether to add a species to the list.

While this administration recognizes the value of critical habitat as a conservation tool, in some cases, designation of critical habitat is not prudent. Revisions to the regulations identify a non-exhaustive list of such circumstances, but this will continue to be rare exceptions.

When designating critical habitat, the regulations reinstate the requirement that areas where threatened or endangered species are present at the time of listing be evaluated first before unoccupied areas are considered. This reduces the potential for additional regulatory burden that results from a designation when species are not present in an area. In addition, the regulations impose a heightened standard for unoccupied areas to be designated as critical habitat. On top of the existing standard that the designated unoccupied habitat is essential to the conservation of the species, it must also, at the time of designation, contain one or more of the physical or biological features essential to the species' conservation.

To ensure federal government actions are not likely to jeopardize the continued existence of listed species or destroy or adversely modify their critical habitat, federal agencies must consult with the U.S. Fish and Wildlife Service and National Marine Fisheries Service under section 7 of the Act. The revisions to the implementing regulations clarify the interagency consultation process and make it more efficient and consistent.

The revisions codify alternative consultation mechanisms that may provide greater efficiency for how ESA consultations are conducted. They also establish a deadline for informal consultations to provide greater certainty for federal agencies and applicants of timely decisions, without compromising conservation of ESA-listed species.

Revisions to the definitions of "destruction or adverse modification," "effects of the action" and "environmental baseline" further improve the consultation process by providing clarity and consistency.

In addition to the final joint regulations, the U.S. Fish and Wildlife Service finalized a separate revision rescinding its "blanket rule" under section 4(d) of the ESA. The rule had automatically given threatened species the same protections as endangered species unless otherwise specified.

The National Marine Fisheries Service has never employed such a blanket rule, so the new regulations bring the two agencies into alignment. The change impacts only future threatened species' listings or reclassifications from endangered to threatened status and does not apply to species already listed as threatened. The U.S. Fish and Wildlife Service will craft species-specific 4(d) rules for each future threatened species determination as deemed necessary and advisable for the conservation of the species, as has been common practice for many species listed as threatened in recent years.

From comments received during the public comment period in making these regulatory changes, concerns were raised regarding the lack of transparency in making listing decisions and the economic impact associated with determinations. Public transparency is critical in all government decision making, and the preamble to the regulation clarifies that the ESA does not prohibit agencies from collecting data that determine this cost and making that information available, as long as doing so does not influence the listing determination.

The final regulations submitted to the Federal Register can be found here: https:// www.fws.gov/endangered/improving_ESA/regulation-revisions.html.

SOURCE: U.S. Department of the Interior. "Trump Administration Improves the Implementing Regulations of the Endangered Species Act." August 12, 2019. https://www.doi.gov/pressreleases/endan gered-species-act.

OTHER HISTORIC DOCUMENTS OF INTEREST

FROM PREVIOUS *HISTORIC DOCUMENTS*

Court Issues Ruling in Opioid Epidemic Trial; Federal Government Releases Funds to Fight Opioid Use

AUGUST 26 AND SEPTEMBER 4, 2019

During the past decade, opioid abuse and overdose deaths in the United States have risen significantly. State and local officials frequently blame the increase on pharmaceutical companies for downplaying the addiction risk associated with prescription opioids as well as doctors who overprescribe such pain medication. In 2019, the state of Oklahoma sought to hold accountable big-name pharmaceutical companies for their role in the opioid crisis that had devastated local communities and drained government coffers. The trial was closely watched by the more than 2,000 plaintiffs in a nationwide consolidated case brought by local governments against pharmaceutical companies, physicians, and distributors. Both the Oklahoma and nationwide cases sought to answer the question of whether the pharmaceutical industry could be held responsible for any part of the U.S. opioid epidemic.

OPIOID OVERDOSE DEATHS RISE

Historically, opioid-based medications, like oxycodone, hydrocodone, and morphine, were prescribed only to those suffering from a terminal illness or to treat extreme pain. In the 1990s, however, doctors began prescribing opioids at a higher rate as their use was widened to include a multitude of afflictions. In 2017, the year for which the most recent comprehensive data are available from the Centers for Disease Control and Prevention (CDC), more than 191 million opioid prescriptions were dispensed in the United States, although the prescribing rate of 58.7 prescriptions per 100 people was at its lowest in more than ten years.

In addition to being widely prescribed to treat almost any type of pain, opioids are highly addictive. According to the Substance Abuse and Mental Health Services Administration, in 2018, 10.3 million Americans aged twelve and older misused opioids, and the majority of those individuals were abusing opioids first prescribed as a pain reliever. Some of the individuals who become addicted to prescription pain medication will later switch to heroin, because it is easier to obtain and less expensive. Those addicted to prescription opioids are forty times more likely than the general population to become heroin addicts. Heroin is sometimes laced with fentanyl, a synthetic drug that is fifty times more potent than heroin and extremely lethal when not used under a doctor's close supervision.

The proliferation of opioid addiction has deadly consequences on the U.S. population. In 2017, the CDC reports there were more than 70,200 overdose deaths in the United States, of which 47,600 involved opioids. According to the Department of Health and Human Services, in 2016 and 2017, 130 Americans died each day from an opioid-related overdose, and these deaths have contributed to a decrease in the average U.S. life expectancy. The number of deaths attributed to opioid-related overdoses has shown few signs of slowing. In the Midwest, an area hit particularly hard by the opioid epidemic, opioid overdoses increased 70 percent from July 2016 through September 2017. Nationwide, from 2010 to 2017, heroin overdose deaths increased fivefold. Public health experts refer to these as "deaths of despair" because they disproportionately impact those without a college degree and veterans. Around 80 percent of opioid-related overdose victims are non-Hispanic whites, and according to the National Institutes of Health (NIH) veterans are twice as likely to die from an overdose as the general population.

The economic impact of the opioid epidemic is estimated at tens of billions of dollars per year. This cost accounts for a number of factors, including state and local government spending to provide services to those addicted to opioids and their families, foster care for children impacted by the crisis, and lost productivity. According to Alan Krueger, a former economic aide to Presidents Bill Clinton and Barack Obama, the opioid crisis could account for more than 40 percent of the decline in the male labor force participation rate from 1999 to 2015 and 25 percent of the decline in the female labor force participation rate over the same time.

CONGRESS, FEDERAL AGENCIES RESPOND TO OPIOID EPIDEMIC

To counteract the growing number of adults falling victim to opioid addiction, federal, state, and local governments enacted programs and legislation aimed at addressing the problem. States have begun passing laws that limit opioid prescribing and are also shifting their law enforcement focus from incarceration to treatment in an effort to decrease demand for opioids. In 2016, Congress passed the 21st Century Cures Act, which provided $1 billion over two years in opioid crisis grants to states. Two years later, in October 2018, the SUPPORT for Patients and Communities Act was signed into law to promote research to find new, less addictive prescription pain medications. The law also expanded the availability of substance abuse treatment for Medicaid recipients. In 2019, the federal government, under the direction of the White House, provided millions of dollars in funds to states, territories, and localities to expand access to treatment for opioid addiction and help state and local governments cope with the crisis.

In 2017, the Department of Justice launched its Opioid Fraud and Abuse Detection Unit to prosecute opioid-related health care fraud. At the same time, it began a three-year pilot program that placed attorneys in twelve jurisdictions around the country who specialize in this type of fraud. In June 2018, the department announced the largest-ever health care fraud enforcement action, with charges against more than 150 nurses, doctors, and other licensed medical professionals for their roles in prescribing and distributing opioid medications.

The most attention-grabbing recent attempts to combat the opioid crisis, however, have come out of state and local governments that have elected to sue major pharmaceutical companies, drug distributors, and even individual physicians, alleging that their marketing and overprescribing techniques drove the opioid crisis. In these cases, the plaintiffs are seeking billions of dollars in damages to cover the cost of services for addressing the opioid epidemic in their communities.

OKLAHOMA WINS FIRST MAJOR PHARMACEUTICAL COMPANY OPIOID CASE

Oklahoma launched the first major opioid lawsuit trial in the United States in June 2017 when the state's attorney general filed suit against thirteen separate pharmaceutical companies for their role in the opioid crisis. From 2015 to 2018, eighteen million opioid prescriptions were written in the state, which has fewer than four million residents. Since 2000, approximately 6,000 Oklahomans died from an opioid overdose.

A majority of the thirteen defendants in *Oklahoma v. Purdue Pharma et al.* settled out of court, but Johnson & Johnson and its subsidiary Janssen Pharmaceuticals chose to go to trial. According to the state, members of the Johnson & Johnson sales team made 150,000 visits to Oklahoma doctors from 2000 to 2011. These visits specifically targeted high-volume prescribers, and the state alleged that the goal of Johnson & Johnson during these visits was to mislead doctors into believing that the opioids were safe to prescribe despite addiction concerns. During the trial, the state described a particular marketing initiative that touted the concept of "pseudoaddiction," the idea that patients requesting early or excessive opioid prescription refills were not always addicted but rather had unmanaged pain that needed to be addressed.

Lawyers for Johnson & Johnson argued that the company could not be held liable for the epidemic because its opioid sales comprise only 1 percent of the market, the drugs it sells are tightly controlled by state and federal agencies, the state had not identified any doctor who was misled by Johnson & Johnson's marketing, and certain products contain a black box warning about addiction as required by government regulations. Furthermore, Johnson & Johnson held that because Janssen no longer made its own opioid pills (after selling the rights to its drugs in 2015) nor did it manufacture hydrocodone or oxycodone, two drugs whose illicit use was driving the epidemic, Janssen cannot be held accountable.

The ruling by Judge Thad Balkman of Oklahoma's Cleveland County District Court was widely anticipated by other governments pursuing or considering similar suits. On August 26, 2019, Judge Balkman ruled that Johnson & Johnson intentionally downplayed the dangers of opioids while overselling their benefits. The company used a "false, misleading, and deceptive marketing campaign designed to convince Oklahoma doctors, patients, and the public at large that opioids were safe and effective for the long-term treatment of chronic, non-malignant pain," the judge wrote. According to Balkman, Johnson & Johnson and Janssen Pharmaceuticals were guilty of perpetuating a "public nuisance" that contributed to the state's ongoing opioid crisis.

Oklahoma was seeking a $17 billion judgment to pay for addiction treatment, drug courts, and other services necessary to assist residents with the opioid crisis through the next few decades. Judge Balkman instead ordered Johnson & Johnson to pay $572 million, an amount later reduced to $465 million due to a mathematical error the judge made in his initial ruling. Oklahoma attorney general Mike Hunter said the ruling "affirmed our position that Johnson & Johnson maliciously and diabolically created the opioid epidemic in our state." Hunter also expressed a desire to appeal the judge's fine, saying, "It is crystal clear under Oklahoma law that once a company is found liable for causing a public nuisance, it must pay what it takes to clean it up until the nuisance is gone."

While promising an appeal, Johnson & Johnson's general counsel and executive vice president, Michael Ullmann, said "neither the facts nor the law support this outcome. We recognize the opioid crisis is a tremendously complex public health issue" and "we have deep sympathy for everyone affected." Sabrina Strong, a lawyer for Johnson & Johnson, said the state could not "sue your way out of the opioid crisis." She added, "Everyone must come together to address this. But J&J did not cause the opioid crisis." The company filed an appeal in December 2019, arguing that the judge improperly applied the public nuisance standard in the case; that appeal was pending as of the time of this writing.

Nationwide Consolidated Case Moves toward Trial

While the Oklahoma case was being tried, more than 2,000 additional cases against drug manufacturers, distributors, and individual physicians brought by cities, counties, and individuals were consolidated by a judicial panel into one case, National Prescription Opiate Litigation. In these cases, the local governments were seeking settlement funds to address the opioid crisis in their communities. The federal court for the Northern District of Ohio was chosen as the venue for all pretrial motions. Once those were heard by Judge Dan Polster, the cases would be sent back to their original courts. The expectation was that many would settle before going to trial. Ohio was the chosen venue because it was the second hardest hit in the nation by the opioid epidemic, the location was geographically convenient for defendants, and the judge had extensive experience with consolidated cases.

The nationwide case accuses drug makers of driving the opioid crisis in search of profit by downplaying addiction and overdose risk. It further accuses distributors—including big names such as CVS, Walgreens, and Walmart—of failing to detect, probe, or report suspicious opioid orders. Companies have argued that their drugs are heavily regulated and require a licensed physician to write a prescription, and they therefore cannot be held liable.

The plaintiffs in the case were consolidated into what is known as a "negotiation class" that allows lawyers to work out the details of a settlement on behalf of every U.S. city and county (unless the city or county opts out). Members of the class are then given the opportunity to vote on the settlement, and if enough approve, the judge signs off and the settlement is finalized. This resolves any other pending lawsuits that are part of the consolidated federal case against companies involved in the settlement and protects the company from future lawsuits by cities or counties at the federal court level. Thirty-seven state attorneys general wrote a letter arguing against the use of the negotiation class, stating that it hurt their bargaining power in separate lawsuits filed in state courts against these companies. The local governments disagreed, arguing that the state should not act as a middleman in a crisis that more heavily impacted local communities. "At this level of government, we are in the best position to serve our local communities and we know what we have spent and what we need for the future," Summit County, Ohio, said in a statement.

OxyContin manufacturer Purdue Pharma and its controlling Sackler family were expected to be part of the consolidated litigation, but they instead reached a settlement in which they agreed to file for Chapter 11 bankruptcy protection, dissolve, transfer all assets to a new company with a board selected by plaintiffs, provide opioid addiction treatment and overdose reversal drugs such as Naloxone at low or no cost, and give plaintiffs $3 billion of the Sacklers' money and billions more of the future revenue of OxyContin sales. In turn, a judge ordered a temporary pause on all state and local government litigation against Purdue and the Sacklers.

Before the first consolidated trials got underway, various motions were filed to stall the proceedings. A group of retailers and distributors named as defendants petitioned the Sixth Circuit Court of Appeals to have Polster removed from the case for alleged bias against the drug industry; that motion was rejected. The Sixth Circuit also rejected an attempt by Ohio attorney general Dave Yost and thirteen other states and the District of Columbia to postpone or dismiss the trial, arguing that it would undermine states' right to litigate on their own and that cities and counties were essentially usurping state authority. (No state was a plaintiff in the consolidated case.)

October 21, 2019, was supposed to mark the start of the federal opioid trial, where Polster would first hear the cases over which his court has jurisdiction, those filed by Cuyahoga and Summit Counties against opioid drug makers in October and December 2017, respectively. However, four defendants in the case—McKesson Corp., Cardinal Health Inc., AmerisourceBergen Corp., and Teva Pharmaceuticals—reached a $260 million settlement with the two counties in lieu of a trial just hours before it was scheduled to start. (Johnson & Johnson, Mallinckrodt, Endo International, and Allergan, who were also listed as defendants, had already reached settlements with the counties.) The settlements with Cuyahoga and Summit Counties did not remove these companies from the larger federal litigation that would be heard in Polster's court, but rather settled only the Cuyahoga and Summit portions of the consolidated case. Additionally, by agreeing to the settlement, Cuyahoga and Summit Counties would lose out on any negotiation class settlement funds.

New trials in the consolidated case were expected to be scheduled by Polster in early 2020.

—Heather Kerrigan

Following is the edited text of Oklahoma v. Purdue Pharma, et al., *decided on August 26, 2019, in which Judge Thad Balkman ruled that the defendants played a role in the state's opioid crisis through their marketing of prescription drugs; and the text of a September 4, 2019, press release from the Department of Health and Human Services on funds distributed to state and local governments to address opioid addiction and treatment.*

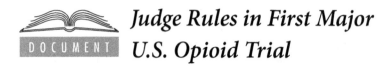 **Judge Rules in First Major U.S. Opioid Trial**

August 26, 2019

[All citations have been omitted.]

IN THE DISTRICT COURT OF CLEVELAND COUNTY

STATE OF OKLAHOMA

Case No. CJ-2017-816
Judge Thad Balkman
State of Oklahoma, ex rel.,
Mike Hunter,

Attorney General of Oklahoma,
            Plaintiff,

vs.

(1)   Purdue Pharma L.P.;

(2)   Purdue Pharma, Inc.;

(3)   The Purdue Frederick Company;

(4)   Teva Pharmaceuticals USA, Inc.;

(5)   Cephalon, Inc.;

(6)   Johnson & Johnson;

(7)   Janssen Pharmaceuticals, Inc.;

(8)   Ortho-McNeil-Janssen Pharmaceuticals, Inc., n/k/a Janssen Pharmaceuticals, Inc.;

(9)   Janssen Pharmaceutica, Inc., n/k/a Janssen Pharmaceuticals, Inc.;

(10) Allergan, PLC, f/k/a Actavis PLC, f/k/a Actavis, Inc., f/k/a Watson Pharmaceuticals, Inc.;

(11) Watson Laboratories, Inc.;

(12) Actavis LLC; and

(13) Actavis Pharma, Inc., f/k/a Watson Pharma, Inc.,
        Defendants.

JUDGMENT AFTER NON-JURY TRIAL

Beginning May 28, 2019, and ending July 15, 2019, the Court conducted a non-jury trial in the above-captioned matter. From the time this action was commenced on June 30, 2017, and through and including today, this Court has been the beneficiary of exemplary professionalism and legal work on the part of counsel for each of the parties—certainly on par with what one would hope for and expect in a case of this magnitude. For that, I wish to express my sincere appreciation of each of you. The Court, having heard testimony of the witnesses sworn and examined in open court, having observed their demeanor and credibility, having reviewed the exhibits admitted into evidence, and being fully advised in the premises, finds as follows:

[The background in the case and overview of Oklahoma's drug crisis has been omitted.]

FINDINGS OF FACT

To the extent any evidence in the record conflicts with one of the facts found below, the Court has weighed the competing evidence and found that the greater weight of the evidence weighs in favor of the facts set forth below.

1.   The State of Oklahoma and the public in general are currently experiencing an opioid crisis and epidemic (herein after referred to as the "Opioid Crisis).

2.   This current stage of the Opioid Crisis was started by and still primarily involves prescription opioids.

3.   Through the mid-1990s, there was no opioid epidemic.

4.   Since at least the mid-1990s, Defendants have marketed, promoted and sold opioid drugs in Oklahoma. During this time period, Defendants specifically manufactured and sold certain of their own branded opioid drugs as a part of its pain franchise, including: (i) Duragesic—a transdermal patch made out of the active pharmaceutical ingredient ("API"), fentanyl; (ii) Ultram and Ultram Extended Release ("ER")—tablets made out of the API, tramadol; (iii) Ultracet—tablets made out of the APIs, tramadol and acetaminophen; (iv) Nucynta and Nucynta ER—tablets made out of the API, tapentadol; (v) Tylenol with Codeine—tablets made out of the APIs, acetaminophen and codine; (vi) Tylox—capsules made out of the APIs, acetaminophen and oxycodone.

5.   Dr. Paul Janssen originally invented fentanyl in the 1950s. Fentanyl is a highly addictive opioid. Fentanyl can always be abused. As a Schedule II opioid comprised of fentanyl, Defendants' Duragesic "has the highest potential for abuse."

[A history of Johnson & Johnson's opioid growing and importing subsidiaries and partners has been omitted.]

17. In 1997, after seeing the success that Purdue had in marketing OxyContin for chronic non-cancer pain, Defendants re-launched their fentanyl-based Duragesic patch for the chronic, non-cancer market as well.

18. Defendants, acting in concert with others, embarked on a major campaign in which they used branded and unbranded marketing to disseminate the messages that pain was being undertreated and "there was a low risk of abuse and a low danger" of prescribing opioids to treat chronic, non-malignant pain and overstating the efficacy of opioids as a class of drug.

19. Defendants' marketing and promotional efforts were designed to reach Oklahoma doctors through multiple means and at multiple times over the course of the doctor's professional education and career in Oklahoma. Examples of such marketing and promotion include, among other things, "education" from Defendants' sales representatives, literature funded by Defendants in medical journals and publications, materials from professional societies/patient advocacy groups, continuing medical education funded by Defendants, unbranded marketing materials, and Defendants' paid speakers. Other avenues included dinners and presentations where doctors spoke to other doctors, partnering with third-party advocacy groups or academic groups to hold seminars, symposiums and conferences. All of these many different efforts were intended to influence the prescribing behavior of physicians and, thus, increase Defendants' profits from opioids.

20. A key element in Defendants' opioid marketing strategy to overcome barriers to liberal opioid prescribing was its promotion of the concept that chronic pain was undertreated (creating a problem) and increased opioid prescribing was the solution. Defendants trained their Oklahoma sales representatives on how to use these campaigns, including through the use of "emotional selling" for opioids by convincing physicians that undertreated pain was harming patients.

21. Another unbranded marketing message Defendants used to accomplish the "[b]ehavior [change]" of "increase[d] opioid use" was that untreated acute pain inevitably would turn into chronic pain. Defendants emphasized this message in their marketing materials that promoted opioids generally as a class of drug.

22. Defendants used the phrase, "pseudoaddiction," to convince doctors that patients who exhibited signs of addiction—e.g., asking for "higher and higher doses" of opioids or

returning to the doctor "early" before a prescription should have run out—were not actually suffering from addiction, but from the undertreatment of pain; and the solution, according to Defendants' marketing was to prescribe the patient more opioids.

[A description of further marketing tactics has been omitted.]

25. As part of Defendants' marketing and advocacy programs aimed at increasing opioid prescriptions, in addition to influencing doctors, Defendants employed strategies to influence a wide range of governmental agencies, through messages aimed at "optimizing the benefits of prescription opioids for pain management [and] minimizing their risks," including the risk of addiction, abuse and diversion.

26. Defendants used a sales force in Oklahoma to promote, market, and sell various types of opioids, including the branded opioid drugs that Defendants, themselves, manufactured . . .

27. Defendants' training of their sales representatives in Oklahoma included teaching sales representatives to avoid the so-called "addiction ditch"—i.e., to avoid the negatives (addiction) and emphasize the positives (efficacy) in sales calls . . .

28. As part of this training, Defendants trained their sales representatives that there was a 2.6% or lower risk of addiction when using opioids prescribed by a doctor. . . .

30. Defendants trained their sales reps to target high-opioid-prescribing physicians, including pain specialists and primary care physicians.

[A description of marketing materials has been omitted.]

33. Defendants did not train their sales representatives regarding red flags that could indicate a "pill mill," including, for example, pain clinics with patients lined up out the door or patients passed out in the waiting room. . . .

35. Defendants' sales representatives called on Oklahoma medical professionals hundreds of thousands of times while selling opioids as evidenced by 35 boxes of call notes from Defendants' Oklahoma sales representatives over the last two decades. . . .

[A description of payments to pain advocacy groups and organizations, the drafting of a "Consensus Statement," and other medical education activities has been omitted.]

44. Defendants' opioid marketing, in its multitude of forms, was false, deceptive and misleading. . . .

46. In 2001, Defendants were advised by Defendants' own hired scientific advisory board that many of the primary marketing messages Defendants used to promote opioids in general, and Duragesic specifically, were misleading and should not be disseminated. Specifically, Defendants were advised not to market opioids, including fentanyl-based Duragesic, using messages related to abuse or with claims about supposedly low abuse potential. Defendants were advised that no data existed that could support these claims, that the data Defendants pointed to (DAWN data) was incapable of supporting these claims, that aggressively marketing OxyContin on the same basis was what had gotten Purdue "in trouble," that minimizing the risk of abuse of Duragesic was "dangerous" due to its lethal nature, and that an increase in Duragesic sales would surely cause an increase in abuse of and addition to the drug. The "Conclusion: Do not include the abuse message. Do not sell opioids on the abuse issue."

47. In 2004, the FDA sent Defendants a letter stating that a professional file card that Defendants used to promote Duragesic ("Duragesic file card") contained "false or misleading claims about the abuse potential and other risks of [Duragesic], and include[d] unsubstantiated effectiveness claims for Duragesic. . . .

[A further discussion of Duragesic and other promotional materials has been omitted.]

52. Defendants additionally executed their strategy of targeting high-opioid-prescribing physicians in Oklahoma, including doctors who ultimately faced disciplinary proceedings or criminal prosecution.

53. Both Drs. Beaman and Mazloomdoost testified that the multifaceted marketing misinformation campaign by the opioid industry, including Defendants, influenced their practices and caused them to liberally and aggressively write opioid prescriptions they would never write today.

54. The increase in opioid addiction and overdose deaths following the parallel increase in opioid sales in Oklahoma was not a coincidence; these variables were "causally linked." Dr. Beaman also testified that, in his opinion, the increase in opioid overdose deaths and opioid addiction treatment admissions in Oklahoma was caused by the oversupply of opioids through increased opioid sales and overprescribing since the late 1990s.

55. Commissioner White testified that the oversupply and "significant widespread rapid increase in the sale of opioid prescription medications" beginning in the mid-1990s caused the "significant rise in opioid overdose deaths" and "negative consequences" associated with opioid use, including addition, opioid use disorder, the rise in NAS, and children entering the child welfare system.

56. With respect to the prescription opioid epidemic in the U.S., on November 1, 2017, the President's Commission on Combatting Drug Addiction and the Opioid Crisis issued its final report and recommendations.

57. The President's Commission on Combatting Drug Addiction and the Opioid Crisis found "Contributors to the Current Crisis" in the U.S. to include, among other things:

- The use of the Porter & Jick letter to make "unsubstantiated claims" by pharmaceutical companies;

- The lack of "[h]igh quality evidence demonstrating that opioids can be used safely for chronic non-terminal pain";

- The use of the phrase, "pain as the fifth vital sign". . . .

- The fact that, "[t]o this day, the opioid pharmaceutical industry influences the nation's response to the crisis. . . .

58. By no later than 2001, "a significant number of Oklahoma physicians, the healthcare community, law enforcement, medical advisory boards, the DUR Board" and others in Oklahoma were "being pushed and pushed and marketed [to] mislead" about opioids by Defendants. . . .

CONCLUSIONS OF LAW

1. In Oklahoma, nuisance law is defined by statute. 50 O.S. 1981 §1, defines a nuisance as follows:

A nuisance consists in unlawfully doing an act, or omitting to perform a duty, which act or omission either:

First. Annoys, injures or endangers the comfort, repose, health, or safety of others; or

Second. Offends decency; or

Third. Unlawfully interferes with, obstructs or tends to obstruct, or renders dangerous for passage, any lake or navigable river, stream, canal or basin, or any public park, square, street or highway; or

Fourth. In any way renders other persons insecure in life, or in the use of property, provided this section shall not apply to preexisting agricultural activities.

50 O.S. §2, states that a public nuisance is "one which affects at the same time an entire community or neighborhood, or any considerable number of persons, although the extent of the annoyance or damage inflicted upon the individual may be unequal."

2. The plain text of the statute does not limit public nuisances to those that affect property. Unlike other states' statutes that limit nuisances to the "habitual use or the threatened or contemplated habitual use of any place," Oklahoma's statute simply says "unlawfully doing an act, or omitting to perform a duty." There is nothing in this text that suggests an actionable nuisance requires the use of or a connection to real or personal property.

3. Supreme Court precedent also supports the conclusion that Oklahoma's nuisance law extends beyond the regulation of real property and encompasses the corporate activity complained of here. . . .

4. However, and in the alternative, in the event Oklahoma's nuisance law does require the use of property, the State has sufficiently shown that Defendants pervasively, systemically and substantially used real and personal property, private and public, as well as the public roads, buildings and land of the State of Oklahoma, to create this nuisance.

5. The State presented substantial evidence—which Defendants did not attempt to dispute—that Defendants' sales representatives were trained in their Oklahoma homes how to spread Defendants' marketing messages; they conducted their deceptive marketing and sales efforts in doctors' offices, hospitals, restaurants, and other venues; they used company cars traveling on State and county roads to disseminate those misleading messages; Defendants paid speakers to deliver Defendants' messages to doctors in their Oklahoma offices; and Defendants sent their messages into the homes of thousands of Oklahomans via computers, smart phones or other devices, all of which involve the use of property, real and personal, to create and exacerbate the public nuisance.

6. The challenged conduct here is Defendants' misleading marketing and promotion of opioids. The state claims that Defendants engaged in a false, misleading, and deceptive

marketing campaign designed to convince Oklahoma doctors, patients, and the public at large that opioids were safe and effective for the long-term treatment of chronic, non-malignant pain. The greater weight of the evidence shows that Defendants did, in fact, engage in such false and misleading marketing and the law is clear that such conduct qualifies as the kind of act or omission capable of sustaining liability under Oklahoma's nuisance law.

7. Defendants promoted their specific opioids using misleading marketing. Among other things, they sent sales representatives into Oklahoma doctors' offices to deliver misleading messages, they disseminated misleading pamphlets, coupons, and other printed materials for patients and doctors, and they misleadingly advertised their drugs over the internet—all of which occurred here in Oklahoma. But Defendants also pervasively promoted the use of opioids generally. This "unbranded" marketing included things like print materials that misleadingly touted the safety and efficacy of opioids as a class of pain medication, as well as online materials that promoted opioids generally. Defendants used and viewed medical education events (including Speakers Bureau sessions and CME opportunities) as promotional endeavors that Defendants leveraged to increase the market for opioids through misleading messaging.

8. According to Defendants' own internal training documents, Defendants concede that "False and Misleading" promotion includes at least the following types of conduct: Broadening of product indication; Data taken out of context; Minimization of safety issues; Omission of material information; Comparative efficacy or safety claims without substantial evidence; and Overstatements of efficacy or safety. The greater weight of the evidence demonstrated that Defendants engaged in promotional activities that violated each one of these rules.

9. Based upon my findings that the Defendants' false, misleading, and dangerous marketing campaigns have caused exponentially increasing rates of addiction, overdose deaths, and Neonatal Abstinence Syndrome, I conclude these are unlawful acts which "annoys, injures, or endangers the comfort, repose, health, or safety of others."

10. The facts show Defendants engaged in false and misleading marketing of both their drugs and opioids generally, and the law makes clear that such conduct is more than enough to serve as the act or omission necessary to establish the first element of Oklahoma's public nuisance law.

11. Accordingly, based on the foregoing, I conclude (a) that Defendants engaged in false and misleading marketing of both their drugs and opioids generally; and (b) this conduct constitutes a public nuisance under extant Oklahoma law.

[A discussion of the First Amendment and freedom of speech has been omitted.]

16. The First Amendment does not protect Defendants' messages which were misleading in that they were told by their own experts that marketing opioids on their abuse potential was dangerous and that Purdue had already shown that such a message was prone to mislead. They were told that the data they cited did not support their claims before they made them, and then again by the FDA after they had already started spreading that misleading message. Accordingly, I conclude that the speech at issue here is commercial in nature and that it is therefore not protected speech under the First Amendment

17. As a matter of law I find that Defendants' actions caused harms and those harms are the kind recognized by 50 O.S. §1 because those actions annoyed, injured or endangered the comfort, repose, health or safety of Oklahomans. This statute requires the State to prove that Defendants' actions caused harm and that those harms are of the kind recognized under the statute. I further find that the State has satisfied its burden of proof and that the Defendants' actions were the cause-in-fact of its injuries.

18. There are no intervening causes that supervened or superseded the Defendants' acts and omissions as a direct cause of the State's injuries, or otherwise defeat a finding of direct and proximate cause.

19. I further find that the facts of this action show by the greater weight of the evidence a public nuisance that "affects at the same time an entire community or neighborhood, or any considerable number of persons, although the extent of the annoyance or damage inflicted upon the individuals may be unequal." There can be no question that this nuisance affects entire communities, neighborhoods, or a considerable number of persons. This nuisance has negatively impacted the state.

20. I further find that the public nuisance created by the Defendants has affected and continues to affect at the same time entire Oklahoma communities and neighborhoods, as well as a considerable number of Oklahomans, although the extent of the harm inflicted upon individual Oklahomans may be unequal. . . .

24. The Court finds that the appropriate remedy to address the Opioid Crisis is the abatement of the nuisance.

[The remainder of the ruling, detailing the abatement of the public nuisance, has been omitted.]

SOURCE: Oklahoma State Courts Network. *State of Oklahoma v. Purdue Pharma et al.* August 26, 2019. http://www.oscn.net/dockets/GetDocument.aspx?ct=cleveland&bc=1044673351&cn=CJ-2017-816&fmt=pdf.

DOCUMENT

White House and HHS Announce Funding to Combat Opioid Crisis

September 4, 2019

Today, the U.S. Department of Health and Human Services (HHS) announced more than $1.8 billion in funding to states to continue the Trump administration's efforts to combat the opioid crisis by expanding access to treatment and supporting near real-time data on the drug overdose crisis.

The Centers for Disease Control and Prevention announced more than $900 million in new funding for a three-year cooperative agreement with states, territories, and localities to advance the understanding of the opioid overdose epidemic and to scale-up prevention and response activities, releasing $301 million for the first year. The Substance Abuse and Mental Health Services Administration awarded approximately $932 million to all 50 states as part of its State Opioid Response grants. By the end of 2019, HHS will have awarded more than $9 billion in grants to states and local communities to help increase access to treatment and prevention services since the start of the Trump administration.

"Thanks to President Trump's leadership and the hard work of so many Americans in local communities, we are beginning to win the battle against the opioid overdose crisis," said HHS Secretary Alex Azar. "Our country is seeing the first drop in overdose deaths in more than two decades, more Americans are getting treatment for addiction, and lives are being saved. At the same time, we are still far from declaring victory. We will continue executing on the Department's 5-Point strategy for combating the opioid crisis, and laying the foundation for a healthcare system where every American can access the mental healthcare they need."

As part of HHS's strategy to combat the opioid crisis, the Centers for Disease Control and Prevention is committed to preventing opioid misuse, overdose, and death and is disseminating resources, messages, and funding. This funding from CDC will help state and local governments track overdose data as closely to real-time as possible and support them in work to prevent overdoses and save lives. Funding for the first year is being awarded to 47 states, Washington, D.C., 16 localities, and two territories. Over the past decade, reporting of mortality data has improved substantially, mainly due to improvements in reporting by state vital records offices. CDC has worked diligently to provide financial and technical assistance to help improve the quality, timeliness, and specificity of surveillance data in states and communities across the nation, and these funds will continue to support this critical work. States may report nonfatal data as quickly as every two weeks and report fatal data every six months.

The State Opioid Response grants from the Substance Abuse and Mental Health Services Administration provide flexible funding to state governments to support prevention, treatment, and recovery services in the ways that meet the needs of their state. HHS has worked to ensure that this grant program, made possible by funding President Trump secured from Congress in 2018, is focused on providing evidence-based treatment, including the gold standard for treating opioid addiction: medication-assisted treatment. These grants have been awarded to all 50 states, Washington, D.C., and U.S. territories. In addition to the approximately $500M released earlier this year, SAMHSA released $932M in continuation funding to support the second year of the State Opioid Response program.

These grants come after the Health Resources and Services Administration, in August, awarded nearly $400 million in grants to community health centers, rural organizations, and academic institutions to help them establish and expand access to substance abuse and mental health services.

Earlier this month, HHS also proposed to modernize regulations that can pose significant barriers to caring for Americans struggling with substance use disorders, including opioid addiction, to make sure they get the effective, coordinated care they need.

Efforts to expand treatment are succeeding: Data suggests approximately 1.27 million Americans are now receiving medication-assisted treatment, out of approximately 2 million Americans with opioid use disorder. Since President Trump took office, the number of patients receiving buprenorphine has increased 28 percent, and the number of naltrexone prescriptions per month has increased 55 percent.

From 2017 to 2018, provisional counts of drug overdose deaths dropped by five percent, and overdose deaths from opioids went down 2.8 percent from 2017 to 2018. The number of individuals reporting pain reliever misuse decreased from 2017 to 2018 by 11 percent, with fewer than 10 million Americans now reporting misuse. Heroin-related opioid use disorder also decreased significantly among young adults.

In April of 2017, HHS announced a 5-Point Strategy to Combat the Opioids Crisis. Those efforts include better addiction prevention, treatment, and recovery services; better data; better pain management; better targeting of overdose reversing drugs; and better research.

SOURCE: U.S. Department of Health and Human Services. "Trump Administration Announces $1.8 Billion in Funding to States to Continue Combating Opioid Crisis." September 4, 2019. https://www.hhs .gov/about/news/2019/09/04/trump-administration-announces-1-8-billion-funding-states-combating-opioid.html.

OTHER HISTORIC DOCUMENTS OF INTEREST

FROM PREVIOUS HISTORIC DOCUMENTS

- President Trump Declares Public Health Crisis; Drug Commission Releases Findings, *2017*, p. 558

CDC and FDA React to Vaping-Linked Lung Illnesses

AUGUST 30 AND SEPTEMBER 11, 2019

Though traditional cigarette smoking among youth and young adults has been in decline for decades, in recent years, public health officials have reported an uptick in electronic cigarette use. In 2019, the Centers for Disease Control and Prevention (CDC) and Food and Drug Administration (FDA) raised alarm about the growing number of young people arriving in emergency rooms and doctors' offices with severe respiratory distress brought on by the use of e-cigarette products. While federal agencies struggled to pinpoint the exact ingredient in e-cigarettes causing lung illnesses and even death, the White House partnered with the FDA to enact a ban on certain e-cigarette products in an attempt to reduce their popularity with young people.

HEALTH IMPACT OF E-CIGARETTE USE

In the spring and summer of 2019, media reports were full of stories about individuals developing serious health issues following the use of e-cigarettes, an umbrella term that includes a number of devices like the e-cigarette itself, vapes, and vape pens, among others. Patients often reported that symptoms, ranging from breathing difficulties and chest pain to high fever and vomiting, began slowly. Most of those arriving at hospitals were young and male; according to federal data, four out of five e-cigarette users reporting a health issue were younger than thirty-five, while those who died after using an e-cigarette product had a median age of forty-five. Many reported that they had used an e-cigarette product containing THC, the psychoactive ingredient in marijuana, before their symptoms began.

While recommending against their use, the CDC and FDA admitted they were struggling to understand exactly which component of e-cigarettes was most harmful. "We are in desperate need of facts," Mitch Zeller, director of the FDA's Center for Tobacco Products, told reporters. Like their traditional counterpart, e-cigarettes contain nicotine, but many also have flavorings and other potentially cancer-causing chemicals. What federal officials did know was that health concerns were rapidly multiplying. By November 2019, there were 2,172 lung injury cases reported nationwide related to e-cigarette use, and forty-two people had died. Many of those affected had irreversible lung damage, and some even required lung transplants. After the first reported e-cigarette-linked death in the United States, CDC director Robert R. Redfield cautioned that "vaping exposes users to many different substances for which we have little information about related harms." He added, "E-cigarettes are not safe for youth, young adults, pregnant women, or adults who do not currently use tobacco products."

By December, early information on the longer-term health impacts of e-cigarette use was released. That month, the *American Journal of Preventative Medicine* published the results of a study that tracked participants for three years. At the start, all participants had no history of diagnosis of respiratory disease. However, by year three, those who used only e-cigarettes had a 30 percent increased risk of developing chronic lung illnesses such as COPD, emphysema, and asthma, compared to those who did not use any nicotine products. Those who used both e-cigarettes and regular tobacco products—what researcher Stanton Glantz, a professor of medicine at the University of California at San Francisco, called "the dominant use pattern among adult e-cigarette users"—had an even higher risk of developing a lung disease. Researchers also reported that switching from conventional smoking to e-cigarettes could lower the risk of developing lung disease, but that very few participants they followed stopped using conventional tobacco in favor of only e-cigarettes.

FEDERAL, STATE OFFICIALS OPEN INVESTIGATIONS

One primary concern among federal and state health officials was the age of e-cigarette users. In 2019, more than one-quarter of high school students admitted to using e-cigarettes in the past thirty days, and more than five million middle and high schoolers said that they used e-cigarette products. Seeking to address the growing health crisis, the CDC, FDA, and other state and federal agencies worked in concert to research devices, ingredients, and contaminants that may lead to respiratory illness. The CDC also called on doctors and other medical professionals to report possible e-cigarette-linked lung disease cases to state health departments to help with data collection.

In an August 30, 2019, joint statement, acting FDA commissioner Ned Sharpless and Redfield said they were working "as quickly as possible, and we are committed to taking appropriate actions as a clearer picture of the facts emerge." They continued, "At this time, the specific substances within the e-cigarette products that cause illness are not known and could involve a variety of substances." In October, the CDC said it believed THC could be the main culprit in health complications, because 78 percent of patients presenting symptoms admitted to using a THC-containing e-cigarette product. However, there was also some indication that a high level of Vitamin E acetate could be to blame. Because the cause was still unclear, "the only way to assure that you are not at risk while the investigation continues is to consider refraining from use of all e-cigarette, or vaping, products," the CDC cautioned.

FEDERAL GOVERNMENT CONSIDERS FLAVORED E-CIGARETTE BAN

While investigations were ongoing, the federal government began taking action to curb youth e-cigarette use. The FDA launched an anti-e-cigarette ad campaign targeting those aged twelve to seventeen titled "The Real Cost." It also continued to issue thousands of warning letters and fines to retailers for the sale of vaping products to minors. In September, the FDA sent a warning letter to JUUL Labs, a well-known e-cigarette product producer, for a variety of its marketing activities, including a presentation at a school where company officials told students that e-cigarettes are less harmful than traditional smoking. The FDA also worked in collaboration with the Federal Trade Commission to have e-cigarette products that looked like juice boxes, cereal, or candy removed from the market.

On September 11, 2019, President Donald Trump announced that he would support an FDA proposal to ban flavored e-cigarette products, saying, "We can't allow people to get sick and we can't have our youth to be so affected." Under the FDA proposal, mint, menthol, fruit, and candy-flavored vaping liquid would all be banned. Department of

Health and Human Services secretary Alex Azar said in a statement that the administration was "making it clear that we intend to clear the market of flavored e-cigarettes to reverse the deeply concerning epidemic of youth e-cigarette use that is impacting children, families, schools and communities." He added, "We will not stand idly by as these products become an on-ramp to combustible cigarettes or nicotine addiction for a generation of youth." Sharpless called the proposal a necessary tool in combating e-cigarette use by young people. "The tremendous progress we've made in reducing youth tobacco use in the U.S. is jeopardized by this onslaught of e-cigarette use. Nobody wants to see children becoming addicted to nicotine," Sharpless said.

As required by law, the FDA proposal went to the Office of Management and Budget, which completed its review on November 4. According to reports in *The Washington Post* and *The New York Times*, in the intervening months, Trump was counseled against signing off on the new rules by advisers who thought the ban could be detrimental to his reelection campaign. An industry trade group, the Vapor Technology Association, ran ads on Fox News, CNN, and MSNBC featuring interviews with individuals stating they would not vote for Trump if he banned e-cigarette products. Those opposing the ban also built a campaign titled We Vape, We Vote, encouraging those who use vaping products to speak out against the ban.

Some public health experts expressed concern that banning certain e-cigarette products could push more youth to traditional tobacco. In the December 2019 issue of the journal *Science*, the authors, all public health experts, cautioned that "the evidence warns against prohibitionist measures. Restricting access and appeal among less harmful vaping products out of an abundance of caution while leaving deadly combustible products on the market does not protect public health. It threatens to derail a trend that could hasten the demise of cigarettes, poised to take a billion lives this century."

It was not until January 2, 2020, that the Trump administration announced that it had finalized a partial flavor ban for most e-cigarette cartridge flavors. Under the regulation, menthol and tobacco flavors were exempt, as were flavored liquid nicotine in any flavor sold in tank-based systems. Azar said the partial ban "seeks to strike the right public health balance by maintaining e-cigarettes as a potential off-ramp for adults using combustible tobacco while ensuring these products don't provide an on-ramp to nicotine addiction for our youth." While promising to take action against those in the industry who failed to comply with the new policy, FDA Commissioner Stephen M. Hahn said the policy "confirms our commitment to dramatically limit children's access to certain flavored e-cigarette products we know are so appealing to them."

Medical groups, like the American Medical Association (AMA), expressed disappointment in the curtailed policy. "If we are serious about tackling this epidemic and keeping these harmful products out of the hands of young people, a total ban on all flavored e-cigarettes—in all forms and at all locations—is prudent and urgently needed," the AMA said in a statement.

—Heather Kerrigan

Following is an August 30, 2019, alert from the Centers for Disease Control and Prevention (CDC) on the lung disease risks associated with e-cigarette use; a statement from CDC director Robert R. Redfield and Food and Drug Administration (FDA) commissioner Ned Sharpless on August 30, 2019, announcing the collaborative effort by the states and federal government to investigate respiratory illnesses as they relate to e-cigarette use; and an FDA press release on September 11, 2019, announcing the Trump administration's backing of a plan to eliminate certain e-cigarette products from the market.

CDC Warns of E-cigarette Dangers

August 30, 2019

Summary

The Centers for Disease Control and Prevention (CDC) is providing: 1) background information on the forms of e-cigarette products, 2) information on the multistate outbreak of severe pulmonary disease associated with using e-cigarette products (devices, liquids, refill pods, and cartridges), and 3) clinical features of patients with severe pulmonary disease. This health advisory also provides recommendations for clinicians, public health officials, and the public based on currently available information.

General Background

E-cigarettes typically contain nicotine, most also contain flavorings and other chemicals, and some may contain marijuana or other substances. They are known by many different names and come in many shapes, sizes and device types. Devices may be referred to as "e-cigs," "vapes," "e-hookahs," "vape pens," "mods," tanks, or electronic nicotine delivery systems (ENDS). Some e-cigarette devices resemble other tobacco products such as cigarettes; some resemble ordinary household items such as USB flash drives, pens, and flashlights; and others have unique shapes. Use of e-cigarettes is sometimes referred to as "vaping" or "juuling." E-cigarettes used for dabbing are sometimes called "dab" pens.

E-cigarettes can contain harmful or potentially harmful substances, including nicotine, heavy metals (e.g., lead), volatile organic compounds, and cancer-causing chemicals. Additionally, some e-cigarette products are used to deliver illicit substances; may be acquired from unknown or unauthorized (i.e., "street") sources; and may be modified for uses that could increase their potential for harm to the user. For example, some e-cigarette pods or cartridges marketed for single use can be refilled with illicit or unknown substances. In addition, some e-cigarette products are used for "dripping" or "dabbing." Dripping involves dropping e-cigarette liquid directly onto the hot coils of an e-cigarette which can result in high concentrations of compounds (e.g., tetrahydrocannabinol [THC] and cannabinoid compounds). Dabbing involves superheating substances such as "budder", butane hash oil (BHO), and "710" that contain high concentrations of THC and other plant compounds (e.g., cannabidiol [CBD]).

Youth, young adults, pregnant women, as well as adults who do not currently use tobacco products should not use e-cigarettes. E-cigarettes containing nicotine have the potential to help some individual adult smokers reduce their use of and transition away from cigarettes. However, e-cigarettes are not currently approved by the Food and Drug Administration (FDA) as a quit smoking aid, and the available science is inconclusive on whether e-cigarettes are effective for quitting smoking.

Outbreak Background

As of August 27, 2019, 215 possible cases have been reported from 25 states and additional reports of pulmonary illness are under investigation. One patient (in Illinois) with a history of recent e-cigarette use was hospitalized with severe pulmonary disease and subsequently died. Although the etiology of e-cigarette-associated pulmonary disease is undetermined, epidemiologic investigations in affected states are ongoing to better characterize the exposures, demographic, clinical, and laboratory features and behaviors of patients. All patients have reported using e-cigarette products. The exact number is currently unknown, but many patients have reported using e-cigarettes containing cannabinoid products such as THC or CBD.

Based on reports from several states, patients have experienced respiratory symptoms (cough, shortness of breath, or chest pain), and some have also experienced gastrointestinal symptoms (nausea, vomiting, or diarrhea) or non-specific constitutional symptoms (fatigue, fever, or weight loss). Symptoms typically develop over a period of days but sometimes can manifest over several weeks. Gastrointestinal symptoms sometimes preceded respiratory symptoms. Fever, tachycardia, and elevated white blood cell count have been reported in the absence of an identifiable infectious disease. Many patients have sought initial care in ambulatory settings, some with several visits, before hospital admission.

Radiologic findings have varied and are not present in all patients upon initial presentation. Bilateral pulmonary infiltrates and diffuse ground-glass opacities have been reported. Many patients required supplemental oxygen, some required assisted ventilation and oxygenation, and some were intubated. Some patients have been treated with corticosteroids with demonstrated improvement. Antimicrobial therapy alone has not consistently been associated with clinical improvement. Assessment for infectious etiologies has been completed in many patients without an identified infectious cause. Several patients from one state have been diagnosed with lipoid pneumonia based on clinical presentation and detection of lipids within bronchoalveolar lavage samples stained specifically to detect oil.

All patients have reported using e-cigarette products and the symptom onset has ranged from a few days to several weeks after e-cigarette use. Within two states, recent inhalation of cannabinoid products, THC or cannabidiol, have been reported in many of the patients. To date, no single substance or e-cigarette product has been consistently associated with illness. CDC is working closely with state health departments to facilitate collecting product specimens for testing at the U.S. FDA Forensic Chemistry Center.

Recommendations for Clinicians

1. Report cases of severe pulmonary disease of unclear etiology and a history of e-cigarette product use within the past 90 days to your state or local health department. Reporting of cases may help CDC and state health departments determine the cause or causes of these pulmonary illnesses.

2. Ask all patients who report e-cigarette product use within the last 90 days about signs and symptoms of pulmonary illness.

3. If e-cigarette product use is suspected as a possible etiology of a patient's severe pulmonary disease, obtain detailed history regarding:

- Substance(s) used: nicotine, cannabinoids (e.g., marijuana, THC, THC concentrates, CBD, CBD oil, synthetic cannabinoids [e.g., K2 or spice], hash oil, Dank vapes), flavors, or other substances

- Substance source(s): commercially available liquids (i.e., bottles, cartridges, or pods), homemade liquids, and re-use of old cartridges or pods with homemade or commercially bought liquids

- Device(s) used: manufacturer; brand name; product name; model; serial number of the product, device, or e-liquid; if the device can be customized by the user; and any product modifications by the user (e.g., exposure of the atomizer or heating coil)

- Where the product(s) were purchased

- Method of substance use: aerosolization, dabbing, or dripping

- Other potential cases: sharing e-cigarette products (devices, liquids, refill pods, or cartridges) with others

4. Determine if any remaining product, including devices and liquids, are available for testing. Testing can be coordinated with the local or state health departments.

5. Consider all possible causes of illness in patients reporting respiratory and gastrointestinal symptoms and of e-cigarette product use. Evaluate and treat for other possible causes of illness (e.g., infectious, rheumatologic, neoplastic) as clinically indicated. Consider consultation with specialists (pulmonary, infectious disease, critical care, medical toxicology) as appropriate.

6. Clinical improvement of patients with severe pulmonary disease associated with e-cigarette use has been reported with the use of corticosteroids. The decision to use corticosteroids should be made on a case-by-case basis based on risks and benefits and the likelihood of other etiologies.

7. Lipoid pneumonia associated with inhalation of lipids in aerosols generated by e-cigarettes has been reported based on the detection of lipid-laden alveolar macrophages obtained by bronchoalveolar lavage (BAL) and lipid staining (e.g., oil red O). The decision about whether to perform a BAL should be based on individual clinical circumstances.

8. Lung biopsies have been performed on some patients. If a lung biopsy is obtained, lipid staining may be considered during pathologic examination, and is best performed on fresh tissue. Routine pathology tissue processing (including formalin-fixation and paraffin-embedding) can remove lipids. Conducting routine tissue processing and histopathologic evaluation is still important. Consider consultation with specialists in pulmonary medicine and pathology to help inform any evaluation plan.

9. Patients who have received treatment for severe pulmonary disease related to e-cigarette product use should undergo follow-up evaluation as clinically indicated to monitor pulmonary function.

Recommendations for Public Health Officials

1. State public health officials should promptly notify CDC about possible cases via VapingAssocIllness@cdc.gov.

2. Contact CDC at VapingAssocIllness@cdc.gov for case classification criteria, reporting guidelines, case investigation forms, and questions about this outbreak.

3. Consider conducting case-finding activities that use existing data sources (e.g., local poison control center, coroner and medical examiner's office, and other applicable surveillance systems including syndromic surveillance). CDC has developed two working syndromic surveillance definitions (one version with specific symptoms and a second focused on e-cigarette product use). CDC will be programming these definitions in CDC's National Syndromic Surveillance Program's BioSense/ESSENCE platform for case-finding within the platform.

4. Consider asking the medical examiner or coroner's office and other pathologists to report possible cases, especially those without an alternative, likely diagnosis. If individuals are identified after death or at autopsy who showed signs of severe pulmonary disease as described above, medical examiners and coroners are encouraged to report the cases to their local or state health department. Thorough sampling of trachea, bronchi, and lung parenchyma with collection of fresh lung tissue for staining of lipids (e.g., oil red O) and submission of formalin-fixed, paraffin-embedded tissues for routine histopathology are recommended. For further consultation, public health officials can contact CDC's Infectious Diseases Pathology Branch at pathology@cdc.gov.

5. State health department officials seeking technical assistance with an epidemiologic investigation can contact CDC at VapingAssocIllness@cdc.gov. State health department officials seeking technical assistance with laboratory testing can discuss with their state health department laboratories or contact CDC at VapingAssocIllness@cdc.gov.

Recommendations for the Public

1. While this investigation is ongoing, if you are concerned about these specific health risks, consider refraining from using e-cigarette products.

2. Regardless of the ongoing investigation, anyone who uses e-cigarette products should not buy these products off the street (e.g., e-cigarette products with THC, other cannabinoids) and should not modify e-cigarette products or add any substances to these products that are not intended by the manufacturer.

3. Regardless of the ongoing investigation, e-cigarette products should not be used by youth, young adults, pregnant women, as well as adults who do not currently use tobacco products. If you use e-cigarette products, monitor yourself for symptoms (e.g., cough, shortness of breath, chest pain) and promptly seek medical attention if you have concerns about your health. CDC and FDA will continue to advise and alert the public as more information becomes available.

4. Adult smokers who are attempting to quit should use evidence-based treatments, including counseling and FDA-approved medications. If you who need help quitting tobacco products, including e-cigarettes, contact your doctor.

5. If you are concerned about harmful effects from e-cigarette products, call your local poison control center at: 1-800-222-1222.

6. We encourage the public to submit detailed reports of any unexpected tobacco or e-cigarette-related health or product issues to the FDA via the online Safety Reporting Portal: https://www.safetyreporting.hhs.govexternal icon.

[The remainder of the CDC release, containing references and locations to receive more information, has been omitted.]

SOURCE: Centers for Disease Control and Prevention. "Severe Pulmonary Disease Associated with Using E-cigarette Products." August 30, 2019. https://emergency.cdc.gov/han/han00421.asp.

FDA and CDC Leaders on E-cigarette Risk Investigations

August 30, 2019

Both the U.S. Food and Drug Administration and the U.S. Centers for Disease Control and Prevention are working tirelessly to investigate the distressing incidents of severe respiratory disease associated with use of e-cigarette products. We were deeply saddened last week to learn of the death of an adult in Illinois who had been hospitalized with a severe respiratory illness following the use of an e-cigarette product. We are working closely with state and local health officials to investigate these incidents as quickly as possible, and we are committed to taking appropriate actions as a clearer picture of the facts emerges.

We've also made it a top priority to communicate with the public about our efforts. Today, we are providing several updates about efforts between FDA, CDC and state health officials to investigate these incidents that have impacted both youth and adults across the country. First, we are updating the number of potential cases of respiratory illnesses reported after use of e-cigarette products. Additionally, we are sharing more details about the work CDC and FDA are undertaking as part of the investigation, including its current status. We are also providing the public and our health partners across the country with information to help mitigate the risk of additional incidents and what health officials and clinicians can do to help us gather as much data as possible to better understand these illness and potential causes.

As of Aug. 27, 2019, 215 possible cases have been reported from 25 states, and additional reports of pulmonary illness are under investigation. States are completing their own investigations and verifications of cases based on CDC's recently released standardized case definition. While some cases in each of the states are similar and appear to be linked to e-cigarette product use, more information is needed to determine what is causing the respiratory illnesses. In many cases, patients reported a gradual start of symptoms, including breathing difficulty, shortness of breath, and/or chest pain before hospitalization. Some cases reported mild to moderate gastrointestinal illness including vomiting and diarrhea, or other symptoms such as fevers or fatigue. In many cases, patients have also acknowledged recent use of tetrahydrocannabinol (THC)-containing e-cigarette products while speaking to healthcare personnel, or in follow-up interviews by health department staff.

Even though cases appear similar, it is not clear if these cases have a common cause or if they are different diseases with similar presentations, which is why our ongoing investigation is critical. CDC and the FDA are providing consultation to state health departments and working closely with them to gather information on any products or substances used. For example, our agencies are working to standardize information collection at the state level to help build a more comprehensive picture of these incidents. This includes investigating the brand and types of e-cigarette products, whether any of them are products that would fall within the FDA's regulatory authority, as well as where they were obtained.

CDC is helping involved states investigate whether the illnesses may be linked to specific devices, ingredients or contaminants in the devices, or substances associated with e-cigarette product use, with the FDA's assistance. Current assistance to states includes deploying CDC staff to Illinois and Wisconsin to assist their state health departments with the respective state investigations; releasing a Clinician Outreach and Communication Activity (COCA) Clinical Action Alert describing this investigation and asking providers to report possible cases to their state health departments; developing and distributing to involved states a standardized case definition, medical chart abstraction form, and case interview questionnaire with input from states who are running investigations; reviewing and providing feedback on data collection and health messaging tools for states; and facilitating information sharing between states with possible cases.

In addition to daily meetings between our federal agencies, as well as frequent communication with state health officials, the FDA has been and will continue to provide laboratory assistance. The FDA has received about 80 samples and continues to receive requests from states to send more samples for the FDA to analyze. The samples represent a variety of different types of products and substances—a number of which contained incomplete information about the product. The FDA is analyzing those samples for their contents, whether they contain nicotine, substances, such as THC or other cannabinoids, or other chemicals and ingredients. The results of that testing will be shared with the respective states to aid in their investigations and will help inform the federal response.

More information is needed to better understand whether there's a relationship between any specific products or substances and the reported illnesses. At this time, there does not appear to be one product involved in all of the cases, although THC and cannabinoids use has been reported in many cases. At this time, the specific substances within the e-cigarette products that cause illness are not known and could involve a variety of substances. We continue to gather information about the names of the products used, where they were purchased, and how the products were used. That information is critical to help determine whether patterns emerge on which we can take additional action. While we continue to gather more information about these incidents and any specific products or substances involved, we also believe it's important to provide the public with useful information to help protect themselves and their loved ones, as well as continue to notify health care professionals about the illnesses, what to watch for, and how to collect and report information on these cases. As part of that commitment, CDC today issued a Health Alert Network (HAN) Health Advisory. The advisory includes the recommendation that while this investigation is ongoing, if you are concerned about these specific health risks, consider refraining from the use of e-cigarette products.

Anyone who does use e-cigarette products should not buy these products off the street (e.g., e-cigarette products with THC or other cannabinoids) and should not modify e-cigarette products or add any substances to these products that are not intended by the manufacturer. Regardless of the ongoing investigation, e-cigarette products should not be used by youth, young adults, pregnant women, and adults who do not currently use tobacco products. If you use e-cigarette products, monitor yourself for symptoms (e.g., cough, shortness of breaths, chest pain) and promptly seek medical attention if you have concerns about your health. CDC and the FDA will continue to advise and alert the public as more information becomes available. Adult smokers who are attempting to quit should use evidence-based treatments, including counseling and FDA-approved medications. If you need help quitting tobacco products, including e-cigarettes, contact your doctor. If you are concerned about harmful effects from e-cigarette products, call your local poison control center at: 1-800-222-1222. We also continue to encourage the public to submit detailed reports of any unexpected tobacco- or e-cigarette-related health or product issues to the FDA via the online Safety Reporting Portal.

As this investigation continues, our agencies remain committed to working as quickly as possible, in collaboration with our state and local public health partners and the clinical community, to find out as much as we can about these cases and potential causes and communicating with the public about these efforts to protect and promote the public health. Our ongoing oversight and educational efforts related to e-cigarettes is critical to our public health mission and, especially, to protecting youth from the dangers of nicotine addiction and tobacco-related disease and death.

The FDA, an agency within the U.S. Department of Health and Human Services, protects the public health by assuring the safety, effectiveness, and security of human and veterinary drugs, vaccines and other biological products for human use, and medical devices. The agency also is responsible for the safety and security of our nation's food supply, cosmetics, dietary supplements, products that give off electronic radiation, and for regulating tobacco products. CDC works 24/7 protecting America's health, safety and security. Whether disease[s] start at home or abroad, are curable or preventable, chronic or acute, or from human activity or deliberate attack, CDC responds to America's most pressing health threats. CDC is headquartered in Atlanta and has experts located throughout the United States and the world.

SOURCE: Food and Drug Administration. "Statement on Federal and State Collaboration to Investigate Respiratory Illnesses Reported after Use of E-cigarette Products." August 30, 2019. https://www.fda.gov/news-events/press-announcements/statement-federal-and-state-collaboration-investigate-respiratory-illnesses-reported-after-use-e.

Trump Administration Supports E-cigarette Product Ban

September 11, 2019

Today, the Trump Administration announced that as part of its ongoing work to tackle the epidemic of youth e-cigarette use, the FDA intends to finalize a compliance policy in the coming weeks that would prioritize the agency's enforcement of the premarket authorization requirements for non-tobacco-flavored e-cigarettes, including mint and menthol, clearing the market of unauthorized, non-tobacco-flavored e-cigarette products. The FDA plans to share more on the specific details of the plan and its implementation soon.

"The Trump Administration is making it clear that we intend to clear the market of flavored e-cigarettes to reverse the deeply concerning epidemic of youth e-cigarette use that is impacting children, families, schools and communities," said Health and Human Services Secretary Alex Azar. "We will not stand idly by as these products become an on-ramp to combustible cigarettes or nicotine addiction for a generation of youth."

Today's announcement comes as preliminary numbers from the National Youth Tobacco Survey show a continued rise in the disturbing rates of youth e-cigarette use, especially through the use of non-tobacco flavors that appeal to kids. In particular, the preliminary data show that more than a quarter of high school students were current (past 30 day) e-cigarette users in 2019 and the overwhelming majority of youth e-cigarette users cited the use of popular fruit and menthol or mint flavors.

"We appreciate President Trump and Secretary Azar's continued support of the agency's efforts to prevent youth use of e-cigarettes, including the bold approach we're announcing today. Once finalized, this compliance policy will serve as a powerful tool that the FDA can use to combat the troubling trend of youth e-cigarette use. We must act swiftly against flavored e-cigarette products that are especially attractive to children. Moreover, if we see a migration to tobacco-flavored products by kids, we will take additional steps to address youth use of these products," said Acting FDA Commissioner Ned Sharpless, M.D. "The tremendous progress we've made in reducing youth tobacco use in the U.S. is jeopardized by this onslaught of e-cigarette use. Nobody wants to see children becoming addicted to nicotine, and we will continue to use the full scope of our regulatory authority thoughtfully and thoroughly to tackle this mounting public health crisis."

Following a rule which became effective August 8, 2016, all electronic nicotine delivery system (ENDS) products were expected to file premarket tobacco product applications with the FDA within two years. ENDS products currently on the market are not being legally marketed and are subject to government action. The compliance policy the FDA anticipates announcing in the coming weeks will outline enforcement policy addressing non-tobacco-flavored e-cigarette products that lack premarket authorization moving forward.

The Trump Administration has demonstrated a deep commitment to preventing youth from using all tobacco products, including e-cigarettes, and the finalization of the compliance policy will be an important step in ongoing work to ensure e-cigarettes are not marketed to, sold to, or used by kids.

The FDA has been holding retailers and manufacturers accountable for marketing and sales practices that have led to increased youth accessibility and appeal of e-cigarettes. For example, the FDA has issued more than 8,600 warning letters and more than 1,000 civil money penalties (fines) to retailers—both online and in brick-and-mortar retail stores—for sales of ENDS and their components to minors. The agency has also issued warning letters—many in collaboration with the Federal Trade Commission (FTC)—that resulted in the market removal of dozens of e-liquid products resembling kid-friendly juice boxes, cereal, and candy. Additionally, the FDA and FTC cited firms that make and sell flavored e-liquids for violations related to online posts by social media influencers on their behalf.

Most recently, on September 9, the FDA issued a warning letter to JUUL Labs Inc. for marketing unauthorized modified risk tobacco products by engaging in labeling, advertising, and/or other activities directed to consumers, including a presentation given to youth at a school. Concurrently, the agency issued a second letter expressing its concern—and requesting additional information—about several issues raised in a recent Congressional hearing regarding JUUL's outreach and mark[et]ing practices, including those targeted at students, tribes, health insurers and employers.

The Administration has also continued to invest in campaigns to educate youth about the dangers of e-cigarette use. Last year, the FDA launched "The Real Cost" Youth E-Cigarette Prevention Campaign—a comprehensive effort targeting nearly 10.7 million youth, aged 12–17, who have used e-cigarettes or are open to trying them. The campaign features hard-hitting advertising on TV, digital and social media sites popular among teens, as well as posters with e-cigarette prevention messages in high schools across the nation.

The FDA in partnership with the Surgeon General joined forces with Scholastic to distribute youth e-cigarette prevention posters and lesson plans to every public and private high school in the U.S.—with additional resources planned for middle school educators throughout the 2019–2020 school year. The agency also released resources for doctors, youth groups, churches, state and local public health agencies, and others on the dangers of youth e-cigarette use and has undertaken efforts to further the discussion and understanding around how to help aid those kids who are already addicted to e-cigarettes quit.

In December 2018, the Surgeon General issued an advisory on e-cigarette use among youth, emphasizing the importance of protecting youth from a lifetime of nicotine addiction and associated health risks in light of the epidemic of youth e-cigarette use.

The FDA, an agency within the U.S. Department of Health and Human Services, protects the public health by assuring the safety, effectiveness, and security of human and veterinary drugs, vaccines and other biological products for human use, and medical devices. The agency also is responsible for the safety and security of our nation's food supply, cosmetics, dietary supplements, products that give off electronic radiation, and for regulating tobacco products.

[Charts on e-cigarette use have been omitted.]

SOURCE: Food and Drug Administration. "Trump Administration Combating Epidemic of Youth E-cigarette Use with Plan to Clear Market of Unauthorized, Non-Tobacco-Flavored E-cigarette Products." September 11, 2019. https://www.fda.gov/news-events/press-announcements/trump-administration-combating-epidemic-youth-e-cigarette-use-plan-clear-market-unauthorized-non.

OTHER HISTORIC DOCUMENTS OF INTEREST

FROM PREVIOUS *HISTORIC DOCUMENTS*

September

Census Bureau Releases Annual Report on Poverty in the United States

SEPTEMBER 10 AND OCTOBER 7, 2019

On September 10, 2019, the U.S. Census Bureau released its annual report on the number of Americans living in poverty. At the same time, it released the supplemental measure of poverty statistics that considers factors the regular Census report does not take into account, such as certain government safety-net programs (the report was re-released on October 7, 2019, with updated data). The September release showed a decrease in the poverty rate to below the pre-recession 2007 level. The supplemental report showed no statistically significant change in the poverty rate from 2017 to 2018. While the White House celebrated the report, some economists cited concern about ongoing income inequality while Democrats and public health experts focused on the growing number of uninsured Americans.

Poverty Rate Declines for Fourth Consecutive Year

The 2019 Census Bureau *Income and Poverty in the United States* report found a decrease in the U.S. poverty rate from 12.3 percent in 2017 to 11.8 percent in 2018. The number of people in poverty was 1.4 million fewer than in 2017. As defined by the Department of Health and Human Services, the 2018 poverty threshold was $25,100 for a family of four or $12,140 for an individual. According to the report, "for the first time in 11 years, the official poverty rate was significantly lower than in 2007, the year before the most recent recession."

The decrease in the rate and number of those in poverty was driven by the increase in the number of Americans finding full-time rather than part-time employment. According to the Census Bureau, 2.3 million more Americans had full-time work in 2018 than in 2017. "We have found quite a big increase in full-time, year-round work that would tend to bring up incomes for working people," said Trudi Renwick, an assistant division chief at the Census Bureau. The Trump administration touted this as proof that the president's economic policies were working. "Employment is the best way out of poverty," said Tomas Philipson, acting head of the White House Council of Economic Advisers. "President Trump's critics wrongly assert that government programs and handouts are the only way to lift people out of poverty, but today's data tells a different story," he added.

The poverty rate decreased in almost every age category, with the exception of those aged sixty-five and older. That group had a poverty rate of 9.7 percent, which was not statistically different from the year prior. Adults aged eighteen to sixty-four had a poverty rate decrease from 11.1 percent to 10.7 percent. Children under age eighteen experienced a decreasing poverty rate from 17.4 percent to 16.2 percent. Despite comprising only 22.6 percent of the population, children made up 31.1 percent of those in poverty in 2018.

The South was the only one of the four Census regions not to experience a decrease in its poverty rate from 2017 to 2018, although the rate of 13.6 percent was not statistically different from the prior year. The South also had the highest poverty rate of the four regions. In the Northeast, the poverty rate was 10.3 percent, or 5.7 million individuals, in 2018, down from 11.3 percent, or 6.3 million people, in 2017. In the Midwest, the poverty rate declined from 11.2 percent in 2017 to 10.4 percent in 2018, with the number falling from 7.6 million to 7 million individuals. And in the West, the poverty rate fell from 11.9 percent in 2017 to 11.2 percent in 2018, but the number of those in poverty—8.7 million— did not decline.

Among black, Asian, and Hispanic racial groups, the poverty rate was not statistically different from 2017 to 2018. In 2018, the poverty rate for blacks was 20.8 percent, or 8.9 million people; for Asians it was 10.1 percent, or 2 million people; and for Hispanics 17.6 percent, or 10.5 million people. The poverty rate for non-Hispanic whites was the lowest of all racial groups at 8.1 percent, or 15.7 million people, in 2018, down from 8.5 percent, or 16.6 million people, in 2017.

The Census Bureau reported that the 2019 number and percentage of shared households—those with one more additional nonhousehold member, spouse, or partner aged eighteen or older (not counting those in school up to age twenty-four)—remained higher than in 2007. Then, 17 percent of households were shared, and in 2019, 19.6 percent of households fell into this category. The number of shared households increased by 410,000 from 2018 to 2019, but the percentage was not statistically different. According to the Census Bureau, it can be difficult to understand how a shared household arrangement impacts poverty. For example, in 2019, 7.6 million adults aged twenty-five to thirty-four lived with their parents and had a poverty rate of 6 percent. If the poverty rate were calculated for these young adults separate from their parents, 34.8 percent would have fallen below the poverty threshold. However, the Bureau reported, "On the other hand, 6.0 percent of families which include at least one adult child (aged 25 to 34) were in poverty in 2018. The poverty rate for these families would have increased to 11.5 percent if the young adult were not living in—and contributing to—the household."

The Census Bureau's calculation of median household income and income inequality drew significant attention from economists. In 2018, median household income was $63,179, which was not statistically different from 2017. Furthermore, from 2017 to 2018, income inequality did not experience a significant change, remaining near its highest level in fifty years. "Median household income today is right where it was in 1999. We've seen two decades with no progress for the middle class," said Justin Wolfers, an economics professor at the University of Michigan. "The economy is producing more than before, but the gains aren't being shared equally," he added. According to Census Bureau data, the top 20 percent of households held more than half of all income in the United States in 2018, with the richest 5 percent holding 23.1 percent of all household income. Since 2007, the income of households earning less than $15,000 fell, while that for households earning more than $250,000 per year grew more than 15 percent.

HEALTH INSURANCE COVERAGE DECLINES

When it releases the report on the number of Americans in poverty, the Census Bureau also issues a second report on health insurance coverage. In 2018, 8.5 percent of individuals lacked health insurance coverage, a slight increase from 7.9 percent in 2017. A total of 27.5 million Americans were uninsured in 2018, including 5.5 million children. According to the report, this was the first increase in the number of uninsured Americans since 2008 to 2009, just before the Patient Protection and Affordable Care Act (ACA) was enacted.

The number of uninsured in 2018 was still lower than it was before the ACA became law, and the number of those enrolled in ACA plans remained relatively steady. Across the country, the sharpest declines were among those covered by public health insurance programs. New York, South Carolina, and Wyoming were the only three states to experience a decline in the uninsured rate, while it rose in eight other states—Alabama, Arizona, Idaho, Michigan, Ohio, Tennessee, Texas, and Washington. The change from 2017 to 2018 was not statistically different in any other state.

The Census Bureau did not state a reason for the decline, noting that there are a variety of factors that can influence health insurance coverage rates, including the strength of the economy because most individuals get their insurance coverage through an employer. Some sought to tie the president's policies to the declining number of Americans with health insurance. They cited the "public charge" restrictions on Medicaid and other forms of public assistance for immigrants who wish to remain in the United States. "People are not only not enrolling, they are coming in [to Medicaid offices] and asking to be disenrolled," said Sara Rosenbaum, a professor of health law and policy at The George Washington University. "Word has gone out if you use Medicaid, then you are a public charge and you're liable not to get a green card," she added. Hispanics had a larger uninsured rate increase than other ethnic groups.

Democrats were quick to blame the drop in health insurance coverage on the December 2017 Tax Cuts and Jobs Act, which zeroed out the ACA tax penalty assessed on those without insurance. Democratic presidential candidate Sen. Bernie Sanders, I-Vt., tweeted, "Mr. Trump lied. He promised to strengthen health care—instead, he has done everything he can to sabotage the Affordable Care Act. The result: Nearly two million people joined the ranks of the uninsured last year." Health groups said it was unlikely that the 2017 change to the individual mandate impacted the 2018 uninsured rate because the penalty was never shown to motivate Americans to purchase insurance and the penalty was still in place until the start of 2019.

Republicans cited affordability as the reason for the increase. Former White House official Brian Blase, who helped develop some of the administration's health care efforts, said the Census Bureau specifically found an increase in the uninsured rate for those earning more than 400 percent of the federal poverty line, the cutoff for ACA subsidies. "People above 400 percent of the poverty line, premiums are really expensive for them," Blase said, pointing to expensive ACA plans that are not an affordable option for some families. ACA-offered health insurance plans have to meet a set of criteria, while the lower-cost options pushed by the Trump administration are not held to the same standards.

SUPPLEMENTAL REPORT FINDS NO CHANGE IN POVERTY RATE

While the official Census poverty estimate accounts for money earned before taxes and includes sources of private and government income such as cash assistance and Social Security, it does not count programs intended to lift Americans out of poverty, including refundable tax credits or the Supplemental Nutrition Assistance Program (SNAP). The official report also does not consider costs related to health care, childcare, housing, or transportation. To account for these factors, every year since 2011 the Census Bureau has released a supplemental poverty report that is thought to provide a more accurate estimate of the number of Americans experiencing poverty.

Released with revised data in October 2019, the supplemental report recorded a poverty rate of 12.8 percent, which was not statistically different from the 2017 rate of

13 percent. In fifteen states and the District of Columbia, the supplemental poverty measure was higher than the official measure, while in twenty-four states it was lower. The remaining eleven states did not have a statistically significant difference. The supplemental poverty rate for most groups was higher than the official rate, with the exception of children who recorded a supplemental rate of 13.7 percent and official rate of 16.2 percent, and cohabitating partner units with a supplemental rate of 13.9 percent and official rate of 24.2 percent.

The supplemental report contained information on the impact of various social programs and the number of individuals kept out of poverty because of the benefits received. The report called Social Security "the most important anti-poverty program" because it kept 27.2 million Americans from falling below the poverty threshold. Refundable tax credits kept 8.9 million Americans out of poverty. SNAP lifted 3.2 million Americans out of poverty, while housing subsidies helped another 3 million people. According to the report, as in years past, "Medical expenses were the largest contributor to increasing the number of individuals in poverty." If medical expenses were subtracted from income, the poverty rate would increase by 2.5 percentage points, placing an additional 8 million Americans below the poverty line.

—Heather Kerrigan

Following are excerpts from the U.S. Census Bureau report on poverty in the United States, released on September 10, 2019; and excerpts from the U.S. Census Bureau supplemental poverty report released on October 7, 2019.

Census Bureau Report on Poverty in the United States

September 10, 2019

[All portions of the report not corresponding to poverty have been omitted. Tables, graphs, footnotes, and references to them have been omitted.]

INTRODUCTION

The U.S. Census Bureau collects data and publishes estimates on income and poverty in order to evaluate national economic trends as well as to understand their impact on the well-being of households, families, and individuals. This report presents data on income and poverty in the United States based on information collected in the 2019 and earlier Current Population Survey (CPS) Annual Social and Economic Supplements (ASEC) conducted by the Census Bureau.

The Census Bureau has been engaged, for the past several years, in implementing improvements to the CPS ASEC. These changes have been implemented in a two-step process, beginning first with questionnaire design changes incorporated over the period of 2014 to 2016, followed by more recent changes to the data processing system. This report is the first time income and poverty measures reflect both data collection and processing system changes. The 2017 and 2018 income and poverty estimates presented in this report are based on the updated processing system and therefore the 2017 estimates may differ from those released in September 2018.

This report contains two main sections, one focuses on income and the other on poverty. Each section presents estimates by characteristics such as race, Hispanic origin, nativity, and region. Other topics, such as earnings and family poverty rates, are included only in the relevant section.

Summary of Findings

- Median household income was $63,179 in 2018, not statistically different from the 2017 median, following 3 consecutive years of annual increases.

- Between 2017 and 2018, the real median earnings of all workers increased 3.4 percent to $40,247.

- The 2018 real median earnings of men and women who worked full-time, year-round increased by 3.4 percent and 3.3 percent, respectively, between 2017 and 2018.

- The number of full-time, year-round workers increased by 2.3 million, between 2017 and 2018. The number of men and women full-time, year-round workers increased by about 700,000 and 1.6 million, respectively.

- The official poverty rate in 2018 was 11.8 percent, a decrease of 0.5 percentage points from 2017. This is the fourth consecutive annual decline in the national poverty rate. In 2018, for the first time in 11 years, the official poverty rate was significantly lower than 2007, the year before the most recent recession.

- The number of people in poverty in 2018 was 38.1 million, 1.4 million fewer people than 2017.

For all demographic groups..., the 2018 median household income estimates were higher or were not statistically different from the 2017 estimates. For most demographic groups ... poverty rates in 2018 were either lower than in 2017 or not statistically different. The only group to experience a statistically significant increase in poverty rates from 2017 to 2018 was people aged 25 or older with no high school diploma.

[The section on income in the United States has been omitted.]

POVERTY IN THE UNITED STATES

Highlights

- The official poverty rate in 2018 was 11.8 percent, down 0.5 percentage points from 12.3 percent in 2017. This is the fourth consecutive annual decline in poverty. Since 2014, the poverty rate has fallen 3.0 percentage points from 14.8 percent to 11.8 percent.

- In 2018, for the first time in 11 years, the official poverty rate was significantly lower than in 2007, the year before the most recent recession.

- In 2018, there were 38.1 million people in poverty, approximately 1.4 million fewer people than 2017.

- Between 2017 and 2018, poverty rates for children under age 18 decreased 1.2 percentage points from 17.4 percent to 16.2 percent. Poverty rates decreased 0.4 percentage points for adults aged 18 to 64, from 11.1 percent to 10.7 percent. The poverty rate for those aged 65 and older (9.7 percent) was not statistically different from 2017.

- From 2017 to 2018, the poverty rate decreased for non-Hispanic Whites; females; native-born people; people living in the Northeast, Midwest, and West; people living inside metropolitan statistical areas and principal cities; people without a disability; those with some college education; people in families; and people in female householder families.

- Between 2017 and 2018, people aged 25 and older without a high school diploma was the only examined group to experience an increase in their poverty rate. Among this group, the poverty rate increased 1.4 percentage points to 25.9 percent, but the number in poverty was not statistically different from 2017.

Race and Hispanic Origin

The poverty rate for non-Hispanic Whites was 8.1 percent in 2018, with 15.7 million individuals in poverty, down from 8.5 percent and 16.6 million in 2017. The poverty rate for non-Hispanic Whites was lower than the poverty rates for other racial groups. . . . Non-Hispanic Whites accounted for 60.2 percent of the total population and 41.2 percent of the people in poverty in 2018.

The poverty rate for Blacks was 20.8 percent in 2018, representing 8.9 million people in poverty. For Asians, the 2018 poverty rate and number in poverty were 10.1 percent and 2.0 million, respectively. The poverty rate for Hispanics was 17.6 percent in 2018, representing 10.5 million people in poverty. Among Blacks, Asians, and Hispanics, neither the poverty rate nor the number in poverty was statistically different from 2017.

Sex

In 2018, the poverty rate for males was 10.6 percent, not statistically different from 2017. The 2018 poverty rate for females was 12.9 percent, down from 13.6 percent in 2017.

The poverty rate in 2018 for women aged 18 to 64 was 12.3 percent, while the poverty rate for men aged 18 to 64 was 9.0 percent. The poverty rate for women aged 65 and older was 11.1 percent, while the poverty rate for men aged 65 and older was 8.1 percent. For people under the age of 18, the poverty rate for girls (16.2 percent) and the poverty rate for boys (16.2 percent) were not statistically different.

Age

Between 2017 and 2018, the poverty rate for people aged 18 to 64 decreased to 10.7 percent, down from 11.1 percent in 2017. There were 21.1 million people aged 18 to 64 in poverty in 2018, down from 21.9 million in 2017. For people aged 65 and older, the 2018 poverty rate was 9.7 percent, representing 5.1 million individuals in poverty. Neither the poverty rate nor the number in poverty was statistically different from 2017 for this age group.

For people under the age of 18, 16.2 percent were in poverty in 2018, down from 17.4 percent in 2017. Approximately 11.9 million individuals under the age of 18 were in poverty in 2018, down from 12.8 million in 2017. People under the age of 18 represented 22.6 percent of the total population in 2018 and 31.1 percent of the people in poverty.

Related children are people under the age of 18 related to the householder by birth, marriage, or adoption and who are not themselves householders or spouses of householders. For related children in 2018, the poverty rate and the number in poverty was 15.9 percent and 11.5 million, down from 17.0 percent and 12.4 million in 2017.

In 2018, 39.1 percent of related children in female householder families were in poverty, down from 41.6 percent in 2017. In 2018, the proportion of related children in poverty was 7.6 percent among married-couple families and 18.7 percent among male householder families. Poverty rates for both groups were not statistically different from 2017.

Among related children under the age of 6, 17.2 percent, or 4.0 million, were in poverty in 2018, down from 18.8 percent and 4.4 million in 2017. About half (47.7 percent) of related children under the age of 6 in families with a female householder were in poverty. This was more than six times the rate of their counterparts in married-couple families (7.8 percent).

Children living in unrelated subfamilies, those whose parents (or parent) are not related by birth, marriage, or adoption to the householder, had a poverty rate of 37.5 percent in 2018, not statistically different from the poverty rate in 2017.

Nativity

The poverty rate for the native-born population decreased to 11.4 percent in 2018, down from 12.0 percent in 2017. The number of native-born people in poverty was 31.8 million in 2018, down from 33.1 million in 2017. Among the foreign-born population, 13.8 percent were in poverty in 2018, representing 6.3 million people. Neither the poverty rate nor the number of foreign-born individuals in poverty were statistically different from the 2017 estimate.

The poverty rate in 2018 for foreign-born naturalized citizens (9.9 percent) was lower than the poverty rates for noncitizens and native-born citizens (17.5 percent and 11.4 percent, respectively). The 2018 poverty rate of 17.5 percent for those who were not U.S. citizens represents 4.1 million individuals in poverty. For both foreign-born naturalized citizens and noncitizens, neither the 2018 poverty rate nor the number in poverty were statistically different from the 2017 estimate.

Region

From 2017 to 2018, the South was the only region not to experience a decline in its poverty rate. The 2018 poverty rate for those in the South was 13.6 percent, representing 16.8 million individuals in poverty, with neither estimate statistically different from 2017. The South had the highest poverty rate in 2018 relative to the other three regions. The 2018 poverty rate and number in poverty for the Northeast was 10.3 percent and 5.7 million, down from 11.3 percent and 6.3 million in 2017. The 2018 poverty rate and number in poverty for the Midwest was 10.4 percent and 7.0 million, down from 11.2 percent and 7.6 million in 2017. Comparing 2017 and 2018, poverty rates declined in the West, while the number in poverty did not. The poverty rate for the West in 2018 was 11.2 percent, down from 11.9 percent in 2017 while the number in poverty was 8.7 million.

Residence

Inside metropolitan statistical areas, the poverty rate and the number of people in poverty in 2018 were 11.3 percent and 31.9 million, down from 11.8 percent and

33.1 million in 2017. Among those living outside metropolitan statistical areas, 14.7 percent, or 6.2 million, were in poverty in 2018, with neither estimate statistically different from 2017.

The 2018 poverty rate for those in principal cities was 14.6 percent, with 15.3 million in poverty, a decline from 15.8 percent and 16.4 million in 2017. Among those living inside metropolitan areas, but not in principal cities, the poverty rate in 2018 was 9.4 percent and the number in poverty was 16.6 million. Neither the poverty rate nor the number in poverty within this group were statistically different from the 2017 estimate.

Work Experience

In 2018, 5.1 percent of workers aged 18 to 64 were in poverty, not statistically different from the 2017 estimate. For those who worked full-time, year-round, 2.3 percent were in poverty in 2018, not statistically different from 2017. Those working less than full-time, year-round had a poverty rate in 2018 of 12.7 percent. While the poverty rate among this group is not statistically different from 2017, the number in poverty is statistically lower, declining to 5.2 million in 2018 from 5.6 million in 2017.

Among those aged 18 to 64 who did not work at least 1 week during the calendar year, 29.7 percent were in poverty in 2018, not statistically different from 2017. Those who did not work at least 1 week in 2018 represented 22.7 percent of all people aged 18 to 64, while they made up 63.2 percent of people aged 18 to 64 in poverty.

Disability Status

For people aged 18 to 64 with a disability, the poverty rate in 2018 was 25.7 percent and the number in poverty was 3.8 million. Neither the 2018 poverty rate nor the number in poverty were statistically different from 2017 estimates. In 2018, among those aged 18 to 64 without a disability, the poverty rate was 9.5 percent and the number in poverty was 17.3 million, down from 9.9 percent and 18.1 million in 2017.

Among people aged 18 to 64, those with a disability represented 7.5 percent of all people, compared with 18.1 percent of people aged 18 to 64 in poverty.

Educational Attainment

In 2018, 25.9 percent of people aged 25 and older without a high school diploma were in poverty, an increase from 24.5 percent in 2017. This was the highest poverty rate among educational groups. . . . Additionally, it was the only group . . . to have a statistically significant increase in poverty from 2017 to 2018. However, the number of people in poverty without a high school diploma (5.7 million) was not statistically different from 2017. The poverty rate for those with a high school diploma but with no college was 12.7 percent, not statistically different from 2017. For those with some college, 8.4 percent were in poverty in 2018, a decline from 9.0 percent in 2017.

Among people with at least a bachelor's degree, 4.4 percent were in poverty in 2018, not statistically different from 2017. Among educational attainment groups, people with at least a bachelor's degree had the lowest poverty rates in 2018. Among those aged 25 and older, 36.0 percent had obtained at least a bachelor's degree in 2018, these individuals represented 15.9 percent of the population aged 25 and older in poverty.

Families

In 2018, the poverty rate for primary families declined from 9.3 percent to 9.0 percent, representing a decrease from 7.8 million to 7.5 million families in poverty. For primary families with a female householder, the poverty rate was 24.9 percent, representing 3.7 million families in 2018, a decline from 26.2 percent and 4.0 million families in 2017.

The poverty rate for married-couple families was 4.7 percent in 2018, representing 2.9 million families. For primary families with a male householder, the poverty rate was 12.7 percent, representing 820,000 families. For unrelated subfamilies, the poverty rate was 33.3 percent, representing 160,000 families. Differences in the poverty rate and number of families in poverty for these family types were not statistically different between 2017 and 2018.

Shared Households

Shared households are defined as households that include at least one "additional" adult, a person aged 18 or older, who is not the householder, spouse, or cohabiting partner of the householder. Adults aged 18 to 24 who are enrolled in school are not counted as additional adults.

In 2019, the number and percentage of shared households remained higher than in 2007, the year before the most recent recession. In 2007, 17.0 percent of households were shared, totaling 19.7 million shared households. In 2019, 19.6 percent of households were shared, totaling 25.2 million shared households. The number of shared households in 2019 was greater than the number in 2018 by 410,000, though the percentage was not statistically different.

It is difficult to assess the precise impact of household sharing on overall poverty rates. An example is young adults living with parents. In 2019, an estimated 7.6 million adults aged 25 to 34 lived with their parents, with a poverty rate of 6.0 percent (when the entire family's income is compared with the threshold that includes the young adult as a member of the family). If poverty status for these individuals had been determined using only the young adult's own income, 34.8 percent of these individuals would have been below the poverty threshold for a single person under the age of 65. On the other hand, 6.0 percent of families which include at least one adult child (aged 25 to 34) were in poverty in 2018. The poverty rate for these families would have increased to 11.5 percent if the young adult were not living in—and contributing to—the household.

Depth of Poverty

Categorizing a person as "in poverty" or "not in poverty" is one way to describe their economic situation. The income-to-poverty ratio and the income deficit or surplus describe additional aspects of economic well-being. While the poverty rate shows the proportion of people with income below the relevant poverty threshold, the income-to-poverty ratio gauges the depth of poverty and shows how close a family's income is to its poverty threshold. The income-to-poverty ratio is reported as a percentage that compares a family's or an individual's income with the applicable threshold. For example, a family with an income-to-poverty ratio of 125 percent has income that is 25 percent above its poverty threshold.

The income deficit or surplus shows how many dollars a family's or an individual's income is below (or above) their poverty threshold. For those with an income deficit, the measure is an estimate of the dollar amount necessary to reach their poverty threshold.

Ratio of Income to Poverty

. . . In 2018, 17.3 million people reported family income below one-half of their poverty threshold. They represented 5.3 percent of all people and 45.3 percent of those in poverty. Approximately 16.0 percent of individuals had family income below 125 percent of their threshold, 20.1 percent had family income below 150 percent of their poverty threshold, and 28.9 percent had family income below 200 percent of their threshold.

Of the 17.3 million people in 2018 with family income below one-half of their poverty threshold, 5.0 million were individuals under the age of 18, 10.1 million were aged 18 to 64, and 2.1 million were aged 65 and older. The demographic makeup of the population differs at varying degrees of poverty. In 2018, people under the age of 18 represented:

- 22.6 percent of the overall population.

- 19.8 percent of people in families with income above 200 percent of their poverty threshold.

- 28.4 percent of people in families with income between 100 percent and 200 percent of their poverty threshold.

- 29.2 percent of people in families below 50 percent of their poverty threshold.

By comparison, people aged 65 and older represented:

- 16.3 percent of the overall population.

- 16.2 percent of people in families with income above 200 percent of their poverty threshold.

- 18.6 percent of people in families between 100 percent and 200 percent of their poverty threshold.

- 12.1 percent of people in families below 50 percent of their poverty threshold.

Income Deficit

The income deficit for families in poverty (the difference in dollars between a family's income and its poverty threshold) averaged $10,452 in 2018, approximately $355 less than the inflation-adjusted income deficit for families in poverty in 2017. The average income deficit was larger for families with a female householder ($11,138) than for married-couple families ($9,789).

The average per capita income deficit was also larger for families with a female house-holder ($3,337) than for married-couple families ($2,735). For unrelated individuals, the average income deficit for those in poverty was $7,502 in 2018. The $7,362 deficit for unrelated women was lower than the $7,688 deficit for unrelated men.

[The sections discussing additional information on income and poverty and sources and estimates have been omitted.]

SOURCE: Census Bureau. "Income and Poverty in the United States: 2018." September 10, 2019. https://www.census.gov/content/dam/Census/library/publications/2019/demo/p60-266.pdf.

Census Bureau Report on Supplemental Poverty Measures

October 7, 2019

[All footnotes, figures, tables (except Table A-2), graphs, and references to them have been omitted.]

INTRODUCTION

Since the publication of the first official U.S. poverty estimates, researchers and policymakers have continued to discuss the best approach to measure income and poverty in the United States. Beginning in 2011, the U.S. Census Bureau began publishing the Supplemental Poverty Measure (SPM), which extends the official poverty measure by taking account of many of the government programs designed to assist low-income families and individuals that are not included in the official poverty measure. This is the ninth report describing the SPM, released by the Census Bureau, with support from the Bureau of Labor Statistics (BLS). This report presents updated estimates of the prevalence of poverty in the United States using the official measure and the SPM based on information collected in 2019 and earlier Current Population Survey Annual Social and Economic Supplements (CPS ASEC).

Highlights

- In 2018, the overall SPM rate was 12.8 percent. This is not statistically different from the 2017 SPM rate of 13.0.

- SPM rates were not statistically different for any of the major age categories in 2018 compared with 2017. SPM rates for children under the age of 18 were 13.7 percent, which is not significantly different than 14.2 percent in 2017.

- The SPM rate for 2018 was 1.0 percentage points higher than the official poverty rate of 11.8 percent.

- There were 15 states plus the District of Columbia for which SPM rates were higher than official poverty rates, 24 states with lower rates, and 11 states for which the differences were not statistically significant.

- Social Security continued to be the most important anti-poverty program, moving 27.2 million individuals out of poverty. Refundable tax credits moved 8.9 million people out of poverty. . . .

[The background discussion has been omitted.]

POVERTY ESTIMATES FOR 2018: OFFICIAL AND SPM

. . . 12.8 percent of people were poor using the SPM definition of poverty, higher than the 11.8 percent using the official definition of poverty with the comparable universe. While the SPM rates were higher than official poverty rates for most groups, the SPM shows lower poverty rates for children and individuals living in cohabiting partner units. Official and SPM poverty rates for individuals living in female reference person units, Blacks, and individuals who did not work were not statistically different.

Census Bureau estimates for the SPM are available back to 2009. Since the SPM's initial production, the SPM rate has been higher than the official poverty rate. . . .

. . . The SPM has ranged from 0.6 to 1.6 percentage points higher than the official measure over this time period.

. . . In 2018, the gap between the official poverty measure and the SPM was largest for individuals aged 65 and older at 3.8 percentage points.

[A section on distribution of income has been omitted.]

Poverty Rates by State: Official and SPM

To create state-level estimates using the CPS ASEC, the Census Bureau recommends using 3-year averages for additional statistical reliability. . . . The 3-year average poverty rate for the United States in 2016–2018 was 12.3 percent with the official measure and 13.1 percent using the SPM.

While the SPM national poverty rate was higher than the official, that difference varies by geographic area. . . .

The 15 states for which the SPM rates were higher than the official poverty rates were California, Colorado, Connecticut, Delaware, Florida, Hawaii, Illinois, Maryland, Massachusetts, Nevada, New Hampshire, New Jersey, New York, Texas, and Virginia. The SPM rate for the District of Columbia was also higher. Higher SPM rates by state may occur for many reasons. Geographic adjustments for housing costs and/or different mixes of housing tenure may result in higher SPM thresholds. Higher nondiscretionary expenses, such as taxes or medical expenses, may also drive higher SPM rates.

The 24 states where SPM rates were lower than the official poverty rates were Alabama, Arkansas, Idaho, Iowa, Kansas, Kentucky, Louisiana, Maine, Michigan, Minnesota, Mississippi, Missouri, Montana, Nebraska, New Mexico, Ohio, Oklahoma, Rhode Island, South Carolina, South Dakota, West Virginia, Wisconsin, and Wyoming. Lower SPM rates could occur due to lower thresholds reflecting lower housing costs, a different mix of housing tenure, or more generous noncash benefits.

The 11 states that were not statistically different under the two measures include Alaska, Arizona, Georgia, Indiana, North Carolina, North Dakota, Oregon, Pennsylvania, Utah, Vermont, and Washington.

The SPM and the Effect of Cash and Noncash Transfers, Taxes, and Other Nondiscretionary Expenses

This section moves away from comparing the SPM with the official measure and looks only at the SPM. This analysis allows one to gauge the effects of taxes and transfers and other necessary expenses using the SPM as a measure of economic well-being. Income used for estimating the official poverty measure includes cash benefits from the government (e.g., Social Security, unemployment insurance benefits, public assistance benefits, and workers' compensation benefits), but does not take account of taxes or noncash benefits aimed at improving the economic situation of the poor. The SPM incorporates all of these elements, adding in cash benefits, and noncash transfers, while subtracting necessary expenses such as taxes, medical expenses, and expenses related to work. An important contribution of the SPM is that it allows us to gauge the potential magnitude of the effect of tax credits and transfers in alleviating poverty. We can also examine the effects of non-discretionary expenses, such as work and medical expenses. . . .

Removing one item from the calculation of SPM resources and recalculating poverty rates shows, for example, that Social Security benefits decrease the SPM rate by 8.4 percentage points, from 21.2 percent to 12.8 percent. This means that with Social Security benefits, 27.2 million fewer people are living below the poverty line. When including refundable tax credits (the Earned Income Tax Credit [EITC] and the refundable portion of the child tax credit) in resources, 8.9 million fewer people are considered poor, all else constant. On the other hand, when the SPM subtracts amounts paid for child support, income and payroll taxes, work-related expenses, and medical expenses, the number and percentage in poverty are higher. When subtracting medical expenses from income, the SPM rate is 2.5 percentage points higher. In numbers, 8.0 million more people are classified as poor.

In comparison to 2017, the 2018 antipoverty impacts of housing subsidies, child support received, unemployment insurance, and workers' compensation decreased, lifting 0.4 million, 0.2 million, 0.2 million, and 0.1 million fewer individuals out of poverty, respectively. Conversely, FICA pushed 0.5 million additional individuals into poverty in 2018 than in 2017.

. . . In 2018, accounting for refundable tax credits resulted in a 6.4 percentage point decrease in the child poverty rate, representing 4.7 million children prevented from falling into poverty by the inclusion of these credits. Subtracting medical expenses, such as contributions toward the cost of medical care and health insurance premiums, from the income of families with children resulted in a child poverty rate 2.3 percentage points higher. For the 65 and older group, SPM rates increased by about 4.0 percentage points with the inclusion of medical expense deductions from income, while Social Security benefits lowered poverty rates by 33.9 percentage points for the 65 and older group, lifting 17.9 million individuals above the poverty line.

Summary

This report provides estimates of poverty using the SPM for the United States. The results illustrate differences between the official measure of poverty and a poverty measure that takes account of noncash benefits received by families and nondiscretionary expenses that they must pay. The SPM also employs a poverty threshold that is updated by the BLS with information on expenditures for food, clothing, shelter, and utilities. Results show higher poverty rates using the SPM than the official measure for most groups, with children being an exception with lower poverty rates using the SPM.

The SPM allows us to examine the effect of taxes, noncash transfers, and necessary expenses on the poor and on important groups within the population in poverty. As such, there are lower percentages of the SPM poverty populations in the very high and very low resource categories than we find using the official measure. Since noncash benefits help those in extreme poverty, there were lower percentages of individuals with resources below half the SPM threshold for most groups. In addition, the effect of benefits received from each program and taxes and other nondiscretionary expenses on SPM rates were examined.

[The remainder of the report, including references and appendices, has been omitted.]

SOURCE: Census Bureau. "The Supplemental Poverty Measure: 2018." October 7, 2019. https://www.census.gov/content/dam/Census/library/publications/2019/demo/p60-268.pdf.

Table A-2 Number and Percentage of People in Poverty by Different Poverty Measures: 2018

(Numbers in thousands. Margin of error in thousands or percentage points as appropriate. For information on confidentiality protection, sampling error, nonsampling error, and definitions, see <https://www2.census.gov/programs-surveys/cps/techdocs/cpsmar19.pdf>)

Characteristic	Number[1] (in thousands)	Official[1]				SPM				Difference	
		Number		Percent		Number		Percent			
		Estimate	Margin of error[2] (±)	Estimate	Margin of error[2] (±)	Estimate	Margin of error[2] (±)	Estimate	Margin of error[2] (±)	Number	Percent
All people	324,356	**38,200**	**794**	**11.8**	**0.2**	**41,420**	**861**	**12.8**	**0.3**	***3,220**	***1.0**
Sex											
Male	159,028	16,820	432	10.6	0.3	19,269	479	12.1	0.3	*2,448	*1.5
Female	165,328	21,380	462	12.9	0.3	22,151	454	13.4	0.3	*772	*0.5
Age											
Under 18 years	73,793	11,924	418	16.2	0.6	10,096	381	13.7	0.5	*–1,828	*–2.5
18 to 64 years	197,775	21,130	479	10.7	0.2	24,151	564	12.2	0.3	*3,020	*1.5
65 years and older	52,788	5,146	206	9.7	0.4	7,174	250	13.6	0.5	*2,028	*3.8
Type of Unit											
Married couple	195,760	10,530	447	5.4	0.2	15,043	526	7.7	0.3	*4,512	*2.3
Cohabiting partners	26,339	6,374	339	24.2	1.0	3,659	267	13.9	0.9	*–2,716	*–10.3
Female reference person	41,543	10,506	475	25.3	1.0	10,390	461	25.0	0.9	–116	–0.3
Male reference person	14,527	1,684	184	11.6	1.2	2,197	214	15.1	1.4	*512	*3.5
Unrelated individuals	46,187	9,105	306	19.7	0.5	10,132	329	21.9	0.6	*1,027	*2.2

Characteristic	Number[1] (in thousands) Estimate	Official[1]				SPM				Difference	
		Number		Percent		Number		Percent			
		Estimate	Margin of error[2] (±)	Estimate	Margin of error[2] (±)	Estimate	Margin of error[2] (±)	Estimate	Margin of error[2] (±)	Number	Percent
Race[3] and Hispanic Origin											
White	248,001	24,984	616	10.1	0.2	27,820	665	11.2	0.3	*2,836	*1.1
White, not Hispanic	195,060	15,742	455	8.1	0.2	16,932	522	8.7	0.3	*1,190	*0.6
Black	42,842	8,891	417	20.8	1.0	8,727	432	20.4	1.0	−164	−0.4
Asian	19,790	2,004	159	10.1	0.8	2,749	220	13.9	1.1	*746	*3.8
Hispanic (any race)	60,095	10,548	403	17.6	0.7	12,216	442	20.3	0.7	*1,667	*2.8
Nativity											
Native-born	278,536	31,878	716	11.4	0.3	32,540	744	11.7	0.3	*662	*0.2
Foreign-born	45,820	6,322	283	13.8	0.6	8,880	344	19.4	0.7	*2,558	*5.6
Naturalized citizen	22,296	2,215	147	9.9	0.6	3,297	193	14.8	0.8	*1,082	*4.9
Not a citizen	23,524	4,107	227	17.5	0.8	5,584	272	23.7	1.0	*1,476	*6.3
Educational Attainment											
Total, aged 25 and older	221,478	21,916	440	9.9	0.2	26,158	576	11.8	0.3	*4,242	*1.9
No high school diploma	21,975	5,693	222	25.9	0.9	6,320	241	28.8	1.0	*627	*2.9
High school, no college	62,259	7,925	255	12.7	0.4	9,272	315	14.9	0.5	*1,347	*2.2
Some college	57,428	4,812	183	8.4	0.3	5,599	218	9.7	0.4	*787	*1.4
Bachelor's degree or higher	79,816	3,486	214	4.4	0.3	4,967	246	6.2	0.3	*1,481	*1.9

(Continued)

(Continued)

Characteristic	Number[1] (in thousands)	Official[1]				SPM				Difference	
		Number		Percent		Number		Percent			
		Estimate	Margin of error[2] (±)	Estimate	Margin of error[2] (±)	Estimate	Margin of error[2] (±)	Estimate	Margin of error[2] (±)	Number	Percent
Tenure											
Owner/mortgage	133,390	5,249	300	3.9	0.2	7,831	383	5.9	0.3	*2,583	*1.9
Owner/no mortgage/rent free	86,285	9,773	411	11.3	0.4	10,146	415	11.8	0.4	*373	*0.4
Renter	104,680	23,179	713	22.1	0.6	23,443	651	22.4	0.5	264	0.3
Residence[4]											
Inside metropolitan statistical areas	281,961	31,978	770	11.3	0.3	36,249	860	12.9	0.3	*4,271	*1.5
Inside principal cities	104,940	15,309	612	14.6	0.5	16,818	689	16.0	0.6	*1,509	*1.4
Outside principal cities	177,021	16,669	614	9.4	0.3	19,431	669	11.0	0.4	*2,762	*1.6
Outside metropolitan statistical areas	42,395	6,222	529	14.7	0.8	5,171	439	12.2	0.7	*–1,051	*–2.5

Characteristic	Number[1] (in thousands) Estimate	Official[1]				SPM				Difference	
		Number		Percent		Number		Percent		Number	Percent
		Estimate	Margin of error[2] (±)	Estimate	Margin of error[2] (±)	Estimate	Margin of error[2] (±)	Estimate	Margin of error[2] (±)		
Region											
Northeast	55,358	5,689	304	10.3	0.6	6,768	339	12.2	0.6	*1,079	*1.9
Midwest	67,630	7,008	378	10.4	0.6	6,223	344	9.2	0.5	*−785	*−1.2
South	123,671	16,786	576	13.6	0.5	17,219	606	13.9	0.5	*432	*0.3
West	77,697	8,716	419	11.2	0.5	11,211	434	14.4	0.6	*2,495	*3.2
Health Insurance Coverage											
With private insurance	217,780	8,376	319	3.8	0.1	12,747	456	5.9	0.2	*4,371	*2.0
With public, no private insurance	78,426	23,520	641	30.0	0.7	21,805	613	27.8	0.7	*−1,714	*−2.2
Not insured	28,150	6,305	279	22.4	0.9	6,868	312	24.4	1.0	*563	*2.0
Work Experience											
Total 18 to 64 years	197,775	21,130	479	10.7	0.2	24,151	564	12.2	0.3	*3,020	*1.5
All workers	152,835	7,781	256	5.1	0.2	10,959	318	7.2	0.2	*3,178	*2.1
Worked full-time, year-round	111,702	2,544	133	2.3	0.1	4,847	214	4.3	0.2	*2,303	*2.1
Less than full-time, year-round	41,133	5,237	213	12.7	0.5	6,112	228	14.9	0.5	*876	*2.1
Did not work at least 1 week	44,940	13,349	354	29.7	0.7	13,191	383	29.4	0.7	−158	−0.4

(Continued)

(Continued)

Characteristic	Number[1] (in thousands) Estimate	Official[1]								SPM								Difference	
		Number		Percent			Number		Percent									Number	Percent
		Estimate	Margin of error[2] (±)	Estimate	Margin of error[2] (±)		Estimate	Margin of error[2] (±)	Estimate	Margin of error[2] (±)								Number	Percent
Disability Status[5]																			
Total 18 to 64 years	197,775	21,130	479	10.7	0.2		24,151	564	12.2	0.3								*3,020	*1.5
With a disability	14,845	3,818	186	25.7	1.1		3,609	187	24.3	1.1								*–209	*–1.4
With no disability	182,010	17,279	391	9.5	0.2		20,500	497	11.3	0.3								*3,221	*1.8

* An asterisk preceding an estimate indicates change is statistically different from zero at the 90 percent confidence level.

[1] Includes unrelated individuals under the age of 15.

[2] The margin of error (MOE) is a measure of an estimate's variability. The larger the MOE in relation to the size of the estimate, the less reliable the estimate. This number, when added to and subtracted from the estimate, forms the 90 percent confidence interval. The MOEs shown in this table are based on standard errors calculated using replicate weights. For more information see "Standard Errors and Their Use" at<https://www2.census.gov/library/publications/2019/demo/p60-266sa.pdf>.

[3] Federal surveys give respondents the option of reporting more than one race. Therefore, two basic ways of defining a race group are possible. A group, such as Asian, may be defined as those who reported Asian and no other race (the race-alone or single-race concept) or as those who reported Asian regardless of whether they also reported another race (the race-alone-or-in-combination concept). This table shows data using the first approach (race alone). The use of the single-race population does not imply that it is the preferred method of presenting or analyzing data. The Census Bureau uses a variety of approaches. Information on people who reported more than one race, such as White and American Indian and Alaska Native or Asian and Black or African American, is available from the 2010 Census through American FactFinder. About 2.9 percent of people reported more than one race in the 2010 Census. Data for American Indians and Alaska Natives, Native Hawaiians and Other Pacific Islanders, and those reporting two or more races are not shown separately.

[4] For the definition of metropolitan statistical areas and principal cities, see <www.census.gov/programs-surveys/metro-micro/about/glossary.html>.

[5] The sum of those with and without a disability does not equal the total because disability status is not defined for individuals in the U.S. armed forces.

Note: Details may not sum to totals due to rounding.

Source: U.S. Census Bureau, Current Population Survey, 2019 Annual Social and Economic Supplement.

OTHER HISTORIC DOCUMENTS OF INTEREST

FROM THIS VOLUME

- State of the Union Address and Democratic Response, p. 41

FROM PREVIOUS *HISTORIC DOCUMENTS*

- Census Bureau Releases Annual Report on Poverty in the United States, *2018*, p. 512
- Members of Congress, President Trump Remark on Tax Code Overhaul, *2017*, p. 671

Federal Officials, UAW, and General Motors Respond to Labor Dispute

SEPTEMBER 14 AND OCTOBER 17, 2019

Between mid-September and late October 2019, General Motors (GM) shuttered plants around the United States after the nearly 50,000-member workforce walked off the job when contract negotiations between the company and International Union, United Automobile, Aerospace, and Agricultural Implement Workers of America, better known as United Automobile Workers (UAW), stalled. The labor dispute was the longest strike against GM in a half-century and came at a time when private sector unions across the country were struggling to attract new members despite public opinion of labor at a sixteen-year high. The strike concluded on October 25, 2019, after UAW members ratified a new contract that provided pay increases and a new employment structure for certain workers but also permanently closed three GM manufacturing plans.

ORGANIZED LABOR'S DECLINE

Union membership reached its peak in the 1950s, when about one-third of the nation's private sector workforce was a member of a labor union. By 2019, according to the Bureau of Labor Statistics, 6.2 percent of the private sector was unionized; unionization rates remained higher in the public sector at 33.6 percent. The decline has been driven by a number of factors, including more manufacturing work moving abroad, a growth in the gig workforce, court rulings, and state legislative action. Twenty-eight states have enacted so-called "right-to-work" laws that prohibit workers from being forced to join a union in their workplace and also give private sector union and nonunion members the option to pay union dues and fees. On one hand, supporters of right-to-work legislation say workers should decide whether to join a union and should not be forced to give up part of their salary to union dues. Opponents, on the other hand, consider the legislation as union-busting activities that hamper the union's ability to advocate on behalf of workers and collectively bargain for higher wages and benefits. According to a study by the liberal think tank Economic Policy Institute, workers in right-to-work states earn an average of 3.1 percent less in hourly wages and also receive fewer benefits.

Recent court action has also favored individual employees over unions. In 2018, the Supreme Court ruled 5–4 in *Janus v. American Federation of State, County and Municipal Employees (AFSCME)* that nonunion public sector workers cannot be forced to pay union fees. This case revolved around "fair share fees" that are paid by nonunion members in unionized workplaces because they benefit from the collective bargaining the union does on the workers' behalf. The Court ruled that these fees infringe on First Amendment rights because the union is negotiating with the government (the employer), thus making the fees a form of political advocacy. "Compelling individuals to mouth support for views they find objectionable violates that cardinal constitutional command, and in most contexts, any such effort would be universally condemned," Justice Samuel Alito wrote for the majority. *Janus* was widely expected to deal a financial blow to public sector unions. However, a year after the decision, a *Politico* analysis found that while the ten large public sector unions they reviewed lost more than 300,000 fee payers, nine reported having more money than before the ruling and, combined, the ten reported an increase of more than 130,000 members.

Despite activity in state legislatures and the courts, as a whole, the American public has an increasingly positive view of labor unions. In 2008, fewer than 50 percent of those polled by Gallup approved of unions. By August 2019, that number increased to 64 percent. According to Gallup, the public view of unions tends to reflect the overall economy and employment. When the unemployment rate is low, union favorability increases, and vice versa. Unions have also been more visibly active over the past few years. In 2018, the number of workers participating in strikes with more than 1,000 workers reached its highest level since the 1980s. A large portion of these walkouts were teacher strikes, though private sector workers have begun protesting in greater numbers, especially as wages at the bottom of the income spectrum have stagnated.

GM Workers on Strike

The UAW is one of the largest private sector unions in the country, but it, too, has been subject to declining membership. In 1979, the union had approximately 1.5 million members. In 2006, that number was 540,000, and the number declined again to 400,000 by 2019. The UAW represents workers from various sectors of the American economy, including those employed by the major Detroit automakers: General Motors (GM), Ford Motor Company, and Fiat Chrysler. Every four years, the UAW engages in contract negotiations with each of these companies, seeking more favorable benefits, working conditions, and pay for their members.

In 2019, talks with GM, one of the world's largest automakers, broke down in mid-September. (Negotiations with the other two manufacturers were temporarily put on hold pending the outcome of the GM talks.) The UAW was pushing GM to reopen the shuttered manufacturing plants in Lordstown, Ohio; Baltimore, Maryland; and Warren, Michigan, and also wanted to end the tiered wages that GM enacted during the recession to save money. Under this structure, those with the company before 2007 could earn a top wage of $31 per hour. Those hired after—approximately one-third of the GM workforce— make far less for the same work. Another 7 percent of the workforce is made up of temporary employees who earn approximately $15 per hour. Workers say this creates significant tension on factory floors. GM was hesitant to agree, and instead wanted to see workers pay more for their health care costs, while at the same time increasing worker pay flexibility and productivity.

With talks at a standstill, at 11:59 p.m. on September 15, one day after the contract between GM workers and the UAW expired, nearly 50,000 GM workers walked off the job. "Today, we stand strong and say with one voice, we are standing up for our members and for the fundamental rights of working-class people in this nation," said union vice president Terry Dittes. "We are standing up for fair wages, we are standing up for affordable, quality health care. We are standing up for our share of the profits," Dittes added. This marked the first major labor action in the United States against the auto industry in more than a decade. The last UAW strike came in 2007 and lasted for three days, costing GM millions of dollars. Two years after that strike, GM filed for bankruptcy protection, which resulted in workers accepting concessions in pay and benefits to allow the automaker to recover. In the intervening years between the bankruptcy and 2019 strike, GM closed factories and worker wages remained relatively stagnant. This was one of the complaints among workers, who pointed to GM's $35 billion in earnings in North America in the three years preceding the strike, little of which they felt trickled down to the workforce.

GM expressed dismay at the decision of the union workers to strike. Its final offer was a $7 billion investment in U.S. plants, the creation of 5,400 jobs, and an increase in pay and benefits. "We presented a strong offer that improves wages, benefits and grows U.S. jobs in substantive ways, and it is disappointing that the U.A.W. leadership has chosen to strike," the company said in a statement. "We have negotiated in good faith and with a sense of urgency. Our goal remains to build a strong future for our employees and our business."

Longest Automotive Strike against GM in Fifty Years

As soon as the strike began, all GM production in the United States at its twelve vehicle assembly factories and twenty-two parts plants stopped. The company announced that it had slightly more than eighty days of inventory available for sale, which, according to financial analysts, could provide a negotiating cushion of at least a week. UAW and GM negotiators met nearly every day over the course of the five-week strike—the longest automotive work stoppage against GM in fifty years.

During the walkout, workers did not receive their regular paychecks but instead were guaranteed only $250 to $275 per week from the union's strike fund. In turn, national and local charity organizations held events for the affected workers and employees of GM suppliers impacted by the labor stoppage, to provide food, information on rent and mortgage assistance, and budgeting strategies. Workers also faced confusion about health care coverage. On September 17, GM initially announced that it would stop providing health insurance for UAW members during the strike, and that the union would instead need to cover the cost of COBRA. (COBRA is temporary health insurance more traditionally offered to workers following a job loss to avoid a lapse in coverage). Following public pushback, on September 26, GM reversed course and announced that it would in fact continue to pay for health insurance and noted that no worker had lost coverage in the intervening nine days.

The strike drew support from high-profile individuals including 2020 Democratic presidential candidates Elizabeth Warren and Joe Biden, who joined workers on the picket lines. In solidarity, the United Steelworkers stopped delivering GM's supplies and the Teamsters union refused to deliver GM cars. "Teamsters and the UAW have a decades-long relationship of having each other's back. And that continues with the UAW's notification that it will go out on strike against General Motors. . . . Our 1.4 million members stand in solidarity with the UAW and will honor their picket lines," said Teamsters general president Jim Hoffa.

The strike came at a trying time for the union internally. Since 2017, a number of UAW executives had been charged in a federal probe with crimes ranging from using union funds for extensive personal spending to bribes and kickbacks. New charges continued to be announced as the union was negotiating. Labor experts questioned whether that could have an impact on how members vote on a new contract. "This is a mystery strike to me," said Gary Chaison, a professor emeritus of industrial relations at Clark University. While it involves "the usual issues: health-care, wages, part-time workers, and so on . . . the corruption charges introduce a new element to this strike—an unpredictable element, to some degree," he said.

AGREEMENT REACHED

On October 16, the UAW announced that it had reached a tentative agreement with GM to end the strike. Provisions included many that the union was seeking. The top wage for full-time hourly employees would increase to $32 per hour within four years, and workers would be able to reach this wage after four years on the job, as opposed to the eight years it took at the time of the agreement. Additionally, GM agreed to create a path for temporary workers to become regular employees with full benefits after three years on the job; previously, these individuals had no job security and no dental or vision insurance. The worker share of health care costs would remain unchanged at around 3 percent, and each full-time worker ratifying the new contract would receive an $11,000 bonus. GM also agreed that it would keep the Detroit-Hamtramck assembly plant open instead of closing it as scheduled in January 2020, where it would now manufacture battery modules and electric trucks. In turn, the union agreed to accept the permanent closure of the Lordstown, Baltimore, and Detroit GM plants. (The company did, however, propose a partnership with an electric vehicle manufacturer who could build a battery plant near the former Lordstown factory that could hire union workers as part of a separate contract.)

The final contract was ratified with 57 percent of the UAW's 41,000 voting members approving the deal. GM welcomed the agreement. "We delivered a contract that recognizes our employees for the important contributions they make to the overall success of the company," said GM chief executive Mary T. Barra. "As one team, we can move forward and stay focused on our priorities of safety and building high-quality cars, trucks and crossovers for our customers," she added. The four-year contract was expected to increase GM labor costs by around $100 million per year. According to economic analysts, GM lost an estimated $1.75 billion during the strike, while employees and workers for GM suppliers lost nearly $1 billion in wages.

—Heather Kerrigan

Following is a September 14, 2019, announcement from the UAW that a strike by GM workers was likely and an October 17, 2019, UAW press release announcing a tentative contract with GM.

UAW Alerts GM and Members to Possible Strike

September 14, 2019

UAW Vice President Terry Dittes released a letter this evening to members announcing that the UAW will not extend the current 2015 Collective Bargaining Agreement but will work without a contract until a course of action is decided by the UAW International Executive Board and the UAW-GM National Council.

"While we are fighting for better wages, affordable quality health care, and job security, GM refuses to put hard-working Americans ahead of their record profits of

$35 billion in North America over the last three years. We are united in our efforts to get an agreement our members and their families deserve."

Source: United Automobile, Aerospace, and Agricultural Implement Workers of America. "After Months of Tough Negotiations, UAW Vice President Terry Dittes Announces No GM Contract Extension; GM Refuses to Put Hard Working American Families before Profits." September 14, 2019. https://uaw.org/months-tough-negotiations-uaw-vice-president-terry-dittes-announces-no-gm-contract-extension-gm-refuses-put-hard-working-american-families-profits.

UAW Announces Tentative Contract Agreement with GM

October 17, 2019

Local General Motors UAW leaders from around the country today announced that the UAW GM National Council voted to accept the Tentative Agreement with General Motors. UAW workers will remain on strike until ratification.

The ratification informational meetings and vote will take place beginning Saturday, October 19 and ending Friday, October 25, 2019. Members should contact their UAW Locals for dates and times for meetings and voting.

"We thank the public for their support during the strike and their continued support as UAW GM members review the tentative agreement," UAW Vice President and Director of the General Motors Department Terry Dittes said. "Ultimately, UAW members will make the decision to ratify the agreement. Their unity and solidarity brought us to this moment."

Source: United Automobile, Aerospace, and Agricultural Implement Workers of America. "UAW GM National Council Votes to Send Tentative Agreement to Members for Ratification." October 17, 2019. https://uaw.org/uaw-gm-national-council-votes-send-tentative-agreement-members-ratification.

OTHER HISTORIC DOCUMENTS OF INTEREST

FROM PREVIOUS *HISTORIC DOCUMENTS*

United States and Saudi Arabia Respond to Attack on Saudi Oil Facilities

SEPTEMBER 15 AND 20, 2019

On September 14, 2019, two of Saudi Arabia's oil installations were damaged in an attack that temporarily halted half of the country's oil production. The largest-ever assault on Saudi oil infrastructure, the incident did not provoke immediate retaliatory action from the United States, one of Saudi Arabia's principal allies, but it did escalate growing tensions between America and Iran, which is believed by the West and Saudi Arabia to be responsible for the attacks.

GROWING TENSIONS BETWEEN SAUDI ARABIA AND IRAN

Relations between Saudi Arabia and Iran have been strained for decades. Tensions between the two countries increased significantly following the Iranian Revolution of 1979, when Iran accused Saudi Arabia of favoring U.S. interests over those of Islamic nations. In January 2016, Sunni-majority Saudi Arabia broke all diplomatic relations with Shia-majority Iran when the latter attacked the Saudi embassy in Tehran following Saudi Arabia's execution of Sheikh Nimr al-Nimr, a Shia cleric.

Various other factors have divided the two countries. Both are major oil and gas exporters, but they have consistently been at odds over energy policy. Saudi Arabia, one of the largest petroleum producers in the world, has advocated keeping oil prices at more moderate levels so as not to provoke Western and other industrial countries from looking for alternative energy sources. Iran, which produces less than half the oil that Saudi Arabia does, has generally pushed for energy-exporting countries to limit production in order to keep world prices high.

Religious and geopolitical differences have also caused the two nations to clash. Saudi Arabia's Sunni Muslim monarchy, established in 1932 and currently ruled by Salman bin Abdulaziz Al Saud and his son, Crown Prince Mohammed bin Salman, has long had strong ties to the United States and the United Kingdom. Conversely, the 1979 Iranian Revolution toppled Iran's monarchy and replaced it with a Shia Islamic Republic, a political system resembling parliamentary democracy, although supervised by a theocracy government and overseen by a supreme leader. Under the leadership of Ayatollah Khomeini, Iran quickly set itself against the West, as well as Sunni Arab states such as Saudi Arabia that were allied with the United States and other Western countries. The country's current leader, Ayatollah Ali Khamenei (who replaced Khomeini as supreme leader upon the latter's death in 1989), has openly expressed his disdain for Saudi Arabia's conservative monarchy, calling it "un-Islamic." Correspondingly, Saudi Arabia regards with suspicion Iran's activities in the Persian Gulf as a transparent and aggressive effort to dominate the Muslim world.

These tensions have been exacerbated by the long-standing alliance between the United States and Saudi Arabia that dates to the 1930s, when full diplomatic relations were established between the two countries. These relations evolved into an alliance first formalized in 1951 with the Mutual Defense Assistance Agreement. In spite of the political differences between the two countries, their relationship as allies has been fairly constant. In fact, both former presidents George W. Bush and Barack Obama had close personal relationships with senior members of the Saudi royal family.

By contrast, the relationship between the United States and Iran has been troubled, and the two nations have had no diplomatic relations since 1980. The 1979–1981 Iran hostage crisis added to a growing estrangement, and Iran's alleged human rights abuses since the Islamic Revolution are believed to have widened that gap. Both countries regard each other with suspicion, often accusing the other of arrogance in the struggle for global dominance.

In 2018, the relationship between the two countries reached new levels of unease when President Donald Trump announced that the United States would pull out of the Joint Comprehensive Plan of Action (JCPOA), a deal reached in 2015 to help prevent Iran from developing a nuclear weapon. Trump criticized a number of aspects of the agreement and expressed his concern that the inspection regime was not tough enough to ensure that the Iranians would not be able to develop a nuclear weapon in the coming years. The president also criticized the agreement because it does not stop Iran from developing ballistic missiles, which can be used to carry nuclear warheads.

In addition to leaving the JCPOA, the United States imposed sanctions that made it increasingly difficult for the Iranians to sell oil in international markets. This, in turn, crippled Iran's economy, which shrank by almost 10 percent in 2019. Iran struck back, first by attacking a number of oil tankers in the Persian Gulf, and then, finally, launching the drone strike against Saudi oil facilities.

Saudi Oil Facilities Attacked

According to the Saudi government, on September 14, 2019, an estimated twenty-five drones and cruise missiles attacked the Khurais oilfield and Abqaiq oil-processing facility. Questions quickly surfaced as to why the Saudi defense system failed to identify the threat, but an investigation found that neither the Saudi nor U.S. systems detected the airstrike because the U.S.-owned Patriot missile system employed by the Saudis was mainly positioned to counter attacks from Yemen. The Saudis have also been accused of mismanaging their Patriot air defense systems, primarily using the systems to protect the royal palaces rather than the country's vulnerable oil infrastructure.

The Houthis, a rebel group based in Yemen, quickly claimed responsibility for the attack, but the United States and Saudi Arabia both indicated a belief that Iran was behind the incident and that the cruise missiles used in the assault had possibly been launched from Iraq. The Saudis claimed that Iranian-made Ya-Ali land-attack missiles were used in the assault. Their range—435 miles—made it unlikely that they were launched from Yemen. The attack also appeared to be launched from a location north of the country, based on the direction of the cruise missiles when they struck, again making Yemen, located south of Saudi Arabia, an unlikely launch site. However, some of the technologies used in the attack, including drones, have long been available to rebel groups supported by Iran.

The oil facility attack came at an unsettled moment for the kingdom, whose economy had been faltering. According to the *Wall Street Journal*, investment into Saudi Arabia was

$16.3 billion as recently as 2011, when oil prices peaked, compared with just $4.2 billion in 2018. This prompted the Saudi government to explore other methods to jump-start its economy, but at least initially, they proved unsuccessful. With two-thirds of the country's earnings still coming from crude oil sales, the attack on the oilfield and processing facility struck at the very heart of the country. According to the *Wall Street Journal*, before the attack the Abqaiq facility had an output of 5.7 million barrels a day, roughly half of the country's total output and approximately 5 percent of the world's oil supply.

UNITED STATES RESPONDS TO THE ATTACK

In a briefing with Chair of the Joint Chiefs of Staff Marine Gen. Joseph F. Dunford, Secretary of Defense Mark T. Esper did not hesitate to blame Iran for the attack, saying that the Iranian regime "is waging a deliberate campaign to destabilize the Middle East" and that the attack marked a "dramatic escalation of Iranian aggression." Esper explained, "It is clear, based on detailed exploitation conducted by Saudi, the United States and other international investigative teams, that the weapons used in the attack were Iranian produced and were not launched from Yemen, as was initially claimed. All indications are that Iran was responsible for the attack."

In a conversation with reporters, President Trump hinted that Iran could be behind the strike but said he was waiting to "get the final results of what we're looking at" to make a final determination, which could then dictate the U.S. response. Iran repeatedly denied any role. On Twitter, the Saudis called the strikes a "terrorist and sabotage attack" that could "threaten the global economy," but they did not make any initial accusations, instead waiting for the completion of an international investigation.

President Trump spoke with the Saudi crown prince following the incident, confirming his "support of Saudi Arabia's self-defense," while at the same time making repeated requests for Iran to begin diplomatic talks. A month later, however, the United States and Saudi Arabia were in discussions about stepping up efforts to protect the kingdom's oil production, including investigating new antidrone technologies and ways to connect Saudi missile defense systems to U.S. systems. Additionally, the U.S. military deployed equipment and personnel to Saudi Arabia, including 2,000 troops, two jet fighter squadrons, and three new antimissile systems.

In the months following the attack, relations between the three countries remained tense. They came to a head in December and January 2019, when Iran and the United States began a series of escalating actions in Iraq, where both countries have troops deployed. On December 31, 2019, Iranian-backed Iraqi militias attacked a U.S. embassy compound in Baghdad. Then, on January 3, 2020, a U.S. airstrike killed Qassem Soleimani, a high-ranking military leader in Iran's Islamic Revolutionary Guard Corps. In response, Iran launched missile strikes at U.S. bases in Iraq. The tit-for-tat strikes raised concerns among some in the United States that the two nations could be headed for war.

—Lyndi Schrecengost

Following is a September 15, 2019, tweet from the Saudi foreign ministry responding to the oil facility attack; and the text of a press briefing by Secretary of Defense Mark Esper and Chair of the Joint Chiefs of Staff Marine Gen. Joseph Dunford Jr., on September 20, 2019, discussing the oil facility attack and possible U.S. response.

Saudi Arabia Responds to Oil Facility Attack

September 15, 2019

Energy Minister Prince Abdulaziz bin Salman: "The terrorist attacks on #Aramco facilities in #Abqaiq and #Khurais are a threat to the world's economy."

SOURCE: Saudi Arabia Foreign Ministry (@KSAmofaEN). Twitter post. September 15, 2019. https://twitter .com/KSAmofaEN/status/1173172151282782209?ref_src=twsrc%5Etfw%7Ctwcamp%5Etweetembed% 7Ctwterm%5E1173172151282782209&ref_url=https%3A%2F%2Firanprimer.usip.org%2Fblog%2F201 9%2Fsep%2F18%2Fsaudi-statements-oil-attacks.

Department of Defense Leaders Discuss Saudi Oil Facility Attack

September 20, 2019

SECRETARY OF DEFENSE DR. MARK T. ESPER: Well, good afternoon, ladies and gentlemen. Gen. Dunford and I just returned from the White House, where we met with the president and his national security team to discuss options to deter Iran's continued aggressive behavior. As we have seen, the Iranian regime is waging a deliberate campaign to destabilize the Middle East and impose costs on the international economy.

In recent months, Iran has increased its military activity through direct attacks and support to its proxies in the region. In the Persian Gulf and Gulf of Oman, which are vital waterways for global commerce, Iran has threatened the safe passage of ships by attacking commercial vessels and illegally seizing a British oil tanker.

In Yemen, Iran is perpetuating war by providing sustained financial support and advanced weapons to the Houthi insurgency. And on June 20th, Iran shot down a United States unmanned aircraft that was flying over international waters.

Despite repeated calls from President Trump to begin diplomatic talks, Iranian aggression continues to increase. In the face of this sustained malign behavior, the United States and other countries have demonstrated great restraint in hopes that Iranian leadership would choose peace, and reverse Iran's steep decline into isolation and economic collapse.

But the attack on September 14th against Saudi Arabian oil facilities represents a dramatic escalation of Iranian aggression. It is clear, based on detailed exploitation conducted by Saudi, the United States and other international investigative teams, that the weapons used in the attack were Iranian produced and were not launched from Yemen, as was initially claimed. All indications are that Iran was responsible for the attack.

The United States has a responsibility to protect our citizens and our interests in the region, and the international community has a responsibility to protect the global economy and international rules and norms. All of this is threatened by Iran's significant escalation of violence.

This week, I have been in dialogue with the Saudi defense minister and other partners about this latest attack. To prevent further escalation, Saudi Arabia requested international support to help protect the kingdom's critical infrastructure. The United Arab Emirates has also requested assistance.

In response to the kingdom's request, the president has approved the deployment of U.S. forces, which will be defensive in nature and primarily focused on air and missile defense. We will also work to accelerate the delivery of military equipment to the Kingdom of Saudi Arabia and the UAE to enhance their ability to defend themselves.

The purpose of the additional defensive support we will provide is as follows. First, to send a clear message that the United States supports our partners in the region. Second, to ensure the free flow of resources necessary to support the global economy. And third, to demonstrate our commitment to upholding the international rules-based order that we have long called on Iran to obey.

As the president has made clear, the United States does not seek conflict with Iran. That said, we have many other military options available should they be necessary.

We urge the Iranian leadership to cease their destructive and destabilizing activities and to move forward on a peaceful, diplomatic path.

Gen. Dunford and I will now take your questions. Thank you.

Q: Mr. Secretary, thank you. You said air and missile defenses primarily. Could you be a little more specific about—are you talking about patriot missiles—and what number of troops are you talking about sending?

GENERAL JOSEPH F. DUNFORD JR.: Yes, so, Bob, Secretary Pompeo just came back this morning, and the Saudis asked for enhanced defensive capabilities. So what we'll do now is take the president's decision; I'll talk to CENTCOM over the weekend; we'll talk with our Saudi partners; and we'll work the details of the deployment, and we'll be able to share that with you next week.

Q: So there's been no decision on specific numbers. . . .
(CROSSTALK)

GEN. DUNFORD: We haven't decided on specific units. Broadly—as the secretary said, it'll be capabilities to enhance their air and missile defense. It's now my job to come back with the—to the secretary with the details of what we believe would meet the Saudi's requirements and is sustainable.

Q: Just—just to follow-up, it wouldn't be—we're not talking about thousands of troops, you're talking about hundreds of troops, and also, just to the secretary, do you think this is going to be enough, or why do you think this will be enough to deter Iran from further attacks?

SEC. ESPER: We think given the state of play now, and then based on whatever assessments we get from Central Command, what the Joint Staff and the chairman do, and other discussions we're having with partners—We have to continually assess that—we think for now, that would be sufficient, but that doesn't mean there could be additional deployments as needed, based on the changing situation.

Q: And on troop numbers?

GEN. DUNFORD: I would say at this point, a moderate deployment, Phil, and we'll have more details for you next week, but—but not ready to share the details.

Q: Not thousands; thousands would be not moderate.

GEN. DUNFORD: That's fair to say, not thousands.

STAFF: Lucas?

(CROSSTALK)

Q: Are there any plans—are there any plans to hold the Lincoln Strike Group any longer than currently planned?

SEC. ESPER: We're not going to discuss any operational details at this time.

STAFF: Barbara?

Q: Does—for either of you. Does this now represent a full U.S. commitment to defend Saudi Arabia and to defend the oil infrastructure of Saudi Arabia?

And for Gen. Dunford in particular, what—your concern about their ability, the Iranian ability to launch swarms of drones at very great distances without any air defense detection of this incoming attack?

GEN. DUNFORD: So what I'd say, Barbara, in terms of what we're doing is, we're contributing to Saudi Arabia's defense. We would be looking, as the secretary said, for other international partners to also contribute to Saudi Arabia's defense.

And with regard to dealing with a specific threat like you just spoke about, you know, no single system is going to be able to defend against a threat like that, but a layered system of defensive capabilities would mitigate the risk of swarms of drones or other attacks that may come from Iran.

SEC. ESPER: I want to double down on the chairman's comments, two ways. First of all, I agree, what we would be deploying to the theater would be what would—what would be a necessary to help support and contribute to the kingdom's defenses. And at the same time, we're calling on many other countries who would also have these capabilities to do two things. First of all, stand up and condemn these attacks; and secondly, look to also contribute defensive capabilities so we can defend those things that I outlined in my remarks, whether it's the infrastructure in Saudi Arabia, and then the broader issues with regard to freedom of the seas, navigation in the Strait, and then the international rules and norms that Iran is clearly violating.

STAFF: Courtney?

Q: So should we take this as, this is the president's decision about the response to the attack in Saudi Arabia, and there's not a kinetic response that we should expect from the United States?

SEC. ESPER: This is the first step we're taking with regard to responding to these attacks. And again, for the reasons I outlined, to help the—bolster the defenses of Saudi Arabia and provide equipment to both the Saudis and UAE; second, to ensure the free flow of commerce though the Strait; and third, to ensure we protect and defend the international rules-based order, and try and convince the Iranians to get back on the diplomatic path.

Q: But the deployment of these kinds of assets can often take days and weeks. Is there—should we expect any other kind of more immediate response from the United States besides. . . .

SEC. ESPER: The United States has a robust presence in the Gulf already. We bolstered it further in May, so we feel quite confident in terms of our own defensive posture and our ability to do anything else as necessary. But that's not where we are right now; right now we're focused on helping the Saudis improve their defenses of that infrastructure.

STAFF: Last question—Nancy?

Q: Mr. Secretary, Chairman Dunford, you've mentioned that the international community should get involved, but you know some allies have questioned whether the attacks were, in fact, launched in Iran. I was wondering if you could give us any sense on whether you will declassify any evidence that shows that those strikes were launched from Iran? And also if you could give us a sense of timeline of when these deployments could start?

SEC. ESPER: So I'll say a few things. First of all, the United States is on the ground in Saudi Arabia, the Saudi Arabians are leading this investigation, and we will keep them in the lead with regard to the forensics. So we need to let that play out and let the evidence play out.

With regard to the partners and allies, first of all, I would commend Secretary Pompeo. He's been on the phone and on the road the past few days, speaking to numerous allies and partners about this incident.

And regardless of where you think it came from, the fact is, the Saudis were attacked by both drones and cruise missiles and are still vulnerable to attack. So asking allies and partners to contribute resources to help them defend themselves and to defend those things I spoke about, I don't think is too much of an ask, given the situation.

GEN. DUNFORD: And we'll work the details, Nancy, over the weekend, and I'll come back to the secretary early next week with some specific recommendations.

Q: But you can confirm that the strike was launched from southwest Iran?

SEC. ESPER: Thank you. Thank you, everyone.

SOURCE: U.S. Department of Defense. "Joint Press Briefing with Secretary of Defense Dr. Mark T. Esper and Chairman of the Joint Chiefs of Staff Marine General Joseph F. Dunford Jr." September 20, 2019. https://www.defense.gov/Newsroom/Transcripts/Transcript/Article/1967413/joint-press-briefing-with-secretary-of-defense-dr-mark-t-esper-and-chairman-of/.

OTHER HISTORIC DOCUMENTS OF INTEREST

FROM THIS VOLUME

▓ President Trump Announces Sanctions against Iran, p. 332

FROM PREVIOUS *HISTORIC DOCUMENTS*

▓ Iranian Nuclear Deal Reached, *2015*, p. 148

Representatives of the United States, United Kingdom, France, Turkey, Iran, and China Address UN General Assembly

SEPTEMBER 24, 25, AND 27, 2019

Nearly all 193 member nations gathered at the United Nations (UN) headquarters in New York City from September 19 to 30, 2019, to address the world stage. Amid a variety of domestic and international crises, leaders espoused their accomplishments, embraced conflicting visions for the future, and pushed for collective action to address worldwide issues. In his third address to the General Assembly, U.S. president Donald Trump again supported a nationalist approach to international relations, rejecting principles of multilateral cooperation promoted by the UN. Other leaders echoed Trump's advocacy for national sovereignty, such as UK prime minister Boris Johnson. Turkish president Recep Tayyip Erdoğan outlined a controversial resettlement strategy for the millions of Syrian refugees living abroad, while Iranian president Hassan Rouhani, in direct response to Trump, spoke about rising tensions in the Middle East, warning world leaders that the region was on the edge of collapse.

TRUMP CONTINUES TO EMBRACE NATIONALISM

As he had in his first two speeches to the General Assembly, Trump delivered a sharp nationalist message and assailed "globalists" in his 2019 remarks. Trump stressed the value of national identity and argued that governments must defend their history, culture, and heritage. "If you want freedom, take pride in your country. If you want democracy, hold on to your sovereignty. And if you want peace, love your nation," he said. Trump argued that "wise leaders put the good of their own people and their own country first." He also declared, "The future does not belong to globalists. The future belongs to patriots. The future belongs to sovereign and independent nations, who protect their citizens, respect their neighbors, and honor the differences that make each country special and unique." At home and abroad, the speech was widely characterized as the president's clearest explanation of his nationalist platform.

Speaking to a body that has long advocated for supporting refugees and migrants, Trump reaffirmed his support for strong borders, a central tenet of his administration. "Many of the countries here today are coping with the challenges of uncontrolled migration," he said. "Each of you has the absolute right to protect your borders." So did the United States, he added. Illegal immigration, Trump argued, is "unfair, unsafe, and unsustainable," and it "undermines prosperity, rips apart societies, and empowers ruthless criminal cartels." Trump framed strong borders as crucial to maintaining "national foundations" and fundamental to the free world's success.

Trump also took aim at international governing bodies, including the UN. Proudly stating that his administration has refused to ratify a UN international treaty, Trump said, "There is no circumstance under which the United States will allow international entities to trample on the rights of our citizens, including the right to self-defense." He also criticized the World Trade Organization (WTO) for being soft on what he viewed as abusive Chinese economic practices. "The second-largest economy in the world should not be permitted to declare itself a 'developing country' in order to game the system at others' expense," Trump said. "For years, these abuses were tolerated, ignored, or even encouraged. Globalism exerted a religious pull over past leaders, causing them to ignore their own national interests. But as far as America is concerned, those days are over."

Beyond the WTO, Trump accused China of failing to liberalize its economy and for engaging in "unfair practices" on trade. Trump championed what he described as the United States' "massive tariffs" on China, imposed "to confront these unfair practices." According to Trump, the tariffs were delivering results. "Already, as a result of these tariffs, supply chains are relocating back to America and to other nations, and billions of dollars are being paid to our Treasury," he said. The president noted that the United States was "absolutely committed to restoring balance to our relationship with China" and that he hoped for "an agreement that would be beneficial for both countries." He added, "But as I have made very clear, I will not accept a bad deal for the American people." He closed his discussion of the U.S.–Chinese relationship with a mention of the ongoing public unrest in Hong Kong. "As we endeavor to stabilize our relationship, we're also carefully monitoring the situation in Hong Kong," Trump said. "How China chooses to handle the situation will say a great deal about its role in the world in the future. We are all counting on President Xi as a great leader."

Trump also focused his ire on Iran, though not as sharply as many observers expected. Days before the international gathering, two major oil facilities in Saudi Arabia were hit by drone strikes for which Yemen's Houthi rebels claimed responsibility. U.S. officials blamed Iran for the attacks, arguing that Rouhani's government was supporting the Houthi rebels. Secretary of State Mike Pompeo called the situation "an unprecedented attack on the world's energy supply" and "an act of war." Yet Trump said relatively little about the strikes. Instead, he tamped down discussion of military conflict, defended his decision to withdraw the United States from the 2015 nuclear agreement, and called on Tehran to give freedom to its people and engage in new talks with the United States. "America is ready to embrace friendship with all who genuinely seek peace and respect," Trump said. "The United States has never believed in permanent enemies. We want partners, not adversaries."

Iran Calls for an End to U.S. Intervention

Rouhani used his remarks to respond directly to Trump and his administration. The Iranian president warned that tensions were high in the Persian Gulf, that the Middle East is "on the edge of collapse," and that a "single blunder can fuel a big fire." He pointed to conflicts in Afghanistan, Iraq, and Syria to argue that the Trump administration could not bring peace to the region, stating instead that peace would only come when America withdrew its troops. "The security of our region shall be provided when American troops pull out," said Rouhani. "Security shall not be supplied with American weapons and intervention."

Rouhani also offered a strong critique of economic sanctions imposed on Iran by the Trump administration. "The Iranian nation will never, ever forget and forgive these crimes," Rouhani promised before declaring that the United States is attempting a "silent killing of a great nation." Rouhani told the General Assembly that Iran would not negotiate with U.S. officials on a new nuclear agreement as long as sanctions remain in place, blaming America for "international piracy" and "merciless economic terrorism." He did suggest that the landmark accord could be a platform for the two countries to talk about other, larger issues but reiterated that "our response to any negotiations under sanctions is negative." Despite the strong rhetoric, some analysts believed Rouhani was attempting to send a signal to the international community that Iran wanted to revive the nuclear deal.

WORLD LEADERS DEFEND GLOBAL COOPERATION

While Trump and others embraced nationalism, many other leaders defended multilateralism and the liberal world order. French president Emmanuel Macron called on the United States and Iran to resume negotiations with other international allies, worrying that "peace is at the mercy of an incident, a miscalculation." Referencing the 2015 nuclear deal, Macron said, "Now more than ever is the time for negotiations among Iran, the United States, the signatories of the J.C.P.O.A. and regional powers, centered on the region's security and stability."

China also defended a globalized economy. China's foreign minister, Wang Yi, in a separate event held during the week, touted the economic benefits of globalization. "Economic globalization as the trend of the times cannot and should not be held back. The free flow of resources enabled by globalization has created tremendous wealth." Wang also stressed that the tariffs that have driven the trade war between the United States and China were harmful to both countries and the international economy. "Neither scapegoating nor initiating a trade war is the right solution" to concerns about globalization, he said. "Trade frictions will only hurt both sides and the whole world."

OTHER NOTEWORTHY REMARKS

Erdoğan appeared at the UN for the first time since proposing a new resettlement policy for refugees displaced by the ongoing civil war in neighboring Syria. Erdoğan's proposal involved creating an expanded "safe zone" in northern Syria where as many as two million people could be relocated. However, this would involve housing the Syrian refugees on Kurdish land, drawing sharp criticisms that Erdoğan was attempting to make a land grab under the auspices of refugee resettlement. Erdoğan has claimed the expanded safe zone will save millions of lives. "Whether with the U.S. or the coalition forces, Russia and Iran, we can walk shoulder to shoulder, hand in hand so refugees can resettle, saving them from tent camps and container camps," he said. The Turkish president also made waves by declaring, "The position of nuclear power should either be forbidden for all or permissible for everyone." He went on to argue that "inequality" between states with nuclear power and those without threatens the global balance.

Johnson delivered a rambling speech espousing the virtues of science, though his speech was largely clouded by domestic turmoil at home. Johnson likened the process of quitting the European Union to Greek mythology. "When Prometheus brought fire to mankind . . . Zeus punished him by chaining him to a Tartarean crag while his liver was pecked out by an eagle," he noted. "And every time his liver regrew the eagle came back and pecked it again. And this went on forever—a bit like the experience of Brexit in the UK, if some of our parliamentarians had their way." Johnson ultimately cut his trip to the

UN short after being rebuked by the British Supreme Court for unconstitutionally suspending parliament.

—Robert Howard

Following are portions of the speeches delivered before the United Nations General Assembly by U.S. president Donald Trump, British prime minister Boris Johnson, French president Emmanuel Macron, and Turkish president Recep Tayyip Erdoğan on September 24, 2019; by Iranian president Hassan Rouhani on September 25, 2019; and by Chinese minister of foreign affairs Wang Yi on September 27, 2019.

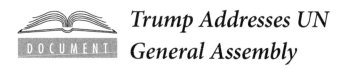

Trump Addresses UN General Assembly

September 24, 2019

Thank you very much. Mr. President, Mr. Secretary-General, distinguished delegates, ambassadors, and world leaders:

Seven decades of history have passed through this hall, in all of their richness and drama. Where I stand, the world has heard from presidents and premiers at the height of the Cold War. We have seen the foundation of nations. We have seen the ringleaders of revolution. We have beheld saints who inspired us with hope, rebels who stirred us with passion, and heroes who emboldened us with courage—all here to share plans, proposals, visions, and ideas on the world's biggest stage.

Like those who met us before, our time is one of great contests, high stakes, and clear choices. The essential divide that runs all around the world and throughout history is once again thrown into stark relief. It is the divide between those whose thirst for control deludes them into thinking they are destined to rule over others and those people and nations who want only to rule themselves.

I have the immense privilege of addressing you today as the elected leader of a nation that prizes liberty, independence, and self-government above all. The United States, after having spent over two and a half trillion dollars since my election to completely rebuild our great military, is also, by far, the world's most powerful nation. Hopefully, it will never have to use this power. . . .

The future does not belong to globalists. The future belongs to patriots. The future belongs to sovereign and independent nations who protect their citizens, respect their neighbors, and honor the differences that make each country special and unique.

It is why we in the United States have embarked on an exciting program of national renewal. In everything we do, we are focused on empowering the dreams and aspirations of our citizens.

Thanks to our pro-growth economic policies, our domestic unemployment rate reached its lowest level in over half a century. Fueled by massive tax cuts and regulations cuts, jobs are being produced at a historic rate. Six million Americans have been added to the employment rolls in under three years.

Last month, African American, Hispanic American, and Asian American unemployment reached their lowest rates ever recorded. We are marshaling our nation's vast energy abundance, and the United States is now the number one producer of oil and natural gas anywhere in the world. Wages are rising, incomes are soaring, and 2.5 million Americans have been lifted out of poverty in less than three years.

As we rebuild the unrivaled might of the American military, we are also revitalizing our alliances by making it very clear that all of our partners are expected to pay their fair share of the tremendous defense burden, which the United States has borne in the past.

At the center of our vision for national renewal is an ambitious campaign to reform international trade. For decades, the international trading system has been easily exploited by nations acting in very bad faith. As jobs were outsourced, a small handful grew wealthy at the expense of the middle class. . . .

We have worked closely with our partners in Mexico and Canada to replace NAFTA with the brand new and hopefully bipartisan U.S.–Mexico–Canada Agreement. . . .

The most important difference in America's new approach on trade concerns our relationship with China. In 2001, China was admitted to the World Trade Organization. Our leaders then argued that this decision would compel China to liberalize its economy and strengthen protections to provide things that were unacceptable to us, and for private property and for the rule of law. Two decades later, this theory has been tested and proven completely wrong.

Not only has China declined to adopt promised reforms, it has embraced an economic model dependent on massive market barriers, heavy state subsidies, currency manipulation, product dumping, forced technology transfers, and the theft of intellectual property and also trade secrets on a grand scale. . . .

The World Trade Organization needs drastic change. The second-largest economy in the world should not be permitted to declare itself a "developing country" in order to game the system at others' expense.

For years, these abuses were tolerated, ignored, or even encouraged. Globalism exerted a religious pull over past leaders, causing them to ignore their own national interests.

But as far as America is concerned, those days are over. To confront these unfair practices, I placed massive tariffs on more than $500 billion worth of Chinese-made goods. Already, as a result of these tariffs, supply chains are relocating back to America and to other nations, and billions of dollars are being paid to our Treasury. . . .

One of the greatest security threats facing peace-loving nations today is the repressive regime in Iran. The regime's record of death and destruction is well known to us all. Not only is Iran the world's number one state sponsor of terrorism, but Iran's leaders are fueling the tragic wars in both Syria and Yemen.

At the same time, the regime is squandering the nation's wealth and future in a fanatical quest for nuclear weapons and the means to deliver them. We must never allow this to happen.

To stop Iran's path to nuclear weapons and missiles, I withdrew the United States from the terrible Iran nuclear deal, which has very little time remaining, did not allow inspection of important sites, and did not cover ballistic missiles.

Following our withdrawal, we have implemented severe economic sanctions on the country. Hoping to free itself from sanctions, the regime has escalated its violent and unprovoked aggression. In response to Iran's recent attack on Saudi Arabian oil facilities, we just imposed the highest level of sanctions on Iran's central bank and sovereign wealth fund.

All nations have a duty to act. No responsible government should subsidize Iran's bloodlust. As long as Iran's menacing behavior continues, sanctions will not be lifted; they will be tightened. Iran's leaders will have turned a proud nation into just another cautionary tale of what happens when a ruling class abandons its people and embarks on a crusade for personal power and riches. . . .

Many of America's closest friends today were once our gravest foes. The United States has never believed in permanent enemies. We want partners, not adversaries. America knows that while anyone can make war, only the most courageous can choose peace.

For this same reason, we have pursued bold diplomacy on the Korean Peninsula. I have told Kim Jong Un what I truly believe: that, like Iran, his country is full of tremendous untapped potential, but that to realize that promise, North Korea must denuclearize.

Around the world, our message is clear: America's goal is lasting, America's goal is harmony, and America's goal is not to go with these endless wars—wars that never end.

With that goal in mind, my administration is also pursuing the hope of a brighter future in Afghanistan. Unfortunately, the Taliban has chosen to continue their savage attacks. And we will continue to work with our coalition of Afghan partners to stamp out terrorism, and we will never stop working to make peace a reality.

Here in the Western Hemisphere, we are joining with our partners to ensure stability and opportunity all across the region. In that mission, one of our most critical challenges is illegal immigration, which undermines prosperity, rips apart societies, and empowers ruthless criminal cartels.

Mass illegal migration is unfair, unsafe, and unsustainable for everyone involved: the sending countries and the depleted countries. And they become depleted very fast, but their youth is not taken care of and human capital goes to waste. . . .

Today, I have a message for those open border activists who cloak themselves in the rhetoric of social justice: Your policies are not just. Your policies are cruel and evil. You are empowering criminal organizations that prey on innocent men, women, and children. You put your own false sense of virtue before the lives, wellbeing, and [of] countless innocent people. When you undermine border security, you are undermining human rights and human dignity.

Many of the countries here today are coping with the challenges of uncontrolled migration. Each of you has the absolute right to protect your borders, and so, of course, does our country. Today, we must resolve to work together to end human smuggling, end human trafficking, and put these criminal networks out of business for good. . . .

One of the most serious challenges our countries face is the specter of socialism. It's the wrecker of nations and destroyer of societies.

Events in Venezuela remind us all that socialism and communism are not about justice, they are not about equality, they are not about lifting up the poor, and they are certainly not about the good of the nation. Socialism and communism are about one thing only: power for the ruling class.

Today, I repeat a message for the world that I have delivered at home: America will never be a socialist country.

In the last century, socialism and communism killed 100 million people. Sadly, as we see in Venezuela, the death toll continues in this country. These totalitarian ideologies, combined with modern technology, have the power to excise [exercise] new and disturbing forms of suppression and domination.

For this reason, the United States is taking steps to better screen foreign technology and investments and to protect our data and our security. We urge every nation present to do the same.

Freedom and democracy must be constantly guarded and protected, both abroad and from within. We must always be skeptical of those who want conformity and control. Even in free nations, we see alarming signs and new challenges to liberty.

A small number of social media platforms are acquiring immense power over what we can see and over what we are allowed to say. A permanent political class is openly disdainful, dismissive, and defiant of the will of the people. A faceless bureaucracy operates in secret and weakens democratic rule. Media and academic institutions push flat-out assaults on our histories, traditions, and values. . . .

As we defend American values, we affirm the right of all people to live in dignity. For this reason, my administration is working with other nations to stop criminalizing of homosexuality, and we stand in solidarity with LGBTQ people who live in countries that punish, jail, or execute individuals based upon sexual orientation.

We are also championing the role of women in our societies. Nations that empower women are much wealthier, safer, and much more politically stable. It is therefore vital not only to a nation's prosperity, but also is vital to its national security, to pursue women's economic development. . . .

There is no circumstance under which the United States will allow international entries [entities] to trample on the rights of our citizens, including the right to self-defense. That is why, this year, I announced that we will never ratify the U.N. Arms Trade Treaty, which would threaten the liberties of law-abiding American citizens. The United States will always uphold our constitutional right to keep and bear arms. We will always uphold our Second Amendment.

The core rights and values America defends today were inscribed in America's founding documents. Our nation's Founders understood that there will always be those who believe they are entitled to wield power and control over others. Tyranny advances under many names and many theories, but it always comes down to the desire for domination. It protects not the interests of many, but the privilege of few. . . .

So to all the leaders here today, join us in the most fulfilling mission a person could have, the most profound contribution anyone can make: Lift up your nations. Cherish your culture. Honor your histories. Treasure your citizens. Make your countries strong, and prosperous, and righteous. Honor the dignity of your people, and nothing will be outside of your reach.

When our nations are greater, the future will be brighter, our people will be happier, and our partnerships will be stronger.

With God's help, together we will cast off the enemies of liberty and overcome the oppressors of dignity. We will set new standards of living and reach new heights of human achievement. We will rediscover old truths, unravel old mysteries, and make thrilling new breakthroughs. And we will find more beautiful friendship and more harmony among nations than ever before.

My fellow leaders, the path to peace and progress, and freedom and justice, and a better world for all humanity, begins at home.

Thank you. God bless you. God bless the nations of the world. And God bless America. Thank you very much.

SOURCE: Executive Office of the President. "Remarks to the United Nations General Assembly in New York City." September 24, 2019. *Compilation of Presidential Documents* 2019, no. 00657 (September 24, 2019). https://www.govinfo.gov/content/pkg/DCPD-201900657/pdf/DCPD-201900657.pdf.

UK Prime Minister Speaks on Dangers of Advances in Technology

September 24, 2019

Mr President, Your Excellencies, Ladies and Gentlemen, faithful late night audience.

It is customary for the British Prime Minister to come to this United Nations and pledge to advance our values and defend our rules, the rules of a peaceful world. From protecting freedom of navigation in the Gulf. To persevering in the vital task of achieving a two-state solution to the conflict in the Middle East. And of course I am proud to do all of these things. But no-one can ignore a gathering force that is reshaping the future of every member of this Assembly. There has been nothing like it in history

When I think of the great scientific revolutions of the past—print, the steam engine, aviation, the atomic age—I think of new tools that we acquired but over which we—the human race—had the advantage, which we controlled. That is not necessarily the case in the digital age. You may keep secrets from your friends, from your parents, your children, your doctor—even your personal trainer—but it takes real effort to conceal your thoughts from Google.

And if that is true today, in future there may be nowhere to hide. Smart cities will pullulate with sensors, all joined together by the "internet of things," bollards communing invisibly with lamp posts, so there is always a parking space for your electric car, so that no bin goes unemptied, no street unswept, and the urban environment is as antiseptic as a Zurich pharmacy.

But this technology could also be used to keep every citizen under round-the-clock surveillance. A future Alexa will pretend to take orders. But this Alexa will be watching you, clucking her tongue and stamping her foot. In the future, voice connectivity will be in every room and almost every object: your mattress will monitor your nightmares; your fridge will beep for more cheese, your front door will sweep wide the moment you approach, like some silent butler; your smart meter will go hustling—if its accord—for the cheapest electricity. And every one of them minutely transcribing your every habit in tiny electronic shorthand, stored not in their chips or their innards—nowhere you can find it, but in some great cloud of data that lours ever more oppressively over the human race. A giant dark thundercloud waiting to burst and we have no control over how or when the precipitation will take place.

And every day that we tap on our phones or work on our ipads—as I see some of you doing now—we not only leave our indelible spoor in the ether. But we are ourselves becoming a resource, click by click, tap by tap. Just as the carboniferous period created the indescribable wealth—leaf by decaying leaf—of hydrocarbons.

Data is the crude oil of the modern economy. . . .

Can these algorithms be trusted with our lives and hopes? . . .

Digital authoritarianism is not, alas, the stuff of dystopian fantasy but of an emerging reality.

The reason I am giving this speech today is that the UK is one of the world's tech leaders—and I believe governments have been simply caught unawares by the unintended consequences of the internet. . . .

We strain our eyes as they come, to make out whether they are for good or bad—friends or foes? AI—what will it mean? Helpful robots washing and caring for an ageing population? Or pink eyed terminators sent back from the future to cull the human race. . . .

And it is a deep human instinct to be wary of any kind of technical progress. In 1829, they thought the human frame would not withstand the speeds attained by Stephenson's rocket, and there are today people today who are actually still anti-science. A whole movement called the anti-Vaxxers, who refuse to acknowledge the evidence that vaccinations have eradicated smallpox, and who by their prejudices are actually endangering the very children they want to protect. And I totally reject this anti-scientific pessimism.

I am profoundly optimistic about the ability of new technology to serve as a liberator and remake the world wondrously and benignly, indeed in countless respects technology is already doing just that. . . .

But how we design the emerging technologies behind these breakthroughs—and what values inform their design—will shape the future of humanity. That is my point to you tonight my friends, my Excellencies—

At stake is whether we bequeath an Orwellian world, designed for censorship, repression and control, or a world of emancipation, debate and learning, where technology threatens famine and disease, but not our freedoms.

Seven decades ago, this General Assembly adopted the Universal Declaration of Human Rights with no dissenting voices, uniting humanity for the first and perhaps only time behind one set of principles. And our declaration—our joint declaration—upholds "freedom of opinion and expression", the "privacy" of "home or correspondence," and the right to "seek . . . and impart information and ideas". Unless we ensure that new technology reflects this spirit, I fear that our declaration will mean nothing and no longer hold.

So the mission of the United Kingdom and all who share our values must be to ensure that emerging technologies are designed from the outset for freedom, openness and pluralism, with the right safeguards in place to protect our peoples.

Month by month, vital decisions are being taken in academic committees, company boardrooms and industry standards groups. They are writing the rulebooks of the future, making ethical judgements, choosing what will or will not be rendered possible. Together, we need to ensure that new advances reflect our values by design.

There is excellent work being done in the EU, the Commonwealth, and of course the UN, which has a vital role in ensuring that no country is excluded from the wondrous benefits of this technology, and the industrial revolution it is bringing about.

But we must be still more ambitious.

We need to find the right balance between freedom and control; between innovation and regulation; between private enterprise and government oversight.

We must insist that the ethical judgements inherent in the design of new technology are transparent to all.

And we must make our voices heard more loudly in the standards bodies that write the rules.

Above all, we need to agree [on] a common set of global principles to shape the norms and standards that will guide the development of emerging technology. . . .

If we master this challenge—and I have no doubt that we can—then we will not only safeguard our ideals, we will surmount the limits that once constrained humanity and conquer the perils that once ended so many lives.

Together, we can vanquish killer diseases, eliminate famine, protect the environment and transform our cities.

Success will depend, now as ever, on freedom, openness and pluralism, the formula that not only emancipates the human spirit, but releases the boundless ingenuity and inventiveness of mankind, and which, above all, the United Kingdom will strive to preserve and advance.

Excellencies, Ladies and Gentlemen, thank you for your kind attention.

SOURCE: UK Prime Minister's Office. "PM Speech to the UN General Assembly: 24 September 2019." September 24, 2019. https://www.gov.uk/government/speeches/pm-speech-to-the-un-general-assembly-24-september-2019.

French President Expresses Nationalism and Climate Change Concerns

September 24, 2019

Thank you very much, Madam President,

Ladies and gentlemen heads of state and government,

Ladies and gentlemen ministers,

Ladies and gentlemen ambassadors,

Dear friends,

We are here for this General Assembly, with the Secretary-General having chosen what is such an important topic, the climate, and we had a meeting on this issue yesterday, at a time when impatience is being expressed everywhere and when everything in the world around us—at any rate, many things—might make us pessimistic.

CLIMATE

We have not met our strict targets, the goals we set ourselves in the battle against global warming and for biodiversity. There are many tensions, at an unprecedented level in certain areas of the world, when you see what has happened again in the Gulf over the past few days, and when you see the challenges facing many of our friends here now, particularly in the Sahel—whose friendly faces I recognize here—and in so many other regions. These conflicts are increasingly tough, painful for civilians, humanitarian personnel, human rights defenders. As David Miliband says, the age of impunity has dawned. Trade tensions are increasing and there are growing concerns about technological changes and their consequences. I do not want to paint a pessimistic picture here, and I know you are tired—you have been listening to many speeches since this morning—so I shall spare you the litany of reasons to despair.

Nevertheless, we have got everything we need to respond to these challenges—everything—and in an unprecedented way. Firstly, we have got the knowledge. Never has world science come together in such a way to describe the challenges we have and anticipate the means of responding to them, from the IPCC to IPBES, to the extent that we are in the process of building on technological revolutions—this has been spelled out. We know a little more each year. We have got the finance, which is not lacking worldwide. We have got the capacity for unmatched innovation which, on many of the issues I have talked about, is also a means of responding to these challenges, of fighting poverty, of stabilizing, of responding to the major changes I have just mentioned. We have got an unprecedented awareness of these present-day ills, [thanks to] our young people, when it comes to the climate or freedoms, and, I must say, our public at large, which has never been as informed as it is now. And we have got a forum, right here, a forum of free states which recognize one another and are supposed to work for the common good and prepare the future of mankind, respond to the current crises, just as we have regional multilateral forums on many subjects or topics when we are dealing with trade or economic cooperation.

So what are we lacking? . . . We lack courage, a great deal of it, frequently, and basically today I simply wanted to tell you that I would like to launch an appeal for a return of courage, on two subjects, simply, to begin with: the courage to build peace and the courage to shoulder responsibility. . . .

IRAN

The first time I spoke to this assembly, I said I firmly believed, on Iran, that the strategy of exerting pressure vis-à-vis the Iran nuclear issue could lead only to a heightening of tensions in the region if it did not, basically, above all, have a clear prospect of a diplomatic solution. In 2018, after the US pulled out of the 2015 Vienna agreement, I proposed a comprehensive framework allowing us to protect the JCPOA and complement it with a wider approach enabling us to address the issues posed by the post-2025 Iran nuclear programme, Iran's role in regional crises and its ballistic programme. What point have we reached today? To America's strategy and the desire of Europe, Russia and China to protect the 2015 Vienna agreement, Iran responded with a strategy of maximum pressure on its regional environment. In this context, tensions have risen constantly over the past few months and the attacks on 14 September against Saudi Arabia were a game changer. Following on from that, today the risk is one of conflagration on the basis of a miscalculation or a disproportionate response. . . . So what do we do? I wholeheartedly believe that, more than ever, it is time for negotiations to be resumed between the United States of America, Iran, the signatories to the JCPOA and the powers in the region first affected by its security and stability.

What must the terms, the objectives of these negotiations be? Firstly, complete certainty that Iran never acquires nuclear weapons. Secondly, an end to the crisis in Yemen. Thirdly, a regional security plan including the other crises in the region and the security of maritime traffic flows. Finally, the lifting of economic sanctions. I am not being naïve in any way, and I do not believe in miracles either. I believe in the courage of building peace, and I know that the United States of America, Iran and all the signatories to the agreement have this courage. . . .

MULTILATERALISM

. . . I do not think that the problems we now have can be resolved by diluting responsibilities or by creating a form of globalization that overlooks the people, and in this respect, I agree with what President Trump said this morning. And I also do not think that the crises we are experiencing can be resolved more effectively by retreating into nationalism. I truly believe in patriotism as long as it is based on love for one's country as well as universal aspirations. I believe deeply in sovereignty as long as it is based on self-determination as well as on the need for cooperation.

What we need to do now, is reinvent what I described in my last speech to you as strong multilateralism. This doesn't mean that our multilateralism is tired, that we are not listening to ourselves anymore, that we are no longer effective, no. It means acknowledging that we will not find a solution by retreating into nationalism, that we will not find a solution without cooperation. This cooperation must however produce concrete results, engage new stakeholders. We have demonstrated the effectiveness of this strong, modern, multilateralism. . . .

The major problem we now have is that we no longer know how to ensure the stability of a world that is increasingly marked by conflict, while we have moved away from the duopoly in which we had lived for decades. There's no longer anyone we can turn to as a last resort to guarantee essential balances. Turmoil is prevailing and we are often too slow to tackle issues effectively. I truly believe that this courage to build peace requires us to reaffirm our values, the values of human rights and the dignity of the human person which must not be undermined by any form of contemporary relativism. Concrete recommitment is needed on all the theatres of operation I have just mentioned in order to build peace and stability and propose concrete solutions to peoples.

And the courage to assume responsibility with respect to many of our challenges: when we talk of contemporary common goods, climate, education, inequality, we can say that we know, we see. We now have many experts who can tell us about and describe in unprecedented detail the situation of our world. If we have grown weaker, it is because we have decided, too often, to challenge the truth, to contest the facts, to take a short-term view, to protect certain interests at times, and this has led to a loss of meaning. . . .

CLIMATE

The climate, too, entails a fight against inequality, and it is another issue that demands courage and responsibility. Basically, there is an ongoing paradox with respect to the climate, which we are all getting used to. In essence, we have offered an outlet for our young people's impatience, we have given them the opportunity to express themselves, we tell them: "We hear you, you're amazing." And then, all too often, we continue on with whatever we were already doing. That will not work.

Here I would like to applaud the commitment of the UN Secretary-General and tell you that when it comes to combating climate change and fighting for biodiversity, we need to move even more forcefully towards concrete action and overhaul our collective organization, the system itself—not just seek to compensate for it or correct it—we must change it ourselves with all of our investors, companies, and societies. First, we must expand our goals. This is vital if we want to have a chance at keeping temperature increases below 2ºC by the end of the century. In order to do that, we must take action in 2020.

In Europe, we must take the necessary decisions in 2020 on carbon taxing, with a higher minimum price and taxation at the borders. While we have not convinced certain partners to comply with this agenda, these courageous decisions are necessary, and they are necessary now. All countries must be more broadly committed to a strategy of carbon neutrality by 2050. Several have joined this coalition. President Piñera has just presented it to you. We must continue to convince others and remain committed to this crucial strategy. India has just indicated its wish to sign on to this agenda and join this coalition. I know how much of a proactive effort China is also making on the climate; it has been substantial in recent years. I know that together, if we commit to carbon neutrality, we can make profound changes and meet our goals. In this regard, COP25 in Chile and COP26 in Europe will be decisive events. The second thing is to achieve consistency in our agendas and our efforts. As I said yesterday, we can't say, "Don't worry, we're doing a great job on everything", while so many countries continue to depend on coal. Everyone—given their constraints and with the help of the international community and good funding, and with respect for every part of our societies, of course—everyone must commit to a strategy of getting out of coal. And major countries must stop funding new polluting facilities in developing countries. Even today, we are still providing export finance and support for projects in so many countries, projects funded by developing countries that involve opening new polluting facilities. In a way, it is like telling developing countries, telling the poorest countries, "Climate change isn't your problem. You can keep on polluting, it's okay for you." That's inconsistent and irresponsible. Let's be honest with ourselves. . . .

I believe in openness and free trade, but only if this free trade is rational and includes the goals of zero carbon and zero deforestation. This means that, in each situation, we need to come up with the right solutions. In each situation, we need to find offsetting measures. But we cannot push certain countries to make efforts and then continue to do business with countries that do not. We cannot keep making statements in this forum and continue to import products that contradict these statements. This will not happen overnight. France itself still imports far too many products that lead to deforestation. Major changes are needed. . . . But if we are not collectively responsible and transparent, and if we refuse consistency between our thoughts and deeds, between our trade and climate agendas, we will never succeed, never. It will take a few years, but we must start now.

There are two climate issues I wish to highlight here before concluding. If we are to win this battle, we need to focus on forests and the ocean. Both of these battles are essential in reducing CO_2 and preserving the balance of biodiversity. In both of these global issues, we are losing the battle.

As far as forests are concerned, yesterday we jointly committed to taking an important step forward in defending the Amazon and African forests—in other words, our planet's primary forest reserves. Several countries made commitments, France among them. I would particularly like to acknowledge the major commitments made by Germany and Norway. This involved major countries, international organizations, non-governmental organizations and most of the countries concerned by the Amazon, if I use language appropriate for this forum. All those who wish to join should join, but we need to make progress. Between now and the Conference of the Parties in Santiago, we will develop extremely effective and pragmatic criteria to invest directly in the field and find useful solutions, with a view to encouraging projects in the fields of reforestation, biodiversity protection and agroecology—projects that contribute to the economic development of the Amazon and African forests in the Congo Basin while preserving forests and supporting our fight to protect biodiversity and combat global warming. . . .

Concerning the oceans, the IPCC report is devastatingly cruel. The facts are blatant, obvious. We are losing the battle. In Biarritz, we began building coalitions with major transport companies, which committed to reducing speed. This is just a beginning. We are far from winning. I would like us to commit—as we are doing for primary forests—to defending the oceans, to supporting new financing and tangible actions, so we can win this battle.

For all of these issues, these are just the first changes, the first steps. And I am telling you now: what we are collectively trying to do is essential. We are collectively trying to change our joint political, economic and social structures, to reduce inequalities—or, even better, to prevent them. In my opinion, given today's growing inequalities, in terms of the climate, opportunities, and education, the right answer is not in the tax agenda in each country. I think the right answer is in education, access to health and inequality prevention policies in each country, as well as in more international cooperation and a robust agenda to fight inequalities. But this requires, fundamentally, an agenda of reconciliation. What we are now seeing is, on the one hand, a constant rhetoric of denunciation—I can hear it. It pushes us to act, but it is no longer sufficient. Denunciation is no longer the issue, we know this. Our forerunners made denunciations 20 years ago; this resulted in groups of experts. So this rhetoric of denunciation is present. On the other hand, among some people, there is a kind of comfort in inaction, a practice of cynicism. And, in the middle, there is a crowded, perhaps clumsy, group of people trying to do things. Let us dare to take strong action. Let us build this agenda of reconciliation together, with our public opinions, with our young people, with our businesses, with our investors and with willing governments, so we can say, "we have the facts, let us continue to look into them and change our practices now"—our practices as consumers, as producers, as investors, as leaders and as citizens, to collectively embark on this agenda of change. But staying within this tandem of denunciation and inaction is pointless. I strongly believe that the courage of shouldering responsibility is about facing facts—saying that there are things that can be done now, and others that will take more time. Because in all of our countries we have producers who are dependent on certain products that are harmful; we have people living in homes that are not fully insulated; people who must travel and pollute while travelling. We cannot blame them. We have to help them change. We have to offer solutions developed through technological innovations, through investment, and through a real agenda to fight social and climate inequalities. This agenda of reconciliation—this is what we need to do. This is what I want to do in France, what we need to develop in Europe, and what we need to build here.

This, ladies and gentlemen, is what I wanted to say to you. I believe in courage and responsibility and, more generally, I believe in the return of courage. In any case, I do not think we have any choice. We must work together. The rulebook has changed. It is less simple than before, and requires more commitment. On all topics related to security, inequality, health and the climate, we know that we will be held accountable. But I do not believe in taking the easy road of pessimism; nor do I believe in division. I believe in our ability to make proposals, think, work together, and build this agenda of reconciliation, which will allow us to again look forward to the future. Thank you.

SOURCE: Embassy of France in Manila. "Speech of French President Emmanuel Macron at the 74th United Nations General Assembly (New York, September 24, 2019)." September 24, 2019. https://ph.ambafrance .org/Speech-of-French-President-Emmanuel-Macron-at-the-74th-United-Nations-General.

Turkish President Addresses UN on Global Challenges

September 24, 2019

President Erdoğan [*spoke in Turkish; English interpretation provided by the delegation*]: On behalf of the Turkish nation and on my own behalf, I salute the General Assembly with the most heartfelt emotion. . . .

Our world today faces many challenges and much pain resulting from injustice on a global scale. . . .

Indeed, the international community is gradually losing its ability to find lasting solutions to such challenges as terrorism, hunger, misery and climate change, all of which threaten the future of all of us. We have no doubt that the theme for the seventy-fourth session of the General Assembly is fitting in that regard: "Galvanizing multilateral efforts for poverty eradication, quality education, climate action and inclusion".

But what is more important than that is to understand what we can achieve together. It is unacceptable to see that one part of the world lives in luxury and enjoys the benefits of prosperity while people in other parts of the world suffer at the hands of poverty, misery and illiteracy. It is painful to see that, while a fortunate minority in the world is discussing such issues as digital technology, robotics, artificial intelligence and obesity, more than 2 billion people are living under the poverty line and 1 billion people are suffering from hunger. We cannot turn our backs on the reality that, until all of us are safe, none of us will be safe.

For many years I have been saying from this rostrum that we cannot leave the fate of humankind to the discretion of a handful of countries. Today I would like to reiterate once again that the world is greater than five countries. It is high time that we change our current mentality, our institutions, organizations and rules. . . .

At a time when 13 people lose their lives every minute owing to air pollution and when global warming threatens our very future, we cannot afford to remain indifferent. First and foremost, we need to strengthen the capacity and efficiency of the United Nations. In particular, we should immediately carry out much-needed fundamental reforms of the Security Council, in line with the principles of justice and equality.

With a proactive and humane foreign policy, Turkey embraces the rest of the world and strives to find justice-based solutions to our problems. It is not without reason that Turkey has earned distinction as the most generous country in terms of humanitarian aid and the country hosting the largest number of displaced persons in the world. . . .

Turkey is the country most affected by the threat of Da'esh, the terrorist organization that has threatened our borders and targeted the very heart of surrounding cities with suicide bombings, killing hundreds of Turkish citizens. Turkey is the country that has inflicted the most important and heaviest blow against the presence of Da'esh in Syria. Through Operation Euphrates Shield, we have neutralized approximately 3,500 Da'esh terrorists and paved the way for that terrorist organization's downfall in Syria. We are also at the forefront of international efforts to identify the terrorists and foreign fighters who come from all over the world to join Da'esh, by imposing entry bans and deportations to and from our country.

At the same time, Turkey is the most generous country today in terms of humanitarian aid and in terms of the ratio between official humanitarian assistance and gross domestic product. We are currently hosting 5 million asylum seekers who are fleeing conflict, starvation and persecution. In other words, there are more asylum-seekers in Turkey than in the combined population of 29 states of the United States, and 3.6 million of them are from Syria. In fact, the number of Syrian brothers and sisters we are currently hosting on our soil is well over half the population of New York City.

We have devoted $40 billion to the asylum seekers over the past eight years. But have we in Turkey received anything? I will tell the Assembly. To date we have received no more than €3 billion from the European Union, not as direct contributions into our national budget but through international organizations. . . .

Unfortunately, the international community has been too quick to forget the journey of survival that they have made, ending either in the dark waters of the Mediterranean Sea or confronted by the security fences stretching along the borders that they are trying to flee. As the Assembly can see, this is the picture of baby Aylan, whose lifeless body washed ashore not so long ago but has already been forgotten. We should never forget that that could happen to any of us. There are many baby Aylans. There are millions of baby Aylans. And we need to take action for them. It is a responsibility to which we must rise. . . .

Today we face three important issues that must be dealt with as we seek to resolve the humanitarian crisis in Syria.

The first is the territorial integrity and political unity of Syria, which depends greatly on an effectively functioning constitutional committee. We met with our Russian and Iranian counterparts in Ankara early last week and, through the Russian summit memorandum, have managed to accomplish most of our goals. When a permanent political solution is reached in Syria, territorial integrity will be restored.

The second important issue is that we must do everything possible to prevent a possible massacre in the city of Idlib and a wave of migration 4 million strong. Despite some setbacks, the agreement we reached with Russia in Sochi on that issue remains valid. Turkey cannot withstand another influx of migration. We therefore expect all countries around the world to support Turkey's efforts to ensure security and stability in Idlib.

The third important issue is the elimination of the PKK-YPG terrorist organization east of the Euphrates, where it occupies one quarter of Syria and seeks to legitimize itself as the so-called Syrian democratic forces. We will not be able to find a permanent solution to the issue of Syria if we fail to deal with all terrorist organizations in the same way.

We remain engaged in talks with the United States with a view to establishing a safe zone within Syria. We intend to establish a peace corridor in Syria, 30 kilometres wide by 480 kilometres long, where we hope, with the support of the international community, to facilitate the settlement of 2 million Syrians. . . .

We will continue to follow the developments relating to the demise of journalist Jamal Khashoggi, who was brutally murdered last year and on whose case the courts have yet to reach a verdict, because we are steadfast in our commitment in that regard.

Another issue that we are heavily invested in is that Egypt's first democratically elected President, Mohamed Morsi, suspiciously lost his life in a court room and his family was not allowed to give him a proper burial. That remains a bleeding wound in our hearts. They have both become a profound symbol of the need for justice and equality in the region.

We also hope that the discussions about Iran's activities, as well as the related threats to that country, will be resolved in a rational manner.

The Palestinian territories today under Israeli occupation have become one of the most striking places of injustice. If the images of an innocent Palestinian woman who was heinously murdered by Israeli security forces on the street just a few days ago will not awaken the global conscience, then we have reached a point where words no longer suffice. . . .

Now, from the rostrum of the General Assembly, I ask those present, where are the borders of the State of Israel? Are they the 1947 borders, the 1967 borders or is there another border of which we must be informed? How can the Golan Heights and the West Bank settlements be seized, just like other occupied Palestinian territories, before the eyes of the world if they do not fall within the official borders of that State? Is the aim of the initiative promoted as the deal of the century to entirely eliminate the presence of the State and the people of Palestine? Is there a thirst for more bloodshed?

All the actors of the international community, in particular the United Nations, should provide concrete support to the Palestinian people beyond mere promises. It is very important in that regard for the United Nations Relief and Works Agency for Palestine Refugees in the Near East to continue its activities effectively. Turkey will continue to stand by the oppressed people of Palestine, as it has always done.

It is also very important for the South Caucasus to cease to be one of the areas of conflict and tension in the world, with a view to achieving a fair and peaceful future. It is unacceptable that Nagorno Karabakh and its surrounding areas, which are Azerbaijani territories, are still occupied despite all the resolutions that have been adopted in that regard.

One of the problems to which the international community has failed to devote enough attention is the Kashmir conflict, which has been awaiting a solution for 72 years. The stability and prosperity of South Asia cannot be separated from the Kashmir issue. Despite the resolutions that the Security Council has adopted, Kashmir remains besieged and 8 million people are still stuck in Kashmir; they cannot leave. In order for the Kashmiri people to look towards a safe future with their Pakistani and Indian neighbours, it is imperative to solve the problem with dialogue and on the basis of justice and equality, instead of with conflict. . . .

Another issue to which the world appears to remain indifferent is the humanitarian tragedy faced by Rohingya Muslims. The independent commission of inquiry, established under the auspices of the United Nations, has recorded the existence of a genocidal intent behind the events perpetrated in Myanmar's Rakhine state. Turkey will continue to carry out initiatives to ensure the security and fundamental rights of the Rohingya people, as well as the humanitarian relief activities it has undertaken since day one.

The invasions, conflicts and terrorist activities that have continued uninterrupted in Afghanistan for almost four decades have also raised challenges at the global level. It is high time for peace and security to be restored. It is up to us to assume that responsibility and to take action.

Today, one of the biggest threats to global peace and stability is the rise in racist, xenophobic, discriminatory and anti-Islamic rhetoric. Muslims are the primary targets of hate speech, discrimination and defamation against their sacred values. . . .

Prejudice, ignorance and bigotry, as well as attempts to marginalize migrants, in particular Muslims, have paved the way for the rise in such morbid tendencies, which can be defeated only by our common will and efforts. As statesmen and stateswomen, it is our fundamental duty to adopt inclusive and tolerant public rhetoric to eradicate the scourge of terrorism once and for all.

I would like to conclude my remarks with the following wishes: freedom for all, peace for all, prosperity for all, justice for all and a peaceful and safe future for all. I wish every success for the work of the seventy-fourth session of the General Assembly. On behalf of my people, I extend greetings to all members with the most heartfelt love and respect.

SOURCE: United Nations. General Assembly. Seventy-fourth Session. 3rd Plenary Meeting. September 24, 2019. https://undocs.org/en/A/74/PV.3.

Iranian President Warns UN of Possible "Collapse" in the Gulf Region

September 25, 2019

President Rouhani [*spoke in Farsi; English text provided by the delegation*]: I would like to congratulate the President on his well-deserved election to lead the General Assembly at its seventy-fourth session, and to wish him and the Secretary-General good luck and every success. . . .

The Middle East is burning amid the flames of war, bloodshed, aggression, occupation and religious and sectarian fanaticism and extremism, a situation in which the oppressed people of Palestine are the biggest victims, as acts of discrimination, the expropriation of land, settlement expansion and killings continue against them. The plans that the United States and the Zionists have imposed on them, such as the deal of the century that recognized Beit Al-Maqdis as the capital of the Zionist regime and the addition of the Syrian Golan to the other occupied territories, are certainly doomed.

In the face of issues such as the destructive plans of the United States, the Islamic Republic of Iran's regional and international assistance and cooperation on security and counter-terrorism have been quite decisive. That approach is clearly exemplified in our cooperation on the Syrian crisis with Russia and Turkey in the Astana format, and our peace proposal for Yemen, based on our active cooperation with the Special Envoys of the Secretary-General, as well as our efforts to facilitate reconciliation talks among the parties in Yemen with four European countries, which resulted in the conclusion of the Stockholm Agreement on Al-Hudaydah port.

I come from a country that has resisted the most merciless economic terrorism and defended its right to independence and the development of science and technology. While imposing extraterritorial sanctions and threats on other nations, the United States Government has tried very hard to deprive Iran of the advantages of participation in the global economy and has resorted to international piracy by misusing the international banking system. . . .

The attitude of the current United States Administration to the nuclear deal, otherwise known as the Joint Comprehensive Plan of Action (JCPOA), not only violates the provisions of Security Council resolution 2231 (2015) but also constitutes a breach of the sovereignty and political and economic independence of all the world's countries. Despite the United States withdrawal from the JCPOA, for a full year Iran remained fully faithful to all of its nuclear commitments under the agreement. Out of respect for the Security Council's resolution, we provided Europe with the opportunity to fulfil its 11 commitments in compensation for the United States' withdrawal. Unfortunately, however, we heard only beautiful words and witnessed no effective measures. It is now clear to all that the United States reneges on all of its commitments, and that Europe is unable, indeed incapable, of fulfilling its commitments. We even adopted a step-by-step approach in implementing paragraphs 26 and 36 of the JCPOA, and we remain committed to our promises in the deal.

However, there is a limit to our patience. When the United States does not respect the resolutions of the Security Council and Europe cannot act, the only option left is to rely on national dignity, pride and strength. They call us to negotiations while they run away from treaties and deals. We negotiated with the current United States Administration at the negotiating table with the Security Council permanent five, Germany and the European Union, but it failed to honour the commitment made by its predecessor. On behalf of my nation and State, I want to announce that our response to any negotiations conducted under sanctions is negative. The Government and people of Iran have remained steadfast against extremely harsh sanctions in the past year and a half and will never negotiate with an enemy that seeks to make Iran surrender with the weapons of poverty, pressure and sanctions. . . .

I would like to make it crystal clear: if the minimum is satisfactory, we will also content ourselves with the minimum, on either side. However, if more is required, more should also be paid. If members stand by their word that they have only one demand for Iran, that is, the non-production and non-utilization of nuclear weapons, that could easily be attained under the supervision of the International Atomic Energy Agency and, more importantly, with a fatwa of the Iranian leader. Instead of a show of negotiation, there should [be] a return to the reality of negotiation. Memorial photographs are at the last stage of negotiations, not the first.

Despite all the obstructions created by the United States Government, we in Iran remain on the path of economic and social growth and prosperity. . . .

The security of our region will be realized when American troops pull out. Security will not be provided by American weapons and intervention. After 18 years, the United States has failed to reduce acts of terrorism. However, the Islamic Republic of Iran managed to terminate the scourge of Da'esh with the assistance of neighbouring nations and Governments. The ultimate way to achieve peace and security in the Middle East involves inward democracy and outward diplomacy. Security cannot be purchased or supplied by foreign Governments. . . .

The solution for peace in the Arabian peninsula, security in the Persian Gulf and stability in the Middle East should be sought inside the region rather than outside it. The issues of the region are too great and important for the United States to be able to resolve. The United States has failed to resolve the issues in Afghanistan, Iraq and Syria and has been the supporter of extremism, Talibanism and Da'eshism. Such a Government is clearly unable to resolve today's more sophisticated issues.

Our region is on the brink of collapse—a single blunder could fuel a conflagration. We will not tolerate the provocative intervention of foreigners. We will respond decisively and strongly to any transgression against, or violation of, our security and territorial integrity. However, the alternative and proper solution for us is to strengthen consolidation among all the nations with common interests in the Persian Gulf and the Hormuz region.

This is the message of the Iranian nation: let us invest in hope towards a better future rather than in war and violence. Let us return to justice, peace, law, commitment and promise and, ultimately, to the negotiating table.

SOURCE: United Nations. General Assembly. Seventy-fourth Session. 5th Plenary Meeting. September 25, 2019. https://undocs.org/en/A/74/PV.5.

Chinese Foreign Minister Announces China's Role in Global Development

September 27, 2019

Mr. Wang Yi (China) [*spoke in Chinese*]: This year marks the seventieth anniversary of the founding of the People's Republic of China. The United Nations was established in 1945 in response to the call of the times. Four years later, the People's Republic of China was founded and the Chinese nation re-emerged before the eyes of the world as a completely reborn nation.

Over the past 70 years, we Chinese have changed our destiny through tireless efforts. Seventy years ago, China put an end to a period in modern history during which the country was torn apart and trampled on. We stood up and became the true masters of our country. Over the past seven decades, China has transformed itself from a closed, backward and poor country with a weak foundation into one that is open and on the move. . . .

The secret behind China's development is our adherence to the centralized, unified leadership of the Communist Party of China, the development path suited to China's national conditions, the fundamental State policy of reform and opening up and a people-centred development philosophy.

Over the past 70 years, China has integrated itself into the global community and made its contribution to the world, boosting world peace and prosperity through its development. Today China has become the leading engine of global development and an anchor of stability for world peace. We are the second-largest funding contributor to both the United Nations and United Nations peacekeeping operations. China has also deployed more peacekeeping personnel than any other permanent member of the Security Council. For more than a decade, China has been a main driver of global growth. We are now pursuing a new round of opening up with higher standards, which I am sure will deliver new opportunities for the world.

As we enter a new era, we Chinese are more confident and capable than ever of achieving a great rejuvenation of the Chinese nation, and we are better positioned than ever to make a greater contribution to humankind. Guided by Xi Jinping Thought on Socialism with Chinese Characteristics for a New Era, China will continue to strive for success and forge ahead. Looking back on the road we have traversed over the past 70 years, we are full of pride. Looking ahead at the journey before us, we are full of confidence in our bright future.

On the diplomatic front, China has travelled a journey of tests and challenges and has remained true to its original purpose. The goal of China's diplomacy has never changed. The Chinese people and the peoples of other countries have always treated each other with sincerity and lent each other mutual support. China and the rest of the world have become stakeholders sharing a common future as their interdependence has increasingly grown. Facing international uncertainties, China will maintain the stability and continuity of its foreign policy and will continue to pursue major-country diplomacy, with distinct Chinese features. We will continue to safeguard world peace and prosperity and promote the development and advancement of humankind.

China is guided by the principle of independence. We will continue to pursue an independent foreign policy of peace. We will neither subordinate ourselves to others nor coerce others into submission. We are firm in upholding China's core national interests and legitimate rights, and we are opposed to the abuse of power and will never yield to pressure. We will remain committed to the basic principles of sovereign equality and non-interference in other country's internal affairs, as enshrined in the Charter of the United Nations. China will never pursue hegemony or seek expansion. Peaceful development, which has long been incorporated into China's Constitution, is the cornerstone of its foreign policy. . . .

China stands for equity and justice. On the international stage, we speak for justice and oppose hegemonism and bullying. We wish to engage others in extensive consultations and joint contributions in pursuit of shared benefits. We call for handling international affairs based on the merits of each particular case, and for settling issues through consultations. As the world's largest developing country, China will always stand firmly with other developing countries in safeguarding their common interests and right to development and in increasing their representation and say in global governance so as to promote democracy in international relations.

China pursues mutually beneficial cooperation. In this globalized world, countries all rise or fall together. A zero-sum mentality and beggar-thy-neighbour policies are recipes for failure. China is committed to fostering an open world economy, upholding the multilateral trading regime of the World Trade Organization and making globalization more open, inclusive, balanced and beneficial to all. We do not seek unilateral security, nor do we put our own interests above those of others. It is our aim to advance our development as part of the development of the global community. We seek to keep the door open, expand shared interests and share opportunities with others through cooperation.

The world today is not a peaceful place. Unilateralism and protectionism are posing major threats to the international order. At a time when the future of the world is at stake, China has never been and will never be an onlooker. As a founding Member of the United Nations, we will work with other countries to build a new type of international relations and a community with a shared future for humankind. We will be resolute in upholding the stature and role of the United Nations, the international system underpinned by the United Nations and an international order anchored on international law.

Facing the headwinds of protectionism, we should not just stand idly by. Erecting walls will not resolve global challenges and blaming others for one's own problems does not work. The lessons of the Great Depression should not be forgotten. Tariffs, and the provocation of trade disputes that upset global industrial and supply chains, undermine the multilateral trading regime and the global economic and trade order. They may even plunge the world into recession.

China is committed to resolving economic and trade frictions and differences in a calm, rational and comprehensive manner, and is willing to demonstrate as much patience and goodwill as necessary. Should the other side act in bad faith or show no respect for equal status or rules in negotiations, we will have to respond as necessary to safeguard our legitimate rights and interests and uphold international justice. . . .

In the face of rampant unilateralism, we should not sit on our hands. For the international order to function, we must abide by laws and rules, and acts that violate international norms can only plunge the world into chaos. The opportunities arising from the new round of scientific and technological revolution are opportunities for the world. The advances thus made should not be monopolized by any single country, and no one should obstruct the efforts of other countries in the name of innovation. It is neither legitimate nor justifiable for any country in a position of power to impose unilateral sanctions or exercise long-arm jurisdiction over other countries, as such practices have no basis in international law and are therefore devoid of legitimacy. Putting one's own interests above the common interests of all other countries is a typical bullying practice that will find no support among the people. . . .

In a world fraught with challenges and mounting risks, China will remain on the side of peace and justice. We will actively explore and apply a Chinese approach to addressing hotspot issues and play a constructive role in upholding international peace and security. China stands for common, comprehensive, cooperative and sustainable security. We hold that disputes should be settled through dialogue and consultation and that common threats should be addressed through international cooperation in the interests of sustaining global peace and common security.

The Iranian nuclear issue affects world peace and security. All the parties involved should work together to uphold the Joint Comprehensive Plan of Action (JCPOA) and ensure that this historic effort is not derailed. Given the growing tensions in the Middle East and the Gulf region, China proposes that the Iranian nuclear issue should be speedily put back on the JCPOA track, the Gulf countries urged to establish a platform for dialogue and consultation, and that countries from outside the region should play a positive role in maintaining security in the region. . . .

Development is the master key to solving all problems. It should be at the centre of the global macro policy framework, with a continued focus on priority areas such as poverty reduction, infrastructure, education and public health. We need to maintain global development cooperation with North-South cooperation as the main channel, supplemented by South-South cooperation. We must build an open world economy and help developing countries better integrate into the global industrial and value chains. Member States should align their medium- and long-term development strategies with the 2030 Agenda for Sustainable Development in an effort to pursue high-quality development. China's Belt and Road initiative aims to achieve high-standard, people-centred development that is open, green and clean. The initiative, which is highly compatible with the 2030 Agenda, has become a road to cooperation, hope and prosperity, delivering real benefits to people the world over. We hope that other countries will seize the development opportunities that it creates to add fresh impetus to their implementation of the 2030 Agenda.

There is global consensus on the need to address climate change, and cutting emissions calls for concerted global efforts. The outcomes of the Climate Action Summit are positive. China, as a co-lead on the nature-based solutions track, has done its part to make that possible. We believe in acting in good faith. We will deliver what we have signed up to, fulfil our obligations and take concrete action to help to build a clean and beautiful world.

China places high importance on the life and health of its people and has always taken a zero-tolerance approach to narcotics. We have put controls on all fentanyl-related substances, a move that goes well beyond the scheduling efforts of the United Nations and demonstrates that China is actively participating in global narcotics control with a keen sense of responsibility. . . .

I would like to conclude with a quote from President Xi Jinping, in which he said,

"Our world is full both of hope and challenges. We should not give up our dreams just because the reality around us is too complicated. We should not stop pursuing our ideals just because they seem out of our reach."

Let us work tirelessly to promote the purposes and principles of the United Nations Charter and together build a community with a shared future for humankind.

SOURCE: United Nations. General Assembly. Seventy-fourth Session. 9th Plenary Meeting. September 27, 2019. https://undocs.org/en/A/74/PV.9.

OTHER HISTORIC DOCUMENTS OF INTEREST

FROM THIS VOLUME

- President Trump Announces Sanctions against Iran, p. 332
- United States and Saudi Arabia Respond to Attack on Saudi Oil Facilities, p. 481

FROM PREVIOUS *HISTORIC DOCUMENTS*

- Trump Addresses the UN General Assembly, *2018*, p. 551

Whistleblower Complaint Filed against President Trump

SEPTEMBER 24 AND 26, 2019

In September 2019, a whistleblower complaint was filed with the intelligence community inspector general alleging that President Donald Trump was using his office to pressure the Ukrainian president into investigating a political rival—former vice president Joe Biden—to influence the outcome of the 2020 presidential election. Trump reportedly also sought the president's assistance in further investigating Russian and potential Ukrainian interference in the 2016 election. The complaint centered on a July phone call between the two leaders but cited actions by other administration officials over several months that contributed to Trump's efforts. The news prompted a second look at the administration's ongoing delays in distributing congressionally approved military aid to Ukraine, leading Democrats to accuse Trump of using the funds as leverage. Trump and his supporters denied any wrongdoing, but the allegations prompted House Speaker Nancy Pelosi, D-Calif., to open a formal impeachment inquiry.

CONGRESS LEARNS OF COMPLAINT, BUT NOT ITS CONTENTS

The existence of the whistleblower complaint was first revealed by House Permanent Select Committee on Intelligence chair Adam Schiff, D-Calif., in mid-September, following a series of communications with the Office of the Director of National Intelligence (ODNI). Schiff and the committee's ranking member, Rep. Devin Nunes, R-Calif., had received a letter from Intelligence Community inspector general Michael Atkinson on September 9 informing them that the complaint had been submitted—without disclosing its contents—and that acting director of national intelligence (DNI) Joe Maguire had failed to report the complaint to Congress. (Under federal law, the intelligence community inspector general has two weeks from the date of a whistleblower complaint's filing to determine whether the complaint is credible and an "urgent concern." If deemed credible, the complaint is forwarded to the DNI, who has one week to provide the House and Senate intelligence committees with a report on the complaint. In this instance, the whistleblower complaint was filed on August 12, giving Maguire a deadline of September 2 to share the complaint with Congress.)

On September 10, Schiff wrote to Maguire, accusing him of breaking the law by not reporting the complaint and demanding that he provide details about its contents. Three days later, ODNI general counsel Jason Klitenic declined Schiff's request for further information. Klitenic said that ODNI consulted with the Department of Justice's Office of Legal Counsel on the matter and determined the complaint was not an "urgent concern" that was "within the responsibility and authority" of Maguire's office. He further stated that the whistleblower statute only requires ODNI to report a complaint to Congress when it involves a member of the intelligence community. Since the complaint in question involved someone outside of the intelligence community, Maguire did not have to relay the matter to Congress. Schiff responded by issuing a subpoena to Maguire to compel him to submit the complaint and any related records to the congressional intelligence committees. In a letter accompanying the subpoena, Schiff wrote that Maguire had "neither the legal authority nor the discretion to overrule a determination" by Atkinson and did "not possess the authority to withhold from the Committee a whistleblower disclosure . . . that is intended for Congress." Schiff added that the "remarkable confluence of factors" could only lead committee members to conclude that "the serious misconduct at issue involves the President of the United States and/or other senior White House or Administration officials." This conclusion, Schiff said, "raises grave concerns" that ODNI and others "are engaged in an unlawful effort to protect the President."

On September 18, *The Washington Post* published a report citing unnamed officials who said the complaint involved communications between Trump and a foreign leader, including some sort of "promise." Trump dismissed the report as "another fake news story" and defended his interactions with foreign leaders as appropriate. Noting that many people across agencies listen into his phone calls, he asked, "Is anybody dumb enough to believe that I would say something inappropriate with a foreign leader while on such a potentially 'heavily populated' call?" Two days later, the *Wall Street Journal* reported that the whistleblower complaint centered on a late-July phone call between Trump and the recently elected Ukrainian president Volodymyr Zelenskyy, during which Trump purportedly pressured Zelenskyy to investigate potential wrongdoing by former vice president Joe Biden and his son Hunter. From 2014 to 2016, the elder Biden repeatedly pressed the Ukrainian government to step up anticorruption efforts and fire the country's prosecutor general, Viktor Shokin, who was widely viewed by Western officials as inactive. Trump and others have alleged that Biden was trying to protect his son, who at the time was a board member for Burisma Holdings, a Ukrainian energy company. The company's owner, a former Ukrainian official, was investigated for money laundering, unlawful enrichment, and other allegations. Pushing Shokin out was a way to ensure Hunter would not face prosecution, Trump and his allies said. However, Ukrainian officials have said Shokin's investigation of Burisma focused on a two-year period before Hunter joined the company and ended before Biden called for the prosecutor general's ouster.

Responding to the latest allegations, Trump insisted his call with Zelenskyy was "totally appropriate." He did not say whether he had pushed for an investigation into the Bidens but did tell reporters "somebody ought to look into that." The president later made a sharper statement on Twitter, declaring, "The Fake News Media and their partner, the Democrat Party, want to stay as far away as possible from the Joe Biden demand that the Ukrainian Government fire a prosecutor who was investigating his son, or they won't get a very large amount of U.S. money, so they fabricate a story about me and a perfectly fine and routine conversation I had with the new President of the Ukraine." Biden told reporters that Trump was "using the abuse of power and every element of the presidency to try to do something to smear me" because "he knows I'll beat him like a drum" in the 2020 election.

DELAYED AID TO UKRAINE RAISES QUESTION OF QUID PRO QUO

With a link between the whistleblower complaint and Ukraine tentatively established, the Trump administration's dealings with its foreign counterparts came under closer scrutiny. Earlier in September, Schiff joined with House Committee on Foreign Affairs chair Eliot Engel, D-N.Y., and House Committee on Oversight and Reform chair Elijah Cummings, D-Md., to request records from the White House and the State Department pertaining to "reported efforts by President Trump, the President's personal lawyer Rudy Giuliani, and possibly others to pressure the government of Ukraine to assist the President's reelection campaign."

Various reports also highlighted repeated delays in the administration's distribution of nearly $400 million in congressionally approved military aid to Ukraine. (The funds were intended to help Ukraine fight pro-Russian separatists.) Administration officials told lawmakers in February and May that they were preparing to distribute the funds, but never did. Then in July, Trump told Office of Management and Budget (OMB) director Mick Mulvaney to delay the distribution of aid again. OMB relayed this directive to the Departments of State and Defense on July 18, instructing agency officials to tell lawmakers the continued delays were due to "interagency processes." The aid was eventually distributed on September 11.

Democrats alleged that Trump was using the military aid as leverage in his efforts to pressure Ukraine. Trump denied there had been a "quid pro quo," stating that he was concerned about ongoing corruption in Ukraine and wanted to ensure it was being addressed before aid was released, even though the Department of Defense certified in May that the country had met congressional requirements to receive the funds. Trump alternatively said he was withholding the aid until European allies increased their assistance to Ukraine. Some Republican lawmakers said the delays were because the administration needed time to assess whether the new president was pro-Russia or aligned with Western interests.

Whistleblower Complaint, Call Transcript Released

On September 24, facing mounting pressure from Congress, the White House released a rough transcript of Trump's July 25 call with Zelenskyy. The document showed that after some discussion of the United States' assistance to Ukraine and the country's interest in procuring more U.S. missiles, Trump told Zelenskyy, "I would like you to do us a favor." Trump then asked Zelenskyy to determine whether the Democratic National Committee's (DNC) server—the one hacked by Russians ahead of the 2016 election—was in Ukraine and examine the cybersecurity firm Crowdstrike, which was paid by the DNC to investigate the hack. (Also underlying this request were allegations made in March 2019 by Ukrainian prosecutor general Yuriy Lutsenko, Shokin's successor, that some Ukrainian officials had interfered in the 2016 election in collaboration with the DNC.) Trump further noted, "There's a lot of talk about Biden's son, that Biden stopped the prosecution and a lot of people want to find out about that," and asked Zelenskyy to "look into it." Zelenskyy promised that his next prosecutor general "will be 100% my person" and "will look into the situation." Trump also repeatedly asked Zelenskyy to meet or speak with Giuliani and Attorney General William Barr to discuss these matters in greater detail.

Two days later, the whistleblower complaint and Atkinson's letter to Congress were declassified and released to the public. "In the course of my official duties, I have received information from multiple U.S. Government officials that the President of the United States is using the power of his office to solicit interference from a foreign country in the 2020 U.S. election," the whistleblower wrote. "This interference includes, among other things, pressuring a foreign country to investigate one of the President's main domestic political rivals." The whistleblower stated that he or she was "not a direct witness to most of the events described" but found their colleagues' reports credible because "in almost all cases, multiple officials recounted fact patterns that were consistent with one another." In addition to recounting several details of Trump's conversation with Zelenskyy that reflected the White House transcript, the whistleblower said that in the days following the call, multiple sources told them that White House officials had "intervened to 'lock down' all records of the phone call, especially the official word-for-word transcript." The complaint also cited multiple conversations between Giuliani and Ukrainian officials throughout the year, including an August meeting that was a "direct follow-up" to Trump's call with Zelenskyy. U.S. special representative for Ukraine negotiations Kurt Volker and U.S. ambassador to the European Union Gordon Sondland reportedly also traveled to Kiev to meet with Zelenskyy and "provided advice" on how to "navigate" the president's demands. Additionally, the whistleblower mentioned the suspension of aid to Ukraine but noted that OMB officials reportedly did not know why aid was being withheld.

Atkinson's letter concluded that the "complainant has reported an 'urgent concern' that 'appears credible.'" He noted the whistleblower had "official and authorized access to the information and sources referenced" and had "subject matter expertise related to much of the material information provided" in the complaint.

REPUBLICANS DEFEND TRUMP; PELOSI PURSUES IMPEACHMENT

Most Republicans in Congress came to Trump's defense. "I've read the transcript in its entirety," said Sen. Charles Grassley, R-Iowa. "It shows that there was no quid pro quo. The Ukrainian president admitted problems with corruption in the country and agreed that the issue at hand warranted looking into further." Others echoed the argument that all Trump had done was to ask Zelenskyy to continue fighting corruption. "This is in context of draining the swamp," said Rep. K. Michael Conaway, R-Tex. Some accused the Democrats of hypocrisy. "Democrats accuse the president of pressuring Ukrainians to take actions that would help himself or hurt his political opponents, and yet there are numerous examples of Democrats doing the exact same thing," said Nunes. But a few Republicans raised concerns about the call. "That conversation is not okay," said Rep. Michael R. Turner, R-Ohio. "And I think it's disappointing to the American public when they read this transcript." Sen. Patrick Toomey, R-Penn., said the exchange was inappropriate but not impeachable.

Democrats disagreed, with pressure mounting on House Speaker Nancy Pelosi, D-Calif., to initiate impeachment proceedings. Schiff told CNN that impeachment could be the "only remedy" if there had been a quid pro quo. Democrats had discussed the possibility of impeachment for months, particularly following the release of Special Counsel Robert Mueller's report, but Pelosi had been reluctant to move forward. On September 24, Pelosi announced a formal impeachment inquiry into Trump, declaring, "The actions taken to date by the president have seriously violated the Constitution." Trump's actions, she went on, amounted to a "betrayal of his oath of office, betrayal of our national security, and betrayal of the integrity of our elections." Trump decried the impeachment inquiry as "PRESIDENTIAL HARASSMENT!" and "witch hunt garbage." House Democrats began issuing subpoenas for the impeachment probe on September 27.

—Linda Grimm

Following is the rough transcript of President Donald Trump's phone call with Ukrainian president Volodymyr Zelenskyy, released by the White House on September 24, 2019; the declassified whistleblower complaint released on September 26, 2019; and Intelligence Community inspector general Michael Atkinson's letter to Congress, released on September 26, 2019, informing them of the whistleblower complaint.

Memorandum of Trump and Zelenskyy Phone Conversation

September 24, 2019

The President: Congratulations on a great victory. We all watched from the United States and you did a terrific job. The way you came from behind, somebody who wasn't given much of a chance, and you ended up winning easily. It's a fantastic achievement. Congratulations.

President Zelenskyy: You are absolutely right Mr. President. We did win big and we worked hard for this. We worked a lot, but I would like to confess to you that I had an opportunity to learn from you. We used quite a few of your skills and knowledge and were able to use it as an example for our elections and yes, it is true that these were unique elections. We were in a unique situation that we were able to achieve a unique success. I'm able to tell you the following; the first time, you called me to congratulate me when I won my presidential election, and the second time you are now calling me when my party won the parliamentary election. I think I should run more often so you can call me more often and we can talk over the phone more often.

The President: [laughter] That's a very good idea. I think your country is very happy about that.

President Zelenskyy: Well yes, to tell you the truth, we are trying to work hard because we wanted to drain the swamp here in our country. We brought in many new people. Not the old politicians, not the typical politicians, because we want to have a new format and a new type of government. You are a great teacher for us and in that.

The President: Well it's very nice of you to say that. I will say that we do a lot for Ukraine. We spend a lot of effort and a lot of time. Much more than the European countries are doing and they should be helping you more than they are. Germany does almost nothing for you. All they do is talk and I think it's something that you should really ask them about. When I was speaking to Angela Merkel, she talks Ukraine, but she doesn't do anything. A lot of the European countries are the same way, so I think it's something you want to look at, but the United States has been very very good to Ukraine. I wouldn't say that it's reciprocal necessarily because things are happening that are not good but the United States has been very very good to Ukraine.

President Zelenskyy: Yes, you are absolutely right. Not only 100%, but actually 1000% and I can tell you the following; I did talk to Angela Merkel and I did meet with her. I also met and talked with Macron and I told them that they are not doing quite as much as they need to be doing on the issues with the sanctions. They are not enforcing the sanctions. They are not working as much as they should work for Ukraine. It turns out that even though logically, the European Union should be our biggest partner but technically the United States is a much bigger partner than the European Union and I'm very grateful to you for that because the United States is doing quite a lot for Ukraine. Much more than the European Union especially when we are talking about sanctions against the Russian Federation. I would also like to thank you for your great support in the area of defense. We are ready to continue to cooperate for the next steps specifically, we are almost ready to buy more Javelins from the United States for defense purposes.

The President: I would like you to do us a favor though because our country has been through a lot and Ukraine knows a lot about it. I would like you to find out what happened with this whole situation with Ukraine, they say Crowdstrike . . . I guess you have one of your wealthy people. . . . The server, they say Ukraine has it. There are a lot of things that went on, the whole situation. I think you're surrounding yourself with some of the same people. I would like to have the Attorney General call you or your people and I would like you to get to the bottom of it. As you saw yesterday that whole nonsense ended with a very poor performance by a man named Robert Mueller, an incompetent performance, but they say a lot of it started with Ukraine. Whatever you can do, it's very important that you do it if that's possible.

President Zelenskyy: Yes, it is very important for me and everything that you just mentioned earlier. For me as a President, it is very important, and we are open for any future cooperation. We are ready to open a new page on cooperation in relations between the United States and Ukraine. For that purpose, I just recalled our ambassador from United States, and he will be replaced by a very competent and very experienced ambassador who will work hard on making sure that our two nations are getting closer. I would also like and hope to see him having your trust and your confidence and have personal relations with you so we can cooperate even more so I will personally tell you that one of my assistants spoke with Mr. Giuliani just recently and we are hoping very much that Mr. Giuliani will be able to travel to Ukraine and we will meet once he comes to Ukraine. I just wanted to assure you once again that you have nobody but friends around us. I will make sure that I surround myself with the best and most experienced people. I also wanted to tell you that we are friends. We are great friends and you Mr. President have friends in our country so we can continue our strategic partnership. I also plan to surround myself with great people and in addition to that investigation, I guarantee as the President of Ukraine that all the investigations will be done openly and candidly. That I can assure you.

The President: Good because I heard you had a prosecutor who was very good, and he was shut down and that's really unfair. A lot of people are talking about that, the way they shut your very good prosecutor down and you had some very bad people involved. Mr. Giuliani is a highly respected man. He was the mayor of New York City, a great mayor, and I would like him to call you. I will ask him to call you along with the Attorney General. Rudy very much knows what's happening and he is a very capable guy. If you could speak to him that would be great. The former ambassador from the United States, the woman, was bad news and the people she was dealing with in the Ukraine were bad news so I just want to let you know that. The other thing, there's a lot of talk about Biden's son, that Biden stopped the prosecution and a lot of people want to find out about that so whatever you can do with the Attorney General would be great. Biden went around bragging that he stopped the prosecution so if you can look into it. . . . It sounds horrible to me.

President Zelenskyy: I wanted to tell you about the prosecutor. First of all, I understand and I'm knowledgeable about the situation. Since we have won the absolute majority in our Parliament; the next prosecutor general will be 100% my person, my candidate, who will be approved, by the parliament and will start as a new prosecutor in September. He or she will look into the situation, specifically to the company that you mentioned in this issue. The issue of the investigation of the case is actually the issue of making sure to restore the honesty so we will take care of that and will work on the investigation of the case. On top of that, I would kindly ask you if you have any additional information that you can provide to us, it would be very helpful for the investigation to make sure that we administer justice in our country with regard to the Ambassador to the United States from Ukraine as far as I recall her name was Ivanovich. It was great that you were the first one who told me that she was a bad ambassador because I agree with you 100%. Her attitude towards me was far from the best as she admired the previous President and she was on his side. She would not accept me as a new President well enough.

The President: Well, she's going to go through some things. I will have Mr. Giuliani give you a call and I am also going to have Attorney General Barr call and we will get to the bottom of it. I'm sure you will figure it out. I heard the prosecutor was treated very badly and he was a very fair prosecutor so good luck with everything. Your economy is going to get better and better I predict. You have a lot of assets. It's a great country. I have many Ukrainian friends, their incredible people.

President Zelenskyy: I would like to tell you that I also have quite a few Ukrainian friends that live in the United States. Actually, last time I traveled to the United States, I stayed in New York near Central Park and I stayed at the Trump Tower. I will talk to them and I hope to see them again in the future. I also wanted to thank you for your invitation to visit the United States, specifically Washington DC. On the other hand, I also want to ensure you that we will be very serious about the case and will work on the investigation. As to the economy, there is much potential for our two countries and one of the issues that is very important for Ukraine is energy independence. I believe we can be very successful and cooperating on energy independence with United States. We are already working on cooperation. We are buying American oil but I am very hopeful for a future meeting. We will have more time and more opportunities to discuss these opportunities and get to know each other better. I would like to thank you very much for your support.

The President: Good. Well, thank you very much and I appreciate that. I will tell Rudy and Attorney General Barr to call. Thank you. Whenever you would like to come to the White House feel free to call. Give us a date and we'll work that out. I look forward to seeing you.

President Zelenskyy: Thank you very much. I would be very happy to come and would be happy to meet with you personally and get to know you better. I am looking forward to our meeting and I also would like to invite you to visit Ukraine and come to the city of Kyiv which is a beautiful city. We have a beautiful country which would welcome you. On the other hand, I believe that on September 1 we will be in Poland and we can meet in Poland hopefully. After that, it might be a very good idea for you to travel to Ukraine. We can either take my plane and go to Ukraine or we can take your plane, which is probably much better than mine.

The President: Okay, we can work that out. I look forward to seeing you in Washington and maybe in Poland because I think we are going to be there at that time.

President Zelenskyy: Thank you very much Mr. President.

The President: Congratulations on a fantastic job you've done. The whole world was watching. I'm not sure it was so much of an upset but congratulations.

President Zelenskyy: Thank you Mr. President bye-bye.

SOURCE: The White House. "Memorandum of Telephone Conversation." July 25, 2019. Declassified September 24, 2019. https://www.whitehouse.gov/wp-content/uploads/2019/09/Unclassified09.2019.pdf.

Whistleblower Complaint to Congressional Intelligence Committees

September 26, 2019

Dear Chairman Burr and Chairman Schiff:

I am reporting an "urgent concern" in accordance with the procedures outlined in 50 U.S.C. §3033(k)(5)(A). This letter is UNCLASSIFIED when separated from the attachment.

In the course of my official duties, I have received information from multiple U.S. Government officials that the President of the United States is using the power of his office to solicit interference from a foreign country in the 2020 U.S. election. This interference includes, among other things, pressuring a foreign country to investigate one of the President's main domestic political rivals. The President's personal lawyer, Mr. Rudolph Giuliani, is a central figure in this effort. Attorney General Barr appears to be involved as well.

Over the past four months, more than half a dozen U.S. officials have informed me of various facts related to this effort. The information provided herein was relayed to me in the course of official interagency business. It is routine for U.S. officials with responsibility for a particular regional or functional portfolio to share such information with one another in order to inform policymaking and analysis.

I was not a direct witness to most of the events described. However, I found my colleagues' accounts of these events to be credible because, in almost all cases, multiple officials recounted fact patterns that were consistent with one another. In addition, a variety of information consistent with these private accounts has been reported publicly.

I am deeply concerned that the actions described below constitute "a serious or flagrant problem, abuse, or violation of law or Executive Order" that "does not include differences of opinions concerning public policy matters," consistent with the definition of an "urgent concern" in 50 U.S.C. §3033(k)(5)(G). I am therefore fulfilling my duty to report this information, through proper legal channels, to the relevant authorities.

I am also concerned that these actions pose risks to U.S. national security and undermine the U.S. Government's efforts to deter and counter foreign interference in U.S. elections.

To the best of my knowledge, the entirety of this statement is unclassified when separated from the classified enclosure. I have endeavored to apply the classification standards outlined in Executive Order (EO) 13526 and to separate out information that I know or have reason to believe is classified for national security purposes.

If a classification marking is applied retroactively, I believe it is incumbent upon the classifying authority to explain why such a marking was applied, and to which specific information it pertains.

The 25 July Presidential phone call

Early in the morning of 25 July, the President spoke by telephone with Ukrainian President Volodymyr Zelenskyy. I do not know which side initiated the call. This was the first publicly acknowledged call between the two leaders since a brief congratulatory call after Mr. Zelenskyy won the presidency on 21 April.

Multiple White House officials with direct knowledge of the call informed me that, after an initial exchange of pleasantries, the President used the remainder of the call to advance his personal interests. Namely, he sought to pressure the Ukrainian leader to take actions to help the President's 2020 reelection bid. According to the White House officials who had direct knowledge of the call, the President pressured Mr. Zelenskyy to, inter alia:

- initiate or continue an investigation into the activities of former Vice President Joseph Biden and his son, Hunter Biden;

- assist in purportedly uncovering that allegations of Russian interference in the 2016 U.S. presidential election originated in Ukraine, with a specific request that the Ukrainian leader locate and turn over servers used by the Democratic National Committee (DNC) and examined by the U.S. cyber security firm Crowdstrike, which initially reported that Russian hackers had penetrated the DNC's networks in 2016; and

- meet or speak with two people the President named explicitly as his personal envoys on these matters, Mr. Giuliani and Attorney General Barr, to whom the President referred multiple times in tandem.

The President also praised Ukraine's Prosecutor General, Mr. Yuriy Lutsenko, and suggested that Mr. Zelenskyy might want to keep him in his position. (Note: Starting in March 2019, Mr. Lutsenko made a series of public allegations—many of which he later walked back—about the Biden family's activities in Ukraine, Ukrainian officials' purported involvement in the 2016 U.S. election, and the activities of the U.S. Embassy in Kyiv. See Part IV for additional context.)

The White House officials who told me this information were deeply disturbed by what had transpired in the phone call. They told me that there was already a "discussion ongoing" with White House lawyers about how to treat the call because of the likelihood, in the officials' retelling, that they had witnessed the President abuse his office for personal gain.

The Ukrainian side was the first to publicly acknowledge the phone call. On the evening of 25 July, a readout was posted on the website of the Ukrainian President that contained the following line (translation from original Russian-language readout):

"Donald Trump expressed his conviction that the new Ukrainian government will be able to quickly improve Ukraine's image and complete the investigation of corruption cases that have held back cooperation between Ukraine and the United States."

Aside from the above-mentioned "cases" purportedly dealing with the Biden family and the 2016 U.S. election, I was told by White House officials that no other "cases" were discussed.

Based on my understanding, there were approximately a dozen White House officials who listened to the call—a mixture of policy officials and duty officers in the White House Situation Room, as is customary. The officials I spoke with told me that participation in the call had not been restricted in advance because everyone expected it would be a "routine" call with a foreign leader. I do not know whether anyone was physically present with the President during the call.

In addition to White House personnel, I was told that a State Department official, Mr. T. Ulrich Brechbuhl, also listened in on the call.

I was not the only non–White House official to receive a readout of the call. Based on my understanding, multiple State Department and Intelligence Community officials were also briefed on the contents of the call as outlined above.

Efforts to restrict access to records related to the call

In the days following the phone call, I learned from multiple U.S. officials that senior White House officials had intervened to "lock down" all records of the phone call, especially the official word-for-word transcript of the call that was produced—as is customary—by the White House Situation Room. This set of actions underscored to me that White House officials understood the gravity of what had transpired in the call.

White House officials told me that they were "directed" by White House lawyers to remove the electronic transcript from the computer system in which such transcripts are typically stored for coordination, finalization, and distribution to Cabinet-level officials.

Instead, the transcript was loaded into a separate electronic system that is otherwise used to store and handle classified information of an especially sensitive nature. One White House official described this act as an abuse of this electronic system because the call did not contain anything remotely sensitive from a national security perspective.

I do not know whether similar measures were taken to restrict access to other records of the call, such as contemporaneous handwritten notes taken by those who listened in.

Ongoing concerns

On 26 July, a day after the call, U.S. Special Representative for Ukraine Negotiations Kurt Volker visited Kyiv and met with President Zelenskyy and a variety of Ukrainian political figures. Ambassador Volker was accompanied in his meetings by U.S. Ambassador to the European Union Gordon Sondland. Based on multiple readouts of these meetings recounted to me by various U.S. officials, Ambassadors Volker and Sondland reportedly provided advice to the Ukrainian leadership about how to "navigate" the demands that the President had made of Mr. Zelenskyy.

I also learned from multiple U.S. officials that, on or about 2 August, Mr. Giuliani reportedly traveled to Madrid to meet with one of President Zelenskyy's advisers, Andriy Yermak. The U.S. officials characterized this meeting, which was not reported publicly at the time, as a "direct follow-up" to the President's call with Mr. Zelenskyy about the "cases" they had discussed.

Separately, multiple U.S. officials told me that Mr. Giuliani had reportedly privately reached out to a variety of other Zelenskyy advisers, including Chief of Staff Andriy Bohdan and Acting Chairman of the Security Service of Ukraine Ivan Bakanov.

I do not know whether those officials met or spoke with Mr. Giuliani, but I was told separately by multiple U.S. officials that Mr. Yermak and Mr. Bakanov intended to travel to Washington in mid-August.

On 9 August, the President told reporters: "I think [President Zelenskyy] is going to make a deal with President Putin, and he will be invited to the White House. And we look forward to seeing him. He's already been invited to the White House, and he wants to come. And I think he will. He's a very reasonable guy. He wants to see peace in Ukraine, and I think he will be coming very soon, actually."

Circumstances leading up to the 25 July Presidential phone call

Beginning in late March 2019, a series of articles appeared in an online publication called *The Hill*. In these articles, several Ukrainian officials—most notably, Prosecutor General Yuriy Lutsenko—made a series of allegations against other Ukrainian officials and current and former U.S. officials. Mr. Lutsenko and his colleagues alleged, inter alia:

- that they possessed evidence that Ukrainian officials—namely, Head of the National Anticorruption Bureau of Ukraine Artem Sytnyk and Member of Parliament Serhiy Leshchenko—had "interfered" in the 2016 U.S. presidential election, allegedly in collaboration with the DNC and the U.S. Embassy in Kyiv;

- that the U.S. Embassy in Kyiv—specifically, U.S. Ambassador Marie Yovanovitch, who had criticized Mr. Lutsenko's organization for its poor record on fighting corruption—had allegedly obstructed Ukrainian law enforcement agencies' pursuit of corruption cases, including by providing a "do not prosecute" list, and had blocked Ukrainian prosecutors from traveling to the United States expressly to prevent them from delivering their "evidence" about the 2016 U.S. election; and

- that former Vice President Biden had pressured former Ukrainian President Petro Poroshenko in 2016 to fire then Ukrainian Prosecutor General Viktor Shokin in order to quash a purported criminal probe into Burisma Holdings, a Ukrainian energy company on whose board the former Vice President's son, Hunter, sat.

In several public comments, Mr. Lutsenko also stated that he wished to communicate directly with Attorney General Barr on these matters.

The allegations by Mr. Lutsenko came on the eve of the first round of Ukraine's presidential election on 31 March. By that time, Mr. Lutsenko's political patron, President Poroshenko, was trailing Mr. Zelenskyy in the polls and appeared likely to be defeated. Mr. Zelenskyy had made known his desire to replace Mr. Lutsenko as Prosecutor General. On 21 April, Mr. Poroshenko lost the runoff to Mr. Zelenskyy by a landslide. See Enclosure for additional information.

It was also publicly reported that Mr. Giuliani had met on at least two occasions with Mr. Lutsenko: once in New York in late January and again in Warsaw in mid-February. In addition, it was publicly reported that Mr. Giuliani had spoken in late 2018 to former Prosecutor General Shokin, in a Skype call arranged by two associates of Mr. Giuliani.

On 25 April in an interview with Fox News, the President called Mr. Lutsenko's claims "big" and "incredible" and stated that the Attorney General "would want to see this."

On or about 29 April, I learned from U.S. officials with direct knowledge of the situation that Ambassador Yovanovitch had been suddenly recalled to Washington by senior State Department officials for "consultations" and would most likely be removed from her position.

Around the same time, I also learned from a U.S. official that "associates" of Mr. Giuliani were trying to make contact with the incoming Zelenskyy team.

On 6 May, the State Department announced that Ambassador Yovanovitch would be ending her assignment in Kyiv "as planned."

However, several U.S. officials told me that, in fact, her tour was curtailed because of pressure stemming from Mr. Lutsenko's allegations. Mr. Giuliani subsequently stated in an interview with a Ukrainian journalist published on 14 May that Ambassador Yovanovitch was "removed . . . because she was part of the efforts against the President."

On 9 May, *The New York Times* reported that Mr. Giuliani planned to travel to Ukraine to press the Ukrainian government to pursue investigations that would help the President in his 2020 reelection bid.

In his multitude of public statements leading up to and in the wake of the publication of this article, Mr. Giuliani confirmed that he was focused on encouraging Ukrainian authorities to pursue investigations into alleged Ukrainian interference in the 2016 U.S. election and alleged wrongdoing by the Biden family.

On the afternoon of 10 May, the President stated in an interview with Politico that he planned to speak with Mr. Giuliani about the trip. A few hours later, Mr. Giuliani publicly canceled his trip, claiming that Mr. Zelenskyy was "surrounded by enemies of the [U.S.] President . . . and of the United States."

On 11 May, Mr. Lutsenko met for two hours with President-elect Zelenskyy, according to a public account given several days later by Mr. Lutsenko. Mr. Lutsenko publicly stated that he had told Mr. Zelenskyy that he wished to remain as Prosecutor General.

Starting in mid-May, I heard from multiple U.S. officials that they were deeply concerned by what they viewed as Mr. Giuliani's circumvention of national security decision-making processes to engage with Ukrainian officials and relay messages back and forth between Kyiv and the President. These officials also told me:

- that State Department officials, including Ambassadors Volker and Sondland, had spoken with Mr. Giuliani in an attempt to "contain the damage" to U.S. national security; and

- that Ambassadors Volker and Sondland during this time period met with members of the new Ukrainian administration and, in addition to discussing policy matters, sought to help Ukrainian leaders understand and respond to the differing messages they were receiving from official U.S. channels on the one hand, and from Mr. Giuliani on the other.

During this same timeframe, multiple U.S. officials told me that the Ukrainian leadership was led to believe that a meeting or phone call between the President and President Zelenskyy would depend on whether Zelenskyy showed willingness to "play ball" on the issues that had been publicly aired by Mr. Lutsenko and Mr. Giuliani. (Note: This was the general understanding of the state of affairs as conveyed to me by U.S. officials from late May into early July. I do not know who delivered this message to the Ukrainian leadership, or when.) See Enclosure for additional information.

Shortly after President Zelenskyy's inauguration, it was publicly reported that Mr. Giuliani met with two other Ukrainian officials: Ukraine's Special Anticorruption Prosecutor, Mr. Nazar Kholodnytskyy, and a former Ukrainian diplomat named Andriy Telizhenko. Both Mr. Kholodnytskyy and Mr. Telizhenko are allies of Mr. Lutsenko and made similar allegations in the above-mentioned series of articles in *The Hill*.

On 13 June, the President told ABC's George Stephanopoulos that he would accept damaging information on his political rivals from a foreign government.

On 21 June, Mr. Giuliani tweeted: "New Pres of Ukraine still silent on investigation of Ukrainian interference in 2016 and alleged Biden bribery of Poroshenko. Time for leadership and investigate both if you want to purge how Ukraine was abused by Hillary and Clinton people."

In mid-July, I learned of a sudden change of policy with respect to U.S. assistance for Ukraine. See Enclosure for additional information.

CLASSIFIED APPENDIX

Supplementary classified information is provided as follows:

Additional information related to Section II

According to multiple White House officials I spoke with, the transcript of the President's call with President Zelenskyy was placed into a computer system managed directly by the National Security Council (NSC) Directorate for Intelligence Programs. This is a standalone computer system reserved for codeword-level intelligence information, such as covert action. According to information I received from White House officials, some officials voiced concerns internally that this would be an abuse of the system and was not consistent with the responsibilities of the Directorate for Intelligence Programs. According to White House officials I spoke with, this was "not the first time" under this Administration that a Presidential transcript was placed into this codeword-level system solely for the purpose of protecting politically sensitive—rather than national security sensitive—information.

Additional information related to Section IV

I would like to expand upon two issues mentioned in Section IV that might have a connection with the overall effort to pressure the Ukrainian leadership. As I do not know definitively whether the below-mentioned decisions are connected to the broader efforts I describe, I have chosen to include them in the classified annex. If they indeed represent genuine policy deliberations and decisions formulated to advance U.S. foreign policy and national security, one might be able to make a reasonable case that the facts are classified.

I learned from U.S. officials that, on or around 14 May, the President instructed Vice President Pence to cancel his planned travel to Ukraine to attend President Zelenskyy's inauguration on 20 May; Secretary of Energy Rick Perry led the delegation instead. According to these officials, it was also "made clear" to them that the President did not want to meet with Mr. Zelenskyy until he saw how Zelenskyy "chose to act" in office. I do not know how this guidance was communicated, or by whom. I also do not know whether this action was connected with the broader understanding, described in the unclassified letter, that a meeting or phone call between the President and President Zelenskyy would depend on whether Zelenskyy showed willingness to "play ball" on the issues that had been publicly aired by Mr. Lutsenko and Mr. Giuliani.

On 18 July, an Office of Management and Budget (OMB) official informed Departments and Agencies that the President "earlier that month" had issued instructions to suspend all U.S. security assistance to Ukraine. Neither OMB nor the NSC staff knew why this instruction had been issued. During interagency meetings on 23 July and 26 July,

OMB officials again stated explicitly that the instruction to suspend this assistance had come directly from the President, but they still were unaware of a policy rationale.

As of early August, I heard from U.S. officials that some Ukrainian officials were aware that U.S. aid might be in jeopardy, but I do not know how or when they learned of it.

SOURCE: House Permanent Select Committee on Intelligence. "Whistleblower Complaint Unclassified." August 12, 2019. Declassified September 26, 2019. https://intelligence.house.gov/uploadedfiles/20190812_-_whistleblower_complaint_unclass.pdf.

Intelligence Community Inspector General Letter on Whistleblower Complaint

September 26, 2019

Dear Acting Director Maguire:

On Monday, August 12, 2019, the Office of the Inspector General of the Intelligence Community (ICIG) received information from an individual (hereinafter, the "Complainant") concerning an alleged "urgent concern," pursuant to 50 U.S.C. § 3033(k)(5)(A). The law requires that, "[n]ot later than the end of the 14-calendar" day period beginning on the date of receipt from an employee of a complaint or information under subparagraph A, the Inspector General shall determine whether the complaint or information appears credible." For the reasons discussed below, among others, I have determined that the Complainant has reported an "urgent concern" that "appears credible."

As you know, the ICIG is authorized to, among other things, "receive and investigate . . . complaints or information from any person concerning the existence of an activity within the authorities and responsibilities of the Director of National Intelligence constituting a violation of laws, rules, or regulations, or mismanagement, gross waste of funds, abuse of authority, or a substantial and specific danger to the public health and safety." In connection with that authority, "[a]n employee of an element of the intelligence community, an employee assigned or detailed to an element of the intelligence community, or an employee of a contractor to the intelligence community who intends to report to Congress a complaint or information with respect to an urgent concern may report such complaint or information" to the ICIG.

The term "urgent concern" is defined, in relevant part, as:

- A serious or flagrant problem, abuse, violation of law or Executive order, or deficiency relating to the funding, administration, or operation of an intelligence activity within the responsibility and authority of the Director of National Intelligence involving classified information, but does not include differences of opinions concerning public policy matters.

The Complainant's identity is known to me. As allowed by law, however, the Complainant has requested that the ICIG not disclose the Complainant's identity at this time. For your information, the Complainant has retained an attorney, identified the attorney to the ICIG, and requested that the attorney be the Complainant's point of contact in subsequent communications with the congressional intelligence committees on this matter.

As part of the Complainant's report to the ICIG of information with respect to the urgent concern, the Complainant included a letter addressed to The Honorable Richard Burr, Chairman, U.S. Senate Select Committee on Intelligence, and The Honorable Adam Schiff, Chairman, U.S. House of Representatives Permanent Select Committee on Intelligence (hereinafter, the "Complainant's Letter"). The Complainant's Letter referenced a separate, Classified Appendix containing information pertaining to the urgent concern (hereinafter, the "Classified Appendix"), which the Complainant also provided to the ICIG and which the Complainant intends to provide to Chairmen Burr and Schiff. The ICIG attaches hereto the Complainant's Letter, addressed to Chairmen Burr and Schiff, and the Classified Appendix. The ICIG has informed the Complainant that the transmittal of information by the Director of National Intelligence related to the Complainant's report to the congressional intelligence committees, as required by 50 U.S.C. § 3033(k)(5)(C), may not be limited to Chairmen Burr and Schiff.

The Complainant's Letter and Classified Appendix delineate the Complainant's information pertaining to the urgent concern. According to the Complainant's Letter, "the actions described [in the Complainant's Letter and Classified Appendix] constitute 'a serious or flagrant problem, abuse, or violation of law or Executive Order," consistent with the definition of an "urgent concern" in 50 U.S.C. § 3033(k)(5)(G).

Upon receiving the information reported by the Complainant, the ICIG conducted a preliminary review to determine whether the report constituted "an urgent concern" under 50 U.S.C. § 3033(k)(5). As part of the preliminaly review, the ICIG confirmed that the Complainant is "[a]n employee of an element of the intelligence community, an employee assigned or detailed to an element of the intelligence community, or an employee of a contractor to the intelligence community." The ICIG also confirmed that the Complainant intends to report to Congress the Complainant's information relating to the urgent concern.

As stated above, to constitute an "urgent concern" under 50 U.S.C. § 3033(k)(5)(G)(i), the information reported by the Complainant must constitute "[a] serious or flagrant problem, abuse, violation of law or Executive order, or deficiency relating to the funding, administration, or operation of an intelligence activity within the responsibility and authority of the Director of National Intelligence involving classified information." Here, the Complainant's Letter alleged, among other things, that the President of the United States, in a telephone call with Ukrainian President Volodymyr Zelenskyy on July 25, 2019, "sought to pressure the Ukrainian leader to take actions to help the President's 2020 reelection bid." U.S. laws and regulations prohibit a foreign national, directly or indirectly, from making a contribution or donation of money or other thing of value, or to make an express or implied promise to make a contribution or donation, in connection with a Federal, State, or local election. Similarly, U.S. laws and regulations prohibit a person from soliciting, accepting, or receiving such a contribution or donation from a foreign national, directly or indirectly, in connection with a Federal, State, or local election. Further, in the ICIG's judgment, alleged conduct by a senior U.S. public official to seek foreign assistance to interfere in or influence a Federal election would constitute a "serious or flagrant problem [or] abuse" under 50 U.S.C. § 3033(k)(5)(G)(i), which would also potentially expose such a U.S. public official (or others acting in concert with the U.S. public official) to serious national security and counterintelligence risks with respect to foreign intelligence services aware of such alleged conduct.

In addition, the Director of National Intelligence has responsibility and authority pursuant to federal law and Executive Orders to administer and operate programs and activities related to potential foreign interference in a United States election. Among other responsibilities and authorities, subject to the authority, direction, and control of the President, the Director of National Intelligence "shall serve as the head of the Intelligence Community, act as the principal adviser to the President, to the [National Security Council], and to the Homeland Security Council for intelligence matters related to national security, and shall oversee and direct the implementation of the National Intelligence Program and execution of the National Intelligence Program budget." Further, the United States Intelligence Community, "under the leadership of the Director [of National Intelligence]," shall "collect information concerning, and conduct activities to protect against . . . intelligence activities directed against the United States."

More recently, in issuing Executive Order 13848, Imposing Certain Sanctions in the Event of Foreign Influence in a United States Election (Sept. 12, 2018), President Trump stated the following regarding foreign influence in United States elections:

> *I, DONALD J. TRUMP, President of the United States of America, find that the ability of persons located, in whole or in part, outside the United States to interfere in or undermine public confidence in United States elections, including through the unauthorized accessing of election and campaign infrastructure or the covert distribution of propaganda and disinformation, constitutes an unusual and extraordinary threat to the national security and foreign policy of the United States.*

Most recently, on July 19, 2019, as part of the Director of National Intelligence's responsibility and authority to administer and operate programs and activities related to potential foreign interference in a United States election, the Director of National Intelligence announced the establishment of the Intelligence Community Election Threats Executive. In the words of then-Director of National Intelligence Daniel R. Coats, who announced the establishment of the new position within the Office of the Director of National Intelligence (ODNI), "Election security is an enduring challenge and a top priority for the IC." A few days later, in an internal announcement for the ODNI, then-Director Coats stated, "I can think of no higher priority mission than working to counter adversary efforts to undermine the very core of our democratic process."

As a result, I have determined that the Complainant's information would constitute an urgent concern, as defined in 50 U.S.C. § 3033(k)(5)(G)(i), provided that I also determine that the information "appears credible," as required by 50 U.S.C. § 3033(k)(5)(B).

Based on the information reported by the Complainant to the ICIG and the ICIG's preliminary review, I have determined that there are reasonable grounds to believe that the complaint relating to the urgent concern "appears credible." The ICIG's preliminary review indicated that the Complainant has official and authorized access to the information and sources referenced in the Complainant's Letter and Classified Appendix, and that the Complainant has subject matter expertise related to much of the material information provided in the Complainant's Letter and Classified Appendix. The Complainant's Letter acknowledges that the Complainant was not a direct witness to the President's telephone call with the Ukrainian President on July 25, 2019. Other information obtained during the

ICIG's preliminary review, however, supports the Complainant's allegation that, among other things, during the call the President "sought to pressure the Ukrainian leader to take actions to help the President's 2020 reelection bid." Further, although the ICIG's preliminary review identified some indicia of an arguable political bias on the part of the Complainant in favor of a rival political candidate, such evidence did not change my determination that the complaint relating to the urgent concern "appears credible," particularly given the other information the ICIG obtained during its preliminary review.

As part of its preliminary review, the ICIG did not request access to records of the President's July 25, 2019, call with the Ukrainian President. Based on the sensitivity of the alleged urgent concern, I directed ICIG personnel to conduct a preliminary review of the Complainant's information. Based on the information obtained from the ICIG's preliminary review, I decided that access to records of the telephone call was not necessary to make my determination that the complaint relating to the urgent concern "appears credible." In addition, given the time consumed by the preliminary review, together with lengthy negotiations that I anticipated over access to and use of records of the telephone call, particularly for purposes of communicating a disclosure to the congressional intelligence committees, I concluded that it would be highly unlikely for the ICIG to obtain those records within the limited remaining time allowed by the statute. I also understood from the ICIG's preliminary review that the National Security Council had already implemented special handling procedures to preserve all records of the telephone call.

Nevertheless, the ICIG understands that the records of the call will be relevant to any further investigation of this matter. For your information, the ICIG has sent concurrently with this transmittal a notice of a document access request and a document hold notice to the White House Counsel to request access to and the preservation of any and all records related to the President's telephone call with the Ukrainian President on July 25, 2019, and alleged related efforts to solicit, obtain, or receive assistance from foreign nationals in Ukraine, directly or indirectly, in connection with a Federal election. The document access request and document hold notice were issued pursuant to the ICIG's authority to conduct independent investigations and reviews on programs and activities within the responsibility and authority of the Director of National Intelligence, which includes the authority for the ICIG to have "direct access to all records, reports, audits, reviews , documents, papers, recommendations, or other materials that relate to the programs and activities with respect to which the Inspector General has responsibilities under this section."

Having determined that the complaint relating to the urgent concern appears credible, I am transmitting to you this notice of my determination, along with the Complainant's Letter and Classified Appendix. Upon receipt of this transmittal, the Director of National Intelligence "shall, within 7 calendar days of such receipt, forward such transmittal to the congressional intelligence committees, together with any comments the Director considers appropriate."

Because the ICIG has the statutory responsibility to "notify an employee who reports a complaint or information" to the ICIG concerning an urgent concern "of each action taken" with respect to the complaint or information "not later than 3 days after any such action is taken," I respectfully request that you provide the ICIG with notice of your transmittal to the congressional intelligence committees not later than 3 days after the transmittal is made to them. In addition, as required by the statute, the ICIG is required to notify the Complainant not later than 3 days after today's date of my determination that the complaint relating to the urgent concern appears credible and that the ICIG transmitted on today's date notice of that determination to the Director of National Intelligence, along with the Complainant's Letter and Classified Appendix.

If you have any questions or require additional information concerning this matter, please do not hesitate to contact me.

Sincerely yours,
Michael K. Atkinson
Inspector General of the Intelligence Community

SOURCE: House Permanent Select Committee on Intelligence. "ICIG Letter to Acting DNI Unclassified." August 26, 2019. Declassified September 26, 2019. https://intelligence.house.gov/uploadedfiles/20190826_-_icig_letter_to_acting_dni_unclass.pdf.

OTHER HISTORIC DOCUMENTS OF INTEREST

FROM THIS VOLUME

FROM PREVIOUS *HISTORIC DOCUMENTS*

October

Peruvian President Dissolves Congress

OCTOBER 1 AND 4, AND DECEMBER 30, 2019

At the end of September 2019, Peruvian leaders found themselves in the midst of a constitutional crisis. President Martín Vizcarra dissolved Congress, claiming it was necessary to overcome opposition lawmakers' resistance to his anticorruption reform measures and new elections. In response, Congress voted to suspend Vizcarra for one year and appealed the president's order to the country's Constitutional Tribunal. Fed up with an ongoing corruption scandal involving dozens of Peruvian lawmakers, the public voiced its support for Vizcarra, as did the police and military. The tribunal ultimately ruled in the president's favor, allowing a legislative election to take place in January 2020.

Corruption Scandal Ensnares Dozens of Politicians

Peru's political turmoil occurred as a wide-ranging corruption scandal continued to unfold across South America. In 2016, Brazilian construction company Odebrecht admitted to bribing public officials and making illegal campaign contributions to lawmakers in exchange for lucrative infrastructure contracts in at least ten countries, including Peru. (The company signed a leniency deal with U.S. and Swiss officials in which it admitted wrongdoing and paid about $2.6 billion in fines. Additionally, seventy-seven company executives plea bargained with the Brazilian authorities. Details from statements made by these executives and the company's confession have since been made public, sending shock waves across the continent.) Company executives confessed to paying about $29 million to Peruvian officials between 2005 and 2014, which helped Odebrecht win roughly $12.5 billion in state contracts. Dozens of lawmakers were accused of accepting bribes or illegal campaign financing from the company, including more than two dozen sitting members of Congress. Keiko Fujimori, leader of the opposition party Popular Force, which held a majority in Congress at the time, was among those facing investigation. Fujimori was arrested in October 2018 for allegedly taking $1.2 million in illegal campaign funding from Odebrecht to support her failed 2011 bid to become president.

Other notable political figures ensnared in the corruption scandal included four former Peruvian presidents. Alejandro Toledo was arrested in the United States in July 2019 on charges that he accepted $20 million in bribes from Odebrecht. Alan García, also accused of taking bribes, committed suicide in April 2019 as police arrived at his home to arrest him. Ollanta Humala resigned the presidency in 2016 after the scandal broke; he and his wife were arrested for allegedly accepting $3 million from Odebrecht to help finance his 2011 campaign. Vizcarra's successor, Pedro Pablo Kuczynski, reportedly received more than $780,000 from Odebrecht through a company he owned while serving as a government minister, while another company for which he served as a director received about $4 million. Kuczynski survived an impeachment effort pursued by lawmakers in December 2017, but he resigned in March 2018 shortly before a second impeachment hearing was scheduled in Congress. As Kuczynski's vice president, Vizcarra was sworn in to serve the remainder of the outgoing president's term.

Construction projects across Peru were halted as the Odebrecht investigations continued, causing tens of thousands of people to lose their jobs and slowing the country's economic growth. Adding to public frustrations with the government, in July 2018, a series of recorded phone conversations involving Peruvian judges indicated that powerful outside players were attempting to influence the justice system and suggested a link between several political parties and organized crime. Fujimori was also implicated in this scandal, which resulted in the firing and resignation of many senior justice officials.

VIZCARRA DISSOLVES CONGRESS

On September 30, Peruvian lawmakers had scheduled a vote to select new members of the country's Constitutional Tribunal. Several of the individuals on Congress's list of nominees had been connected to the Odebrecht scandal or accused of other criminal acts. The incoming roster of tribunal members would be responsible for ruling on a habeas corpus petition for Fujimori's release, among other key cases. To prevent Congress from voting on the candidates, Vizcarra called for a vote of confidence in his government. Congress declined to take up his proposal, instead moving to consider the tribunal nominees. At that point, Vizcarra dissolved the legislature and announced a new legislative election would be held on January 26, 2020.

Vizcarra said the dissolution was necessary because the opposition lawmakers who controlled Congress had repeatedly rebuffed his attempts to call a new election and had blocked his efforts to implement anticorruption reforms. (Most recently, Vizcarra put forward a bill earlier in September that called for snap elections, but lawmakers declined to consider it. The year prior, the president threatened to dissolve Congress and call a new election if lawmakers did not move his anticorruption measures forward.) "The closure seems a democratic solution to the problem that's been plaguing the country for three years," Vizcarra said. "Let the people finally decide who is right." Vizcarra also said that opposition lawmakers' actions—or inaction—showed "the shamelessness into which the parliamentary majority has fallen, completely divorced from the will of the Peruvian people." From a constitutional standpoint, Vizcarra argued that by refusing to conduct a vote of confidence, Congress had effectively rejected his government. Peru's Constitution allows the president to dissolve the legislature if the government loses two votes of confidence in one Congress. Since Kuczynski's government previously lost a vote of confidence in Congress, Vizcarra claimed the sitting lawmakers met this two-vote threshold.

The president had built a solid base of popular support among Peruvians who were tired of the ongoing scandals and fed up with opposition lawmakers, and rallies were held in cities across the country to show support for Vizcarra's dissolution of Congress. Various public opinion polls showed that somewhere between 70 percent and 80 percent of Peruvians approved of the president's action. Police and military leaders also affirmed their support for the president, issuing statements that they continued to recognize Vizcarra as the president and commander in chief.

CONGRESS SUSPENDS THE PRESIDENT

Opposition lawmakers accused Vizcarra of attempting a coup and of using the stalled anticorruption measures as an excuse to take executive action that would consolidate his power. Some lawmakers refused to leave the congressional chamber after his announcement, sparking public protests outside the building. "Vizcarra is trying to dissolve the

Congress like any dictator," said Congressman Juan Sheput. Pedro Olaechea, the president of Congress, said Vizcarra "had to dissolve Congress with this appearance of legality because otherwise he was definitely facing impeachment." In fact, several lawmakers introduced a motion to impeach the president, but they did not have enough votes to push the measure forward. Instead, the opposition voted to suspend Vizcarra for one year, claiming he had been morally incapacitated. Congress then named Vice President Mercedes Aráoz as acting president. "I accept this with fortitude," Aráoz said. "It is one of the most difficult decisions I have made in my life."

Aráoz's contested tenure was brief, however; she resigned as interim president and vice president on October 1. "The fundamental reason for my resignation is that the constitutional order has been broken in Peru," she wrote in her resignation letter to Congress. She pledged to continue "working to protect the rule of law, respect the democratic order, the independence of the State's powers, and dialogue and consensus as the best ways to achieve development of Peru" as a citizen. Aráoz also cited a statement issued by the Organization of American States (OAS) earlier in the day, which called into question her appointment as interim president. In that statement, the OAS declared that "it is the responsibility of the Constitutional Court of Peru to rule on the legality and legitimacy of the institutional decisions adopted, as well as on the differences that may exist in the interpretation of the Constitution." The organization also called for parties involved in the turmoil to "make gestures that favor calm in the face of the crisis." The OAS further commended the scheduling of a new election, noting that "the final decision rests with the Peruvian people, in whom lies the sovereignty of the nation. It is fair that the political polarization in the country will be resolved by the people at the polls."

Vizcarra continued to defend his "pretty important decisions" to dissolve the legislature, stating on October 4 that his actions "scrupulously respect our democracy and our Constitution" while "thinking about what is best for the country." The president said that lawmakers' political maneuverings were "distractions" and "take away our time and ability to focus on devoting ourselves to what is really important." He called for all parties to "get past this stage of confrontation" and "put all of our effort into what is really relevant: sustainable growth for all Peruvians."

Olaechea filed an appeal with the Constitutional Tribunal on October 10, asking for Congress's closure to be revoked because the president had exceeded his constitutional authority. Court members ruled on January 15, 2020, that Olaechea's case was unfounded and affirmed that Congress's dissolution had been constitutional.

Opposition Parties Lose Congressional Majority

The legislative election proceeded as scheduled on January 26. The OAS and the European Union (EU) deployed election monitors to observe the vote. Josep Borrell, the EU's high representative for foreign affairs and security police, noted that the election was taking place "at a critical political juncture" for Peru. "It is the first time that anticipated elections are organised in the context of heated institutional debates, including on anticorruption reforms," he said.

More than 2,300 candidates across twenty-one parties stood in the poll. A quick vote count conducted by Ipsos indicated that Popular Force received roughly 7 percent of the vote, giving it fewer than twenty seats in Congress. By comparison, the party won more than 36 percent of the vote in Peru's last parliamentary election in 2016, giving it 73 of the 130 congressional seats. The American Popular Revolutionary Alliance (APRA), an opposition party considered to be Popular Force's biggest ally in Congress, also suffered significant losses. Ipsos noted that with less than 3 percent of the vote, APRA was likely to lose its party registration and would not get any seats in Congress. None of the other parties emerged with a majority, although several centrist groups picked up seats. Centrist party Popular Action was the top vote getter at about 10 percent, while the center-right Progress Alliance and centrist *Partido Morado* each won about 8 percent of the vote. Analysts have speculated that the increase in centrist congressmembers could help Vizcarra push his anticorruption proposals through, since centrists are more likely to support those measures than opposition parties.

Following the election, Vizcarra said he wanted to establish with the new Congress "a responsible, mature relationship that seeks a consensus that benefits Peru." Analysts noted the president will need to work quickly because the next general election—for both president and members of Congress—will take place in April 2021, and neither Vizcarra nor the newly elected lawmakers will be eligible to run for reelection at that time. Observers also noted that many of the lawmakers who lost their seats in Congress could face prosecution in 2020, since they will no longer enjoy immunity from prosecution.

—Linda Grimm

Following is a statement issued by the Organization of American States on October 1, 2019, commenting on political developments in Peru; Second Vice President Mercedes Aráoz's resignation letter, submitted on October 1, 2019; excerpts of remarks delivered by President Martín Vizcarra on October 4, 2019, during which he discussed his dissolution of Congress; and a press release issued by the European Union on December 30, 2019, announcing the deployment of its election observation mission in Peru.

Statement of the OAS General Secretariat on the Situation in Peru

October 1, 2019

It is the political responsibility of the General Secretariat of the Organization of American States (GS/OAS) to ensure compliance with the effective exercise of representative democracy as the basis of the rule of law and constitutional regimes. In this case, the GS/OAS considers that it is the responsibility of the Constitutional Court of Peru to rule on the legality and legitimacy of the institutional decisions adopted, as well as on the differences that may exist in the interpretation of the Constitution, depending on the actions and positions expressed to the Court by political actors.

It is a constructive step that the elections have been called according to the constitutional deadlines and that the final decision rests with the Peruvian people, in whom lies the sovereignty of the nation. It is fair that the political polarization in the country will be resolved by the people at the polls.

The GS/OAS also considers it desirable for the parties to make gestures that favor calm in the face of the crisis. It is essential that the public is not exposed to violence in a context of conflict and political fragility seen in recent months through different points of possible escalation of sectoral conflicts that, although they are outside the current crisis, could further complicate the situation.

The GS/OAS remains at the disposal of Peruvian political actors if they decide to request support for solutions according to the rule of law and the constitutional order of the country.

SOURCE: General Secretariat of the Organization of American States. "Statement of the OAS General Secretariat on the Situation in Peru." October 1, 2019. https://www.oas.org/en/media_center/press_release.asp?sCodigo=E-073/19.

Second Vice President Aráoz Resigns Post

October 1, 2020

Through this communication I inform you of my decision to irrevocably resign the office of Second Vice President of the Republic, which I've held since July 2016 by popular election. The fundamental reason for my resignation is that the constitutional order has been broken in Peru.

Regarding the suspicion in the office of Sr. Martín Alberto Vizcarra Cornejo, as constitutional president of the Republic, under Legislative Resolution No. 006-2019-2020-CR dated September 30, 2019, as well as the office of the same functions as the undersigned, I decline the conferred responsibility by resigning the office of Vice President of the Constitutional Republic.

Before the request of the Organization of American States (OAS) for the Constitutional Court to decide the constitutionality of the adopted measure by Sr. Martín Vizcarra to dissolve the Congress of the Republic, I considered that there are no minimum conditions to exercise the office given to me by the Congress of the Republic.

Throughout my life and public career, I have always put my principles and legality before my personal interests or my policies' popularity. I am convinced that in Peru we have millions of citizens who want to build solid and independent institutions, and the way to do it is defend them.

As a citizen, I will continue working to protect the rule of law, respect the democratic order, the independence of the State's powers, and dialogue and consensus as the best ways to achieve development of Peru.

SOURCE: Mercedes Aráoz (@MecheAF). Twitter post. October 1, 2020. Translated by SAGE Publishing. https://twitter.com/MecheAF/status/1179221001936211968.

President Vizcarra on Dissolution of Congress, National Priorities

October 4, 2019

In this last week, we made pretty important decisions, we affirm that they all scrupulously respect our democracy and our Constitution, they have been difficult decisions, but thinking about what is best for the country and all Peruvians. . . .

The distractions, the political entrapments, they take away our time and ability to focus on devoting ourselves to what is really important. We hope that with the decision we have made, with the process started for congressional elections on January 26, we can get past this stage of confrontation and we can put all of our effort into what is really relevant: sustainable growth for all Peruvians. . . .

Together we can change the country, achieve progress and growth and so leave our children, our grandchildren, growth and better conditions. Thus, we continue this effort despite difficult moments and with certainty that we are coming out of it, making the most appropriate decisions for all Peruvians. . . .

SOURCE: Presidency of the Republic of Peru. "Presidente Vizcarra: Las decisiones que tomó el Gobierno han sido respetando la Constitución y la democracia y por el bien del Perú." October 4, 2019. Translated by SAGE Publishing. https://www.gob.pe/institucion/presidencia/noticias/52156-presidente-vizcarra-las-decisiones-que-tomo-el-gobierno-han-sido-respetando-la-constitucion-y-la-democracia-y-por-el-bien-del-peru.

EU Announces Election Observation Mission to Peru

December 30, 2019

Following the invitation of the Peruvian authorities, the European Union is deploying an Election Observation Mission (EOM) to Peru to observe the anticipated congressional elections due to take place on 26 January 2020. Reflecting the EU's long-standing commitment to supporting credible, transparent and inclusive elections in Peru, the EU has previously deployed an EOM to the general elections in both 2011 and 2016.

Josep Borrell, High Representative of the Union for Foreign Affairs and Security Policy and Vice-President of the European Commission, has appointed Leopoldo López Gil, Member of the European Parliament, as Chief Observer of the EU Election Observation Mission to Peru.

High Representative and Vice President Josep Borrell stated: "These elections are taking place at a critical political juncture for Peru. It is the first time that anticipated elections are organised, in the context of heated institutional debates, including on anti-corruption reforms. With this electoral observation mission, the European Union wants to make a meaningful contribution to this process."

Mr. López Gil declared: "I feel honoured to lead the EU Election Observation Mission to Peru. The EU has observed all previous general elections since 2011 and has provided important recommendations to strengthen the democratic framework. I am hopeful that our observation will contribute to an inclusive, credible and transparent election and that the recommendations our mission will make will further feed the debate on how to continue making progress on strengthening democracy in Peru."

The Electoral Observation Mission's core team, consisting of nine analysts, arrived in Lima on 17 December and will stay in the country until the completion of the electoral process. On 26 December, the core team was joined by 50 long-term observers who were deployed on 30 December across the country.

Shortly after the day of the elections, the mission will issue a preliminary statement of its findings during a press conference in Lima. A final report, including recommendations for future electoral processes, will be presented to the Peruvian Government after the finalisation of the electoral process.

SOURCE: European Union. European External Action Service. "Peru: European Union Deploys an Election Observation Mission." December 30, 2019. https://eeas.europa.eu/headquarters/headquarters-homepage/72634/peru-european-union-deploys-election-observation-mission_en.

OTHER HISTORIC DOCUMENTS OF INTEREST

FROM THIS VOLUME

- OAS Conducts Election Audit in Bolivia, p. 615

FROM PREVIOUS *HISTORIC DOCUMENTS*

- Paniagua on His Inauguration as President of Peru, *2000,* p. 924
- Fujimori on Capture of Peruvian Shining Path Leader, *1992,* p. 860
- Drug Summit Agreements at Cartagena, Colombia, *1990,* p. 117

Supreme Court Allows Sandy Hook Families to Sue Remington

OCTOBER 4 AND 18, 2019

In a November 2019 ruling, the U.S. Supreme Court rejected an appeal by gun manufacturer Remington to review a lower court's decision that would allow a lawsuit brought by families of the victims of the Sandy Hook Elementary School shooting to proceed against the company. The case could now move forward in Connecticut's state superior court, with a trial expected to begin in 2021. The outcome could have repercussions for other victims of gun violence across the country who seek restitution from gun manufacturers.

SANDY HOOK FAMILIES SUE GUN MANUFACTURER

In December 2012, Adam Lanza killed twenty first-graders and six adults at Sandy Hook Elementary in Newtown, Connecticut. Two years later, the families of nine victims and one survivor filed a lawsuit in Connecticut state superior court against Remington Arms Co., the manufacturer of the Bushmaster AR-15 style rifle, one of the guns used in the massacre. In their case, *Soto v. Bushmaster*, the families argued that the gun should not have been sold because it is a military-style weapon and entrusting it to the public "involved an unreasonable risk of physical injury to others." Specifically, the plaintiffs said Remington was in violation of the state's unfair trade practices law because it "knowingly marketed and promoted the Bushmaster XM15-E2S rifle for use in assaults against human beings." According to the suit, Remington targeted its products to disturbed young men using phrases such as "consider your man card reissued" and "the opposition will bow down." They said that Remington marketed the AR-15 "as a highly lethal weapon designed for purposes that are illegal—namely, killing other human beings." Remington sought to have the case moved to federal court, which the company argued would be a more appropriate venue. Some law experts explained that moving the case to federal court might also give Remington a more favorable outcome. Ultimately, a U.S. District Court judge sent it back to the state court.

After the case was sent back to the lower court, Remington sought to have it dismissed. The gun manufacturer argued that the lawsuit was in direct violation of the 2005 Protection of Lawful Commerce in Arms Act, which protects gun manufacturers and sellers from prosecution when their weapons are used to commit crimes. There are exceptions to the law, however, including one that allows lawsuits filed on the grounds that the gun manufacturer or seller knowingly violated state or federal law in how it marketed or sold the product. In April 2016, Superior Court judge Barbara Bellis rejected Remington's request to dismiss the case, saying that the law "does not prevent lawyers for the families of Sandy Hook victims from arguing that the AR-15 semi-automatic rifle is a military weapon and should not have been sold to civilians."

In October 2016, Judge Bellis heard the case of *Soto v. Bushmaster* and issued her ruling. She declared that the case hinged not on the marketing but on whether the gun manufacturer could have knowledge that the user of its product would misuse it. According to her ruling, the 2005 law prohibits suits brought "for the harm solely caused by the criminal or unlawful misuse of firearm products or ammunition products by others when the product functioned as designed and intended." She dismissed the case, but the plaintiffs appealed. In March 2019, a divided Connecticut Supreme Court upheld the appeal, writing that the plaintiffs are "entitled to have the opportunity to prove their wrongful marketing allegations."

In turn, Remington filed *Remington Arms Co. v. Soto*, an appeal to the U.S. Supreme Court to dismiss the case. The National Rifle Association (NRA), twenty-two House members, ten states, and other gun rights groups filed legal briefs in support of Remington. In its filing with the Court, Remington argued that if the lawsuit were allowed to proceed, it could put gun manufacturers "out of business by unlimited and uncertain liability for criminal misuse of their products." It rejected arguments by the Sandy Hook families that "the illegal marketing proximately caused their injuries, which arise from the terror, pain and suffering, and death of the victims of the Sandy Hook Elementary School shooting."

SUPREME COURT RULES FOR SANDY HOOK FAMILIES

On November 12, 2019, the U.S. Supreme Court ruled in *Remington Arms v. Soto*, denying the request to hear Remington's appeal to review the Connecticut Supreme Court's decision. That ruling would allow the lawsuit against Remington to move forward. The justices made no comments on the case.

Sandy Hook families celebrated the decision. "The families are grateful that the Supreme Court upheld precedent and denied Remington's latest attempt to avoid accountability," said Josh Koskoff, the attorney representing the plaintiffs. "We are ready to resume discovery and proceed towards trial in order to shed light on Remington's profit-driven strategy to expand the AR-15 market and court high-risk users at the expense of Americans' safety," Koskoff added. "We're glad to see the case move forward," said Neil Heslin and Scarlett Lewis, whose son was killed at Sandy Hook. In response to those who felt the case was politically motivated, Heslin and Lewis said, "It's solely and strictly about the marketing of Remington products. Gun control is really not what the lawsuit is about. It's about the marketing and advertising, accountability, and responsibility."

Gun rights organizations slammed the decision. "Lawsuits that deflect attention away from mental illness and criminals in order to blame inanimate objects won't reduce violent crime or make anyone safer," said Jason Ouimet, executive director of the National Rifle Association (NRA) Institute for Legislative Action. "The firearm on which citizens and first responders rely isn't the actual problem; the sociopath who steals and misuses a firearm against innocent people is the real problem," Ouimet said.

After the Supreme Court's ruling, the case could move into the pretrial discovery phase, where the plaintiffs and defendants exchange information. Lawyers representing the Sandy Hook families requested internal documents from Remington, including market research, e-mails, and other communications materials on the company's marketing strategy. "We'll want to ask questions to find out what was behind the decision-making for the marketing that was so aggressive and reckless," said Koskoff. Judge Bellis announced in December 2019 that the case would go to trial in September 2021.

The case will be closely watched across the country by others challenging the 2005 gun manufacturer shield law. At the time the Supreme Court chose not to hear Remington's appeal, many lawsuits were working their way through the courts but few had gone to trial. "Gun manufacturers throughout the country should be on notice that they'll need to answer for their reckless business practices in the courts," said Eric Tirschwell, managing director of litigation and national enforcement policy for Everytown Law, a firm focused on gun safety. "This reaffirms that the gun industry is not above the law."

Congress, White House Respond to Mass Shootings

According to the Gun Violence Archive, since Sandy Hook, more than 2,000 mass shootings took place in the United States (any incident where at least four people other than the perpetrator are shot), with 417 of those occurring in 2019. These included one of the deadliest mass shootings in U.S. history, which took place on August 3, 2019, at an El Paso, Texas, Walmart and left twenty-two people dead, as well as the May 31 attack at a Virginia Beach government building where twelve were killed. Each incident renewed calls for Congress to act either to pass legislation to protect the rights of gun owners or limit gun ownership.

In February 2019, the House passed 240–190 a bill that would require background checks for all commercial gun sales, including sales online or at gun shows. Democrats said that shifting public attitudes in favor of background checks along with growing youth activism for gun safety regulations since the shooting at a Parkland, Florida, high school in February 2018 pushed lawmakers to pass the legislation. "Every day, there's a group of young people up here campaigning for expansion of background checks," said Rep. Mike Thompson, D-Calif. Some Republicans, however, said that the legislation considered in the House would threaten the rights of gun owners and have little to no impact on mass shootings. "It's one more step towards federalized gun registration and ultimately gun confiscation," said Rep. Steve Scalise, R-La., who was shot at a congressional baseball practice in 2017. According to a September NPR/PBS NewsHour/Marist Poll, 55 percent of adults found it important to control gun violence, while only 39 percent felt it was more important to protect gun rights. Eighty-three percent said Congress should require background checks for gun purchases at gun shows and other private sales; only 14 percent disagreed with such legislation.

The day after passing the background check bill, on February 28, the House passed a second gun control measure. Dubbed the "Charleston loophole" bill, it would close a gap in the background check system that enables some firearms to be transferred by gun dealers to the purchaser before a background check is complete. Supporters argued that such a regulation could have stopped Dylann Roof from buying the gun he used to kill nine people in 2015 at the Mother Emanuel Church in Charleston, South Carolina. The bill passed, 228–198. "Closing this Charleston loophole is a common sense and pragmatic solution with bipartisan support," said Rep. Joe Cunningham, D-S.C. "We as elected officials have a duty to right the wrong because nothing begets nothing and if we change nothing then nothing at all will change," he added. Neither bill was considered on the Senate floor.

Without action in the Senate, the Trump administration worked to enact gun control provisions. This included a ban on bump stocks, attachments that allow semiautomatic weapons to fire like automatic weapons. The Department of Justice issued the rule in December 2018, giving owners ninety days either to destroy or turn in the attachments before the ban officially went into effect in March 2019. The rule was challenged by gun rights groups, but the Supreme Court denied a request to block the bump stock ban.

President Donald Trump also endorsed so-called "red flag laws" that allow law enforcement or family members to request that a temporary court order be issued to immediately remove guns from an individual who is deemed a danger to themselves or others. "We must make sure that those judged to pose a grave risk to public safety do not have access to firearms, and that if they do, those firearms can be taken through rapid due process," the president said. "That is why I have called for red-flag laws, also known as extreme-risk protection orders." The laws are in use in seventeen states and the District of Columbia. Despite support for such laws among both parties in Congress and the public, a red flag law was not passed by either chamber in 2019.

—Heather Kerrigan

Following are excerpts from the Brief in Opposition and Reply for Petitioners in the case of Remington Arms Co. v. Soto, *submitted by Sandy Hook victims' families on October 4, 2019, and Remington on October 18, 2019, respectively.*

Sandy Hook Families Submit Brief to Supreme Court on Remington Case

O c t o b e r   4 ,   2 0 1 9

[Footnotes and in-text citations have been omitted.]

IN THE SUPREME COURT OF THE UNITED STATES

No. 19-168

Remington Arms Co., LLC,
et al., Petitioners,

v.

Donna L. Soto, Administratrix
of the Estate of Victoria L. Soto,
et al., Respondents

**On Petition for a Writ of
Certiorari to the Supreme
Court of Connecticut**

BRIEF IN OPPOSITION

[Names and addresses of respondents have been omitted.]

QUESTION PRESENTED

Respondents, who are plaintiffs below, allege that petitioners violated the Connecticut Unfair Trade Practices Act (CUTPA) when they knowingly marketed and promoted the Bushmaster XM15-E2S rifle for use in assaults against human beings. Respondents allege that the illegal marketing proximately caused their injuries, which arise from the terror, pain and suffering, and death of the victims of the Sandy Hook Elementary School shooting.

The Protection of Lawful Commerce in Arms Act preempts certain civil actions against manufacturers and sellers of firearms and ammunition. But it expressly does not prohibit "action[s] in which a manufacturer or seller of a [firearm] knowingly violated a State or Federal statute applicable to the sale or marketing of the product."

The question presented is whether the Connecticut Supreme Court erred in determining that respondents' claims under CUTPA constitute, within the meaning of Section 7903(5)(A)(iii), a violation of "a State * * * statute applicable to the sale or marketing" of the XM15-E2S.

[The tables of contents and authorities have been omitted.]

INTRODUCTION

Respondents are administrators of the estates—in many cases the parents—of children and teachers slaughtered at Sandy Hook Elementary School in 2014. The Sandy Hook victims were slain in a commando-style assault on the school. Their killer's weapon of choice was a Bushmaster XM15-E2S rifle, manufactured and marketed by petitioners. The XM15-E2S was designed for military combat, specifically to inflict maximum lethal harm on the enemy. Petitioners' marketing emphasized precisely those characteristics of the firearm. In words and images, petitioners touted the XM15-E2S as a combat-tested weapon that would bestow the power to "perform under pressure" and "single-handedly" conquer "forces of opposition."

Following the massacre at Sandy Hook, respondents sued petitioners in Connecticut state court under the Connecticut Unfair Trade Practices Act (CUTPA). As narrowed by the Connecticut Supreme Court, the gravamen of their claim is that petitioners chose to market the assaultive qualities, military uses, and lethality of the XM15-E2S, and that this advertising focus inspired the killer's actions and encouraged him to choose a weapon that would maximize the mayhem he could inflict.

Petitioners filed a motion to strike on the ground that respondents' claims were preempted by the Protection of Lawful Commerce in Arms Act (PLCAA), 15 U.S.C. 7902(a), which generally preempts state claims against firearms manufacturers based on alleged misuse of a firearm by third parties. In rejecting that threshold motion, the Connecticut Supreme Court held that respondents had adequately pled a claim falling within the PLCAA's express statutory exemption, which covers "action[s] in which a manufacturer or seller of a qualified product knowingly violated a State or Federal Statute applicable to the sale or marketing of the product." The court did not, however, decide the ultimate question of the PLCAA's applicability, which will depend on whether respondents prove that petitioners knowingly violated CUTPA and whether the challenged conduct proximately caused the harms respondents allege. The case has been remanded for discovery and further proceedings.

The Connecticut Supreme Court's interlocutory decision is not within this Court's certiorari jurisdiction under 28 U.S.C. 1257(a). Nor does it present a question worthy of this Court's review. Petitioners' claim of a conflict with federal court of appeals decisions is contrived. The Connecticut Supreme Court's carefully reasoned decision is faithful to the text, structure, and purposes of the PLCAA. And petitioners' assertion that the decision will unleash a flood of litigation is groundless hyperbole. Certiorari should be denied.

STATEMENT OF THE CASE

1. On December 14, 2012, Adam Lanza used a Bushmaster XM15-E2S rifle to shoot his way into Sandy Hook Elementary School in Connecticut and take the lives of 20 young children and six adults. Upon entering the school, the shooter first deployed the XM15-E2S to kill two school staff members and wound two others. He next entered a first-grade classroom, where he fatally shot 15 children and two adults. He then moved to another first-grade classroom, where he fatally shot five children and two adults. In the second classroom, nine children were able to escape only when he paused to reload. The assault took less than five minutes.

2. The Protection of Lawful Commerce in Arms Act bars certain suits against gun manufacturers and sellers. The PLCAA provides that "[a] qualified civil liability action may not be brought in any Federal or State court," and defines a "qualified civil liability action" as "a civil action * * * brought by any person against a manufacturer or seller of a qualified product, or a trade association, for damages, punitive damages, injunctive or declaratory relief, abatement, restitution, fines, or penalties, or other relief, resulting from the criminal or unlawful misuse of a qualified product by the person or a third party." The XM15-E2S is a "qualified product" within the meaning of the PLCAA.

But the PLCAA does not shield all conduct of gun manufacturers and sellers. As relevant here, Section 7903(5)(A)(iii) excludes from the scope of a preempted "qualified civil liability action" any "action in which a manufacturer or seller of a qualified product knowingly violated a State or Federal statute applicable to the sale or marketing of the product, and the violation was a proximate cause of the harm for which relief is sought." That provision has been referred to as the "predicate exception" because it allows lawsuits that are predicated on violations of other statutes.

3. In 2014, respondents filed suit in Connecticut state court against petitioners, the makers and marketers of the XM15-E2S used at Sandy Hook Elementary School.

Respondents' complaint alleges that petitioners violated the Connecticut Unfair Trade Practices Act, which confers a right of action for personal-injury damages on any person harmed by "unfair methods of competition and unfair or deceptive acts or practices in the conduct of any trade or commerce." The complaint alleges that petitioners' unlawful marketing of the XM15-E2S contributed to the deaths of the Sandy Hook victims by inspiring the shooter's conduct and by causing him to select a particularly deadly weapon for his attack.

As the complaint explains, petitioners chose to market the XM15-E2S as a highly lethal weapon designed for purposes that are illegal—namely, killing other human beings. For example, petitioners published promotional materials that promised "military-proven performance" for a "mission-adaptable" shooter in need of the "ultimate combat weapons system." One Bushmaster product catalogue showed soldiers moving on patrol through the jungle, armed with Bushmaster rifles, and stated that "[w]hen you need to perform under pressure, Bushmaster delivers." Despite evidence that rifles like the XM15-E2S have become the weapon of choice for mass shooters, petitioners' advertising continued to exploit the fantasy of an all-conquering lone gunman, proclaiming: "Forces of opposition, bow down. You are single-handedly outnumbered." Petitioners reinforced those messages by specifying in advertisements that high-capacity 30-round magazines are "standard" equipment on the XM15- E2S; by contrast, petitioners' hunting and competition rifles are sold with 5- or 10-round magazines.

The complaint alleges that petitioners' illegal marketing motivated the shooter's attack and caused him to choose the XM15-E2S rather than another weapon to carry it out. The shooter was obsessed with the military and had expressed a desire to join the elite Army Rangers unit. But when he turned eighteen, he did not enlist; rather, he acquired the XM15-E2S, which his mother had purchased for him. On the day of the Sandy Hook Elementary School attack, he handpicked the XM15-E2S from a home arsenal that included assorted other firearms and swords. The complaint alleges that he chose the XM15-E2S "for its military and assaultive qualities, * * * in particular its efficiency in inflicting mass casualties," and "because of its marketed association with the military."

4. a. The Connecticut trial court determined that the PLCAA does not bar respondents' CUTPA claims. In reaching that conclusion, the court relied on the Second Circuit's interpretation of the predicate exception in *City of New York v. Beretta USA Corp.*, 524 F.3d 384 (2d Cir. 2008). Because CUTPA had been applied to the sale or marketing of firearms in the past, it could fall within the predicate exception under the Second Circuit's analysis, which the Connecticut court adopted. The court concluded, however, that respondents lacked standing to bring CUTPA claims under state law because they had not alleged "at least some business relationship with the defendant[s]."

b. The Connecticut Supreme Court reversed as to state-law standing but agreed with the lower court's ruling that this action is not categorically barred under the PLCAA. The court ruled that respondents had standing to bring their particular CUTPA claims because of the direct relationship between the alleged wrongdoing and respondents' injuries. ("If the defendants' marketing materials did in fact inspire or intensify the massacre, then there are no more direct victims than these plaintiffs."). The court was clear that its decision in that regard was limited to the facts before it: "We need not decide today whether there are other contexts or situations in which parties who do not share a consumer, commercial, or competitor relationship with an alleged wrongdoer may be barred, for prudential or policy reasons, from bringing a CUTPA action." The court also ruled that respondents' CUTPA claims surmounted a variety of other state-law hurdles, including the applicable statute of limitations.

After examining CUTPA in detail and confirming that respondents' claims could proceed under state law, the Connecticut Supreme Court turned to the PLCAA's predicate exception. On that issue, the court agreed with the trial court that the instant suit alleges a violation of "a State or Federal statute applicable to the sale or marketing of the [qualified] product."

First, looking to the statutory text, the Connecticut Supreme Court rejected petitioners' interpretation of "applicable," under which the predicate exception would cover only actions alleging violations of firearm-specific statutes. The court explained that if Congress "had intended to limit the scope of the predicate exception to violations of statutes that are directly, expressly, or exclusively applicable to firearms," then Congress "easily could have used such language, as it has on other occasions." The court noted that CUTPA and other unfair trade practices laws had long been used to govern firearms sales and marketing—that is, those statutes had been "applied" to firearm sales and marketing in the past. The court reasoned that Congress was "presumed to be aware that the wrongful marketing of dangerous items such as firearms for unsafe or illegal purposes traditionally has been and continues to be regulated primarily" through laws like CUTPA "rather than by firearms specific statutes."

Second, the court reviewed Congress's statement of findings and purposes and the legislative history of the PLCAA. The court explained that the PLCAA was designed to protect the ability "of firearms sellers to market their wares legally and responsibly," and to curtail "the rising number of instances in which municipalities and 'anti-gun activists' filed 'junk' or 'frivolous' lawsuits targeting the entire firearms industry." But the court found support in the legislative history for Congress's intent to allow a defendant to "be held liable for violating a statute during the production, distribution, or sale of firearms." . . . And the court drew a stark contrast between the "novel" and "frivolous" suits that the PLCAA was designed to prevent and respondents' suit, in which "the private victims of one specific incident of gun violence seek compensation from the producers and distributors of a single firearm on the basis of alleged misconduct in the specific marketing of that firearm." Throughout its opinion, the court emphasized that its conclusion regarding the predicate exception extended only to the particular CUTPA allegations stated in petitioners' complaint. . . .

Three dissenting justices found respondents' reading of the statutory text "reasonable" and turned to legislative history as an aid in interpreting the predicate exception. The dissent acknowledged that the legislative history is "extensive" and "mixed," but ultimately concluded that "the legislative debate * * * supports an interpretation of predicate statutes as those specifically regulating the sale or marketing of firearms," of which CUTPA was not one.

5. The proceedings below tested only the sufficiency of the pleadings, and, as to the PLCAA, narrowly addressed the meaning of "applicable to the sale or marketing of firearms" in the predicate exception. Accordingly, the Connecticut Supreme Court remanded the case for further proceedings, remarking that it "d[id] not know whether the plaintiffs will be able to prove th[eir] allegations to a jury. Under Connecticut procedure, petitioners retain the right to move for summary judgment. The issues to be decided in such a motion, or at trial, may include the meaning of other aspects of the PLCAA as well as the sufficiency of respondents' CUTPA evidence.

ARGUMENT

I. This Court Lacks Jurisdiction.

A. This Court has jurisdiction to review only "[f]inal judgments or decrees rendered by the highest court of a State." Under that rule, "[t]o be reviewable * * * a state-court judgment must be * * * final as an effective determination of the litigation and not of merely interlocutory or intermediate steps therein."

The Connecticut Supreme Court's interlocutory decision remanding the case for further proceedings is not "final" under Section 1257(a). That court reviewed a ruling on petitioners' motion to strike, affirmed the trial court's judgment in part and reversed it in part, and "remanded for further proceedings according to law." Although those "further proceedings" may eventually lead to a final judgment reviewable in this Court, the decision below is not a final judgment because it neither finally accepts nor finally rejects petitioners' PLCAA defense. This Court has never understood Section 1257(a) to authorize review of such intermediate rulings, and this is surely not the case in which to rewrite the rules governing the Court's jurisdiction.

B. Petitioners acknowledge the interlocutory posture of the case but nonetheless urge this Court to go out of its way to grant review. In general, Section 1257 "preclude[s] reviewability * * * where anything further remains to be determined by a State court," no matter "how dissociated" from the federal issue presented to this Court. The Court has treated interlocutory state-court decisions as final for jurisdictional purposes only in exceptional circumstances that are not remotely presented here.

The four exceptions to the usual rule that this Court cannot review a state high court's decision remanding for further proceedings are described in *Cox Broadcasting Corp. v. Cohn*. Petitioners do not contend that the first three *Cox* exceptions apply. Nor does the fourth. That exception is implicated only "where [1] the federal issue has been finally decided in the state courts [2] with further proceedings pending in which the party seeking review * * * might prevail on the merits on nonfederal grounds, thus rendering unnecessary review of the federal issue by this Court, * * * [3] reversal of the state court on the federal issue would be preclusive of any further litigation," and [4] "a refusal immediately to review the state court decision might seriously erode federal policy." The decision below fails at least the first and fourth prongs of that exception. . . .

II. The Decision Below Does Not Warrant This Court's Review.

The Connecticut statute at issue in this case forbids marketing products in a way that promotes their criminal misuse. . . . Respondents allege that petitioners knowingly violated that statute. And the Connecticut Supreme Court ruled that the statute is, under the specific facts here, "applicable" to the marketing of the XM15-E2S used in the Sandy Hook mass shooting, within the meaning of the PLCAA's predicate exception. That narrow ruling is in line with every other court to have addressed the PLCAA, and it is correct on the merits. Accordingly, even if this Court had jurisdiction to decide this case, review would be unwarranted. . . .

[Additional information in the argument that Remington's request does not require review has been omitted.]

C. The Interlocutory Decision Below Will Not Have The Broad Effects That Petitioners Claim.

Petitioners and their amici assert that this Court's immediate review is necessary to avoid "a flood of lawsuits across the country that will wreak ruin on the entire firearms industry." Those assertions about the consequences of the decision below are hyperbolic in the extreme.

By its plain terms, the PLCAA does not foreclose any and all liability for the firearms industry. Rather, in creating a predicate exception to preemption, Congress contemplated that a very limited set of suits could proceed against manufacturers and sellers. The Connecticut Supreme Court responsibly followed the line that Congress itself drew—and so there is no reason for concern that any litigation will proceed that Congress chose to bar.

Indeed, the decision below is quite narrow. The Connecticut Supreme Court declined to adopt a rule under which even every CUTPA claim would satisfy the predicate exception. Instead, the court confined its ruling to the claims before it, which "allege only that one specific family of firearms sellers advertised one particular line of assault weapons in a uniquely unscrupulous manner, promoting their suitability for illegal, offensive assaults"—exactly "th[e] sort of specific, narrowly framed wrongful marketing claim * * * that Congress did not intend to immunize." . . .

Petitioners are also wrong to suggest that the decision below will expose gun manufacturers and sellers to "claims under broad unfair trade practices laws existing in all 50 states." In fact, most other States' consumer protection laws would not permit suit by a victim of gun violence. Even if such a suit were possible, claims brought under other state laws also would have to surmount a host of potential state-law impediments, including statutes of limitations, exclusivity provisions, and statutory carve-outs (such as CUTPA's exemption provision, see Pet. App. 215a). And, as the present case illustrates, the PLCAA itself puts yet other barriers in the way of such suits, including the requirement under the predicate exception that a statutory violation be knowing and that such a violation be "a proximate cause of the harm for which relief is sought."

Accordingly, petitioners' claims of industry-ending liability are baseless. . . .

CONCLUSION

The petition for a writ of certiorari should be denied.

[The respondents' names and addresses have been omitted.]

SOURCE: Supreme Court of the United States. *Remington Arms Co. v. Soto.* Brief in Opposition. https://www.supremecourt.gov/DocketPDF/19/19-168/118198/20191004151558181_19-168BriefIn Opposition.pdf.

Remington Asks Supreme Court to Review Request to End Lawsuit

October 18, 2019

[Footnotes and in-text citations have been omitted.]

IN THE SUPREME COURT OF THE UNITED STATES

No. 19-168

Remington Arms Co., LLC,
et al., Petitioners,

v.

Donna L. Soto, Administratrix
of the Estate of Victoria L. Soto,
et al., Respondents

On Petition for a Writ of
Certiorari to the Supreme
Court of Connecticut

REPLY FOR PETITIONERS

[Names and addresses of petitioners and a statement on corporate disclosure, along with the tables of contents and authorities, have been omitted.]

REPLY FOR PETITIONERS

Respondents ignore that the Connecticut Supreme Court acknowledged lower courts are "divided" due to "the difficulties that the federal courts have faced in attempting to distill a clear rule or guiding principle from the predicate exception" to the Protection of Lawful Commerce in Arms Act ("PLCAA"). The decision below exacerbated this conflict. Although federal courts of appeals previously had faced difficulties, they nevertheless uniformly rejected the "capable of being applied" test adopted below.

Unsurprisingly, this wrong test led to the wrong result. Respondents' lawsuit is exactly the kind of case arising from a criminal's misuse of a firearm that "may not be brought in any Federal or State Court" under the PLCAA. Respondents use a general deceptive trade practices statute to implausibly claim that a firearms manufacturer's advertising caused a criminal's mass shooting. And that claim is even more implausible here, where the shooter (1) did not even purchase the gun, and (2) had "severe and deteriorating internalized mental health problems."

As experts predicted, the ruling below is already being used as a roadmap to evade the PLCAA. This Court's review is needed now to avoid costly litigation against the firearms industry that "may not be brought" in any court.

A.   The Decision Below Exacerbates An Acknowledged Division of Authority

1. The sharply split 4–3 decision below recognized that lower courts are "divided" and have had "difficulties *** distill[ing] a clear rule or guiding principle from the predicate exception." Yet respondents—who champion that decision—wrongly pretend that this conflict is "contrived."

Exacerbating the preexisting confusion, the Connecticut Supreme Court adopted the broadest possible reading of the PLCAA's predicate exception: the "capable of being applied" test. The Second Circuit rejected this test precisely because it "leads to a far too-broad reading" that "would allow the predicate exception to swallow the statute." The Ninth Circuit also rejected this test as "too broad" in light of the predicate exception's enumerated examples.

2. Respondents incorrectly portray the decision below as a "quite narrow" one, "confined *** to the claims before it," and under which not "even every *CUTPA* claim would satisfy the predicate exception."

The Connecticut Supreme Court's own articulation of its holding refutes this: "*CUPTA qualifies as a predicate statute.*" And the decision below adopted "the plaintiff's interpretation of the statutory language"—the "capable of being applied" test. The court admitted this was a "*broad* reading" that covers "state consumer protection laws."

Neither respondents nor the court below can insulate that decision from review by disingenuously asserting that its broad statutory interpretation concerned only "one specific family of firearms sellers" and "one particular line" of firearms. Tellingly, respondents spend pages defending the broad "capable of being applied" test, despite their efforts elsewhere to argue that the court never even adopted it.

The "capable of being applied test"—which was rejected by the Second and Ninth Circuits—has been given new vigor. This further entrenches confusion over whether this sweeping test or a firearm-specific-statute test that is in line with the PLCAA's plain language and expressed purpose should be followed.

3. The outcome of the question presented would have been different in the Ninth Circuit.

Ileto expressly declined to construe the predicate exception to "cover[] all state statutes that *could be applied* to the sale or marketing of firearms." Instead, it concluded that "Congress had in mind *only* *** statutes that regulate manufacturing, importing, selling, marketing, and using *firearms* or that regulate the *firearms industry*." General deceptive trade practices statutes fall within neither category, as they do not regulate firearms specifically. This tracks Judge Berzon's appraisal that the Ninth Circuit held the predicate exception is limited to "firearm-specific" laws. If Judge Berzon misunderstood Judges Graber and Reinhardt's majority holding, that only *reinforces* the lower court's confusion.

Ileto also held that statutes capable of "judicial evolution" do not qualify as predicate statutes. Even the Connecticut Supreme Court has recognized that CUTPA's standards are "elusive" and "flexible"—the hallmarks of a statute permitting judicial evolution.

Similarly, the public nuisance statute that *Ileto* held was not a predicate statute would qualify under the decision below. Just as CUTPA applies to "the conduct of any trade or commerce," California's public nuisance statute has "been applied" to the conduct of those engaged in commerce.

B. The Decision Below is Wrong

1. Respondents fail to demonstrate that the "capable of being applied" test adopted below is supported by the PLCAA's statutory text and structure. And they offer no response to the Second Circuit's criticism that this broad test "would allow the predicate exception to swallow the statute."

The PLCAA's statutory structure, as exemplified by the predicate exception's enumerated examples, shows that Congress used "applicable" to encompass statutes regulating only firearms specifically. "'Just as Congress' choice of words is presumed to be deliberate' and deserving of judicial respect, 'so too are its structural choices.'"

Respondents ignore the "well-worn" canon *noscitur a sociis*—cited by petitioners and the dissent below. Under this canon, "a word is known by the company it keeps—to 'avoid ascribing to one word a meaning so broad that it is inconsistent with its accompanying words, thus giving unintended breadth to the Acts of Congress." So "'[a] word is given more precise content by the neighboring words with which it is associated.'"

Here, the predicate exception's enumerated examples apply specifically to firearms, confirming "both the presence of company that suggests limitation and the absence of company that suggests breadth." Respondents contend that the first example is not firearm-specific, positing that it encompasses *all* "record-keeping requirements." But they omit the rest of the statutory phrase: "any record required to be kept under Federal or State law *with respect to the qualified product*." "[Q]ualified product" means "firearm" or "ammunition."

Respondents similarly err by claiming that the examples are just "belt-and-suspenders." This argument assumes the contested premise (the broadest possible interpretation of the predicate exception). And it is wholly implausible. If Congress meant for the word "applicable" to broadly encompass all laws possibly capable of being applied to firearms, Congress would not have needed to enumerate much *narrower* examples specific to firearms. That is precisely why the Ninth Circuit explained "there would be no need to list examples at all" if Congress had created a "capable of being applied" test. . . .

2. Respondents also cannot reconcile their interpretation with Congress's manifest policy to shield the firearms industry from abusive lawsuits based on the criminal acts of third parties.

First, respondents argue that the PLCAA was designed only to stop "common law" claims. Respondents have no answer, though, to the fact that such an atextual limitation would render (1) much of Congress's definition of covered actions inoperative and (2) other exceptions superfluous. Moreover, a statute like CUTPA that proscribes "unfair or deceptive" conduct, is broader than a common-law tort. Accordingly, as the claims here illustrate, plaintiffs can easily use these statutes to evoke exotic theories based on "judicial evolution."

Second, both respondents and the decision below note that CUTPA has previously been used in litigation against the firearms industry. But even if that were true, the PLCAA's coverage cannot turn on this. As its text confirms, the PLCAA was designed to curb abuses of *existing* law—not just hypothetical future ones. That is why the statute required covered, then-pending lawsuits to be "immediately dismissed."

3. Finally, should this Court turn to legislative history, lawsuits prompting the PLCAA relied on legal theories and causes of action similar to the claim here. Legislators, regardless of whether they supported or opposed the PLCAA, agreed that marketing statutes would not satisfy the predicate exception. . . .

C.   This Court Has Jurisdiction To Review The Decision Below, And The PLCAA's Protections Would Be Eviscerated Without Review Now

Respondents incorrectly suggest that this Court lacks jurisdiction. Respondents' position would lead to the untenable consequence that this Court could *never* review an erroneous state court decision allowing a case to go to trial that "may not be brought" in the first place under the PLCAA.

The Court plainly has jurisdiction under the fourth category of cases recognized by *Cox Broadcasting Corp v. Cohn*, and its progeny. And the Court should grant review now, as the PLCAA's protections against costly litigation will be lost if this suit proceeds any further. The PLCAA is not a factual defense to be applied only after a case is tried to conclusion.

1.a. Under the first prong of the relevant *Cox* test, the federal issue "has been finally decided in the state court[]." The Connecticut Supreme Court held that "CUPTA qualifies as a predicate statute" under the PLCAA. It does not matter that the federal issue may turn on the meaning of a "*single word*." . . .

b. Under the fourth prong of the relevant *Cox* test, delay in reviewing this important issue would "seriously erode federal policy." . . .

2. This Court's review of this exceptionally important federal policy is needed now. Respondents ignore the numerous experts who predicted that the decision below would be used as a roadmap to evade the PLCAA. Instead, respondents level the baseless charge that petitioners are being "hyperbolic in the extreme." But the experts have already been

proven right. Less than one month ago, the District of Nevada relied on the decision below to conclude that *Nevada's* Deceptive Trade Practices Act satisfies the PLCAA's predicate exception. Similar cases have been filed or revived around the country.

This Court's review is needed now to resolve an acknowledged division of authority, preserve Congress's protections in the PLCAA, and prevent widespread costly litigation that harms First and Second Amendment rights.

CONCLUSION

The petition for a writ of certiorari should be granted.

[The names and addresses of the petitioners have been omitted.]

Source: Supreme Court of the United States. *Remington Arms Co. v. Soto*. Reply for Petitioners. https://www.supremecourt.gov/DocketPDF/19/19-168/119458/20191018123650970_Remington%20Cert%20Reply.pdf.

OTHER HISTORIC DOCUMENTS OF INTEREST

FROM PREVIOUS *HISTORIC DOCUMENTS*

Responses to the Political and Humanitarian Crisis in Haiti

OCTOBER 9 AND 17, NOVEMBER 1, AND DECEMBER 6, 2019,
AND JANUARY 12, 2020

In 2019, Haiti experienced a weakening economy, a major corruption scandal involving President Jovenel Moïse, and a period of political instability that left the country without a functioning government for nearly one year. Anger over these developments led to months of demonstrations that effectively shut down public services and hampered aid delivery, exacerbating a humanitarian crisis in a country still reeling from a deadly 2016 hurricane. During this time, the United Nations (UN) launched a new mission in Haiti to help bring political stability. The UN also monitored the protests and police response to them, in addition to boosting aid efforts to reach a growing number of food-insecure Haitians.

A Poor Economy Weakens

According to the World Bank Group, Haiti is the poorest country in the western hemisphere. Government corruption and instability, weak infrastructure, and high vulnerability to natural disasters have hampered the country's ability to improve its economy. These factors have also contributed to a worsening financial situation, which included a record high inflation rate of 17 percent and government deficit of $450 million in 2019. (Haiti's external debt was forgiven after the 2010 earthquake but has since grown to about $2.7 billion.) The value of Haitian currency (the gourde) has also dropped dramatically. In 2014, the exchange rate was roughly forty gourdes to one U.S. dollar, but by the end of 2019, it cost more than ninety-six gourdes to buy one U.S. dollar. At the same time, the cost of basic goods has risen, with some observers estimating prices have doubled since 2004. Adding to these challenges, Haiti experiences periodic blackouts and fuel shortages due to the government's inability to pay fuel suppliers. Access to affordable fuel is crucial due to the country's unreliable electrical grid; gas is needed to run generators that power homes and businesses, in addition to fueling transportation.

Many observers link Haiti's current economic troubles to the conclusion of Venezuela's PetroCaribe program in March 2018. That program allowed Caribbean countries to purchase low-cost oil and defer payments on 40 percent of what they bought for up to twenty-five years, with an interest rate as low as 1 percent. Participating countries, including Haiti, could sell this oil domestically to generate funds for government initiatives, such as investments in infrastructure, hospitals, and public assistance programs. When Venezuela ended PetroCaribe, Haiti had to buy all of its fuel on the more expensive Caribbean and U.S. markets.

Other observers say the roots of the crisis lay in the government's 2017 seizure of a fuel ship after a Haitian company and two others decided to import fuel on their own, rather than work through the government. Officials threatened legal action against the companies, and a few months later Moïse gave the Bureau of Monetization Programs and Development Aid a monopoly over fuel imports. Since then, observers say, the government has mismanaged the bidding process for fuel contracts. The government tried to raise the price of gasoline in July 2018 to help offset Haiti's financial woes but backed down from the proposal after several days of violent protests against the increases. The chaos prompted the resignation of Moïse's first prime minister, Jack Guy Lafontant, who faced a vote of no confidence in parliament over his alleged mismanagement of the price hike.

In March 2019, the International Monetary Fund (IMF) agreed to give Haiti an interest-free $229 million loan on the condition that the government reduce its deficit, implement social protection programs, and approve a budget. Without a functioning government, Haiti has not been able to receive IMF funds or other offers of international aid.

President Implicated in Embezzlement of State Funds

The slow pace of disaster recovery and a lack of improvements across the country raised questions about where and how the PetroCaribe money was being spent. In November 2017, a Senate anticorruption commission released a report accusing government officials and private businesses of embezzling funds from the program through fraudulent contracts, project overpayments, and other schemes. The report recommended charges be filed against two former prime ministers, several former government ministers, and some private-business owners. The commission's findings, ongoing fuel shortages, and attempted price hikes fed frustrations and antigovernment sentiment among Haitians, which, in the second half of 2018, bubbled over into public demonstrations that remain ongoing. Many protesters call themselves "PetroChallengers."

In October 2018, Moïse announced the Haitian Superior Court of Auditors and Administrative Deputies would investigate the corruption allegations. The court examined the government's management of the PetroCaribe funds between 2008 and 2016, spanning six governments under three different presidents. An initial report on the court's investigation was released in January 2019. It confirmed that roughly $2 billion in PetroCaribe funds had been misappropriated, implicating fifteen former ministers and other government officials in the scandal. Outraged Haitians took to the streets in a major demonstration the following month, effectively shutting down the country for ten days as public transportation halted and schools and businesses closed. The protesters demanded to know where the embezzled funds had gone and called for Moïse's resignation. The president refused to step down, saying he "will not leave the country in the hands of armed gangs and drug traffickers." He also blamed Prime Minister Jean-Henry Céant, successor to Lafontant, for the ongoing economic crisis, claiming he had failed to deliver on promises including new agreements to spur domestic and foreign investment in Haiti.

On May 31, the court of auditors issued a second report. Among the findings, the auditors concluded that Moïse had received approximately $2 million in questionable payments for road rehabilitation projects in 2014 and 2015 through his company Agritrans, with some payments made shortly before he registered as a presidential candidate. (Moïse was elected in November 2016 and took office in February 2017.) In one instance, the auditors found, Haiti's public works ministry issued two contracts to two different companies—one of which was Agritrans—for the exact same road reconstruction project. "For the court, giving a second contract for the same project . . . is nothing less than a scheme to embezzle funds," the auditors wrote. Moïse denied the allegations, telling Haitians during a press conference on June 12, "Your president, whom you voted for, is not guilty of corruption." He said those who had misused state funds would be "brought to justice in a fair, equitable trial without political persecution." The protests escalated sharply following the report's release, with demonstrators setting up roadblocks, burning tires, and throwing stones at buildings and cars. The UN Office of the High Commissioner of Human Rights (OHCHR) later stated that forty-one people were killed and another one hundred injured in this flare of tensions.

In parliament, opposition lawmakers initiated an effort to impeach the president, claiming Moïse had committed "crimes of high treason" and accusing him of corruption, misappropriation of funds, and more than twenty-five constitutional violations. An impeachment vote was held in the Chamber of Deputies (the lower house of parliament) on August 22 but failed by an overwhelming margin. Only 61 of the chamber's 119 deputies were present, and of those, only 3 voted to impeach Moïse.

PRIME MINISTER RESIGNS

While the corruption allegations swirled, Moïse and his supporters struggled to maintain a government. On March 21, 2019, Céant resigned after he was censured by parliament for failing to make any progress to improve the economy and living conditions for Haiti. The country had effectively been without a functional government since then. Jean-Michele Lapin, former minister of culture, was tapped to serve as acting prime minister following Céant's departure. On April 9, Moïse nominated Lapin to assume the office's full responsibilities, but some questioned whether Lapin had enough experience and economic understanding to pull Haiti out of crisis. Some opposition leaders refused to discuss forming a new government with Moïse, regardless of his nominee for prime minister. The Senate ultimately failed three times to vote on Lapin's nomination, his proposed government, and his general policy statement, also known as a political program. (Both the Senate and the Chamber of Deputies must approve nominees for prime minister as well as ratify their proposed government and political program.)

With Lapin's nomination dead, Moïse proposed on July 22 that Fritz William Michel become prime minister. As with Lapin, some opposition members argued that Michel and his proposed cabinet ministers lacked experience, adding that they did not reflect the consensus government Haitians were demanding. Although the Chamber of Deputies accepted Michel and ratified his general policy statement on September 3, the Senate failed at least five times to approve him as prime minister. On two occasions, September 11 and September 23, a group later described by the UN as "opposition militants, some of them armed and abetted by a small number of senators," stormed the Senate chamber and disrupted debate.

PROTESTS SHUT DOWN COUNTRY; POLICE ACCUSED OF EXCESSIVE FORCE

Demonstrations flared again in September as inflation continued to climb and fuel shortages worsened. Thousands of people protested across the capital, Port-au-Prince, and further road blockades, tire fires, looting, and riots caused schools, businesses, and public services to shut down. Protest leaders pledged to keep the country shut down until Moïse resigned and demonstrations continued almost daily through mid-October. According to OHCHR, at least forty-two people died and eighty-six were injured during this period of demonstrations.

Around this time, several reports surfaced accusing the Haitian National Police of using excessive force against protesters. In early October, Haiti's national Network for the Defense of Human Rights accused the police of using repressive tactics and called for an investigation into their efforts to dispel demonstrators. A separate report by Amnesty International alleged police used live ammunition against protesters who were unarmed or had "less-lethal ammunition," in addition to firing tear gas at peaceful protesters and beating others. On November 1, OHCHR said that "[r]eports indicate[d] that security forces were responsible" for nineteen of the forty-two deaths recorded between mid-September and mid-October, including at least one journalist. OHCHR also expressed concerns about "the impact that the closure of judicial institutions and other public institutions is having in the country," citing an "alarmingly high number of detainees in prolonged pre-trial detention" as one example.

Amid the chaos, Moïse delivered a national address to Haitians on September 25. Declaring Haiti at a "political crossroads," he called for Haitians to "gather our courage" and "cast aside our divisions." He proposed conducting a national dialogue with opposition groups and forming a unity government. "If you don't want to do this for yourselves, let's do it for Haiti," he said. Moïse added that the disruption and destruction caused by the protests were not allowing the government to collect the revenue it needs to function; however, he said, he "will not respond to violence with violence."

UN Swaps Peacekeeping for Political Mission

Meanwhile, the UN ended its fifteen-year peacekeeping mission in Haiti, replacing it with a new, integrated office with a political mission designed to "strengthen political stability and good governance in Haiti through support of an inclusive national dialogue." The peacekeeping mission, known as the United Nations Mission for Justice Support in Haiti (MINUJUSTH), concluded on October 15, with the new United Nations Integrated Office in Haiti (BINUH), initiating operations on October 16. BINUH was led by a special representative and was charged with assisting Haiti to plan elections, provide human rights training to the National Police, combat gang violence, ensure compliance with international human rights obligations, and strengthen its justice system. In a statement on October 17, UN secretary-general António Guterres reaffirmed "the continuous commitment of the United Nations to support the Haitian people on their path to peace and development, through a new partnership." He also expressed concern about "the current political crisis and its adverse impact on the security situation and the lives of Haitians," and he called for "all Haitian stakeholders to engage in genuine dialogue and prevent a further escalation in violence that threatens to reverse stability gains."

Various UN officials noted the political instability and unrest that were contributing to the humanitarian crisis in Haiti. "Since the beginning of the school year in September, most children across Haiti have been unable to go to school," said an OHCHR spokesperson. "Roadblocks and violence have meant that people, particularly in regions outside the capital, have had serious difficulty accessing food, drinking water, medicine and fuel. The health sector has been hit particularly hard, with shortages of electricity, fuel, supplies, and the inability of many medical personnel to reach their places of work." The UN's ability to distribute aid was also affected, officials said, though the organization reported that several program offices had been able to deliver some medical supplies, fuel, and food aid to certain areas in mid-October. On December 6, the World Food Programme announced it was "scaling up" operations to provide emergency food assistance to 700,000 Haitians and issued an appeal for the international community to contribute $62 million to support its efforts. Roughly 3.7 million Haitians needed "urgent food assistance," it said, with about 1 million people "suffering severe hunger."

LEGISLATIVE TERMS EXPIRE

On January 13, 2020, the terms of one-third of Haitian senators, the entire Chamber of Deputies, and many local officials expired. Haiti was due to hold elections for these positions in October 2019, but the vote was cancelled due to the political crisis and parliament's inability to approve the required electoral law for the vote. With only ten senators remaining, Moïse declared the end of Haiti's Fiftieth Parliament, marking the fourth time the country would be governed without a sitting legislature. Moïse now had the ability to rule by decree until the end of his term in 2022. The president tweeted that this situation represents "a historic opportunity" to "come together to initiate the reforms" that will transform Haiti into a "servant state" and end the "ongoing crisis undermining the future of this country."

—Linda Grimm

Following is a report submitted by UN secretary-general António Guterres to the Security Council on October 9, 2019, on the political, humanitarian, and security situation in Haiti, as well as benchmarks for the UN's new political mission; a statement by Guterres on October 17, 2019, on the UN's new mission and the situation in Haiti; a press briefing conducted by the UN Office of the High Commissioner for Human Rights on November 1, 2019, on the country's humanitarian crisis; a press release issued by the World Food Programme on December 6, 2019, announcing an increase in food assistance to Haiti; and a tweet posted by President Jovenel Moïse on January 12, 2020, on opportunities for political change.

DOCUMENT

UN Secretary-General's Report on the Situation in Haiti

October 9, 2019

[I. Introduction has been omitted.]

II. Significant developments

A. Political situation and related security developments

The reporting period was characterized by protracted, and to date unsuccessful, negotiations on the confirmation of a new government, a failed attempt to impeach the President of Haiti, Jovenel Moïse, in the Lower Chamber of Parliament, and a looming constitutional crisis caused by the failure to organize elections in time to renew the current legislature, whose term expires on 13 January 2020. Against this backdrop of political crisis, the security situation remained volatile, as the opposition organized several violent actions during the month of September and armed criminal gangs continued to pose a threat to public order.

Haiti has remained without a functional government since the resignation on 21 March 2019 of Mr. Moïse's second Prime Minister, Jean-Henry Céant, following his censure by the Lower Chamber of Parliament. On 22 July, after three failed attempts by the Senate to hold the vote on the general policy statement of the proposed government to be led by his third appointed Prime Minister, Jean-Michel Lapin, Mr. Moïse announced the nomination of a fourth Prime Minister, Fritz William Michel. . . . Whereas the Lower Chamber endorsed the general policy statement of Prime Minister-designate Mr. Michel, on 3 September, consultations between the Executive and the Senate on the confirmation of this fourth government have yet to conclude. On 11 and 23 September, attempts by the Senate to consider the proposed government degenerated into mayhem as opposition militants, some of them armed and abetted by a small number of senators, entered the Senate chamber, preventing the session from taking place. On the latter occasion, two civilians were injured after a senator from the leading Parti Haïtien Tèt Kale discharged his personal weapon in front of Parliament. Subsequent allegations of corruption levied against Mr. Michel appeared to have lessened the prospects of his confirmation, and on 25 September, in an address to the nation, Mr. Moïse proposed the formation of a government of national unity to overcome the current impasse. Several opposition leaders rejected the President's proposal and continued to call for protests, almost on a daily basis, to demand his resignation. On 4 October, thousands of protesters marched in the streets of Port-au-Prince, at least 2,000 of whom—including a number of opposition parliamentarians—gathered in front of MINUJUSTH headquarters in Tabarre (West Department). A delegation of officials among the protesters delivered a letter, addressed to the Secretary-General, to draw his attention to what they described as an explosive situation unfolding in the country.

Honouring a procedural agreement made on 26 June in order to placate the parliamentary opposition and accelerate the process through which a new government would be approved, the Speaker of the Lower Chamber, Gary Bodeau, allowed the body to hold a debate on the motion to impeach Mr. Moïse for "having violated at least 25 articles of the Constitution", and on the basis of allegations of corruption and fraud. In a report issued in May, the Superior Court of Audit identified Agritrans, a company led by Mr. Moïse prior to his election, as having been implicated in the alleged mismanagement of PetroCaribe funds. Following two prior sessions dedicated to the debate, on 22 August, the impeachment motion was defeated by a vote of 53 against, 3 in favour, and 5 abstentions. Opposition parliamentarians considered the vote to have been held illegally, given the turnout of Lower Chamber parliamentarians below the two-thirds quorum (80 parliamentarians), which is required by the Constitution to hold a vote on the impeachment of a sitting President.

In August, one year after the emergence of the "PetroChallengers" movement and its call for accountability concerning the alleged mismanagement of funds received by the Haitian State through the PetroCaribe agreement, demonstrations were organized to encourage the Superior Court of Audit to issue a third report on the 23 per cent of authorized projects not covered in its reports of 31 January and 31 May, and to call for a public trial to be held to shed light on the allegations. The movement is also increasingly vocal in demanding the resignation of Mr. Moïse, perceived by many to be an obstacle to the holding of a trial.

Elections to renew the entire Lower Chamber and one third of the Senate were constitutionally mandated to take place by the end of October 2019. Parliament's failure to approve a new electoral law and budget prior to the end of the legislative year on 9 September, together with the absence of political agreement on a new composition of the Provisional Electoral Council, made it materially impossible to hold elections in 2019, as the electoral body would need between five and six months to organize them. With the term of all Lower Chamber parliamentarians and at least a third of Senators ending on 13 January 2020, the likelihood of a constitutional crisis has significantly increased. In the event of its occurrence, it will be paramount to ensure that the parameters within which Mr. Moïse will be allowed to rule by decree until a new parliament is elected and seated are well defined and transparent. . . .

The protracted political crisis and tense security environment continued to have an adverse impact on the country's economy. The national currency (gourde) has lost 37.6 per cent of its value against the United States dollar over the past 12 months, inflation is now estimated at 19.1 per cent, and gross domestic product is projected to have contracted by over 1 per cent during the recently concluded fiscal year. In the agricultural sector, the effect of localized droughts and low rainfall on aggregate crop production was exacerbated by gang members driving farmers away from their productive land. This has added strain on households, which is reflected by an increase in the index of severe food insecurity in rural areas, from 17 percent in 2018 to 49.5 per cent since the end of April 2019. Moreover, the ongoing impasse in the effort to confirm a new government continues to impede the passing of important legislative texts, including the 2018–19 and 2019–20 budget laws, as well as the electoral law. In the absence of a fully functioning government and with no budget approved, several bilateral and multilateral donors, including the International Monetary Fund and the Inter-American Development Bank, continue to withhold budgetary support from Haiti.

Even though the challenges Haiti faces are understood by all actors, there has been no progress towards the holding of an inclusive and comprehensive national dialogue to lead the country out of the current multidimensional crisis. Since the expiration of the mandate of the committee to facilitate an inter-Haitian dialogue in May, no new serious initiatives towards dialogue have been undertaken.

B. Humanitarian situation

The significant decline in agricultural output linked to prolonged periods of drought in the Artibonite and North-East Departments and the continued rise in the price of basic food staples (19 per cent over the past 12 months) have contributed to further worsening of the food security situation in Haiti, including the nutritional status of Haitian children. Some 39,000 children under 5 years of age are projected to suffer from acute malnutrition in 2019. In August, the Central Emergency Relief Fund allocated $5 million from its rapid response window to enable humanitarian actors to respond to the country's urgent food security and nutrition needs. Through the 2019 Humanitarian Response Plan, which, as of 18 September was 21 percent funded ($26.2 million received of $126.2 million required), humanitarian organizations seek to aid the 1.3 million most vulnerable people. . . .

[The following page containing information about crisis simulations and the UN's response to Haiti's cholera outbreak has been omitted.]

III. Mandate implementation

[Section A, containing information on community violence reduction in Haiti, has been omitted.]

B. Security and police development (benchmarks 1, 4, 5 and 6)

Street demonstrations, which had largely subsided during the reporting period, increased in frequency and violence during the month of September, with confrontations occurring between protesters and the national police on 20 and 23 September in Port-au-Prince. The past months have also been marked by a continued increase in major crime trends and gang-related incidents. The number of reported homicides for 2019 has increased by 17 per cent compared with 2018, with 698 cases between 1 January and 8 October, against 594 for the same period last year. Two thirds of the homicides were recorded in the West Department, where gang-related criminality is most prevalent. In addition, 34 police officers were killed between 1 January and 24 September 2019, compared with 17 during the entirety of 2018. The rise in criminality is creating danger zones in areas such as the Port-au-Prince neighbourhood of Martissant, where the population has begun to protest the free rein of armed criminals who act with complete impunity, in defiance of State authority. The negative crime trends place an additional burden on a national police force already struggling to honour payments to service providers and meet the basic needs of officers, thereby limiting its operational capacities and forcing its leadership to make difficult operational choices. . . .

[Sub-items twenty through twenty-three, providing information on recruitment, regional office construction, and gender-based violence prevention, have been omitted.]

The results of the second evaluation of the strategic development plan for the national police, 2017–2021, conducted with support from MINUJUSTH, showed continued progress. Such progress notwithstanding, the persistent political crisis, the lack of government engagement and donor fatigue contributed to an overall low implementation rate of 34.5 per cent. Of the 133 priority actions contained in the plan, 2 have been completed, 103 are ongoing and 28 have yet to begin.

Whereas progress in national police development over the past 15 years of peacekeeping presence is evident, maintaining the momentum of continued growth and professionalization will require greater attention by national authorities and the international community to resourcing the police. Addressing the acute equipment needs of the police, which lacks both ammunition and armoured vehicles, is urgent. The expansion of territorial coverage, the strengthening of operational capacities—specifically with regard to crime prevention, crowd control, criminal intelligence and investigation—and increasing the representation of women in the national police, should remain the focus of the next mission.

C. Justice and anti-corruption (benchmarks 1, 2, 5, 6 and 10)

In spite of the negative impact that the security situation has had on the functioning of the Port-au-Prince court of first instance, significant progress was made in reducing the rate of prolonged pretrial detention in the jurisdiction, in large part as a result of stronger leadership and more effective collaboration among judicial actors, through the penal chain committee, in handling penal cases. During the month of July, all 76 cases transferred to the Court were processed in real time by the prosecutor's office, investigating judges closed 79 cases, and the Court held 29 judgment sessions, closing 23 cases. During the reporting period, the legal aid offices supported by MINUJUSTH contributed to the release of 34 adults and 18 minors. Overall, the number of pretrial detainees in the Port-au-Prince jurisdiction has decreased by 14 per cent since October 2017.

Delays continued in the installation of the National Council on Legal Aid, the body tasked with providing legal assistance to the most vulnerable, following the promulgation of the Legal Aid law on 26 October 2018. The State has yet to define its national legal assistance strategy, draft a related action plan and allocate funding to implement it.

MINUJUSTH and UNDP supported the Ministry of Justice and Public Security through the recruitment of a consultant to draft the strategic plan, which will provide the National Council with the tools to establish 18 legal aid offices nationwide. . . .

Important progress has been made with regard to the administration of justice, the functioning of judicial institutions and legislative reform since October 2017. Through the joint rule of law programme, MINUJUSTH and UNDP supported the Superior Council of the Judiciary in developing a five-year strategic plan for 2018–2023 and elaborating a report on the state of the judiciary. Internal oversight and accountability mechanisms have been strengthened both within the Ministry and the Council. The former conducted a nationwide inspection of 18 offices of prosecutors, five appellate courts, over 100 tribunaux de paix and 18 offices of prison clerks between December 2018 and June 2019. The latter published the first results of the vetting of magistrates. Furthermore, all seats on the Supreme Court and the Council have been filled.

With respect to legislative reform, the adoption and promulgation of the Legal Aid law will, gradually, allow access to justice for the most vulnerable. Despite the efforts by MINUJUSTH and its partners, the Criminal Code and the Code of Criminal Procedure, as well as the draft organic law of the Ministry of Justice and Public Security, have yet to be debated in Parliament. Their passing and promulgation will constitute key priorities for the new Office. Furthermore, the Mission forged a partnership with the United Nations Office on Drugs and Crime and the State's anti-corruption unit to build the capacities of judicial actors in the fight against corruption. The partnership will enable the assessment of the current 10-year national anti-corruption strategy, and the drafting of a new one.

Nonetheless, the full achievement of justice and rule of law benchmarks will require a long-term effort and sustained engagement by both the national authorities and the international community. Such long-term institution-building would benefit from the adoption of a nationally owned rule of law reform road map, so as to be effective and sustainable. . . .

[Section D, describing progress on corrections benchmarks, has been omitted.]

E. Human rights (benchmarks 4, 5, 6, 7, 8 and 9)

The appointment of a Minister Delegate for human rights and the fight against extreme poverty in September 2018 reinvigorated the work of the Inter-Ministerial Committee on Human Rights and enhanced State compliance with reporting obligations to international human rights mechanisms. During the reporting period, the Inter-Ministerial Committee finalized Haiti's midterm report as part of the universal periodic review, detailing progress made in the implementation of the recommendations accepted by Haiti during the second cycle of the universal periodic review, in 2016. On 30 July, the Office of the Prime Minister discussed the report with representatives of ministries, public institutions, including the Office of the National Human Rights Ombudsperson, and civil society organizations. In addition, a first draft of the national action plan on human rights was finalized in July, and is pending endorsement by the Executive, following consultations with representatives of public institutions and civil society organizations.

During the two-year mandate of MINUJUSTH, the capacity of the national human rights institution to function independently and protect citizens significantly improved. It released its first public annual report since 2013, which included 20 recommendations to State authorities on a broad range of human rights issues. The confirmation of the A status of the national human rights institution by the Global Alliance of National Human Rights

Institutions, in May 2019, further showed international recognition for its efforts to comply with the principles relating to the status of national institutions for the promotion and protection of human rights (the Paris Principles). The human rights institution also increased its public advocacy on critical human rights issues, and progress was observed in the implementation of its recommendations by national authorities, notably in relation to the reduction of prolonged pretrial detention. Finally, as a result of capacity-building support provided through the joint rule of law programme, the human rights institution is finalizing the drafting of its 2019–2024 internal strategy, as well as a manual on internal rules and regulations.

The Mission continued to strengthen the capacities of civil society organizations, notably by facilitating trainings on human rights monitoring and reporting, as well as on partnerships between remote communities and local authorities in promoting human rights, and by conducting advocacy sessions on the implementation of the recommendations accepted by Haiti during the second cycle of the universal periodic review, in 2016, and the preparation of the civil society report for the next cycle of the universal periodic review, in 2021. Special emphasis was put on the role of civil society in advocating the ratification by Parliament of the Convention against Torture and Other Cruel, Inhuman or Degrading Treatment or Punishment and in combating the discrimination faced by women electoral contenders. . . .

Throughout its two-year mandate, MINUJUSTH has monitored the authorities' response to four other major instances of serious human rights violations: the killing, arbitrary arrests and forced disappearance of civilians during police operations in October and November 2017, in Lilavois and Grand Ravine, respectively; the beating to death of a disabled 25-year-old man by a police officer in La Victoire, in December 2017; and numerous abuses allegedly committed by the national police during anti-government protests in July, October and November 2018 and February 2019. In the light of the absence of concrete judicial developments to establish accountability and bring justice to the victims of these high-profile cases, advocacy for stronger accountability mechanisms and justice for all victims will remain a key feature of the mandate of BINUH. . . .

[Section F, detailing election preparations, and Section IV, discussing mission transition planning, have been omitted.]

V. New benchmarks

. . . After a process of consultation that included the strategic workshop held in Port-au-Prince in September, six new benchmarks and 25 indicators have been identified to measure progress towards sustainable stability after the deployment of BINUH. . . . The benchmarks and indicators are grounded in the 2030 Agenda for Sustainable Development, the realization of which would put Haiti on a definite path of peace and prosperity. . . .

The benchmarks represent objectives for the Haitian people and their national institutions to pursue over the horizon of the next two to three years so as to improve the structural foundations of stability and social cohesion. The benchmarks have been informed by national priorities set by the Government of Haiti, the preliminary results of national dialogue processes and the most recent national development strategies. . . .

Given the current fluid political environment and the pending formation of a new government, continued, multisectoral consultations, led by BINUH leadership, will ensure that the objectives behind these benchmarks enjoy as broad a national understanding and ownership as possible. BINUH and the Government of Haiti will agree on the specific targets for each indicator in 2020 and 2021. . . . BINUH will also seek to establish a monitoring and data collection mechanism on progress against the benchmarks, in partnership with the government and the country team and drawing on existing data collection mechanisms for the Goals.

While the benchmarks are not a tool for assessing the performance of the United Nations in the country, they reflect the initial foundation for the establishment of system-wide critical priorities that the United Nations presence in the country will work towards over the next years. Support for their achievement will be delivered to national actors in an integrated manner by BINUH and the country team, taking into account their distinct capacities and comparative advantages, namely the mission's political and advisory role and the programmatic role of agencies, funds and programmes. . . .

[Sections VI through VIII have been omitted. They contain information on the UN's drawdown and closure of MINUJUSTH, conduct and discipline of UN staff in Haiti, and mission costs.]

IX. Observations

The upcoming cessation of MINUJUSTH activities and the departure of its personnel will mark the first time since 2004 that Haiti will not have the presence of a United Nations peacekeeping operation on its soil. Over the past 15 years, the women and men of MINUSTAH and MINUJUSTH have worked closely with national authorities, civil society, national and international partners and the rest of the United Nations system to help solidify political and stability gains, as well as develop and professionalize the national police, in order to foster an environment conducive to the development of the country. . . .

As the United Nations prepares to embark upon a new partnership with Haiti, the country stands at a delicate moment. The protracted multidimensional crisis with which it has been contending since July 2018 shows little sign of abatement or resolution. The increasingly fraught and violent nature of Haiti's political context has led to the virtual paralysis of most State institutions, including Parliament. The continued decline of its economy, exacerbated by the activities of criminal gangs operating at strategic points between ports and agricultural lands and urban centres, has contributed to a general increase in food insecurity and a marked deterioration in the living conditions of an ever-growing swathe of the population.

The need for a broad-based and comprehensive inter-Haitian dialogue to remove political blockages, revitalize the economy and recast the terms of the Haitian social contract has never been more acute. I urge all actors to set aside their differences and particular interests to work together to overcome the increasingly preoccupying situation, as only then will Haiti be able to resume its progress towards sustainable development and the achievement of the 2030 Agenda. The articulation and conduct of such a process would likely require a degree of external facilitation, to which the United Nations, through my Special Representative, stands ready to contribute. The United Nations Integrated Office in Haiti, the United Nations country team and other international partners are poised to support a range of political and economic reform initiatives which might derive from such a dialogue.

Impunity continues to hamper progress towards improved governance and genuine accountability. Despite the investigations by police and judicial authorities, 11 months after the extreme violence in La Saline, which resulted in at least 26 killings, the alleged disappearance of 12 persons, and a number of cases of gang rape, negligible progress has been made to ensure justice for the victims. No judicial proceedings have been initiated against those police officers and State officials who are alleged to have been complicit in the violence. I deplore that no legal proceedings have been initiated in relation to the Grand Ravine killings and other serious violations committed in the past two years.

The pervasive sense of impunity, whether with regard to corruption or human rights violations, perpetuates a lack of trust in judicial institutions and State authorities, reinforcing a widespread sense of insecurity. The scenes of violence and the allegations of corruption that have affected Parliament over the past months, as political actors struggled to obtain confirmation of not one, but two, governments, are regrettable. Outcomes in the fight against corruption continue to lag. Judicial proceedings on the ongoing embezzlement cases have produced little in the way of prosecutions. It is time that the debate on corruption and reform give rise to concrete measures to tackle the iniquities that are eroding Haiti's institutions and detracting from its domestic and international image.

Addressing the question of impunity, through the continued reform of the justice system, the uprooting of corruption and the unfailing prosecution of the perpetrators of human rights violations, will be paramount to restoring Haitian citizens' confidence in their political and economic elites and persuading them to reengage through democratic and peaceful means in the building of their collective future. I encourage the government to adopt a road map for rule of law and justice reforms so as to outline national priorities and ensure sustainable long-term development of the sector. I also encourage the Executive and the Superior Council of the Judiciary to ensure the strict upholding of the legal requirements controlling the integrity and credentials of judges and thus provide for the appointment and confirmation of a greater number of qualified magistrates who deliver effective justice services to the population. In addition, BINUH, the United Nations country team and international partners will continue to provide technical and financial support to the work undertaken by the legal aid offices, as well as to the implementation of the State-provided legal aid programme.

As national authorities have fully assumed sole responsibility for the provision of security across the country, and as the Haitian National Police now relies exclusively on its own capacities to conduct operations, it is imperative that the national police be well resourced and equipped in order to fulfil its mandate. Even though BINUH will continue to support the development of its technical capacities, without adequate specialized assets such as armoured vehicles and airlift and aerial reconnaissance capabilities, the task of the national police will remain arduous. It is imperative that the investments made by so many international partners in developing the police force not be squandered, so that it can continue to develop as an exemplary, apolitical, professional force.

As the work of the new United Nations presence in Haiti is set to begin, I express my continued commitment to the Haitian people for an effective, impactful and consequential engagement of the United Nations system on the ground. This requires the integration of the political and advisory capacities of BINUH and the programmatic and technical assistance capacities of the country team in the service of a common priority objective that cuts across the peace and security, human rights and development pillars. Together, these capacities, along with full national ownership and accountability, will support the country's vision for stability and prosperity. . . .

[Annexes have been omitted.]

SOURCE: United Nations Mission for Justice Support in Haiti. "Report of the Secretary-General on the United Nations Mission for Justice Support in Haiti." October 9, 2019. https://undocs.org/en/S/2019/805.

UN Secretary-General Statement on the End of Peacekeeping Operations in Haiti

October 17, 2019

As the United Nations peacekeeping mission in Haiti came to an end on 15 October, the Secretary-General reaffirms the continuous commitment of the United Nations to support the Haitian people on their path to peace and development, through a new partnership.

The United Nations Integrated Office in Haiti (BINUH), which started operations on 16 October, and the UN country team that has always accompanied Haiti, will integrate their activities to support national efforts to bring about lasting stability and the implementation of the 2030 Agenda for Sustainable Development.

The Secretary-General recognizes the contributions of the United Nations Stabilization Mission in Haiti (MINUSTAH) and the United Nations Mission for Justice Support in Haiti (MINUJUSTH) to the country's progress towards stabilization. He expresses the deepest respect to the memory of the 188 UN military, police and civilian personnel who lost their lives in Haiti since 2004. He also praises the vital contribution of the UN development and humanitarian partners to the fulfilment of the missions' mandates.

The Secretary-General is concerned by the current political crisis and its adverse impact on the security situation and the lives of Haitians. He urges all Haitian stakeholders to engage in genuine dialogue and prevent a further escalation in violence that threatens to reverse stability gains. He calls on the Haitian National Police, which has assumed full responsibility for the security and protection of the Haitian people, and building upon the support provided by MINUSTAH and MINUJUSTH over the past years, to discharge its duties with due regard for all people and their human rights.

While continuing to uphold all ongoing efforts for the elimination of cholera, which has seen significant progress, and the resolution of pending cases of sexual exploitation and abuse, the Secretary-General reiterates the unyielding commitment of the United Nations to Haiti's stability and prosperity.

[French version has been omitted.]

SOURCE: United Nations Secretary-General. "Statement Attributable to the Spokesman for the Secretary-General—on the End of the United Nations Peacekeeping Mission in Haiti and the Start of Operations of BINUH." October 17, 2019. https://www.un.org/sg/en/content/sg/statement/2019-10-17/statement-attributable-the-spokesman-for-the-secretary-general-the-end-of-the-united-nations-peacekeeping-mission-haiti-and-the-start-of-operations-of-binuh-scroll-down.

UN High Commissioner for Human Rights Briefing on Haiti

November 1, 2019

We are deeply concerned about the protracted crisis in Haiti, and its impact on the ability of Haitians to access their basic rights to healthcare, food, education and other needs.

At least 42 people have died and 86 have been injured as tensions have escalated since the latest round of protests began on 15 September, according to information verified by our office. The vast majority suffered gunshot wounds. Reports indicate that security forces were responsible for 19 of the deaths while the rest were killed by armed individuals or unknown perpetrators. Among those killed was at least one journalist. Nine other journalists were injured and many have reportedly been threatened. We urge all actors to refrain from targeting journalists and respect the freedom of the media to report on the situation.

Since the beginning of the school year in September, most children across Haiti have been unable to go to school. Roadblocks and violence have meant that people, particularly in regions outside the capital, have had serious difficulty accessing food, drinking water, medicine and fuel. The health sector has been hit particularly hard, with shortages of electricity, fuel, supplies, and the inability of many medical personnel to reach their places of work. We are also concerned about the impact that the closure of judicial institutions and other public institutions is having in the country, especially on vulnerable groups. For example, the alarmingly high number of detainees in prolonged pre-trial detention has further increased due to the closure of many local courts for security reasons.

We urge all parties to avoid hampering the functioning of hospitals and to facilitate access to healthcare, as well as the delivery, including through humanitarian channels, of food and medicine for individuals in prisons, orphanages and other vulnerable groups such as people living with disabilities.

We welcome the launching of investigations by the General Inspectorate of the Haitian National Police into allegations of human rights violations by police and stress the need for investigations to be thorough, transparent and independent, with a view to ensuring accountability, justice and truth for victims and their families—including through judicial action.

It is crucial that all actors take measures to support and advance peaceful solutions to the many grievances that have led Haitians to take to the streets repeatedly over the past 16 months. We stand ready to support attempts at meaningful and inclusive resolution to the current situation and alleviate the suffering of the people of Haiti.

SOURCE: From "Press Briefing Note on Haiti Unrest," November 1, 2019, by United Nations Office of the High Commissioner for Human Rights, ©2019 United Nations. Reprinted with the permission of the United Nations. https://www.ohchr.org/EN/NewsEvents/Pages/DisplayNews.aspx?NewsID=25247&LangID=E.

World Food Programme Announces *Increased Aid to Haiti*

December 6, 2019

PORT-AU-PRINCE The United Nations World Food Programme (WFP) has announced it is scaling up its operation to provide emergency food assistance to 700,000 people. To reach them and deliver common humanitarian services, WFP is appealing for US$62 million.

One in three Haitians, or 3.7 million people, need urgent food assistance, including 1 million suffering severe hunger according to a nationwide study conducted in August by the CNSA (National Coordination for Food Security) with support from WFP and the Food and Agriculture Organization of the United Nations.

"Poor Haitian families face a very dramatic situation. WFP and its partners are doing their utmost to reach a growing number of vulnerable people with emergency assistance," said Miguel Barreto, WFP Regional Director for Latin America and the Caribbean, who is on a field mission to Haiti until the 7th of December.

Millions of Haitians have been hit hard by rising prices, a weakening local currency, and a drop in agricultural production. Social and civil unrest over the past three months rendered many main roads impassable too, further restricting access to food for poorer households. Recently, a slight improvement in security allowed WFP to deliver food assistance to families cut off since September.

Over the past three weeks, nearly 23,000 people have received emergency food assistance in the Nord-Ouest department, defined by the government's report as the most food insecure in the country. WFP provides families with enough food for a month.

WFP is also expanding distributions and providing cash and vouchers to other departments affected by food insecurity. In November, 67,000 people were given cash so as local markets recover, households can purchase food locally. So far in 2019, WFP has met the emergency food needs of 138,000 people across the country. New distributions and deliveries will be organized whenever the security situation allows.

The unrest has hampered humanitarian organizations' efforts too. Transport of WFP food to many vulnerable communities, particularly using the main roads between the capital Port-au-Prince and Artibonite and across southern Haiti, has been affected.

"Despite these challenges, we are committed to ensure the continuity of our assistance. It's heart-warming to see schools reopening and children able to attend class, as we also provide them with a hot meal. For poor families, it is often the only meal they eat in a day," said Barreto.

WFP's school feeding programme provides meals to 300,000 children annually in 1,200 schools nationwide. It is considered the largest food safety net in Haiti but only 60 percent of schools have reopened since the turmoil began three months ago.

To reach areas difficult or impossible to access by road, WFP launched a three-month air operation in late November. A chartered Mi8-AMT helicopter is providing reliable transport for cargo and staff from the entire humanitarian community. It can carry up to 22 passengers or 4 tons of cargo.

For WFP, investing in sustainable solutions is key to addressing the root causes of food insecurity in Haiti. WFP significantly increased its support to local agriculture in line with Government plans to revitalize the agriculture sector as a means of tackling food insecurity.

SOURCE: World Food Programme. "World Food Programme Ramping Up to Reach 700,000 with Emergency Operations in Haiti." December 6, 2019. © World Food Programme, 2019. https://www.wfp .org/news/world-food-programme-ramping-reach-700000-emergency-operations-haiti-0.

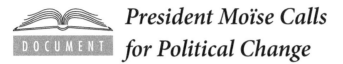

President Moïse Calls for Political Change

January 12, 2020

This institutional vacuum is a historic opportunity for the actors to come together to initiate the reforms that must lead to the transformation of this predatory state into a servant state that will put an end to this ongoing crisis undermining the future of this country.

SOURCE: President Jovenel Moïse (@moisejovenel). Twitter post. January 12, 2020. Translated by SAGE Publishing. https://twitter.com/moisejovenel/status/1216589858518568961.

OTHER HISTORIC DOCUMENTS OF INTEREST

FROM PREVIOUS *HISTORIC DOCUMENTS*

United Nations and President Moreno Call for Peace during Protests in Ecuador

OCTOBER 11 AND 15, AND NOVEMBER 29, 2019

Ecuadorian president Lenín Moreno's introduction of unpopular austerity measures in October 2019 sparked nationwide protests against policies projected to have a disproportionate impact on lower-income people. Riots and violent clashes between protesters and police resulted in at least nine deaths and injured hundreds more, prompting United Nations (UN) officials to call for calm and investigations into potential abuses by the country's security forces. After ten days of unrest, Moreno and leaders of Ecuador's indigenous groups—who had been the driving force behind the protests—negotiated a deal that ended the unrest and laid the foundation for new proposals to address the country's financial challenges.

MORENO INTRODUCES AUSTERITY MEASURES

Ecuador's economy is closely linked to the commodities market given the country's wealth of oil and mineral resources. Moreno's predecessor, President Rafael Correa, sought to expand development of these resources—in addition to borrowing heavily from China— to fund extensive spending on public programs and services during his time in office. With the global drop in oil prices and the beginning of China's economic slowdown around 2014, the government began introducing some austerity measures to shrink Ecuador's ballooning public debt as funds dried up. (Ecuador's estimated budget deficit was $3.6 billion in 2019.)

When Moreno was elected, he was expected to continue many of Correa's policies, but upon taking office, he began to distance himself from the former president and pursue a different course to stabilize Ecuador's economy. This included striking an agreement with the International Monetary Fund (IMF) in March 2019 under which Ecuador could receive a $4.2 billion loan if the government implemented a series of ambitious reforms to cut its deficit and rein in spending. (The IMF is generally unpopular with Latin American politicians such as Correa as well as with the public. Many people blame austerity measures imposed as part of agreements with the IMF for their personal financial hardships.)

On October 2, 2019, Moreno announced an end to government-provided fuel subsidies, saying that Ecuador could no longer afford them. The subsidies had been in place for roughly forty years and were estimated to cost the government about $1.3 billion per year. "It's necessary to correct grave economic errors," Moreno said in his announcement. "In the region, the only country with this fuel subsidy is Venezuela. And you'll agree with me, it's not a good example to follow." The fuel subsidy elimination was one of several reforms Moreno's government had developed to save Ecuador more than $2 billion a year and meet the IMF agreement's terms. Other reforms included plans to reduce the public work-force, privatize some government functions, impose higher taxes on businesses making more than $10 million a year, cut wages for new contracts in public sector jobs by 20 per-cent, and require that public workers donate one day's worth of earnings to the govern-ment each month.

Reforms Lead to Protests

Ecuadorians responded angrily to Moreno's announcement, with many indigenous, poor, and working-class people claiming they would be the hardest hit. Without the fuel sub-sidies, the cost for regular fuel rose about 30 percent while diesel fuel prices more than doubled. Rising fuel prices in turn prompted speculation and quickly caused the cost of other consumer goods to rise. These increases, the people argued, were not affordable, particularly considering that Ecuador's minimum wage is $394 per month.

Frente Unitario de los Trabajadores (a central organizing body for trade unions), the Confederation of Indigenous Nationalities of Ecuador (CONAIE), Popular Front (a group representing various labor unions and social movements), and the Federation of University Students of Ecuador called for nationwide protests against the fuel price hike and pro-posed austerity measures. Taxi, bus, and truck drivers organized a national transport strike and led initial protests in Quito and the coastal city of Guayaquil on October 3, blocking roads and bridges in these major cities. The strike was called off the next day fol-lowing talks with the government, but the protests continued under the leadership of stu-dent and labor unions, human rights groups, and CONAIE. Moreno declared a two-month state of emergency on October 4 to "ensure citizens' security and avoid chaos."

Early reports indicated protests were mostly peaceful, though some demonstrators burned tires and threw rocks or other objects at police vehicles. Violence soon broke out, however, with rioters attacking dozens of public and private buildings on October 7. Demonstrators vandalized the National Assembly building in Quito, forcibly entered the office of the comptroller general, destroyed property at a major dairy and several rose plantations, and caused the shutdown of a major oil production facility in the Amazon region. Other reports said demonstrators were throwing petrol bombs. Indigenous people blocked roads in Ecuador's Andean region, cutting some cities and towns off from the rest of the country. (Supplies reportedly had to be airlifted to Ecuador's third-largest city, Cuenca, because of the blockade.) "[This] is not a protest of social dissatisfaction faced with a government decision but the looting, vandalism and violence show there is an organised political motive to destabilise the government," Moreno declared, while reaf-firming he would not restore the fuel subsidies. The president announced he was relocat-ing the capital from Quito to Guayaquil due to security concerns.

Moreno also accused Correa of plotting a coup against him in collaboration with Venezuelan president Nicolas Maduro. (Moreno's break with Correa's policies and his push to reinstate term limits that precluded the former president from running again cre-ated a major rift between the once-allied men. Correa had been living in Belgium since leaving office in 2017, in what some believe was an effort to avoid prosecution for nearly thirty corruption charges—allegations that Correa claimed are nothing more than Moreno's attempt to smear him.) Officials in Argentina, Brazil, Colombia, El Salvador, Guatemala, Paraguay, and Peru appeared to support Moreno's claim by accusing Maduro of "actions aimed at destabilizing our democracies." Juan Guaidó, the opposition leader turned legislature-declared president of Venezuela, claimed that "a group financed by Maduro's accomplices in America, taking advantage of the most vulnerable, seeks to end the country's stability." Correa said the allegations were "nonsense" and called for a new election to address the unrest. Maduro also said the allegations were absurd but applauded Ecuador's "popular insurrection" against the IMF.

Protests continued apace, with CONAIE taking primary leadership of the demonstrations. (Indigenous groups have long been a force for change in Ecuador. Since 1997, indigenous-led protests had pushed three presidents out of office.) The people demanded that Moreno end the state of emergency, reinstate the fuel subsidies, and repeal other reforms introduced as part of the IMF deal. Riots also continued. On October 8, demonstrators briefly forced themselves into the National Assembly building before police pushed them back out using tear gas. Several other government buildings were reportedly damaged, and indigenous people took over two water treatment facilities. Moreno responded by imposing a curfew around government buildings as well as airports, oil refineries, and other critical infrastructure. Two days later, protesters captured ten police officers near a cultural center in Quito that was being used as an organizing point for indigenous protesters. The officers were paraded across a stage in the city, and some were forced to carry the coffin of an indigenous activist who protesters claimed was killed by a police-fired tear gas canister. The officers were released later that evening. Facing fresh riots on October 12, Moreno deployed troops to patrol the streets of Quito and announced a twenty-four-hour curfew. Protesters had set fire to the national comptroller's office and a television station, and they reportedly pushed into the office of *El Comercio* newspaper.

UN Appeals for Calm

The chaos in Ecuador drew the UN's attention. During the UN's daily press briefing on October 10, a spokesperson said that Secretary-General António Guterres was "concerned about the recent developments in Ecuador" and "calls on all actors to reduce tensions, avoid acts of violence and exercise maximum restraint." The spokesperson said the Ecuadorian government had asked the UN to "facilitate a dialogue with different civil society sectors," and that the UN "stands ready to consider a role in support of dialogue if its engagement is accepted by all the relevant parties."

The rioting and frequent clashes between police and protesters also raised concerns about potential human rights violations. A team from the UN Office of the High Commissioner for Human Rights was dispatched to Ecuador between October 21 and November 8 to speak to people who were injured in the protests and riots and those who witnessed the conflict. Based on the data they collected, team members concluded that at least 9 people had been killed during the unrest and another 1,507 injured, including 435 members of the security forces. More than 1,300 people had been detained, the team found, noting that many arrests had been arbitrary. The team said it had received reports "of use of force by law enforcement officials that was not in conformity with international norms and standards, including unnecessary and disproportionate use of force," such as frequent incidents in which the police and military fired tear gas and pellet rounds directly at protesters at very close range. The team acknowledged the Public Prosecutor's Office had opened seventeen investigations into alleged abuse of force, and the police had another thirty-one investigations in progress but called for independent investigations into every reported death and serious injury. The team also urged the Ecuadorian government to "promote a participatory approach to decision-making, ensuring the enjoyment by people of their right to participate in public affairs." A "strategy of participation," the team said, "should be extended to economic and fiscal measures—including on proposals of austerity measures—and especially with the communities likely to be worst affected." Commenting on the team's findings, High Commissioner for Human Rights Michelle Bachelet said, "Last month's unrest had a high human cost. People should be able to express their grievances without fear of being hurt or arrested. At the same time, it is important that protestors do not resort to violence." Bachelet also observed that "social and economic inequality remains a structural barrier for development for vast sectors" of Ecuadorian society. "It is of paramount importance that society as a whole, with the Government as a guiding force, embark together in search of paths of mutual understanding with the aim of constructing an inclusive, multicultural and peaceful society," she said.

GOVERNMENT, PROTESTERS STRIKE A DEAL

After about a week of protests and riots, Moreno signaled a willingness to talk and soon offered to begin direct negotiations with CONAIE. The group initially stated that it would not participate in a dialogue with the government until Moreno reinstated fuel subsidies. Finally, on October 12, CONAIE agreed to negotiations. The two sides came together on October 13 for nearly four hours of televised negotiations moderated by a local UN representative and the Episcopal Conference. In the end, the government agreed to restore the fuel subsidies, promising to substitute the measure with "a new one that has mechanisms for directing its resources to the people who need it most," and CONAIE agreed to end the protests. The deal's announcement was celebrated in the streets, but some urged caution until the details of the new measure were worked out. Even CONAIE noted that "this isn't over until the agreement is fully completed." Moreno signed a decree restoring the fuel subsidies on October 14. He has also pledged to create a new commission of indigenous leaders and other social groups that would be charged with developing proposals for reducing Ecuador's debt.

Addressing a crowd in Quito the next day, Moreno acknowledged that his government had failed to anticipate Ecuadorians' reaction to the fuel subsidy repeal. "We thought it was going to be a simple reaction, as has always occurred . . . without hurting others, without breaking the law, without destroying our beloved cities," he said. Moreno explained that he repealed the subsidy because "Ecuadorian money, the subsidies we give, leave the country in the hands of corrupt people" and because it advantaged "those who have money; those who have high-end vehicles; those in manufacturing." The repeal was intended to "redirect those resources for the benefit of Ecuadorians," he said. However, Moreno acknowledged, "the right thing, the moment I spoke with the indigenous brothers, was to find peace" and reinstate the fuel subsidy. "Now comes a decree that most favors the poor, the most helpless, the most forgotten among the forgotten."

—Linda Grimm

Following is a UN news article published on October 11, 2019, about Secretary-General António Guterres's view of the situation in Ecuador; excerpts from a speech delivered by President Lenín Moreno on October 15, 2019, in which he discussed the fuel subsidy repeal; and a press release issued by the UN Office of the High Commissioner for Human Rights on November 29, 2019, about the findings from a UN investigation into alleged human rights violations during the unrest.

UN Offers to Support Dialogue in Ecuador

October 11, 2019

Amid violent street protests that have rocked Ecuador's Government, fomenting a political crisis, the UN Secretary-General has voiced his concern, saying the Organization is standing by to help mediate if politicians can agree to sit down for talks.

In a statement given by his deputy-Spokesperson to correspondents in New York, António Guterres called on all actors to reduce tensions, avoid acts of violence, and exercise maximum restraint.

For more than a week, thousands of protesters have held anti-Government rallies, ignited by President Lenín Moreno's announcement of an end to fuel subsidies which have seen prices rise dramatically.

The President's decision to cut decades-old fuel subsidies, combined with tax and labour reforms, have led to street protests led largely by indigenous activists. With police firing tear gas at the crowds, and protesters fighting back, at least five have been killed, and hundreds of others wounded, according to media reports.

On Thursday the United Nations confirmed the Organisation has received a request from the Government of Ecuador to facilitate a dialogue with different civil society actors to deescalate tensions: "The United Nations stands ready to consider a role in support of dialogue if its engagement is accepted by all the relevant parties," said the UN chief's statement.

After declaring a state of national emergency last week, President Moreno has relocated the Government away from the capital Quito, to the country's coastal city of Guayaquil. On Thursday, he reportedly refused protesters' demands to reverse his reform measures.

Mr. Guterres reaffirmed that the UN system and the Episcopal Conference are supporting preliminary talks with the authorities and different civil society sectors.

On Thursday, the UN rights office in the region (ACNUDH) called for swift and independent investigations into the deaths of victims reported thus far, aiming to prevent any further fatalities—reaffirming an appeal made on Sunday for protesters' rights to demonstrate peacefully to be upheld.

"The violent acts or crimes of some should not be attributed to others whose behaviour is peaceful," the statement read. Authorities must "guard the rights to freedom of expression, opinion, and peaceful assembly and participation in public affairs."

In a message on social media, the UN office in Ecuador has called on the country to maintain, "now more than ever, its attitude of peace, solidarity and respect."

Source: United Nations News. "Ecuador: UN 'Stands Ready' to Support Talks, in Bid to End Political Turmoil." October 11, 2019. https://news.un.org/en/story/2019/10/1049121.

President Moreno Addresses the Fuel Subsidy Repeal

October 15, 2019

Today there is no reason for joy, there is no celebration. There have been confrontations between Ecuadorians. Never again may a situation like this happen. Because if you are wrong or fooled once, it can be the other's fault. But if you are fooled twice, it's your fault. I totally admit to not seeing everything coming. (After the elimination of fuel subsidies.)

We thought it was going to be a simple reaction, as has always occurred, complying with the Constitution, protesting as is the right of each Ecuadorian. But without hurting others, without breaking the law, without destroying our beloved cities, without destroying the heritage that the people have worked for with much effort. And many times, the most weak, the most humble, are the most sacrificed. . . .

I made that decision because Ecuadorian money, the subsidies we give, leave the country in the hands of corrupt people. And then we also knew that the reason drug traffickers have installed their operation centers and laboratories on the border is because they receive our subsidized gasoline. That is to say, we are paying for the manufacturing of cocaine, which destroys and hinders the future of our children, and of young people all over the world.

I made that decision because those most taken advantage of are those who have money; those who have high-end vehicles; those in manufacturing, instead of using electricity, use diesel. That's why I made the decision! To redirect those resources for the benefit of Ecuadorians.

Everyone has the right to protest. But one should always think about doing the right thing. And the right thing, the moment I spoke with the indigenous brothers, was to find peace. . . .

I am a man of my word. I promised to repeal that decree! I kept my word! Now keep yours. Because we are in conversations to prepare the new Decree. To make better the conditions of the first.

Friends: the dialogue is continuing because it is the best way to find the truth. No one should believe he is the owner of the truth. The owner of the truth has already gone to Belgium. Now we are the ones who believe that it's important to listen to others, that it's important to hear us, that the knowledge of all is important.

Dear compatriots: how blind we were! Clearly the (office of) intelligence failed us. How blind we were not to see that it was a guerilla war. They were here, hundreds of Venezuelans filtered with the good people. They came in with Venezuelans who fled a despotic regime that now also victimizes Ecuadorians, and have left poor villages tormented and in hunger, in desperation, and loss.

We fulfill what we promised: Repealed the decree. Now comes a decree that most favors the poor, the most helpless, the most forgotten among the forgotten. Now the decree is coming, when we finish talks, to agree. So that no one complains. . . .

Dear friends: now come justice and strength. Reconciliation, yes! Clearly, yes. With justice, judging the guilty. Reconciliation, yes, with justice! Now I make decisions for a better future for Ecuadorians, to be able to live in peace! . . .

SOURCE: President of the Republic of Ecuador. "Por el Trabajo, por el Futuro, por la Familia." October 15, 2019. Translated by SAGE Publishing. https://www.presidencia.gob.ec/wp-content/uploads/downloads/2019/10/2019.10.15-POR-EL-TRABAJO-FUTURO-Y-FAMILIA.pdf.

UN High Commissioner for Human Rights Urges Peace, Calls for Investigations

November 29, 2019

UN High Commissioner for Human Rights Michelle Bachelet on Friday urged all actors in Ecuador to engage in dialogue to prevent new conflicts and forge an inclusive, peaceful society with full respect for its multicultural nature.

The High Commissioner also called for independent, impartial and transparent investigations into allegations of human rights violations and abuses committed in Ecuador during the protests from 3 to 13 October—including killings, violations of international norms and standards on the use of force, arbitrary detentions, as well as looting and destruction of public and private property.

Following an invitation by the Government of Ecuador, the UN Human Rights Office sent a mission to the country from 21 October to 8 November. The High Commissioner thanked the Ecuadorian authorities for their openness to international scrutiny, for their collaboration and for the information provided by national authorities and state institutions to the human rights mission.

The purpose of the mission was to collect first-hand information and identify possible human rights violations and abuses that occurred in the context of the protests that broke out in response to austerity measures, such as the elimination of subsidies for fuel, and a package of economic and fiscal proposals.

The team met with high-level officials from all branches of Government, with civil society representatives, indigenous groups, journalists, unionists, health sector workers, and businesses, among others. In total, the mission interviewed 373 people, including 83 individual victims. The team also visited three detention centres and conducted field visits in Chimborazo, Tungurahua, Cotopaxi and Guayas Provinces.

According to information received by the team, over 11 days of social unrest, at least nine people died and 1,507 were injured, including 435 members of security forces. Reportedly, 1,382 people were detained. There are allegations that many of these people were arbitrarily detained.

"Last month's unrest had a high human cost," the High Commissioner said. "People should be able to express their grievances without fear of being hurt or arrested. At the same time, it is important that protestors do not resort to violence."

The team received reports from victims and witnesses of use of force by law enforcement officials that was not in conformity with international norms and standards, including unnecessary and disproportionate use of force. Law enforcement officials included the police and the military, which was deployed following the declaration of a state of exception.

Victims and witnesses informed the team that teargas and pellet rounds were regularly shot by the security officers directly at the protesters at very close range, causing hundreds of injuries, and possibly some of the deaths.

While acknowledging that the Public Prosecutor's Office and the Police have opened 17 and 31 investigations respectively, the UN Human Rights chief stressed the importance of investigating the circumstances of all deaths and serious injuries. She added that it is imperative that the internal protocols regarding the use of force for law enforcement officials are reviewed and that the authorities ensure they comply with international norms and standards.*

Some protestors also resorted to violence and unidentified individuals have been accused of inciting and using violence. Riots, roadblocks, looting, attacks on dozens of ambulances, arson and destruction of public and private property, cutting off water supplies, and damage to oil production facilities were all used as means of expressing dissent. According to official reports, more than 400 police and military officers were held against their will and subjected to harassment and ill-treatment.

According to figures provided by civil society organizations, there were more than 100 attacks on journalists, carried out both by security officers and by protestors. Media outlets' signals were cut, particularly in El Arbolito in Quito on 10 October, and one of their headquarters was raided by the police—indicating a deliberate effort to hinder the ability to both impart and receive information, which is a key aspect of the right to freedom of expression and opinion. Violent groups burned the Teleamazonas building and attacked the El Comercio newspaper.

On a number of occasions, unidentified individuals who the organisers of the protests said were unknown to them were allegedly responsible for either inciting violence or for carrying out acts of violence themselves. The UN Human Rights Office team was informed that the Public Prosecutor's Office has opened inquiries into these cases.

Bachelet also called on the authorities to refrain from statements and other actions that may lead to stigmatization of indigenous peoples and foreigners, as well as of journalists and political opponents, exposing them to additional risks of physical harm.

A worrying pattern identified by the mission was the very high number of alleged arbitrary detentions. Mass arrests were carried out throughout the crisis, and in several cases without any evidence against specific individuals. A number of victims and witnesses reported cruel, inhuman or degrading treatment during their arrests to the UN human rights team. In addition, there are allegations that in many cases, due process was not followed: detainees were held incommunicado, transferred to unauthorized places of detention, and access to lawyers was often delayed or obstructed. According to information from the Government and the Public Prosecutor's Office, 80 percent of those detained were subsequently released, in most cases without charges. The remaining 20 percent were charged on an array of counts ranging from contraventions, assault, and illegal association through to terrorism charges. According to the authorities, this last charge was laid against at least 30 people accused of setting fire to the building of the Office of the State Comptroller General.

"The Government should ensure that those released without charges are not left with an adverse record against them as a result. By the same token, those who have been charged should enjoy a fair trial and proper treatment in accordance with international standards," the High Commissioner said. "A comprehensive package of reparations should also be provided for the victims. People not only have the right to truth, but also to remedy, which include guarantees of non-recurrence. Without these, the feeling of frustration and injustice will prevail."

Regarding the triggers of the crisis, the UN Human Rights Office strongly recommends that the Government promote a participatory approach to decision-making, ensuring the enjoyment by people of their right to participate in public affairs.** Such a strategy of participation should be extended to economic and fiscal measures—including on proposals of austerity measures—and especially with the communities likely to be worst affected. This would be in line with the view of the UN Committee on Economic, Social and Cultural Rights which recommended that Ecuador ensure that any economic decisions affecting people should be taken in a transparent manner and in consultation with the affected population.***

The historical and persistent discrimination against indigenous peoples should also be a matter of concern and priority for the Government. The High Commissioner urged the authorities to do their outmost to identify effective measures to deal with this problem, and to recognise that it is a barrier to overcoming structural economic inequalities.

"Social and economic inequality remains a structural barrier for development for vast sectors of society, who have felt left behind for generations and do not see positive prospects for the future," Bachelet said. "It is of paramount importance that society as a whole, with the Government as a guiding force, embark together in search of paths of mutual understanding with the aim of constructing an inclusive, multicultural and peaceful society."

*https://www.ohchr.org/en/professionalinterest/pages/useofforceandfirearms.aspx

**https://www.ohchr.org/Documents/Issues/PublicAffairs/GuidelinesRightParticipatePublic Affairs_web.pdf

***https://tbinternet.ohchr.org/_layouts/15/treatybodyexternal/Download.aspx?symboln o=E%2fC.12%2fECU%2fCO%2f4&Lang=en

SOURCE: From "Ecuador: Bachelet Calls for Dialogue to Prevent Conflict and Create an Inclusive Society," November 29, 2019, by United Nations Office of the High Commissioner for Human Rights, ©2019 United Nations. Reprinted with the permission of the United Nations. https://www.ohchr.org/EN/NewsEvents/Pages/DisplayNews.aspx?NewsID=25368&LangID=E.

OTHER HISTORIC DOCUMENTS OF INTEREST

FROM THIS VOLUME

Chilean Leaders and UN Respond to Unrest

OCTOBER 19, 21, AND 28, NOVEMBER 8, AND
DECEMBER 13, 2019

The Chilean government's October 2019 announcement of subway fare increases sparked nationwide protests on a scale not seen since the fall of former dictator Augusto Pinochet. The rate hike provided a catalyst for Chileans to take action against systemic income inequality in the country, with protesters' demands ranging from a higher minimum wage to a new constitution. They also called for the resignation of President Sebastián Piñera, who initially responded to the unrest by declaring a state of emergency but later announced social reforms and new cabinet ministers. Clashes between police and protesters prompted allegations of excessive use of force, and an investigation by the United Nations (UN) Office of the High Commissioner for Human Rights (OHCHR) found evidence of human rights abuses committed by security personnel.

SUBWAY FARE HIKE SPARKS UNREST

Chile is widely viewed as having one of the strongest and most stable economies in Latin America, but it also has the highest rate of income inequality among the Organisation for Economic Co-operation and Development's (OECD) thirty-five mostly developed member countries. The OECD reports that wealth is largely concentrated among the top 10 percent of Chileans, who earn 26.5 times the country's average income. According to Chile's National Statistics Institute, half of the country's workers earn $550 a month or less. Chileans have increasingly voiced dissatisfaction with the rising cost of living and low wages, as well as low-paying pension programs. The country's partial privatization of health care and education has driven up the costs of these services, making them unaffordable for many poor and working-class Chileans.

Amid this economic backdrop, the government announced at the beginning of October 2019 that rush hour fares for the Santiago metro system—which transports about three million Chileans per day—would increase by thirty pesos, or roughly 4 percent. (Fares had been increased by twenty pesos in January.) Officials said the increase was necessary due to fluctuating currency exchange rates, but this explanation failed to quell Chileans' frustrations. Public anger over the increase was exacerbated by Minister of Economy Juan Andrés Fontaine's assertion that anyone who was upset about the rising fares could wake up earlier to pay a lower rate.

On October 7, one day after the price increase took effect, students in Santiago began staging fare evasion protests. In most instances, students jumped over turnstiles in the metro stations to avoid paying the higher rate. But protests intensified the following week, with students reportedly destroying turnstiles and ticket machines, knocking down metal gates, and otherwise vandalizing subway stations. Clashes between students and police were also reported.

STATE OF EMERGENCY DECLARED AS PROTESTS ESCALATE

The students' demonstrations eventually spilled out onto the streets of downtown Santiago and began drawing Chileans of all ages. Protests escalated on October 18, as police used water cannon and tear gas to disperse Chileans who had erected barricades in the streets. The office of an electricity company was set on fire, and officials shut down the city's entire metro system following reports that nearly every subway station had been attacked. Government leaders' use of sharp rhetoric to describe the protests further inflamed tensions. Piñera said Chile was "at war with a violent enemy" while Interior Minister Andrés Chadwick called the protesters "criminals." Transportation Minister Gloria Hutt initially declared the fare hike would not be reversed; however, the price increase was suspended two days later due to the public outcry.

Yet demonstrations continued, with protesters' demands growing to include Piñera's resignation, an increased minimum wage, changes to the pension system, and the drafting of a new constitution. (Chile's current constitution was developed in 1980 under the dictator Augusto Pinochet.) The majority of protests were peaceful, with many Chileans banging spoons against cooking pots in a form of popular protest known as a *cacerolazo*, but there were also reports of looting and rioting. Metro stations, grocery stores, public buses, and gas stations were set on fire, as were the offices of the newspaper *Mercurio*. Clashes between protesters and police were frequent, and police reportedly used tear gas, water cannon, rubber bullets, and pellets to break up the crowds. By October 21, eleven people had been killed in incidents connected to the protests, including at least three people who died in fires set by rioters. Schools were closed and hundreds of flights out of Santiago Airport were cancelled.

Piñera declared a state of emergency in Santiago and several surrounding provinces and communes on October 19. The president cited "serious and recurrent attacks and assaults against stations and premises of the Metro of Santiago, against the public order and the citizens' safety, as well as against public and private properties" that had "severely affected the free circulation and the safety of the inhabitants" of Santiago as the reason for his declaration. He blamed the violence on "genuine criminals" who did not respect their fellow Chileans. He also sought to reassure the people that the government was listening. "I am fully aware of the difficulties and shortages affecting many of our fellow citizens, and I want to point it out clearly: that contributing to solving their problems, creating opportunity opportunities and helping them fulfill their dreams is the lodestar, the essential lodestar that guides each of the acts of our Government," he said. Piñera added that the government would "call for a transversal dialogue and is going to make all the efforts within our reach to mitigate and relieve the situation of our fellow citizens." As a result of the declaration, curfews were imposed in twelve cities and tens of thousands of troops were deployed across the country, including an estimated 20,000 soldiers assigned to the Santiago area.

The state of emergency was lifted on October 27, two days after a massive protest that saw more than one million people gather in the streets of Santiago. The demonstration was reportedly the largest since Chile had restored its democracy after the Pinochet regime's downfall. Thousands more Chileans protested in major cities across the country.

SECURITY FORCES ACCUSED OF HUMAN RIGHTS VIOLATIONS

Allegations of human rights abuses committed by Chilean police and troops emerged soon after the protests escalated. On October 24, UN High Commissioner for Human

Rights Michelle Bachelet issued a statement noting that at least eight people had been killed, several dozen had been injured, and more than 1,900 people had been arrested in connection with the protests. "The authorities must act in strict accordance with international human rights standards," Bachelet said, continuing, "It is essential that all actions, by the authorities and by protestors, that have led to injury or death, are subjected to independent, impartial and transparent investigations." Bachelet called for immediate dialogue to end the crisis and urged all parties to avoid making the situation worse. "The use of inflammatory rhetoric will only serve to further aggravate the situation, and risks generating widespread fear," she said, adding that "any application of the state of emergency must be exceptional and rooted in law."

On October 24, Chile's National Human Rights Institute reported that it had filed nearly seventy legal actions against security personnel for these alleged abuses, which included five killings and twelve accusations of sexual violence. The institute also reported numerous allegations of torture, verbal and physical abuse, and the use of live ammunition against protesters. A later statement from UN human rights experts noted that "the high number of wounded and the way in which non-lethal weapons have been used seems to indicate that the use of force was excessive and violated the requirements of necessity and proportionality."

At the invitation of the Chilean government, an OHCHR team arrived in the country on October 28 to begin investigating the human rights situation on the ground and the allegations against security personnel. The team spent the first three weeks of November collecting information from seven regions in Chile. In its resultant report, the team concluded that "the police and army failed to adhere to international human rights norms and standards relating to management of assemblies and the use of force." The team "documented 113 specific cases of torture and ill-treatment, and 24 cases of sexual violence against women, men, and adolescent girls and boys, perpetrated by members of the police and army," the report stated, noting that the National Human Rights Institute had filed criminal complaints in hundreds more cases. Of the twenty-six deaths being investigated in connection with the protests, the report said, at least two cases involved the use of live ammunition "in the absence of any risk to the lives of civilian or military personnel and against people who were not participating in acts of violence." In addition, the report found that Chilean officials had information regarding the extent of injuries resulting from the protests as early as October 22, but "those responsible failed to adopt effective, prompt and timely measures to end the use of less-lethal weapons, especially anti-riot shotguns using pellets. Prompt action by the relevant authorities could have prevented other people suffering serious injuries."

GOVERNMENT ANNOUNCES REFORMS, CONSTITUTIONAL REFERENDUM

Piñera met with leaders of opposition parties on October 22 to try to find a way to quell the protests. Several organizations boycotted the meeting, including the Socialist Party, which is the country's largest opposition group. Regardless, the government said the president would announce a new social agenda after the meeting. Unveiled later that day, the new social agenda included proposals to raise the minimum wage, boost the basic pension amount by 20 percent, impose higher taxes on wealthier Chileans, reduce lawmakers' and government officials' salaries, lower the cost of medicines for the poor, and cancel a planned increase in electricity rates. Many protesters and other critics said the plan did not go far enough to address systemic inequality, and some noted the proposals relied on increased public funding rather than requiring greater contributions from private companies. According to a poll released by Cadem on October 27, 80 percent of Chileans did not believe the president's proposals were sufficient, and Piñera's approval rating had dropped to 14 percent.

Piñera next moved to dismiss his entire cabinet on October 27. He announced new ministers of the interior, finance, economy, labor, national assets, and sports the next day, along with a new general secretariat of the presidency and general secretariat of the government. Piñera said that Chile had changed, so the government must change with it. "Our Government has listened to the strong and clear message of the Chileans, who ask for and deserve a fairer and caring Chile," he said. The president also highlighted his proposed social agenda, acknowledging that it would not solve all of Chile's problems but was an important first step and would bring "significant relief" to the people. Additionally, Piñera said he had asked the Ministry of Social Development and Family to organize an inclusive national dialogue through which the government would solicit Chileans' input on the country's major challenges and solutions to its problems.

As protests continued unabated into November, the government took a step further. On November 15, after two days of debate and negotiation in the National Congress, lawmakers agreed to hold a constitutional referendum in April 2020. The referendum would ask voters if they want a new constitution and, if so, whether the new constitution should be written by everyday citizens or a group comprised of both lawmakers and regular Chileans. If Chileans vote in favor of a new constitution, the writers would be selected in October 2020, in conjunction with regional and municipal elections. The writers would have nine months to draft the document. Once the document was published, a separate vote would be held to approve or reject the proposed text. "We are responsible for many of the injustices, inequities and abuses that Chileans have pointed out to us," said Senate president Jaime Quintana. "This is a peaceful and democratic exit to the country's crisis." Piñera signed a decree on December 27 that set the constitutional referendum for April 26, 2020.

Ongoing Protests

Although many protesters celebrated the referendum agreement as a sign that the structural changes they want to see in Chile's governance are coming, students vowed to continue demonstrating to keep up pressure on the government. In the early days of 2020, fresh student protests prompted officials to suspend university entrance exams in sixty-four locations across the country, where students had blocked testing centers, vandalized classrooms, or burned exam papers. Student union groups claim the university admissions system, of which the entrance exams are a symbol, gives an advantage to wealthier students, who live in better neighborhoods and have access to better schools.

—Linda Grimm

Following is President Sebastián Piñera's declaration of a state of emergency on October 19, 2019; a statement issued by UN High Commissioner for Human Rights Michelle Bachelet on October 21, 2019, calling for a dialogue to end the violence in Chile; remarks by Piñera on October 28, 2019, during which he announced new cabinet ministers; a statement by UN human rights experts on November 8, 2019, suggesting Chilean authorities used excessive force against protesters; and a press release issued by the UN Office of the High Commissioner for Human Rights on December 13, 2019, about human rights abuses in Chile.

DOCUMENT ## *State of Emergency Declaration*

October 19, 2019

Dear fellow citizens:

In the face of the serious and recurrent attacks and assaults against stations and premises of the Metro of Santiago, against the public order and the citizens' safety, as well as against public and private properties that we have experienced in recent times in the city of Santiago which have severely affected the free circulation and the safety of the inhabitants of the city of Santiago and which have also massively disrupted the public order, and making use of the power conferred to me as the President of Chile by the Constitution and the Law, I have decreed the State of Emergency in the Provinces of Santiago and Chacabuco as well as in the communes of Puente Alto and San Bernardo in the Metropolitan Region.

For these purposes I have appointed Major General Javier Iturriaga del Campo as Chief of the National Defense according to that stated in our legislation regarding the State of Emergency.

The objective of this State of Emergency is very simple, but very meaningful: to ensure the public order, to ensure the tranquility of the inhabitants of the city of Santiago, to protect the public and private assets and, above all, to guarantee the rights of all and each one of our fellow citizens which have been seriously violated by the action of genuine criminals who do not respect anything or anybody, who are willing to destroy such a useful and necessary entity which is the Metro, and who, additionally, do not respect neither the rights nor the freedoms of their fellow citizens.

In addition to that, as we have announced today, we have invoked the Law of National Security through complaints which seek the objective that such persons who have committed those most serious criminal acts face justice and assume their responsibilities.

In a democracy, a rule of law as the one all Chileans have built with such an effort in our country, there must not be space at all for the violence or the crime we have seen recently in our city.

As President I am fully aware of the difficulties and shortages affecting many of our fellow citizens, and I want to point it out clearly: that contributing to solving their problems, creating opportunity opportunities and helping them fulfill their dreams is the lodestar, the essential lodestar that guides each of the acts of our Government.

The increase which occurred regarding the prices of the Metro fares is according to the law; it copes with the increase that occurred in the price of the dollar, the price of oil, and it was determined by a panel of experts as provided by the law.

But I quite understand and do sympathize with many of my fellow citizens affected by this kind of increase. For this reason, in the following days our Government is going to call for a transversal dialogue and is going to make all the efforts within our reach to mitigate and relieve the situation of our fellow citizens who have been affected by this increase in the price of the Metro ticket, so as to be able to contribute to the most vulnerable and the most needed receiving the help they need.

I want to conclude these words sincerely thanking the Carabiniers of Chile and the Chilean Fire Department for their dedication, for their sacrifice, for the commitment they have demonstrated to defend our security, to defend our city, to defend our rule of law.

And also to make a strong call to all men and women of good will in our country, which are the immense majority of the Chileans, to fully unite against the unleashed violence, against the very serious crime we have faced recently, which have caused so much harm to our country and, mainly, to our most vulnerable sectors and to our middle class.

I am convinced that with the unity of all the Chileans in a difficult world as the one we are living in these times, Chile shall be able to carry on progressing, to continue contributing to solve problems, to go on promoting a better quality of life and contributing so that all our fellow citizens are able to enjoy a fuller and happier life.

This is the reason that makes me wake up very early every morning and go to bed very late every night, since that is the duty I feel towards my fellow citizens as President of Chile.

Thank you very much.

SOURCE: Government of Chile. "President Piñera Decrees State of Emergency in the Provinces of Santiago and Chacabuco as Well as in the Communes of San Bernardo and Puente Alto so as to Regularize the Public Order." October 19, 2019. Translated by SAGE Publishing. https://prensa.presidencia.cl/discurso .aspx?id=103651.

UN High Commissioner for Human Rights Calls for Dialogue in Chile

October 21, 2019

The UN High Commissioner for Human Rights Michelle Bachelet on Monday urged all political and civil society actors in Chile to engage in immediate dialogue and to avoid further polarizing the situation with words or deeds, following the violence and unrest that have gripped the country over the past few days.

At least eight people have died so far, with some reports suggesting the number may be as high as 13. In addition, according to the National Human Rights Institution, a further 44 people have been injured, nine of them seriously, and 283 people have been detained in the context of the protests. According to the Ministry of Interior, the number detained is 1,906.

"I'm deeply disturbed and saddened to see the violence, destruction, deaths and injuries that have occurred in Chile over the past five days," Bachelet said. "It is essential that all actions, by the authorities and by protestors, that have led to injury or death, are subjected to independent, impartial and transparent investigations."

The High Commissioner warned that "the use of inflammatory rhetoric will only serve to further aggravate the situation, and risks generating widespread fear."

"The authorities must act in strict accordance with international human rights standards, and any application of the state of emergency must be exceptional and rooted in law,"

Bachelet said. "There are disturbing allegations of excessive use of force by security and armed forces, and I am also alarmed by reports that some detainees have been denied access to lawyers, which is their right, and that others have been mistreated while in detention."

"In addition, dozens of members of the security forces themselves are reported to have been injured," she said.

"In the interest of the nation, I urge the Government to work with all sectors of society to find solutions that can help calm the situation and address the grievances of the population. I also urge all those planning to take part in protests later today and going forward, to do so peacefully," she said.

Bachelet also called on the authorities "to ensure that the rights of individuals to freedom of expression and peaceful assembly are respected."

"There needs to be open and sincere dialogue by all actors concerned to help resolve this situation, including a profound examination of the wide range of socio-economic issues underlying the current crisis," she added.

SOURCE: From "Bachelet Urges 'Immediate Dialogue' to Resolve Crisis in Chile," October 21, 2019, by United Nations Office of the High Commissioner for Human Rights, ©2019 United Nations. Reprinted with the permission of the United Nations. https://www.ohchr.org/EN/NewsEvents/Pages/DisplayNews.aspx?NewsID=25179&LangID=E.

President Piñera Announces New Cabinet Ministers

October 28, 2019

Dear fellow citizens, dear Ministers, a very good afternoon:

We have experienced very difficult days, we have lived between the pain and the hope, and we have encountered the best and also the worst of human nature.

On the side of pain, the brutal wave of violence, of wickedness and of destruction unleashed by small organized groups which have destroyed things that have cost us so much to build: they have destroyed, looted and set fire to the Metro of Santiago, supermarkets, stores, shops, public buildings, SMEs, small shops and even modest homes in the whole country. Not only have these unfortunate events caused a huge damage to the property of the State and of the people, but they have also caused a huge damage to the soul of our country.

But the most painful has been, without doubt, the loss of human lives. I express my total condolences to and my solidarity with the relatives of those who lost their lives. Our thoughts and our prayers are with you.

This violence should never be accepted in a civilized society, it must be directly condemned by all the democrats and it must be duly sanctioned by Justice, applying all the instruments of the State and with full respect for everybody's Human Rights.

The democracy not only has the right, but also the duty to defend itself from its adversaries, applying all the instruments granted by the democratic order, the Constitution and the law and respecting, indeed, in every moment, under any circumstances, the human rights of all citizens. For that we know we have to modernize and strengthen our democratic institutions and to modernize and strengthen our citizen intelligence and security system.

I want to acknowledge and thank the selfless and difficult task that the Carabiniers of Chile and the Investigation Police have carried out so as to safeguard the public order, to protect the citizens' security, to protect their freedom and their rights, as well as to our Armed Forces during the State of Emergency that, as from today, has been lifted in the whole territory of our country.

Not only the Government but our Armed Forces and the law-enforcement forces also have a solid and strong commitment to Human Rights. And if they have committed abuses or violations, they should be investigated by the Prosecutors and solved by the Justice.

Additionally, and so as to guarantee protection and transparency, from the first day we have provided all the support to the National Institute of Human Rights it is able to comply with its important role and we have requested the United Nations High Commissioner for Human Rights and Human Rights Watch to send missions to Chile, so they are able to know the situation of Human Rights in situ, since we have nothing to hide. . . .

But let's go to the hope. On the hope side are those gorgeous peaceful demonstrations through which millions and millions of Chileans, across our country, have been able to express themselves. Similarly, the acts of solidarity as well as the virtuous conducts of responsibility and civic commitment we have known about and which have arisen spontaneously from our society.

Our Government has listened to the strong and clear message of the Chileans, who ask for and deserve a fairer and caring Chile, a Chile with more dignity and without abuse, a Chile with more equal opportunities and fewer privileges, as well as a more prosperous Chile and a Chile in peace. And for that, we must remember in these days, it is fundamental to act with responsibility, to strengthen the capacity of growth of our economy, which is what generates more and better employment, one that allows improvement in salaries and pensions, one that allows the creation of opportunities so everybody is able to develop his or her talents, one that allows us a social system which protects and provides guarantees of dignity to all our fellow citizens and is also what healthily finances the public expenditure and, most notably, the social expenditure. . . .

Some days ago our Government proposed to all Chileans an extensive, sound and challenging Social Agenda. Extensive because it addresses many highly sensitive areas in the life of Chileans; sound because it benefits the greatest majority of our fellow citizens, with a very special emphasis on the most vulnerable ones, in women, in the middle class and in senior adults; and also challenging because it will require an enormous financing effort by the State.

Among the pillars of this Social Agenda it must be emphasized:

- An increase in the pensions which will benefit almost 2 million Chileans
- The creation of a Catastrophic Health Insurance Policy
- A lower price for medicaments
- A higher Guaranteed Minimum Income for our workers
- Higher Contributions and Taxes by higher income sectors
- A strengthened Criminal Defender's Office for the victims of crimes
- Greater territorial equity among different communes of our country

- The stabilization and freezing of electric energy prices, and we hope that soon we will be able to include urban highway fees

- A reduction in the allowances and in the number of members of the Parliament as well as of the higher salaries of the Public Administration.

We know that these measures do not solve all the problems, but we also know that they are a first and important step and that it will translate into a significant relief from the needs and shortages and a major contribution towards the improvement of the living standard of the Chileans, but, above all, they will reflect the strong determination of our Government and the serious commitment of all of us toward a Chile with greater justice and social equity.

Chilean men and women:

Chile is not the same country that we had a couple of weeks ago; Chile changed and the Government also has to change to face these new challenges and these new times.

For these reasons I want to share with you some changes in the Cabinet that backs this President.

- **Ministry of Interior:** Gonzalo Blumel, public vocation since his younger age. He worked in the Municipality of Futrono, he was part of the Jóvenes al Servicio de Chile (JSCH), he helped in the Fundación Avanza Chile and until now he has been serving as General Secretary of the Presidency. He is 41 years old.

- **General Secretariat of the Presidency:** Felipe Ward, Deputy of the district of Calama from 2006 until 2018. As from March 11, 2018, he has been serving as Minister of National Assets. Lawyer, with vast professional experience in the public sector. He is 47 years old.

- **General Secretariat of the Government:** Karla Rubilar, expert in Public Health, served as a surgeon in diverse consulting rooms. She has extensive experience in the public service. At present she is Major of the Metropolitan Region, apart from having served as Deputy during three periods as from the year 2005 by the District of Conchalí, Huechuraba and Renca. She is 42 years old.

- **Ministry of Finance:** Ignacio Briones, his professional vocation has always been focused on public policies and economy, finance and institutionality. He served as Ambassador of Chile before the Organización de Cooperación y Desarrollo Económico (OCDE) (Organisation for Economic Co-operation and Development). At present he serves as Dean of the School of Government of the University Adolfo Ibáñez. He is 46 years old.

- **Ministry of Economy:** Lucas Palacios, with great public vocation, he served as council member of the commune of Puente Alto and he was advisor to the Budgets Office. He also served as Under Secretary of Public Works. Poet and musician by profession. He also served as executive secretary of the Asociación de Municipalidades de la Pre Cordillera de la Región de la Araucanía (Association of Municipalities of the Lower Ranges of the Araucania Region). He is a Commercial Engineer. As from March 11, 2018, he has been serving as Under Secretary of Public Works. He is 45 years old.

- **Ministry of Labor:** María José Zaldívar, she has an extensive career in social security and in the occupational and health safety areas, forged from her services rendered in the Social Security Superintendence, where she worked as report lawyer, attorney and superintendent. As of 2014 she has been serving as general manager of the Corporación de Investigación, Estudio y Desarrollo de la Seguridad Social (CIEDESS) and in March 2018 she took the position of Under Secretary of Social Welfare. Degree in History, lawyer and Master in Public Law. At present she serves as Under Secretary of Social Welfare. She is 44 years old.

- **Ministry of National Assets:** Julio Isamit, student of the Instituto Nacional José Miguel Carrera, where he was executive secretary of the student center in 2006. As a university student, he was an active leader and participated in the Centro de Estudios Res Pública, which he chaired from 2011 until 2015. He is a lawyer and from March 11, 2018, he has been serving as Chief of Cabinet of the Ministry of the General Secretary of the Presidency. He is 30 years old.

- **Ministry of Sports:** Cecilia Pérez, lawyer by profession, she was a council member of the commune of Florida from the year 2000 until the year 2010. She was Under Secretary of Women's Affairs and Major of the Metropolitan Region. After that, she helped form the Fundación Avanza Chile and at present she is Minister General Secretary of the Government. She was Vice President and General Secretary of the Renovación Nacional party for 3 years. She is 43 years old.

I want to express my appreciation from the bottom of the soul to the Ministers who are leaving this Cabinet today: Andrés Chadwick, Felipe Larraín, Juan Andrés Fontaine, Nicolás Monckeberg and Pauline Kantor. For a long time I have known their capacities and their personal merits, but I have come to know something remarkably valuable which is their great vocation for the public service, their high commitment to the Chileans and their unwavering commitment to Chile. I appreciate and thank from the bottom of the soul their dedication and their generosity, and I owe a great debt of gratitude to you.

The great challenge we face, and not only our Government, but all the Chilean men and women of good will, is to learn the lesson of these last two weeks, heal the wounds on the body and the soul of our society and channel the energy and the hope of our citizens who do not want to destroy everything, and on the contrary, want to build something much better and want to walk the paths of progress, justice and peace.

To achieve this, it is fair and necessary to listen and to listen with a lot of humility, with great attention and with a sense of urgency to the strong and sound message of the people.

For this reason I have asked the Minister of Social Development and Family, Sebastián Sichel, to help organize a dialogue that emerges from the society, from the communities, an extensive, free, respectful dialogue among all the Chileans, a dialogue that reaches all the communes and corners of our country and to which all are able to contribute, in which all are able to participate so as to be able to build for us, for our children, for our grandchildren and for those who will come afterwards, who we do not know and yet we have the commitment to leave them a better country. . . .

As President of all the Chileans I will make all the efforts, I will not spare any sacrifice and I will give the best of myself, as I know that all the Ministers will do and also most of my fellow citizens, to lead our country through these paths of challenges, along these paths of future. . . .

SOURCE: Government of Chile. "President Piñera nombra nuevos ministros." October 28, 2019. Translated by SAGE Publishing. https://prensa.presidencia.cl/discurso.aspx?id=133961.

UN Experts Condemn Excessive Use of Force, Violence in Chile

DOCUMENT

November 8, 2019

UN human rights experts have condemned the excessive use of force by security forces in Chile during the recent weeks of protests.

At least 20 people are reported to have been killed and about 1,600 hurt, including police officers, during protests that began in early October over rising transport costs, and deeply entrenched inequality. A state of emergency was declared in a number of provinces on 19 October amid escalating violence. Thousands of people have also been detained, including children and adolescents.

"Violence can never be the answer to people's social and political demands, the high number of wounded and the way in which non-lethal weapons have been used seems to indicate that the use of force was excessive and violated the requirements of necessity and proportionality," said the experts who are appointed by the Human Rights Council and serve in their personal capacities

The experts are also deeply concerned by reports of the excessive use of force against individuals before detention and reports of abuses perpetrated against children, ill-treatment and beatings that could constitute torture. There have also been reports of sexual violence against women, men and adolescents, including practices such as forced stripping, touching and rape in detention. "Women and children have been actively participating in the ongoing protests and the State must address their specific protection concerns," the experts said.

The independent experts rejected all acts of violence committed by private individuals, reminding that "the Government of Chile has an obligation not only to respect human rights but to protect people against violent acts committed by private individuals. It must allow protests to take place by isolating those who resort to violence, while guaranteeing that everyone in the country can enjoy their rights."

The independent experts welcomed the decision of the authorities to invite a mission from the UN Human Rights Office to the country. The mission will assess the human rights situation related to protests and the state of emergency in Chile, including the identification of the main patterns of human rights violations, the analysis of the response of Chilean state institutions as well as the causes related to the protests.

Finally, the experts have engaged in correspondence with the authorities and discussed their expressed willingness to pursue and determine the responsibilities in cases of human rights violations, in particular those committed by agents of the State.

Source: From "Chile: UN Experts Condemn Excessive Use of Force and Acts of Violence in Recent Protests," November 8, 2019, by United Nations Office of the High Commissioner for Human Rights, ©2019 United Nations. Reprinted with the permission of the United Nations. https://www.ohchr.org/EN/NewsEvents/Pages/DisplayNews.aspx?NewsID=25269&LangID=E.

UN Reports on Human Rights Violations by Chilean Police and Army

December 13, 2019

The Office of the UN High Commissioner for Human Rights, in a report on Chile published on Friday, says that during the recent mass protests and state of emergency the police and army failed to adhere to international human rights norms and standards relating to management of assemblies and the use of force.

The 30-page report was produced by a UN Human Rights Office team which spent the first three weeks of November researching the situation across seven regions of Chile. It details extensive allegations—including specific examples—of torture, ill-treatment, rape and other forms of sexual violence by the police against people held in detention, many of whom appear to have been detained arbitrarily. In all, according to official figures, more than 28,000 people were detained between 18 October and 6 December, although the great majority have been released.

The team met with, and received extensive cooperation from, a wide number of local and national authorities. It also received significant assistance from the National Human Rights Institute and the Office of the Children's Ombudsperson, and met with over 300 members of civil society.

The team carried out 235 interviews with victims of alleged human rights violations—including injured and detained protestors and their family members—and conducted 60 interviews with police officers, including some of those injured during the protests. It was granted free access to hospitals and health centres, to interview people injured during the demonstrations. It was also given rapid and unhindered access to places of detention, including police stations and prisons, as well as to people deprived of liberty whom it wished to interview in private, and to relevant reports and records.

The report says that information gathered from a variety of sources indicates "the police has regularly failed to distinguish between people demonstrating peacefully and violent protesters."

During its mission, the team documented 113 specific cases of torture and ill-treatment, and 24 cases of sexual violence against women, men and adolescent girls and boys, perpetrated by members of the police and army. It notes that the National Human Rights Institution has filed criminal complaints relating to hundreds more such cases.

The Office of the Public Prosecutor has indicated there are ongoing investigations into 26 deaths that occurred in the context of the protests, and the UN Human Rights Office says it has verified information concerning 11 of those 26 cases. Of these, the report says, four cases involved "arbitrary deprivation of life and other unlawful deaths involving State agents." In two of these cases, it says, "lethal force, in the form of live ammunition, appears to have been used in the absence of any risk to the lives of civilian or military personnel and against people who were not participating in acts of violence. This contravenes international norms and standards on the use of force and may, depending on the circumstances, amount to an extrajudicial execution."

The report cites the Ministry of Justice figure of 4,903 people injured up to 10 December, including 2,792 police officers, but notes other sources suggest higher numbers of injured. It states that there had been "unnecessary and disproportionate use of less-lethal weapons, in particular anti-riot shotguns, during peaceful demonstrations and/or outside the context of violent confrontations between demonstrators and security forces. This has resulted in a high number of people being injured, including passers-by and people who were not committing violent acts but just protesting peacefully."

"The alarmingly high number of persons with injuries to their eyes or faces (approximately 350) provides a strong basis to believe that 'less-lethal weapons' have been used improperly and indiscriminately, against international principles on minimizing the risk of injury," the report says. It notes that while eye injuries mainly resulted from shotgun pellets, some cases were "due to the use of chemical irritants, in particular tear gas and, in some instances, from impacts from tear gas canisters."

The report states that the authorities "had information regarding the extent of the injuries as early as 22 October. However, those responsible failed to adopt effective, prompt and timely measures to end the use of less-lethal weapons, especially anti-riot shotguns using pellets. Prompt action by the relevant authorities could have prevented other people suffering serious injuries." However, the report also notes recent decisions by various courts of appeal around the country which have limited the use of shotguns in peaceful demonstrations, and have also limited or prohibited the use of tear gas in certain circumstances or places (for example, in hospitals).

Among a number of recommendations to the Chilean State, the report recommends it "immediately end the indiscriminate use of anti-riot shotguns to control demonstrations." It also calls for tear gas only to be used "when strictly necessary and never inside education and health establishments," adding that police officers should receive clear instructions on the proper use of tear gas, including by ensuring that tear gas canisters "are always fired at a high angle and never horizontally, according to international standards."

The report notes how "different State institutions have taken measures to ensure investigations of alleged human rights violations; to ensure prompt access to lawyers for detainees; access to services for victims; and to provide comprehensive, regular and accessible information to the public. Rulings have been issued by tribunals to protect those persons exercising their rights, including to peaceful assembly." The National Human Rights Institution and the Ombudsperson for Children's Rights, in particular, "have effectively and in a timely manner carried out their mandate to protect human rights."

The report notes in its conclusions that the demonstrations that have taken place in Chile "have multiple root causes, including social and economic inequality." It says that "the majority of those who have exercised the right to assembly during this period, have done so in a peaceful manner. However, there have been numerous attacks against security forces and their premises. Both during and outside of demonstrations, there was also significant looting and destruction of property."

"There are reasonable grounds to believe that, from 18 October onwards, a high number of serious human rights violations have been committed," it states. "These violations include excessive or unnecessary use of force that led to unlawful killings and injuries, torture and ill-treatment, sexual violence, and arbitrary detentions."

"The management of assemblies by the police has been carried out in a fundamentally repressive manner," the report says, adding that "certain human rights violations, in particular the improper use of less lethal weapons and cases of ill treatment, are recurrent over time and space." . . .

Source: From "UN Human Rights Office Report on Chile Crisis Describes Multiple Police Violations and Calls for Reforms," December 13, 2019, by United Nations Office of the High Commissioner for Human Rights, ©2019 United Nations. Reprinted with the permission of the United Nations. https://www.ohchr.org/EN/NewsEvents/Pages/DisplayNews.aspx?NewsID=25423&LangID=E.

OTHER HISTORIC DOCUMENTS OF INTEREST

European Union, Lebanese Prime Minister, and U.S. Leaders Remark on Protests in Lebanon

OCTOBER 25 AND 29, AND DECEMBER 20, 2019

The protests in Lebanon near the end of 2019 were unlike any the country had seen before. This youth-driven, nonsectarian, and largely peaceful grassroots movement prompted hundreds of thousands of people to take to the streets and squares all across the country to protest what they saw as long-standing political corruption and express their desire for a unified Lebanon. Their cause elicited the support of governments around the world.

Tensions Build across Lebanon

Tensions had been building for years in a country that had witnessed deteriorating public services, economic decline, and profiteering and corruption from its government. With one of the world's highest debt to gross domestic product (GDP) ratios, the import-dependent country's economy had stagnated and was facing collapse. The tipping point for mass protests against the government was the October 17 announcement that new taxes would be imposed, including a $6 monthly fee on calls on free messaging apps such as WhatsApp.

Demonstrations were unique in that they crossed gender, age, class, and religious lines. The diverse group of protesters called for unity across all segments of Lebanese society. Indeed, the identifying chant of their movement was "All Means All," a reference to the nonsectarian nature of their motives and demands. And, in its early days, the movement appeared to be as much a celebration as a protest, with people of all faiths and ages waving national flags, chanting, and dancing in the streets.

Although by no means exclusively a youth movement, some young Lebanese believed they had particular cause to feel that their country did not care about them. Many are educated and multilingual, yet they had been forced to leave Lebanon, immigrating to places where they could find jobs. Protesters claimed that Lebanon's political elite had stolen billions of dollars from them, aided by laws that allow bank secrecy.

Infrastructure issues have long plagued the country, including water shortages, unclean water, and no sustainable waste management plan. Garbage regularly overflows from landfills and clutters the streets. Electricity is cut off during the day—for eight hours or more—and Internet is unreliable because the state-owned telecommunications company had not been able to pay its international bills. Other critical services are unreliable or absent. For instance, a fire that burned a large swath of a forest could have been limited, but the government failed to maintain the firefighting helicopters that might have contained the blaze. In fact, major wildfires throughout the country have displaced hundreds of people and caused extensive damage to wildlife. But some protesters also took issue with broader political issues, such as the tendency of the political elite to blame refugees for Lebanon's woes, particularly inveighing against the country's 1.5 million Syrian refugees.

While specific grievances were many, protesters were also keen to address the underlying system that had led to these problems in the first place—namely, a sectarian, power-sharing system that caused many divisions in the past. Established following the 1989 Taif agreement, Lebanon's political system allocates political authority based on the religious affiliation of the person holding office. Lebanon's president must be a Maronite Christian, the prime minister a Sunni Muslim, and the speaker of parliament a Shiite Muslim. But Lebanon has eighteen recognized sects, and critics of the system believe it entrenches political patronage and pits citizens against each other. In addition, Hezbollah, a Shia Islamist parliamentary party and armed militia supported by Iran, has at times destabilized the politics of the country.

The civil disobedience aspect to the protest was evident, as protesters set up makeshift tents to block traffic in main thoroughfares and slept in public squares, all in an effort to get the current government to step down. In fact, the reclaiming of public space was a visible sign of the protesters' unity. In Beirut, all the roads into Martyr's Square were blocked, creating a pedestrian-only area where people could visit food stalls and tents set up by civil society groups.

As reported in an article by *The New York Times*, Nizar Hassan, cohost of the Lebanese Politics Podcast, commented, "If you want to give this a name, it would be the 'uprising of dignity'—people taking back their dignity because it's so humiliating to be a citizen of Lebanon under this ruling class."

LEBANESE GOVERNMENT RESPONDS TO MOUNTING PRESSURE

The international response to the protests in Lebanon was generally sympathetic. Solidarity protests were held in major European cities, as well as in North America and Australia. Writing from Lebanon, David Hale, U.S. under secretary of state for political affairs, remarked that the protests were "largely peaceful" and reflected the "Lebanese people's longstanding and frankly legitimate demand for economic and institutional reform, better governance, and an end to endemic corruption." He urged the country's political leaders to undertake meaningful, sustained reforms. This was echoed in more philosophical terms by António Guterres, the United Nations secretary-general, who addressed what was happening in Lebanon as part of a wave of similar demonstrations around the world. He wrote on October 25, "It is clear that there is a growing deficit of trust between people and political establishments, and rising threats to the social contract. The world is also wrestling with the negative impacts of globalization and new technologies, which have increased inequalities in societies."

While the proposed WhatsApp tax was quickly scrapped just hours after the protests began, there remained many other unresolved and incendiary issues. The protests pushed Lebanese prime minister Saad Hariri to meet with ambassadors from several countries, as well as representatives from the Arab League, China, and the United Nations, to discuss various proposed reforms, which included halving officials' salaries, reducing the deficit by $3.4 billion in 2020, giving $160 million in housing loans, and setting up an anticorruption committee. The representatives, who formed the International Support Group for Lebanon, encouraged political leaders to engage in an open dialogue with its country's citizens. But the planned package of reforms, which Hariri announced on October 21, did little to appease the protesters.

Two weeks into the protests, the movement got a boost when Hariri announced he was submitting his resignation, saying he had hit a "dead end" in negotiations with the protesters. However, views on Hariri's resignation were mixed. Some felt Hariri, who leads the Sunni-backed Future Movement, was part of the problem, and they welcomed his resignation, believing it would entail an overhaul of power. Others expressed concern that his withdrawal from government would give more muscle to corrupt opponents and to Hezbollah. Hariri—whose own father was assassinated in 2005, allegedly at the behest of foreign powers, when he was prime minister—blamed Iran and Hezbollah for causing turmoil in the region.

Just prior to his announcement, hundreds of Hezbollah men attacked protesters and destroyed their encampments, retreating only when security forces arrived on the scene. And while protesters had been demanding a government comprised of independent experts rather than sectarian representatives, some argued that this would be no more than a public relations victory, leaving the old *modus operandi* firmly in place. Although Hariri stepped down, other longtime politicians targeted by the protesters remained in power.

President Michel Aoun, in a speech on October 31, stressed the government's commitment to fighting corruption, eliminating terrorists, and returning Syrian refugees to the country. However, just two weeks later he called for an end to the protests, claiming they were in violation of international law and were like "stabbing the nation with a dagger."

Protests Turn Violent

While the protest movement strived for peaceful negotiations, violence soon erupted when supporters of Hezbollah, as well as the Hezbollah-allied Amal Movement, began attacking protesters. Hezbollah leader Hasan Nasrallah justified these actions by claiming that the protests were not "spontaneous," but rather funded by foreign embassies and countries. The military was dispatched to restore calm, a seemingly neutral peacekeeping buffer between the protesters and Hezbollah radicals.

But by the sixth week of the protest, the tide had turned, spurred on in part by the killing of Alaa Abou Fakhr on November 12. Fakhr, a Lebanese national, had attended the protest in Khalde with his wife and child. Unarmed, he was shot by a soldier who was attempting to clear a path for an army convoy. Later in the month, protesters gathered outside of the U.S. embassy in opposition to U.S. interference in Lebanon after Hezbollah claimed that U.S. meddling had delayed the formation of a new cabinet. On November 24, Hezbollah and Amal supporters burned civil society tents, trashed cars, and caused extensive property damage. When the Lebanese army intervened this time, it was with tear gas and flash grenades.

Months of protest had further weakened the country. Many local businesses were forced to stop paying their employees full salaries. Banks were limiting withdrawals to $200 a week, and there were major shortages and price hikes in gasoline, food, medical, and other vital supplies. The service sector had been crippled, in some cases dangerously so. Both private and public hospitals could not pay staff, because the government still owed them money. Lack of capital had caused the cost of imported medicine and medical equipment to skyrocket. Meanwhile, clashes were now occurring more frequently between security forces and the protesters, which appeared to substantiate President Donald Trump's claim that the country's armed forces had been infiltrated by Hezbollah. Security forces were using tear gas, water cannon, and metal fence barriers in their confrontations with demonstrators. As peaceful protest gave way to increased violence and rioting, the Lebanese Red Cross and Civil Defense began to report hundreds of injuries.

New Government Formed

As the protests wore on, the country's ruling parties failed to find a viable compromise candidate, and it was clear they were still reluctant to give up long-held privileges. President Aoun postponed a series of meetings that seemed prepared to reinstate Hariri. On January 21, 2020, Lebanon's government announced that Hassan Diab—a relatively unknown sixty-one-year-old computer engineering professor and former education minister with connections to Hezbollah—would be the country's new prime minister. But Diab did not appeal to protesters; they felt they were simply exchanging one bad choice for another. For many of Lebanon's citizens, the situation by year's end had reached a critical point, which Diab plaintively articulated: "We are facing the most difficult and dangerous stage in the history of Lebanon. We are facing a disaster."

A government dominated by Hezbollah, which is considered a terrorist group by the United States, United Kingdom, and other countries, was viewed negatively by some of Lebanon's allies, and threatened to invite international sanctions. The Trump administration placed a temporary hold on security aid destined for Lebanon amid these concerns; the money was ultimately released in December.

When asked if the United States would work with a government dominated by Hezbollah, Secretary of State Mike Pompeo was noncommittal at first. "We're prepared to engage, provide support, but only to a government that's committed to reform," he said. Later, Pompeo stated more strongly, "The test of Lebanon's new government will be its actions and its responsiveness to the demands of the Lebanese people to implement reforms and to fight corruption."

—Lyndi Schrecengost

Following is a statement by the European Union's high representative on October 25, 2019, responding to developments in the Lebanon protests; an October 29, 2019, press release from the Lebanese government announcing the prime minister's resignation; and a December 20, 2019, statement by Under Secretary of State for Political Affairs David Hale calling for the safety of protesters and formation of a new government.

DOCUMENT   *EU Responds to Protests in Lebanon*

October 25, 2019

The European Union is a close long-term partner of Lebanon and has followed with great attention the events taking place in the past days. The EU stands with Lebanon and is committed to the stability of the country and the region.

The EU supports the reform objectives that Prime Minister Hariri and the Government have outlined.

We are confident that the authorities will respond swiftly and wisely to legitimate aspirations of the Lebanese people by implementing much-needed and long-awaited structural and transformative reforms.

As we've discussed many times with our Lebanese partners, the fight against corruption, the implementation of good governance and of just and socially responsible reform measures is the first priority. In this regard the EU expects an inclusive dialogue on reforms and remains fully committed to the objectives agreed at the 2018 CEDRE conference.

The EU appreciates the overall non-violent nature of the protests and encourages the security forces to continue their policy of restraint.

The EU reaffirms its support to Lebanon and its people, and its commitment to the unity, sovereignty, stability, political independence and territorial integrity of Lebanon.

SOURCE: Council of the European Union. "Declaration by the High Representative on Behalf of the EU on the Latest Developments in Lebanon." October 25, 2019. © European Union, 2019. https://www.consilium.europa.eu/en/press/press-releases/2019/10/25/declaration-by-the-high-representative-on-behalf-of-the-eu-on-lebanon.

DOCUMENT   *Lebanese Prime Minister Resigns*

October 29, 2019

Prime Minister Saad Hariri announced the submission of the resignation of the government to H.E. President General Michel Aoun and the Lebanese people from all strata in response to the will of many Lebanese whom went to the squares to demand change and a commitment to the need to provide a safety net that protects the country at this historic moment. The Prime Minister called on all Lebanese to put the interest and safety of Lebanon, the protection of civil peace, and prevention of economic deterioration over anything else.

Prime Minister Al-Hariri's statement came in a speech addressed at four o'clock in the afternoon to the Lebanese people from the "House of the Center," which reads as follows:

> Thirteen days ago, the Lebanese people had been waiting for a decision to provide a political solution to stop the deterioration, and I tried throughout that period to find a way through which we could listen to the voice of the people and protect the country from security, economic and living risks. Today, I speak frankly to you, I have reached a dead end, and it is imperative that we cause a positive shock to face the crisis. I will head to Baabda Palace to present the resignation of the government to His Excellency President General Michel Aoun and the Lebanese people in all regions in response to the will of many Lebanese who went to the squares to demand change and as a commitment to the need to provide a safety net that protects the country at this historic moment.
>
> My appeal to all Lebanese is to advance Lebanon's interest and safety, protect civil peace, and prevent economic decline over anything else. To all partners in political life, I say: Our responsibility today is how to protect Lebanon and prevent the arrival of fires. Our responsibility is how to boost the economy, and there is a serious opportunity that must not be lost.
>
> I tender my resignation at the disposal of His Excellency the President and all the Lebanese. Jobs come and go; what's important is the country's dignity and safety.

Also, I say: "No one is bigger than the nation," May Allah protect Lebanon, May Allah protect Lebanon, long live you and Lebanon.

Source: Government of Lebanon. "PM Hariri Submits His Resignation to the President of the Republic and to All Lebanese People." Translated by SAGE Publishing. October 29, 2019. http://www.pcm.gov.lb/arabic/subpg.aspx?pageid=13514.

State Department Leader Calls for Security for Protesters

December 20, 2019

Good morning everyone I am in Lebanon today, at the request of Secretary of State Pompeo, to meet with Lebanese leaders to discuss the current situation here.

My visit reflects the strength of the partnership between our two countries.

I am here to encourage Lebanon's political leaders to commit to and to undertake meaningful, sustained reforms that can lead to a stable, prosperous, and secure Lebanon. And that was the content of the conversation that I just had with President Aoun.

It is time to put aside partisan interests and act in the national interest, advancing reforms and forming a government that is committed to undertake those reforms and capable of doing so. We have no role in saying who should lead and comprise such a cabinet. Or indeed any cabinet.

The unified, non-sectarian, and largely peaceful protests over the last 65 days reflect the Lebanese people's longstanding and frankly legitimate demand for economic and institutional reform, better governance, and an end to endemic corruption.

America calls on the security forces to continue to guarantee the safety of protesters as they engage in peaceful demonstrations, and for restraint by all. Violence has no place in civil discourse.

America wants Lebanon and its people—all of its people—to succeed, and we will remain a committed partner in that effort.

Thank you very much.

Source: U.S. Embassy in Lebanon. "Statement by U/S of State for Political Affairs David Hale Developments in Lebanon." December 20, 2019. https://lb.usembassy.gov/statement-by-u-s-of-state-for-political-affairs-david-hale-developments-in-lebanon.

OTHER HISTORIC DOCUMENTS OF INTEREST

FROM PREVIOUS *HISTORIC DOCUMENTS*

Treasury Secretary Addresses Budget Deficit; President Signs FY 2020 Spending Bills

OCTOBER 25 AND DECEMBER 20, 2019

In October, the Department of the Treasury announced that the federal budget deficit for fiscal year (FY) 2019 had reached $984 billion. That marked the fourth consecutive deficit increase but was lower than the original Trump administration estimation that the deficit would have topped $1 billion by the end of the fiscal year. Some members of Congress and economists raised alarm that the federal government was spending at an unsustainable rate, but those concerns were not reflected in either the two-year budget deal reached between the White House and Congress or the two FY 2020 spending bills.

FEDERAL DEFICIT NEARS $1 TRILLION

While campaigning for president, Donald Trump promised that he would eliminate the federal deficit, the gap between spending and revenue, within eight years. As president, however, the deficit increased nearly 50 percent from his inauguration in January 2017 through the end of FY 2019. From FY 2018 to FY 2019, the deficit grew 26 percent to $984 billion. The increase was driven largely by federal borrowing to compensate for the administration's tax and spending policies. The president sought, and Congress agreed to, large increases in military spending from an average of around $600 billion per year to more than $700 billion in 2019. To secure additional funding for the military, the president also allowed for funding increases in domestic programs such as Social Security and Medicare.

Another contributor to the growing deficit was a decrease in revenue. In FY 2019, which ended in September, federal spending grew twice as fast as tax revenue. Tax revenue had been decreasing since the December 2017 Tax Cuts and Jobs Act was signed into law, cutting about $1.5 trillion in taxes. "The biggest factor was the tax cuts, which gave a short-term sugar high but now are just contributing to a larger deficit," said Robert L. Bixby, executive director of the Concord Coalition, a group that promotes fiscal responsibility. "We don't have an economy that's going to grow its way out of this problem," he added. When it was selling the legislation to Congress and the American public, the administration promised the new law would not impact the deficit. "Not only will this tax plan pay for itself, but it will pay down debt," Treasury secretary Steven Mnuchin said in 2017. However, according to *The New York Times*, tax revenue was more than $400 billion short in fiscal years 2018 and 2019 than what the Congressional Budget Office (CBO) had predicted before the law was passed.

The increase in the federal deficit somewhat contradicted normal deficit patterns. Traditionally, when the economy is strong and unemployment is low, as it had been throughout the first three years of the Trump administration, the federal deficit decreases because fewer Americans seek federal safety-net benefits. "This is the first time in our history that we are seeing a boom in the economy at the same time deficits are rapidly rising. It's alarming," said Marc Goldwein, senior policy director for the Committee for a Responsible Federal Budget, a group that promotes reducing the federal deficit. G. William Hoagland, senior vice president at the Bipartisan Policy Center, said the deficit was "unprecedented in peacetime during a growing economy."

In an October 25 statement announcing the FY 2019 deficit, Mnuchin focused many of his remarks on the strength of the economy. "President Trump's economic agenda is working: the Nation is experiencing the lowest unemployment rate in nearly 50 years, there are more jobs to fill than there are job seekers, and Americans are experiencing sustained year-over-year wage increases," he said. He further placed the onus for fixing the deficit problem on Congress. "In order to truly put America on a sustainable financial path, we must enact proposals—like the president's 2020 budget plan—to cut wasteful and irresponsible spending," Mnuchin said.

The CBO predicted that the federal deficit would top $1 trillion in FY 2020 and could stay above that mark for the next decade. Economists speculated that the only reason why the deficit did not reach $1 trillion in FY 2019 was because of the tariffs imposed by the Trump administration on China and some other nations. According to the Department of the Treasury, the government collected nearly $71 billion in tariffs, up 70 percent from the previous year. The last time the federal deficit reached above $1 trillion was from 2009 to 2012 as the United States was coming out of the Great Recession and the federal government was spending at higher levels to encourage economic growth.

Budget Deal Inked

Despite the ballooning deficit, in August Congress negotiated and passed, and the president signed, a two-year budget deal that was expected to further increase the federal deficit. "Our nation's leaders are in debt denial, running up red ink all while ignoring trillions of dollars in shortfalls for Social Security, Medicare, and other programs that many millions of Americans rely upon," said Mitch Daniels, cochair of the Center for a Responsible Federal Budget. "We are at a turning point—without action now to phase in reforms over the coming years, Americans will face a much different future than the one that was promised," Daniels said. The president, however, tweeted that the deal was "phenomenal for our Great Military, our Vets, and Jobs, Jobs, Jobs!"

Some of the most conservative deficit hawks on Capitol Hill decried the spending increase. "I'm worried about the staggering debt we're leaving for our children and grandchildren," said Sen. Rick Scott, R-Fla. But others celebrated the bipartisan nature of the work done. "Today we saw an example of how government should work. Democrats and Republicans put partisanship aside and came together in favor of securing a stronger future for American families and upholding the full faith and credit of the United States," said House Budget Committee chair Rep. John Yarmuth, D-Ky. Many Republicans, who wanted only an increase in defense spending, pushed their colleagues to vote for the budget deal, recognizing that this compromise was likely the best possible in a divided Congress. "As our adversaries grow stronger, critical gaps remain in our ability to counter expansion, influence campaigns, and direct acts of violence toward America and our allies around the world," said Senate majority leader Mitch McConnell, R-Ky., on the Senate floor before the budget deal vote took place. "This bipartisan funding deal is the opportunity—the only opportunity on the table—to continue filling in those gaps, before it's too late," he added.

The budget deal passed the House by a vote of 284–149 and the Senate 67–28; Republican support was relatively weak in both chambers. The two-year $2.7 trillion agreement does not fund federal agencies but rather sets the parameters for the congressional appropriations committees to do their work. The deal permanently eliminated the Budget Control Act of 2011, which imposed caps on both defense and nondefense spending. As part of the deal, defense spending would increase approximately 3 percent while nondefense spending would rise around 4 percent. Initially, the president wanted to cut domestic spending while vastly increasing military funds, but Congress rejected the idea and the White House and Congress reached a compromise to increase both. The debt ceiling—the limit on how much the federal government can borrow—was also suspended through July 2021 as part of the budget deal.

President Trump Signs FY 2020 Spending Bills

While the budget deal did not eliminate the threat of a federal government shutdown if Congress failed to pass an FY 2020 budget, it did make the prospect somewhat less likely. Congress required two continuing resolutions to fund the government after the new fiscal year began on October 1; however, in December the two chambers were able to pass two separate funding packages containing all twelve regular appropriations bills. One bill package had funding for security-related programs, while the other covered domestic programs, foreign aid, tax breaks, and other miscellaneous items. The total $1.4 trillion in spending gave $738 billion to the military and $632 to nondefense agencies, up $22 billion and $27 billion, respectively, from the prior fiscal year. The bill included $1.375 billion for border barrier construction, in line with what was provided in FY 2019, but lower than the president's $5 billion request. Congress chose not to backfill the $3.6 billion previously diverted by the Trump administration from military construction projects to border wall construction, and it also did not seek to eliminate the administration's ability to reprogram funding for other parts of the wall. It instead left that decision to the courts, where a number of lawsuits were ongoing challenging the White House decision to move funds set aside for other defense projects to the southern border barrier. The FY 2020 funding legislation also raised the legal age to purchase tobacco from eighteen to twenty-one and eliminated three taxes that would have paid for Obamacare; the elimination is expected to add $373 billion to the federal deficit over the next ten years.

President Trump signed the pair of funding bills before midnight on December 20 to avert a federal shutdown. In his signing statement, the president said, "The government funding bills I just signed into law contain big victories for my Administration and the American people. They enable us to continue to advance our pro-growth, pro-worker, pro-family, America First agenda." Both Republicans and Democrats claimed victory in the annual funding fight. Sen. Richard Shelby, R-Ala., chair of the Senate Appropriations Committee, said the package included an important "increase in defense funding and the largest pay raise in a decade for our men and women in uniform." Democrats celebrated money set aside for gun violence prevention research, a pay raise for federal civilian workers, and additional funds for climate research and to combat the opioid crisis. "I am particularly proud that House Democrats prevailed in securing historic investments For the People, including record funding levels for Head Start and lifesaving medical research at NIH, and in funding priorities vital to our shared security, like gun violence prevention research and election security grants to states," said Rep. Nita Lowey, D-N.Y., chair of the House Appropriations Committee.

—Heather Kerrigan

Following is an October 25, 2019, statement by Department of the Treasury secretary Steven Mnuchin and Office of Management and Budget acting director Russell Vought on the FY 2019 federal deficit; and President Donald Trump's December 20, 2019, FY 2020 appropriations legislation signing statement.

Treasury and OMB Leaders Comment on Federal Deficit

October 25, 2019

[Footnotes have been omitted.]

U.S. Treasury Secretary Steven T. Mnuchin and Office of Management and Budget (OMB) Acting Director Russell Vought today released the final budget results for FY 2019. The deficit in FY 2019 was $984 billion, $205 billion more than in the prior fiscal year but $16 billion less than forecast in the FY 2020 Mid-Session Review (MSR). As a percentage of GDP, the deficit was 4.6 percent, 0.8 percentage point higher than the previous year.

"President Trump's economic agenda is working: the Nation is experiencing the lowest unemployment rate in nearly 50 years, there are more jobs to fill than there are job seekers, and Americans are experiencing sustained year-over-year wage increases," said U.S. Treasury Secretary Steven T. Mnuchin. "In order to truly put America on a sustainable financial path, we must enact proposals—like the President's 2020 budget plan—to cut wasteful and irresponsible spending."

"Americans from all walks of life are flourishing again thanks to pro-growth policies enacted by this Administration," said Acting OMB Director Russ Vought. "By providing a responsible fiscal path forward and pursuing pro-growth reforms, President Trump's agenda will make America's economic expansion enduring. That's why the President's Budget included more deficit reduction than any administration in history—saving $2.8 trillion over 10 years."

SUMMARY OF FISCAL YEAR 2019 BUDGET RESULTS

Year-end data from the September 2019 Monthly Treasury Statement of Receipts and Outlays of the United States Government show that the deficit for FY 2019 was $984 billion, $205 billion higher than the prior year's deficit. As a percentage of GDP, the deficit was 4.6 percent, an increase from 3.8 percent in FY 2018.

The FY 2019 deficit was $107 billion less than the estimate of $1,092 billion in the FY 2020 Budget (Budget), and $16 billion less than the estimate of $1,001 billion in the MSR, a supplemental update to the Budget published in July.

Governmental receipts totaled $3,462 billion in FY 2019. This was $133 billion higher than in FY 2018, an increase of 4.0 percent, above expectations from the Budget, but $10 billion below the MSR estimate. As a percentage of GDP, receipts equaled 16.3 percent, 0.1 percentage point lower than in FY 2018 and 1.1 percentage points below the average over the last 40 years. The nominal increase in receipts for FY 2019 can be attributed primarily to higher social insurance and retirement receipts, net individual income tax receipts, customs duties, net corporation income tax receipts, and excise taxes, partially offset by lower deposits of earnings by the Federal Reserve, and other miscellaneous receipts.

Outlays grew in FY 2019, but by less than expected in the Budget and the MSR. Outlays were $4,447 billion, $339 billion above those in FY 2018, an 8.2 percent increase. As a percentage of GDP, outlays were 20.9 percent, 0.7 percentage point higher than in the prior year, and 0.3 percentage point higher than the 40-year average of 20.6 percent. Contributing to the dollar increase over FY 2018 were higher outlays for Medicare, Social Security, Defense, and interest on the public debt.

Total Federal borrowing from the public increased by $1,052 billion during FY 2019 to $16,803 billion. The increase in borrowing included $984 billion in borrowing to finance the deficit, as well as $67 billion in net borrowing related to other transactions such as changes in cash balances and net disbursements for Federal credit programs. As a percentage of GDP, borrowing from the public grew from 77.5 percent of GDP at the end of FY 2018 to 79.1 percent of GDP at the end of FY 2019.

To coincide with the release of the Federal Government's year-end financial data, the Treasury's Bureau of the Fiscal Service has updated Your Guide to America's Finances (Your Guide) with this new data. Your Guide was launched in 2019 to make federal financial information transparent and accessible to all Americans. It presents a snapshot of the trillions of dollars collected and spent by the Federal Government each year and provides useful context for those numbers. Your Guide also clarifies common questions such as the difference between the deficit and the debt through user-friendly explanations, charts, and visualizations.

Table 1. Total Receipts, Outlays, and Deficit (in billions of dollars)

	Receipts	*Outlays*	*Deficit*
FY 2018 Actual	3,329	4,108	−779
Percentage of GDP	16.4%	20.2%	−3.8%
FY 2019 Estimates:			
2020 Budget	3,438	4,529	−1,092
2020 Mid-Session Review	3,472	4,473	−1,001
FY 2019 Actual	3,462	4,447	−984
Percentage of GDP	16.3%	20.9%	−4.6%

NOTE: Detail may not add to totals due to rounding.

Below are explanations of the differences between estimates in the MSR and the year-end actual amounts for receipts and agency outlays.

FISCAL YEAR 2019 RECEIPTS

Total receipts for FY 2019 were $3,462.2 billion, $10.1 billion lower than the MSR estimate of $3,472.3 billion. This net decrease in receipts was the net effect of lower-than-estimated collections of customs duties, social insurance and retirement receipts, individual income taxes, estate and gift taxes, and other miscellaneous receipts, partially offset by higher-than-estimated collections of corporation income tax receipts, deposits of earnings by the Federal Reserve, and excise taxes. Table 2 displays actual receipts and estimates from the Budget and the MSR by source.

- Individual income taxes were $1,717.9 billion, $1.2 billion lower than the MSR estimate. This decrease was the net effect of lower withheld payments of individual income tax liability of $4.4 billion, lower nonwithheld payments of $0.4 billion, and lower-than-estimated refunds of $2.4 billion.

- Corporation income taxes were $230.2 billion, $9.0 billion above the MSR estimate. This difference was the net effect of higher-than-expected payments of 2019 corporation income tax liability of $10.8 billion and higher-than-estimated refunds of $1.9 billion.

- Social insurance and retirement receipts were $1,243.1 billion, $2.7 billion lower than the MSR estimate.

- Excise taxes were $98.9 billion, $0.9 billion above the MSR estimate.

- Estate and gift taxes were $16.7 billion, $0.7 billion below the MSR estimate.

- Customs duties were $70.8 billion, $10.9 billion below the MSR estimate.

- Miscellaneous receipts were $84.6 billion, $4.6 billion below the MSR estimate. This was the net effect of lower-than-expected collections of various fees, penalties, forfeitures, and fines of $8.6 billion, in large part due to a reduced number of customs, commerce, and antitrust settlement agreements; partially offset by higher-than-expected deposits of earnings by the Federal Reserve System of $4.0 billion.

FISCAL YEAR 2019 OUTLAYS

Total outlays were $4,446.6 billion for FY 2018, $26.4 billion below the MSR estimate. Table 3 displays actual outlays by agency and major program as well as estimates from the Budget and the MSR. The largest changes in outlays from the MSR were in the following areas:

Department of Agriculture — Outlays for the Department of Agriculture were $150.1 billion, nearly $5.1 billion lower than the MSR estimate.

Outlays for the Farm Service Agency were $4.2 billion lower than estimated in the MSR, primarily due to slower-than-expected outlays from the Market Facilitation Program. Outlays for the Office of the Secretary were about $1 billion below the MSR estimate, due to slower than anticipated enrollment in the Wildfire and Hurricane Indemnity Program Plus disaster program.

Outlays in the Supplemental Nutrition Assistance Program (SNAP) were $1.9 billion lower than estimated in MSR due to declining participation. In July 2019, SNAP served 36.3 million people, nearly two million fewer than July 2018, and 4.5 million fewer than projected. Outlays for the Risk Management Agency were $4.2 billion higher than anticipated in the MSR primarily because USDA is allowing producers to defer premium payments until after harvest. Forest Service outlays were about $1.3 billion below the MSR estimate, primarily because the 2019 fire season was less severe than anticipated.

Department of Commerce — Outlays for the Department of Commerce were $11.3 billion, $2.1 billion lower than the MSR estimate.

This difference is primarily due to lower-than-expected outlays for the 2020 Decennial Census due to lower operational expenses and slower-than-expected hiring. Lower-than-expected outlays in the National Oceanic and Atmospheric Administration due to delays in certain weather satellites also contributed to the lower outlay rate.

Department of Defense — Outlays for the Department of Defense were $654.0 billion, $3.9 billion lower than the MSR estimate.

This difference is mostly due to lower-than-expected outlays for activities such as operation and maintenance contracts ($3.8 billion), Air Force research, development, test and evaluation contracts ($3.4 billion), and Military Construction projects ($0.7 billion); as well as higher-than-anticipated burden-sharing contributions from partner countries ($0.4 billion). These differences were partially offset by higher-than-expected outlays from accounts including Air Force miscellaneous procurement programs ($1.8 billion), Navy and Air Force Working Capital activities (1.2 billion), Army National Guard personnel ($0.7 billion), and Navy personnel ($0.5 billion).

Department of Education — Outlays for the Department of Education were $104.4 billion, $1.9 billion lower than the MSR estimate.

Outlays for the Hurricane Education Recovery account were $1.5 billion lower than anticipated for three reasons. Puerto Rico, the largest grantee, drew down their funds more slowly than anticipated due to contracting and capacity issues. Slower than usual Restart spending slowed down the anticipated phase 2 process of the Restart program. Similarly, Emergency Assistance to Institutions of Higher Education grantees were unable to spend all of their requested funds by the statutory deadline due to the nature of their projects which involve mostly construction or repairs.

In the Pell Grant program, outlays were $1.2 billion higher than projected in the MSR, due to faster-than-expected disbursement patterns.

For the Federal Direct Student Loan program, because of changes in the mix of activity in direct student loans, $2.7 billion less in positive subsidy outlays for the 2017 loan cohort were recorded in 2019 than estimated in the MSR, primarily due to reduced Consolidation loan volume compared to original estimates.

Department of Health and Human Services — Outlays for the Department of Health and Human Services (HHS) were $1,213.8 billion, $2.2 billion lower than the MSR estimate.

Outlays for Medicaid were $3.6 billion above the MSR estimate. The difference was primarily the result of higher-than-anticipated benefits spending during the second half of the year.

Outlays for Medicare Part A were $1.5 billion lower than the MSR estimate due in part to lower utilization of inpatient hospital services and lower than estimated skilled nursing facility utilization among Medicare beneficiaries. Outlays for Medicare Part B were $3.1 billion higher than the MSR estimate which is likely due to higher utilization of outpatient services. Federal contributions to Medicare Part B were $1 billion higher than the MSR estimate which is also likely due to higher than anticipated utilization of outpatient services.

The actual outlays for other health programs was $3.2 billion lower than what was projected in MSR. This is primarily due to the absence of an appropriation for Cost-Sharing Reductions (–$2 billion).

Actual outlays for Temporary Assistance for Needy Families (TANF) were $1.2 billion lower than what was projected in MSR. TANF was initially extended on short-term bases in appropriations bills, and in January 2019, its authorization was extended through June 2019. Legislation extending the program through the end of 2019 was not signed until July 5, 2019, causing a delay in the availability of funding. At the time that the MSR estimate was developed, HHS believed the states would compensate for this delay so that total outlays at the end of the fiscal year would be consistent with prior years. However, states did not spend the funding as anticipated.

Department of Homeland Security — Outlays for the Department of Homeland Security were $56.3 billion, $2.4 billion lower than the MSR estimate.

Approximately $1.7 billion of the difference is driven by the Federal Emergency Management Agency (FEMA). FEMA's Disaster Relief Fund MSR outlay estimate differential accounts for $570 million of the overestimate, which can be attributed to the difficulty in determining when a grantee may draw down disaster funds. FEMA overestimated Urban Area Security Initiative outlays for the same reason. Finally, the government shutdown impacted outlays for facility maintenance, IT systems, and security contracts. Approximately $635 million of the difference is due to U.S. Coast Guard (USCG), driven by a combination of a late year appropriation, which delayed the timeline for normal issuance of contracts. Additionally, USCG's large unobligated carryover related to emergency funding remaining from 2018 and new emergency funding in 2019 has been spent down slower than a usual project, which was not adequately captured in the MSR estimate.

Department of Justice — Outlays for the Department of Justice were $35.1 billion, $4.8 billion lower than the MSR estimate. The Department's difference is predominately due to large differences in both the Crime Victims Fund (CVF) and the Asset Forfeiture Program (AFP).

Outlays for the CVF were $1.4 billion lower than estimated in MSR due to a slower-than-anticipated draw down of funds made available in prior fiscal years. Outlays by the AFP were $1.2 billion lower than anticipated in MSR due to an unanticipated lag in victim payments. Additionally, outlays were lower across many accounts due to delayed enactment of 2019 appropriations.

Department of the Treasury — Net outlays for the Department of the Treasury were $689.5 billion, $8.4 billion higher than the MSR estimate.

The increase was attributable primarily to dividend payments from Fannie Mae and Freddie Mac (the GSEs) on their Senior Preferred Stock that were $5.0 billion less than projected, increasing net outlays relative to MSR due to a reduction in offsetting receipts.

This change is the result of an agreement, announced after the MSR was released, that increases the level of capital the GSEs are permitted to retain.

In addition, payment where certain tax credits exceed liability for corporate tax was $4.3 billion higher than projected in MSR. This change is a result of larger refund payments in May and June than were anticipated in MSR.

Net outlays for intragovernmental interest transactions with non-budgetary credit financing accounts were $2.1 billion higher than projected, including $4.4 billion in lower-than-projected interest paid to credit financing accounts and $6.5 billion in lower-than-anticipated receipts of interest from credit financing accounts. (Interest received from credit financing accounts is reported in Treasury's aggregate offsetting receipts.)

These amounts were partially offset by lower outlays for interest on the public debt, which is paid to the public and to trust funds and other government accounts. Interest on the public debt was $4.2 billion lower than the MSR estimate, due primarily to lower-than-projected interest paid to the public, particularly on inflation-protected and shorter-maturity securities.

Department of Veterans Affairs — Outlays for the Department of Veterans Affairs (VA) were $199.6 billion, $4.6 billion lower than the MSR estimate.

Veterans Health Administration outlays were $2.7 billion less than projected in MSR. The primary driver was an inadvertent adjustment in MSR estimates of medical services outlays by $2.1 billion due to the timing of obligations. The next largest contributor was a $0.5 billion decrease in the Veterans Choice Program, driven by the accelerated transition from the Veterans Choice Program to the VA Medical Community Care program.

Outlays for Departmental Administration were $1.7 billion less than projected in MSR. The primary driver is approximately $0.8 billion less in the supply fund due to an error in calculating MSR outlay projections. The VA Electronic Health Record contributed to the difference due to later than anticipated contract awards reducing the portion of outlays from 2019 and increasing outlays into 2020.

The decrease in benefits programs is due to reduced claim payments based on the number of claimants.

International Assistance Programs — Outlays for International Assistance Programs were $23.6 billion, $1.4 billion higher than the MSR estimate.

This difference is largely due to net outlays for Foreign Military Sales that were $3.1 billion higher than the MSR estimate due to lower-than-anticipated receipts received from foreign governments for weapons purchases. This difference can be attributed to variables associated with the contracting and sale of defense articles and services. The higher Foreign Military Sales outlays were partially offset by lower-than-estimated outlays from Foreign Military Financing grants.

National Aeronautics and Space Administration — Outlays for the National Aeronautics and Space Administration were $20.2 billion, $1.1 billion lower than the MSR estimate. The NASA mission areas with the largest variances are Science, Deep Space Exploration, and LEO and Spaceflight Operations. Outlays were lower than anticipated due to delays due to the government shut down and Congressional reporting requirements; program schedule delays; and new contracts that outlay at slower rates than has been typical.

Federal Deposit Insurance Corporation — Net outlays for the Federal Deposit Insurance Corporation were −$7.5 billion, $1.7 billion lower than the MSR estimate. The difference was almost entirely due to lower-than-estimated outlays from the Orderly Liquidation Fund.

United States Postal Service — Net outlays for the United States Postal Service were –$1.0 billion, $1.0 billion lower than the MSR estimate, due mostly to non-personnel operating, capital, and transportation expenses that were lower than anticipated in MSR.

Undistributed Offsetting Receipts — Undistributed Offsetting Receipts were –$247.8 billion, $1.5 billion lower than the MSR estimate (higher collections).

Interest received by trust funds was $1.2 billion lower than the MSR estimate. The difference was due largely to Medicare interest earnings, which were $1.8 billion higher than the MSR estimate. This intragovernmental interest is paid out of the Department of the Treasury account for interest on the public debt and has no net impact on total Federal Government outlays.

SOURCE: U.S. Department of the Treasury. "Mnuchin and Vought Release Joint Statement on Budget Results for Fiscal Year 2019." October 25, 2019. https://home.treasury.gov/news/press-releases/sm806.

President Trump Signs FY 2020 Appropriations Bills

December 20, 2019

The Government funding bills I just signed into law contain big victories for my administration and the American people. They enable us to continue to advance our progrowth, proworker, profamily, America-first agenda.

These bills will help us rebuild and invest in the military, with a $22 billion increase in defense spending (to $738 billion in fiscal year 2020), a pay raise of 3.1 percent for the troops, and the establishment of the United States Space Force. At the same time, the bills enable us to help our veterans by robustly funding the Department of Veterans Affairs (VA), and ensuring America's veterans receive the best choice in their care between VA, the community, telehealth, and urgent care.

The legislation increases access to affordable and high-quality childcare for American families. It also expands apprenticeships and workforce development programs and extends the paid parental leave tax credit and the work opportunity tax credit, providing grant incentives for businesses to hire and retain well-qualified employees.

The legislation builds on criminal justice reform efforts by providing $75 million for my Administration's historic criminal justice reform initiative, the First Step Act.

We continue to defend America's most vulnerable, the unborn. The legislation preserves all pro-life protections like the Hyde Amendment, rejects Senator Jeanne Shaheen's anti-life amendment that could have increased funding for pro-abortion organizations; and rejects all anti- life riders in the partisan versions of these bills that originally passed the House, including one that would have undermined my administration's pro-life title X rule.

The legislation preserves my authorities to build the wall on our southern border, and it prevents attempts to slash and cap ICE detention beds, as well as efforts to defund and block my administration's successful strategies and use of available law enforcement tools, which have produced dramatic reductions in illegal border-crossings.

We have now also repealed the Obamacare medical device tax, which threatened access to cutting-edge devices that save lives and enhance the quality of life for all Americans. We also eliminated the Obamacare "Cadillac tax," which would have imposed a 40 percent tax on 1 in 5 employers in 2022, ultimately placing severe financial burdens on employees.

Taken together, the Government funding bills guarantee that critical priorities—investing in the military, ensuring Americans are more prosperous and healthy, delivering border security, engaging on criminal justice reform, and defending life—will be met in the upcoming year.

SOURCE: Executive Office of the President. "Statement on Signing Fiscal Year 2020 Appropriations Legislation." December 20, 2019. *Compilation of Presidential Documents* 2019, no. 00879 (December 20, 2019). https://www.govinfo.gov/content/pkg/DCPD-201900879/pdf/DCPD-201900879.pdf.

OTHER HISTORIC DOCUMENTS OF INTEREST

FROM THIS VOLUME

FROM PREVIOUS *HISTORIC DOCUMENTS*

President Trump Announces Death of ISIL Leader

OCTOBER 27, 2019

Islamic State of Iraq and the Levant (ISIL) leader Abu Bakr al-Baghdadi's life came to a violent end following a U.S. military raid carried out October 26–27, 2019, in northwest Syria. Tracked by military dogs and cornered by U.S. special operations forces at the end of a dead-end tunnel, the self-styled caliph detonated a suicide vest, killing himself, two women (also wearing suicide vests that had not detonated), and three children, reportedly his own, who were with him. There were no U.S. casualties.

Baghdadi's Radicalism

Born in the central Iraqi city of Samarra into a religious Sunni Arab family, Baghdadi's birth name was recorded as Ibrahim Awad Ibrahim al-Badri, but he was known by many names. Abu Bakr al-Baghdadi was his *nom de guerre*; he would later claim descent from the Quraysh tribe (the tribe of Muhammad and therefore a prerequisite for becoming a caliph), but this link has not been substantiated.

It is unclear precisely when Baghdadi became radicalized, but there were early signs of a developing predilection. Relatives referred to the teenaged Baghdadi as "the believer" due to the long hours he spent at the local mosque memorizing the Koran, as well as his tendency to rebuke those whom he believed had deviated from Islamic law. Shy and unprepossessing, he would join the Muslim Brotherhood in his youth. After moving to Baghdad in the early 1990s, Baghdadi acquired both undergraduate and graduate degrees in Islamic studies.

International experts believe the chaos of post-2003 Iraq most likely played a role in shaping Baghdadi's extremist and violent radicalism. Following the U.S. invasion that toppled Saddam Hussein, Baghdadi first showed up on U.S. radar when it was discovered that he had helped found an Islamist insurgent group called *Jamaat Jayah Ahi al-Sunnah was-l-Jamaah*, responsible for attacks on U.S. troops and their allies. In early 2004, he was interned as a civilian, along with other future al Qaeda leaders, in the city of Fallujah, Iraq, and then taken to a detention center at Camp Bucca, in the southern part of the country.

Some recent scholarship indicates that American-run detention centers such as Camp Bucca were breeding grounds for Islamic militancy, places where detainees could easily form contacts and nurture networks. Baghdadi's behavior while there—delivering sermons, leading prayers, and even mediating in prison disputes—led him to be considered a "low-level threat" by the U.S. military, resulting in his release after just ten months.

Baghdadi joined the Mujahideen Shura Council (MSC) in 2006, and when MSC was renamed the Islamic State of Iraq (ISI)—also known as al Qaeda in Iraq—he became the general supervisor of the ISI's *sharia* (or law) committee. Following the death of his predecessor, Abu Omar al-Baghdadi, Baghdadi was declared the leader of ISI in May 2010. In

April 2013, after ISI merged with the al-Nusra Front, Baghdadi renamed the terrorist group ISIL.

Baghdadi's Rise to Power

In 2011, ISI began a campaign of conquest that led to its takeover of significant parts of Iraq and Syria. It was able to do this in part because the U.S. military had left Iraq, and Syria was in the throes of a civil war. Following the death of al Qaeda leader Osama bin Laden in Pakistan in 2012, Baghdadi appeared to accelerate violent retaliatory actions across Iraq, including raids, suicide attacks, and roadside bombings.

Baghdadi's rise to prominence led to his designation by the U.S. Department of State as a Specially Designated Global Terrorist. By 2011, he had a $25 million price on his head. In 2014, Baghdadi took to a pulpit in a mosque in Mosul, Iraq, to outline his vision for what was a rapidly expanding terrorist organization with an extreme and often brutal ideology.

Baghdadi was responsible for many atrocities and human rights violations, including organized rape, floggings, systematic executions, and the genocide of the Yazidis in Iraq. Under his leadership, he executed one of the deadliest terrorist attacks in Sri Lanka. Baghdadi was also implicated in the fate of American humanitarian aid worker Kayla Mueller. Although it was reported that Mueller had been killed in an anti-ISIL airstrike in February 2015, others have claimed that she was murdered by ISIL.

Baghdadi was able to stay off the grid for years, successfully eluding capture and keeping himself hidden for so long it was often rumored he was dead or wounded. He rarely appeared on video and avoided all electronic devices. However, in April 2019, he released a rare video recording. It was a critical moment for ISIL, as the group had lost its territory in Iraq and Syria—largely due to a counteroffensive organized by the United States and its allies in the region—and Baghdadi's whereabouts were unknown. Baghdadi reasserted his authority and made clear that ISIL's vision had not changed. Although the so-called caliphate in Iraq and Syria had been destroyed, it is believed that there are many thousands of fighters left who have gone underground in places as diverse as Australia and Algeria.

Baghdadi Killed in U.S. Raid

On October 27, 2019, President Donald Trump announced in a nationally televised address that the U.S. military had carried out a "dangerous and daring nighttime raid" to capture or kill Baghdadi. According to the president, Baghdadi's whereabouts became known to the United States a couple of weeks before the attack. U.S. commandos in turn trained for a raid of the ISIL leader's compound, which they undertook on October 26, 2019, at approximately 5:00 p.m. Eastern.

Deeming Baghdadi's killing the "top national security priority of my administration," President Trump was jubilant, saying, "He died like a dog. He died like a coward. The world is now a much safer place." It appeared that only a few members of Congress had learned of the raid before its announcement, prompting House Speaker Nancy Pelosi, D-Calif., to complain that the Russians had been informed of the operation, but not the country's own congressional leadership. She called on the president to present a clear strategy for defeating ISIL. Some also questioned if there was a connection between the action against Baghdadi and Trump's earlier decision to withdraw troops from Syria, a move some analysts warned could pave the way for an ISIL resurgence.

After he was killed, Baghdadi was buried at sea and afforded Islamic rites. In an audio recording that aired on October 31, 2019, ISIL's media arm, Amaq, confirmed the death of Baghdadi while at the same time announcing his successor, Abu Ibrahim al-Hashimi al-Qurayshi.

—Lyndi Schrecengost

Following is the text of President Donald Trump's statement on October 27, 2019, announcing the death of ISIL leader Abu Bakr al-Baghdadi.

President Trump Announces Death of Abu Bakr al-Baghdadi

October 27, 2019

The President. Last night the United States brought the world's number-one terrorist leader to justice. Abu Bakr al-Baghdadi is dead. He was the founder and leader of ISIS, the most ruthless and violent terror organization anywhere in the world.

The United States has been searching for Baghdadi for many years. Capturing or killing Baghdadi has been the top national security priority of my administration. U.S. Special Operations forces executed a dangerous and daring nighttime raid in northwestern Syria and accomplished their mission in grand style. The U.S. personnel were incredible. I got to watch much of it.

No personnel were lost in the operation, while a large number of Baghdadi's fighters and companions were killed with him. He died after running into a dead-end tunnel, whimpering and crying and screaming all the way. The compound had been cleared by this time, with people either surrendering or being shot and killed. Eleven young children were moved out of the house and are uninjured. The only ones remaining were Baghdadi in the tunnel, and he had dragged three of his young children with him. They were led to certain death.

He reached the end of the tunnel as our dogs chased him down. He ignited his vest, killing himself and the three children. His body was mutilated by the blast. The tunnel had caved in on it, in addition. But test results gave certain immediate and totally positive identification. It was him.

The thug who tried so hard to intimidate others spent his last moments in utter fear, in total panic and dread, terrified of the American forces bearing down on him. We were in the compound for approximately 2 hours, and after the mission was accomplished, we took highly sensitive material and information from the raid, much having to do with ISIS origins, future plans, things that we very much want.

Baghdadi's demise demonstrates America's relentless pursuit of terrorist leaders and our commitment to the enduring and total defeat of ISIS and other terrorist organizations. Our reach is very long. As you know, last month, we announced that we recently killed Hamza bin Laden, the very violent son of Usama bin Laden, who was saying very bad things about people, about our country, about the world. He was the heir apparent to Al Qaida.

Terrorists who oppress and murder innocent people should never sleep soundly, knowing that we will completely destroy them. These savage monsters will not escape their fate, and they will not escape the final judgment of God. Baghdadi has been on the run for many years, long before I took office. But at my direction, as Commander in Chief of the United States, we obliterated his caliphate, 100 percent, in March of this year.

Today's events are another reminder that we will continue to pursue the remaining ISIS terrorists to their brutal end. That also goes for other terrorist organizations. They are, likewise, in our sights. Baghdadi and the losers who worked for him—and losers they are—they had no idea what they were getting into. In some cases, they were very frightened puppies. In other cases, they were hardcore killers. But they killed many, many people. Their murder of innocent Americans—James Foley, Steven Sotloff, Peter Kassig, and Kayla Mueller—were especially heinous. The shocking publicized murder of a Jordanian pilot, a wonderful young man—spoke to the King of Jordan; they all knew him, they all loved him—he was burned alive in a cage for all to see. And the execution of Christians in Libya and Egypt, as well as the genocidal mass murder of Yazidis, rank ISIS among the most depraved organizations in the history of our world.

The forced religious conversions, the orange suits prior to so many beheadings, all of which were openly displayed for the world to see, this was all that Abu Bakr al-Baghdadi—this is what he wanted. This is what he was proud of. He was a sick and depraved man, and now he's gone. Baghdadi was vicious and violent, and he died in a vicious and violent way, as a coward, running and crying.

This raid was impeccable and could only have taken place with the acknowledgement and help of certain other nations and people. I want to thank the nations of Russia, Turkey, Syria, and Iraq. And I also want to thank the Syrian Kurds for certain support they were able to give us. This was a very, very dangerous mission.

Thank you, as well, to the great intelligence professionals who helped make this very successful journey possible. I want to thank the soldiers, and sailors, airmen, and marines involved in last night's operation. You are the very best there is anywhere in the world. No matter where you go, there is nobody even close.

I want to thank General Mark Milley and our Joint Chiefs of Staff, and I also want to thank our professionals who work in other agencies of the United States Government and were critical to the mission's unbelievable success.

Last night was a great night for the United States and for the world. A brutal killer, one who has caused so much hardship and death, has violently been eliminated. He will never again harm another innocent man, woman, or child. He died like a dog. He died like a coward. The world is now a much safer place.

God bless America. Thank you.

[A question-and-answer session with reports has been omitted.]

Source: Executive Office of the President. "Remarks on the Death of Islamic State of Iraq and Syria (ISIS) Terrorist Organization Leader Abu Bakr al-Baghdadi and an Exchange with Reporters." October 27, 2019. *Compilation of Presidential Documents* 2019, no. 00757 (October 27, 2019). https://www.govinfo.gov/content/pkg/DCPD-201900757/pdf/DCPD-201900757.pdf.

OTHER HISTORIC DOCUMENTS OF INTEREST

FROM THIS VOLUME

FROM PREVIOUS *HISTORIC DOCUMENTS*

November

OAS Conducts Election
Audit in Bolivia

NOVEMBER 10 AND 11, AND DECEMBER 4, 2019

Bolivian president Evo Morales stepped down in November 2019 after the Organization of American States (OAS) released a report finding serious irregularities and evidence of vote count manipulation during the country's latest general election. A subsequent slew of resignations among high-ranking officials put Senate vice president and opposition leader Jeanine Añez Chavez in line to become interim president until new elections could be called. This entire period was marked by continual unrest, as both pro- and anti-Morales Bolivians took to the streets to make their voices heard.

A POPULAR PRESIDENT LOSES SUPPORT

After becoming Bolivia's first indigenous president in 2006, Morales earned a reputation as a champion of the country's native populations and the poor. He gained tremendous public support for his successful efforts to grow the Bolivian economy, leveraging revenues from the commodities boom, international investments, and redistribution of the country's natural gas wealth to improve infrastructure in poor communities and lift millions of people out of poverty. However, an economic slowdown—coinciding with the global decline in oil and natural gas prices—and a growing perception that Morales was attempting to consolidate power eroded his popularity. In addition to stacking the courts and electoral bodies with loyalists and increasing prosecution of political opponents, Morales tried in 2016 to eliminate presidential term limits. (During his first term, Morales oversaw the development of a new Bolivian Constitution that included a two-term limit for presidents. His successors had been limited to one five-year term.) When voters rejected his proposed constitutional amendment in a public referendum, Morales appealed the outcome to the Constitutional Court. The court overturned the vote, ruling that term limits infringed upon the president's human rights. Morales subsequently stated his intent to run for a fourth term in 2019.

ELECTION MARRED BY FRAUD ALLEGATIONS

The general election took place on October 20. Of the nine registered presidential candidates, Carlos Mesa emerged as Morales's primary opponent. Mesa had briefly served as president from 2003 to 2005, following the resignation of former president Gonzalo Sánchez de Lozada amid widespread public protests and strikes. He was the chosen candidate of Civic Community, a political coalition of centrist parties that had come together in 2018 to challenge Morales's campaign for a fourth term.

The Supreme Electoral Tribunal released a preliminary vote count several hours after the polls closed. With about 80 percent of votes recorded, Morales did not appear to have enough support to win the first round outright. (In order to avoid a second-round vote, presidential candidates must either win more than 50 percent of the vote or receive between 40 percent and 50 percent of the vote *and* be at least 10 percent ahead of their closest opponent.) Then the tribunal suddenly stopped publishing results for almost twenty-four hours. When the tribunal released its next update on the evening of October 21, Morales was projected to win a first-round victory by a narrow margin of votes over Mesa.

The results reversal and the suspicious interruption in the tribunal's reporting immediately prompted allegations of vote tampering and triggered major public protests. Mesa and his supporters released documentation they claimed provided evidence of election fraud, including records that showed more votes were counted in some precincts than there were eligible voters. "This government is trying to block the path to a second round," said Mesa. (Analysts had projected that if a second-round vote occurred, the other seven candidates would throw their support behind Mesa, making a Morales victory less likely.)

Morales declared himself the winner on October 24, an outcome confirmed by the official results released the following day. The Supreme Electoral Tribunal reported that Morales won 46.8 percent of the vote compared to Mesa's 36.7 percent, meaning the president had narrowly avoided a second-round poll. Tribunal officials acknowledged the results may be challenged. "We are aware of the critical situation we find ourselves in," said María Eugenia Choque, tribunal president. "With my heart in my hand, we are open to any audit." Manuel González, leader of OAS's election observation mission in Bolivia, said he was "profoundly concerned" by the "drastic" reversal, which he called "inexplicable." He added that OAS would prepare a comprehensive report on the election's conduct that would likely conclude a second-round vote was warranted. Officials in Argentina, Brazil, Colombia, the European Union, and the United States called for a second round. Morales allies, including officials in Mexico, Nicaragua, and Venezuela, recognized the results and congratulated the president.

The official results were rejected by Mesa and other opposition leaders, and they called for protests to continue. Morales responded by urging his supporters to block access points to Bolivian cities to keep antigovernment protesters at bay. Some Bolivians formed a type of neighborhood watch in their communities to help protect against vandals and riots as tensions escalated. Altercations between Morales supporters and antigovernment protesters were reported, as were clashes between protesters and police. Several local electoral tribunal offices were set on fire. Support for the president began to wear thin as protests continued. On October 31, a letter released by the army, air force, and navy declared that nearly 3,000 officers refused to intervene in the unrest and would not stop antigovernment protesters. "The armed forces of the state will never take up arms against the people," the letter stated. "Our weapons will only be raised to defend our people, our Constitution and our laws." There were also reports that several police units had mutinied and joined the protests.

OAS Audit Finds Irregularities, Flaws in Election

With election fraud allegations swirling and unrest paralyzing the country, the Bolivian government agreed on October 30 to cooperate with an OAS audit "of the electoral integrity" of the general election. "We have nothing to hide," Morales declared. OAS dispatched a team of thirty-six specialists—including electoral attorneys, statisticians, IT specialists, handwriting experts, and others—to Bolivia. The team was charged with conducting "a proper audit of the official vote count in the elections of October 20, along with verification of the tally sheets, statistical aspects, the electoral process, and the chain of custody."

Mounting public pressure prompted the OAS team to issue a preliminary report on its findings on November 10. The results were damning. In one instance, the team found irregularities in 23 percent of a sample of more than 300 tally sheets, which are used by polling place workers to manually count votes. "In some cases, it was confirmed that all the tally sheets in a center had been completed by the same person," the report said. "Sometimes, that person turned out to be the MAS representative accredited as the party's delegate in the voting center concerned." (MAS refers to the Movement Towards Socialism party, which is the political party of Morales.) The team also found evidence of forged signatures on the tally sheets. They speculated that "even more irregularities would surface" if the team had more time to review additional documentation.

The OAS team also found flaws in the two different systems used to transmit election results. (The first of these systems was called the Preliminary Election Results Transmission System, or TREP, and was designed to provide an initial quick count of votes on Election Day. The second system was meant to provide the final, official vote count.) Best practices for system software testing and authentication were not followed, the team wrote, and test data were found mixed in with actual tally sheets from election day. Furthermore, an outside user was able to gain access to the vote-counting server through an application that would have enabled them to alter data. The team also found that when the transmission of preliminary results resumed on the evening of October 21, the data were being redirected from TREP's primary server to two other servers that were not overseen by Bolivia's Civic Registry Service, which manages the initial count of election results. This was particularly concerning, the team wrote, because there were approved backup servers under the Civic Registry Service's control that were not used and there was "no valid technical explanation" for why those backups had not been used instead of external equipment. The use of external servers would have made it possible for someone to manipulate the data and falsify records. "This is extremely serious and impacts the transparency of the process," the team wrote. Also concerning to the team was a lack of documentation about the transmission interruption. "There is no document with the life cycle of the incident relating to the interruption of the TREP, which might explain what happened and the root cause of it. Nor is there a detailed record of the persons who acted at that moment and the role they played."

Other irregularities included OAS's finding that the official counts for Potosí and Chuquisaca states were not conducted on the premises of established electoral facilities. Instead, tally sheets were driven to locations that were three hours and one and a half hours away, respectively. Electoral officials told OAS this was done because the original facilities were "ill-suited" to conduct the counting process due to protests and riots occurring at the time. However, OAS noted that party delegates were not informed of the location change and thus were unable to witness the official vote count. Furthermore, the team observed that local electoral tribunals lacked standardized organizational procedures for processing tally sheets. Another portion of the audit report contained a detailed analysis of the last 5 percent of the vote count, which the team concluded showed a "highly unlikely trend." The team's analysis showed a steep increase in support for Morales as these votes were counted while votes for Mesa dropped off. "Morales average vote share increased by over 15% compared to the previous 95%, while Mesa's average vote share plunged by about the same percentage. This pattern is highly unusual," the report said.

Considering all of these irregularities and flaws, the OAS team concluded that it "cannot validate the results of this election and therefore recommends another electoral process. Any future process should be overseen by new electoral authorities to ensure the conduct of credible elections." The team's final report, released on December 4, affirmed the initial findings of "intentional manipulation" and "serious irregularities." These findings "do not allow for certainty about the margin of victory of the candidate Evo Morales over the candidate Carlos Mesa," OAS said. "What can be affirmed is that there has been a series of intentional operations aimed at altering the will expressed at the polls."

MORALES RESIGNS

Responding to the preliminary OAS report, Morales denied wrongdoing but announced that new elections would be held, prior to which lawmakers would choose new members of the Supreme Electoral Tribunal. However, the audit findings had already started a chain of events that saw remaining support for Morales crumble in a matter of hours. Gen. Williams Kaliman, leader of the Bolivian Army, voiced the military's support for the protesters and called on Morales to resign. Indigenous groups and labor unions also withdrew their support for the president, and the attorney general ordered an investigation into tribunal members' conduct. High-ranking MAS officials, including Senate president Adriana Salvatierra Arriaza and Chamber of Deputies president Victor Borda, resigned. Protesters ransacked Morales's home and broke into the homes of other MAS officials. (Borda's house was among those set on fire. His brother was also kidnapped.)

Morales and Vice President Alvaro Garcia Linera announced their resignation later that day. Morales accused Mesa and protest leader Luis Fernando Camacho of conspiring against his government, declaring that "the world and our Bolivian patriots repudiate the coup." Officials in Mexico echoed sentiments that a "coup" had ousted Morales and granted the former president asylum. Some Bolivians remained loyal to Morales and descended on La Paz to demonstrate their ongoing support. The OAS General Secretariat issued a statement cautioning against "any unconstitutional resolution of the situation" and calling for peace. The General Secretariat also urged Bolivian lawmakers to meet to "name new electoral authorities to guarantee a new electoral process," adding that it was important for law enforcement officials to investigate "the commission of crimes" related to the October 20 vote.

On November 12, Senate vice president and opposition leader Jeanine Añez Chavez declared herself interim president before the Plurinational Legislative Assembly. MAS lawmakers boycotted the legislative session during which Añez was to be confirmed, but the Constitutional Court affirmed her posting. "I assume the presidency immediately and will do everything necessary to pacify the country," Añez said, adding a promise that she would quickly call new elections. Añez began naming her new cabinet ministers on November 13. The same day, Gen. Carlos Orellana Centellas was named the new commander of the armed forces and pledged to take orders from Añez as interim president.

Fresh protests broke out following Añez's confirmation, with Morales supporters calling for her to step down. On November 14, Añez signed a decree granting troops immunity for actions taken in a "legitimate defense or state of necessity" as they worked to calm the unrest. The decree raised concerns that Añez was opening the door to human rights abuses—concerns magnified by subsequent clashes between security forces and protesters that resulted in nine deaths. On November 23, the Plurinational Legislative Assembly unanimously passed a bill annulling October election results and preventing Morales from running in a new poll. In return, Añez agreed to revoke the immunity decree and withdraw troops from most protest areas, among other things. Añez signed the bill into law on November 24. The Supreme Electoral Tribunal announced in early January 2020 that a new election will take place on May 3, 2020.

—Linda Grimm

Following is the preliminary election audit report released by the Organization of American States (OAS) on November 10, 2019; a statement issued by the OAS General Secretariat on November 11, 2019, on the situation in Bolivia; and a press release from OAS on December 4, 2019, publishing the final election audit report.

Report on OAS Audit of General Elections in Bolivia

November 10, 2019

[All graphs and charts have been omitted.]

Background

On October 30, the OAS General Secretariat and the Government of the Plurinational State of Bolivia signed the agreements relating to the analysis of the electoral integrity of the elections held on October 20. Those documents established that the Government would provide every facility needed to perform a proper audit of the official vote count in the elections of October 20, along with verification of the tally sheets, statistical aspects, the electoral process, and the chain of custody. It was likewise agreed that the authorities would provide the OAS experts with full access to their installations, as well as any information regarding the elections that the team considered relevant.

At the same time, it was established that the audit would focus on Election Day (October 20) and on subsequent stages and that, upon completing its analysis, the group of specialists would deliver a report to the Secretary General, who would remit it to the Government of Bolivia. In addition, in order to ensure both maximum seriousness and rigor, it was established that the conclusions would be binding upon the parties to the process.

On instructions from the Secretary General, a team was formed consisting of 36 specialists of 18 different nationalities, including electoral attorneys, statisticians, I.T. experts, document specialists, handwriting experts, experts in chain of custody and experts in electoral organization. The group of experts and auditors arrived in Bolivia on October 31 and began their activities on November 1.

The purpose of the electoral integrity analysis was to acquire detailed insight into the processes involved in the vote count, the transmission of preliminary results, the official tally, and the chain of custody of electoral materials, so as to verify, on the basis of that information, the integrity and reliability of the electoral results of October 20, 2019.

To achieve that objective, the technical team proceeded to audit the following:

A.   The authenticity and reliability of the vote count records (tally sheets) and of the data input into the electoral results transmission system and the official count system.

B.   The Plan for comprehensive custody of all electoral materials (tally sheets, ballots, voters register).

C.   Infrastructure and operation of the I.T. systems used to transmit preliminary results and the official count.

D.   Uploading flows of the data on preliminary electoral results and the official count.

The team worked continuously, compiling, systematizing, and analyzing information through to November 9. In addition, more than 250 complaints regarding the electoral process were received, both physically and via an e-mail address established for that purpose. Based on the work of the various audit teams, preliminary findings are as follows:

PRELIMINARY FINDINGS

Finding: Flawed transmission systems for both preliminary election results and the final count.

Electoral Results Transmission System

1)   The BO1 server had not been contemplated as part of the technological infrastructure for the Preliminary Election Results Transmission System (TREP). It was used despite the absence of the corresponding monitoring agent. According to reports by the audit company, it was provided at the request of the Supreme Electoral Tribunal (TSE) in order to facilitate consultations.

 Based on the analysis conducted by our experts, this equipment was not used for the purpose conveyed to the team. It was used, from the beginning of the day's work on October 20, 2019 until 7:40 p.m. on the same day (when the interruption occurred) for the flow of information related to the Preliminary Election Results Transmission (TREP) System workstations.

2)   The OAS audit detected that the flow of transcription information following the interruption was re-directed to a server (BO20) that was not included among those contemplated for the TREP in the cloud nor to the physical equipment of the National Information Technology Directorate (DNTIC). Furthermore, it was not overseen by the audit company, by Civic Registry Service (SERECI) officials, or by technical personnel of the DNTIC, but, rather, by an external person. No mention of this server was made in the reports given to us by the Tribunal and everyone involved omitted to mention its existence until it was detected by the OAS auditors.

 When he was interviewed (after the discovery), the technical head of the DNTIC acknowledged knowing about this server (BO20) and denied that it was he who had ordered the change of flow, adding that it had not been he who controlled or oversaw it either.

 It is strange that the dataflow should be re-directed to an extraneous network that had neither been contemplated nor documented. There is also no valid technical explanation for the non-usage of the perimeter servers controlled by the audit company. This is extremely serious and impacts the transparency of the process.

3) To re-direct the flow of information generated in SERECI to the (BO20) server, the Internet Protocol (IP) address to which the 350 machines used in SERECI were directed was altered. This occurred even though there were servers in the TREP network that were ready and overseen by the audit company inside the network.

4) Contrary to the technological arrangements that had been made, the tally sheet flow reached the main server in the TREP via two separate routes that were not monitored by the audit company. After the information flow had been interrupted and traffic re-directed to the BO20 server, the information went directly to the public IP of the TREP's primary server, which constitutes very poor practice. There is no reason why the flow should elude audit company oversight.

5) From a breakdown of the data in the reports given to OAS technical experts by the TSE, it transpires that there was an established infrastructure of principal perimeter servers and their respective contingency equipment. During the interviews conducted with technical personnel in the electoral tribunal and the contractor, no explanation was forthcoming about why, when the BO1 server stopped functioning, and perimeter servers were available in excellent working condition (according to the audit company's reports), the decision was taken to change the IP for 350 computers instead of using the servers provided for that purpose. This is a highly serious matter, in addition to it occurring right in the middle of an electoral process.

6) According to the information provided by the electoral authority, there was one principal BO2 server, one for publishing (BO3) and the corresponding contingency. Curiously enough, the BO3 server was not used for publication as had been planned. The OAS Audit managed to ascertain that the BO3 contingency server does not have the same number of logs as the principal BO2 server. In other words, they do not have the same information in their databases as one would expect.

7) There is no document with the life cycle of the incident relating to the interruption of the TREP, which might explain what happened and the root cause of it. Nor is there a detailed record of the persons who acted at that moment and the role they played. The OAS audit team asked for documentation of the log and all those interviewed denied the existence of such documentation.

8) What were found were leftovers from out-of-date databases and other versions of the app in perimeter servers, which is contrary to best practice.

9) META DATA (data of images received from cellphones) were not kept, even though they are vital for transparency in a process of this nature.

10) The app did not restrict the transmission of tally sheets to equipment with the correct date. Furthermore, it is impossible to secure computers belonging to the user (volunteer) who registered to send the tally sheet. For that reason, tally sheets were received with dates that do not fall within the TREP life cycle.

11) According to OAS audit findings, no record was kept of the hash value in the software freeze log. That is bad practice.

12) Based on the OAS auditors' observations:

- Not all (100%) of the data flows of the TREP were monitored;
- Infrastructure was not overseen by or familiar to the SERECI technician in charge;
- Key infrastructure components were not specified;
- A server was used that was not part of the TRP "BO1" or "BO" infrastructure;
- Traffic was re-directed to a network of servers extraneous to the TREP and the Official "BO20" Count;
- TREP perimeter servers were not properly used, because they were side-stepped.

Conclusion:

It is not possible to certify the accuracy of the TREP.

Official count:

1) Best practices were not followed.

2) The following software tests were not carried out:

- Unit testing;
- Integration testing;
- Regression testing.

3) The tests lacked a formal software acceptance process:

- Cases in which the software is used
- Cases in which formal testing of the software is performed.

4) Authentication was weak, allowing someone to take control and perform administrator functions, due to:

- Deficient implementation of the multiple authentication function (several sessions can be opened using the same code)
- A new tab could be opened in the navigator before closing the previous one (without authentication).
- When the previous person working withdrew, even though he or she had closed the application, it was possible to gain access with her or his user name without authentication (even to roles permitting validation of tally sheets).

5) The database reset to zero value procedure did not follow basic security requirements:

- A formal deletion procedure was conducted;
- Later on the head of the company gained unrestricted access to the databases;
- When the single database was already in zero, a new deletion was performed from Departmental Electoral Tribunals (TEDs).

6) Software integrity was ignored:
   - Software was frozen without keeping a record of the hash values
   - The software was recompiled in the middle of the process, causing integrity to be lost
   - The change violated core security principles by going directly into the production environment

7) The test data contaminating the production environment were not removed:
   - No arrangements were made to ensure a sterile environment at the start of the process. Test data (tally sheets, for instance) were found in the computers of the Departmental Electoral Tribunal of La Paz mixed up with Election Day tally sheets.

8) TREP tally sheets found their way Into the OFFICAL COUNT:
   - TREP tally sheets (in a setting in which the network was damaged and manipulated) were included in the Official Count.
   - From a server in a damaged network (the TREP BO2 server), contact was made with the Official Count network in order to transfer data.
   - The number of TREP tally sheets directly included in the official count is 1,575.

9) The provider of the app gained direct remote access to the server:
   - Virtual Private Networks (VPN) were allowed access to Official Count servers.

10) Evidence of the election was not kept:
   - To this day, the provider and principal actor involved in an investigation into incidents in a disputed election are in absolute possession of the data and nobody else can access them without their authorization. This is contrary to best practices in the handling of incidents and violates the chain of custody.
   - There is no official preservation of election data that could later be the subject of judicial proceedings.
   - The apps used to access databases by persons operating from Bolivia suffer from the authentication shortcomings described earlier (assumption of an administrator function without having to perform authentication procedures).

11) A flaw in the calculation algorithm known as "*flat computado*":
   - There was a flaw in the "*flat computado*" algorithm, revealing a lack of testing. Apart from that, the flaw could cause an incomplete tally sheet. That flaw could not be corrected using the app. The head of the company had to be given unrestricted (maximum privileges) access (through SQL commands) to solve the problem. That poses a high risk for data integrity.

12) Direct access to the database was provided without going through the app:
   - During the process, direct access was given to modify data in the database via SQL commands (which allow data to be changed without using the app). That is unacceptable in an electoral process and jeopardizes data integrity.

- One of the reasons why that form of access was granted was to (as officials put it) reverse the annulment of tally sheets.

13) A single person (the person in charge of the software provider) performed the following functions:
   - Designing, developing, testing, and implementing the software.
   - During the election the same person:
     - Recompiled the software;
     - Applied no change management, testing, or security procedure;
     - Accessed the database with maximum data-changing privileges;
     - Retained exclusive control over the servers, databases, and the app.
     - As a result of the above, broke the chain of custody since the incident.

14) The audit company did not monitor data integrity:
   - It was not assigned that task.

Conclusions

As a result of the above, the process was contrary to best practices and failed to abide by security standards.

The audit company publicly acknowledged the weaknesses and irregularities. Nevertheless, it failed to describe the redirecting of the server in the cloud (BO20).

Given all the irregularities observed, it is impossible to guarantee the integrity of the data and certify the accuracy of the results.

Finding: forged signatures and alteration of tally sheets.

The OAS technical team performed handwriting analyses of 333 questionable tally sheets. To obtain that sample, the team selected the voting tables in which the MAS obtained 99% of the votes, as well as the successive tables, that is, those in the same voting center.

Expert analysis showed irregularities in 78 tally sheets (23% of the sample). In some cases, it was confirmed that all the tally sheets in a center had been completed by the same person. Sometimes, that person turned out to be the MAS representative accredited as the party's delegate in the voting center concerned. Likewise, several tally sheets were found in which the government party obtained 100% of the votes. In some of those documents, the fields for opposition parties had not even been filled in with a "0". In some of those voting tables, moreover, attendance was 100%, which is practically impossible.

The OAS experts asked the Plurinational Electoral Body (OEP) for the original tally sheets and materials used at voting tables to perform more in-depth expert analysis. Tables were found for which the signatures on the original tally sheet did not match those of the copies. The signatures of the panel members (*jurados*) shown on the tally sheets were also cross-checked against those on the worksheets, as a result of which cases emerged in which the signatures of the six panel members on the worksheet document had been forged.

Conclusions

It should be borne in mind that the irregularities we have pointed out are those we observed in a short period of time. It is also important to point out that it was not possible to analyze the original tally sheets for the departments of Potosí, Chuquisaca, and Santa Cruz as part of the documentation had been burned. In all likelihood, given more time to process documentation, even more irregularities would surface.

Finding: Deficient chain of custody

A team of 18 experts of 13 different nationalities was deployed in 5 departments in Bolivia: Cochabamba, Pando, Beni, Tarija, and La Paz, with a view to verifying conditions relating to Departmental Tribunals and the chain of custody of electoral material. Part of the team in La Paz was assigned to the same tasks relating to voting abroad.[1] The OAS was unable to deploy specialists to the departments of Chuquisaca, Oruro, Potosí, and Santa Cruz because of road blocks and lack of security.

At a meeting with nine Departmental Electoral Tribunals (TED), the OAS team heard of a number of post-election incidents caused by unrest, such as the burning down of electoral facilities (TEDs and SERECI), pillaging in political party offices, and demonstrations. In particular, some sensitive and non-sensitive material was burned in Chuquisaca, Beni, Pando, Potosí, and Santa Cruz.

The OAS experts compiled information from 894 original tally sheets, selected on the basis of a statistical sample. The experts verified the contents of the tally sheets and compared them with the final count and voter registry lists. From that analysis it emerged that 176 of the tally sheets in the sample had been counted in Argentina and 38.07% were inconsistent with the number of citizens casting a vote. That is to say, the tally sheets showed a higher number of votes than voters on the voter registration lists.

In the departments of Chuquisaca and Potosí, the tally sheet counts were conducted in places other than those established by each TED plenary. In Chuquisaca, they were conducted in the municipality of Zudañez (an hour and a half's drive from the TED); in Potosí, they were conducted in the municipality of Llallagua (three hours away from the TED). In both cases, the OAS was told that this change had come about at the initiative of the TED, which argued that the original sites were ill-suited to continue the process, given the conditions at the time. While those conditions might have justified the change of locality, according to party delegates, they were not informed in time of the changes and so were unable to witness the official vote count in the new premises.

Under the Interagency Cooperation Agreement signed by the Supreme Electoral Tribunal (TSE) and the Security Forces (Bolivian Police and Armed Forces), the latter had an obligation to provide protection for the transfer of the envelopes taken by electoral notaries to the Departmental Electoral Tribunals (TEDs). However, OAS experts ascertained that in none of the five departments are there signed records or other evidence certifying any actions relating to the transfer of electoral material (Envelope A) either on Election Day or in the post-electoral stage, not even for the material transferred from the headquarters.

Information compiled in the departments showed, moreover, that there is no specific protocol for custody of the Official Tally (Envelope A) after it is received in the Departmental Electoral Tribunals. The experts ascertained that there are no standardized organizational procedures for tally sheets in the various TEDs.

Conclusions

Currently, the controls needed in respect of the chain of custody of sensitive electoral material do not exist. The fact that some electoral records were burned illustrates the lack

---

[1] Overseas voting took place in 33 countries, for 341,000 Bolivians resident abroad.

of protection, the absence of appropriate precautions, and poor coordination between the TEDs and the security forces.

Given that there is no possibility of recounting votes in Bolivia, protection of tally sheets is vital for providing guarantees for the electoral process. Monitoring of whoever handles the tally sheets and of the place they are kept at any one time is crucial.

When handling sensitive documentation, it is essential to note everything irregular and out of the ordinary. The electoral authority needs to keep records so that documents can be traced, particularly when unforeseen events take place. That did not happen in these elections.

Finding: Highly unlikely trend shown in the last 5% of the vote count.

For the following exercise, both TREP and Official Count data were analyzed.

Analysis of Trend in the TREP

The first figure shows a distribution of 33,000+ voting tables at the time when the tally sheets were transmitted to the TSE. The distribution is normal.

The next figure plots a similar distribution but this time by the time stamp for when the tally sheets were "verified" by the TSE. The second chart is "bimodal" with a second spike late at night. That second spike is also visible if we use the approval (aprobador_ date) time-stamp instead. See below.

Here the second spike has moved further to the right, and the accompanying time stamp reveals a threshold that represents about the last 5% of the cumulative vote count.

Consequently, there are two especially interesting moments in this election. First, the moment when processing of the tallies reaches 81%, just before the TSE stops reporting progress with the vote count. That is the moment when an abnormal number of tally sheets are uploaded in the TREP system, coming from a server that was unknown at the time. The second moment is when the processing of tally sheets in the TREP system reaches 95%, as shown in the following charts.

Each point in the graph above is a voting table plotted against its MAS vote share and the time at which its acta was transmitted to the TSE. The red vertical line is the 81% cumulative vote count. The blue smoothed average vote trend line is right along 46% for most of the night until the line curves upwards starting at the 81% mark and trends even more sharply up at the end of the distribution.

The next figure removes the individual voting table from the graph so that the trend is more clearly visible.

The jump is marked and this is again the case if one consider a 95% threshold (see below).

Clearly the MAS did very well in the final 5% of the cumulative vote. By contrast, the next two graphs show the Comunidad Ciudadana (CC) vote share using the 81% and 95% thresholds respectively.

In the last 5% of the count, 290,402 votes were counted. Of those, Morales won 175,670, that is to say 60.5% of the votes, while Mesa obtained only 69,199 votes, that is to say, 23.8%. In other words, Morales average vote share increased by over 15% compared to the previous 95%, while Mesa's average vote share plunged by about the same percentage. This pattern is highly unusual.

Analysis of Trends in the Official Count System.

The charts shown below reflect the decline of the candidate for Comunidad Ciudadana and the rise of the candidate of the MAS.

The final 5% of the data entered into the final count came from six departments (La Paz, Cocachamba, Oruro, Potosí, Chuquisaca, and Beni). While La Paz and Cochabamba are overrepresented because of the number of voting tables they have, the curve should not be so marked.

Taking statistical projections into account, it is possible that candidate Morales came in first and candidate Mesa second. However, it is statistically unlikely that Morales obtained the 10% difference needed to avoid a second round.

Conclusions of the preliminary findings

In the four factors reviewed (technology, chain of custody, integrity of the tally sheets, and statistical projections), irregularities were detected, ranging from very serious to indicative of something wrong. This leads the technical audit team to question the integrity of the results of the election on October 20, 2019.

As regards I.T. aspects, serious security flaws were discovered in both the TREP (Preliminary Election Results Transmission) and final count systems. In addition, a clear manipulation of the TREP system was discovered, which affected the results of both that system and the final count.

The existence of 1,575 TREP tally sheets in the final count corresponds to approximately 350,000 votes. The first round margin of victory is fewer than 40,000 votes. Therefore, an irregularity on that scale is a determining factor in the outcome. For those reasons, the audit team is unable to confirm a first round victory.

The manipulations of the I.T. system are of such magnitude that they should be investigated in depth by the Bolivian State in order to get to the bottom of them and determine who is responsible for such a serious situation.

The existence of physically altered tally sheets and forged signatures also undermines the integrity of the official count.

Of the 176 tally sheets in the sample that had been counted in Argentina, 38.07% were inconsistent with the number of citizens casting a vote. That is to say, the tally sheets showed a higher number of votes than voters on the voter registration lists.

Taking statistical projections into account, it is possible that candidate Morales came in first and candidate Mesa second. However, it is statistically unlikely that Morales obtained the 10% difference needed to avoid a second round.

The OAS technical personnel were given the information and access needed to do their job.

The audit team cannot validate the results of this election and therefore recommends another electoral process. Any future process should be overseen by new electoral authorities to ensure the conduct of credible elections.

Finally, the audit team will continue to process information and the more than 250 complaints received regarding the electoral process, with a view to producing the final report, which will contain a series of recommendations. Nevertheless, the preliminary findings are conclusive.

SOURCE: General Secretariat of the Organization of American States. "Statement of the Group of Auditors Electoral Process in Bolivia." November 10, 2019. http://www.oas.org/documents/eng/press/Electoral-Integrity-Analysis-Bolivia2019.pdf.

OAS General Secretariat Statement on the Situation in Bolivia

November 11, 2019

Facing the political and institutional crisis in Bolivia, the General Secretariat of the Organization of American States (OAS) rejects any unconstitutional resolution of the situation.

The General Secretariat calls for peace and respect for the Rule of Law.

In that sense, the General Secretariat requests an urgent meeting of the Plurinational Legislative Assembly of Bolivia to ensure the institutional functioning and to name new electoral authorities to guarantee a new electoral process.

It is also important that justice continues to investigate existing responsibilities regarding the commission of crimes related to the electoral process held on October 20, until they are resolved.

SOURCE: General Secretariat of the Organization of American States. "Statement of the OAS General Secretariat on the Situation in Bolivia." November 11, 2019. https://www.oas.org/en/media_center/press_release.asp?sCodigo=E-101/19.

OAS Releases Final Audit Report

December 4, 2019

The General Secretariat of the Organization of American States (OAS) presented today the final report of the audit conducted on the general elections held on October 20 in Bolivia. The conclusion is that there was "intentional manipulation" and "serious irregularities" that make it impossible to validate the results originally issued by the Bolivian electoral authorities.

The full report and its annexes are available here http://www.oas.org/fpdb/press/Audit-Report-EN-vFINAL.pdf.

The Secretary General of the OAS, Luis Almagro, said "the final audit report represents the integrity of the work of the Organization. It was an evolutionary process that began many months ago, and at each step of which the Organization fulfilled its task with responsibility, affinity to its values and principles, and adherence to the different agreements signed with the Bolivian government. The Bolivian people and their government needed certainty regarding their electoral process and for that they requested the support of the Organization. Neither they nor the rest of the OAS member states deserved any response other than the exceptional and professional work of the audit team reflected in this report."

The report confirms that the intentional manipulation of the elections took place in two areas. First, the audit detected changes in the minutes and the falsification of the signatures of poll officials. Second, it was found that in the processing of the results the data flow was redirected to two hidden servers and not controlled by personnel of the Supreme Electoral Tribunal (TSE), which made it possible to manipulate data and falsify minutes.

To this are added serious irregularities, such as the lack of protection of the acts and the loss of sensitive material. The report also details a significant number of errors and indices.

The audit findings also reveal the partiality of the electoral authority. The members of the TSE, who were tasked with ensuring the legality and integrity of the process, allowed the flow of information to be diverted to external servers, destroying all confidence in the electoral process.

The conclusion of the report is that "the manipulations and irregularities indicated do not allow for certainty about the margin of victory of the candidate Evo Morales over the candidate Carlos Mesa. On the contrary, based on the overwhelming evidence found, what can be affirmed is that there has been a series of intentional operations aimed at altering the will expressed at the polls."

The report contains 96 pages of analysis and more than 500 pages of annexes. The annexes contain hundreds of documents that support and substantiate the audit findings, and support the analysis and conclusions of the report, including:

- calligraphic analysis of more than 220 poll reports

- documents signed by officials of the electoral body

- reference to 37 indexed lists of citizens authorized to vote (the audit team has a copy of the complete lists, but will not publish them because it contains personal information of Bolivian citizens)

- registration of the reception of the more than 200 complaints and communications with information received from citizens

- 11 requests for information

The final audit report presented today responds to a request from the Government of the Plurinational State of Bolivia, embodied in an agreement signed on October 30 to conduct "an analysis of electoral integrity of the elections." The work was carried out between November 1 and 9 by a team of 36 specialists and auditors of 18 nationalities including: electoral lawyers, statisticians, computer experts, specialists in documents, calligraphy, chain of custody and electoral organization.

SOURCE: General Secretariat of the Organization of American States. "Final Report of the Audit of the Elections in Bolivia: Intentional Manipulation and Serious Irregularities Made It Impossible to Validate the Results." December 4, 2019. https://www.oas.org/en/media_center/press_release.asp?sCodigo=E-109/19.

OTHER HISTORIC DOCUMENTS OF INTEREST

FROM PREVIOUS HISTORIC DOCUMENTS

International Court of Justice Announces Proceedings against Myanmar

NOVEMBER 11 AND 14, 2019

On November 11, 2019, The Gambia filed a lawsuit at the United Nations (UN) International Court of Justice (ICJ) formally accusing Myanmar of genocide against Rohingya Muslims. The two countries are signatories to the 1948 Genocide Convention, which requires that nations both prevent genocide in their own countries and punish such atrocities committed in other nations. Though well-documented crimes against the Rohingya people span decades, rising hostility and violence targeting the country's minority Muslim population in recent years have fueled a massive and historic humanitarian crisis. Until The Gambia brought the case before the ICJ, grave human rights violations by Myanmar's military had largely been unmitigated.

THE GAMBIA FILES LAWSUIT SEEKING PROVISIONAL MEASURES

The Gambia's forty-six-page legal submission to the court in The Hague, Netherlands, detailed the deliberate, widespread, and systematic destruction of Rohingya communities in Myanmar. The filing also asserted that Myanmar's military was conducting a campaign of ethnic cleansing against the Rohingya people, in violation of various provisions of the 1948 Convention on the Prevention and Punishment of the Crime of Genocide (also known as the Genocide Convention). The Genocide Convention, to which both The Gambia and Myanmar are party, not only prohibits states from committing genocide, but also compels all signatories to prevent and punish such crimes. While the case could take years to reach a final ruling, The Gambia requested the ICJ to order provisional measures "as a matter of extreme urgency" that Myanmar cease ongoing genocidal acts, refrain from destroying evidence, allow for "the safe and dignified return" of those who have been forcibly displaced, and ensure "respect for their full citizenship and human rights and protection against discrimination, persecution, and other related acts."

The Gambia, a small West African nation with a large Muslim population, filed the suit on behalf of the fifty-seven-member Organization of Islamic Cooperation, which is funding the team of international law experts handling the case. Having only recently emerged from a repressive dictatorship, The Gambia has its own, difficult history of human rights violations. The Gambia's attorney general and minister of justice, Abubacarr M. Tambadou, assumed leadership of the case having previously served as special assistant to the prosecutor of the International Criminal Tribunal dealing with the 1994 genocide in Rwanda. In an interview with *The New York Times,* Tambadou said, "The world failed Rwanda when the international community did not prevent the genocide while it was unfolding." He went on to state that "the treatment of the Rohingya is illustrative of the international community's failure to prevent genocide in Myanmar. . . . The world cannot stand by and do nothing." After filing The Gambia's lawsuit, Tambadou told reporters, "The aim is to get Myanmar to account for its action against its own people: the Rohingya."

The Rohingya people are a Muslim ethnic minority who have faced decades of repression under successive Myanmar governments. For years, the Rohingya have existed in apartheid-like conditions with restrictions on marriage, employment, access to health care and education, and freedom of movement. Although the Rohingya have lived within Myanmar for generations, the government largely treats them as illegal immigrants from neighboring Bangladesh. It does not recognize the Rohingya as citizens, or even as an ethnic group, effectively making them stateless. The government does not even recognize the term *Rohingya,* and many government officials refuse to say the word. Before August 2017, most of the estimated one million Rohingya in Myanmar lived in the Rakhine state, where widespread poverty, poor infrastructure, and scarce employment opportunities exacerbated tensions with the dominant ethnic Buddhist group.

The Gambia's submission to the ICJ stated that "in the early hours of 9 October 2016, a small number of Rohingya, armed mainly with sticks, knives and a few firearms, reacting to Myanmar's persecution of the group, attacked three border guard police posts in northern Rakhine state." Shortly afterward, the military, known as the Tatmadaw, launched what it described as "clearance operations." Conflict intensified after August 25, 2017, when Rohingya militants attacked police across northern Rakhine state, killing several officers. In response, the military escalated a sweeping campaign of mass murder, rape, and arson against Rohingya communities that resulted in the deaths of at least 6,700 people in the first month, according to Doctors Without Borders. Satellite imagery confirms several hundred villages were burned and bulldozed, with new military facilities built in their place. Claiming the Tatmadaw had genocidal intent, The Gambia's submission noted that preceding the attacks, military officials were "prime operatives" in a "pervasive campaign of dehumanisation" on social media. This targeted violence triggered an exodus of more than 740,000 Rohingya refugees. Most crossed into neighboring Bangladesh, while others traveled to Indonesia, Malaysia, and Thailand. Nearly one million Rohingya now live in sprawling refugee camps, while several hundred thousand remain displaced inside Myanmar.

The Gambia's lawsuit argues that these actions against the Rohingya people were carried out with intention to destroy the Rohingya as a group, and that Rohingya communities and individuals remaining in Myanmar face "real and significant danger" of further genocidal acts. It draws heavily from the results of an independent fact-finding mission conducted by the UN Human Rights Council in 2018, which established clear and consistent patterns of severe human rights abuses and serious violations of international humanitarian law. The mission presented a comprehensive analysis of indicators of genocidal intent, concluding "the actions of those who orchestrated the attacks on the Rohingya read as a veritable check-list," and that the "State of Myanmar breached its obligation not to commit genocide under the Genocide Convention." The mission contends that the country's state counselor and effective prime minister, Aung San Suu Kyi, had not used her "de facto power or moral authority to stem or prevent the unfolding events or to protect the civilian population." It stressed that accountability must come from the international community and made specific recommendations to investigate and prosecute military officials in an international criminal tribunal.

The Gambia's filing marked the first time since the court was established in 1946 that a country without any direct connection to the crimes in question has used the Genocide

Convention to bring a case to the ICJ. Officials in The Gambia reasoned that a UN member state could bring legal actions against another state over breaches of international law. The case is also significant because it marks the first time the ICJ is investigating genocide claims without relying on findings from another tribunal, as it did to support its 2007 ruling in the case of *Bosnia and Herzegovina v. Serbia and Montenegro*. The case is not a criminal one against individual perpetrators but rather will result in a legal determination of responsibility for genocide, governed by provisions in the UN Charter, the ICJ Statute, and the Genocide Convention.

The Gambia's actions were praised by the international community and human rights organizations. "Gambia's genocide case unlocks a long overdue legal process to credibly examine Myanmar's countless atrocities against the Rohingya," said Param-Preet Singh, associate international justice director at Human Rights Watch. In December, the governments of Canada and the Netherlands announced "their obligation to support The Gambia before the ICJ, as it should concern all of humanity." The United Kingdom also expressed support for the case.

Aung San Suu Kyi Leads Myanmar Defense

Once an international icon of moral leadership and a Nobel Peace Prize winner, Suu Kyi rapidly lost credibility and tarnished her global reputation by refusing to intervene in or authorize an investigation of the Rohingya crisis. She repeatedly dismissed international criticism and denied most allegations of targeted military-led violence targeting the Rohingya, claiming the Tatmadaw was trying to protect the country against insurgent threats from Rohingya militants.

Although it is unprecedented for a political leader to assume such a role, Suu Kyi led her country's defense during hearings before the ICJ in December. U Myo Nyunt, party spokesperson for Suu Kyi's National League for Democracy (NLD), told Reuters that Suu Kyi decided to take on the case herself because The Gambia "accused [her] of failing to speak out about human rights violations." Her decision to lead Myanmar's defense was popular among the country's Buddhist majority and supported by the NLD and parliament. Still, some representatives of Myanmar's ethnic groups viewed her decision as an attempt to consolidate political support in the country, while securing trust in the military. Ethnic Chin human rights activist Cheery Zahau expressed this sentiment to Radio Free Asia, saying, "Instead of going to the ICJ to defend the country, she should be working to make fundamental changes to stop rights violations on the ground and to protect citizens." On November 28, three ethnic armed organizations and their respective political wings issued a statement of support for The Gambia's case against Myanmar.

In her opening statement before the ICJ, Suu Kyi outlined decades of tensions between the Rohingya Muslim and Buddhist communities and lamented that the case brought against her country was "an incomplete and misleading factual picture in Rakhine state and Myanmar." She added, "It would not be helpful for the international legal order if the impression takes hold that only resource-rich countries can conduct adequate domestic investigations and prosecutions." Throughout the hearing, she continued to reject charges of genocide and asserted, "If war crimes have been committed by members of Myanmar's defense services, they will be prosecuted through our military justice system." Suu Kyi maintained that military forces were acting in the interest of stability and argued that while it could not be ruled out that the Tatmadaw had used disproportionate force, "surely, under the circumstances, genocidal intent cannot be the only hypothesis."

On January 23, 2020, the court unanimously ruled to approve The Gambia's requested provisional measures. The ICJ mandated that Myanmar submit a report of all actions taken to comply with the provisional measures within four months and provide updates every six months until a final ruling is reached. While the ICJ has no means to enforce its rulings, under the UN Charter, all UN member states must abide by ICJ decisions to which they are party, and in the event of noncompliance, can be referred to the UN Security Council.

ICC Authorizes Investigation

While the ICJ can establish state responsibility for international crimes, the International Criminal Court (ICC) has a mandate to investigate, establish criminal responsibility, and prosecute individuals. Shortly after The Gambia submitted its case to the ICJ, the ICC authorized an investigation into alleged crimes against humanity committed against Rohingya by Myanmar. The November 14 announcement set a significant precedent in expanding the jurisdiction of the ICC. Although Myanmar is not party to the Rome Statute that established the court in 2002 and does not recognize its authority, the court intends to exercise jurisdiction for crimes committed by Myanmar within ICC member state Bangladesh, including the displacement of Rohingya refugees. The ICC's announcement noted that court officials had received comments supporting an investigation from hundreds of thousands of victims of Myanmar's alleged crimes. "Victims unanimously insist that they want an investigation by the Court and many of the consulted alleged victims 'believe that only justice and accountability can ensure that the perceived circle of violence and abuse comes to an end,'" the court stated.

The ICC authorization allows prosecutors to collect evidence that could ultimately form the basis for summons to appear or arrest warrants for Myanmar's military leaders. However, without a referral by the UN Security Council, the ICC cannot address the full scope of crimes committed, and thus the ICJ remains the international community's most viable option to establish judicial qualification of the violence as genocide.

—Megan Howes

Following is a press release issued by the International Court of Justice on November 11, 2019, announcing The Gambia's initiation of legal proceedings against Myanmar; and an announcement by the International Criminal Court on November 14, 2019, that justices had authorized an investigation into Myanmar's alleged crimes against the Rohingya.

The Gambia Files Legal Proceedings against Myanmar

November 11, 2019

The Republic of The Gambia ("The Gambia") today instituted proceedings against the Republic of the Union of Myanmar ("Myanmar") before the International Court of Justice, the principal judicial organ of the United Nations, alleging violations of the Convention on the Prevention and Punishment of the Crime of Genocide (the "Genocide Convention") through "acts adopted, taken and condoned by the Government of Myanmar against members of the Rohingya group."

Specifically, The Gambia argues that

> from around October 2016 the Myanmar military (the "Tatmadaw") and other Myanmar security forces began widespread and systematic "clearance operations"—the term that Myanmar itself uses—against the Rohingya group. The genocidal acts committed during these operations were intended to destroy the Rohingya as a group, in whole or in part, by the use of mass murder, rape and other forms of sexual violence, as well as the systematic destruction by fire of their villages, often with inhabitants locked inside burning houses. From August 2017 onwards, such genocidal acts continued with Myanmar's resumption of "clearance operations" on a more massive and wider geographical scale.

The Gambia contends that these acts constitute violations of the Genocide Convention. It states that it has made this claim known to Myanmar since September 2018, but that Myanmar has continued to deny any wrongdoing.

The Applicant seeks to found the Court's jurisdiction to entertain this dispute on Article 36, paragraph 1, of the Statute of the Court and on Article IX of the Genocide Convention, to which both States are parties.

In its Application, The Gambia

respectfully requests the Court to adjudge and declare that Myanmar:
— has breached and continues to breach its obligations under the Genocide Convention, in particular the obligations provided under Articles I, III (a), III (b), III (c), III (d), III (e), IV, V and VI;
— must cease forthwith any such ongoing internationally wrongful act and fully respect its obligations under the Genocide Convention, in particular the obligations provided under Articles I, III (a), III (b), III (c), III (d), III (e), IV, V and VI;
— must ensure that persons committing genocide are punished by a competent tribunal, including before an international penal tribunal, as required by Articles I and VI;
— must perform the obligations of reparation in the interest of the victims of genocidal acts who are members of the Rohingya group, including but not limited to allowing the safe and dignified return of forcibly displaced Rohingya and respect for their full citizenship and human rights and protection against discrimination, persecution, and other related acts, consistent with the obligation to prevent genocide under Article I; and
— must offer assurances and guarantees of non-repetition of violations of the Genocide Convention, in particular the obligations provided under Articles I, III (a), III (b), III (c), III (d), III (e), IV, V and VI.

The Application also contains a request for the indication of provisional measures, seeking to protect the rights of the Rohingya group and those of The Gambia under the Genocide Convention, and to prevent the aggravation or extension of the dispute pending the final judgment of the Court. The Gambia thus asks the Court to indicate the following provisional measures:

Myanmar shall immediately, in pursuance of its undertaking in the Convention on the Prevention and Punishment of the Crime of Genocide of 9 December 1948, take all measures within its power to prevent all acts that amount to or contribute to the crime of genocide, including taking all measures within its power to prevent the following acts from being committed against member[s] of the Rohingya group: extrajudicial killings or physical abuse; rape or other forms of sexual violence; burning of homes or villages; destruction of lands and livestock, deprivation of food and other necessities of life, or any other deliberate infliction of conditions of life calculated to bring about the physical destruction of the Rohingya group in whole or in part;

Myanmar shall, in particular, ensure that any military, paramilitary or irregular armed units which may be directed or supported by it, as well as any organizations and persons which may be subject to its control, direction or influence, do not commit any act of genocide, of conspiracy to commit genocide, or direct and public incitement to commit genocide, or of complicity in genocide, against the Rohingya group, including: extrajudicial killing or physical abuse; rape or other forms of sexual violence; burning of homes or villages; destruction of lands and livestock, deprivation of food and other necessities of life, or any other deliberate infliction of conditions of life calculated to bring about the physical destruction of the Rohingya group in whole or in part;

Myanmar shall not destroy or render inaccessible any evidence related to the events described in the Application, including without limitation by destroying or rendering inaccessible the remains of any member of the Rohingya group who is a victim of alleged genocidal acts, or altering the physical locations where such acts are alleged to have occurred in such a manner as to render the evidence of such acts, if any, inaccessible;

Myanmar and The Gambia shall not take any action and shall assure that no action is taken which may aggravate or extend the existing dispute that is the subject of this Application, or render it more difficult of resolution; and

Myanmar and The Gambia shall each provide a report to the Court on all measures taken to give effect to this Order for provisional measures, no later than four months from its issuance.

SOURCE: International Court of Justice. "The Republic of The Gambia Institutes Proceedings against the Republic of the Union of Myanmar and Asks the Court to Indicate Provisional Measures." November 11, 2019. https://www.icj-cij.org/files/case-related/178/178-20191111-PRE-01-00-EN.pdf.

ICC Authorizes Investigation into Situation in Myanmar

November 14, 2019

On 14 November 2019, Pre-Trial Chamber III of the International Criminal Court ("ICC" or the "Court") authorised the Prosecutor to proceed with an investigation for the alleged crimes within the ICC's jurisdiction in the Situation in the People's Republic of Bangladesh/ Republic of the Union of Myanmar ("the situation in Bangladesh/Myanmar").

ICC Pre-Trial Chamber III is composed of Judge Olga Herrera Carbuccia, Presiding, Judge Robert Fremr, and Judge Geoffrey Henderson.

This authorisation follows the request submitted on 4 July 2019 by the Prosecutor to open an investigation into alleged crimes within the ICC's jurisdiction committed against the Rohingya people from Myanmar.

The Chamber also received the views on this request by or on behalf of hundreds of thousands of alleged victims. According to the ICC Registry, victims unanimously insist that they want an investigation by the Court and many of the consulted alleged victims "believe that only justice and accountability can ensure that the perceived circle of violence and abuse comes to an end." The Chamber recognised all the individuals and organisations that assisted, guided and advised alleged victims throughout this process.

The Chamber concluded that the Court may exercise jurisdiction over crimes when part of the criminal conduct takes place on the territory of a State Party. While Myanmar is not a State Party, Bangladesh ratified the ICC Rome statute in 2010. Upon review of the available information, the Chamber accepted that there exists a reasonable basis to believe widespread and/or systematic acts of violence may have been committed that could qualify as the crimes against humanity of deportation across the Myanmar-Bangladesh border and persecution on grounds of ethnicity and/or religion against the Rohingya population. The Chamber found no need to assess whether other crimes within the Court's jurisdiction may have been committed, even though such alleged crimes could be part of the Prosecutor's future investigation.

Noting the scale of the alleged crimes and the number of victims allegedly involved, the Chamber considered that the situation clearly reaches the gravity threshold. According to the supporting material, an estimated 600,000 to one million Rohingya were forcibly displaced from Myanmar to neighbouring Bangladesh as a result of the alleged coercive acts. Noting the victims' views, the Chamber agreed with the Prosecutor that there are no substantial reasons to believe that an investigation into the situation would not be in the interests of justice.

Consequently, Pre-Chamber III authorised the commencement of the investigation in relation to any crime, including any future crime, as long as: a) it is within the jurisdiction of the Court, b) it is allegedly committed at least in part on the territory of Bangladesh, or on the territory of any other State Party or State accepting the ICC jurisdiction, c) it is sufficiently linked to the situation as described in the present decision, and d) it was allegedly committed on or after the date of entry into force of the Rome Statute for Bangladesh or other relevant State Party.

Next steps: The Office of the Prosecutor will start collecting the necessary evidence from a variety of reliable sources, independently, impartially, and objectively. The investigation can take as long as needed to gather the required evidence. If sufficient evidence would be collected to establish that specific individuals bear criminal responsibility, the Prosecutor would then request Judges of Pre-Trial Chamber III to issue either summonses to appear or warrants of arrest. The responsibility to enforce warrants of arrest issued by an ICC Chamber remains with States. States Parties to the Rome Statute have a legal obligation to cooperate fully with the ICC. Other States may be invited to cooperate with the ICC and may decide to do so on a voluntary basis.

Source: International Criminal Court. "ICC Judges Authorise Opening of an Investigation into the Situation in Bangladesh/Myanmar." November 14, 2019. https://www.icc-cpi.int/Pages/item.aspx?name=pr1495.

OTHER HISTORIC DOCUMENTS OF INTEREST

FROM PREVIOUS *HISTORIC DOCUMENTS*

- United Nations and Myanmar Leaders Respond to Rohingya Crisis, *2017*, p. 99
- Pro-Democracy Leader Aung San Suu Kyi Wins Seat in Burmese Parliament, *2012*, p. 197

FBI Releases Report on Hate Crime Statistics; Federal Agency Recommends Anti–Hate Crime Strategies

NOVEMBER 12 AND 13, 2019

In its annual report on hate crime statistics, the Federal Bureau of Investigation (FBI) announced an increase in the number of bias-motivated attacks against individuals, but a decrease in property crimes. The data corresponded with other reports from advocacy groups, specifically showing an increase in physical and verbal assaults against Latinos, Jews, the disabled, and transgender individuals. Following the report's release, the U.S. Commission on Civil Rights submitted a report calling on Congress and other federal agencies to undertake measures to address the rise in hate crimes.

HATE CRIMES AGAINST INDIVIDUALS TREND UPWARD

On November 12, 2019, the FBI released its annual report, *Hate Crime Statistics*, detailing the number of bias-motivated crimes committed against individuals and property in 2018. Based on the FBI definition, a hate crime is a "criminal offense against a person or property, motivated in whole or in part by an offender's bias against a race, religion, disability, sexual orientation, ethnicity, gender, or gender identity." Overall, hate crimes decreased 0.8 percent from 2017 to 2018. Crimes against property were down 19 percent, while those involving the physical or verbal assault of a person were up 11.7 percent and hit a sixteen-year high. A total of 4,571 hate crimes were committed against people in 2018. Intimidation crimes rose 13 percent, aggravated assaults 4 percent, and simple assaults 15 percent.

Of the single-bias hate crimes reported to the FBI, 57.5 percent were motivated by race, ethnicity, or ancestry. Of those, 46.9 percent were against African Americans, the lowest share since the first year the FBI published hate crime data in 1992. Another 20.2 percent of crimes were motivated by religious bias. Seventeen percent of hate crimes were motivated by sexual orientation, 2.4 percent by gender identity, 2.3 percent by disability, and 0.7 percent by gender. "Unfortunately, we did have a 37 percent increase in disability categories, mainly in the anti-physical—that increased by 87.5 percent. And in the gender identity category, we had a 41.2 percent increase. Primarily that included a 34 percent increase in anti-transgender and a 100 percent increase in anti-gender non-conforming," said Scott Rago, section chief at the FBI. "There's a diversifying base of groups that are being targeted. We're getting back to more violence," said Brian Levin, director of the Center for the Study of Hate and Extremism at California State University.

One of the most striking facts to come out of the FBI report was the increase in bias-motivated murders, which rose from fifteen in 2017 to twenty-four in 2018, the highest number since the FBI began tracking these statistics. "After about a 30% increase over the last few years, hate crimes overall took a pause (last year) but the more violent types of hate crimes did not. So under this stable exterior, we see a shuffling of the type of offenses and the types of victims," said Levin. "We're seeing a leaner and meaner type of hate crime going on," he added.

The FBI cautions against comparisons or drawing conclusions from its annual hate crime statistics because of known omissions. Police departments are not required to report hate crimes to the FBI, though the group has made an effort to encourage more voluntary reporting. Of all reporting agencies in 2018, 87 percent reported no hate crimes, including the entire states of Alabama and Wyoming. Underreporting has been a long-running problem with the data. For example, the murder of Heather Heyer during the Unite the Right rally in Charlottesville, Virginia, in 2017 was prosecuted as a hate crime but never recorded in the official hate crime statistics. Furthermore, according to the Bureau of Justice Statistics, more than half of all victims of hate crimes do not report the incident to police. "Nearly every expert on hate crimes agrees it's under-reported," said Daniel Elbaum, the chief advocacy officer for the American Jewish Committee. And, he added, "It's really hard to tackle a problem until you have a handle on how large of a problem it is."

LATINOS, JEWISH COMMUNITY EXPERIENCE RISE IN VIOLENCE

In 2018, incidents targeting Latinos were up but those against Muslims and Arab Americans were down, tracking with national surveys that show Americans are now more concerned with immigration than terrorism. "Attacks against Muslims peaked around 2016 when terrorism was the concern. Now immigration is the number one issue and Latinos are being targeted," said Levin. "We're seeing the swapping of one derided group in the social-political arena for another," he added. A total of 485 hate crimes against Latinos were reported to the FBI in 2018, the highest level since 2010 and an increase from 430 in 2017.

Some blamed President Donald Trump's anti-immigrant rhetoric and southern border policies for the uptick. "There's a direct correlation between the hate speech and fear-mongering coming from President Trump and the right wing of the Republican Party with the increase in attacks against Latinos," said Domingo Garcia, national president of the League of United Latin American Citizens. "President Trump frequently refers to Latinos in the most hateful and bigoted ways, and words matter," said Janet Murguia, head of the Latino civil rights group UnidosUS. "President Trump should be aware that in the community's mind, he bears some responsibility for the increase in hate crimes against Latinos," she said.

Muslims and Arab Americans experienced 270 reported attacks, the lowest level since 2014. The Council on American–Islamic Relations disputed this, saying that it recorded more than 1,600 hate crimes against Muslims in 2018. "We don't know the full scope of anti-Muslim hate crimes and other hate crimes," said Robert McCaw, the council's director of governmental affairs, noting that bullying at schools or discrimination in the workplace are not reported to the FBI. Arab American groups similarly blamed the White House for the ongoing violence. "The Trump administration has advanced policies, and the president has trafficked in rhetoric, targeting the same communities that have also experienced a surge of hate violence," said Maya Berry, executive director of the Arab American Institute.

Some of the most high-profile crimes reported in 2018 targeted the Jewish community. Of the crimes motivated by religious bias, 57.8 percent were anti-Semitic attacks, and 11 of the 24 total hate-motivated murders occurred at the Tree of Life Synagogue in

Pittsburgh, Pennsylvania. Those crimes continued into 2019. Although complete FBI data will not be available until November 2020, a review of early 2019 data by the Center for the Study of Hate and Extremism showed that crimes against the Jewish community in the cities of Los Angeles, New York, and Chicago were on their way to historically high levels. In Los Angeles, in the first ten months of the year, there were 58 anti-Semitic hate crimes, compared with 29 during the first ten months of 2018. In New York, 229 anti-Semitic crimes were recorded from January 1 through December 30, 2019, up from 185 in 2018. Chicago had a 46 percent increase through November 1, 2019, as compared to the prior year. "It is unacceptable that Jews and Jewish institutions continue to be at the center of religion-based hate crime attacks," said Anti-Defamation League CEO Jonathan Greenblatt.

U.S. COMMISSION ON CIVIL RIGHTS
RELEASES REPORT ON HATE CRIMES

One day after the FBI released its hate crime statistics, the U.S. Commission on Civil Rights (USCCR) made public *In the Name of Hate*, a report reflecting on the rise in hate crimes in the United States and making recommendations to Congress, the White House, and other federal agencies and law enforcement bodies to address the situation. "As this report reflects, the nation urgently needs leadership against hate, promoting respect for the dignity of all persons in our communities. None of us is immune to the harm of hate, and we all deserve and benefit from commitment to confronting and eliminating this toxicity that threatens America's promise of equity and justice," said Catherine E. Lhamon, chair of the commission.

Specifically, the report called on Congress to pass legislation that would encourage police departments to better identify and investigate hate crimes and report those incidents to the FBI. "The need for improved data collection and reporting is astonishing, and the absence of effective data hamstrings any effective response that we as a nation might have," Lhamon said. While the USCCR did not call for passage of a specific piece of legislation, at the time of the report's release the Jabara-Heyer NO HATE Act, named for two individuals killed in hate-motivated attacks, was pending in the Senate. That bill would increase funding for hate crime reporting and investigations. The USCCR called on the Department of Justice to provide resources, both financial and otherwise, to police departments to improve their cultural competency and sensitivity in dealing with bias-motivated crimes. "Developing effective policies, procedures, and responses to hate crimes can reduce overall crime, while simultaneously building relationships and trust between law enforcement and communities who feel targeted by acts of hate," the report stated. The report also recommended that the Trump administration reinstate groups within the Department of Homeland Security that analyze domestic terrorism and reauthorize grants for groups that counter white supremacy. "We live in deeply dangerous times, and we have had an insufficient government response to that danger," said Lhamon.

—Heather Kerrigan

Following is a summary of the Federal Bureau of Investigation's annual hate crime statistics, released on November 12, 2019; and the text of the executive summary of a briefing report issued by the United States Commission on Civil Rights on November 13, 2019, recommending strategies to combat the rise in hate crimes.

FBI Releases Annual
Hate Crime Statistics

November 12, 2019

Today the FBI released *Hate Crime Statistics, 2018*, the Uniform Crime Reporting (UCR) Program's latest compilation about bias-motivated incidents throughout the nation. The 2018 data, submitted by 16,039 law enforcement agencies, provide information about the offenses, victims, offenders, and locations of hate crimes.

Law enforcement agencies submitted incident reports involving 7,120 criminal incidents and 8,496 related offenses as being motivated by bias toward race, ethnicity, ancestry, religion, sexual orientation, disability, gender, and gender identity. Please note the UCR Program does not estimate offenses for the jurisdictions of agencies that do not submit reports. Highlights of *Hate Crime Statistics, 2018*, follow. (Due to rounding, percentage breakdowns may not add to 100.0 percent.)

Victims of Hate Crime Incidents

There were 7,036 single-bias incidents involving 8,646 victims. A percent distribution of victims by bias type shows that 59.6 percent of victims were targeted because of the offenders' race/ethnicity/ancestry bias; 18.7 percent were targeted because of the offenders' religious bias; 16.7 percent were victimized because of the offenders' sexual-orientation bias; 2.2 percent were targeted because of the offenders' gender identity bias; 2.1 percent were victimized because of the offenders' disability bias; and 0.7 percent were victimized because of the offenders' gender bias.

There were 84 multiple-bias hate crime incidents, which involved 173 victims.

Offenses by Crime Category

Of the 5,566 hate crime offenses classified as crimes against persons in 2018, 46.0 percent were for intimidation, 34.0 percent were for simple assault, and 18.4 percent were for aggravated assault. Twenty-four (24) murders and 22 rapes were reported as hate crimes. The remaining 39 hate crime offenses were reported in the category of *other*.

There were 2,641 hate crime offenses classified as crimes against property. The majority of these (71.0 percent) were acts of destruction/damage/vandalism. Robbery, burglary, larceny-theft, motor vehicle theft, arson, and other offenses accounted for the remaining 29.0 percent of crimes against property.

Two hundred eighty-nine (289) additional offenses were classified as crimes against society. This crime category represents society's prohibition against engaging in certain types of activity such as gambling, prostitution, and drug violations. These are typically victimless crimes in which property is not the object.

Known Offenders

In the UCR Program, the term *known offender* does not imply that the suspect's identity is known; rather, the term indicates that some aspect of the suspect was identified, thus distinguishing the suspect from an unknown offender. Law enforcement agencies specify the number of offenders and, when possible, the race of the offender or offenders as a group. Beginning in 2013, law enforcement began reporting whether suspects were juveniles or adults, as well as the suspect's ethnicity when possible.

Of the 6,266 known offenders, 53.6 percent were White, and 24.0 percent were Black or African American. Other races accounted for the remaining known offenders: 1.3 percent were Asian; 1.0 percent were American Indian or Alaska Native; 0.3 percent were Native Hawaiian or Other Pacific Islander; and 6.9 percent were of a group of multiple races. The race was unknown for 12.9 percent.

Of the 5,349 known offenders for whom ethnicity was reported, 29.9 percent were Not Hispanic or Latino, 8.9 percent were Hispanic or Latino, and 1.6 percent were in a group of multiple ethnicities. Ethnicity was unknown for 59.5 percent of these offenders.

Of the 5,589 known offenders for whom ages were known, 84.7 percent were 18 years of age or older.

Locations of Hate Crimes

Law enforcement agencies may specify the location of an offense within a hate crime incident as 1 of 46 location designations. In 2018, most hate crime incidents (25.7 percent) occurred in or near residences/homes. More than 18 percent (18.7) occurred on highways/roads/alleys/streets/sidewalks; 9.2 percent occurred at schools/colleges; 5.3 percent happened at parking/drop lots/garages; and 3.7 percent took place in churches/synagogues/temples/mosques. The location was reported as other/unknown for 11.2 percent of hate crime incidents. The remaining 26.1 percent of hate crime incidents took place at other or multiple locations.

Source: Federal Bureau of Investigation. "FBI Releases 2018 Hate Crime Statistics." November 12, 2019. https://ucr.fbi.gov/hate-crime/2018/resource-pages/hate-crime-summary.

Civil Rights Commission Issues Report on Strategies to Reduce Hate Crimes

DOCUMENT

November 13, 2019

[All sections not included in the Executive Summary, as well as footnotes, have been omitted.]

EXECUTIVE SUMMARY

Reports of hate crimes have been steadily increasing over the past several years, particularly against certain groups; there were reports of 6,121 incidents in 2016 and 7,175 incidents in 2017 (a 17 percent increase)—making 2017 the highest year to date of reported incidents to the FBI since it began collecting data in 1995. Hate crime experts are unsure if this increase reflects a rise in hate incidents, a willingness on the part of victims to report, or better reporting practices by law enforcement (or a combination of these factors); regardless, these crimes have lasting and far-reaching effects for victims, their communities, and for the nation.

The Commission's research shows that many Americans are negatively impacted by these heinous crimes and are fearful of a rising sentiment of hate and bigotry in the United States. In response to increased reports of hate crimes including horrific acts of violence the Commission voted to investigate the federal government's role in combating hate crimes. In particular, the Commission examined three areas: (1) local law enforcement's reporting practices of hate crimes statistics and federal policies to encourage greater participation in reporting hate crimes; (2) federal prosecution and enforcement of hate crimes laws; and (3) the prevention of hate crimes. On May 11, 2018, the Commission held a briefing where it received written and oral testimony from impacted community members, legal and academic experts, federal and local law enforcement officials, and members from the public. The Commission also sent formal requests for information to relevant federal government officials at the U.S. Departments of Justice and Education, and to five local law enforcement agencies the Commission selected for the agencies' hate crimes reporting practices. The Commission also conducted extensive qualitative and quantitative research regarding the impact of hate crimes and bias-motivated incidents on targeted communities in the United States since the passage of the Matthew Shepard and James Byrd Jr. Hate Crimes Prevention Act (HCPA) in 2009.

The FBI defines a hate crime as "a traditional offense like murder, arson, or vandalism with an added element of bias." Federal hate crimes—also called bias crimes—are offenses where a perpetrator willfully causes bodily injury or through use of fire or a dangerous weapon or explosive device, willfully causes or attempts to cause bodily injury to any person because of the actual or perceived race, ethnicity, national origin, religion, gender, gender identity, sexual orientation, or disability status of any person. Federal hate crimes law also prohibits bias-based damage to religious property or interference with the right to practice one's religion, using force or threats of force to interfere with federally protected activities (such as education and public accommodations) or to interfere with access to housing, because of bias-based motivation.

A majority of states have passed hate crime statutes that allow for an additional penalty or sentence enhancement if prosecutors prove beyond a reasonable doubt that the crime was motivated by bias. These statutes can vary from state to state in terms of scope and coverage regarding, for example, which groups are protected, and whether the statutes mandate compiling of hate crime statistics by local law enforcement.

Congress has determined that the reverberating injuries that hate crimes inflict in our democratic society justify a special response. The Supreme Court has held that the systemic effects of hate crimes are substantial enough to justify the use of enhanced sentences against offenders found guilty in hate crimes cases. In addition to legal liability, from a policy standpoint, enhanced punishments for hate crimes are also often seen as symbolically important because these laws send a "message to society that criminal acts based upon hatred will not be tolerated." Therefore, to address the gap in protection left by some states, Congress passed the HCPA in 2009, to protect victims who were targeted because of their actual or perceived race, color, religion, national origin, sexual orientation, ethnicity, gender identity, disability, or gender.

Violent hate crimes are often more brutal than other crimes: compared to perpetrators of similar non-hate crimes, perpetrators of hate crimes use extreme violence more often. During 2011–2015, about 90 percent of reported hate crimes involved violence and of those, 29 percent were serious violent crimes, compared to 25 percent of violent non-hate crime victimizations falling into the category of being serious. When comparing hate crime victims to non-hate crime victims, researchers find that hate crime victims are significantly more likely to report being fearful, expect to be targeted for additional victimizations, are more likely to experience employment issues, suffer from health issues, have difficulties overcoming the victimization, and suffer from post-traumatic stress disorder. Georgetown Law Professor Frederick Lawrence asserts that the subsequent effects of the crime may be heightened since "bias crime victim[s] cannot reasonably minimize the risk of future attacks because [they are] unable to change the characteristic that made [them] a victim." Since hate crimes are often intended "to not just harm the victim, but to send a message of intimidation to an entire community of people," these targeted communities experience hate crime in "a manner that has no equivalent in the public response to a parallel crime." These crimes leave entire communities feeling threatened, attacked, and can also stoke tensions between and within communities following a crime.

The Hate Crimes Coalition, a group of over 50 civil rights, religious, education, and professional organizations, contends that many hate crimes are the result of perpetrators holding white supremacy ideologies, and states that "[w]hite supremacy is un-American and unacceptable." The coalition discusses an increase of reported hate crimes and bias-motivated incidents over the past several years and that the acts of racism, anti-Semitism, Islamophobia, and hatred toward LGBT communities experienced by individuals and communities and "underline[] an essential fact . . . that hate crimes are a national problem, deserving of priority attention . . . [and] the federal government has an essential leadership role to play in confronting acts of violence motivated by prejudice—and in promoting anti-bias initiatives for schools, communities, and law enforcement officials." The Civil Rights Division of the Department of Justice in the current Administration has stated its agreement with these principles, highlighting on its website and in Attorney General speeches and presentations a priority focus on hate crime enforcement. It has also prosecuted a number of hate crimes cases.

One of the greatest challenges to understanding the severity and magnitude of hate crimes is the lack of sufficient data. The passage of HCPA was an important step in confronting bigotry, increasing public awareness, and improving law enforcement's responses to hate violence, but without national data and police training to accurately identify and report hate crimes, preventing these incidents in the first place is substantially more challenging. Currently, the best sources of data come through the annual FBI's Uniform Crime Reporting (UCR) Hate Crime Statistics and the Bureau of Justice Statistics' National Crime Victimization Survey (NCVS). The UCR program relies upon voluntary reporting from local, state, and federal law enforcement, and as such, only perceived by victims to be motivated by an offender's bias against their actual or perceived identity provides a snapshot of the extent of hate crimes. In contrast, the NCVS measures crimes or group characteristic. While neither of these data sets are without limitations, this report discusses that, taken together, they provide some insight into the increase of hate violence in the United States.

Developing effective policies, procedures, and responses to hate crimes can reduce overall crime, while simultaneously building relationships and trust between law enforcement and communities who feel targeted by acts of hate. The Department of Justice states that "[o]f all crimes, hate crimes are [the] most likely to create or exacerbate tensions, which can trigger larger community-wide racial conflict, civil disturbances, and even riots." Furthermore, these crimes can then impede the work of law enforcement and prosecutors in investigating, prosecuting, and preventing all crime. The "recognition and reporting of hate crimes and incidents is critical to raising awareness of the problem, acknowledging to victims the pain bias actions cause, and helping police and prosecutors better understand where and how such incidents occur." While policies alone cannot eradicate hate, effective laws and responses to hate violence by law enforcement officials send a message to targeted communities that these crimes and the threat they pose will be addressed and send a message to perpetrators that their actions are not condoned. At the time of this writing, recent hate crimes resulting in the death of people of color, such as the mass shooting in El Paso, Texas, demonstrate the ongoing urgency and the work that is needed to prevent bias-based attacks on individuals and communities. Further, the Commission also explored the increase in hate incidents in American schools and in the public realm, along with current and potential civil rights tools that may be used to protect students and others against hateful, hostile, or threatening speech, including online speech, within the bounds of the First Amendment. . . .

Findings:

- Hate crimes are increasing in America according to available evidence. Much of the evidence reflects massive underreporting of hate crimes.

- Many Americans are negatively impacted by hate crimes and are fearful of the heightened expression of hate and bigotry in the United States.

- Effective laws for, reporting of, and responses to hate violence by law enforcement officials send a message to targeted communities that these crimes and the threat they pose will be addressed through appropriate training of law enforcement officers and increased availability of resources.

- As of the time of this writing, 46 states and the District of Columbia have some form of hate crime statute, leaving Arkansas, Georgia, South Carolina, and Wyoming as states without such statutes.

- While bullying does not necessarily reach the level of a hate crime, these incidents are significant for educators, researchers, parents, and students to pay attention to and actively work with students to prevent.

Recommendations:

- Congress should pass legislation and provide adequate funding that would incentivize local and state law enforcement to more accurately report hate crimes to the FBI, and promote greater transparency and accountability, which would aid in building community trust.

- Congress should also pass legislation to ensure that federal law enforcement agencies collect and report their hate crime data to the FBI and that states are accurately reporting hate crime data they receive from local law enforcement agencies in their jurisdiction.

- The Trump Administration should reinstate groups within DHS who analyze the threat of domestic terrorism and reinstate grants awarded to groups who counter white supremacist terror.

- Law enforcement agencies that do not yet engage in this practice should start investigating "hate incidents" even if they do not escalate to meet the legal definition of a crime. Documenting and investigating hate and bias incidents may aid in the prevention of hate crimes and enhance public trust and safety.

- State legislators should pass legislation that clearly defines hate crimes and hate incidents.

SOURCE: U.S. Commission on Civil Rights. "In the Name of Hate: Examining the Federal Government's Role in Responding to Hate Crimes." November 13, 2019. https://www.usccr.gov/pubs/2019/11-13-In-the-Name-of-Hate.pdf.

OTHER HISTORIC DOCUMENTS OF INTEREST

FROM THIS VOLUME

FROM PREVIOUS *HISTORIC DOCUMENTS*

UN and United States Remark
on Deadly Unrest in Iran

In November 2019, Iran experienced its worst period of public unrest in almost forty years. Prompted by the government's announcement of fuel price increases and petrol rations, the protests spanning the country demonstrated the people's growing dissatisfaction with Iran's struggling economy—one that has been hard hit by U.S. economic sanctions. The government quickly cracked down on protesters, shutting down Internet access and deploying the Islamic Revolutionary Guard Corps (IRGC) to restore order. U.S. and United Nations (UN) officials condemned the violence and urged the government to protect its citizens' human rights.

Iran Announces Hike in Fuel Prices, Petrol Rationing

At midnight on November 15, the Iranian government announced that it was increasing fuel prices by 50 percent, introducing monthly petrol rations, and cutting fuel subsidies. Effective immediately, the changes included a sixteen-gallon-per-month limit on fuel purchases for private vehicles, with additional charges incurred if an Iranian bought fuel over that limit.

The plan was developed by Iran's Supreme Council of Economic Coordination, led by President Hassan Rouhani, Speaker of Parliament Ali Larijani, and Chief Justice Ebrahim Raisi. These officials and other government leaders said it was necessary to raise fuel prices to generate funds that could be used to support Iran's poorest citizens. Mohammad Baqer Nobakht, leader of Iran's Plan and Budget Organization, said that revenues from the program would be distributed as monthly cash assistance to roughly 18 million households. Many analysts said Iran needed the money to offset the impact of economic sanctions reimposed by the United States in 2018 upon withdrawing from the Joint Comprehensive Plan of Action nuclear agreement. The International Monetary Fund reported that Iran's gross domestic product shrank by nearly 5 percent in 2018 as a result of sanctions and projected it would shrink by another 9.5 percent in 2019. The country's oil exports had been cut in half; inflation and unemployment continued to increase; and Iranian currency, the rial, lost at least 50 percent of its value. Low- and middle-income Iranians were the hardest hit, particularly as the cost for basic goods skyrocketed. The Statistical Centre of Iran reported in November 2019 that food and beverage prices, for example, had increased by 61 percent over the prior year.

Fuel is cheaper in Iran than in most countries, even accounting for the price increase, but many Iranians shared concerns on social media that their average incomes were too low to be able to afford the increase. Others expressed surprise at the announcement, though some acknowledged that the government's recent reintroduction of fuel cards had been a sign of things to come.

SECURITY FORCES CRACK DOWN ON PROTESTS

Iranians began taking to the streets the next day to protest against the fuel price increases and petrol rations. Analysts noted that while the new fuel program may have provided a catalyst for unrest, dissatisfaction with the country's economic situation—and the perceived role of government corruption in Iran's financial woes—had been simmering for years. Protests and strikes had periodically broken out across the country since late 2017.

The protests that began on November 16 were initially peaceful, with drivers leaving their vehicles on highways and demonstrators blocking roads. But they soon turned violent. Hundreds of buildings were looted, set on fire, or otherwise damaged. Interior Minister Abdolreza Rahmani Fazli later reported that more than 700 banks, 140 public buildings, 9 religious centers, 70 petrol stations, and more than 300 vehicles were damaged during protests. He also said that 50 military bases had been attacked. Official estimates placed the number of protesters between 120,000 and 200,000. Fazli said that protests had occurred in 29 of Iran's 31 provinces. Media reports suggested that many of these protests occurred in towns and cities with larger populations of poor and working-class Iranians and that most protesters were young males who were unemployed or low-income.

The government's subsequent crackdown on protesters was swift and brutal. The IRGC and the volunteer Basij militia were dispatched to assist local police and security forces in quieting the unrest. Videos and eyewitness reports indicated that in many instances the IRGC and other security officials fired live ammunition at mostly unarmed protesters to break up demonstrations. One widely reported incident occurred in the city of Mahshahr on November 18. Protesters had taken control of the city and its surrounding suburbs by blocking main roads into and out of the area. Local law enforcement reportedly failed to disperse the crowds, at which point the IRGC was deployed. Witnesses told reporters and human rights groups that upon arriving at a suburban roadblock, IRGC troops immediately shot dozens of protesters, killing several of them. One protester who was armed allegedly shot at the troops while others fled to a nearby marsh. The IRGC troops pursued and surrounded the protesters before opening fire and killing anywhere from 20 to 100 people. Reports indicated that the bodies of the dead were taken by the IRGC and only returned to their families for burial after they signed agreements not to hold memorial services or talk to the media.

The full scope of the protests and the crackdown that ensued were difficult to assess due to the government's shutdown of Internet services, which also began on November 16. A government spokesperson said the Internet would be restored in provinces where "there are assurances the Internet will not be abused." He acknowledged that "people have faced difficulties" as a result of the shutdown but said the bigger concern was "maintaining the country's peace and stability." The government began restoring Internet connectivity on November 21.

Iranian officials accused "foreign enemies" of organizing the protests. Supreme Leader Ayatollah Ali Khamenei called protesters "thugs" and said the security crackdown was a justified response to enemy interference. "The counter-revolution and Iran's enemies have always supported sabotage and breaches of security and continue to do so," Khamenei said. "Unfortunately, some problems were caused, a number of people lost their lives and some centers were destroyed." The commander of the Basij militia declared that "America's plot failed," while the IRGC said that several detained protest leaders held dual citizenship or had other connections to foreign governments. The Fars News Agency further claimed that some protesters had been paid to destroy property.

U.S. officials decried the violence. "We condemn strongly any acts of violence committed by this regime against the Iranian people and are deeply concerned by reports of several fatalities," said Secretary of State Mike Pompeo. He called for the government to "immediately restore the ability of all Iranians to access a free and open Internet," warning that "the world is watching." He also reiterated the United States' position: "The Iranian people will enjoy a better future when their government begins to respect basic human rights, abandons its revolutionary posture and its destabilizing foreign policy in the region, and behaves simply like a normal nation." On Twitter, President Donald Trump wrote, "Iran has become so unstable that the regime has shut down their entire Internet System so that the Great Iranian people cannot talk about the tremendous violence taking place within the country." The U.S. Department of the Treasury imposed new sanctions on Communications Minister Mohammad Javad Azari-Jahromi for leading "widescale internet censorship" during the unrest and later sanctioned two Iranian judges for their role in suppressing "freedoms of speech and assembly" during the period of unrest.

The UN Office of the High Commissioner for Human Rights (OHCHR) also weighed in, with a spokesperson saying officials were "deeply concerned by reported violations of international norms and standards on the use of force, including the firing of live ammunition, against demonstrators in Iran." The OHCHR called on "Iranian authorities and security forces to avoid the use of force to disperse peaceful assemblies and in cases in which an assembly is violent to restrict the use of force to the greatest extent possible," while also urging protesters to "carry out demonstrations peacefully." The spokesperson further noted that Iran is party to the International Covenant on Civil and Political Rights, a binding treaty that requires governments to respect the rights to freedom of expression and peaceful assembly and association.

CASUALTY COUNTS, REPORTS OF ABUSES GROW

As Internet connectivity was restored and new details emerged, the estimated casualty counts began to grow. The UN reported on November 22 that as many as 106 people had been killed and 1,000 arrested amid the unrest but also noted various reports that suggested higher tallies. On December 6, the OHCHR issued a press release providing updated numbers and accounts of security officials' actions. "All in all, the picture now emerging from Iran is extremely disturbing," said High Commissioner for Human Rights Michelle Bachelet, who also "expressed alarm at the continuing lack of transparency about casualties and the treatment of thousands of detainees."

According to the OHCHR, roughly 200 Iranians had been killed, including thirteen women and twelve children. At least 7,000 people had been arrested in twenty-eight provinces since the beginning of the protests. The office was "extremely concerned about their physical treatment, violations of their right to due process, and the possibility that a significant number of them may be charged with offences that carry the death penalty, in addition to the conditions under which they are held." The OHCHR cited reports that many detainees did not have access to a lawyer, were held in overcrowded prisons in "harsh conditions," and that some were denied medical attention. The release also noted allegations that detainees were being tortured for information.

Furthermore, OHCHR said there appeared to be evidence of "multiple violations" of the International Covenant on Civil and Political Rights. Security forces reportedly used water cannon, tear gas, batons, and live ammunition against unarmed protesters. "Verified video footage indicates severe violence was used against protesters, including armed members of security forces shooting from the roof of a justice department building in one city, and from helicopters in another," Bachelet said. "We have also received footage which appears to show security forces shooting unarmed demonstrators from behind while they were running away, and shooting others directly in the face and vital organs—in other words shooting to kill. These are clear violations of international norms and standards on the use of force, and serious violations of human rights." The OHCHR acknowledged some conflicting reports about whether some protesters had been armed but declared that it "does not in any way justify such an indiscriminate, horrifying and deadly reaction by the security forces."

A mid-December report by Amnesty International placed the number of dead at 304 Iranians and echoed OHCHR's findings of abuse by security forces. Iranian officials claimed such numbers were "fabricated" and declined to release official casualty counts. "Any casualty figures not confirmed by the government are speculative and unreliable, and in many cases part of a disinformation campaign waged against Iran from outside the country," said Alireza Miryousefi, a spokesperson for Iran's UN mission.

Then on December 23, Reuters published an exclusive report citing data provided by three officials within Iran's Ministry of Interior that showed roughly 1,500 people had been killed. This number included at least 17 teenagers and about 400 women, as well as some police officers and soldiers. Reuters said the data were based on information collected by the officials from the security forces, morgues, hospitals, and coroners.

These grim tallies appeared to validate characterizations of the 2019 protests as the worst and most violent unrest seen in Iran since the Islamic Revolution of 1979.

Uncertainty Ahead for Iranian Regime

Analysts speculate the fuel price increases and the government's crackdown on protests will significantly reduce Rouhani's support, making it more likely that a hardline candidate will succeed him as president in 2021. Meanwhile, the Iranian government has again become the focus of public ire following the accidental shootdown of Ukraine International Airlines Flight PS752 in January 2020, which killed dozens of Iranians, and an apparent effort to cover-up the incident.

—Linda Grimm

Following are comments made by U.S. secretary of state Mike Pompeo about the protest situation in Iran during a press briefing on November 18, 2019; a press briefing conducted by the UN Office of the High Commissioner for Human Rights (OHCHR) on November 19, 2019, on the situation in Iran; and a press release issued by OHCHR on December 6, 2019, reporting on the number of dead and wounded, as well as rights abuses by Iranian security forces.

U.S. Secretary of State Comments on Situation in Iran

November 18, 2019

[The following statement and Q&A with reporters have been excerpted from a longer press briefing transcript.]

Good afternoon, everyone. I have several statements I want to make today, starting with a statement about the Islamic Republic of Iran.

The United States is monitoring the ongoing protests in Iran closely. We condemn strongly any acts of violence committed by this regime against the Iranian people and are deeply concerned by reports of several fatalities. We've been at that since the beginning of this administration.

The Islamic Republic must cease violence against its own people and should immediately restore the ability of all Iranians to access a free and open Internet. The world is watching.

The Iranian people will enjoy a better future when their government begins to respect basic human rights, abandons its revolutionary posture and its destabilizing foreign policy in the region, and behaves simply like a normal nation.

The choice is clearly with the regime.

Continuing with Iran, President Rouhani recently announced that Iran will begin uranium enrichment activities at the Fordow facility. Therefore, the United States will terminate the sanctions waiver related to the nuclear facility at Fordow, effective December 15th, 2019. The right amount of uranium enrichment for the world's largest state sponsor of terror is zero.

Iran originally constructed Fordow as a fortified, underground bunker to conduct secret uranium enrichment work, and there is no legitimate reason for Iran to resume enrichment at this previously clandestine site. Iran should reverse its activity there immediately.

Iran's supreme leader is reverting to his tried-and-true method of using nuclear brinksmanship to extort the international community into accepting the regime's destabilizing activity. The United States rejects this approach completely and calls on all nations to do the same.

The only viable way forward is through comprehensive negotiations that address the full range of Iran's threats in their entirety. Iran's most recent action is yet another clear attempt at nuclear extortion that will only deepen its political and economic isolation from the world. . . .

QUESTION: Mr. Secretary, first on Iran. How do you balance your support for the Iranian people and the request to topple their government—or sorry, the request to hold their government accountable, and your support for them that has been seen and criticized by the Iranian regime as interference? . . .

SECRETARY POMPEO: We—I remember how the previous administration treated the Iranian people. I remember the signs that said, "Are you with us? Are you with the regime?" I don't think anybody in the world has any doubt about where this administration stands. We want Iran to be a normal nation, and we want the people there to have the freedoms to which they're entitled, and we want the—we want the regime's monies to be spent on things that benefit the Iranian people, not proxy forces in Iraq, not underwriting Hizballah, not conducting assassination campaigns throughout Europe. We want the Iranian regime to behave like a normal nation, to take care of their people, and I think that is what you are hearing and seeing in these protests that are taking place in the Islamic Republic of Iran over these past few days.

SOURCE: U.S. Department of State. "Secretary Michael R. Pompeo Remarks to the Press." November 18, 2019. https://www.state.gov/secretary-michael-r-pompeo-remarks-to-the-press.

UN Office of the High Commissioner for Human Rights Briefing on Iran

DOCUMENT

November 19, 2019

We are deeply concerned by reported violations of international norms and standards on the use of force, including the firing of live ammunition, against demonstrators in Iran during the protests that began on Friday and have continued into this week. We are especially alarmed that the use of live ammunition has allegedly caused a significant number of deaths across the country.

While the fact that there have been some deaths has been acknowledged by the authorities, including by Ayatollah Khamenei, it has been extremely difficult to verify the overall number. However, Iranian media and a number of other sources suggest dozens of people may have been killed and many people injured during protests in at least eight different provinces, with over 1,000 protesters arrested. Overall, protests have reportedly been held in 40 or more towns and cities across the country, but again details have been hard to verify because of the shutdown of the internet late on Saturday.

We urge the Iranian authorities and security forces to avoid the use of force to disperse peaceful assemblies and in cases in which an assembly is violent to restrict the use of force to the greatest extent possible, especially actions that are likely to cause serious injury or loss of life. This includes issuing clear instructions to the security forces to abide by international norms and standards on the use of force, including ensuring that firearms are used only in cases of an imminent threat to life or of serious injury and only when less extreme measures are insufficient to address such a threat.

We also urge protesters to carry out demonstrations peacefully, without resorting to physical violence or destruction of property.

As Iran is a State party to the International Covenant on Civil and Political Rights, we call on the Iranian authorities to respect the right to freedom of expression, and the right to peaceful assembly and association, as laid down in the Covenant, which is a binding international treaty.

We also call on the Government to immediately re-establish Iranians' access to the internet, as well as other forms of communication, which allow for freedom of expression and access to information.

While noting the serious economic challenges the country is experiencing, including in the context of sanctions imposed by the United States, we urge the Iranian Government to engage in meaningful dialogue with various actors in the country about the socio-economic challenges the population is facing, and to collectively work with a cross-section of society towards a sustainable resolution to these issues.

As so many other popular protests across the world have illustrated all too clearly in recent weeks and months, simply responding with harsh words and an iron fist raises a significant risk not only of violating international norms and standards but also of seriously aggravating the situation to everyone's disadvantage, including the Government's.

Protests of this nature and on this scale are an indication of deep-rooted and often well-founded grievances, that cannot simply be brushed aside.

SOURCE: From "Press Briefing on Iran," November 19, 2019, by United Nations Office of the High Commissioner for Human Rights, ©2019 United Nations. Reprinted with the permission of the United Nations. https://www.ohchr.org/EN/NewsEvents/Pages/DisplayNews.aspx?NewsID=25311&LangID=E.

UN High Commissioner for Human Rights Calls on Iran to Address Human Rights Violations

December 6, 2019

As more information gradually filters out of Iran in the wake of the recent protests, the UN High Commissioner for Human Rights Michelle Bachelet on Friday expressed alarm at the continuing lack of transparency about casualties and the treatment of thousands of detainees, as well as continuing arrests reported to be taking place across the country.

At least 7,000 people have reportedly been arrested in 28 of Iran's 31 provinces since mass protests broke out on 15 November, and the High Commissioner said she is "extremely concerned about their physical treatment, violations of their right to due process, and the possibility that a significant number of them may be charged with offences that carry the death penalty, in addition to the conditions under which they are held."

During the five days of demonstrations, which according to official Government sources involved between 120,000 and 200,000 protestors, the UN Human Rights Office has information suggesting that at least 208 people were killed, including 13 women and 12 children. There are also reports, which the UN Human Rights Office has so far been unable to verify, suggesting more than twice that number killed.

"In such circumstances, with so many reported deaths, it is essential the authorities act with far greater transparency," Bachelet said. "They must undertake prompt, independent and impartial investigations into all violations that have taken place, including the killing of protesters and reported deaths and ill-treatment in custody. And those responsible must be held accountable. There appear to be multiple violations of the International Covenant on Civil and Political Rights, which Iran has ratified and is obliged to uphold."

Security forces responded to the protests with water cannon, tear gas, batons, and in some cases live ammunition against unarmed demonstrators who posed no imminent threat of death or serious injury. According to reports, members of the Basij militia and the Islamic Revolutionary Guard Corps (IRCG) were involved in shooting protestors.

"Verified video footage indicates severe violence was used against protesters, including armed members of security forces shooting from the roof of a justice department building in one city, and from helicopters in another," Bachelet said. "We have also received footage which appears to show security forces shooting unarmed demonstrators from behind while they were running away, and shooting others directly in the face and vital organs—in other words shooting to kill. These are clear violations of international norms and standards on the use of force, and serious violations of human rights."

In what appears to be one of the worst incidents, which took place on 18 November, the High Commissioner said her Office had received information partially corroborating reports that Iranian security forces used machine guns against protesters in Jarahi Square in Mahshahr—including against people fleeing the area and people hiding in nearby reedbeds—resulting in at least 23 people killed, and possibly many more.

As well as protestors, it is reported that bystanders in the street and people watching from their homes were also hit with bullets during the Mahshahr incident. "There are conflicting reports about whether or not there were one or more armed people among the protestors," Bachelet said. "But this does not in any way justify such an indiscriminate, horrifying and deadly reaction by the security forces."

The UN Human Rights Office has received numerous reports of ill-treatment against those arrested, including with the apparent aim of extracting forced confessions, and State television has broadcast the "confessions" of some detainees alleged to be protest leaders and people affiliated with anti-government groups or foreign States. According to the deputy chief of the IRGC, those who have "openly confessed they were doing mercenary work" will face severe punishment.

"Many of the arrested protesters have not had access to a lawyer, meaning due process is not being respected," Bachelet said. "We also have reports of severe overcrowding and harsh conditions in detention centres, which in some cities include military barracks, sports venues and schools in addition to official detention facilities. There are also reports that individuals who were wounded or otherwise injured during the crackdown are being denied medical treatment in detention."

She expressed concern at reports of intimidation of journalists trying to report on the situation both inside and outside the country, with family members of Iranian journalists working for news channels based outside Iran reportedly summoned and threatened with reprisals by intelligence officials.

"All in all, the picture now emerging from Iran is extremely disturbing," Bachelet said. "I urge the authorities to immediately release from detention all protestors who have been arbitrarily deprived of their liberty, and to ensure their right to due process, including access to a lawyer of their choosing during the investigative stage. In the event of further protests, I urge the Government to respect Iranians' right to exercise freedom of expression, peaceful assembly and association and, in addition to investigating the violations that have already occurred, to restrict the use of force to the greatest extent possible, as provided for under the relevant international norms and standards."

SOURCE: From "Bachelet Calls on Iran to Address Multiple Human Rights Violations in Context of Recent Protests," December 6, 2019, by United Nations Office of the High Commissioner for Human Rights, ©2019 United Nations. Reprinted with the permission of the United Nations. https://www.ohchr .org/EN/NewsEvents/Pages/DisplayNews.aspx?NewsID=25393&LangID=E.

OTHER HISTORIC DOCUMENTS OF INTEREST

FROM THIS VOLUME

FROM PREVIOUS HISTORIC DOCUMENTS

President and Defense Leaders on U.S. Engagement in Afghanistan

NOVEMBER 28 AND DECEMBER 12, 2019

After a three-year legal battle with the federal government, on December 9, 2019, *The Washington Post* published the results of its investigation into the costs and consequences of U.S. involvement in Afghanistan. The six-part investigation, known as the Afghanistan Papers, recounted in detail how the U.S. government, including senior political and military leaders, systematically misled the public about the war's true costs and the odds of victory. Military officials and President Donald Trump tried to downplay the report's findings, noting ongoing successes in combating terrorist groups operating in the region along with progress on talks to secure a peace agreement with the Taliban. Yet despite such assurances, the Afghanistan Papers symbolized a watershed moment for the longest-running war in American history and sparked calls on Capitol Hill for future investigations.

THE AFGHANISTAN PAPERS

On December 9, 2019, *The Washington Post* published the Afghanistan Papers, a six-part investigation into U.S. involvement in Afghanistan. The report's findings began bluntly, stating in the very first sentence that "senior U.S. officials failed to tell the truth about the war in Afghanistan throughout the 18-year campaign, making rosy pronouncements they knew to be false and hiding unmistakable evidence the war had become unwinnable." Through more than 400 interviews with top U.S. officials and more than 2,000 pages of documents, reporters outlined how the American government systematically misled the public about the U.S. strategy in Afghanistan.

The report's title positioned the investigation as a modern-day Pentagon Papers, the groundbreaking report that documented a systematic campaign of lying about progress in Vietnam and helped bring about an end to the war. The *Post*'s Afghanistan investigation focused on six different subjects: how U.S. officials misled the public about the war in Afghanistan, the lack of a clear war strategy across multiple administrations, the failure of U.S. efforts to rebuild the war-torn country, how corruption was tolerated and rampant, how the U.S. military trained inept and incompetent security forces, and how the American government failed to end opium production in the South Asian country.

Amid the revelations were candid descriptions from officials in decision-making capacities about the myriad of missteps facing the United States and confessions about misleading the American public. "We were devoid of a fundamental understanding of Afghanistan—we didn't know what we were doing," Douglas Lute, a three-star general and former White House Afghan czar under the Bush and Obama administrations, told government interviewers. Lute asked, "What are we trying to do here? We didn't have the foggiest notion of what we were undertaking." Bob Crowley, an army colonel who served as a senior counterinsurgency adviser to U.S. military commanders in 2013 and 2014, told government interviewers, "Every data point was altered to present the best picture possible." He added, "Surveys, for instance, were totally unreliable but reinforced that everything we were doing was right and we became a self-licking ice cream cone."

Together, the cost of the war as presented in the Afghanistan Papers was staggering. An estimated 43,000 Afghan civilians were killed, as were more than 64,000 Afghan soldiers and police; approximately 42,100 Taliban fighters; 2,300 U.S. military personnel; 3,814 U.S. contractors; and 1,145 North Atlantic Treaty Organization (NATO) and coalition troops. The financial toll for the United States exceeded $1 trillion.

President Trump Touts U.S. Success in Afghanistan

Days before the report was published, the president traveled to Bagram Airfield in Afghanistan to visit troops stationed there for the Thanksgiving holiday. At a briefing following a meeting with Afghan president Ashraf Ghani Ahmadzai, President Trump focused largely on American progress in the region, discussing U.S. and Afghani efforts to fight the Islamic State of Iraq and the Levant (ISIL) and to bring stability to Afghanistan through engaging in peace talks with the Taliban.

President Trump stressed that on both objectives, the United States had achieved "tremendous success." He said of ISIL, "We've hit them very, very hard. And they're down to literally hundreds as opposed to thousands." The president said that despite having thousands of fighters in the past, "now they're down to hundreds. Probably 200 left. And we're scouting them out. So we'll be down to very little, if anything, in a very short period of time." Trump stressed the U.S. desire to "make a deal" with the Taliban. The president later promised that the military conflict with ISIL and the political conflict with the Taliban "will be over with very soon."

Trump also addressed a planned troop drawdown. "At the same time, we're bringing down the number of troops substantially. But we're able to, because of the weaponry and all of the things that we have in place. We can do, actually, more damage with even fewer troops," the president said. He did not give a clear number or goal for the drawdown, only stating that "we'll be down at a number that's very—it's a good number. And we're going to stay until such time as we have a deal or we have total victory. And they want to make a deal very badly." When pressed by reporters, Trump hinted at cutting the number of troops down to 8,600 but was noncommittal, saying only that it was being considered but "we can do much better than that."

Other U.S. officials similarly pointed to "significant progress" on both degrading ISIL and establishing peace talks. "The troops here, and Afghan troops and international troops, have all put a significant amount of pressure on ISIS, particularly in Nangarhar," Chair of the Joint Chiefs of Staff Mark A. Milley said. "Their numbers have been treaded and dwindled significantly. Organizationally, they have not been destroyed, but they have been severely hurt. And that pressure will continue," he added. On peace talks with the Taliban, Milley stressed the administration's desire for success, which then will lead to "Afghan-to-Afghan dialogue in the not-too-distant future."

President Ahmadzai praised American involvement in his country and the "remarkable partnership" between the U.S. and Afghan governments. "I'd like to thank you for your leadership and for your determination both on the South Asia strategy that made this possible and on your very principled decisions regarding putting limits on the type of peace that would ensure the gains of the past years and ensure your security and our freedom," Ahmadzai said. The briefing closed with the U.S. president stressing that Americans were "leading it all the way" in establishing a safer, more prosperous Afghanistan, but he called on others in the region to assist in that goal. "We want other players in this area to help. They don't like ISIS either. They don't like Al Qaida either. And they have to help also. You have countries that are right nearby that are very big, that have power, and they should be doing some of the work too, not just the United States," Trump said.

U.S. Defense Officials Reaffirm Commitment to Transparency and Diplomatic Solution in Afghanistan

The Washington Post investigation did little to alter the position of the Trump administration. After the investigation was published, U.S. officials again downplayed the situation in Afghanistan and denied purposefully misleading the American public. Assistant to the Secretary of Defense for Public Affairs Jonathan R. Hoffman, together with Joint Staff vice director Rear Adm. William D. Byrne Jr., in a Department of Defense press briefing days after the investigation went public, stressed that the "top-line view" from the administration is that "the future in Afghanistan is one that is going to be through a diplomatic solution with all parties." Hoffman argued the U.S. government has succeeded in helping build up Afghanistan's military and political institutions as part of "a continuing commitment from our partners and allies to support the Afghans as we go through this process." In particular, Hoffman pointed to the recent elections as an example of the success achieved by coalition forces. The fact that the Afghan government was "able to conduct a relatively violence-free election was one of the major goals and major accomplishments of the year for our allies," Hoffman said.

Hoffman also sought to reaffirm the administration's commitment to being transparent and open with the American public. Asked for what "assurances" the administration could give the American people that they were being truthful in light of the Afghanistan Papers' revelations, Hoffman said the administration will "always endeavor to be . . . open and transparent with the American people." He continued, "This department has attempted to be honest, open, transparent in all of its actions with the American people." According to Hoffman, "The American people have a right to understand what's going on overseas, and what our military is doing. And our forces and our military men and women deserve to have that transparency as well." Hoffman reiterated that the administration was working toward facilitating a "diplomatic solution" for the Afghani people. Pressed by a reporter to explain the administration's desired "conclusion," Hoffman said that the U.S. government will focus on building up Afghani security forces but that the Afghani people "need to work with the other parties in the country to come to a diplomatic solution." He concluded, "That's the path that we've set out, that we're helping the Department of State pursue, and that's the stated goals of this administration right now."

Bipartisan Calls for Investigations

Outside of the administration, lawmakers, veterans, and experts expressed shock and anger at the Afghanistan Papers. For some, the revelations were frustratingly familiar, more evidence of missteps that many knew but did not publicly acknowledge. On Capitol Hill, leaders from both parties called for investigations. Sen. Richard Blumenthal, D-Conn., a member of the Senate Armed Services Committee, said public hearings should be held with Defense Secretary Mark Esper and other officials. "We must end the vicious, lethal cycle of misinformation and unspecified, unsupported strategies," Blumenthal said. "The

Senate Armed Services Committee should hold hearings on the state of the Afghanistan conflict and the infuriating details & alleged falsehoods reported today," Sen. Josh Hawley, R-Mo., a member of the committee, wrote on Twitter.

—Robert Howard

Following are remarks by President Donald Trump, chair of the Joint Chiefs of Staff Mark A. Milley, and Afghan president Ashraf Ghani Ahmadzai on November 28, 2019, on U.S. policy and progress in Afghanistan; and remarks from a Department of Defense press briefing by Assistant to the Secretary of Defense Jonathan Hoffman and Rear Adm. William Byrne on December 12, 2019, on work being done by the United States in Afghanistan.

DOCUMENT

President Trump and Chair Milley Remark on U.S. Involvement in Afghanistan

November 28, 2019

President Trump. Well, thank you very much. It's great to be in Afghanistan with our troops. And we had a wonderful Thanksgiving lunch. It was abbreviated a little bit, but we served lunch and had lunch. And these are great people, and it's also wonderful to be with the President of Afghanistan. And, President Ghani, thank you very much. It's an honor.

We have a lot of things to talk about, many, many things. We've had tremendous success in the last few months with our military, as you know. ISIS has been very, very badly hit, very severely hit. We had al-Baghdadi down in a different part to the world, and we took him out. That was the father of ISIS, the founder. And he was trying to rebuild it, and that didn't work out too well for him.

But we had tremendous success with ISIS over the last 3 to 4 months, and we're down to a very small number. And likewise, with Al Qaida, we're down to a very small number. And the Taliban wants to make a deal. We'll see if they make a deal. If they do, they do. And if they don't, they don't. That's fine. But we've had tremendous success.

And I think what I'd like to do—and perhaps, General, if you could say just a couple of words before President Ghani. Tell them about how we've literally decimated ISIS in Afghanistan, also Al Qaida in Afghanistan, if you would.

Chairman of the Joint Chiefs of Staff Mark A. Milley, USA. Sure, absolutely, Mr. President. And, President Ghani, good to see you again. And we had a great meeting earlier today.

And as you know, Scott Miller and the troops here, and Afghan troops and international troops, have all put a significant amount of pressure on ISIS, particularly in Nangarhar. And they've been hurt bad. Their numbers have been treaded and dwindled significantly. Organizationally, they have not been destroyed, but they have been severely hurt. And that pressure will continue.

And as the President mentioned, there's ongoing talks with the Taliban, and hopefully, those will be successful. And hopefully we'll then lead to Afghan-to-Afghan dialogue in the not-too distant future.

So I think there's been some significant progress, Mr. President. And I thank Scott Miller and the Ambassador. And the entire team of U.S. forces here, in combination with the Afghan National Security Forces, has done a great job.

So thanks for your support.

President Trump. Good. Thank you very much, General.

And, Scotty, do you want to just mention how much—what we're left with? You're down to very small numbers with ISIS, and also you're down to very, very small with Al Qaida. Do you want to mention that?

North Atlantic Treaty Organization Resolute Support Mission Commander Gen. A. Scott Miller, USA. Mr. President, with the Afghan forces, particularly over the last 30 days of this—although it's been a long fight—we've seen a—quite a few surrenders by Daesh/ISIS fighters, as well as their families, coming out of southern Nangarhar, which, as everybody knows, that's a—been a tough set of terrain for the United States of America and Afghanistan.

Since 2001, it was a safe haven for bin Laden in the early days, and it's been a pretty remarkable military operation, as well as the following operations with the Afghans.

President Ghani. Equally with Al Qaida South Asia.

President Trump. Yes. We've made that tremendous progress though over the last, I would say, 6 months. And we've really, with respect to ISIS and Al Qaida. And we've hit them very, very hard. And they're down to literally hundreds as opposed to thousands. They had many thousands a short while ago, and now they're down to hundreds. Probably 200 left. And we're scouting them out. So we'll be down to very little, if anything, in a very short period of time.

Great job, by the way. Great job.

Gen. Miller. Thank you, sir.

President Trump. Appreciate it, Scotty.

Mr. President, please.

President Ghani. Well, Mr. President, it's a great honor and pleasure to welcome you. Let me first pay tribute to the Americans who paid the ultimate sacrifice. From 2001, 2,298 Americans—might be one or two difference—paid the ultimate sacrifice. We salute their courage and their determination for your security and our freedom.

Since you've been President, the number has been 52. So it's been a tremendous change. Afghan security forces are taking the lead now in most of operations. I would like to pay tribute to General Miller and to Ambassador Bass for their remarkable partnership with their problem solving and our security forces. Our team is here; has gone from strength to strength.

I'd like to thank you for your leadership and for your determination both on the South Asia strategy that made this possible and on your very principled decisions regarding putting limits on the type of peace that would ensure the gains of the past years and ensure your security and our freedom.

President Trump. Right. Well, as you know, for a period of time, we've been wanting to make a deal, and so have the Taliban. Then, we pulled back. We were getting close, and we pulled back. We didn't want to do it because of what they did. It was not a good—it was not a good thing they did with the killing a soldier. They knew he was a soldier, but he was a solider, an American soldier from Puerto Rico. And they killed him. They killed a United Nations soldier. And they also killed—they killed a total of 12 people. They thought that was good negotiating power. I said, "No, that's bad negotiating power." That was not good what they did.

And since then, we've hit them so hard, they've never been hit this hard. In the history of the war, they have not—never been hit this hard.

And they want to make a deal. So we'll see what happens. If they make it, fine. If they don't make it, that's fine.

We're going to be able to do everything we're doing and actually more. And, at the same time, we're bringing down the number of troops substantially. But we're able to, because of the weaponry and all of the things that we have in place. We can do, actually, more damage with even fewer troops.

So we're going to—we're bringing it down very substantially. And we'll be down at a number that's very—it's a good number. And we're going to stay until such time as we have a deal or we have total victory. And they want to make a deal very badly.

So we're dealing with—this is really for the media, I guess, more than anybody, because the President knows what I'm saying. Again, the Taliban wants to make a deal. And we're meeting with them, and we're saying it has to be a cease-fire. They didn't want to do a cease-fire, but now they do want to do a cease-fire, I believe. And it will probably work out that way. And we'll see what happens. But we've made tremendous progress.

But the thing I'm most proud of—because you could look at Taliban and say they're fighting for their land; you could look at, you know, others and say they're fighting for other things. But we know what ISIS is fighting for, and we know what Al Qaida is fighting for. And we have them down to a very small number of people. So—and that won't be—that will not be a longlasting fight. That will be over with very soon.

So we've made a lot of progress, and, at the same time, we're drawing down our troops. And by the way, the same thing in Syria. I have to tell you, there was false reporting in *The New York Times* and some of the others yesterday.

We—as you know, we did withdraw from Syria; except, we kept the oil. And we're doing a little scattered fighting, because we had some areas where ISIS was a little prevalent and gaining some traction. And we sent some troops in and pretty much wiped it out. But we have left—for the most part, we've left, but we've kept the oil. And by keeping the oil, we don't have the enemy getting the oil. And the oil is what fueled the enemy. In this case, it was ISIS.

And so in addition to—in addition to what we did 2 weeks ago, which was pretty remarkable, the—what that group of young people was able to do very rapidly and very surgically, we are only in an area where we're keeping the oil and knocking out certain small groups of ISIS as it reforms. We don't want to—as it—as it reforms, it gets back, it tries to get back.

But we also knocked out—Mr. President, as you know, we knocked out the number-two person who became the number-one person. And now we have our sights on the number-three person, who's going to be the number-one person, if he wants it. You know, it's not a good job. *[Laughter]* I don't think he wants it. Maybe he doesn't want it so badly. He's not acting too quickly.

So we've had tremendous success. And we've had tremendous success here, especially over the last period of 6 months to a year. So it's very nice to be with be with you.
  [. . .]

Q. Has the U.S. restarted peace talks with the Taliban?

President Trump. No, we're talking to the Taliban. Yes.

Q. Are you prepared to withdraw even without a deal?

Q. And will you include the Afghan—

President Trump. I would never say a thing like that. You wouldn't want me to say a thing like that. But I could just say this: We haven't had so much success in this—in this country, in this area. We haven't had success like this probably from the beginning, certainly as it relates to ISIS and Al Qaida, which is a very primary aim. But we've had very good success in talks with the Taliban.

Q. You said that you're, at this point, pulling out troops. How many troops are currently in Afghanistan? And what is the plan for—

President Trump. Well, we'll give you those numbers later, but we'll get down to a certain number. I'm not sure I want to give you that number, to be honest. But it's a very big difference. But because of new weaponry and technology, we're able to do actually more with fewer troops.

Q. You had mentioned 8,600. Is that not the number anymore, sir?

President Trump. It's a number that people are talking about, yes.

Q. And is that the number you're talking about?

President Trump. Yes, it is, for now. And then, we can do much better than that.

Q. Would you like to get it lower, sir?

President Trump. We can go much further than that. But we'll have it all covered.
  You know, this is a country where, for whatever reason, they reform, they regenerate. And we don't want that to happen. And we also have the support of a lot of other countries, by the way. We have a lot of help from a lot of other countries. But don't let anybody tell you that's it's anybody else, because we're leading it all the way.

Q. What is the greatest challenge—

President Trump. And frankly—and frankly, that's one of the things. We—look, we're in an area of the world—we're 8,000 miles away. Some of us—I guess, most of us came here together. We want other players in this area to help. They don't like ISIS either. They don't like Al Qaida either. And they have to help also. You have countries that are right nearby that are very big, that have power, and they should be doing some of the work too, not just the United States.
  Thank you very much, everybody.

Source: Executive Office of the President. "Remarks Following a Meeting with President Ashraf Ghani Ahmadzai of Afghanistan and an Exchange with Reporters at Bagram Airfield, Afghanistan." November 28, 2019. *Compilation of Presidential Documents* 2019, no. 00834 (November 28, 2019). https://www .govinfo.gov/content/pkg/DCPD-201900834/pdf/DCPD-201900834.pdf.

Department of Defense Holds
Briefing on Afghanistan

December 12, 2019

ASSISTANT TO THE SECRETARY OF DEFENSE JONATHAN R. HOFFMAN: Hey, good morning, everybody. Thank you for being here today, and thank you to all those who made it out to our holiday event yesterday—good to talk to many of you.

[An outline of Defense Department leadership's upcoming schedule has been omitted.]
   With that, Rear Admiral Byrne and I are happy to take your questions.
   [. . .]

Q: Thank you. The "Afghanistan Papers" were published by *The Washington Post* earlier this week. So in light of that, can either of you tell us what has been the progress—the military progress in Afghanistan over the course of the year?

   And if so, could you give specific—give examples, such as have they been able to take additional ground, or have they been able to get their casualties into check so they can have a sustainable casualty numbers for the future, something like that?

MR. HOFFMAN: OK, I'll take that first crack at that and then if the admiral has some operational views on that. With regard to Afghanistan, I think the top-line view from the department, from the administration, has been that the future in Afghanistan is one that is going to be through a diplomatic solution with all parties. And so we've continued to look into that and to work toward that.

   To do so, we've been working with the Afghan Security Forces and able to build up their capabilities, and we have seen that increase over the last year; we've seen the number of students that go through those programs; we've seen the success of their—the safety of the elections and how those elections were conducted; and the number of major attacks was minimal and that's a—to great credit to the Afghan Security Forces in doing that. And what we've also seen is a continuing commitment from our partners and allies to support the Afghans as we go through this process.

   So we've seen that happen over the last year, but we're still looking and focusing on trying to get to a diplomatic solution in a timely manner.

ADM. BYRNE: Yeah, I'm not going to get into specifics with respect to metrics, but Gen. Miller, the commander on the ground, is satisfied with the force posture that he has currently in order to meet the mission, which is counterterrorism, and training, advising and assisting our Afghan partners.

Q: Well to follow up, with all due respect, I wasn't asking about the goal of the diplomatic solution, I was ask—I want—I would like to hear a snapshot of the military progress that we've seen, and I would love to hear from Gen. Miller but he hasn't spoken to us recently.

   So could somebody talk about just a review of the year, militarily what has our—what have our allies done to progress in Afghanistan—or have they not? Have they lost ground, have they lost numbers?

MR. HOFFMAN: Well, I mean, I would just point you back to the Afghan Security Force. I think the fact that they're able to conduct a relatively violence-free election was one of the major goals and major accomplishments of the year for our allies, for partners; that we've been able to train—I don't—I can get you the training numbers, but the amount of training that we've done with them is obviously one of the major goals and major things that we've been working on, that they've been able to increase that training and that they've been able to deploy a force that was—that had the capability to protect their population and have a relatively violence-free election, I think that's one of the major accomplishments. So—all right, we'll go right. . . .

[. . .]

Q: Thank you. *The Washington Post* also reported that for 20 years, defense officials have altered statistics to give a sense of false progress in Afghanistan. What assurances can you give that this department will provide accurate information about Afghanistan, going forward?

MR. HOFFMAN: So one, I would quibble with the idea that we weren't providing it in the past. I think what we see from the report from *The Washington Post* is, looking at individuals giving retrospectives years later on what they may have believed at the time.

This department has attempted to be honest, open, transparent in all of its actions with the American people. And I think that you can see is the fact that these interviews that make up the basis of this report, the *Washington Post* report, were interviews that were given to Congress' special investigator on this, with the intention of being public.

So I don't follow that interviews given with the purpose of going to Congress and going to the American people, show any sign of being dishonest.

I know from this administration, from this secretary, that we will always endeavor to be as open and transparent with the American people, and to show our work and be honest about it.

The number of—the American people have a right to understand what's going on overseas, and what our military is doing. And our forces and our military men and women deserve to have that transparency as well.

Q: If I could follow up, in the reporting, which as far as I know no one has disputed the accuracy of the statements, public officials have said one thing in private and a very different thing in public. Given these were the Obama and Bush administrations.

But given this difference between what they're saying in public and private, why should the American public trust anything that the military says about Afghanistan?

MR. HOFFMAN: So once again, I can just speak for this administration and this department today. And the fact that we're going to continue to be open, transparent and honest with the American people. That's the direction that I have from the secretary, and that's the direction that all of us have.

And also, I'd point out, once again, those statements appeared for the most part to be people looking back retrospectively on things that they had said previously—and using hindsight to speak to comments they had made. So (inaudible).

Q: You just said that transparency and open about what's happening overseas, and that it's the right of the American people to hear it. However, ever since Gen. Miller has assumed command, he's never given a Pentagon press briefing.

There's been no information. I've asked for over a year, when this briefing's going to happen. I've sent e-mails saying, when are you going to do a briefing? Gotten silence. When is the Pentagon press corps going to hear from the commander of Resolute Support about the Afghanistan war?

MR. HOFFMAN: OK, I can take that for action. I was not familiar that you had that request in. I'll be happy to take it and talk to the general. I will note that he was on the Hill briefing Congress on this. . . .

Q: In a closed hearing, though.

MR. HOFFMAN: He was briefing the American people's representatives on what's going on in Afghanistan. So I—but I understand your point and it—it's a fair question and I'll be happy to take that.

Q: So I have two questions. First, on—a follow up on Afghanistan. You said the future of Afghanistan is a diplomatic solution. After 19 years of war fighting against Taliban, millions of dollars of spending and thousands of casualties, is that the conclusion, that you ended up with, a diplomatic solution with Taliban?

MR. HOFFMAN: I think right now, what we've—in Afghanistan, we have worked to a position where we've been helping the Afghan Security Forces reach to where they have—and capabilities to handle their defensive needs and we're going to continue to help them to grow that, but that—they need to work with the other parties in the country to come to a diplomatic solution.

That's the path that we've set out, that we're helping the Department of State pursue, and that's the stated goals of this administration right now.

Source: U.S. Department of Defense. "Department of Defense Press Briefing by Assistant to the Secretary of Defense Jonathan Hoffman and Rear Admiral William Byrne." December 12, 2019. https://www.defense.gov/Newsroom/Transcripts/Transcript/Article/2039359/department-of-defense-press-briefing-by-assistant-to-the-secretary-of-defense-j.

Other Historic Documents of Interest

From previous *Historic Documents*

December

House Passes Articles of Impeachment against President Trump; President Responds

DECEMBER 3, 17, AND 18, 2019

After months of investigation and days of debate, on December 18, 2019, President Donald Trump became the third sitting president in U.S. history to be impeached. The party-line vote in the House of Representatives was followed by a trial in the Senate, where the president was acquitted of wrongdoing. Throughout the process, the president and his Republican allies in Congress remained defiant, categorizing the Democratic impeachment proceedings as a "hoax" and "witch hunt," as a politically motivated attempt to remove a duly elected president from office. Democrats remained firm in their conviction that the president had attempted to use his office to curry political favor and prevent Congress from using its constitutional authority to investigate the alleged crimes.

DEMOCRATS LAUNCH IMPEACHMENT INQUIRY

After former Federal Bureau of Investigation (FBI) director Robert Mueller released the findings of his investigation into possible coordination between the Trump campaign and Russian government and attempts by the president to impede the investigation, speculation was rampant about whether House Democrats would try to impeach President Trump. Speaker Nancy Pelosi, D-Calif., remained cautious about how to proceed, but the push for impeachment from within the Democratic Party reached a fever pitch after a whistleblower complaint alleged that President Trump attempted to condition foreign aid to Ukraine on that country's announcing an investigation into 2020 Democratic presidential candidate and former vice president Joe Biden. According to the complaint, during a July 25, 2019, phone call with Ukrainian president-elect Volodymyr Zelenskyy, Ukraine requested additional aid from the United States to bolster its military strength in its ongoing fight with Russian-backed separatists in Ukraine. The president, in turn, requested the investigation into matters dealing with Biden, his son Hunter, and a Ukrainian energy company named Burisma Holdings. President Trump denied any wrongdoing, and the White House declassified a rough transcript of the call on September 24 as proof.

The allegation that the president may have tried to coerce a foreign government into investigating a political rival appeared to push Pelosi to act. On September 24, 2019, the Speaker announced a formal impeachment inquiry into the president's conduct that Pelosi said revealed a "betrayal of his oath of office, betrayal of our national security and betrayal of the integrity of our elections." She added, "The actions taken to date by the president have seriously violated the Constitution." President Trump would be the fourth president in U.S. history to face impeachment. Former presidents Andrew Johnson and Bill Clinton were impeached by the House but acquitted by the Senate; President Richard Nixon resigned before impeachment proceedings began. The impeachment inquiry permitted congressional committees to investigate whether there was any wrongdoing by the president that rose to the level of the impeachment standard outlined in the Constitution: "The President, Vice President, and all civil Officers of the United States, shall be removed from Office on Impeachment for, and Conviction of, Treason, Bribery, or other high Crimes and Misdemeanors." The start of the inquiry itself did not mean the president had been impeached, only that the House could present and vote on articles of impeachment at a future date.

On Twitter, President Trump, who was at the annual convening of the United Nations General Assembly in New York, called the decision "PRESIDENTIAL HARASSMNENT!" He added, "Such an important day at the United Nations, so much work and so much success, and the Democrats purposely had to ruin and demean it with more breaking news Witch Hunt garbage. So bad for our Country!" In Washington, White House press secretary Stephanie Grisham tied the announcement to Democratic congressional inaction on other issues vital to Americans. The inquiry "destroyed any chances of legislative progress for the people of this country by continuing to focus all their energy on partisan political attacks," Grisham said.

House Votes to Formalize Impeachment Proceedings

After Pelosi's announcement, the House Intelligence Committee began holding closed-door hearings as part of its investigation into the president's conduct. This was a key point of contention among Republicans, who criticized the Democrats for doing their work out of the view of the American public. Furthermore, they said, in past presidential impeachments the full House voted to authorize the inquiry. Without that vote, Republicans argued, the work of the committee would be invalid.

In response, five weeks after Pelosi's announcement, on October 31, the House debated a bill to formalize the impeachment inquiry and set the rules for the work of the House committees. During debate, Rep. Jim McGovern, D-Mass., chair of the Rules Committee, said if Congress failed to "hold this president accountable, we will be ceding our ability to hold any president accountable." He continued, "The obstruction from this White House is unprecedented. It's stunning. We don't know if Trump will be impeached, but the allegations are as serious as it gets." On the other side of the aisle, Republicans both defended the president and criticized their Democratic colleagues. House minority whip Steve Scalise, R-La., delivered his remarks next to a sign that read "37 DAYS OF SOVIET-STYLE IMPEACHMENT PROCEEDINGS." House minority leader Kevin McCarthy, R-Calif., said there was nothing the president did during his phone call with the leader of Ukraine "that is wrong or impeachable." He also urged Democrats, "Give the people back their power. Let them choose the next leader of the free world. Follow the principles of our Constitution. And do not dilute our democracy by interfering in elections from Washington."

The final vote tally to formalize the impeachment inquiry fell almost entirely along party lines, 232–196. The president responded on Twitter that it was the "Greatest Witch Hunt In American History." The resolution passed by the House allowed the public phase of the impeachment inquiry to begin and established the procedures that would guide the work. It gave the House Intelligence Committee the ability to release transcripts of closed-door testimony that had already taken place. It also gave Republicans on the Intelligence and Judiciary Committees the opportunity to subpoena documents and witnesses, so long as the chair of the committee or a majority of the committee members agreed. It further provided for the White House to participate in the inquiry by questioning witnesses once the Judiciary Committee began its work.

House Holds Public Impeachment Hearings

In the impeachment proceedings against President Trump, the Intelligence Committee started the formal process, then presented its findings to the Judiciary Committee, which was tasked with drafting formal articles of impeachment, if needed. During its work, the Intelligence Committee held public and closed-door hearings over the span of two weeks, listening to testimony from current and former federal officials. In the first week, former U.S. ambassador to Ukraine Marie Yovanovitch, acting U.S. ambassador to Ukraine William Taylor, and Deputy Assistant Secretary of State for European and Eurasian Affairs George Kent told the committee that the president frequently relied on the advice of private citizens and his personal attorney, Rudy Giuliani, to guide his foreign affairs decision making. During the second week, Lt. Col. Alexander Vindman, a member of the National Security Council, testified that he heard the July 25 call and said Trump asked the Ukrainian president for a political favor. Also testifying were Kurt Volker, the former special envoy to Ukraine, and Gordon Sondland, a donor to the president's inaugural committee and former U.S. ambassador to the European Union, both members of Trump's team handling Ukraine policy. Both previously testified in closed-door hearings that President Trump had not conditioned the release of Ukraine aid on an investigation into Hunter Biden. In their public testimony, they sought to amend those remarks and instead insisted that the president wanted Ukraine to announce the investigation before aid would be released. Volker, who was invited by Republicans, testified, "In hindsight, I now understand that others saw the idea of investigating possible corruption involving the Ukrainian company, 'Burisma,' as equivalent to investigating former Vice President Biden." He added, "I saw them as very different—the former being appropriate and unremarkable, the latter being unacceptable." The Intelligence Committee released its draft report on the findings of its investigation on December 3.

The Judiciary Committee began its public hearings the following day. The White House was invited to participate, but refused. Each day of hearings opened with wrangling between the two parties over the process and whether Democrats were attempting to subvert the power of the president and Republican members of Congress. The first hearing was intended to present the constitutional grounds for impeaching the president. Democrats called three law professors as their witnesses: Noah Feldman of Harvard, Pamela Karlan of Stanford, and Michael Gerhardt of the University of North Carolina. Republicans called one witness: Jonathan Turley, a law professor at The George Washington University. Turley called the proceedings a "dangerous precedent" and said the Democrats were seeking to impeach Trump "without a clear criminal act." While admitting that Trump's actions on Ukraine may have been ill-advised, Turley said, "There is no case law that would support a claim of corrupt intent in such comments to support a bribery charge." The other three witnesses were united in their belief that the president's actions represented an impeachable offense. "The president's serious misconduct, including bribery, soliciting a personal favor from a foreign leader in exchange for his exercise of power, and obstructing justice and Congress are worse than the misconduct of any prior president, including what previous presidents who faced impeachment have done or been accused of doing," said Gerhardt.

The committee held its second public hearing on December 9 to review the Intelligence Committee report. As witnesses, the committee called counsel for the Judiciary Committee's Democrats Barry Berke, counsel for the Intelligence Committee's Democrats Daniel Goldman, and Stephen Castor, counsel for Republicans on both the Judiciary and Intelligence Committees. Goldman characterized President Trump's behavior as "a clear and present danger to our free and fair elections and to our national security," while Castor called Democratic arguments in favor of impeachment "baloney." Castor noted that most of the witnesses called by Democrats on the Intelligence Committee had no firsthand knowledge of the call with Ukraine and were merely making presumptions about the president's intent. At the conclusion of the ten-hour hearing, Rep. Jerry Nadler, D-N.Y., said the president had put his own interests before those of the country, which was a clear "danger to our democracy." Rep. Doug Collins, R-Ga., said that contrary to the argument presented by Democrats, the "facts are not agreed to," and that the House Democrats' work amounted to the first partisan impeachment inquiry in U.S. history.

At the direction of Speaker Pelosi, Democrats ultimately drafted two articles of impeachment against President Trump. Article I accused the president of "abusing his high office to enlist a foreign power in corrupting democratic elections," while Article II charged the president with "unprecedented, categorical and indiscriminate defiance of subpoenas issued by the House of Representatives."

Judiciary Committee Considers Articles of Impeachment

On December 11, the House Judiciary Committee began a two-day public markup session to debate the two articles of impeachment against President Trump. During fourteen hours of debate, Democrats and Republicans on the committee sparred over the two articles and at times personally attacked each other. Six amendments were introduced during debate, including one by Democrats seeking to replace Trump's middle initial "J" with his full middle name, "John." Republicans introduced five amendments, each of which failed on a party-line 17–23 vote. The first came from Rep. Jim Jordan, R-Ohio, who wanted to eliminate the first article of impeachment, saying it "ignores the truth, it ignores the facts, it ignores what happened, and what has been laid out for the American people over the last three weeks." He also introduced an amendment to eliminate the last eight lines of each article, essentially removing the Democrats' conclusion that the president should be impeached. "They are afraid they cannot beat him at the ballot box so they're going to do this rigged, rushed, and wrong impeachment process," Jordan said. Rep. Andy Biggs, R-Ariz., sought to amend the article language to indicate that the president's actions were lawful because he was concerned about corrupt practices in Ukraine and that the underlying argument for impeachment was invalid because the aid was eventually released. Rep. Guy Reschenthaler, R-Pa., wanted to eliminate Article II, alleging that Democrats treated the president unfairly in their handling of the impeachment inquiry. Democrats responded that they provided the White House and the president plenty of opportunities to participate, but they refused.

Rep. Matt Gaetz, R-Fla., suggested a highly contentious amendment to replace language in Article I stating that Joe Biden was a "political opponent" with a line about "a well-known corrupt company, Burisma, and its corrupt hiring of Hunter Biden." Republicans accused Joe Biden of using the office of the vice president to protect Burisma from corruption investigations in order to allow the younger Biden to profit from his association with the company. Debate over the amendment became personal, with Gaetz pointing to a *New Yorker* article alleging that Hunter Biden was a known cocaine user, saying, "It's a little hard to believe that Burisma hired Hunter Biden to resolve their international disputes when he could not resolve his own dispute with Hertz rental car over leaving cocaine and a crack pipe in the car." In turn, Democrats made loosely veiled references to Gaetz's arrest for drunk driving. "The pot calling the kettle black is not something we should do," said Rep. Hank Johnson, D-Ga.

Nadler ended the committee's debate around 11:00 p.m. Eastern on December 12 before a vote could be held, angering Republicans who expected to vote that night. "I want members on both sides of the aisle to think about what has happened over the last two days and to search their consciences before they cast their final votes," Nadler said before gaveling out. "That was the most bush league play I have ever seen in my life," said Representative Collins, the committee's ranking Republican. He accused the committee chair of delaying the vote to ensure it was held at a more favorable time. "They want the prime time hit," he said. Democrats defended the decision, saying the vote was too consequential for the country to hold it at night.

The committee came back into session the morning of December 13 for a final vote. "Today's vote highlights the pettiness of last night's delay and the folly of articles of impeachment that allege no crime and establish no case," said Collins. "While it's already clear that Democrats broke their own promises to rig this outcome, what will become more obvious in the coming days and years is that Democrats gravely abused their power," he said. Ultimately, the committee voted 23–17 along party lines to send the two articles of impeachment for consideration before the full House. "Today is a solemn and sad day," said Nadler after the vote. "For the third time in a little over a century and half, the House Judiciary Committee has voted articles of impeachment against the president, for abuse of power and obstruction of Congress. The House will act expeditiously," Nadler added. At the White House, the president called it a "very sad thing for our country" but "good for me politically."

Full House Passes Articles of Impeachment

With the two articles of impeachment passed out of the Judiciary Committee, on December 17, the House Rules Committee met to set the parameters for floor debate. The committee agreed to allow for six hours of debate, divided equally between the two parties. There would be no amendments allowed during debate of the articles, and a vote would take place immediately following debate. With the rules set, Pelosi announced that on December 18, the House would "exercise one of the most solemn powers granted to us by the constitution," and consider the two articles of impeachment.

The same day the Rules Committee met, President Trump sent a six-page letter to Pelosi urging her to end the impeachment inquiry. "I write to express my strongest and most powerful protest against the partisan impeachment crusade being pursued by the Democrats in the House of Representatives. This impeachment represents an unprecedented and unconstitutional abuse of power by Democrat Lawmakers, unequaled in nearly two and a half centuries of American legislative history," the letter begins. "It is time for you and the highly partisan Democrats in Congress to immediately cease this impeachment fantasy and get back to work for the American People. While I have no expectation that you will do so, I write this letter to you for the purpose of history and to put my thoughts on a permanent and indelible record," the president wrote, calling the impeachment a "partisan attempted coup" that would backfire on Democrats during the November 2020 presidential election. As he had frequently done since the impeachment inquiry began, the president defended his call with Zelenskyy, noting that the transcript released by the White House vindicated him. "You are turning a policy disagreement between two branches of government into an impeachable offense—it is no more legitimate than the Executive Branch charging members of Congress with crimes for the lawful exercise of legislative power," Trump wrote, adding, "History will judge you harshly as you proceed with this impeachment charade."

The morning of December 18, the full House debated and approved the rules package along party lines and then entered into debate on the actual articles of impeachment. Once debate concluded, the House would hold two separate votes, one on each article. A simple majority was required to impeach the president. Pelosi opened the impeachment debate, urging members to vote in favor of both articles. "Today, as speaker of the House, I solemnly and sadly open the debate on the impeachment of the president of the United States," Pelosi said. "If we do not act now, we would be derelict in our duty. It is tragic that the president's reckless actions make impeachment necessary. He gave us no choice," the Speaker added. Representative Collins opened debate for his party. "This is a poll-tested impeachment about what actually sells to the American people. Today is going to be a lot of things. What it is not is fair. What it is not is about the truth," Collins said. "Why do we keep calling this a solemn occasion when you've been wanting to do this ever since the gentleman was elected?" he asked.

From there, debate alternated between the two parties and members gave brief speeches of no more than a couple of minutes. Democrats defended the investigation and treatment of the president and sought to cast the vote as a necessity to protect democracy. "No one came to Congress to impeach a president," said Rep. Ben Ray Luján, D-N.M., but what the president did was "so blatantly wrong that ignoring his abuses of power would be abdicating the oath we made to protect this country and uphold our Constitution." Rep. John Lewis, D-Ga., called the vote "a sad day," adding, "When you see something that is not right, not just, not fair, you have a moral obligation to say something, to do something." Rep. Ted Lieu, D-Calif., warned that impeachment would be a permanent stain on the president's record but said it sent a message that "no one is above the law."

Republicans, however, dismissed the articles of impeachment as a politically motivated stunt. "This day is about one thing and one thing only. They hate this president. They hate those of us who voted for him. They think we are stupid. They think we made a mistake. They think Hillary Clinton should be president and they want to fix that," said Rep. Chris Stewart, R-Utah. Rep. Bill Johnson, R-Ohio, mirrored Lewis's remarks, calling it "a sad day for America" before asking for a moment of silence for the millions of Americans who voted for the president. Others quoted Scripture. "When Jesus was falsely accused of treason, Pontius Pilate gave Jesus the opportunity to face his accusers," said Rep. Barry Loudermilk, R-Ga. "During that sham trial, Pontius Pilate afforded more rights to Jesus than the Democrats have afforded this president in this process," Loudermilk said.

The final vote was held around 7:00 p.m. Eastern, at the same time the president was taking the stage for a campaign rally in Battle Creek, Michigan. In the House, the first article of impeachment passed by a vote of 230–197–1, with two Democrats voting against the article and one Democrat, Rep. Tulsi Gabbard, D-Hawaii, voting "present." The second article also passed, 229–198–1, with three Democrats voting against the measure and Gabbard again voting "present." No Republicans voted in favor of impeachment. In Battle Creek, the president celebrated the Republican Party's ability to hold together. "The Republican Party has never been so united as they are right now," he said, noting that he was confident the Senate would "do the right thing" and acquit him.

Senate Debates, Rejects Articles of Impeachment

Historically, once the House passes articles of impeachment, they are quickly turned over to the Senate, which holds a trial to decide whether the president should be removed from office. That trial is presided over by the chief justice of the Supreme Court and gives each party equal time to present its case either in defense of or against the president. After the vote in the House, however, Pelosi indicated an intent to delay sending the articles of impeachment to the Senate, fearing that Republicans would not hold a fair trial. This drew the ire of Republicans, who accused the Speaker of unnecessarily delaying progress. It was not until January 10, 2020, when Pelosi announced that she had asked Nadler "to bring to the Floor next week a resolution to appoint managers and transmit articles of impeachment to the Senate." That resolution passed on January 15, and the trial in the Senate began on January 21.

House impeachment managers and the president's legal team were each given up to twenty-four hours to present their case. At the end, senators would be allowed to submit written questions to the prosecution and defense, and then a final vote would be held. A two-thirds majority was needed to remove Trump from office. On February 5, the Senate voted 52–48 to reject Article I and 53–47 to reject Article II. Sen. Mitt Romney, R-Utah, was the lone Republican to join all Democrats in voting in favor of impeachment. The president shall "be, and is hereby, acquitted of the charges," Chief Justice John Roberts said at the conclusion of the two votes. The following day, in a lengthy White House address, the president held up a copy of *The Washington Post* with the words "Trump Acquitted" on the front page. He celebrated his victory, calling the inquiry "evil, it was corrupt, it was dirty cops, it was leakers and liars."

—Heather Kerrigan

Following is the Preface of the House Intelligence Committee's report on the impeachment inquiry, released on December 3, 2019; a December 17, 2019, letter from President Donald Trump to Speaker Nancy Pelosi, D-Calif., expressing opposition to the articles of impeachment; the articles of impeachment against President Trump, debated in the House of Representatives on December 18, 2019; Speaker Pelosi's statement on the House floor in support of impeachment on December 18, 2019; and the December 18, 2019, floor statement of Rep. Doug Collins, R-Ga., opposing impeachment.

House Intelligence Committee Releases Report on Impeachment Investigation

DOCUMENT

December 3, 2019

[All sections not pertaining to the Preface, as well as all footnotes, have been omitted.]

This report reflects the evidence gathered thus far by the House Permanent Select Committee on Intelligence, in coordination with the Committee on Oversight and Reform and the Committee on Foreign Affairs, as part of the House of Representatives' impeachment inquiry into Donald J. Trump, the 45th President of the United States.

The report is the culmination of an investigation that began in September 2019 and intensified over the past three months as new revelations and evidence of the President's misconduct towards Ukraine emerged. The Committees pursued the truth vigorously, but fairly, ensuring the full participation of both parties throughout the probe.

Sustained by the tireless work of more than three dozen dedicated staff across the three Committees, we issued dozens of subpoenas for documents and testimony and took more than 100 hours of deposition testimony from 17 witnesses. To provide the American people the opportunity to learn and evaluate the facts themselves, the Intelligence Committee held seven public hearings with 12 witnesses—including three requested by the Republican Minority—that totaled more than 30 hours. . . .

* * *

As this report details, the impeachment inquiry has found that President Trump, personally and acting through agents within and outside of the U.S. government, solicited the interference of a foreign government, Ukraine, to benefit his reelection. In furtherance of this scheme, President Trump conditioned official acts on a public announcement by the new Ukrainian President, Volodymyr Zelensky, of politically-motivated investigations, including one into President Trump's domestic political opponent. In pressuring President Zelensky to carry out his demand, President Trump withheld a White House meeting desperately sought by the Ukrainian President, and critical U.S. military assistance to fight Russian aggression in eastern Ukraine.

The President engaged in this course of conduct for the benefit of his own presidential reelection, to harm the election prospects of a political rival, and to influence our nation's upcoming presidential election to his advantage. In doing so, the President placed his own personal and political interests above the national interests of the United States, sought to undermine the integrity of the U.S. presidential election process, and endangered U.S. national security.

At the center of this investigation is the memorandum prepared following President Trump's July 25, 2019, phone call with Ukraine's President, which the White House declassified and released under significant public pressure. The call record alone is stark evidence of misconduct; a demonstration of the President's prioritization of his personal political benefit over the national interest. In response to President Zelensky's appreciation for vital U.S. military assistance, which President Trump froze without explanation, President Trump asked for "a favor though": two specific investigations designed to assist his reelection efforts.

Our investigation determined that this telephone call was neither the start nor the end of President Trump's efforts to bend U.S. foreign policy for his personal gain. Rather, it was a dramatic crescendo within a months-long campaign driven by President Trump in which senior U.S. officials, including the Vice President, the Secretary of State, the Acting Chief of Staff, the Secretary of Energy, and others were either knowledgeable of or active participants in an effort to extract from a foreign nation the personal political benefits sought by the President.

The investigation revealed the nature and extent of the President's misconduct, notwithstanding an unprecedented campaign of obstruction by the President and his Administration to prevent the Committees from obtaining documentary evidence and testimony. A dozen witnesses followed President Trump's orders, defying voluntary requests and lawful subpoenas, and refusing to testify. The White House, Department of State, Department of Defense, Office of Management and Budget, and Department of Energy refused to produce a single document in response to our subpoenas.

Ultimately, this sweeping effort to stonewall the House of Representatives' "sole Power of Impeachment" under the Constitution failed because witnesses courageously came forward and testified in response to lawful process. The report that follows was only possible because of their sense of duty and devotion to their country and its Constitution.

Nevertheless, there remain unanswered questions, and our investigation must continue, even as we transmit our report to the Judiciary Committee. Given the proximate threat of further presidential attempts to solicit foreign interference in our next election, we cannot wait to make a referral until our efforts to obtain additional testimony and documents wind their way through the courts. The evidence of the President's misconduct is overwhelming, and so too is the evidence of his obstruction of Congress. Indeed, it would be hard to imagine a stronger or more complete case of obstruction than that demonstrated by the President since the inquiry began.

The damage the President has done to our relationship with a key strategic partner will be remedied over time, and Ukraine continues to enjoy strong bipartisan support in Congress. But the damage to our system of checks and balances, and to the balance of power within our three branches of government, will be long-lasting and potentially irrevocable if the President's ability to stonewall Congress goes unchecked. Any future President will feel empowered to resist an investigation into their own wrongdoing, malfeasance, or corruption, and the result will be a nation at far greater risk of all three.

* * *

The decision to move forward with an impeachment inquiry is not one we took lightly. Under the best of circumstances, impeachment is a wrenching process for the nation. I resisted calls to undertake an impeachment investigation for many months on that basis, notwithstanding the existence of presidential misconduct that I believed to be deeply unethical and damaging to our democracy. The alarming events and actions detailed in this report, however, left us with no choice but to proceed.

In making the decision to move forward, we were struck by the fact that the President's misconduct was not an isolated occurrence, nor was it the product of a naïve president. Instead, the efforts to involve Ukraine in our 2020 presidential election were undertaken by a President who himself was elected in 2016 with the benefit of an unprecedented and sweeping campaign of election interference undertaken by Russia in his favor, and which the President welcomed and utilized.

Having witnessed the degree to which interference by a foreign power in 2016 harmed our democracy, President Trump cannot credibly claim ignorance to its pernicious effects. Even more pointedly, the President's July call with Ukrainian President Zelensky, in which he solicited an investigation to damage his most feared 2020 opponent, came the day after Special Counsel Robert Mueller testified to Congress about Russia's efforts to damage his 2016 opponent and his urgent warning of the dangers of further foreign interference in the next election. With this backdrop, the solicitation of new foreign intervention was the act of a president unbound, not one chastened by experience. It was the act of a president who viewed himself as unaccountable and determined to use his vast official powers to secure his reelection.

This repeated and pervasive threat to our democratic electoral process added urgency to our work. On October 3, 2019, even as our Committee was engaged in this inquiry, President Trump publicly declared anew that other countries should open investigations into his chief political rival, saying, "China should start an investigation into the Bidens," and that "President Zelensky, if it were me, I would recommend that they start an investigation into the Bidens." When a reporter asked the President what he hoped Ukraine's President would do following the July 25 call, President Trump, seeking to dispel any doubt as to his continuing intention, responded: "Well, I would think that, if they were honest about it, they'd start a major investigation into the Bidens. It's a very simple answer."

By doubling down on his misconduct and declaring that his July 25 call with President Zelensky was "perfect," President Trump has shown a continued willingness to use the power of his office to seek foreign intervention in our next election. His Acting Chief of Staff, Mick Mulvaney, in the course of admitting that the President had linked security assistance to Ukraine to the announcement of one of his desired investigations, told the American people to "get over it." In these statements and actions, the President became the author of his own impeachment inquiry. The question presented by the set of facts enumerated in this report may be as simple as that posed by the President and his chief of staff's brazenness: is the remedy of impeachment warranted for a president who would use the power of his office to coerce foreign interference in a U.S. election, or is that now a mere perk of the office that Americans must simply "get over"?

* * *

Those watching the impeachment hearings might have been struck by how little discrepancy there was between the witnesses called by the Majority and Minority. Indeed, most of the facts presented in the pages that follow are uncontested. The broad outlines as well as many of the details of the President's scheme have been presented by the witnesses with remarkable consistency. There will always be some variation in the testimony of multiple people witnessing the same events, but few of the differences here go to the heart of the matter. And so, it may have been all the more surprising to the public to see very disparate reactions to the testimony by the Members of Congress from each party.

If there was one ill the Founders feared as much as that of an unfit president, it may have been that of excessive factionalism. Although the Framers viewed parties as necessary, they also endeavored to structure the new government in such a way as to minimize the "violence of faction." As George Washington warned in his farewell address, "the common and continual mischiefs of the spirit of party are sufficient to make it the interest and duty of a wise people to discourage and restrain it."

Today, we may be witnessing a collision between the power of a remedy meant to curb presidential misconduct and the power of faction determined to defend against the use of that remedy on a president of the same party. But perhaps even more corrosive to our democratic system of governance, the President and his allies are making a comprehensive attack on the very idea of fact and truth. How can a democracy survive without acceptance of a common set of experiences?

America remains the beacon of democracy and opportunity for freedom-loving people around the world. From their homes and their jail cells, from their public squares and their refugee camps, from their waking hours until their last breath, individuals fighting human rights abuses, journalists uncovering and exposing corruption, persecuted minorities struggling to survive and preserve their faith, and countless others around the globe just hoping for a better life look to America. What we do will determine what they see, and whether America remains a nation committed to the rule of law.

As Benjamin Franklin departed the Constitutional Convention, he was asked, "what have we got? A Republic or a Monarchy?" He responded simply: "A Republic, if you can keep it."

Adam B. Schiff
Chairman, House Permanent Select Committee on Intelligence

SOURCE: House Permanent Select Committee on Intelligence. "The Trump-Ukraine Impeachment Inquiry Report." December 3, 2019. https://intelligence.house.gov/uploadedfiles/the_trump-ukraine_impeachment_inquiry_report.pdf.

President Trump Sends Letter to Speaker Pelosi Arguing against Impeachment

December 17, 2019

Dear Madam Speaker:

I write to express my strongest and most powerful protest against the partisan impeachment crusade being pursued by the Democrats in the House of Representatives. This impeachment represents an unprecedented and unconstitutional abuse of power by Democrat Lawmakers, unequaled in nearly two and a half centuries of American legislative history.

The Articles of Impeachment introduced by the House Judiciary Committee are not recognizable under any standard of Constitutional theory, interpretation, or jurisprudence. They include no crimes, no misdemeanors, and no offenses whatsoever. You have cheapened the importance of the very ugly word, impeachment!

By proceeding with your invalid impeachment, you are violating your oaths of office, you are breaking your allegiance to the Constitution, and you are declaring open war on American Democracy. You dare to invoke the Founding Fathers in pursuit of this election-nullification scheme—yet your spiteful actions display unfettered contempt for America's founding and your egregious conduct threatens to destroy that which our Founders pledged their very lives to build. Even worse than offending the Founding Fathers, you are offending Americans of faith by continually saying "I pray for the President," when you know this statement is not true, unless it is meant in a negative sense. It is a terrible thing you are doing, but you will have to live with it, not I!

Your first claim, "Abuse of Power," is a completely disingenuous, meritless, and baseless invention of your imagination. You know that I had a totally innocent conversation with the President of Ukraine. I then had a second conversation that has been misquoted, mischaracterized, and fraudulently misrepresented. Fortunately, there was a transcript of the conversation taken, and you know from the transcript (which was immediately made available) that the paragraph in question was perfect. I said to President Zelensky: "I would like you to do us a favor, though, because our country has been through a lot and Ukraine knows a lot about it." I said do us a favor, not me, and our country, not a campaign. I then mentioned the Attorney General of the United States. Every time I talk with a foreign leader, I put America's interests first, just as I did with President Zelensky.

You are turning a policy disagreement between two branches of government into an impeachable offense—it is no more legitimate than the Executive Branch charging members of Congress with crimes for the lawful exercise of legislative power.

You know full well that Vice President Biden used his office and $1 billion dollars of U.S. aid money to coerce Ukraine into firing the prosecutor who was digging into the company paying his son millions of dollars. You know this because Biden bragged about it on video. Biden openly stated: "I said, 'I'm telling you, you're not getting the billion dollars' . . . I looked at them and said: 'I'm leaving in six hours. If the prosecutor is not fired, you're not getting the money.' Well, son of a bitch. He got fired." Even Joe Biden admitted just days ago in an interview with NPR that it "looked bad." Now you are trying to impeach me by falsely accusing me of doing what Joe Biden has admitted he actually did.

President Zelensky has repeatedly declared that I did nothing wrong, and that there was No Pressure. He further emphasized that it was a "good phone call," that "I don't feel pressure," and explicitly stressed that "nobody pushed me." The Ukrainian Foreign Minister stated very clearly: "I have never seen a direct link between investigations and security assistance." He also said there was "No Pressure." Senator Ron Johnson of Wisconsin, a supporter of Ukraine who met privately with President Zelensky, has said: "At no time during this meeting . . . was there any mention by Zelensky or any Ukrainian that they were feeling pressure to do anything in return for the military aid." Many meetings have been held between representatives of Ukraine and our country. Never once did Ukraine complain about pressure being applied—not once! Ambassador Sondland testified that I told him: "No quid pro quo. I want nothing. I want nothing. I want President Zelensky to do the right thing, do what he ran on."

The second claim, so-called "Obstruction of Congress," is preposterous and dangerous. House Democrats are trying to impeach the duly elected President of the United States for asserting Constitutionally based privileges that have been asserted on a bipartisan basis by administrations of both political parties throughout our Nation's history. Under that standard, every American president would have been impeached many times over. As liberal law professor Jonathan Turley warned when addressing Congressional Democrats: "I can't emphasize this enough . . . if you impeach a president, if you make a high crime and misdemeanor out of going to the courts, it is an abuse of power. It's your abuse of power. You're doing precisely what you're criticizing the President for doing."

Everyone, you included, knows what is really happening. Your chosen candidate lost the election in 2016, in an Electoral College landslide (306–227), and you and your party have never recovered from this defeat. You have developed a full-fledged case of what many in the media call Trump Derangement Syndrome and sadly, you will never get over it! You are unwilling and unable to accept the verdict issued at the ballot box during the great Election of 2016. So you have spent three straight years attempting to overturn the will of the American people and nullify their votes. You view democracy as your enemy!

Speaker Pelosi, you admitted just last week at a public forum that your party's impeachment effort has been going on for "two and a half years," long before you ever heard about a phone call with Ukraine. Nineteen minutes after I took the oath of office, *The Washington Post* published a story headlined, "The Campaign to Impeach President Trump Has Begun." Less than three months after my inauguration, Representative Maxine Waters stated, "I'm going to fight every day until he's impeached." House Democrats introduced the first impeachment resolution against me within months of my inauguration, for what will be regarded as one of our country's best decisions, the firing of James Comey (see Inspector General Reports)—who the world now knows is one of the dirtiest cops our Nation has ever seen. A ranting and raving Congresswoman, Rashida Tlaib, declared just hours after she was sworn into office, "We're gonna go in there and we're gonna impeach the motherf****r." Representative Al Green said in May, "I'm concerned that if we don't impeach this president, he will get re-elected." Again, you and your allies said, and did, all of these things long before you ever heard of President Zelensky or anything related to Ukraine. As you know very well, this impeachment drive has nothing to do with Ukraine, or the totally appropriate conversation I had with its new president. It only has to do with your attempt to undo the election of 2016 and steal the election of 2020!

Congressman Adam Schiff cheated and lied all the way up to the present day, even going so far as to fraudulently make up, out of thin air, my conversation with President Zelensky of Ukraine and read this fantasy language to Congress as though it were said by me. His shameless lies and deceptions, dating all the way back to the Russia Hoax, is one of the main reasons we are here today.

You and your party are desperate to distract from America's extraordinary economy, incredible jobs boom, record stock market, soaring confidence, and flourishing citizens. Your party simply cannot compete with our record: 7 million new jobs; the lowest-ever unemployment for African Americans, Hispanic Americans, and Asian Americans; a rebuilt military; a completely reformed VA with Choice and Accountability for our great veterans; more than 170 new federal judges and two Supreme Court Justices; historic tax and regulation cuts; the elimination of the individual mandate; the first decline in prescription drug prices in half a century; the first new branch of the United States Military since 1947, the Space Force; strong protection of the Second Amendment; criminal justice reform; a defeated ISIS caliphate and the killing of the world's number one terrorist leader, al-Baghdadi; the replacement of the disastrous NAFTA trade deal with the wonderful USMCA (Mexico and Canada); a breakthrough Phase One trade deal with China; massive new trade deals with Japan and South Korea; withdrawal from the terrible Iran Nuclear Deal; cancellation of the unfair and costly Paris Climate Accord; becoming the world's top energy producer; recognition of Israel's capital, opening the American Embassy in Jerusalem, and recognizing Israeli sovereignty over the Golan Heights; a colossal reduction in illegal border crossings, the ending of Catch-and-Release, and the building of the Southern Border Wall—and that is just the beginning, there is so much more. You cannot defend your extreme policies—open borders, mass migration, high crime, crippling taxes, socialized healthcare, destruction of American energy, late-term taxpayer-funded abortion, elimination of the Second Amendment, radical far-left theories of law and justice, and constant partisan obstruction of both common sense and common good.

There is nothing I would rather do than stop referring to your party as the Do-Nothing Democrats. Unfortunately, I don't know that you will ever give me a chance to do so.

After three years of unfair and unwarranted investigations, 45 million dollars spent, 18 angry Democrat prosecutors, the entire force of the FBI, headed by leadership now proven to be totally incompetent and corrupt, you have found NOTHING! Few people in high position could have endured or passed this test. You do not know, nor do you care, the great damage and hurt you have inflicted upon wonderful and loving members of my family. You conducted a fake investigation upon the democratically elected President of the United States, and you are doing it yet again.

There are not many people who could have taken the punishment inflicted during this period of time, and yet done so much for the success of America and its citizens. But instead of putting our country first, you have decided to disgrace our country still further. You completely failed with the Mueller report because there was nothing to find, so you decided to take the next hoax that came along, the phone call with Ukraine—even though it was a perfect call. And by the way, when I speak to foreign countries, there are many people, with permission, listening to the call on both sides of the conversation.

You are the ones interfering in America's elections. You are the ones subverting America's Democracy. You are the ones Obstructing Justice. You are the ones bringing pain and suffering to our Republic for your own selfish personal, political, and partisan gain.

Before the Impeachment Hoax, it was the Russian Witch Hunt. Against all evidence, and regardless of the truth, you and your deputies claimed that my campaign colluded with the Russians—a grave, malicious, and slanderous lie, a falsehood like no other. You forced our Nation through turmoil and torment over a wholly fabricated story, illegally purchased from a foreign spy by Hillary Clinton and the DNC in order to assault our democracy. Yet, when the monstrous lie was debunked and this Democrat conspiracy dissolved into dust, you did not apologize. You did not recant. You did not ask to be forgiven. You showed no remorse, no capacity for self-reflection. Instead, you pursued your next libelous and vicious crusade—you engineered an attempt to frame and defame an innocent person. All of this was motivated by personal political calculation. Your Speakership and your party are held hostage by your most deranged and radical representatives of the far left. Each one of your members lives in fear of a socialist primary challenger—this is what is driving impeachment. Look at Congressman Nadler's challenger. Look at yourself and others. Do not take our country down with your party.

If you truly cared about freedom and liberty for our Nation, then you would be devoting your vast investigative resources to exposing the full truth concerning the FBI's horrifying abuses of power before, during, and after the 2016 election—including the use of spies against my campaign, the submission of false evidence to a FISA court, and the concealment of exculpatory evidence in order to frame the innocent. The FBI has great and honorable people, but the leadership was inept and corrupt. I would think that you would personally be appalled by these revelations, because in your press conference the day you announced impeachment, you tied the impeachment effort directly to the completely discredited Russia Hoax, declaring twice that "all roads lead to Putin," when you know that is an abject lie. I have been far tougher on Russia than President Obama ever even thought to be.

Any member of Congress who votes in support of impeachment—against every shred of truth, fact, evidence, and legal principle—is showing how deeply they revile the voters and how truly they detest America's Constitutional order. Our Founders feared the tribalization of partisan politics, and you are bringing their worst fears to life.

Worse still, I have been deprived of basic Constitutional Due Process from the beginning of this impeachment scam right up until the present. I have been denied the most fundamental rights afforded by the Constitution, including the right to present evidence, to have my own counsel present, to confront accusers, and to call and cross-examine witnesses, like the so-called whistleblower who started this entire hoax with a false report of the phone call that bears no relationship to the actual phone call that was made. Once I presented the transcribed call, which surprised and shocked the fraudsters (they never thought that such evidence would be presented), the so-called whistleblower, and the second whistleblower, disappeared because they got caught, their report was a fraud, and they were no longer going to be made available to us. In other words, once the phone call was made public, your whole plot blew up, but that didn't stop you from continuing.

More due process was afforded to those accused in the Salem Witch Trials.

You and others on your committees have long said impeachment must be bipartisan—it is not. You said it was very divisive—it certainly is, even far more than you ever thought possible—and it will only get worse!

This is nothing more than an illegal, partisan attempted coup that will, based on recent sentiment, badly fail at the voting booth. You are not just after me, as President, you are after the entire Republican Party. But because of this colossal injustice, our party is more united than it has ever been before. History will judge you harshly as you proceed with this impeachment charade. Your legacy will be that of turning the House of Representatives from a revered legislative body into a Star Chamber of partisan persecution.

Perhaps most insulting of all is your false display of solemnity. You apparently have so little respect for the American People that you expect them to believe that you are approaching this impeachment somberly, reservedly, and reluctantly. No intelligent person believes what you are saying. Since the moment I won the election, the Democrat Party has been possessed by Impeachment Fever. There is no reticence. This is not a somber affair. You are making a mockery of impeachment and you are scarcely concealing your hatred of me, of the Republican Party, and tens of millions of patriotic Americans. The voters are wise, and they are seeing straight through this empty, hollow, and dangerous game you are playing. I have no doubt the American people will hold you and the Democrats fully responsible in the upcoming 2020 election. They will not soon forgive your perversion of justice and abuse of power.

There is far too much that needs to be done to improve the lives of our citizens. It is time for you and the highly partisan Democrats in Congress to immediately cease this impeachment fantasy and get back to work for the American People. While I have no expectation that you will do so, I write this letter to you for the purpose of history and to put my thoughts on a permanent and indelible record.

One hundred years from now, when people look back at this affair, I want them to understand it, and learn from it, so that it can never happen to another President again.

Sincerely yours,
DONALD J. TRUMP
President of the United States of America

SOURCE: Executive Office of the President. "Letter to the Speaker of the House of Representatives on the Articles of Impeachment against the President." December 17, 2019. *Compilation of Presidential Documents* 2019, no. 00871 (December 17, 2019). https://www.govinfo.gov/content/pkg/DCPD-201900871/pdf/DCPD-201900871.pdf.

Articles of Impeachment against President Trump

DOCUMENT

December 18, 2019

Articles of Impeachment Against Donald John Trump

{House Resolution 755, One Hundred Sixteenth Congress, First Session}

CONGRESS OF THE UNITED STATES OF AMERICA,

IN THE HOUSE OF REPRESENTATIVES,

December 18, 2019.

RESOLUTION

Resolved, That Donald John Trump, President of the United States, is impeached for high crimes and misdemeanors and that the following articles of impeachment be exhibited to the United States Senate:

Articles of impeachment exhibited by the House of Representatives of the United States of America in the name of itself and of the people of the United States of America, against Donald John Trump, President of the United States of America, in maintenance and support of its impeachment against him for high crimes and misdemeanors.

ARTICLE I: ABUSE OF POWER

The Constitution provides that the House of Representatives "shall have the sole Power of Impeachment" and that the President "shall be removed from Office on Impeachment for, and Conviction of, Treason, Bribery, or other high Crimes and Misdemeanors". In his conduct of the office of President of the United States—and in violation of his constitutional oath faithfully to execute the office of President of the United States and, to the best of his ability, preserve, protect, and defend the Constitution of the United States, and in violation of his constitutional duty to take care that the laws be faithfully executed—Donald J. Trump has abused the powers of the Presidency, in that:

Using the powers of his high office, President Trump solicited the interference of a foreign government, Ukraine, in the 2020 United States Presidential election. He did so through a scheme or course of conduct that included soliciting the Government of Ukraine to publicly announce investigations that would benefit his reelection, harm the election prospects of a political opponent, and influence the 2020 United States Presidential election to his advantage. President Trump also sought to pressure the Government of Ukraine to take these steps by conditioning official United States Government acts of significant value to Ukraine on its public announcement of the investigations. President Trump engaged in this scheme or course of conduct for corrupt purposes in pursuit of personal political benefit. In so doing, President Trump used the powers of the Presidency in a manner that compromised the national security of the United States and undermined the integrity of the United States democratic process. He thus ignored and injured the interests of the Nation.

President Trump engaged in this scheme or course of conduct through the following means:

(1) President Trump—acting both directly and through his agents within and outside the United States Government—corruptly solicited the Government of Ukraine to publicly announce investigations into—

(A) a political opponent, former Vice President Joseph R. Biden, Jr.; and

(B) a discredited theory promoted by Russia alleging that Ukraine—rather than Russia—interfered in the 2016 United States Presidential election.

(2) With the same corrupt motives, President Trump—acting both directly and through his agents within and outside the United States Government—conditioned two official acts on the public announcements that he had requested—

(A) the release of $391 million of United States taxpayer funds that Congress had appropriated on a bipartisan basis for the purpose of providing vital military and security assistance to Ukraine to oppose Russian aggression and which President Trump had ordered suspended; and

(B) a head of state meeting at the White House, which the President of Ukraine sought to demonstrate continued United States support for the Government of Ukraine in the face of Russian aggression.

(3) Faced with the public revelation of his actions, President Trump ultimately released the military and security assistance to the Government of Ukraine, but has persisted in openly and corruptly urging and soliciting Ukraine to undertake investigations for his personal political benefit. These actions were consistent with President Trump's previous invitations of foreign interference in United States elections.

In all of this, President Trump abused the powers of the Presidency by ignoring and injuring national security and other vital national interests to obtain an improper personal political benefit. He has also betrayed the Nation by abusing his high office to enlist a foreign power in corrupting democratic elections.

Wherefore President Trump, by such conduct, has demonstrated that he will remain a threat to national security and the Constitution if allowed to remain in office, and has acted in a manner grossly incompatible with self-governance and the rule of law. President Trump thus warrants impeachment and trial, removal from office, and disqualification to hold and enjoy any office of honor, trust, or profit under the United States.

ARTICLE II: OBSTRUCTION OF CONGRESS

The Constitution provides that the House of Representatives "shall have the sole Power of Impeachment'" and that the President "shall be removed from Office on Impeachment for, and Conviction of, Treason, Bribery, or other high Crimes and Misdemeanors". In his conduct of the office of President of the United States—and in violation of his constitutional oath faithfully to execute the office of President of the United States and, to the best of his ability, preserve, protect, and defend the Constitution of the United States, and in violation of his constitutional duty to take care that the laws be faithfully executed—Donald J. Trump has directed the unprecedented, categorical, and indiscriminate defiance of subpoenas issued by the House of Representatives pursuant to its "sole Power of Impeachment". President Trump has abused the powers of the Presidency in a manner offensive to, and subversive of, the Constitution, in that:

The House of Representatives has engaged in an impeachment inquiry focused on President Trump's corrupt solicitation of the Government of Ukraine to interfere in the 2020 United States Presidential election. As part of this impeachment inquiry, the Committees undertaking the investigation served subpoenas seeking documents and testimony deemed vital to the inquiry from various Executive Branch agencies and offices, and current and former officials.

In response, without lawful cause or excuse, President Trump directed Executive Branch agencies, offices, and officials not to comply with those subpoenas. President Trump thus interposed the powers of the Presidency against the lawful subpoenas of the House of Representatives, and assumed to himself functions and judgments necessary to the exercise of the "sole Power of Impeachment'" vested by the Constitution in the House of Representatives.

President Trump abused the powers of his high office through the following means:

(1) Directing the White House to defy a lawful subpoena by withholding the production of documents sought therein by the Committees.

(2) Directing other Executive Branch agencies and offices to defy lawful subpoenas and withhold the production of documents and records from the Committees—in response to which the Department of State, Office of Management and Budget, Department of Energy, and Department of Defense refused to produce a single document or record.

(3) Directing current and former Executive Branch officials not to cooperate with the Committees—in response to which nine Administration officials defied subpoenas for testimony, namely John Michael "Mick" Mulvaney, Robert B. Blair, John A. Eisenberg, Michael Ellis, Preston Wells Griffith, Russell T. Vought, Michael Duffey, Brian McCormack, and T. Ulrich Brechbuhl.

These actions were consistent with President Trump's previous efforts to undermine United States Government investigations into foreign interference in United States elections.

Through these actions, President Trump sought to arrogate to himself the right to determine the propriety, scope, and nature of an impeachment inquiry into his own conduct, as well as the unilateral prerogative to deny any and all information to the House of Representatives in the exercise of its "sole Power of Impeachment'". In the history of the Republic, no President has ever ordered the complete defiance of an impeachment inquiry or sought to obstruct and impede so comprehensively the ability of the House of Representatives to investigate "high Crimes and Misdemeanors". This abuse of office served to cover up the President's own repeated misconduct and to seize and control the power of impeachment—and thus to nullify a vital constitutional safeguard vested solely in the House of Representatives.

In all of this, President Trump has acted in a manner contrary to his trust as President and subversive of constitutional government, to the great prejudice of the cause of law and justice, and to the manifest injury of the people of the United States.

Wherefore, President Trump, by such conduct, has demonstrated that he will remain a threat to the Constitution if allowed to remain in office, and has acted in a manner grossly incompatible with self-governance and the rule of law. President Trump thus warrants impeachment and trial, removal from office, and disqualification to hold and enjoy any office of honor, trust, or profit under the United States.

Speaker of the House of Representatives.

SOURCE: U.S. Congress. "Articles of Impeachment against Donald John Trump." H. Res. 775. December 18, 2019. https://www.congress.gov/116/bills/hres755/BILLS-116hres755enr.pdf.

Speaker Pelosi Opens Debate on Articles of Impeachment

December 18, 2019

Ms. PELOSI. Madam Speaker, I thank the gentleman for yielding and for his tremendous leadership in helping us honor the Constitution of the United States.

I also extend my gratitude to Chairman SCHIFF, who will be presiding later in the day.

Madam Speaker, this morning and every morning when we come together, Members rise and pledge allegiance to the flag. Every day, all across America, children in school, members of the military, officials, and those civilly engaged, also pledge allegiance to the flag.

Let us recall what that pledge says: "I pledge allegiance to the flag of the United States of America, and to the Republic for which it stands, one nation under God, indivisible, with liberty and justice for all."

"The Republic for which it stands" is what we are here to talk about today: "a republic, if we can keep it."

We gather today, under the dome of this temple of democracy, to exercise one of the most solemn powers that this body can take: the impeachment of the President of the United States.

No Member, regardless of party or politics, comes to Congress to impeach a President; but every one of us, as our first act as a Member of Congress, stood on this historic House floor, before our beautiful American flag, and raised our hands in this sacred oath: "I do solemnly swear that I will support and defend the Constitution of the United States against all enemies, foreign and domestic. . . . So help me God."

For 230 years, Members have taken that sacred oath, which makes us custodians of the Constitution.

When our Founders declared independence and established our new Nation, they crafted a system of government unlike any ever seen before: a republic, starting with the sacred words, "We the People."

For centuries, Americans have fought—and died—to defend democracy for the people. But, very sadly, now, our Founders' vision of a republic is under threat from actions from the White House. That is why, today, as Speaker of the House, I solemnly and sadly open the debate on the impeachment of the President of the United States.

If we do not act now, we would be derelict in our duty. It is tragic that the President's reckless actions make impeachment necessary.

He gave us no choice.

What we are discussing today is the established fact that the President violated the Constitution.

It is a matter of fact that the President is an ongoing threat to our national security and the integrity of our elections: the basis of our democracy.

Hundreds of historians, legal scholars, and former prosecutors—regardless of party—have stated that the President committed impeachable offenses. . . .

[A letter submitted for the record from former federal prosecutors has been omitted.]

Ms. PELOSI. Madam Speaker, what we are discussing today is the established fact that the President, again, violated the Constitution.

It is a matter of fact that the President is, again, an ongoing threat to our national security. And the testimony of decorated war heroes, distinguished diplomats, and patriotic, career public servants—some the President's own appointees—over the past weeks have told us this.

The President used the power of his public office to obtain an improper personal, political benefit at the expense of America's national security. When the President weakens a democratic ally that is advancing American security interests by fighting an American adversary, the President weakens America.

This abuse of power also jeopardizes the integrity of our elections. All Americans agree that American voters should choose our President, not some foreign government.

The Founders understood that it is profoundly corrosive for our democracy for a President to invite interference in our elections.

As George Washington, our Nation's patriarch, under whose gaze we stand today, warned: "History and experience prove that foreign influence is one of the most baneful foes of republican government"—George Washington.

Sadly, the American people have witnessed further wrongs of the President, which necessitate the second Article of Impeachment: obstruction of Congress.

When the President's wrongdoing was revealed, he launched an unprecedented, indiscriminate, and categorical campaign of defiance and obstruction. Never before in the history of our Nation have we seen a President declare—and act as if—he is above the law.

The President even goes so far as to say and act on this absurdity when he says: "Article II says I can do whatever I want."

No, it doesn't.

That recklessness is a profound violation of the Constitution and our Republic, which endure because of our system of separation of powers: three coequal branches, each a check and balance on the others—"a republic," again, "if we can keep it."

The Founders' great fear of a rogue or corrupt President is the very reason why they enshrined impeachment in the Constitution.

As one Founder, William Davie of North Carolina, warned, unless the Constitution contained an impeachment provision, a President might spare no efforts or means whatever to get himself reelected.

Another Founder, George Mason, insisted that the President who procured his appointment in the first instance through improper and corrupt acts might repeat his guilt and return to power.

We in Congress, Article I, the legislative branch, must stand up and make clear to the American people and to all people who this body still stands by the principles enshrined in the Constitution and defended by generations of Americans.

Last week, in observance of the 75th anniversary of the Battle of the Bulge, Members traveled to that hallowed ground to express our gratitude to the heroes who sacrificed everything to secure victory of freedom over tyranny, not just for America but for the world. The veterans of that battle, who are in their nineties, told us how, after the war was won, the Europeans whom they liberated would ask: Why did you risk—you don't know us—and give your lives to save us? We are not Americans.

Our men would say: We came here to fight for you not because you are Americans but because we are Americans.

As our beloved Elijah Cummings, our Oversight Committee chair, our North Star, said when he announced his support of this action: "When the history books are written about this tumultuous era, I want them to show that I was among those in the House of Representatives who stood up to lawlessness and tyranny."

He also said, almost prophetically: When we are dancing with the angels, the question will be: What did we do to make sure we kept our democracy intact?

Elijah has since passed on. Now, he is dancing with the angels.

I know that he and all of us here are very proud of the moral courage of Members who want to honor the vision of our Founders for a republic, the sacrifice of our men and women in uniform to defend it, and the aspirations of our children to live freely within it.

Today, we are here to defend democracy for the people. May God bless America.

SOURCE: U.S. Congress. House. "Impeaching Donald John Trump, President of the United States, for High Crimes and Misdemeanors." H. Res. 755. 116th Congress, 1st Session. *Congressional Record.* vol. 165, no. 205, daily ed. (December 18, 2019): H12131–H12133. https://www.govinfo.gov/content/pkg/CREC-2019-12-18/pdf/CREC-2019-12-18-house.pdf.

Representative Collins Speaks in Opposition to Impeachment

December 18, 2019

Mr. COLLINS of Georgia. Madam Speaker, I yield myself such time as I may consume.

Madam Speaker, we are here today to enter into a debate that should surprise no one. This has not been a surprise, and it is not even something that we would not have thought about. From the very moment that the majority party in this House won, the inevitability that we would be here today was only a matter of what date they would schedule it, nothing else.

In fact, how it even began to look even further was, on September 24, the Speaker announced an impeachment inquiry even before seeing the call transcript that we are going to hear so much about today.

You know, it is not about what this body can do and its constitutional oath, and there has been a lot of "constitutional" and "Founders" thrown around and will be all day today. But there is one thing that I will mention all along, and that is, also, the Founders were very concerned about a partisan impeachment in which politics or the majority, who have their strength, can do what they want to do, regardless of any facts.

In fact, I have said it before, and I will say it again, I do not believe, no matter what was said today and even what has been said—this is not a solemn occasion. When you go looking for something for 3 years, and especially this year since January, you ought to be excited when you find it, but they can't because I know what has now happened. It took me till last night, but I was thinking about it. Why do we keep calling this a solemn occasion when you have been wanting to do this ever since the gentleman was elected? The President came forward and did what he saw fit for the American people, but yet they wanted to impeach him. And it hit me. Now I know.

The reason they wanted to is now they are realizing what I told them and have been telling them for the last few weeks, that the clock and the calendar are terrible masters. The clock and the calendar are terrible masters. They do not care about anything except getting the time done and the calendar fixed. They do not care about facts. They do not care about time. And one day, the clock and the calendar will hang along this body in a very detrimental way.

How do I know this? Because one of our Members, Ms. TLAIB, said on the night she was sworn in: We are going to impeach.

Well, you know the rest. In May 2019, AL GREEN said: I am concerned if we don't impeach this President, he will get reelected.

That is probably the most prescient thing said by the majority in the last year is that they said: We can't beat him if we don't impeach him.

There is a reason behind the impeachment. Even Speaker PELOSI said it would be dangerous to leave it to voters to determine whether President Trump stays in office. Really? After we just said the Pledge of Allegiance, we go back to the Speaker's own words and she said it would be dangerous to leave it to the voters.

I will tell you right now, Madam Speaker, we on the Republican side have no problem taking our case to the majority and to the people of this country because they elected Donald Trump, and it is a matter for the voters, not this House, not in this way, not in the way this is being done. It has trampled everything this House believes in.

I said it yesterday, and I believe this to be true today, I will fight this on process, which has been deplorable, to use a word of the majority. It has been awful.

The calendar and the clock make it impressive that we actually do it quickly. We don't care about rules. We don't care about minority hearing days. We don't care about giving the opportunity for witnesses to be called because the chairman gets to determine what is relevant. Wow, that is pretty good. Let the accuser determine what is relevant to the one being accused.

The people of America see through this. The people of America understand due process, and they understand when it is being trampled in the people's House.

You see, it is also not a matter of process, which will be discussed today. It is a matter of actual facts. I will fight the facts all day long because what we have found here today is a President who did not do as being charged. In fact, they had to go to abuse of power, this amorphous term that you are going to hear many arguments about that abuse of power, except for one thing, the call itself, the two parties say no pressure. Nothing was ever done to get the money. In fact, they didn't even know the money was held.

But there is something that very much bothers me about the facts. There were five meetings—we will hear about those today—in which there was never a linkage made. There was one witness who is depended on over 600 times in the majority's report that, in the end, after questioned, had to say: Well, that was my presumption of what was happening.

You see, this is an impeachment based on presumption, basically also a poll-tested impeachment on what actually sells to the American people.

Today is going to be a lot of things. What it is not is fair. What it is not is about the truth. What is true today, and I just heard it just a moment ago in the articles themselves where it said—and the Speaker, I believe, actually talked about this, that the President weakened a foreign leader.

Do you know what the truth of the matter is, Madam Speaker? The most interesting and deplorable thing that I have heard over the last few weeks is the actual attack by the majority on President Zelensky because they realize the whole crux of their case is that if he was not pressured, their house of cards falls. By the way, it has already fallen.

But if we can't show pressure, then we either have to call him a liar, a world leader, or we have to make up names to call him. That is exactly what happened in the Judiciary Committee when a Member of the majority actually compared him to a battered wife. That is below the dignity of this body, to take a world leader and, when he doesn't make your case for you, to belittle him, especially, as is going to be often said by the majority, that they are in the middle of a hot war with Russia.

You see, President Trump actually did give them offensive weapons. President Trump did nothing wrong. We are going to talk about that all day long today.

We went on process, and we went on facts. Why? Because the American people will see through this.

Before I close this first part, I will have to recognize that even the minority leader in the Senate recognizes that the House did not do their job because he can't make the case to his own Members so he is having to ask for witnesses, ask for more time. You see, and even yesterday, it was sort of funny. I thought it was hilarious that the minority leader in the Senate went out and did a press conference and said: They denied my witnesses. They denied my requests.

Well, welcome to the club, Mr. SCHUMER. That is exactly what has happened over here for the last 3 months.

Today, we are going to talk a lot about impeachment. We are going to talk a lot about our President. We are going to talk about two Articles of Impeachment, abuse of power because they can't actually pin anything of factual basis on him—the President did nothing wrong in this issue—and then they are going to talk about obstruction of Congress.

You know, obstruction of Congress, as I have said before, is like petulant children saying we didn't get our way when we didn't ask the right way, and we didn't actually go after it and try to make a case.

You know why, Madam Speaker? The clock and the calendar are terrible masters. The majority will own that problem today because to the clock and the calendar, facts don't matter. The promises to the base matter, and today is a promise kept for the majority—not a surprise, a fact.

Madam Speaker, I reserve the balance of my time.

SOURCE: U.S. Congress. House. "Impeaching Donald John Trump, President of the United States, for High Crimes and Misdemeanors." H. Res. 755. 116th Congress, 1st Session. *Congressional Record.* vol. 165, no. 205, daily ed. (December 18, 2019): H12133–H12134. https://www.govinfo.gov/content/pkg/CREC-2019-12-18/pdf/CREC-2019-12-18-house.pdf.

OTHER HISTORIC DOCUMENTS OF INTEREST

Response to Controversial Indian Citizenship Law

DECEMBER 9, 11, 12, 13, AND 22, 2019

The Indian parliament passed a new citizenship law in December 2019 that quickly faced international condemnation and domestic protests for its anti-Muslim nature. The law, called the Citizenship Amendment Bill (CAB, also known as the Citizenship Amendment Act—CAA), is a cornerstone of Prime Minister Narendra Modi's Hindu-nationalist agenda and establishes a religion test to determine whether illegal migrants in India can become citizens. The law showed favor to all of South Asia's major religions except Islam, leading members of the more than 200 million Muslims living in India, along with the international community, to label it discriminatory. The new law sparked widespread domestic protests as tens of thousands rioted in three states across India's northeast. The government responded with military force, violently clashing with protesters.

CONTROVERSIAL CITIZENSHIP LAW PASSES INDIAN PARLIAMENT

On December 11, 2019, the Indian parliament passed a controversial citizenship law, sending the measure to Prime Minister Modi's desk to be signed into law. The measure established a religious test for migrants who want to become citizens, allowing government officials to use religion as a criterion for determining whether illegal migrants in India can be fast-tracked for citizenship. The bill specifically included provisions to allow members of all of the major religions of South Asia except Islam to be fast-tracked, leading many Muslim and religious leaders to label the bill as discriminatory and dangerous. The bill is a cornerstone of Modi's Hindu-nationalist agenda to promote and emphasize India's Hinduism identity. The country is approximately 80 percent Hindu, with a large Muslim minority.

The citizenship law came on the heels of several other measures that chipped away the rights of many Muslims living in India. In May, Modi and his ruling Bharatiya Janata Party won a landslide reelection on a far-right Hindu-nationalist platform. Shortly afterward, the government established a program in the northeastern state of Assam forcing all 33 million residents to produce evidence that they or their ancestors were Indian citizens. As a result, more than 2 million people, many of them Muslims and lifelong residents of India, were left off the state's citizenship rolls. The ruling party saw the measure as an example for the rest of the country and publicly expressed a desire to expand the citizenship requirement to other states.

Modi's government also stripped away autonomy and statehood for Kashmir, India's only Muslim-majority state. And a month before parliament passed the controversial citizenship test, the nation's highest court handed Hindu fundamentalists a major victory, allowing them to build a new temple over the ruins of a demolished mosque in the city of Ayodhya, a major flashpoint for Muslim and Hindu clashes. Many saw the series of measures to restrict citizenship for Muslims as undermining India's commitment to a secular democracy, which was enshrined in the nation's constitution in 1976 via the forty-second amendment.

Modi Defends Law, Attacks Critics

Modi and his government defended the law by saying it would protect human rights and religious freedom. "The bill provides expedited consideration for Indian citizenship to persecuted religious minorities already in India from certain contiguous countries," said Raveesh Kumar, a spokesperson for the foreign ministry. "It seeks to address their current difficulties and meet their basic human rights. Such an initiative should be welcomed, not criticized by those who are genuinely committed to religious freedom," Kumar continued.

Modi delivered a sharper defense of the law. During a combative speech a few weeks after the law was signed, Modi singled out critics and opposing politicians for "spreading lies" and accused demonstrators of trying to destroy the country through vandalism and bloodshed. "Respect the Parliament!" Modi called out to his supporters. "Respect the Constitution! Respect the people elected by the people! I challenge the ones who are spreading lies. If there is a smell of discrimination in anything I have done, then put me in front of the country." Modi argued that the law was meant only to extend citizenship to religious minorities fleeing persecution in three Muslim-majority countries—Afghanistan, Bangladesh, and Pakistan— and said it would not be used against Indian citizens. "If we haven't asked your religion for previous policies, why would we ask your religion for this policy?" Modi asked. "We never asked their religion. We only saw the poverty of the poor and gave them a home." Referring to the law, Modi added, "I want to clarify once again that the C.A.A. is not going to take away anybody's citizenship. It is about giving citizenship to those facing discrimination."

International Community, Humans Rights Groups Condemn the Law

Despite the reassurances that the law would not be abused, the Indian government faced swift international backlash and protests at home. Muslim leaders and human rights organizations immediately condemned the move, worrying that the legislation would make it easier to incarcerate and deport Muslim residents, even those whose families have been in India for generations. Other leaders positioned the bill as a direct threat to India's secular democracy. Rahul Gandhi, the leader of the opposition Indian National Congress party, said, "India belongs to everybody—all communities, all religions, all cultures." Another party leader, Shashi Tharoor, called the bill an "all-out assault on the very idea of India."

The United States Commission on International Religious Freedom (USCIRF) expressed serious concerns, while Congress questioned the intent of the law. Referencing the law, the USCIRF said, "The CAB enshrines a pathway to citizenship for immigrants that specifically excludes Muslims, setting a legal criterion for citizenship based on religion. The CAB is a dangerous turn in the wrong direction; it runs counter to India's rich history of secular pluralism and the Indian Constitution, which guarantees equality before the law regardless of faith." The statement pointed to the recent series of Hindu-nationalist policies pushed by Modi as a sign that the state was working to marginalize Muslims. "In conjunction with the ongoing National Register of Citizens (NRC) process in Assam and nationwide NRC that the Home Minister seeks to propose, USCIRF fears that the Indian government is creating a religious test for Indian citizenship that would strip citizenship from millions of Muslims," the group said. The commission further suggested that the United States should explore sanctions on India to curb its efforts to marginalize Muslims. "If the CAB passes in both houses of parliament, the United States government should consider sanctions against the Home Minister and other principal leadership." Congress expressed similar concerns. The United States House Committee on Foreign Affairs questioned the intent, and stated, "Any religious test for citizenship undermines this most basic democratic tenet."

Leading international bodies shared similar worries about possible discrimination under the new law. The United Nations High Commissioner for Human Rights (UNHCHR) called the law "fundamentally discriminatory in nature" days after it cleared both houses of parliament. "The amended law would appear to undermine the commitment to equality before the law enshrined in India's constitution and India's obligations under the International Covenant on Civil and Political Rights and the Convention for the Elimination of Racial Discrimination, to which Indian is a State party, which prohibit discrimination based on racial, ethnic, or religious grounds. Although India's broader naturalization laws remain in place, these amendments will have a discriminatory effect on people's access to nationality," the UNHCHR said. The UNHCHR reiterated the United Nations' commitment to human rights, especially for immigrants and those fleeing persecution. "All migrants, regardless of their migration status, are entitled to respect, protection, and fulfilment of their human rights," the body said. According to the group, "While the goal of protecting persecuted groups is welcome, this should be done through a robust national asylum system that is premised on the principle of equality and non-discrimination, and which applies to all people in need of protection from persecution and other human rights violations, with no distinction as to race, religion, national origin or other prohibited grounds."

PAKISTAN, BANGLADESH, AND AFGHANISTAN RESPOND AS PROTESTS ERUPT ACROSS INDIA

Neighboring countries, specifically Pakistan, Bangladesh, and Afghanistan—three countries Modi singled out as seeking to persecute religious minorities—expressed concern that the law was discriminatory and would strain relations between their respective countries and India. Pakistani prime minister Imran Khan criticized the act as a "discriminatory law" and argued that it would violate "bilateral agreements and understandings between India and Pakistan, particularly those on security and rights of minorities in the respective countries." Bangladeshi minister of foreign affairs A. K. Abdul Momen said the bill could weaken India's standing as a secular nation and denied that minorities were facing religious persecution in his country. "Within India, people are facing many problems," Momen said, adding, "We don't understand why [the Indian government] did it. It was not necessary." Former Afghan president Hamid Karzai urged Modi to treat all minorities equally, saying, "We don't have persecuted minorities in Afghanistan." Instead, because of the Afghanistan conflict, "the whole country is persecuted," Karzai said. "We have been in war and conflict for a long time. All religions in Afghanistan, Muslims and Hindus and Sikhs, which are our three main religions, have suffered."

In India, protests erupted. Tens of thousands of protesters rioted in three states across India's northeast after the law was passed. Demonstrations spread to Mumbai, Chennai, Varanasi, Guwahati, Hyderabad, Bhopal, Patna, Pondicherry, and the capital, New Delhi. Some of the protests were violent. Protesters set two train stations on fire, clashed with security forces, blocked national highways, burned vehicles, and attacked the home of the highest-ranking government official in the capital of Assam. The Indian government responded with a swift crackdown. Government officials imposed a curfew, deployed additional military officials and security forces, shut down the Internet, limited the number of people who could assemble, and clashed with protesters. In New Delhi, some police officers beat unarmed students with wooden poles, while in Assam, they shot and killed two protesters. The show of force only angered and emboldened the protesters, who included not only Muslims worried about being further marginalized but also progressives, young people, students, Indians of other faiths, and Indians who believed a secular government is fundamental to India's identity and future.

In the aftermath, experts warned that the citizenship law greatly escalated India's gradual slide to authoritarianism and Hindu nationalism under Modi. Some drew parallels to Myanmar's 1982 citizenship law, which excluded the Rohingya people when it allowed for citizenship for "indigenous races" only, setting the stage for the violence against the Rohingya that followed. Yet amid the concerns, others saw in the mass demonstrations a reawakening of India's secular democracy. Images of tens of thousands of people from diverse backgrounds marching in the streets chanting the preamble to the constitution of India and its promises of social, political, and economic justice and freedom of thought, expression, and belief brought optimism to many and reinvigorated the Indian people's federal spirit.

—Robert Howard

Following is a statement from the U.S. Commission on International Religious Freedom delivered on December 9, 2019, after the lower house of the Indian parliament passed the Citizenship Amendment Bill; a tweet posted by Prime Minister Narendra Modi on December 11, 2019, celebrating the bill's passage; the full text of the Citizenship Amendment Bill as of December 12, 2019; a statement by United Nations High Commissioner for Human Rights spokesperson Jeremy Laurence on December 13, 2019, expressing concern about the Indian citizenship bill; and excerpts of a campaign speech delivered by Prime Minister Modi on December 22, 2019, in which he defended the bill.

DOCUMENT

U.S. Commission Responds to India's Citizenship Bill

December 9, 2019

The U.S. Commission on International Religious Freedom (USCIRF) is deeply troubled by the passage of the Citizenship (Amendment) Bill (CAB), originally introduced by Home Minister Amit Shah, in the Lok Sabha (the lower house of the Indian Parliament) given the religion criterion in the bill. The CAB will now move to the Rajya Sabha (Indian Parliament's Upper House). If the CAB passes in both houses of parliament, the United States government should consider sanctions against the Home Minister and other principal leadership.

The CAB enshrines a pathway to citizenship for immigrants that specifically excludes Muslims, setting a legal criterion for citizenship based on religion. The CAB is a dangerous turn in the wrong direction; it runs counter to India's rich history of secular pluralism and the Indian Constitution, which guarantees equality before the law regardless of faith. In conjunction with the ongoing National Register of Citizens (NRC) process in Assam and nationwide NRC that the Home Minister seeks to propose, USCIRF fears that the Indian government is creating a religious test for Indian citizenship that would strip citizenship from millions of Muslims.

The Lok Sabha first passed the CAB in January 2019, but due to protests, the government withdrew it before it could be voted on by the Rajya Sabha. Both houses of parliament must ratify a bill before it can become law. The BJP included the passage of the CAB as part of its manifesto released ahead of its overwhelming electoral victory in May 2019.

SOURCE: U.S. Commission on International Religious Freedom. "USCIRF Raises Serious Concerns and Eyes Sanctions Recommendations for Citizenship (Amendment) Bill in India, Which Passed Lower House Today." December 9, 2019. https://www.uscirf.gov/news-room/press-releases-statements/uscirf-raises-serious-concerns-and-eyes-sanctions.

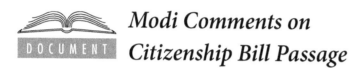

Modi Comments on Citizenship Bill Passage

December 11, 2019

A landmark day for India and our nation's ethos of compassion and brotherhood! Glad that the #CAB2019 has been passed in the #RajyaSabha. Gratitude to all the MPs who voted in favour of the Bill. This Bill will alleviate the suffering of many who faced persecution for years.

SOURCE: Narendra Modi (@narendramodi). Twitter post. December 11, 2019. https://twitter.com/narendramodi/status/1204788395613966336.

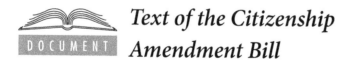

Text of the Citizenship Amendment Bill

December 12, 2019

THE CITIZENSHIP (AMENDMENT) BILL, 2019

(As Passed by the Houses of Parliament)

A

BILL

further to amend the Citizenship Act, 1955.

BE it enacted by Parliament in the Seventieth Year of the Republic of India as follows:—

1. (1) This Act may be called the Citizenship (Amendment) Act, 2019.

(2) It shall come into force on such date as the Central Government may, by notification in the Official Gazette, appoint.

2. In the Citizenship Act, 1955 (hereinafter referred to as the principal Act), in section 2, in sub-section (1), in clause (b), the following proviso shall be inserted, namely:—

"Provided that any person belonging to Hindu, Sikh, Buddhist, Jain, Parsi or Christian community from Afghanistan, Bangladesh or Pakistan, who entered into India on or before the 31st day of December, 2014 and who has been exempted by the Central Government by or under clause (c) of sub-section (2) of section 3 of the Passport (Entry into India) Act, 1920 or from the application of the provisions of the Foreigners Act, 1946 or any rule or order made thereunder, shall not be treated as illegal migrant for the purposes of this Act;".

3. After section 6A of the principal Act, the following section shall be inserted, namely:—

'6B. (1) The Central Government or an authority specified by it in this behalf may, subject to such conditions, restrictions and manner as may be prescribed, on an application made in this behalf, grant a certificate of registration or certificate of naturalisation to a person referred to in the proviso to clause (b) of sub-section (1) of section 2.

(2) Subject to fulfilment of the conditions specified in section 5 or the qualifications for naturalisation under the provisions of the Third Schedule, a person granted the certificate of registration or certificate of naturalisation under sub-section (1) shall be deemed to be a citizen of India from the date of his entry into India.

(3) On and from the date of commencement of the Citizenship (Amendment) Act, 2019, any proceeding pending against a person under this section in respect of illegal migration or citizenship shall stand abated on conferment of citizenship to him:

Provided that such person shall not be disqualified for making application for citizenship under this section on the ground that the proceeding is pending against him and the Central Government or authority specified by it in this behalf shall not reject his application on that ground if he is otherwise found qualified for grant of citizenship under this section:

Provided further that the person who makes the application for citizenship under this section shall not be deprived of his rights and privileges to which he was entitled on the date of receipt of his application on the ground of making such application.

(4) Nothing in this section shall apply to tribal area of Assam, Meghalaya, Mizoram or Tripura as included in the Sixth Schedule to the Constitution and the area covered under "The Inner Line" notified under the Bengal Eastern Frontier Regulation, 1873.'.

4. In section 7D of the principal Act,—

(i) after clause (d), the following clause shall be inserted, namely:—

"(da) the Overseas Citizen of India Cardholder has violated any of the provisions of this Act or provisions of any other law for time being in force as may be specified by the Central Government in the notification published in the Official Gazette; or";

(ii) after clause (f), the following proviso shall be inserted, namely:—"Provided that no order under this section shall be passed unless the Overseas Citizen of India Cardholder has been given a reasonable opportunity of being heard.".

5. In section 18 of the principal Act, in sub-section (2), after clause (ee), the following clause shall be inserted, namely:—

"(eei) the conditions, restrictions and manner for granting certificate of registration or certificate of naturalisation under sub-section (1) of section 6B;".

6. In the Third Schedule to the principal Act, in clause (d), the following proviso shall be inserted, namely:—

'Provided that for the person belonging to Hindu, Sikh, Buddhist, Jain, Parsi or Christian community in Afghanistan, Bangladesh or Pakistan, the aggregate period of residence or service of Government in India as required under this clause shall be read as "not less than five years" in place of "not less than eleven years"'..

SOURCE: Lok Sabha. "The Constitution (Amendment) Bill, 2019, as Passed by Both Houses." December 12, 2019. http://164.100.47.4/BillsTexts/LSBillTexts/PassedBothHouses/citizenship-47%20of%2019.pdf.

UN Human Rights Group Expresses Concern about India's Citizenship Legislation

DOCUMENT

December 13, 2019

We are concerned that India's new Citizenship (Amendment) Act 2019 is fundamentally discriminatory in nature.

The amended legislation seeks to expedite citizenship for religious minorities— naming specifically only Hindus, Sikhs, Buddhists, Jains, Parsis and Christians—fleeing persecution in Afghanistan, Bangladesh and Pakistan, who have been resident before 2014. But it does not extend the same protection to Muslims, including minority sects.

The amended law would appear to undermine the commitment to equality before the law enshrined in India's constitution and India's obligations under the International Covenant on Civil and Political Rights and the Convention for the Elimination of Racial Discrimination, to which India is a State party, which prohibit discrimination based on racial, ethnic or religious grounds. Although India's broader naturalization laws remain in place, these amendments will have a discriminatory effect on people's access to nationality.

All migrants, regardless of their migration status, are entitled to respect, protection and fulfilment of their human rights. Just 12 months ago India endorsed the Global Compact for Safe, Regular and Orderly Migration, which commits States to respond to the needs of migrants in situations of vulnerability, avoiding arbitrary detention and collective expulsions and ensuring that all migration governance measures are human rights–based.

While the goal of protecting persecuted groups is welcome, this should be done through a robust national asylum system that is premised on the principle of equality and non-discrimination, and which applies to all people in need of protection from persecution and other human rights violations, with no distinction as to race, religion, national origin or other prohibited grounds.

We understand the new law will be reviewed by the Supreme Court of India and hope it will consider carefully the compatibility of the law with India's international human rights obligations.

In the meantime, we are concerned at reports that two people have died and many including police officers have been injured in the Indian states of Assam and Tripura as people protest against the Act. We call on the authorities to respect the right to peaceful assembly, and to abide by international norms and standards on the use of force when responding to protests. All sides should refrain from resorting to violence.

SOURCE: From "Press Briefing on India," December 13, 2019, by United Nations Office of the High Commissioner for Human Rights, ©2019 United Nations. Reprinted with the permission of the United Nations. https://www.ohchr.org/EN/NewsEvents/Pages/DisplayNews.aspx?NewsID=25425&LangID=E.

DOCUMENT

Modi Responds to Citizenship Bill Concerns in Campaign Speech

December 22, 2019

Prime Minister Shri Narendra Modi today kicked off the BJP's campaign for the upcoming Delhi assembly elections by addressing a mega rally at Ramlila Maidan. Amid the chants and slogans of people, PM Modi said unity in diversity is the hallmark of India. "Ramlila Maidan is a historic place. I can see an end to uncertainties on your faces," he said to the residents of unauthorized colonies.

Congratulating residents of unauthorized colonies, PM Modi said, "Even after several decades after Independence, a large section of population in Delhi had to face fear, uncertainty, deceit & false electoral promises. Illegal, sealing, bulldozer and a cut-off date—life of a large population in Delhi was confined around these words. I am happy that the BJP and the government have had the opportunity of bringing a new dawn in the lives of 40 lakh people of Delhi."

In a scathing attack on the Congress Party, Prime Minister Modi said that they gave land to VVIPs, while his party gave land to the people of Delhi. He also attacked the ruling Aam Aadmi Party government and said that it was doing nothing to provide clean water to the people of Delhi.

PM Modi during his speech at the Ramlila Maidan said that earlier governments did nothing to expand the metro network. He added that the fourth phase of Delhi Metro was stalled unnecessarily by the previous government. "25 km of new metro route added annually in last five years, it was 14 km earlier. In the last five years, we've made unprecedented development in Delhi Metro. We also built the Peripheral Expressway to decongest Delhi," he said.

The Prime Minister addressed the Citizenship Amendment Act issue that has caused massive protests across India and said that fake news and misinformation regarding the act is being spread to provoke people by the Congress and its cronies.

Assuring everyone that Modi Government not stripping anyone of their rights, PM Modi highlighted, "Some political parties are spreading rumours, they are misleading people and inciting them. I want to ask them, when we authorized the unauthorized colonies, did we ask anyone their religion? Did we ask which political party they support? Did we ask for documents from 1970, 1980?"

PM Modi hit out at the opposition parties for spreading rumours about elaborate paperwork in [order] to prove Citizenship in the CAA. He said his government never put the restriction of paperwork when it provided welfare schemes to the poor. "Hindus, Muslims, Sikhs, Christians all were benefitted, everyone who lives here was benefitted. We have never asked anyone if he goes to temple or mosque when it comes to implementing our schemes. We are dedicated to the mantra of 'Sabka Saath, Sabka Vikas'," he added furthermore.

In a furious attack on the violent protests against the CAA, PM Modi said, "Hate me but don't hate India. Burn my effigies but don't burn a poor man's auto-rickshaw. What will you get from beating poor people, poor drivers and policemen." He asserted that the police is there to always help the people and attacking them is not justified. 33,000 police personnel laid down their lives during work since independence but now being attacked mercilessly.

Citing no rules framed about NRC, PM Modi remarked, "There have been multiple rumours about NRC too. NRC was implemented in Assam after the Supreme Court order. There are no rules that have been framed, it has not been introduced in Parliament. While we are giving you your right with the unauthorized colonies bill, will we then try and snatch your right?"

Training his guns at the Congress party, PM Modi said, "Politicians belonging to 100-year old political parties are not voicing for peace. Now that the people of the country have dismissed them, they have gone back to their old measures of divide and rule. Citizenship law and NRC have nothing to do with Indian Muslims and there is no detention centre in the country."

PM Modi while reassuring that no one's citizenship is threatened, said, "Who understands the pain of refugees better than people of Delhi? CAA, in fact, provides citizenship to the religiously persecuted minorities from Pakistan, Afghanistan and Bangladesh. CAA is not to take away citizenship, it is to give citizenship to people." He requested the youth of the country to read the Act in detail and told them not to fall prey to the rumors of detention-centers being spread by Urban Naxals and Congress.

The Prime Minister attacked the Congress for opposing the Citizenship Amendment Act and named few of its leaders who once supported the Act. He also quoted ex-PM Manmohan Singh's remarks in support of giving citizenship to persecuted minorities from Bangladesh.

PM Modi said that during the tenure of his government, India's relationship with Gulf countries had improved. He highlighted that Muslim countries released many Indian prisoners, and Saudi increased Hajj quota because of India's growing ties with the Islamic nations.

He appealed to people to contribute in Swachh Bharat Abhiyan and urged everyone to stop using single-use plastics. Several party leaders and karyakartas were present at the event.

SOURCE: Narendra Modi. "PM Modi Addresses a Huge Public Rally in Delhi's Ramlila Maidan." December 22, 2019. https://www.narendramodi.in/pm-modi-addresses-public-meeting-at-ramlila-maidan-in-delhi-22-dec-19-547719.

OTHER HISTORIC DOCUMENTS OF INTEREST

FROM PREVIOUS *HISTORIC DOCUMENTS*

Settlement Reached with PG&E Wildfire Victims

DECEMBER 9 AND 17, 2019

In 2017 and 2018, devastating wildfires swept through parts of California, forcing residents from their homes, destroying tens of thousands of structures, and killing dozens of people. According to state investigators, poorly maintained equipment owned by utility company Pacific Gas and Electric (PG&E) was to blame in some of the worst blazes. In December, PG&E announced that it reached a $13.5 billion settlement to compensate the victims of these fires. The announcement came on the heels of two earlier, smaller settlements with insurance providers and municipal governments, all of which were vital for the company to stay on track to emerge from Chapter 11 bankruptcy protection by June 2020.

PG&E Equipment Causes Deadly Wildfires

In 2017 and 2018, California experienced some of the most deadly and destructive wildfires ever recorded. In 2017, according to the California Department of Forestry and Fire Protection (CAL FIRE), it responded to 7,117 individual fires that burned more than 500,000 acres. The following year, it responded to 6,284 fires that burned more than 875,000 acres. During those two years, 150 individuals were killed. "Fueled by drought, an unprecedented buildup of dry vegetation and extreme winds, the size and intensity of these wildfires caused the loss of more than 100 lives, destroyed thousands of homes and exposed millions of urban and rural Californians to unhealthy air," CAL FIRE said.

One of these fires was the deadly Camp fire that started on November 8, 2018. That fire was the most expensive single natural disaster in the world in 2018 and eliminated nearly the entire town of Paradise, California. Eighty-six people were killed in the fire, and more than 13,000 homes were destroyed. According to investigations by CAL FIRE and the California Public Utilities Commission, it was PG&E's equipment that caused the blaze. The commission reported that one transmission tower in particular sparked at the origination of the fire. PG&E last climbed the tower for inspection and maintenance in 2001, contrary to its own company policy that requires regular maintenance on any equipment with recurring problems. Investigators said if adequate maintenance had been performed, the issues would have been identified and "its timely replacement could have prevented the ignition of the Camp fire." PG&E did not dispute the findings of the investigation.

PG&E Files for Bankruptcy Protection, Settles Claims

A spate of lawsuits were filed by victims, insurance companies, and local governments against PG&E related to its role in the 2018 Camp fire and various 2017 wildfires in Northern California. In turn, in January 2019, the company filed for Chapter 11 bankruptcy protection to allow it to continue operating while addressing the liabilities related to the fires. As part of the filing, the company would be required to settle claims, restructure its own organization, and propose changes to its operations with the intent of avoiding future wildfires. Each action required the approval of a bankruptcy court. The company needed to emerge from bankruptcy protection by June 2020 to qualify for coverage under a newly established state fund that would better protect utilities from losses incurred after wildfires ignited by their aging transmission lines.

The first settlement was announced in June 2019. This $1 billion agreement was entered into with eighteen cities, counties, districts, and public agencies related to claims arising from the 2017 and 2018 fires, as well as the 2015 Butte fire in Amador County (two people were killed, and around 800 homes and other structures were damaged or destroyed in that fire). In September, PG&E reached an $11 billion settlement with insurers who had already paid out claims to their customers arising from the 2017 Northern California fires and 2018 Camp fire. The company also set up a separate $105 million Wildfire Assistance Fund to help those who were displaced during the 2017 and 2018 fires and needed help with housing or other personal matters related to relocation.

PG&E ANNOUNCES VICTIM SETTLEMENT

On December 9, 2019, PG&E announced its biggest settlement of the year. It would give $13.5 billion to fire victims to compensate for any losses not otherwise covered by an insurance company. The compensation package was intended to cover claims arising from 2017 Northern California fires, the Camp fire, and the Ghost Ship fire, the latter of which was not caused by a wildfire but which in 2016 killed thirty-six people living in a warehouse in Oakland. (The families of the victims claimed faulty PG&E equipment was to blame, but that has been disputed in investigations.)

PG&E CEO Bill Johnson said in a statement that the company's goal in the settlement had been "getting wildfire victims fairly compensated, especially the individuals. . . . We want to help our customers, our neighbors and our friends in those impacted areas recover and rebuild after these tragic wildfires." He added that the company would "continue to make the needed changes to re-earn the trust and respect of our customers, our stakeholders and the public. We recognize we need to deliver safe and reliable energy service every single day—and we're determined to do just that." Robert Julian, a lawyer representing the victims, welcomed the settlement. "We are pleased that PG&E has finally admitted that the victims' losses exceed $13.5 billion, and that PG&E is responsible," he said.

Like the others before it, the settlement still needed the approval of a bankruptcy judge; the company also asked Gov. Gavin Newsom to weigh in. On December 13, 2019, Governor Newsom rejected the settlement and the company's reorganization plans submitted as part of the $13.5 billion settlement. Newsom said the plan does "not result in a reorganized company positioned to provide safe, reliable, and affordable service to its customers," adding that the settlement gave the company "limited ability to withstand future financial and operational headwinds." According to Newsom, "PG&E, as we know it, cannot persist and continue." He continued, "Everybody objectively acknowledges and agrees with that. It has to be completely transformed."

In a December 17 court hearing on the settlement, the state's attorneys said the governor did not necessarily oppose the settlement; he rather felt that it was not in line with a new state wildfire law and wanted to see additional changes from the company. The changes sought by Newsom included replacing the entire board of directors, setting aside more funds for upgrades to the company's transmission system, and a provision to make it easier for state or local governments to take over the utility and turn it into a nonprofit or customer cooperative if the company failed to meet expectations. The judge ultimately rejected Newsom's finding and allowed the $13.5 billion settlement to move forward. Victims were given until the end of the year to apply for compensation.

At the same hearing, a separate $1.675 billion settlement was proposed between the state and PG&E. This agreement would require shareholders to cover the cost of PG&E's legal fees related to fire claims, rather than its 16 million customers. The settlement would set aside around $1.625 billion for those legal fees. The remainder would go toward fire avoidance activities such as vegetation management, safety town halls, and enhanced data sharing. "We remain deeply sorry about the role our equipment had in tragic wildfires in recent years, and we apologize to all those affected. None of us wants to see another catastrophic wildfire in the communities we call home. This settlement agreement underscores our commitment to learning from the past and doing what's right for safety in the future," said Johnson. That settlement was approved, and in fact increased to $2.1 billion in early 2020. The company will next move toward submitting and seeking approval for additional restructuring plans before it is allowed to emerge from bankruptcy protection.

2019 Wildfire Season

Over the past decade, the wildfire season in California has become longer and more intense. According to CAL FIRE, climate change is a major driver. "Warmer spring and summer temperatures, reduced snowpack, and earlier spring snowmelt create longer and more intense dry seasons that increase moisture stress on vegetation and make forests more susceptible to severe wildfire," the group said. These climate change–driven issues are compounded by the Santa Ana and Diablo winds, which are not new phenomena, but with the right conditions can make wildfires even more dangerous.

Even so, as compared to the two years before it, the 2019 wildfire season in California was less destructive. According to CAL FIRE, 259,823 total acres were burned by 7,860 wildfires. Only three individuals were killed and 732 structures damaged or destroyed. The state attributed this to both pre–fire season preparation and luck. Winter and spring brought a sizeable snowpack and rainfall, which helped keep vegetation from drying out. Early in the year, fire crews undertook vegetation management, like controlled burns, brush removal, and trench digging to slow wildfire spread. Governor Newsom also approved the release of additional funds to pre-place fire teams in strategic locations once the fire season began so they could both watch for new blazes and respond promptly. Once fire season was underway, local governments were faster to order resident evacuations as fires neared, as opposed to years past when they took a wait-and-see approach, fearful of creating traffic jams that would trap people in their cars in fire zones.

Another contributing factor was fire safety plans submitted to the state by the three largest utility companies—PG&E, Southern California Edison, and San Diego Gas & Electric—that included planned blackouts. The companies felt these plans could help avoid new wildfires sparked by their equipment. The state approved these plans, and they were initially welcomed by many individuals. However, on October 26, PG&E cut power to around three million residents, some of whom were left without power for almost a week (Edison and San Diego Gas & Electric were more limited in their blackout application). Public anger grew when it became apparent that PG&E power lines, transformers, and poles may have sparked a number of the 2019 fires, including the Kincade fire, the largest of the year. Even so, PG&E stood by its decision. "The reason we do this, as we've said many times, is for public safety. We continue to believe it's the right thing to do," said Andrew Vesey, PG&E chief executive for utility operations.

—Heather Kerrigan

Following is a December 9, 2019, statement from Pacific Gas & Electric (PG&E) on its $13.5 billion proposed settlement to compensate California wildfire victims; and a December 17, 2019, announcement from the California Public Utilities Commission regarding a separate $1.675 billion agreement with PG&E related to its liability for the 2017 and 2018 wildfires.

PG&E Announces $13.5 Billion Wildfire Victim Settlement

December 9, 2019

PG&E Corporation and Pacific Gas and Electric Company (together, "PG&E") have agreed to a settlement with the Official Committee of Tort Claimants (TCC) and with firms representing individual claimants who sustained losses from the 2015 Butte Fire, 2017 Northern California Wildfires and 2018 Camp Fire. The settlement agreement is valued at approximately $13.5 billion and has the support of the TCC. The settlement will resolve all claims arising from those fires, including the 2017 Tubbs Fire as well as all claims arising from the 2016 Ghost Ship Fire in Oakland.

The settlement is subject to a number of conditions and is to be implemented pursuant to PG&E's Chapter 11 Plan of Reorganization (the "Plan"), which is subject to confirmation by the Bankruptcy Court in accordance with the provisions of the Bankruptcy Code.

Bankruptcy Court approval of the settlement agreement would put PG&E on a sustainable path forward to emerge from Chapter 11 by the June 30, 2020, deadline to participate in the State of California's go-forward wildfire fund.

"From the beginning of the Chapter 11 process, getting wildfire victims fairly compensated, especially the individuals, has been our primary goal. We want to help our customers, our neighbors and our friends in those impacted areas recover and rebuild after these tragic wildfires," said CEO and President of PG&E Corporation Bill Johnson.

"We appreciate all the hard work by many stakeholders that went into reaching this agreement. With this important milestone now accomplished, we are focused on emerging from Chapter 11 as the utility of the future that our customers and communities expect and deserve."

"There have been many calls for PG&E to change in recent years. PG&E's leadership team has heard those calls for change, and we realize we need to do even more to be a different company now and in the future. We will continue to make the needed changes to re-earn the trust and respect of our customers, our stakeholders and the public. We recognize we need to deliver safe and reliable energy service every single day—we're determined to do just that."

"Finally, we share the state's focus on helping mitigate the risk of future wildfires and we will continue to do everything we can to help reduce those risks across our system," concluded Johnson.

Previous Settlements

This new agreement is the third major settlement that PG&E has achieved in its Chapter 11 case. PG&E previously reached settlements with two other major groups of wildfire claim holders including a $1 billion settlement with cities, counties and other public entities, and an $11 billion agreement with insurance companies and other entities that have already paid insurance coverage for claims relating to the 2017 and 2018 wildfires.

PG&E's Updated Plan of Reorganization

With all major wildfire claims now on a path to be resolved and the total amount of wildfire liabilities determined, PG&E will now amend and finalize its Plan, which will satisfy all wildfire claims in accordance with Assembly Bill 1054 (AB 1054) and otherwise comply with all requirements of the Bankruptcy Code. The company remains on track to obtain regulatory approval and Bankruptcy Court confirmation of its Plan in advance of the June 30, 2020, statutory deadline set by AB 1054 for participation in the state's go-forward wildfire fund.

In addition, PG&E has received over $12 billion of equity backstop commitments to support the settlement and its Plan.

SOURCE: Pacific Gas and Electric. "In Final Major Settlement, PG&E Reaches Agreement to Resolve Individual Claims Relating to the 2017 and 2018 Wildfires and the 2015 Butte Fire; PG&E Has Now Reached Settlements with All Major Groups of Wildfire Claimants." December 9, 2019. https://www.pge .com/en/about/newsroom/newsdetails/index.page?title=20191209_in_final_major_settlement_pge_ reaches_agreement_to_resolve_individual_claims_relating_to_the_2017_and_2018_wildfires_and_ the_2015_butte_fire.

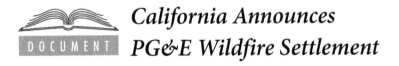

California Announces
PG&E Wildfire Settlement

December 17, 2019

The California Public Utilities Commission's (CPUC) Safety and Enforcement Division, following a months-long investigation, today filed a proposed settlement addressing issues involving the role of Pacific Gas and Electric Company's (PG&E) facilities in igniting fires in its service territory in 2017 and 2018. This includes wildfires that occurred in 2017 in Butte, Calaveras, Lake, Mendocino, Napa, Nevada, Sonoma, and Yuba Counties, and the deadly 2018 Camp Fire.

The proposed settlement is available at www.cpuc.ca.gov/wildfiresinfo under "Staff Investigations."

The proposed settlement between the CPUC's Safety and Enforcement Division, the CPUC's Office of the Safety Advocate, the California Coalition of Utility Employees

(CUE), and PG&E, prevents the utility from recovering $1.625 billion in wildfire-related costs from ratepayers and would fund an additional $50 million by PG&E shareholders in system enhancements and community engagement initiatives to strengthen its electric operations and maintenance in an effort to mitigate the risk of wildfires. This amounts to a total financial obligation by PG&E shareholders of $1.675 billion.

Today's filing sets in motion the next steps, which include review by an Administrative Law Judge, a 30-day comment period, and public review by the CPUC's Commissioners. Parties have 30 days to comment on the proposed settlement. Any final settlement must be considered and approved by the CPUC's Commissioners at a public Voting Meeting. Members of the public can comment on the proposed settlement by emailing public .advisor@cpuc.ca.gov and referring to proceeding number I.19-06-015.

The $50 million in shareholder-funded system enhancements would include vegetation management and electric operations-focused initiatives, system-wide analyses, community engagement-focused initiatives, and transparency and accountability-focused initiatives. Among other things, the initiatives would include:

- PG&E Officers conducting regular Town Hall meetings to share safety and utility service-related information with, and gather feedback from, members of the community.

- Quarterly public reporting on electric maintenance work.

- Semi-annual meetings with local government planning, public works, emergency services, and fire leadership to exchange feedback and information regarding ongoing wildfire safety activities.

- Up to $5 million in shareholder funds to the California Foundation for Independent Living Centers for a pilot program to help alleviate some disruptive impacts for, and support the safety and welfare of, vulnerable customers before, during, and after disasters and Public Safety Power Shut-off (PSPS) events.

- Funding of up to $10 million to aid in the development of non-diesel generators capable of meeting a range of use cases including (but not limited to) planned outages, unplanned outages, and temporary micro-grids for PSPS events.

The parties involved in the proposed settlement have requested expedited approval by the CPUC's Commissioners so that PG&E's Chapter 11 bankruptcy case can be resolved by June 30, 2020, enabling the utility to participate in the state's special wildfire fund to pay future wildfire claims.

The CPUC regulates services and utilities, safeguards the environment, and assures Californians' access to safe and reliable utility infrastructure and services. For more information on the CPUC, please visit www.cpuc.ca.gov.

SOURCE: California Public Utilities Commission. "CPUC Staff File Proposed $1.675 Billion Settlement after Investigation of 2017–18 Catastrophic Wildfires." December 17, 2019. http://docs.cpuc.ca.gov/PublishedDocs/Published/G000/M322/K538/322538773.PDF.

OTHER HISTORIC DOCUMENTS OF INTEREST

Ethiopian Prime Minister Awarded Nobel Peace Prize

DECEMBER 10, 2019

Since 1901, the Nobel Peace Prize has been awarded 100 times to 134 laureates, both individuals and organizations. In his will establishing the prize, Alfred Nobel outlined three types of peace work that could qualify for the award: contributions to fraternity between nations, to the abolition or reduction of standing armies, or to the holding and promotion of peace congresses. On December 10, 2019, the Nobel Committee presented the annual award to Ethiopian prime minister Abiy Ahmed. The committee praised Ahmed's implementation of domestic reforms as well as his active engagement in peace efforts across eastern and northeastern Africa—particularly Ethiopia's rapprochement with neighboring Eritrea.

AHMED RECEIVES AWARD FOR PEACE DEAL WITH ERITREA

The Nobel Committee reported that it considered the nominations of 304 candidates for the 2019 peace prize, of which 223 were individuals and 78 were organizations. Although the names of the nominees are not officially made public until fifty years after the award is presented, nominating entities sometimes reveal the names of their favored candidates, and bookmakers around the globe frequently publicize the odds of potential recipients. Leading contenders for the 2019 award were predicted to include Ahmed; teenage climate activist Greta Thunberg; New Zealand prime minister Jacinda Ardern; Reporters without Borders; Greek prime minister Alexis Tsipras; North Macedonian prime minister Zoran Zaev; and Raoni Metuktire, the chief of an indigenous Brazilian tribe and environmental activist working to protect the Amazon.

On October 11, 2019, Berit Reiss-Andersen, the chair of the Norwegian Nobel Committee, announced the 2019 Nobel Peace Prize would be awarded to Ahmed "for his efforts to achieve peace and international cooperation, and in particular for his decisive initiative to resolve the border conflict with neighbouring Eritrea." The announcement explained the prize was "meant to recognize all the stakeholders working for peace and reconciliation in Ethiopia and in the East and Northeast African regions" and noted Ahmed's active contributions to these "peace and reconciliation processes." Highlighted efforts included Ahmed's participation in the normalization of diplomatic relations between Eritrea and Djibouti, assistance in mediating talks between Kenya and Somalia over disputed maritime territory, and "key role" in Sudan's drafting of a new constitution "intended to secure a peaceful transition to civil rule." The committee further praised Ahmed for seeking to "promote reconciliation, solidarity, and social justice" among Ethiopia's ethnic groups and initiating "important reforms that give many citizens hope for a better life and a brighter future," such as releasing thousands of political prisoners, reducing media censorship, and lifting the state of emergency imposed by his predecessor,

Prime Minister Hailemariam Desalegn. The Nobel Committee acknowledged that "much work remains in Ethiopia," with challenges including escalating ethnic strife, but said that Ahmed was "the person who in the preceding year has done the most to deserve the Nobel Peace Prize for 2019."

Award Decision Questioned by Human Rights Groups, Other Observers

Ending Ethiopia's violent twenty-year dispute with Eritrea and reestablishing relations between the two neighbor countries was one of Ahmed's most significant early accomplishments as prime minister. On June 5, 2018, Ahmed agreed to "fully accept and implement" the terms of a peace agreement reached in 2000, following a nasty two-year war that killed roughly 80,000 people. Although Ethiopia had signed the treaty at the end of the war, its government had refused to recognize an international boundary commission's ruling on disputed border territory and maintained a troop presence in areas the commission said belonged to Eritrea. "No war, no peace" between the two countries meant they did not maintain a trade or transport relationship, nor did they engage diplomatically. By finally accepting all of the treaty's terms, Ethiopia also agreed to grant certain border lands to Eritrea and withdraw its troops. The Nobel Committee deemed Ahmed's acceptance of the commission's ruling "an important premise for the breakthrough" in Ethiopia–Eritrea relations. Ahmed and Eritrean president Isaias Afeworki officially declared an end of hostilities on July 9, 2018. The two countries subsequently reopened their respective embassies and their land border, restored flights, and allowed direct phone calls between their citizens. The easing of tensions with Ethiopia, and later the government of Somalia, in turn prompted the United Nations (UN) Security Council to lift sanctions on Eritrea in November 2018.

Ahmed had also moved quickly to accelerate initial reform efforts in Ethiopia upon becoming prime minister in April 2018, following the embattled Desalegn's resignation. In addition to the domestic accomplishments highlighted by the Nobel Committee, Ahmed invited opposition leaders to return from exile, welcomed UN High Commissioner for Human Rights Zeid Ra'ad al-Hussein back to Ethiopia, fired senior prison officials for alleged human rights abuses, streamlined cabinet-level positions and named new ministers, and promised to hold free and competitive elections in 2020.

However, some human rights groups, activists, and other observers questioned whether Ahmed deserved the peace prize, with many critics noting the peace deal with Eritrea had not been fully implemented. Human Rights Watch (HRW) was among the organizations reporting that daily life had not changed for Eritreans. "Eritrea's borders remain closed, the border between the two countries has not been demarcated, and the exodus of Eritreans fleeing the brutal restrictions imposed by their government continues," HRW said in a statement. In one example, the group cited the government's continued conscription of many Eritreans into permanent military service—a program officials had claimed was necessary due to ongoing border disputes with Ethiopia. Others reported that Ethiopians crossing the border, often while transporting construction materials or other goods, had been arrested without explanation and in some cases had been beaten. The border demarcation process has also been slow to progress, and Eritrea has reportedly reclosed parts of the border it had opened after the peace deal was announced.

Ethiopia was also in the midst of an uptick in ethnic unrest. A fresh wave of protests started two weeks after the Nobel Committee's announcement after a prominent political activist and opponent of Ahmed's claimed the police—possibly with the prime minister's consent—had tried to facilitate an attack against him. At least sixty-seven people were killed in protest-related violence before the activist called for calm. Ahmed was criticized for not cutting short a trip to Russia (he was attending a summit of African leaders) to return to Ethiopia and for not responding to the violence at home for several days.

The Nobel Committee sought to acknowledge such concerns in its prize announcement. "No doubt some people will think this year's prize is being awarded too early," the announcement read. "The Norwegian Nobel Committee believes it is now that Abiy Ahmed's efforts deserve recognition and need encouragement. The Norwegian Nobel Committee hopes that the Nobel Peace Prize will strengthen Prime Minister Abiy in his important work for peace and reconciliation."

Some observers also took note that the Nobel Committee had declined to award the 2019 Nobel Peace Prize to Eritrea's Afeworki as well as to Ahmed. (In some years, the peace prize has been awarded to multiple individuals, such as in 2018 when Denis Mukwege, a gynecological surgeon from the Democratic Republic of the Congo, and Nadia Murad, an Iraqi woman forced into sexual slavery by the Islamic State of Iraq and the Levant, won for their respective work to end the use of sexual violence as a weapon of war.) At the same time, analysts said Afeworki's exclusion was unsurprising given that he leads a repressive military dictatorship and has been accused by the UN of "systematic, widespread and gross human rights violations." The Nobel Committee did appear to acknowledge Afeworki in the prize announcement, stating, "Peace does not arise from the actions of one party alone. When Prime Minister Abiy reached out his hand, President Afwerki grasped it, and helped to formalise the peace process between the two countries."

AHMED OUTLINES HIS VISION OF PEACE

After receiving the peace prize during a ceremony in Oslo on December 10, Ahmed delivered his Nobel lecture. He began by accepting the award "on behalf of Ethiopians and Eritreans, especially those who made the ultimate sacrifice in the cause of peace." Ahmed also acknowledged "my partner, and comrade-in-peace, President Isaias Afeworki, whose goodwill, trust, and commitment were vital in ending the two-decade deadlock between our countries."

Ahmed then reflected on his experience as a young soldier in Ethiopia, describing one battle that left him the only surviving member of his military unit. "War is the epitome of hell for all involved," he said. "I know because I have been there and back." Ahmed spoke about the tremendous cost of the conflict between Ethiopia and Eritrea, not just in terms of casualties but the "untold numbers of families broken." The conflict "permanently shattered communities on both sides," he said. "Massive destruction of infrastructure further amplified the post-war economic burden. Socially, the war resulted in mass displacements, loss of livelihoods, deportation and denationalization of citizens."

Ahmed said that he and Afeworki had been able to achieve peace because "we understood our nations are not the enemies. Instead, we were victims of the common enemy called poverty." He and Afeworki "recognized that while our two nations were stuck on old grievances, the world was shifting rapidly and leaving us behind. We agreed we must work cooperatively for the prosperity of our people and our region." Ahmed declared, "Today, we are reaping our peace dividends," as families are reunited, diplomatic relations are restored, and air and telecommunications services are reestablished. The prime minister said he and Afeworki were also focusing on joint infrastructure projects "that will be a critical lever in our economic ambitions."

Ahmed said he viewed peace as "a labor of love" and something that must be nurtured. He likened the process of achieving and sustaining peace to planting trees. "Just like trees need water and good soil to grow, peace requires unwavering commitment, infinite patience, and goodwill to cultivate and harvest its dividends. Peace requires good faith to blossom into prosperity, security, and opportunity." He added that peace can be cultivated and shared with others "if we choose to remove our masks of pride and arrogance. When our love for humanity outgrows our appreciation of human vanity then the world will know peace." He further explained that his vision of peace is rooted in the philosophy of Medemer, which "signifies synergy, convergence, and teamwork for a common destiny." Ahmed said he thinks of Medemer as a social compact for Ethiopians to "build a just, egalitarian, democratic, and human society" by combining resources to achieve collective survival and prosperity. "I truly believe peace is a way of life," he said. "War, a form of death and destruction."

ADDITIONAL NOBEL AWARDEES

The Nobel Prize is also given out in the categories of physiology or medicine, physics, chemistry, literature, and economic sciences. In the physiology or medicine category, the award was given jointly to William G. Kaelin Jr., Sir Peter J. Ratcliffe, and Gregg L. Semenza for discovering how cells can sense and adapt to changing oxygen availability. The Nobel Prize in Physics was split between James Peebles, who was recognized for his contributions to the field of physical cosmology, and Michel Mayor and Didier Queloz, who jointly discovered an exoplanet (a planet outside our solar system) orbiting a solar-type star within the Milky Way galaxy. The chemistry prize was awarded to John B. Goodenough, M. Stanley Whittingham, and Akira Yoshino for their contributions to the development of the first lithium-ion battery. Two Nobel Prizes in Literature were awarded. The 2018 prize was given to Olga Tokarczuk, a Polish author recognized by the committee "for a narrative imagination that with encyclopedic passion represents the crossing of boundaries as a form of life." (Announcement of the 2018 prize had been postponed by the Swedish Academy, a panel of writers and scholars responsible for awarding the Nobel Prize in Literature, following a sexual assault scandal involving an academy member's spouse.) The 2019 literature prize went to Austrian author Peter Handke "for an influential work that with linguistic ingenuity has explored the periphery and the specificity of human experience." The economic sciences prize, established in 1968, was given to Abhijit Banerjee, Esther Duflo, and Michael Kremer for developing experimental research methods to better understand and alleviate global poverty.

—Linda Grimm

Following is the Nobel lecture delivered by Ethiopian president Abiy Ahmed on December 10, 2019, upon being awarded the Nobel Peace Prize.

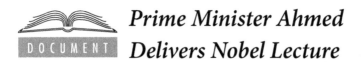

Prime Minister Ahmed
Delivers Nobel Lecture

December 10, 2019

Your Majesties, Your Royal Highnesses,

Distinguished members of the Norwegian Nobel Committee,

Fellow Ethiopians, Fellow Africans, Citizens of the World

Ladies and Gentlemen,

I am honored to be here with you, and deeply grateful to the Norwegian Nobel Committee for recognizing and encouraging my contribution to a peaceful resolution of the border dispute between Ethiopia and Eritrea.

I accept this award on behalf of Ethiopians and Eritreans, especially those who made the ultimate sacrifice in the cause of peace. Likewise, I accept this award on behalf of my partner, and comrade-in-peace, President Isaias Afeworki, whose goodwill, trust, and commitment were vital in ending the two-decade deadlock between our countries. I also accept this award on behalf of Africans and citizens of the world for whom the dream of peace has often turned into a nightmare of war.

Today, I stand here in front of you talking about peace because of fate. I crawled my way to peace through the dusty trenches of war years ago. I was a young soldier when war broke out between Ethiopia and Eritrea. I witnessed firsthand the ugliness of war in front-line battles.

There are those who have never seen war but glorify and romanticize it.

They have not seen the fear,

They have not seen the fatigue,

They have not seen the destruction or heartbreak,

Nor have they felt the mournful emptiness of war after the carnage.

War is the epitome of hell for all involved. I know because I have been there and back. I have seen brothers slaughtering brothers on the battlefield. I have seen older men, women, and children trembling in terror under the deadly shower of bullets and artillery shells.

You see, I was not only a combatant in war. I was also a witness to its cruelty and what it can do to people. War makes for bitter men. Heartless and savage men.

Twenty years ago, I was a radio operator attached to an Ethiopian army unit in the border town of Badme. The town was the flashpoint of the war between the two countries. I briefly left the foxhole in the hopes of getting a good antenna reception. It took only but a few minutes. Yet, upon my return, I was horrified to discover that my entire unit had been wiped out in an artillery attack. I still remember my young comrades-in-arms who died on that ill-fated day. I think of their families too.

During the war between Ethiopia and Eritrea, an estimated one hundred thousand soldiers and civilians lost their lives. The aftermath of the war also left untold numbers of families broken. It also permanently shattered communities on both sides. Massive destruction of infrastructure further amplified the post-war economic burden. Socially, the war resulted in mass displacements, loss of livelihoods, deportation and denationalization of citizens.

Following the end of active armed conflict in June 2000, Ethiopia and Eritrea remained deadlocked in a stalemate of no-war, no-peace for two decades. During this period, family units were split over borders, unable to see or talk to each other for years to come. Tens of thousands of troops remained stationed along both sides of the border. They remained on edge, as did the rest of the country and region. All were worried that any small border clash would flare into a full-blown war once again.

As it was, the war and the stalemate that followed were a threat for regional peace, with fears that a resumption of active combat between Ethiopia and Eritrea would destabilize the entire Horn region.

And so, when I became Prime Minister about 18 months ago, I felt in my heart that ending the uncertainty was necessary. I believed peace between Ethiopia and Eritrea was within reach. I was convinced that the imaginary wall separating our two countries for much too long needed to be torn down. And in its place, a bridge of friendship, collaboration and goodwill has to be built to last for ages.

That is how I approached the task of building a peace bridge with my partner President Isaias Afeworki.

We were both ready to allow peace to flourish and shine through. We resolved to turn our "swords into plowshares and our spears into pruning hooks" for the progress and prosperity of our people. We understood our nations are not the enemies. Instead, we were victims of the common enemy called poverty. We recognized that while our two nations were stuck on old grievances, the world was shifting rapidly and leaving us behind. We agreed we must work cooperatively for the prosperity of our people and our region.

Excellencies, Ladies and Gentlemen,

Today, we are reaping our peace dividends. Families separated for over two decades are now united. Diplomatic relations are fully restored. Air and telecommunication services have been reestablished. And our focus has now shifted to developing joint infrastructure projects that will be a critical lever in our economic ambitions. Our commitment to peace between our two countries is iron-clad.

One may wonder, how it is that a conflict extending over twenty years, can come to an amicable resolution. Allow me to share with you a little about the beliefs that guide my actions for peace.

I believe that peace is an affair of the heart. Peace is a labor of love.

Sustaining peace is hard work. Yet, we must cherish and nurture it.

It takes a few to make war, but it takes a village and a nation to build peace.

For me, nurturing peace is like planting and growing trees. Just like trees need water and good soil to grow, peace requires unwavering commitment, infinite patience, and goodwill to cultivate and harvest its dividends. Peace requires good faith to blossom into prosperity, security, and opportunity.

In the same manner that trees absorb carbon dioxide to give us life and oxygen, peace has the capacity to absorb the suspicion and doubt that may cloud our relationships. In return, it gives back hope for the future, confidence in ourselves, and faith in humanity.

This humanity I speak of, is within all of us. We can cultivate and share it with others if we choose to remove our masks of pride and arrogance. When our love for humanity outgrows our appreciation of human vanity then the world will know peace.

Ultimately, peace requires an enduring vision. And my vision of peace is rooted in the philosophy of Medemer. Medemer, an Amharic word, signifies synergy, convergence, and teamwork for a common destiny. Medemer is a homegrown idea that is reflected in our political, social, and economic life.

I like to think of "Medemer" as a social compact for Ethiopians to build a just, egalitarian, democratic, and humane society by pulling together our resources for our collective survival and prosperity.

In practice, Medemer is about using the best of our past to build a new society and a new civic culture that thrives on tolerance, understanding, and civility.

At its core, Medemer is a covenant of peace that seeks unity in our common humanity. It pursues peace by practicing the values of love, forgiveness, reconciliation, and inclusion.

Excellencies, Ladies and Gentlemen,

I come from a small town called Beshasha, located in the Oromia region of Western Ethiopia. It is in Beshasha that the seeds of Medemer began to sprout. Growing up, my parents instilled in me and my siblings, an abiding faith in humanity. Medemer resonates with the proverb, "I am my brother's keeper. I am my sister's keeper." In my little town, we had no running water, electricity, or paved roads. But we had a lot of love to light up our lives. We were each other's keepers. Faith, humility, integrity, patience, gratitude, tenacity, and cooperation coursed like a mighty stream. And we traveled together on three country roads called love, forgiveness, and reconciliation.

In the Medemer idea, there is no "Us and Them." There is only "US" for "We" are all bound by a shared destiny of love, forgiveness, and reconciliation. For the people in the "Land of Origins" and "The 13 Months of Sunshine," Medemer has always been second nature.

Ethiopians maintained peaceful coexistence between the followers of the two great religions because we always came together in faith and worship.

We, Ethiopians, remained independent for thousands of years because we came together to defend our homeland.

The beauty of our Ethiopia is its extraordinary diversity. The inclusiveness of Medemer ensures no one is left behind in our big extended family.

It has also been said, "No man is an island." Just the same, no nation is an island. Ethiopia's Medemer-inspired foreign policy pursues peace through multilateral cooperation and good neighborliness.

We have an old saying: "yoo ollaan nagayaan bule, nagaan bulanni." It is a saying shared in many African languages, which means, "For you to have a peaceful night, your neighbor shall have a peaceful night as well."

The essence of this proverb guides the strengthening of relations in the region. We now strive to live with our neighbors in peace and harmony.

The Horn of Africa today is a region of strategic significance. The global military superpowers are expanding their military presence in the area. Terrorist and extremist groups also seek to establish a foothold. We do not want the Horn to be a battleground for superpowers nor a hideout for the merchants of terror and brokers of despair and misery. We want the Horn of Africa to become a treasury of peace and progress. Indeed, we want the Horn of Africa to become the Horn of Plenty for the rest of the continent.

Excellencies, Ladies and Gentlemen,

As a global community, we must invest in peace. Over the past few months, Ethiopia has made historic investments in peace, the returns of which we will see in years to come. We have released all political prisoners. We have shut down detention facilities where torture and vile human rights abuses took place. Today, Ethiopia is highly regarded for press freedom. It is no more a "jailor of journalists." Opposition leaders of all political stripes are free to engage in peaceful political activity. We are creating an Ethiopia that is second to none in its guarantee of freedoms of expression. We have laid the groundwork for genuine multiparty democracy, and we will soon hold a free and fair election.

I truly believe peace is a way of life. War, a form of death and destruction. Peacemakers must teach peace breakers to choose the way of life. To that end, we must help build a world culture of peace.

But before there is peace in the world, there must be peace in the heart and mind. There must be peace in the family, in the neighborhood, in the village, and the towns and cities. There must be peace in and among nations.

Excellencies, ladies, and gentlemen: There is a big price for enduring peace.

A famous protest slogan that proclaims, "No justice, no peace," calls to mind that peace thrives and bears fruit when planted in the soil of justice.

The disregard for human rights has been the source of much strife and conflict in the world. The same holds in our continent, Africa.

It is estimated that some 70 percent of Africa's population is under the age of 30. Our young men and women are crying out for social and economic justice. They demand equality of opportunity and an end to organized corruption. The youth insist on good governance based on accountability and transparency. If we deny our youth justice, they will reject peace.

Standing on this world stage today, I would like to call upon all my fellow Ethiopians to join hands and help build a country that offers equal justice, equal rights, and equal opportunities for all its citizens.

I would like to especially express that we should avoid the path of extremism and division, powered by politics of exclusion.

Our accord hangs in the balance of inclusive politics.

The evangelists of hate and division are wreaking havoc in our society using social media. They are preaching the gospel of revenge and retribution on the airwaves.

Together, we must neutralize the toxin of hatred by creating a civic culture of consensus-based democracy, inclusivity, civility, and tolerance based on Medemer principles.

The art of building peace is a synergistic process to change hearts, minds, beliefs and attitudes, that never ceases.

It is like the work of struggling farmers in my beloved Ethiopia. Each season they prepare the soil, sow seeds, pull weeds, and control pests. They work the fields from dawn to dusk in good and bad weather. The seasons change, but their work never ends. In the end, they harvest the abundance of their fields.

Before we can harvest peace dividends, we must plant seeds of love, forgiveness, and reconciliation in the hearts and minds of our citizens. We must pull out the weeds of discord, hate, and misunderstanding and toil every day during good and bad days too.

I am inspired by a Biblical Scripture which reads: "Blessed are the peacemakers, for they shall be called the children of God."

Equally I am also inspired by a Holy Quran verse which reads: "Humanity is but a single Brotherhood. So, make peace with your Brethren."

I am committed to toil for peace every single day and in all seasons.

I am my brother's keeper. I am my sister's keeper too.

I have promises to keep before I sleep. I have miles to go on the road of peace.

As I conclude, I call upon the international community to join me and my fellow Ethiopians in our Medemer-inspired efforts of building enduring peace and prosperity in the Horn of Africa. . . .

I thank you!

SOURCE: The Nobel Foundation. "Forging a Durable Peace in the Horn of Africa." December 10, 2019. © The Nobel Foundation. https://www.nobelprize.org/prizes/peace/2019/abiy/109716-lecture-english.

OTHER HISTORIC DOCUMENTS OF INTEREST

FROM THIS VOLUME

FROM PREVIOUS HISTORIC DOCUMENTS

U.S. Leaders Remark on Iraq Embassy Attack and Airstrikes

DECEMBER 30 AND 31, 2019

In October 2019, Iraqis rallied across their country, speaking out against endemic corruption, high unemployment, dire public services, and foreign interference from Iran. Those protests—and the government's subsequent crackdown—forced the prime minister to resign, but demonstrators continued to advocate for deeper political change and an end to foreign influence in domestic politics. In late December 2019, Iraqis, upset over foreign influence in their country, stormed past security forces and broke into the heavily guarded compound of the U.S. embassy in Baghdad. American officials responded swiftly to the embassy attack. Defense officials announced the United States would shift additional forces to the region and launch additional airstrikes in Iraq and Syria against the Iranian-backed Iraqi military.

PROTESTS ERUPT ACROSS IRAQ CALLING FOR POLITICAL CHANGE

On October 1, 2019, violent protests erupted across Iraq as demonstrators poured into the streets, angered by poor public services, rampant corruption, and high unemployment. The protests were sparked by a decision by the prime minister to remove the popular counterterrorism chief, but the ouster ignited tensions that had simmered for months. The unrest lasted several days and amounted to the largest display of public anger at Prime Minister Adel Abdul Mahdi and his cabinet since they took office a year earlier.

The situation escalated overnight. The government took drastic measures to bring the mass demonstrations under control, imposing a curfew, shutting down the Internet to make it more difficult for protesters to organize, and dispatching additional security forces to the capital. As demonstrators marched from Baghdad's Tahrir Square to the Green Zone, Iraqi security forces opened fire, killing fourteen. The government's response fueled additional anger, sparking new protests outside of the capital and drawing international condemnation. As protests spread outside of Baghdad to the country's southern and central provinces, Mahdi convened a national security meeting and released statements underscoring his support for both the protesters' "legitimate concerns" and for the security forces trying to keep order. Amid the pressure, Mahdi promised to reshuffle his cabinet and launch efforts to reduce unemployment.

Protests continued throughout the fall, and at least 400 people were killed in the demonstrations against the Iraqi government. The ongoing protests, the government's response, and the prime minister's refusal to call new elections put intense pressure on Mahdi to resign, which he did in late November.

UNITED STATES LAUNCHES AIRSTRIKES IN IRAQ AGAINST IRANIAN-BACKED GROUPS

As the political crisis in Iraq deepened, the tug-of-war between the United States and Iran spilled into public view. After an American contractor was killed in a rocket attack in Iraq, American officials retaliated with airstrikes against five targets in Iraq and Syria controlled by an Iranian-backed paramilitary group, Kataib Hezbollah. Twenty-four were killed. The retaliation involved direct strikes on Iranian proxies, an escalation over previous American retaliations and a shift in how the United States had been operating in Iraq.

American officials, speaking at a press briefing after the attacks, said the airstrikes were a "decisive response" to "weeks and weeks" of Iranian-backed aggression that had put Americans at risk. "Today, what we did was take a decisive response that makes clear what President Trump has said for months and months and months, which is that we will not stand for the Islamic Republic of Iran to take actions that put American men and women in jeopardy," Secretary of State Mike Pompeo said. "We will always honor that commitment to take decisive action when that takes place, and we continue to demand that the Islamic Republic of Iran act in a way that is consistent with what I laid out, back in May of 2018, for what it is that we expect Iran to do so that it can rejoin the community of nations," Pompeo concluded.

Secretary of Defense Mark Esper echoed Secretary Pompeo's comments. "The Department of Defense took offensive actions in defense of our personnel and interests in Iraq by launching F-15 Strike Eagles against five targets associated with Kata'ib Hezbollah, which is an Iranian-sponsored Shiite militia group. The targets we attacked included three targets in Western Iraq and two targets in Eastern Syria that were either command and control facilities or weapons caches for Kata'ib Hezbollah," Esper explained. "The strikes were successful." Esper also stated that he and Secretary Pompeo discussed with President Donald Trump the option of future attacks. "In our discussion today with the President, we discussed with him other options that are available. And I would note also that we will take additional actions as necessary to ensure that we act in our own self-defense and we deter further bad behavior from militia groups or from Iran," Esper explained.

Senior Department of State officials, speaking anonymously to discuss in-depth strategy, framed the president's decision to launch airstrikes as a defensive action meant to deter Iranian aggression. "We are not looking for any conflict in the Middle East. These were defensive strikes. But we are not going to let Iran get away with using a proxy force to attack American interests, and we will hold Iran accountable for these attacks, which we have done," one official said. The same official said the airstrikes were meant to support Iraqi demonstrators. "We are standing with the Iraqi people. You've seen the protests in Iraq. They are tired of the corruption from the political class," that official continued. "What we are also seeing regionally—the protests in Iran, the protests in Iraq, and the protests in Lebanon are a consistent rejection of the Iranian model of undermining sovereignty, endemic corruption, weaponizing sectarian grievances, and destabilizing the region broadly."

The senior officials also warned other nations, primarily Russia, not to support Iran. "Now is not the time for governments to be doing any sort of military exercises with this regime. We think now is the time to be sanctioning the Iranian leadership for the human rights abuses that it has committed against its own people and to be diplomatically isolating the regime in every way possible," an official said. The official also cautioned Iran or its proxies against escalating the conflict. "If there's any further escalation, it lies directly at the feet of Iran's proxies in Iraq, not on us," the official said.

PROTESTERS STORM THE U.S. EMBASSY

The airstrikes sparked one of the most serious political crises in years for the United States in Iraq, stoking anti-Americanism and turning the focus from Iran's influence in local politics to America's. The American airstrikes put Washington squarely in the focus of public hostility and reduced the attention on Tehran and its proxies almost overnight. Iraqi leaders accused the United States of violating their state's sovereignty and worried that increasing tensions could escalate into a proxy war between the United States and Iran on Iraqi soil.

The crisis reached its peak two days after the strikes when protesters broke into the U.S. embassy in Baghdad and set fires inside the compound. Thousands of protesters, including some militia members from Kataib Hezbollah and other fighters overseen by the Iraqi military, swarmed the Green Zone and the U.S. embassy, breaching the fortified compound's outside walls. The protesters withdrew quickly and did not enter the main embassy buildings but joined thousands of demonstrators outside of the compound. The crowd, chanting "Death to America," demanded that the United States remove its forces from Iraq and vowed to camp indefinitely outside of the compound. American personnel, including U.S. ambassador Matt Tueller, were safe, and there were no plans to evacuate the embassy, the Department of State announced.

The embassy attack was unlike previous demonstrations against either the United States or Iran. Experts believed that the demonstrators had received some sort of permission from Iraqi security officials because of their ability to breach the walls of one of the most heavily guarded zones in the Middle East. Others argued that the presence of protesters and militia members in the fortified Green Zone underscored Iran's continued ability to exert a powerful influence over the Iraqi government and the host government's inability to control the militias. Still others believed that the limited scope of the attack—protesters were not in the compound for long, did not reach the main embassy structures, and did not clash directly with American forces or personnel—revealed that the government may have allowed the militias to vent their frustrations with the United States with minimal damage.

U.S. GOVERNMENT OFFICIALS RESPOND

American officials responded quickly to the embassy attack. Esper announced that the United States was taking measures to secure American personnel in the region. "We have taken appropriate force protection actions to ensure the safety of American citizens, military personnel and diplomats in country, and to ensure our right of self-defense," Esper said. Esper also announced that the United States had deployed additional forces to the region and called on the Iraqi government to help secure American personnel. "As in all countries, we rely on host nation forces to assist in the protection of our personnel in country, and we call on the Government of Iraq to fulfill its international responsibilities to do so. The United States continues to support the Iraqi people and a free, sovereign, and prosperous Iraq," he said.

President Trump immediately laid blame for the protests with Iran. "Iran killed an American contractor, wounding many. We strongly responded, and always will," Trump said. "Now Iran is orchestrating an attack on the U.S. Embassy in Iraq. They will be held fully responsible. In addition, we expect Iraq to use its forces to protect the Embassy, and so notified!" The statements from both Trump and Esper raised fears of a proxy war between the United States and Iran on Iraqi soil. Even as tensions gradually eased over the coming weeks, the episode punctuated how close the region was to armed conflict and highlighted how Iraq, wracked by months of protests, crippled by political paralysis and without a prime minister, threatened by renewed terrorism, and squeezed between two regional powers, maintained only a tenuous hold on peace within its own state.

—Robert Howard

Following is the text of a press briefing by Secretary of State Mike Pompeo and Secretary of Defense Mark Esper on December 30, 2019, responding to protests at the U.S. embassy in Iraq; a December 30, 2019, press briefing from senior State Department officials on U.S. airstrikes in Iraq and Syria; and a December 31, 2019, statement by Secretary Esper on operations to defend U.S. personnel in Iraq.

Secretaries of State and Defense Address Protests near U.S. Embassy in Iraq

December 30, 2019

SECRETARY POMPEO: Good evening. Myself, with Secretary Esper, Chairman of the Joint Chiefs of Staff Milley, came here to Florida today to brief the President on the activities that have taken place in the Middle East over the course of the last 72 hours.

I will leave to Secretary Esper to talk about the military activity, but I want to put it in the context of our policy with respect to the Islamic Republic of Iran. The attacks that took place against an Iraqi facility threatened American forces. This has been going on now for weeks and weeks and weeks. This wasn't the first set of attacks against this particular Iraqi facility and others where there were American lives at risk.

And today, what we did was take a decisive response that makes clear what President Trump has said for months and months and months, which is that we will not stand for the Islamic Republic of Iran to take actions that put American men and women in jeopardy.

We will—we will always honor that commitment to take decisive action when that takes place, and we continue to demand that the Islamic Republic of Iran act in a way that is consistent with what I laid out, back in May of 2018, for what it is that we expect Iran to do so that it can rejoin the community of nations.

And with that, I'll turn it over to the Secretary of Defense.

SECRETARY ESPER: Thank you. As we reported earlier today, the Department of Defense took offensive actions in defense of our personnel and interests in Iraq by launching F-15 Strike Eagles against five targets associated with Kata'ib Hezbollah, which is an Iranian-sponsored Shiite militia group. The targets we attacked included three targets in Western Iraq and two targets in Eastern Syria that were either command and control facilities or weapons caches for Kata'ib Hezbollah.

The strikes were successful. The pilots and aircraft returned back to base safely. I would add that, in our discussion today with the President, we discussed with him other options that are available. And I would note also that we will take additional actions as necessary to ensure that we act in our own self-defense and we deter further bad behavior from militia groups or from Iran. Thank you.

SOURCE: U.S. Embassy and Consulates in Iraq. "Press Briefing by Secretary of State Mike Pompeo and Secretary of Defense Mark Esper." December 30, 2019. https://iq.usembassy.gov/press-briefing-by-secretary-of-state-mike-pompeo-and-secretary-of-defense-mark-esper.

State Department Officials Discuss Airstrikes in Iraq and Syria

December 30, 2019

MODERATOR: Hey, everybody. Thanks for joining us. Happy New Year, happy 2020. I have a couple of people that all of you know very well. On the phone, we have [Senior State Department Official One], [Senior State Department Official Two], and we have [Senior State Department Official Three]. We will, of course, allow for time for question and answers.

And I think what I'm going to do is just turn it over right away to [Senior State Department Official One] and let him give some opening statements. But if you have specific questions on Syria, we have [Senior State Department Official Two], and we have [Senior State Department Official Three] for Iraq questions. And of course, [Senior State Department Official One] can answer everything Iran-related.

Okay, [Senior State Department Official One].

SENIOR STATE DEPARTMENT OFFICIAL ONE: All right, sorry, it was on mute. Thank you, [Moderator], and thanks everybody for joining us. I think it's essential to understand that the strikes that the President ordered yesterday, those are—it was a defensive action designed to protect American forces and American citizens in Iraq, but it is also aimed at deterring Iran.

It is clear that under the nuclear deal, Iran was able to run and finance an expansionist foreign policy, and we are trying to restore deterrence against Iran's regional aggression, against its missile proliferation around the region that finds its way into conflicts, as we have seen recently in Iraq. In the past two months alone, there have been 11 attacks on Iraqi bases that host coalition forces. And then the most recent attack, which was a barrage of rockets on the base near Kirkuk, killed one U.S. citizen and injured American and Iraqi soldiers.

So President Trump and Secretary Pompeo have been making clear for some time now that we will not tolerate this sort of behavior, not tolerate attacks on U.S. citizens, its military, or our allies. And it was just a few weeks ago that Secretary Pompeo, on December 13th, said—he reminded "Iran's leaders that any attacks by them, or their proxies . . . that harm Americans, our allies, or our interests will be answered with a decisive U.S. response."

That was delivered yesterday. And it shows that the President has done a very good job of balancing and calibrating our diplomatic efforts in terms of our foreign policy in Iran, Iraq, Syria, and also backing that up with the hard power.

And we are not looking for any conflict in the Middle East. These were defensive strikes. But we are not going to let Iran get away with using a proxy force to an attack—to attack American interests, and we will hold Iran accountable for these attacks, which we have done.

We are standing with the Iraqi people. You've seen the protests in Iraq. They are tired of the corruption from the political class. You have Iraqi soldiers and American soldiers who have fought and died for a sovereign and independent Iraq, and the Iraqi protesters are demanding it. And that's why we support their demands. They do not want to see Iraq fall under the domination or the influence of the ayatollah and his cronies, Qasem Soleimani and others.

What we are also seeing regionally—the protests in Iran, the protests in Iraq, and the protests in Lebanon are a consistent rejection of the Iranian model of undermining sovereignty, endemic corruption, weaponizing sectarian grievances, and destabilizing the region broadly. And so—since May of 2018, I would refer you to Secretary Pompeo's speech in May of 2018. He also said that all Iranian-commanded forces must leave Syria. And it's important to recognize that the strikes were conducted not only in Iraq but also in Syria, and I'd like to have [Senior State Department Official Two] speak a little bit about that.

SENIOR STATE DEPARTMENT OFFICIAL TWO: Sure. As [Senior State Department Official One] just said, it's been longstanding U.S. policy, reiterated by the President to Congress, Mike Pompeo, and the rest of us many times publicly, that all Iranian-commanded forces—which would include, in our view, KH—leave Syria. They are a threat to our interests and to those of many of our partners and allies in the region.

Secondly, we have seen attacks by Iranian-supported or Assad-supported elements against American or coalition forces or our partners on the battlefield, the SDF, repeatedly since 2017 inside Syria. Finally, we do see threat streams and threatening activities by all of these forces that are of concern to us from a force protection standpoint.

But lastly, again, as [Senior State Department Official One] indicated, this shows that we can respond not just in Iraq, but we can respond anywhere that we think it makes sense to us and to the interests and security of our partners and allies in dealing with this threat to the region.

Thank you.

MODERATOR: [Senior State Department Official Three.]

SENIOR STATE DEPARTMENT OFFICIAL THREE: I have nothing to add. Excuse me.

MODERATOR: All right. So now we have some time for some questions. We're going to just pause for a moment while everyone queues up.

OPERATOR: And ladies and gentlemen, as a reminder, if you do have a question, please press 1 then 0 on your touchtone phone. You'll hear a tone indicating you've been placed in queue. You may remove yourself from the queue by repeating the 1 then 0 command. If you are using a speakerphone, please pick up your handset before pressing any buttons.

Again, if you have questions, please press 1 then 0 on your touchtone phone at this time. One moment, please, for our first question.

MODERATOR: For our first question, can you open the line of Kim Dozier?

OPERATOR: One moment, please.

QUESTION: (Inaudible) there was also a report that the Iraqi prime minister, the for-mer—resigned prime minister, asked the U.S. not to go ahead with these strikes. How do you respond to that, and what do you fear they might do?

SENIOR STATE DEPARTMENT OFFICIAL THREE: Kim, it's always a pleasure to hear from you, but I didn't hear the first part of the—this is [Senior State Department Official Three] by the way. I did not hear the first part of your question.

QUESTION: Trying again. Kim Dozier at *Time* asking—there were reports that the for-mer Iraqi prime minister had asked the U.S. not to go ahead with these strikes, and now Iraqi officials are vaguely warning of some sort of consequences. What do you fear those consequences might be, and why did you go ahead with the strikes?

SENIOR STATE DEPARTMENT OFFICIAL THREE: Well, Kim, this is [Senior State Department Official Three] again. We don't have any fears in this regard, but we have warned the Iraqi Government many times, and we've shared information with them, to try to work with them to carry out their responsibility to protect us as their invited guests. The U.S. Military is there, as you know, upon the invitation of the Iraqi Government, and the U.S. diplomatic presence there is there as well at the—under the agreement with the Iraqi Government. So it's their responsibility and duty to protect us, and they have not taken the appropriate steps to do so.

MODERATOR: Okay. For our next question, can we go to Alexandra von Nahmen from Deutsch Welle?

OPERATOR: One moment, please, while I open your line. One moment.

QUESTION: If I may—

OPERATOR: And Alexandra, your line is open. Go ahead.

QUESTION: Okay, thank you so much for doing this. I have two questions, if I may. Are you not concerned that the airstrikes could lead to further escalation on the ground, tak-ing into account how unstable the situation in Iraq is right now and considering the new threats from the Iranian proxies that they are going to respond?

And the second question is the Iranian foreign minister reacted to the airstrikes dur-ing his visit in Moscow, where he met with the Russian foreign minister to discuss broker-ing a peace deal for the region. Could you comment on that, on both talks? Thank you so much.

SENIOR STATE DEPARTMENT OFFICIAL ONE: Well, we—the State Department and the Defense Department—regularly update our threat assessment. There have been—as I mentioned earlier, you've had 11 attacks against Iraqi bases that host coalition forces in just the last two months, and so it's very important that we not tolerate that kind of behav-ior, because if we don't respond, it will invite further aggression. And so if you're going to have in place a deterrent effect, this is the kind of action that is required. President Trump directed our Armed Forces to respond in a way the Iranian regime will understand. And this is the language they speak, and so we're confident about that.

And the second question was about—what was it?

SENIOR STATE DEPARTMENT OFFICIAL TWO: The Moscow meeting.

SENIOR STATE DEPARTMENT OFFICIAL ONE: Oh, Moscow. There was a Reuters report recently out that had the regime having murdered 1,500 of its own citizens. You have thousands that were injured and well north of 8,000 innocent Iranians have been put into jail for protesting—basic human rights, demanding basic human rights.

Now is not the time for governments to be doing any sort of military exercises with this regime. We think now is the time to be sanctioning the Iranian leadership for the human rights abuses that it has committed against its own people and to be diplomatically isolating the regime in every way possible.

I would just ask those nations that don't—they are sending a very clear message to the Iranian people that they're siding with their oppressors and their murderers.

MODERATOR: Okay. For our next question, we'll go to Julian Borger with *The Guardian*.

OPERATOR: Thank you. And ladies and gentlemen, as we open up your lines, please allow me a moment to locate and open up your line before you ask your question. And Julian, your line is open. Go ahead.

QUESTION: Hi, thanks very much for doing this. You talk about 11 attacks over the last couple of months. Does this, in your mind, represent a campaign, an Iran-directed campaign to go after coalition forces? And how tight would you characterize Iranian control over KH?

SENIOR STATE DEPARTMENT OFFICIAL ONE: I'll give you sort of my answer—this is [Senior State Department Official One]—to the second part of your question, and ask [Senior State Department Official Three] to answer the first part. On September 11th of 2018, the White House issued a statement saying that we do not make a distinction between the Iranian regime and any of its proxies that they organize, train, and equip. And Kitaib Hizballah certainly is an entity that the regime organizes, trains, and equips, and as a consequence, we took the necessary action. And so this idea—I mean, Iran has been—it has been a feature of Iran's expansionist foreign policy to conduct deniable attacks. We are not giving Iran the fiction of deniability any longer.

SENIOR STATE DEPARTMENT OFFICIAL THREE: This is [Senior State Department Official Three]. I would say that this obviously is a campaign. Back in May of this year, the Secretary visited Baghdad and very dramatically and publicly said that we were very concerned about new credible threats against us by the Iranians—excuse me—and their proxies in Iraq and elsewhere throughout the region. And I think over the following months, you saw this come to pass, and so now, unfortunately, we've seen Iraqis and Americans killed because of it. And if there's any further escalation, it lies directly at the feet or Iran's proxies in Iraq, not on us.

MODERATOR: All right, for our next question, can we go to Jennifer Hansler from CNN.

OPERATOR: Thank you. One moment please. And Jennifer, your line is open.

QUESTION: Thank you. Thanks for doing the call. Could you talk us through a little bit of the conversations you had ahead of this strike with Iraqi officials and in the—approximately a day since the strikes have taken place? Has the Secretary of State spoken to anyone in the Iraqi Government?

SENIOR STATE DEPARTMENT OFFICIAL THREE: Jennifer, this is [Senior State Department Official Three]. We have frequent and robust exchanges with the Iraqi Government about these threats, and have for some time. And we absolutely told them that we were going to be taking action against this particular attack.

SENIOR STATE DEPARTMENT OFFICIAL ONE: And we have also—we have been—this is [Senior State Department Official]—we've been voicing our concerns over these kinds of attacks against bases that are hosting coalition forces. We've voiced our concerns with senior Iraqi Government officials repeatedly. We have asked them to arrest and bring to justice the perpetrators. And as [Senior State Department Official Three] said, the Iraqi Government needs to ensure the safety of American forces, and there's just been too many attacks, attempted attacks against American and Iraqi forces.

MODERATOR: Okay, before we move to our next question, I just want to reinforce that this is being provided on background. So our next question will be Joel Gehrke from *Washington Examiner*.

OPERATOR: Thank you, and Joel, your line is open.

QUESTION: Hi. Thanks for doing this. I wondered—we're talking about this just a few days after China and Russia conducted joint drills with Iran in the Gulf. Do you assess that China, for instance, has provided any kind of strategic support to Iran of the sort that would embolden Iran to launch this campaign of attacks that you observe against bases where there are U.S. forces located?

SENIOR STATE DEPARTMENT OFFICIAL THREE: No, we have not seen that level of assistance.

MODERATOR: Okay. Moving on to our next question, could you open the line of Lahav Harkov from *Jerusalem Post*?

OPERATOR: One moment, please. And here we are, and your line is open. Go ahead, please.

QUESTION: Is this a one-time thing, a response to the sort of specific attack on specific U.S. interests and that killed a civilian, et cetera? Or is this a sort of—marks a sort of a return by the U.S. to play a more active role?

SENIOR STATE DEPARTMENT OFFICIAL ONE: We don't preview future military action. We don't discuss our military options. Since May, we have moved an additional 14,000 troops to the region. We have established the International Maritime Security Initiative. We've enhanced our intelligence, surveillance, and reconnaissance assets, which we know has helped to disrupt and deter many of the attacks that Iran had been plotting, either by land, sea, or air. And then now we have the President responding decisively with military strikes yesterday in both Iraq and Syria. So we're very pleased with the response package that we've put in place, the overall enhancing our force posture, but we have also deepened Iran's economic crisis over this same period, and over the same period we have also weakened Iran's proxies financially.

SENIOR STATE DEPARTMENT OFFICIAL TWO: And [Senior State Department Official Two]. In short, we're not returning to the front in the Middle East. We never left it.

MODERATOR: Okay, thanks. For our next question could we turn to Nick Schifrin from PBS?

OPERATOR: Your line is open. Go ahead, Nick.

QUESTION: Hey, guys. Thanks very much for doing this. For [Senior State Department Official One], you just listed some of the steps that you guys have taken, some of the major steps you guys have taken over the last few months. You also used the word "restore deterrence." Have you had any concerns or has there been any concerns at all that the lack of response to the attack in Saudi Arabia on the oil fields and the lack of response to the U.S. drone being shot down has lost some deterrence?

And to [Senior State Department Official Three], to go back to Kim's question, do you have any concerns about the Iraqi Government's statements of negativity since this attack, and that will impact your overall relationship with the Iraqi Government? Thanks.

SENIOR STATE DEPARTMENT OFFICIAL ONE: Thanks, Nick. I'll do the first one. I think Iran, from about 2007 until about 2017, was able to run an expansionist foreign policy without negative consequence, and when President Trump came into office he took an entirely different approach. We don't believe that we—that we need to be telling our allies in the region that they need to share it with Iran. So we reversed that policy. We started sanctioning Iran. We have now had—I think we're at or over 1,000 individuals and entities that have been sanctioned during this period. We are trying to reverse the gains that Iran enjoyed prior to this administration. And obviously this is the work of many months and years. Our sanctions have only been in place—because the President got out of the Iran deal in May, we had a six-month wind-down period, and so we didn't have all of our sanctions in place—it's been within a year.

So we have had enormous success even in that short period of time to try to re-establish deterrence, because Iran, they were in compliance with the Iran nuclear deal. That's a low bar for compliance. And while they were in compliance, there was an incentive for countries to look the other way on Iran's ballistic missile testing, their missile proliferation, their regional aggression, the hostage taking. And so now we are taking a comprehensive approach to the entire range of threats that Iran presents, and we're able to do that because we are outside of the nuclear deal and we're much better postured to achieve our national security objectives this way than inside the deal.

And I'll ask [Senior State Department Official Three] to answer the second part.

SENIOR STATE DEPARTMENT OFFICIAL THREE: Yeah, the question was about whether we're concerned about Iraqi politicians' statements condemning us instead of Hizballah. We're disappointed with those statements. We're disappointed that every time that Kitaib Hizballah controls and moves weapons and people on behalf of the Iranians, there's no condemnation. Every time Hizballah represses protestors peacefully out there in the streets, there's no condemnation. Every time Hizballah sends fighters off into Syria without the authorization of the Iraqi Government, there's no condemnation. Yeah, it's disappointing. But it's moments like this when you see people's true colors.

MODERATOR: Okay. For the next question, can we turn to Bryant Harris from Al-Monitor?

OPERATOR: Your line is open. Go ahead.

QUESTION: Hey, thanks so much for doing the call. Two questions. Number one, I think the Iraqis initially claimed that the attack on the base was from the Islamic State, so can you just kind of lay out how you arrived at the determination that it was Kitaib Hizballah? And number two, earlier this year, in June I believe, you submitted a legal opinion to Congress that said the 2001 and 2002 AUMFs could be used against Iran in the context of defending U.S. forces in Iraq from Iranian proxies. Do you at this point in time have any plans to retaliate against Iran itself for the recent attacks? Thank you.

SENIOR STATE DEPARTMENT OFFICIAL ONE: Yeah, can you give us the second question one more time? Because obviously the AUMF does permit us to operate defensively, and so in this case, we were attacked by a militia in Iraq, and then we took strikes as a matter of self-defense, which is consistent with the AUMF.

With respect to the first question on—we know that KH was responsible for the attacks. But we—but we're not worried about our confidence level on that one. Kitaib Hizballah is very well armed and trained by Iran, and they are responsible for many of these attacks against American troops and Iraqi troops.

MODERATOR: All right, we have time for one more question. We'll go to Amanda Macias from CNBC.

OPERATOR: Amanda, your line is open. Go ahead, please.

QUESTION: Thank you. I just wanted to go back to the sanctions issue. So despite the near-1,000 sanctions on Iran, they've still been able to carry out attacks and even sophisticated attacks that we saw earlier this year with the oil tanker. So I just wanted to get your analysis on this one more time that you do think that these economic sanctions are working on Iran.

SENIOR STATE DEPARTMENT OFFICIAL ONE: The nature of modern terrorism is terrorists enjoying asymmetric advantage in any theater, and so Iran uses modern terrorism. And we have never claimed that our sanctions will eliminate the asymmetric capability of your modern terrorists.

What we are doing is denying the regime the revenue that it needs to run an expansionist foreign policy. We are also—and by that policy, Iran has less money to spend today than it did three—almost three years ago when we came into office. There have been front-page stories in *The New York Times* and *The Washington Post* in March and in May documenting how our sanctions are financially weakening Iran's proxies. That is going to continue. There will be more sanctions to come.

Iran's economic problems and challenges are going to compound in 2020. They're already deep into a recession. And we're also seeing Iran come under greater diplomatic isolation. The leaders of Germany, the UK, and France condemned Iran's attack on Saudi Arabia on September 14th. Prime Minister Johnson called for Iran to come to the negotiating table to address the challenge of Iran's missile proliferation. That has been our position as well for some time.

I think over the life of the Iran nuclear deal, because the missile proliferation has been neglected, we have been accumulating risk of a conflict in the Middle East, and we are now focused very aggressively against Iran's missile program, its missile testing. We've sanctioned many of the individuals and entities that are responsible for Iran's missile program, and we invite other countries to do the same.

MODERATOR: All right. That's all the time we have. Just a reminder this briefing was provided on background, and in the transcript that we'll put out later, our speakers will be referred to as Senior State Department Official One, Two, and Three. Thank you for joining the call and thanks to our briefers for being part of this.

SENIOR STATE DEPARTMENT OFFICIAL TWO: Thank you all.

SENIOR STATE DEPARTMENT OFFICIAL ONE: Thank you.

SOURCE: U.S. Department of State. "Senior State Department Officials on U.S. Airstrikes in Iraq and Syria." December 30, 2019. https://www.state.gov/senior-state-department-officials-on-u-s-airstrikes-in-iraq-and-syria.

Defense Secretary Details Personnel Protection Efforts in Iraq

December 31, 2019

The Department of Defense is working closely with the Department of State to ensure the security of our Embassy and personnel in Baghdad. We have taken appropriate force protection actions to ensure the safety of American citizens, military personnel and diplomats in country, and to ensure our right of self-defense. We are sending additional forces to support our personnel at the Embassy. As in all countries, we rely on host nation forces to assist in the protection of our personnel in country, and we call on the Government of Iraq to fulfill its international responsibilities to do so. The United States continues to support the Iraqi people and a free, sovereign, and prosperous Iraq.

SOURCE: U.S. Department of Defense. "DOD Statement on Iraq from Secretary Esper." December 31, 2019. https://www.defense.gov/Newsroom/Releases/Release/Article/2048868/dod-statement-on-iraq-from-secretary-esper.

OTHER HISTORIC DOCUMENTS OF INTEREST

FROM THIS VOLUME

- President Trump Announces Sanctions against Iran, p. 332

FROM PREVIOUS *HISTORIC DOCUMENTS*

- U.S. and Iraqi Officials on New Iraqi Leadership, *2014*, p. 315
- Iraq Conducts Elections amid Tenuous Security Environment, *2013*, p. 109
- President Obama Releases New Defense Strategy, *2012*, p. 3

Index

NOTE: Page references with (table) refer to tables.